Nineteenth-Century Literature Criticism

Guide to Gale Literary Criticism Series

When you need to review criticism of literary works, these are the Gale series to use:

If the author's death date is: **You should turn to:**

After Dec. 31, 1959
(or author is still living)

CONTEMPORARY LITERARY CRITICISM

for example: Jorge Luis Borges, Anthony Burgess,
William Faulkner, Mary Gordon,
Ernest Hemingway, Iris Murdoch

1900 through 1959

TWENTIETH-CENTURY LITERARY CRITICISM

for example: Willa Cather, F. Scott Fitzgerald,
Henry James, Mark Twain, Virginia Woolf

1800 through 1899

NINETEENTH-CENTURY LITERATURE CRITICISM

for example: Fyodor Dostoevsky, Nathaniel Hawthorne,
George Sand, William Wordsworth

1400 through 1799

LITERATURE CRITICISM FROM 1400 TO 1800
(excluding Shakespeare)

for example: Anne Bradstreet, Daniel Defoe,
Alexander Pope, François Rabelais,
Jonathan Swift, Phillis Wheatley

SHAKESPEAREAN CRITICISM

Shakespeare's plays and poetry

Antiquity through 1399

CLASSICAL AND MEDIEVAL LITERATURE CRITICISM

for example: Dante, Homer, Plato, Sophocles, Vergil,
the Beowulf Poet

Gale also publishes related criticism series:

BLACK LITERATURE CRITICISM

This three-volume series presents criticism of works by major black writers of the past two hundred years.

CHILDREN'S LITERATURE REVIEW

This series covers authors of all eras who have written for the preschool through high school audience.

DRAMA CRITICISM

This series covers dramatists of all nationalities and periods of literary history.

POETRY CRITICISM

This series covers poets of all nationalities and periods of literary history.

SHORT STORY CRITICISM

This series covers the major short fiction writers of all nationalities and periods of literary history.

ISSN 0732-1864

R

Volume 35

Nineteenth-Century Literature Criticism

Excerpts from Criticism of the
Works of Novelists, Poets, Playwrights,
Short Story Writers, Philosophers, and Other
Creative Writers Who Died between 1800
and 1899, from the First Published Critical
Appraisals to Current Evaluations

Joann Cerrito
Paula Kepos
Editors

Tina Grant
Drew Kalasky
Jelena O. Krstović
Mark Swartz
Lawrence J. Trudeau
Associate Editors

 Gale Research Inc. · DETROIT · LONDON

STAFF

Joann Cerrito, Paula Kepos, *Editors*

Tina Grant, Drew Kalasky, Jelena O. Krstović, Mark Swartz, *Associate Editors*

David J. Engleman, Rogene M. Fisher, Judy Galens, Christine Haydinger, Alan Hedblad, Elisabeth Morrison, James Poniewozik, Debra A. Wells, *Assistant Editors*

Jeanne A. Gough, *Permissions & Production Manager*
Linda M. Pugliese, *Production Supervisor*
Paul Lewon, Maureen Puhl, Camille Robinson, Jennifer VanSickle, *Editorial Associates*
Donna Craft, Rosita D'Souza, Sheila Walencewicz, *Editorial Assistants*

Victoria B. Cariappa, *Research Manager*
Maureen Richards, *Research Supervisor*
Mary Beth McElmeel, Tamara C. Nott, *Editorial Associates*
Andrea B. Ghorai, Daniel J. Jankowski, Julie K. Karmazin, Robert S. Lazich, Julie Synkonis, *Editorial Assistants*

Sandra C. Davis, *Permissions Supervisor (Text)*
Maria L. Franklin, Josephine M. Keene, Denise Singleton, Kimberly F. Smilay, *Permissions Associates*
Brandy Johnson, Michele Lonoconus, Shelly Rakoczy, Shalice Shah, *Permissions Assistants*

Margaret A. Chamberlain, *Permissions Supervisor (Pictures)*
Pamela A. Hayes, *Permissions Associate*
Amy Lynn Emrich, Karla Kulkis, Nancy M. Rattenbury, Keith Reed, *Permissions Assistants*

Mary Beth Trimper, *Production Manager*
Mary Winterhalter, *Production Assistant*

Arthur Chartow, *Art Director*
C. J. Jonik, Nicholas Jakubiak, *Keyliners*

Contents

Preface   vii

Acknowledgments   xi

Preface

Since its inception in 1981, *Nineteenth-Century Literature Criticism* has been a valuable resource for students and librarians seeking critical commentary on writers of this transitional period in world history. Designated an "Outstanding Reference Source" by the American Library Association with the publication of its first volume, *NCLC* has since been purchased by over 6,000 school, public, and university libraries. The series has covered more than 300 authors representing 26 nationalities and over 15,000 titles. No other reference source has surveyed the critical reaction to nineteenth-century authors and literature as thoroughly as *NCLC*.

Scope of the Series

NCLC is designed to serve as an introduction for students and advanced readers to the authors of the nineteenth century, and to the most significant interpretations of these authors' works. The great poets, novelists, short story writers, dramatists, and philosophers of this period are frequently studied in high school and college literature courses. By organizing and reprinting the enormous amount of commentary written on these authors, *NCLC* helps students develop valuable insight into literary history, promotes a better understanding of the texts, and sparks ideas for papers and assignments. Each entry in *NCLC* presents a comprehensive survey of an author's career or an individual work of literature and provides the user with a multiplicity of interpretations and assessments. Such variety allows students to pursue their own interests; furthermore, it fosters an awareness that literature is dynamic and responsive to many different opinions.

Every fourth volume of *NCLC* is devoted to literary topics that cannot be covered under the author approach used in the rest of the series. Such topics include literary movements, prominent themes in nineteenth-century literature, literary reaction to political and historical events, significant eras in literary history, prominent literary anniversaries, and the literatures of cultures that are often overlooked by English-speaking readers.

NCLC continues the survey of criticism of world literature begun by Gale's *Contemporary Literary Criticism (CLC)* and *Twentieth-Century Literary Criticism (TCLC)*, both of which excerpt and reprint commentary on authors of the twentieth century. For additional information about *TCLC, CLC,* and Gale's other criticism series, users should consult the Guide to Gale Literary Criticism Series preceding the title page in this volume.

Coverage

Each volume of *NCLC* is carefully compiled to present:

- criticism of authors, or literary topics, representing a variety of genres and nationalities
- both major and lesser-known writers and literary works of the period
- 7-10 authors or 4-6 topics per volume
- individual entries that survey critical response to each author's work or each topic in literary history, including early criticism to reflect initial reactions; later criticism to represent any rise or decline in reputation; and current retrospective analyses.

Organization of This Book

An author entry consists of the following elements: author heading, biographical and critical introduction, list of principal works, excerpts of criticism (each preceded by an annotation and followed by a bibliographic citation), and a bibliography of further reading.

- The **author heading** consists of the name under which the author most commonly wrote, followed by birth and death dates. If an author wrote consistently under a pseudonym, the pseudonym will be listed in the author heading and the real name given in parentheses on the first line of the biographical and critical introduction. Also located at the beginning of the introduction to the author entry are any name variations under which an author wrote, including transliterated forms for authors whose languages use nonroman alphabets.

- The **biographical and critical introduction** outlines the author's life and career, as well as the critical issues surrounding his or her work. References are provided to past volumes of *NCLC* and to other biographical and critical reference series published by Gale, including *Children's Literature Review, Contemporary Authors, Dictionary of Literary Biography, Drama Criticism, Poetry Criticism, Short Story Criticism,* and *Something about the Author.*

• Most *NCLC* entries include **portraits** of the author. Many entries also contain reproductions of materials pertinent to an author's career, including manuscript pages, title pages, dust jackets, letters, and drawings, as well as photographs of important people, places, and events in an author's life.

• The list of **principal works** is chronological by date of first book publication and identifies the genre of each work. In the case of foreign authors with both foreign-language publications and English translations, the title and date of the first English-language edition are given in brackets. Unless otherwise indicated, dramas are dated by first performance, not first publication.

• **Criticism** is arranged chronologically in each author entry to provide a perspective on changes in critical evaluation over the years. All titles of works by the author featured in the entry are printed in boldface type to enable the user to easily locate discussion of particular works. Also for purposes of easier identification, the critic's name and the publication date of the essay are given at the beginning of each piece of criticism. Unsigned criticism is preceded by the title of the journal in which it appeared. Publication information (such as publisher names and book prices) and parenthetical numerical references (such as footnotes or page and line references to specific editions of works) have been deleted at the editors' discretion to provide smoother reading of the text.

• Critical excerpts are prefaced by **annotations** providing the reader with information about both the critic and the criticism that follows. Included are the critic's reputation, individual approach to literary criticism, and particular expertise in an author's works. Also noted are the relative importance of a work of criticism, the scope of the excerpt, and the growth of critical controversy or changes in critical trends regarding an author. In some cases, these annotations cross-reference excerpts by critics who discuss each other's commentary.

• A complete **bibliographic citation** designed to facilitate location of the original essay or book follows each piece of criticism.

• An annotated list of **further reading** appearing at the end of each author entry suggests secondary sources on the author. In some cases it includes essays for which the editors could not obtain reprint rights.

Cumulative Indexes

• Each volume of *NCLC* contains a cumulative **author index** listing all authors who have appeared in the following Gale series: *Contemporary Literary Criticism, Twentieth-Century Literary Criticism, Nineteenth-Century Literature Criticism, Literature Criticism from 1400 to 1800,* and *Classical and Medieval Literature Criticism.* Topic entries devoted to a single author, such as the entry on the textual reconstruction of James Joyce's *Ulysses* in *TCLC* 26, are listed in this index. Also included are cross-references to the Gale series *Poetry Criticism, Drama Criticism, Short Story Criticism, Children's Literature Review, Authors in the News, Contemporary Authors, Contemporary Authors Autobiography Series, Dictionary of Literary Biography, Concise Dictionary of American Literary Biography, Something about the Author, Something about the Author Autobiography Series,* and *Yesterday's Authors of Books for Children.* Useful for locating authors within the various series, this index is particularly valuable for those authors who are identified by a certain period but who, because of their death dates, are placed in another, or for those authors whose careers span two periods. For example, Fyodor Dostoevsky is found in *NCLC,* yet Leo Tolstoy, another major nineteenth-century Russian novelist, is found in *TCLC* because he died after 1899.

• Each *NCLC* volume includes a cumulative **nationality index** which lists all authors who have appeared in *NCLC* volumes, arranged alphabetically under their respective nationalities, as well as Topics volume entries devoted to particular national literatures.

• Each new volume in Gale's Literary Criticism Series includes a cumulative **topic index,** which lists all literary topics treated in *NCLC, TCLC, LC 1400-1800,* and the *CLC* Yearbook.

• Each new volume of *NCLC,* with the exception of the Topics volumes, contains a **title index** listing the titles of all literary works discussed in the volume. The first volume of *NCLC* published each year contains an index listing all titles discussed in the series since its inception. Titles discussed in the Topics volume entries are not included in the *NCLC* cumulative index.

A Note to the Reader

When writing papers, students who quote directly from any volume in Gale's Literary Criticism Series may use the following general forms to footnote reprinted criticism. The first example pertains to material drawn from periodicals, the second to material reprinted from books.

[1] T. S. Eliot, "John Donne," *The Nation and the Athenaeum,* 33 (9 June 1923), 321-32; excerpted and reprinted in *Literature Criticism from 1400 to 1800,* Vol. 10, ed. James E. Person, Jr. (Detroit: Gale Research, 1989), pp. 28-9.

[2] Clara G. Stillman, *Samuel Butler: A Mid-Victorian Modern* (Viking Press, 1932); excerpted and reprinted in *Twentieth-Century Literary Criticism,* Vol. 33, ed. Paula Kepos (Detroit: Gale Research, 1989), pp. 43-5.

Suggestions Are Welcome

In response to suggestions, several features have been added to *NCLC* since the series began, including annotations to excerpted criticism, a cumulative index to authors in all Gale literary criticism series, entries devoted to criticism on a single work by a major author, more extensive illustrations, and a title index listing all literary works discussed in the series since its inception.

Readers who wish to suggest authors or topics to appear in future volumes, or who have other suggestions, are cordially invited to write the editors.

ACKNOWLEDGMENTS

The editors wish to thank the copyright holders of the excerpted criticism included in this volume, the permissions managers of many book and magazine publishing companies for assisting us in securing reprint rights, and Anthony Bogucki for assistance with copyright research. We are also grateful to the staffs of the Detroit Public Library Complex, and University of Michigan Libraries for making their resources available to us. Following is a list of copyright holders who have granted us permission to reprint material in this volume of *NCLC*. Every effort has been made to trace copyright, but if omissions have been made, please let us know.

COPYRIGHTED EXCERPTS IN *NCLC,* VOLUME 35, WERE REPRINTED FROM THE FOLLOWING PERIODICALS:

Acta Germanica, v. 17, 1984. © Verlag Peter Lang GmbH, Frankfurt am main 1984. All rights reserved. Reprinted by permission of the publisher.—*boundary 2,* v. XII, Fall, 1983. Copyright © *boundary 2,* 1983. Reprinted by permission of the publisher.—*Children's Literature Association Quarterly,* v. 14, Spring, 1989. © 1989 Children's Literature Association. Reprinted by permission of the publisher.—*CLIO,* v. 16, Winter, 1987 for "Obedience, Struggle, and Revolt: The Historical Vision of Balzac's 'Father Goriot' " by James Smith Allen. © 1987 by Robert H. Canary and Henry Kozicki. Reprinted by permission of the author.—*Education Theatre Journal,* v. 24, October, 1972. © 1972 University College Theatre Association of the American Theatre Association. Reprinted by permission of the publisher.—*Essays in Criticism,* v. XV, July, 1965 for "Wuthering Heights" by F. H. Langman. Reprinted by permission of the editors of *Essays in Criticism* and the author.—*French Forum,* v. 9, January, 1984. Copyright 1984 by French Forum, Inc. Reprinted by permission of the publisher.—*The German Quarterly,* v. LIV, May, 1980. Copyright © 1980 by the American Association of Teachers of German. Reprinted by permission of the publisher.—*The Hudson Review,* v. XXII, Summer, 1969. Copyright © 1969 by The Hudson Review, Inc. Reprinted by permission of the publisher.—*The Journal of the Midwest Modern Language Association,* v. 19, Spring, 1986. Reprinted by permission of the publisher.—*Nineteenth-Century Fiction,* v. 20, June, 1965 for "The Ironic Vision of Emily Brontë" by John E. Jordan; v. 21, March, 1967 for "Control of Sympathy in 'Wuthering Heights' " by John Hagan; v. 25, December, 1970 for "The Strangeness of 'Wuthering Heights' " by Arnold Krupat. © 1965, 1967, 1970 by The Regents of the University of California. All reprinted by permission of The Regents and the respective authors.—*NOVEL: A Forum on Fiction,* v. 3, Fall, 1969. Copyright NOVEL Corp. © 1969. Reprinted with permission.—*Orbis Litterarum,* v. 45, 1990. Reprinted by permission of the publisher.—*Russian Literature Triquarterly,* n. 9, 1974. © 1974 by Ardis Publishers. Reprinted by permission of the publisher.—*Studies in the Novel,* v. I, Fall, 1969. Copyright 1969 by North Texas State University. Reprinted by permission of the publisher.—*Studies in Romanticism,* v. V, Winter, 1966. Copyright 1966 by the Trustees of Boston University. Reprinted by permission of the publisher.—*Theology,* v. LXXVIII, January, 1975 for "Kingsley as Novelist" by P. G. Scott. Reprinted by permission of SPCK and the author.—*The Victorian Newsletter,* n. 68, Fall, 1985 for "The Waif at the Window: Emily Brontë's 'Bildungsroman' " by Annette R. Federico. Reprinted by permission of *The Victorian Newsletter* and the author.—*Victorian Studies,* v. VIII, March, 1965 for "Charles Kingsley and the Literary Image of the Countryside" by Gillian Beer; v. 21 Autumn, 1977 for "Charles Kingsley's Fallen Athlete" by Henry R. Harrington. Both reprinted by permission of the Trustees of Indiana University and the respective authors.

COPYRIGHTED EXCERPTS IN *NCLC,* VOLUME 35, WERE REPRINTED FROM THE FOLLOWING BOOKS:

Affron, Charles. From *Patterns of Failure in "La Comédie Humaine."* Yale University Press, 1966. Copyright © 1966 by Yale University. All rights reserved. Reprinted by permission of the publisher.—Ahearn, Edward J. From *Rimbaud: Visions and Habitations.* University of California Press, 1983. © 1983 by The Regents of the University of California. Reprinted by permission of the publisher.—Apter, T. E. From "Romanticism and Romantic Love in 'Wuthering Heights'," in *The Art of Emily Brontë.* Edited by Anne Smith. London: Vision Press, 1976. © 1976 Vision Press. All rights reserved. Reprinted by permission of the publisher.—Auerbach, Erich. From *Mimesis: The Representation of Reality in Western Literature.* Translated by Willard R. Trask. Princeton University Press, 1953. Copyright 1953, renewed 1981 by Princeton University Press. Reprinted by permission of the publisher.—Balzac, Honoré de. From *Honoré de Balzac: Pére Goriot.* Translated by A. J. Krailsheimer. Oxford University Press, Inc., 1991. © A. J. Krailsheimer 1991. All rights reserved.—Belinsky, V. G. From *Selected Philosophical Works.* Foreign Languages Publishing House, 1948.—Bellos, David. From *Honoré de Balzac: Old Goriot.* Cambridge University Press, 1987. © Cambridge University Press 1987. Reprinted with the permission of the publisher and the author.—Black, Michael. From *The Literature of Fidelity.* Chatto & Windus, 1975. © Michael Black 1975. Reprinted

Honoré de Balzac

Le père Goriot

(Also wrote under the pseudonym Lord R'hoone and Horace de Saint-Aubin) French novelist, short story writer, dramatist, essayist, and editor.

The following entry presents criticism of Balzac's novel *Le père Goriot* (1835; *Old Goriot;* also translated as *Father Goriot*). For discussion of his complete career, see *NCLC,* Volume 5.

INTRODUCTION

Balzac is generally regarded as the greatest nineteenth-century French novelist, and *Le père Goriot* is acknowledged as his finest achievement. Written as part of the *Comédie humaine,* a series of novels in which Balzac sought to create a highly detailed, comprehensive history of the "manners and customs" of his era, *Le père Goriot* juxtaposes the opulent world of Parisian aristocracy with the dinginess of a middle-class boardinghouse in a powerful exposé of the vapid values of the upper class and the destructive emphasis on money in post-Revolutionary society. Critics consider this novel a landmark in the development of literary Realism, praising its precise depiction of both the appearance and mood of Balzac's time.

Although Balzac had published several novels in the early 1830s, he first alluded to the *Comédie humaine* in 1835, shortly after completing *Le père Goriot,* and critics speculate that he conceived of the plan to unify his work as a single series while writing this novel. The first mention of *Le père Goriot* is found in an undated entry in Balzac's notebook: "Subject of Father Goriot—A brave man—middle-class boarding-house—600 franc income—wasting himself for his daughters who both have 50,000 franc incomes—dying like a dog." In a letter to his mistress and future wife, Madame Hanska, dated 18 October 1834, he expressed his optimism about the work: " 'Le père Goriot,' a master work! the painting of a sentiment so great that nothing can exhaust it, neither rebuffs, nor wounds, nor injustice; a man who is *father,* as a saint, as a martyr is Christian." Balzac considered *Le père Goriot* his greatest achievement and hoped that it would rescue him from ever-present financial pressure which resulted from a series of disastrous business ventures and was compounded by his extravagant lifestyle. The work first appeared in the periodical *Revue de Paris* in four installments from December 1834 through February 1835 and was an immediate popular success, surpassing even Balzac's high expectations. The first issue, 14 December, sold out overnight, and an additional fifty thousand copies were printed. Critics unanimously condemned the work, finding its realistic, frank depiction of the evils in Parisian society both cynical and immoral. Subsequent editions of the work contained prefaces in which Balzac responded

to such criticism, contending that an honest portrait of society necessitates the inclusion of vice.

Le père Goriot relates the dual story of the degradation of Jean-Joachim Goriot, a retired vermicelli merchant, and the social education of Eugène de Rastignac, a poor but aristocratic young man. It begins when Rastignac arrives in Paris, where his family has sent him to study law. He encounters a variety of Parisian personalities at his boardinghouse—Maison Vauquer—among them Monsieur, known as "Père," Goriot. After being introduced to aristocratic society, Rastignac learns that Goriot has two wealthy and beautiful daughters and that he sacrificed his fortune to provide them with enormous dowries, thus ensuring their acceptance into the upper class. The novel focuses on Goriot's obsessive paternal devotion, which compels him to sell all his belongings to meet his daughters' continuing requests for money despite their neglect of his emotional needs. Goriot's declining economic status is reflected in both his movement to increasingly sordid apartments and the rapid deterioration of his health and appearance. His death struggle, ostensibly caused by self-hatred following his failure to meet his daughters' financial demands, is the occasion of his devastating revelation that his daughters do not love him. His tragedy is compounded by their absence at his funeral to which they send only their empty carriages and servants. Goriot's plight serves as a poignant lesson to Rastignac, who must choose between the middle-class existence of an honest lawyer and the luxurious but amoral milieu to which his lineage entitles him. Repelled by the middle class as represented by the Maison Vauquer, Rastignac decides to remain among the aristocracy, knowing that his integrity and morality may well be an impediment to his success there. The novel closes with Rastignac's challenge to Parisian society: "It's between the two of us now!"—spoken from Père Lachaise cemetery where he has just buried Goriot.

Balzac's presentation of Paris and its inhabitants through the eyes of Rastignac enabled him to convey his own impressions of the city. His portrayal of post-Revolutionary society exposes the superficial values of the upper classes and the corresponding breakdown of traditional French values, illustrated most clearly in his depiction of the weakening family structure. Goriot's outburst, "Money is life itself, it's the mainspring of everything," emphasizes the alienating effects of a materialist society in which greed supplants love and respect. The breakdown of the family is presented not only in Goriot's situation but also in the novel's subplots: Victorine Taillefer, a virtuous young woman living at the Maison Vauquer, is senselessly rejected by her father, and Rastignac abuses his family's generosity to hasten his entry into high society.

Critics note that the realism of Balzac's portrait of society is augmented by his use of history. Through their involvement in major events of French history, the characters gain a historical specificity. Goriot, for example, made his fortune during the Revolution, a period of unprecedented economic opportunity for the middle class, while his rejection by his daughters is due in part to the increasing emphasis on aristocratic lineage following the restoration of the Bourbon monarchy in 1815. Critics view this conception of a connection between personal and cultural history as the key to understanding Balzac's characterization. His understanding of environment as both an extension and a molding force of personality has led many critics to praise his examination of, in the words of Sandy Petrey, the "interpenetration of the collective and the individual." *Le père Goriot* is also the first novel in which Balzac incorporated characters that had appeared in earlier novels, a technique he continued to use throughout the remainder of the *Comédie humaine.* Balzac's contemporaries often expressed boredom with his reappearing characters, and some even suggested that this device was only an excuse to leave his novels unfinished. *Le père Goriot* in particular was criticized for its ambiguous ending because Rastignac's future is left uncertain. Recent critics, however, have praised both the openness of *Le père Goriot*'s conclusion and Balzac's characterizations. Mary Susan McCarthy, for example, has interpreted such recurring characters in Balzac's fiction as "the tool by which we gain a mastery of the total work and the point of departure for our highly creative reading."

Balzac considered himself "Secretary of the Age," honest-ly recording the essential features of his society, and critics have unanimously praised his powers of acute observation as his greatest artistic strength. However, his contemporaries, while lauding his accuracy, were shocked by his cynical depiction of the "ugly" side of life. Noting its similarities to *King Lear,* many interpreted *Le père Goriot* as a "*Lear* without Cordelia," emphasizing the absence of a moral weight to balance the selfishness and depravity of the principal characters. Later nineteenth-century critics differed in their acceptance of immorality as a necessary aspect of verisimilitude. Twentieth-century attention to *Le père Goriot* has stressed its value as both a historical document and one of the first important Realist novels. Stressing this aspect of the novel, Petrey has described it as "practically a one-volume illustration of the Realist aesthetic."

Leslie Stephen   (essay date 1874)

[*Many scholars consider Stephen among the most important English literary critics of the Victorian era. He has been praised for his moral insight and judgment, as well as for his intellectual vigor—although some have charged that his criticism is deficient in aesthetic and formal analysis. The key to Stephen's moral criticism is his theory that all literature is nothing more than an imaginative rendering, in concrete terms, of a writer's philosophy or beliefs. It is the role of criticism, he contends, to translate into intellectual terms what the writer has told the reader through character, symbol, and event. More often than not, Stephen's analysis passes into biographical judgment of the writer rather than the work. In the following excerpt, he condemns* Le père Goriot *as excessively melodramatic.*]

The characteristic peculiarities of Balzac's novels may be described as the intensity with which he expresses certain motives, and the vigour with which he portrays the real or imaginary corruption of society. Upon one particular situation, or class of situations, favourable to this peculiar power, he is never tired of dwelling. He repeats himself indeed, in a certain sense, as a man must necessarily repeat himself who writes eighty-five stories, besides doing other work, in less than twenty years. In this voluminous outpouring of matter the machinery is varied with wonderful fertility of invention, but one sentiment recurs very frequently. The great majority of Balzac's novels, including all the most powerful examples, may thus be described as variations on a single theme. Each of them is in fact the record of a martyrdom. There is always a virtuous hero or heroine who is tortured, and, most frequently, tortured to death by a combination of selfish intrigues. The commonest case is, of course, that which has become the staple plot of French novelists, where the interesting young woman is sacrificed to the brutality of a dull husband; that, for example, is the story of the *Femme de Trente Ans,* of *Le Lys dans la Vallée,* and of several minor performances; then we have the daughters sacrificed to the avaricious father, as in *Eugénie Grandet;* the woman sacrificed to the imperious lover in the *Duchesse de Langeais;* the immoral beauty sacrificed to the ambition of her lover in the *Splendeurs et Misères des Courtisans;* the mother sacrificed to the dissolute son in the *Ménage de Garçon;* the woman of political ambition sacrificed to the contemptible intriguers opposed to her in *Les Employés;* and, indeed, in one way or other, as subordinate character or as heroine, this figure of a graceful feminine victim comes into nearly every novel. Virtuous heroes fare little better. Poor Colonel Chabert is disowned and driven to beggary by the wife who has committed bigamy; the luckless curé, Birotteau, is cheated out of his prospects and doomed to a broken heart by the successful villany of a rival priest and his accomplices; the Comte de Manerville is ruined and transported by his wife and his detestable mother-in-law; Père Goriot is left to starvation by his daughters; the Marquis d'Espard is all but condemned as a lunatic by the manœuvres of his wife; the faithful servant Michu comes to the guillotine; the devoted notary Chesnel is beggared in the effort to save his scapegrace of a master; Michaud, another devoted adherent, is murdered with perfect success by the brutal peasantry, and his wife dies of the news; Balthazar Claes is the victim of his devotion to science; and Z. Marcas dies unknown and in the depths of misery as a reward for trying to be a second Colbert. The old-fashioned canons of poetical justice are inverted; and the villains are dismissed to live very happily ever afterwards, whilst the virtuous are slain outright or sentenced to a death by slow torture. Thackeray, in one or two of his minor stories, has touched the same note. The history of Mr. Deuceace, and especially its catastrophe, is much in Balzac's style; but as a rule, our English novelists shrink from anything so unpleasant.

Perhaps the most striking example of this method is the *Père Goriot.* The general situation may be described in two words, by saying that Goriot is the modern King Lear. Mesdames de Restaud and de Nucingen are the representatives of Regan and Goneril; but the Parisian Lear is not allowed the consolation of a Cordelia; the cup of misery is measured out to him drop by drop, and the bitterness of each dose is analysed with chemical accuracy. We watch the poor old broken-down merchant, who has impoverished himself to provide his daughters' dowries, and has gradually stripped himself, first of comfort, and then of the necessaries of life, to satisfy the demands of their folly and luxury, as we might watch a man clinging to the edge of a cliff and gradually dropping lower and lower, catching feebly at every point of support till his strength is exhausted, and the inevitable catastrophe follows. The daughters, allowed to retain some fragments of good feeling and not quite irredeemably hateful, are gradually yielding to the demoralizing influence of a heartless vanity. They yield, it is true, pretty completely at last; but their wickedness seems to reveal the influence of a vague but omnipotent power of evil in the background. There is not a more characteristic scene in Balzac than that in which Rastignac, the lover of Madame de Nucingen, overhears the conversation between the father in his wretched garret and the modern Goneril and Regan. A gleam of good fortune has just encouraged old Goriot to anticipate an escape from his troubles. On the morning of the day of expected release Madame Goneril de Nucingen rushes up to her father's garret to explain to him that her husband,

the rich banker, having engaged all his funds in some diabolical financial intrigues, refuses to allow her the use of her fortune, whilst, owing to her own misconduct, she is afraid to appeal to the law. They have a hideous tacit compact, according to which the wife enjoys full domestic liberty, whilst the husband may use her fortune to carry out his dishonest plots. She begs her father to examine the facts in the light of his financial experience, though the examination must be deferred, that she may not look ill with the excitement when she meets her lover at the ball. As the poor father is tormenting his brains, Madame Regan de Restaud appears in terrible distress. Her lover has threatened to commit suicide unless he can meet a certain bill, and to save him she has pledged certain diamonds which were heirlooms in her husband's family. Her husband has discovered the whole transaction, and, though not making an open scandal, imposes some severe conditions upon her future. Old Goriot is raving against the brutality of her husband, when Regan adds that there is still a sum to be paid, without which her lover, to whom she has sacrificed everything, will be ruined. Now old Goriot had employed just this sum—all but the very last fragment of his fortune—in the service of Goneril. A desperate quarrel instantly takes place between the two fine ladies over this last scrap of their father's property. They are fast degenerating into Parisian Billingsgate, when Goriot succeeds in obtaining silence and proposes to strip himself of his last penny. Even the sisters hesitate at such an impiety, and Rastignac enters with some apology for listening, and hands over to the countess a certain bill of exchange for a sum which he professes himself to owe to Goriot, and which will just save her lover. She accepts the paper, but vehemently denounces her sister for having, as she supposes, allowed Rastignac to listen to their hideous revelations, and retires in a fury, whilst the father faints away. He recovers to express his forgiveness, and at this moment the countess returns, ostensibly to throw herself on her knees and beg her father's pardon. She apologises to her sister, and a general reconciliation takes place. But before she has again left the room she has obtained her father's endorsement to Rastignac's bill. Even her most genuine fury had left coolness enough for calculation, and her burst of apparent tenderness was a skilful bit of comedy for squeezing one more drop of blood from her father and victim. That is a genuine stroke of Balzac.

Hideous as the performance appears when coolly stated, it must be admitted that the ladies have got into such terrible perplexities from tampering with the seventh commandment, that there is some excuse for their breaking the fifth. Whether such an accumulation of horrors is a legitimate process in art, and whether a healthy imagination would like to dwell upon such loathsome social sores, is another question. The comparison suggested with *King Lear* may illustrate the point. In Balzac all the subordinate details which Shakespeare throws in with a very slovenly touch are elaborately drawn, and contribute powerfully to the total impression. On the other hand, we never reach the lofty poetical heights of the grander scenes in *King Lear.* But the situation of the two heroes offers an instructive contrast. Lear is weak, but is never contemptible; he is the ruin of a gallant old king, is guilty of no degrading compliance, and dies like a man, with his 'good biting falchion' still grasped in his feeble hand. To change him into Goriot we must suppose that he had licked the hand which struck him, that he had helped on the adulterous intrigues of Goneril and Regan from sheer weakness, and that all his fury had been directed against Cornwall and Albany for objecting to his daughters' eccentric views of the obligation of the marriage vow. Paternal affection leading a man to the most trying self-sacrifice is a worthy motive for a great drama or romance; but Balzac is so anxious to intensify the emotion, that he makes even paternal affection morally degrading. Everything must be done to heighten the colouring. Our sympathies are to be excited by making the sacrifice as complete, and the emotion which prompts it as overpowering as possible; until at last the love of children becomes a monomania. Goriot is not only dragged through the mud of Paris, but he grovels in it with a will. In short, Balzac wants that highest power which shows itself by moderation, and commits a fault like that of an orator who emphasizes every sentence. With less expenditure of horrors, he would excite our compassion more powerfully. After a time the most highly-spiced meats begin to pall upon the palate. (pp. 326-33)

> Leslie Stephen, "Balzac's Novels," in his Hours in a Library, *Smith, Elder, & Co., 1874, pp. 299-348.*

Frederick Wedmore (essay date 1890)

[*Wedmore was an English journalist, critic, and novelist. In the following excerpt, he discusses Balzac's depiction of paternal self-sacrifice in* Le père Goriot.]

In a preface to a book not of his compiling—the *Répertoire de la Comédie Humaine,* by Messieurs Cerfberr and Christophe, which to the student is quite as necessary a possession as Monsieur de Lovenjoul's *Histoire des œuvres de H. de Balzac,*—Monsieur Paul Bourget, has expressed, very happily, the commonsense opinion that more than half of Balzac's triumph in the portraiture of the soul, in the portraiture of Society, was due to divination, to an intellectual second sight. Philarète Chasles—I think it was—had said so before him. A *"voyant"* had been the word. Monsieur Bourget puts it strongly, of course, when—alluding to Balzac's continual literary busyness—he says, in round terms, *"Balzac n'a pas eu le temps de vivre."* He is strictly accurate in adding that "the experience of this master of exact Literature was reduced to a minimum; but this minimum sufficed for him." "To the comparatively small number of *data* with which his observation had furnished him, he applied an analysis so intuitive that he discovered, behind the limited materials, the deep forces—the generative forces, if one may so call them."

Of course to do this, in some measure—to call the great out of the little: to divine much, where not much may be perceived or experienced—is ever the function of high novelist or dramatist—of the creative writer. But Balzac is an instance of such capacity to a very peculiar degree. In his treatment of love affairs no doubt divination counted. Yet Balzac, in his own person, knew something of Love—he had, at the least, come very near to it before he

was middle-aged: long before it was Madame de Hanska who occupied him the most. He knew nothing of paternity: there was no personal experience of that relationship to fall back upon as a guide. Yet of all passions, the one which he has described with the very fullest power is that passion of paternal self-sacrifice which made Père Goriot the creature, the slave, the ever-watchful and protecting genius of his child.

Few writers have been greater than Balzac in the exhibition of the moral qualities: no one has been more careful that they shall be presented with dignity, hedged in with honour, though the possessors of them need sometimes to be shown as of lives sordid and saddened, as of manners ungainly, of aspect almost repulsive. No fear, in any case, for the esteem in which we are to hold them. The flag is kept by Balzac spotless above the mire. Yet the width of Balzac's sympathy and the depth of his penetration must have made him, for his own part, as tolerant as he makes his Popinot in *L'Interdiction,* which we read for the portrait of a just, keen judge, a man of practical charity, never tired of well-doing.

I have classed, by implication, among "moral qualities," le Père Goriot's devotion to his daughters. Yet I know that he carried it to excess. I know that in his case devotion o'erreached itself, and that it fell "o' the other side." For, when to sacrifice himself has become to le Père Goriot a thing of habit, we behold him, in his daughters' interests, the ardent helper of their intrigues. They have been badly used, in some sort: they must be assisted to their consolations: at all costs, they must be made happy. Of course, the thought is repulsive. But when did le Père Goriot move in guarded circles solely—hear only words of goodness and discretion? When did he have the privilege of profiting by the examples of a blameless life, in an ideal Society, or in a world of politic restraint? We must take him for what he is—an ill-balanced, ill-educated soul, faulty, lovable: a lonely widower, in an obscure boarding-house, willingly stripping himself that the darlings of his heart may go in purple and fine linen. His surroundings have been base; the counsels of his companions, for all their outward respectability, dark and mean; his conceptions of Life—of some of its good things—were very limited, and must have been apt to be gross. He is ennobled, at all events, by the profundity of his affection.

The affection that le Père Goriot lavished was never in any sense returned. His daughters tolerated him. Scarcely even that. He was nothing but an unpresentable old man, who in his youth had made a fortune by astuteness and industry and successful dealings in vermicelli. He had educated his children—Anastasie and Delphine—and they had been enabled to contract marriages which were brilliant, instead of happy. He assisted Delphine in her loves, and Anastasie in her difficulties. It was not in either of them to dispense with his services, but they broke his heart by their neglect. Though both of them had been married in prosperity, they belonged to very different worlds. It was fitting that they should see each other but seldom; yet only accident prevented them from meeting at his death-bed—they might have quarrelled in his presence; they had done so before; and that had been one of his fears. At the last, it was impossible for Delphine to arrive. She fancied she was ill, and would not come. Then she would come, but must have money for her father; and Monsieur de Nucingen, her husband, must allow it her. He refused. She fainted. "*Mes filles, mes filles! Je veux les voir!*" had to be called in vain. Delphine's maid-servant came instead; and, when le Père Goriot was no longer conscious, Anastasie burst into the garret with her tardy tears and the repentance of an hour. Ingratitude has its degrees.

The keeper of the boarding-house—to whom Père Goriot owed a trifle she was uncertain of receiving—grudged him the sheets in which to die. But Rastignac and the young Bianchon—Delphine's lover, and his friend, a student of medicine—saw that a certain decency was kept: that a certain consideration—which Humanity, even when it is penniless, may conceivably claim—was paid to the obscure failure, who was passing away. The last sounds that le Père Goriot uttered, the last expressions that stirred upon his face, were sounds, expressions, of grateful, even joyous, recognition of what he thought to be his daughter's presence. The signs came from out of the depths—from out of the depths of his being. A day or two later the empty carriages of le Père Goriot's sons-in-law followed, in state and chilly ceremony, the humble hearse which bore him to his grave. The loving-kindness of the family that he had made, extended even so far as that.

There should be pointed out, in **Le Père Goriot,** as characteristic of Balzac—and nowadays there needs to be pointed out particularly—the unflinching fashion in which he attacks the difficult scene. At least one living writer, highly valued amongst us, expends a half of his dexterity in knowing what he must avoid. The "*scène à faire*"—in Monsieur Sarcey's phrase—is for him only the scene to be bridged across and passed over. It is the triumph of the great as distinguished from the clever—it is the triumph, one allows, of Mr. Thackeray, in *Vanity Fair*—to approach with fearlessness the critical moment, and, having been true already, to be truest of all there. Much of the other work may have been observant chronicle—the work now is revelation. The death scene in **Le Père Goriot** is of just that order.

Balzac—for all his vivid and immediate appreciation of the work of his own brain—would have considered it pretentious, perhaps, to have called this book a tragedy. A romance he is careful not to call it. What he calls it is a drama: "not that this history is *dramatic* in the usual sense of the word; though, when the work is accomplished"—he speaks on its first page—"some tears, perhaps, will have been shed, *intra muros, et extra.*" Will it be understood, he asks himself, beyond the limits of Paris? He is doubtful. "The details of these scenes, displaying observation and so much local colour, can scarcely be appreciated, except within the illustrious valley, so full of sufferings that are real, and of joys that are often false." And he puts his sordid boarding-house in the Rue Neuve-Sainte-Geneviève; since that, above all other streets, "*est comme un cadre de bronze, le seul qui convienne à ce récit.*" No one knows better than Balzac into what catacombs he is descending—to show there, not empty skulls, indeed, but "dried-up hearts."

Directly round Père Goriot moves, then, the sordid life of the boarding-house: Madame Vauquer, its mistress; the young Rastignac, gifted, ambitious, poor; Vautrin, whose "last incarnation" is elsewhere written of—a being of mysterious fascination, of magic influence, of horrible relationships—one or two elderly or middle-aged women, with tired eyes and withered mouths; and a certain Victorine Taillefer, sometimes hopeful because she is young, but whose life, whose very type, indeed, suggests, at present, only a narrow destiny, a limited personal experience. She lacked, Balzac reminds us, "the very making of a woman—frocks and love-letters." So much for the interior. Outside the boarding-house, surges, of course, Paris— the sense of its nearness and of its infinity—of its ambitions, triumphs, failures, intrigues—never quite lost, and sometimes very dominant. For the troubled figure of le Père Goriot, a stormy background—an immense and appropriate vista. (pp. 69-75)

> *Frederick Wedmore, in his* Life of Honoré de Balzac, *Walter Scott, 1890, 145 p.*

W. D. Howells   (essay date 1895)

[*Howells was the chief progenitor of American Realism and an influential literary critic during the late nineteenth and early twentieth centuries. He stands as one of the major literary figures of his era; having successfully weaned American literature from the sentimental Romanticism of its infancy, he earned the popular sobriquet "the Dean of American Letters." In the following excerpt, he criticizes the "exaggerated passions" of* Le père Goriot, *denying that it deserves to be called a novel.*]

[A] great master may sin against the "modesty of nature" in many ways, and I have felt this painfully in reading Balzac's romance—it is not worthy the name of novel—**Le Père Goriot,** which is full of a malarial restlessness, wholly alien to healthful art. After that exquisitely careful and truthful setting of his story in the shabby boarding-house, he fills the scene with figures jerked about by the exaggerated passions and motives of the stage. We cannot have a cynic reasonably wicked, disagreeable, egoistic; we must have a lurid villain of melodrama, a disguised convict, with a vast criminal organization at his command, and

> So dyed double red

in deed and purpose that he lights up the faces of the horrified spectators with his glare. A father fond of unworthy children, and leading a life of self-denial for their sake, as may probably and pathetically be, is not enough; there must be an imbecile, trembling dotard, willing to promote even the liaisons of his daughters to give them happiness and to teach the sublimity of the paternal instinct. The hero cannot sufficiently be a selfish young fellow, with alternating impulses of greed and generosity; he must superfluously intend a career of iniquitous splendor, and be swerved from it by nothing but the most cataclysmal interpositions. It can be said that without such personages the plot could not be transacted; but so much the worse for the plot. Such a plot had no business to be; and while actions so unnatural are imagined, no mastery can save fiction from contempt with those who really think about it. To Balzac it can be forgiven, not only because in his better mood he gave us such biographies as *Eugénie Grandet,* but because he wrote at a time when fiction was just beginning to verify the externals of life, to portray faithfully the outside of men and things. It was still held that in order to interest the reader the characters must be moved by the old romantic ideals; we were to be taught that "heroes" and "heroines" existed all around us, and that these abnormal beings needed only to be discovered in their several humble disguises, and then we should see every-day people actuated by the fine frenzy of the creatures of the poets. How false that notion was few but the critics, who are apt to be rather belated, need now be told. Some of these poor fellows, however, still contend that it ought to be done, and that human feelings and motives, as God made them and as men know them, are not good enough for novel-readers. (pp. 205-06)

> *W. D. Howells, "Criticism and Fiction," in his* My Literary Passions: Criticism & Fiction, *1895. Reprint by Kraus Reprint Co., 1968, pp. 193-282.*

George Saintsbury   (essay date 1907)

[*Saintsbury has been called the most influential English literary historian and critic of the late nineteenth and early twentieth centuries. His numerous literary histories and studies of European literature have established him as a leading critical authority. Saintsbury adhered to two distinct sets of critical standards: one for the novel and the other for poetry and drama. As a critic of novels, he maintained that "the novel has nothing to do with any beliefs, with any convictions, with any thoughts in the strict sense, except as mere garnishings. Its substance must always be life not thought, conduct not belief, the passions not the intellect, manners and morals not creeds and theories. . . . The novel is . . . mainly and firstly a criticism of life." As a critic of poetry and drama, Saintsbury was a radical formalist who frequently asserted that subject is of little importance, and that "the so-called 'formal' part is of the essence." In the following excerpt, he praises* Le père Goriot *as an exhibition of Balzac's best qualities.*]

Le Père Goriot perhaps deserves to be ranked as that one of Balzac's novels which has united the greatest number of suffrages, and which exhibits his peculiar merits, not indeed without any of his faults, but with the merits in eminent, and the faults not in glaring, degree. It was written (the preface is dated 1834) at the time when his genius was at its very height, when it had completely burst the strange shell which had so long enveloped and cramped it, when the scheme of the *Comédie Humaine* was not quite finally settled (it never was that), but elaborated to a very considerable extent, when the author had already acquired most of the knowledge of the actual world which he possessed, and when his physical powers were as yet unimpaired by his enormous labour and his reckless disregard of "burning the candle at both ends." Although it exhibits, like nearly all his work, the complication of interest and scheme which was almost a necessity to him, that complication is kept within reasonable bounds, and managed

with wonderful address. The history of Goriot and his daughters, the fortunes of Eugène de Rastignac, and the mysterious personality and operations of Vautrin, not only all receive due and unperplexed development, but work upon each other with that correspondence and interdependence which form the rarest gift of the novelist, and which, when present, too commonly have attached to them the curse of over-minuteness and complexity. No piece of Balzac's Dutch painting is worked out with such marvellous minuteness as the Pension Vauquer, and hardly any book of his has more lifelike studies of character.

It would, however, not be difficult to find books with an almost, if not quite, equal accumulation of attractions, which have somehow failed to make the mark that has been made by *Le Père Goriot.* And the practised critic of novels knows perfectly well why this is. It is almost invariably, and perhaps quite invariably, because there is no sufficiently central interest, or because that interest is not of the broadly human kind. Had Goriot had no daughters, he would undoubtedly have been a happier man (or a less happy, for it is possible to take it both ways); but the history of his decadence and death never could have been such a good novel. It is because this history of the daughters—not exactly unnatural, not wholly without excuse, but as surely murderesses of their father as Goneril and Regan—at once unites and overshadows the whole, because of its intensity, its simple and suasive appeal, that *Le Père Goriot* holds the place it does hold. That it owes something in point of suggestion to *Lear* does not in the least impair its claims. The circumstances and treatments have that entire difference which, when genius is indebted to genius, pays all the score there is at once. And besides, *Lear* has offered its motive for three hundred years to thousands and millions of people who have been writing plays and novels, and yet there is only one *Père Goriot.*

It is, however, a fair subject of debate for those who like critical argument of the nicer kind, whether Balzac has or has not made a mistake in representing the ex-dealer in floury compounds as a sort of idiot outside his trade abilities and his love for his daughters. That in doing so he was guided by a sense of poetical justice and consistency—the same sense which made Shakespeare dwell on the ungovernable temper and the undignified haste to get rid of the cares of sovereignty that bring on and justify the woes of Lear—is undeniable. But it would perhaps not have been unnatural, and it would have been even more tragic, if the *ci-devant* manufacturer had been represented as more intellectually capable, and as ruining himself in spite of his better judgment. On this point, however, both sides may be held with equal ease and cogency, and I do not decide either way. Of the force and pathos of the actual representation, no two opinions are possible. There is hardly a touch of the one fault which can be urged against Balzac very often with some, and sometimes with very great, justice—the fault of exaggeration and phantasmagoric excess. Here at least the possibilities of actual life, as translatable into literature, are not one whit exceeded; and the artist has his full reward for being true to art.

Almost equally free from the abnormal and the gigantic is the portraiture of Rastignac. Even those who demur to the description of Balzac as an impeccable chronicler of society must admit the extraordinary felicity of the pictures of the young man's introduction to the drawing-rooms of Mesdames de Restaud and de Beauséant. Neither Fielding nor Thackeray—that is to say, no one else in the world of letters—could have drawn with more absolute vividness and more absolute veracity a young man, not a *parvenu* in point of birth, not devoid of native cleverness and "star," but hampered by the consciousness of poverty and by utter ignorance of the actual ways and current social fashions of the great world when he is first thrown, to sink or swim, into this great world itself. We may pass from the certain to the dubious, or at least the debatable, when we pass from Rastignac's first appearance to his later experiences. Here comes in what has been said . . . as to the somewhat fantastic and imaginary, the conventional and artificial character of Balzac's world. But it must be remembered that for centuries the whole structure of Parisian society has been to a very great extent fantastic and imaginary, conventional and artificial. Men and women have always played parts there as they have played them nowhere else. And it must be confessed that some of the parts here, if planned to the stage, are played to the life—that of Madame de Beauséant especially.

It is Vautrin on whom Balzac's decriers, if they are so hardy as to attack this most unattackable book of his at all, must chiefly fasten. It was long ago noticed—indeed, sober eyes both in France and elsewhere noticed it at the time—that the criminal, more or less virtuous, more or less terrible, more or less superhuman, exercised a kind of sorcery over minds in France from the greatest to the least at this particular time, and even later. Not merely Balzac, but Victor Hugo and George Sand, succumbed to his fascinations; and after these three names it is quite unnecessary to mention any others. And Balzac's proneness to the enormous and gigantesque made the fascination peculiarly dangerous in his case. Undoubtedly the Vautrin who talks to Rastignac in the arbour is neither quite a real man nor quite the same man who is somewhat ignominiously caught by the treachery of his boarding-house fellows; undoubtedly we feel that with him we have left Shakespeare a long way behind, and are getting rather into the society of Bouchardy or Eugène Sue. But the genius is here likewise, and, as usual, it saves everything.

How it extends to the minutest and even the least savoury details of Madame Vauquer's establishment, how it irradiates the meannesses and the sordidnesses of the inhabitants there are those who have read know. . . . Let it only be repeated, that if the rarest and strangest charms which Balzac can produce are elsewhere, nowhere else is his charm presented in a more pervading and satisfactory manner. (pp. xi-xiv)

> *George Saintsbury, in a preface to* Old Goriot
> *by Honoré de Balzac, J. M. Dent & Sons, 1907,*
> *pp. xi-xiv.*

George E. Downing   (essay date 1932)

[*In the following excerpt, Downing examines the technical aspects of the detailed presentation of Maison Vauquer and praises Balzac's ability to harmonize setting and characterization.*]

Le Père Goriot is certainly one of the best examples of the Balzacian novel, and one that illustrates most transparently our author's method of working. A letter to Mme Balzac, written toward the end of September, 1834, indicates his own satisfaction in the novel: ". . . c'est une œuvre plus belle encore qu'*Eugénie Grandet;* du moins, j'en suis plus content." One feels that this is a more honest statement in its pride than the one in a letter to Mme Hanska, in which he implies doubts about the merit of the book. He there says that although his readers—friends and enemies alike—are calling *Le Père Goriot* better than all of his previous work, he is unable to judge it for himself. Obviously circumstances combined to bring out *Le Père Goriot* at exactly the proper moment. André Le Breton notes [in *Balzac, l'homme et l'oeuvre,* 1905] that Balzac in the middle and late thirties was at the height of his powers: before 1832, his observation inclined to superficiality; after 1840, it was more and more falsified by contact with his own personality. But in 1834–35 his creative force was brought to bear upon a plot which would immediately suggest Balzacian treatment. He thus describes the story to Mme Hanska: "La peinture d'un sentiment si grand que rien ne l'épuise, ni les froissements, ni les blessures, ni l'injustice; un homme qui est *père* comme un *saint, un martyr est chrétien.*" He revels in the story. The massing and piling-up of detail after detail, insult after insult, *douleur* after *douleur,* is Balzac at his best. Perhaps, says Jules Bertaut [in *Le Père Goriot de Balzac,* 1928], an incident in real life is responsible for the story: Balzac often needed an actual occurrence to start his mind on its journey to an imagined world. The same author quotes an undated note by Balzac which outlines the plot: "Sujet du Père Goriot.—Un brave homme—pension bourgeoise—600 fr. de rente—s'étant dépouillé pour ses filles qui toutes deux ont 50,000 fr. de rente, mourant comme un chien." It would be interesting to know how long this bare outline remained in Balzac's mind before it was elaborated into the structure of the completed novel.

Bertaut continues his discussion of the plot with conjectures as to its origin. The theme, the suffering of a parent at the hands of ungrateful children, is, of course, an old one, an example of the classical themes that often fascinated Balzac. But for the grave and majestic paternal love of classical treatments he substituted a peculiarly nineteenth-century romantic-realistic monomania, and thus enlivened a theme which had grown into a conventional formula. It is worth noticing that the same turn was being given to established formulas in French painting contemporary with Balzac. The classicism of Corot is very apparent in his versions of the landscape-painting of Poussin and Claude: this no one could deny. Yet his developed style, which is clear in the 1830's, usually throws a romantic veil over the clarity of his predecessors' conceptions of nature, and a veil whose tremulousness is based upon that careful, realistic study of light which makes Corot a precursor of the Impressionists. Doubtless the proportions of classicism, romanticism, and realism are different in Corot from what they are in Balzac. One might more readily connect the author of *Le Père Goriot* with Daumier and Courbet;

but the work of Daumier and Courbet also, being French, has classical strains. There is more obviously a touch of what is northern and grotesque in the passions which control Balzac's novels. More conscious classicists than Balzac felt this; thus, Bertaut quotes Saint-Marc Girardin: "La monomanie attriste ou fait rire, selon les goûts, mais elle n'attire pas." But whatever the specific sources for the plot of *Le Père Goriot,* there is no reason to deny that its classical universality was understood by its author.

What is more, the fire of his energy as a creator fused, for him, the disparate elements whose simultaneous appearance in a single work worried his critics. Thus, to such criticisms of *Le Père Goriot* as the one which appeared under the initials "I. C. T." in the *Constitutionnel,* he replied: "Le père Goriot est comme le chien du meurtrier qui lèche la main de son maître quand elle est teinte de sang: il ne discute pas, il ne juge pas, il aime." Balzac's reply to W. D. Howells, if he could have made one, would probably have had much the same ring. The separate parts of the story are of a piece, however curious may be the blend they represent of what we are pleased to call classical, or romantic, or realistic. It is only for the sake of discussion that one searches out their diverse parentage. Balzac's agents for the fusion, not only of the material of the novel itself, but also of the modes of thought which are characteristic of the author, are the passions which control his characters: in *Le Père Goriot,* Goriot's love for his daughters and Rastignac's ambitions. Through such passions we realize what to Balzac was *truth.*

It is upon the reality of life as he sees it that he insists at once; and whether his truth is classical, romantic, or realistic, it is first of all Balzacian. The reality of the story to Balzac is impressed upon the reader in the opening paragraph of *Le Père Goriot:* "Après avoir lu les secrètes infortunes du père Goriot, vous dînerez avec appétit en mettant votre insensibilité sur le compte de l'auteur, en le taxant d'exagération, en l'accusant de poësie. Ah! sachez-le: ce drame n'est ni une fiction, ni un roman." There follows immediately the arresting, italicized break into English: "*All is true,* il est si véritable, que chacun peut en reconnaître les éléments chez soi, dans son cœur peut-être." And after this, Balzac spares neither himself nor the reader. The turns of the screw come with mechanical fatality, and we see Père Goriot sink farther and farther into his grave with each new spadeful of earth thrown upon him by his daughters.

The concrete point of departure in *Le Père Goriot* for Balzac's technique of truth, his presentation of his particular and peculiar version of the "slice of life," is the *pension bourgeoise.* Balzac wanted not only to tell the story of Père Goriot but to fill that pigeonhole in the **Comédie humaine** which the bourgeois boarding-house represents in the life of Paris. And he has stuffed it full, risking tediousness and the loss of the reader's interest. After the first exciting and objective description of the *pension* itself, the details which bring it back to life are trivial per se, but the whole is convincing and complete. For after all, are not the lives of the *pensionnaires* a series of little nothings? And so the plays upon words, the commonplaces on life, the little economies of Mme Vauquer, all mount to a telling effect. Any-

one who has lived in a boarding-house will recognize the atmosphere. Jokes that never die, complaints against the absent landlady, compliments for her in her presence, roomers with their various peculiarities (one knows what each will do under any given circumstances)—these are the things Balzac emphasizes. And these form the life of a *pension*—not only of Mme Vauquer's, but of any French *pension* and of any American boarding-house.

Probably the classical tinge to Balzac's realism shows in no way more clearly than in the claims to universality with which he invests his observations. The Pension Vauquer does not merely fill the boarding-house pigeonhole in Paris. Balzac says of it: "Une réunion semblable devait offrir et offrait en petit les éléments d'une société complète." This representative character is implied in other ways. Père Goriot himself is a universal type: Balzac bids his readers look around and see that this is so. The women of the story are also types. There is Mme de Beauséant, the good aristocrat, Mme de Restaud, the flighty one; Mme Vauquer, the penny-pinching landlady; Victorine Taillefer, the saintly young girl. In *Le Père Goriot* there are fourteen important generalizations regarding women, which demonstrate Balzac's pride in his knowledge of them. Other generalizations, about sixty-five in all, are also interesting; they include nine on human nature, ten on young men (Rastignac represents one type), fourteen on the sociological features of Paris, four on sociology in general, and sixteen others that one cannot classify without becoming needlessly didactic.

It is through Balzac's intimate living with his characters that they become universal types; and, in the same vein, even his materialism has a personal force. His conception of man as an animal and his fondness for animalisms are well illustrated in *Le Père Goriot.* There are forty-three important animalisms, many of which will be treated later in relation to characterization. Money is also a great force in the story. There are thirty-six references to money, other than mere passing allusions. Even Père Goriot, symbol of paternal love, and therefore, one would think, not entirely materialistic, says "L'argent, c'est la vie." There are several interesting references to exact amounts. The forced reduction of Goriot's rent, in fact, forms a tap in his abasement: when Goriot first comes to live in the *pension,* he pays one hundred francs a month; later, he moves to the next floor above, and pays seventy-five; finally, he moves again, and pays only forty-five francs. The exact amounts even of tips are given. We find several business transactions, notably that by which Goriot raises the money for his daughter's ball dress, and that dishonest one by which the Baron de Nucingen is to become wealthy.

The sociological features of the story are no less typically Balzacian: for example, the contrasting of different social levels. Nearly every time that Rastignac returns to the *pension* after having been in Parisian society, or goes out into the world from the Rue Neuve-Sainte-Geneviève, the contrast is made. (It will be remembered that this practice of making a character act as a shuttle between two milieux is a common one with Balzac.) For instance, during the scene in which Rastignac dines with Mme de Nucingen in the apartment she has furnished for him, Balzac says: "Ce dernier contraste entre ce qu'il voyait et ce qu'il venait de voir, dans un jour où tant d'irritations avaient fatigué son cœur et sa tête, détermina chez Rastignac un accès de sensibilité nerveuse." Some of the most interesting sociological references are those to Paris, personified in various ways. There are more than a dozen of these. The idea is a favorite one with Balzac: to picture Paris as an executioner, or as a stream that overwhelms rich and poor, young and old. (pp. 138-42)

The transition from Balzac's rendering of a heartlessly impartial Paris to the Balzacian conception of realistic impersonality is short. Our author thinks of his characters as swept along by the march of events; he apparently expresses little sympathy for them; yet, by piling up events against them, he deepens their wounds, effectively enlisting the sympathy of the reader. The death of Goriot will illustrate. The old man lies in his room, listening for his daughters who do not come. Here we should certainly expect the author to soften his hard blows, if he does so anywhere. Not in the least. Bianchon launches into a discussion of the characteristics of the disease and the possible circumstances of Goriot's death, according to the form the fever may take. The reader may possibly be struck with the inappropriateness of the discussion, but not so Balzac. Here is a turn of the screw which is mercilessly pressing Goriot. It is a fact, it happened, it must be stated—and Balzac understands its effectiveness.

Such monumental building of a scene is only one instance of the solidity of Balzac's writing in *Le Père Goriot.* We have firm ground upon which to proceed from the beginning. The first sixteen pages of the novel (in the Conard edition) are concerned with a description of the *pension* and its environs, a comprehensive picture indeed. Although the narrative does not at once introduce the reader into the back court of the house, this area is nevertheless described, even to its dimensions ("large d'environ vingt pieds"). The typical prospectus which Mme Vauquer sent out is quoted. Balzac's mocking, heavy humor adds to the exposition two significant details: the sign over the gate reading "Pension bourgeoise des deux sexes et autres"; and the statue of Cupid painted with apparent irrelevance on the garden wall.

Le Père Goriot is noteworthy for the number of important reappearing characters which it includes, and for references to other stories. In both of these ways the novel is solidified. The diamonds of Mme de Restaud, for example, form an important link with the earlier novel, *Gobseck.* And *Le Père Goriot* prepares the ground for many other stories; its characters are given a start which carries them into other phases of the *Comédie humaine.* Among the most important reappearing characters are Mme de Beauséant, Horace Bianchon, Vautrin (properly called Jacques Collin), Nucingen (husband and wife), Maxime de Trailles, and Derville. The most important of all, and one of the great creations of the *Comédie humaine,* is Rastignac, who reappears in twenty-one other novels. There are, in all, thirty-five reappearing characters. Thus, *Le Père Goriot* is in the very heart of the *Comédie humaine,* and it is not surprising that several authorities recommend

our seeking an introduction to that comprehensive work by reading this novel first.

The outstanding technical elements in *Le Père Goriot* are those to which the reader has by now become accustomed. As already suggested, the total exposition forms a large part of the novel. On a somewhat rough estimate of the proportions of exposition and narration, the former occupies about one-third of the whole.

The Balzacian types of detail and their varied uses are best studied in the many descriptions. The examination of detail in *Le Père Goriot* takes us at once to the *pension bourgeoise.* In the famous opening description, Balzac has a very definite method of approach. First we are introduced into the quarter in which the *pension* is located; then we come into the street. We stop a moment before the gate. Next we go into the little garden, which we examine along with the court at the back. Soon we enter the house, and are conducted from bottom to top systematically. In this progression, detail after detail is added with cumulative effect. As for the quarter: "L'homme le plus insouciant s'y attriste comme tous les passants, le bruit d'une voiture y devient un événement, les maisons y sont mornes, les murailles y sentent la prison. . . . Nul quartier de Paris n'est plus horrible, ni, disons-le, plus inconnu." The street is "un cadre de bronze" for the story to be told. Presently the keynote of the *pension* is struck thus in the description of the dining-room: "Enfin, là regne la misère sans poësie; une misère économe, concentrée, râpée."

The whole of the interior is in harmony with this note, even to the ironic pictured wall paper of the salon— representing the feast given to Ulysses' son. The salon exhales an "odeur de pension," but is elegant and perfumed in comparison to the dining-room. The furniture of that scene of cheer is described in one breath as "vieux, crevassé, pourri, tremblant, rongé, manchot, borgne, invalide, expirant." The carafes on the sideboard are sticky, and the cat drinks the milk out of the bowl of the *pensionnaires.* The walls of the dining-room are faded and exhibit the strange patterns left by dirty fingers; the napkins of the boarders are wine-spotted; and the tablecloth is so dirty that one can write his name on it with his fingernail.

Balzac gets deeper and deeper into his description and gives "unrelated bits" whose only purpose is to solidify and complete the picture. Thus we learn that the wall paper presents scenes from *Télémaque,* in which the most important personages are colored; the plates in the dining-room are thick, bordered with blue, and were made in Tournai; there is a barometer out of which a priest comes when it rains.

The long description of the *pension* irritates Faguet, who complains [in *Balzac,* 1913] that Balzac describes for the sake of describing, and remarks that the *pension* explains, as environment, only the character of Mme Vauquer. Stanley L. Galpin points out [in "The Influence of Environment in *Le Père Goriot*" in *MLN* XXXII (1917)], however, that the Pension Vauquer formed most of the environment of Rastignac; and that the contrast of the luxury of Parisian society with the squalor of the *pension* played a large part in arousing his worldly ambition and therefore is directly responsible for his resolve, "A nous deux maintenant!" It might further be said that it is the total weight of Balzac's descriptions, together with their completeness, which provides the *raison d'être* as well as the background for certain peculiar movements of his characters.

After having created the *pension,* Balzac passes easily to the characters who live in it. Here his will to harmonize is given full sway. When Mme Vauquer enters, he says that she is "en harmonie avec cette salle où suinte le malheur." Again: "Son jupon de laine tricotée, qui dépasse sa première jupe faite avec une vieille robe, et dont la ouate s'échappe par les fentes de l'étoffe lézardée, *résume* le salon, la salle à manger, le jardinet, *annonce* la cuisine et *fait pressentir* les pensionnaires." Mme Vauquer belongs to that type of "women who have had their troubles." After keynoting her as a part of the house, its personification in fact, Balzac continues to add harmonious details. The animalisms are interesting. Mme Vauquer is as fat as a church rat, and has a nose (another Balzacian nose!) like the beak of a parrot.

Père Goriot himself is given a keynote shortly after his first entrance on the stage, although this keynote is more in the nature of a prophecy than a description of the old man as we first meet him. Balzac says: "Ce devait être une bête solidement bâtie, capable de dépenser tout son esprit en sentiment."

The animalisms used in connection with Goriot are probably the most persuasive in the novel; given in succession, they show clearly his decline. He is called, in order, "un vieux matou," "un mollusque," "une bête brute," "un vieux rat sans queue" though with an "œil d'aigle"; his love for his daughters is "canine," and he wants to be "le petit chien à leurs genoux." We read, "Le père Goriot saisit cette parole du vol comme un chien saisit un mouvement de son maître." He calls himself "un vieux loup," but later "un chien qui crève." Finally, he loses all hope and says, "Mourrai-je donc comme un chien?" and on his deathbed "il pousse des cris plaintifs et inarticulés à la manière des animaux qui ont une grande douleur à exprimer." Obviously, these animalisms symbolize a progressive derogation.

Another of Balzac's methods for harmonizing his characters is by the use of gestures and of glances full of meaning. These are frequently combined with animalisms, which may be conventional or not. Rastignac has the eyes of a lynx, which go along with his "ténacité méridionale." Vautrin often looks at people with "un de ces regards par lesquels cet homme semblait s'initier aux secrets les plus cachés du cœur." Sometimes his eyes burned like those of a wildcat. He bounds like a lion. On one occasion, he makes "un mouvement de joie semblable à la sourde expression d'un pêcheur qui sent un poisson au bout de sa ligne." The *regard* of Père Goriot is, above all, *niaïs,* and he has a way of raising his head, usually bowed, when he hears people talking about him. The summary of all of the boarders in the Pension Vauquer is striking, as concerns their expressions: these faces are cold, hard, and inexpressive, defaced like wornout money. Later, they are all said to resemble oysters on a rock.

Balzac, as usual, has accumulated topical references in *Le Père Goriot,* in order to give historical background for the story. Salient details of this type are the mention of the warships "le Vengeur" and "le Warwick," together with "l'armée de la Loire," and the various pieces being played in Parisian theaters. Other details are brought in purely to furnish local color. Perhaps the best example of this trick is the *diorama* business, which the author uses with telling effect in creating the atmosphere of his *pension. . . .* A cruel play upon this word furnishes a turning of the screw in the final wind-up of the story. Both of these types of detail—whether suggesting historical or local color—are scattered; no attempt is made to bring them into focus, for they are merely background. Another type of scattered detail is found in the little mannerisms with which Balzac endows his characters. There is Mme Vauquer's habit of pronouncing the word *tilleul "tieuille,"* as well as Poiret's inane, parrot-like repetition of what some one else has said.

There are a few "documents" in which the assumed style is perfect. One of the best is the prospectus for the Pension Vauquer:

> MAISON VAUQUER. "C'était, disait-elle, une des plus anciennes et des plus estimées pensions bourgeoises du pays latin. Il y existait une vue des plus agréables sur la vallée des Gobelins (on l'apercevait du troisième étage), et un *joli* jardin, au bout duquel s' ÉTENDAIT une ALLEE de tilleuls."

The two long letters, one from Rastignac's mother and one from his sister Laure are again excellent examples of the successful use of an assumed style.

A few other minor points should be mentioned. In accord with Balzac's zeal for documentation is the criminal slang or argot used picturesquely by Vautrin. Then too, the names of some of the characters are obviously chosen to fit the person. If we change Michonneau to Michonnette, and Poiret to Poireau, as Christophe does in the novel, we have, respectively, a little old loaf of bread and a wart.

The style of the novel is, for the most part, simple. It is the usual thing, of course, with Balzac, to write clearly and swiftly when he is taken up with narrative; but in *Le Père Goriot,* the exposition is lucid too. There are, however, exceptions to this statement. Take for instance this thought: "Si les mélancoliques ont besoin du tonique des coquetteries, peut-être les gens nerveux ou sanguins décampent-ils si la résistance dure trop. En d'autres termes, l'élégie est aussi essentiellement lymphatique que le dithyrambe est bilieux." This is the sort of heavy technical language that makes two readings necessary to grasp a not very important meaning. Again, the writing may become ponderously scientific: "Sans doute les idées se projettent en raison directe de la force avec laquelle elles se conçoivent, et vont frapper là où le cerveau les envoie, par une loi mathématique comparable à celle qui dirige les bombes au sortir du mortier." But these are exceptions. Generally, the writing is swift and transparent: we recall Lamartine's statement that what is felt vividly is written quickly. (pp. 143-48)

George E. Downing, "A Famous Boarding-House: 'Le Père Goriot'," in Studies in Balzac's Realism *by E. Preston Dargon and others, The University of Chicago Press, 1932, pp. 136-50.*

An excerpt from *Le père Goriot*

When [Rastignac] reached the rue Neuve-Sainte-Geneviève he ran up to his room, came down with ten francs for the cabby, and went into the disgusting dining-room, where he saw the eighteen diners feeding like animals at a trough. He was revolted at the sight of such wretchedness and the appearance of the room. The transition was too abrupt, the contrast too complete, not to arouse in him cravings of boundless ambition. On the one hand the fresh and charming images of the most elegant society, young and lively figures in a setting composed of marvels of art and luxury, minds fired with passion and poetry; on the other, dismal pictures edged with grime, faces on which passions had left behind only their strings and mechanism. The lesson which the fury of a woman scorned had wrung from Madame de Beauséant, her specious offers came back into his memory, and this misery was commentary enough. Rastignac resolved to open up two parallel lines of advance in his assault on fortune, to rely both on knowledge and love, to be a learned doctor of law and a man of fashion. He was still very much a child! These two lines are asymptotes which can never meet.

Honoré de Balzac, in his Père Goriot, *translated by A. J. Krailsheimer, Oxford University Press, 1991.*

Martin Turnell (essay date 1950)

[*An English critic, Turnell wrote many studies of French literature and translated the works of Jean-Paul Sartre, Guy de Maupassant, Blaise Pascal, and Paul Valéry. In the following excerpt, he contests evaluations of* Le père Goriot *as Balzac's masterpiece, criticizing the work as sentimental and melodramatic.*]

The view that *Le Père Goriot* is Balzac's masterpiece seems to be common to his admirers and to hostile critics like Leslie Stephen and Henry James who both wrote damaging essays on him. This is a matter on which the critic has no right to temporize. I must therefore record my own opinion that far from being a masterpiece, it is as a whole one of the worst of Balzac's mature works, that it is mainly interesting as an illustration of his most characteristic vices as a novelist and that the chief reason for examining it in detail is to try to correct some of the exaggerated estimates of previous writers.

Nearly all Balzac's novels open with a factual statement which is apparently intended to prepare the way for the curious obsessions of which his characters are the victims:

Madame Vauquer, née de Conflans, est une vieille femme qui, depuis quarante ans, tient à Paris une pension bourgeoise établie rue Neuve-Sainte-Geneviève, entre le quartier latin et le faubourg Saint-Marcel.

[Madame Vauquer, *née* de Conflans, is an old woman who for forty years has run a middle-class Paris boarding-house which stands in the Rue Neuve-Sainte-Geneviève between the Latin Quarter and the Faubourg Saint-Marcel.]

On the next page we find the first attempt to link physical squalor and human misery:

Les particularités de cette Scène pleine d'observation et de couleur locale ne peuvent être appréciées qu'entre les buttes Montmartre et les hauteurs de Montrouge, dans cette illustre vallée de plâtras incessamment près de tomber et de ruisseaux noirs de boue; vallée remplie de souffrances réelles, de joies souvent fausses, et si terriblement agitée, qu'il faut je ne sais quoi d'exorbitant pour y produire une sensation de quelque durée.

[The details of this Scene which is full of observation and local colour can only be appreciated between the rising ground of Montmartre and the heights of Montrouge in the illustrious valley of broken bricks and mortar always on the verge of collapse and streams black with mud; a valley filled with real suffering and joy which is often false and so terribly agitated that it needs a suggestion of the extravagant to create any impression of permanency.]

Whatever his critics may think, Balzac liked to insist on the realism or supposed realism of his work, and it is no accident that the word *observation* turns up in the first sentence of this characteristically melodramatic passage. *Tomber* is a key word. The spectacle of buildings on the point of collapse looks forward to the moral collapse of Balzac's simple, worthy merchant. *Terriblement* and *exorbitant* are both tell-tale words. For here, as surely as in **L'Illustre Gaudissart,** the novelist seems without realizing it to point out exactly what he intends to do. A drama is about to unfold in which compared with normal standards the emotions will appear 'exorbitant' and which will (he hopes) strike the reader as 'terrible'.

A few pages later he switches from the exterior to the interior of the *pension*:

Cette première pièce exhale une odeur sans nom dans la langue, et qu'il faudrait appeler l'*odeur de pension.* Elle sent le renfermé, le moisi, le rance; elle donne froid, elle est humide au nez, elle pénètre les vêtements; elle a le goût d'une salle où l'on a dîné; elle pue le service, l'office, l'hospice.

[The first room exudes a nameless odour which should be called *the boarding-house smell*. It is an airless, mouldy, rancid smell; it gives you a chilly feeling; it is damp to the nostrils; it seeps into your clothes; it has the taste of a room where people have been eating; it stinks of meals, the pantry, the poor-house.]

The use of the present tense both in this and in the first passage that I quoted is intentional. The novelist's aim is to convince us that this *pension* still exists, that we have only to go as far as the Rue Neuve-Sainte-Geneviève to see the sign, 'MAISON VAUQUER: Pension Bourgeoise des deux sexes et autres', and arrive at the scene of the 'terrible drama' which he is about to relate. And the piling up of adjectives and images of physical decay does in the end give us a sickening sense of the stench of the building.

Balzac, we know, was convinced that once he had established the physical existence of the milieu—his preoccupation with 'atmosphere' is [a] link with the writers of 'detective fiction'—he could make its inhabitants seem equally real to us:

> Aussi le spectacle désolant que présentait l'intérieur de cette maison se répétait-il dans le costume de ses habitués, également délabrés. Les hommes portaient des redingotes dont la couleur était devenue problématique, des chaussures comme il s'en jette au coin des bornes dans les quartiers élégants, du linge élimé, des vêtements qui n'avaient plus que l'âme. Les femmes avaient des robes passées, reteintes, déteintes, de vieilles dentelles raccommodées, des gants glacés par l'usage, des collerettes toujours rousses et des fichus éraillés.

> [Thus the desolate spectacle presented by the interior of the house was reflected in the residents' clothes which were equally dilapidated. The men wore frock coats whose colour had become problematic, shoes of the kind that are thrown out in the fashionable quarters of the city, worn linen, garments of which there was nothing left but the soul. The women wore dresses which were faded, redyed, faded again, old lace which had been mended, gloves which were shiny with use, collars which were always brownish and frayed shawls.]

The most important word in the passage is *désolant*. It illustrates the novelist's habit of working certain words—particularly words suggesting decay—with the result that they attract other words with similar associations. *Désolant* leads to *délabrés* which somehow evokes the *couleur problématique,* the *linge élimé* and the 'robes passées, reteintes, déteintes . . . des fichus éraillés'. This is apparently what M. Blanchot means by 'the paroxysmal unfolding of idea-characters and idea-situations' or 'the hallucinatory dance' of words. No doubt there is an internal logic about the process, a progressive withdrawal into the spectral world of the **Comédie humaine,** but the value of this form of creation is less evident.

In another place we are told: 'M. Poiret était une espèce de mécanique.' *Mécanique* was a favourite word of Balzac's, and it explains why we so often have the sensation that his characters are marionettes whose gestures, repeated over and over again, have a hypnotic effect which reminds us of a nightmare. They are grotesque and somehow frightening, but you feel that at any moment the springs may give way and the whole apparatus collapse into a mass of metal, rag and sawdust.

Balzac uses the same factual approach when he introduces Goriot himself:

> Le père Goriot, vieillard de soixante-neuf ans environ, s'était retiré chez madame Vauquer, en 1813, après avoir quitté les affaires.

> [Old Goriot, an old man of about sixty-nine, had gone to live at Madame Vauquer's in 1813 after retiring from business.]

In another passage he strikes a familiar note:

> Il devint progressivement maigre; ses mollets tombèrent; sa figure, bouffie par le contentement d'un bonheur bourgeois, se rida démesurément; son front se plissa, sa mâchoire se dessina . . . le bourgeois gros et gras . . . semblait être un septuagénaire hébété, vacillant, blafard.

> [He became steadily thinner; his calves fell; his face, puffy with the satisfaction of bourgeois happiness, became immeasurably wrinkled; his forehead furrowed; you could see the contours of his jaw . . . the big fat bourgeois looked like a man of seventy—dazed, shaky, wan.]

A few pages later we read:

> Le commerce des grains semblait avoir absorbé toute son intelligence. S'agissait-il de blés, de farines, de grenailles, de reconnaître leur qualité . . . Goriot n'avait pas son second. . . . Sorti de sa spécialité, de sa simple et obscure boutique . . . il redevenait l'ouvrier stupide et grossier, l'homme incapable de comprendre un raisonnement, insensible à tous les plaisirs de l'esprit, l'homme qui s'endormait au spectacle, un de ces Dolibans parisiens, forts seulement en bêtise.

> [The grain trade seemed to have absorbed the whole of his intelligence. When it came to judging the quality of corn, flour, tailings, Goriot had no equal. . . . Once he was off his special subject and away from his dark, simple shop he became the common stupid workman, the man who was incapable of following an argument or experiencing any of the pleasures of the mind, the man who fell asleep at the theatre, one of those Parisian Dolibans whose stupidity is their only endowment.]

There is no reason why a novelist should not put simple souls into his books, but his characters are after all the instruments which he uses to express a particular experience and we cannot be indifferent to the fact that the choice of a sentimentalized figure like Goriot is the sign of a defective view of life. For this account of his limitations is the prelude to the main theme of the book—the obsession with his daughters which brings him to destruction. We learn that after the death of a wife 'who was the object of a religious wonder to him, a boundless love'

> . . . le sentiment de la paternité se développa chez Goriot jusqu'à la *déraison*.

> [. . . with Goriot the sense of fatherhood was developed to the point of unreason.]

Again:

> L'éducation de ses deux filles fut naturellement *déraisonnable*.

> [The education of his daughters was naturally unreasonable.]

In order to be sure that we are well prepared for what is to come, Balzac cannot resist the observation:

> Ice se termine l'exposition de cette obscure mais *effroyable* tragédie parisienne.

> [Here ends the prologue to this obscure, but appalling Parisian tragedy.]

Nor is the background of the book more impressive. The reflections of Mme de Beauséant and Vautrin on 'life' are distressing in their banality:

> Vous saurez alors ce qu'est le monde, une réunion de dupes et de fripons.

> Vous croyez à quelque chose de fixe dans ce monde-là! Méprisez donc les hommes et voyez les mailles par où l'on peut passer à travers le réseau du Code. Le secret des grandes fortunes sans cause apparente est un crime oublié, parce qu'il a été proprement fait.

> [You'll find out then what the world's like—a collection of gulls and rogues.

> You believe in something unchanging in that world! Come, despise men and look for the loopholes by which one can get round the law. The secret behind all the great fortunes which have no apparent cause is a crime which was forgotten because it was properly carried out.]

The arrest of Vautrin shows Balzac at his worst:

> Le lendemain devait prendre place parmi les jours les plus extraordinaires de l'histoire de la maison Vauquer.

> Le forçat évadé jeta sur Eugène le regard froidement fascinateur que certains hommes éminemment magnétiques ont le don de lancer, et qui, dit-on, calme les fous de dans les maisons d'aliénés. Eugène trembla furieux tous ses membres.

> [The next day was destined to take its place among the most extraordinary in the history of the Maison Vauquer.

> The escaped convict shot a coldly fascinating glance at Eugène—the sort of glance which belongs to certain men who are in a high degree magnetic and which is said to soothe raging lunatics in asylums. Eugène trembled in every limb.]

Then comes the actual arrest:

> Le chef alla droit à lui, commença par lui donner sur la tête une tape si violemment appliquée, qu'il fit sauter la perruque et rendit à la tête de Collin toute son horreur. Accompagnées de cheveux rouge brique et courts qui leur donnaient un épouvantable caractère de force mêlée de ruse, cette tête et cette face, en harmonie avec le buste, furent intelligemment illuminées comme si les feux de l'enfer les eussent éclairées. . . . Collin devint un poète infernal où se peignirent tous les sentiments humains moins un seul, celui du repentir. Son regard était celui de l'archange déchu qui veut toujours la guerre.

> [The chief of police went straight up to him and began by giving him such a violent blow on the head that it knocked off his wig and restored to Collin's head all its horror. Covered with short brick-red hair which gave them an appalling character of strength mixed with cunning, the head and face which matched the body were intelligently lighted up as though the fires of hell had shone on them. . . . Collin became a poet of the nether regions in whom one saw all human feelings with a single exception—repentance. His look was that of the fallen archangel who always wants war.]

There would be no point in dwelling on this curious exhibition if the passages were not taken from what is generally regarded as one of the great French novels and if Vautrin had not been described by some critics as 'a great creation'. It is a perfect example of Balzac's Light Programme manner. For this is crude melodrama as distinct from what I have called Balzac's highly personal melodrama. Vautrin is a borrowing from the *roman frénétique* which has been transported bodily into the novel.

It is, perhaps, only fair to add that it is the story not so much of Vautrin as of Goriot's insensate passion for his daughters which has excited the admiration of critics on both sides of the Channel. Comparisons between Goriot and Lear have become commonplaces of criticism. Nor are they always as favourable to Shakespeare as one might expect. It was once claimed for **Eugénie Grandet** that it shows us a particular miser in a particular French province in the nineteenth century while in *L'Avare* Molière managed to give us no more than a picture of the Miser in abstract terms. Something of the same sort has been said of **Le Père Goriot.** In their comparisons, Balzac's critics have been at pains to point out that Goriot is a 'modern' Lear—a Marxist critic has recently called him a 'bourgeois' Lear—with the implication that he knows more about the detailed workings of the human mind than Shakespeare.

Turn to some characteristic passages and the comparison at once ceases to be even credible:

> 'Mon Dieu! pleurer, elle a pleuré?'

> 'La tête sur mon gilet,' dit Eugène.

> 'Oh! donnez-le-moi,' dit le père Goriot. 'Comment! il y a eu là des larmes de ma fille, de ma chère Delphine, qui ne pleurait jamais étant petite! Oh! je vous en achèterai un autre, ne le portez plus, laissez-le-moi.'

> 'Mes filles, mes filles! Anastasie, Delphine! je veux les voir. Envoyez-les chercher par la gendarmerie, de force! la justice est pour moi, tout est pour moi, la nature, le Code civil. Je proteste! La patrie périra si les pères sont foulés aux pieds. Cela est clair. La société, le monde, roulent sur la paternité, tout croule si les enfants n'aiment pas leurs pères. Oh! les voir, les entendre, n'importe ce qu'elles me diront, pourvu que j'entende leur voix, ca calmera mes douleurs. . . .'

> ['God! cry, she cried?'

'With her head on my waistcoat,' said Eugene.

'Oh! give it to me,' said old Goriot. 'What! my daughter's tears were there, my dear Delphine who never cried when she was little. Oh! I'll buy you another one. Don't wear it any more. Let me have it.'

'My daughters, my daughters! Anastasie, Delphine! I want to see them. Send the police to bring them by force! Justice is on my side. Everything is on my side—nature and the law. I protest! The country will perish if fathers are trampled underfoot. That's quite clear. Society and the world are founded on fatherhood. Everything will collapse if children don't love their fathers. Oh! just to see them, to hear them speak. It doesn't matter what they say, if only I could hear their voices it would ease my pain.']

There are many more pages in the same strain. It scarcely seems necessary to evoke the name of the greatest poet to place this cataract of words or Balzac's curious sentimentality in their true perspective. One critic [F. R. Leavis] has suggested that Shelley's *Cenci* is a more suitable term of comparison; and in both works we find the same hysteria, the same lack of feeling for language and the same surrender to the most dubious form of inspiration. (pp. 228-35)

> *Martin Turnell, "Balzac," in his* The Novel in France, *Hamish Hamilton, Ltd., 1950, pp. 209-46.*

Erich Auerbach   (essay date 1953)

[*Auerbach was a German-born American philologist and critic. He is best known for his* Mimesis: Dargestellte Wirklichkeit in der abendländischen Literatur (Mimesis: The Representation of Reality in Western Literature), *a landmark study in which he explores the interpretation of reality through literary representation. The breadth of Auerbach's learning is evident in the scope of the work: he begins with an examination of literary imitation in the Bible and Homer and progresses through literary history to an explication of the works of such modern writers as Marcel Proust and Virginia Woolf. In the following excerpt from* Mimesis, *he praises Balzac's "atmospheric realism" as a significant contribution to the development of modern realism.*]

Balzac, who had as great a creative gift [as Stendhal] and far more closeness to reality, seized upon the representation of contemporary life as his own particular task and, together with Stendhal, can be regarded as the creator of modern realism. He was sixteen years younger than Stendhal, yet his first characteristic novels appeared at almost the same time as Stendhal's, that is, about 1830. To exemplify his method of presentation we shall first give his portrait of the pension-mistress Madame Vauquer at the beginning of **Le Père Goriot** (1834). It is preceded by a very detailed description of the quarter in which the pension is located, of the house itself, of the two rooms on the ground floor; all this produces an intense impression of cheerless poverty, shabbiness, and dilapidation, and with the physical description the moral atmosphere is suggested. After

the furniture of the dining room is described, the mistress of the establishment herself finally appears:

Cette pièce est dans tout son lustre au moment où, vers sept heures du matin, le chat de Mme Vauquer précède sa maîtresse, saute sur les buffets, y flaire le lait que contiennent plusieurs jattes couvertes d'assiettes et fait entendre son *ronron* matinal. Bientôt la veuve se montre, attifée de son bonnet de tulle sous lequel pend un tour de faux cheveux mal mis; elle marche en traînassant ses pantoufles grimacées. Sa face vieillotte, grassouillette, du milieu de laquelle sort un nez à bec de perroquet; ses petites mains potelées, sa personne dodue comme un rat d'église, son corsage trop plein et qui flotte, sont en harmonie avec cette salle où suinte le malheur, oùs'est blottie la spéculation, et dont Mme Vauquer respire l'air chaudement fétide sans en être écœurée. Sa figure fraîche comme une première gelée d'automne, ses yeux ridés, dont l'expression passe du sourire prescrit aux danseuses à l'amer renfrognement de l'escompteur, enfin toute sa personne explique la pension, comme la pension implique sa personne. Le bagne ne va pas sans l'argousin, vous n'imagineriez pas l'un sans l'autre. L'embonpoint blafard de cette petite femme est le produit de cette vie, comme le typhus est la conséquence des exhalaisons d'un hôpital. Son jupon de laine tricotée, qui dépasse sa première jupe faite avec une vieille robe, et dont la ouate s'échappe par les fentes de l'étoffe lézardée, résume le salon, la salle à manger, le jardinet, annonce la cuisine et fait pressentir les pensionnaires. Quand elle est là, ce spectacle est complet. Agée d'environ cinquante ans, Mme Vauquer ressemble à toutes les femmes *qui ont eu des malheurs.* Elle a l'œil vitreux, l'air innocent d'une entremetteuse qui va se gendarmer pour se faire payer plus cher, mais d'ailleurs prête à tout pour adoucir son sort, à livrer Georges ou Pichegru, si Georges ou Pichegru étaient encore à livrer. Néanmoins elle est *bonne femme au fond,* disent les pensionnaires, qui la croient sans fortune en l'entendant geindre et tousser comme eux. Qu'avait été M. Vauquer? Elle ne s'expliquait jamais sur le défunt. Comment avait-il perdu sa fortune? "Dans les malheurs," répondaite-elle. Il s'était mal conduit envers elle, ne lui avait laissé que les yeux pour pleurer, cette maison pour vivre, et le droit de ne compatir à aucune infortune, parce que, disait-elle, elle avait souffert tout ce qu'il est possible de souffrir.

(The room is at its brilliant best when, about seven in the morning, Madame Vauquer's cat enters before its mistress, jumps up on the buffet, sniffs at the milk which stands there in a number of bowls covered over with plates, and emits its matutinal purring. Presently the widow appears, got up in her tulle bonnet, from beneath which hangs an ill-attached twist of false hair; as she walks, her wrinkled slippers drag. Her oldish, fattish face, from the middle of which juts a parrot-beak nose, her small, plump hands, her figure as well filled out as a churchwarden's, her loose, floppy bodice, are in harmony with the room, whose walls ooze misfortune, where speculation cowers, and whose warm and fetid air Madame Vauquer breathes without nausea. Her face, as chilly as a first fall frost, her wrinkled eyes, whose expression changes from the obligatory smile of a ballet-girl to the sour scowl of a sharper, her whole person, in short, explains the pension, as the pension implies her person. A prison requires a warder, you could not imagine the one without the other. The short-statured woman's blowsy *embonpoint* is the product of the life here, as typhoid is the consequence of the exhalations of a hospital. Her knitted wool petticoat, which is longer than her outer skirt (made of an old dress), and whose wadding is escaping by the gaps in the splitting material, sums up the drawing-room, the dining room, the little garden, announces the cooking and gives an inkling of the boarders. When she is there, the spectacle is complete. Some fifty years of age, Madame Vauquer resembles all women *who have had troubles*. She has the glassy eye, the innocent expression of a bawd who is about to make a scene in order to get a higher price, but who is at the same time ready for anything in order to soften her lot, to hand over Georges or Pichegru if Georges or Pichegru were still to be handed over. Nevertheless, she is *a good woman at heart*, the boarders say, and they believe, because they hear her moan and cough like themselves, that she has no money. What had Monsieur Vauquer been? She never gave any information about the deceased. How had he lost his money? "In troubles," she answered. He had acted badly toward her, had left her nothing but her eyes to weep with, this house for livelihood, and the right to be indulgent toward no manner of misfortune because, she said, she had suffered everything it is possible to suffer.)

The portrait of the hostess is connected with her morning appearance in the dining-room; she appears in this center of her influence, the cat jumping onto the buffet before her gives a touch of witchcraft to her entrance; and then Balzac immediately begins a detailed description of her person. The description is controlled by a leading motif, which is several times repeated—the motif of the harmony between Madame Vauquer's person on the one hand and the room in which she is present, the pension which she directs, and the life which she leads, on the other; in short, the harmony between her person and what we (and Balzac too, occasionally) call her milieu. This harmony is most impressively suggested: first through the dilapidation, the greasiness, the dirtiness and warmth, the sexual repulsiveness of her body and her clothes—all this being in harmony with the air of the room which she breathes without distaste; a little later, in connection with her face and its expressions, the motif is conceived somewhat more ethically, and with even greater emphasis upon the complementary relation between person and milieu: *sa personne explique la pension, comme la pension implique sa personne;* with this goes the comparison to a prison. There follows a more medical concept, in which Madame Vauquer's *embonpoint blafard* as a symptom of her life is compared to typhoid as the result of the exhalations in a hospital. Finally her petticoat is appraised as a sort of synthesis of the various rooms of the pension, as a foretaste

of the products of the kitchen, and as a premonition of the guests; for a moment her petticoat becomes a symbol of the milieu, and then the whole is epitomized again in the sentence: *Quand elle est là, ce spectacle est complet*—one need, then, wait no longer for the breakfast and the guests, they are all included in her person. There seems to be no deliberate order for the various repetitions of the harmony-motif, nor does Balzac appear to have followed a systematic plan in describing Madame Vauquer's appearance; the series of things mentioned—headdress, false hair, slippers, face, hands, body, the face again, eyes, corpulence, petticoat—reveal no trace of composition; nor is there any separation of body and clothing, of physical characteristics and moral significance. The entire description, so far as we have yet considered it, is directed to the mimetic imagination of the reader, to his memory-pictures of similar persons and similar milieux which he may have seen; the thesis of the "stylistic unity" of the milieu, which includes the people in it, is not established rationally but is presented as a striking and immediately apprehended state of things, purely suggestively, without any proof. In such a statement as the following, *ses petites mains potelées, sa personne dodue comme un rat d'église . . . sont en harmonie avec cette salle où suinte le malheur . . . et dont Mme Vauquer respire l'air chaudement fétide . . .* the harmony-thesis, with all that it includes (sociological and ethical significance of furniture and clothing, the deducibility of the as yet unseen elements of the milieu from those already given, etc.) is presupposed; the mention of prison and typhoid too are merely suggestive comparisons, not proofs nor even beginnings of proofs. The lack of order and disregard for the rational in the text are consequences of the haste with which Balzac worked, but they are nevertheless no mere accident, for his haste is itself in large part a consequence of his obsession with suggestive pictures. The motif of the unity of a milieu has taken hold of him so powerfully that the things and the persons composing a milieu often acquire for him a sort of second significance which, though different from that which reason can comprehend, is far more essential—a significance which can best be defined by the adjective demonic. In the dining-room, with its furniture which, worn and shabby though it be, is perfectly harmless to a reason uninfluenced by imagination, "misfortune oozes, speculation cowers." In this trivial everyday scene allegorical witches lie hidden, and instead of the plump sloppily dressed widow one momentarily sees a rat appear. What confronts us, then, is the unity of a particular milieu, felt as a total concept of a demonic-organic nature and presented entirely by suggestive and sensory means.

The next part of our passage, in which the harmony-motif is not again mentioned, pursues Madame Vauquer's character and previous history. It would be a mistake, however, to see in this separation of appearance on the one hand and character and previous history on the other a deliberate principle of composition; there are physical characteristics in this second part too (*l'œil vitreux*), and Balzac very frequently makes a different disposition, or mingles the physical, moral, and historical elements of a portrait indiscriminately. In our case his pursuit of her character and previous history does not serve to clarify either of them but rather to set Madame Vauquer's darkness "in the right light," that is, in the twilight of a petty and trivial demonism. So far as her previous history goes, the pension-mistress belongs to the category of women of fifty or thereabouts *qui ont eu des malheurs* (plural!); Balzac enlightens us not at all concerning her previous life, but instead reproduces, partly in *erlebte Rede,* the formless, whining, mendaciously colloquial chatter with which she habitually answers sympathetic inquiries. But here again the suspicious plural occurs, again avoiding particulars— her late husband had lost his money *dans les malheurs*— just as, some pages later, another suspicious widow imparts, on the subject of her husband who had been a count and a general, that he had fallen on LES *champs de bataille.* This conforms to the vulgar demonism of Madame Vauquer's character; she seems *bonne femme au fond,* she seems poor, but, as we are later told, she has a very tidy little fortune and she is capable of any baseness in order to improve her own situation a little—the base and vulgar narrowness of the goal of her egoism, the mixture of stupidity, slyness, and concealed vitality, again gives the impression of something repulsively spectral; again there imposes itself the comparison with a rat, or with some other animal making a basely demonic impression on the human imagination. The second part of the description, then, is a supplement to the first; after Madame Vauquer is presented in the first as synthesizing the milieu she governs, the second deepens the impenetrability and baseness of her character, which is constrained to work itself out in this milieu.

In his entire work, as in this passage, Balzac feels his milieux, different though they are, as organic and indeed demonic unities, and seeks to convey this feeling to the reader. He not only, like Stendhal, places the human beings whose destiny he is seriously relating, in their precisely defined historical and social setting, but also conceives this connection as a necessary one: to him every milieu becomes a moral and physical atmosphere which impregnates the landscape, the dwelling, furniture, implements, clothing, physique, character, surroundings, ideas, activities, and fates of men, and at the same time the general historical situation reappears as a total atmosphere which envelops all its several milieux. It is worth noting that he did this best and most truthfully for the circle of the middle and lower Parisian bourgeoisie and for the provinces; while his representation of high society is often melodramatic, false, and even unintentionally comic. He is not free from melodramatic exaggeration elsewhere; but whereas in the middle and lower spheres this only occasionally impairs the truthfulness of the whole, he is unable to create the true atmosphere of the higher spheres—including those of the intellect. (pp. 468-73)

> *Erich Auerbach, "In the Hôtel de la Mole," in his* Mimesis: The Representation of Reality in Western Literature, *translated by Willard R. Trask, 1953. Reprint by Princeton University Press, 1968, pp. 454-92.*

W. Somerset Maugham (essay date 1954)

[*Maugham was an English dramatist, short story writer, and novelist who is considered a skilled, cynical satirist.*

Best known for his autobiographical novel Of Human Bondage, *Maugham also achieved popular success with such plays as* Caesar's Wife, The Breadwinner, *and* Our Betters. *In the following excerpt, he explains why he considers* Le père Goriot *Balzac's best novel.*]

George Sand rightly said that each of Balzac's books was in fact a page of one great book, which would be imperfect if he had omitted that page. In 1833 he conceived the idea of combining the whole of his production into one whole under the name of *La Comédie Humaine.* When it occurred to him, he ran to see his sister: "Salute me," he cried, "because I'm quite plainly (*tout simplement*) on the way to become a genius." He described as follows what he had in mind: "The social world of France would be the historian, I should be merely the secretary. In setting forth an inventory of vice and virtues, in assembling the principal facts of the passions, in painting characters, in choosing the principal incidents of the social world, in composing types by combining the traits of several homogeneous characters, perhaps I could manage to write the history forgotten by so many historians, the history of manners and customs." It was an ambitious scheme. He did not live to carry it to completion. It is evident that some of the pages in the vast work he left, though perhaps necessary, are less interesting than others. In a production of such bulk, that was inevitable. But in almost all Balzac's novels there are two or three characters which, because they are obsessed by a simple, primitive passion, stand out with extraordinary force. It was in the depiction of just such characters that his strength lay; when he had to deal with a character of any complexity, he was less happy. In almost all his novels there are scenes of great power, and in several an absorbing story.

If I were asked by someone who had never read Balzac to recommend the novel which best represented him, which gave the reader pretty well all the author had to give, I should without hesitation advise him to read *Le Père Goriot.* The story it tells is continuously interesting. In some of his novels, Balzac interrupts his narrative to discourse on all sorts of irrelevant matters, or to give you long accounts of people in whom you cannot take the faintest interest; but from these defects *Le Père Goriot* is free. He lets his characters explain themselves by their words and actions as objectively as it was in his nature to do. The novel is extremely well constructed; and the two threads, the old man's self-sacrificing love for his ungrateful daughters, and the ambitious Rastignac's first steps in the crowded, corrupt Paris of his day, are ingeniously interwoven. It illustrates the principles which in *La Comédie Humaine* Balzac was concerned to bring to light: "Man is neither good nor bad, he is born with instincts and aptitudes; the world (*la société*), far from corrupting him, as Rousseau pretended, perfects him, makes him better; but self-interest then enormously develops his evil propensities."

So far as I know, it was in *Le Père Goriot* that Balzac first conceived the notion of bringing the same characters into novel after novel. The difficulty of this is that you must create characters who interest you so much that you want to know what happens to them. Balzac here triumphantly succeeds and, speaking for myself, I read with added enjoyment the novels in which I learn what has become of certain persons, Rastignac for instance, whose future I am eager to know about. Balzac himself was profoundly interested in them. He had at one time as his secretary a man of letters called Jules Sandeau, who is chiefly known in literary history as one of George Sand's many lovers: he had gone home because his sister was dying; she died, and he buried her; and on his return Balzac, having offered his condolences and asked after Sandeau's family, said, so the story goes: "Come, that's enough of that, let's get back to serious things. Let's talk of Eugénie Grandet." The device which Balzac adopted (and which, incidentally, Sainte-Beuve in a moment of petulance roundly condemned) is useful because it is an economy of invention; but I cannot believe that Balzac, with his marvellous fertility, resorted to it on that account. I think he felt that it added reality to his narrative, for in the ordinary course of events we have repeated contacts with a fair proportion of the same people; but more than that, I think his main object was to knit his whole work together in a comprehensive unity. His aim, as he said himself, was not to depict a group, a set, a class or even a society, but a period and a civilization. He suffered from the delusion, not uncommon to his countrymen, that France, whatever disasters had befallen it, was the centre of the universe; but perhaps it was just on that account that he had the self-assurance to create a world, multicoloured, various and profuse, and the power to give it the convincing throb of life.

Balzac started his novels slowly. A common method with him was to begin with a detailed description of the scene of action. He took so much pleasure in these descriptions that he often tells you more than you need to know. He never learned the art of saying only what has to be said, and not saying what needn't be said. Then he tells you what his characters look like, what their dispositions are, their origins, habits, ideas and defects; and only after this sets out to tell his story. His characters are seen through his own exuberant temperament and their reality is not quite that of real life; they are painted in primary colours, vivid and sometimes garish, and they are more exciting than ordinary people; but they live and breathe; and you believe in them, so intensely indeed that when he was dying he cried: "Send for Bianchon. Bianchon will save me." This was the clever, honest doctor who appears in many of the novels. He is one of the very few disinterested characters to be met with in *La Comédie Humaine.*

I believe Balzac to have been the first novelist to use a boarding-house as the setting for a story. It has been used many times since, for it is a convenient way of enabling the author to present together a variety of characters in sundry predicaments, but I don't know that it has ever been used with such happy effect as in *Le Père Goriot.* We meet in this novel perhaps the most thrilling character that Balzac ever created—Vautrin. The type has been reproduced a thousand times, but never with such striking and picturesque force, nor with such convincing realism. Vautrin has a good brain, will-power and immense vitality. These were traits that appealed to Balzac, and ruthless criminal though he was, he fascinated his author. It is worth the reader's while to notice how skilfully, without giving away a secret he wanted to keep till the end of the

A contemporary illustration of Père Goriot.

book, he has managed to suggest that there is something sinister about the man. He is jovial, generous and good-natured; he has great physical strength, he is clever and self-possessed; you cannot but admire him, and sympathize with him, and yet he is strangely frightening. He obsesses you, as he did Rastignac, the ambitious, well-born young man who comes to Paris to make his way in the world; but you feel in the convict's company the same uneasiness as Rastignac felt. Vautrin is a great creation.

His relations with Eugène de Rastignac are admirably presented. Vautrin sees into the young man's heart and proceeds subtly to sap his moral sense: true, Eugène revolts when he learns to his horror that Vautrin has had a man killed to enable him to marry an heiress; but the seeds are sown.

Le Père Goriot ends with the old man's death. Rastignac goes to his funeral and afterwards, remaining alone in the cemetery, surveys Paris lying below him along the two banks of the Seine. His eyes dwell on that part of the city in which reside the denizens of the great world he wishes to enter. "*A nous deux maintenant,*" he cries. It may interest the reader, who has not felt inclined to read all the novels in which Rastignac plays a part, more or less conspicuous, to know what came of Vautrin's influence. Madame de Nucingen, old Goriot's daughter, and the wife of the rich banker, the Baron de Nucingen, having fallen in love with him, took and expensively furnished for him an apartment, and provided him with money to live like a gentleman. Since her husband kept her short of cash, Balzac has not made clear how she managed to do this: perhaps he thought that when a woman in love needs money to support a lover she will somehow manage to get it. The Baron seems to have taken a tolerant view of the situation, and in 1826 made use of Rastignac in a financial transaction in which a number of the young man's friends were ruined, but from which he, as his share of the swag, received from Nucingen four hundred thousand francs. On part of this he dowered his two sisters, so that they could make good marriages, and was left with twenty thousand francs a year: "The price of keeping a stable," he told his friend Bianchon. Being thus no longer dependent on Madame de Nucingen, and realizing that a liaison that lasts too long has all the drawbacks of marriage, without its advantages, he made up his mind to throw her over and become the lover of the Marquise d'Espard, not because he was in love with her, but because she was rich, a great lady and influential. "Perhaps some day I'll marry her," he added. "She'll put me in a position in which at length I shall be able to pay my debts." This was in 1828. It is uncertain whether Madame d'Espard succumbed to his blandishments, but if she did, the affair did not last long, and he continued to be the lover of Madame de Nucingen. In 1831 he thought of marrying an Alsatian girl, but drew back on discovering that her fortune was not so great as he had been led to believe. In 1832, through the influence of Henry de Marsay, a former lover of Madame de Nucingen, who, Louis Philippe being then King of France, was a Minister, Rastignac was made Under Secretary of State. He was able, while holding this office, largely to increase his fortune. His relations with Madame de Nucingen apparently continued till 1835 when, perhaps by mutual agreement, they were broken off; and three years later he married her daughter Augusta. Since she was the only child of a very rich man, Rastignac did well for himself. In 1839 he was created a Count and again entered the Ministry. In 1845 he was made a peer of France and had an income of three hundred thousand francs a year (£ 12,000), which for the time was great wealth.

Balzac had a marked predilection for Rastignac. He endowed him with noble birth, good looks, charm, wit; and made him immensely attractive to women. Is it fanciful to suggest that he saw in Rastignac the man he would have given all but his fame to be? Balzac worshipped success. Perhaps Rastignac was a rascal, but he succeeded. True, his fortune was founded on the ruin of others, but they were fools to let themselves be taken in by him, and Balzac had little sympathy with fools. Lucien de Rubempré, another of Balzac's adventurers, failed because he was weak; but Rastignac, because he had courage, determination and strength, succeeded. From the day when, at Père La Chaise, he had flung his challenge in the face of Paris, he had let nothing stand in his way. He had resolved to conquer Paris; he conquered it. Balzac could not bring himself, I fancy, to regard Rastignac's moral delinquencies with censure. And after all, he was a good sort: though ruthless and unscrupulous where his interests were concerned, he was to the end ever willing to do a service to the old friends of his poverty-stricken youth. From the beginning, his aim had been to live in splendour, to have a fine house with a host of servants, carriages and horses, a string of mistresses and a rich wife. He had achieved his

aim: I don't suppose it ever occurred to Balzac that it was a vulgar one. (pp. 128-33)

> *W. Somerset Maugham, "Balzac and 'Le Père Goriot',"* in his The Art of Fiction: An Introduction to Ten Novels and Their Authors, *1954. Reprint by Doubleday & Company, Inc., 1955, pp. 109-34.*

C. Hobart Edgren   (essay date 1957)

[*In the following essay, Edgren suggests that the final paragraphs of* Le père Goriot *have been misunderstood and that Rastignac's challenge to Parisian society demands reinterpretation as a sign of his moral rectitude.*]

A satisfactory interpretation of Balzac's **Père Goriot** would depend, it seems to this writer, on a reading of the final two paragraphs of the work in relation to the whole structure. Majority opinion would have us read the novel as a tragedy in which Eugène de Rastignac [in the words of E. K. Brown] "develops unexpected traits of ambition, covetousness and vanity under the pressure of the luxurious and corrupt life of the capital" of France. On this basis, we see Eugène at the end of the tale mature in the ways of the world, ready to enter the "humming hive" of corrupt society, eager to get out of it everything that he desired in terms of personal satisfaction and gratification, militant in his own belief that he would not allow society to manipulate him as it had old Goriot. His education was now complete; he had made the "proper" connections and was well on his way in Parisian society, corrupt though it be. This interpretation, acceptable to most readers of Balzac, seems to the present writer to misinterpret and misconstrue the fundamental influence of Father Goriot on the life of Eugène, in terms of the latter's "education."

There is, then, another reading of the final two paragraphs of this work that results in a more fundamental consistency with the total structure. In reality, this is a story of a young man of twenty-one years of age who undergoes a significant change from naïveté to purpose under the influence of a totally new environment. In the course of events, as we watch Eugène in his contacts with Goriot, Goriot's daughters, Delphine and Anastasia, Vautrin and the Viscountess, it becomes apparent that his "education" will lead him in one of two directions: that exemplified by the Mephistophelean Vautrin, who urged him to succeed at any cost, or that poignantly revealed by the miserable life and death of Père Goriot, about whom Eugène makes the significant observation: "He's the superior of us all." The influence of Vautrin, aided and abetted as it is by the additional pernicious influence of the modern Lear's two ungrateful daughters, is at first a strong one upon Eugène, but he is finally able to overcome it:

> . . . Eugène had examined his conscience too gravely that day; and the arrest of Vautrin, revealing to him the depth of the abyss into which he had almost fallen, had too much reinforced his nobler feelings and his sense of delicacy; he could not yield to the caressing way in which the baroness was trying to refute the scruples of his honor.

On the other hand, the ennobling influence of old Goriot awakens Eugène ultimately to a more wholesome view of life, its duties and obligations and perhaps even its true meaning. Listening to the lamentations of the dying old man, Eugène concludes: "There is a God! Oh, yes! There is a God and He has made a better world for us to go to, or this earth of ours is without meaning. If it hadn't been so tragic I should break out weeping, but I feel such a sense of oppression over my heart and my stomach." To the ungrateful and callous daughters, who will not attend their father's dying moments, Eugène speaks reproachfully: "Even if you were at the point of death . . . you should drag yourself to your father's side." Their ingratitude is completed, in Eugène's mind, when the girls send two carriages with armorial bearings, empty, to follow the funeral procession to Père la Chaise. It is at this point that Eugène "dropped . . . the last of his youthful tears," and declared, as he viewed "the region of that high society in which he had sought to make his way . . . , 'Between us the battle is joined hence-forward.' " He had now determined that the society that had brought old Goriot to this pitiful end was evil and corrupt and worth battling against. Of this world he had earlier remarked to a friend: "Whatever evil you hear of society, believe it; there is no one, not even a Juvenal, who could paint the horror of it, covered though it be with gold and precious stone."

With this in mind, the final paragraph of the novel is not to be read ironically, but literally. "And as a first act in challenge of Society, Eugène went to dine with the Baroness de Nucingen." Would it not be perfectly logical that, after determining to battle the corrupt Parisian society that had ruthlessly driven old Goriot to his death, he should decide to begin that battle in the life of Delphine, the Baroness de Nucingen, with whom he was deeply in love? In time he might be able to convince her of the corruption of the society in which she lived and moved, the influence of which had led to her unconscionable ingratitude toward her father.

This interpretation would argue, then, that considered as a whole and a work in itself, the novel, *Père Goriot,* is not a tragedy but rather a work of limited seriousness in which the central character, Eugène de Rastignac, in a new environment, moves from naïveté to knowledge and experience, from innocent drifting to purposeful living.

> Eugene, now wholly alone, took a few steps to gain the highest point in the cemetery, and looked out on Paris winding its length along the two banks of the Seine, in which its lights were beginning to be reflected. His eyes were fixed almost avidly on the area between the column in the Place Vendome and the dome of the Invalides, the region of that high society in which he had sought to make his way. Upon this humming hive he cast a look which seemed already to suck the honey from it, and he gave utterance to these portentous words: "Between us the battle is joined henceforward."
>
> And as a first act in challenge of Society, Eugene went to dine with the Baroness de Nucingen.
>
> (pp. 393-94)

C. Hobart Edgren, "On Balzac's 'Père Goriot'," in Notes and Queries, Vol. 4, No. 9, September, 1957, pp. 393-94.

P. J. Yarrow   (essay date 1957)

[*In the following essay, a defense of* Le père Goriot *against current criticism, Yarrow accuses Martin Turnell of misrepresentation in his emphasis on Goriot rather than Rastignac as the focus of the novel. For Turnell's comments, see the essay dated 1950, above.*]

'The view that **Le Père Goriot** is Balzac's masterpiece,' writes Mr. Martin Turnell in his *Novel in France* (1950), 'seems to be common to his admirers and to hostile critics like Leslie Stephen and Henry James who both wrote damaging essays on him. This is a matter on which the critic has no right to temporize. I must therefore record my opinion that far from being a masterpiece, it is as a whole one of the worst of Balzac's mature works, that it is mainly interesting as an illustration of his most characteristic vices as a novelist and that the chief reason for examining it in detail is to try to correct some of the exaggerated estimates of previous writers.'

Mr. Turnell's low opinion of **Le Père Goriot,** and of Balzac's works in general, has remained unchallenged. This is unfortunate: Mr. Turnell's opinion, though unfair, cannot safely be ignored. As a contributor to *Scrutiny* and the author of several volumes on French literature, Mr. Turnell has acquired considerable standing as a critic. Nor is his condemnation of Balzac unique: Mr. Leavis has slated **Goriot** in *The Great Tradition;* and the fact that the B.B.C., normally so sensitive to centenaries, completely ignored the centenary of Balzac's death in 1950, seems to indicate that the British public in general cares as little for Balzac as Mr. Turnell. His judgment, therefore, seems to deserve more serious examination that it has so far received.

Mr. Turnell, then, finds the following weaknesses—typical of Balzac—in **Le Père Goriot**:

(1) It is melodramatic. 'The arrest of Vautrin shows Balzac at his worst . . . It is a perfect example of Balzac's Light Programme manner. For this is crude melodrama . . . Vautrin is a borrowing from the *roman frénétique* which has been transported bodily into the novel.' Moreover, the 'preoccupation with "atmosphere" is another link with the writers of "detective fiction".'

(2) The characters are weak. 'In another place we are told: "M. Poiret était une espèce de mécanique." *Mécanique* was a favourite word of Balzac's, and it explains why we so often have the sensation that his characters are marionettes whose gestures, repeated over and over again, have a hypnotic effect which reminds us of a nightmare. They are grotesque and somehow frightening, but you feel that at any moment the springs may give way and the whole apparatus collapse into a mass of metal, rag and sawdust.' And of Goriot, Mr. Turnell writes: 'There is no reason why a novelist should not put simple souls into his books, but his characters are after all the instruments which he uses to express a particular experience and we cannot be indifferent to the fact that the choice of a sentimentalized

figure like Goriot is the sign of a defective view of life. For this account of his limitations is the prelude to the main theme of the book—the obsession with his daughters which brings him to destruction.' He denies that Goriot is comparable with Lear: 'One critic [i.e. Leavis] has suggested that Shelley's *Cenci* is a more suitable term of comparison; and in both works we find the same hysteria, the same lack of feeling for language and the same surrender to the most dubious form of inspiration.'

(3) The criticism of society is inadequate: 'The reflections of Mme de Beauséant and Vautrin on "life" are distressing in their banality.'

Now, in the first place, Mr. Turnell misrepresents the novel. Despite the title, the main theme is not the story of Goriot and his daughters, which is only one strand, though an important one, in a complex web. The central character in the book is, of course, Rastignac; and the novel is essentially the story of his introduction to society—a *Bildungsroman,* in fact. Goriot, except in the introductory section of the book, is seen through Rastignac's eyes and in relation to him. Considered as the story of Goriot, the novel is full of irrelevancies and digressions; seen as the story of Rastignac, it appears as a beautifully balanced work—'la réunion de plusieurs sujets autour d'une idée directrice,' as Bardèche puts it—as a novel in which a central theme informs every part, every character and every episode—in fact, as a work having 'organisation', in the sense in which Mr. Leavis uses the word.

The central character, then, is Rastignac, and the central theme is society. At the opening of the novel, Rastignac is a young man just beginning his career in Paris; in the course of the story, he comes to realise the nature of society, and his attitude to it crystallises. Around him are grouped a number of characters, each illustrating a different aspect of society or a different attitude to life. The essential symbolism of the novel is summed up thus by Balzac: 'Il avait vu les trois grandes expressions de la société: l'Obéissance, la Lutte et la Révolte; la Famille, le Monde et Vautrin. Et il n'osait prendre parti. L'Obéissance était ennuyeuse, la Révolte impossible, et la Lutte incertaine.'

Obedience—that is to say, morality and comparative poverty—is symbolised by Rastignac's family and by the majority of the inmates of the Maison Vauquer—Poiret, Mme Couture, Mme Vauquer, and Bianchon. Rastignac's family and Mme Couture show us the noble, idyllic side of this attitude; they exemplify uncomplaining devotion to one's task, the 'poésie du devoir', to borrow a phrase of Vigny's: Poiret and Mme Vauquer show its sordid side. Rastignac's mother, aunt, and sisters are content to live on their small estate in the country, with an income of 3,000 francs a year, over a third of which is sent to Rastignac, who can count on them to make further sacrifices, willingly and uncomplainingly, should he wish. Mme Couture is a widow living on a small pension, generous enough to look after a distant relative, Victorine Taillefer. Poiret, on the other hand, has been a minor civil servant, performing some necessary, but sordid, task; and he is now living in poverty-stricken retirement, ignoble, besotted, and revolting. His relevance to Rastignac's life is emphasised by Vautrin: 'Le travail, compris comme vous le

comprenez en ce moment, donne, dans les vieux jours, un appartement chez maman Vauquer, à des gars de la force de Poiret.' With Poiret may be grouped Mme Vauquer, the type of the boarding-house-keeper, slovenly, stingy, a purveyor of squalid lodgings and indifferent meals, ready to increase her profits by petty acts of dishonesty, and incapable of a disinterested thought or deed.

All these, whether honest or dishonest, contented or discontented, are failures in society. Bianchon, however, represents contented, uncomplaining devotion to duty, and is destined to be a success. He is a philosopher: 'Moi,' he says, 'je suis heureux de la petite existence que je me créerai en province, où je succéderai tout bêtement à mon père. Les affections de l'homme se satisfont dans le plus petit cercle aussi pleinement que dans une immense circonférence. Napoléon ne dînait pas deux fois, et ne pouvait pas avoir plus de maîtresses qu'en prend un étudiant en médecine quand il est interne aux Capucins. Notre bonheur, mon cher, tiendra toujours entre la plante de nos pieds et notre occiput; et, qu'il coûte un million par an ou cent louis, la perception intrinsèque en est la même au dedans de nous.' Bianchon's outlook is that which Balzac regards as the wisest. Rastignac, who chooses another course, urges him at the end of the book to go on as he has begun: 'Mon ami, va, poursuis la destinée modeste à laquelle tu bornes tes désirs. Moi, je suis en enfer, et il faut que j'y reste. Quelque mal que l'on te dise du monde, crois-le! Il n'y a pas de Juvénal qui puisse en peindre l'horreur couverte d'or et de pierreries.' Bianchon, in fact, is the antithesis of Rastignac, as Lucien de Rubempré, in *Illusions Perdues,* is the antithesis of d'Arthez and his companions. Bianchon and Rastignac, the attraction of hard work and the appeal of an easy fortune, are both, of course, sides of Balzac himself.

Rastignac would like to be a Bianchon, but he cannot: he lacks perseverance, he is dazzled by the splendour of society, and he recoils from the mediocrity which is all that hard work, as Vautrin points out, can be expected to bring him. The other courses open to him, then, are *Révolte* and *Lutte.* This is where Vautrin comes in. His rôle in the novel is essential and threefold. First and foremost, he symbolises the attitude of revolt; and his arrest, which Mr. Turnell characterises as crude melodrama, is necessary to show that this attitude cannot succeed, that crime does not pay. (Incidentally, it also provides an opportunity for bringing out the degradation of Poiret and Mlle Michonneau—for *Le Père Goriot* is a very close-knit novel.) Second, he observes and comments on society, and, in fact, fulfils a function akin to that of the chorus in a Greek tragedy. And, lastly, he is the evil genius of Rastignac, the tempter, to whose wiles, however, Rastignac does not quite succumb.

There remains, then, the third attitude, that of struggle, that of the adventurer in society, which is the one Rastignac finally adopts. He is not sufficiently noble to follow the example of Bianchon; not sufficiently evil to sell himself to Vautrin. He chooses the middle course, that of weakness, symbolised in the novel by the various society ladies, dandies and adventurers he meets, by Rastignac himself, and by Mlle Michonneau. There is no idealisation in the novel either of the society which Rasitgnac wishes to enter, or of the means by which success in it is to be won. Indeed, Balzac stresses that between *Lutte* and *Révolte*, between the criminal like Vautrin and the successful member of society, there is no clear moral distinction to be drawn. 'Il vit le monde comme il est: les lois et la morale impuissantes chez les riches, et vit dans la fortune *l'ultima ratio mundi.*'

The picture of society we are given—and there is no reason to doubt its truth: Balzac had had two or three years' experience of it when he wrote **Goriot,** and in the main his account tallies with that of his contemporary, Stendhal—is not an attractive one. Society life is a desperate struggle for existence, and its various facets are illustrated in the novel by different characters. Social success is not happiness: luxury and glamour involve a desperate need for money, which overrides all scruples. As Goriot's daughters bleed their father, so Rastignac bleeds his mother and sisters. The key to success is hypocrisy and opportunism; even love must be used as a means to an end. Mme de Nucingen's love for Rastignac originates in her desire to gain entry into a higher social sphere; his love for her—a 'passion de commande', Balzac calls it—springs from his desire to make his way in the world; Adjuda-Pinto abandons Mme de Beauséant to make a profitable marriage. For the men, in general, a love affair is a source of financial profit. Genuine feeling is a weakness and a danger: hence the downfall of Mmes de Beauséant and de Langeais. Women, being less skilled in controlling their emotions than men, are more unhappy: it is not Ajuda-Pinto or Montriveau or Maxime de Trailles or Marsay who suffer, but their mistresses—Mme de Beauséant, Mme de Langeais, Mme de Restaud and Mme de Nucingen; and if the last two suffer less from love than the two former, it is because their love is less pure, less disinterested. But success, even by the cold-blooded exploitation of human emotion, is uncertain; and, in contrast to Mme de Beauséant and Mme de Langeais, who are too sincere to succeed, we are shown Mlle Michonneau, the ex-courtesan or *femme entretenue,* whose attempt to exploit human passions has brought her to the same ignominious degradation to which a lifetime of debasing drudgery has brought Poiret. There is no certain receipt for success in life.

The more deeply involved with society Rastignac becomes, the less unselfish and disinterested he is; and the stages of his moral deterioration are skilfully depicted. He begins by being determined to make his way by hard work; then he resolves to combine study with social life, but the compromise is impossible: having made up his mind to work all night to make up for lost time, he feels tired and goes to bed. He visits Mme Restaud, and, humiliated by his poverty, takes a cab he cannot afford; he champions Goriot, but mulcts his own family in order to set up as a man of fashion. Vautrin shows him that he must choose between hard work and mediocrity, or wealth achieved by more or less dishonourable means. Rastignac recoils from the crime Vautrin proposes, and resolves to make his fortune by means of Mme de Nucingen; but, as his need for money grows, Vautrin's proposition proves more and more attractive to him: and though he never quite succumbs to the temptation, he does go so far as to flirt with

Victorine Taillefer in the midst of his courtship of Mme de Nucingen. When he finds Mme de Nucingen determined to go to Mme Beauséant's ball, despite her father's illness, he is shocked, but too selfish to try to dissuade her: she would never forgive him. After Goriot's death, the book ends with Rastignac, disillusioned, defying society: 'Et pour premier acte de défi qu'il portait à la Société,' notes Balzac, ironically, 'Rastignac alla dîner chez madame de Nucingen.'

A study of society, then—a complex and penetrating study—such is this novel, in which the story of Goriot is one episode, giving Rastignac an insight into the true nature of society, and illustrating the exploitation of family affections for selfish ends and the defeat of genuine emotion by society. In neither respect is Goriot an isolated phenomenon. Mme de Beauséant and Mme de Langeais are also there to show the vulnerability of genuine feeling; and the retirement of Mme de Beauséant and the death of Goriot run parallel, and together terminate the book. That the two events are intended to be grouped together is made clear by Rastignac, who is common to both, and who also draws the moral: 'Comment les grands sentiments s'allieraient-ils, en effet, à une société mesquine, petite, superficielle?' Similarly, Goriot and his daughters are not the only example of the exploitation of affection by self-interest. 'Si elles [i.e. society ladies in general] ne savent pas se vendre,' says Vautrin, 'elles éventreraient leurs mères pour y chercher de quoi briller.' Goriot's devotion is paralleled by the sacrifices of Rastignac's family, and Rastignac compares himself to Goriot's daughters. 'De quel droit maudirais-tu Anastasie?' he asks himself; 'tu viens d'imiter pour l'égoïsme de ton avenir ce qu'elle a fait pour son amant! Qui d'elle ou de toi, vaut mieux?' In contrast, we have Victorine Taillefer, the devoted daughter, whose affection is spurned by her father and brother.

The Goriot episode brings us to the second main point—that Goriot is much less sentimentalised, that Balzac's attitude to him is much less uncritical, than Mr. Leavis and Mr. Turnell suggest. Vautrin is made to class Goriot, along with gamblers, collectors and gourmands, as an 'homme à passions'—a warning, surely, that we are not to take his sublimity too seriously. Balzac has no illusions about his character. He is a sentimental fool—'une bête solidement bâtie, capable de dépenser tout son esprit en sentiment.' In everything but his own line of business he is a fool; his person is unprepossessing, and his speech and habits are common; and he is not a particularly good man—he made his fortune by gross profiteering, and he ruins a competitor for playing a trick on him. He has no insight into his daughters' minds: he is either convinced that they do not love him at all, or that their affection is equal to his own, neither of which is true. It is symbolic that, at the end, after railing against them immoderately—'Ce sont des infâmes des scélérates; je les abomine, je les maudis; je me relèverai, la nuit, de mon cercueil pour les remaudire'—he should die caressing the heads of Rastignac and Bianchon, in the belief that they are his daughters.

His love for his daughters has, of course, its sublime side; but Balzac, if at one moment he refers to him as 'ce Christ de la Paternité', clearly indicates that there is a reverse side too. Goriot's love is not only excessive, but blind and foolish as well. He has spoilt his daughters, and still spoils them—as when he encourages Delphine's liaison with Rastignac (his motives, incidentally, are not unselfish: he will see more of her if she loves Rastignac). He has brought his misfortunes on his own head, like an Aristotelian hero: 'Je suis un misérable, je suis justement puni. Moi seul ai causé les désordres de mes filles, je les ai gâtées.' He is possessive, too: 'Je veux mes filles! je les ai faites! elles sont à moi !' he cries on his deathbed; and he hates his sons-in-law who have taken his daughters from him: 'Le gendre est un scélérat qui gâte tout chez une fille, il souille tout.' And this last sentence is not the only hint in the novel that there is an element of sexual aberration in his love. It was not until after the death of his wife that his paternal fondness began to be excessive, we are told; and he is made to say: 'Mes filles, c'était mon vice à moi; elles étaient mes maîtresses, enfin tout!' He wants physical contact with them: 'Est-ce bon de se frotter à sa robe, de se mettre à son pas, de partager sa chaleur!' In Delphine's presence, he behaves like a lover: 'Il se couchait aux pieds de sa fille pour les baiser; il la regardait longtemps dans les yeux; il frottait sa tête contre sa robe; enfin il faisait des folies comme en aurait fait l'amant le plus jeune et le plus tendre.'

There is no reason to suppose that Balzac does not mean to imply sexual aberration. He does not elsewhere shrink from it: Lesbianism is the subject of *La Fille aux Yeux d'Or,* and *Sarrazine* deals with a young man who finds that the opera singer with whom he has fallen in love is really a *castrato.* And are we not meant to infer potential abnormality in Vautrin? If Racine had to provide Hippolyte with a mistress, in order that his coldness to Phèdre should not incur the lewd gibes of the *petits-maîtres* of his day, it is unlikely that Balzac, of all people, could be oblivious of the fact that he had exposed Vautrin—with his indifference to women, and his tenderness towards handsome young men (the 'très beau jeune homme qu'il aimait beaucoup' and Rastignac in this novel, and Lucien de Rubempré in *Splendeurs et Misères*)—to a similar charge. It seems clear, then, that Balzac has deliberately made Goriot's paternal affection excessive, abnormal, and unhealthy.

Balzac's conception of the relations between parents and children is, thus, not a romantic or sentimental one. As he sees Goriot's faults, so he analyses the causes which have weakened the ties between him and his daughters—causes which can estrange any children from their parents. *First,* marriage; for, if Goriot's daughters have been unable to offer their father an apartment in their houses, it is chiefly through the opposition of their husbands. Here Goriot's daughters are in no way exceptional. 'Ici', says Mme de Beauséant, 'la belle-fille est de la dernière impertinence avec le beau-père, qui a tout sacrifié pour son fils. Plus loin, un gendre met sa belle-mère à la porte.' *Second,* the fact of moving in different social milieux. 'Ce père Doriot,' to quote Mme de Beauséant again, 'n'aurait-il pas été une tache de cambouis dans le salon de ses filles?' And Goriot tells us that his daughters, after their brilliant marriages, 'commençaient à rougir de moi. Voilà ce que c'est que de bien élever ses enfants.' *Third,* parental possessiveness. It

is generally accepted nowadays that it is unwise for married children to live with their parents. This, in effect, is what Delphine de Nucingen points out to Rastignac, when she says: 'Voyez-vous? quand mon père est avec nous, il faut être tout à lui. Ce sera pourtant bien gênant quelquefois.' 'Eugène,' continues Balzac, 'qui s'était senti déjà plusieurs fois des mouvements de jalousie, ne pouvait pas blâmer ce mot, qui renfermait le principe de toutes les ingratitudes.'

Leslie Stephen compares Anastasie and Delphine to Goneril and Regan; but it is clear from the foregoing that the comparison cannot be made. Goriot's daughters have both good and bad qualities. They are selfish, having been spoiled, for which Goriot has only himself to blame; but they are not heartless. They do not love their father as he would like; but there is a good deal that can be said on their behalf. They have been brought up to move in a different social sphere; and no child could satisfy the demands of a nature such as Goriot's. Filial ingratitude is partly a defence against parental oppressiveness, and it is no accident that the only devoted child in this book is Victorine Taillefer, who has known no parental affection at all. But Goriot's daughters *do* love their father, and they are capable of genuine feeling. Mme de Restaud is genuinely in love with Maxime de Trailles, and her grief at her father's deathbed is sincere. Mme de Nucingen refuses to give up her one chance of satisfying her social ambitions, when her father is ill; but she is kind-hearted, and fond of her father and sister. She is the more affectionate of the two, says Goriot; and when her sister confesses her troubles, 'Madame de Nucingen la saisit à plein corps, la baisa tendrement, et l'appuyant sur son coeur:—Ici, tu seras toujours aimée sans être jugée, lui dit-elle.' It is not their fault that they cannot go to their father's deathbed; and if they extract money from him, it is because they have no other resource in face of the demands of their social ambitions and the exigencies of their lovers—and if they have lovers and are unhappy in their marriages, it is because their father indulgently allowed them to choose their own husbands. All their faults can be traced back to the fact that their faith has spoilt them.

Goriot and his daughters, then, are painted neither wholly white nor wholly black; and their relations are realistically analysed. Their problem is potentially that of all parents and children; but only with a father like Goriot can all the potentialities become actual, which is a justification of Balzac's choice of character.

In conclusion, then: a complex study of society, and of the various attitudes one may adopt towards it; and a careful study, with universal implications, of the relations between parents and children—those are the two main themes of the novel; and they are superbly handled. The skilful use of contrast (between the glamour of society and the squalor of the boarding house, between the outward splendour of its members and their inward wretchedness, between the life of Goriot and that of his daughters); the masterly alternation of the scenes of high life with those set in the maison Vauquer; the excellence of the descriptions, of the narrative, of the characters (Rastignac, Mme Vauquer, Mme de Beauséant, and Goriot's daughters, for example, not to mention Goriot himself); and the delicate analysis of human motives and relationships (e.g. the liaison between Delphine and Rastignac, the friendship of Mme de Beauséant and Mme de Langeais, besides the relations between Goriot and his daughters) all contribute to make this a great novel. (pp. 363-73)

P. J. Yarrow, " 'Le Père Goriot' Re-considered," in Essays in Criticism, *Vol. VII, No. 4, October, 1957, pp. 363-73.*

Herbert J. Hunt   (essay date 1959)

[*Hunt was an English educator and critic who wrote several studies of nineteenth-century French literature as well as a biography of Balzac. In the following excerpt, he discusses* Le père Goriot, *focusing on Balzac's use of recurrent characters and the novel's association with other stories in which its characters appear.*]

All Balzac's previous efforts appear to converge on [*Le père Goriot*], and all of his favourite themes to be caught up in it. It is, most conspicuously, his third great study of a monomania, though here the emphasis is shifted. The ex-manufacturer of vermicelli, Jean-Joachim Goriot, is not, like Félix Grandet and Balthazar Claës, an egocentric whose mania inflicts unmerited suffering on his family. He himself is the victim of the idolatrous love he bears his two daughters, a passion natural enough in its origins, since it is the transference to them of a 'religious adoration' formerly lavished on his now defunct wife, but one which in course of time has become exclusive, uncritical, monstrous. It has expressed itself originally in the expensive education he has provided for them, in the marriages he has arranged for each of them according to her taste: Anastasie to the Comte de Restaud, on account of her 'aristocratic leanings', Delphine to the Alsatian banker, Nucingen, in order to satisfy her craving for wealth and display. Its growth in monstrosity is measured by the way in which, after having made over to them the bulk of his wealth for their dowries, he strips himself by degrees of all he has left in order to gratify their whims or extricate them from embarrassment. Knowing our Balzac . . . , we should expect him to translate this denudation into terms of money and status: Goriot's gradual ascent from well-furnished first-floor to shabby garret in the boarding-house he occupies, the deterioration in dress and appearance, and the rising hostility and scorn which this degeneration inspires in his landlady and her other lodgers. It is more dramatically illustrated in a scene in which Goriot is discovered twisting up his plate before selling it for the precious metal it contains. When he has mortgaged even his meagre annuity and cannot bleed himself any further for his rapacious daughters, his distraught mind leaps to impossible schemes—he will sell himself, he, a septuagenarian, as a substitute conscript or, decrepit as he is, rush to Odessa to corner wheat supplies and resume his manufacture of Italian paste.

The reward which this plebeian King Lear reaps is that he has a Regan and a Goneril, but no Cordelia. Anastasie and Delphine are ashamed of their father. He is excluded from their lives and homes, and reduced to the humilia-

tion of loitering in streets and parks to watch their comings and goings, overjoyed to catch a glimpse of them as they pass by. His squalid garret is only lit up by their presence when they want to extract more money from him. Viewed sympathetically, as Balzac of course does view it, this infatuation has all the intensity of religious devotion. In fact Goriot's willing self-martyrdom for his strumpets of daughters is such that Balzac does not shrink from referring to him as 'ce Christ de la paternité'. Goriot himself says:

> Quand j'ai été père, j'ai compris Dieu. Il est tout entier partout, puisque la création est sortie de lui. Monsieur, je suis ainsi avec mes filles. Seulement j'aime mieux mes filles que Dieu n'aime le monde, parce que le monde n'est pas si beau que Dieu, et que mes filles sont plus belles que moi.

Viewed from the ethical angle, the passion of this man, who shows himself ready to equip Delphine's lover with a luxurious *garçonnière,* so that he may be allowed to bask in the reflected warmth of their illicit joys, would be profoundly immoral were it not so patently pathological:

> J'aime les chevaux qui les traînent, et je voudrais être le petit chien qu'elles ont sur leurs genoux. Je vis de leurs plaisirs.

At dinner in the flat he has furnished for Eugène de Rastignac, he embarrasses the lovers by his ecstatic fawnings:

> Il se couchait aux pieds de sa fille pour les baiser, il la regardait longtemps dans les yeux; il frottait sa tête contre sa robe; enfin il faisait des folies comme en aurait fait l'amant le plus jeune et le plus tendre.

Indeed this canine devotion is so extreme in its manifestations that it has something of the flavour of an unnatural vice. The penalty he pays for it is atrocious. 'Il aimait jusqu'au mal qu'elles lui faisaient'; but when the rapacity and mutual hatred of the two sisters have brought him to his death-bed he is at last forced to acknowledge what in fact he realized all along, despite the fanaticism which has driven him to find excuses for them and blame their husbands or lovers for the callousness they have shown: namely, that they have not an atom of real affection for him. His delirious ravings, when he lies yearning for a last glimpse of them, mark the climax of the book: moments of clear-sightedness when he admits their worthlessness and his own guilt in corrupting them; invocation of the law to protect the rights of fathers and compel his daughters to visit him—'Envoyez-les chercher par la gendarmerie, de force!'; denunciation of marriage which robs a father of his children. Reproaches and entreaties, maledictions and endearments pour from him tumultuously; yet this drawn-out agony ends with his delusion reinstated.

As an example of one of 'ces horribles supplices infligés dans l'intérieur des familles . . . aux âmes douces par les âmes dures', *Le père Goriot* is pre-eminently a 'Scene of Private Life'; but it is so perfectly merged into the Parisian setting that one can only approve of Balzac's earlier decision to include it in the Parisian life category, even though he rescinded that decision in 1845. Goriot is scarcely conceivable save as a denizen of Paris. His martyrdom only attains its morbid grandeur in relation to the two social *milieux* which are set over against each other as two opposite poles throughout the story. One is the 'Pension Vauquer', whose fly-blown mediocrity, like that of the quarter in which it is situated, is so tellingly conveyed in the opening pages of the novel that it has become the very type of the middle-class boarding-house, with its dilapidated and greasy furnishings, its stale smells, its odious landlady—'sa personne explique la pension, comme la pension implique sa personne'—and its motley and vulgar crowd of lodgers and daily boarders. The other is the superb Faubourg Saint-Germain residence of Mme de Beauséant, the heroine of *La Femme abandonnée.* Thanks to his self-denudation Goriot lives as the most penurious and the most despised of Mme Vauquer's paying-guests. Through his daughters he is indirectly linked to Mme de Beauséant's salon, for Anastasie, by virtue of her marriage, has access to it, while Delphine would sell her soul—and bleed her father white—to be admitted there. Moreover, between these two *milieux* oscillates the person on whom the action of the story is pivoted—the impecunious young Gascon noble, Eugène de Rastignac. Financed by self-denying parents to study law and win his spurs by hard work, he decides to take the short cut to prosperity by exploiting his social privileges—his kinship with the influential Mme de Beauséant—and by using women as stepping-stones to fortune. 'Le démon du luxe le mordit au cœur.' A snub from Anastasie de Restaud throws him into the arms of her sister, Delphine de Nucingen, so that, later, he is able to rise to wealth as an associate in the Alsatian banker's shady speculations.

And so another theme is interwoven with the King Lear one: that of a decent and honourable young man corrupted by ambition, and learning to dispense with scruples. Although the process of corruption is only in its beginnings in *Le père Goriot,* and although Rastignac remains a sympathetic figure throughout by virtue of his kindness to the old man, the steps in his moral downfall are clearly designated. He exploits the generosity of his mother and sisters, at home in the Angoûmois, for money to start his campaign for the conquest of society. He seizes his chance to catch Delphine on the rebound when she is cast off by a former lover. As is frequent with Balzac's heroes, his first advances to her are prompted by cold calculation—'Le mors est mis à ma bête, sautons dessus et gouvernons-la.' Then the 'passion de commande' becomes a genuine one, though it can be little more than sensual. His wooing of Delphine is closely associated with the sympathy and protection he accords to Goriot; but the further he advances in her favour and the more intimately he becomes involved in the threefold drama enacted between father and daughters, the more certain does he grow of the arrant selfishness of both women. In Delphine's case the crucial moment occurs when he finds himself obliged to confront her with the choice of attending Mme de Beauséant's ball, on which her heart is set, or of consoling her father in his last moments. She attends the ball. Yet he never has the courage to break with her. He overcomes the nausea he feels, and after escorting Goriot to his pauper's grave, continues his liaison with her. He has fully realized that Paris is a wicked city and that conscience and kindliness must be stifled in the effort to conquer it. But conquer it he will: '*À nous deux maintenant!*' This challenge, which he utters as he gazes down on it from the cemetery of Père-Lachaise, has become famous. In bringing Rastignac to such a decision Balzac fulfils the promise implied in the introduction to *La Fille aux yeux d'or.* While de Marsay remains for the present the symbolical representative of 'le flibustier en gants jaunes', Rastignac is, so to speak, the working model of the type. Over against him stands the gay but hard-working medical student, Horace Bianchon, who takes his meals at the Pension Vauquer; a close friend of Rastignac, and like him sympathetic and charitable to Goriot; but holding himself aloof from any compromise with the forces of evil.

> —As-tu lu Rousseau? Rastignac asks him at one juncture.
>
> —Oui.
>
> —Te souviens-tu de ce passage où il demande à son lecteur ce qu'il ferait au cas où il pourrait s'enrichir en tuant par sa seule volonté un vieux mandarin, sans bouger de Paris? . . . s'il était prouvé que la chose est possible et qu'il te suffit d'un signe de tête, le ferais-tu?

Bianchon needs little reflection before he gives his emphatic reply: 'Eh bien! non.'

One might well imagine that, with the Goriot and the Rastignac themes thus intertwined, the author of *Le père Goriot* had material enough to keep his readers interested. But, in these early years and even later, he was scarcely able to conceive of an 'histoire parisienne', however close its correspondence to life as he saw it, without setting it against a melodramatically sinister background. Ferragus and the Thirteen here give way to a new invention, that of the arch-criminal Jacques Collin, alias Trompe-la-Mort, who lives in the Pension Vauquer as the coarse and jovial Vautrin. Balzac had several models to pose for him as he fashioned Vautrin, among them Vidocq, the ex-convict turned policeman who was chief of the French *brigade de sûreté* from 1811 to 1827 and again from 1831 to 1832, and whose *Mémoires* of 1828-9, unscrupulously 'revised' by Émile Morice and Lhéritier de l'Ain, had given the world a highly coloured account of his violent and varied career. It was apparently through meeting Vidocq, in company with Sanson, son of the executioner of Louis XVI, at a dinner given by the philanthropist Benjamin Appert in April 1834 that Balzac got the idea of developing *Le père Goriot,* originally intended as a simple *nouvelle,* and making of it the complex work it had become by the autumn of that year. Vautrin is a diabolic, but not unsympathetic figure, destined to play a prominent part in later stories. Sent to the galleys for a forgery for which, though innocent, he shouldered the responsibility, he had escaped and made himself the leader and financier of the Parisian criminal world. He has declared organized war upon society. Homosexually inclined, he becomes interested in Eugène de Rastignac, divines the struggle going on inside him between innate rectitude and the urge to succeed at all cost, and offers to smooth out his path by marrying him to another lodger at the Pension Vauquer, the pale and passive Victorine Taillefer, after arranging the death by duel of her brother, who stands between her and the inheritance of an immense fortune.

Eugène rejects the bargain with righteous horror, even though Vautrin, before he is ferreted out and arrested by the Paris police, carries out the plan for assassination with brutal efficiency. His unmasking through the agency of two other lodgers at the pension, its sudden invasion by armed policemen, and Vautrin's cool self-mastery when it is a question of avoiding being killed 'while resisting arrest', go to make a well-told chapter eminently fitted for a *roman policier.* But Vautrin has found his way into *Le père Goriot* not merely as a means for adding still stronger seasoning to an already pungent story. He inherits something of the symbolic role of the characters in *La Peau de chagrin,* whilst yet appearing as a very real and vivid scoundrel, with his brick-red hair, concealed by a powdered wig, his dyed whiskers, his robust physique, resonant voice, piercing eyes and penetrating intelligence. He is to Rastignac what Mephistopheles is to Faust, and serves not only as a tempter, but also as a mentor who gives Rastignac an objective view of the alternative ways of life between which he is hesitating: laborious mediocrity and callous opportunism. Or, more exactly, he foresees the choice Rastignac will make of the second of these two ways, and puts a further alternative to him: the choice between candid and hypocritical unscrupulousness. His contempt for society is based on the contrast, already emphasized in *Le Code des gens honnêtes* and *Les Marana,* between that sort of criminality which openly flouts the laws and ends up on the scaffold, and the respectable roguery which wins wealth, fame and consideration. Vautrin echoes Balzac's own fulminations against Paris, a mud-pit of which he says 'ceux qui s'y crottent en voiture sont d'honnêtes gens, ceux qui s'y crottent à pied sont des fripons'. Alternatively, with Fenimore Cooper in mind, he sees Paris as

> une forêt du Nouveau-Monde, où s'agitent vingt espèces de peuplades sauvages . . . qui vivent du produit que donnent les différentes chasses sociales; vous êtes [he is talking to Rastignac] un chasseur de millions. Pour les prendre, vous usez de pièges, de pipeaux, d'appeaux. Celui qui revient avec sa gibecière bien garnie est salué, fêté, reçu dans la bonne société.

This then is the choice which the cynic of the Pension Vauquer proposes to the aspirant to honours and fortune:

> Savez-vous comment on fait son chemin ici? Par l'éclat du génie ou par l'adresse de la corruption. Il faut entrer dans cette masse d'hommes comme un boulet de canon, ou s'y glisser comme une peste. L'honnêteté ne sert à rien.

It is a view of things which impresses Eugène so much the more because he has already listened to similar sentiments expressed by the bruised and disillusioned Claire de Beauséant:

> Le monde est infâme et méchant. . . . Plus froidement vous calculerez, plus avant vous irez. Frappez sans pitié, vous serez craint. N'acceptez les hommes et les femmes que comme des chevaux de poste que vous laisserez crever à

chaque relais, vous arriverez ainsi au faîte de vos désirs.

'Vous arriverez.' In spite of his youthful compunction, that is Rastignac's one aim. He is appalled at Vautrin's outspokenness, though in the end he learns that Vautrin is right. But he still wishes to make his way by means which soothe and drug the conscience. The challenge he flings to the city of Paris from Père-Lachaise leads to no great heroic gesture, but merely to a cosy dinner with Delphine de Nucingen. M. Félicien Marceau puts the matter bluntly: Rastignac makes his way as a 'gigolo'.

Le père Goriot is universally acclaimed as one of Balzac's greatest novels, for the complexity of its structure, the realism with which it lays bare certain permanent features in social manners and conduct, and the vividness and truth of its characterization, a truth which must be admitted if, while allowing for the fact that Goriot and Vautrin transcend the bounds of normal human verisimilitude, one reflects on the wide range of representative personalities the book offers—from the superior ladies of the Faubourg Saint-Germain to the simple-hearted slavey of the Pension Vauquer; from insolent dandies like Maxime de Trailles to the imbecile little rentier and informer Poiret; from the voracious and squabbling Goriot sisters to the shrill and treacherous Mlle Michonneau. But a memorable innovation in *Le père Goriot* gives it a special importance in the history of Balzac's work. It is the first novel in which he consciously and systematically applies a device which constitutes one of the most original features of the *Comédie Humaine*—the use of recurrent characters.

According to [Balzac's sister] Laure Surville, this idea— *relier tous ses personnages pour en former une société complète*—came one day to Balzac with all the effulgence of a revelation. 'Saluez-moi, nous dit-il joyeusement [as he burst into his sister's flat], car je suis tout bonnement en train de devenir un génie.' The date of this inspiration is uncertain. 'Vers 1833', says Laure, 'lors de la publication de son *Médecin de campagne*'. Although the idea must have been simmering for a considerable period, he did not begin to apply it deliberately till the autumn of 1834, when writing *Le père Goriot.* In the preface to the first edition in book form (March 1835), he attributed the device to scruples arising from criticism made of his earlier works. Their morality had been so much called in question that he would permit himself only one new 'mauvaise femme' in *Le père Goriot*—Delphine de Nucingen, and keep to the ration of erring women, Mme de Beauséant, Lady Brandon, the Comtesse de Restaud and the Duchesse de Langeais, already offered to the public. The statement is undoubtedly ironic, for his obvious aim was to give a stronger flavour to his 'Études de Mœurs' by establishing as it were a pool of characters, families and *milieux,* so that he might move from one to another in different novels, throwing the limelight on each one in turn while leaving the others in the shade. The more easily might the impression be created of a closely knit society in which, as in real life, the reader would continually be coming upon people he had met before, whose family connections and personal history he would know in part, and whose every appearance would increase the store of knowledge he already possessed about them.

This he proceeded to do in *Le père Goriot* and subsequent works. Not content with this, in his new editions of former works he made continual changes, replacing anonymous or named persons with more familiar ones, and so bringing into circulation a world of fictitious people in whom readers tend to become so interested that they have blessed the enterprise of Cerfberr and Christophe (1887) and Fernand Lotte (1952) in compiling their respective 'Repertory' and 'Dictionary' of Balzacian characters. Thanks to these compilations a reader of any novel of Balzac may obtain full information about the antecedents and future career of any character appearing in it.

This ingenious device has of course not escaped criticism. He applied it in the main to his Parisian Scenes, and the constant reappearance of the same figures and the same families, such as the aristocratic Grandlieus, Granvilles and Sérisys, the society queens like the Duchesse de Maufrigneuse, the Marquise d'Espard, Mme Firmiani, the middle-class Popinots, Birotteaus, Crottats, and Camusots, and the same usurers, bankers, courtesans, etc., has given rise to the not very convincing objection that we have here a singularly small world to represent the teeming population of Paris. But certainly the system has some weak points. The retrospective substitution of names demanded greater care and attention than Balzac was able or willing to spare. The merging of two originally independent characters sometimes created difficult psychological problems. For instance, it was only in the course of composing *Le père Goriot* that he decided to equate his newly invented careerist, who thus makes his first appearance in the Paris of 1819, and whom he originally intended to call Eugène de Massiac, with the blasé opportunist of *La Peau de chagrin,* the Rastignac whom we have seen giving advice to Raphaël de Valentin in the late eighteen-twenties. Also Balzac involved himself in sometimes inextricable chronological difficulties, as anyone will realize who attempts to work out a satisfactory time-sequence in *Gobseck, César Birotteau* and *La Femme de trente ans,* a work to which the principle of recurrent personages was not consistently applied until 1842. And furthermore, to read the life-story of such and such a character, for example Andoche Finot, Émile Blondet and the poet Canalis, in Cerfberr and Christophe or Lotte, can be irritating to one who knows by what sudden impulses, by what hesitant and fitful steps, by what shifts of amalgamation and modification Balzac brought them into his repertory. A more fascinating study is that of the appearance and development of the recurrent characters in Balzac's own conception, but that involves the task of collating manuscripts, proofs and successive editions of the works.

On the other hand the device has inestimable value in tying the different works together. Each one, although perfectly complete in itself, explains and enriches the other, just as each new appearance of a character reveals a fact at which a previous appearance had only hinted, and takes the reader backwards or forwards to the beginning, the middle or the end of his career. For with the *Comédie Humaine,* unlike the 'roman-fleuves' of our own century, there can be no steady, no simultaneous march forward in time of all the characters. On the contrary, as Balzac was to observe in the Preface to *Une Fille d'Ève* (1839):

> . . . il en est ainsi dans le monde social. Vous rencontrez au milieu d'un salon un homme que vous avez perdu de vue depuis dix ans; il est premier ministre et capitaliste; vous l'avez connu sans redingote . . . puis vous allez dans un coin de salon, et là quelque délicieux conteur de société vous fait, en une demi-heure, l'histoire pittoresque des dix ou vingt ans que vous ignoriez. . . . Il n'y a rien qui soit d'un seul bloc dans ce monde; tout y est mosaïque.

Such a method puts each novel, and each character, in perspective; and behind the mass of separate novels, one glimpses a sort of hinterland, in which people are moving, developing and changing as they do in real life.

No better example than *Le père Goriot* can be cited of this enrichment of one novel by episodes and reminiscences absorbed into it from previous ones, or of the illusion of depth and fullness it derives therefrom. In the first flush of enthusiasm for his new-found device, Balzac incorporated into this novel lengthy enumerations of the social celebrities he had created one by one in the course of four years. To this somewhat mechanical expedient he was often to resort in later novels. But far more ingenious and salutary is the way in which, by the reappearance of certain personages, other fictions are assumed into the novel. Claire de Beauséant, whom *La Femme abandonnée* had shown as a recluse in Normandy, nursing her wounds before finding a new lover, is moved backward into 1819 at a moment when her first lover, the Marquis d'Ajuda-Pinto, is mustering up courage to take a wife and desert her: she serves as Rastignac's kindly and noble-hearted cicerone in the brilliant society of which she is a leader. The Duchesse de Langeais, at the climax of her misunderstanding with Montriveau (Balzac's chronology is weak here), plays her part as a malicious, then a sympathetic friend of Claire, and also is called on to give Rastignac such sketchy knowledge of Goriot's past as polite society possesses. Henri de Marsay, the elegant philanderer from *La Fille aux yeux d'or,* the events of which were situated in 1815, lurks in the background as the sated lover of Delphine de Nucingen whom Rastignac replaces. Mme de Restaud, the unfaithful wife who, in *Les Dangers de l'inconduite,* has pawned the family jewels for the sake of her lover, now expressly named as the profligate Maxime de Trailles, is transformed into Anastasie, Goriot's elder daughter. De Restaud's discovery of her transactions with Gobseck, his intervention, and the implacable firmness with which he forces her to sign away her fortune in favour of her eldest son, together with the refusal of Delphine's husband, the Baron de Nucingen, to relax his grip on his wife's marriage portion, determine the final paroxysm and death-throes of Goriot—while at the same time offering some slight attenuation of the daughters' guilt in failing to appear at his death-bed. And so *Le père Goriot* achieves additional significance by virtue of its relationship with the previous stories. And to them can be added several others. In the early versions of *Le père Goriot* Lady Brandon, from *La Grenadière,* made a momentary appearance, and was not to be excluded from it until 1843. Likewise *L'Auberge rouge* soon became permanently linked with it, since the banker Taillefer, father of the pathetic Victorine, was given in 1836 the role of the murderer, formerly named Mauricey, in that story. Moreover Balzac had only to give Taillefer's name to the Amphitryon of the Bacchanalian orgy in *La Peau de chagrin* for a second link to be forged between that novel and *Le père Goriot.* The *Étude de Femme* of 1830 was also to be brought into its orbit in its later editions, the careless lover who sends a love-letter to the wrong woman being identified with Rastignac, while the rightful recipient of the letter naturally becomes Delphine de Nucingen.

Le père Goriot met with resounding success which filled Balzac with jubilation. As a kind of postscript he rewrote *Les Dangers de l'inconduite,* now virtually a satellite story, and published it as *Papa Gobseck* in November 1835. The lawyer whom Gobseck has befriended, and who is a witness of the Restaud conflict, is identified with the Derville of *Le colonel Chabert.* The usurer himself is magnified into a figure worthy to stand beside Grandet, Claës and Goriot as the incarnation of a devouring passion which in its turn reaches its culmination in the delirium of a death-bed. For this, and no less for the fact that Balzac has now achieved an equilibrium by the perfect blending of his social and philosophical themes, in such wise that the latter, though present, do not obtrude, we may well endorse the judgment of M. Lalande in his study of *Gobseck:* 'En 1835, le génie de Balzac arrive à sa maturité.' (pp. 86-98)

> *Herbert J. Hunt, in his* Balzac's Comédie Humaine, *University of London, The Athlone Press, 1959, 506 p.*

Donald Fanger   (essay date 1965)

[*Fanger is an American educator and critic. In the following excerpt, he discusses narrative technique and characterization, concluding with an analysis of the role of Vautrin.*]

Le Père Goriot, published in 1835, represents a crucial stage in the development of Balzac's work. Here his mythology in its double sense—as idea and as form—may be seen to crystallize. His technical mastery is secure, and that enabling device of the *Comédie humaine,* the *retour des personnages,* is first put to work here. The city, society, and money are first fully invoked in the central roles they will henceforth fill—the Parcae of the Balzacian world. *Le Père Goriot* is nothing less than the cornerstone of the vast edifice to whose completion he gave the remaining decade and a half of his life. By any standards it is an intricately plotted, highly compressed book, and just because it is so, the need—remarked by Henry James and many others—to take Balzac in bulk, rather than in small doses, is in large measure obviated. For there is in this book a bulk of matter that its physical slenderness belies. What makes this possible is a consistency of heightening (not unlike that of Shakespeare, to whose Lear Goriot offers a conscious parallel) which creates a total atmosphere of myth, a decorum akin to that of poetic drama—and it inheres not in the speeches but in the particular character of the narration, one might almost say of the narrator.

The distinction is of some importance; while a narrative always implies a narrator, in the way that a chair implies a chairmaker, the implication may be fostered or weakened, as the literary strategy requires. Balzac's beginning, with its present-tense immediacy and its total objectivity, seems to promise an uncompromising realism: "Madame Vauquer, née de Conflans, is an elderly woman who, for the last forty years, has kept a family boardinghouse in the Rue Neuve-Sainte-Geneviève between the Latin Quarter and the Faubourg Saint-Marceau." Yet a dozen lines later, we find our attention distracted by the narrator's assurances that, however overworked the word "drama" may be, "it must be used here; not that this story is dramatic in the true sense of the word, but by the time it is finished some tears may perhaps have been shed—*intra muros* and *extra*." The author steps forward as stage manager, reminding us that the drama exists, already finished; what we are to see are the workings-out of several interrelated destinies toward an end already known, if not yet revealed. The time perspective is indicated; the geographical one, dependent as it is on "local color," is similarly announced in the rhetorical question, "Will it [the novel] be understood outside Paris?" and the response, "One may doubt it." The voice assuring us that "this drama is neither fiction nor romance" gives repeated evidence of a concern with its proper reception. Erich Auerbach [in *Mimesis,* 1953] has brilliantly analyzed the description that follows of the boardinghouse and its mistress, showing how "the motif of the unity of a milieu has taken hold of [Balzac] so powerfully that the things and the persons composing a milieu often acquire . . . a sort of second significance which, though different from that which reason can comprehend, is far more essential—a significance which can best be defined by the adjective demonic," so that "every milieu becomes a moral and physical atmosphere." What is perhaps of equal interest is the author's preparation of the reader for such multiple significances. In this case, Balzac informs us, "The Rue Neuve-Sainte-Geneviève especially is like a bronze frame, the only one befitting this story, for which the mind must be prepared by gloomy colors and heavy thoughts." To the interior lighting corresponds an exterior one, and these monitory emphases on the emotional tone of the story, as on its significance, have the important function of reminding the reader of his role as spectator: they are invitations to see, understand, and judge, rather than to participate in the action.

This preparation of the reader's intelligence is a constant feature in Balzac. "Nothing could be more dismal than the sight of this sitting-room," he writes in introducing the famous catalogue of the interior of the Maison Vauquer, in which the personality of place fuses with that of its mistress; and one wonders whether, in view of what follows, this is not supererogatory. The same technique, however, has wider functions. Besides underlining a given aspect of the physical scene, as above—or even of the spiritual one, as when Balzac refers to the lodgers as "these narrow minds"—it can on occasion furnish an orientation obtainable in no other way. Rastignac, well into his education by now, resolves "to open two parallel lines of attack on success, to lean on knowledge and on love, to be a learned jurist and a man of fashion." "He was still very much a child!" Balzac comments: "These two lines are asymptotes, which can never meet." In editorializing, Balzac limits the reader's freedom of judgment by guiding it; yet this is no simple didacticism. What keeps it from being that is one's overriding awareness that the world in which the action takes place is, though an interpretation of reality, so complete a one that it must have its own laws, its own iron necessities. Made constantly aware that he is witnessing *un passé déjà accompli,* the reader cannot resent the historian's underlining of critical junctures.

The narrator, then, is the chorus to the drama he presents. Like the chorus in Greek tragedy, he announces the exigencies of Fate, the limits of possibility. As chorus, too, he may color present action by invoking—like the shadow it casts before—the future. In the Balzacian world, where things have their destinies as well as men, we see futurity hanging over them. Balzac completes the description of the wretchedness of the Vauquer furniture by noting: "If it is not yet filthy, it is spotted; if it has neither holes nor tatters, it is going to fall into pieces from decay." The same is true even of secondary characters: when Rastignac goes to the Marquis d'Ajuda-Pinto to reclaim his cousin's letters, Balzac tells us of the marquis: "He seemed to wish to talk to Eugene, to question him about the ball or about the Viscountess, or perhaps to confess to him that he was already in despair about his marriage, as he was later known to be." And when he describes Anastasie, brilliant in her diamonds, he takes care to add in passing: "She was wearing them for the last time."

If the future represents one form of potentiality, there are others as well, which the narrator as chorus will emphasize. Sometimes this emphasis comes by way of analogy, as when the conventions of graphic art are invoked to ratify the disposition of the novelist's figures. Thus, among the lodgers of Madame Vauquer, Balzac notices in singling out Goriot for attention that on him "a painter, like the teller of this story, would have made all the light of his picture fall." Again: "Victorine was like one of those naive paintings of the Middle Ages in which all accessories are neglected by the artist, who has reserved the magic of his calm and proud brush for the face, yellow in tone, but in which heaven seems to be reflected with its golden tones." But there are other sorts of potentialities, which depend more strictly on the force of the subjunctive: "If the excitement of a ball had reflected its rosy tints in that pale face; if the ease of an elegant life had filled out and colored those cheeks, already slightly hollow; if love had lit up those sad eyes, Victorine could have rivaled the loveliest girls."

From such comparisons of what is with what might be, it is only a short step to the use of metaphor and symbol. Thus, describing the boardinghouse, Balzac underlines in passing a symbol that will come to dominate a whole aspect of his story; having mentioned a statue of the God of Love, he notes that in its peeling and scaly surface "those fond of symbols might perhaps discover an allegory of Parisian love." Paris itself appears in two main metaphorical guises, each suggestive of a side of its mythical character. The first is contrasted with the Paris of *comme il faut* and stresses the wonder and the variety that the metropolis contains: "But Paris is a veritable ocean. Throw in the plummet, you will never know its depth. Survey it, describe it? Whatever care you take in surveying and describing it, however numerous and curious the explorers

of this sea may be, there will always be a virgin realm, an unknown cavern, flowers, pearls, monsters, something unheard of, overlooked by the literary divers." Midway through the book, the metaphor is taken up again; the money received from his mother and sisters leaves Rastignac "free for fifteen months to sail the Parisian ocean and devote himself to the woman trade, or to fishing fortune from it." The other metaphor is Vautrin's, and it will serve as a base for the multifarious intrigues of *Splendeurs et misères des courtisanes* (as well as for Dumas' later *Les Mohicans de Paris*):

> Paris, you see, is like a forest in the New World where a score of savage tribes operate—the Illinois, the Hurons, who live on the proceeds offered by the different social classes. You are a hunter of millions; to capture them you employ snares, limed twigs, decoys. There are several ways of hunting. Some hunt dowries . . . some fish for consciences, others sell their clients bound hand and foot. The man who comes back with his gamebag well stocked is hailed, feted, received into good society.

The speaker of these lines, it should be noted, is himself the choicest example of symbolic heightening in the novel; partly for this reason, partly because of his thematic connections with later books, discussion of him is deferred for separate treatment. What we may notice meanwhile, in completing this survey of the special functions of the narrator as chorus, is the way he manages to present character itself as symbol. It is not a question of Balzac's identifying Goriot as "this Christ of Paternity" or of his having Bianchon find on him the identifying marks of "an Eternal Father." Such allusions, among which we might include the marks of Judas on Mademoiselle Michonneau, suggest an erratic religious light playing about the action, underlining the fateful nature of the ethical issues—but finally applying only to the action itself. In the process of characterization, they are only metaphors, casually invoked and casually dropped. More important by far is the way Balzac makes each of his characters symbolize a whole army of his fellows and explain them, or be explained by them. Here it is customary to invoke the parallel Balzac set forth in his preface between the varieties of social man and the species of the animal kingdom: "The differences between a soldier, a worker, an administrator, a lawyer, an idler, a scholar, a statesman, a trader, a sailor, a poet, a poor man, a priest, are, although more difficult to seize, as considerable as those which distinguish the wolf, the lion, the ass, the vulture, the shark, the seal, the lamb, etc."

Certainly the invocation is justified. Madame Vauquer, Balzac says in introducing her, "resembles all *women who have had their troubles.*" Poiret, the only comic character in the book, is classified with elaborate care: only after "the great family of simpletons" has been surveyed does he emerge as "a bureaucratic ninny," and the traits of his species explain his part in the betrayal of Vautrin. "Such natures are almost all alike"—this is the Balzacian axiom. Proclaiming it in his characterization of Goriot, however, he adds by way of explanation: "At the heart of almost all of them you find a sublime sentiment." With such a remark, we are at the point where sociological classification merges with a more personal one; we are reminded that Balzac's principal characters hold a dual citizenship, in the historical Paris and in the mythical, Balzacian one. Thus Delphine's anxiety to be received by Madame de Beauséant is explained by the former, by her being a parvenue. But when, deploying against Rastignac "all the resources of feminine diplomacy as practiced in Paris," she is nevertheless pictured as sincere, the explanation derives rather from the myth: "Women are always true, even in the midst of their greatest hypocrisies, because they are yielding to some natural sentiment."

Behind each figure rise the legions of the class he represents. Rastignac is introduced as "one of those young men accustomed to work by poverty." His reaction to the snubs of Madame de Restaud is explained not in terms of his individual psychology, but of his class's: "When a young man of his age is treated with scorn, he flares up, flies into a rage, and shakes his fist at all society; he seeks revenge, but at the same time doubts himself." Even his self-divisions are typical. Thus in speaking of them, Balzac can refer to "all the instincts, good and bad, of the two or three men that make up a young Parisian." In such ways, the narrator is not only guide but philosopher, pointing through and beyond the characters he presents to the main lines of a world that they incarnate and interpret, but one that he interprets also. To Rastignac's dawning awareness of the nature of Parisian society, the narrator adds his own ratification: "He saw the world as it is—laws and moral judgments powerless among the rich—and saw in success the *ultima ratio mundi.*" Ultimately, this freedom of narrative comment welds together the realistic and the melodramatic planes of the work by its modulations between emotional coloring and documentary objectivity, between harbingers of futurity and disclosures of potentiality, between symbolic presentation and passages of rationalization. The result is a richness of narrative texture that can accommodate in a single paragraph the flat summary, "In his heart of hearts [Rastignac] had surrendered completely to Vautrin," and the lurid but not artistically unjustified picture of the result, "Desperation lent him new beauty, and he shone with all the fires of the hell he carried within him." But such suppleness could not be the work of the narrator as chorus alone; it is made possible as well by the skill of the narrator as architect, by the unremitting pace of his narrative and the multiple tensions resulting from contrasting variations on a few key themes. It is the passion in great works that gives them life, Balzac had said; but he also knew the value of structure and "the first law of literature . . . the necessity for contrasts."

Contrast had been a central principle in Balzac's writing from his earliest pseudonymous productions, and his use of it shows constant efforts at refinement. A whole school of writing—to which he himself inclined for a while—had, at the height of the romantic period, enshrined the crudest kind of contrast as the basis for its productions; the character of this *école frénétique* is strongly enough suggested by the title of Jules Janin's parodistic *L'Ane mort et la femme guillotinée.* No novel, of course, is without its internal contrasts—but they may be implicit and ironic or explicit and intentionally emphasized. The second of these two manners was more common in the romantic period

and followed naturally from that penchant for the depiction of strong feelings which the eclectic Balzac most notably shared with his contemporaries. Passionate people produce passionate contrasts. Further, the very act of definition always emphasizes the contrast of the area defined with the areas adjacent to it—and Balzac, as the great definer of social types, by underlining their salient characteristics also underlined their sharpest differences. Despite his periodic protests about the leveling of mores in French society, Paris remained for him always "the home of contrasts." As he was consistent in proclaiming, "In Paris, extremes meet through the passions. Vice is perpetually joining the rich man to the poor there, and the great to the humble." So it is not surprising to find *Le Père Goriot,* one of Balzac's most carefully constructed books, built around this "first law of literature," in both the architecture of its scenes and that of its themes.

The scenes in the novel number some twenty-four, taking "scene" roughly in its theatrical usage, to designate directly presented actions, diversely located. Their succession is characterized by a regular alternation between scenes in the boardinghouse and those outside it. Thus, at the end of the lengthy exposition (marked by the sentence, "Such was the general situation in the boardinghouse at the end of November 1819"), the first scene is that of the ball chez Madame de Beauséant, presented through Rastignac's retrospective musing on his return and contrasted strikingly with the poverty of the two scenes that follow: Rastignac's discovering Goriot in the act of twisting his silver service, and the boarders during a typical day. The next two scenes take Rastignac to the aristocratic houses of Mesdames de Restaud and de Beauséant, between which Balzac underlines the contrast: "He had seen the luxury which a Mademoiselle Goriot was bound to love, the gilding, the expensive objects prominently displayed, the unintelligent luxury of the newly rich, the squandering of the kept woman. This fascinating picture was suddenly eclipsed by the imposing Beauséant mansion." Right after this, his return to the boardinghouse produces an important effect: "The transition was too abrupt, the contrast too complete, not to develop in him an ambition beyond measure." Two scenes at the boardinghouse follow, with documents and exposition interpolated, and Rastignac once more visits the Beauséant house, where he meets Delphine—only to be struck, on his return home, by an even crueler contrast. Visiting Goriot for the first time in his room, Eugene "could not repress a start of astonishment in seeing the awful hole the father lived in, after having admired the finery of his daughter."

As contrasting scenes of squalor and luxury continue to alternate, Rastignac's reactions become more pronounced, his attraction to the fashionable world more passionate, his revulsion to poverty more instinctive and physical. When, on the heels of Vautrin's arrest, he is led to the luxurious new bachelor apartment that Delphine and her father have arranged for him, "this last contrast between what he saw now and what he had just seen made his overwrought nerves give way." Moreover, as the book draws to a close, the scenes become shorter, until the effect produced by this acceleration becomes almost one of montage. The climax comes when Rastignac has hurried home from the sumptuous ball of his retiring tutor in strategy to the squalid deathbed of his tutor in sentimental generosity; and here the narrator is again at pains to underline what is already dramatically evident. With the fruitless visits to Goriot's two daughters, the scene shifts for the last time to the Vauquer establishment, and from there to the cemetery of Père-Lachaise, where the fidelity of Rastignac is set in relief against the callousness of the daughters, represented by the empty carriages, marked with the Restaud and Nucingen arms, which join the funeral procession.

The alternation of scenes is thus calculated to sustain the maximum dramatic effect in the recurring contrasts of atmosphere. But scenic structure is only the scaffolding of a novel; well managed, it facilitates the full orchestration of key themes. Bardèche has noted of the early Balzac that, even before he had any experience to guide him, he showed a vivid sense of the illumination his characters might be made to lend each other. We see this same sense, now highly developed, at work from the beginning of *Le Père Goriot.* So in the preliminary canvass of Madame Vauquer's lodgers, he sets apart Rastignac and Victorine: "Two figures there formed a striking contrast with the mass of boarders and habitués." Beyond this initial contrast, of course, Rastignac and Victorine take their places in a continuum representing varieties of child-parent relationships, a coninuum that is itself only one of several sets of themes with contrasting variations. These themes may be grouped according to Rastignac's climactic awareness of "the three great expressions of society: Obedience, Struggle, and Revolt; the Family, the World, and Vautrin."

The primacy of the family is sufficiently indicated by the title of the book; it is that basic element of society which represents the social ties of uncorrupted nature and so serves as a barometer, measuring the degree of social corruption in terms of its corrosion of family ties. It is no accident that "this obscure but dreadful Parisian tragedy" reveals parallels to *King Lear:*

> "Oh! well, yes, their father," replied the Viscountess, "a father, a good father who, they say, gave each of them five or six hundred thousand francs to secure their happiness by marrying them well, and kept only eight or ten thousand livres of income for himself, two homes where he would be adored and made much of. Inside of two years his sons-in-law had banished him from their society as if he were the lowest of outcasts."

Perhaps even more strongly than in *King Lear,* pathos is produced by temporal contrast: each character's past is invoked to lend illumination and pathos to the present. Thus when Goriot first appears in the exposition, it is in 1813—six years before the main action of the book takes place—and the successive stages of his ascent, floor by floor, to cheaper rooms in the boardinghouse reveal the ebbing of his fortune; and the ebbing of his fortune is made to symbolize his fading prospect of family happiness. Already in the beginning the dominant connection is underlined between the themes of family and money: Goriot, still relatively affluent, unpacks his silver service, which recalls to

him "the solemnities of his domestic life." Ardently devoted to his wife (whose nature, characteristically, "contrasted sharply with his" and who might, had she lived, have cultivated "that inert nature"), on her death we are told how he transferred all his affection to his two daughters, "who, at first, fully satisfied all his emotional demands." The brief period of past happiness is recalled more than once at moments of extreme tension; it colors the whole tragedy of Goriot and gives it its pathos.

If Goriot represents the indulgent father wounded by the neglect of his daughters, a contrasting picture is offered in the situation of Victorine Taillefer, whose father is insensible alike to the deathbed entreaties of his wife on the girl's behalf and to the eloquent pleas for recognition from Victorine herself. And both of these situations, which Balzac identifies as essentially Parisian, form a further contrast with that of Rastignac and his family in the provinces. This, significantly, is pictured immediately on the heels of the recital of Goriot's history, as Rastignac has pieced it together from his inquiries. The Rastignac family is shown as harmonious, unified, and affectionate; his mother and sisters are generously ready to scrape together the money he requests—and he, on his part, receives the money with a noteworthy consciousness of its value to them. This awareness of others sets him apart from the Goriot daughters, even as he himself is perceiving the outward similarity of their situations: "Your mother has broken up her jewels!" he says to himself. "Your aunt has doubtless wept as she sold some of her keepsakes! What right have you to condemn Anastasie? Out of egoism, you have just done for your future what she did for her lover! Of the two of you, who is the better?" And Balzac adds, "He experienced that noble secret remorse, whose merit is rarely appreciated by men when they judge their fellows but which often makes the angels of heaven absolve the criminal condemned by earthly justice."

Three sets of parents and children, then: Goriot, Taillefer, Rastignac, whose fates are all connected and serve as commentaries on one another. Two loveless women between whom Rastignac hesitates: Delphine de Nucingen and Victorine Taillefer. And a corresponding series of spiritual relationships: Rastignac, more than either of Goriot's real children, stands to him as a son and is so called. "Papa Vautrin," as he calls himself, similarly stands to Rastignac as a would-be spiritual father (Rastignac senior being, for all practical purposes, out of the picture), and goes so far as to offer to make him his heir: "If I have no children . . . I'll will you my fortune!" Vautrin further boasts the largest possible spiritual family, in the midst of a society where the rule tends to be every man for himself. "Is there one of you," he asks the startled lodgers, "who can say, as I can, that he has ten thousand brothers ready to do anything for him?"

The conclusion to which all these examples tend is that genuine family ties are impossible in Paris. It is implicit in Balzac's description of the scene in which the Duchesse de Langeais summarizes the history of Goriot and his family situation: "Tears glistened in Eugene's eyes. He had recently felt renewed by the pure and holy influence of family affection, was still under the spell of youthful beliefs,

Mme Hanska.

and this was only his first day on the battlefield of Parisian civilization." The whole adverbial tendency of this statement is toward a future in which Rastignac's familial susceptibilities will be less tender, as his membership in Parisian civilization becomes less tentative, more conscious and more willed. For society is struggle, in which the sole consideration, and the most important weapon, is money. Whatever the goal of the struggle—power or love—money comes to be the *sine qua non.* In the course of the novel, this theme encroaches gradually on the others, but it is present from the first. When the lodgers are introduced, we are told how much rent each pays. The unfolding of Goriot's tragedy—and of his daughters'—is a demonstration of the pathetic hollowness of the Parisian equation of love and money. Rastignac's own imperative need to realize a fortune is ascribed to his desire to settle a dowry on the sisters he loves, who are made to sacrifice what little they have as a sort of down payment. His abortive pact with the devil, Vautrin, turns on the question of money, is sealed with his acceptance of a loan, and has in view the fortune Victorine will inherit when her brother is murdered. Vautrin himself is betrayed for money. Goriot, even in death, is pursued by the money question in the arrangement of his pauper's funeral—"in an age," as Balzac notes ironically, "where religion is not rich enough to pray gratis." And the pathos of the closing scene in the cemetery includes the significant detail of Rastignac's having to borrow twenty sous from the menial Christophe in order to tip the gravediggers.

The larger tragedy of the book, centering on Rastignac, has to do with the nature of Parisian society where, as

Rastignac soon concludes, "success is virtue." That society is twice analyzed in the book—by Madame de Beauséant and by Vautrin. The former explains the power of fashionable women, and the ways of exploiting them, in which the cardinal rule is the concealment of all true emotions, on pain of losing all. Her concluding summary is that the world is "an assembly of fools and knaves," and her concluding advice is, "Take care that you belong to neither class." In resolving to follow this advice, Rastignac decides to pursue two simultaneous paths, to be a "learned jurist" and "a man of fashion." But Balzac is quick to comment on the impossibility of such a course, and Rastignac's gradual abandonment of his studies follows shortly. Madame de Beauséant's picture of society is true, but her suggestion that it is possible to avoid joining one of its two camps is wishful thinking. The analysis given by Vautrin is more terrifying precisely because it is so completely without sentimentality. "He has told me bluntly," Rastignac muses, "what Madame de Beauséant was telling me in more polished fashion." In Vautrin's analysis, the emphasis is on money: "Do you know what you need, the way you're going? A million, and at once." But Vautrin goes beyond money, as he goes beyond sentiment and beyond morality; his arguments rest on the belief that "there are no principles; there are only events." Therefore he can speak "with the superiority of a man who, after examining the state of things here below, has seen that there are only two choices: either a stupid obedience or revolt." His arguments impress Rastignac, who muses afterwards: "This brigand has told me more about virtue than I ever learned before from men or books." Yet he ends his meditations with a characteristic evasion: "Hell! My head is swimming. I don't want to think about anything; the heart is a good guide." Only at the end of the book will the choice he has made be declared. The final contrast is between that "last tear of his youth" which he buries with Goriot and his "first act of challenge to society" in going to dine with Madame de Nucingen. He has chosen to follow, if not join, the party of revolt, whose legendary spokesman now calls for attention.

Vautrin is the "vertebral column" of this book no less than of the series that includes it: he is the principal carrier of mystery, the most flamboyant figure of melodrama, the most consistent embodiment of religious themes; he is the most complex symbol and perhaps the most complex character; certainly he is the Balzacian character par excellence, compact of energy, will, and passion to the point of transcendence; at once the rebel and revolt itself. It is not for nothing that we find his name taken as a common noun in Balzac's startling series, "the Family, the World, and Vautrin." He is, in short, the most striking guide to the various levels of the Balzacian universe, for he exists on every one of them.

Vautrin is introduced, in the exposition, as "the man of forty," a figure of transition between the two young lodgers "carried away by the whirlwinds of Parisian life" and the others, "those old men indifferent to everything that didn't touch them directly"; he is the only figure in his prime. We learn that he is amiable, but that this amiability serves to fend off any intimacy; that he is affluent and ready to lend money; that he is an expert locksmith; that he dyes his sideburns; that he returns late each night with the aid of a master key. All this suggests either the criminal or the policeman (and it is well to remember, as Vautrin's own final "incarnation" will show, that in the popular novel of Balzac's time the two were often interchangeable). There is nothing to contradict either possibility in the hints that we are dealing with an extraordinary nature, tending toward omniscience, if not omnipotence: "He knew everything, moreover: ships, the sea, France, foreign countries, business, men, events, laws, great houses, and prisons. . . . His eye, like that of a stern judge, seemed to penetrate to the heart of all questions, to probe all consciences, to divine all feelings." One may, it is true, doubt the judgment of a narrator who finds evidence of "an imperturbable sang-froid which bespoke a man who would not hesitate to commit a crime to get out of a dubious position" in the way in which the man spat; and one notices what seems a crude heightening in the reference to the "fearful depth" of his character. The closing observation, however, tends to be more matter-of-fact: "Often a burst of invective worthy of Juvenal, by which he seemed to delight in scoffing at laws, in scourging high society and proving its inconsistency, suggested that he held some grudge against the social system, and that he had in his background some carefully buried secret."

Oddly enough, in this book, where he functions most consistently *as a character* beneath all the symbolic trappings and melodramatic heightening, the personal reasons for this attitude are not given in any fullness. We learn from Inspector Gondureau that Vautrin first ran afoul of the law in a manner that made his conviction "something that brought him no end of honor in his own set. . . . He agreed to take another man's crime upon himself, a forgery committed by a handsome young man of whom he was very fond, a young Italian, a bit of a gambler, who later entered military service, where his record has been spotless." But already the hints of homosexuality are sufficiently telling in the passing reference to the young Italian's beauty, as in the sole slip that Vautrin makes in the course of the book, when he exclaims to the handsome Rastignac: "I'm fond of you, as sure as my name is Cheat—(good God!)—Vautrin." Gondureau says flatly that Vautrin does not like women, and Vautrin himself tends to confirm this in offering to make Rastignac his heir "if I have no children—which is likely, since I'm not anxious to plant slips of myself here." "Is that being a friend to a man?" he goes on: "But I'm fond of you. I have a passion for devoting myself to another. I've done it before. . . . Well, for me—and I know life inside out—there exists only one true sentiment, friendship between man and man. Pierre and Jaffier, there you have my passion." When he has put Rastignac into a drunken sleep, he moves him so that he may sleep comfortably and "kisses him warmly on the forehead"; and it is difficult not to see in his words when captured—" 'Goodbye, Eugene,' he said in a gentle and sad voice that contrasted strikingly with the rough tone of his earlier speeches"—[in the words of Félicien Marceau in *Balzac et son monde,* 1955] the "sad sweetness of loves that might have been."

Vautrin's personal relations with Rastignac on this level are all relations *manquées,* doomed by the student's

strength of will and cut short by his own summary removal from the scene. Nor is this, in any case, their most significant level. Vautrin gives few indications (beyond paying fifteen extra francs a month for a gloria at dessert) of being primarily a sensualist. His campaign of seduction is waged with consummate artistry, but on a larger field. His homosexuality does not obviously affect his actions; it serves to complete his outlawry—since all the other criminals in Balzac have more socially acceptable sexual ties— rather than to define it. Vautrin's attempted seductions are, first of all, more general temptations; whatever else there may be is deferred: "You're wondering, why this devotion? Well, I'll tell you sometime; I'll whisper it sweetly into your ear." Thus Balzac refers to him more than once as, simply, "the tempter" or "this fierce logician"; the latter is particularly significant because the temptations that Vautrin strews in Rastignac's path have in view (literally, at least) nothing more personal than an ideological change of allegiance. Balzac's emphasis on "the seductive arguments which he had sown in the heart of the student" finds its counterpart in the scene where Vautrin offers him financial aid but refuses to press the advantage to secure Rastignac's assent to his proposition regarding Victorine: "But listen!" he says, "I have my delicacy, like any other man. Don't make up your mind now. You're a little off balance, you have debts. I don't want it to be passion or desperation that decides you to come over to me, but reason."

Nonetheless, Vautrin's speeches are a striking combination of social analysis and arguments *ad hominem*. If his analysis of "the present state of your social disorder" coincides largely with Balzac's, it is still an interested one, and the longest exposition of it, in Vautrin's first tête-à-tête with Rastignac, ends with a proposition from which he stands to gain 200,000 francs. The second one—when he lends Rastignac the 3,500 francs—shows a similar progress from an insistence on seeing "the world as it is" to a display of personal temptations: "Ah! if you wanted to become my pupil, I would make you achieve all your ambitions. You would not form a desire but what it would be instantly satisfied—anything you might wish: honors, wealth, women." Always the point of view remains the same: "I am taking the inventory of your desires in order to put the question to you." The result is that Rastignac accepts the lessons without accepting the tutelage; he will not compromise his freedom of action; nor will he abandon the residue of sentimentality, the vestiges of those qualities that Madame de Beauséant praises in him ("You have seemed to me to be kind and noble, unspoiled and open, in this world where such qualities are so rare") at the very moment of his decision to abandon them.

"What kind of a man are you, then?" Rastignac asks Vautrin. The answers are various. "I am what you call an artist," he says at one point—and one recalls Balzac's view of the artist as a usurper of God's attributes in Vautrin's homage to Cellini, from whose memoirs, he says, "I have learned to imitate Providence, which kills us at random, and to love the beautiful wherever it may be found." In engineering the death of young Taillefer, Vautrin is as good as his word, and Balzac himself takes every opportunity to suggest, somewhat melodramatically, Vautrin's possession of providential powers. His magnetic eyes are forever casting "glances by which this man seemed to penetrate the best-hidden secrets of the heart"; he is forever divining the thoughts of those around him; and at the moment at table when Bianchon alludes, too late, to the treachery of Vautrin's betrayer, "His magnetic glance fell like a ray of sunlight on Mademoiselle Michonneau, and this spurt of will made her legs buckle."

Behind the exercise of these powers, and behind Vautrin's very conception of providence, we find his conviction that there are no principles, only events; we move in a sphere beyond good and evil, the sphere of the superman. "I do not accuse the rich in favor of the people," he tells Rastignac; "man is the same at the top, at the bottom, in the middle. For every million head of this human cattle, there are ten sharp fellows who put themselves above everything, even laws; I am one of them. You, if you are a superior man, go straight ahead with your head high." As for him, "When I have resolved on something, God alone is strong enough to stop me." One recalls Balzac's statement about criminals' possessing many of the qualities that make great men. Vautrin, on one side, is the apotheosis of this romantic view. He is related in passing to Juvenal, Diogenes, Cromwell, Don Quixote, the Pierre of *Venice Preserved,* Cellini, and Rousseau ("whose pupil I am proud to be"). He boasts that he has never betrayed anyone, that his devotion to his friends and comrades is unwavering, as theirs to him; he operates a sort of welfare scheme for convicts, in which he shows himself strikingly more honest with money than any of the respectable characters in the book. That all these marks of the romantic tradition of the outlaw have their origin in the romantic interpretation of Milton's Satan is of particular significance because of the numerous ways in which Balzac deliberately invokes an identification of Vautrin with his legendary exemplar. Vautrin the man is aggrandized to include the tradition at its fullest, and undergoes in the process an assumption to religious heights.

In elevating Vautrin to the level of religious mythology, Balzac does not cease to betray a divided attitude toward him, but the divisions are here appropriately magnified. On the positive side there is the fact that the initials of Vautrin's given name, Jacques Collin, are those of Jesus Christ; and what might seem farfetched in itself is bolstered by his sobriquet, Cheat-Death, as well as by the story of his sacrificial suffering in taking on himself the crime of another. These hints, of course, are in the final analysis ironic. In a letter answering criticisms of this character, Balzac took pains to emphasize the biblical portrayal of Satan as the most beautiful of the angels, and though Vautrin is hardly presented as being physically beautiful, he has a clearly Satanic grandeur that derives from the Balzacian equation of evil with excess and passion. We see this in his being called constantly tempter and demon; in his emblem of revolt, carried to such extremity; in his continually smiling "diabolically" and manifesting his "infernal genius." One may even find an echo of Milton's "Better to reign in hell than serve in heaven" in Vautrin's "Everything or nothing! That is my motto." His campaign against Rastignac is put into this perspective by Balzac in speaking of "the seductive arguments which he

had sown in the heart of the student to corrupt him." And the hints in his own speech are progressively less veiled. Thus, referring to those who practice honesty and altruism, he speculates sardonically on "the wry faces of these fine people if God should play us the bad joke of staying away from the last judgment." More pointedly, he tells Rastignac, "You would be a fine catch for the devil," tempts him with promises of wealth and power, and predicts that "in a few days you will be ours." Thus it is that when Rastignac momentarily yields, he is presented as "made even more beautiful by his despair, and shining with all the fires of the hell in his heart." Similarly Vautrin, at the moment of his arrest, becomes "an infernal poem, expressing all human emotions except one—repentance. His look was that of the fallen archangel who desires eternal war."

It is true that Balzac calls him in this book "typical of a whole degenerate nation, of a people savage and logical, brutal and supple," but the proof of this, and the sense of its horror, is unstressed. It could hardly be otherwise when the whole context of the novel renders Vautrin's counter-charge so persuasive: "There is less infamy in the brands on our shoulders than in your hearts, you flabby members of a rotting society: the best among you wouldn't resist me." Twelve years later, Balzac was to write that Vautrin represented "corruption, prison, social evil in all its horror," and to add, surprisingly, that there was "nothing gigantic about him"! But by then Vautrin had reappeared in a new avatar. In the daylight world of Parisian society, his corruption could hardly eclipse that of society; in the later works, the focus is on the nocturnal underworld itself, and Vautrin is rejudged against the background of his own subsociety, where the flamboyance of the action puts all the characters on the same scale. In *Le Père Goriot,* by contrast, Vautrin, while playing an important part in the action, lends it a new dimension by his very outrance. In the extremity of his antisocial persuasion, he carries the social analysis of the book to a pitch attainable in no other way; and in so doing, he justifies the terror as Goriot does the pity of tragedy. This is perhaps more than a conventional character might be able to do. Balzac, at least, declines any such attempt and, by keeping biographical details to a bare minimum and heightening the transcendental aspects of Vautrin, makes him a presence almost more than a personage. In the later books he remains this, but the perspective changes: the dimension he lends to *Le Père Goriot* becomes the scale of the whole presented world as we move from mixed drama to pure melodrama, from a recognition of the ubiquity of masks to a view of the world behind them. (pp. 38-56)

Donald Fanger, "Balzac: The Heightening of Substance," in his Dostoevsky and Romantic Realism: A Study of Dostoevsky in Relation to Balzac, Dickens, and Gogol, *Cambridge, Mass.: Harvard University Press, 1965, pp. 28-64.*

Catharine H. Savage   (essay date 1966)

[Savage is an American educator, critic, and poet who has published studies of such prominent French authors

*as André Gide and Roger Martin du Gard. In the fol-
lowing essay, she notes that the self-serving behavior of
Rastignac and Vautrin is not censured by Balzac, concluding that* Le père Goriot *is an "ethically schizophrenic" novel that reflects the moral indecisiveness of Balzac's society.*]

The ambivalent position of Honoré de Balzac with respect
to the bourgeoisie which he depicts in the **Comédie humaine** has recently been noted. On the one hand, from the
time of his first mature novels, he espoused the conservative bourgeois values which he inherited and which, both
at their best and their worst, were those of his age, particularly from the reign of Louis-Philippe. On the other hand,
he castigated these values, impatient with their inherent
limitations, with their adulteration in post-revolutionary
France, and with the mediocrity from which they seemed
to be inseparable. The complement to this contradictory
position is an ambivalent attitude towards the romantic
character as Balzac conceived and re-created it. I should
like to show this ambivalence towards the romantic
hero—the anti-bourgeois—as it is expressed in *Le Père
Goriot* (1834) and to suggest on this basis a judgment of
Balzac.

In *Le Père Goriot,* Eugène de Rastignac and Vautrin are
both conceived of romantically and have a romantic role
to play. Rastignac is, it has been observed, akin to Julien
Sorel: the young, ambitious, individualistic provincial who
yearns for success and who is ready to fight his personal
Napoleonic battles in Paris in order to impose himself.
Without at first being aware of what success in society requires from a young man, he is eager to learn and ready
to adjust his inherited values—those of a conservative,
modest nobility—to whatever new ones are requisite, with
few exceptions. The models whom he chooses (such as
Maxime de Trailles) may be puny compared to the colorful Byronic figures or to the Imperial heroes whom Stendhal and Vigny wished to emulate; nonetheless his attitude is that of the apprentice who would learn to conquer.
Vautrin, who acts as mentor to Eugène, even when the latter chafes under his influence, is a romantic outlaw who
has chosen the underside of society in which to achieve individual conquest. Having attained a sort of success—
independence, power, imposition of will—he enjoys the
position of *noli me tangere.* By his revolt which he culti-
vates, he maintains the Byronic strain; by his hidden action on society, he demonstrates the social power and superiority which Julien Sorel had felt he must achieve and
which, under a different guise, Rastignac covets.

Both of these heroes are traitors to the conservative bourgeoisie and nobility. By his gradual abandonment of family social codes and traditional values, Rastignac betrays
the most solid segment of the social order in favor of the
values of the *arriviste.* Vautrin participates in the undermining of the entire French society, by favoring the rebel,
finding loopholes for the ambitious, and weakening in others whom he considers the elect the ethical and social scruples which prevent them from realizing themselves. With
no sense of responsibility to the collectivity, he preaches
the rule of the strong in the social jungle, of which he gives
a realistic appraisal, corresponding closely to that which
the aristocratic Mme de Beauséant makes. His rebellion

is based on his belief in the hypocrisy of society, which has
neither order nor virtue except through chance or stupidity and which masks its vices behind thrift and self-respect,
traditionally associated with bourgeois virtue since the
seventeenth century. This revolt derives likewise from his
extremist view of man's corruption, which is reminiscent
of Joseph de Maistre and Bonald. Vautrin plays the role
of the disabused romantic who has seen, as he says, "les
profondes déceptions du contrat social." He proposes simply, then, that one accept the bourgeois's own code,
"Chacun pour soi," "Enrichissez-vous," and so forth, and
thus makes an explicit moral program out of the worst features of France, at the expense of tottering traditional values.

These two heroes, whose romanticism is neither as languishing nor as grandiose as that of heroes of earlier decades but who show the same *culte du moi* and the same
antisocial impulses as the Renés and the Laras, are placed
in a plot structure centered on a middle-class drama and
revolving around a threat to traditional values. As in
César Birotteau, where Balzac is concerned with bourgeois commercial probity, and in *Le Lys dans la Vallée,*
which is a paean to feminine virtue, the novelist is seeking
to embody and defend a conception of virtue and order.
That the old man who incarnates the principle is stupid
and sentimental to the point of being destructive and anti-
social himself does not outweigh the praise which Balzac
explicitly gives to him in the novel and the recognition
which the author accords here and elsewhere to the sa-
credness of love and paternity. If his unwise love contributes to his own ruin and the instability of those around
him, it is precisely by reference to a notion of order, reason, and justice that he is to be judged, and finally judges
himself, like the broken Lear—although still more sinned
against than sinning. A phrase of the père Goriot himself,
who is qualified as a "saint," "le Christ de la paternité,"
will serve to summarize the author's attitude toward the
central question of social ethics: "la justice est pour moi,
tout est pour moi, la nature, le code civil. Je proteste. La
patrie périra si les pères son foulés aux pieds. Cela est clair.
La société, le monde roulent sur la paternité, tout croule
si les enfants n'aiment pas leurs pères."

It is certain that Balzac's intention was to support this
point of view in *Le Père Goriot,* as, in his other novels
dealing with society, he wished to defend traditional social
order. This is, then, the standard by which the characters
should be judged within the book. One would expect Balzac so to order his plot and build his characters that they
would be seen in light of this standard, be judged, and fall
or stand according to their merit—thus offering the "grande leçon" which according to Balzac, the author who fulfills his task nobly must present. Some of the secondary
figures are so judged, and the structure makes this clear.
The Goriot daughters, particularly the Comtesse de Restaud, who have the role of representing extreme vanity
and rebellion against discipline and filial duty, do not long
hide from the reader their pettiness and mercenary motives. Balzac puts them into situations where they, like
their husbands, appear weak, interested, and egotistical.
As the novelist unveils more and more of their private
lives, they are shown increasingly wanting, both to us and

to their father, who is led at last to admit their ingratitude. When they are set against one another in a vicious quarrel, it becomes clear that lack of gratitude towards their father is coupled with hate for each other. The final scene—Goriot's funeral, at which only empty carriages with their seals of nobility follow in the funeral procession—is a well-calculated stroke, expressing in a graphic symbol their hollowness, their abandonment of their father and of the concept of duty. This detail, which Balzac happily refrains from commenting on, is consistent with the previous balance of judgments accumulated against them. Here, the structure of the novel reveals the author's intentions—made explicit elsewhere—and carries them out.

If we apply this mode of analysis to the two heroes who are in the foreground of the novel as frequently as the père Goriot himself, we see that they are not dealt with in the same consistent manner. Although Balzac's announced conservatism should have led him to blame pointedly the growing excesses and the compromises of the young man, Rastignac remains clearly the darling of his creator. Eugène's ambitions—to dress well, to dance in the best salons, to win the love of beautiful women and the respect of Parisian dandies—are projections of Balzac's own desires, as his correspondence reveals them; he speaks of them here in the warm tones of sympathy. Eugène maintains throughout grace and charm, as well as much of his candor and generosity and ability to be shocked. This cannot be regarded as a justification of his behavior in society, but rather betrays the intention of the novelist to make him win the reader's approval in spite of his ill-controlled ambition. In no place does the author blame the fundamental program of Rastignac; at most he shows that some of the steps in it—the calculated liaison with Delphine, the use of his family's money, the accepting of Goriot's garçonnière—are not pretty. As Vautrin and Mme de Beauséant have described society to Eugène, he has seen that ambition is the only possible mode of existence for him, and that all means which favor success in this mode, such as money, women, and cynicism, are justified.

There are, it is true, important scruples which Balzac allows to Rastignac and which play an important role in the plot. When Vautrin proposes to him the bargain by which Vautrin will have Victorine Taillefer's brother killed by a duelist obligated to him so that Victorine will inherit her father's fortune and Eugène may marry her, dividing his gain with Vautrin, the young man protests, horrified. The fact that he is sincerely shocked is shown by his subsequent attempt to warn Taillefer. Here, Rastignac appears as a representative of social virtues. Yet he is sorely tempted, in spite of himself, to accept the bargain, and is prevented from succumbing only by the fortune of winning in gambling a sum sufficient to sustain him a while longer. One must mention likewise in his favor the sincere concern which he shows for Goriot. As he is moved by his fellow-boarder's plight and shocked by the daughters' attitude, the reader sees the situation through his eyes and shares this feeling of blame. This is particularly true as the old man approaches death; and Rastignac's blame for the neglectful daughters and sons-in-law is dramatized in the scenes where he tries to persuade them to visit their fa-

ther's bedside. By contrast with them, he is put in a favorable light.

Nevertheless, this evidence of virtue and these *beaux gestes* which Balzac places in evidence in his plot, particularly the dramatic devotion which Rastignac shows to the dying Goriot, are placed in a structure which in the main condemns Rastignac and shows that he is capable of cynicism, and that he can be successfully tempted. He is one of those who prefer to "aller à la fortune" rather than to retain the essential social virtue of probity. Although his cynicism is not unmitigated by generosity and his selfishness is not entire, like that of the Marquis d'Ajuda-Pinto, most of his disinterested actions are performed at no great cost to himself, often in fact with an advantage accruing. It has been remarked that his weaning of money from his mother and sisters to pay for his entrée into the Faubourg Saint-Germain forms a structural counterpoint to the Goriot daughters' extortion of money from their father, although there are differences in attitude. In a sympathetic portrait, Balzac attributes to Eugène's mother and sisters such pure motives and generous sentiments that his accepting their money for ambitious projects they would not approve cannot but look villainous, in spite of his assertions that he wishes to assist his family. Likewise he is in frequent contrast to Bianchon, the modest, honest medical student who refuses to "tuer le mandarin," that is, to make use of others for his own gain. P. J. Yarrow has observed [in "*Le Père Goriot* Reconsidered" in *Essays in Criticism* VII (Oct. 1957)] in this connection, "Bianchon's outlook is that which Balzac regards as wisest." Though Eugène finally refuses Vautrin's proposal, he coldly plans to make love to Delphine so as to get her to favor his entrance into society. The fact that Rastignac will remain with Delphine for some time does not change the motivation of his original decision. And while blaming the conduct of the daughters towards their father, he does not hesitate to pursue his liaison, to accompany Delphine to the ball for which she abandons her dying father, and to go dine with her the very evening of the funeral. His education is being completed, Balzac announces. His final words, the famous challenge to Paris, "A nous deux maintenant," are justly cited as the expression of his dominant attitude and of that of an entire generation. It is the admission that many of his scruples, if not all, having had their day, are now buried like the père Goriot. His glance from the Père-Lachaise seems to suck the "miel" of Paris. Rastignac has joined the party of those who trample underfoot the old codes and who thus hasten the death of order and the consecration of a romantic disorder in personal and social morals.

Balzac's attitude towards Vautrin is even more revealing. Following a successful thriller pattern, the novelist presents Vautrin as a mysterious, powerful character, whose past (unlike Eugène's and Goriot's) remains unrevealed to the reader, with the exception of a few details, and who appeals by his clandestine role and his forceful manner. It is only gradually that he is disclosed to us as an ex-convict and as a sort of Mephistopheles who reveals the secrets of the world and proposes cynically the exploitation of all possibilities. Principally by his efforts to arrange the marriage of Eugène and Victorine, which necessitates a murder, he takes on his most vicious light. The author composes for Vautrin's feminine victim, Victorine Taillefer, a figure of utter innocence and goodness. Her story too forms a counterpoint to the Goriot plot, with a reverse situation: unjustly deprived of her heritage by a capricious and cruel father, she maintains her sentiment of obedience and filial devotion and prays only that she may see him and receive some sign of his recognition. By making Vautrin the agent of an action which will plunge her into grief, and by maintaining her throughout as an angelic figure, Balzac makes Vautrin play a villain's role. The murdered brother is not an innocent victim, like Madame de Beauséant, but Vautrin's manner of doing away with him is not exonerated thereby; and even the fact that the fatal duel brings about the reconciliation of Victorine and her father cannot justify either Vautrin's action or his attitude towards it, namely that he believes himself to have the right to dispose of another's life.

Thus, a considerable segment of the plot structure assigns to Vautrin the role of evil counselor and evil doer, which his speeches likewise seem to warrant. Again, however, as in the case of Eugène, Balzac is inconsistent in his treatment of Vautrin, to such an extent that this villain (corresponding to the villain of the melodrama and the *roman noir*) becomes a hero. His antisocial action, directed at society in general or at a particular individual, is glossed over through passages which show the appeal of his character. The novel abounds in incidents and statements which present him favorably, and these are not sufficiently counterbalanced by critical qualifications. In the initial description of him, the reader is impressed with his superior force and knowledge. This impression is corroborated by what we read of the opinions and reactions of the other boarders. His piercing eye, which discloses no secrets of his own, seems to delve to the depths of others' souls and to lift the veil from reality (a vision to which Balzac himself pretended and with which he could not fail to sympathize). Moreover, Vautrin's claims to tell the truth to Eugène are vindicated by the empirical accuracy and apparent justification of what he says about society. As we have seen, Balzac emphasizes that Vautrin, sober in most ways, does not *create* vice, but merely takes advantage of others' vices and of the loopholes in the law. With his own sort of sincerity, he even clothes his scheme against Victorine in the guise of a just action to redress the wrongs done to her. One of the few facts we have of his past is that he originally went to prison for an action of which he was innocent but which he confessed—for motives of his own. He appears to be altruistic towards Eugène also, though it becomes increasingly clear that he does want to use Eugène in order to make a fortune for both of them, and that perhaps he is attracted to Eugène for unsound reasons.

It becomes even more apparent in the episode of Vautrin's arrest that the novelist does not allow any of his faults to detract from his stature; paradoxically, he has the *beau rôle*. Were it not for the Taillefer murder, we could say without hesitation that all sympathy would be for Vautrin. Even as the plot stands—with the duel and the arrest occurring nearly simultaneously in a series of *coups de théâtre*—Balzac directs most of the reader's sympathy toward Vautrin. He presents an impressive image of human power. By contrast with Mlle Michonneau and Poiret, he seems dignified and humane; by contrast with Mme Vauquer, honest and generous. The reactions of the other boarders, while primitive, echo ours: they believe only with great difficulty that he is a criminal at all, and find in him, despite his dramatic disclosure as Jacques Collin, the elements of a true gentleman, "un bon homme tout de même," who presents a contrast with the pettiness of the stool pigeons and the brutal machinery of the law. He emerges marked with a criminal's brand but nevertheless master of his soul and superior to the society which, mindless of his *belle âme,* seizes him.

Our last glimpse of Vautrin is thus, as Balzac left it, a favorable one. This composition, and the technique of virtually condoning Eugène's ambition by an indulgent presentation, reveal profound attitudes of the novelist and, perhaps, of his generation, and cannot be dismissed as simply concessions to popular taste, concern with an accurate portrayal of types, or fascination with exciting characters. It is true that he countered attacks against his immorality and depiction of vice by asserting that virtue being uniform and vice various, the latter was necessarily more interesting for the novelist. He affirmed that "les honnetes gens dont la vie est sans drame" could not suffice as characters, and that edifying literature would never change the morals of society. Furthermore, he noted, vice is attractive and must be so presented. This is a defense of his subject matter; it cannot be a defense of the author's attitude to it. Furthermore, his creation of figures such as Mme de Mortsauf, Ursule Mirouët, and the Baronne Hulot show what imaginative force he could give to the portrait of virtue. He could have developed the story of Vautrin and that of Rastignac (with its "true confession" element) without putting the two heroes in an ultimately favorable light, revealing by style and vocabulary his bias in their favor, and letting the balance of the fictional material lean in their favor. There is here a real ambivalence which expresses Balzac's own hesitations between the values of order, middle-class virtue, and conservatism on the one hand, and the values of individualistic, anarchical Romanticism on the other.

I suggest that this inconsistency is a flaw in Balzac's fictional achievement in *Le Père Goriot* and a weakness in his moral outlook. He did not *intend* to propose to us a standard of ambiguity or relativism, a new "Est-il bon? est-il méchant?" In his exhaustive study, Guyon has shown how, after an early period of unorthodoxy and liberalism in politics, Balzac had evolved a solid conservative position by 1833 from which he would no longer depart in his theoretical statements. As he expressed it in 1842, he was writing in the light of "deux Vérités éternelles: la Religion, la Monarchie, deux nécessités que les événements contemporains proclament, et vers lesquelles tout écrivain de bon sens doit essayer de ramener notre pays." In *Le Père Goriot* as in other novels, he may have wished to show conflicting elements of society—"grandeur et décadence," "splendeurs et misères"—but not a conflicting attitude on his part, nor a contradictory morality. But being himself unsure, wavering between a romantic ideal of grandeur and a conservative ideal of discipline and order, he projected this hesitation into *Le Père Goriot* and made his novel ethically schizophrenic. He wished to retain both the figure of the suffering Père Goriot who, though mediocre, is great ("sublime") by virtue of his incarnation of a sacred principle, and the lone, superior hero Vautrin who transcends the society which misunderstands him. The novel can come, then, to no conclusion; it cannot carry out the implied purpose which is the castigation of vice and the "defense and illustration" of virtue. Many readers [such as Martin Turnell in *The Novel in France,* 1951] have felt that the novel was ill-structured because it hesitates between Eugène's story (with Vautrin) and the principal, or at least original, drama, that of Goriot. I suggest that these two plots could have been reconciled and indeed are close to being so by theme and by scenic technique, but that they remain separate because of their conflicting ethic, and that thus they allow in the novel a cloudiness which has disturbed a number of readers.

Unlike some modern instances of paradox and ambivalence in literature, this cloudiness is essentially romantic because it reveals a reluctance to choose and to accept moral responsibility. In spite of his program of realism in art and conservatism in politics, Balzac remained a romantic, not only because of the romantic elements on which he continued to base much of his fiction, but also because, much as his predecessor Rousseau, he wished to hold unreconcilable positions. The refusal to choose in *Le Père Goriot* creates an indecisive work which is the mirror of a confused age. (pp. 104-12)

> *Catharine H. Savage, "The Romantic 'Père Goriot',"* in Studies in Romanticism, *Vol. V, No. 2, Winter, 1966, pp. 104-12.*

Charles Affron   (essay date 1966)

[*Affron is an American educator and critic. In the following excerpt, he traces the decline of Goriot and examines its causes.*]

Le Père Goriot, offers us an excellent framework within which to judge the effects of destructive passion. A panorama encompassing many aspects of society as seen through the eyes of a central character, the novel is organized like a lesson. Rastignac is the schoolboy, and life the curriculum. The reader, along with this character, learns that true, blinding love is a decided liability in the real world. Rastignac, at the novel's end, can defy Paris with confidence. Sobered of his illusions, he begins his attack on life, firm in the conviction that he will not make the elementary errors committed by the failures who appear in the novel. With a mentor like Vautrin and the graphic examples of Goriot and Madame de Beauséant before his eyes, Rastignac extracts meaning from the lesson.

Perhaps the most accurate appraisal of Goriot and of his passion is made by the Duchess of Langeais, as she recounts the old man's story to Rastignac. The Duchess, whose ill-fated love life is described in the novel bearing her name, is herself destroyed by passion. Her observations on one of love's victims are therefore particularly interesting. They bear a great measure of personal conviction, a sympathy reinforced by her own experience.

> Our heart is a treasure; empty it all at once and you are ruined. We no more forgive a sentiment for revealing itself completely than we do a man who has not a penny to his name. This father had given everything. For twenty years he had given his entrails, his love; he had given his fortune in one day. The lemon well squeezed, his daughters left the rind on the street corner.

The Duchess of Langeais perceives that the lover is doomed when the object of his affection does not reciprocate. As the self is irretrievably spent, the lover is inevitably dehumanized. The image of the squeezed lemon is especially well chosen, suggesting at once the bitterness of Goriot's lot and the nonhuman form he has assumed. The Duchess of Langeais describes the heart as a treasure, but she might describe it more accurately as a luxury. Goriot's initial mistake is allowing himself to be ruled by the dictates of his most urgent paternal instinct. By satisfying the every wish of his daughters, he jeopardizes his utility and puts a term to the role that he can play in their lives. Since his whole identity is contained in his fatherhood, when he can no longer fulfill the function of that position, he has destroyed himself. Having despoiled himself of all material advantage, Goriot is no longer useful to a system that is so completely oriented toward wealth. As the Duchess of Langeais states, the world simply does not pardon a poor man. Sentiment and feeling are judged solely on a monetary standard. Love must in some way be made tangible in the pragmatic Balzacian universe. Put in its most primitive terms, Goriot, when he has no more money to give his daughters, can no longer love them according to their needs. He has outlived his usefulness, thrown away his fortune, the only arm he had for defense, and is left with a single possession, his passion. The pressed lemon is a brutally precise image of Goriot, denied his function in life, emptied of his vitality.

Seen in this light, the old man's ravings, when Madame de Restaud comes to ask him for money, take on a horrible kind of logic. As we later learn during the deathbed scene, Goriot is always aware of the truth. He realizes the nature and extent of his importance to his daughters, and one can understand his frustration when forced to miss the opportunity of affirming his paternity. His beloved Nasie, from whose house he is excluded and whose visits to him have become increasingly rare, asks him for money, help, these two materializations of his affection. He offers to rob, to kill, to sell his own body, but then admits the futility of such gestures.

> All right, I must die, all I can do is die. Yes, I am no longer good for anything. I am no longer a father, no! She asks, she needs, and I, wretch, I have nothing! Ah, you invested in annuities, old scoundrel, and you had daughters! But don't you love them? Die, die like the dog that you are! What, I am less than a dog, a dog would not act thus!

Goriot sees his very humanity menaced by his inability to satisfy the needs of Anastasie. Without money, his passion cannot express itself. Since his whole life is consecrated to this passion, he has lost his raison d'être. Truly, he is less than a dog.

The process of his dehumanization establishes one of the dominant tonalities in the novel. The example he sets for Rastignac is a vivid one, and it is characterized by willful self-destruction and the perversion of life. . . . [Balzac] expresses this both symbolically and explicitly. He is determined to present the ambiguity of Goriot's position in most unambiguous terms. He bends his whole rhetoric to the task of exposing the paradox of Goriot's ennobling self-degradation. This is a constant problem facing Balzac, a price he must pay for attempting to straddle the real and the ideal worlds. The images tend to emphasize Goriot's animality and distortion of life, while his nobility is suggested through implication and reflection.

The final condition of Goriot takes on stature through its inevitability. According to Goriot's definition of paternity, the better he fulfills the role, the quicker he will reach the end of his resources and therefore cease to be a father. This is a bitter irony. Having abdicated the other aspects of his personality, he has nothing upon which to rely, literally no other identity. He has lost all personality by striving for the ultimate expression of fatherhood. "He saw that his daughters were ashamed of him, that they loved their husbands, and that he would be detrimental to his sons-in-law. He had then to sacrifice himself. He sacrificed himself because he was a father; he committed an act of self-banishment." In his exaggerated desire to be the perfect father, he denies his existence and puts his paternity in fatal jeopardy. We are once again reminded of the contiguity of nobility and degradation.

The novel shows Goriot during his decline; the reader is permitted to examine the symptoms of his disease in their ugliest, most rotten phase. In a flashback, however, Balzac describes the changes that have occurred in Goriot's life, showing the gradual absorption of his personality into his passion. As is to be expected, the author carefully attaches the moral changes to very obvious physical ones, thus mirroring and magnifying the more subtle traits of personality in their easily discernible concretizations. With an ironic touch, the financial decline of Goriot's fortune is symbolized, inversely, by his inglorious rise in the Pension Vauquer. Beginning in a quite comfortable apartment on the building's first floor, he meets his fate in an incredibly miserable attic, barely furnished and virtually exposed to the elements. The author's ambivalence to Goriot is implicit in this position. Goriot's alienation from humanity is reflected in his eschewal of civilizing comforts. He discards the objects that represent men's mastery over their environment and differentiate them from animals. And yet, this literal rise in the pension puts him closer to heaven, the realm of ideals, where love has its only relevance. Thus, Balzac astutely presents contrary viewpoints in this single, versatile image, incidentally stressing Goriot's animality by an inference to his spirituality.

The changes in the hero's physical aspect, however, contain no germ of an increased spirituality. The flesh remains the flesh, and its corruption signals the physicality of passion. When Goriot first arrives at the Pension Vauquer, he is still an attractive man, one who has aged gracefully. With the loss of his fortune and separation from his daughters, he progressively crumbles into ruin. Physical discomfort and emotional chagrin take their toll, the years avenge themselves, and Goriot comes to truly merit the appellation *père*. "He became thinner and thinner; the calves of his legs grew flabby, his face, swollen by bourgeois happiness, became tremendously wrinkled; his forehead was creased, his jaw stood out. During his fourth year at Rue Neuve-Sainte-Geneviève, he no longer resembled himself." Nature refuses to tolerate this useless being, and Goriot is forced to pay a heavy price for the meager fruits of his passion. The self-indulgent illusions that protected him during the youth of his daughters cannot stand the shock of such total unhappiness. He is thus a pauper in two ways—a stranger to both the happy father and extremely comfortable bourgeois who had come to live at the Pension Vauquer, four years previously.

Balzac translates this surrender of life into the distortion of a nonhuman image. Goriot's abdication of self is voluntary and absolute, symbolized in the incident concerning his dead wife's luncheon service. One day, Madame Vauquer sees Goriot fondling a gilded plate and learns that it was the very first gift he had received from his wife. He treasures it as he does no other object in the world. Expressing himself with his habitual exaggeration, Goriot says: "You see, Madame, I would prefer to scratch the earth with my nails than to part with this." The connection between Goriot and the plate serves two purposes. His visceral commitment functions as a premonition of his increasing animality, and the eventual sacrifice of the object shows the extent of his spiritual suicide, his dehumanization. In the sacrifice of his will, his common sense, he offers up his being on the altar of passion. The luncheon service is sold for his daughters. "He held fast to it as to his life." Disposing of the plates, which he had first pounded and bent out of shape, is the symbolic act which summarizes his life. His personality is warped, graceless, literally pounded out of shape, and he himself is destroyed by his passion. He is a failure as a human being. Since he virtually no longer exists, the act of giving away the precious luncheon service can be performed without compunction. Having already given away his life, the object most important to that life has lost its value.

Vautrin successfully analyzes the true character of Goriot, even though he mistakes paternal affection for an old man's romantic dalliance. In fact, the two are closely related. Vautrin, with his penetrating eye, his tremendous experience, and his unerring instinct for the truth, plumbs the depths of Goriot's soul. "People like that seize an idea and never let go. They are only thirsty for a certain water taken at a certain fountain, and it is often foul; to drink there, they would sell their wives, their children, they would sell their soul to the devil." The emphasis on instinct in the reference is not gratuitous. All is passionately unleashed instinct with Goriot; reason and judgment no longer play roles in his existence. Every breathing moment is now consecrated to the frustrated love for his daughters. Blinded to all proporation, alien to the system into which he was born, his religion is paternity and his goddesses are Delphine and Anastasie. Why should he hesitate to sell his soul for his faith? Goriot is not loath to admit the fact that he has actually sold his soul, if not to the devil, then to his daughters. "Actually . . . what am I? A poor cadaver whose soul is wherever my daughters are." Goriot has done high treason to the human race. His previously discussed outburst of self-damnation, in which he esteems himself lower than a dog, takes on grim significance when one considers it in relation to another self-evaluation, made under less hysterical circumstances. Goriot is determined to explain his personality to Rastignac and spares no grizzly detail. One does not doubt for a moment the failure of this man who passionately disposes of his humanity. "I love the horses which draw them and I would like to be the little dog that they hold on their laps." Goriot envies the horses and dogs which are more important to Delphine and Anastasie than their father. His failure as a human being is illustrated no more graphically than in these few words. Balzac's pity for Goriot is tempered by this character's epic disloyalty to other men. The author, obsessed by the power of the human will, by the transcendental nature of human beings, can feel only intense loathing for this creature during such moments of debasement.

Ruthlessly pursuing the seeds of this debasement Balzac uncovers the shocking truth that feeds Goriot's passion. He provides further evidence of the character's degradation, attesting to the shabbiness of his ungenuine paternity. Goriot at once personifies fatherhood and is supremely unfit to be a father. He is therefore unfaithful to the cause he most fervently serves, further disqualifying himself from humanity. In his relationship to Delphine and Rastignac, gleefully sharing the secret of their romance and so anxious to live near his daughter's young lover, Goriot bears a striking resemblance to the typical maid of the typical *lorette*. In this case, the *lorette* is Rastignac, and the wealthy keeper is Delphine Nucingen, née Goriot. But an ulterior motive explains Goriot's wholehearted approbation of the Eugène-Delphine liaison. He wishes vicariously, and perhaps not so vicariously, to share in the sensuality of the young lovers. He craves physical proximity to his daughter and basks in the affection that reigns in the love nest that is Rastignac's apartment. If one can, for a moment, forget the image of the wronged, Learlike father, Goriot's actions emerge in all their luridness.

> The whole evening was spent in childishness, and old Goriot was not the least mad of the three. He lay down at his daughter's feet in order to kiss them; he looked for a long time into her eyes; he rubbed his head against her dress; finally he did all the foolish things that the youngest and tenderest lover would have done.

With a heavy hand, Balzac describes the unusual fatherly passion of Goriot, which has deep roots in overt eroticism. Because of this, Goriot lies outside the pale of those particular values that function within the Balzacian universe. The father is no longer true to his role. His passion is pushed to such an extreme that it does not fit into the area prescribed by the rules of paternity. A father who makes mistresses out of his daughters has clearly lost sight of his role in society. He has consciously let his exaggerated passion lead him to his doom. "My daughters were my vice, they were my mistresses, in a word, they were everything!" Goriot is unbecoming to his species; he falls into the obliv-ion reserved for all the incongruents of *La Comédie humaine.*

Goriot, however, is more than a crazed old man delighting in the pleasure of seeing and touching his daughters. His sacrifice is one of those noble but vain gestures of defiance against the pettiness of normal existence. Balzac has the profoundest respect for the figure of the outcast and therefore assigns Goriot to the same category designated for the noble Madame de Beauséant. Rastignac, who has observed at close hand the agonies of these two characters, comments on their similarity. " 'Madame de Beauséant flees, this one dies,' he said. 'Beautiful souls cannot remain for long in this world. How, in fact, can great sentiments find a place in a society that is petty, small, superficial'." These creatures, so tortured by their passions, are truly beautiful souls. They have nothing to do with a world that excludes their sentiments, their sublime gestures, their dedication.

Madame de Beauséant is the sum of grace, beauty, generosity, a product of all that the author considers best in the aristocracy. In spite of these traits, or perhaps because of them, she is destroyed by the same vulnerability that spells the failure of Goriot. Wearing her heart on her sleeve, she neglects to hide her love for the dandy Ajuda-Pinto from a very curious Parisian society. Her first mistake, however, is to permit herself a genuine love in a world where love must eventually bow to money. She misjudges her possibilities for happiness, thus leaving herself open to the hard gaze of a ruthless world. Giving a ball on the very night she learns of Ajuda-Pinto's intention to marry the wealthy Mademoiselle de Rochefide, she must bare her grief to her guests, undergoing a kind of public failure. She, like Goriot, is offered up by society as a propitiatory sacrifice to the voracious machine of existence.

The most interesting aspect of the Goriot-Beauséant relationship is the way in which it illustrates the basic duality of purpose that runs through *La Comédie humaine,* a duality that incidentally controls the dramatic progression of *Le Père Goriot.* Praise and damnation, failure and success are constantly shifting polarities for the author, controlled by his shifting balance between the real and the ideal. Janus-like, he is often neutralized by the simultaneity with which he views the fact of past evidence and the ideal of future potential. Thus, he faces an unalterable paradox in his feelings about Goriot, the "Christ of Paternity" who yearns for his daughters' caresses as he lies in their laps like a dog. The major burden of suggesting the old man's capacity for beautification, spiritual success, sublimation through love, falls upon Madame de Beauséant. We are confronted with the author's irresistible attraction to the mirror of character reflection, which so clearly reveals his philosophical ambivalence and his literary obsession with antithesis. Madame de Beauséant suffers in noble silence, fully cognizant of the risk she runs in submitting to sincere love and ready to accept her harsh failure. At the ball, she pridefully exhibits her life, somehow knowing that the cause of her sacrifice, her glowing human sincerity, is infinitely more important than her defeat. Goriot, a victim of the underside of passion, expires on a filthy bed, in a paroxysm of madness atrociously com-

pounded by lucidity. The apotheosis of Madame de Beauséant is an exultant mixture of courage and resignation.

> "Let's go downstairs. I do not want them to
> think that I am crying. I have eternity before me,
> I will be alone, and no one will ask me to account
> for my tears. Yet another glance at this room."
> She stopped. Then, after having hidden her eyes
> for a moment with her hand, she dried them,
> bathed them with clear water and took the stu-
> dent's arm. "Onward," she said.

Madame de Beauséant has a superabundance of nobility,
enough so that she can lend some to miserable old Goriot,
her brother in passion. Her ability to transfigure worldly
failure casts an uplifting light upon her fellow martyr,
thereby mitigating the animality and degradation that, by
contrast, her noble presence has imposed upon him.

Madame de Beauséant and Goriot define Rastignac's
world with a set of contiguous, and in some ways identical,
extremes. This unity within diversity is the kind of device
that appeals to Balzac, enabling him to suggest the paradoxes of existence within a single literary framework and
to remain consistent to an established tonality. Thus, he
can posit the crisis of Rastignac's life in terms of two characters who are dear to the young man, who resemble each
other, and who represent two kinds of failure in the eyes
of the world. Madame de Beauséant, through her spiritu-
alization, and Goriot, through his degradation, prove to
Rastignac the uselessness of passion, the self-destructive
effects of sincere love. He sees before his eyes a saint and
a subhuman creature. In the last pages of the novel he is
shuttled from Goriot's bedside, to the ball of Madame de
Beauséant, and then back again to witness the old man's
death agony. Life is explained to him spatially and conceptually, and his final choice is described in the same way.
Rastignac, standing on the highest point of the cemetery,
Père-Lachaise, sheds his final tear, buries his sincerity
with Goriot, dies to the world of the passionate, and challenges Paris with what must be a premonition of success.
Set on the path by the omniscient Vautrin, led to this place
of death by the saint and the groveling dog, he leaves behind his heart and is ready to face the world on its own
terms. (pp. 58-68)

> *Charles Affron, in his* Patterns of Failure in
> "La Comédie Humaine," *Yale University
> Press, 1966, 148 p.*

Peter Brooks   (essay date 1969)

[*Brooks is an American educator and critic. In the following essay, he views the novel as a series of metaphors
uniting widely divergent contexts.*]

The melodrama of **Père Goriot** is patent enough: the novel
turns on secrets and mysteries, false identities and masked
relationships, lurid and grandiose events; its moment of
moral crisis involves a murder disguised as a duel (arranged by a disguised escaped convict), while the protagonist lies unconscious from a potion of drugged wine. The
narrative tone consciously adopts the breathlessness of
melodrama from the opening page, where the narrator
claims for his tale the label of "drama . . . despite the abu-

sive and contorted manner in which it has been used," adding that his drama is no fiction, but rather the drama of
the real, for "All is true." The essential mode of the novel
is melodramatic, and all its tropes correspond to this
mode: in particular, the characters' attitudes are "sublime" and "immense," their gestures of heroic proportions, hyperbolic.

Eugène de Rastignac's first social call is structured around
two verbal gestures, the first of which opens doors, produces a sense of belonging, and a flood of light on society;
the second, obscurity, rejection, and a permanent barring
of passages. If his arrival is obviously a nuisance to the
Comtesse Anastasie de Restaud (who is receiving her
lover, Maxime de Trailles), when the Comte de Restaud
enters she introduces Rastignac with the "magic" phrase,
that he is "related to Mme la Vicomtesse de Beauséant by
the Marcillac": a formulation which is a "stroke of the
wand" opening "thirty compartments in the brain of the
young man from the Midi" and restoring to him "all his
prepared wit"; which provides a "sudden light" to make
him "see clear in the air of high society." The Comte de
Restaud is then all polite attention, and discusses ancestors until Rastignac announces his acquaintanceship with
someone he has just perceived leaving the Hôtel de Restaud, Père Goriot: "At the mention of this name, prettified
with the sobriquet *père,* the Comte, who had been attending to the hearth, threw his tongs into the fire as if they
had burned his hands, and stood up. 'Sir, you could have
said Monsieur Goriot,' he cried." In a moment, Rastignac
perceives that there has again been a stroke of the wand,
but one that has had the "inverse effect" of "related to
Mme la Vicomtesse de Beauséant." The subject is
changed, Rastignac's departure hastened: and upon his
leaving the Hôtel, we hear the Comte give his valet the
order that they will never again be at home to Monsieur
de Rastignac.

Rastignac has seemingly, without his or our quite knowing how, made an unseemly social gesture, committed
what he qualifies as a "gaucherie." Such an outcome of a
first venture into society by a young provincial would seem
to be too banal to merit further comment: we appear to
be well established on the plane of comedy of manners,
witnessing a scene which could be found, doubtless with
greater subtlety, in Marivaux or Richardson, Jane Austen,
Stendhal, Henry James, E. M. Forster—any of those novelists whose attention and efforts at representation are directed to the texture of social life, the significant gestures
of actors on the public stage of society. Balzac indeed refers us to this stage and this texture when he talks of the
"magical effect" of social formulae, the importance of an
omitted "monsieur," or when, a few pages later, he comments that Rastignac has made progress in that "Parisian
code which no one talks about but which constitutes a
high social jurisprudence which, well learned and well
practiced, leads to everything."

Yet the crudity of Balzac's rendering—the excess of the
Comte's reaction, the hyperbolic speed of Rastignac's
complete acceptance and complete rejection—is troublesome: the social gestures he dramatizes seem the motions
of the bull in the china closet, where more is broken than

need be to make the "point" about Rastignac's social inexpertise. In fact, Balzac's social gestures do not really have the volume and opacity of those we find in a novel of manners: there, gestures are counters which have value in terms of a system, a social code which forms their context and assigns their meaning. If the first magic phrase, "related to Mme la Vicomtesse de Beauséant by the Marcillac," seems a reasonable equivalent to any social identification found in Jane Austen or Stendhal or Forster, his disastrous mention of Père Goriot cannot be assimilated to Emma's insult to Miss Bates, Julien Sorel's failure to change into silk stockings for dinner, or Leonard Bast's confusions with an umbrella. These refer us to the code, in terms of which they are inappropriate, embarrassing, wrong. Rastignac's gaffe is other, it is charged in a different manner; it is more than socially inappropriate or wrong, because it evokes a context other than the social; it is potentially revolutionary. It is in fact the unwitting first draft of a metaphor which is inadmissible because literally destructive of the manners of the social upper class. And to understand how this is so is to understand why Balzac is not simply writing bad (unsubtle, crude, melodramatic) comedy of manners, but something else, something we might indeed accurately call "melodrama of manners."

The "Parisian code" which Rastignac must master is only on the surface a code of manners. This is already suggested in the preliminary circumstances of his visit to the Restaud: he stumbles into a dark passage, overhears voices, and the sound of a kiss, from a hidden staircase, then sees Père Goriot almost run down by the Comte de Restaud's carriage, then given a greeting of "forced consideration" by the Comte. Such circumstances go beyond the idiom of social comedy to call into play mystery and melodrama. And Rastignac's mistaken verbal gesture cannot fit within the framework of manners; it raises other, threatening questions. He discovers why in the course of his next social call, on Mme de Beauséant: Goriot is the publicly repudiated and secretly exploited father of Anastasie de Restaud, as also of Delphine de Nucingen, a man who has been banished from his daughters' drawingrooms where he appeared "a spot of grease," but is frequently called to the backstairs for cash. Rastignac's mention of Goriot in the Restaud drawingroom has indeed had the effect of a "grease-spot," because it is the juxtaposition of a public social style and its unavowable genetic and financial substructure. Rather than simply committing a social impropriety, Rastignac has cut through the very texture of social life to what lies beneath, the greasy, unspeakable substratum which is supposed to remain hidden.

A metaphor, according to I. A. Richards, is a "transaction between contexts," and Rastignac has precisely violated the single context of codified social manners, has unconsciously conjugated together two contexts which must remain separate. The draft metaphor must be conjured away by the Restaud because it is dangerous, revolutionary in the manner of all metaphor because the transaction brings a certain merging of the two contexts, an end to their sharp differentiation in a new fusion, a new unitary vision of the whole—a vision whereby, in this case, society is no longer Society, a closed system of manners, but a layered

structure, where what is at the top can and must be explained by what is underneath it, and precedent to it.

Rastignac's draft metaphor cannot in fact be conjured away: the whole novel is in a sense structured on it, and moves toward clear articulation of it—articulation which belongs to the hero and expresses the clear vision of society on which he is to found his personal comportment. The most decisive formulation of the metaphor comes during Mme de Beauséant's final ball, where Anastasie de Restaud and Delphine de Nucingen are decked in diamonds bought or redeemed with their father's last money, while he lies dying in the meanest room of the Pension Vauquer: Rastignac "saw then beneath the diamonds of the two sisters the pallet where Goriot lay stretched in pain." The essential words here are *beneath,* which expresses the relation of superstructure to substructure, the way the display of wealth of an arriviste upper class is furnished by the exploitation of labor and commerce; and *saw,* which suggests that the economic reality is visible through the veneer of manners, the substructure implicit in the superstructure: and Society hence threatened by the organization of society.

The image is, like Rastignac's gaffe in the Restaud drawingroom, crude, gross—a direct, unsubtle metaphor expressing a basic relationship; and there are countless others in the same style, in the mouth of the narrator and almost all of the characters. Clearly, such metaphors would be out of place in the worlds of Stendhal, Jane Austen, or James. Yet they are clearly constitutive of Balzac's world: he has earned the right to use them because they are the tropes that correspond to the melodramatic mode he has chosen to exploit. The same necessities govern mode and tropes: Balzac is not attempting to represent a drama within the social code, nor trying to render the texture of social intercourse and the interplay of individual destinies on the social stage; he aims rather at uncovering and dramatizing the structures of society, its basic governing relationships, and the play of individuals in terms of the forces and structures, horizontal and vertical, which define the total organization of the human commimity, and the true dimensions of the human experience. Like the novelist of manners, he is attracted to the social sphere that yields the most significant gestures: the highest. His careers are exemplary. But for Balzac (and there is doubtless an historical cause here, in the French Revolution's destruction of *le monde,* Society in its eighteenth-century sense) this sphere can never be understood alone: its meaning is gained from juxtaposition to its substructure. Therefore the theater of Balzac's drama cannot have the closure and self-containment of the true novel of manners: it must be metaphoric, based on a drama of interacting contexts. His whole method, that is, must be analogous to his metaphors: it must juxtapose different contexts and show their interpenetration, it must reveal the copresence of superstructure and substructure, articulate the governing relationships. And therefore the manners dramatized cannot themselves have the opacity, volume, fixity and sublety of those in a true novel of manners: they must always reach toward the total structuration, call into question the autonomy of the context in which they seem to exist, become charged with a significance which splits the frame of comedy of manners. Hence a melodrama of manners: a drama of hyperbolic gestures, of supersignificances.

It is the Duchesse de Langeais, calling on Mme de Beauséant when Rastignac arrives to pay his visit, who strikes the theme of the lesson of morality these two noble ladies give to the young provincial: "Society is a mudhole, let us try to stay on the heights." The image is ramified on all levels in the novel. Paris, Rastignac concludes after Vautrin's first lesson in the ethics of success, is morally a mudhole; to which we must juxtapose Mme de Beauséant's remark that Delphine de Nucingen "would lap up all the mud there is between the rue Saint-Lazare [quarter of rich bourgeois like Nucingen] and the rue de Grenelle [in the Faubourg Saint-Germain] to gain entry to my drawingroom." Literally, Paris is again a mudhole, and if you cross it on foot you get your boots dirty, which is what happens to Rastignac on the way to visit Mme de Restaud (and while waiting in the antechamber, he has occasion to compare his own to Maxime de Trailles' impeccable boots). "Staying on the heights" means, among other things, taking a carriage, and this too has immediate moral ramifications: " 'And an odd sort of mudhole,' replied Vautrin. 'Those who get dirty in a carriage are honorable men, those who get dirty on foot are crooks.' " To go into the streets of Paris is a descent, the descent of a woman like Anastasie who after the ball goes to seek the usurer Gobseck, a condition generalized by Vautrin as a continual vertical movement: "Yesterday at the top of the wheel at a Duchess' . . . this morning at the bottom of the ladder at the moneylender's: that is the Parisienne." Near the start of the novel, the narrator evokes the start of Dante's journey when he compares approach to the rue Neuve-Sainte-Geneviève (where the Pension Vauquer is located) to entry into the Catacombs: "as, with each step, light diminishes and the chant of the guide goes hollow. . . ."

The novel reposes on its two most widely separated terms, both horizontally and vertically: the Pension Vauquer and the Faubourg Saint-Germain, the worlds inhabited respectively by Goriot and by Mme de Beauséant (and, potentially, Goriot's daughters). It is Rastignac who almost daily experiences the distance between the two, who journeys from one to the other. The ethical experience of the novel is constructed on his returns from the upper world to the lower, the journeys (mostly night journeys) which bring to consciousness his moral choices, and the possible formulae for permanently leaving one world for the other. Upon his return from his first visit to Mme de Beauséant, hesitating between the career in the law he has initiated and the splendors of society to which he has been exposed, he makes a decision to "open two parallel trenches leading to fortune, to brace himself both on learning and on love, to be a learned doctor of laws and an *homme à la mode*." To which the narrator comments that parallel lines never meet.

Something more germane to the necessary approach is suggested by the tailor whom Rastignac convokes after remarking how poorly his suits compare to Maxime de Trailles', a tailor who considers himself "a hyphen between young men's present and their future." A hyphen is the beginning of a relationship, of a juxtaposition and a passage; it is related to metaphor, to the construction of a ladder out of the mudhole. And construction is imperative: Rastignac's progress cannot be uniquely one in awareness about society, the consciousness of its structuration which allows him at the end to formulate the metaphor juxtaposing Goriot's deathbed and the sisters' diamonds; it depends on the fabrication of his own metaphor of action, one which will allow him to excape the confines of one context and penetrate within the other. Consciousness and construction are in fact interdependent: as soon as Rastignac acts, he understands; as soon as he understands, he acts again. The two are mutually elucidating, and like all of Balzac's parvenus, Rastignac moves with exemplary, hyperbolic, melodramatic speed.

But the metaphor presupposes for its construction (as the hyphen for its insertion) a median term, a "vehicle," which, in Balzac's universe, is inevitably money. Money, Rastignac discovers as soon as he starts to open his parallel trenches, is the *"ultima ratio mundi"*: what we might call the eisenoplastic power of society, enabling one to perform the transaction between contexts. And yet, the acquisition of money implies a choice of means which, according to Vautrin's exposition of society, is an absolute and total commitment of the self: there can be no parallel trenches because virtue is indivisible—it either is or isn't—and Rastignac is summoned to choose between two great symbolic attitudes toward society, Obedience and Revolt. Paradoxically, the vehicle of metaphorical passage, money, threatens to lead beyond metaphor to a symbolic reduction of life to one of two mutually exclusive gestures.

Vautrin, critic of "a gangrened society," disciple of Rousseau in the manner of Sade, is in fact a moral absolutist, and it is the "puritanism" of his ethics which tends for a time to make of Rastignac's choice a symbolic moral melodrama or even allegory. His proposition to Rastignac is restated by Rastignac to Bianchon in a gross analogy: if one could become rich simply by willing the death of one unknown and aged mandarin in China, should one accept? This simplifies accurately: Rastignac need only consent to Vautrin's assumption of the role of Providence; Vautrin will have young Taillefer killed in a duel, Victorine Taillefer will become her rich father's sole heir—and she is already in love with Rastignac. Vautrin assumes a Mephistophelean guise, and the moral problem is reduced to its simplest, most grandiose form: temptation. " 'What kind of a man are you,' cried Eugène, 'you were created to torment me.' " The moral crisis and climax of the novel is a *Walpurgisnacht* where the hero, sotted by drugged wine, listens to his tempter's projects without being able to summon the force to protest, a nightmare realm where gesture cannot be made to accord with intention, where crime can only be assented to, and unconsciousness finally takes over to create a gap in time, Rastignac awakening only at eleven o'clock the next morning, to find that all has been consummated.

We ought surely to see in Rastignac's drugged lethargy a metaphor of his essential moral passivity: he has at least analogically killed the mandarin. Yet the melodrama is so arranged that Rastignac will never have to face the "bargain" effectuated in his name (Vautrin is hauled off to prison), and the threat to his metaphorical construction posed by Vautrin's symbolic reduction is conjured away. Indeed, Rastignac's response to Vautrin's symbolic alternatives is always a refusal of choice: to Obedience and Revolt he adds a third term, Struggle. And Struggle is precisely the effort to answer the two primary symbolic gestures with metaphor, with a constructive, mediative effort which rejects exclusive commitment to one or the other.

This effort will take the form of a transaction between love and money. "I don't want to think about anything," Rastignac concludes after Vautrin's first temptation, "the heart is a good guide." He calls on this principle to reach the decision not to profit from the crime committed by marrying Victorine Taillefer. But we should not be the dupes of this decision: what in fact comes to save Rastignac as he walks in the Luxembourg struggling with his conscience is the recollection of a message transmitted by Goriot just before the previous evening's crisis, that Goriot has taken and furnished an apartment which will serve as a place of rendezvous with Delphine de Nucingen: "He remembered the confidences made by Père Goriot the previous evening, he remembered the apartment chosen for him near Delphine, in the rue d'Artois: he took out her letter again, reread it, kissed it. 'Such a love is my anchor to windward,' he said to himself." Such is his Beatrix, his salvation offered: the apartment of the rue d'Artois, scene of his liaison with Delphine, is the means of constructing a liaison to the "heights." When he is in the apartment, struck by momentary guilt at the evidence of the expenses incurred by Goriot in furnishings, he resolves his moral struggles with the grandiose phrase, "I will be worthy of all this." Worthy, that is, of "this complete luxury, these beautiful dreams realized, all this poetry of a young and elegant existence." Delphine is defined by this poetry of luxury; she is an object whose price is set by her accessory objects, the "luxury of the courtesan," as Rastignac qualifies it: or as her husband puts it in *La Maison Nucingen,* she is "the representation of [my] fortune, an indispensable *thing.*" Rastignac's first meeting with her led to the gaming tables, and the first kiss she bestowed was a reward for winning seven thousand francs to pay her debts. The success of his courtship is assured when he has obtained for her an invitation to Mme de Beauséant's ball: "he went promptly to see Delphine, happy to be able to procure her a joy the price of which he would undoubtedly receive."

Delphine is Rastignac's appropriate and necessary *rite de passage:* the luxury/love she incarnates constitute both the solution to Rastignac's moral dilemma and the necessary mediating term in his passage from the Pension Vauquer to what we know, from subsequent novels, will be the highest positions imaginable. Ex-Goriot, banker's wife, ambitious of promotion into the Faubourg Saint-Germain, she is the perfect realization of "Parisian love," the fusion of love and money to the point where they are indistinguishable, so that Rastignac's ambition and acquisitiveness can always be translated into terms of love (solving the moral predicament posed by Vautrin by taking "the heart" as his "guide"), and his love for her immediately translated into cash and position (solving his problem of transition: and in a completely literal sense, it is

Delphine's husband who will make Rastignac's fortune). Each of the two terms "means" the other; Rastignac saying love also says money, and begins to construct his ladder, his metaphor.

It is to this construction that Rastignac returns at the last, when, after accepting all his disillusionments about Delphine's character, after facing the menace of the absurd posed by Goriot's death agony, he stands on the heights of Père Lachaise cemetery following Goriot's burial, and looks down on Paris. The final passage is preceded by a metaphor of a baroque complication and excess announcing the end of Rastignac's youth: "he looked at the grave and buried there his last tear of youth, a tear brought forth by the sacred emotions of a pure heart, one of those tears which, from the earth where they fall, rebound into the heavens." After this last gesture of mediation with the celestial, and the moral realm, Rastignac is spiritually complete for his encounter with the real antagonist:

> Alone now, Rastignac took a few steps toward the height of the cemetery and saw Paris lying serpentine along the two banks of the Seine, where lights were starting to shine. His eyes focused almost avidly between the column of the Place Vendôme and the dome of the Invalides, the dwelling place of that good society into which he had tried to penetrate. He threw at this murmuring hive a glance which seemed in advance to suck out its honey, and spoke these grandiose words: "Now between the two of us!"

> And as first act in the challenge hurled at Society, Rastignac went to dine at Mme de Nucingen's.

Metaphor and melodrama reach a perfectly controlled climax in symbolic action. Rastignac's situation—standing on the heights of Père Lachaise, a mountain of the Parisian dead, another, immobilized Paris (the theme is developed by Balzac at the end of *Ferragus*), facing and looking down on the Paris of the *beau monde* stretched out with a contained reptilian energy along the Seine between the two commanding beacons of the Vendôme column and the Invalides—is excessively grandiose, already a gesture of disproportion, but of necessary disproportion and excess because it allows Rastignac to perform a summary operation upon Paris and Society. The city becomes a beehive which his glance possesses in its vital richness, sucking its honey, extracting its wealth. So hypostasized and vivified, Paris can be turned into the antagonist and called to arms. Yet the challenge, the act of defiance, is an act within society—as its institution in his going to dine at Delphine's shows; not Revolt, but again Struggle, which aims not at overthrow but at possession. Or rather: it is Rastignac's melodramatic metaphoric command of Paris from the heights of Père Lachaise, and the grandiose and excessive terms in which he expresses what is literally a *vision* of reality, that permit his gesture to make the passage from revolt to possession, which subsume the former to the latter because society has been seized in its totality and its essence, in a gathering together of all its structures, movements, implications into essential metaphors.

The formation of gross, encompassing metaphors which give summary representations of an immediate intellectual

Père Lachaise cemetery. Detail from an engraving by Jacques Guignet.

grasp of society, and the exploitation of a technique of juxtaposition of masses, hyperbolic forces, including the grandiose and disproportionate gesture—a technique of melodrama—are interdependent and central to Balzac's representation of society, which addresses itself, not to the texture of gestures and voices which we call manners, but to a totality of understanding, a sense of the structuration of the whole, and the place of each human gesture, motive, decision within it. It is wrong to seek here a subtle unfolding of a problem of ethics and comportment within a system of manners. The virtues of the melodrama of manners are different: it continually refers us through manners, below and beyond them, not only to psychology, but to society conceived as the theoretical totality of human relationships, passions, gestures, as a total economy. Hence scrutiny of any particular of reality will lead through the surface to the center, to a "truer" reality, and finally to the vital unitary principles.

Much has been said—most strikingly by Erich Auerbach in *Mimesis*—about the relations of people to things in Balzac: how, especially in the celebrated preliminary description of the Pension Vauquer, the objects amongst which man lives announce him, imply him, define him. The adjectives applied to the furniture of the Pension already people a human world: the furniture is "proscribed," placed in the Pension "as the debris of civilization are put

in the Hospital of Incurables"; chairs are "dismembered," or, in a suite of adjectives which moves from the objective to the completely vitalized, "old, cracked, rotted, wobbly, gnawed, one-armed, one-eyed, invalid, expiring." What we should also perceive is how, as description of objects opens onto the human condition, description of people inevitably leads to questions about the mysteries of passion lying behind their appearance, the structure of melodrama implicit in their faces in the form of interrogations. "The boarders gave a premonition of dramas finished or in action," the narrator announces. Then, in his account of Mlle Michonneau, after five lines of description, he suddenly passes to the interrogatory: "What acid had stripped this creature of her female forms? she must once have been pretty and well-made: was it vice, sorrow, greed? had she loved too much, had she been a wardrobe dealer or simply a courtesan? Was she expiating the triumphs of an insolent youth . . . ?" And with Poiret, after thirteen lines of description: "What work could have so shrivelled him up? what passion had blackened his bulbous face . . . ?"

The real, or more precisely the intelligent human glance directed at the real in the act of possession by description, inevitably leads to interrogations, to the sense of something behind, of a mystery and a drama to be elucidated. The technique rapidly passes beyond "realism," because the real—in the sense of the concrete, the apparent, the immediately seizable—slips from our grasp, loses its solidity and opacity, opens up depths that cannot be dealt with by sight alone, which rather demand vision. Reality is both the scene of a drama for Balzac, and the mask of the real drama; and in almost every Balzacian narrative there comes a moment when the prose "takes off " (or indeed "turns on"), when appearances are passed through or reabsorbed in something else, in a vision of the total human melodrama. Hence the characters' gestures refer us, not to the contexture of other gestures, the structure of appearances we call "manners," but to the implications behind gestures, to another "true" reality both masked by and implicit in what we ordinarily call reality. A striking instance occurs in Balzac's tale **Facino Cane:** "And he made a frightening gesture of extinguished patriotism and disgust for things human." This is very literally a gesture—a movement of the hand; yet it is obvious that no movement of the hand could "really" be charged with such significance, could contain so much meaning. The gesture as such in fact virtually disappears, is eclipsed and obliterated by the meanings which the visionary narrator can read in it: the signifier, one might say in the terms of linguistics, is destroyed by the signified.

In this sense, it is apparent that virtually all gesture in Balzac is by essence metaphoric: it constantly constructs on the basis of the real, out of the real, the implications of a truer, more significant superdrama, a melodrama which is merely figured in the domain of the actual, by "real" gestures which appear finally as shadows both concealing and speaking of the true drama. And this is as accurate a description of Rastignac's disastrous verbal gesture in the Hôtel de Restaud as it is of Facino Cane's wave of the hand: because Rastignac creates a transaction between two contexts, rending the texture of manners, he locates the drama in a world *beyond,* which is first of all the world of true, because total, social structurations, then the realm of the true, central, emotional and moral drama of the novel. The same can evidently be said for Rastignac's moral drama, where the effort to transact between different contexts becomes—as Vautrin's statement of the problem, and Vautrin's mythic dimensions, force us to see—an effort to transact between two great symbolic gestures toward society. The final gesture in Père Lachaise expresses the successful metaphorical operation performed on Paris and society and allows us—and Rastignac himself—to see his career as hyperbolic, exemplary, the very type of the truth.

The world, said Claudel, is before us like a text to be deciphered. But whereas for Claudel each discrete particle of reality can in the end directly be related to—because in the end it directly emanates from—a spiritual unity, in Balzac the final reality, and the way to it, are more elusive. We open first onto the melodrama of social experience, and the mystery of passion; particulars of reality both speak of this mystery and conceal it, hence call forth the questing effort to understand, and then finally to go beyond to the organizing unitary principles in the realm of the spirit. Rhetorically, we pass from description to increasingly audacious efforts to construct metaphors for the total organization of society, the total human experience, and the forces which shape and determine all experience. It is of course the *Oeuvres philosophiques* that provide the final metaphors of the unitary forces: the electric power of the will in animating the world, the "fecundation of matter by spirit," as Béguin accurately states it—Balzac's "angelism," straining toward the ultimate metaphor predicted by Louis Lambert: "Perhaps one day the reverse of the *Et Verbum caro factum est* will be the summary of a new Scripture proclaiming: *And flesh will be made Spirit, it will become the Word of God.*" Even within the frame of the single novel **Père Goriot,** however, one can detect the development of one such principle—and one of Balzac's central metaphors—in the interiorization of the novel's melodrama, the melodrama of the spirit. The form this takes is implicit in the title: it is the drama of paternity, of creation, of the incarnation of the mind.

"When I became a father," says Goriot, "I understood God. He is complete everywhere, since all creation came from him. Sir, so am I with my daughters." This immediately transcends the level of what we ordinarily think of as vicarious existence to move into a higher realm, that of the creator who lives in his creation: not simply *through* the other, but *in* an otherness which is a new realization of the self, a new objectification of the mind, a metaphor of the ego. Vautrin, whose motto is "there are no principles, only events, there are no laws, only circumstances," understands that such a lack of clearly visible laws of organization leaves the superior being a large liberty to invent them: "I will take upon myself the role of Providence," he proposes to Rastignac; "I will force the will of God." And it is Vautrin who explicitly carries the metaphor to its next stage, that of literary creation: "I am a great poet. I don't write my poems, they consist in actions and sentiments." Rastignac is the necessary scene of this poem, the vehicle for the realization of Vautrin's dreams of creation, the metaphor by which the Word is made flesh: "A man is ev-

erything or nothing. He is less than nothing when he is named Poiret, you can squash him like a bedbug, he's flat and he stinks. But a man is a god when he looks like you; he is no longer a machine covered with skin but a theater where the most beautiful emotions are acted out. . . ."

The sterility implied in Vautrin's homosexuality is hence transmuted into creative fertility, the power to make life, the arrogation to himself of the role of Providence, the temptation to godhead. His dream of a patriarchal society in the southern United States is to be realized through the ascension of Rastignac to the highest social sphere: two poems, indeed, to be written from one intellect with the same metaphor—Rastignac-as-beauty translated into Rastignac-as-money (Victorine Taillefer's dowry). Yet his relation to his creature-metaphor will be thwarted: man will fall off from his creator, be unequal to his conceptions (or: free from his intentions), and institute distance between the two of them—or else, as will be the case with Vautrin's second protégé, Lucien de Rubempré in **Splendeurs et misères des courtisanes,** betray God. (A more successful self-deification is achieved by the usurer Gobseck, but only because he is miserly, self-contained, sterile, and never attempts a creation: he is finally a poet figure after Mallarmé, pure inviolable *logos* never made flesh.) Goriot too is betrayed by his creation, and in his deathbed monologue this "genius of fatherhood" reinvents Hamlet's interdiction of marriage: "Fathers, tell the Assembly to make a law on marriage! . . . No more marriages!" Marriage is accursed because it destroys the vertical, genetic relationship of father and child, creator and creature, to substitute for it a horizontal social relation which, the novel has amply demonstrated, is a denatured contract, a barter, a commerce, institutionalized prostitution. In his final rantings, Goriot reverts to another, precedent, primary social organization: "I protest. The nation will perish if fathers are trodden underfoot. That is clear. Society, the world turn on paternity. . . ."

Society does not perish; it rather succumbs to secularization, class stratification, commercialism, legalism, the play of means and modes of production and their superstructure in manners: the whole network of relations which the novel has sought metaphors to express. And hence it opens up possibilities for the grandiose personal gesture aimed toward a reorganization, a new principle of unity, a new metaphor of governing creation: the erection of self to godhead we find in Vautrin—and a number of other Balzacian monomaniac geniuses—and in Balzac himself, in his presence as creator, in the drama of his insane effort to "compete with the Civil Registry," to know and to conquer the drama of life through the melodrama of this fictional metaphors, to recreate the discrete particles of the real in a synthetic spiritual vision. In "the long prison of his labor," as Henry James called it, he engendered creations with profligacy, spawned metaphors of the spirit made flesh, only to find, like Vautrin (punishment for the sin of aspiring to Godhead?) that the creations ramified in independence, grew vital on their own: that his characters performed what Béguin calls an "insurrection" against their creator, an insurrection which accounts for the sense of novelistic freedom that James found in Balzac, the way he gives each character "the long rope, for acting [himself] out."

This of course is the destiny of any valid work of art, which must always live in a state of insurrection, in a declaration of independence from its creator. It is a destiny that can perhaps provide a last elucidation of metaphor and the melodrama of manners as Balzac uses them. The struggle to organize the mass of metaphors of the *Comédie humaine* calls into play new metaphorical efforts—new transactions between ever larger contexts, and the ever-renewed attempt to work through such transactions to essential structurations, to the basic drama, and ultimately to the principles of all creation—which finally have the effect of making the whole opus an exacerbated nerve center where a touch on one strand provokes reactions through many different chains, where one particular object, or person, or destiny can constantly be seen in other contexts, in terms of something else, in a chain of metaphoric mutations. This may suggest a final explanation of why Balzac's mode can only be melodramatic, a theater where everything is pushed toward the grandiose, the hyperbolic, the sublime. (pp. 213-28)

> Peter Brooks, "Balzac: Melodrama and Metaphor," in The Hudson Review, Vol. XXII, No. 2, Summer, 1969, pp. 213-28.

Ronald Berman   (essay date 1969)

[*Berman is an American educator and critic. In the following excerpt, he examines* Le père Goriot *as a novel whose success depends on literary conventions rather than strict realism.*]

Père Goriot is our classic of realism—if reality attaches only to the truths of economics. We know how much a loaf of bread costs at the Maison Vauquer and how much a room on the third story; we know how much a pair of white kid gloves costs, how much an attorney can sell himself for, and how much can be gotten for selling someone else. The book is alive with such evaluations, forcing us at every moment to pause, calculate, compare and acknowledge that everything has its price and is therefore part of a system. Yet it has been often remarked that this is a weakness of Balzac. His obsession with raw facts could not be reduced to novelistic form and intrudes upon the narrative in a way that, to invoke Stendhal, is like a pistol shot at an opera. Worse, his concern with "science" imposes a peculiar theoretical strain upon his writing. It is one of the great ironies that Balzac sought to establish his view of social life by evidence that no one can any longer take seriously. When he goes to what were the truths of nineteenth-century thought he satisfies us least because those truths are now considered illusions, if not ideological falsehoods.

Harry Levin notes in *The Gates of Horn* that Balzac was an intellectual captive to "the animal magnetism of Mesmer, the physiognomy of Lavater, the phrenology of Gall." These systems are not easily yoked to the novelistic form, for the true *métier* of that form is psychology. The novel resists categories. Thus character in *Père Goriot* is often in danger of becoming mere symptom. The "curious

monstrosities" of the Vauquer household fit into a system of metaphor rather than of personality: Monsieur Poiret, for one, is "like a kind of machine"; Mademoiselle Michonneau, skeletal and withered, is described as the waste product of the aging process, a kind of *exemplum* of biological necessity; Victorine is "like a shrub, transplanted to unfavorable soil, the leaves of which are dying." What is a scientific analogy for one century is a myth for another. Vautrin, the modern reader observes, is a walking bundle of proverbial symptoms, the red hair as indicative of passion as the Galenic choleric humor, the blazing eye as hypnotic as that of the ancient Mariner. Goriot himself is placed by the pseudoscience of somatotypes:

> Besides, his long square nose, and the large and salient calves of his legs prognosticated moral qualities, the existence of which was confirmed by the good old fellow's moon-shaped and ingenuously foolish face.

The tone is unserious, but the information is certainly offered seriously.

Throughout the narrative the literary agents study each other against the norms of pseudoscience: the medical students at the Maison Vauquer observe Goriot's fall into misery and measure "the top of his facial angle" to comprehend the experience of grief; Rastignac looks at Vautrin and sees "the cold and fascinating gaze that is the gift of certain men of eminently magnetic temperament and is said to have the power of conquering madmen in insane asylums." When offered as literally true and realistic these observations lose all credibility. The problem is that Balzac tries to be most realistic—if not scientific—while using intellectual materials which have by now become totally unconvincing. We are at our most impatient when invited to contemplate the bumps on Goriot's forehead, or the externals which impose so faithfully upon Vautrin the forms of nineteenth-century forensic medicine. In short, criminology, biology, and phrenology may have been at one time guideposts of intellectual discernment, but they now seem to lack even the most elementary clues to character.

The greatness of *Père Goriot* would seem not to depend on the "scientific" norms to which it addresses itself. The intellectual systems that sustain the book are now dead, but the book manages to speak to us in our own critical language. Paradoxically, we are most convinced of *Père Goriot's* fidelity to reality by its literary norms. We become aware, for example, that this is a specifically *literary* book, that it urges us continually to break out of the circumstances of social life and contrast them with standards derived from wider and deeper experience. The book does this in several ways: by the use of rhetorical exaggeration and allusiveness; by a systematic inversion of values; and by the imposition of ideas derived from other books. It is covered with a thick layer of literary patterns.

There are different ways of being realistic about objects. The two bottles of champagne that Madame Vauquer declines to offer Vautrin "would cost twelve francs." That is the only life they have, as counters in her highly limited imagination. She prudently offers to substitute for them some bottles of her despicable homemade cordial (as prudently refused by her lodgers, who are aware of its laxative quality) and the matter of their existence is closed. The determination of these objects is simple and finite. In the flat and well-delineated world of economic realities they are simply the equivalent of twelve francs. On the other hand, the pair of white gloves envied by Rastignac "at six francs a pair" are the indispensable marks of an identity he wishes passionately to assume. As he stands waiting for the carriage to take him to his destiny in the Rue De Grenelle he is man unclothed, the thing itself "without any umbrella, in his black coat, white waistcoat, yellow gloves, and patent leather boots." His provincial outfit has been the emblem of his social success, if not of his total human value. The desired pair of white gloves translates the outfit into something else, and Rastignac becomes aware that he is worse than naked. Perhaps Balzac's acquaintance with *King Lear* was more thorough than we imagine, for it is at this moment, in the middle of a storm, that the hero reflects on appearance in a world of reality. It is a neat reversal. Man clothed and unclothed can also be the subject of comedy—a human comedy, to be sure.

Rastignac's subsequent ride through Paris becomes a *rite de passage*. With evident premeditation Balzac dispatches him to the drawing-room of Madame de Beauséant in a carriage which still contains some sprigs of orange blossom, remnants of the wedding it has just served. That the ride costs ten francs is inconsequential; what matters is its allusiveness. As the "vulgar bridal equipage" rattles into the courtyard before lackeys "solemn as judges" he becomes a convert to the truth of Paris. The mocking transformations, the half-symbolic allusions go far beyond a literal sense of what is realistic. From the provincial outfit which reflects his social nakedness, to the "blind rage" of his self-hatred, to the symbolic ride in the bridal coach through the city of man, to the courtyard itself, a version of the Heaven he wishes to scale, all the details of realistic narrative transform themselves to something more inclusive. The event is easily managed in the sense that a scene is quietly moved by ponderous and well-oiled machinery beneath the stage. But in order to write about these simple actions a great deal of literary machinery is involved: from the intimations of the voyage perilous to the explicit figure of Paris as a "labyrinth" (as it is called by Madame de Beauséant) the events occur within the framework of literary tradition. To be simply realistic is to particularize, but here and in many other instances Balzac is intent upon universalizing. The allusions are brief but precise; they are the common stock of mythical and therefore psychological experience. As for the mode, there is considerable utility to *diminuendo*. The "quest" of Rastignac is from this moment endowed with a particular irony, for it is a parody of the heroic.

Surely one of the most meaningful and impressive verbal patterns imposed on the narrative is that supplied by Madame de Beauséant: "I give you my name to use, like the silken thread of Ariadne, in the labyrinth you are trying to enter." She is a variant of the mythos of Fortune—and Rastignac is a man looking for the right gods to adore. The labyrinth is one of the dominant metaphors of the book, and not only because it suggests an equivocal resemblance between Rastignac and the amoral figure of Theseus. If we

recall the opening, we will note that the buildings on the Rue Neuve-Sainte-Geneviève are "like those of a prison." One does not *locate* this area, but, as in *Bleak House,* one comes upon it by accident, "straying in this direction." It is not only the most unpleasant but the most "unfamiliar" of all Parisian quarters. Almost casually, the main aspects of the myth are sketched in: intricacy, strangeness, a sense of involuntary progression to a point of meaning. Balzac's summation is explicit to the point of making comment superfluous:

> The Rue Neuve-Sainte-Geneviève is like a bronze frame, the only one in keeping with my tale, for which the minds of my readers cannot be too well prepared by somber colors and somber thoughts, just as, step by step, the daylight wanes and the song of the guide grows hollow as the pilgrim descends to the Catacombs. This is a true comparison. . . .

The defining analogy for which Balzac searches, that of the Catacombs, invokes at once the figure of an infinitely deceiving maze of passageways and that of the quest for some kind of meaning. It is an analogy applied to the entire life of Paris, a figure used by Vautrin, by Rastignac, and most often by Balzac himself. When the author describes Rastignac's intention to impose upon the Nucingen household the same kind of *troika* arrangement as that governing the Restauds, he writes that the ideal novelistic vehicle for this might be a derivative of the ancient but satisfying metaphor: "the crooked ways through which an ambitious man of the world drives his conscience when he tries to skirt along the edge of evil and succeeds in saving appearances and compassing his ends." When Madame de Nucingen is considering the pleasures of yielding to Rastignac the metaphor once again resurfaces, this time with a pronounced moralistic form deriving from the medieval *topoi:* "a young libertine, she found so much pleasure in straying through the flowery paths of love that she lingered gladly to study all its charms, to feel its thrills, and suffer herself to be caressed by its chaste breezes." Whether as an analogy or an allegory the figure will never relinquish its hold upon the narrative. The characters are seen persistently in figural terms, "straying" through the labyrinthine moral and material circumstances of their lives. When the last invocation of this figure appears we should recognize the tensions by now inherent in its use: "His eyes fixed themselves almost eagerly upon the space between the Place Vendôme and the Dôme des Invalides, *upon the center of the great world he had longed to penetrate*" (italics mine). With this summation of a very ancient figure the book closes, but not before warning us that all the meanings suspended in that figure are meant to be balanced against each other. (pp. 7-10)

If we stop to consider how many other books are addressed directly or obliquely by Balzac in the course of this narrative we find that they constitute a small library. Some of these books are used continuously and furnish guiding themes and germinal metaphors. Some are used in specific instances, inviting us to transfer our attention from one text to another. In both cases the text of **Père Goriot** must be viewed through the text of the book it addresses. Our responses are intentionally complicated and thickened by this method.

One of the most obvious examples is the death-bed scene which transfers attitudes and motifs from *King Lear*. It raises the subject of bourgeois tragedy to another plane altogether. Another well-known parallelism is that between *Père Goriot* and the Gospels, the latter imposing upon the former a pattern of the sufferings of Christ. This is not to mention what might be called biblical commonplace:

> "That old bat always makes me shiver," said Bianchon to Vautrin in a low voice, speaking of Mademoiselle Michonneau. "I am studying Gall's system, and I think she has the bumps of a Judas."

It would of course be folly to think literally in these terms, and to evoke the image of the Betrayal for the capture of Vautrin. Yet we should note that Bianchon's insight is convincing not because it has been authenticated by phrenology, but because it is precisely unscientific and intuitive. It gathers its force from the story it suggests, for the mystery of her character, like that of Vautrin, is impossible to communicate as a "realistic" conception. The imposition of Judas upon Gall allows Balzac to suggest souls as well as characters.

The text is full of explicit stage-directions. Two of the most important are concerned with analogues of character:

> "The devil!" said the painter, "he would make a splendid model!"

> In order to describe the expression of this Christ among fathers, it is necessary to seek a comparison in those pictures in which the princes of the palette have represented the sufferings endured by the Saviour of men for the salvation of the world.

The suggestions of a "model" and a "comparison" and the representational quality of the "palette" point to a formal quality of the narrative. What is really being stated is that a thing ought not to be viewed in itself. Particularly where the Christian mythos is involved, and at those points where values are being suggested, Balzac's method is to involve the reader's sense of the universal—and even to create it.

The Bible of course is not the only vehicle for this intention. I would venture a guess that *Paradise Lost* supplies its own "model" of the "poet of infernal genius, who . . . wore the look of a fallen archangel resolved for war." The temptations of Rastignac are related, I suggest, either to this specific source or to the vast, inchoate body of Christian tradition. Certainly of a more demonstrable order are those allusions made to contemporary literature. Certain writers are introduced briefly to point an allusion: Chateaubriand, Bernardin de Saint-Pierre, Arlincourt, Guilbert de Pixérécourt. Their function is to underline a specific attitude, as when Madame Vauquer says of a drama called *Le Mont Sauvage*: "it is so pretty that we cried like so many Magdalens of Elodie, under the linden trees last summer, and it is moral too. . . ." The allusion gives us some sense of what is worthy of her grief—and of her ethi-

cal responsiveness. Mesmer and Gall are invoked for the apparatus of their theories on evil. Anthropologists like Geoffroy Saint-Hilaire make their presence felt, giving to the narrative its theoretical form of evolutionary development and natural selection.

Balzac's use of *Paul et Virginie* is somewhat more complicated and will perhaps be clarified by passages in apposition:

> "There," said he crossing his arms, "is a scene that would have inspired that good Bernardin de Saint-Pierre, the author of *Paul et Virginie*. Youth is very beautiful, Madame Couture!—Sleep, my poor boy," said he to Eugène; "fortune comes sometimes when we are sleeping.—Madame," he resumed, addressing the widow, "what I find so attaching and so attractive in this young man is the knowledge that his soul is as beautiful as his face. See, isn't he like a cherub, leaning on the shoulder of an angel? He is really worthy of being loved!"

> What need, indeed, had these young people of riches or learning such as ours? Even their necessities and their ignorance increased their happiness. . . . Thus grew these children of nature. No care had troubled their peace, no intemperance had corrupted their blood, no misplaced passion had depraved their hearts. Love, innocence, and piety possessed their souls; and those intellectual graces were unfolding daily in their features, their attitudes, and their movements. Still in the morning of life, they had all its blooming freshness; and surely such in the garden of Eden appeared our first parents. . . .

The cosmic drama which overshadows *Père Goriot*—the drama of temptation, fall, and transformation—has after all its point of origin in Genesis. *Paul et Virginie*, sentimental as it is, contributes strikingly to the mythos of *Père Goriot*. In the "forest" of Paris, we are reminded of the "garden" of the beginning; the preparations for a murder are confronted with the "innocence" of the state of grace; the primitivism of the bestial is contrasted to a primitivism specifically beyond history. In short, we are referred to *Paul et Virginie* in order to complicate and refine our responses. We are forced to read Vautrin's remarks within the atmosphere of Saint-Pierre's envisioning. The more we turn over the pages of *Paul et Virginie* the more we see how themes hinted at in *Père Goriot* are made explicit in the work to which it refers so obliquely. The essential point is that both books describe a state of nature: one does this in a way sentimental and serious, the other in a way ironic and indirect. But the power of irony lies in the fact that it is derivative, that it implies a vision corruptible enough to utilize. There is of course one more difference worth noting. Where *Paul et Virginie* is almost mindlessly sentimental, Vautrin is enormously complex. The balance of his feeling, his sensuality, and his contempt is made exquisitely plain in the remark I have quoted. In a way he is a literary critic.

This is by no means to exhaust the list of literary relationships. In order to imply the moral weakness of Rastignac under temptation Balzac contrasts him with the Alceste of Molière and the Jeanie Deans of Sir Walter Scott, both literary models of moral strength. In order to portray his increasing psychological disintegration Balzac invokes the character of *"Le Distrait"* in La Bruyère. The comic elements of this "character" become attached to our conception of Rastignac. Menalcas goes through Paris in a whirlwind of confusion, mistaking persons, confounding objects, blind to his own interests, absorbed in some interior dialogue that imprisons him. Much the same can be said metaphorically of Rastignac, who goes from the Maison Vauquer to the gaming tables, from the Mont-de-Piété to the home of the Nucingens with all the blind haste and moral ignorance of that figure, which for an ironic moment, he once again brings to life in its satiric fullness.

The great books of the Enlightenment are not addressed specifically, yet they seem to permeate the story. When Balzac observes toward the end of *Père Goriot* that Rastignac's "education was approaching its completion" he is utilizing a conception made famous by Rousseau and Voltaire. Rastignac is certainly one of the great figures of *paideia;* his is a personality which forms itself in relation to the social truths by which it is circumscribed. There is of course an irony displayed—his education involves a contradiction between the individual and the citizen, a contradiction made famous by *Emile.* Rousseau observed of the "natural" man (of whom Vautrin is a representative figure) that he lives for himself: he is the whole unit of existence as opposed to the artificial entity of the state. It is toward this dangerous condition that Rastignac progresses; in other words, the very things feared by Rousseau as forms of moral alienation are exposed (and perhaps mordantly accepted) by Balzac as characteristic of social life.

Perhaps the most penetrating of the literary references in *Père Goriot* is addressed to this specific problem. At one point Vautrin reminds us of his own literary ancestry: "My passion is the same as that of Pierre and Jaffeir, and I know *Venice Preserved* by heart." One may presume that Balzac knows this drama thoroughly, and the reader of *Père Goriot* is well advised to become familiar with it. It is not often, in the novel, that a character gives us such explicit stage-directions concerning the interpretation we are likely to formulate about him.

If there is one phrase that reverberates through Otway's tragedy that phrase is "Nature." And it is always used in the same way, to indicate the violent abuse of individual being by civilized corruption. When Pierre describes the origin of society to Jaffeir he sounds like nothing so much as Vautrin instructing Rastignac:

> JAFFEIR. I'm thinking, Pierre, how that damned
>   starving quality
> Called honesty, got footing in the world.
> PIERRE. Why, pow'rful villainy first set it up,
> For its own ease and safety; honest men
> Are the soft, easy cushions on which knaves
> Repose and fatten. Were all mankind villains,
> They'd starve each other; lawyers would want
>   practice,
> Cut-throats rewards; each man would kill his
>   brother

> Himself; none would be paid or hanged for murder.
> Honesty was a cheat invented first
> To bind the hands of bold deserving rogues,
> That fools and cowards might sit in power,
> And lord it uncontrolled above their betters.
> JAFFEIR. Then honesty is but a notion?
> PIERRE. Nothing else;
> Like wit, much talked of, not to be defined.

Venice Preserved offers a definitive picture of the relationship of Vautrin and Rastignac: the preceptor who is on the side of "Nature" and the pupil striving to formulate his experience. The rhetorical violence of the play suits the mood constructed by Balzac; its passion and anger at the state of society underlie the animosity of both the novelist and his creations. Most important, there is a great divide in *Venice Preserved* between the authenticity of "natural" man and the tyranny of culture. It is an opposition central to the dialogues of Vautrin.

There are of course some vast differences. As the object of parody—and in a central sense all the literary models mentioned in *Père Goriot* are parodied—its grandiloquence is transformed into something more modern and subtle: heroic friendship reappears as homosexuality and sensibility becomes a loathsome form of physical responsiveness. We are expected to draw upon this tragedy for our own responses to Vautrin, and to divide ourselves in the ambiguous way it indicates. It too is a drama of decadence, and it offers to the intellect the dangerous consolations of unleashed feeling and amoral action. It offers as well what has been called the sense of an ending—the operatic finale of *Venice Preserved* shows the whole edifice of human organization toppled by its own weight. The story that begins with the apologetics of philosophy ends in the fact of anarchy.

In summary, I have been trying to indicate the extent of Balzac's interest in literary patterns. The strategy of *Père Goriot* is, I suggest, to filter through its own text the analogies of its intellectual sources. Its mode, finally, is that of comparison. When Balzac uses these sources it is to impose upon the event at hand some consciousness of a larger and often more ironic meaning. His depiction of Victorine—"like an artless picture of the Middle Ages"—brings to our consciousness a disturbing reminder of the lost state of innocence. She becomes part not of a social circumstance but of a moral tradition. When Balzac uses this simile he invokes the nameless "artist" of the Middle Ages to crystallize in painterly detail, in the failure of mere objectivity, the attitude which he is trying to bring forth. He is at the limits of his descriptive power, but not nearly at the limits of his powers of analogy.

The literary mode of *Père Goriot* tells us a good deal about those limits. In his ceaseless strife with representation Balzac periodically addresses a truth beyond the objective. "This Christ among fathers" takes his place in a literary scheme and in a structure of values to which, eventually, the truths of realism are inconsequential. His great antithesis, who "wore the look of a fallen archangel resolved for war," is equally part of a grand dialectic. This dialectic will eventually dissolve the temporal world so painstakingly constructed by the author himself. The story does not remain a bourgeois drama but becomes a commentary on its sources. When Balzac pauses, late in the narrative, to reach for the kind of truth that descriptive power can hope to reveal, it is with a graceful sense of failure: "It is necessary," he writes, "to seek a comparison." That, in a sense, has been the mode of *Père Goriot;* the depth of its metaphors and the breadth of its literary analogies are comparisons in action. (pp. 11-16)

Ronald Berman, "Analogies and Realities in 'Père Goriot'," in Novel: A Forum on Fiction, *Vol. 3, No. 1, Fall, 1969, pp. 7-16.*

Anthony Winner (essay date 1981)

[*Winner is an American educator and critic. In the following excerpt, he examines Balzac's conception of character as a "collection of private energy with public form."*]

In Balzac's major fiction it is precisely the framework provided by internalized social realities that structures the historical validity and mundane effectiveness of character. Balzac consistently depicts social processes, roles, and aspirations as inseparable from meaningful individuality. Even the moral, quasi-allegorical types with which, for example, *La Cousine Bette* abounds are realized dramatically through their involvement in a social setting whose motives and cues for action include class ideology, the economics of love and lust, and the expectations of mundane power. As Georg Lukács has argued [in *Studies in European Realism,* 1950], the dynamics of individual psychology are usually particularized versions of general social processes. Balzac appoints himself secretary to a world in which neither ideal sentiments nor principles can be staged. Both the earthly drama and its dramatis personae act out a realistic pragmatism akin to that advocated by the diabolic empiricist Vautrin. This drama, of course, is intended to demonstrate truths outside itself: to be a vehicle for Balzac's conservative, if sentimental, Catholic and Royalist beliefs. But these beliefs rarely possess dramatic force; their message is often segregated into moralistic asides, and their truth risks becoming an abstract premise rather than a source of compelling action.

Given Balzac's intense concern with social drama, the interplay between good and evil is forced to adopt the often ambiguous parts provided by economic and political issues. In a sense the blurring of moral distinctions is the price exacted by the narrative patterns social life grants the writer. Rephrasing absolute definitions within the empirical data of manners and history, Balzac protects his plots and characters against the alternations that so often turned the fiction of his parent generation into a set of vertiginous gyrations between absolutism and dailiness. *La Comédie humaine* grows out of and well beyond the grub-street Gothicism and historical-sentimental romances that were the popular fare of Balzac's youth and that he himself helped turn out: a fiction prone to see human action as always teetering upon the brink of sensationalistic extremity, only weakly attached to the mediations and complex stabilities of social existence. Responding to the exceptional stimuli with which their authors bombarded

them, the characters in such fiction were repeatedly cast out of earthly time and place into uncharted realms. Development, community, and even the type of particularized exemplary behavior common to *Clarissa* and *La Nouvelle Héloïse* were carried away in the rebound of many late eighteenth- and early nineteenth-century romantic fables into sheer emotion or action. Such figures as Werther and Victor Frankenstein—at the beginning and the end of the period—unable to integrate their desires with the circumstantial limits of probable social life, sought their truths elsewhere: the feeling heart, and with it the possibility of domestic loving, reacted to commonplace frustrations by passionate rebellion; the curious mind, and with it the possibility of temporal education, veered off from conventional curricula to confront primal mystery.

Balzac retains much of the melodrama of these plots, but he desires to bring it within the pale of his society. "All is true," as the epigraph to *Le Père Goriot* announces, but at the same time home truths are truer. What is wrong with Gothic romances and their like is not the implausibility of their basic action but the implausible implications fostered by their ahistorical, asocial settings. Folk tale, legend, and myth are true; circumstantial data are real. The two together fuse energetically to create what Balzac terms drama. Well-dressed Mohicans stalk Paris streets, combining the force of the primal with the activities of public life; mythic beauties, clothed as fashionable girls with eyes of gold, stroll Paris parks, joining the transcendent scope of amatory romance to the topical fascination of society's mating games.

Yet the drama Balzac stages is complicated and enriched by his awareness of the ambiguities that result when final truths are costumed in everyday garments. At times he seems unwilling to subject the largesse of romance to the minutiae of the novel. Though he reworks the basic method of Scott's historical fiction—the grounding of absolutism in the plausible field of earthbound common life—Balzac's attitude toward the process is more deeply divided than that of the Waverley novelist. While Scott's allegiance is sometimes claimed by the absolute, his moral perspective usually follows the example of Cervantes in tempering the ideal to the real. The borderland becomes a setting for the deflating contrast between highland extremity and the moral heroism of those who are learning to forego the elixir of epic gestures for the more nourishing manners of civil life. Such translation frequently strikes Balzac as potential trivialization. The relocation of the glories and perils of supreme deeds within the conventions of social order risks setting in motion something like a chemical reaction that will alter and compromise the nature of the former. Both within individual works and in his career-long rush from one type of fiction to another, from philosophic or pastoral romance to novelized epic to novel of manners, Balzac tries to satisfy at once and by turns elemental truths and sociohistorical realities. The banker Nucingen enters at one moment as a rather silly cuckold, a figure of fun and fractured French; at another he is glorified through the tactics of mythopoeic finance into a Napoleon of speculation hurling his armies of stockholders into an epic fray. If all is true, both are true accounts. But even Balzac's enthusiastic dramaturgy cannot quite avoid a tainting and confusing conflation of the two. The novelistic alchemy that creates price war out of real war gives off a certain atmosphere of diminishment. Being in his way both a militant hero-worshiper and a Christian moralist, Balzac often seems to be deploring the socialization he desires.

Such duality, of course, is shared by Scott, Stendhal, and many other novelists of the period. But Balzac goes further than any other in making the tension between the mythic and the Marxian, melodrama and manners, the essential ground of character. The protagonists of his worldly—as opposed to pastoral or philosophic—novels tend to vacillate between the dictates of moral idealism and the practical rewards of social action. Their drama unfolds within the narrative emphases of what Vautrin calls "secret history." Near the end of *Les Illusions perdus,* that satanic arch-empiricist chides the suicidal Lucien de Rubempré for his ignorance of this crucial subject.

> You don't seem very strong in History. There are two Histories: official History, those lies one is taught . . . then secret History, which contains the true causes of events, a shameful story. . . . Have you studied the means whereby the Médicis, simple merchants, came to be Grand Dukes in Tuscany? . . . Well, young man, they became Grand Dukes in the same way Richelieu became Minister. If you had sought in history for the human causes of events instead of learning lists by heart, you would have drawn from them precepts for your own career.

As a principle of character creation, secret history explains Balzac's focus on the inner circumstances—psychology would be a misleading term—that lead men to become social types, the private motivation that (in a favorite phrase) makes of each "one of those who." The narrative key signature is a version of the gospel according to Goethe's Mephistopheles: in the beginning was the act, the deed, not the word. "Principles don't exist, only events," as Vautrin tells Rastignac. Or, in the words of Norman Mailer [in *Advertisements for Myself,* 1959], as much a disciple of Balzac as Lucien becomes of Vautrin: "It is the actions of men and not their sentiments which make history." For Balzac, a character's private life is a uniquely shaped, and thus obscure or hidden, epitome of the general issues of sociohistory; and such history is the sum and interaction of private lives. Only insofar as the individual is and makes history is he a properly dramatic subject. And individuals can be subspecies within the natural drama of history only insofar as they internalize its goals and processes.

Le Père Goriot is an exemplary outgrowth of this general view. In a celebrated passage, the narrator explains that his protagonist, Eugène de Rastignac, "had seen the three great expressions of society [history in action]: Obedience, Struggle, and Revolt; the Family, Society life [*le Monde*], and Vautrin. He dared not take sides. Obedience was dull, Revolt impossible, and Struggle uncertain." Obedience, the morally ideal life that Balzac usually portrays in pastoral terms, equates actions and sentiments, and hence lacks the dramatic tension of secret history.

If there are exceptions to the Draconian laws of the Parisian code, they are to be found in solitude, in men who are never led astray by social doctrines, who live near some clear, fleeting, but ever-running brook; who, faithful to their green shades, are happy to listen to the language of the infinite written all about them and which they discover in themselves as they wait patiently for their heavenly wings while commiserating the earthbound. But Eugène, like most young men who have had a foretaste of splendor, wanted to dash fully armed into the lists of the worldly; having espoused its fever, he perhaps felt in himself the force to dominate it, though without knowing either the means or the end of his ambition. . . . As yet he had not shaken off completely the fresh and sweet ideas that surround like foliage a country childhood. He had continually hesitated to cross the Paris Rubicon.

Balzac's narrative voice speaks from the Paris side. While clearly more experienced and probing than Rastignac's, it nonetheless agrees that society offers dramatic struggle: a conflict that obscures the ideal, the purity of which is left behind in the sentimental stasis of a better but less engaging realm.

The drama rests in Rastignac's rite of passage from provincial inexperience to tainting experience, from a kind of archetypal innocence to a mixed state wherein ideals are subject to social pragmatism. As Eugène walks back to his shabby boardinghouse after one of his first encounters with the glitter of high society, he speculates:

> "If Madame de Nucingen takes me up, I'll teach her how to manage her husband. The husband is in the gold market, he could help me to get a fortune at one stroke." It was not put as crudely as this; he was not yet worldly enough to sum up a situation, understand it, and calculate its possibilities. These ideas floated on the horizon like feathery clouds; and though they hadn't as yet the spirit of Vautrin's, still, if they had been tested in the crucible of conscience, they wouldn't have yielded anything very pure. By a series of such compromises men reach that moral laxity to which our age subscribes. More rarely than ever before do we come upon those upright men of fine will who never bend before evil and to whom the slightest deviation from the straight path seems a crime—such magnificent images of probity as have inspired two masterpieces: Molière's *Alceste* and more recently Walter Scott's Jenny [*sic*] Dean and her father. Perhaps a work of opposite intention, painting the devious ways by which an ambitious man of the world games with his conscience as he tries to skirt round evil, so as to achieve his goal while preserving appearances, would be no less fine, no less dramatic.

Rastignac develops out of the tense intermingling of pure moral standards with society's impure options. By itself, the young man's demoralizing immersion in the facts of life would satisfy only reader curiosity about social mechanics; told from the vantage of rigid probity, the story would have the flatness of moralistic fable. Balzac, however, gives equal reality to worldly ambition and to the truths of conscience.

Rastignac is energy without form or direction, a tabula rasa on which Goriot's spiritual truth and Vautrin's immoral pragmatism will be imprinted. By the end, the protagonist becomes both a hero of compromise and a compromised hero. He must achieve some kind of parity among selfhood, a worldly identity, and soul. To do this, the extremes of obedience and revolt must be bent to intermediate purposes. The man we see at the conclusion is a socially and morally ambiguous creation, his education points to nothing so clear as a middle way, nothing so deterministic as a pivot of embattled forces. For Balzac's idea of society, compounding realistic curiosity and moral condemnation, is radically uncertain; and Rastignac's character becomes the character of this uncertainty.

The terms of Eugène's initiation and education, of the moral deflation of his potentialities into character, are implicit in the portraits of his two opposing models. Both Goriot and Vautrin are larger than the sociohistory in which they appear. At the same time, both are rendered partially grotesque by their real-life context. In essence, Goriot embodies Family and Obedience, but his exemplary devotion, placed within a corrupting social frame, seems not quixotic but vaguely pathological. When the old man finances a bachelor's flat for Rastignac's affair with his daughter, Delphine's pleasure fills him with ecstasy. He clasps her in an embrace "so savage, so frantic," that she cries out:

> "Oh! you're hurting me!"
>
> "Hurting you!" he said turning pale. He looked at her with a more than human expression of grief. To paint as it should be painted the face of this Christ among Fathers, we should have to search among the images created by the princes of the palette to depict the passion suffered on the world's behalf by the Savior of mankind. Goriot gently kissed the girdle his fingers had pressed too tightly. . . .
>
> Eugène, overwhelmed by the man's inexhaustible devotion, looked at him with the naive admiration that in the young constitutes faith.

Goriot is the absolute manifestation of one of the postures taken by sentiment in popular fiction: the proof of heart and feeling through suffering. Yet the tone and form of his passion deflate his divine model. Instead of the inevitable, serious parody involved in any earthly imitation of a supreme essence, we have a trivializing transposition into alien terms. The occasion and the grief are grotesquely incommensurate. Instead of exalting the fond father, the allusions to Christ (and elsewhere to Lear) tend to ridicule him. Balzac, of course, obviously partakes in the youthful ingenuousness of Rastignac's faith, clearly views the old man as an archetype. Yet this estimate is more than balanced by the validity granted the social perspective that sees Goriot as bathetic or absurd. The father's adoration is compromised both by its objects, the crass daughters, and by its medium, cash. At times the Christ among fathers appears a lapdogish, even a salacious, figure. As a character rather than an archetype the warring gyrations of his deathbed harangue portray him as a crazed and baf-

fled spirit trying to reconcile earthly facts with ideal expectations.

> Ah! how stupid fathers are! I loved them [the daughters] so much that I kept going back to them like a gambler to the gaming table. My daughters, that was *my* vice; they were my mistresses. . . . I want to see them. Send the police, the troops to look for them! Justice is on my side, everything's on my side: nature, the civil code. I protest. The country will perish if fathers are trodden underfoot. That's obvious. Society, the great world, turns on fatherhood; everything collapses if children don't love their fathers. (Balzac's italics)

The Avant-Propos as well as numerous asides stress Balzac's belief in the familial ideals Goriot garbles. But what makes the father's maddened inconsequences so dramatically impressive is not the spectacle of martyred truth, not the echoes of the romantic theme of absolutism trapped within the finite, but rather the inner view of pathetically mismatched contexts. Ideals are not malleable; transported across the Rubicon of social psychology, they foster a state nearer to psychopathology than to sanctity. Balzac anticipates the kind of loosely Manichaean perspective sometimes discovered in Kafka. When in *The Trial* Joseph K. finds the examining magistrate's law books to be cheap pornography, the scene can be read as an illustration of the principle that what in the spiritual realm might be a work devoted to the Virgin would become erotic trash if brought into the material world. Goriot's ideal paternity, carried into a fallen society, is transmogrified into a gambler's letch for the jackpot of love.

Witnessing the change, Rastignac experiences an almost Gothic violation of his "fresh and sweet" country notions. As in *Oliver Twist* a few years later, society is marked as a Gothic institution. But whereas Dickens presents Oliver as essentially invulnerable, as morally and psychically exempt from the horrors around him, Balzac presents the cumulative shocks to Rastignac's innocence as an education in the Gothic nature of social things: an education necessary to the development of realistic character. Earthly selfhood is the result of a brave gamble, though in spiritual life gambling is wrong. Delphine acts both as the agent of and the prize offered by the game. When she insists that Eugène share the money she wins at the tables, he resists "like a virgin." "But the baroness having told him, 'I'll take you for my enemy if you aren't my accomplice,' he took the money." Desiring, even loving, Delphine, he must play the game. Yet all the while he is "appalled." Typically, when Delphine attends the society ball rather than her dying father, Rastignac's conscience names her an "elegant parricide."

The gap between truth and social reality is the burden of Madame de Beauséant's and Vautrin's dark sayings. Eugène "saw the social world as an ocean of mud; whoever ventured in would be in it up to the neck. 'They commit only shabby crimes,' he said to himself, 'Vautrin is greater.'" There is no institutional equivalent to revolt; only the name, Vautrin. The archcriminal stands against all aspects of the social contract. As in his arrangements for the death of Victorine's brother, he is a demonic stage manager. More usually he is a demonic commentator, a raw voice: "stick to your principles as little as to your words. When they're asked for, sell them. . . . Principles don't exist, only circumstances. The superior man weds himself to events and circumstances in order to control them. If there were fixed principles and laws, people wouldn't keep changing them as they change shirts." Vautrin's accuracy in painting the muddy realities of the Parisian code suggests a fallen omniscience. Given a world that debases Goriot's gold into filthy lucre, moreover, Vautrin's revolt indicates a model for authenticity. Rastignac is tempted.

But Balzac deflates "Cheat Death" and his absolute revolt no less than Goriot and his absolute obedience. The former trivializes Satan no less than the latter defames Christ. Despite his uncompromising words, Vautrin conforms to Madame de Beauséant's social prescription: "if you have any true feeling, hide it like a treasure." Vautrin's identity with revolt is his treasure; to live in society he must hide it. He must live disguised, blurring his exemplary force, squandering his truth. Undisguised, he could not be included among Madame Vauquer's boarders, who represent "in miniature the elements of the whole social order." As part of this order, Vautrin is reduced to a petty demon, "the man of forty with dyed whiskers . . . one of those whom the vulgar call a 'bright spark'." If one of those, then not unique. In his sardonic mock courtship of the dowdy landlady, in his sentimental, homosexually toned inveigling of his "dear child" Rastignac, and perhaps most clearly in his falling victim to the trap baited by the dull Poiret and the faded Mademoiselle Michonneau, Vautrin shrinks to the mean measure of the society whose meanness he so often makes the butt of sallies "worthy of Juvenal."

Even in the scene of his arrest, his finest moment, Vautrin's archetypal evil must give way to social common sense.

> All hope of flight was cut off . . . [The Inspector] gave him so brusque a rap on the head that his wig leapt off, revealing Collin's head in all its horror. Along with the brick-red short hair that gave him the terrifying quality of force mixed with cunning, his head and face and torso as well were clearly lit up as if by the fires of hell. Each of the onlookers understood Vautrin in his entirety: his past, his present, his future, his ruthless doctrines, his religion of selfish pleasure, the regality conferred on him by the cynicism of his thoughts and deeds, the force of a nature capable of anything. . . . He sprang back with a movement of such ferocious energy, he roared so, that he tore cries of terror from all the boarders. . . . Collin understood his danger when he saw the glint of the cocked guns, and suddenly gave proof of the highest human power. Horrible and majestic sight! . . . The drop of cold water that froze his rage was an insight swift as lightning.

Pure immorality might qualify Vautrin as Rastignac's mentor in an immoral world. But the transition from regal Satanism to cunning criminality, no matter how majestic from the viewpoint of normal willpower, underscores the pragmatic omnipotence of marshaled society. Absolute sincerity of being grandly gives way to a simple gesture of self-preservation that even a bureaucratic cog like Poiret can understand. Vautrin's high rhetoric of condemnation lapses into the grossness of criminal cant, and as this happens Rastignac becomes aware that the diabolic brio has always included a shabby social note.

> The prison, with its manners and language, its stark transitions from the facetious to the horrible, its appalling grandeur, its vulgar familiarity, its baseness, was suddenly made plain . . . in this man who was no longer a man but the type of a whole degenerate nation, a savage, logical race, brutal and slippery. In a single moment Collin became a hellish poem in which were painted all human feelings, save one: repentance. His expression was that of a fallen archangel bent on eternal war. Rastignac lowered his eyes, acknowledging his criminal kinship as an expiation of his own wicked thoughts.

Vautrin is carried off, still exhibiting the double meaning of an absolute pulsation of primal energy and the worldly diffusion of such energy into baseness.

Rebounding from the dual impossibility of utter revolt and social disfranchisement, Rastignac turns to Delphine and her father. Through his love he wants to satisfy both ambition and goodness. But Delphine's blandishments also turn the poetry of pure feeling into the crass prose of fact; she inextricably confuses love and gold. "Eugène had questioned himself very seriously that day, and Vautrin's arrest, in showing him the depths of the abyss into which he had nearly rolled, had so strongly reinforced his noble feelings and his delicacy that he could not yield to this caressing refutation of his generous ideas. A profound sadness bore him off." Yet to reject Delphine is to reject ambition, to return to the unworldly, static life on the other side of the Rubicon. As earlier, in taking his share of Delphine's winnings, now too Rastignac is led to compromise his principles.

A saddened accommodation with what exists becomes the hallmark of Rastignac's emerging character, of his personal share in the confusing tension between the mundane and the moral that typifies social reality. Goriot and Vautrin, uncontained by the ambiguities shrouding the young man, appear as rootless emigrés from earlier sentimental and Gothic fiction. Their primary colors serve nonetheless as contrasts to the chiaroscuro of Rastignac's existence. For him to follow either would be to remain forever a provincial in regard to the issues Balzac presents as real life; for him to revolt against the dense texture of such life would be to deny all vestige of the humanity Balzac presents as possible in this world. After Goriot's funeral, in the concluding passage, Rastignac agrees to struggle for selfhood upon the unclear terrain Balzac has mapped out.

> Rastignac, left alone, took a few steps towards the topmost part of the cemetery and saw Paris spread crookedly along the banks of the Seine where lights were beginning to sparkle. His gaze centered almost avidly on the space between the Place Vendôme and the dome of Les Invalides. There lived the beau monde into which he had wished to penetrate. He cast on this humming hive a glance which seemed already to be suck-

ing its honey, and uttered these high-flown words:

"Now I'm ready for you!" [*A nous deux mainte-nant!*]

And, as the first act in the challenge he was launching at society, Rastignac went to dine with Madame de Nucingen.

Earlier, announcing his own course to the decent young Doctor Bianchon, Eugène had in a muted fashion taken over the role of instructor in realities: "go, stick to the modest fate your desires harbor. Me, I'm in hell, and I must stay there. Whatever evil you're told about society, believe it! No Juvenal could paint the horror beneath the gold and jewels."

Not only is Rastignac's hell less absolute, less literal, than Vautrin's, but he himself is clearly no evil figure. Why, then, must he agree to act on hell's terms? Balzac's answer is implicit both in the use of Delphine's married name and in the dueling challenge Eugène flings down at Parisian society. In society, the ideal is always married to the real; the approach to love's pure gold is through adultery with the banker's wife. In general, throughout Balzac's world, duels and gambling retain their romantic function: they transpose epic scope into the socially probable acts of individuals, serve as moments of heightened being that the heroic adventurer can store up against the historical loss of his occupation. Energy, for Balzac, as for many of his inheritors, is both a potentially criminal, antisocial force and an essential component of meaningful identity. In *La Comédie humaine* the only field open to expressions of energy is that offered by a sociohistory that blunts, diffuses, and often debases. Goriot and Vautrin both compromise the archetypal good and evil they incarnate, but because they are defined more by these pure categories than by social cross-purposes, they stand forth as epitomes, not historical characters. Their force being an outgrowth of their essence, they are not permitted the kinds of tensions and complications of motive that permit an individual such as Rastignac to taste the rich realities of the world Balzac dramatizes. They cannot conform to Georg Lukács's fine description: "The Balzac characters, complete within themselves, live and act within a concrete, complexly stratified social reality and it is always the totality of the social process that is linked with the totality of the character. . . . these individual destinies are always a radiation of the socially typical, of the socially universal, which can be separated from the individual only by an analysis *a posteriori.*"

Rastignac's situation reverses that of his two models. Their purity of meaning precludes any fundamental modification, any incorporation into social typicality. He lacks fixed essence, is only a potentiality. For him the complex contradictions of social processes provide a modus operandi through which he can define his self. Dinner with Delphine, Madame de Nucingen, and all it represents give shape to the previously amorphous energy and values of the nondescript provincial on the make. The character Rastignac develops both responds to and contends with a world in which the voices of his exemplars have become intermingling and uncertain echoes. The young man's ed-

ucation makes him a specific instance of the abstract, polemic category Gide terms the Balzacian ideal. But the tangled emotions, aspirations, and circumstances that go to make up Rastignac's character do not create "purity and continuity of line"; the pattern they produce is anything but consistent. The model Eugène imitates in his concluding duelist's challenge is as inconclusive as the nature of the society he is calling out to fight; indeed, it depends on the ambiguity of that nature for its form and practical meaning. His character exemplifies "secret history": the struggle between individual and social motives in the creation of meaning and interpretation. Balzac fulfills the promise of privileged insight he makes at the beginning: "Eugène de Rastignac . . . was one of those young men molded by the misfortune of having to work; from their earliest years they know the hopes their families set on them and prepare a fine destiny by calculating from the start the range of their studies, adapting them in advance to the future development of society so as to be the first to exploit it." Worldly reality and individual temperament interact to stage the drama of character. Balzac's idea of character takes form from the field of hidden pressures, the public corruptions and private pathologies, the deviations from value and conjunctions of need that constitute his vision of society. And in this sense the Balzacian ideal of the binding unity of character edges toward a substitution of social process for what Locke termed reflection—the inner, God-given process that holds together sensations and defines the identity of self and soul. (pp. 10-27)

An excerpt from *Le père Goriot*

"Oh, God, since you know the misery and suffering I have endured; since you know how often I have been stabbed in the back throughout this time that has aged me, broken me, changed me, turned my hair white, why do you make me go on suffering today? I have fully expiated my sin of loving [my daughters] too dearly. They have exacted revenge in full for my affection, they have tortured me like executioners. Yes, indeed, fathers are so stupid! I loved them so dearly that I went back to them like a gambler to the gaming table. My vice was my daughters; for me they were mistresses, everything. They were both always needing some finery or other. Their maids would tell me, and I would give it to them to earn a welcome! But all the same they gave me a few little lessons on social behaviour. Oh! Their patience soon ran out. They were beginning to be ashamed of me. That's what comes of giving one's children a good education. But at my age I couldn't go back to school. (God, this pain is terrible! Doctors! doctors! if they could open my head up it wouldn't hurt so much!) My daughters, my daughters, Anastasie, Delphine! I want to see them! Send the police after them, force them to come! Justice is on my side, everything is on my side, nature, civil law. I protest. The country will perish if fathers are trampled down. That's obvious. Society, the world, turns on fatherhood, everything breaks up if children don't love their fathers."

Honoré de Balzac, in his Père Goriot, translated by A. J. Krailsheimer, Oxford University Press, 1991.

*Anthony Winner, "Balzac's 'Le Père Goriot':
The Character of Society," in his* Characters
in the Twilight: Hardy, Zola, and Chekhov,
University Press of Virginia, 1981, pp. 9-27.

James Smith Allen   (essay date 1987)

[*Allen is an American educator and critic who has written extensively on nineteenth-century French history
and culture. In the following essay, he studies the depiction in* Le père Goriot *of three figures of importance to
the* Comédie humaine: *the ambitious young man, the social victim, and the social rebel.*]

Since Honoré de Balzac announced his intention "to write
the history long neglected by so many historians, that of
manners and mores," his novels have been valued for their
completeness and accuracy of observation. Balzac's contemporaries George Sand and Friedrich Engels praised
the novelist's historical vision at a moment when his fiction was generally held in low esteem. In time one tendency of critical commentary has taken seriously Balzac's
claim to have been "more historian than novelist." Most
recently Nora Stevenson, Georges Pradalié, Jean-Hervé
Donnard, and Ronnie Butler actually have attempted to
assess the historical authenticity of the master's novels.
Practicing professional historians still refer to the author's
fictional work for its rich store of information about social
structure, economic development, political conflict, and
intellectual trends, while the critical literature on the historicity of Balzac's novels continues to grow in size and
sophistication. Indeed, *The Human Comedy* is among the
best sources available for a social history of France from
1815 to 1848.

Balzac certainly had social as well as literary considerations in mind while composing *Father Goriot.* In 1834 he
scribbled in his notebook, "Subject of Father Goriot—a
brave man—middle-class boarding-house—600 franc income—wasting himself for his daughters who both have
50,000 franc incomes—dying like a dog." For the author,
the novel was to consist of an accurate depiction of a poor
man whose paternal role in the family, an important element of social order, was subject to the destructive influence of money. But as he hurriedly composed the novel
concurrently with his mystical *Séraphita* to meet publishers' deadlines, working as much as eighteen hours a day,
Balzac took time to write Mme. Hanska of its intended
moral qualities as well: "the portrait of an affection so
great nothing exhausts it, neither turmoil, nor injury, nor
injustice; a man who is *father* as a *saint, a martyr is Christian*" (Balzac's emphasis). The idea occurred to Balzac to
employ his main character's monomaniacal affection for
his daughters to portray a "Christ of Paternity." As a result, *Father Goriot* was meant to incorporate at least two
disparate elements: social observation and human passion.
At the height of his creative powers, Balzac wanted to
create a novel that was exclusively neither sociological nor
moral in intention, but a combination of the two that won
the acclaim of his reading public when it was published serially in the *Revue de Paris* from December 1834 to February 1835 and in two separate editions in 1835.

Nevertheless, *Father Goriot* is more than what the author

intended and what his audience consciously valued. More
specifically in this novel, Balzac outlined in formal terms
a social "myth" elaborated later in *The Human Comedy.*
Like his character Eugène de Rastignac, a major figure in
nearly three dozen novels by Balzac, the author "had seen
the three great expressions of society: Obedience, Struggle,
and Revolt." In these aspects of society reflecting the destruction of the Old Regime, the establishment of bourgeois society, and the imminent threat of open social conflict, Balzac created a complex plot linking Goriot and his
ungrateful daughters with Rastignac's ambitions for a
place in the new social order of Paris and with Vautrin's
rebellion against the repressive character of the Constitutional Monarchies. What this novel depicts, in its interwoven narrative structure with the three stories of Goriot,
Rastignac, and Vautrin played out together, are the historical themes touched upon in *The Wild Ass' Skin* (1831)
and *Eugénie Grandet* (1834), among other earlier works,
and developed later in the remainder of *The Human Comedy.* In his novels Balzac portrayed what he and many of
his contemporaries perceived to be the decline of traditional stability represented by an Old Regime society
based on property and inherited status. In its place was the
tenuous legitimacy of the bourgeois hierarchy based on
nonlanded wealth and acquired status. The result, for Balzac and others, was a tendency towards social dissolution,
the awareness of which is well portrayed in *Father Goriot.*
Here the author established central character types—
Rastignac the dandy, Goriot the victim, and Vautrin the
rebel—figures of major literary proportions enmeshed in
a drama of historical significance at the heart of *The
Human Comedy.*

The point of convergence in *Father Goriot* is the Vauquer
boarding-house, a squalid pension in Paris on the rue
Neuve-Sainte-Geneviève where the novel's principal action occurs in 1819-1820. Under one roof lives "an apparent collection . . . in miniature [of] the elements of a complete society," a society apart consisting almost exclusively of bourgeois *déclassés.* Each inhabitant *as a social type,*
including the three main characters, has come down in the
world as a consequence of the historical transition from
land to income as the principal criterion determining social rank in post-revolutionary France. Balzac's careful
descriptions of the house, "a boarding house for men,
women and others," provides an important clue to this
problem: like the boarders, it had seen better days since
the end of the Old Regime. Although it may have been
built specifically for lodging in the eighteenth century, the
Vauquer boarding-house was at one time clean, neat, and
fresh, like the epigram above the front door heralding Voltaire. Balzac's elaborate details point out the house's material decline since the 1789 revolution. The novel stresses
this suggestive deterioration and identifies the house with
Mme. Vauquer, the dowdy landlady whose aristocratic
maiden name, de Conflans, tells how far she has sunk despite her forty thousand francs. Her boarders are more
clearly dispossessed of their former status by their loss of
income; Mme. Couture, the wealthiest, is the pensioned
widow of a Republican commissary-general, Mr. Poiret a
retired petty functionary during the Empire, and Mlle.
Michonneau an elderly spinster living on a contested
thousand-franc annuity. Poverty has reduced these people

to social outcasts, defaced like worn-out coins and rejected like Victorine Taillefer whose father, the banker of ill-gotten wealth in *The Wild Ass' Skin,* has completely disowned her. Just as Mme. Vauquer is appropriate to the boarding house—"her whole person explains the lodging house"—so are the lodgers at the bottom of the Parisian bourgeois social structure.

Here in the Vauquer pension is portrayed Goriot's decline and death. Like the others, he too has suffered from historical change as a retired noodle manufacturer living on a slim pension whose income and social position sink with each successive move to upper-story rooms. His once immense fortune he has divided between his two selfish daughters who no longer recognize him as their father. By giving away all his money out of a less-than-disinterested affection, Goriot has sacrificed his place in the world for the sake of his personal and social ambition and for this daughters' love and their well-placed marriages—all of which depend upon his limited sources of money. As a resident of the Vauquer boarding house, Goriot shares in this bourgeois community in miniature that is suggestive of a historic decline. Here Goriot's social martyrdom resembles that of a bourgeois King Lear: where Lear dooms himself and his kingdom by the division of affection and power between Goneril and Regan, Goriot wastes his love and fortune on Anastasie de Restaud and Delphine de Nucingen, his socially established but self-centered daughters. But, in his position and character, Lear is tragic while Goriot, the petty bourgeois without a Cordelia, is only pathetic. Goriot is, in effect, a victim of his inordinate passion to make his daughters happy at any cost, but also of the social gap he creates between himself and the objects of his affection. His misery, the novel suggests, would have been averted had he not allowed them to marry into the upper classes of society. *Father Goriot*'s tragedy lies not solely in the fate of its wretched main character; it belongs as well to the changing distinctions between classes, and, more, to the shift from traditional to more modern criteria in determining the social hierarchy. A careful look at Goriot reveals this more clearly.

How Goriot came to his status, the narrative indicates, began with the spectacular profits he made during the First Republic when military needs provided an enormous demand for grain. While bread was scarce Goriot monopolized the Parisian noodle trade and profited by his privy information as the president of his section. Gouging the market at the highest possible prices, Goriot built his fortune on the misfortunes of others. Like his respectability, his wealth was a deception, an illusion hiding the man's true nature.

> Beyond his immediate concerns, his modest and forgotten shop on the front step of which he stood during his idle hours, his shoulder leaned against the door frame, he became once more the stupid and crass worker, the man incapable of comprehending an argument, insensitive to all pleasures of the mind, the man who slept at the theater, one of those Parisian dolts, remarkable only for idiocy.

With his rapid fortune and false esteem in the world, Goriot compounded his social deception by endowing his daughters for 1.6 million francs. His fortune exhausted except for a modest but comfortable pension, Goriot retired to the Vauquer lodgings. But in his ambition and affection for his daughters, Goriot persisted in giving away what little money he had left to finance their extravagant whims. Once "a clever wolf " he became "a cowering dog." By the novel's end Goriot had returned to the social nadir of Paris from which he had risen.

Most significant in Goriot's rise and fall is the fact that he succeeded in marrying off his daughters to the upper classes of Parisian society. "Goriot placed his daughters among the angels, and necessarily above himself." After his wife's death, the ambitious man transferred his intense sentiments to his daughters and did his utmost to promote their social accomplishments with special tutors. When the girls were old enough, they were left to choose their own husbands; and with their father's fortune and encouragement, they aimed high.

> Courted for her beauty by the Comte de Restaud, Anastasie had aristocratic penchants which led her to leave her father's house in order to throw herself into the higher spheres of society. Delphine loved money: she married Nucingen, a banker of German origin who became a baron of the Holy Roman Empire. Goriot remained a merchant of noodles.

What resulted from Goriot's extraordinary commercial success and social ambition, in spite of his shopkeeper's mentality, was a self-imposed exile from his daughters when they married far above their station in life. Father and daughters were no longer of the same social class. The novel is thus a portrayal of the effects of this distance between father and children. As time passes, Goriot is increasingly excluded from his daughters' homes until he is closed out completely as a social embarrassment to them. To see his daughters he must wait outside the gates of their homes for their carriages to pass. Anastasie, now among aristocrats, rejects her father to the point of refusing entrance to Rastignac after he mentions her father during a previous visit. Her sister Delphine tolerates Goriot for ulterior motives; she wishes to realize the very last of her father's money. Similarly, she sees Goriot as a means of using the titled Rastignac, her father's only friend in the boarding-house, to gain access to the salons of the Faubourg Saint-Germain over her sister's snobbish resistance. Meanwhile, to meet the bills his daughters incur, Goriot moves to cheaper quarters, from 100 to 74 and finally to 45 francs a month, details which the narrative faithfully documents in Goriot's social decline.

What kills Goriot in the end is not his daughters' cruel repudiation of his monomaniacal affection for them, even though they induce his final trauma by their petty quarrel over the last of his money; Goriot collapses in the midst of their jealous exchanges, unable to bear the pain of their rejection of his love and torn by his lack of money to buy back their sentiments. Complains Goriot to Rastignac near the end, "My latest lack of money has crushed my heart." But it is significant that Goriot is actually killed by social distance in his family, between him and his daughters and between Delphine and Anastasie. The source of their argument is Delphine's bitterness over the fact that she is not married to a French title like her sister and hence is not admitted to aristocratic salons as a bourgeoise. "They are killing me," moans Goriot as they bicker in their social resentment. They do not attend their father's death or funeral because they would have to confront each other again, indifferent to their father as much in their different acquired stations in life as in their genuine heartlessness.

Thus, what the novel depicts in its structure is a portrait of more than a "Christ of Paternity" destroyed by a neurotic passion for his selfish daughters, as generally understood. *Father Goriot*'s structure offers an underlying explanation for his martyrdom: Goriot is the victim of a society whose false respect for money enabled him to purchase his ambitions in life with his ill-gotten gains. His daughters rich and esteemed in the new social order, the impoverished Goriot is cut off from the objects of his love. He can no longer share in his daughters' love now that they have risen in the new social hierarchy. Goriot is destroyed by his mania, obviously, but the novel sets this self-destruction in the context of changing criteria in the determination of social rank and the widening gap perceived between classes in post-revolutionary France.

This view of Goriot's passion as a historical as well as a human phenomenon is also witnessed by Balzac's decision initially to include the novel among his *Scenes of Parisian Life.* Certainly the meaning of Goriot's fate is expressed in the narrative in more explicit terms than the implicit meaning of the main character's *déclassé* status. Balzac or, more precisely, the implied neo-legitimist narrator, insists upon complementing his fictional construction with the heavy-handed lesson he draws from Goriot's domestic tragedy. "Society, the world revolves around fatherhood," Goriot mutters on his death bed. "All is destroyed if children do not love their fathers." To Balzac the conservative writer welcomed to the salons of political reactionaries, no greater condemnation of his time could be made than this view of society's most essential element, the family. The narrative blames Goriot's illicit fortune, his social ambition, and his unwise affection for their part in the disorder; but it also points accusingly at his selfish daughters, their financial extravagances, and their preoccupations with social status. But this explicit moral in Goriot's martyrdom, drawn by the narrative, remains overshadowed by the new function of money in the social relations portrayed in the rest of the novel.

A similar view of bourgeois Paris exists in the figure of Jacques Collin, alias Death's Defier (*Trompe-la-Mort*), the Mr. Vautrin of the Vauquer boarding house. This "sphinx in a wig" is an escaped convict, the leader of the Society of Ten-Thousand organized to help the families of criminals. An exciting underworld figure added to the novel for more than interest, Vautrin performs an important function in his revolt, stemming from his views of Parisian society, that relates thematically to Goriot's story. Where Goriot's decline and death make him a social victim, Vautrin's unscrupulous scheming and cynical commentary emphasize the social dissolution that Balzac saw as inevitable when all the Goriots had died. Comments the critic Philippe Bertault [in *Balzac and the Human Come-*

dy, 1963], "This pirate is the typical outlaw, the personification of anti-social passion," for Vautrin is in open war with his world and makes no pretense of his rebellion. The product of a hypocritical and tenuous legal system that accused and punished him for a forgery he did not commit, Vautrin embodies the spirit of revolt in nineteenth-century France that, for Balzac, lacked the stabilizing authority apparent in the Old Regime.

The narrative identifies the origin of his virulent reaction to bourgeois society. Vautrin's revolt is less an unreasoned and self-seeking than a considered and justified response to an already unprincipled situation. In his monologues, he analyzes the perversion that results from the introduction of money into social manners and morals as well as in the determination of class. "If you ever probe the hearts of women in Paris, you will find there the creditor before the lover," he tells Rastignac. How this perversion in human conduct touches him personally appears in his unjust incarceration. In an implicit reference to his own crime and punishment, Vautrin generalizes: "Those who get about by carriage are gentlemen, those who get about on foot are cads. Have the hard luck to get caught swiping whatever, you are displayed at the square of the Palais de Justice as a curiosity. Steal a million, you are pointed out in the salons as a virtue." He resents the middle-class conception of law and order that is as much a mockery of justice as its conception of ethics is a perversion of morality, all of which have been reduced to a matter of wealth. In the hypocrisy of bourgeois principle and authority, the narrative partially justifies, despite or perhaps because of Balzac's own neo-legitimist convictions, Vautrin's rebellion.

Consequently, the narrator's attitude towards Vautrin expressed in the novel is ambivalent, a mixture of grudging respect and guarded suspicion. On the one hand, Balzac, the implied author, fears this man reputedly based on Vidocq, the former convict turned police chief whose memoirs were published in 1828. The views Vautrin advocates in his conversations with Rastignac are aimed at shocking the reader sensitive to basic Judeo-Christian precepts. "There are no principles, there are only occasions," Vautrin remarks. "There are no laws, there are only circumstances: the superior man espouses occasions and circumstances in order to control them." On the other hand, despite this obvious distrust, the narrator retains a frequently sympathetic tone. In fact, the jocular escaped convict stands in marked contrast to the jaded boarders in the Vauquer pension, especially in his concern for Goriot and Victorine. Except for Vautrin and perhaps Rastignac, "hardly any of the characters troubled himself to verify whether the misfortune alleged by one of them was either false or true." His cynicism aside, Vautrin manifests with the greatest force this sympathy for others.

From the novel's ambivalent tone, between Vautrin's analysis of the bourgeoisie and his revolutionary response, arises Vautrin's role as social rebel. He is a nineteenth-century urban version of the twentieth-century rural figures [described by Eric Hobsbawm in *Bandits,* 1969] on the margin of society "whom the lord and state regard as criminals, but who remain within peasant society, and are considered by their people as heroes, as champions, avengers, fighters for justice." These bandits appeared mostly, but not exclusively, in agricultural settings in a transitional economy. In effect, they reflect "the disruption of an entire society, the rise of new classes and social structures, the resistance of entire communities or peoples against the destruction of its way of life." Although social banditry is, by definition, a more recent rural phenomenon, *Father Goriot* presents Vautrin in a remarkably similar light, as a social rebel with largely altruistic intentions, at least for the socially displaced. Despite his apparent lack of principles, Vautrin actually represents the retribution for the victims of recent historical change, for all the Goriots in nineteenth-century Paris. The novel clarifies the ambiguous tone in this latter element of Vautrin's formal function. Besides his leadership of the Society of Ten-Thousand, Vautrin takes up Victorine's quest for her rightful inheritance. When she tells him of her prayers to change her father's heart, Vautrin responds,

> But that is not enough. You must have a friend who will take it upon himself to tell off that blackguard, a savage who is worth, they say, three millions, and who is not giving you a dowry . . . *O women innocent, miserable and harried* . . . that is what you are! In a couple of days I will see to your affairs and all will come out right.

True to his word, Vautrin finds a means, however devious, to provide the dowry Victorine deserves. Justice is done despite her ungenerous middle-class father. The narrative, speaking of his generosity, approves of Vautrin's handiwork, especially in light of the hypocritical counterscheming on the part of the police to apprehend him—more for the bounty on his head than for the sake of duty. The dignity of his farewell speech to the other lodgers suggests Vautrin's status as a nineteenth-century Parisian "Robin Hood."

Also in the context of his role as social rebel in the novel is Vautrin's relationship to Rastignac. Here again he is as much the protector of the uninformed as the tempter of the innocent. Accordingly, he tells Rastignac,

> A quick fortune is the problem that at this moment fifty thousand young men who find themselves in your situation are trying to resolve. You are just one in that number. Consider the efforts that you have to make and the fierceness of the combat. You must eat each other like spiders in a jar, given that there are not fifty thousand good positions. Do you know how one makes his way here? By the stroke of genius or by the exercise of corruption.

Vautrin offers Rastignac the road of corruption in a desperate social struggle. Encouraging the impoverished aristocrat to marry Victorine, the Mephistophelean figure endeavors to make his fortune by killing Victorine's brother, the only major obstacle to the young woman's substantial dowry. Balzac's fearful conservative reservations aside, the novel portrays Vautrin as a positive agent of social justice in an unjust society; the rebel intends to restore the aristocrat, with traditional esteem and modern wealth, to his rightful position in the world, and to place the dutiful

daughter in a proper relationship to her father, whatever Vautrin's personal gains in the arrangement.

In this way the novel clarifies the implied author's ambivalence toward Vautrin; the figure's essentially conservative ends conflict with his revolutionary means. Although he stands on the margins of Parisian society, "a man beyond the law," he lives rightly in the center of the Vauquer boarding-house whose other residents he defends in his war on the newly empowered middle-classes, until he is betrayed by two of his own people, Poiret and Michonneau, who inform the police of his activities. But with Rastignac's repudiation of Vautrin's offer, the novel finally casts Vautrin in a decidedly negative light. Despite his larger role in *Father Goriot*'s fictional structure, reflected in his social rebellion and his thematic relationship to Goriot's fate, Vautrin embodies the anarchy dreaded by the nineteenth-century neo-legitimist behind the narrative.

If Vautrin attracts and repulses to the extreme, Eugène de Rastignac, his elusive prodigy, remains consistently appealing, notwithstanding his moments of weakness. The novel's frequent contrast in tone toward the experienced convict and the innocent youth emphasizes their important relationship in *Father Goriot.* In the extended narrative attention paid to his social activities, Rastignac often overshadows Vautrin's revolt and Goriot's martyrdom, even though they all relate thematically in the novel's elaborate structure. Logically, Rastignac embodies many of the same themes created in the roles played by Goriot and Vautrin. Clearly evident in Rastignac's function in the work are the decline of acquired status and landed wealth, the establishment of bourgeois ethics and standards of rank, and the real possibility of revolt in the resulting loss of social and political legitimacy. In the impoverished aristocrat's quest of fortune in an urban middle-class world, the novel portrays the difficulties posed by the historical context of France during the Constitutional Monarchies. Indeed, as a historical reality, the poor provincial student establishing his future in the city furnishes one of the most appropriate subjects of realistic nineteenth-century fiction, as it does for many novels in *The Human Comedy.*

Like his counterparts, "the lions of Paris" and Adolphe Thiers (the journalist-turned-politician on whom he is partially based), Rastignac comes to Paris from Gascony to make his and his family's fortune. His provincial aristocratic parents share 1,200 of their 3,000 franc-a-year income to support him through law school in the hopes that he will succeed by his talent and hardwork in a middle-class liberal profession. "The uncertain future of this large family . . . rested on him." His need for money to complement his titled esteem underlies Rastignac's attempt to establish himself in an essentially bourgeois society; the new criteria in determining social status have usurped the traditional values of privilege and forced the displaced aristocrat to seek a fortune commensurate with his title. For months Rastignac, as a proper bourgeois, lives at the Vauquer pension and shares the *déclassé* status of Goriot and the other boarders because he, too, lacks the requisite income. Before long Rastignac realizes the limitations of this difficult road to the rank he feels he deserves. As

Vautrin points out, competition among middle-class pro-
fessionals in a slowly industrializing economy demands
genius or corruption. But the ingenuous Rastignac
chooses another route, the fashionable salons where his
good name and well-placed relatives will help him on
more quickly, as the narrative makes clear: "If at first he
had wanted to throw his whole person into work, [he was]
seduced early by the necessity to create connections[;] he
noticed how much influence women have in social life, and
[he] decided suddenly to throw himself into the world, ultimately to capture there his protectresses." Rastignac
soon throws over his law studies for a more glamorous fortune sought through Mme. de Beauséant, a distant cousin,
whose salon is among the most celebrated in Paris. "To
be admitted to these golden gatherings equalled an established claim to high nobility. In showing himself in this society, the most exclusive of all, he had conquered the right
to be accepted everywhere." The influence of an exclusive
social class, as well as the protection of women, seemed
to offer Rastignac the lingering advantages of Old Regime
nobility in nineteenth-century France.

With his first visit to Mme. de Beauséant, a true woman
of the world, Rastignac begins to see as well the importance of women to his bourgeois social ambitions of gaining a fortune appropriate to his title. As his wise cousin
advises him, "You see, you will be nothing here if you do
not have a woman who interests herself in you. You must
have her young, rich, elegant." She invites him to a ball
where he becomes immediately infatuated with the possibilities of Anastasie de Restaud, ironically enough a social
deception as the daughter of the former noodle manufacturer. Wealthy and married to a French count, she embodies the ultimate in Rastignac's aspirations in a new social world. But when he sees her preoccupations with another lover, he compromises on her sister Delphine de Nucingen, another false ideal with only her husband's money
and purchased foreign title to offer her new lover. Despite
his knowledge of her plebeian origins and her social limitations, Rastignac persists in his quest of Delphine and the
vast sums of money available through her husband the
banker. "To have a mistress is an almost royal position,
he told himself, this is the mark of power." A wealthy
woman did indeed signify a particular kind of royal power
in social Paris: the middle-class power denied the Old Regime aristocrat in the nineteenth century.

But Rastignac is handicapped in this adventure by his
poverty. He must have more money to put on a decent appearance, so he writes home to his family for what little
they can afford in addition to their already generous sacrifices. Rationalizing his decision, Rastignac sees the money
he squeezes from his struggling family as an investment
in the future. "These frightful sacrifices were going to
serve him as a ladder in order to come up to Delphine de
Nucingen," he thinks in justification of his self-serving request as his worldly education advances. Already he has
begun to compromise his moral sensibility for the sake of
getting on in the new Parisian social setting. Rastignac is
not far from taking to heart the cynical advice Mme. de
Beauséant offers early in the novel: "The more coldly you
calculate, the further you will go. Strike without mercy,
you will be feared. Accept men and women only as post

horses that you destroy at each relay, you will come thus
to the attainment of your goals." Rastignac's imposition
on his family for the sake of winning part of Delphine's
money, an impossible scheme, comes close to Vautrin's
advice as well, to cut his way through society like a cannon
ball.

With Vautrin's unscrupulous offer, the next lesson in his
social education in Paris, Rastignac faces the central
moral dilemma of his need for money. How conscious he
is of this problem is evident to Horace Bianchon, his well-
principled friend in medical school, as they discuss an anecdote from Rousseau's *Confessions.* Asks Horace,

> "Do you remember the passage where he asks
> his reader what he would do in the situation in
> which he could enrich himself by killing in
> China by his sole wish an old mandarin, without
> moving from Paris?"
>
> "Yes."
>
> "Eh! Well?"
>
> "Bah! I am on my thirty-third mandarin."

Vautrin later offers Rastignac an analogous situation: to
enrich himself by the murder of Victorine's brother, neither a mandarin nor in China, but a bourgeois on the other
side of Paris. Although he is saved from a decision by
Vautrin's arrest, Rastignac has fewer qualms about taking
Goriot's money in his quest for Delphine: he decides to accept a hide-away that Goriot finances despite the old
man's obvious poverty. He makes the same kind of compromise in escorting Delphine to Mme. de Beauséant's
ball as Goriot lies dying at the Vauquer boarding-house.
Implicitly, by his wish, he profits by "killing" Goriot instead.

But it is only with Goriot's death and his daughters' callous neglect to attend his death bed and funeral for the
sake of their petty social rivalry that Rastignac's Parisian
education is completed. Like Vautrin's invitation to corruption, Goriot's domestic tragedy teaches Rastignac of
Delphine's personal deception and the changes taking
place in the social order in which money has determined
not only social status but also human feeling. In lieu of
corruption and victimization, Rastignac chooses struggle.
"He had seen the three great expressions of society: Obedience, Struggle, and Revolt; the Family, the World, and
Vautrin." In the end, standing next to Goriot's grave in
Père Lachaise cemetery, looking across Paris to the Faubourg Saint-Germain, Rastignac directs a challenge to the
city in a tacit recognition of the loss of the social order of
the eighteenth century, the tenuous legitimacy of the nineteenth, and the tendency towards revolt in the immediate
future. But his final line, "Now it is between you and me,"
is no more revolutionary than Rastignac's plans to dine
with Delphine after the funeral. Only now he is aware of
the rebels and the victims fostered by the society he lives
in. He goes to Delphine deliberately because he knows
that otherwise he will be crushed like Goriot or thrown
in jail like Vautrin, if not forgotten in the Vauquer boarding-house. In effect, he has no choice as a historical figure
in nineteenth-century Paris.

Thus Balzac establishes in *Father Goriot* three major figures of typal importance in *The Human Comedy.* In Goriot he portrays the social victim, in Vautrin the social rebel, and in Rastignac the ambitious young man in society. As Balzac plays out their stories together in and near the Vauquer pension, he creates a fictional structure of clear historical significance. Goriot dies as a result of the new role of money that enabled him to buy the distance between himself and his beloved daughters; Vautrin revolts as a result of the perversion of middle-class manners and morals protected by repression; and Rastignac struggles on in the knowledge of the victims and rebels, of their relationship to the problem of survival and power in the Paris of the Constitutional Monarchies. What Balzac portrays in *Father Goriot,* with its typed characters and fictional constructs, is the historical context of nineteenth-century France: the loss of the tradition and privilege of the Old Regime as perceived by his contemporaries, the new middle-class hierarchy and the role of money in determining its structure, and the pervasive fear of revolt by the many displaced social elements that resulted. With the forms and themes of *Father Goriot,* as they matured in *The Human Comedy* after Balzac's early imitations of Walter Scott's novels, the author clearly established a conception of his period both as a novelist and as a historian.

Moreover, this particular achievement was entirely appropriate to a larger historical context of political, economic, and intellectual developments, even though Balzac's vision, as studied here, remained focused almost exclusively on the social changes of the 1820s and the 1830s. Goriot, Vautrin, and Rastignac in fact responded to only part of their historical situation; they faced much more than a new social hierarchy. Politically, the legitimacy of both the Restoration and July Monarchies remained disputed by strong Liberal, Republican, and Bonapartist forces. The disruption of the July 1830 Revolution was matched even more profoundly, perhaps, by the less startling changes in the French economy in the same period. French manufacturing began to adopt new forms of energy, power, machinery, materials, and organization, in textiles especially, to transform many sleepy bourgs into noisy, crowded industrial cities. The Parisian population exploded, as well, for related economic reasons; declining rural industrial and collective agricultural activities added a major push to the already considerable pull of seasonable employment opportunities in France's largest city. Here, too, was the lure for many well-heeled provincial youths who sought in Paris professional careers whose failure led many men to the creative activity associated with the Romantic movement. Like Balzac who came from Tours, most young authors challenging the neo-classical verities of an earlier generation of writers were not Parisian, at least not until much later and then only by adoption.

Thus the world of *Father Goriot,* the world of both its characters and its author, coincided with some remarkable historical changes, many of which are not altogether evident in the work. Appropriate historically in both its form and content, Balzac's novel may well concern more than the new social hierarchy and its criteria for determining class standing. But this selectivity of historical vision in no way diminishes its value or that of the novel. All volumes in *The Human Comedy* remain valuable sources, as literary works and as historical documents, that have yet to be studied adequately by historians, even though many new historical approaches to literature generally have been well explored recently. For example, Natalie Zemon Davis, Emmanuel Le Roy Ladurie, and Bonnie Smith have expanded considerably the domain of history by their creative use of literary sources in their study of historical myth, rural life, and bourgeois domesticity, respectively. Subject to and perhaps because of the many difficulties in determining meaning that such a protean intellectual achievement poses, Balzac's fiction surely promises insight into the nature of France in the first half of the nineteenth century, especially in the careful study of specific works such as *Father Goriot. The Wild Ass' Skin, Eugénie Grandet, Lost Illusions,* and *Cousin Bette* all deserve similar treatment not only as distinguished novels, but also as equally impressive historical visions worthy of the historian's attention. Study of individual works, not just within *The Human Comedy* but particularly in their own right, can shed considerable light as sources of truly creative historical understanding of a complex and important period in modern French history. (pp. 103-16)

> *James Smith Allen, "Obedience, Struggle, and Revolt: The Historical Vision of Balzac's 'Father Goriot'," in* CLIO, *Vol. 16, No. 2, Winter, 1987, pp. 103-19.*

David Bellos   (essay date 1987)

[In the following excerpt, Bellos surveys Balzac's representation of historical events and the role of money in post-Revolutionary society.]

Balzac locates the action of *Old Goriot* at a quite precise historical moment, the winter of 1819-20. Secondly, he communicates through the stories he tells a quite broad interpretation of the course of French history in the earlier nineteenth century. The purpose of Balzac's use of historical reference in the novel is similar to his reasons for using as much authentic geographical, financial and material detail as he could, that is to say to beguile his readers into suspending their disbelief and treating imaginary characters as if they were real. But the historical rootedness of *Old Goriot* also serves another purpose, and that is to give a solid foundation to the novel's overall argument about history and its implied warning for the future of French society.

In the early nineteenth century, history and literature were not perceived, as they are now, as radically different enterprises. Michelet's aim, in his monumental *Histoire de France* (1832–47), was to recount the development of the French nation as if it were a novel; and the aims of Sir Walter Scott and Victor Hugo (in *Notre-Dame de Paris*) were to write novels that were properly historical. History, for Balzac, did not belong outside the novel, but was at the very centre of his activity as a writer of fictions. He took the view that as a novelist he could write history that was more properly historical than history proper; here is how he puts his case in the 1842 introduction to *The Human Comedy:*

Reading those dry and rebarbative listings of facts called *histories,* who has not noticed that writers have forgotten, in all ages, in Egypt, in Persia, in Greece, in Rome, to give us a history of how life is lived? . . . French Society was to be the historian, I was to be but the secretary. By drawing up the inventory of vices and virtues, gathering together the principal facts of the passions, painting characters, choosing the principal events of Society, composing types by combining features drawn from several similar characters, perhaps I would manage to write that history forgotten by so many historians, the history of how life is lived. With much patience and much courage, I would complete, for nineteenth-century France, the book that we all miss, the book which Rome, Athens, Tyre, Memphis, Persia, India have unfortunately not left us on their civilisations.

Old Goriot does not belong to the literary genre of the historical novel, as does *Notre-Dame de Paris,* and it contains no real historical characters. But it does claim to be an 'histoire des mœurs' (translated above as 'history of how life is lived') and its stories are made to seem quite remarkably specific to a particular moment in historical time. Balzac creates that sense of historical specificity in two principal ways. First, he gives his characters past lives which engage with major and minor events in French history. Secondly, he gives some of his characters an awareness of—but no involvement in—the current events of 1819. It is quite difficult for modern readers to notice this modest, erudite and surprisingly extensive inscription of history in the text, because we have become ignorant with the passing of time. What are scholarly footnotes for us were living allusions to the readers of the *Revue de Paris*: but one guesses that even they could learn some of their own recent history from **Old Goriot.**

Jean-Joachim Goriot worked for a pasta-maker before the French Revolution of 1789. His employer fell victim by chance to the first uprising, which means to say he was executed, like many others, for no known reason. All the violence of those turbulent days is brought out in Balzac's almost offhand account of how Goriot was able to buy the business he worked for. He profited from the Revolution and belonged to the new middle class whose interests it served in the longer term. Under the revolutionary government, the sixty 'districts' of Paris were reorganised into 48 'sections', corresponding to the modern *arrondissements* and *quartiers.* Out of calculation ('gros bon sens', 'plain good sense') rather than conviction, Goriot became president of his section, the Halle aux Blés (grain market), and was thus in a position to manipulate prices during the famine of 1792–3—which, Balzac hints, may have been an artificial famine actually created by profiteers like Goriot. Citizen Goriot grew rich, not out of a straightforward crime of the sort that Vautrin proposes to Rastignac, but out of shady deals in a period when, historically, there was much scope for shady deals. The veracity of this background information has already been underpinned in the novel by the memory of la Duchesse de Langeais, whose mother's estate-manager had sold Goriot quantities of grain at high prices. But the Duchesse is an aristocrat, a member of the class which the Revolution had sought to

destroy, and she harbours an inherited resentment against the revolutionaries of the Committee of Public Safety, calling them 'coupeurs de têtes', 'head-choppers', assuming that they were corruptly involved in the profiteering of tradesmen like Goriot; and she continues to resent Napoleon, the 'usurper', whose name she mutilates, as did all his aristocratic enemies, to Buonaparte.

These historical references situate Goriot and la Duchesse de Langeais solidly within French history. The doting father does not come from nowhere; he comes from the class of people who were in the right place at the right time to make a fortune out of nothing. But after 1815 when, with the defeat of France at Waterloo, Napoleon's empire came to an end and the Allies reimposed the old Bourbon monarchy in the person of Louis XVIII, Goriot's revolutionary past became a liability. His sons-in-law may reject him for personal, psychological and financial reasons, but their rejection is firmly anchored, in Balzac's account, in the historical reality of the restoration of the monarchy and the accompanying reaction of the right-wing aristocracy against former revolutionaries and the middle classes. 'Vous comprenez bien', 'You won't fail to grasp', says la Duchesse de Langeais to the student Rastignac, and through him to us,

> que, sous l'Empire, les deux gendres ne se sont pas trop formalisés d'avoir ce vieux Quatrevingt-treize chez eux; ça pouvait encore aller avec Buonaparte. Mais quand les Bourbons sont revenus, le bonhomme a gêné monsieur de Restaud, et encore plus le banquier.

> (that under the Empire, the two sons in law didn't make any bones about having that old man of 1793 in their homes; under Bonaparte that was still alright. But when the Bourbons came back, the old man was an embarrassment to Restaud, and even more to the banker.)

No significant gaps are left in Goriot's life-story, which is worked out as a historically plausible life engaging with the major political changes which took place in France between the 1780s and 1819. But history also enters **Old Goriot** in the opposite way—as a comic rigmarole perceived by Madame Vauquer, a woman of such little brain that she is wrong in every judgement she makes (about the false comtesse d'Ambermesnil . . . , about Goriot's sexual tendencies . . . , about Vautrin right up to his arrest, even about her own boarding-house in the comical prospectus). When did she lose her husband? 'Dans les malheurs' ('in the troubles') . . . is all she will say; we may surmise, in the French Revolution (Madame Vauquer, aged about fifty in 1819, would have then been in her twenties), seen not as history but as a nuisance. She sees the massive upheavals of France, from the height of the Revolution in 1792 to the defeat of Napoleon at Waterloo, as a routine backdrop to the main business of life, namely food; her comic lament on the loss of five boarders at once is a parody of broad common sense:

> Car, vois-tu, nous avons vu Louis XVI avoir son accident, nous avons vu tomber l'Empereur, nous l'avons vu revenir et retomber, tout cela était dans l'ordre des choses possibles . . . on

peut se passer de roi, mais il faut toujours qu'on
mange.

(Because, you know, we've been through Louis
XVI having his mishap [decapitated by guillotine on 21 January 1793], the fall of the Emperor
[Napoleon I capitulated against overwhelming
forces at Fontainebleau on 4 April 1814, exiled
to Elba], we've seen his return [landed at Cannes
on 1 March 1815 and reassembled French forces
for 100 days] and fall a second time [defeated at
Waterloo by Wellington and Blücher, 18 June
1815], all that was in the order of things
possible . . . You can do without a king, but
people can't do without eating.)

For once Madame Vauquer is speaking a sort of truth
here. France had indeed done without a king from 1793
to 1805 (when it acquired an Emperor), but it had not
done without eating except in the dire famine which had
made Goriot's fortune. So her lament is both a comic version of history, and a version of Balzac's own claim, quoted above at length, that what mattered was not the 'dry
and rebarbative listings of facts called *histories'*, but the
history of life as it is lived—eating and all.

Rastignac has no past life in French history, of course,
since he is only nineteen, but he is the heir to a family
whose past misfortunes, accounting for the young man's
poverty, are typical of a whole social class. Rastignac's father is the nephew of an eighteenth-century naval com-
mander (a colleague of Restaud's grandfather: the world
is small!) and the family's fortune, bar the lands it owns
south of Angoulême, disappeared overnight when the
Revolution nationalised without compensation the enterprise in which the money was invested, the Compagnie des
Indes, a colonial trading company modelled on the British
East India Company. The entire family history given . . .
is fictional, except the existence of the Compagnie des
Indes (actually called the *Nouvelle Compagnie des Indes*
from 1785) and its suppression, amidst a scandal involving
several members of the Convention (revolutionary government) in 1793–4. Many formerly wealthy families of the
landed aristocracy were impoverished by revolutionary
confiscations: Rastignac, whose parents were lucky
enough not to have been forced into emigration or executed at the height of the Terror (1793–4), when the cry in
Paris was 'les aristocrates à la lanterne!' ('hang the aristocrats from the lamp-posts!') is in this respect intended to
represent a social group which was historically significant
in the period after Waterloo, and still alive in the 1830s.

On his restoration to the throne in 1815 (after a short-lived
restoration in 1814, interrupted by Napoleon's escape
from Elba), Louis XVIII adopted a constitution heavily
influenced by the English model, which allowed for a parliament, though with stringent restrictions on the right to
vote in parliamentary elections. The first parliament was
overwhelmingly reactionary; but in 1818 elections were
held which brought into parliament l'abbé Grégoire, a former member of the Convention which had voted Louis
XVI's death sentence, and weakened considerably the
king's hold on his government. There were disturbances
in the streets of Paris—and Balzac's medical student, Horace Bianchon, was there:

I say, the medical student continued, as he came
out of Cuvier's lecture at the Zoological Garden,
I've just seen that Michonneau woman and that
chap Poiret chatting on a bench with a fellow I
saw in the disturbances last year near the Chamber of Deputies, and who looked to me like a
man from the police dressed up as an ordinary
citizen.

It is almost as if Balzac were trying to give away secrets.
Were those 1818 riots the work of police agents, provoking trouble to justify more repressive measures? Bianchon
nearly says so, but not quite. But the authenticity of this
fictional character is somehow guaranteed, in the conventions now clearly established by Balzac, by his apparently
uninvolved presence at an earlier historical event, and his
attendance at the celebrated lectures on palaeontology
(the first fossils had been discovered at the end of the eighteenth century, and a whole new subject was coming alive)
given by Cuvier, attended in reality by many hundreds of
young men in 1819, including Honoré de Balzac.

Bianchon is a youthful liberal, and he reads a liberal newspaper, *Le Pilote*. Curiously, it is precisely when Balzac's
historical memory fails him in some way—*Le Pilote* was
not founded until 1821, though it was run, as Balzac says,
by Tissot—that he steps in as narrator, explaining how
Bianchon could have got news of Taillefer's son's death so
quickly. However, the possible view that Bianchon's suspicions of shady dealings in the elections and disturbances
of 1818 derive from his political leanings to the left is
much more neatly dealt with by a parallel implication in
the sermon that Vautrin gives Rastignac, since Vautrin
may be suspected of almost anything but liberalism. [The]
criminal holds out to the law student the prospect of becoming a public prosecutor by the age of forty—but only
if he performs 'quelques-unes de ces petites bassesses poli-
tiques, comme de lire sur un bulletin Villèle au lieu de
Manucl' ('one of those squalid little political favours, like
reading Villèle [Minister without portfolio in 1820, Finance Minister 1821, Prime Minister 1822] in place of
Manuel [elected to parliament in 1818, member of the liberal opposition, expelled from parliament in 1823] on a
voting slip').

To the extent that Balzac has anything to say about the
details of French political history, he does so indirectly,
by allusions that have become imperceptible to all but
scholarly eyes. To readers of the *Revue de Paris*, these references to the events of 1818 must already have been
somewhat obscure, but we must assume that Balzac intended them to situate his fiction in the half-remembered
history of nearly twenty years before. In this sense his
work is comparable to that of Cuvier, restoring a living
and intelligible shape to the petrified fragments of an age
now lost, writing a kind of archaeology of social life which
included a memory of political events, but also many hum-
bler reminiscences: songs (like those which Vautrin
hums), plays at Paris theatres, books read by characters,
all these cultural objects used by characters in *Old Goriot*
carry their own date with them, and bring not a vague
sense of a grandiose national past, but a feeling of the recent past as it was lived in daily life.

Old Goriot is rooted in a specific historical moment the

better to give a sense of the broad trends of historical change in the period following the enormous and unprecedented upheavals of the French Revolution and Napoleon's adventure. Balzac's view, by and large, is that things were getting worse; his huge and detailed panorama of French society in the earlier nineteenth century is unmistakably a story of decline.

It would be wrong to assume that Balzac did not believe at all in progress, to which so many of his contemporaries were passionately attached; but he compares the 'forward movement' of French civilisation to the progression of the chariot of the Indian idol Juggernaut, crushing spectators and worshippers beneath its wheels. **Old Goriot,** like many other novels by Balzac, is more concerned with the moral and human consequences of historical change than with any long-term benefits of nineteenth-century 'progress'.

The lives of Rastignac, Delphine and Anastasie are made to seem 'modern' in the novel by Balzac's inclusion of other elements specifically labelled as belonging to the past. He comments as narrator that he cannot put at the centre of a novel of modern life characters like Molière's Alceste or Scott's Jenny Deans, 'magnificent images of probity', because such 'rectangular souls' have disappeared from the modern world. But Balzac does sketch in at least one such upright figure on the rural periphery of modern urban life, Rastignac's mother, who reminds the young man of older, better ways in the letter she writes him:

> Mon bon Eugène, crois-en le cœur de ta mère, les voies tortueuses ne mènent à rien de grand. La patience et la résignation doivent être les vertus des jeunes gens dans ta position.

> (My dear Eugene, believe it from your mother's heart, devious paths lead to nothing great. Patience and resignation should be the virtues of young people in your position.)

And the warm, innocent fun of the letter from his sister Laure serves to show Rastignac and the reader that in a world based on the older values expressed by his mother, emotions can still be true and pure.

The letters constitute Rastignac's own past—a happy childhood in the country—and also the past of the novel, a lost age of innocence. The Goriot family can also look back to a time of 'paradise', not in the country, but in the commercial centre of Paris:

> Mon paradis était rue de la Jussienne . . . Je crois les voir en ce moment telles qu'elles étaient . . . Bonjour, papa, disaient-elles . . . Elles me caressaient gentiment . . . Quand elles étaient rue de la Jussienne, elles ne raisonnaient pas, elles ne savaient rien du monde, elles m'aimaient bien.

> (My paradise was in the rue de la Jussienne . . . I can see them now as they were then . . . Good morning, daddy, they would say . . . They cuddled me sweetly . . . When they were at the rue de la Jussienne, they didn't argue, they knew nothing of the world, they liked me.)

The Goriot children, like Rastignac, have grown up into a world which seems worse than what went before. This is not the only way of understanding what it means to grow up. By including his characters' childhoods and presenting them as a lost paradise, Balzac provides a natural human dimension to his overall view of history as decline. The field Rastignac enters with his challenge to Paris . . . does not seem likely to be the scene of heroic exploits which would change the general direction of history.

It is easy to see why the mood of 1819–20 might have been one of pessimism. Four years previously, France had been humiliated at Waterloo, Paris had been occupied by Russian, Austrian and English troops for a short period, and the monarchy, swept away in the Revolution of 1789, had been restored in the person of Louis XVIII, an obese and impotent old man; and the constitution through which he ruled had been virtually dictated by England. But these events are only alluded to in **Old Goriot** by Madame Vauquer, and they have little enough to do with the way the novel presupposes and accounts for the sense of historical decline.

In looking back at the period of his own youth with the advantage of fifteen years' hindsight, Balzac could hardly fail to understand it in terms of what had happened between 1819 and 1834. Louis XVIII died in 1824, and was succeeded by his brother who took the title of Charles X. His regime became increasingly autocratic and biased towards the Church; a movement of opposition, coupled with a wave of intellectual ferment in the later 1820s, culminated in a revolt, sparked off by clumsy repressive measures, which was so mishandled by Charles X that in the course of three days (27–9 July 1830) the royal troops were defeated by the people of Paris and the King fled to England. Three young politicians (a lawyer, Adolphe Thiers, and two bankers, Périer and Laffitte) cleverly averted the danger of a Republic being once again proclaimed in France by bringing back to the throne an exiled member of the junior branch of the royal family, Louis-Philippe d'Orléans. The new king was much less regal than his predecessors, styled himself 'roi des Francais' not 'roi de France', and lived very much like any wealthy member of the middle classes. He used his power to serve the interests not of the aristocracy, but of the commercial and financial bourgeoisie: his finance minister, Guizot, concluded his first budget speech with the famous exhortation: 'Enrichissez-vous par le travail et par l'épargne!', ('Grow rich through work and savings!').

By the time Balzac wrote **Old Goriot,** it had become very clear that under the July Monarchy of Louis-Philippe there would be no limit set on the social and political power of the moneyed middle classes. That movement of society must have been much less clear in 1819, when the aristocracy had only recently been restored to its positions of power. So when Balzac has Vautrin persuade Rastignac that wealth is the *'ultima ratio mundi'* ('the ultimate root of social life'), or when he has Goriot exclaim that 'monnaie fait tout' ('money does everything'), he is, in a way, *inventing* the past that is needed to make a sense of the present of 1834, a past which contains the origins of the present in a quite explicit way.

Old Goriot offers one very obvious explanation for the decline of human values which it presupposes between the lost paradise of childhood and the modern world (which is in this sense 1834 just as much as 1819), and that is the rule of money. Unlike English novelists of the same period, Balzac is not describing directly or indirectly the effects of the Industrial Revolution: what had begun to happen in the textile mills of the Lille region and in the ironworks at Le Creusot (all much later, and on a smaller scale, than in Manchester or Glasgow) does not impinge on Balzac's Paris, and the working classes have only a marginal existence in *The Human Comedy*—as servants (Christophe, Sylvie and Thérèse in *Old Goriot*) or as the anonymous, distant victims of Nucingen's crookery. What Balzac charts is the rise of commerce and banking, of the middle men, like Goriot and Nucingen, who constitute the middle class of pre-industrial, capitalist society.

Though the rule of money cannot be separated from the rise of the middle classes, the picture Balzac gives of the deleterious effect of the rule of money in *Old Goriot* cannot be construed simply as an attack on the rise of the middle classes. The principal victim of the harsh, money-grabbing society he depicts is none other than the principal representative of the new commercial bourgeoisie, a profiteer and speculator of the first post-revolutionary generation; and one of the main beneficiaries of the novel's action is a hereditary aristocrat. This is not done to turn back the clock; but it makes *Old Goriot* a novel written, in a way, against the flow of the historical movement which it demonstrates.

Old Goriot is no doubt historically accurate in showing how far the middle classes still had to go, in 1819, to achieve social dominance. Even if it is money that makes things go round, and even if the Goriots and the Nucingens have plenty of it, what they want to do with it—for their offspring, especially, but also for themselves—is to acquire the prestige of aristocracy, of the aristocracy that had been impoverished, decimated and exiled after 1789 and restored, cautiously, by Napoleon after 1805 (when Nucingen bought the title of Baron), and vindictively by the Bourbon monarchy in 1814 and 1815. The aristocracy, for its part, would like to keep itself quite distinct from the bourgeoisie—it is after all a class defined by breeding, not by occupation or wealth—but few of its members can afford to do so: in *Old Goriot,* only the Beauséants can really choose the company they receive, since only they have kept their great wealth as well as their name. But even the great lady of this noble house (whose name recalls the standard of the Knights Templar, Beaucéant) leaves the scene of Paris, defeated by a poignant instance of the rule of money, her lover's greed for the fortune of the Rochefide heiress.

It is this historical situation alone, a bizarre situation in which two antagonistic social classes, separated by centuries of mutual scorn, by a violent revolution and by a less violent but no less vindictive restoration, come together behind the scenes and in marriage contracts in order to pretend to survive as distinct classes, which allows the plot of *Old Goriot* to make any sense at all; conversely, this plot, in which Rastignac's noble name has a cash value, in which an invitation to Madame de Beauséant's ball is worth as much to Delphine as Restaud's diamonds are worth to Anastasie, must be seen not only as a representation, but as an interpretation of French social history in the Restoration and July Monarchy periods.

What *Old Goriot* argues by demonstration is that the rule of money would destroy the aristocracy from within more surely than the revolutionary expropriations and executions had done. The noble Rastignac will use his inheritance (that is to say, his name) to pursue a special kind of middle-class career: he will succeed as the lover of a trader's daughter married to a banker. The world will be controlled by the Nucingens, the Gobsecks and by adroit manipulators such as Rastignac, not by the Beauséants or the Restauds, except insofar as they connive with the rulers of money. Readers who, whether in the wake of Marx or of his opponents, see history in terms of economic power, must presumably see *Old Goriot* as giving a generally correct interpretation of history. But Balzac's personal attitude towards the trends he depicts is by no means simple, and to some extent it is simply confused.

As a middle-class writer of the Restoration and July Monarchy period, Balzac was as much in thrall to the prestige of the aristocracy as any of his characters. (He adopted the particle of nobility, 'de', in 1830, after the July Revolution, and later had a coat of arms painted on the door of the tilbury he could not afford.) Madame de Beauséant is more than a representative of a dying class, she is truly a *grande dame* for the novelist, and he requires the reader to admire and pity her:

> les personnes les plus élevées ne vivent pas sans chagrins, comme quelques courtisans du peuple voudraient le lui faire croire.
>
> (persons of the highest rank do not live without sadness, as some lickspittles of the populace would like to make it believe)

The grandeur and the suffering of the true aristocrat are values, in the structure of *Old Goriot,* as much as the hard work of the grain-trader, as much as the purity of the Rastignacs' family feelings. The narrator claims at the start that the story he has to tell is a tragedy: 'cette obscure mais effroyable tragédie parisienne' ('this obscure but terrible Parisian tragedy'). Seen as an interpretation of history, Goriot is not a tragedy of the aristocracy in decline, or a tragedy of the bourgeois defeated by his own creation, or a tragedy of the destruction of family bonds: it is a tragedy of all three at once, all three broken by the rule of money. In this way, the novel mobilises the reader's sympathy for values belonging to quite different social classes and historical moments. Like some literary vacuum-cleaner, *Old Goriot* sweeps up aristocratic prestige, commercial speculation, a belief in the family, an admiration for strength even in crime, sentimental attachment to rejected children and even religious sentiment. Partly sincere, partly inherited, partly opportunistic, the novel's amalgam of values, embodied in the character (but not explicitly in the consciousness) of Rastignac is to be seen not so much as the representation, but as the creation of the value-structure or ideology of the modern, moneyed middle class. (pp. 67-80)

David Bellos, in his Honoré de Balzac: Old Goriot, *Cambridge University Press, 1987, 103 p.*

Sandy Petrey (essay date 1988)

[*In the following excerpt, Petrey explores the various meanings of fatherhood in* Le père Goriot, *emphasizing that the social conventions governing relationships take precedence over biological claims to kinship.*]

In one of its many applications of the standard techniques for novelistic realism developed in the eighteenth century, the text of Balzac's *Le Père Goriot* attributes its origin to the discoveries made by one of its characters. According to this device, the information about Goriot's past life given the reader comes from Eugène de Rastignac's research into his fellow pensioner's background. "Without the observations to which his curiosity led him and the skill with which he gained entry to the drawing rooms of Paris, this tale would not display the colors of truth it no doubt owes to his astute mind"; "Rastignac wanted to learn about the earlier life of père Goriot and assembled reliable information." Functioning like a footnote to a legitimately historical narrative, such accreditations are a classic means for speciously asserting the referential status of a nonreferential work.

Rastignac's first information about Goriot's biography comes during his celebrated visit to the vicomtesse de Beauséant, when he listens to a long speech by Mme de Langeais. Here, too, classic realist techniques accumulate and multiply to insist with great firmness that Goriot's biography is uniquely the effect of history. By killing his employer, the French Revolution put Goriot in a position to profit from the grain shortages to come. By aggravating those shortages, the Revolution made his profit immense. Because his wealth then permitted the marriages desired by his two daughters, every moment in the ascendant phase of Goriot's life was directly due to the situation of France at the time it was lived.

Goriot's descending phase was just as tightly connected to vast historical movements. Under the Bourbon Restoration, the nonaristocratic source of their wealth became an intolerable embarrassment to Goriot's daughters. In an effort to conceal their newly unacceptable origins, they first forced their father to give up his life in trade, then tried to hide his existence altogether by refusing to let him be seen with them. Elevated by the Revolution, Goriot was abased by its aftermath. Rastignac's discoveries about his neighbor's biography perfectly exemplify the realist commitment to continuously displaying interpenetration of the collective and the individual.

Several factors thus combine to accord special generic importance to the duchesse de Langeais's speech to Rastignac. *Le Père Goriot,* which is practically a one-volume illustration of the realist aesthetic, grounds itself in the knowledge Rastignac begins to acquire by listening to that speech. Furthermore, Rastignac's instruction is organized around the fundamental insight into human existence in society that Lukács and Auerbach have brilliantly situated at the core of French realism. As a model of the texture of realist prose, the duchesse de Langeais's speech should—if [my] argument is valid—also be a model of realist preference for constative over referential expression.

This preference is not only manifest but takes the arresting form of dissolving all referential authority attributed to the quintessential form of verbal reference, a proper name. In telling Goriot's story, Mme de Langeais calls him indifferently Loriot, Foriot, Doriot, Moriot, and Goriot. Her reaction to Rastignac's insistence on the proper name's proper form is a paradigm for her entire speech.

> "I seem to recall that this Foriot . . ."
>
> "Goriot, Madame."
>
> "Yes, this Moriot was president of his section during the Revolution."

The man whose existence should in theory solidify his linguistic designation disappears as his name becomes not a sign attached to a referent but a word spinning off multiple variants on its own indeterminacy. In recounting the biography of a person destroyed by history, Mme de Langeais makes history destroy the word that gave him identity as well. Where there was an individual and a verbal specification of his individuality, there is now an absence fortuitously coupled to verbal slippage. Rastignac's (and the reader's) initiation into the truth of Goriot is an imperious demonstration that Loriot, Moriot, Doriot, and Foriot do not allow truth to impede their exuberant play.

The referential is the language of objective reality, the constative that of social conventions. Mme de Langeais's annihilation of "Goriot" is a compelling display of the priority of conventions over reality in determining the shape of realist communication. Goriot's existence is of no value in stabilizing his identification because the dominant ideology has decreed that his existence no longer counts. As a constative term, "Goriot" is subject to Austin's Rule A.1, that there must exist a conventional procedure having conventional effect for words to do things [J.L. Austin, *How to Do Things with Words,* 1975]. Since conventional procedures under the Restoration were not those of the Revolution, "Goriot" does not name a human being but detonates consonantal fission. Like the words of Louis XVI when the National Assembly refused his decree of abolition, the name of Goriot was an empty noise because historical conditions had abolished its referential authority. When "the present king of France" regained its denotational force, "Goriot" became a denotational nightmare.

The character of the historical conditions evacuating the proper name is apparent in two other elements of Mme de Langeais's speech, her double reference to Goriot as an old Ninety-three, "ce vieux Quatre-vingt-treize," and her designation of Napoleon as "Buonaparte." The latter, pronounced as the Italian words *buona parte* (or, for the absolute legitimists, *buon a parte*) and the form of the emperor's name preferred by Restoration notables, is a striking instance of play with a signifier undermining a referent. Besides refusing to accord Napoleon the royal and imperial privilege of designation by his given name, the surname "Buonaparte" denied that the emperor of the French was even French. Like Doriot and Moriot, *Buonaparte* has the characteristically constative power of transferring words' sense from the nature of their referents to the ideology of their users.

"Quatre-vingt-treize," Mme de Langeais's most thorough deformation of "Goriot," simultaneously situates ideology in its historical matrix and defines its constative effect. Referentially an allusion to the Revolution's bloodiest year, Mme de Langeais's "Quatre-vingt-treize" is nevertheless taken away from a year to be applied to a man. What actually happened during the year is irrelevant to the meaning of its name, which comes from the set of ideologically molded procedures allowing it to produce a conventional effect. The referent can shift from a unit of time to a person because referential dependability is irrelevant to constative validity. In Balzac's realist discourse, the sentence "so the heart of that poor Ninety-three bled" is not a variant on the surrealist game of *cadavre exquis* but a demonstration that even piteous human suffering cannot prevent lexical drift. For a constative vision of the world, any set of phonemes can substitute for any other so long as conventional agreements recognize the substitution's legitimacy.

Goriot-Moriot-Foriot-Doriot-Loriot-Quatre-vingt-treize: no name is more authoritative than any other because each expresses the vision of the namer instead of the existence of the named. So dramatic a shift in the verbal func-

tion of a proper noun, coming in a passage so crucial to the development of realist fiction, acquires even greater moment because of the strong associations between conventional views of proper nouns and conventional views of realist discourse. As theorists of language from the Greeks to Derrida have pointed out, proper nouns are in important and persuasive ways the best evidence for the thesis that the function of words is to designate things that are not words. Whereas the truth value of a sentence such as "This is a man" depends at least in part on the purely conventional agreements defining the word "man," that of "This is Jean-Joachim Goriot" ought to admit no such ambiguity. Like all other proper nouns, "Jean-Joachim Goriot" has not a definition but a referent, and the intraverbal problematics of words with definitions should not in theory apply to it.

In the duchesse de Langeais's speech, however, the proper noun inaugurates a series of transmutations that confound efforts to protect any verbal category from the metonymic phantasmagoria of signifiers in eruption. When the firmest of all linguistic units becomes loose and flighty, it is impossible to imagine how realist language could achieve its traditional task of conveying the reality of a world prior to language. Is Goriot Goriot, Moriot, or Quatre-vingt-treize? Was Napoleon the emperor of France or an Italian peasant with a comic name? Simply by virtue of the fact that they can be asked, those questions preclude definitive

Jean de Margonne's château at Saché where Balzac wrote Le père Goriot.

answers. Their formulation in itself conveys the Austinian thesis that conventions rather than reality define an utterance as true or false.

The proper noun is of course one among many manifestations of a convention with incalculable social consequences, that of paternity. What makes a noun proper is the Name of the Father, and that Name's central contribution to societies' survival has been a dominant theme of European research in the human sciences for the better part of this century. Let Jacques Lacan [in *The Language of the Self,* 1968] illustrate: "It is in the *name of the father* that we must recognize the support of the Symbolic function which, from the dawn of history, has identified his person with the figure of the law." Furthermore, in common with the referential vision of language in general, the social impact of the Name of the Father depends on its supposed connection to an objective fact, the engendering power of heterosexual intercourse. The duchesse de Langeais's aristocratic contempt for the name of a commoner is also an implicit philosophical argument against the referentiality of names in general.

The antipaternal implications in the "Goriot" slippages are of course accented by the fact that, in a text entitled *Le Père Goriot,* the Name of the Father has been "Goriot" from the moment the reader began to read. That association, reinforced in the vast majority of cases where the word *Goriot* appears, is especially strong during Rastignac's instruction, which began when he asked for information about "un père" and was interrupted before he could specify which father he had in mind. In apposition throughout the novel, "le père" and "Goriot" are inextricable when the latter dissolves into nothingness.

The former had actually preceded it, for the principal effect of the "père Goriot" syntagm is to eliminate paternity from the paternal sign that inaugurates it. What happens to "Goriot" on the level of the signifier is prepared and completed by what happens to "père" on the level of the signified: instead of the Name of the Father, the father's name becomes a pejorative insult whose mere utterance is enough to expel Rastignac from the Restaud home forever. Introduction of the character who bears *the* paternal term specifies that he does so as a sign of his abasement ("a former manufacturer . . . who let himself be called père Goriot") and time after time the text specifies that Goriot's sobriquet is contemptibly inferior to a simple "monsieur" ("père Goriot, who around this time was respectfully named monsieur Goriot"). When Mme de Langeais dismembers the second component of *père Goriot,* she merely does to the father's proper name what the novel has done to his common name from its opening words.

Lacan again: "The primordial Law . . . is revealed clearly enough as identical to an order of Language. For without kinship nominations, no power is capable of instituting the order of preferences and taboos which bind and weave the yarn of lineage down through succeeding generations." As if in illustration of Lacan's point, other "kinship nominations" join that of fatherhood in bathetic disarray when Rastignac learns Goriot's history from his aristocratic informants. When *père* no longer means *père,* the words for

the relationships the Father institutes lose their self-identity as well. Here is Mme de Beauséant on Goriot's daughters: "Her sister is no longer her sister; these two women renounce each other as they renounce their father."

If the text does present kinship terms as equivalent to themselves, it is to display the ignorance of those who believe the equivalency holds. Goriot, "believing his daughters would remain his daughters," makes himself their hapless victim. Kinship terms in *Le Père Goriot* cannot affirm what Lacan calls "the primordial Law" because there is no "order of language" when words' analytic relationship has been destroyed, when A does not equal A, "her sister is no longer her sister," and daughters remain daughters nowhere except in the unbalanced imagination of a pathetic old man.

Even when the paternal lexicon is most insistently exalted, its context just as insistently compromises it. At one point in Rastignac's instruction, Mme de Beauséant accords *father* the anaphoric repetition associated with paeans to the most high: "yes, their father, the father, a father, a good father." The occasion for this exuberance, however, is a sentence that denies the devotion attached to the name the vicomtesse so devoutly repeats, Rastignac's "they renounced their father!" Analogously, when Rastignac returns from Mme de Beauséant's to Mme Vauquer's, he expresses his new admiration for Goriot in a sentence that seems to resituate the Name of the Father and other kinship nominations in their rightful place: "Ah! my good neighbor, I am still a son and brother as you are a father." Given that the occasion of Rastignac's feeling of filial and fraternal smugness is that he has just written letters designed to wrench from his family more money than they can afford to give him, however, his "son and brother" are as dizzying as any other kinship term. "I am a son and brother as you are a father" does not correct but highlights the catastrophic uncertainty of fatherhood throughout Balzac's text.

A last example, one deserving its final position: also on his return to the Vauquer pension, Rastignac learns the result of Bianchon's phrenological examination of Goriot's skull. In Bianchon's words, "I tested his head, there's a single bump, the one for paternity, we've got an *Eternal* Father" (Balzac's emphasis). God the Father enters the text, capital letters and all, as yet another name for Goriot-Doriot-Moriot-Loriot-Quatre-vingt-treize. Whether manifested on earth or in heaven, the Name of the Father is in *Le Père Goriot* a word that cannot stand still long enough to mean something.

Lacan, Barthes, Claude Lévi-Strauss, and the other French thinkers who have emphasized the contribution of the paternal function to successfully organizing social existence have an immense body of social theory from which to take proofs of their point. Phallocentric conceptualization of the human condition is a venerable tradition, one that acquired special prominence during the Restoration's militant struggle against the Revolution. The idea of the king as father of the French, tirelessly reiterated during and after the Bourbons' return, was so ideologically persuasive a point because it suggested that the Revolution had been a crime against Nature rather than an insurrection against a regime. In conservative thought, the Revolution did not overthrow a political system but attacked the order of the world, the order manifest in the indubitably universal and eternal institution of the family.

Paternal dissolution in *Le Père Goriot* is consequently a game with deadly implications, for the Name of the Father was associated, explicitly and interminably, with the survival of the state. Among the sociopolitical thinkers who illustrate this equation, Louis-Gabriel-Amboise, vicomte de Bonald, deserves special mention. Besides publishing many thousands of pages to repeat that the family units *father, mother, child* are and must be the ground for the social units *power, minister, subject,* Bonald was unfailingly aware that none of these units could preserve themselves if the words for them were subject to historical or cultural alteration: if the Father is to rule, his Name must not vary.

The following passage is from an essay Bonald entitled "De l'origine du langage" in which he argued that language could not have developed and changed through the ages because its original and endless perfection is necessary to express the original and endless perfection of the social order.

> Society was in its beginnings, as it will be until its final days, composed of three *necessary persons, father, mother, child,* or, to generalize these persons and their names so that they refer to public society, *power, minister, subject.* . . . Society was therefore complete or *finished* in its beginnings. . . . Thus society was in no way able to form language; rather language, the expression of society, necessarily had to be, in its beginnings, complete or finished like society.

In view of the deconstructive points that have been made about writing in recent decades, it is worth noting parenthetically that Bonald extends this argument in a companion essay entitled "De l'origine de l'écriture." Like spoken language, writing was for Bonald complete and perfect at its origin, for only thus could the perfection of society be codified and preserved. *Ecriture,* for recent critics the essence of antireferential autonomy, was for the vicomte de Bonald the essence of referential authority, that which showed its majesty at its birth "by fixing and making forever unchangeable the text of the divine laws, fundamental and primitive."

Bonald's straightforward identification of the stability of language with that of society and of both with the sovereign position of the Father suggests momentous consequences in the duchesse de Langeais's wayward consonants and the textual play they recapitulate. At issue is the underpinning of Restoration ideology, the natural justification of the social hierarchy inherited from the past. In a book that made assimilation of the natural and the social its founding gesture by taking as its title *Analytical Essay on the Natural Laws of the Social Order,* Bonald identified the contemporary equivalents of *father, mother, child* as *royalty, nobility, Third Estate.* This identification, prepared by the announcement that a revolution was going to end, makes destruction of the Name of the Father intolerably seditious. Madame de Langeais's deformation of Goriot the name, like textual denigration of Goriot the father, can without strain be understood as contesting the Restoration's survival as a social and political order.

Yet Mme de Langeais's corruption of the Name of the Father is not a diegetic variant of the famous authorial paradox which Marxist critics from Engels to the present have associated with Balzac. Unlike her creator, this aristocratic character falls short of condemning the ideology she wants to defend. For—unlike the vicomte de Bonald—she seems to sense that the natural and the social coincide only when society determines that Nature counts. Although the same natural fact of procreation naming Goriot also names the duchesse de Langeais, she herself is in no danger of becoming Gangeais-Dangeais-Mangeais-Fangeais. In the case of her name, language is what Bonald considered it, a rock-solid articulation of what was in the beginning, is now, and ever shall be.

It is in fact the Name of the Father that gives Mme de Langeais the right to dismember the father's name. As not just a commoner but a commoner enriched by the Revolution, Goriot represents everything the Restoration understood as a crime against Nature. Dissemination of Goriot's name therefore *corrects* an aberration instead of effecting one, affirms social conventions while scorning objective truth and the verbal stability it requires. This unrelenting assault on the referential leaves the constative intact. "Goriot" is variable because the dominant ideology does not incorporate it, because the conventional procedures including such a name are not pertinent to what Mme de Langeais's community recognizes as the world. (pp. 83-92)

[The] abolition of Antithesis which Barthes attributes to *Sarrasine* is at the same time a demonstration that verbal antithesis holds so long as a verbal community accepts it. The contrast between "Goriot" and "madame la duchesse de Langeais" develops the demonstration by instituting an antithesis no conceivable referential semantics can underwrite. Rastignac's inaugural lesson on the patronym's nullity simultaneously manifests the constative's majesty.

Preparation for the lesson was a thorough display of how kinship nominations function without reference to kinship. Rastignac is at Mme de Beauséant's for two reasons, because his aunt believed that the vicomtesse would respond to a letter of introduction and because the Restauds have just kicked him out of their house. Each reason shows that the names for relationships are capable of doing things only when the relations they name allow them to perform. "After shaking the branches of the family tree" in response to her nephew's request for information about "the kinship ties that might still be reattached," Rastignac's aunt Marcillac concludes that Mme de Beauséant would be the least frosty if asked for help. What matters is not the kinship nomination but the conventions it elicits. Like "Goriot," "Rastignac" and "Marcillac" name only what their listeners determine.

Thanks to Mme de Beauséant's graciousness, Rastignac is admitted to the Restaud household: "By calling himself madame de Beauséant's cousin, he received an invitation from that woman." Note the typically constative form Rastignac's activity takes. It is "by calling himself " an aristocrat that he obtains his invitation, extended so that his hostess will be able to perform the same kind of gratifying speech act as her guest. Mme de Restaud uses the presence of Mme de Beauséant's cousin to invoke the conventional procedure of aristocratic denomination and produces a constative exemplum. Monsieur de Restaud and Maxime de Trailles look at Eugène with undisguised and unbearable contempt until Mme de Restaud makes this introduction.

> "This gentleman," she went on, introducing Eugène to the comte de Restaud, "is monsieur de Rastignac, who is related to madame la vicomtesse de Beauséant through the Marcillac family; I had the pleasure of seeing him at her last ball."
>
> *Related to madame la vicomtesse de Beauséant through the Marcillac family:* these words, spoken almost emphatically by the countess . . . had a magical effect; the count abandoned his coldly ceremonial manner and greeted the student. . . .
>
> Even Comte Maxime de Trailles looked at Eugène with concern and suddenly abandoned his impertinent manner. This wave of the sorcerer's wand (*ce coup de baguette*), due to the powerful intervention of a name, opened new sections in the Southerner's brain and brought back all the witty things he had meant to say. A sudden light let him see clearly in the atmosphere of Parisian society, still shadowy for him.

"Magical effect . . . the sorcerer's wand . . . the powerful intervention of a name . . . see clearly in the atmosphere of Parisian society": such expressions are in accord with Austin's dual conviction that the things words do are wonderful and that the wonders are created by the words' users. Like a magic wand, identification of Eugène's family alters the nature of the world and produces a man where there was a void. Like the performance of a marriage, this metamorphosis occurs only because the formula that produces it figures in one of the conventional procedures by which a collectivity organizes itself. Eugène simultaneously becomes somebody and understands how society functions because both changes depend on a single set of rules.

The irrelevance of facts to application of those rules becomes apparent when Eugène asks his hosts about Goriot. What speech does remains magic, but its power is now destructive rather than creative. The man produced by one set of words is annihilated by another. "In pronouncing the name of père Goriot, Eugène had waved a magic wand (*avait donné un coup de baguette magique*), but this time the effect was the opposite of that produced by these words: related to madame de Beauséant." The striking aspect of the power to negate in Eugène's "père Goriot" is that the kinship those words invoke is incomparably more solid than that underlying the power to produce in "related to madame de Beauséant." Mme de Restaud should not need to "shake the branches of the family tree" to learn that she is related to her father. At issue, however, are conventions rather than facts, constative authority rather than objective accuracy. Because Restoration norms pre-

clude a countess with a plebeian father, the name of the comtesse de Restaud's father must disappear from the discourse in which she figures. Banishment is Eugène's punishment for using referential speech in a setting from which reference is excluded.

Madame de Beauséant, when Eugène first names his relationship to her, reiterates the exclusion. After thinking of his hostess as "my cousin," the provincial visitor puts the thought into words, to devastating effect.

> "Cousin," responded Eugène.
>
> "What!" said the vicomtesse, flashing a look of freezing contempt at him.
>
> Eugène understood her "What." He had learned so many things in three hours that he was on the alert.

The most important thing Eugène has learned is that words' factuality is irrelevant to their nominative function. If he is Mme de Beauséant's cousin, it is due not to blood but to sufferance, not to his family but to his interlocutor. A mood change is enough to convert the vicomtesse's "What!" into "Well now, cousin" and to have her introduce Mme de Langeais to "monsieur de Rastignac, a cousin of mine." The narrative voice subsequently ratifies this introduction by describing Mme de Beauséant's reaction to "her cousin." The degree of kinship in kinship nominations has nothing to do with a fact, everything to do with an attitude.

Like "père" and "Goriot," therefore, "cousin" undergoes the same metonymic fission that Barthes found in *Sarrasine*. And, like *Sarrasine, Le Père Goriot* suggests in a multitude of ways that words' capacity for fission does not in the least affect their solidity when society has something for them to do. Instead of endlessly proliferating, the metonymy is rigorously controlled in a clear illustration of why Wittgenstein contended that at any given moment there is indeed a last house on the road. When Mme de Beauséant formally recognizes Eugène as her cousin in the paradigmatically performative sentence "I give you my name," his identity becomes as firm as Goriot's is shaky. The rest of the novel (like much of the rest of *La Comédie humaine*) shows him capitalizing on a kinship term whose power is undiminished by previous insistence on its referential undecidability. In theaters and concert halls, at balls and receptions, in the aristocratic faubourg Saint-Germain and the bourgeois chaussée d'Antin, Mme de Beauséant's fellows and imitators perpetuate the truth of Rastignac's relationship to her. "He had a status in society by virtue of being the recognized cousin of madame de Beauséant," and his position is no less real for depending not on the descriptive accuracy of *cousin* but on the constative authority of *recognized.*

Cousin therefore joins all the text's other kinship nominations as a word that does things in conformity with Austin's argument that collective conventions are the sole ground for the things done. The precise degree of Rastignac's relationship to Mme de Beauséant is immaterial, for blood determines his social position no more than it establishes Goriot's paternity. If *cousin* works while *père* becomes an insult, if "Rastignac" names a force while

"Goriot" quivers and dissipates, the reason is a collectively accepted protocol rather than a referentially established difference. The names that count in *Le Père Goriot* are constative affirmations of social position, and the defining trait of all constative affirmations is their dissociation from objective reality.

The realist constative has emptiness at its core but solidity on its surface, and Rastignac is acutely aware that the solidity of his own identity requires a great deal of money. When Vautrin jokingly calls him "monsieur le marquis," Rastignac's response is angry but perceptive. "Here, to be a real marquis, you've got to have a hundred-thousand-livre income." In Rastignac's mind, a real marquis is the product not of the familial origin that ought to confer the title but of enough money to buy the things with which the title is associated. Those things elicit the appropriate social response, and social response constitutes the entirety of constative identity. Really to be a marquis means not having the right father but displaying the right signs.

On acquiring what he considers a sufficient amount of money, Rastignac undergoes an inner as well as an outer transformation. The strong phallic overtones in description of what money does to Rastignac are a powerful indication of of what is at stake in any such conversion. "The instant money slips into a student's pocket, there is erected in him a fantastic column that is his support. . . . Unheard of phenomena take place in him, he wants to do everything and can do everything. . . . All Paris belongs to him." The corollary is obvious. Without money, there is no fantastic column and hence no phallic identity. Madame de Beauséant took only a first step when she gave Eugène her name and allowed him to be her cousin. "Really" to bear such a kinship nomination requires money as well as indulgence, and Vautrin is correct when he points out over and over that money is what Eugène lacks. In *Sarrasine,* the mysterious figure in the Lanty household is a man because money gives him the right to be what he chooses. In *Le Père Goriot,* Eugène's poverty constrains him to struggle endlessly in order to retain the aristocratic position to which his birth in theory entitles him.

In both cases, money and identity combine in a univocal statement of constative truth, for the money Eugène must have is not that which buys things but that which establishes position. Or, more accurately, the things money buys are not objects but signs, conventional features of a conventional procedure that functions in exactly the same way as such verbal sequences as "related to madame la vicomtesse de Beauséant through the Marcillac family." The hundred-thousand-franc income Rastignac believes necessary for a real marquis is essential because the things bought on such an income are immediately *interpreted.* They signify by virtue of their position in a clear semiotic structure. Their constitutive function in producing status derives from their capacity to elicit determinate hermeneutic operations from those before and for whom they are displayed

Identifying money as the pivot around which the Balzacian universe revolves is of course hardly a new insight. A huge and powerful body of criticism, Marxist and non-

Marxist, has demonstrated money's centrality to the characters, plots, and style of the *Comédie humaine.* The contribution of a speech-act perspective is not to show that money talks in Balzac but to heighten attention to what it says. Riches are needed to sustain a social role, to be a real marquis, to be what one is supposed to be even without money. According to Restoration ideology, an objective event, the fact of birth, creates the identity that social discourse incorporates into its naming procedures. By repeatedly showing that birth is not pertinent to identity, Balzacian insistence on money widens the gap between social discourse and objective facts. Besides condemning him to hunger, Goriot's poverty also makes him something other than a father. Besides clothing him, Rastignac's wealth makes him Rastignac. The things money buys are the significant features of an insistently constative language.

On his expulsion from the Restaud home, Rastignac lists the objects he needs in order to remain in Parisian society. That he is also cataloging semiotic units is evident in the list's conclusion, a vulgar outburst against Goriot and the negative impact of his name. "Can I go out into society when, to get around properly, I need a heap of carriages, polished boots, indispensable trinkets, gold chains, white kid gloves that cost six francs for the mornings and countless yellow gloves for the evenings? Silly old père Goriot!" What leads from gloves, boots, carriages, and golden chains to Goriot, from commodities to a name? It is the common status of the commodities and the name as incantatory formulas given power by the collective response they evoke. To counteract the effect of a name, Rastignac needs things, and his associative processes are puzzling only if we mistakenly assume that things and names are qualitatively distinct. As a sign was responsible for his expulsion from a social milieu, so signs can effect his reintegration. The imperative to be wealthy comes from the social hermeneutics attendant on display of wealth.

Vautrin understands this perfectly. As he explains to Rastignac, the actual possession of riches is irrelevant. What matters is that other people assume that riches are possessed: "So if you want to make your fortune fast, you must already be rich, or look like you are (*être déjà riche, ou le paraître*)." The venerable distinction between *être* and *paraître* is now an equation. When statements are constative rather than referential, being and appearing are merged.

The fantastic column that money erects in Rastignac is in direct opposition to the fantastic void produced in Goriot by lack of money. Phallic identity and phallic dissolution have the same cause, the medium society uses to evaluate the goods circulating within it. The Name of the Father has become the Balance of the Account, and the Father stops being himself when he loses the wherewithal to keep money's circulation active and vigorous. Rastignac needs money to signify his identity as a full member of aristocratic society, Goriot to signify his position as a father. Procreation has no more to do with paternity than with aristocracy, for every social category is the effect of social performance. Goriot's laments that he can no longer be a father because he has no money to give his children furnish the novel's most sustained illustration of fatherhood's absolute prerequisite.

What is the conventional procedure that has the conventional effect of paternity? Goriot's answer is the novel's: to be a father is to participate actively in the socially regulated exchange of goods. "Fathers must always give in order to be happy. Always giving is what makes you a father"; "I'm not good for anything now, I'm not a father anymore! No! She's asking me, she needs something! And I'm a poor wretch who doesn't have anything"; "Money is life. It does everything." Those and countless comparable outbursts convey a single message. Because giving makes one a father, not giving makes one something else. Far from the natural result of an objective fact, fatherhood is in *Le Père Goriot* a fortuitous intersection in the supremely unnatural process of monetary circulation.

When he learns that his daughter Anastasie is being forced to surrender control of her fortune to her husband, Goriot vows to prevent so monstrous a transgression by kidnapping the Restauds' oldest son. This criminal project is envisioned in terms reminiscent of those with which Rastignac conceptualizes aristocracy. Whether the goal is to be a real father or a real marquis, money is essential to achieving it.

> "Nasie, you can rest easy. Oh, so he cares about his heir! Good, good. I'll take his son who, blast it all, is my grandson. I've got a right to see the kid, I suppose? I'll put him in my village. I'll take care of him, don't worry about that. I'll make him surrender, the monster, by telling him, 'The fight's on! If you want your son back, give her property back to my daughter and let her do what she wants.' "

> "My father!"

> "Yes, your father! Ah, I'm a real father."

For Goriot—"he cares about his *heir*"—monsieur de Restaud is vulnerable not because he loves his son but because he needs a person to whom his money will be conveyed. Goriot claims the right to kidnap that person because his own paternity is threatened by his daughter's loss of the money he gave her. In both families, the father is "real" only if he transmits money to his child. In Goriot's apostrophe to M. de Restaud, "If you want your son back, give her property back to my daughter," *son, daughter,* and *property* are lexically as well as pragmatically substitutes for one another in a system of kinship nominations completely dissociated from birth. If they are to remain fathers, Goriot must retrieve Anastasie's wealth and Restaud must preserve his heir. The kidnapping scenario sees one father as having money but no child and the other as having a child but no money. Neither condition is "real" paternity because neither permits the socioeconomic activity on which paternity depends.

A constative vision of the paternal function also animates *Le Père Goriot*'s crucial subplot, which concludes when Victorine Taillefer's father officially recognizes that she is his daughter. Referentially, Victorine's familial situation is never in doubt. In Mme de Couture's words, father and daughter are physically so alike that their relationship is

self-evident to whoever sees them together. "I don't know how he can deny she's his, she looks exactly like him." Referential facts do not count, however, for M. Taillefer refuses the constative act of naming Victorine his child. "Without saying his daughter," he leaves Victorine in an unbearable limbo where her name and family are not hers.

When Vautrin's scheme for killing M. Taillefer's son succeeds, Victorine's referential condition remains the same but her constative identity is transmuted. Her father calls her his daughter, and the name she acquires produces a radically different existence. "Her father is forced to adopt her" for the same reason M. de Restaud would have to return Anastasie's money if Goriot carried out his kidnapping, because fathers cannot be fathers unless they transmit funds to their children.

Vautrin said as much when he originally outlined his Taillefer scheme to Rastignac. "Père Taillefer . . . has an only son he wants to leave his property to, at Victorine's expense. . . . If God's will were to take his son from him, Taillefer would welcome his daughter back; he'd want an heir of some kind—a stupid but natural desire—and I know he can't have any more children."

As with the Restauds, so with the Taillefers: "child" is another word for "heir." The act by which M. Taillefer recognizes Victorine is the consequence of the paternal imperative to assure that money reaches its intended recipient. He undertakes the performative process of making Victorine his daughter (recall the curious sentence "her *father* is forced to *adopt* her") so that he can continue to perform his own identity as a socially recognized father.

Fatherhood's definition as a convention not a condition receives its most poignant formulation during Goriot's death agony. The dying man realizes that his children were his children and he their father only because speech acts performed the relationship, because "they *said* they were my daughters, and they *recognized* me as their father" (my emphasis). It is as as Mme de Beauséant's "recognized cousin" that Rastignac becomes a force, and it is for lack of the same recognition that Goriot becomes a void. As the creation of a conventional procedure, identity cannot survive the procedure's withdrawal.

Goriot's dying vision of the wonders of devotion that would be worked around his deathbed if he were still rich is his understanding that paternity is never performed except according to the protocols accepted by society. "Oh, if I were rich, if I had kept my fortune, if I hadn't given it to them, they'd be here, they'd keep my cheeks wet with their kisses! I'd be living in a huge house, I'd have beautiful rooms, servants, my own fire, and they'd be all teary, with their husbands and their children. I'd have all that. But nothing. Money gives everything, even daughters."

This passage is something besides another textual condemnation of the venal Parisian world in which the most sacred human obligations are ignored if they offer no financial gain. Negative moral commentary takes the form of affirmative financial vision. If poverty takes children away, wealth produces them: "Money gives everything, even daughters." The man whose paternity is unverifiable would with money be a man whose paternity is constantly enacted by children and grandchildren following every convention of filial love and devotion, all of them eager to plant their adoring kisses on their father's cheek.

In a supremely laconic sentence—"But nothing"—Goriot describes what paternity actually is. With much more expansive rhetoric, he describes what it would be if he had kept his money. Although the final section of **Le Père Goriot** is entitled "The Death of the Father," what dies is only the referential concept of fatherhood. The constative definition remains authoritative, as Goriot unknowingly demonstrates in maxims that validate paternity as a convention while destroying it as an absolute. "A father must always be rich"; or "Il faut toujours se faire valoir." *Se faire valoir* has the ambiguity that Barbara Johnson points out [in *The Critical Difference*, 1980] in the key Austinian terms *perform* and *act*. All three verbs simultaneously signify something real and something false, all refer at the same time to a fact and its imitation. Goriot's death agony is a long meditation on the irresoluble duality of *se faire valoir*. While ceasing to mean anything in itself, fatherhood retains the power to mean everything provided the correct conventional procedures are applied. The nothingness in which Goriot dies because he believed the family was a natural unit does not blind him to the plentitude of filial love as a sanctioned social performance.

As the supreme vehicle for collective sanctions, money invigorates paternity with the same demonstrativeness that poverty displays in evacuating it. The dying Goriot remembers as well as fantasizes occupying the father's place. "So when some of those sophisticated people whispered in my son-in-law's ear: 'Who's that man?' 'He's the father with the money, he's rich.' 'The devil you say!' and they looked at me with the respect due the money." Although it was not elicited by paternity, the respect Goriot received when he was rich was solid and real. The paternal word in "father with money" commands homage no less strongly than that in "father without a sou" repels it. Valorized by an attribute society finds worthy, the father and his name are awesome. (pp. 92-102)

Proof of fatherhood's conventionality is cruel in the conventional methods that this father advocates to bring his children to his deathbed. As an exemplary performative utterance, Goriot's "I protest" invokes the institutional system empowered to recognize protests as legitimate. The father must therefore plead for constative assertion of his paternity in the very process of proclaiming that paternity is a referential absolute requiring no systemic ratification. To be efficacious, this protest must be sustained by the *social* forces whose pertinence to *natural* duties the protest intends to deny. Simply by virtue of the terms in which it is made, Goriot's call for help is an admission of defeat.

The call concludes with a vision of society's utter dissolution. "The country will perish if fathers are trampled under like this. . . . Society, the world depends on fatherhood." Those apocalyptic sentences assume a definition of paternity incompatible with a biography showing time and again that what counts is not the Father but the Name. Although society is indeed based on fatherhood, it is also based on the principle that the force of all such foundational words comes not from their reference but

from their function. Goriot dies alone because his paternity is a natural fact in a world where social facts are supreme.

The marriage ceremony, one of Austin's original examples of performative speech, is in **Le Père Goriot** one of the clearest demonstrations of fatherhood's conventionality. Every attempt to define the family as natural must elide the fact that all families originate in an artificial ceremony varying with the norms of the group in which it takes place. Most naturalistic visions of the family obscure the elision. Goriot makes it explicit by crying out that (natural) families can endure only if (conventional) marriages are forbidden. The consequence is a bitter irony. In defense of the family, Goriot pleads that there be no more marriages, which is of course to plead that there be no more families. Nowhere is paternity's constative definition more apparent than in Goriot's absurd demand for prohibition of the convention that legitimates paternity as a value. "Fathers, tell the legislature to pass a law about marriage! In the end, you can't let your daughters marry if you love them. The son-in-law is a scoundrel who spoils everything about a daughter, he makes everything dirty. No more marriages! they take our daughters away from us, and we don't have them when we die. Pass a law about the death of fathers!" The paradox in this appeal for marriages to be outlawed is the same as that in the appeal for children to be made filial. Each assertion of natural duty is addressed to a conventional institution, in this case the legislature. To urge that marriage be outlawed is to admit that the paternity that marriage authorizes is also subject to repeal. Goriot's "No more marriages!" demands at one and the same time that he be respected as a father and that the social practice making fatherhood respectable be abolished. In the terms of Austin's Rule A.1, Goriot has the impossible desire to eliminate a conventional procedure while keeping its conventional effect whole and pure.

In Goriot's view, his sons-in-law destroyed his position as a father by taking away his daughters. But his daughters' alienation simply confirms that the family is not a given but a creation, not the will of God but the custom of a community. As only constative speech can express the effects of a communal custom, Goriot's exaltation of *father* and denigration of *son-in-law* is a hysterical misapprehension. The word *son-in-law* is unmistakably the product of a conventional procedure; it proclaims what the word *father* obscures, that there is no family apart from social validation of the names for its members. To become a father, one does something; to become a son-in-law, one says something. The distinction is objectively real but practically inconsequential, for neither what is done nor what is said signifies in and of itself. Acts and words alike acquire semantic content only within a social matrix, and within Goriot's social matrix procreation is value-free.

Goriot's dying plea that marriage be outlawed is prompted by the same concepts that produced Austin's inaugural suggestion that marriage be carefully contemplated. For both men, marriage is a clear demonstration that human existence and the words expressing its nature are a matter of pure convention. For Austin, the demonstration was the underpinning for a philosophical system. For Goriot, it was fatal refutation of the belief that some things stand independently of the forms in which a collectively represents them.

Marriage and the son-in-law reveal society's actual structure for Mme de Langeais as well. While telling Rastignac about Goriot's past life, the duchess defines the "drama of the son-in-law" as a central motif of their decadent world.

> "Heavens," said madame de Langeais, "yes, that seems quite horrible, and yet we see it every day. Isn't there a reason? Tell me, my dear, have you ever thought about what a son-in-law is? He's a man for whom the two of us will raise a dear little creature bound to us in a thousand ways, who will for seventeen years be the joy of the family, what Lamartine would call its white soul, and who will become its plague. . . . I hear people ask what there is dramatic in society today; but the drama of the son-in-law is frightful, not to mention our marriages, which have become really stupid things."

Mme de Langeais's statement that marriage transforms the family's "soul" into its "plague" invites development. The soul gives life, the plague death. When marriage dissolves the thousand bonds keeping the daughter in her place, therefore, the family comes to an end. Yet that end is also a beginning, for one family's death is another's birth. Mme de Langeais bumps into the same quandary as Goriot. Every father must begin as a son-in-law if he is to deserve the paternal name; the son-in-law unseating the father perpetuates his position. There are contradictory answers to Mme de Langeais's "have you ever thought about what a son-in-law is?" If a daughter's marriage destroys the family, it also creates it, and neither the negative nor the positive function is conceivable without the other.

Because a family that already exists must be dissolved for another family to come to be, no family can lay claim to irrevocable integrity. The actual horror of the son-in-law is that, by exposing the family as a conventional effect, he reveals the conventional base of existence as a whole. "The drama of the son-in-law is frightful" because it suggests that the Name of the Father is nothing more than the effect of a ceremony. Madame de Langeais implies as much by defining the family as a performance, as a "drama" in which roles are assumed and can thus be abandoned. "What there is dramatic in society today" is everything in society today, an agglomeration of identities that hold only so long as they are enacted.

Mme de Langeais's insistent repetition of "drama" recalls the lexical imperative concerning that word in the first paragraph of *Le Père Goriot*: "It is necessary to use the word drama here." This necessity rapidly produces a sentence containing five occurrences of the word to characterize Mme Vauquer's boarders. "These boarders induced presentments of completed or on-going dramas; not those dramas played before footlights and painted canvas but living, mute dramas, frozen dramas that stirred the heart to warmth, continuous dramas." Although the principal purpose of *drama* in that sentence is to make the common Balzacian announcement that a pending narrative is fascinating and momentous, the word's theatrical sense is crucial. *Le Père Goriot* is a constant equivocation between different kinds of dramatic performance, those that have artificial trappings and those that are lived. The Vauquer pension is the stage for serial changes of roles culminating in the message that no role can command adherence unless it is well scripted and well played. The apparent oxymoron in "living dramas" vanishes when the novel recapitulates a socially imposed scenario that writes Goriot out with the same authoritative control employed to write Rastignac in.

Immediately after she copies the narrative voice by repetitively foregrounding the word "drama," the duchesse de Langeais starts her dismemberment of the word "Goriot." The transition is effortless because the two operations develop a single concept of lexical validity. Like the drama of the son-in-law, that of the father is a sustained demonstration that language names convincingly only when what it names is coherent social practice.

Among Mme Vauquer's boarders, the man who affirms the performative nature of his identity is the man most comfortable with the performance's result, Vautrin. He alone has taken a name with no natural origin in a father, and he alone states with assurance that his name is a fact: "Who am I? Vautrin." So ringing an affirmation is inconceivable from Goriot-Moriot-Loriot and the other characters at Mme Vauquer's, none of whom shares Vautrin's awareness that signs are arbitrary. In Vautrin's vision of the world, the conventional procedure of bearing a name can be dispensed with altogether if the requisite conventional effect is achieved without it. "If I succeed, nobody will ask 'Who are you?' I'll be monsieur Four-Million."

Vautrin's disregard for the Father is such that he prepares this comical reduction of identity to whatever circulates in society by a double announcement that he will become monsieur Four-Million by leading "the patriarchal life." The patriarch is not he who bears the Name of the Father but he who knows that the Name needs the Father not at all. Again money is the synecdoche for all the means that society employs as evaluative tools, and again positive evaluation in no way entails the actual presence of its supposed cause.

Vautrin, who has "more than ten thousand *brothers*" (my emphasis), extends his concept of the Father's arbitrariness to other kinship nominations as well. His paternal solicitude for Eugène produces an adoption procedure including this succinct lesson on social truth: "There are no principles, there are only events; there are no laws, there are only circumstances." In Austinian terms, there are no facts, there are only conventions. The contrast between "Vautrin" and "Goriot" is between a name that is explicitly a sign and a name pretending to adhere to a reality. The latter's dissipation encapsulates the text's lessons on the gulf between referential accuracy and constative validity.

Banal though it is to address Rastignac's situation between the two father figures "père Goriot" and "papa Vautrin," the contrast between the proper names "Goriot" and "Vautrin" prompts comparison of the paternal words "père" and "papa." "Père" is the father in his majesty, the word taken by all those who occupy the exalted paternal position from God through the king to a peasant providing a hut for his family. "Papa" is a familiar colloquialism, a spoken term that expresses an attitude rather than a position, a relationship rather than an autonomy. To appreciate the difference, imagine Lacan and other recent theorists expounding on the sociopsychological ramifications of "le nom du papa" instead of "le nom du père."

That so childish a term as *papa* cannot convey the weighty messages attached to *père* was obvious to Pierre Larousse. The article "papa" in the *Grand dictionnaire universel* distinguishes "Aryan" languages from those heard "among the Negroes of Africa" in part by pointing out that in European speech *papa* and *maman* "are heard exclusively in children's speech." Advanced civilizations require an advanced term to name the paternal function, and *papa* just does not measure up.

Yet it is *père* that collapses in **Le Père Goriot,** a failure defining Rastignac's filial options as a choice between reference and solidity. "Goriot" and "père" have firm existential reality behind them and nevertheless they evaporate. "Vautrin" and "papa" are oral performances without referential claims, yet their impact on Eugène is decisive. Like the distinction between *gendre* and *père,* that between "Goriot" and "Vautrin" inexorably demonstrates that meaning is a conventional effect best produced when words openly accept that their only reference is to what they themselves do.

Eugène's performance will not, however, replicate Vautrin's. The difference comes to the fore in Rastignac's deformation of Vautrin's statement on the options available to any member of a social group, which is to say to any human being. In his own view, Vautrin speaks "with the superiority of a man who, after examining things here below, saw that there were only two courses to take: either dumb obedience or revolt." Later, after Vautrin's arrest and the onset of Goriot's fatal illness, Rastignac converts his mentor's dyad into a triplet. "He had seen the three great expressions of society: Obedience, Struggle, and Revolt; the Family, Paris (*le monde*), and Vautrin." The choice between acceptance and revolt has acquired a third term, struggle against society but by its rules. That is the course Rastignac takes, and his progress on it is a sustained illustration of the realist constative in operation.

Rastignac personifies the two-term schema of obedience and revolt as the family and Vautrin, as the father and the criminal. The former embodies meaning as a referential derivation, the latter as a creative poetics. Vautrin's name is what he makes it, but by making it without attending to social rules he risks losing it. His arrest and unmasking are a debaptism in which society reasserts the supremacy of its own procedures for identifying its members. In Vautrin's case, socially enacted identification even has the material, corporeal form of the convict's "T.F." brand on his shoulder. As it erases the name Goriot was born to, so society erases the name Vautrin came to. Neither objective reality nor individual creativity stands against against a collectivity's will to insure that its conventions have their prescribed effect.

Rastignac's consciousness of the power inherent in the collective will is apparent when he defines Obedience, Struggle, and Revolt as "the three great expressions of society." Even revolt against it is one of society's expressions of itself. Despite its awesome grandeur, Vautrin's resolution to withhold obedience does not provide an escape from the dominion of communal practices. The name he took for himself is in a series with two supremely social entities, the family and Parisian society, as so many articulations of a transcendent whole no part of which can violate the protocols keeping the whole together. The name "Vautrin" disappears because it threatened the laws of social cohesion.

Rastignac ultimately determines that the same fate will not overtake "Rastignac," a sign that will be ratified by all the procedures requisite for it to have effect. Unlike Vautrin, Rastignac obtained his name through a process recognized as valid by his fellows. Unlike Goriot, Rastignac behaves as though aware that recognition of validity does not proceed automatically from the facts it claims to endorse. The man who conquers society as "the recognized cousin of madame de Beauséant" is the man who understands that the road to conquest has already been laid out for him.

The paternal names "Goriot" and "Vautrin" are complementary violations of constative protocols. Based on reference alone, "Goriot" vanishes when society shows that reference is not pertinent to identity. Based on individual prowess alone, "Vautrin" vanishes when society reaffirms the principle that individuals are not to be confused with monads. "Rastignac" survives because it confirms the community's right to name without implying that the ground for such a right must lie outside the community exercising it. The third term Rastignac adds to Vautrin's dyad is less a middle way than a dialectical transcendence. Obedience and Revolt come together in Struggle, which combines the former's acceptance of social rules with the latter's conviction that the rules need no objective validity.

Considered in relation to verbal reference and verbal play, the realist constative is the same kind of dialectical transcendence. It too recognizes the arbitrariness of social expression without positing a space beyond the constraints imposed by society's need to express. The family, *le monde,* and Vautrin: in its indeterminate senses of "world" and "society"—of the whole and the part—the central term *monde* powerfully conveys the text's vision of an all-inclusive conventionality. What society performs *is* the world for its members, and no good comes of contemplating facts not collectively recognized as factual.

Just after his meditation on society's three great expressions, Rastignac turns his thoughts to the family's apparent insulation from the society it also expresses. "In his thoughts he was borne back into the bosom of his family. He recalled the pure emotions of that calm life, remembered the days he spent surrounded by those who cherished him. Conforming to the natural laws of the domestic hearth, those dear creatures found a full, unbroken happiness, without anxieties." For my purposes, two factors are crucial in this pastoral interruption of Rastignac's social education. First, the family is defined as a natural rather than a created institution, and its *natural* laws promise endless contentment to all who obey them. Second (as is so often the case with pastoral escapes), Rastignac unhesitatingly refuses the perfect life offered by obeying natural laws. The full, unbroken happiness without anxieties is spurned, for Rastignac's vision of familial bliss leads directly to his decision to profane the family by ignoring Delphine's duty to her dying father in order to take her to the Beauséant ball. The family is everything society is not, but what is not society can appeal only to the imagination. In terms of their narrative impact, the pure joys of familial contentment are as hollow as the paternal vocabulary in the syntagm "père Goriot." Without practical consequence of any kind, Rastignac's idyllic vision of family life constitutes at most a formulaic banality.

Family life therefore has great representational value but no constative force. Nothing social contributes the solidity necessary for familial language to ground a being. The same opposition between constative and representational value organizes Eugène's reaction to the death of Goriot, "a being who, for Eugène, *represented* Fatherhood" (my emphasis). That quotation comes during an extended textual demonstration that the father's death and the disappearance of his name do not in any way disrupt the normal course of social exchange. Eating, drinking, talking, and joking go on without hindrance from Goriot, who—in the ultimate metonymic spin-off of Loriot-Moriot-Foriot-Doriot-Quatre-vingt-treize—becomes with his dying breath "a little deathorama." The figure who represents Fatherhood with a capital *F* for Eugène is deprived of the constative identity necessary to represent anything whatever to a group larger than one.

And a group much larger than one is Eugène's choice after he buries Goriot and enters the constative universe par excellence, a world in which signification never claims to be anything other than collective performance. Rastignac's Père Lachaise scene—in its memorialization of a Jesuit, the name of the setting is the novel's final display of paternity's irrelevance to the paternal lexicon—continues the development begun by adding Struggle to Vautrin's Obedience or Revolt. In tacit confirmation of that continuity, the defiant "A nous deux" with which Rastignac goes down to Paris repeats the words of those who represent the family and its rejection, père Goriot and papa Vautrin. Here too the third term transcendently affirms how collectivities mean, here too the "challenge he hurled at Society" also venerates Society's right to its capital letter. When the novel's closing words recount Rastignac's move from Goriot's grave to Delphine's table, the Father is definitively severed from the conventions organizing social coexistence and validating social nomination.

The unnarrated Nucingen dinner with Goriot fresh in his grave corresponds to the narrated Beauséant ball with Goriot writhing on his deathbed. Both social functions substitute for the paternal function, both ratify Name and Law while the Father dies and decays. The Nucingen dinner obliterates Goriot but begins production of the identity that will eventually make Rastignac a count, a minister, and a peer of France with an annual income of 300,000 francs. The Beauséant ball obliterates Goriot but incorporates Rastignac among Paris notables, transforms Del-

phine from a woman of no consequence to a woman of substance, and displays Anastasie in the diamonds necessary for her to remain a woman of honor. It is on the Father's dilapidation that the power of the Name is consolidated.

Rastignac senses as much when he considers that the presence of Goriot's daughters at the Beauséant ball entails absence from their dying father's side. On Delphine: "He felt that she was capable of walking on her father's corpse to get to the ball." On Anastasie: " 'She has,' said Rastignac, 'made collateral of her father's death'." The father's corpse, the father's death, the daughters' ball: annihilation of the family's origin is the precondition for its members' denomination by their community. The conventional procedures producing the conventional effect of identity unfold in the absence of the figure that identity theoretically evokes.

Read in the context of the ball during which the Father dies, the dinner following his burial is a postdiegetic suggestion of the process through which the Name circulates. The coincidence of Rastignac's ascent with Goriot's disappearance summarizes the dual thematics of constative identity. Dramatically and definitively separated from the father, the paternal function attaches firmly to society. Without connection to any individual, denomination is inextricable from a collectivity. Rastignac's stellar performance in Restoration Paris begins as one component of a sustained textual argument that success depends on nothing more than skillful manipulation of the conventions a community recognizes as its own. (pp. 103-13)

> *Sandy Petrey, "The Father Loses a Name: Constative Identity in 'Le Père Goriot',"* in her Realism and Revolution: Balzac, Stendhal, Zola, and the Performances of History, *Cornell University Press, 1988, pp. 83-122.*

FURTHER READING

Adamson, Donald. *"Le père Goriot:* Notes Towards a Reassessment." *Symposium* XIX No. 2 (Summer 1965): 101-14.
    Addresses the critical debate of the previous two decades, focusing on Balzac's method of characterization, the novel's so-called "banal" view of life, and the difficulty of determining whether Rastignac or Goriot is the intended protagonist.

Ahearn, Edward J. "Vautrin's Hundred." In his *Marx and Modern Fiction,* pp. 119-63. New Haven, Conn.: Yale University Press, 1989.
    Comparison of formal and thematic aspects of *Le père Goriot* and William Faulkner's *Absalom, Absalom!,* emphasizing their treatment of economic, familial, and sexual issues.

Besser, Gretchen R. "Lear and Goriot: A Re-evaluation." *Orbis Litterarum* XXVII No. 1 (1972): 28-36.

Investigates similarities of plot, character, and structure between *Le père Goriot* and *King Lear.*

Bourque, Joseph H. "Latent Symbol and Balzac's *Le père Goriot.*" *Symposium* XXXII No. 4 (Winter 1978): 277-88.

Examines the symbolic implications of eating in *Le père Goriot.*

Conner, J. Wayne. "On Balzac's *Goriot.*" *Symposium* VIII No. 1 (Summer 1954): 68-75.

Suggests possible prototypes for the Goriot character and sources for his name.

Houston, John Porter. "Balzac and *La comédie humaine.*" In his *Fictional Technique in France, 1802-1927: An Introduction,* pp. 26-46. Baton Rouge: Louisiana State University Press, 1972.

Assesses Balzac's creation of fictional time in *Le père Goriot.*

Krailsheimer, A. J. Introduction to *Le père Goriot,* by Honoré de Balzac, pp. vii-xviii, Oxford: Oxford University Press, 1991.

Discusses the historical context of *Le père Goriot,* Balzac's integration of setting and characterization, and his use of dramatic irony.

Maurois, André. "Balzac: *Le père Goriot.*" In his *The Art of Writing,* pp. 91-103. Translated by Gerard Hopkins. London: The Bodley Head, 1960.

Analyzes Rastignac, Vautrin, and Goriot as exemplifications of Balzac's own personality.

McCarthy, Mary Susan. "Mastery of *La comédie humaine*: The Reappearing Character." In her *Balzac and his Readers: A Study in the Creation of Meaning in "La comédie humaine,"* pp. 93-136. Columbia: University of Missouri Press, 1982.

Uses Wolfgang Iser's reception theory to explore the ways in which Balzac guides the reading process. In her analysis of *Le père Goriot,* McCarthy focuses on the importance of recurring characters in the reader's determination of meaning.

Oliver, E. J. "*Le père Goriot.*" In her *Honoré de Balzac,* pp. 53-68. New York: Macmillan, 1964.

Discusses the relationships among the characters, emphasizing that Vautrin brings out the worst in Rastignac, while Goriot brings out the best.

Prendergast, Christopher. "The Official History and the Secret History." In his *Balzac: Fiction and Melodrama,* pp. 173-87. London: Edward Arnold, 1978.

Explains the melodramatic elements of *Le père Goriot,* focusing on Balzac's reversal of the conventional role of the father in melodramatic fiction.

Pugh, Anthony R. "*Le père Goriot.*" In his *Balzac's Recurring Characters,* pp. 57-87. Toronto: University of Toronto Press, 1974.

A thorough examination of possible sources for Balzac's technique of recurring characters as well as a discussion of its role in *Le père Goriot.*

Sobel, Margaret. "Balzac's *Le père Goriot* and Dickens's *Dombey and Son*: A Comparison." *Rice University Studies* 59 No. 3 (Summer 1973): 71-81.

Studies the fathers in both novels as examples of their respective creators' fascination with characters dominated by obsessive feelings or unnatural passion.

Stowe, William S. "Interpretation: *Le Père Goriot* and *The American.*" In his *Balzac, James, and the Realistic Novel,* pp. 21-55. Princeton, N.J.: Princeton University Press, 1983.

Uncovers the parallel between Rastignac's search for truth in Parisian society and the reader's efforts to interpret the novel.

Suck, Titus T. "The Paternal Signifier: The Monetary Metaphor in Balzac's *Le père Goriot.*" Romantic Review LXXXI No. 1 (January 1990): 25-44.

Examines Balzac's depiction of a society in which economic power has replaced the father figure as the source of authority.

Additional coverage of Balzac's life and career is contained in the following sources published by Gale Research: *Nineteenth-Century Literature Criticism,* Vol. 5 and *Short Story Criticism,* Vol. 5.

Bonaventura

German novelist.

INTRODUCTION

Bonaventura is the pseudonym of the author of *Nachtwachen (The Night Watches of Bonaventura),* a short novel published at the end of 1804 that satirizes the philosophical and cultural currents of the early nineteenth century. Scholars have suggested a number of possible identities for Bonaventura, but there has been no consensus. This question, along with the complex, enigmatic events of the novel and the extreme nihilism of its protagonist, has given *The Night Watches* a reputation as a uniquely mysterious work.

Aside from the facts of publication, nothing about Bonaventura or the writing of *The Night Watches* is known. The periodical *Zeitung für die elegante Welt* published a prose work in July 1804 that later became the eighth chapter of the novel. The complete work appeared in *Journal von neuen Deutschen original Romanen,* published by F. Dienemann in the Saxon town of Penig. The novel is narrated mostly by the watchman Kreuzgang, a bitter and sarcastic character who reveals details of his personal history in the course of sixteen "night watches." According to Kreuzgang, he is the son of an alchemist and a gypsy, who buried him as a baby and instructed a shoemaker to unearth him. As a young man, he established himself as a poet, but after incarceration in an insane asylum he stifled his artistic aspirations and took his post as a watchman. In this capacity, he is able to observe a number of strange—and apparently unrelated—nocturnal events, including an adulterous rendezvous, an attempted suicide, and the live burial of a nun who has just given birth. Kreuzgang augments his narration with tales from his past, philosophical observations, and bizarre, spontaneous images. The novel closes with Kreuzgang exhuming the corpse of his father.

Most of the scholarship related to *The Night Watches* centers on the issue of authorship. Beliefs about the identity of Bonaventura inevitably affect the interpretation of the work, and critical assessments vary with each new hypothesis. Because Friedrich Schelling, the German Romantic philosopher, had written verse under the pseudonym Bonaventura in 1802, many initially assumed him to be the author of *The Night Watches.* His refusal to discuss the work perhaps fueled these suspicions, and for most of the nineteenth century he was widely believed to have written it. Gradually, scholars came to believe that Schelling's overall philosophy was too religious and optimistic to be reconciled with the despair and irony that pervade *The Night Watches,* and with this recognition came a renewed critical interest in investigating the novel's strangeness and in

establishing Bonaventura's identity. Among the names that have since been suggested are E. T. A. Hoffmann, a popular composer and novelist whose works explore darker aspects of humanity; August Klingemann, a minor author and theater director whose journalistic writings show a stylistic affinity with Bonaventura; Caroline Schlegel-Schelling, whose marriages to Schelling and to August Wilhelm Schlegel would have given her access to the philosophical and cultural debates that arise in *The Night Watches;* Friedrich Wetzel, a minor poet and tragedian whose writings often allude to the works of many of the same authors cited by Bonaventura; and Clemens Brentano, whose dramas and stories often contain satire comparable to that of *The Night Watches.* The methods of determining the identity of Bonaventura have continued to increase in sophistication in the twentieth century. These include statistical analyses of grammar and vocabulary that are similar to those used in determining the authorship of works attributed to William Shakespeare.

Many commentators have found *The Night Watches* to be formally chaotic, noting that the presentation of events defies chronological order, the narrator often shifts without warning, and the blending of genres is often bewildering. In this respect the novel has been compared to Laurence Sterne's *Tristram Shandy* (1760), an English novel with which the German readers were familiar. Like Sterne's work, *The Night Watches* capriciously incorporates elements borrowed from a variety of genres, including the bildungsroman or apprenticeship novel, the epistolary novel, classical tragedy, and the marionette show—a popular form of entertainment at the time. In *"The Nachtwachen von Bonaventura": A Structural Interpretation* (1965), the first major work in English to discuss the novel, Jeffrey L. Sammons sought to dispel the impression that the *The Night Watches* lacks a coherent organization. According to Sammons, the lapses in chronological order and the abrupt stylistic shifts are necessitated by thematic concerns, and he views the work as being composed of five successive cycles, each moving from satire to nihilism. Gerald Gillespie, who translated *The Night Watches* into English in 1971, similarly defended its organization as appropriate to its intention when he maintained, "Not a simplistic plot line, but the development of interlocking motif patterns determines the narrative rhythm."

A character type found in European literature as far back as the seventeenth century, the night watchman was commonly employed to express the author's beliefs about society with ruthless objectivity. Kreuzgang disparages religion, traditional concepts of romatic love, and the cultural and political opinions of the average citizen. He also mocks the writings of such prominent philosophic and literary figures as Johann Gottlieb Fichte and August von Kotzebue. According to Gillespie, the work is a powerful reaction against the German Romantic movement's idealization of nature, humanity, and artistic sensibilities. Because of his nihilistic outlook, critics have compared Kreuzgang to the protagonist of Fyodor Dostoevsky's *Zapiski iz podpol'ya* (1864; *Notes from Underground*). Indeed, like Dostoevsky's underground man, Kreuzgang endorses complete indulgence in hate, doubts the possibility of salvation through religion, art, or love, and exults in the degradation of humanity. While some critics have taken the final word of the novel, "Nichts!" ("Nothing!"), as confirmation of Kreuzgang's unyielding nihilism, others perceive an element of hope in the mocking tone of the novel, noting that satire assumes the possibility of remediation. Such critics contend that the sustained tension between idealism and despair in *The Night Watches* is the source of its literary achievement.

Jeffrey L. Sammons   (essay date 1965)

[*Sammons is an American critic and educator best known for his writings on Heinrich Heine. In the following excerpt, he depicts the narrative structure of* The Night Watches *as consisting of five successive cycles, each moving from satire to nihilism.*]

A superficial glance at the *Nachtwachen* as a whole reveals the fact that the work is divided into sixteen night-watches. This must now be our starting point, because if an analysis of the external structure . . . is possible at all, we must somehow be able to make sense out of the order of the night-watches. This is particularly the case because the work is a fictional biography told entirely out of chronological order, and it is just this apparently arbitrary rearrangement of materials which invites our curiosity. The basic outlines of the watchman's biography are these: he was conceived on Christmas Eve by a gypsy woman; his father was an alchemist who had succeeded in exorcising the devil, and the latter stood godfather to the child (center portion of XVI); the gypsy buried the boy in a casket in the earth and directed a shoemaker to find him, enabling the watchman to grow up as a shoemaker-poet in the tradition of Jakob Böhme and Hans Sachs (first part of IV); he acquires a certain reputation as a poet, but his behavior at a trial for satirical slander lands him in the madhouse (VII); his stay there (IX) leads to a love affair with another inmate who dies in childbirth (XIV); he is expelled from the madhouse and becomes a marionetteer, but the troupe is broken up as politically dangerous, so he obtains a post as a night-watchman (XV). In this post he is deprived of his horn and prohibited from singing for announcing the Day of Judgment (VI); he becomes involved in a quarrel between a dying atheist and the Church (I, II, and part of III), he interferes with and prevents an adulterous tryst (III), he listens to the life story of an unhappy, mad Spaniard (latter part of IV), and retells the story in a different style (V); he recounts the suicide of an unsuccessful author (VIII), is present as a nun is buried alive for having given birth to a child (X) and tells the life story of the child's father (XI); endeavors to prevent a suicide, which turns out to be merely play-acting (XII), pays a visit to an art museum with appropriate satirical comments (XIII), and finally enters a cemetery where he learns of his ancestry and opens his father's grave (remainder of XVI).

Thus the true chronological order of the night-watches is as follows: XVI, IV, VII, IX, XIV, XV, VI, I, II, III, (IV), V, VIII, X, XI, XII, XIII, (XVI). It seems that it is this apparently helter-skelter arrangement which has convinced the critics that the work was written without plan or form. To be sure, there are definite chronological difficulties. The original impression of the reader that he is accompanying the watchman on his rounds cannot be sustained. Night-watch X clearly takes place on a winter night in which a beggar freezes to death, while the first sentence of XIII places the action at the vernal equinox. Thus the effect of successive night-watches, which we have clearly in I, II, and III, is not maintained. More serious is the frequently observed problem of the watchman's horn; in II he uses his horn as an "antipoeticum", and in III he blows his horn as part of his intervention in the adulterous situation, but in VI he relates how he lost the right to blow the horn altogether. One solution to this problem would be to abandon any attempt to regard I, II, and III as related in the present, and to place VI chronologically between III and IV. Equally possible, however, is that it is merely a slip on the part of the author, which one need not erect into a theory of technical incompetence, for such mistakes in detail appear in the works of the most careful of writers. In any case, however, any attempt to resolve this anomaly as an irony of the author would lead away from the nature of the work: Bonaventura does not play with his materials simply to exhibit his artistic sovereignty. Furthermore, we cannot regard all the night-watches as having taken place previous to the narration, for it seems necessary to regard the final chapter as subsequent to the telling of the earlier biographical events, in which the watchman gives no evidence of being aware of his ancestry. In the satirical speculation concerning his descent from the devil and "einer eben kanonisirten Heiligen", one gets the impression that at this point in his narrative the watchman is ignorant of his family background.

In the face of such evidence of carelessness, is it possible also to find evidence that the *Nachtwachen* is indeed a planned and organized work? Those of us whose profession it is to read literary works over and over again until we are as sure as we can be of the character of their content do well to remember that fiction is after all essentially a linear art; that is, a work is presumably written to be read from front to back, once. It will be useful to ask if any indication of organization appears to the reader upon such a first reading. Despite the numerous assertions of all critics to the contrary, it seems to me that there are at least two such indications. The first is the juxtaposition of IV and V wherein the same story is told twice . . . [This] juxtaposition fairly demands interpretation within the context of the work, and thus is an indication of organizational intent. A second such indication is the tension created between IX and XIV. Night-watch IX begins:

> Es freut mich daß ich in den vielen Dornen
> meines Lebens doch wenigsten Eine blühende
> volle Rose fand; sie war zwar so von den Sta-

In a 1985 study by the German critic Horst Flieg, Ernst Klingemann was suggested to be the author of The Night Watches.

In 1903 the German critic Richard M. Meyer suggested E. T. A. Hoffmann as the author of The Night Watches.

In 1912 the German scholar Erich Frank suggested Clemens Brentano as the author of The Night Watches.

Friedrich Schelling, who published poetry under the pseudonym Bonaventura, was long believed to be the author of The Night Watches.

cheln umschlungen, daß ich sie nur mit blutiger Hand und entblättert hervorziehen konnte; doch aber pflükte ich sie, und ihr sterbender Duft that mir wohl. Diesen einen Wonnemonat unter den übrigen Winter- und Herbstmonden verlebte ich—im Tollhause.

The chapter ends: "Für meinen Wonnemonat im Tollhause spare ich ein anderes Nachtstück auf". The importance of the event to which this remark points, the love affair in XIV, will be discussed at length below. It is sufficient to note here that Bonaventura is aware, as he writes IX, of what will take place later. Thus we are able to see that the author has the plan of the work more or less clearly in mind. He does not set down in random order the first thing that occurs to him. As we look at the work more closely, we are able to find other evidence of the author's awareness of the structure as a whole. In the first night-watch he refers briefly to his own career as a poet, which is however not described until VII. Similarly, in II he remarks, "und doch war ich Poet, Bänkelsänger, Marionettendirekteur und alles dergleichen Geistreiches nach einander", which points ahead not only to the contents of VII but also of XV. The gypsy woman who appears on the woodcut in IV indicates the author's awareness of the watchman's antecedents as they are to be revealed in XVI. The stranger who appears in X is mentioned only with these words: "Plötzlich stieß ich auf jemand in Mantel—was ich von ihm erfuhr, gehört in die folgende Winternacht; was ich that, noch in diese", and indeed, his story is told in XI. From all this the suspicion grows that we have in fact a planned, thought-out narrative and not a random *jeu d'esprit;* these passages far outweigh the evidence of carelessness noted above. The critics who deny this have, I fear, not themselves tried their hand at constructing a consistent fictional narrative.

With all this evidence in hand, we are obliged once again to look at the work as a whole, this time in the order in which it is presented to us. At the risk of redundancy we must again describe the content of the night-watches, because both the chronological rearrangement and the wealth of detail make it imperative that the contents of the work be kept clearly in mind in the course of the discussion which follows.

Under threatening night skies the watchman introduces us to the town poet, who works at night in order to escape his creditors, and to a dying atheist surrounded by his grieving family as well as to a frustrated priest who roars threats of hell-fire and damnation into the dying man's ears. This situation develops into a scene of grisly slapstick as priests disguised as devils endeavor to kidnap the body; they are foiled by the dead man's brother, and the Church exploits popular superstition in order to cover up the situation. Shortly thereafter the watchman foils a pair of adulterers, delivering them with heavy irony into the hands of the dry, bloodless husband. Then the watchman meets a Spaniard whose unhappy love affair has led him to a terrible crime, but for years he has inexplicably been prevented from taking his own life. The story is told twice, first by the Spaniard in the form of a marionette play with the characters of the *Commedia dell' Arte,* and then again by the watchman in sober prose (I-V).

Next the watchman tells the story of the commotion he caused by announcing the Day of Judgment on the last night of the century; he then reaches into his own past and describes how his satirical writings and ballads landed him first in prison and then in the madhouse; following this he recounts the suicide of the town poet, who hangs himself upon receipt of his rejected tragedy (VI-VIII).

Now the watchman returns again to satire, describing the inmates of the madhouse, including one who believes himself to be God the Creator; following this is a chapter containing three vignettes: in quick succession we see a beggar freezing to death, the wedding of a young man at the same time as the funeral of his abandoned love, and a violently misanthropic porter who directs the watchman to the burial of an Ursuline who has given birth to a child. The watchman then tells part of the story of the father of that child (IX-XI).

A fourth time the watchman turns to satire, describing a character who prides himself on acquiring the external trappings of great men, and narrating his own blunder in attempting to dissuade an actor who as merely practising a suicide scene. This is followed by a "Dithryrambus über den Frühling" and a visit to an art museum, in which the statues seem to come to life in a bitter phantasy. Then comes the great and gripping chapter which describes his own love affair in the madhouse (XII-XIV). He reaches again into his past to describe his career as a marionetteer, and closes the work with the scene in the cemetery, where he meets his mother and watches the remains of his father dissolve into nothingness (XV-XVI).

My purpose in retelling the story in this fashion has been to show what I believe is structurally the case in this work; that it is basically cyclical in nature. Obviously this cyclical structure is neither completely symmetrical nor rigidly consistent, but nonetheless it appears that we have the same type of progression repeated five times: a beginning which is essentially satirical, frequently abounding in commentary, based on materials either out of the watchman's past or from the night-watches themselves; this satirical display then gradually leads into a situation which is catastrophic in character, in which the satirical elements yield to an increasing nihilism and a muted or repressed despair, and the comedy to an acrid and barely relieved bitterness. These five catastrophes—the Spaniard's tale of love and crime, the suicide of the poet, the young man whose beloved is buried alive, the tragic end of the watchman's moment of happiness in the madhouse, and the final outburst of total nihilism in the cemetery—are the points of demarcation for the structure of the **Nachtwachen.** Each time the catastrophe is told, it is as though the author had taken a breath, and we find ourselves once again in the relatively harmless realm of satire, as the process begins anew, but each time we are increasingly in the shadow of the preceding horror; the satire becomes less occasional and more existential in impact, the comedy more hollow, until finally the responses of the reader are crushed under the increasing weight of nihilism and he is able to comprehend the outburst in the concluding chapter. This is basically the external structure of the **Nachtwachen,** and it will be useful to look in detail at each of the five sections which I have postulated.

If we return again to our method of inquiring after the impression left by a first reading, certainly it would seem reasonable to find the reader in a state of bewilderment after having perused I-V. Perhaps the impression given by this section taken alone, a first impression, of course, accounts for the insistence of critics upon the disorganized quality of the work, for it is only when seen from the perspective of the work as a whole that the motifs of this section fall into place. We are introduced to the town poet in I and II, and he is apostrophized in I by the watchman, yet he appears here only as the stimulus for satirical and bitter observations and does not become a central figure until VIII. Nor are we really aware of the depth of bitterness in the watchman's remarks until more of the fabric of his soul has been unfolded for us. Upon a first reading, such a remark as:

> Ich bannte diesen poetischen Teufel in mir, der am Ende immer nur schadenfroh über meine Schwäche aufzulachen pflegte, gewöhnlich durch das Beschwörungsmittel der Musik. Jezt pflege ich nur ein paarmal gellend ins Horn zu stoßen, und da geht's auch vorüber

is greeted with amusement; we admire the cleverness of his "anti-poeticum". In the course of time the matter takes on a darker cast.

As for the phantasmagoria surrounding the death of the atheist, it requires a certain amount of attention on the part of the reader to make out just what is going on. But when we have untangled the mystifications, the devilish priests masquerading as devils, and the compounded embarrassment of the Church, which, in order to avoid identification of the dead priest, claps his severed head into a locked reliquary and thus inadvertently gives rise to the dangerous belief that the devil has been killed, we believe we have merely extravagant comedy at the expense of the Church. We have not yet seen enough of the ubiquitous motif of the mask, the *Larve,* to be aware of the implications of the scene.

Our bafflement grows when faced with the extended anecdote of frustrated adultery. Not only does the scene appear to have nothing whatever to do with the foregoing, but in addition irony is piled upon irony so that it is difficult to say just what is being satirized. Basic to the situation is the ancient motif of adultery behind the back of a deserving cuckold,

> ein Wesen . . . , von dem ich anfangs zweifelhaft blieb, ob es ein Mensch oder eine mechanische Figur sey, so sehr war alles Menschliche an ihm verwischt, und nur bloß der Ausdruck von Arbeit geblieben.

But the watchman is by no means a partisan of the adulterous pair:

> Der Mann ließ es sich recht angelegen sein im rhetorischen Bombast, und sprach in einem Athem von Liebe und Treue; das Frauenbild dagegen zweifelte gläubig, und machte viel künstlichen Händeringens;

these are characters under the spell of the fashionable literature so despised by the watchman: the wife speaks in the jargon of popular Romanticism, and the lover has "die Moral voöllig, dem Geiste der neuesten Theorien gemäß, abgewiesen". The watchman interferes in this miserable triangle by delivering the couple to the mercies of the unworthy husband, thus serving a morality to which one might have thought him in opposition, considering his admiration of the atheist in I and II. Added to this is the openig section of IV, where the watchman in relatively warm and sentimental tones tells us something about his childhood in a style quite different from the frenetic satire which precedes. And to top off the confusion, we then have a story which is told twice.

Before turning to that problem, it is important to assert now that this confusion is only apparent. In fact, the night-watches I-V serve as an introduction to the whole work, and it is not an exaggeration to say that the whole *Gehalt* of the **Nachtwachen** is contained, one way or another, in these chapters, a fact which, however, can only be appreciated once the entire work has been assimilated. Bonaventura's deep disgust with the literary and intellectual climate of his age, exhibited here in the three anecdotes described above, pervades the work, and it is only its existential quality which has not yet been made clear. We shall see eventually that both the story of the atheist and the ironies of the anecdote of adultery are indicative of the total decay of values which the work finally asserts. The two most pervasive motifs of the **Nachtwachen,** the mask and the marionette, are introduced in their characteristic context in these chapters. The way in which these matters are subsequently developed will be the subject of later sections of this study. It is sufficient here to assert that they are contained in embryo in this first cycle.

The story which is told twice is that of a Spanish gentleman who falls in love with an unknown lady, but while he is searching for her, his brother marries her. The disappointed lover then arranges for his brother to kill his wife and her page out of jealousy, and then to take his own life. Filled with bitter remorse, he perpetually endeavors to commit suicide, but is restrained by some unidentifiable force. In IV, this tale is told as a marionette play, in which the wooden lack of free will of the characters is described and the place of fate taken by Hanswurst, whose blundering prevents the gentleman from pursuing his love: "Jener will ihr nachstürzen, rennt aber, weil der Marionettendirektor hier ein Versehen macht, sehr hart gegen den Hanswurst". His inability to take his own life is also ascribed to a clumsiness on the part of the director.

> dann greift er, ohne ein Wort weiter zu sagen, ebenfalls nach dem Degen, um auch sich selbst, zu guter lezt, hinterherzusenden; doch in diesem Augenblicke reißt der Drath, den der Direktor zu starr anzieht, und der Arm kann den Stoß nicht vollführen und hängt unbeweglich nieder.

There is a distinct satirical element in this passage; whether or not the marionette play is a satire on Schiller's *Braut von Messina,* as has been both asserted and denied, is difficult to decide, but surely the contemporary theater is under the lash here. The import of the marionette itself is traditionally satirical, and the author of the **Nachtwachen** gives the motif additional force. . . . [The] really striking aspect of the matter [is] the juxtaposition of this chapter with retelling of the story in the following night-watch.

This time the watchman tells the story during the day, as a cure for insomnia:

> Da konnte ich nun nichts bessers thun, als mir meine poetisch tolle Nacht in klare langweilige Prosa übersetzen, und ich brachte das Leben des Wahnsinnigen recht motivirt und vernünftig zu Papiere, und ließ es zur Lust und Ergözlichkeit der gescheuten Tagwandler abdrucken.

This he does in a manner which has no parallel elsewhere in the work. . . . The characters now have names; the Spanish setting is clearly presented; Don Juan's emotional responses, such as his feelings upon seeing Ines for the first time, are described in detail, psychological observations are made, the tale is complicated by the growth of an unspoken love between Don Juan and Ines, etc. For a moment we are tempted to say that the story, first told satirically and bitterly from the perspective of Don Juan's madness, is here given psychological depth and realistic coloring. But soon we realize that this cannot be; not only does it make no structural sense in the work as a whole, but we have seen that the watchman himself speaks of the second narration with the utmost contempt. We are driven to argue that the second narration is in fact inferior to the first, that the psychology presented is not a deeper insight but a superficial explanation for an action that is in actual fact wooden, cold, and not subject to free will, that emotions are not real but simply painted on and built in, and that the director of life (i.e., God), is an incompetent fumbler. Why then is the tale told twice?

Whatever the conscious intention of the author might have been, surely this juxtaposition serves as a graphic elucidation of Bonaventura's method. For it underlines the fact that he is not writing phantasy, and at bottom he is not writing satire. Every aspect of the work is a reflection of a reality such as is presented in V, but a reality stripped of its illusion and deception, cleaned of emotion, meaning and the delusion of free will, such as is presented in IV. The story told in IV is truer than the same story told in V, and this is the kind of truth, extracted from the outward appearance of the world as a whole, which will pervade the entire work. There is no need for further explanation, no need to retranslate the subsequent narration "so recht zusammenhängend und schlechtweg . . . , wie andre ehrliche protestantische Dichter und Zeitschriftsteller"; it has been done once, and the method, when seen against the background of the whole work, becomes abundantly clear. Seen from this standpoint, it is evident that the juxtaposition of IV and V properly belongs in the introductory section, indeed, rounds it off as a unity.

When we leave the unsettling implications of IV and V, we find ourselves in the somewhat more breathable atmosphere of satire in VI. There is great comedy in the Day of Judgment hoax which the watchman creates out of pure

whimsy, comedy directed against both the hypocrisy of society and the gullibility of the townspeople. From the point of view of external structure there is little to be said about this chapter. But it must be kept in mind that the satire of VI stands in the shadow of what we have learned from the first cycle. The very universality of the satire, directed against king, nobility, jurists, clergymen, and the whole range of society, gives us pause, for who escapes the reckoning? Only the town poet, the watchman's alter ego in the garret, and a man whose satirical curiosity transcends the pretended earnestness of the moment, so that he takes his own life to see if it is still possible in the last moments of Creation.

In VII we pick up a strand of biography which was begun in IV. A brief comparison of these two passages will be useful here. . . . In IV, using as a fiction a book of woodcuts which describe his life, he draws vignettes out of his childhood as the shoemaker's foundling, emphasizing especially his interest in Böhme and Hans Sachs, and he describes the shoemaker's astonishment at the boy's gifts and open-hearted response to nature. In VII this idyll of childhood is left behind, as the boy's poetic gifts and peculiarity of viewpoint lead him into frustration. His "Leichenrede" upon the birth of a child, dilating upon the physical fact that the human being begins to die as soon as he is born, is misunderstood and used as a funeral eulogy. A general satire upon the necessity of asses in the world is taken personally by a citizen, and the young man lands in prison. He fares no better in his subsequent career as a *Bänkelsänger;* his satirical ballads bring libel suits upon him. His defense in court is an attack upon the morality of judges in general, and the bewildered judges see no other recourse than to have the young man committed to the madhouse. So ends his poetic career.

The following night-watch describes the end of another career, that of the local author already mentioned in I, II, and VI. The connection with the preceding night-watch is clear enough, for it is just such an end that the watchman has escaped by abandoning his poetic vocation. Already in I he has observed:

> Aber ich habe diese Beschäftigung [die Dichtung] aufgegeben gegen ein ehrliches Handwerk, das seinen Mann ernährt. . . . Nachtwächter sind wir zwar beide; schade nur daß dir deine Nachtwachen in dieser kalt prosaischen Zeit nichts einbringen, indeß die meinigen doch immer ein Uebriges abwerfen. Als ich noch in der Nacht poesirte, wie du, mußte ich hungern, wie du, und sang tauben Ohren; das letzte thue ich zwar noch jetzt, aber man bezahlt mich dafür. O Freund Poet, wer jezt leben will, der darf nicht dichten!

The bitterness which is caused by this capitulation and symbolized by the horn used to repress "diesen poetischen Teufel in mir" is sufficiently clear. But the poet, though he belongs "zu den Idealisten, die man mit Gewalt durch Hunger, Gläubiger, Gerichtsfrohne u.s.w. zu Realisten bekehrt hatte", remains true to his vocation, despite starvation, and concentrates on a tragedy entitled *Der Mensch* which will demask the world and reveal it for what it is. The tragedy is rejected, and the poet hangs himself with the string from the package in which it is returned. There is no real differentiation in style or content between that which the poet is supposed to have written and the watchman's own mode of expression. The poet is in a very real sense the watchman's alter ego; he has remained with the career with which the watchman began, and represents the end to which the watchman would necessarily have come had he not given up poetry.

Here a second section of the work closes naturally. We have begun with a general satire exposing the world as a whole; we have recapitulated the watchman's own poetic career and its violent collapse and then, by way of both of commentary and of deepening the unhappy significance of both presentations, we are witness to the miserable end of a poet who has combined an attempt to pursue his career with a realization of the shattering insights presented in VI. It is perhaps here more than at any other point in the work that we are tempted to agree with Josef Nadler that the *Nachtwachen* is by no means a Romantic book; for the watchman's abdication from Parnassus and the implication that poetry is impossible in the world he describes, rather runs counter to the Romantic faith in the permanent and real value of poetry in the total existence of man. On the other hand, we will come to see, as a modification of this view, that the values of poetry have some permanence in the context of the work.

The ninth night-watch begins and ends with a reference to the most important single event in the watchman's life, his love affair in the madhouse, but, true to the pattern of the work which we have identified, this most shattering of all his experiences is postponed to XIV. Here we are back in the realm of satire again, as the various inmates are enumerated and described. The chapter is a kind of *Narrenschiff* in reverse; the fools, instead of being flayed themselves, are used as a stick with which to beat the world, for it is the unreasonableness of the world which has brought most of them to this pass.

Here it is worth saying that IX is unquestionably the weakest chapter in the book. The satirical possibilities of describing a set of twenty inmates of a madhouse are limitless, but Bonaventura's ordinarily rich imagination is simply not up to it. Of the nineteen inmates excluding the watchman, Nos. 1, 7, and 8 are also shipwrecked poets, while No. 5 is an orator whose speeches were too sensible and comprehensible. This preoccupation with the problem of the *Literat* in a work of universal satire is a bit parochial. Nos. 12, 13, 14, and 15 "sind Variazionen über denselben Gassenhauer, die Liebe", without any effort to characterize them even briefly. No. 18, who pursues the mathematical impossibility of finding a final number, may be a reference to a contemporary personage, but if so, it has escaped the attention of the editors, and means nothing to the uninformed reader. The remark made upon No. 17, who concentrates upon his own nose: "Vertiefen sich doch oft ganze Fakultäten über einen einzigen Buchstaben, ob sie ihn für ein α oder ω nehmen sollen", is insipid wit. If the continued accusations of the critics that Bonaventura is careless and lacks the will to artistic perfection have any validity, it is here in this night-watch.

On the positive side is the monologue of the Creator, who holds a ball in his hand as a symbol of the world and discourses regretfully upon the use man has made of Creation. The spark of the divine which he put in mankind was a mistake, and now he is at a loss as to what to do: "Am besten ich warte überhaupt mit der Entscheidung bis es mir einfällt einen jüngsten Tag festzusetzen und mir ein klügerer Gedanke beikommt—". We have already been introduced, by implication, to the blundering God, in the person of the director of the marionette play in IV. Here we see essentially the same view from the perspective of God, rather than of man: the God who has spoiled his Creation by his own poor management expresses his contempt for the worthlessness and baseless intellectual pride of mankind. For the author the situation is a delicious vehicle for satire.

We must take note of the fact, however, that all the while the ground for satire has been sliding out from under our feet. For it is expected of the satirist that he have a fairly firm footing upon his own ideal, or, put in another way, he makes fun of imperfect superficial aspects of a world which is sound at the core, aspects which can be corrected by bringing them back into harmony with the ideal. Bonaventura himself is aware of this, for he begins VIII with a comment on the subject:

> Bösartig aber werden sie [die Dichter] sobald sie sich erdreisten ihr Ideal an die Wirklichkeit zu halten, und nun in diese, mit der sie gar nichts zu schaffen haben sollten, zornig hineinschlagen. . . . Für den Maasstab ihres Ideals muß alles zu klein ausfallen, denn dieser reicht über die Wolken hinaus und sie selbst können sein Ende nicht absehen, und müssen sich nur an die Sterne als provisorische Grenzpunkte halten.

A satirical view of jurists presupposes a firmly held attitude toward justice; of adulterers, toward morality; of theologians, toward a proper religious attitude, etc. But in the course of the work this ideal ground begins to dissolve in the acid of the watchman's existential observations. Justice has no meaning if free will is denied, as it has been in IV; morality and religion have no base if God is an incompetent and fumbler who does not even know his own mind, as appears in IX. Gradually, with each succeeding cycle, the satire which opens the cycle becomes increasingly abysmal. . . . [We] will see immediately that the realm of satire is abandoned sooner in this section than in the two preceding, for the events of the next two night-watches throw an increasing pall of horror over these chapters.

The tenth night-watch contains three causally unconnected anecdotes told in succession. . . . [All three anecdotes turn upon the same dichotomy of love and death.]

The first anecdote concerns a beggar who fights off slumber to keep from freezing to death in the cold night. The watchman considers whether or not to wake him, and finally consigns him to death. This is not the first shock of its kind in the *Nachtwachen*—the suicide in the Day of Judgment scene, which is directly the result of the watchman's prank, is another—but it is the most powerful. I do not know of a single parallel to this scene in the literature of the time, in Germany or out, and I believe one would have to go far into the nineteenth century before finding a comparable example of such programmatic callousness. The horror is compounded in the accusation which the watchman makes against Death after the event:

> O mörderischer Tod, der Bettler hatte noch eine Erinnerung an das Leben und die Liebe—die braune Locke seines Weibes hier unter den Lumpen auf der Brust; du hättest ihn nicht würgen sollen,—und doch—.

This leads to a monologue asserting that it is only the dream of love and the longing for it which has value, an idea which is picked up again under a somewhat different aspect in XVI.

The second anecdote describes a wedding which takes place in the same house as a funeral; the dead girl, "die weiße Braut", who has died of a broken heart after being abandoned by the groom, is contrasted with the successful bride, "eine rothe Rose". It has long been recognized that both the motifs and the situation are in the ballad tradition; there is in fact a specific reference to Bürger's "Lenore". But the importance of the brief phantasy lies in the juxtaposition of love and death again, with the hint that the dead girl has had the more fortunate experience.

Once these matters have been dealt with, we enter upon a situation which carries over into the next night-watch. The porter of an Ursuline cloister directs the watchman to a pageant of horror, in which a nun is buried alive as a punishment for having given birth to a child. This porter, we will come to see, is to some extent another alter ego of the watchman. A thoroughgoing misanthropist, he displays his dismay at mankind by putting his bitter questions to a bird which has been taught to respond with the one word "Mensch". In the face of the scene itself, in which the solemn pomp of the ceremony, the intimated quiet ecstasy of the victim, and the nocturnal, Gothic setting underline the horror of the situation, the watchman responds with a frenetic "Lauf durch die Skala". The events here described have created a pressure of terror which brings even the watchman to the edge of madness.

The eleventh night-watch serves as background explanation of the foregoing. It contains the tiny *Novelle* of a blind boy whose sight is restored by a miracle of medicine. In his sightless world he has become attached to a foster sister who sings to him; in a fierce twist of irony, however, the mother vows to give her adopted daughter to the Church if by some miracle the boy's sight should be restored. The short chapter ends in a gripping description of the boy's first experience of sight, which quite overwhelms him: "O Nacht, Nacht, kehre zurük! Ich ertrage all das Licht und die Liebe nicht länger!"

It is a commonplace to remark that one of the supreme literary arts is the art of omission, the art of knowing what to leave out, thus preparing for the reader himself the joy or shock of discovery. That XI is a pure, one might even say, textbook example of this literary device, ought to be almost too obvious to mention. Yet even this chapter, in my opinion one of the strongest in the work, has been used as evidence for the putative incompetence of the author: it is asserted that the author lacked the artistic patience

to finish the story! This is a result of an over-serious view of the opening remarks of XII (which of course again returns to the realm of satire), where the author puckishly states:

> Es geht nun einmal höchst unregelmäßig in der Welt zu, deshalb unterbreche ich den Unbekannten im Mantel hier mitten in seiner Erzählung. . . . So gebe ich nach romantischen Stoffen hungernden Autoren mein Wort, daß sich ein mäßiges Honorar mit seinem Leben erschreiben ließe—sie mögen ihn nur aufsuchen und seine Geschichte beenden lassen.

This is of course only an intended mystification which serves to draw the reader's attention to the artistic skill displayed in XI. We are easily able to supply the remainder: after the boy's sight is regained, his love for the girl who sang to him deepens, but his mother must carry out her vow to make her a nun. The young man pursues his love affair behind the walls of the cloister, and the result is the tragic scene described in X. To have told this story, some elements of which are fairly common coin in the literature of the period, would have been banal; to leave it to the reader's imagination seems to me to indicate a fine sense of structure on the part of the author. Here, as in the first cycle, we are given as a final chapter explanatory background after the significant aspect of the situation has been described.

Actually with the exception of the description of boyhood in IV (with which XI has certain affinities), there is no other passage in the **Nachtwachen** which displays more warmth, human compassion and even sentimentality than this night-watch. But just like the psychologically motivated tale in V, it is all basically illusion and delusion, for this sweet story of love and a medical miracle ends in frustration, death, and nameless horror. In order that we should be in no doubt on this point, the frustration, death, and nameless horror are described to us *first*. We have come to the end of another cycle.

By now we know what to expect on the heels of the foregoing: a renewed burst of satire, and this is what we get in XII. The terrible tales which have just been told have by no means obviated the possibility for pure comedy, for we now meet a character who could have come from the pen of Heine himself. This creature, having discovered that he has "Kants Nase, Göthens Augen, Lessings Stirn, Schillers Mund und den Hintern mehrerer berühmter Männer", has managed also to acquire Kant's shoes, Goethe's hat, Lessing's wig and Schiller's nightcap, in which outfit he entertains society by weeping like Kotzebue and sneezing like Tieck; and someone has informed him that his imitation of Goethe's walk "amüsire ihn mehr, als Göthens neueste Schriften". The whole scene is a clever slap at the imitative, popular authors of the time; only perhaps its point is somewhat blunted for us by our recognition that Bonaventura's own work has clearly derivative aspects, and perhaps there is some self-irony involved, for it is just such self-irony which is the next order of business.

There is something basically impertinent about true satire, for it implies the attitude that the world is a pack of fools and only the satirist himself has the right attitude toward things. But we have already observed the fact . . . that Bonaventura's satire lacks a solid base of positive conviction. Under these circumstances, is it possible that the satirical watchman should himself escape the lash? Not if the author is writing a consistently structured work. And indeed, it is now the watchman's turn to be the victim of delusion. For now he comes upon an apparent suicide attempt; to dissuade this gentleman, the watchman delivers an "Apologie des Lebens", which itself is a thinly-veiled rehearsal of the meaninglessness of human life. But the supposed suicide is only a practicing actor attempting to work himself into a "mäßiges Rasen" (a magnificently significant oxymoron), and for once the watchman himself has been gulled. The ironies of this passage are inextricably intertwined. The apparent suicide scene is in a sense fake, but so is the burden of the watchman's "Apologie des Lebens", which is in fact just the opposite of what it claims to be, and although this double deception calls forth from the watchman an even more violent diatribe against the fraudulence of the world, the situation on which it is based is at bottom totally insignificant, for, after all, why should not the actor improve his skill in this fashion? In a sense the limits of satire have been reached at this point; the satire has turned upon itself, and the satirist himself has been caught in the web of it.

The chapter which follows is the most difficult in the entire book. It falls clearly into two parts: a "Dithyrambus über den Frühling", and a scene in a small art museum. From the structural point of view, problems abound in this chapter, some of which do not admit of a clear solution. Although we have been accustomed to think of the night-watches as taking place in the frozen stillness of winter, XIII describes "die Tag- und Nachtgleiche des Frühlings". The "Dithyrambus" itself, however, presents no insuperable difficulties; we are in the atmosphere of the Creator's monologue of IX and the misanthropic observations of the porter in X. The book of nature can be read joyfully until we come to man himself, who seems to contradict the logic of nature: "Kannst du es nimmer lösen, warum alle deine Geschöpfe träumend glücklich sind, und nur der Mensch wachend dasteht und fragend—ohne Antwort zu erhalten?" Thus this passage fits into the pattern which has been taking shape in the **Nachtwachen** thus far. The scene in the museum immediately thereafter is more complex. It begins as follows: a dilettante climbs upon the pedestal of a Venus di Medici, "mit gespiztem Munde und fast thränend, um, wie es schien, ihr den Hintern, als den bekanntlich gelungensten Kunsttheil dieser Göttin, zu küssen". It is evident that on one level the watchman is busy grinding his satirical axes; he blasts the impiety of the modern age and its supercilious view toward the remnants of a more harmonious past. But the satire is by now totally integrated with more fundamental problems. . . . There is a curious parallel between the use of the word "Göttertorso" here and the word "Naturtorso" occurring in the cold wintry night in which the beggar freezes to death. Of that night the watchman says: "Der kalte Tod steht in ihr"; it is a night in which life has been amputated from nature, as it were. The statues of the gods have undergone amputation also; many of their limbs are missing, so that they are the wreckage of a piety which has long since lost its relevance. The modern age, by resurrecting these remnants of a lost relevance, has committed an absurd sacrilege, represented symbolically by the incapacity of modern experts to restore the missing limbs in any convincing manner, and conceptually by the modern substitution of intellectual analysis for naive religious devotion: " . . . unsere moderne Kunstreligion betet in Kritiken, und hat die Andacht im Kopfe, wie ächt Religiöse im Herzen". Certainly it would have been more pious to leave the statues buried in the earth.

What would seem to be implied here is the pervasive view held by early modern Europe of classical antiquity as a Golden Age, in comparison with which modern men are hypercivilized pygmies. But this is in fact not the case, for the art of the ancients is in fact a distortion of nature. Nature left to herself produces not ideal beauty, but disharmony and distortion; if nature had begun with the perfect little toe of Apollo's statue, it would undoubtedly have gone on to produce a cripple. Earlier, in the "Creator's" monologue, we are told that the step from nature to the construction of images of the gods represents a diminution of natural piety:

> In der einen Sekunde, die sie [die Puppe, d.h., der Mensch] das goldene Zeitalter nannte, schnizte sie Figuren lieblich anzuschauen und baute Häuserchen darüber, deren Trümmer man in der andern Sekunde anstaunte und als die Wohnung der Götter betrachtete.

But the idea of the "Naturtorso" mentioned in X is in some sense adumbrated in the "Dithyrambus über den Frühling" in this nightwatch, where we see how the continuum of nature breaks off abruptly and incomprehensibly at the point where man enters the picture. What, then, is the proper object of harmonious piety? The intellectual constructions of modern man? No. The sculptured images of the Golden Age? No. Nature? No. We see that Bonaventura has shattered the pattern of reality so that man has no truly religious recourse left to him.

That this train of thought should drive the watchman again to the edge of terror is thus not surprising; in the candlelight the statues seem to come to life, but it is only the meaningless movement of a "Torso". (pp. 33-54)

For some time now we have been waiting for the "Wonnemonat im Tollhaus" which was promised to us in IX. At the beginning of XIV Bonaventura takes note of our expectation:

> Kehre mit mir zurück ins Tollhaus, du stiller Begleiter, der du mich bei meinen Nachtwachen umgiebst.—Du erinnerst dich noch an meine [sic] Narrenkämmerchen, wenn du anders den Faden meiner Geschichte—die sich still und verborgen, wie ein schmaler Strom, durch die Fels- und Waldstücke, die ich umher aufhäufte, schlingt—nicht verloren hast.

In the madhouse the watchman meets an old acquaintance: a girl who played Ophelia to the watchman's Hamlet, and who was so impressed by "die mächtige Hand des Shakespear", that her histrionic madness became real, and it became necessary to commit her. Here the watchman, who fears and distrusts love, nevertheless falls in love with her, much against his will. For a time it seems possible to make a compromise with the hollow world in which he is so uneasy. But this final opportunity is torn away from him, for Ophelia gives birth to a dead child and then dies herself. Thus the fourth cycle ends in a tragedy of profound proportions. But it is not Ophelia's tragedy, for in death she recognizes the only possibility of recovering her true identity: "Gottlob daß ich aus dem Stücke herauskomme und meinen angenommenen Namen ablegen kann; hinter dem Stücke geht das Ich an!" It is the watchman's tragedy, for out of the depth of his melancholy insights he has made an existential leap, a sort of investment in compromise, and he lands—just where he was before. The flicker of hope which of all things in his life showed the most promise turned out to be also hopeless illusion. Any remaining possibility for the watchman to rejoin the human race and accommodate himself to the human condition has now been permanently eradicated.

It is clear and evident that this chapter is not only the catastrophic culmination of the fourth cycle, according to the pattern we have described, but that it is also the climax of the *Nachtwachen*. . . . [All] the previous thirteen night-watches have been moving in the direction of this one, circuitously, cyclically, but inexorably. In a sense, it is XIV which, under these circumstances, defines the nature of the whole work, for from this point on the watchman's position can no longer be open to doubt; the rest is commentary.

Thus it follows that to a certain extent XV and part of XVI are epilogue. The fifteenth night-watch resumes the thread of the watchman's biography, describing his career as a marionetteer. The chapter is replete with satire; we have already had a slap at the chaos of the French Revolution, and now the lash is directed against the other political extreme, the official panic which the Revolution caused in Germany. A performance of "Judith and Holofernes" arouses the populace to demand the head of the local mayor; although the watchman succeeds in quieting the mob, the marionette equipment is confiscated as politically dangerous and the director hangs himself. The narrative brings the biography up to the present, for it is after this event that the narrator becomes a watchman.

But the position of true satire has long since been abandoned, and we see how quickly it fades into the catastrophic gloom which the work has presented with increasing frequency. Not only the unhappy death of the director and the additional failure in the watchman's career, but also the re-introduction of the marionette motif, with which the watchman quiets the mob by denying free will, show that satire and comedy are not and can no longer be the operative force in the work.

The final night-watch contains three anecdotes, all of which, appropriately enough, turn on the question of the meaning of death. The first is a dream of the watchman stimulated by the appearance of a poet whom he meets wandering through the cemetery. The poet attempts to write a poem on immortality, using, ironically enough, a skull as a writing table. As he calls forth a vision of the Day of Judgment, the graves open, but the dead refuse to move. "Wie, ist denn kein Gott!" (pp. 54-7) is his horrified cry. The second describes a strange character who claims to be able to see a vision of the dead person above the grave as the body has not decomposed. He has returned for a tryst with his dead beloved. This passage certainly seems influenced by the vision which Novalis calls up in his third "Hymne an die Nacht"; the difference is, however, that Novalis' vision is an intimation of immortality, whereas here the vision gradually fades along with the decomposition of the body into nothingness.

The third anecdote of XVI supplies the final piece to the biographical puzzle. In the cemetery the watchman meets an old gypsy woman, who introduces him to the grave of his father and informs him of the circumstances of his birth. The gypsy opens the grave for him, and there he sees the body of his father undecomposed. For a moment the watchman believes he can infer a last possibility of permanence in the face of nothingness. But as he attempts to tear apart his father's hands which are folded in a position of prayer, the whole body collapses at once into dust and ashes. It is the final catastrophe, the final victory of death over love, the final evidence for the meaninglessness of being:

> Ich streue diese Handvoll väterlichen Staub in die Lüfte und es bleibt—Nichts!
>
> Drüben auf dem Grabe steht noch der Geisterseher und umarmt Nichts!
>
> Und der Wiederhall im Gebeinhause ruft zum letztenmale—Nichts!

Thus, true to the pattern of the work, this final section ends in a catastrophe which expressly puts the proper label on all the catastrophes preceding, and on the world which has been described here: *Nichts*.

It has been my purpose in this chapter to identify a pattern in the order of the sixteen night-watches. We have found that there is such a pattern, a movement from satire to nihilistic catastrophe, repeated five times over, and we have at least had a suggestion that this pattern is a key to the structure and meaning of the work as a whole. (pp. 54-7)

> *Jeffrey L. Sammons, "The Sequence of the Sixteen Night-Watches," in his "The Nachtwachen Von Bonaventura": A Structural Interpretation, Mouton & Co., 1965, pp. 33-57.*

Gerald Gillespie   (essay date 1971)

[*Gillespie is an American educator, critic, and translator whose English version of* The Night Watches *helped establish its international reputation. In the following excerpt from his introduction to that work, Gillespie discusses its primary aesthetic and philosophical concerns.*]

No one has ever convincingly identified the actual author of the bitter and bizarre work *Nachtwachen* which appeared in 1804 under the pseudonym Bonaventura. It is thus a mark of the book's unusual power that it eventually entered the German literary canon of our century when, as the unknown Bonaventura predicted, there would be a general turning to the grotesque and absurd out of the logic of our cultural development. Since the *Nachtwachen* draw the gloomiest consequences inherent in Romantic pessimism and radically attack all German idealism, I feel justified in attaching Mario Praz' well-known phrase also to this most agonized of the many black outpourings of that age in Germany. The term is more than approximately suited to an odd narrator whose name Kreuzgang, from the spot where he was found as a baby, is one of several punning allusions to his cross or anguish. Whatever disagreements still may arise over the interpretation of puzzling moments in the book, one point ought to be clear by this day—that we get nowhere judging Bonaventura by the literary values which he himself so vehemently dismisses. This holds especially for the sublime, governing concepts of the age of Goethe. 'Humanity' Bonaventura exposes as a tragic lie; despite its perplexing splendours, 'nature' possesses for him no ultimate meaning except as a model of horror. Accordingly, to conclude that the *Nachtwachen* presents a disjointed turmoil of diatribes and ghastly scenes amounts only to a misleading truism. Dismay on our part over a seeming lack of 'organic' growth obliquely acknowledges that the work is not moored in the bedrock of theodicy, but rather in an oppositional attitude with its own coherent aesthetic.

Of course, anyone has a perfect right to reject such a challenge on religious or philosophic grounds as perverse and therefore 'impossible'. The historical impediments to receptivity to Bonaventura are by far less weighty. Each reader will grasp features of the work's structural complexity variously, according to his own familiarity with literature of the period; however, because romantic themes and devices have deeply affected modern writing, most details in the *Nachtwachen* possess a basic resonance in themselves. The work is obviously a mosaic, but it is not necessary to know about romantic adulation of the *fragment* as a formal principle in art to sense how Bonaventura, through skilful arrangement, produces turbulence, irregularity, and anxiety, a jaggedness which is the objective correlative to the flow of events in a chaotic universe, and mirrors the quirky logic of Kreuzgang's perceptions. Not a simplistic plot line, but the development of interlocking motif patterns determines the narrative rhythm. Initiated readers will recognize further that this motivic variation also permits a running commentary on romantic and earlier thought, for the work almost bursts with allusions, parodies, paraphrases, quotations, and names. These bits and pieces of cultural heritage are elements subordinate in a particular mentality. The essence of this cerebral control is that it excludes peace of mind. Through the very process of manipulating supernatural references and constructing myths which interpret himself and the world, Bonaventura's impetuous fantasy leaps beyond any faith to a dead end.

As Jeffrey Sammons has pointed out [in *The Nachtwachen Von Bonaventura: A Structural Interpretation,* 1965], the sixteen 'vigils' or 'night watches' fall roughly into a series of groups, each progressing from satire to despair and tragedy, while the work as a whole intensifies cycle by cycle with unrelenting consistency toward the spiritual catastrophe in its final chapter. In the earlier chapters, the narrator is noticeably more a commentator on happenings he witnesses, or acts as a listener while others relate various stories. But he becomes increasingly involved with, and speaks more and more of and for, himself so that the work as a whole progressively turns into a self-revelation. Sammons sees 'a kind of structural counter-point'—on the one hand—'as an external form a cyclical movement boring ever deeper into the empty core of the universe'; on the other, 'the convergence of two lines of presentation: the intellectual content . . . and the personality of the watchman'. His suggestive analysis enhances Dorothee Sölle-Nipperdey's study of the *Nachtwachen* as a process of 'unmasking' which renders any simple kind of identification impossible. The narrator's ironic distance and personal alienation go together because the *ego* is one of the book's chief subjects, as well as its principal instrument for probing the nature of existence. The misanthropes and cynics in it who do exchange a few signs of recognition share only their knowledge of the world's perversity. Otherwise the watchman, like the sub-narrators, really engages in a lonely monologue, as the final page drastically underscores. What is more, the oppressive realities of transitoriness and eternity shape the meaning of any sentimental development; the entire pattern of individuation and the ages of Man is reduced to a mechanical model. Bonaventura presents human experience as truncated segments in a nightmare. The juxtaposition of these facts in a kind of spacial arbitrariness expresses the aimless, crushing monotony of existence.

If we feel Bonaventura's despair to be genuine, one of the first questions must then be why this impulse did not disrupt his book, an attempt, after all, at communication, from which we could perhaps infer some hope for meaning. Pointing to his numerous references to a lost age of faith or innocence, Sölle-Nipperdey posits that the author must have regarded death as a passage to rebirth for corrupt humankind and sought purification through the anguish of absolute loss of belief; that his denial of God almost possessed mystical potential as a form of mortification; but that in trying to test the inextinguishable reality of divine love through negation, he drifted from an eschatological yearning into nihilistic despair as his subject overwhelmed him. I shall return later to how Bonaventura actually interprets the romantic paradigm of a development from unconsciousness or a golden age, modelled on the myth of Man's expulsion from Eden. The immediate matter is the implication that the *Nachtwachen* may be to some extent an artistic, through the human, failure, if the author was defeated in his purpose and lured into the abyss. Though ably argued, Sölle-Nipperdey's theory suspiciously rests on the traditional assumption that every artist sets out, necessarily and properly, to express final trust in a higher order. It so happens, however, that Kreuzgang consistently defines the true artist's role otherwise, and the critic must resort to the notion of the governing 'spirit' of the narration to override its explicit statements through the narrator. Yet we could not imagine a spokesman more ready and able to expose the deficiencies of his own viewpoint, more bent on unmitigated disillusionment!

Indeed, Kreuzgang—so far as we can tell by internal evidence—is the highest ironist in the book's world, and the cause of his suffering is that he cannot honestly detect the sway of any supreme Author worthy of reverence. English-speaking readers will be interested by his frequent allusions to the darker insights of Shakespeare. It would be no exaggeration to define the art of the *Nachtwachen* as an attempt to portray life as 'a tale told by an idiot, full of sound and fury, signifying nothing'. The particular character of that Nothing which obsesses Bonaventura requires careful scrutiny. Notable in this connection is that he never despises genuine artists, of whom he mentions more than a dozen in passing; true artistry is virtually the only value he respects. And since the sixteen night watches formulate their message in large measure by means of literary quotation and reference to the arts and the artist problem, creative consciousness may be regarded as the framework containing the author's nihilism. On one level, the book tells of the narrator's struggle against prosaic life. Neither Bonaventura as author nor Kreuzgang as fictive speaker, however, aims simply at manifesting his own artistic sovereignty over a world his mind invents or interprets. Apparent arbitrariness may be the compositional method, but romantic irony is not the rationale; such a triumph of the ego in the Fichtean sense is denied as a delusion. I shall trace the steps in this simultaneous statement on delusion and disillusionment shortly. The *Nachtwachen* reveal a remarkable economy in the way they present a fictional biography purposely out of order, a general indictment against the world, and a manifesto of an art of despair deserved by decadence.

If we reconstruct the rough chronology of experiences to make it clear in prosaic terms—an act which naturally contravenes the spirit as well as actual sequence of the work—we gain this approximate picture: The narrator was conceived on Christmas when his gypsy mother and necromancer father fatefully interrupted the latter's conjuration of the devil. His mother put him in a casket at a crossroads so that a gullible, pious shoemaker would find him while treasure-hunting. Raised in the image of the mystic Jakob Böhme and the Mastersinger Hans Sachs, both cobblers (and folk figures idealized by the German romantics), young Kreuzgang begins to lose his innocence through overacute intellect. His social satire as a budding poet lands him rather soon in the madhouse. There he succumbs to love for Ophelia, the insane actress who had once played opposite him in *Hamlet* but lost her own identity and became her rôle. Her death in childbirth on a ghostly storm-lit night elicits one of the two tears which the narrator ever manages to shed. The next drops for the confiscated puppet Hanswurst (Clown), with whom he associates himself while employed as a marionette master after his release from the asylum. The authorities disband the troupe as a political threat during the unrest attending the French Revolution, for the traditional puppet play of Judith and Holofernes incites the peasants to violent rebellion. At this juncture, the defeated poet takes a steady job as nightwatchman, in which we actually first meet him in the book's opening chapters where he becomes involved in the struggle between a confident, dying atheist and a cruel, corrupt church. And it is during his career as watchman that the various minor stories occur or are told. There is his interference with an adulterous couple whom he turns over to the pedantic husband, an execution-loving judge, simply in revenge for the hollow romantic clichés they use to mask their lust; his hearing of the story of the incestuous fratricide Don Juan, and retelling of it; the piteous suicide of the town's unsuccessful poet, who hangs himself with the cord from the returned manuscript of his tragedy entitled *Man;* the secret burial alive of an Ursuline nun who has borne a child, followed by the history of the young father who curses his own recovery of physical sight, which helped precipitate the disaster; the attempt to dissuade from suicide a person who proves to be an actor diligently studying his part; a visit to an art museum, with sardonic commentary on modern adulation of antiquity; and finally, Kreuzgang's discovery of his own ancestry and opening of his father's grave. The above condensation regrettably must omit many choice details of which there is such a rewarding abundance. (pp. 1-6)

[The watchman introduces] the unanswerable question why man has the misfortune of appearing as observer-participant in this colossal drama under the ultimate sign of entropy. For, once we accept that the cosmos is running downhill toward extinction, nature is then only a cruel sketch broken off without meaningful continuation; and because man has lost his primitive protective naiveté, all he can now know is the echo of his own thoughts trapped within a dying system. The book fully grants the existence of a *natura naturans,* but its whole motion is unmasked as a hideous nightmare. In the final chapter, the watchman rails against the creation such as he views it:

> '. . . diese Myriaden von Welten sausen in allen ihren Himmeln nur durch die gigantische Naturkraft, und diese schreckliche Gebärerin, die alles und sich selbst mitgeboren hat, hat kein Herz in der eigenen Brust, sondern formt nur kleine zum Zeitvertreib, die sie umher verteilt—'

> [. . . these myriads of worlds roar through all their heavens only by the gigantic force of nature, and this terrifying spawner who has spawned everything and herself with it, has no heart in her own breast, but for a pastime only forms little ones which she passes around.]

[The] similarity of attributes (terrible, monstrous, self-generating and self-consuming) indicates that the ego is also a model for the entire universe in Bonaventura's eyes. His several references to evolution never affirm even remotely the idea of an expansion of consciousness within the whole of created nature as a gradual triumph of the spirit; rather he seems to view the overall organic development of consciousness simply as the product of an enclosed system, somewhat in analogy to individuation within one's skin. The human beings who appear with 'hearts' are simply outgrowths of evolution. That the development of sentiments means useless tragedy is only an unfortunate fact of no consequence to the system. With a lack of concern equal to that of a puppet master in assigning destinies (or playing stories), nature has spawned hearts.

Bonaventura's gaze into the abyss of nature remarkably resembles the anguished perception of Goethe's Werther, in the letter of August 18, concluding:

> '. . . mir untergräbt das Herz die verzehrende Kraft, die in dem All der Natur verborgen liegt; die nichts gebildet hat, das nicht seinen Nachbar, nicht sich selbst zerstörte. Und so taumle

ich beängstigt. Himmel und Erde und ihre we-
benden Kräfte um mich her: ich sehe nichts als
ein ewig verschlingendes, ewig wiederkäuendes
Ungeheuer.'

[. . . my heart is undermined by the consumptive power which lies hidden in the entirety of
nature; which has formed nothing which did not
destroy its neighbour, destroy itself. And so I
reel anguished. Heaven and earth and their interacting forces about me: I see nothing but an
eternally devouring, eternally regurgitating
monster.]

The related fear that life is a ridiculous puppet spectacle
occurs in Werther's letter of January 20:

'Ich spiele mit, vielmehr ich werde gespielt wie
eine Marionette und fasse manchmal meinen
Nachbar an der hölzernen Hand und schaudere
zurück.'

[I play away, rather I am played with like a marionette and sometimes grasp my neighbour by
his wooden hand and recoil shuddering.]

Bonaventura does not draw back from this threat to
Storm-and-Stress and, next, Romantic spirits. Rather
than mitigate the primal horror of existence, which is ordinarily subordinated in the standard German poetic cos-
mology of organic development, he calls in question any
rationalization of suffering endured by the 'heart'. Thus
Jakob Böhme's concept of a contest in the very processes
of the universe between Love and Hate may be as familiar
in the *Nachtwachen* as it is generally in German Romanticism. But instead of hinting at some ultimate transfigura-
tion of life, Bonaventura announces a triumph of darkness
and hate. One of the watchman's more elaborate references to this struggle within his own personality is a perverse variation upon the metaphor of the marriage of
Heaven and Earth. He muses—

daß eben der Teufel selbst, um dem Himmel
einen Possen zu spielen, sich während einer dun-
keln Nacht in das Bette einer eben kanonisierten
Heiligen geschlichen, und da mich gleichsam als
eine lex cruciata für unsern Herrgott nieder-
geschrieben habe, bei der er sich am Welt-
gerichtstage den Kopf zerbrechen solle.'

[that the very devil himself, in order to play
a trick on heaven, slipped into the bed of a just
canonized saint during a dark night and inscribed me there as it were as a *lex cruciata* for
our Lord God, over which He should break His
head on the Judgment Day.]

Lex cruciata refers to the law of biological inheritance and
is, of course, another pun on cross, for Kreuzgang. In the
grisly recognition scene of the final nightwatch, of which
I intend to speak again, the narrator hears from his mother the maxim of their kind. It is a total reversal of romantic
values and of the sense of the romantic vision of evolution:
'Es ist größer, die Welt zu hassen, als sie zu lieben.'

[It is greater to hate the world than to love it.]

This negativism appears logically in the several models for
the supreme artist of such a vexatious creation. One of the

God-figures is the inmate at the insane asylum in IX who
thinks he is the Creator. Of course, on several levels of
meaning, the madhouse is a representation of micro- and
macro-cosmic relationships. In the 'Monolog des wahn-
sinnigen Weltschöpfers', a pathetic, indecisive person expresses views which are, ambiguously, the acknowledged
product of mental aberration. Reviewing his work, this
self-appointed God is sorry that he created the world in
which man is a misfit by virtue of endowment with a misleading, hurtful spark of divinity. But though he admits
that he has bungled, he is equally confused as to what remedy to apply, beyond letting the race muddle along with
its delusions in the chaos, until he can bring himself to ap-
point a day of final judgment, i.e., ultimate extinction. The
idea of having to grant men their overweening dream of
immortality and therefore tolerate them for eternity
frightens the mad creator. He is already quite annoyed
that man's inquisitive probing through science encroaches
on his own lordly prerogatives. The other important God-
figure is, of course, the marionette director, who can quite
arbitrarily pull a wire and decide a destiny. By contrast,
he appears to be a powerful, indifferent demiurge; his theatre is characterized by the ridiculous gestures and harsh
laughter of clowns. Nonetheless, like the frustrated town
poet, he kills himself over the loss of his private universe
which gets out of control, that is, which mirrors the primitive relationships of the bigger world accurately enough
to trigger violence, with its repercussions.

Shifting our focus slightly, we can consider these hyper-
trophic egos also as variations upon the ego-model in
Kreuzgang's nightmare. On one level, each figure's story
is a case of extreme loneliness, an exclusion from and of
'normal' life—which they bitterly expose. On another
level, the respective suicide or insanity indicates the direction in which consciousness develops as it expands in the
drive for absolute supremacy. The trend is toward perversion and even annihilation—all creation is tragic through
its own inherent principle. The idea of entropy seems to
imply the correlative of suicide for the identity within its
universe. In this sense, the final cry of the book is simultaneously a moment when Nothingness overwhelms Kreuzgang and when his mind merges with the universal process
and end of being.

Obviously, we are dealing here with a complex picture, because the *Nachtwachen* repeatedly portrays men as helpless dolls and the narrator himself often senses being a
puppet. Bonaventura incorporates in the dense space of
150 pages all important phases in the development of the
marionette theme in German since the reaction to Enlightenment rationalism. Scorning popular and lower forms of
theatre—including puppet plays and fairytales—as manifestations of the barbaric, retrograde, and superstitious in
the folk, critics such as Gottsched had tried to banish
Hanswurst from the stage. It seemed necessary if they
were to lift art to a classical, ethical, progressive plane. But
the German pre-romantics soon rallied to the defence of
folk theatre and the clown. For young Goethe and Storm-
and-Stress generally, the puppet acquired new literary
value as a symbol variously of an outside, dead society; or
of the frustrated genius and the arbitrariness of the powers
of fate operating against his freedom. In Tieck's *William*

Lovell and in early Romanticism, the marionette expressed a subjective fatalism on the part of the aspiring class of artists, their fear of the existence of a mechanical world instead of one governed by the dynamic natural processes with which their creative theory was linked. The marionette play thus provided a pattern of gestures for a new kind of style. Finally, the Romantic concept of the 'organic' began to exclude the idea of a dynamic or irrational unfolding in favour of transcendental significance in art. Mature Romantic irony, or the control by art over life, introduced a perspective for the genius not as a Storm-and-Stress Prometheus in chains, but as a sublime puppeteer. The primitivism of the marionette form permitted allegorical manipulation of the author's creatures. Eventually, it became evident that such an emphasis upon a shaping idea would tend to equalize necessity and freedom for a fictive protagonist. This meant the inevitable nullification of the tragic hero's individualism based on dynamic qualities, and here was the basis for the growth of the late Romantic *Schicksalstragödie* (fate drama) in which man is a pawn of dark forces. Needless to say, the attitude behind such plays also contributed its measure to the eventual formation of German Naturalist drama, for it was easy to leap from inherent obscure factors such as a curse to various allegedly scientific factors of determinism.

The basis for the dignity of the tragic hero was shattered. Thus—as Bonaventura precociously says in several places overleaping Naturalistic realism—comedy replaces tragedy, and as a corollary, the puppet becomes the highest form of actor, for his wooden gestures are closest in essence to those of ancient masked drama. In this connection, I shall now turn to that aspect of Bonaventura's work which may most intrigue present-day readers. They cannot fail to notice that he develops the story of Don Juan's incestuous and fratricidal mania in V explicitly on the Oedipal pattern, or arrives at the watchman's birth trauma in a circuitous approach to the root of evil. In the grisly discovery of XVI, the narrator states:

> 'Welch ein helles Licht nach dieser Rede in mir aufging, das können sich nur Psychologen vorstellen; der Schlüssel zu meinem Selbst war mir gereicht, und ich öffnete zum ersten Male mit Erstaunen und heimlichem Schauder die lang verschlossene Tür—da sah es aus wie in Blaubarts Kammer, und es hätte mich erwürgt, wäre ich minder furchtlos gewesen. Es war ein gefährlicher psychologischer Schlüssel!'

> [What a clear light dawned in me after this speech, that only psychologists can imagine; the key to my Self was tendered me, and for the first time I opened with astonishment and secret trembling the long-barred door—the inside looked like Bluebeard's chamber, and it would have strangled me had I been less fearless. It was a dangerous psychological key!]

This weird final night watch is intended to symbolize the embodiment of contesting forces in him, rather than be a confessional revelation. Throughout the book sexual drives are regarded as among the mechanisms which make puppet-humanity perform its farcical tragedy. It is plain that Bonaventura had absorbed many implications of general Romantic psychology, on which Freud and Jung and others later built with slight modifications, the way Darwin and the Naturalists built on Romantic biology, with its thesis of evolution. In fact, both fields of study were already unified in advanced Romantic thought. An outline must suffice here. The idea that individuation recapitulated and continued evolution was widespread around 1800. Leading scientists accepted the appearance of matter out of the void, organic life out of matter, and spiritual life within organic nature as a meaningful process. Many regarded the growth of the human being as an analogous pattern of emergence from unconsciousness to consciousness. In illustration, I will cite the opening line of *Psyche: Zur Entwicklungsgeschichte der Seele* (1846) by the eminent biologist Carl G. Carus: 'Der Schlüssel zur Erkenntnis vom Wesen des bewußten Seelenlebens liegt in der Region des Unbewußtseins.' Bonaventura is not novel because he recognizes the existence of shaping impulses behind the façade of the ego, but because he casts doubt on the meaningfulness of the whole scheme of life from top to bottom. He certainly senses the depths of the mind—but as an abyss. Hence although the book's structure suggests formally the psychoanalytic release of repressed materials, it advances to just the opposite outcome expected of a therapeutic process. The acquisition of self-knowledge cannot effect any conventional normalization here, since in learning to hate a hateful universe, paradoxically, the watchman exemplifies its very perversity. He himself grasps the strange unity of defiance and defeat, while denying that unity tragic stature.

The romantic quest for a key to both inner and outer knowledge led many like the subjective idealist Friedrich Schelling through nature philosophy to metaphysical symbolization. But among the truly new directions in the early nineteenth century for interpreting the given 'facts' about the life patterns of the creature *homo sapiens,* the most productive comparisons we can draw are with troubled contemporaries of the romantics such as Heinrich von Kleist and Georg Büchner.

In his famous essay 'Über das Marionettentheater', Kleist proposes that man can return to a state of 'grace' only by reapproaching himself from his hidden side. The image of the astonishingly agile bear who can outfence a rational opponent is one of his many hints that unconscious factors will restore man's lost balance. He also identifies grace with the unconsciousness of puppets' movements. Their unreflecting, physical purity suggests the paradise from which man has fallen by virtue of tasting of the tree of knowledge. The paradigm of an ascending restoration is the sequence: 'marionette' (total unconsciousness), 'man' (sentimental split), 'god' (total consciousness indistinguishable from spontaneous nature). Kleist resembles Bonaventura in denying the validity of Kantian moral imperatives arrived at through rational abstraction, but is unlike him in often glorifying nature's deep promptings, laws which are Dionysian rather than Apollonian. While the unconscious is implicit in Bonaventura's model of man as puppet, he envisions no regaining of a golden age or state through its agency. The story of being ends with *Mensch: eine Tragödie,* as the town poet summed it up. Bonaventura may take for granted that hidden springs impel human beings and that their dreams are distorted releases of inner psychic movement. But just as he is nauseated by modern humanity's sentimental projections into the ruins of a primal era (e.g., Greek antiquity), so he impatiently repudiates psychological realism as a mere deceptive surface painting and exposes instead the unauthentic view of society of itself as a moral order and of men of themselves as sentimental personalities. Perhaps the only significant moments when he seems to exult in dark impulses are the several anarchistic gestures in the book; for example, there is the boy in VI who shoots himself during the watchman's false alarm of an onrushing apocalypse just to see whether he can avoid participating in God's grand finale to time! In brief, Bonaventura regards communal life as an amoral pyramid of structured power, which wears the mask of 'society', and human history as a process of deformation from barbaric splendour to grotesque farce.

This ethical rage brings him closer to the sphere of Büchner, who also was concerned over the compulsiveness of human actions and the villainous oppression of man by man through manipulation of the natural drives in the social order. Giving way to nihilistic despair, Bonaventura does not, however, balance his own vision of grinding ennui and transitoriness with a programme of revolutionary redemption. His cry that the clown must replace the tragic victim remains strictly an artistic, rather than a social manifesto, anticipating certain elements in the aesthetic of the grotesque and absurd today. His puppet theatre is a compact and obvious microcosm based on the older world theatre—over whose metaphors he so often and so negatively broods. But in associating the unconscious or mechanical aspects of existence with the idea of an arbitrary assignment of human beings to particular roles, he deals a double blow, on the one hand to theodicy, and on the other, to the concept of progress deriving therefrom under the guise of organic laws or dialectical processes. The secular interpretive problem of the nineteenth century may be illustrated by the quarrel of Herbert Spencer and Thomas Huxley over the meaning of evolution. The former thought its cruel mechanisms should be allowed to operate freely so as to guarantee a 'healthy' society through survival of the fittest. The latter held that all vital progress was, on the contrary, based on a struggle against greater nature for moral evolution, that civilization was a laboriously cultivated garden cut out of the jungle. Bonaventura, in a third position as nihilist, neither attempts to justify the laws of the jungle, nor can honestly believe that the special garden is anything more than a delusion, excited by the fundamental natural force for continuing life blindly.

It was noted that the narrator's ramblings and flashbacks, as he reworks the materials of his life, bear some analogy to psychoanalysis. The work evinces perhaps an even more pertinent foreshadowing of later psychological thought. Bonaventura gradually defines the emergence in his narrator's tormented intellect of a life-denying force, what Freud termed the death wish. In outline, Kreuzgang states that illusion is inherent in life itself; life continues through the masking of things in Apollonian light and colour. Truth, he decides, is thus an attack on the deception

of being. Significant is that the watchman, as satirist, does not himself escape the trap but must also become ridiculous. His encounter with Ophelia leads to no affirmation of a meaning; rather he admits the folly of his love affair. Similarly, he admits being taken in by the compulsion to talk a seeming suicide out of rejecting life; the party turns out to be an actor practising his role of despair, for which he lacks any personal feeling. Such double deceptions only underscore the fraudulence of the world. No sure hold is left, when the cynic too is so easily victimized. The prescription given by the asylum doctor in IX is less or no thinking at all. The mind, in exposing the system of the universe to be empty and absurd, drifts into its fateful orientation to Nothingness through an effort to rebel against the alleged enslavement by the vital instincts and drives.

The conflict between good and evil or love and hate in the genesis of the watchman is no longer just the familiar theme from Storm and Stress to explain the turbulence of wild heroes who live out in themselves the struggle between nature and perversion. Bonaventura's attitude toward nature is disturbingly ambivalent. Though he acknowledges its piercing beauty, he is horrified by the grim inevitability of absolute extinction under its vernal mask. Ultimately, the mechanical, heartless, frozen triumph—hence Kreuzgang's obsession with the motifs of death as rigidity and fragmentation and mutilation, as in his dream of the ancient gods in the museum, or his vignette of the dying beggar in winter. The former are called a 'Göttertorso', the latter a 'Naturtorso', and the entire work is ridden with expressions such as 'stump' for 'limb' and the like Everything, both biological entities and art are perceived to be returning to the realm of lifelessness, disorganization. Men's works, such as the entire glory of Greek civilization, become finally broken bits and sheer dust.

In view of our actual state of consciousness, Bonaventura proposes, only a savage marionette play is artistically true. Jarry's *Ubu Roi* and Valle-Inclán's aesthetic of the *esperpento* are independent recapitulations of the same thought in the early twentieth century. In an historical sense, however, current repetitive exponents of absurdity are doing what Bonaventura fiercely denounced in the then contemporary sentimental literature—they are providing a warm bath of self-pity, a new commercialized escape for jaded masses robbed of gripping beliefs and any authenticity. The negation of the formal message itself is the logical step which Bonaventura never took. Though numerous modern artists have indeed progressed to the point of half-hearted attempts at creating art which 'denies' art, only total silence and abstinence from creative activities would fulfil the nihilistic trend. Even 'happenings' and ostentatious 'destructions' of work are merely evasions, without any forthright facing of the dilemma of a dead-end. Obviously, as a Kreuzgang might well have noticed, the modern artistic community hangs on to its illusions, its life; only certain of its members are committing literal or figurative suicide, though many find a solution in insanity, and several tenacious camps of thriving, professional 'illusionists' can be named. Bonaventura's rejection of freewill sets him off, of course, from any existentialists who—in agreement with Sartre—conceive of a godless world but insist man must accept his moral freedom and create values. In

Bonaventura, man remains, despite any acquired knowledge of his condition or attempt at meaningful engagement, inevitably and hopelessly the dupe of godless nature. Unlike Brechtians who scourge man's criminality and then revert to a faith in an ultimate solution—betraying hereby their underlying kinship to bourgeois idealists—Bonaventura breaks off with an anguished cry but no answer to the reality of bestial habits.

As Dürrenmatt says, somewhat belatedly, when the world grows absurd in our eyes, tragedy must metamorphose into farce. Hence, as the *Nachtwachen* already proposed, Hanswurst replaces Hamlet. Of course, Bonaventura's harsh laughter is a defence against the consequences of a loss of identify. It is a retreat from the senseless world into total isolation vis-à-vis chaos. An inversion of values must follow such inversion into oneself. The narrator's mother expresses the work's internal logic in this 'oracular' dictum:

> 'Es ist größer, die Welt zu hassen, als sie zu lieben; wer liebt, begehrt, wer haßt, ist sich selbst genug und bedarf nichts weiter als seinen Haß in der Brust und keinen dritten!'

> [It is greater to hate the world than to love it; he who loves desires, he who hates is sufficient unto himself and needs nothing beyond the hate in his breast and no third party.]

We see the aftermath of the Kantian relegation of all authority to the inherent structures of the mind, and of the post-Kantian attempt to create an ego philosophy capable of embracing total responsibility for the patterns of the perceived universe and man's own special situation. The fragmentation process of European individualism is effectively completed in the statement cited above: the single unit of being is sundered from all organic human relationships which depend on 'love', that is, emotional acceptance. If one thinks 'too much', the book often enough shows, it becomes very difficult to submit to the social context or the notions of 'health' which social structure imposes. The alienated begin to insist more defiantly on retiring into private mental worlds; many to the extent of being classified as 'sick'. Bonaventura knows that romantic introspection is leading to this impasse and that he himself, as a representative analyst of man, is penetrating into disagreeable, once better hidden recesses of the human mind. In this sense, his book compresses into a rapid series of scenes and discourses a set of 'discoveries' which, historically, have occurred in various guises to mystics in different nations and epochs. Bonaventura's fundamental ideas might be summarized as follows: That by its very nature the human self must, in the course of things, discover its own limitations as a speck of consciousness attached to a dying animal within a doomed system. That even the products of the brain, that transitory organ which is the fountainhead of all human achievement, evil, and pretension, constitute only a phantasmagoria without validity or permanence. That mankind brings forth the mysterious script of the world theatre through the interaction of minds in a collective tragedy, but both for the single *persona* and for all *dramatis personae* during the life of our species, the script is nightmarishly and futilely finite:

'Was ist nun dieser Palast, der eine ganze Welt und einen Himmel in sich schließt; dieses Feenschloß, in dem der Liebe Wunder bezaubernd gaukeln; dieser Mikrokosmus, in dem alles, was groß und herrlich, und alles Schreckliche und Furchtbare im Keine nebeneinander liegt, der Tempel gebar und Götter, Inquisitionen und Teufel; dieses Schwanzstück der Schöpfung—das Menschenhaupt!——die Behausung eines Wurmes.—O, was ist die Welt, wenn dasjenige, was sie dachte, nichts ist und alles darin nur vorüberfliegende Phantasie!—Was sind die Phantasien der Erde, der Frühling und die Blumen, wenn die Phantasie in diesem kleinen Rund verweht, wenn hier im innern Pantheon alle Götter von ihren Fußgestellen stürzen und Würmer und Verwesung einziehen. O, rühmt mir nichts von der Selbständigkeit des Geistes—hier liegt seine zerschlagene Werkstatt, und die tausend Fäden, womit er das Gewebe der Welt webte, sind alle zerrissen, und die Welt mit ihnen.'

[What now is this palace which can enclose a whole world and a heaven; this fairy castle in which love's wonders enchantingly delude; this microcosm in which all that is great and splendid and everything terrible and fearsome reside together in embryo, which brought forth temples and gods, inquisitions and devils; this tailpiece of the creation—the human head!—shelter for a worm!—Oh, what is the world if that which it thought is nothing, and everything in it only transitory fantasy!—what are the fantasies of earth, spring and the flowers, if the fantasy in this little orb is scattered as dust, if here in the inner Pantheon all gods crash from their pedestals, and worms and decay take possession! Oh, do not vaunt to me in any way of the autonomy of the spirit—here lies its battered workshop, and the thousand threads with which it spun the tissue of the world are all rent and the world with them.]

Regarding tragedy as the highest genre, Schopenhauer saw the artist's function as a piercer of the veil of Maya, as a definer of the idea of Man, consciousness momentarily redeeming itself from bondage to life. While Bonaventura ostensibly denies tragedy, he actually substitutes in its place a modern existential anguish. He does not, then, directly anticipate Nietzsche's more positive cry for authenticity of suffering in an attempt to transcend even the idea of Man. The sole point of contact is that, in both cases, the philosophic preparation for any chance for 'truth' is the rigorous denunciation and rejection of Man, including the masses of deluded egos in their common separate dreams. The puzzling irreality of human 'identity' is explored. Applying Northrup Frye's theory of modes [stated in his *Anatomy of Criticism,* 1957], we have to do with a seeming deadend in literature after a long steady descent from High to Low mimesis, when protagonists no longer appear capable of playing even the roles of 'ironic comedy' or of parodying 'tragic irony'. In Bonaventura, to transpose Frye, 'One notes a recurring tendency on the part of ironic comedy to ridicule and scold an audience assumed to be hankering after sentiment, solemnity, and the triumph of fidelity and approved moral standards.' But we also already have in the watchman 'a character who, with the sympathy of the author or audience, repudiates such a society to the point of deliberately walking out of it, becoming thereby a kind of *pharmakos* [scapegoat] in reverse'; that is, we witness 'an ironic deadlock in which the hero is regarded as a fool or worse by the fictional society, and yet impresses the real audience as having something more valuable than his society has.' We are, in short, compelled to take sides by joining in the irony, no matter how ambiguous our position remains on so choosing. There are signs of an urge in such irony for a return to myth, and alienation itself is made into a quester story with enigmatic suggestiveness. Nausea, exile, insanity, rebellion, forlornness, and many other negative attributes invest the new actor with a symbolic aura—even though no one may have a ready key to meaning.

This kind of truth shatters old norms. If suffering is to remain authentic and not degenerate into mock sensibility, only sardonic, self-critical art can cope with it. Lessing had fleetingly probed demonic laughter as an expression of despair in extremity (Odoardo) and misanthropy (Tellheim), but Bonaventura makes it into a chief weapon with his myth of its invention by the devil, a theme which recurs in Baudelaire. It is given to mankind as a reaction of doubt in the face of absurd facts. The artist is destined to make his pact with the powers of darkness, forced to side against life with its implied subservience to a hypothetical Creator who permits the monstrosities of reality. Truth makes common cause metaphorically with the devil, and the artist finds his own face contorted in the grimace of all inmates of hell. (pp. 13-26)

(The identity of Bonaventura as the respected Romantic theater critic and director August Klingemann, who first produced Goethe's *Faust,* was discovered virtually simultaneously during the 1970s by two German scholars: Jost Schillemeit, *Bonaventura: Der Verfasser der "Nachtwachen"* (Munich, 1973); and Horst Fleig, *Sich versagendes Erzählen,* Beilage (Göppingen, 1974). The anonymous **Night Watches** marked the boundary between Klingemann's youthful ventures in narrative fiction and his mature career in Brunswick as an influential reshaper of the nineteenth-century dramatic canon.—G.G., 1992)

> *Gerald Gillespie, in an introduction to* Die Nachtwachen des Bonaventura: The Night Watches of Bonaventura, *edited and translated by Gerald Gillespie, University of Texas Press, 1971, 1-26.*

Ellis Finger   (essay date 1980)

[*In the following essay, Finger examines Kreuzgang's personality for what it reveals about Bonaventura's life and beliefs.*]

The remarkable prose work of 1805, **Nachtwachen,** contains many passages which exhibit a gifted and self-assured narrative inventiveness by the still-unknown Bonaventura. But there is one four-chapter sequence (NW X-XIII) which stands apart by virtue of an unusually bold display of shifting perspectives, elusive character connections, and jumbled chronologies of incident and recollec-

---

> ### An excerpt from *The Night Watches*
>
> What wouldn't I give to be able to narrate with the same nice coherence and directness as other honest Protestant poets and magazine writers, who become great and splendid in so doing and exchange their golden ideas for golden realities. It simply has not been granted to me, and the brief, simple murder story has cost me sweat and toil enough and, none the less, still looks shaggy and motley enough.
>
> Unfortunately I was corrupted in my young years, and as it were already in the bud, for in contrast to the way other scholarly boys and promising youths make it their business to become more and more clever and reasonable, I have constantly had a special predilection for folly and tried to bring about absolute confusion in myself just so as, like our Lord God, to achieve a fine and complete chaos, out of which afterwards opportunely, whenever it occurred to me, a tolerable world could be arranged.—Indeed, it even sometimes strikes me in over excited moments that the human race has botched even chaos and been too precipitate in organizing; and on this account, then, nothing can come to rest at its appropriate place and the Creator will have to set about as soon as possible deleting and nullifying the world as a miscarried system. . . .
>
> (translation by Gerald Gillespie)

tion. Besides being one of the richest series of encounters in the entire novel, it also shows the writer's widest range of emotional and atmospheric moods, extending from the morbid, icy tones of winter's deathliness to the joyous affirmations occasioned by the rebirth of spring. And most importantly, it reveals to fine advantage the organizing principle chosen by Bonaventura to give shape to his book: the constant presence of the narrator-watchman, Kreuzgang, not merely as observer and chronicler of actions around him, but more incisively, in his tendency to color, to reshape and even to transform these events by the force of his personality and by the occasional interplay of his own life history.

The opening images in NW X flow quickly. After making note of several persons visible in the icy landscape (a sleepwalker on the church tower, a beggar struggling for warmth and sleep, members of a wedding party and funeral procession, strangely linked by a love triangle), Kreuzgang comes to a cloaked figure who waits outside the St. Ursula Abbey. He hears the man's tale (its contents conspicuously withheld until the following chapter) and then moves on to the entrance, where the porter greets him and leads him to a darkened section of the church. Here he witnesses the immurement of a nun who has just given birth. After the execution, he receives the woman's child from the porter and carries it outside to the waiting man ("der Unbekannte im Mantel"), who is the rightful father. In NW XI Kreuzgang interposes, in first-person narration, the marvelous tale of how this man had been born blind, educated to the beauties of song and poetry by his tutor, Maria (apparently the very woman who had just been put to death for bearing his child), and later given his sight by a special operation. His ecstatic account of viewing his first sunrise (without question one of the few altogether joyous passages in the book, with moving tribute to nature's loveliness) is muted only by the reminder of the prior pledge by his parents to consecrate Maria's life to God if he were granted his sight. Kreuzgang breaks off the man's account at its peak of intensity and shifts in NW XII to a totally new subject and tone, indulging briefly in several matters of social and literary satire. But in NW XIII he replays the situation of the earlier passage, now working from the personal standpoint of his own life and not that of the interposed character: once again we find a hillside ascent, a spectacular sunrise and a glorious sense of rebirth, inspired by this moment of the vernal equinox. And once again Kreuzgang shatters the created mood by turning abruptly to a scathing satire on man's failure to accept his role as the centerpiece of creation.

In sum, this is a stunning sequence of occurrences. But the real value of this segment as an indicator of how Bonaventura constructed his book does not lie in the substance of the reported events; rather, it is the active participation of the narrator in these events and his creative shaping of them, practically to the point of using his own presence and experience as a sounding board to give them their final resonance and timbre. This influence exerts itself in several important ways: by deferring the stranger's tale until after the circumstances of his child's birth have been given, Kreuzgang places the man's account of his childhood in direct sequence with this infancy of his own offspring; the altered chronology also shows his parents' gesture of thanksgiving in respect to Maria to have resulted in separation and death, thus casting a painful irony over the joyous attainment of sight. More immediately to the point, Kreuzgang weakens the boundary between himself and the life history he reports, first by retaining the first-person vantage point for the interpolated tale (conspicuously, the only such instance in the novel) and second, by transferring the exact setting and tone of the stranger's tale to his own perspective in NW XIII. In doing so, he tends to draw the details of this encounter into the orbit of his own life and to create a sense of common ground between himself and the cloaked figure.

It is this final point that brings us to our real matter of concern: by focusing first on this four-chapter segment, I wish to isolate at the very outset the very troublesome and altogether crucial relationship between Kreuzgang and the many surrounding figures whose lives, actions and experiences give substance to his book. In the course of his manuscript, Kreuzgang offers periodic glimpses of his past, showing considerable interest in the business of self-portrayal. And several of his major interpolations drawn from the lives of others are marked by this same preoccupation. How these two spheres are joined and what this connection tells us about the author's (Bonaventura's) creative impulses in large part determine how we are to approach the subtleties of this text and how successful we are to be in meeting its many challenges. On the basis of this initial overview, I would like to offer two working hypotheses as framework for continuing discussion: first, that the prevailing character of this book—the author's design in writing it and the compelling claims it makes on the reader's responses—is confessional and biographical; and sec-

Title page for the first publication of The Night Watches. *The year of publication is given as 1805, though the novel actually came out at the end of the previous year.*

ond, that the full spectrum of self-portrayal given us for interpretation is to be sought in the delicate interplay between Kreuzgang's fragmented life history and those major interpolations in which he involves himself to an unusual degree.

Despite strong concern for the confessional tone of this novel, my aims are really quite different from any of the past attempts to establish authorship. Instead of reworking the scant and misleading clues about the historical identity of Bonaventura, I am much more interested in studying the manifest efforts by his fictional character, Kreuzgang, to sort out the fragments of his life history, to chart his intellectual and spiritual position in life, and to grapple with unspoken aspects of his character by means of the kindred histories which he often bonds to the torso of his own biography. To compensate for the uncertainty about the actual author, we have within the text itself a life-portrayal which is richly detailed, systematically complete, and delicate in artistic and psychological shadings. These nuances of personality include not only the periodic insights into character such as we find in the final graveyard scene, but also the excursions by Kreuzgang into matters of self-depiction and the pervasive preoccupation throughout the text, by narrator and author alike, with the membrane-like boundary which mediates between narrative fictions and private truths.

As a starting point let us consider the above paradox of Bonaventura's continuing obscurity vis-à-vis the strong confessional impulse evident in the narrator's methods. This paradox is more than simply a vexing side-issue in Bonaventura studies; its causes lie fundamentally within the style of the novel: the darkened, opaque atmosphere maintained in many of the vigils; the frequent use of masks and cloaks to shield identities while conveying actions [The critic adds in a footnote: "The important image of the cloak serves a double purpose: to underscore the theme of concealment and to tie in certain secondary figures with the core of Kreuzgang's confessions."]; the truncated and often evasive manner of self-portrayal stipulated by Kreuzgang in many of his recollections; and the frequent shifts and modulations given several of the episodes interpolated into his notebooks. In sum, very much of what Kreuzgang presents for view seems to issue from the contradictory desire to achieve self-depiction while at the same time safeguarding the privacy of experience.

One of the best illustrations of how this principle operates is Kreuzgang's first entrance into the storehouse of his past (NW IV). His choice of woodcuts as the proper vehicle for addressing the reader says much about the necessary blend of openness and secrecy that he seeks to preserve. He limits us to several isolated poses, thus compressing the richness of birth and childhood to a few emblematic tableaux. The chosen scenes, furthermore, are drained of coloration and nuance by virtue of stark monochromatic imprints. Fineness of detail is deliberately avoided; bold slashes of light and dark create outlines at the expense of interpretive embellishment. When he does include verbal summations, they concentrate on such general qualities as poetic leanings, fascination for nature, and curiosities about the secrets of life; specific facts of learning, of growth, and of the home environment are left unexplained. And more frequently he puts aside all "Betrachtungen," arguing the inappropriateness of such statements to the chosen medium of the woodcut: "der Künstler [hat] die Grenzen seiner Kunst nicht im mindesten . . . überschreiten wollen." His acceptance of these self-imposed boundaries causes him to omit entirely his commentary to one woodcut because it speaks too openly of his own personal qualities: "Weiter mag ich nicht im Erklären gehen, weil in dem Holzschnitte von meiner eigenen Originalität zuviel die Rede ist." Thus, this first entry into the autobiographical sphere is marked by a strong desire to establish a confessional sub-structure in his book and by an equally strong determination to do so in an elliptical, suggestive manner.

This distinctive way of seeing and depicting his past, it should be carefully noted, also characterizes his view of surrounding events in the opening sections of the novel. Indeed, the similarities between the graphic properties of the woodcut and the visual atmosphere of the first three night-watches are striking. Here, too, we find a pervasive *chiaroscuro* of light effects set against the darkness of the night. The moon playing mysteriously from behind clouds; lightning flickering remotely on the horizon, then exploding in incandescent bolts as the storm arrives; the eery glimmer of candles in the home of the libertine; the faint lamplight in the cathedral which illuminates Kreuzgang's "Lebensbuch": each in its own way creates a sense of partial, fleeting visibility. Rapid changes from light to dark allow only momentary glimpses of the shapes around him. Consequently, the scenes he records have this same blunted, suggestive quality of the woodcut: figures are shown in profile, sketched in simple outlines rather than described; faces appear as carnival masks ("Karnevalslarven") and not as individual, personal identities. In keeping with this visual style, the poet—soon to become so importantly entwined with Kreuzgang's life—is first observed as a vaporous shadow on the wall of his room, thus reducing the complexities of his artistic existence to a two-dimensional, colorless silhouette.

Much later in the book Kreuzgang acknowledges this manner of vision and concedes its closeness to how he observes his world and how he registers these observations in his writing. Sensing the reader's expectation of greater accuracy and completeness of detail, he pleads his inability to use such a style: "leider . . . fehlen mir die Farben in der Nacht dazu, und ich kann nichts als Schatten und luftige Nebelbilder vor dem Glase meiner magischen Laterne hinfliehen lassen." With this statement, the shadowy quality of vision, yielding blunted and half-recognizable images, becomes something more than simply an aspect of mood or atmosphere; it stands as one of several important statements of stylistic method which lay the groundwork of communication between narrator and reader. Strikingly, the very same manner of vision is applied to the autobiographical segment of his notebooks, falling conspicuously just before his second lengthy digression into his past: "Schmeicheln werde ich nicht, denn ich male in der Nacht, wo ich die gleissenden Farben nicht anwenden kann und nur auf starke Schatten und Drucker mich einschränken muss." This use of practically identical wording to join the two spheres of the novel—the incidental figures and events encountered during his vigils and the private, interior world of memory and experience—is an important indication that similar kinds of narrative and descriptive techniques operate on both planes.

This connection is kept visible as further statements of narrative method come forth, many of which are addressed to the crucial question of self-portrayal. In two such passages, Kreuzgang retains the principles noted earlier with the woodcuts, favoring elliptical, even twisted and fragmented lines of depiction over straightforward accuracy of detail. And again, the same kinds of descriptive techniques are applied to surrounding incidents and to Kreuzgang's own life-history. He once takes up the autobiographical thread of his story in this very manner, "vor dem Spiegel meiner Einbildungskraft sitzend." But the resulting self-portrait is so distorted by aberrations that instead of a true likeness, he gets little more than a figurative rendering of several facets of his personality: "eine Grazie, eine Meerkatze, und en face den Teufel." In one of Kreuzgang's views of his kinsman, the poet, this same image emerges as a conscious and deliberate technique of depicting the outer world: "Der Tragiker hielt das schöne Antlitz des Lebens mit eiserner Faust unverrückt vor seinen grossen Hohlspiegel, worin es sich in wilde Züge verzerrte und gleichsam seine Abgründe offenbarte in den Furchen und hässlichen Runzeln, die in die schönen Wangen fielen; so zeichnete er's ab." And in one further pair of statements, the very same structuring technique is applied to the autobiographical segment of the book and to the outer episodes which Kreuzgang witnesses and records. As if, once again, to join stylistically these two spheres of reference, he stresses the jumbled, incoherent nature of his own biography ("verwirrt und toll genug geschrieben"), then designates exactly the same qualities as the ordering mechanism for the interpolated episodes: "Was gäbe ich doch darum, so recht zusammenhängend und schlechtweg erzählen zu können, wie andre ehrliche protestantische Dichter. . . . Mir ists nun einmal nicht gegeben. . . . [ich] habe im Gegenteile stets eine besondere Vorliebe für die Tollheit gehabt, und es zu einer absoluten Verworrenheit in mir zu bringen gesucht. . . . "

Through these statements we get a firmer grasp on the kind of self-portrait which seems to be taking shape. Kreuzgang's continuing interest in the fragments of his past keeps the autobiographical framework clearly in view. But the sketchy summations he offers us rarely break free of the calculated maskings we noted earlier with the woodcuts. Yet even as he concedes the self-imposed restrictions of these sketches, he points the way toward a second source of personal depiction: the cast of peripheral figures and the settings and embellishments he gives their tales. A final indicator of such an expansive portrayal of his "history" comes just before the Ophelia episode in NW XIV. He begs the reader to recall his arrival in the madhouse several chapters earlier (NW IX), then speaks of the intervening chapters as a decorative landscape through which the unbroken line of his story flows like a stream: "Du erinnerst dich noch an mein Narrenkämmerchen, wenn du anders den Faden meiner Geschichte—die sich still und verborgen, wie ein schmaler Strom, durch die Fels- und Waldstücke, die ich umher aufhäufte, schlingt—nicht verloren hast." We should take his words as a figurative device and not as a blanket view of every interpolation as part of an all-inclusive life history. But this image, like many similar phrases cited earlier, suggests an enlargement of the character study undertaken by Kreuzgang, spreading outward from the fragments of his own biography and extending to many of the more important secondary tales.

To pursue further the workings of this expansive depiction, three segments will be considered in detail: two involving secondary figures for whom Kreuzgang shows special sympathies and one episode from his own biography—the Ophelia tale. As a group, they confirm the manner of portrayal noted earlier: maskings and concealments in respect to personal truths, balanced by the tendency to project himself into the life circumstances he encounters around him. The effect is a blurring of the lines which separate the actual biography, its surfaces guarded and veiled, from the secondary plots, many of which probe deeply into the emotional lives of the participants. As these interlockings between narrator and subject become more clearly established, we are led beyond the conspicuous scaffold-ing of Kreuzgang's self-depiction and—to enlarge now upon our original hypothesis—we begin to catch glimpses of the far more substantial mortar-work of a composite life history spread across many different segments of the novel. This larger portrayal draws upon specific situations, character groupings, family bonds, love relationships, and intellectual positions which, we must also suppose, stand in some correlation to the hidden emotional life of our author.

By far the most important of the secondary figures is the poet. Unlike all the others, he is pictured several different times, with unusually thorough attention given to his death and to the manuscript of his drama, *Der Mensch*. He is present in Kreuzgang's earliest observations, and themes raised by his death—located at the exact mid-point of the book—reverberate through many of the tangent episodes. Frequent statements of common purpose by Kreuzgang create distinctive bonds between himself and this spiritual kinsman. And the closeness of his own background to the poetic profession establishes both parallels and contrasts to this figure, thereby amplifying the important issue of the writer's vocation and his options for literary expression.

We are shown two very different sides of the poet's work. He first appears in the rather conventional pose of lyric bard, his eyes uplifted to the heavens and his soul exposed to the ravages of the storm. Far removed from the mundane cares of daily routine, he favors the nighttime solitude of his lofty garret. But he is not spared the agony of having his grandiose dreams trivialized by the inadequate resources of language: "Da fliegt der Geist von Pole zu Pole, glaubt das ganze Universum zu überflügeln, und wenn er zuletzt zur Sprache kommt—so ist es kindisch Wort, und die Hand zerreisst rasch das Papier." By the time we progress to his drama, these frustrations have mounted, twisting his dreams of immortality into the cynical critiques of a world-weary nihilist. His earlier transcendence above worldly needs has now been shattered by the very insufficiencies he had sought to surmount. He faces squarely the impairments of life and speaks despairingly and bitterly of its hopelessness for him.

There seems little doubt that Bonaventura used this characterization to elaborate his profile of the poetic life, the major sections of which are located in his narrator's biography. He created enough parallels between Kreuzgang and the poet that their experiences convey similar aspirations, difficulties, and style of expression—even to the point of having the final word spoken by each be the same: "Nichts." The prominence of these vocational references throughout the text makes it likely that the complete profile, its various aspects spread across several passages, mirrors in some way the experience of Bonaventura himself. And among its most provocative features is the difference between Kreuzgang's grudging accommodation to the disparities of life and the poet's refusal to continue living in face of such overwhelming odds. This difference is foreshadowed by Kreuzgang's earliest statements: he chides the poet affectionately, first discounting the empty idealism of his hymns and later cautioning him against an uncompromising stance toward life's failings. On both counts, he sees a kind of extremism doomed to defeat. To this highmindedness he opposes his own pragmatic response—the stentorian voice of criticism as a kind of strident "antipoeticum" and the cynic's laughter as antidote to otherwise unbearable conditions. Throughout his commentary on the poet's life, we sense that Kreuzgang is actually describing potential dangers which he himself has faced and overcome. His lead phrase, "Ich war einst deinesgleichen," turns many of his subsequent remarks into a kind of indirect self-analysis, with probable ramifications also for Bonaventura's efforts to measure his personal literary career. In this larger scheme, the poet's death presents itself as a figurative termination of two extremes—idealistic lyricism and self-consuming nihilism—as pivotal stations along the way toward the seasoned maturity of Bonaventura's present posture, represented through some sense of likeness by Kreuzgang. Elements of nihilism survive, as do moments of lyrical exaltation. But the life-threatening extremism of each is eliminated with the poet's symbolic suicide.

Many of the themes surrounding the poet's death appear also with the attempted suicide victim in NW IV-V: the rewriting of intensely personal anguish in the expressionless, cold movements of marionettes; the featured role of the farcical Hanswurst to enact the most serious of subjects, the prominence of suicide in both episodes—once as fact and once as a painful incapacity; and the conspicuous use of theater props such as the tragic dagger. And to leave no doubt as to the relatedness of the passages, two examples of verbal repetition further solidify the bond. As prelude to his tale of fraticide the speaker chooses Mozart: "Zuerst gibt es eine Mozartsche Symphonie von schlechten Dorfmusikanten exekutiert, das passt so recht zu einem verpfuschten Leben. . . . " Virtually the same phrasing appears in Kreuzgang's address to the poet: "Drollig bleibt es allerdings, dass du als eine Mozartsche Stimme in ein schlechtes Dorfkonzert mit eingelegt bist. . . . " Similarly, near identical wording is used to characterize the tragi-comic effect of the two lives. "Das alles [the brother rivalry] ist so sonderbar, dass man nicht weiss, ob man's ernsthaft oder lustig nehmen soll" and "ich weiss nicht ob ich deine [the poet's] Himmelsfahrt komisch oder ernsthaft nehmen soll."

Kreuzgang takes special pains to join this episode also to the framework of his biography, perhaps even exceeding the sense of kinship given his portrayal of the poet. Throughout his early description of the stranger, affectionate forms of address are common: "mein Mann," "Freund," "Kamerad." An exceptional involvement in the man's fate is shown by his hushed response to the gestures of suicide; he experiences a moment of intense dread almost as if the life in question were his own. The man's first entrance, furthermore, is marked by the cloak imagery, which Kreuzgang often uses to connect himself with several of the important figures he encounters: first appearing as "eine grosse männliche Gestalt in einen Mantel gehüllt," the intruder moves to the sepulchre and throws off his hood ("warf . . . den Mantel von sich") to reveal his true visage. To underscore these surface connections which Kreuzgang gives the setting of this tale, there are two additional framing devices which suggest with striking persuasiveness that Kreuzgang intended that the episode be placed in sequence with his own biography. When surprised by this intrusion, he had been occupied with the early chapters in his "Lebensbuch," presented as a series of woodcuts. In relating his own history, Kreuzgang's companion also chooses to recast his experiences in a kind of wood carving, using marionettes: "Ich finde es . . . recht wohl getan seine [i.e. his own] Geschichte in Holz zu schnitzen." In back of this verbal transition is their common desire to mask the true complexion of experience with stylized gesture and stiff facade. Kreuzgang's framing of this episode concludes in his retelling of the man's tale, with an introductory note which is almost identical to the preface he gave his own "Lebensbuch" one chapter earlier. In NW IV: "heute führte es mich auf meine eigene Geschichte, und ich blätterte, gleichsam aus Langerweile, mein Lebensbuch auf"; and in NW V: "ich musste den hellen prosaischen Tag . . . durchwachen und mich in dem bürgerlichen Leben . . . langweilen."

These many embellishments by which the episode is joined to Kreuzgang's biography draw the substance of the man's tale into close connection with the confessional impulses of the book. As was the case with the poet, the narrator once again leads us beyond the core of his own history, establishing well-marked tangents to other areas of experience. Although the literal facts of this tale lack the ring of a truthful representation, the underlying motives could well be tied, as Kreuzgang's framing of the tale would suggest, to emotional scars and personal sorrows from the author's past. Through such a reading, we find evidence of a rivalry between two brothers or friends who compete for the love of the same woman. Latent animosities are aroused and culminate in the irreparable break of friendship, shown figuratively by the murderous blow. And most importantly, we see the protagonist so utterly torn by remorse over his deed that he wishes only for a suicidal death which he cannot complete.

In both interpolations, images of theater and puppetry serve the speakers as means of expressing the deepest truths about their lives. With these secondary characters, such stock contrivances are not unexpected. But it is surprising that Kreuzgang should turn to the same devices in coming to grips with that segment in his life which has unquestionably the greatest emotional importance for him. Between his work as a political satirist (NW VII) and his time with the marionette troupe (NW XV), he is confined to a madhouse. Here he experiences the only love mentioned in his memoirs and witnesses the gruesome results of his brief desire to father a child. These are pivotal events in his biography, giving force to his cynical convictions. But the account he gives of this fruitless love is thickly disguised: he reduces the complexities of personality, sentiment and motive to the theatrical setting of Hamlet and Ophelia. Role and mask are taken up by both as they explore their attraction to each other. Their vows of love, their exchange of intimacies, and the consummation of their bond are confused by the reversal of identity and role, of truth and fiction. But the final sadness of their union rises up in horror to dwarf the play-like preliminaries of a theatrical love as Kreuzgang recoils from the stillborn child and the mad lament of the mother, herself on the verge of death. The brutal fact of this loss is in itself pathetic; but perhaps even more overpowering for Kreuzgang is his recollection of it, phrased now in narrative terms which concede that the entire episode was "played out" with real identities masked and with true feelings narrowed to fit contrived roles.

The essential issues of this passage—Kreuzgang's life-affirming love and the crushing effect of the deaths—lead us to the ultimate question debated by Bonaventura through the voice of his narrator: the value of the individual struggle in face of senseless circumstance. And as we turn now to consider his response, we begin to grasp the full scope of his refracted self-study, spread among several of the secondary figures whose lives Kreuzgang reports. To see the many sides of this difficult final question, it is necessary to go beyond the narrator's own biography and to weigh the related incidents which in one form or another illustrate the tenets he expounds.

In many of Kreuzgang's encounters, suicide looms as a major theme. His own nihilism comes close to justifying, even forcing upon him such a logical imperative. His bleak estimation of man's lot seems often to allow no other recourse but suicide. At several points he addresses this theme directly. The arguments he offers pro and con and the final verdict he reaches are crucial to an understanding of Bonaventura's own outlook.

In the icy wasteland of NW X, Kreuzgang faces this choice with a beggar in danger of freezing to death. Questioning whether he should awaken him and bring him to shelter, he weighs the crucial issue of life's value: "Beim Teufel ich weiss es ja nicht was besser ist—Sein oder Nichtsein!" In this instance he leans toward the latter, but with the twisted reasoning that society no longer merits this life which it has so rudely barred from its privileged circle: " . . . die Brüder haben den Joseph verstossen, und verschliessen tückisch die Gaben, die du [Mutter Natur] ihm, wie den andern Kindern reichst.—O die Brüder sind es nicht wert, dass Joseph unter ihnen wandle!—Er mag entschlummern." A much more serious denial of life's worth comes at the close of the Ophelia episode. Upon finding his child dead in the arms of its mother, Kreuzgang suppresses all feeling of remorse, viewing the death instead as welcome refutation of his earlier terror over the emptiness of eternity: " 'Gottlob, es gibt einen Tod, und dahinter liegt keine Ewigkeit!' Sprach ich unwillkürlich." But here, too, his initial response—prompted more by the extreme context of his dream than by his actual feelings—is altered in his later grief over his lover's death: "Ich stand stürmisch aufgereizt neben dem Lager und in mir machte es sich zornig Luft, wie zu einem wilden Gelächter—ich erschrak, denn es wurde kein Gelächter, sondern die erste Träne, die ich weinte." This heartfelt grief counterbalances his earlier self-reproach for wishing to propagate this flawed humankind, thus showing some measure of trust in the beauty of life. A similar kind of affirmation, though still somewhat askew, comes at the end of the episode with the suicidal brother (NW IV). Having heard the man's tale of guilt and shame, Kreuzgang considers inflicting the coup de grâce which the fellow is incapable of administering himself: "Hier endete der Mann,

und in mir stieg die heisse Sehnsucht auf, dem armen Schlaflosen das wohltätige Opium mit eigener Hand zu reichen, und ihm den langen süssen Schlaf, nach dem sein heisses überwachtes Auge vergeblich schmachtete, zuzuführen." Kreuzgang's many pronouncements of nihilism and his frequent unmaskings of illusionary rewards of life would suggest no reluctance to perform this "service." But he does hesitate, deciding surprisingly to preserve the chance that the fellow will regain his desire to live: "Doch fürchtete ich, dass in dem entscheidenden Augenblick sein Wahnsinn von ihm weichen könnte, und er, sterbend, das Leben, eben um der Vergänglichkeit willen, wieder liebgewinnen möchte."

The poet's death is to be viewed from several perspectives. At first Kreuzgang reacts in his predictable manner, rehearsing the absurdity of life and congratulating his friend for having summoned the courage to make his final exit. But later he shows genuine compassion for his death, as he discovers the drawing of a childhood scene which held the man's attention just as he died. His pose accentuates the power of this beauty in his past and his imperfect efforts to continue it through his art. Thus the scornful negativism of his drama, quoted at length by Kreuzgang, is somewhat muted by this passing moment of joy and his brief recollection of life's potential loveliness.

Two similar passages elsewhere in the book corroborate this theme. In Kreuzgang's account of his own childhood, he gives a glowing portrayal of his early learning and curiosities. He is enlivened by the mysteries of his world and responsive to its charms. The despondency and sarcasm of his later years seem far removed from this tranquility. Very much the same mood is evoked by the blind youth in NW XI. Although the world's visual beauty is closed to him at first, he is given access by Maria to a poetic and musical splendor unattainable by most. And his impassioned description of his first sunrise proclaims a sanguine world-view very much different from what we normally hear from Kreuzgang. It may be argued that Kreuzgang allows these moments of hope only to set off more severely his nihilism. But the accumulated strength of these related passages also has the opposite effect of establishing a counterbalance to his usual gloom and stridency. Added to his denial of suicide as a valid response to life's ills, it makes his nihilistic claims something less than total, allowing the possibility, at least, of a hopeful confidence in man's lot.

This balance of nihilism and hope is seen to best advantage in the final chapter. The somber graveyard setting is further darkened by Kreuzgang's speech on the worthlessness of the lives he sees commemorated around him. His cynicism peaks at his father's grave, where he praises the decay by which the follies of kings, philosophers and lovers are leveled to dust. In his closing act of defiance, he unclasps his father's hands, which had been folded in Christian penitence. With this symbolic denial of divine grace, the corpse crumbles to nothingness, giving rise to Kreuzgang's despairing cry with which the novel ends: the reverberant "Nichts!"

But to offset this gloom there is considerable buoyancy in Kreuzgang's earlier discovery of his parentage and of the diabolical influence of his life. The facts of this discovery are shattering to him—he labels them "gefährlich"—but the joy of coming to final knowledge about himself outweighs the disturbing truths he confronts. His mother reads from his palm all the stages of his life—presumably a recapitulation of the materials he has just finished documenting in his book. She then goes beyond his first recorded memory (the alchemist unearthing the "treasure box"), explaining how the devil's eye governed the moment of impregnation. His stunned response is marked by awe and delight: "Welch ein helles Licht nach dieser Rede in mir aufging, das können nur Psychologen vorstellen; der Schlüssel zu meinem Selbst war mir gereicht, und ich öffnete zum ersten Male mit Erstaunen und heimlichem Schauder die lang verschlossene Tür—."

As Sammons has noted [in *The Nachtwachen Von Bonaventura: A Structural Interpretation,* 1965], this moment of insight is more symbolic than real. This knowledge explains much to Kreuzgang about his sinister leanings and the eccentric course of his life. But it adds little of substance to what we have seen previously of his character and life history. Somehow the forcefulness of his response is not quite justified by the content of these revelations. But if we view the passage as a figurative statement, the terms of his discovery are indeed major, constituting the conclusive portion of the novel's biographical framework. Kreuzgang's cry of elation over this final "key" extends beyond this one discovery and refers to the completion of his life history made possible by this knowledge. To summarize the pivotal value of this passage: in the flow of the novel, this is the last piece of information given in the segmented biography of the narrator; but in the natural chronology of his life, it stands first, coming just before the series of woodcuts described in NW IV. This final chapter thus has the unifying effect of closing the circle of background circumstance which serves as basis for Kreuzgang's self-portrayal.

The deliberateness of this structure, together with the genuine sense of discovery and self-cognition which Bonaventura causes his narrator to express, raises the issue of an analogue between what Kreuzgang attains through this "finishing" of his tale and what Bonaventura has now accomplished in his completion of the novel. We have found that much of what Kreuzgang presented as personal depiction served as scaffolding for a greatly more elaborate portrayal spread across many of the secondary figures of the book. The contours of this larger canvas, we supposed, refer in some hidden and subtle way to aspects of Bonaventura's life. We must also suppose that Kreuzgang's words of delight over seeing his life history complete are prompted by some comparable sense of achievement by our author. With his book now finished, he has successfully laid out the harsh terms of his scornful world view. He has vented his rage against numerous targets, some specific to his literary world and others drawn from the general social realm. Most importantly—if Kreuzgang's example is an accurate guide—he has grappled with the mass of his private experience and worked toward a fictional rendering of his origins, his growth, and his present posture in life. And he has done so in a finely nuanced style that safeguards the privacy of this inner world. Through his narrator's voice he made clear his intent to try the difficult art

of self-portrayal and stipulated the boundaries to be observed in depictions of personal truths. He now speaks his satisfaction with both undertakings, again with Kreuzgang's words as his vehicle. (pp. 282-95)

Ellis Finger, "Bonaventura Through Kreuzgang: 'Nachtwachen' as Autobiography," in The German Quarterly, *Vol. LIV, No. 3, May, 1980, pp. 282-97.*

Rado Pribić   (essay date 1984)

[*In the following essay, Pribić explores the causes and effects of Kreuzgang's feelings of alienation.*]

Alienation which is a condition of being an outsider in a state of isolation and estrangement can be found in many characters of world literature. Friedrich Schiller in 1793 for the first time delineated the concept of alienation and dehumanization in his twenty-seven *Briefe über die aesthetische Erziehung des Menschen,* and Hegel's *Phänomenologie des Geistes* (1807) presented the first exhaustive and systematic treatment of this universal predicament of man and prepared the ground for both Marx and twentieth-century Existentialism.

So far, scholars and thinkers agree that the alienation has inward and outward sources and agents, and expresses itself in various ways. It emerges from man's awareness of being different and terminates in conscious separation from someone or something with whom or with which one should be united.

One of the best and earliest examples of an alienated protagonist in all of world literature is Kreuzgang the hero of the German Romantic novel **Nachtwachen** by Bonaventura. **Nachtwachen** appeared in 1804 in the rather obscure periodical *Journal von neuen Deutschen Original Romanen* which was edited by the small publishing house F. Dienemann und Comp. in the little known Saxon town of Penig.

In spite of vague origins, the nihilistic concept in the novel began to fascinate literary critics. Beginning with Fritz Strich and Hermann August Körff, who first underscored the nihilistic-pessimistic aspect of early German Romanticism, Bonaventura's **Nachtwachen** has been time and again quoted as the gloomiest and most blatant example of nineteenth-century nihilism.

In sixteen night-watches, Kreuzgang, the watchman, ponders over his enigmatic ambivalent personality. He comments on various events he either witnessed or learned about from others—referring to social, moral, ethical, and aesthetic problems, and he indulges in metaphysical quests. But all he detects on both the rational and irrational levels is chaos, decay, meaninglessness, and emptiness.

Kreuzgang believes that there is nothing lofty and sublime in man's nature and endeavors, rather, he takes the position that men are immoral, deceitful, vain, and vicious. The entire history of humanity, according to Kreuzgang, is nothing but "a silly novel in which there are a few sorry characters and a great number of wretched ones."

Bonaventura's watchman calls his era a "heartless time,"

a "vacillating era" in which everything is leveled and in a state of confusion. He gives the following description of the general dilemma:

> In einem schwankenden Zeitalter scheut man alles Absolute und Selbständige; deshalb mögen wir denn auch weder ächten Spaß, noch ächten Ernst, weder ächte Jugend noch ächte Bosheit mehr leiden. Der Zeitkarakter ist zusammengeflikt und gestoppelt wie eine Narrenjakke, und was das Ärgste dabei ist—der Narr, der darin stekt, mögte ernsthaft scheinen.

Looking at the sources of Kreuzgang's alienation, one can find them in four major areas: 1) in the transitional historical period in which Kreuzgang lived, 2) in Kreuzgang's lack of family ties, 3) in the protagonist's intellect, and 4) in the mass-oriented and dehumanizing environment of a large city.

Let us now take a brief look at these sources. First, Kreuzgang lives at the turn of the eighteenth to nineteenth-century. It is a period of changes, of insecurity, of popular revolutions, and of the Napoleonic wars. The French Revolution of 1789 did not nearly satisfy man's hopes and expectations. Referring to this event Kreuzgang criticizes the monstrous bloodshed which plunged the Republic into despotism and diluted the concept of brotherhood. He calls the Revolution "die große Tragikomödie, in der ein König unglücklich debütirte und der Hanswurst, als Freiheit und Gleichheit lustig Menschenköpfe, statt der Schellen schüttelte."

Instead of leading man toward the ideal state of liberty, equality, and fraternity, the Revolution unleashed man's cruelty, viciousness, his desire for power, and revealed an alarming lack of mutual understanding. It created a "frivolous period" with no absolute or autonomous values.

The next source of estrangement can be found in the lack of family ties. Kreuzgang grew up as an outsider; he never married and never had children of his own. As a substitute for missing human contact and love he used the brothel.

Kreuzgang was brought up by a pious shoemaker-poet who, while digging for a treasure, found the infant in a casket. To be sure, Kreuzgang's relationship to his foster father is not disagreeable, yet the shoemaker contributed little to shape the boy's personality and did not secure his position in society. Musing about his mysterious descent and his strange character, which became a source of permanent disturbances, the protagonist finally drew the whimsical conclusion that the devil himself had fathered him with a recently canonized saint.

Kreuzgang's own predicament is best conveyed by the epigone's complaint in the twelfth night-watch:

> . . . was soll ein Mensch, der nicht schon im Mutterleibe eine Krone auf dem Haupte trägt, oder mindestens, wenn er aus dem Eie gekrochen, an den Äesten eines Stammbaums das Klettern lernen kann, in dieser Welt anfangen, wenn er weiter nichts mitbringt als sein naoktos Ioh und gesunde Glieder.

The third source of Kreuzgang's alienation is his acute intellect. From the shoemaker's diary one learns about

Kreuzgang's urge to discover the phenomena of the objective world and to strive for an answer to questions which lie beyond knowledge and proof. The universities, which Kreuzgang apparently attended in order to achieve this goal, did not satisfy his craving; for in his letter to his love Ophelia he complains about "fingierten Wahnsinn" and "metaphysische Spitzfündigkeiten" which he brought back from there.

Kreuzgang is very much aware that intellect is responsible for his overly critical attitude as well as his unwillingness to make a commitment, which entails a lack of communication. In a mental asylum a physician diagnoses Kreuzgang's condition as an "exaggerated intellectual debauchery" and prescribes "little or no thinking at all."

The last major source of alienation is the dwelling in a large city. Not only does the city disrupt man's contact with nature, it also corrupts his morale, creates social discrepancies and turns old values upside down. But most of all, it makes man indifferent and destroys true human feelings. Strolling through the sleeping town, the shuddering Kreuzgang listens to his lonely footsteps; he feels like a prince in an enchanted city where an evil power had transformed every living being into stone. Eventually, he finds refuge in graveyards, old churches and monasteries.

The alienation which emerges from the above-mentioned sources affects the protagonist's personality as well as his relation to his fellow man and his society. In this author's mind, the most striking manifestation of alienation is the protagonist's self-alienation, i.e. his awareness of the disparity between his precise nature and its realization under given circumstances.

Kreuzgang observes various incompatibilities of his character and a strong tendency to perceive everything from two different aspects. He considers himself more rational than reason itself, yet, at the same time, he declares everything rational as absurd. He prays in the brothel and laughs in the church; he weeps while watching comedies and cannot refrain from malicious thoughts when reading solemn works; he regards life as an exile between birth and death and writes, on the other hand, an apology for life; he feels free and sound as long as he hates, and turns into a sick slave because he loves. Kreuzgang's self-alienation reaches such a degree that he no longer discerns whether he or his fellow man is topsy-turvy.

Kreuzgang comments:

> Dieser verdammte Widerspruch in mir geht so weit, daß z.B. der Papst selbst beim Beten nicht andächtiger sein kann, als ich beim blasphemiren, da ich hingegen wenn ich recht gute erbauliche Werke durchlese, mich der boshaftesten Gedanken dabei durchaus nicht erwehren kann.

Finally, he compares himself with a "widersinnig gestimmten Seitenspiele, auf dem daher niemals in einer reinen Tonart gespielt werden kann."

The feeling of otherness brings along another type of alienation, namely the separation from his fellow man. Kreuzgang gradually detects that he is surrounded by people who are stupid and vain, have no inventiveness and resemble one another like a flock of sheep. These people reject everyone who differs from their model and do not hesitate to pronounce their fellow man insane, when he attempts to express his own ideas. Man's mind pivots upon clothing, positions, success, and material gains, but disregards man himself.

Kreuzgang concludes that men are absolutely incompetent. Their heads are everything but the shrine of mind and wit. They are "in doppelter Hinsicht nur Surrogate von Köpfen anzusehen, und stehen da oben nur gleichsam wie die Knöpfe auf Thürmen, zum bloßen Schlusse der Gestalt."

Kreuzgang sees man as an absolute failure, "ein satirischer Beitrag zu den Fehlgriffen des Genies." Man's life is like "eine mozartsche Symphonie von schlechten Dorfmusikanten exekutirt," and man is not only a poor player, but he is the least talented one.

According to Kreuzgang, beside stupidity man's most conspicuous traits are immorality and viciousness. Man does filthy things, wallows in mud and corrupts others, but he is not ashamed of it. He has no compunction to humiliate, hurt, and bully his fellow man, and he always looks down upon others, uses them as doormats, or considers them houseflies. Civilization has not made man better, it only created a greater variety of sensation and taught him how to slaughter on a larger scale. Man's viciousness has almost no limitations. It begins with the cruelty of parents to children. In the eleventh night-watch Kreuzgang, who himself was abandoned by his mother, tells the story of a blind boy whose mother dedicated a parentless waif to heaven, making her son unhappy and causing the death of the girl.

However, man reveals an admirable versatility to camouflage his true character; Kreuzgang sees man as a hypocrite. Man pretends to be honest and just, but is a rogue at the bottom of his heart. He displays a broad outlook and speaks about ideals, yet he would not raise his little finger to achieve these ideals.

The protagonist's negative reaction to the experiences with people may be traced back to his childhood. The highly susceptible Kreuzgang often embarrassed his foster father with sophisticated questions that the simple man was unable to answer. The shoemaker's apprentices teased the boy because he was different and did not fit into their pattern. This created the first gulf between Kreuzgang and his fellow man. Kreuzgang's later career became a train of failures, for people continued to misunderstand him. His birthday oration was interpreted as a funeral speech and his whimsical satire on a donkey was perceived as a personal insult by a high official. His criticism of jurisprudence, his reference to the discrepancy between law and morality and his call for observance of the spirit of the law were declared by the judges as utterances of a madman.

Kreuzgang is so disgusted with people's wickedness and wretchedness that, for a short time, he even plays Hamlet out of rage over mankind. He finally draws the conclusion that God should destroy men and surrender them to oblivion, for neither heaven nor hell will accept them; for hell they are too evil, for heaven too boring.

In *Nachtwachen* alienation from men is also accompanied by alienation from society. Kreuzgang observes many elements in the society of which he disapproves. The society enslaves men. It does not tolerate bold actions and ideas nor does it permit deviations from the established norms. For society fears that "Menschen dieses Schlages, wenn sie emporkämen, würden feindseelig sich äussern, und als eine Pest, ein Erdbeben oder Gewitter unter das Volk fahren, und ein gutes Stück von dem Planten aufreiben und zu Pulver verbrennen."

If man dares to point out the cracks in the fabric of society, if he tries to manifest his own will, society will throw mountains over him under which he can only shake himself in fury, without harming the social structure. Such a mountain is, for instance, the madhouse where society herds those whose ideas do not harmonize with its fundamentals. Society prefers good machines to bold spirits; it values hands and feet higher than heads, for the state has need only of one single head, but of a hundred arms.

The above-discussed sources and manifestations of alienation suggest that the author, hiding behind the pseudonym Bonaventura, perceived elements of alienation as a central feature of human nature. At the root of all alienation there is uprootedness, intellectual curiosity, man's heightened consciousness, and the unrest of freedom. As long as man perceives his inner and outer world as a harmonious unity and identifies himself with his age and environment, alienation remains a dormant agent. Yet, as soon as the unity grows weak as a result of negative perceptions and experiences, man begins to rebel against his environment and indulges in painful self-analysis. Eventually he will exaggerate his individualism and trigger the feeling of otherness, loneliness, frustration and powerlessness, i.e. activate the inherent propensity to alienation.

No matter how hard Kreuzgang tries to reconcile individual freedom with life in the community, the norms of society force him into isolation. At the end, Kreuzgang's inner alienation from society is absolute. In order to survive, however, he makes concessions and accepts the job of a night watchman which is far below his intellectual capacities. He turns into a passive spectator who refuses to assume responsibility for the events around him. (pp. 21-8)

> *Rado Pribić, "Kreuzgang: The Alienated Hero of the 'Nachtwachen',"* in Acta Germanica, *Vol. 17, 1984, pp. 21-8.*

Thomas F. Barry   (essay date 1986)

[*In the following essay, Barry compares the nihilism of* The Night Watches *to philosophic currents in early nineteenth-century Germany.*]

The Nightwatches was issued as No. 7 of the third year of the obscure *Journal von neuen deutschen Romanen* edited by the small publishing house of F. Dienemann in the town of Penig, Saxony, a firm which specialized in the minor works of German Romantic authors. The title page of the journal reads 1804, whereas the title page of the novel itself indicates the year 1805. It was signed with the popular Romantic pseudonym of Bonaventura. The secondary literature has been concerned for the most part with the attempt to establish the true identity of the author. If we accept the rather convincing evidence presented by Jost Schillemeit in his 1973 book, *Bonaventura. Der Verfasser der Nachtwachen,* the writer is August Klingemann (1777-1831), a lesser known poet, dramatist, and theater director, and not Schelling, Hoffmann, Jean Paul, or any of the other more famous German Romantics to whom scholars have attributed authorship. The text consists of the 16 nightly rounds of the narrator Kreuzgang during which he relates the events of his life that have led him to his solitary, nocturnal wanderings. It is a highly ironic work which takes pointed satiric jabs at individual and societal hypocrisy, the excesses of German Idealist philosophies, and the pretensions of classical-romantic art. As Jeffrey Sammons suggests [in *The Nachtwachen Von Bonaventura: A Structural Interpretation,* 1965], however, the nightwatchman's narrative moves through several cycles from satire, through profound feelings of despair, and finally to a devastating, nihilistic vision of human existence. Kreuzgang's observations present, as Dorothee Sölle-Nipperdey points out, a progressive unmasking of illusions that reveals a cosmos devoid of meaning and purpose. *The Nightwatches* exposes the Leibnizian-Enlightenment view of a universe which is in a divinely-inspired harmony and is "the best of all possible worlds" to disclose an essentially Romantic, Schopenhauerian creation which is mindless and irrational. It represents a view which is—with its image of an absurd cosmos—far ahead of its time, as Gerald Gillespie suggests [in "Bonaventura's Romantic Agony: Prevision of an Art of Existential Despair," *Modern Language Notes* 85 (1970)], existential in its theme and import. Whoever the author may have been, he/she was in sensibility a kind of eighteenth-century Samuel Beckett, achieving a similar blend of ironic humor and desperate nihilism. Quite different from the nature idealization or nostalgic melancholy of his/her English or French Romantic counterparts, the author of *The Nightwatches* presents an insane vision of the universe in which traditional notions of the relationship between self and world are dissolved. In the following discussion, I would like to examine the issue of Kreuzgang's madness and his loss of an existential orientation to reality with particular regard to the roots of his crisis in the philosophical idealism of Johann Gottlieb Fichte (1762-1814) and the pessimistic philosophy of Arthur Schopenhauer (1788-1860).

Born to a gypsy mother and an alchemist/necromancer father at (as his name suggests) a crossroads—the traditional burial place for suicides—Kreuzgang seems fated to suffer the lot of the insane and the displaced. He is burdened with a hyperintellect and it is this acute consciousness that leads to his madness and alienation. There are, however, two aspects to this insanity: the feigned "madness" of the clown/fool and the true madness of the individual who has genuinely lost contact with reality. At the end of the seventh nightwatch, Kreuzgang is sentenced by a court to confinement in a mental asylum for the "crime" of having heralded the Last Judgment during his nightly rounds and having disturbed the rest as well as the consciences of the

sleeping townfolk: ". . . I was to be numbered among the *mente captis* and my offense had to be considered as the result of a partial insanity, for which reason they would have to deliver me over to the madhouse without further ado." His offense here is typical of the unmasking of the individual and societal hypocrisy he sees around him, an example of the satirical thrust which pervades much of the novel. As a result of his trumpeting of the divine Final Summons, the order of society is disrupted and the mask which hides its corruptness is torn away:

> Oh, how can I describe how before me on the stage the people ran into one another and in confusion and in their fear prayed and cursed and moaned and howled; and how the disguise fell from the countenance of every mask on this great ball collapsed by the trumpet's summons. . . .

This satiric gesture of unmasking informs many of the novel's episodes as in the first sections when he witnesses the attempt by several priests in devil's masks to steal the corpse of an unrepentent freethinker, thus revealing the hypocrisy of the church. In the third nightwatch he exposes the deceit of an adulterous couple who mask their lust with romantic clichés: "The man was quite absorbed in rhetorical bombast and spoke in one breath of love and troth; the woman figure, in contrast, credulously doubted and managed a lot of artificial handwringing." Such incidents reveal Kreuzgang to be "mad" in the sense that he adopts the role of a clown or fool figure. Indeed, he is labeled as such for his calling of the pseudo-Last Judgment: ". . . and I was regarded out of the highest mercy only as a fool. . . . " When he works with a marionnette troupe later on, he claims that his chief specialty is that of the clown. His madness must be considered here to be double-edged, much in the manner that say Erasmus's fool figure, for example, is presented in his *In Praise of Folly,* that is, Kreuzgang's insanity is eminently sane in that his bizarre actions reveal the unacknowledged madness of those about him. The nightwatchman's behavior as foolishness/clownishness allows him the pose of innocence which informs his social criticism. Clown and fool images—the Hanswurst figure, the wooden-headed marionnettes, or the Columbine character from the *commedia del arte* tradition—predominate in *The Nightwatches* and serve as the vehicle for its ironic humor. More importantly, however, the mocking laughter of Kreuzgang's ironic poses affords him a measure of emotional distance, an antidote, as we shall see, to the insights into existence which threaten him with genuine insanity.

As the nightwatchman himself points out on several occasions, the satiric laughter of the fool can easily and quickly shift into the demonic, hysterical laughter of the truly insane: "I was, however, suddenly touched in my good mood, the way a violently laughing man finally breaks into tears. . . . " Laughter is his mode of relating to the world yet it is a fragile defense which borders on the tears of the desperate: "Nothing really beats laughing, and I value it almost as highly as other refined people do crying, although a tear can easily be coaxed to light . . . even by vehemently persistent laughing alone." For Kreuzgang, crying is an emotional release which signals defeat and despair and this collapse of the defenses of the self is an experience which he seeks to avoid at all costs. He actually sheds genuine tears only on two occasions in the novel: once when Ophelia, his love with whom he acts in *Hamlet* when in the madhouse, dies during childbirth, and once when his beloved Hanswurst marionnette is confiscated by the authorities for being politically subversive. The nightwatchman's laughter as a gesture of emotional distance generates a defensive gap between his thoughts and feelings and thus protects him from the horrible vision of the universe which his over-acute intellect yields him. The mocking laughter of the clown/fool is aggressive and aimed at exposing the falsity of others, that is, at a world which is out of balance and in which the self is stable. The passive tears of the madman are the expression of a world in which the self is profoundly dislocated. Both are present in the character of Kreuzgang and the borderline between the two is a thin one. As Sammons suggests in his study of the narrative structure of *The Nightwatches,* the cycles of satire-despair-nihilism become more bleak in the course of the text, the satire and comedy giving way to a perception of reality so dark that the distinction between the nightwatchman's laughter and crying becomes a very fine one at best.

The author of *The Nightwatches* had clearly assimilated the nihilistic implications present in the philosophical idealism of Kant-Fichte-Schopenhauer, especially the latter two. As a result of Kant's so-called "Copernican revolution" in epistemology, the "reality" we perceive becomes a subjective phenomenon, the product of human categories of perception and cognition. There is still an absolute reality—the noumenal "thing-in-itself"—but it remains unknowable in human terms. Such notions as absolute value, truth, or even the existence of a divinity must be bracketed; the "reality" we know may be predictable but it is relative and intersubjective. Absolute reality, although unknowable, continues, however, as an essentially stable or static entity; it is still assumed and constitutes the other to which the self can relate. In the Fichtean critique of the Kantian system, the "thing-in-itself" as objective entity is held to be an unwarranted assumption. The absolute ego posits—on a level prior to the consciousness of the individual's empirical ego—a non-ego as a necessary precondition for self-consciousness. In other words, so that it may come to know itself, the absolute ego generates the other, the non-ego. The static and dualistic Kantian universe becomes in Fichte monistic; "reality" is dynamic mental process, the product of the continuous positing of the non-ego by the absolute ego. Kant's noumenon, which provided in absolute terms a stable reference point for the self, is dissolved and consciousness is left alone with itself, engaged in an ongoing act of creation. The alienation of the self from reality present in Kant's idealism is intensified in the Fichtean system; consciousness is now profoundly disoriented, deprived of any reference point. This notion—consciousness cast adrift in a sea of nothingness—is the lesson the author of *The Nightwatches* learned from Kant and Fichte and it is the experience of this nothingness which seems to drive Kreuzgang to the edge of madness.

Kreuzgang mentions Fichte by name once during his stay in the mental asylum when he comments on a speech given by one of the other patients who fancies himself the (insane) creator of the universe:

> It is almost dangerous for us other fools to tolerate this titan among us, for he has his consistent system just as well as Fichte and basically has an even smaller opinion of man than the latter, who sunders him from heaven and hell, but in compensation compresses everything classic round about into the little I (which any tiny boy can cry out), as into a pocket format.

The other implicit references to the Fichtean system are not so ironically humorous. In a letter to his love Ophelia—who can no longer distinguish between her role and her real self—he alludes to the Kantian-Fichtean school and claims that this time (as opposed to his fool or clown role) his madness is truly real:

> But do not let yourself be deceived by this, idol, for this time I am really mad—so very much does all reside in ourselves and outside of us there is nothing real; indeed, according to the newest school we do not know whether we are in fact standing on our feet or on our heads, except that we have assumed the first by ourselves on trust and faith.

In another letter, his allusions become more grim:

> I had now ceased thinking everything else and was only thinking myself! No object was to be found round about but the great dreadful I which feasted on itself and in devouring constantly regenerated itself. I was not sinking, for there was no longer space; just as little did I seem to float upward. Variety had disappeared simultaneously with time, and there reigned a horrible, eternally void tedium. Beyond myself, I tried to annihilate myself—but I remained and felt myself immortal!

The allusion Kreuzgang makes is clearly to Fichte's absolute ego and its constant mental dynamism. With the loss of any objective other to which the self can relate, a "thing-in-itself," consciousness becomes dislocated, thrown into an endless void of nothingness. In the 10th nightwatch—when Kreuzgang witnesses the burial alive of an Ursuline nun who has given birth to a child—there is an almost lyrical, yet chilling interlude ("Run through the musical Scale") in which existence is described as a disorienting dance of masks. All reality is dissolved and even the individual's sense of identity is exposed as a mere chimera, an illusion of an illusion:

> Does no I stand in the mirror, when I step before it—am I only the thought of a thought, the dream of a dream—can you not help me find my body, and will you always be shaking your bells when I think they are mine? Hoo! It is indeed terribly lonely in the ego, when I clasp you tight, you masks, and I try to look at myself—everything echoing sound with the disappeared note—nowhere substance, and yet I see—that must be the Nothing that I see!—Away, away from the I—only dance on, you masks!

Both in spirit and in tone, this and the other passages in

The Nightwatches which examine the implications of Fichtean thought for an understanding of the individual self, echo the thoughts and sentiments expressed in Fichte's own *The Vocation of Man* of 1800. It is one of his so-called popular writings—addressed to the general educated public—in which he presents the idealist philosophy that he had explicated in his *Theory of Science* of 1794 for the professional philosopher. The second section of this text is entitled "Knowledge" and is presented in the form of a dialogue between "Spirit"—representing Fichte's position—and the "I"—who is intended to voice the responses of the popular reader. In one of the summaries of what it has learned from the "Spirit," the "I" expresses the essence of the Fichtean critique of the Kantian system with its assumption of a noumenal world:

> All attempts to conceive of an absolute connection between things *in themselves,* and the *I in itself* are but attempts to ignore our own thought,—a strange forgetfulness of the undeniable fact that we can have no thought without having thought it. A thing *in itself* is a thought. . . .

Fichte contends that Kant's noumenon is itself a projection of the human faculty of understanding just as Kant himself had claimed of phenomenal "reality." What remains is pure thought, consciousness, the ceaseless mental activity of the absolute ego. As the "I" of the dialogue again summarizes, it has learned its lesson well, the same lesson that Kreuzgang has also assimilated:

> . . . by all that thou has hitherto said, there is nothing, absolutely nothing but presentations,—modes of consciousness, and of consciousness only. But a presentation is to me only the picture, the shadow, of a reality; in itself it cannot satisfy me, and has not the smallest worth.

Consciousness is here cast adrift into nothingness; reality is reduced to dynamic process, a dance of masks, illusions, pictures. The "I" of Fichte's text reacts in much the same manner as Bonaventura's Kreuzgang, with almost the same images as occur in the "Run through the musical Scale" passage cited earlier:

> There is nothing enduring, either out of me, or in me, but only ceaseless change. I know of no being, not even my own. There is no being. I myself absolutely know not, and am not. Pictures are:—they are the only things which exist, and they know of themselves after the fashion of pictures: pictures which float past without there being anything past which they float; which by means of like pictures, are connected with each other: pictures without anything which is pictured in them, without significance and without aim. I myself am one of these pictures; nay, I am not even this, but merely a confused picture of the pictures. All reality is transformed into a strange dream, without a life which is dreamed of, and without a mind which dreams it; into a dream which is woven together in a dream of itself

Fichte's text approaches here what could easily be read as the major teachings of Eastern philosophy; the speech of the "I" resembles passages from the Hindu *Upanishads* or the lessons of a Zen Buddhist master; the perceived world is *māyā*, illusion, including the sense of an individual identity. This parallel to Eastern thought is not mere coincidence. The German Romantics were the first to write grammars of Sanskrit and to begin translations of major Hindu and Buddhist texts. Schopenhauer, as we shall see, was profoundly influenced by Eastern religions and incorporated certain ideas into his own philosophy. In Eastern cultures, where familial identification often precedes individual identity, the ego is a liability, a myth which promotes only suffering. Western cultures, on the other hand, are characterized (as Spengler suggested) by the Faustian striving of the individual and thus the "I" of Fichte's dialogue experiences a sense of loss and despair. The alienation of consciousness from any traditional Western notion of "reality" or ego identity is clear in the above section of Fichte's text and it is this dislocation of the self which brings or nearly brings Kreuzgang to the point of true insanity, as he suggests in another of his letters to the doomed Ophelia:

> Do not ponder over things so deeply, my dear, for they are of such intricate nature that they could easily lead you to the madhouse! It is all role, the role itself and the play actor who is behind it, and in him in turn his thoughts and plans and enthusiasms and buffooneries—all belongs to the moment and swiftly flees, like the word on the comedian's lips.—All is even but theatre. . . .

The motif patterns in *The Nightwatches,* such as the above allusion to the *theatrum mundi* metaphor, all suggest this Fichtean vision of a consciousness dislocated from any notion of a stable universe of substance and meaning. Kreuzgang's playing of Hamlet to his love's Ophelia in the madhouse or the frequent motif of the mask indicate an interpretation of existence in which all distinctions between fact and fiction, actor and role, cannot be separated; all concepts of reality that could provide a sense of orientation for the self dissolve into a phantasmagoria of images that, in Western terms, are symptomatic of psychotic disorientation. There are other motif patterns which suggest a severely disturbed sense of self. The pervasive marionnette/puppet images and the frequent allusions to human behavior as being mechanical symbolize on a philosophical level Fichte's thesis of the endless, mental activity of the absolute ego but on the level of the individual psyche, they imply a grossly distorted view of the self. Finally, there is another dominant motif pattern in the text—the images of dismemberment and mutilation—which suggest graphically (and literally) a consciousness that is dislocated.

Although *The Nightwatches* of Bonaventura predates Arthur Schopenhauer's 1818 *The World as Will and Idea,* it seems to prefigure the pessimistic manner in which this dour philosopher revised the Fichtean system. Schopenhauer's notion of the Will with its continual creation and destruction of the forms or images that make up the illusory "reality" we perceive represents an organic or biological version of Fichte's absolute ego with its constant mental dynamism. The Will continually gives birth to and devours itself in endless cycles in which each individual existence—as another of the illusory images or presentations—is without meaning. In *The Nightwatches* this process is reflected in the frequent use of the biological image of digestion and organic dissolution. We find such a Schopenhauerian vision of existence in the "Clown's Prologue to the Tragedy: Man" written by the tragic poet whom Kreuzgang meets on his nightly rounds:

> Everything is Nothing and vomits itself up and gulps itself greedily down, and even this self-devouring is an insidious sham, as if there were something whereas, if the choking were to cease, precisely the Nothing would quite plainly make its appearance and all would be terrorstruck before it; by this cessation, fools understand "eternity"; but it is the real Nothing and absolute death, since life on the contrary, only arises through a continual dying.

Such a view, as the text continues, could easily bring about a true insanity: "If one were ready to take the like consideration seriously, it could easily lead to the madhouse; but I take it merely as Clown. . . ." Again the distancing irony of the clown/fool serves as a buffer for this knowledge which later, in a philosopher like Nietzsche, would prompt the terrible wisdom of Silenus, the satyr follower of Dionysus: that it is best never to be born or to die as quickly as possible. Kreuzgang is, for the most part, successful in adopting this posture of the clown, at least until the final scene of the novel when he digs up his father's grave in an attempt to find his true heritage and finds—in true Schopenhauerian (and Shakespearean) fashion—the ultimate wisdom of the worm. In the following passage from his last nightwatch, he seems to combine the ideas of Fichte and Schopenhauer in a final vision of the futility of existence:

> Oh, what is the world if that which it thought is nothing, and everything in it only transitory fantasy! What are the fantasies of earth, spring and the flowers, if the fantasy in this little orb is scattered as dust, if here in the inner Pantheon all gods crash from their pedestals, and worms and decay take possession!

Schopenhauer's answer to this dilemma was the solution found in many Eastern religions: the quietistic withdrawal from the world, a denial of the desire which causes pain and suffering. By the end of *The Nightwatches,* Kreuzgang has renounced all that is human, all desire, love, and feeling, so that he may respond to the great nothingness of the universe with the mocking laughter of the clown/fool:

> Wimper no longer—these myriads of worlds roar through all their heavens only by the gigantic force of nature, and this terrifying spawner who has spawned everything and herself with it, has no heart in her own breast, but for a pastime only forms little ones which she passes around— cleave to these and love and coo so long as these hearts still hold together!—I refuse to love and will remain quite cold and frozen so as, if possible, to be able to laugh away when the giant's hand crushes me, too! . . .

Kreuzgang's laughter is ironic and seeks to generate emotional distance with respect to a universe which is perceived as being inhuman and absurd in its essence. As such it suggests a Schopenhauerian denial of desire and emotion, although its tone is clearly one of defiance in the face of defeat. This gesture of rebellion—as assertion of the self—is, of course, not at all consistent with the Buddhist notion of the denial of desire that Schopenhauer intended. It is an indication, however, of the extent to which Kreuzgang's stability of self is threatened by the terrible vision of existence that he perceives. Toward the end of the novel, the sense of despair and horror is at such a point of tension that the distinction between his foolish laughter and the desperate tears/laughter of the madman is a fine one indeed. Because the narrative of *The Nightwatches* is told as a series of flashbacks which lead up to the point at which the text begins, it is clear that the nightwatchman does not slip over into the disabling state of the permanently insane. The reader, however, comes to realize in the course of the text that Kreuzgang's ironic stance of the clown/fool is intimately related—as with the opposite sides of a coin—to the threat of genuine madness he experiences.

As Sammons has suggested, *The Nightwatches* is not a psychological novel in a strict sense. The text does not give the reader insight into childhood or other early environmental factors which might have produced the nightwatchman's bizarre personality. He is obviously well-read and the influences on his view of the world are philosophical and artistic. As a character, Kreuzgang is more of an abstract figure, a kind of intellectual Everyman, intended as an illustration of the consequences for the individual of the trends current in German Idealism. These consequences are not, however, depicted solely on an abstract, intellectual plane, but rather in terms of the emotional effect on the perspective of the character. This is a major reason why the novel transcends the boundaries of German Romanticism and points to the attitudes of modern existential writers and thinkers with the latter's radical insistence on the individual's intellectual *and* emotional response to the dilemma of human existence. The pessimism and nihilism present in the thought of Kant-Fichte-Schopenhauer engender an experience of consciousness as being profoundly dislocated in a universe which is absurd, indifferent to human suffering. The issue of the nightwatchman's madness, as we have seen, focuses precisely on this issue. Kreuzgang's madness as the ironic stance of the clown/fool is a gesture of defiance and defense in view of the threatening vision of existence expressed in the ideas of the above philosophers and to this extent the novel may be termed psychological. One might term *The Nightwatches* a prophetic portrait of the individual in the modern age. The close association of irony and madness in the character of the nightwatchman is predictive of similar tensions to be found in post-romantic authors, ranging from Thomas Mann to Samuel Beckett, John Barth, and Thomas Pynchon. (pp. 50-8)

Thomas F. Barry, "Madness and the Disoriented Self in Bonaventura's 'Nightwatches'," in The Journal of the Midwest Modern Language Association, *Vol. 19, No. 1, Spring, 1986, pp. 50-8.*

FURTHER READING

Blackall, Eric A. "A Visit to the Madhouse." In his *Novels of the German Romantics,* pp. 209-20. Ithaca N.Y.: Cornell University Press, 1983.

Describes *The Night Watches* as "a work of uncanny, disturbing, and profound poetry and significance, a collection of apocalyptic visions combined with gruesomely nihilistic reflections, serious and comic, moving and grotesquely absurdist at the same time."

Brough, Neil and Kavanagh, R. J. "Kreuzgang's Precursors: Some Notes on *The Nachtwachen des Bonaventura.*" *German Life and Letters* n.s. XXXIX, No. 2 (April 1986): 173-92.

Examines the use of the nightwatchman as a literary device.

Brzović, Kathy. "*Nachtwachen von Bonaventura:* A Critique of Order." *Monatshefte* 76, No. 4 (Winter 1984): 380-95.

Views Kreuzgang as a relatively unbiased observer of mainstream society.

——. *Bonaventura's "Nachtwachen": A Satirical Novel.* Studies in Modern German Literature, edited by D. G. Brown, Vol. 36. New York: Peter Lang, 1990, 159 p.

Interprets the novel as a satire "narrated from the standpoint of a persecuted, but unrepentant satirist." Brzović focuses on several episodes exemplifying Kreuzgang's reaction to German society.

Davies, Paul. "Why Mozart in the *Nachtwachen?*" *Forum for Modern Language Studies* XXIII, No. 3 (July 1987): 265-73.

Identifies several implicit and explicit references to Wolfgang Amadeus Mozart in the text of *The Night Watches,* maintaining that music is held in high regard by Kreuzgang.

——. "Bad Iambics and Assonance: A Note on the Puppet Play in Bonaventura's *Nachtwachen* and Friedrich Schlegel's *Alarcos.*" *Michigan Germanic Studies* XIV, No. 1 (Spring 1988): 30-4.

Suggests that the verse spoken during the puppet play in the fourth chapter of *The Night Watches* is meant as a satire upon the use of language in Schlegel's drama *Alarcos.*

——. "Musical Analogies and Their Contexts in Bonaventura's *Nachtwachen.*" *Orbis Litterarum* 45, No. 1 (1990): 71-83.

Cites references to music in the novel as "evidence of Bonaventura's tendency to think in terms of music."

Gillespie, Gerald. "Night-Piece and *Tail-Piece:* Bonaventura's Relation to Hogarth." *Arcadia* 8, No. 3 (1973): 284-95.

Examines the influence of the English painter and engraver William Hogarth on German culture, describing the final chapter of *The Night Watches* as a narrative rendition of Hogarth's etching *Tail-Piece.*

——. "Kreuzgang in the Role of Crispin: *Commedia dell'arte* Transformations in *Die Nachtwachen.*" In *Herkommen und Erneuerung: Essays for Oskar Seidlin,* edited by Gerald Gillespie and Edgar Lohner, pp. 185-200. Tübingen, Germany: Max Niemeyer Verlag, 1976.

Examines "the pattern of *commedia dell'arte* elements with which, among others, the book establishes the peculiar ambiance of its opening chapters."

Hunter, Rosemarie. "*Nachtwachen von Bonaventura* and *Tristram Shandy.*" *Canadian Review of Comparative Literature* 1, No. 3 (Autumn 1974): 218-34.

Contends that there are many formal similarities between the two novels, while their philosophical and social themes differ greatly.

Kavanagh, R. J. "Bonaventura Unmasked—Again?" *German Life and Letters* n.s. XL, no. 2 (January 1987): 97-116.

Recapitulates the theories that emerged during the 1980s regarding the identity of Bonaventura.

Neuswanger, Russell. "On Laughter in Bonaventura's *Nachtwachen.*" *German Life and Letters* n.s. XXX, No. 1 (October 1976): 15-24.

Relates instances of laughter to larger themes of death and despair in *The Night Watches.*

Pribić, Rado. *Bonaventura's "Nachtwachen" and Dostoevsky's "Notes from the Underground": A Comparison in Nihilism.* Munich, Germany: Verlag Otto Sanger, 1974, 155 p.

Observes similarities in narrative strategy and philosophical outlook in the novels.

Sammons, Jeffrey L. "In Search of Bonaventura: The *Nachtwachen* Riddle: 1965-1985." *The Germanic Review* LXI, No. 2 (Spring 1986): 50-6.

Examines the state of scholarship on *The Night Watches.* focusing on inquiries into its authorship.

Emily Brontë

Wuthering Heights

(Full name Emily Jane Brontë. Also wrote under the pseudonym Ellis Bell) English novelist and poet.

The following entry presents criticism of Brontë's novel *Wuthering Heights* (1847). For discussion of her complete career, see *NCLC,* Volume 16.

INTRODUCTION

Wuthering Heights is considered one of the most powerful and original works of Victorian literature. While Brontë incorporated into her work the horror and mystery of a Gothic novel, the remote setting and passionate characters of a Romantic novel, and the social criticism of a Victorian novel, she transformed these traditions, informing her work with what Derek Traversi described as her "intensely personal imaginative power." In this story of extraordinary love and revenge, Brontë demonstrated the conflict between elemental passions and civilized society, resulting in a compelling work that has attracted generations of readers and commentators alike.

Aside from brief stays at various boarding schools, both as pupil and teacher, Brontë lived most of her life in her father's secluded parsonage at Haworth in Yorkshire, the locale of *Wuthering Heights.* Her time away from home was generally lonely and unhappy; biographers indicate that she clearly preferred a reclusive lifestyle amidst the primitive beauty of the moors. As young children, she and her siblings Charlotte, Anne, and Branwell wrote stories and poems about the imaginary lands of Angria and Gondal. Emily continued writing poems about Gondal into her adult years, as well as writing a number of poems on various other subjects. The paucity of biographical information on Brontë has led biographers to speculate on the sources of *Wuthering Heights;* many observers have marvelled that such a reserved, introverted person could have created a work of such passion and imagination. Uncertain about the time frame in which *Wuthering Heights* was written, biographers suggest Brontë may have been developing her only novel for several years before its publication. Brontë, under the pseudonym Ellis Bell, published *Wuthering Heights* together with Anne's first novel, *Agnes Grey,* in 1847.

Wuthering Heights chronicles the effect of the orphan Heathcliff on his adoptive family, the Earnshaws of Wuthering Heights, and on the neighboring Linton family. Bringing the foundling home after a trip to Liverpool, Mr. Earnshaw announces that Heathcliff will be treated as a member of the family, causing jealousy on the part of his young son, Hindley. Earnshaw's daughter Catherine, however, finds in Heathcliff a best friend and kindred soul. The two characters are linked by a spiritual bond of pre-

ternatural strength as they grow up together in the midst of the raw beauty of the Yorkshire moors. Mr. Earnshaw's unexpected death marks the beginning of a cycle of conflict and turmoil at Wuthering Heights. Hindley, as the new head of the household, oppresses Heathcliff, relegating him to the role of servant. Catherine eventually befriends the neighboring Linton family of Thrushcross Grange and soon becomes enchanted with their wealth and sophistication. In spite of her bond with Heathcliff, she chooses to marry Edgar Linton, whose refinement and delicate physical beauty stand in stark contrast to the degraded, unkempt Heathcliff, whom Catherine describes as "an arid wilderness of furze and whinstone." Critics concur that, by marrying Edgar, Catherine betrays herself as well as Heathcliff, creating an emotional unrest which prevents her from finding contentment as Edgar's wife. When Catherine and Heathcliff attempt to resume their friendship after the wedding, Edgar's jealous response leads to a violent confrontation between the two men. This confrontation sends Catherine into a delirious rage, which is followed by a severe illness and eventually death. Despairing over the loss of Catherine, and embittered by Hindley's oppression of him, Heathcliff resolves to seek revenge on both the Lintons and the Earnshaws. He ultimately gains legal control of both Wuthering Heights and Thrushcross Grange, but in the end he loses his will to force both families into subservience. He dies after twenty years of unrelieved grieving for Catherine, confident that he will be reunited with her after death. Despite Heathcliff's determined efforts to inflict misery on the Earnshaws and the Lintons, the novel ends with a sense of hope and resolution in the promise of marriage between Catherine's daughter, Cathy Linton, and Hindley's son, Hareton Earnshaw, the last descendant of the Earnshaw family.

While acknowledging the force and originality of *Wuthering Heights,* contemporary critics reacted to the novel with shock and distaste. Many early reviewers assumed that Ellis Bell was a man and praised the author's courage in depicting such desolation and anguish; but when it was determined that Bell was a woman, James H. Kavanaugh asserts, "critical attitudes tended to change from camaraderie to condescension. The writer was chided for her lack of mature feminine discretion." Commentators objected to the depiction of unrelenting cruelty, and several reviewers even insisted that the novel, with its portrayal of brutality and insightful depiction of a male character, could not have been written by a woman, and that it must have been the work of Emily's brother, Branwell. Charlotte Brontë defended her sister in her preface to the 1850 edition of *Wuthering Heights,* arguing that the rough language and manners portrayed in the work were realistic. At the same time, however, she apologized for the dark vision of life presented in the book, also noting Emily's reclusive lifestyle as evidence of her eccentric worldview. These remarks on Brontë's isolation, combined with much commentary that focused on the spiritual and supernatural overtones of her novel, established an image of the writer as a solitary mystic.

Commentators observe that Brontë achieved the extraordinary intensity of her novel by combining fierce animal imagery, depictions of raw violence, supernatural elements, and the vivid and powerful characterizations of Catherine and Heathcliff. Dream motifs figure prominently in *Wuthering Heights* as well, and critics also stress the importance of windows as symbolic vehicles of spiritual entrance and escape in the novel. Technically, Brontë's work is noted for two prominent attributes: a highly schematized structure that is reflected in the symmetrical pedigrees of the Earnshaws and the Lintons, and a narrative method featuring dual narrators and an intricate arrangement of narratives-within-narratives. Lockwood, a temporary tenant of Thrushcross Grange, relates the story to the reader after hearing it from household employee Nelly Dean, who in turn has heard much of the story from other characters in the novel. Critics note Brontë's suggestion of bias in every narrator; Nelly's account, for example, is influenced both by her conventional morality and by personal motives, and she is openly unsympathetic to the novel's chief protagonists, Catherine and Heathcliff. Some commentators suggest that Nelly represents the author's sentiments, while others argue that Brontë identified with Catherine and Heathcliff and intended Nelly as a villainous character. Lockwood is also a problematic narrator; his understanding of the people of Wuthering Heights is superficial and his interpretations of their actions are often incorrect. The complexity of Brontë's narrative method and the ambiguity of her intent have engendered widespread critical debate since the novel's publication.

Many scholarly discussions of *Wuthering Heights* center on its oppositions, for example, the pitting of the civilized and refined values of Thrushcross Grange against the primitive and natural values of Wuthering Heights. Thus, Heathcliff is often interpreted as a representative of natural man or pure passion whose ideological foil in the story is Edgar Linton; by choosing Edgar over Heathcliff, then, Catherine is frequently understood to be embracing civilized values and rejecting natural ideals. Readings featuring the dialectic between spiritual and material, as well as between a number of economic and social systems operative in the novel, also proliferate, creating a variety of interpretations that underscores both the profundity and the thematic ambiguity of Brontë's work. Some commentators attribute the ambiguous quality of *Wuthering Heights* to Brontë's own ambivalence toward her subject, maintaining, for example, that it is not possible to ascertain whether the novel's conclusion is meant to affirm the values associated with Wuthering Heights or those linked with Thrushcross Grange. Thomas Vogler, representing one current trend in Brontë studies, suggests that Brontë did not intend to endorse one way of life over the other. He maintains that "the novel is about the problem of contrasted vision itself, perhaps even about the impossibility of adopting decisively one or the other mode of vision." The myriad critical approaches to *Wuthering Heights* indicate the difficulty of discerning its meaning, but scholars consistently conclude that it has attained the status of a literary classic, and that Brontë is among the finest novelists of the nineteenth century.

The Eclectic Review   (review date 1851)

[*In the following review, the critic praises Brontë's depiction of scenery in* Wuthering Heights, *but asserts that the novel's characters are exaggerated and unsympathetic, and the situations unbelievable.*]

That [*Wuthering Heights*] has considerable merit we admit. The scenery is laid in the North, the bleak, moorish, wild, character of which is admirably preserved. Ellis Bell was evidently attached to her native hills. She was at home amongst them; and there is, therefore, a vividness and graphic power in her sketches which present them actually before us. So far we prefer no complaint, but the case is different with the *dramatis personœ.* Such a company we never saw grouped before; and we hope never to meet with its like again. Heathcliff is a perfect monster, more demon than human. Hindley Earnshaw is a besotted fool, for whom we scarce feel pity; while his son Hareton is at once ignorant and brutish, until, as by the wand of an enchanter, he takes polish in the last scene of the tale, and retires a docile and apt scholar. The two Catherines, mother and daughter, are equally exaggerations, more than questionable in some parts of their procedure, and absurdly unnatural in the leading incidents of their life. Isabella Linton is one of the silliest and most credulous girls that fancy ever painted; and the enduring affection and tenderness of her brother Edgar are so exhibited as to produce the impression of a feeble rather than of a virtuous character. Of the minor personages we need say nothing, save that, with slight exceptions, they are in keeping with their superiors.

As the characters of the tale are unattractive, so the chief incidents are sadly wanting in probability. They are devoid of truthfulness, are not in harmony with the actual world, and have, therefore, but little more power to move our sympathies than the romances of the middle ages, or the ghost stories which made our granddames tremble. (p. 227)

> *"Wuthering Heights and Agnes Grey," in* The Eclectic Review, *n.s. Vol. 1, February, 1851, pp. 222-27.*

Arthur Symons   (essay date 1918)

[*An English critic, poet, dramatist, short story writer, and editor, Symons gained initial notoriety during the 1890s as one of the leading figures of the Decadent movement in England, eventually establishing himself as an important critic of the modern era. His* The Symbolist Movement in Literature *(1899) provided his English contemporaries with an appropriate vocabulary with which to define their new aesthetic—one that communicated their concern with dreamlike states, imagination, and a reality that exists beyond the boundaries of the senses. In the following essay, Symons praises the passion and intensity of* Wuthering Heights, *deeming it an unforgettable work.*]

It is exactly one hundred years to a month—I write in August—since Emily Brontë was born; she was born in August, 1818, and died December 19th, 1848, at the age of thirty. The Stoic in woman has been seen once only, and that in the only woman in whom there is seen the paradox of passion without sensuousness. She required no passionate experience to endow her with more than a memory of passion. Passion was alive in her as flame is alive in the earth. Her poems are all outcries, as her great novel, *Wuthering Heights,* is one long outcry. Rossetti, in 1854, wrote: "I've been greatly interested in *Wuthering Heights,* the first novel I've read for an age, and the best (as regards power and style only) for two ages, except 'Sidonia.' But it is a fiend of a book. The action is laid in hell—only it seems places and people have English names there." He is not altogether right in what he says, and yet there is hell in the heart of Heathcliff, that magnificent and malevolent gipsy, who, to my mind, can only be compared with Borrow's creations in *Lavengro* and *The Romany Rye*—such as the immortal Jasper Petulengro and Ursula, and with the lesser creations of Meredith's in *The Adventures of Harry Richmond.*

When Charlotte says of Emily that what "her mind had gathered of the real concerning the people around her was too exclusively confined to their tragic and terrible traits, out of which she created Earnshaw and Catherine, and that having formed these beings, she did not know what

she had done," there is no doubt that on the whole she is right. For these spirits are relentless and implacable, fallen and lost spirits, and it is only in this amazing novel that I find maledictions and curses and cries of anguish and writhings of agony and raptures of delight and passionate supplications, such as only abnormal creatures could contrive to express, and within the bounded space of the moors, made sad by sombre sunrises and glad by radiant sunsets. It is sad, colored, and desolate, but when gleams of sunlight or of starlight pierce the clouds that hang generally above it, a rare and sunny beauty comes into the bare outlines, quickening them with living splendor.

In the passionately tragic genius of Emily I find a primitive nature-worship; so strangely primitive that that wonderful scene of mad recrimination between the dying Catherine and the repentant Heathcliff, when she cries, "I forgive you! Forgive me!" and he answers: "Kiss me again; and don't let me see your eyes. I forgive what you have done to me. I love *my* murderer—but *yours?* How can I?" is almost comparable with a passage in *Macbeth,* where Banquo speaks of "the temple-haunting martlet" and its loved masonry, which preludes Lady Macbeth's entrance from under the buttresses as the delicate air bears witness to the incarnate murder that swarms, snake-like, hidden under grass. Something of Emily's saturnine humor comes into the mouth of the Calvinistic farm-servant, whose jests are as grim and as deadly and as plague-like as the snow-storms that make winter unendurable.

Yes, this creature had, in herself and in her imagination, something solitary and sorrowful—that of a woman who lived, literally, alone—and whose genius had no scorn. She, who believed in the indestructible God within herself, was silenced for ever; herself and her genius which had moved as a wind and moved as the sea in tumult, and moved as the thunderclouds in fury upon the tragical and perilous waters of passion that surround "the topless towers" of *Wuthering Heights.*

In one who, like Emily Brontë, was always dying of too much life, one can imagine the sensitive reticences, the glowing eyes, and the strain of the vehemences of that inner fire that fed on itself, which gave her her taciturnity. "It is useless to ask her; you get no answers. The awful point was that, while full of ruth for others, on herself she had no pity; the spirit was inexorable to the flesh; from the trembling hand, the unnerved limbs, the fading eyes, the same service was exacted as they had rendered in health" [Charlotte Brontë].

"The spirit inexorable to the flesh"—there is the whole secret of what in her life was her genius. Alone with herself—with her soul and her body—she allows herself no respite: for she was always of an unresting nature. So in the words of Pater—who told me of his enormous admiration for her prose—"we are all *condamnés à mort avec des sursis indéfinis;* we have our interval, and then our place knows us no more." How she spent these "intervals" must be for ever unknown. Not in high passions, I imagine, nor in wisdom, nor in care for material things; but in moods of passion, in intellectual excitement, in an inexhaustible curiosity, in an ironical contemplation "of the counted pulses of a variegated, dramatic life." But never, I am certain, was she ever capable—as she watches the weaving and unweaving of herself—of the base corruption of what his existence was to Beardsley. "That he should be so honest with his fear," I have written of him, "that he should sit down before its face and study it feature by feature: that he should never turn aside his eyes for more than one instant, make no attempt to escape, but sit at home with it, travel with it, see it in his mirror, taste it in the sacrament: that is the marvellous thing, and the sign of his fundamental sincerity in life and art."

Emily Brontë's passionate and daring genius attains this utmost limit of Tragedy, and with this a sense—an extreme sense—of the mystery of terror which lurks in all the highest poetry as certainly in her lyrical prose; a quality which distinguishes such prose and verse from all that is but a little lower than the highest. Her genius is sombre in the sense that Webster is, but much less dramatic. Neither his tragedies nor her novel are well-constructed; and in her case something is certainly lacking; for her narrative, is dominated by sheer chance, and guided by mere accident. And I think that she, with her sleepless imagination, might have said as the child Giovanni in Webster's Tragedy says: "I have not slept these six nights. When do the dead walk?" and is answered: "When God shall please." When in disguise she sings of the useless rebellions of the earth, rarely has a more poignant cry been wrenched out of "a soul on the rack"—that is to say, since Santa Teresa sang:—

> A soul in God, hidden from sin,
> What more desires for thee remain,
> Save but to love, and love again
> And, all on flame, with love within,
> Love on, and turn to love again?

than this stanza:

> O! dreadful is the shock—intense the agony—
> When the ear begins to hear, and the eye begins
>   to see;
> When the pulse begins to throb, the brain to
>   think again,
> The soul to feel the flesh and the flesh to feel the
>   chain.

At times there is a tragic sublimity in her imagination, which gathers together, as it were, the winds from the world's four quarters, that howled in winter nights across the moor around the house she lived in. Indeed, the very storm of her genius hovers in the air between things sublime and things hideous. "There never was such a thunderstorm of a play," said Swinburne on Cyril Tourneur's *Revenger's Tragedy*. I am inclined to add: "There never was such a thunderstorm of a novel as *Wuthering Heights*." And it is blood-stained with the blood of the roses of sunsets; the heavy atmosphere is sultry as the hush and heat and awe of midnoon; sad visions appear with tragic countenances, fugitives try in vain to escape from the insane brooding of their consciences. And there are serviceable shadows; implacable self-devotions and implacable cruelties; vengeances unassuaged; and a kind of unscrupulous ferocity is seen not only in Heathcliff but in one of his victims. And there are startling scenes and sentences that, once impressed on the memory, are unforgettable; as

scarlet flowers of evil and as poisonous weeds they take root in one. (pp. 546-47)

Arthur Symons, "Emily Brontë," in The Nation, *New York, Vol. XXIII, No. 21, August 24, 1918, pp. 546-47.*

Boris Ford   (essay date 1938)

[*In the following essay, Ford provides an analysis of the tone and structure of* Wuthering Heights. *He acknowledges contentions by other commentators that the characters of the novel are oppressively morbid and cruel, but asserts that Brontë achieved an admirable balance between good and evil.*]

By common consent there is something wrong with *Wuthering Heights,* and greater nonsense has been written in an effort to bring this blemish to light than has been occasioned by perhaps any other novel. In fact, *Wuthering Heights* has now become the *enfant terrible* of the English Novel, and critics hurry past with little more than a furtive glance at this regrettable deviation from the norm of sanity and health. A. A. Jack, for example, writes in the Cambridge History:

> It is not desirable to read; to take *Wuthering Heights* from the shelf is to prepare for oneself no pleasure.

If this is being rather more frank than most commentators, that is the only point of difference. The prevailing opinion is that the novel is most oppressive—'It is undoubtedly too morbid and humorless to reach the highest excellence,' and that the bleakness of the Yorkshire moors would be sufficiently cathartic without introducing Heathcliff as well. Charlotte Brontë, who cannot be accused of lacking sympathy, found herself forced to say:

> Whether it is right or advisable to create beings like Heathcliffe, I do not know: I scarcely think it is.

But one cannot help feeling that, if the matter were made one of 'right or advisable,' it would not be Emily who would be condemned, but Charlotte herself, who created the mad Mrs. Rochester:

> It was a discoloured face—it was a savage face. I wish I could forget the roll of the red eyes and the fearful blackened inflation of the lineaments! . . . [she] was purple: the lips were swelled and dark; the brow furrowed; the black eyebrows widely raised over the bloodshot eyes.

The point is, of course, that few people object to Mrs. Rochester because she only exists in the assertion, she is not realized artistically and consequently never impinges on the imagination; whereas Heathcliff arouses various kinds of disapproval, from disgust to fear, precisely because he is so vividly present to the emotions of the reader.

That anyone could create such a character as Heathcliff, a man who 'stands unredeemed; never once swerving in his arrow-straight course to perdition,' naturally leads to observations about Emily Brontë herself. The most respectable of these appear in *The Common Reader;* Virginia Woolf at any rate appreciates *Wuthering Heights,* even if she seems not to understand it fully. She writes:

> Emily was inspired by some more general conception. The impulse which urged her to create was not her own suffering or her own injuries. She looked out upon a world cleft into gigantic disorder and felt within herself the power to unite it in a book. The gigantic ambition is to be felt throughout the novel—a struggle, half thwarted but of superb conviction, to say something through the mouths of her characters which is not merely "I love" or "I hate" but "we, the whole human race" and "you, the eternal powers . . . " the sentence remains unfinished.

When one considers how unsympathetic Virginia Woolf might be expected to find *Wuthering Heights,* the somewhat mystical tone of her remarks will not appear unnatural; but, unnatural or not, it seems highly improbable that Emily Brontë did any looking out 'upon a world cleft into gigantic disorder,' and though it is no doubt very hard to understand how she could have written such a novel, little can be gained by attempting to explain the phenomenon. Explanations tend to become vulgar, and Miss Romer Wilson, whose biography of Emily Brontë is entitled *All Alone,* expends considerable energy in distorting the facts when she writes:

> There is Emily at Haworth, exiled from love, with a man's soul in her female body, hell tormenting her, poetry adding to the torment.

Actually, in the thirty years she lived, Emily Brontë pursued an entirely normal existence, which was not in the least romantic or in the smallest degree interesting, one would have supposed, to creative biographers. Contrary to the impression that one might get from the novel, she does not appear to have been in any way gloomy or pessimistic. In 1845, while writing her novel, she wrote in the second of her two scraps of diary:

> I am quite content for myself: not as idle as formerly, altogether as hearty, and having learnt to make the most of the present and long for the future with the fidgetiness that I cannot do all I wish; seldom if ever troubled with nothing to do, and merely desiring that everybody could be as comfortable as myself and as undesponding, and then we should have a very tolerable world of it.

Her tranquillity was conditional, however, upon her remaining at Haworth, and of the few years when she was sent away to school, Charlotte writes:

> The change from her own home to a school, and from her own very noiseless, very secluded, but unrestricted and unartificial life to one of disciplined routines was what she failed in enduring. Her nature was too strong for her fortitude. Every morning, when she woke, the visions of home and the moors rushed on her, and darkened and saddened the day that lay before her. Nobody knew what ailed her but me. I knew only too well. In this struggle her health was quickly broken: her white face, attenuated form, and failing strength threatened rapid decline. I felt in my heart she would die if she did not go home.

This nostalgia, which contributes to the main theme of the novel, informs much of Emily Brontë's poetry:

> There is a spot, 'mid barren hills,
> Where winter howls, and driving rain;
> But, if the weary tempest chills,
> There is a light that warms again.

But on the whole the poems do not offer much biographical interest, but rather are remarkable for a fine normality and an emotional strength not common in Victorian verse. This can be seen very clearly if one compares **"Remembrance"** with the relevant parts of *In Memoriam.* Emily Brontë is obviously writing with her finger on a keen experience, and she reveals an unwillingness to sentimentalize and indulge her emotion that makes her a much more masculine poet than most of her male contemporaries.

But the distinction of her best poems, however indisputable it may be, can hardly compare with that of the novel. From the first page to the last one is aware of a rigid control and a clarity of execution that are truly remarkable. There is no trace at any point of emotional indulgence, and this in a work which operates throughout at very considerable pressure. A short quotation may serve to enforce this point. The scene is the death of Frances, Hindley's wife:

> . . . but one night, while leaning on his shoulder in the act of saying she thought she should be able to get up tomorrow, a fit of coughing took her—a very slight one—he raised her in his arms; she put her two hands about his neck, her face changed, and she was dead.

The delicate assurance of this passage does not depend upon the use of an emotive vocabulary; the words, in contrast to the situation described, are colourless, and force attention above all on the precision of the movement. Up to 'a fit of coughing took her' the prose runs smoothly, with Frances convincing herself that she is now better; but with the dash, the prose takes on a quivering and panting motion, and then as it were loses its balance, and falls. And it is because the staple of the prose of *Wuthering Heights* is of this quality that one has confidence in asserting with D. H. Lawrence that 'it is a great book.'

Wuthering Heights, it should be quite evident, is not an unpleasant novel, and one of the main purposes of this analysis will be to demonstrate that it is in fact a very precisely balanced structure of 'pleasant' and 'unpleasant,' 'normal' and 'abnormal.' Far from giving way to melodrama and self-indulgence, Emily Brontë relegates all the potentially unhealthy elements to their place in the artistic whole, and the novel moves continually towards a resolution of perfect tranquillity. At the centre of *Wuthering Heights* lies, of course, the relationship between Cathy and Heathcliff; for the second half of the book there is a closely allied theme, the relationship between Catherine and Hareton, the latter theme acting, in its similarity to the former, as a commentary, though upon a very different emotional plane. There are in addition several subsidiary themes which serve to determine and qualify the attitude to be adopted by the reader. The novel is almost entirely recounted by two observers, Mrs. Dean and Lockwood, for much the greater part by the former. Lockwood, in fact, has no more than the first and the last words, and for the rest he merely listens to Mrs. Dean's story as a representative of a world foreign to the events that take place. As such he tends to be both uncomprehending and insensitive; he explains, for instance, that his search for solitude is to help him forget an unsuccessful love-affair:

> While enjoying a month of fine weather at the sea-coast, I was thrown into the company of a most fascinating creature: a real goddess in my eyes, as long as she took no notice of me. I "never told my love" vocally; still, if looks have language, the merest idiot might have guessed I was head over ears . . .

The vulgarity of this is enforced by the flat and lifeless prose; and the absurdity of Lockwood's passion helps to bring out by contrast the significance of the Cathy-Heathcliff relationship. Lockwood's response, at subsequent points in the novel, is more or less what the response of the ordinary reader might be expected to be. At first unsympathetic, he is by the end entirely reconciled to all that has taken place. He has not long made the acquaintance of Heathcliff and Wuthering Heights before he feels that

> The dismal spiritual atmosphere of the place overcame, and more than neutralised the glowing physical comforts around me; and I resolved to be cautious how I ventured under the rafters a third time.

Having thus recorded the natural reaction of an observer as yet unacquainted with the deeper cross-currents of emotion, Lockwood tends to suspend judgment until the end of the novel.

Mrs. Dean's function in the novel cannot be so simply stated; she may be said to act as Chorus with the difference that she offers a point of view which is not altogether disinterested. As raconteuse she naturally has to move upon a plane of normal and sometimes trivial consciousness that excludes her to some extent from the emotional atmosphere of the Cathy-Heathcliff relationship; but this apart, she represents the maximum objectivity possible to any active participant in the events described. Her essential qualifications appear when Lockwood says to her:

> "Excepting a few provincialisms of slight consequence, you have no marks of the manners which I am habituated to consider peculiar to your class. I am sure you have thought a great deal more than the generality of servants think. You have been compelled to cultivate your reflective faculties for want of occasions for frittering away your life in silly trifles."
>
> Mrs. Dean laughed.
>
> "I certainly esteem myself a steady, reasonable kind of body," she said; "not exactly from living among the hills and seeing one set of faces, and one series of actions, from year's end to year's end; but I have undergone sharp discipline, which has taught me wisdom; and then, I have read more than you would fancy, Mr. Lockwood. You could not open a book in this library that I have not looked into, and got something out of also . . . "

The key-words—'think,' 'reflective faculties,' 'steady,' 'reasonable,' 'sharp discipline,' 'wisdom'—emphasize the essential normality, the spiritual poise which informs the whole novel. And it is important that Mrs. Dean's 'wisdom' is not an exclusively rural heritage, and comes 'not exactly from living among the hills'; it is also derived from a wide reading, and it is this which endows her with a width and generosity of opinion that contrast very strongly with the narrow calvinism of old Joseph, who says to Heathcliff:

> "Aw hed aimed tuh dee, where Aw'd served fur sixty year . . . "

If Lockwood is not to be trusted as a commentator, he being almost a foreigner, nor is Joseph, who is too exclusively part of the environment to offer any semblance of impartiality.

The central theme, as has been suggested, is the relationship between Cathy and Heathcliff. Emily Brontë, however, has no particular concern with the surface appearance of this relationship, but insists throughout on its inner tension. To Mrs. Dean, Cathy is explicit:

> "This is for the sake of one [Heathcliff] who comprehends in his person my feelings to Edgar [Cathy's future husband] and myself. I cannot express it; but surely you and everybody have a notion that there is or should be an existence beyond you. What were the use of my creation if I were entirely contained here? My great miseries in this world have been Heathcliff's miseries; and I have watched and felt each from the beginning: my great thought in living is himself. If all else perished, and he remained, I should still continue to be; and if all else remained, and he were annihilated, the universe would turn to a mighty stranger: I should not seem a part of it. My love for Linton is like the foliage in the woods: time will change it, I'm well aware, as winter changes the trees. My love for Heathcliff resembles the eternal rocks beneath: a source of little visible delight, but necessary. Nelly, I *am* Heathcliff. He's always, always in my mind: not as a pleasure, any more than I am always a pleasure to myself, but as my own being. So don't talk of our separation again: it is impracticable . . . "

Elsewhere she says:

> "Whatever our souls are made of, his and mine are the same."

And Heathcliff, speaking of the dead Cathy, says:

> "I *cannot* live without my life! I *cannot* live without my soul!"

Though the point should not be much laboured, there exists a distinct similarity between these passages and the one by Charlotte describing Emily's enforced absence from Haworth; and the comparison serves to emphasize the non-personal nature of the Cathy-Heathcliff relationship.

The key-sentence in the first passage quoted is 'My love for Heathcliff resembles the eternal rocks beneath.' This imagery drawn from nature, and particularly from its sterner elements, is recurrent in the descriptions of Heathcliff. Mrs. Dean describes him as being 'hard as whinstone,' and when he and the refined Edgar appear together, she says that 'The contrast resembled what you see in exchanging a bleak, hilly, coal country for a beautiful fertile valley.' Cathy is even more outspoken, and describes him as an 'arid wilderness of furze and whinstone.' But, in contrast with the 'red eyes and the fearful blackened inflation of the lineaments' of Mrs. Rochester, Heathcliff is presented as being physically quite attractive. Lockwood finds that 'he has an erect and handsome figure,' and Mrs. Dean says that 'his manner was even dignified: quite divested of roughness, though too stern for grace.' In so far as Heathcliff is abnormal, if that is the right word, it is an abnormality that tends to lie below the level of social deportment. Cathy says:

> "Pray don't imagine that he conceals depths of benevolence and affection beneath a stern exterior! He's not a rough diamond—a pearl-containing oyster of a rustic: he's a fierce, pitiless, wolfish man."

Heathcliff himself relates how he has 'taught him [his son] to scorn everything extra-animal as silly and weak'; and later he says: 'It's odd what a savage feeling I have to anything that seems afraid of me.' And finally Isabella, his wife, contributes to the impression of the non-human element in Heathcliff, when she asks: 'Is Mr. Heathcliff a man? If so, is he mad? And if not, is he a devil?'

With the death of Cathy, however, what was once latent now emerges, and Heathcliff ceases to be dignified. Mrs. Dean relates how, just before her death, he 'foamed like a mad dog'; and he himself says: 'You know, I was wild after she died.' The balanced relationship is now broken up, and a great contrast is evident between Cathy and Heathcliff. Mrs. Dean says of the former:

> . . . hers [was the hush] of perfect peace. Her brow smooth, her lids closed, her lips wearing the expression of a smile; no angel in heaven could be more beautiful than she appeared. And I partook of the infinite calm in which she lay; my mind was never in a holier frame than while I gazed on that untroubled image of Divine rest . . . To be sure, one might have doubted, after the wayward and impatient existence she had led, whether she merited a haven of peace at last. One might doubt in seasons of cold reflection; but not then, in the presence of her corpse. It asserted its own tranquillity.

As for Heathcliff, Mrs. Dean finds him 'leant against an old ash tree.' After talking to him, she relates:

> He dashed his head against the knotted trunk; and, lifting up his eyes, howled, not like a man, but like a savage beast getting goaded to death with knives and spears.

The contrast is not only one of verbal description, but also of movement; the Cathy passage runs very smoothly and evenly, and reflects the 'tranquillity'; whereas the Heathcliff passage is lumpy and awkward to read, generally uneasy in motion. The contrast persists, by implication, till the end of the novel. Heathcliff's behaviour remains weird and unnatural. He now bends all his energies towards bringing under one control the two properties of Wuthering Heights, where he has lived, and Thrushcroft Grange, where Cathy lived with her husband, Edgar Linton. This undertaking, symbolizing his desire to be re-united with Cathy, obsesses him, and he lets nothing stand in his way. He shows, for instance, considerable subtlety and brutality in arranging the marriage between Linton, his son, and Catherine, to whom Thrushcroft Grange will belong on the death of Edgar. The essential clue to his behaviour is supplied by Catherine, who says to him:

> "Mr. Heathcliff, *you* have *nobody* to love you; and, however miserable you make us, we still have the revenge of thinking that your cruelty arises from your greater misery!"

But, once the mundane union has been effected, Heathcliff subsides. He goes and looks at Cathy in her coffin—' "I saw her face again—it is hers yet" '—and says to Mrs. Dean:

> "She [Cathy] has disturbed me, night and day through eighteen years—incessantly—remorsely—till yesternight; and yesternight I was tranquil. I dreamt I was sleeping the last sleep by that sleeper, with my heart stopped and my cheek frozen against hers."

He now has 'a single wish,' and his 'whole being and faculties are yearning to attain it.' The ordinary physical demands of life have no more interest for him: ' "I have to remind myself to breathe—almost to remind my heart to beat!" ' He moves nearer and nearer towards the unspecified goal; ' "I'm too happy, and yet I'm not happy enough. My soul's bliss kills my body, but does not satisfy itself." ' And finally Mrs. Dean relates:

> Mr. Heathcliff was there—laid on his back. His eyes met mine so keen and fierce, I started; and then he seemed to smile . . . he was dead and stark!

He is buried, as he had demanded, with Cathy; and the final cadence comes with the small boy's story:

> "They's Heathcliff, and a woman, yonder under t' Nab," he blubbered, "un' Aw darnut pass 'em."

The level on which the Cathy-Heathcliff relationship has moved, and its depersonalized character, make it seem entirely fitting that it should attain equilibrium and tranquillity only with the death of the two persons concerned.

The structure of ***Wuthering Heights,*** as has been shown by C.P.S. in a Hogarth pamphlet, is truly remarkable for the degree to which it seems to have been artificially constructed, with minute attention paid to details of apparent irrelevance. Analysis reveals, however, that this is not a symptom of misapplied energy and interest in Emily Brontë, but is precisely what gives the novel its coherence. The stresses and contradictions inherent in the Cathy-Heathcliff theme just analysed are reflected in varying ways in all the relationships of the novel; heredity, above all, plays a structural and unifying rôle that merits some attention at this point. The fundamental conflict emerges in the contrast between the two estates, between Thrush-croft Grange—'a splendid place carpeted with crimson, and crimson-covered chairs and tables,' and Wuthering Heights—'the floor was of smooth white stones; the chairs high-backed, primitive structures, painted green.' Thrush-croft Grange is the home of the Lintons, and Edgar and Isabella Linton, together with Frances, stand for refinement and delicacy. In contrast there are Hindley and Cathy Earnshaw and Heathcliff, all of whom were brought up in Wuthering Heights, and develop very roughly and without the civilized graces. In comparison with the 'beautiful fertile valley' of Edgar, Heathcliff is a 'bleak, hilly coal country.' As a girl Cathy was a 'wild, wicked slip,' but, after staying for some time with the Lintons, she returns 'a very dignified person'; the Linton environment tends to eradicate from her the wilder elements that remain in Heathcliff. There are two inter-marriages: Heathcliff marries Isabella, and Cathy marries Edgar. The former marriage is a complete failure; Heathcliff shatters Isabella, and their son, Linton, is utterly spineless and wastes away rapidly. The second marriage is more successful; Mrs. Dean believes that Cathy and Edgar 'were really in possession of deep and growing happiness.' Their daughter is Catherine, of whom Mrs. Dean says:

> Her spirit was high, though not rough, and qualified by a heart sensitive and lively to excess in its affections. That capacity for intense attachments reminded me of her mother: still she did not resemble her; for she could be as soft and mild as a doe, and she had gentle voice and pensive expression: her anger was never furious: her love never fierce; it was deep and tender.

The implications of these marriages and their offspring are fairly general. The first emphasizes the incompatibility of the Heathcliff and Isabella elements. And the second reveals that there exists a potential sympathy between the two conflicting houses; Cathy, her nature modified by a stay at Thrushcroft Grange, marries Edgar with comparative success, and their daughter meets with as great approval as Heathcliff's son with contempt from Mrs. Dean. And finally there is Hareton, the son of Frances and Hindley, Cathy's brother. Up till the age of about seventeen, Hareton is almost a replica of Heathcliff, though the Frances influence renders him more subdued, she being an insignificant and frail person. Mrs. Dean says that Heathcliff 'appeared to have bent his malevolence on making him [Hareton] a brute'; and not long before Heathcliffe dies, he says:

> "Hareton seemed a personification of my youth, not a human being . . . his startling likeness to Catherine [Cathy] connected him fearfully with her . . . Hareton's aspect was the ghost of my immortal love, of my wild endeavours to hold my right, my degradation, my pride, my happiness, and my anguish . . ."

The differences between the two main themes, Cathy-Heathcliff and Catherine-Hareton, lie, very generally, in the fact that the former is wilder and more Lawrencian. For instance, Cathy and Heathcliff do not marry; Cathy tells Mrs. Dean that their relationship has no need for sanctions of that kind, and that it is not likely to be affect-ed by her marriage to Edgar. And the same applies to Heathcliff's marriage to Isabella, Edgar's sister. In fact the Cathy-Heathcliff relationship is handled in neither sexual nor even particularly human terms. On the other hand, the Catherine-Hareton theme moves on a plane of normal procedure; at the end of the novel they are about to be married. And this distinction between the two themes is of fundamental importance: the Catherine-Hareton relationship is the projection into the sphere of ordinary behaviour of the Cathy-Heathcliff relationship; it is the expression in conventional social terms of the main spiritual conflict. As in the description of Catherine quoted above, on the one hand the anger is 'furious' and the love 'fierce,' on the other everything is 'soft and mild,' 'gentle,' and 'pensive.'

Between Catherine and Hareton, however, there is no such immediate sympathy as there was between Cathy and Heathcliff. The former relationship being, as has been suggested, a counterpart of the latter, it develops from outside itself. Cathy dies in giving birth to Catherine, and so, just as from this moment she and Heathcliff are separated and only very slowly re-united, similarly there exists from the first a lack of sympathy between Catherine and Hareton which is only gradually overcome. At their first meeting she mistakes him for a servant, and he retorts:

> "I'll see thee damned before I be *thy* servant."

Heathcliff's struggle to unite the two estates involves marrying his son, Linton, to Catherine, and this naturally throws her further apart from Hareton. But, once the marriage has taken place (Linton dies almost immediately) and Heathcliff feels himself moving ever closer to Cathy, intimacy between Catherine and Hareton springs up rapidly. And, significantly linking up with Mrs. Dean's remarks about her literary education, it is in teaching Hareton to read and appreciate her books that Catherine gives impetus to this relationship. Mrs. Dean says:

> His honest, warm, and intelligent nature shook off rapidly the clouds of ignorance and degradation in which it had been bred; and Catherine's sincere commendations acted as a spur to his industry.

It is this relationship which meets with Mrs. Dean's approval. Her comments on Heathcliff and Cathy are fundamentally sympathetic, but none the less qualified. After Cathy has told her of her feelings for Heathcliff—' "Nelly, I *am* Heathcliff!" '—she says that she 'was out of patience with her folly!'; and after Cathy's death she says:

> Retracing the course of Catherine Linton, I fear we have no right to think she is [happy in the other world]; but we'll leave her with her Maker.

And when she finds Heathcliff in the grounds, and sees him dash 'his head against the knotted trunk,' she observes that 'It hardly moved my compassion.' But of Hareton and Catherine she says:

> The crown of all my wishes will be the union between these two. I shall envy no one on their wedding-day: there won't be a happier woman than myself in England!

But the 'union between these two' symbolises also the final union of Cathy and Heathcliff. The close sympathy between the two themes now emerges clearly. When Heathcliff dies, Hareton 'sat by the corpse all night, weeping in bitter earnest.' The resolution into tranquillity with which the Cathy-Heathcliff theme ends is paralleled in the Hareton-Catherine theme. As Mrs. Dean tells Lockwood that the latter are going to live at Thrushcroft Grange, they return from a walk.

> "They are afraid of nothing," I [Lockwood] grumbled, watching their approach through the window. "Together, they would brave satan and all his legions."
>
> As they stepped onto the door-stones, and halted to take a last look at the moon—or, more correctly, at each other, by her light—I felt irresistibly impelled to escape them . . .

Lockwood, whose sympathies are now fully engaged, goes to find the graves of Edgar, Cathy and Heathcliff.

> I lingered round them, under that benign sky: watched the moths fluttering among the heather and hare-bells; listened to the soft wind breathing through the grass; and wondered how anyone could ever imagine unquiet slumbers for the sleepers in that quiet earth.

The even and balanced movement of the prose, and the particularity of the description, bring the novel to a close on a note of great calm and completeness. Suggestions of the novel being 'terrible,' or not 'enjoyable,' are now seen to be possible only as a result of stubborn misreading; unfortunately this appears to be the sanctioned way of reading *Wuthering Heights.* (pp. 375-89)

> *Boris Ford, in a review of "Wuthering Heights," in* Scrutiny, *Vol. VII, No. 1, June, 1938, pp. 375-89.*

W. Somerset Maugham   (essay date 1948)

[*Maugham was an English dramatist, short story writer, and novelist who is considered a skilled, cynical satirist. Best known for his autobiographical novel* Of Human Bondage *(1915), Maugham also achieved popular success with such plays as* Caesar's Wife *(1922),* Our Betters *(1923), and* The Breadwinner *(1930). In the following excerpt, he describes some imperfections in the narrative technique of* Wuthering Heights, *but praises the novel's power and mystery.*]

It is evident that Charlotte [Brontë] did not quite know what to make of *Wuthering Heights;* she had no notion that her sister had produced a book of astonishing originality and one compared with which her own were commonplace. She felt compelled to apologize for it. When it was proposed to republish it she undertook to edit it. "I am likewise compelling myself to read it over, for the first time of opening the book since my sister's death. Its power fills me with renewed admiration; but yet I am oppressed: the reader is scarcely ever permitted a taste of unalloyed pleasure; every beam of sunshine is poured down through black bars of threatening cloud; every page is surcharged with a sort of moral electricity; and the writer was unconscious of all this—nothing could make her conscious of it." And again:

> If the auditor of her work, when read in manuscript, shuddered under the grinding influence of natures so relentless and implacable—of spirits so lost and fallen; if it was complained that the mere hearing of certain vivid and fearful scenes banished sleep by night, and disturbed mental peace by day, Ellis Bell would wonder what was meant, and suspect the complainant of affectation. Had she but lived, her mind would of itself have grown like a strong tree—loftier, straighter, wider-spreading—and its matured fruits would have attained a mellower ripeness and sunnier bloom; but on that mind time and experience alone could work; to the influence of other intellects it was not amenable.

One is inclined to think that Charlotte little knew her sister. *Wuthering Heights* is an extraordinary book. It is a very bad one. It is a very fine one. It is ugly. It has beauty. It is a terrible, an agonizing, a passionate book. Some have thought it impossible that a clergyman's daughter who led a retired, humdrum life and knew few people and nothing of the world could have written it. This seems to me absurd. *Wuthering Heights* is wildly romantic: now romanticism eschews the patient observation of realism; it revels in the unbridled flight of the imagination and indulges, sometimes with gusto, sometimes with gloom, in horror, mystery, fearful passions and deeds of violence. It is an escape from reality. Given Emily Brontë's character . . . and fierce, repressed passions, which what we know of her suggests, *Wuthering Heights* is just the sort of book one would have expected her to write. But on the face of it, it is much more the sort of book that her scapegrace brother Branwell might have written, and a number of people have been able to persuade themselves that he had either in whole or in part in fact done so. One of them, Francis Grundy, wrote: "Patrick Brontë declared to me, and what his sister said bore out the assertion, that he wrote a great part of *Wuthering Heights* himself. . . . The weird fancies of diseased genius with which he used to entertain me in our long talks at Luddendenfoot, reappear in the pages of the novel, and I am inclined to believe that the very plot was his invention rather than his sister's." On one occasion two of Branwell's friends, Dearden and Leyland by name, arranged to meet him at an inn on the road to Keighley to read their poetical effusions to one another, and this is what Dearden some twenty years later wrote to the Halifax *Guardian:*

> I read the first act of *The Demon Queen;* but when Branwell dived into his hat—the usual receptacle of his fugitive scraps—where he supposed he had deposited his manuscript poem, he found he had by mistake placed there a number of stray leaves of a novel on which he had been trying his 'prentice hand.' Chagrined at the disappointment he had caused, he was about to return the papers to his hat, when both friends earnestly pressed him to read them, as they felt a curiosity to see how he could wield the pen of a novelist. After some hesitation, he complied with the request, and riveted our attention for about an hour, dropping each sheet, when read

into his hat. The story broke off abruptly in the middle of a sentence, and he gave us the sequel, *viva voce,* together with the real names of the prototypes of his characters; but, as some of these persons are still living, I refrain from pointing them out to the public. He said he had not yet fixed upon a title for his production, and was afraid he would never be able to meet with a publisher who would have the hardihood to usher it into the world. The scene of the fragment which Branwell read, and the characters introduced in it—so far as they developed— were the same as those in *Wuthering Heights,* which Charlotte Brontë confidently asserts was the production of her sister Emily.

Now this is either a pack of lies or it is true. Charlotte despised and within the bounds of Christian charity hated her brother; but as we know, Christian charity has always been able to make allowances for a lot of good honest hatred, and Charlotte's unsupported word cannot be accepted. She may, as people often do, have persuaded herself to believe what she wanted to believe. The story is circumstantial, and it is odd that anyone for no particular reason should have invented it. What is the explanation? There is none. It has been suggested that Branwell wrote the first four chapters, and then, drunk and doped as he was, gave it up, whereupon Emily took it over. The argument adduced is that these chapters are written in a more stilted style than the rest of the novel. That I cannot see. The whole book is very badly written in the pseudo-literary manner that the amateur is apt to affect. When the amateur, and it must be remembered that Emily Brontë had never written a book before, sits down to write he thinks he must use grand words rather than ordinary ones. It is only by practice that he learns to write simply. The main part of the story is told by a Yorkshire servant and she expresses herself in a way that no human being could. Emily Brontë was perhaps aware that she was putting words into Mrs. Dean's mouth that she could hardly have known, and to explain it makes her say that she has in the course of her service had the opportunity to read a number of books, but even at that the pretentiousness of her discourse is appalling. She never *tries* to do a thing, but *endeavors* or *essays,* she never *leaves* a room but *quits* it, she never *meets* anybody but *encounters* him. I should have said that whoever wrote the first chapters wrote the rest, and if in the early ones there is somewhat more pomposity in the writing I surmise that this is owing to a not unsuccessful attempt on Emily's part to show that Lockwood was a silly, conceited young man.

I have read somewhere the conjecture that if it was Branwell who wrote the beginning of the novel his intention was to make Lockwood take a much greater part in the action. There is indeed a hint that he was attracted by the younger Catherine, and it is obvious that if he had fallen in love with her a complication would have been added to the intrigue. As it is, Lockwood is merely a nuisance. The novel is very clumsily constructed. But is this surprising? Emily Brontë had never written one before and she had a complicated story to tell dealing with two generations. This is always a difficult thing to do because the author has to give some sort of unity to a narrative that concerns

two sets of characters and two sets of events; and he must be careful not to allow the interest of one set to overshadow the interest of the other. He has also to compress the passage of years into a period of time that can be accepted by the reader with a comprehensive glance as one seizes in a single view the whole of a vast fresco. I do not suppose that Emily Brontë deliberately thought out how to get a unity of impression into a straggling story, but I think she must have wondered how to make it coherent, and it may have occurred to her that she could best do this by making one character narrate the long succession of events to another. It is a convenient way of telling a story, and she did not invent it. Its disadvantage is, as I pointed out just now, that it is almost impossible to maintain a conversational manner when the narrator has to *tell* a number of things, descriptions of scenery for instance, which no sane person would think of doing. And of course if you have a narrator (Mrs. Dean) you must have a listener (Lockwood). It is possible that an experienced novelist might have found a better way of telling the story of *Wuthering Heights,* but I cannot persuade myself that if Emily Brontë used it it was because she was working on a foundation of someone else's invention.

But more than that, I think that Emily Brontë's method might have been expected of her when you consider her extreme, her morbid shyness and reticence. What were the alternatives? One was to write the novel from the standpoint of omniscience, as for instance *Middlemarch* and *Madame Bovary* were written. I think it would have shocked her harsh, uncompromising virtue to tell the outrageous story as a creation of her own; and if she had, moreover, she could hardly have avoided giving some account of Heathcliff during the years he spent away from Wuthering Heights, years during which he managed to acquire an education and make money. She couldn't do this because she simply didn't know how he had done it. The fact the reader is asked to accept is hard to believe, and she was content to state it and leave it at that. Another alternative was to have the story narrated to her, Emily Brontë, by Mrs. Dean, say, and tell it then in the first person; but I suspect that that too would have brought her into a contact with the reader too close for her quivering sensibility. By having the story in its beginning told by Lockwood and unfolded to Lockwood by Mrs. Dean she hid herself behind, as it were, a double mask. The Rev. Patrick Brontë told Mrs. Gaskell a story which in this connection has some significance. When his children were young, desiring to find out something of their natures which their timidity concealed from him, he made each one in turn put on an old mask, under the cover of which they could answer more freely the questions he put to them. When he asked Charlotte what was the best book in the world she answered: The Bible; but when he asked Emily what he had best do with her troublesome brother Branwell, she said: "Reason with him; and when he won't listen to reason, whip him."

And why did Emily need to hide herself when she wrote this powerful, terrible book? I think because she disclosed in it her innermost instincts. She looked deep into the well of loneliness of her heart and saw there undisclosable secrets which, notwithstanding, her impulse as a writer drove her to unburden herself of. It is said that her imagination was kindled by the weird stories her father used to tell of the Ireland of his youth and by the tales of Hoffman which she learned to read when she went to school in Belgium and which she continued to read, we are told, back at the parsonage seated on a hearthrug by the fire with her arm around Keeper's neck. Charlotte was at pains to state that Emily, whatever she had heard of them, had no communication with the people round her who might be supposed to have suggested the characters of her novel. I am willing to believe that this is true, and I am willing to believe that she found in the stories of mystery and horror of the German romantic writers something that appealed to her own fierce nature; but I think she found Heathcliff and Catherine Earnshaw in the hidden depths of her own soul. It may be that in the lesser characters—Linton and his sister, Earnshaw's wife and Heathcliff's—objects of her disdain for their weakness and frailty, she found hints in persons she had known, but readers seldom give an author credit for a power of invention and it is just as likely that she created them out of her own overbearing and contemptuous imagination. I think she was herself Catherine Earnshaw, wild, tempestuous, passionate; and I think she was Heathcliff.

Is it strange that she should have put herself into the two chief characters of her book? Not at all. We are none of us all of a piece; more than one person dwells within us, often in uneasy companionship with his fellows; and the peculiarity of the writer of fictions is that he has the power to objectify the diverse persons of which he is compounded into individual characters: his misfortune is that he cannot bring to life characters, however necessary to his story they may be, in which there is no part of himself. It is not only not uncommon for an author writing his first novel, as *Wuthering Heights* was, to make himself his principal character, it is not uncommon either that in his theme there will be something of wish-fulfilment. It becomes then a confession of the reveries, on solitary walks or in wakeful hours at night, in which he has imagined himself saint or sinner, great lover or great statesman, heroic general or cold-blooded murderer; and it is because there is a lot of absurdity in most people's reveries that there is a great deal of nonsense in most writers' first novels. I think *Wuthering Heights* is just such a confession.

I think Emily Brontë put the whole of herself into Heathcliff. She gave him, I think, her violent rage, her sexuality, vehement but frustrated, her passion of unsatisfied love, her jealousy, her hatred and contempt of human beings, her cruelty, her sadism. . . . There is [a] curious incident related by Charlotte's friend, Ellen Nussey: "She enjoyed leading Charlotte where she would not dare go of her own free will. Charlotte had a mortal dread of unknown animals, and it was Emily's pleasure to lead her into close vicinity, and then tell her of how and what she had done, laughing at her horror with great amusement." I think Emily loved Catherine Earnshaw with Heathcliff's masculine, purely animal love, and I think she laughed, as she had laughed at Charlotte's fears, when as Heathcliff she kicked and trampled on Earnshaw and dashed his head repeatedly against the stone flags, and I think she laughed when, as Heathcliff, she hit the younger Catherine in the

face and heaped humiliations upon her; I think it gave her a thrill of release when she bullied, reviled and browbeat the persons of her invention because in real life she suffered such bitter mortification in the company of her fellow creatures; and I think, as Catherine, doubling the rôles, as it were, though she fought Heathcliff, though she despised him, though she knew him for the evil thing he was, she loved him with her body and soul, she exulted in her power over him, she felt they were kin (as indeed they were if I am right in supposing they were both Emily Brontë), and since there is in the sadist often something of the masochist too, she was fascinated by his violence, his brutality and his untamed nature.

But I have said enough. *Wuthering Heights* is not a book to talk about; it is a book to read. It is easy to find fault with it; it is very imperfect; and yet it has what few novelists can give you, power. I do not know a novel in which the pain, the ecstasy, the ruthlessness, the obsessiveness of love have been so wonderfully described. *Wuthering Heights* reminds me of one of those great pictures of El Greco in which in a somber, arid landscape under dark clouds heavy with thunder, long, emaciated figures in contorted attitudes, spellbound by an unearthly emotion, hold their breath. A streak of lightning flitting across the leaden sky gives a final touch of mysterious terror to the scene. (pp. 126-34)

W. Somerset Maugham, "Emily Brontë and 'Wuthering Heights',' in his Great Novelists and Their Novels: Essays on the Ten Greatest Novels of the World, and the Men and Women Who Wrote Them, *The John C. Winston Company, 1948, pp. 115-34.*

Arnold Kettle   (essay date 1951)

[*Kettle is an English critic and educator specializing in social history and literature. His works include* Karl Marx, Founder of Modern Communism *(1963);* Communism and the Intellectuals *(1965); and (with V. G. Hanes)* Man and the Arts: A Marxist Approach *(1968). In the following essay, he analyzes the historical context of* Wuthering Heights, *concluding that the conflicts in the novel do not stem from abstract forces, but from concrete struggles between classes in nineteenth-century capitalist society.*]

Wuthering Heights, like all the greatest works of art, is at once concrete and yet general, local and yet universal. Because so much nonsense has been written and spoken about the Brontës and because Emily in particular has been so often presented to us as a ghost-like figure surrounded entirely by endless moorland, cut off from anything so banal as human society, not of her time but of eternity, it is necessary to emphasize at the outset the local quality of the book.

Wuthering Heights is about England in 1847. The people it reveals live not in a never-never land but in Yorkshire. Heathcliff was born not in the pages of Byron, but in a Liverpool slum. The language of Nelly, Joseph and Hareton is the language of Yorkshire people. The story of *Wuthering Heights* is concerned not with love in the abstract but with the passions of living people, with property-ownership, the attraction of social comforts, the arrangement of marriages, the importance of education, the validity of religion, the relations of rich and poor.

There is nothing vague about this novel; the mists in it are the mists of the Yorkshire moors; if we speak of it as having an elemental quality it is because the very elements, the great forces of nature are evoked, which change so slowly that in the span of a human life they seem unchanging. But in this evocation there is nothing sloppy or uncontrolled. On the contrary the realization is intensely concrete: we seem to smell the kitchen of Wuthering Heights, to feel the force of the wind across the moors, to sense the very changes of the seasons. Such concreteness is achieved not by mistiness but by precision.

It is necessary to stress this point but not, of course, to force it to a false conclusion. The power and wonder of Emily Brontë's novel does not lie in naturalistic description, nor in a detailed analysis of the hour-by-hour issues of social living. Her approach is, quite obviously, not the approach of Jane Austen; it is much nearer to the approach of Dickens. Indeed, **Wuthering Heights** is essentially the same kind of novel as *Oliver Twist*. It is not a romance, not (despite the film bearing the same title) an escape from life to the wild moors and romantic lovers. It is certainly not a picaresque novel and it cannot adequately be described as a moral fable, though it has a strong, insistent pattern. But the pattern, like that of Dickens's novel, cannot be abstracted as a neat sentence: its germ is not an intellectualized idea or concept.

Emily Brontë works not in ideas but in symbols, that is to say concepts which have a significance and validity on a level different from that of logical thought. Just as the significance of the workhouse in *Oliver Twist* cannot adequately be conceived in merely logical terms but depends on a host of associations—including its physical shape and colour—which logical analysis may penetrate but is unlikely adequately to convey, so the significance of the moors in **Wuthering Heights** cannot be suggested in the cold words of logic (which does not mean that it is illogical). The symbolic novel is an advance on the moral fable just in the sense that a symbol can be richer—can touch on more of life—than an abstract moral concept.

The opening sentence of the *Social Contract* gives a simple example: "Man was born free, but everywhere he is in chains." Of the two statements in this sentence the first is abstract, the second symbolic. And the impact of the second on our imagination is greater than that of the first for this very reason. (If one were concerned to go deeper into the matter one might suggest that Rousseau *knew* that man was in chains but merely speculated that he had been born free.) Now, whereas the symbolism of the moral fable (and the fable is itself a kind of extended symbol) is inherently limited by the abstract concept behind it, the symbolism of **Wuthering Heights** or the good part of *Oliver Twist* is the expression of the very terms in which the novel has been conceived. In fact, it *is* the novel and the novel stands or falls by its validity, its total adequacy to life.

Wuthering Heights is a vision of what life in 1847 was like.

Whether it can be described as a vision of what life as such—all life—is like is a question we will consider later. It is, for all its appearance of casualness and the complexity of its family relationships, a very well-constructed book, in which the technical problems of presentation have been most carefully thought out. The roles of the two narrators, Lockwood and Nelly Dean, are not casual. Their function (they the two most 'normal' people in the book) is partly to keep the story close to the earth, to make it believable, partly to comment on it from a common-sense point of view and thereby to reveal in part the inadequacy of such common sense. They act as a kind of sieve to the story, sometimes a double sieve, which has the purpose not simply of separating off the chaff, but of making us aware of the difficulty of passing easy judgments. One is left always with the sense that the last word has not been said.

The narrators do not as a rule talk realistically, though sometimes Nelly's part is to slip into a Yorkshire dialect that 'places' what she is describing and counteracts any tendency (inherent in symbolic art) to the pretentious. At critical points in the narrative we are not conscious of their existence at all; there is no attempt at a limiting verisimilitude of speech. They do not impose themselves between us and the scene. But at other times their attitudes are important.

One of the subtleties of the book is the way these attitudes change and develop; Lockwood and Nelly, like us, learn from what they experience, though at first their limitations are made use of, as in the very first scene when the expectations of the conventional Lockwood are so completely shocked by what he finds at Wuthering Heights. He goes there, he the normal Victorian gentleman, expecting to find the normal Victorian middle-class family. And what he finds—a house seething with hatred, conflict, horror—is a shock to us, too. The attack on our complacency, moral, social and spiritual, has already begun.

The centre and core of the book is the story of Catherine and Heathcliff. It is a story which has four stages. The first part, ending in the visit to Thrushcross Grange, tells of the establishing of a special relationship between Catherine and Heathcliff and of their common rebellion against Hindley and his régime in Wuthering Heights. In the second part is revealed Catherine's betrayal of Heathcliff, culminating in her death. The third part deals with Heathcliff's revenge, and the final section, shorter than the others, tells of the change that comes over Heathcliff and of his death. Even in the last two sections, after her death, the relationship with Catherine remains the dominant theme, underlying all else that occurs.

It is not easy to suggest with any precision the quality of feeling that binds Catherine and Heathcliff. It is not primarily a sexual relationship. Emily Brontë is not, as is sometimes suggested, afraid of sexual love; the scene at Catherine's death is proof enough that this is no platonic passion, yet to describe the attraction as sexual is surely quite inadequate. Catherine tries to express her feelings to Nelly (she is about to marry Linton).

> 'My great miseries in this world have been
> Heathcliff's miseries, and I watched and felt
> each from the beginning: my great thought in

living is himself. If all else perished, and *he* remained, *I* should still continue to be; and if all else remained, and he were annihilated, the universe would turn to a mighty stranger: I should not seem a part of it. My love for Linton is like the foliage in the woods: time will change it, I'm well aware, as winter changes the trees. My love for Heathcliff resembles the eternal rocks beneath: a source of little visible delight, but necessary. Nelly, I *am* Heathcliff! He's always, always in my mind: not as a pleasure, any more than I am always a pleasure to myself, but as my own being.'

and Heathcliff cries, when Catherine is dying: "I *cannot* live without my life, I *cannot* live without my soul." What is conveyed to us here is the sense of an affinity deeper than sexual attraction, something which it is not enough to describe as romantic love.

This affinity is forged in rebellion and, in order to grasp the concrete and unromantic nature of this book, it is necessary to recall the nature of that rebellion. Heathcliff, the waif from the Liverpool slums, is treated kindly by old Mr. Earnshaw but insulted and degraded by Hindley. After his father's death Hindley reduces the boy to the status of a serf. "He drove him from their company to the servants, deprived him of the instructions of the curate, and insisted that he should labour out of doors instead; compelling him to do so as hard as any other hand on the farm." The situation at Wuthering Heights is wonderfully evoked in the passage from Catherine's journal, which Lockwood finds in his bedroom:

'An awful Sunday!' commenced the paragraph beneath. 'I wish my father were back again. Hindley is a detestable substitute—his conduct to Heathcliff is atrocious—H. and I are going to rebel—we took our initiatory step this evening.

All day had been flooding with rain; we could not go to church, so Joseph must needs get up a congregation in the garret, and, while Hindley and his wife basked downstairs before a comfortable fire—doing anything but reading the Bibles, I'll answer for it—Heathcliff, myself, and the unhappy plough-boy, were commanded to take our Prayer-books, and mount: were ranged in a row, on a sack of corn, groaning and shivering, and hoping that Joseph would shiver too, so that he might give us a short homily for his own sake. A vain idea! The service lasted precisely three hours: and yet my brother had the face to exclaim, when he saw us descending, "What, done already?" On Sunday evenings we used to be permitted to play, if we did not make much noise; now a mere titter is sufficient to send us into corners!

"You forget you have a master here," says the tyrant. "I'll demolish the first who puts me out of temper! I insist on perfect sobriety and silence. Oh, boy! was that you? Frances darling, pull his hair as you go by: I heard him snap his fingers." Frances pulled his hair heartily, and then went and seated herself on her husband's knee: and there they were, like two babies, kissing and talking nonsense by the hour—foolish palaver

that we should be ashamed of. We made ourselves as snug as our means allowed in the arch of the dresser. I had just fastened our pinafores together, and hung them up for a curtain, when in comes Joseph on an errand from the stables. He tears down my handiwork boxes my ears and croaks—

"T' maister nobbut just buried, and Sabbath no o'ered, and t' sound o' t' gospel still i' yer lugs, and ye darr be laiking! Shame on ye! Sit ye down, ill childer! There's good books enough if ye'll read em! sit ye down, and think of yer sowls!" Saying this, he compelled us so to square our positions that we might receive from the far-off fire a dull ray to show us the text of the lumber he thrust upon us. I could not bear the employment. I took my dingy volume by the scroop, and hurled it into the dog-kennel, vowing I hated a good book. Heathcliff kicked his to the same place. Then there was a hubbub!

"Maister Hindley!" shouted our chaplain. "Maister, coom hither! Miss Cathy's riven th' back of 'Th' Helmet O' Salvation,' un Heathcliff's pawsed his fit into t' first part o' 'T' Brooad Way to Destruction.' It's fair flaysome, that ye let 'em go on this gait. Ech! th' owd man wad ha' laced 'em properly—but he's goan!"

Hindley hurried up from his paradise on the hearth, and seizing one of us by the collar, and the other by the arm, hurled both into the back kitchen, where, Joseph asseverated, "owd Nick" would fetch us as sure as we were living, and, so comforted, we each sought a separate nook to await his advent.'

This passage reveals, in itself, a great deal of the extraordinary quality of **Wuthering Heights.** It is a passage which, in the typical manner of the novel, evokes, in language which involves the kind of attention we give to poetry, a world far larger than the scene it describes, and evokes it through the very force and concreteness of the particular scene. The rebellion of Catherine and Heathcliff is made completely concrete. They are not vague romantic dreamers. Their rebellion is against the régime in which Hindley and his wife sit in fatuous comfort by the fire whilst they are relegated to the arch of the dresser and compelled for the good of their souls to read the *Broad Way to Destruction* under the tutelage of the canting hypocrite Joseph. It is a situation not confined, in the year 1847, to the more distant homesteads of the Yorkshire moors.

Against this degradation Catherine and Heathcliff rebel, hurling their pious books into the dog-kennel. And in their revolt they discover their deep and passionate need of each other. He, the outcast slummy, turns to the lively, spirited, fearless girl who alone offers him human understanding and comradeship. And she, born into the world of Wuthering Heights, senses that to achieve a full humanity, to be true to herself as a human being, she must associate herself totally with him in his rebellion against the tyranny of the Earnshaws and all that tyranny involves.

It is this rebellion that immediately, in this early section of the book, wins over our sympathy to Heathcliff. We know he is on the side of humanity and we are with him just as we are with Oliver Twist, and for much the same reasons. But whereas Oliver is presented with a sentimental passivity, which limits our concern, Heathcliff is active and intelligent and able to carry the positive values of human aspiration on his shoulders. He is a conscious rebel. And it is from his association in rebellion with Catherine that the particular quality of their relationship arises. It is the reason why each feels that a betrayal of what binds them together is in some obscure and mysterious way a betrayal of everything, of all that is most valuable in life and death.

Yet Catherine betrays Heathcliff and marries Edgar Linton, kidding herself that she can keep them both, and then discovering that in denying Heathcliff she has chosen death. The conflict here is, quite explicitly, a social one. Thrushcross Grange, embodying as it does the prettier, more comfortable side of bourgeois life, seduces Catherine. She begins to despise Heathcliff's lack of 'culture.' He has no conversation, he does not brush his hair, he is dirty, whereas Edgar, besides being handsome, "will be rich and I shall like to be the greatest woman of the neighbourhood, and I shall be proud of having such a husband." And so Heathcliff runs away and Catherine becomes mistress of Thrushcross Grange.

Heathcliff returns, adult and prosperous, and at once the social conflict is re-emphasized. Edgar, understandably, does not want to receive Heathcliff, but Catherine is insistent:

> 'I know you didn't like him,' she answered, repressing a little the intensity of her delight. 'Yet, for my sake, you must be friends now. Shall I tell him to come up?'
>
> 'Here,' he said, 'into the parlour?'
>
> 'Where else?' she asked.
>
> He looked vexed, and suggested the kitchen as a more suitable place for him. Mrs. Linton eyed him with a droll expression—half angry, half laughing at his fastidiousness.
>
> 'No,' she added after a while; 'I cannot sit in the kitchen. Set two tables here, Ellen: one for your master and Miss Isabella, being gentry, the other for Heathcliff and myself, being the lower orders. Will that please you, dear? . . . '

And from the moment of Heathcliff's reappearance Catherine's attempts to reconcile herself to Thrushcross Grange are doomed. In their relationship now there is no tenderness, they trample on each other's nerves, madly try to destroy each other; but, once Heathcliff is near, Catherine can maintain no illusions about the Lintons. The two are united only in their contempt for the values of Thrushcross Grange. "There it is," Catherine taunts Edgar, speaking of her grave, "not among the Lintons, mind, under the chapel roof, but in the open air, with a headstone." The open air, nature, the moors are contrasted with the world of Thrushcross Grange. And the contempt for the Lintons is a *moral* contempt, not a jealous one. When Nelly tells Heathcliff that Catherine is going mad, his comment is:

> 'You talk of her mind being unsettled. How the devil could it be otherwise in her frightful isolation? And that insipid paltry creature attending her from *duty* and *humanity!* From *pity* and *charity!* He might as well plant an oak in a flower-pot, and expect it to thrive, as imagine he can restore her to vigour in the soil of his shallow cares!'

The moral passion here is so intense, so deeply imbedded in the rhythm and imagery of the prose, that it is easy to be swept along without grasping its full and extraordinary significance. Heathcliff at this point has just perpetrated the first of his callous and ghastly acts of revenge, his marriage to Isabella. It is an act so morally repulsive that it is almost inconceivable that we should be able now to take seriously his attack on Edgar Linton, who has, after all, by conventional, respectable standards, done nobody any harm. And yet we *do* take the attack seriously because Emily Brontë makes us. The passion of the passage just quoted has the quality of great poetry. Why?

We continue to sympathize with Heathcliff, even after his marriage with Isabella, because Emily Brontë convinces us that what Heathcliff stands for is morally superior to what the Lintons stand for. This is, it must be insisted, not a case of some mysterious 'emotional' power with which Heathcliff is charged. The emotion behind his denunciation of Edgar is *moral* emotion. The words "duty" and "humanity," "pity" and "charity" have precisely the kind of force Blake gives such words in his poetry.

They are used not so much paradoxically as in a sense inverted but more profound than the conventional usage. Heathcliff speaks, apparently paradoxically, of Catherine's "frightful isolation," when to all appearances she is in Thrushcross Grange less isolated, more subject to care and society, than she could possibly be with him. But in truth Heathcliff's assertion is a paradox only to those who do not understand his meaning. What he is asserting with such intense emotional conviction that we, too, are convinced, is that what he stands for, the alternative life *he* has offered Catherine is more natural (the image of the oak enforces this), more social and more moral than the world of Thrushcross Grange. Most of those who criticize Heathcliff adversely (on the grounds that he is unbelievable, or that he is a neurotic creation, or that he is merely the Byronic satan-hero revived) fail to appreciate his significance because they fail to recognize this moral force. And as a rule they fail to recognize the moral force because they are themselves, consciously or not, of the Linton party.

The climax of this inversion by Heathcliff and Catherine of the common standards of bourgeois morality comes at the death of Catherine. To recognize the revolutionary force of this scene one has only to imagine what a different novelist might have made of it.

The stage is all set for a moment of conventional drama. Catherine is dying, Heathcliff appears out of the night. Two possibilities present themselves: either Catherine will at the last reject Heathcliff, the marriage vow will be vindicated and wickedness meet its reward; or true love will triumph and reconciliation proclaim the world well lost. It is hard to imagine that either possibility ever crossed Emily Brontë's mind, for either would destroy the pattern of her book, but her rejection of them is a measure of her moral and artistic power. For instead of its conventional potentialities the scene acquires an astonishing moral power. Heathcliff confronted with the dying Catherine, is ruthless, morally ruthless: instead of easy comfort he offers her a brutal analysis of what she has done.

> 'You teach me now how cruel you've been—cruel and false. *Why* did you despise me? *Why* did you betray your own heart Cathy? I have not one word of comfort. You deserve this. You have killed yourself. Yes, you may kiss me, and cry: and wring out my kisses and tears: they'll blight you—they'll damn you. You loved me—then what *right* had you to leave me? What right—answer me—for the poor fancy you felt for Linton? Because misery and degradation, and death, and nothing that God or Satan could inflict would have parted us, *you,* of your own will, did it. I have not broken your heart—*you* have broken it; and in breaking it you have broken mine. So much the worse that I am strong. Do I want to live? What kind of living will it be when you—oh, God! would *you* like to live with your soul in the grave?'

It is one of the harshest passages in all literature, but it is also one of the most moving. For the brutality is not neurotic, nor sadistic, nor romantic. The Catherine-Heathcliff relationship, standing as it does for a humanity finer and more morally profound than the standards of the Lintons and Earnshaws has to undergo the kind of examination Heathcliff here brings to it. Anything less, anything which smudged or sweetened the issues involved, would be inadequate, unworthy. Heathcliff knows that nothing can save Catherine from death but that one thing alone can give her peace, a full and utterly honest understanding and acceptance of their relationship and what it implies. There is no hope in comfort or compromise. Any such weakness would debase them both and make a futile waste of their lives and death. For Heathcliff and Catherine, who reject the Lintons' chapel roof and the consolations of Christianity, know, too, that their relationship is more important than death.

In the section of the book that follows Catherine's death Heathcliff continues the revenge he has begun with his marriage to Isabella. It is the most peculiar section of the novel and the most difficult because the quality of Heathcliff's feeling is of a kind most of us find hard to comprehend. All normal and healthy human feeling is rejected. He cries:

> 'I have no pity! I have no pity! The more the worms writhe, the more I yearn to crush out their entrails! It is a moral teething; and I grind with greater energy, in proportion to the increase of pain.'

"It is a moral teething"—the phrase is both odd and significant, giving as it does the answer to our temptation to treat this whole section as a delineation of pathological neurosis. Heathcliff becomes a monster: what he does to Isabella, to Hareton, to Cathy, to his son, even to the wretched Hindley, is cruel and inhuman beyond normal thought. He seems concerned to achieve new refinements of horror, new depths of degradation. And we tend to feel, perhaps, unless we read with full care and responsiveness, that Emily Brontë has gone too far, that the revenge (especially the marriage of Cathy and Linton Heathcliff) has o'erflown the measure.

And yet it is only one side of our minds, the conscious, limited side that refers what we are reading to our everyday measures of experience that makes this objection. Another side, which is more completely responding to Emily Brontë's art, is carried on. And the astonishing achievement of this part of the book is that, despite our protests about probability (protests which, incidentally, a good deal of twentieth-century history makes a little complacent), despite everything he does and is, we continue to sympathize with Heathcliff—not, obviously, to admire him or defend him, but to give him our inmost sympathy, to continue in an obscure way to identify ourselves with him *against* the other characters.

The secret of this achievement lies in such a phrase as "it is a moral teething" and in the gradually clarifying pattern of the book. Heathcliff's revenge may involve a pathological condition of hatred, but it is not at bottom merely neurotic. It has a moral force. For what Heathcliff does is to use against his enemies with complete ruthlessness their own weapons, to turn on them (stripped of their romantic veils) their own standards, to beat them at their own game. The weapons he uses against the Earnshaws and Lintons are their own weapons of money and arranged marriages. He gets power over them by the classic methods of the ruling class, expropriation and property deals. He buys out Hindley and reduces him to drunken impotency, he marries Isabella and then organizes the marriage of his son to Catherine Linton, so that the entire property of the two families shall be controlled by himself. He systematically degrades Hareton Earnshaw to servility and illiteracy. "I want the triumph of seeing *my* descendant fairly lord of *their* estates! My child hiring their children to till their father's lands for wages." (This is a novel which, some critics will tell you, has nothing to do with anything as humdrum as society or life as it is actually lived.) And what particularly tickles Heathcliff's fancy is his achievement of the supreme ruling-class triumph of making Hareton, the boy he degrades, feel a deep and even passionate attachment towards himself.

Heathcliff retains our sympathy throughout this dreadful section of the book because instinctively we recognize a rough moral justice in what he has done to his oppressors and because, though he is inhuman, we understand *why* he is inhuman. Obviously we do not approve of what he does, but we understand it; the deep and complex issues behind his actions are revealed to us. We recognize that the very forces which drove him to rebellion for a higher freedom have themselves entrapped him in their own values and determined the nature of his revenge.

If ***Wuthering Heights*** were to stop at this point it would still be a great book, but a wholly sombre and depressing one. Man would be revealed as inevitably caught up in the meshes of his own creating; against the tragic horror of

Heathcliff's appalling rebellion the limited but complacent world of Thrushcross Grange would seem a tempting haven and the novel would resolve itself into the false antithesis of Thrushcross Grange/Wuthering Heights, just as in *Oliver Twist* the real antithesis becomes sidetracked into the false one of Brownlow/Fagin. But *Wuthering Heights,* a work of supreme and astonishing genius, does not stop here. We have not done with Heathcliff yet.

For at the moment of his horrible triumph a change begins to come over Heathcliff.

> 'It is a poor conclusion, is it not?' he observed, having brooded a while on the scene he had just witnessed: 'an absurd termination to my violent exertions? I get levers and mattocks to demolish the two houses, and train myself to be capable of working like Hercules, and when everything is ready and in my power, I find the will to lift a slate off either roof has vanished! My old enemies have not beaten me; now would be the precise time to revenge myself on their representatives: I could do it, and none could hinder me. But where is the use? I don't care for striking; I can't take the trouble to raise my hand! That sounds as if I had been labouring the whole time only to exhibit a fine trait of magnanimity. It is far from being the case: I have lost the faculty of enjoying their destruction, and I am too idle to destroy for nothing.

> 'Nelly, there is a strange change approaching: I'm in its shadow at present.'

and he goes on to speak of Cathy and Hareton, who "seemed a personification of my youth, not a human being." "Hareton's aspect was the ghost of my immortal love; of my wild endeavour to hold my right; my degradation, my pride, my happiness and my anguish." When Nelly asks "But what do you mean by a *change,* Mr. Heathcliff?" he can only answer "I shall not know that till it comes," he said "I'm only half conscious of it now." Once more the stage is set for a familiar scene, the conversion of the wicked who will in the final chapter turn from his wickedness. And once more the conventional must look again.

The change that comes over Heathcliff and the novel and leads us on to the wonderful, quiet, gentle, tentative evocation of spring of the final sentence, is a very subtle one. It has something of the quality of the last two acts of *The Winter's Tale* but is much less complete, less confident. Mr. Klingopulos in his interesting essay on *Wuthering Heights* [in *Scrutiny,* Vol. XIV] has commented on the ambiguous nature of this final tranquillity. I do not agree with his analysis but he has caught the tone most convincingly. Heathcliff, watching the love of Cathy and Hareton grow, comes to understand something of the failure of his own revenge. As Cathy teaches Hareton to write and stops laughing at his ignorance we too are taken back to the first Catherine.

Cathy and Hareton are not in the novel an easy re-creation of Catherine and Heathcliff, they are, as Mr. Klingopulos remarks, different people, even lesser people, certainly people conceived on a less intense and passionate scale than the older lovers. But they do symbolize the continu-

ity of life and human aspirations, and it is through them that Heathcliff comes to understand the hollowness of his triumph. It is when Hareton, who loves him, comes to Cathy's aid when he strikes her that the full meaning of his own relationship with Catherine comes back to him and he becomes aware that in the feeling between Cathy and Hareton there is something of the same quality. From the moment that Cathy and Hareton are drawn together as rebels the change begins. For now for the first time Heathcliff is confronted not with those who accept the values of Wuthering Heights and Thrushcross Grange but with those who share, however remotely, his own wild endeavours to hold his right.

Heathcliff does not repent. Nelly tries to make him turn to the consolations of religion.

> 'You are aware, Mr. Heathcliff,' I said, 'that from the time you were thirteen years old, you have lived a selfish, unchristian life; and probably hardly had a Bible in your hands during all that period. You must have forgotten the contents of the Book, and you may not have space to search it now. Could it be hurtful to send for some one—some minister of any denomination, it does not matter which—to explain it, and show you how very far you have erred from its precepts; and how unfit you will be for its heaven, unless a change takes place before you die?' 'I'm rather obliged than angry, Nelly,' he said, 'for you remind me of the manner in which I desire to be buried. It is to be carried to the churchyard in the evening. You and Hareton may, if you please, accompany me: and mind, particularly, to notice that the sexton obeys my directions concerning the two coffins! No minister need come; nor need anything be said over me.—I tell you I have nearly attained my heaven, and that of others is altogether unvalued and uncoveted by me.'

One sentence here, in its limpid simplicity, especially evokes the state of mind Heathcliff has come to. He speaks of the manner in which he wishes to be buried. "It is to be carried to the churchyard in the evening." The great rage has died in him. He has come to see the pointlessness of his fight to revenge himself on the world of power and property through its own values. Just as Catherine had to face the full moral horror of her betrayal of their love, he must face the full horror of his betrayal too. And once he has faced it he can die, not nobly or triumphantly, but at least as a man, leaving with Cathy and Hareton the possibility of carrying on the struggle he has begun, and in his death he will achieve again human dignity, "to be carried to the churchyard in the evening."

It is this re-achievement of manhood by Heathcliff, an understanding reached with no help from the world he despises, which, together with the developing relationship of Cathy and Hareton and the final sense of life reborn in springtime, gives to the last pages of *Wuthering Heights* a sense of positive and unsentimental hope. The Catherine-Heathcliff relationship has been vindicated. Life will go on and others will rebel against the oppressors. Nothing has been solved but much has been experienced. Lies, complacencies and errors, appalling errors, have been revealed. A veil has been drawn from the conventional face of bourgeois man; he has been revealed, through Heathcliff, without his mask.

Above all, the quality of the feeling that binds Catherine and Heathcliff has been conveyed to us. Their love, which Heathcliff can without idealism call immortal, is something beyond the individualist dream of two soul-mates finding full realization in one another; it is an expression of the necessity of man, if he is to choose life rather than death, to revolt against all that would destroy his inmost needs and aspirations, of the necessity of all human beings to become, through acting together, more fully human. Catherine, responding to this deep human necessity, rebels with Heathcliff but in marrying Edgar (a 'good' marriage if ever there was one) betrays her own humanity; Heathcliff, by revenging himself on the tyrants through the adoption of their own standards makes more clear those standards but betrays too his humanity and destroys his relationship with the dead Catherine whose spirit must haunt the moors in terror and dismay.

Only when the new change has come over Heathcliff and he again recognizes through Hareton (and remotely, therefore, through Catherine herself) the full claims of humanity can Catherine be released from torment and their relationship re-established. Death is a matter of little importance in *Wuthering Heights* because the issues the novel is concerned with are greater than the individual life and death. The deaths of Catherine and Heathcliff are indeed a kind of triumph because ultimately each faces death honestly, keeping faith. But there is no suggestion that death itself is a triumph: on the contrary it is life that asserts itself, continues, blossoms again.

Mr. David Wilson in his excellent essay on Emily Brontë [*Modern Quarterly,* 1947] to which I am deeply indebted (though I do not agree with all of his interpretation) suggests an identification, not necessarily conscious in Emily Brontë's mind, of Heathcliff with the rebellious working men of the hungry 'forties' and of Catherine with that part of the educated class which felt compelled to identify itself with their cause. Such a formulation, suggestive as it is, seems to me to be too far removed from the actual impact of *Wuthering Heights* as a novel, to be satisfactory. But Mr. Wilson has done a valuable service in rescuing *Wuthering Heights* from the transcendentalists and in insisting on the place of Haworth (generally assumed to be a remote country village) in the industrial revolution and its attendant social unrest. The value of his suggestion with regard to Heathcliff and Catherine seems to me in the emphasis it gives to the concrete, local particularity of the book.

It is very necessary to be reminded that just as the values of Wuthering Heights and Thrushcross Grange are not simply the values of *any* tyranny but specifically those of Victorian society, so is the rebellion of Heathcliff a particular rebellion, that of the worker physically and spiritually degraded by the conditions and relationships of this same society. That Heathcliff ceases to be one of the exploited is true, but it is also true that just in so far as he adopts (with a ruthlessness that frightens even the ruling class itself) the standards of the ruling class, so do the human

values implicit in his early rebellion and in his love for Catherine vanish. All that is involved in the Catherine-Heathcliff relationship, all that it stands for in human needs and hopes, can be realized only through the active rebellion of the oppressed.

Wuthering Heights then is an expression in the imaginative terms of art of the stresses and tensions and conflicts, personal and spiritual, of nineteenth-century capitalist society. It is a novel without idealism, without false comforts, without any implication that power over their destinies rests outside the struggles and actions of human beings themselves. Its powerful evocation of nature, of moorland and storm, of the stars and the seasons is an essential part of its revelation of the very movement of life itself. The men and women of *Wuthering Heights* are not the prisoners of nature; they live in the world and strive to change it, sometimes successfully, always painfully, with almost infinite difficulty and error.

This unending struggle, of which the struggle to advance from class society to the higher humanity of a classless world is but an episode, is conveyed to us in *Wuthering Heights* precisely because the novel is conceived in actual, concrete, particular terms, because the quality of oppression revealed in the novel is not abstract but concrete, not vague but particular. And that is why Emily Brontë's novel is at the same time a statement about the life she knew, the life of Victorian England, and a statement about life as such. Virginia Woolf, writing about it, said:

> That gigantic ambition is to be felt throughout the novel, a struggle half thwarted but of superb conviction, to say something through the mouths of characters which is not merely 'I love' or 'I hate' but 'we, the whole human race' and 'You, the eternal powers . . .' the sentence remains unfinished.

I do not think it remains unfinished. (pp. 139-55)

Arnold Kettle, "Emily Brontë: 'Wuthering Heights'," *in his* An Introduction to the English Novel: To George Eliot, Vol. I, *Hutchinson's University Library, 1951, pp. 139-55.*

B. H. Lehman   (essay date 1955)

[*In the following essay, Lehman explores* Wuthering Heights *in terms of its style, narrative structure, and character depiction.*]

The easy assertion that *Wuthering Heights* is a Gothic tale can no longer be taken seriously. The story, abstracted into a skeleton plot, is indeed as absurd and improbable as any Gothic story, or, for that matter, as Hamlet's story, both of which it resembles in the use of haunted precincts, the usurpation of rights and property, the tendency to leap into graves, abrupt deaths, passion, and the rationalizing of elemental revenge impulses into a righting of wrongs. The scraps which are dissolved into the work may have come from the prodigalities of the Gothic novel, or from "The Bridegroom of Barna" in *Blackwood's,* or from Byron's tales, or from Shakespeare, or they may have been found in the world from which Emily said "Charlotte will bring it all home to me." The materials include bits from Charlotte's "mad Methodist Magazines full of miracles and apparitions and preternatural warnings, ominous dreams, and frenzied fanaticisms," along with such local memories as those of old William Grimshaw, hero of the Methodist Haworth Round, who had a son and a daughter who filled his house with the poor and the adopted, and farmed his glebe by setting Methodist preachers expert in Yorkshire to labor between exhortations, whose son drank himself to degradation as did Hindley Earnshaw. These are there and also the commercial-age tale of John Walker and his nephew Jack from the Halifax neighborhood.

Of the material, too, is the moor. There are those who hold that the book was moor-born, that the subject of the book is the moor, that the genius of the book is the genius of awesome place. Certainly the moor is there, as a reality and a condition of realities. It is never directly described, yet rock ribs its surface, for Cathy has noted and for her own purposes mentions the fact. Its surface within narrow range is various in form and color: paths and pits and rolling stretches and ridges, trees and heather and grass and birds, the moor cock and the wild duck, and those ousels that went about nest building in spite of Heathcliff—he had stood motionless so long while Cathy was dying. It is there at all hours, in all lights, in all weathers. Sometimes it is so quiet water is heard far off in Gimmerton beck and again the storm roars. The wind stirs gently the trees near the grange but it has slanted the stunted firs at the Heights. The moor, changing from season to season but constant from year to year, rises real in the mind because Heathcliff crosses it, and Cathy remembers it, and Nelly Dean looks out on it. But the moor cannot be the subject of the work. It does not dominate the lives lived upon it. It conditions them as any environment does, in special ways arising from its character and quality; and those that are native to it fit it well, and Heathcliff who is a foreigner has with it an inner affinity perceived by us at large and in a special sense by Cathy when she says to Isabella he is all "furze and whinstone." Most of all, had Emily Brontë felt the moor to be her subject she would have ended with it. Yet as we move to the close the moor is outside the circle of illumination, only its benign manifestations are heard or seen as at a distance; under the slant firs bent with storms Nelly Dean sits with her work; and in the last sentence the moor has become that universal thing earth, the grave of all. The moor, we are reminded, is not all furze and whinstone: violence and terror and stark fortitude seem to have an especial appropriateness in that landscape; but of old time the Lintons were merry in their crimson and white and gold drawing room and gay in their park, and Heathcliff and Cathy as children happy on the Heights, and now Hareton and Catherine are taking a good-night look at one another by the moon's light; these moods also are appropriate on the moor. In this juxtaposition, then, of sleepers in the quiet earth and the retrospect and prospect upon an adorable life, we come close, I believe, to the subject of *Wuthering Heights.*

If now we more closely observe the novel, it must strike us that certain universal modes of being pervade it. One— the march of the generations—is inherent in the nature of life itself. In the Linton and Earnshaw families, three gen-

erations, with differing fullness of portraiture of course, come before our view, and in the happy prelude to nest building in which we glimpse Hareton and Catherine at last, there is promise of another. One remembers the ousels building a nest while Heathcliff waited the word that ended his hope of nest making with Cathy in this world. But more notable still, we are told that the Earnshaws are an ancient stock and reminded that generations bygone are laid away in the Linton vaults in Gimmerton church. The line vanishes in the past, it emerges to view in the future. The generations rise and fall, each with its vicissitudes. The elder Lintons appear to have lived a delightful life till fever killed them; all went smoothly at farmer Earnshaw's with such minor excitements as the father's bringing home a gypsy-looking waif. The next generation lived in stress and storm and fire, which hung threateningly over the third, till the death of Heathcliff, following his ecstatic withdrawal from violence and revenge, made all things fair. These variations have been going on time out of mind; no man knows through what aeons to come they will continue. The condition of them is birth and death and an interval between.

In *Wuthering Heights* no great ado is made about birth, even when a mother's death is its immediate cost; and, with Hindley's imported wife Frances chirping at everything but weepily afraid of dying to set the perspective, death is taken as naturally as birth. It is of the nature of things and on the moor one knows what that is. Nelly Dean not only observes the seasons and birds and man at nest building. She also lays out the dead and washes the newborn. Between these end events human beings may

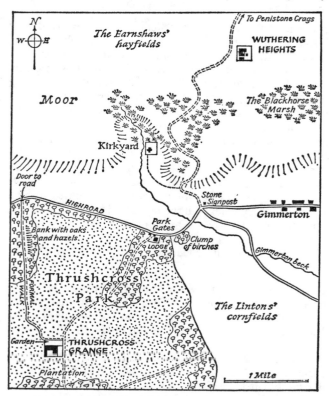

A map of the locale of Wuthering Heights.

shine like the moonbeams or the frost, or burn like fire or the lightning, as Cathy implies. But in any case the generations rise, fulfill their destinies, and go down. To the absurdities and improbabilities that fill the interval we call living, set thus in the endless pattern of life itself, there accrues something of necessity, something of simplicity. That Hareton and Catherine, not without Heathcliff's recognition, rediscover in themselves the promptings that assure that endlessness, assuages, even consoles. Those "Twain / Rule in this realm"; Fortinbras has the dying voice. End of Hamlet, end of Lear! But with a difference. We partake deeply of tranquillity among the household activities at the Heights before we stand in Gimmerton churchyard where the moss is spread on the tombstones, where among the heath and harebells the moth flutters away its brief vitality, where the wind moves so softly among the leaves of common grass.

These images of less elaborated forms of existence serve to remind us that those who sleep in the grave were beset in consciousness by other modes, peculiar to the human, and for the human more or less universal in the era. At first glance property seems to absorb into itself all the manifestations of society. There are the estates of the Lintons and the Earnshaws, the sum laid aside for Isabella's dowry, and in Heathcliff the force that remorselessly, or at least mercilessly, usurps them. Then toward the end we learn that Zillah is storing her labors' wage and supposes Nelly Dean to be doing the same, and throughout the book there are present the process and effect of livings earned from the land at the Heights. But property is only one element in a play of forces, though perhaps a primary one. Pride, power, and freedom are inextricably involved with property.

In the book as it comes before us, we at the very outset have this interplay dramatically realized. Mr. Lockwood has apologized for his

> "... perseverance in soliciting the occupation of Thrushcross Grange: I heard yesterday," he says, "you had had some thoughts—"

> "Thrushcross Grange is my own, sir," [Heathcliff] interrupted, wincing. "I should not allow any one to inconvenience me, if I could hinder it—walk in!"

The note here struck is sounded again by Nelly Dean soon after she begins her story: Hindley—a boy of fourteen— blubbers aloud because the fiddle bought him as a present, bundled in Mr. Earnshaw's greatcoat with the little gypsy, has been crushed, and Cathy spits out her ill-humor at the stupid little thing because her riding whip has been lost. For Hindley, young Heathcliff remained from that emotional moment a threat to his rights, the more so since, as the months passed, Mr. Earnshaw developed and did not conceal a growing partiality for the waif, and Heathcliff himself to get what he wanted—a sound pony on one occasion—boyishly and justifiably blackmailed Hindley into giving over. Hindley's hurt pride, soothed in the three years' absence which gave him freedom and power, manifested itself again only after he came into his inheritance. Then, awakened by his wife's dislike of Heathcliff, the old hatred took those frightening forms which ended in mak-

ing the boy a bitter oaf. Hindley brought him "so low" that Cathy confides in Nelly, "It would degrade me to marry Heathcliff now," and Heathcliff overhearing vanishes.

Thus, inconspicuously arising from the broken fiddle the stream of events moves on through the degradation of Hareton, Hindley's son, as well as of Hindley himself, and Wuthering Heights becomes Heathcliff's property. Then Isabella's dowry. Then Thrushcross Grange. But none of the property is a pleasure in possession or is attained for the pleasure of possession. And only the first with a pure motive of revenge; the others come into Heathcliff's hands as the result of blind, wild striking out against the Lintons who, in the person of Edgar, have drawn to themselves his loved Cathy. With those he loved—and that he could have loved everyone and was not admitted to is a powerfully moving tragic fact about him—Heathcliff was not a fighter for possessions. "When," he says to Nelly in his delectable report of the experience he shared with Cathy at the drawing-room windows of the Lintons', "When would you catch me wishing to have what Catherine wanted?" He was a boy when he said that and thought of Cathy as his sister. Later looking back on himself enslaved by those who had land and wealth, of a race that gets on without either, he sought freedom which his blood bespoke and he vaguely understood but fiercely felt it was to be had by land and wealth. Possession was power; with power he would soothe *his* hurt pride, greater than Hindley's had ever been by as much as he is more passionate than that pallid Earnshaw, by as much as a lost Cathy is greater than a lost fiddle. He had destroyed, because the glory lurking in the world had been destroyed for him; but at last he can say, "I have lost the faculty of enjoying their destruction, and I am too idle to destroy for nothing"; and a little later, "... how to leave my property I cannot determine! I wish I could annihilate it from the face of the earth."

The property was nothing, come into possession, especially to a gypsy nature. The wish to annihilate is touched of course in its intricate causes with the vengeful desire to deprive the Lintons and the Earnshaws in perpetuity, but there is an emergent sense in Heathcliff that property held on to is itself a villain, frustrating whatever is immediate and tender, whatever alleviates because the nerves sing; he fears it for Hareton and young Catherine, as they go about with his Cathy's eyes, gleaming at one another. Himself, he has come into a vast emptiness, populated only by Cathy's image—on the flagstone, in every cloud, in every tree, filling the air at night. When he might have used property to move upon his true object, he did not have it or its blessing; at last that object is beyond reach by such means, and he relaxes his grasp. He does not make a will. Let the tried forms of this little world reassert themselves, the inheritance fall by law. The habited responses, engendered in a given milieu, which rescue mortal men in crises have never been his; although he only now gives up to the little world's law, he has always been a foreigner. Direct and fiercely intelligent, he can for certain uses grasp the mechanism of a property civilization with its respectabilities; but though he is imaginative and tender, he is too passionate to seize the essences concealed in the elaborations of such a civilization or to make fruitful use of either. In his aspect, his blood, and his predicament, there is something of Othello, something of Medea. It is not chance that when the history is done, Heathcliff's blood is eliminated entirely. For all his accidental affinity with furze and whinstone, he was an extravagant and erring stranger from the first, against whom subtle and obscure as well as forthright barriers were set up. However it may be in that other world where he and Cathy walk side by side to the terror of a little boy and some sheep, the evolved, the homogeneous manner of life on the moors will have less of pain, the vicissitudes turn in narrower range now he is gone. The intense and terrible years are over, the simple life-giving routines for which Nelly Dean has stood symbol reassert themselves.

It is, in nature, not a permanent equilibrium, since, in nature, that is impossible. Other intrusion may at any time upset it. There is a suggestion of this in Lockwood's presence: he casts an appraising and speculative eye on young Catherine's nubile beauty. But his observation and his very tentative thoughts of marriage merely confirm what is otherwise more richly asserted.

The subject Emily Brontë finds in her material is no less than a vision of life renewing itself: however tortured by conventions and property, however tormented by the collision of such as Cathy and Heathcliff, it fulfills itself in mere being, in love which is the lure of begetting. The love of Cathy and Heathcliff is a tragic tale, defeated in the flesh and symbolically fixed upon union beyond the flesh, either in the ashes of the grave with a pair of coffin sides removed, or in the spectral presences that may, for all that has been said or seen, veritably haunt the ways their bodies walked. But in the dreadful story the ravaged and ravaging central figures are sealed off at last with the affirmation "youth again, love again, life again, and peace at last always." The vision of life extending both before and after the tragic episode is deep and comic in the full sense that the whole book makes for well-being, reassures us of the one indispensable thing: The life stream will continue.

For Emily Brontë the novelist the problem then was how, with so dreadful a story to tell, with the disastrous collision, the ravaging passion, and no help from Christian consolation, to end with this affirmation? The answer was Nelly Dean and the broken doubling-back line of the narrative.

These were marvelous intuitions. For, before everything else, the world of these events must be a solid world, perceived by every sense in every activity characteristic of it, the violence and the dreadfulness embedded in the familiar and the habitual. In Emily Brontë's mind it was real: C. P. Sanger has demonstrated the exactness and the thoroughness of the chronology in itself and with respect to seasonal phenomena in nature, the soundness of the use of the very intricate law of land and that of money and goods involved in the property transfers, and the supporting force of the symmetrical pedigrees of the Earnshaws and the Lintons. For Emily Brontë, too, the household routines were immediate to the mind's eye; she had spent half her days ironing, cooking, cleaning. And the moor! Virginia Woolf to the contrary notwithstanding, Emily

Brontë had observed nature as accurately as Dorothy Wordsworth and painted it as minutely as Tennyson. For this book, her unconscious art rejected minuteness and the accuracy of minuteness, save upon revealing occasion; but that no one ever saw more particularly the things evoked, witness her water-color drawing of her pet merlin-hawk, which in spite of the unclosed claw on bough impresses the bird experts of this Audubonic age; or witness her pencil sketch of the great stricken pine in the garden of the Pensionnat Héger, a minute and accurate rendering infused with the very spirit of pine tree.

It was all real indeed to Emily Brontë. Merely to affirm that world—with its astonishing people and its scenes that banished Charlotte's sleep by night—would be to invite dismissal: to hear said, after all it was only a tale. Besides, no ordinary recounting with the interest fixed on the main events could possibly draw our attention for full value to the familiar and habitual living as it goes on in those houses. Yet it was that very routine with which one might hope to anchor the wild and violent story and prepare for the last stage, the final mood. The personal narrative on the principle of "Part of which I was, all of which I saw," would do, provided a servant properly articulated in both households could at once be a mere narrator and an unawarely peasant-shrewd but book-literate woman of all-round endowment and of the most undeniable sanity and steadiness. What she reported, who could question? Yet there were difficulties. Should such a servant write the story, she would vanish as a person; her natural penlessness would turn her into nothing, if one gave her pen. She must talk. And there were of course things she could not herself have seen. So much the better then! For some could be reported by the letter method, which had seemed so vivifying for whole novels, and when necessary the narrator could report what had been reported to her, thus giving added solidity to the world of the story, since in effect more pairs of eyes than one had seen. For example, there is that picture one means to give of the drawing room at Thrushcross Grange, that will best be seen first by the unaccustomed eyes of young Heathcliff in Cathy's exciting company, and through casements, a magical cave of light and color undeserved by its squabbling children. A servant would only see it as a place to dust, with tables to bring up for tea, and fires to mend, as Nelly Dean later will see it; she would only think of the children as naughty; whole ranges of suggestion and implication that belong to young Heathcliff do not belong to Nelly. Much is gained by various glimpses. Furthermore, this book-read servant would be able to report the speech of her masters, but she could also mimic Joseph, and he with his finely shaded Calvinistic Methodism must be there as the ineffectual orthodox Christian commentary upon these events that spin themselves as though Christ had never died upon the Cross. Another difficulty: a paragon of servants and a ruminating and capacious-memoried woman, would she not be too good to be true? Well, let her be something of a busybody; curiosity is common enough in servants and a positive blessing in people who tell stories. She may pry and even snoop at keyholes, and intrude in the affairs of grownups, having minded them and their business when they were little. Of course, though she peeps and intrudes, she fancies herself above doing that, so she will have misgivings and moments of self-reproach; yet the folk artist in her likes to get things straight, so she will not be very hard on herself. She can have other realizing touches: to keep her job she learns to accommodate herself, and calls it learning to be less touchy; she enjoys giving people a piece of her mind upon occasion, but she plays safe; she takes pride in her reading; she has traveled as far as the coal country. And then she will have not only a native's sense of the moor but a servant's: she will have gone about her work in all weathers, and will see the moor practically, with a weather-wise eye, landscapes oftenest in terms of weather or ground to cover, and as often as not from indoors: that is as life on the moor really is. There will be no descriptions as in Walter Scott's novels. Also, in a servant's view furniture and utensils are for use, and she will speak of them as in use. That too will avoid descriptions, and the pictures will be varied but not miscellaneous. It seems a happy idea altogether. And Nelly Dean becomes a personality as she grows in the mind imagining the novel that is to be written. In her abundance and heartiness and usefulness in tending the hearth (how often we see her at that), she is an unwavering symbol of life lived to the best of its possibilities, a sensible soul, as she calls herself, most objective in reporting haunted rooms and ghosts, the maker of order out of disorder. A marvelous intuition that became a triumphant realization.

Still there remained that problem that Nelly Dean in her nature would never take up a pen and write the story. Perhaps the broken doubling-back line of narrative had already occurred to Emily Brontë, or perhaps it suggested itself as a solution of this problem. In any case, there it is. Thirty-five years before Henry James wrote *The Portrait of a Lady*, almost twice as many years before Joseph Conrad lifted James's "most superior intelligence" out of the story, made him a narrator in the oblique method, and experimented with the presentation of events in a rearranged chronology with the object of deepening the perspective and building up ever more solidly, stone by stone, the universe in which his people moved, Emily Brontë discovered for herself that way of achieving a unified effect in terms of a subject perceived to be inherent in a given material.

The defect of instrumentality for the doubling-back narrative in **Wuthering Heights** does not lie in Nelly Dean. It arises from the fact that Mr. Lockwood is not the more sensitive consciousness of the two who are reviewing the events, that he listens not because he is interested in what he hears but because he is bored with the condition into which he has got himself, that he has deficient appreciation of Nelly's gifts, and that, returning to Gimmerton casually as he does, it is unbelievable that he would have bothered to set the story down, though it is credible that at the end, confronting Cathy and Heathcliff in the one situation he is ever likely to share with them, he should for a moment rise to the occasion in the beautiful words with which the book ends. For the rest, though he has a seeing eye, he is a petty man, an ineffectual "romantic" who fancies he wants solitude, love, reality, and actually lives firmly enmeshed in the false secondary code that crystallizes from wealth, leisure, and negligible natural equipment. Whether he is so because Emily Brontë did not fully understand the possibilities his blank space in her plan of-

fered her, or because her unconscious mind gave her no help with the city man whose background so far as she knew it was deeply distasteful to her, or because she was betrayed by an incidental impulse to show so disliked a specimen to disadvantage, it is impossible to guess. Certainly, for whatever reason, Lockwood was uncongenial to her genius. He contributes few of those small inevitable indications which as they accumulate make the texture of the work as it comes from Nelly's tongue.

In this matter of Mr. Lockwood the realization is not triumphant, but the intuition was marvelous nevertheless. Because, in spite of Lockwood's inappropriate nature, Emily Brontë draws from him values of highest importance to her total effect. First of all, Lockwood's initial view of the household at the Heights shows us that strange place with its wire-drawn tensions as it looks from the outside to one who knows nothing of motives, of past history, of present strains. Lockwood comes upon it unprepared, and we receive through his report an impression of objective existence that startles, as Nelly Dean could never give it at the outset without an artful trick or a rhetorical heightening that would be uncharacteristic of one so folk-bred. Further, when before beginning her story Nelly Dean speaks of conditions at the Heights and of Heathcliff, the fact of a second observer reassures us of their objective existence in spite of the strangeness. In addition, offering us first this picture of an advanced condition of affairs in the story eliminates the possibility that we shall go astray in our expectation after Heathcliff leaves the moor and nothing is heard of him: he is set by this means permanently in the center of the book, where he belongs from first sentence to last. Yet the arrangement allows Emily Brontë to keep well in hand the subject of the work, which transcends him and his story. Also, when on Lockwood's second visit to the Heights he is stormbound, his dream in Cathy's bed not only brings, through Heathcliff's reactions to it, a very advanced state of being into the present, but affords us—precisely because it is a dream—a rational possibility with respect to ghosts and a necessary early account of the unnatural phenomena which crackle in this charged atmosphere. And it sets before us in unearthly connection the room in which Heathcliff is to be found dead. Altogether, the method deepens the perspective in place by setting London and the watering places on the periphery of the world, as the insisted-upon succession of the generations deepens the perspective in time, and works thus to achieve, the more because of Lockwood's intonation as of a man slumming, that isolation which is procured in great drama by raising the central figures to kingly or other high distinction. Finally, only Lockwood—an outsider and a city man—could note for us the carving above the principal door at Wuthering Heights: the crumbling griffins and the shameless little boys. It is of the highest importance that these should be noted. The monsters are breaking down, taking under the weather suaver lines, going off bit by bit in the wind and the rain to be part of the quiet earth. Those shameless little boys signify most certainly that, however it may strike a sophisticated city man, these passionate loves of Heathcliff and Cathy have no accent on the mechanics of sex; and this—the little boys affirm—is intended, is not a result of ignorance or evasion or neglect.

But the chief value drawn from Lockwood is, when we remind ourselves of the subject of the book, to be found in the concluding doubling-back upon the story when he returns to settle his rent obligation. In direct linear narrative, it would have been impossible to report with suitable emphases of delight and gaiety the emergent love of Catherine and Hareton while we were daily more engaged by Heathcliff's mounting ecstasy, as sleepless and foodless he makes his extraordinary transition into death. On the other hand, to have held that phase up for report after Heathcliff's burial would have necessitated hurry and overcompression, since Heathcliff's weight in the book is such that we should be impatient of what might, so presented, seem an addendum. In any case, the subject being what it is, and the ultimate resolution being in terms of humanity itself and not of a few human beings, it is indispensable that we should have both matters put before us simultaneously, and all the while feel thoroughly the mood and temper of the new life, now going on at the Heights, presently to be lived at the Grange. In the last pages all this is managed without awkwardness. The awkwardness in the earlier stretches is only to be expected. These devices were unexampled, and Emily Brontë herself was new at the craft.

I have used the word intuition, but it may have been more logical powers of the mind that found these ways to reality and the form of reality in narrative prose. Charlotte, in 1848, wrote to Emily's publisher that Ellis might next attempt the essay, which can be a reasoning mode. M. Héger, the only unconfused and genuinely able mind that knew Emily, thought of her as gifted for the writing of history (*Wuthering Heights* is as a fact created in a sound historical setting), and he wrote: "She would have been . . . a great navigator. Her powerful reason would have deduced new spheres of discovery from the knowledge of the old; and her strong, imperious will would never have been daunted by opposition or difficulty . . . " It *may* have been reason that operated in these important matters we have examined.

But for the rest, what complex and delicate, what energetic, subtle effects, accumulating by the hundred, are used to render these deep-drawn and widely derived materials, subjected to the subject, externalized in characters the most vivid, in events at once the most universal and the most starkly individual! Whatever the reason may have had to do with the plan of the work, in this regard the multifarious unconscious creative activity worked magic. Direct and simple in impression, profound yet enchantingly integumented, the most central impulses moving in the slightest phrases, *Wuthering Heights* has the effect of poetry, for perhaps all that is essential in the poetic process was involved in the making of the book. The thousand minute correspondences, the innumerable resonances of the unearthly and earthy, the balances inconspicuously set and finely varied, the rejections no less than the inclusions—all make at last for a unified intensity of effect. The book is literature, but it is like a great music, as Emily loved it. *Wuthering Heights* is a work both of intuitive and of conscious mastery. In its technical devising, however, it is not a work of practiced mastery. How could it be? The novel was only at the end of its first century, and Emily

Brontë, essaying what had never yet been essayed, was writing her first novel. (pp. 3-17)

B. H. Lehman, "Of Material, Subject, and Form: 'Wuthering Heights'," in The Image of the Work: Essays in Criticism by B. H. Lehman and others, University of California Press, 1955, pp. 3-17.

F. R. Leavis on the Brontë family and *Wuthering Heights*:

The genius, of course, was Emily . . .[*Wuthering Heights*] seems to me a kind of sport. It may, all the same, very well have had some influence of an essentially undetectable kind: she broke completely, and in the most challenging way, both with the Scott tradition that imposed on the novelist a romantic resolution of his themes, and with the tradition coming down from the eighteenth century that demanded a plane-mirror reflection of the surface of 'real' life.

F. R. Leavis, in his The Great Tradition, *Doubleday and Company, Inc., 1948.*

Derek Traversi   (essay date 1963)

[*Traversi is an English-born educator and critic. In the excerpt below from a revised edition originally published in 1963, he discusses the two themes he considers primary in* Wuthering Heights: *the relationship between Catherine and Heathcliff, and the contrast between the two houses, Wuthering Heights and Thrushcross Grange.*]

No nineteenth-century novel . . . is less derivative in its essential content, or answers more fully to an intimate vision [than *Wuthering Heights*]. In its fundamental as distinct from its accidental qualities, *Wuthering Heights* is an exploration of human passion at different levels and of the effect exercised by the interplay of these levels upon human life in its individual and social aspects alike. Creative or destructive in their consequences, making for life or death, basic human emotions are presented in a state of purity and concentration; no other novel of the Victorian period has penetrated so far into the depths of passion, or followed with such unrelenting logic to their ultimate consequences the intensity of its operations. The very novelty of the enterprise accounts for the remoteness of the book, at its most successful moments, from the greater part of the normal devices of the novelist. The novel, as Emily Brontë's great contemporaries conceived it, dealt primarily with the analysis of characters in their mutual relationships and in their attitude to external events; but the beings who dominate *Wuthering Heights* draw their life from sources at once simpler and deeper, more obscure and less differentiated, than those with which the novel is traditionally concerned. Purged of all accidental qualities, indivisible in essence and too self consistent to undergo change, their function is that of elements which can only, in their relations with the similar entities around them, destroy or suffer destruction. The result is a unique imaginative creation which, largely ignoring the moral and social assumptions of the contemporary novel, aspires rather to the severe simplicity of ancient tragedy.

The presence of the distinctive power which animates *Wuthering Heights* is felt whenever the emotions of the chief characters are deeply involved. No doubt there are moments—as when Catherine is described 'dashing her head against the arm of the sofa, and grinding her teeth so that you might fancy she would crash them to splinters'—when passion fails to make its presence felt through the crudity of its expression; but they are not, taken by and large, characteristic. The romantic melodramas with which Emily Brontë was certainly familiar owed their success almost invariably to effects created by ambiguity and mistiness, to lack of precision and vague suggestiveness. Romantic emotion of this type is felt rather than seen, is always rather a possibility than a tangible reality. In *Wuthering Heights,* the exact opposite normally occurs. Although the events described may frequently strike us as incredible, they are related in the great majority of cases with vivid clarity and precision. The qualities by which the writing is differentiated from the commonplaces of romantic sensibility are nowhere more apparent than in the opening description of Heathcliff's house and its surroundings. Wuthering Heights is described, as the narrator Mr Lockwood sees it, through a series of exact, vivid touches. The exposition, careful, orderly, and even slightly pedantic, as befits the speaker, rises almost imperceptibly to the deeply poetic reference to 'the range of gaunt thorns all stretching their limbs one way, as if craving alms of the sun', so that this evocation of the spirit of place does not strike the reader in any way as an intrusion. Above all, the temptation to exploit the poetic note is firmly resisted and the description of the interior which follows, where firmness in the grasp of detail and the stress laid on the normality of the setting ('The apartment and furniture would have been nothing extraordinary as belonging to a homely northern farmer') belongs to a type of writing diametrically opposed to romantic sensationalism. The same concrete imagination makes itself felt even in Lockwood's account of his highly theatrical dream, where if anywhere we might have expected the strained romantic note to impose a lack of precision, but where, in fact, the illusion of reality is maintained through a sense of physical pain that borders on the intolerable: 'Terror made me cruel; and, finding it useless to attempt shaking the creature off, *I pulled its wrist on to the broken pane,* and rubbed it to and fro till the blood ran and soaked the bedclothes.' In such a passage the peculiar intensity of Emily Brontë's romanticism—if we may continue to use the word for lack of a better—achieves its effect through a remarkable and characteristic immediacy. The capacity to effect an intimate fusion between the thing seen, or the felt sensation, and its imaginative interpretation, to write the visible and tangible with the intensity proper to poetry, has enabled her to raise a melodramatic story to the level of a profoundly personal creation.

To understand the true inspiration of *Wuthering Heights* we need, in short, to set aside the machinery of romantic passion and consider more closely what are in fact the two central themes of the novel. These themes, which correspond to aspects of it which we might call respectively 'personal' and 'social', stand in the closest relationship to one another. The first or 'personal' theme, by which the whole tragedy is illuminated, concerns the love of Catherine Earnshaw for Heathcliff, and of Heathcliff in turn for her. The relationship between these two is based, no doubt, on the familiar romantic conception of irresistible passion. Like so many pairs of romantic lovers, Catherine and Heathcliff are, so to speak, consecrated one to another, each feeling his or her passion to be the consuming reality of existence. The expression of this love is marked, however, by an intensity which finds perhaps its most significant manifestation in Catherine's attempt to explain her feelings to Nelly Dean:

> I cannot express it; but surely you and everybody have a notion that there is or should be an existence of yours beyond you. What were the use of my creation, if I were entirely contained here? My great miseries in this world have been Heathcliff's miseries, and I watched and felt each from the beginning: my great thought in living is himself. If all else perished, and *he* remained, I should still continue to be; and if all else remained, and he were annihilated, the universe would turn to a mighty stranger: I should not seem a part of it. My love for Linton is like the foliage in the woods: time will change it, I'm well aware, as winter changes the trees. My love for Heathcliff resembles the eternal rocks beneath: a source of little visible delight, but necessary. Nelly, I *am* Heathcliff! He's always, always in my mind: not as a pleasure, any more than I am always a pleasure to myself, but as my own being.

The spirit which animates this passage is undeniably personal to Emily Brontë. It is a spirit of concentration, from which considerations of sentiment or pleasure, in the common acceptance of the terms, have been excluded. The entire weight of feeling is focused upon a relationship deliberately stripped of the accidents of personality. The simple affirmation 'I *am* Heathcliff', to which the whole speech leads, states a necessity based rather upon the true being, the essential nature of the speaker, than upon any transitory impulse of desire. False or sentimental emotions are invariably involved in verbiage to make them appear greater, more genuine than they really are; but here the statement of passion is presented in all its bareness, expressed with a sharp, defined clarity that is its own guarantee of truth. It is in such a spirit that it calls for our response.

If we pause to consider more closely the manner in which Catherine tries to define the emotion which dominates her being we shall be forced to the conclusion, fundamental for an understanding of the spirit in which the novel was conceived, that there is about it a quality which can properly be called religious. Once again a fundamental opposition with normal romantic feeling is implied. The outstanding characteristic of romantic sentimentality is its self-centredness, we might even say its egoism. For the romantic, emotion tends to be its own justification, the intense kindling of feeling a guarantee of spiritual value. With Catherine this is not so. She bases her defence of her attitude to Heathcliff on a recognition that the individual is not sufficient to himself, that his or her experience thirsts for completion through vivifying contact with another existence: 'What were the use of my creation, if I were entirely contained here?' The emphasis so placed on the idea of creation, and upon that of the end of existence, is profoundly typical. The nature of Emily Brontë's experience of life, here perhaps expressed more directly than elsewhere, was religious in type: religious not merely in the sense of the rather indefinite 'mysticism' which has often been conceded to her on the strength of isolated passages in her poems, but in an awareness, at once more clear-cut and more open to definition, of the necessary incompleteness of all the elements that go to make up human nature in its time-conditioned state. It is upon this awareness, and not upon phrases which, taken in isolation, may mean everything or nothing, that any estimate of the religious significance of Emily Brontë's work must rest. It strikes us less, perhaps, as an experience than as the intense recognition of a need. The spirit in which *Wuthering Heights* was conceived, though absolutely distinct from that of Christian mysticism, can only be interpreted as a thirst for religious experience. From a profound sense of the finite and dependent nature of man ('surely you and everybody have a notion that there is or should be an existence of yours beyond you'), there arises the desire to make contact with a reality by which the self may be completed. In the light of this desire the world of mere external presentation—in so far as it remains merely external, unrelated to the spiritual intuition born of this consuming metaphysical passion—appears empty, and the very sense of this emptiness can properly be related to an experience of religious desolation: 'If all else perished, and *he* remained, I should still continue to be; and if all else remained, and he were annihilated, the universe would turn to a mighty stranger: I should not seem a part of it.'

The consequences of the emotion so expressed extend, in the contrast which the novel so consistently stresses between Heathcliff and Linton, and between Catherine's feelings for them both, to the moral order. Linton may be held, in a certain sense, to symbolize the superficial graces of civilized life, in which Heathcliff is totally lacking. It is perfectly natural that Catherine should be attracted to Linton. Courtesy, charm, and urbanity are all qualities worthy to be admired, and it is on their account that she is, at a certain level of her nature, impelled to respond to Linton's affection; but, as she herself recognizes, it is not the deepest part of her nature which is thus involved: 'My love for Linton is like the foliage in the woods: time will change it, I'm well aware, as winter changes the trees. My love for Heathcliff resembles the eternal rocks beneath: a source of little visible delight, but *necessary.*' Once more the conflict between two types of feeling is stated with a simplicity fundamentally intellectual in its sense of definition, which emphasizes the absence of all purely transitory or sentimental considerations. In the contract between the *agreeable* and the *necessary,* between emotions which serve at best to adorn life and others whose absence is felt to be equivalent to spiritual death, we can observe once more the peculiar inspiration of the book, and our judgement of it as a whole is likely to depend upon our reaction to these words.

It is not surprising that this reaction has differed notably from reader to reader. Behind such passionate utterances as this of Catherine there lies a moral problem of the utmost seriousness. This problem follows from the presence in *Wuthering Heights* of the spiritual content whose nature we have just indicated, and Emily Brontë was perfectly conscious that it existed. We feel its presence clearly when we follow, through the eyes of Nelly Dean, whose common sense offers throughout a necessary counterweight, a relevant though not a final comment, the process of reasoning by which Catherine is urged to abandon Heathcliff. Reflection, aided by Nelly, presents Heathcliff as what he undeniably is: a brutal creature whom she could certainly abandon with social advantage to marry the young, rich, and attractive Edgar Linton. Nelly, guided by her inherent good nature and by her long if not particularly imaginative experience of life, maintains that Edgar is a good match, that he is, socially speaking, acceptable and likely to bring her to normal domestic happiness, whereas her devotion to Heathcliff can only end in disaster and degradation. All this is undoubtedly true, relevant to the complete understanding of a novel which presents the destructive consequences, as well as the transforming ectasies, of passion; but the impressive simplicity of Catherine's reply is sufficient evidence that it is not all the truth. 'He' [Heathcliff] 'is more myself than I am. Whatever our souls are made of, his and mine are the same; and Linton's is as different as a moonbeam from lightning, or frost from fire.' Once more, we are conscious of being raised from normal social considerations to the world of essential passions with which, in their transforming and destructive operation, Emily Brontë is finally concerned.

Considered in the light of the central passion which thus animates the novel, it becomes easier to respond to its second main theme: that conveyed in the contrast between the two houses which between them divide the action, Wuthering Heights and Thrushcross Grange, Wuthering Heights clearly reflects the character of Heathcliff, who owns it; we might, indeed, call Heathcliff its human incarnation. Severe, gloomy, and brutal in aspect and atmosphere, firmly rooted in local tradition and custom, it is an appropriate background for the life of bare and primitive passion to which its owner is dedicated. Thrushcross Grange, the home of the Lintons, is in every respect different. It reflects a conception of life at first sight altogether more agreeable, more human than that set against it; a conception, indeed, which can attract the approval of Nelly Dean's common sense and so is not to be despised, but which, when closely observed, shows signs of decadence. Like Wuthering Heights, though with very different results, Thrushcross Grange answers to the character of its owners. Judged from a superficial standpoint, the Lintons seem to possess refinement, kindness, an amiability which makes life tolerable; but a closer inspection shows that the exclusion of Heathcliff's intense if self-concerning passion is not altogether a proof of moral strength. Beneath the surface of refinement exhibited by the Lintons in their ancestral surroundings exist moral flaws which play a part of the utmost importance in the development of the tragedy.

There is in the early pages of the novel a most significant

moment in which Thrushcross Grange and those who dwell in it are seen from the outside, from the standpoint of external and critical observers. At this moment Heathcliff and Catherine, still young children, climb up—acutely aware of themselves as intruders—to look into the illuminated windows of the Linton mansion. Their first glimpse of this strange new world produces an impression of contemptuous hostility which will always remain with them. They observe that the Linton children, far from feeling happy in their luxurious home, are in fact quarrelling bitterly over a lap-dog, itself a symbol of pampered indulgence, which each desires to handle and pet:

> And now, guess what your good children were doing? Isabella—I believe she is eleven, a year younger than Cathy—lay screaming at the farther end of the room, shrieking as if witches were running red-hot needles into her. Edgar stood on the hearth weeping silently, and in the middle of the table sat a little dog, shaking its paw and yelping; which, from their mutual accusations, we understood they had nearly pulled in two between them. The idiots! That was their pleasure! to quarrel who should hold a heap of warm hair, and each begin to cry because both, after struggling to get it, refused to take it. We laughed outright at the petted things; we did despise them!

The contempt apparent in Heathcliff's words represents the attitude of a soul in which the fundamental passions are still intensely alive for a world which claims to be superior but is in reality trivial, selfish, and empty. The emphasis laid upon the soft and clinging luxury in which the Lintons live, protected by bull-dogs and obsequious servants from the intrusion of the inferior world outside, is calculated to produce an impression of excessive sweetness and decay: 'We saw—ah! it was beautiful—a splendid place carpeted with crimson, and crimson-covered chairs and tables, and a pure white ceiling bordered by gold, a shower of glass-drops hanging in silver chains from the centre, and shimmering with little soft tapers.' The sight of so much luxury undoubtedly makes a certain appeal to the children, strikes them from outside as 'beautiful'. It corresponds, indeed, to a sense of social graciousness which the Heathcliff world is the poorer for lacking; but it also rouses in the youthful intruders from this other world a feeling of repudiation which the behaviour of the dwellers in this 'paradise' can only intensify. The 'gold', the crimson carpets and chair-coverings which serve to deaden, to mollify the impact of life, the slightly unreal prettiness of the 'shower of glass-drops hanging in silver chains', and the barely defined sense of exquisite decadence in the reference to the 'little soft tapers' burning in the room: all these, seen through eyes already dedicated to passionate sincerity, point to a contrast which lies at the very heart of the novel.

The contrast, indeed, is carried in similar terms into the main body of the story. When Catherine, as a grown woman, brings Edgar Linton (whom in her superficial attraction for exactly this kind of luxury, she has married) the news of Heathcliff's return and asks if she is to bring him into the parlour, the appropriate setting of gentility, he looks 'vexed' and suggests 'the kitchen as a more suit-

able place' for him. By so doing he conforms to the nature of his own world, which has created an elaborate system of social distinctions to deaden the impact, at once vivifying and destructive, of essential passion; but Catherine, true to the promptings of her deeper nature, replies by instructing Nelly to prepare two tables, 'one for your master and Miss Isabella being gentry; the other for Heathcliff and myself, being of the lower orders'. To the social distinction thus stressed by the Lintons as human, civilizing, and repudiated as irrelevant, life-denying by Catherine, correspond a number of findings in the moral order which belong to the book's very substance. The most significant of these throw an adverse light upon the Linton claim to superiority of character. 'Pettish', 'silly', 'whining', 'envious' are the adjectives applied to Edgar by Catherine; and Emily Brontë is at some pains to relate them to the world of pampered luxury in which the family are represented as living. It is no accident that the man who, as a child, had been protected by bull-dogs from the intrusion into the family property of two harmless children calls upon his servants, after attempting to retire himself, to eject his hated rival from his house. As we come to know the Lintons better, we find beneath their richly and essentially unformed character refinement undoubtedly, but also selfishness, meanness, and even a cruelty which, although very different from Heathcliff's brutality, is hardly less inhuman in some of its manifestations.

It is in part his reaction against the debased civilization represented by the Lintons that induces Heathcliff to embark upon the destructive activity which finally brings him to his death.

For it is, after all, destruction, a dedication to death, that results from Catherine's faith and Heathcliff's sombre intensity. To see in *Wuthering Heights* no more than a plain contrast between civilized decadence and primitive vitality would, indeed, be too simple. Beneath Catherine's love for Heathcliff lies a genuine conflict, a clash of different levels of passion which ends by consuming her. The part of her nature which craves civilized, social fulfilment is sufficiently attracted by the agreeable aspects of life in the society of the Lintons to marry Edgar and become part of the family. She herself never refuses the name of 'love' to her feeling for Edgar. Yet this love—and here we return to the deeper content of the novel, its exploration of the conflicting depths of personality—can satisfy only the more superficial part of her nature. All that is most powerful and permanent in her repudiates Linton, impels her to return to Heathcliff; through the whole of her story we are faced with the contrast between the 'foliage' which changes and the 'eternal rocks' beneath. Yet the foliage, though in no sense fundamental, represents a reality, even—on its own level—a necessity, which cannot be ignored without simplifying unduly the profound balance of conflicting sensations upon which the novel rests.

Wuthering Heights represents, in other words, not the statement of a 'naturalist' thesis, or a return to primitive instinct, but a genuine clash of emotional states; and it is the clash, not the thesis, or even any attempt at resolution, that gives the novel its unique character and power. This clash, indeed, animates one of the most surprising and beautiful passages of the book. In it Cathy, daughter of Catherine and Edgar Linton, and thereby heiress to two conflicting outlooks, describes a discussion between herself and the sickly son of Heathcliff and Isabella Linton:

> One time, however, we were near quarrelling. He said the pleasantest manner of spending a hot July day was lying from morning till evening on a bank of heath in the middle of the moors, with the bees humming dreamily about among the bloom, and the larks singing high up over head, and the blue sky and bright sun shining steadily and cloudlessly. That was his most perfect idea of heaven's happiness: mine was rocking in a rustling green tree, with a west wind blowing, and bright white clouds flitting rapidly above; and not only larks, but throstles, and blackbirds, and linnets, and cuckoos pouring out music on every side, and the moors seen at a distance, broken into cool dusky dells; but close by great swells of long grass undulating in waves to the breeze; and woods and sounding water, and the whole world awake and wild with joy. He wanted all to lie in an ecstacy of peace; I wanted all to sparkle, and dance in a glorious jubilee. I said his heaven would be only half alive; and he said mine would be drunk: I said I should fall asleep in his; and he said he could not breathe in mine, and began to grow very snappish.

Here once more we may detect the intense operation of that peculiar spiritual emotion which Emily Brontë imparted to her characters. The emotion is of the same type as we find in the most personal of her poems. It is characteristic of the essentially religious nature of her inspiration that what begins as a discussion of the best way of passing a hot summer's day turns rapidly into a comparison between two contrasted ideas of the nature of celestial happiness. If Linton appears to be concerned with no more than 'the *pleasantest* manner' of passing a July day, whereas Catherine begins by transforming 'pleasant' into 'perfect' and thereby shifts the conception of felicity to quite another level, the implied difference can be defined in strictly literary terms. It is underlined, above all, by the contrasted choice of adjectives in the two parts of the speech. For Linton the bees hum 'dreamily', the sun shines 'steadily' and 'cloudlessly' in the sky; the ideal which attracts him, and which finds reflection even in the tranquil immobility of the prose rhythm in the parts of Cathy's speech which refer to him, is one of stillness, passivity, peace. It is only when she sets against it her own thirst for identification with a world in which vitality finds expression in an increasing emotional tempo that the tone of the speech is transformed: for she imagines herself 'rocking' at the heart of a world in motion, with the wind 'blowing' and the clouds 'flitting rapidly above' and all this leads up to an overpowering vision of the birds—not of one kind alone, like Linton's larks invisibly suspended in the heights of a uniform blue sky, but innumerable and diversified in species—'pouring out music on every side', whilst the grass is 'undulating' to the breeze, the water 'sounding', and 'the whole world *awake* and *wild* with joy'.

What is at stake here, as well as two different reactions to natural beauty, is a clash between two opposed conceptions of life, each of which gives, by contrast, added meaning to its opposite. For Linton Heathcliff, life tends to peace, calm passivity; for Cathy, it consists in active identification with the surrounding world. Yet the fact that Cathy's emotion is so powerful as to sweep aside the impression of passivity left by Linton cannot alter the fact that both emotions formed a part of Emily Brontë's intuition of life, that Catherine's identification with the forces of universal motion tended as its end towards a peace and quiescence which, if not that of Linton, is none the less implied in the novel. That its authoress felt *both* emotions, that her own creative impulse rested upon the balance, the tension set up between them, is sufficiently clear from this passage and from others which abound in the book. If her characteristic reaction to nature was one of eager and active acceptance, it is also true that she sought through and beyond this acceptance an intuition of permanence which was essentially contemplative. The impulse to unite these two necessities of her nature is the true source of the inspiration of her novel.

This craving for unity expressed itself in **Wuthering Heights** through the stress repeatedly laid upon yet another element, itself romantic in origin, of the emotional make-up of the novel: the tendency to see human life and individual passions in the shadow of death. The presence of death is felt intensely in **Wuthering Heights,** at times as something against which the protagonists react with all the force of their passionate energies, and at times as a profoundly evocative intuition of peace. The two attitudes need to be seen in relation to one another if we are not to simplify excessively the true nature of the emotion which the novel conveys. The death of Mr Earnshaw and the final lingering of the narrator over the graves of the sleepers 'in that *quiet* earth', characteristic as they are of Emily Brontë, no doubt owe part of their inspiration to an attraction for the idea of peace through dissolution which can be associated with adolescent emotion. They do not, however, stand alone. For a proper estimate of their importance we need to recall other and closely associated phrases which point to emotions of a more complex kind. When Nelly Dean, after Mr Earnshaw's death, hears the children comforting each other for their loss, she makes, indeed, her own sentimental comment—'no person in the world ever pictured heaven so beautifully as they did in their innocent talk'; but the comment is not the last word, and the next sentence comes as the intrusion of a more real and more truly tragic experience, as unexpected as it is profoundly moving in its simplicity: 'While I sobbed and listened, I could not help wishing we were all there *safe* together.' The end of Heathcliff, too, stands in the closest relation to a tragedy in which life and death, the exclusive fulfilment of passion and the self-destruction which inevitably accompanies it, are inextricably fused. If he appears at the end of the novel to have found a kind of peace in death, one of his last phrases recalls once more that his was no simple slipping into unconsciousness, no surrender to the craving for fictitious repose: 'My soul's bliss kills my body, but does not satisfy itself.' The phrase is Emily Brontë's, but the spirit of metaphysical passion which animates it, the consuming desire for a completeness unattainable in time but implied by temporal experience, is not—when due allowance has been made for the world of differences which separated her from Christian belief—

altogether remote from that of religious experience. (pp. 261-72)

Derek Traversi "The Brontë Sisters and 'Wuthering Heights'," in From Dickens to Hardy, *edited by Boris Ford, revised edition, 1963. Reprint by Penguin Books, 1982, pp. 256-73.*

John E. Jordan   (essay date 1965)

[*Jordan is an American critic and educator. In the following excerpt, he illustrates the complexity of* Wuthering Heights *by demonstrating Brontë's use of irony.*]

[The whole structure of **Wuthering Heights**] is a fabric of ironies. On the very first page we are introduced to the isolated moorland setting as "a perfect misanthropist's heaven"; yet in this misanthropic setting is developed one of the strongest affirmations of human values in English literature. The whole introductory section is a sort of comedy of errors. The primary irony of the book is that the slightly ridiculous Lockwood, who has come to the country professedly seeking solitude and who declares that "a sensible man ought to find sufficient company in himself," yet cannot stay away from his only neighbors and devotes all of his attention to their affairs. Otherwise there would have been no book! This same conceited, sophisticated character is promptly put into humiliating combat with dogs and terrified by a ghost. He is the city slicker in the haunted house.

It is really very funny, if we stop to think about it. But we are only half invited to do so. The atmosphere is charged, as with wry economy Emily Brontë makes the comedy serve to forward the predominantly serious tone of the book. The spectral experience which Lockwood tries to laugh off actually stripped him to primitive realities: "Terror made me cruel; and, finding it useless to attempt shaking the creature off, I pulled its wrist on to the broken pane, and rubbed it to and fro till the blood ran down and soaked the bedclothes: still it wailed." Surely it is ironical that the cultured Lockwood should be brought to this, and that *he* should be the means of establishing contact with the spirit world—that the visitation for which Heathcliff had so longed should be vouchsafed to Lockwood. What are we to deduce: The affinity of opposites, the perversity of things, or the "blessedness" of those who expect little? All of these ironies are there, and all are elaborated throughout the novel.

Alerted by this obvious play of irony in the introduction, we look for more of it in the structure of the novel. The first line consists of nothing but a date: "1801"—suggesting that the story belongs significantly to a certain time. And time is important in it; Emily has managed her calendar well and run out the generations precisely. Yet the date might almost as well have been 1701—Joseph's canting piety would simply have been Puritan instead of Methodist. The efforts of Arnold Kettle and others to make this novel a commentary on Victorian capitalism are not persuasive. It does not have that kind of contemporary relevance. The precise opening date is one of its ironies. For the famous last line of the novel reflects upon the enduring "sleepers in that quiet earth," clearly transcending

time. Let us pass the other curious irony of that beautiful, serene closing speech's coming from Lockwood, and consider this time-eternity opposition in the first and last passages. Emily's point is not simply that the course of the story goes from now to eternity, but that the two are ironically inseparable, and that a narrative which runs a carefully consistent chronological course is at the same time on the edge of timelessness.

Even the box within a box within a box "point of view" of the novel, which has been criticized by Somerset Maugham as clumsy and praised by Dorothy Van Ghent as a device for obtaining both psychological familiarity and dream-like freedom, has an ironic function. It provides a commentary on the limitations of the different narrators. The outer box, Lockwood's narrative, contains the most easy play of conscious irony. Lockwood begins with a mocking sparkle of double meanings. Gayly superior, he calls the glowering Heathcliff "a capital fellow," the sour Cathy an "amiable hostess" and a "beneficent fairy," and the surly group at the Heights a "pleasant family circle." It seems as if Emily means to imply that possession of a capacity for irony certifies an intelligent reporter. Lockwood is a conceited fop, a spoiled product of civilization against whom the primitive energies of the moors can show to advantage; but he is no fool. Like a juryman, Lockwood is qualified as an unprejudiced observer in part by virtue of his ignorance of the story he is to transmit—in itself an ironical point—and in part by his knowledge of the world which makes him able to flit ironically detached from this crude moorland spectacle. His intentional irony, however, soon turns to unintentional, as his ignorance manifests itself and his creator displays her independent vision. He innocently asks young Cathy if "her favourites" are among a furry heap which he takes to be kittens but which turns out to be a pile of dead rabbits. The mistake is amusing, but there is an ironical relevance in his question. Are her favorites among the soft ones of the world, literally the Lintons? Are the soft ones always doomed to the fate of the rabbits? These are questions at the center of the novel.

Actually, of course, Cathy is to find a favorite among the sturdy and enduring, the moderated Heathcliff who is Hareton. This irony is compounded by the inability of Lockwood, who is among the slick ones of this world, to perceive the inevitable appropriateness of their union. When he prematurely jumps to the conclusion that Cathy and Hareton are married, he regrets that "she has thrown herself away upon that boor from sheer ignorance that better individuals existed"—by which he means himself. And one of the delightfully ironic strands of the novel is the hypothetical relationship between Cathy and Lockwood. He warns himself to "beware the fascination that lurks in Catherine Heathcliff's brilliant eyes," is flattered by Nelly's hopes that maybe he will marry her young mistress, and finally consoles himself for his neglect by remarking, "Living among clowns and misanthropists, she probably cannot appreciate a better class of people when she meets them." Cathy is not for the likes of him, and it is a measure of his limitation that he cannot perceive the fact.

Nelly Dean, on the other hand, partly because she is closer to the story and partly because she is less sophisticated, displays in the narrative of her inner box less conscious irony. When she does recognize or countenance an ironical discrepancy between appearance and reality, she does so with little of Lockwood's flippancy. The nearest she comes is when she describes Cathy's stolen visits to Wuthering Heights: "I remarked a fresh colour in her cheeks and a pinkness over her slender fingers; instead of fancying the hue borrowed from a cold ride across the moors, I laid it to the charge of a hot fire in the library." Or when she notes Heathcliff's return: "He is reformed in every respect, apparently: quite a Christian: offering the right hand of fellowship to his enemies all around!" Plainly she has her doubts. Or when she wryly labels as a "self-complaisant conviction" Catherine's calling herself "an angel." She uses irony more solemnly when, with few illusions as to the realities of the situation, but a humane desire to spare Mr. Linton, she implores Cathy to tell her dying father that "she should be happy with young Heathcliff." This is the irony of pretending, the futile little gesture of closing one's eyes.

Most of the time, however, Nelly's ironies are chiefly Emily's. It is hard to say how much the canny Mrs. Dean means her comforting remark to her fading master: "people who do their duty are always finally rewarded." How much does Miss Brontë mean it? In a sense the novel supports the notion of cosmic justice: the good—or the more orthodox—are ultimately victorious. The demonic spirit literally dissipates, and innocent flowers are once more planted at the Heights. But the cost has been great and the way devious. Old Mr. Earnshaw did his Christian duty by befriending an orphan waif and brought upon his house destruction. Nelly points up this irony: "It hurt me to think the master should be made uncomfortable by his own good deed." Later she puts the idea in a somewhat ambiguous frame: " 'But where did he come from, the little dark thing, harboured by a good man to his bane?' muttered Superstition, as I dozed into unconsciousness." Superstition mutters, Nelly wonders, and Emily queries. The contention that "people who do their duty are always finally rewarded" is ironically ambiguous. Rewarded how? What do they deserve, people who just do their duty? Heathcliff condemns the futility of Edgar's attending Catherine "from *duty* and *humanity!* From *pity* and *charity!*" Maybe the rewards of this life come directly or indirectly to or through those who have the energy and the vision to transcend duty. Is the "reward" to the dutiful Mr. Earnshaw and the dutiful Mr. Linton misery unto the second and third generation, or the purgation which ultimately rejuvenates their families? Emily Brontë does not stay for an answer on the matter.

Sometimes Nelly is sublimely unconscious of the irony of her statements. She complacently remarks of young Linton's reception at the Heights: "I'll console Mr. Edgar by acquainting him with the turn Heathcliff's humour has taken"—when the whole pattern is scarcely consoling. She is amusingly belatedly aware of the irony of her feeling when she was looking for her lost Cathy and it gave her "delightful relief to observe, in hurrying by the farmhouse, Charlie, the fiercest of the pointers, lying under a window, with swelled head and bleeding ear"—an odd cause of delight.

When Nelly says of Cathy's persistence in wanting to see the world outside of the Grange, "It's a pity she could not be content," probably *she* means it. Certainly this defense of a cloistered virtue has ironic overtones for Emily Brontë. Whether or not she was personally content with limited horizons, and thought she was wise to be so, she does not approve such conduct in her characters. Penistone Crags must be visited, because they are there. Only the weakling Linton is querulously content to stay put. Cathy leaves her paradise, but she is really better off for it in the long run—the paradox of the Fortunate Fall. Heathcliff, who is several times equated with the Devil, is at his most satanic when he tempts Cathy to disobey her father and leave the Grange Park. For in so doing she realized the serpent's scriptural prediction: she acquired the knowledge of good and evil, and she became as one of the gods. She gained power over Heathcliff:

> "I know he has a bad nature," said Catherine: "he's your son. But I'm glad I've a better, to forgive it; and I know he loves me, and for that reason I love him. Mr. Heathcliff, *you* have *nobody* to love you; and, however miserable you make us, we shall still have the revenge of thinking that your cruelty arises from your greater misery. You *are* miserable, are you not? Lonely, like the devil, and envious like him? *Nobody* loves you—*nobody* will cry for you when you die! I wouldn't be you!"

This scene is a remarkably complex moment. Emily Brontë has quite skillfully kept the reader's sympathies with Heathcliff; we recognize that in a sense Cathy cannot come close to reaching or even understanding the power of Heathcliff's passion. He has been loved, as she can never be loved. And he is loved, by a spirit which will not cry but rejoice at his death, or at his parting that veil the living call death. On this level Cathy's speech is ironically hollow. Yet not without reason does Heathcliff in his reply call her a "witch." She has a kind of supernatural perception; on another level she is right. Heathcliff is miserable and cruel, and the kind of revenge she offers him is to pity him: "I wouldn't be you!" Thus she wins something of the same kind of victory over him that Prometheus does over his torturer, Jupiter, in Shelley's *Prometheus Unbound:*

> For Justice, when triumphant, will weep down
> Pity, not punishment, on her own wrongs,
> Too much avenged by those who err (I, 403-405).

This is not the revenge of impotence, although many have thought so and will think so, just as Earth thought that the pitying Prometheus was surrendering when he withdrew his curse:

> Misery, Oh misery to me,
> That Jove at length should vanquish thee (I, 306-307).

Cathy is weak, and yet she is strong. In ways she is almost a parody of her mother, and this speech almost a ludicrous parallel to the elder Catherine's rebuke to Heathcliff:

"I wish I could hold you," she continued bitterly, "till we were both dead! I shouldn't care what you suffered. I care nothing for your sufferings. Why shouldn't *you* suffer? I do!"

And yet Cathy's perception is richer than her mother's. Her love may be a sort of maternal perversion, a ridiculous and incomprehensible thing. But that is the character of love: it "suffereth long, and is kind," it "is not puffed up" and it "seeketh not its own." Catherine is selfish in her passion. As Albert J. Guerard has well pointed out, she expects to have both Heathcliff and Edgar, and elects to die rather than compromise.

On this level it is apparent that the relation of Cathy to her mother and of Hareton to Heathcliff is that of the Olympians to the Titans, that cultural progress which Keats hails in *Hyperion:*

> So on our heels a fresh perfection treads,
> A power more strong in beauty, born of us
> And fated to excel us, as we pass
> In glory that old Darkness (II, 212-215).

Cathy and Hareton are both physically and spiritually more beautiful than Catherine and Heathcliff, who themselves "pass in glory" the "old Darkness" of primordial energies to which they are akin. That most readers tend to prefer the elder pair merely attests to the well-known attractiveness of the improper. Of course it may suggest that Emily Brontë, like Milton, was "of the Devil's party without knowing it." But I don't think so. I believe that she was having her cake on one level and eating it on another. We are supposed to see both that Cathy is a ludicrously weak echo of her brilliant mother and that she becomes a finer human being. Catherine guilefully plays a double role and cheats two men. Cathy innocently sacrifices herself for one man and is the means of saving another. Cathy is, as Lockwood puts it, "not an angel," and her motives are not all lofty. Blindness and pettiness blend ironically with generosity and goodness when she tells Nelly

> And I'm certain Linton would recover quickly if he had me to look after him. I'm older than he is, you know, and wiser: less childish, am I not? And he'll soon do as I direct him, with some slight coaxing. He's a pretty little darling when he's good. I'd make such a pet of him, if he were mine. We should never quarrel, should we, after we were used to each other? Don't you like him, Ellen?

The final question is ludicrous. Linton is thoroughly unlikeable, as the reader and everybody in the story except Cathy agrees. He is beyond salvation.

Although Cathy's sacrifice does Linton little good, it is not futile, because of the satisfaction it gives her father and the contribution it makes to her own growth. When Linton dies Heathcliff, acting as a chorus for Emily, asks Cathy, "How do you feel, Catherine?"

> "He's safe, and I'm free," she answered: "I should feel well—but," she continued, with a bitterness she couldn't conceal, "you have left me so long to struggle against death alone, that I feel and see only death! I feel like death!"

This symbolizes a sort of death for her, and she goes through a "Center of Indifference" before she finds the "Everlasting Yea" with Hareton, the affirmation which Lockwood grumblingly notes at the end of the story: "*They* are afraid of nothing. . . . Together they would brave Satan and all his legions." They have done so, and they have won. Had Cathy been "content" to stay at Thrushcross Grange she would never have won Hareton, the Caliban of the Chaos she made whole. She ought no more to have been "content" to stay at Thrushcross Grange than her mother to have been content to go there to marry Edgar. The elder Catherine knew that she belonged to Heathcliff, but she sold herself to the amenities of the Lintons; she took the easy way, the false way. She tried to deny her destiny, and to deny the essence of love by making it only possessive, only selfish:

> I've no more business to marry Edgar Linton than I have to be in heaven; and if the wicked man in there had not brought Heathcliff so low, I shouldn't have thought of it. It would degrade me to marry Heathcliff now; so he shall never know how I love him: and that, not because he's handsome, Nelly, but because he's more myself than I am. Whatever our souls are made of, his and mine are the same; and Linton's is as different as a moonbeam from lightning, or frost from fire.

Cathy's speech, "I'm certain Linton would recover quickly if he had me to look after him" might well have proved to be true if Catherine had said it of Heathcliff.

The futility of Nelly's efforts to protect Cathy from her destiny are of a piece with the futility of all the efforts in the book to warn Isabella against Heathcliff or keep Catherine and Heathcliff apart. From some points of view, it is "a pity" that Isabella and Catherine could not have been more reasonable, more amenable, more restrained, more prudent. And yet one suspects that Emily agreed with Blake that "Prudence is a rich, ugly old maid courted by Incapacity," and "He who desires but acts not, breeds pestilence." The irony is therefore double. It is partly the irony of the "best laid plans of mice and men," the pathetic puniness of rational efforts to control the lives of men. The more Catherine and Nelly warn Isabella, the more determined she is to contravene them. Edgar's effort to come to a showdown with Heathcliff and to throw out of Catherine's life that "moral poison" resulted in her belatedly making a clear choice for Heathcliff and effectively throwing Edgar out: "I'd rather see Edgar at bay than you." For, although Edgar had all propriety and domestic virtue on his side, he picked a time when Catherine was trying to protect Isabella and to effect a sort of equilibrium that would neutralize Heathcliff and bring peace and happiness to all. And the "poison" he sought to remove was as necessary to Catherine as another was to Rappaccini's daughter. Thus, this is partly the irony of the wrong-headedness of the world's wisdom, the comic irony of presumption and misplaced effort, of the flea climbing the hind leg of an elephant, with rape on its mind. Experience teaches not only that the best-laid plans "gang aft agley," but that often they were not such good plans anyway. Nelly could but dimly see all this: she felt the pity of futility, but was too proper to recognize the pity of propriety.

Other narrators have quite different irony quotients. The innermost boxes in the complicated "point of view" are those occupied by narrators who tell Nelly what she tells Lockwood that she cannot know from her own observation. The most important of these—Heathcliff, Isabella, and Zillah—cover a wide range of perceptivity. Heathcliff, particularly in his youth, is often involved in ironies beyond his comprehension, as when he roundly declares, "I'd not exchange, for a thousand lives, my condition here, for Edgar Linton's at Thrushcross Grange"—an exchange which much of his later life is spent in partly effecting. Miss Brontë neatly underlines the irony of his returning as a master to "the same room into which he had been ushered, as a guest, eighteen years before: the same moon shone through the window; and the same autumn landscape lay outside." The novelist broadens the scope of this ironical parallel by having Heathcliff say when Nelly brings him his blond weakling son: "You've brought it, have you? Let us see what we can make of it." That neuter pronoun reminds us of old Earnshaw's tumbling out a dark boy: "you must e'en take it as a gift of God; though it's as dark almost as if it came from the devil." Both men make what they can "of it," neither what he had hoped. The blond as well as the dark lad acts as if he had come "from the devil," and neither is taken "as a gift of God." If Hindley (Hind-ly, Hind-sightedly?) had so treated Heathcliff, he would not have seemed to Catherine degraded, and she would probably have married him and saved both of them. I cannot agree with Richard Chase that "to Emily Brontë, their marriage is unthinkable." It was desirable, even fatally necessary, and that it did not come about is one of the ironies of the book, one in the early part of which Heathcliff is an unwitting participant. Ironically, he stayed in his unobserved position long enough to overhear Catherine say that it would degrade her to marry Heathcliff, not long enough to hear her add that she loved him and was one with him.

The later Heathcliff, as a result of his mysterious maturation, is the most aware character in the book, alert to ironies and taking an intellectual pleasure in them: "I want the triumph of seeing *my* descendant fairly lord of their estates: my child hiring their children to till their father's lands for wages." For that reason he will be "*very* kind" to Linton, although he despises and hates him. He delights in the double irony of Hareton's reversed position and his ignorant acceptance of it: "And the best of it is, Hareton is damnably fond of me!" He even indulges in sarcasm, telling the innocent Cathy, "You suppose papa is highly esteemed and respected then?"—and asserting that he "has a mind to be hospitable" when he is making Nelly and Cathy prisoners in order to force the latter's marriage to his son. Heathcliff is also well aware of the irony of the "poor conclusion" of his revenge: "It will be odd if I thwart myself."

Isabella, of course, has a much smaller role, but she is the chief source of information about her marriage, and as a narrator she suddenly springs forth as an ironic voice. We had scarcely been aware of her before. We saw her first fighting with her brother over a lap dog, and next fighting with Catherine over Heathcliff: she seems a spoiled, weak sentimentalist, with no perception of reality. Then she runs off with Heathcliff, and against his contempt, in the irony of her position as an unloved bride, she acquires strength and some bitter clarity of vision. This marriage, along with that of Cathy and Linton, has been criticized as the implausible result of overplotting, a too-neat working out of the revenge motif. Both marriages can probably be defended on the prosaic grounds of proximity and the scarcity of available mates—this society naturally has the inbreeding of a remote tribe. I would suggest also that they are part of the ironic pattern of the book. This irony is partly literary: the Isabella-Heathcliff relationship is a caricature of the romantic damsel and the Byronic hero—Lady Caroline Lamb's designation of Byron as "mad, bad, and dangerous to know" fits Heathcliff quite well. Furthermore, the very perversity of these marriages is thematic. Isabella becomes a sort of spokesman for the doctrine of perversity. "Catherine," she says, "had an awfully perverted taste to esteem him [Heathcliff] so dearly, knowing him so well." She hates her husband so much that she declares, "I'd rather he suffered *less,* if I might cause his sufferings." And she holds, "It is preferable to be hated than loved by him." Isabella is no longer the simple romantic miss. Out of these unions of opposites comes a kind of illumination. Through them Cathy and Isabella suffer, but through them they grow. Still, Isabella has grown, like so many others in the book, with a twist—we remember Heathcliff's famous speech when Hareton comes under his control: "And we'll see if one tree won't grow as crooked as another, with the same wind to twist it!" Isabella no longer sees Heathcliff in a romantic aura; she perceives the irony of her infatuation. She does not yet see Heathcliff clearly nor perceive the irony of her values. She tells Hindley, "When I recollect how happy we were—how happy Catherine was before he came—I'm fit to curse the day." She believes this, Nelly probably accepts it, but for Emily Brontë it is surely ironic.

Zillah has an interesting function. She is the most detached of the narrators; even Lockwood, although an outsider, is personally more involved. Zillah "always refused to meddle." Her role as a narrator is to present an ironic counterpoint to the partial accounts of Nelly Dean, who always meddled. Young Cathy is much less angelic in Zillah's portrait. Yet Emily Brontë does not leave Zillah alone in her objectivity, but makes her say

> However, I took care there should be no further
> scorning at my good-nature: ever since, I've been
> as still as herself; and she has no lover or liker
> among us: and she does not deserve one.

The irony of this is that even in her own version Zillah has shown little "good-nature." She is the hired instrument: "I was not going to disobey the master," "I didn't wish to lose my place, you know." And we may remember, what clergyman's daughter Emily certainly knew, that Zillah means "darkness," and that she was a descendant of Cain, the mother of Tubal-Cain, "father of all such as forge copper and iron," and the wife of Lamech, famous for the Curse of Lamech: "If Cain shall be avenged sevenfold, truly Lamech seventy and sevenfold" (Genesis, 4:24).

It is hard to believe that her presence in the story is not related to the revenge motif, which begins early when the boy Heathcliff tells Nelly, "I'm trying to settle how I shall pay Hindley back. I don't care how long I wait, if I can only do it at last." Zillah entered Heathcliff's employ, took the "place" she so valued, after Hindley's death, at the time that Heathcliff's revenge got full play in twisting Hareton as Hindley had twisted him. And she simply "left," without any reason offered, when the spiritualized Heathcliff had lost interest in revenge. Is it to consider too curiously to note that the other servant at Wuthering Heights, loyally attached to the Earnshaws and disapproving of Heathcliff even while he served him, was named Joseph? For the Biblical Joseph was, in his generous treatment of his brothers, the first important Old Testament character clearly to repudiate revenge. I'm not sure that Emily Brontë deliberately connected Yorkshire Joseph with his patriarchal namesake—perhaps not. If she did so, it was certainly with tongue in cheek, and the first conflict of Joseph and Zillah which we see takes on ironic dimensions: Joseph sicks the dogs on Lockwood for stealing his lantern, and Zillah rescues the hapless guest.

Thus from Lockwood to Zillah the narrative boxes provide some ironic cross-references. Another significant level of irony in the novel is that inherent in the paradoxical combinations, concretized in the series of marriages and carried pervasively is the metaphoric structure: the union of hard and soft, of frost and fire, of lightning and moonbeam, the oak in the flower pot, the sea in the horse trough, the "good things lost amid a wilderness of weeds." Although this note is complex, it is in large measure the irony which seems part of the human condition, the perversity of men and things. Thus, young Heathcliff's efforts to improve his appearance result in his being called a coxcomb and ultimately getting thrashed. Catherine's slapping Edgar is the catalyst that makes them lovers. Heathcliff automatically catches the falling Hareton and thus unintentionally benefits his enemy. Catherine marries Edgar partly to "aid Heathcliff to rise." Catherine wants the window open for "a chance of life" and nearly gets her death. Hindley's attempt upon Heathcliff's life results in his own injury. Joseph "contributed much to . . . [Hareton's] deterioration, by a narrow-minded partiality" for him. Cathy sincerely swears never to do anything to vex her father, just before embarking upon renewed relations with the Heights which will vex him. Edgar dies comforting himself with the vain hope of providing for Cathy through her liaison with Linton. Hareton's efforts to improve himself by learning to read result in his being laughed at. Hareton weeps at the death of Heathcliff, which brings him release and restores him to his heritage.

All of these events have something in common with the *peripeteia,* the reversal of tragedy. There is an inevitable note of pity and fear in the perversity of things. But life remains a comedy to the man who thinks, and despite all the powerful feeling in her book, Emily Brontë writes like a woman who thinks. The prevalent undertone is comic irony, brought to the surface in the characterizations of the foppish Lockwood and the sanctimonious Joseph, according to Nelly "the wearisomest self-righteous Pharisee that ever ransacked a Bible to rake the promises to himself

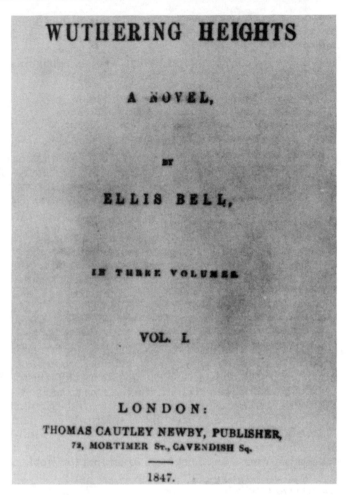

Title page of the first edition of Wuthering Heights.

and fling the curses to his neighbors." Joseph is a parody of the canting, bigoted Methodism in Emily's experience, but his comedy also has some of the same sort of ironic relevance that the monologue of the drunken porter does in *Macbeth.* When the children are spurning his pious books, he calls out: "Maister, coom hither! Miss Cathy's riven th' back off 'Th' Helmet o' Salvation,' un' Heathcliff's pawsed his fit into t' first part o' 'T' Brooad Way to Destruction!' ". And so he had.

E. M. Forster has put **Wuthering Heights** among those works of prophecy which call for "a suspension of the sense of humor." Biblical prophecy, I submit, calls for no such suspension—see particularly Ezekiel and Jonah— and neither does Emily Brontë. The reason we do not laugh at her in the high moments of romantic excess is that we are always comfortably close to laughing with her. The account of Heathcliff's reaction to Catherine's death is such a moment:

> He dashed his head against the knotted trunk;
> and, lifting up his eyes, howled, not like a man,
> but like a savage beast being goaded to death
> with knives and spears.

The image is perilously laughable, yet we are supposed to take it seriously. We do so, partly because we have been conditioned to a sort of grudging admiration of the Titanic vitality which could not find satisfaction within normal human compass, and partly because three pages earlier we had been reminded humorously that Nelly is telling this to Lockwood:

> Do you believe such people *are* happy in the other world, sir? I'd give a great deal to know. I declined answering Mrs. Dean's question, which struck me as something heterodox.

And Heathcliff's speech just before this head-dashing scene had in it elements of irony which for all their intensity still suggest a wry smile. When he learns that Catherine died peacefully: "Why, she's a liar to the end!" And he declares, "I *cannot* live without my life!" Emily means this literally, and yet she is clearly alert to the punning play.

Is there not a kind of cosmic irony in all this that fits Emily Brontë's demand that we, in Mr. Lockwood's words, "extract wholesome medicines from Mrs. Dean's bitter herbs"? For this is a complex tale, complexly told, and there is more to it than meets the eye. Miss Brontë knew her Shakespeare; she is at pains to make a specific reference to *King Lear* in the second chapter and it has been suggested that Heathcliff owes something to Edmund; probably he also owes something to Hamlet. It is interesting to note the bird imagery. Nelly says Heathcliff's history is "a cuckoo's" and "Hareton has been cast out like an unfledged dunnock!" Catherine warns Isabella that Heathcliff would crush her "like a sparrow's egg" and Nelly adds that he is "a bird of bad omen." Perhaps Emily Brontë was amusing herself with the implication that it takes a wiser man than Lockwood to see that the problem before us is the ironic one of knowing a hawk from an Earnshaw. (pp. 5-18)

> *John E. Jordan, "The Ironic Vision of Emily Brontë," in* Nineteenth-Century Fiction, *Vol. 20, No. 1, June, 1965, pp. 1-18.*

F. H. Langman   (essay date 1965)

[*In the excerpt below, Langman assesses the critical response to* Wuthering Heights. *He particularly notes discussions of Brontë's style, her method of narration, and her treatment of the themes of love and cruelty in the novel.*]

On the prose style of *Wuthering Heights,* [Dorothy] Van Ghent speaks of 'an excess everywhere present in language' [*The English Novel—Form and Function*]. Mark Schorer makes a stylistic analysis of more subtlety and substance, but he too declares that the novel has an 'almost impossibly inflated style' ["Fiction and the 'Analogical Matrix'," *Kenyon Review* (1949)]. Confronted by such opinions, it seems necessary to say flatly that the novel's style is not uncontrolled, excessive, and unchanging. On the contrary, it combines force and variety with an almost unfaltering control over tone and imagery.

To give substance to these assertions, I shall point to the flexibility and variety of the prose, and the skill with which it is modulated. Consider, for example, the long paragraph on the second page, describing the parlour at the Heights.

This paragraph establishes the scene of much of the ensuing action: all the details of furniture are solidly there, and the house is shown to be not unduly rough but well kept and as refined as might be expected of its place and time. The effect is, before the story begins, to anchor it to a reality of time and place, to give it this stable location as distinct from the resonant suggestiveness of the outdoor landscape:

> One end . . . reflected splendidly both light and heat from ranks of immense pewter dishes, interspersed with silver jugs and tankards, towering row after row, on a vast oak dresser, to the very roof. The latter had never been underdrawn: its entire anatomy lay bare to an enquiring eye, except where a frame of wood laden with oatcakes and clusters of legs of beef, mutton, and ham, concealed it.

The writing here is precise and methodical (it follows the gaze of the 'enquiring eye' up the rows of shining utensils, from there along the rafters, then down again along the fire place wall), but it is not highly charged. The chief impression it gives is that it is accurate, dependable. The thorough detail and workmanlike exposition give an assurance that sanity and a sense of actuality lie behind the passages of extraordinary poetic writing for which the novel is usually noted. Poetic intensity may mark the style of the high points: but the strength of the whole is a prose strength.

The strength of the whole is worth insisting on, because in concentrating attention upon the love of Catherine and Heathcliff most critics lose too much of the novel's abundant life. [G. D.] Klingopulos writes:

> As an Elizabethan play stands or falls by the quality of the poetry at its crises of meaning, so *Wuthering Heights* may be said to justify itself by the quality of some half-dozen or so speeches of Catherine's and Heathcliff's which are as direct and as highly organised in word and rhythm as poetry. In such speeches the novel establishes the reality of its subject matter. ["The Novel as Dramatic Poem: *Wuthering Heights,*" *Scrutiny* XIV, No. 4]

The criterion offered here seems unacceptably narrow for the judgment of an Elizabethan play; applied to a novel it surely won't do at all. The interest of *Wuthering Heights* may centre in the passages of most intense emotion, but they possess their intensity, they convince, only by their place in the whole. I should say, instead, that the novel convinces us of its reality—of its being serious and meaningful—by the firmness of its structure and the integrity of its prose, and that the scenes of intense emotion can only be understood and judged in relation to many passages of a quieter strength.

To indicate the nature of that strength I should like to refer to the passage, too long to quote here, which describes the death of Mr. Earnshaw. The passage, beginning 'But the hour came, at last, that ended Mr. Earnshaw's troubles', is at the end of Chapter V.

In this passage, the dramatic effect is beautifully restrained: the surprise is not for the reader, who has been warned by the first sentence, but for the characters only. Attention is thus turned not to the fact that death comes but to the way that it comes. And the nature of the old man's death, as it comes through in the writing, generates a moving and significant symbolism. It is a quiet death, a lapsing out at the completion of a well-lived cycle. In this, it forms a contrast to the premature, painful deaths of Catherine, Hindley, and, later Heathcliff, and to the sterile wasting-away of Edgar. The passage begins with two brief and limpid sentences, rhythmically slow. October—the end of Autumn, the closing of the year. Evening. The orchestrated, subdued suggestions are at work relating human destiny to the universal pattern of closing cycles, gently persuading our minds to accept such a close as inevitable and natural. The third sentence evokes the setting within which death is to be contemplated. It conveys the isolation of humanity within the unliving universe, and hence the mystery of life—isolation, not, while men can draw into community ('we were all together'), loneliness. (Heathcliff and Catherine die essentially alone.) The natural world, brought in by the wind, is heard as 'wild and stormy' yet not positively hostile—it is not cold. Within the house, the grouping suggests the inter-relations of the people. The servants are in the same room, not separated from the family yet not quite of it, seated at a remove. Cathy leans against her father's knee, Heathcliff rests his head in her lap. The scene is immensely touching, but without a drop of sentimentality. It is quite clean of the kind of embarrassment we might fear from Dickens in such a place. The calm and peace are inherent in the established regularity of the household under the old man's mastership. At the same time, we are made conscious that the moment of calm is, after all, only momentary. It is one of Cathy's rare moments of quietness and contrition. In her retort—'Why cannot you always be a good man, father?'—there is a reminder of her usual nature: it is subdued here, but not glossed over, not made angelic for the sake of the scene.

The passage gets much of its strength from its function as a centre of the organisation or pattern of the whole novel, from the way significances draw together in it and run out again to make inter-relations with all that follows. The old man's dying brings to a close a period of stability in the little community of the Heights. Cathy's moment of recalcitrance is a sign of the restlessness which will impel the new generation to seek other satisfactions and to break the discipline of the old settled way of life. 'Restlessness' may be too vague a term. What I mean is that the generation of Cathy and Heathcliff have become aware of their energies and emotions in a way unknown to their elders, and require more developed values than the simple pieties they have been taught. Cathy's question—'Why cannot you always be a good man?'—is more than an exhibition of her pertness. It has a shrewdness, a knowledge that human character is complex and not simply black or white, that her father's question wholly lacks—'Why canst thou not always be a good lass, Cathy?'

To describe the novel as a 'dramatic poem' is thus unsatisfactory, because it leads to an undervaluing of Emily Brontë's specific strength as a *novelist:* her command of the wide resources of narrative prose. Another indication

of this command is given by her flexible and organic use of humour. The first chapters provide a clear illustration. It is important to get the tone of these chapters right. The weather is the principal means of creating 'atmosphere' in these chapters: by a series of suggestions it sets our expectations in a particular key; it prepares us for the nightmare with all its implications that follows in Chapter III, by making us see and feel the premature darkness, the cold, the isolating, suffocating snow. At the same time a more complex effect is achieved. The tone of the chapters is not wholly grim. The bitterness of the elements presses as a threat behind a lighter, almost farcical element, as Lockwood makes a fool of himself, first at tea and then in his impetuous flight from his boorish hosts. Lockwood's first dream has the same quality, half comedy, half melodrama, which establishes it as an ordinary nightmare to set off the poignant reality of the second dream.

In Cathy's diary the comic note is different. Like her drawing of Joseph, her description of his sermon evinces a quality often overlooked in assessments of her personality. She is one of the few characters with a sense of humour. Moreover it is not of the frivolous facetious sort displayed by Lockwood. A genuine comic verve comes out in the vitality of her sentences:

> While Hindley and his wife basked downstairs before a comfortable fire—doing anything but reading their Bibles, I'll answer for it— Heathcliff, myself, and the unhappy ploughboy, were commanded to take our Prayer books, and mount: we were ranged in a row, on a sack of corn, groaning and shivering, and hoping that Joseph would shiver too, so that he might give us a short homily for his own sake. A vain idea! The service lasted precisely three hours; and yet my brother had the face to exclaim, when he saw us descending, 'What, done already?'

Wit of this sort has a certain maturity: it is poised—'the unhappy ploughboy'—and shrewd—'doing anything but reading their Bibles'. Catherine's rebelliousness shows itself here as the humorous reaction of a sympathetic and sensible nature against bullying sentimentality and cant. There is more than the common childish response to love-making in her scorn of Hindley and his Frances.

Passages like this make Catherine quite different from the figure the critics tend to describe. The real Catherine comes across as fully human, sprightly, lovable. She is essentially normal and even, in the first part of the book, normative. From the start she is too vital a person to be limited by the conditions others impose for their own convenience: 'her spirits were always at high-water mark'. And she is essentially joyous, with an expansive sense of life: 'singing, laughing, and plaguing everybody who would not do the same'.

The real Heathcliff is evoked by more elusive means; but he too emerges, at least as a child, as more human than those around him, more sensitive, more responsive. Lacking Catherine's vivacity, he has nevertheless the most vivid perception of it:

> 'Afterwards, they dried and combed her beautiful hair, and gave her a pair of enormous slip-

pers, and wheeled her to the fire; and I left her, as merry as she could be, dividing her food between the little dog and Skulker, whose nose she pinched as he ate . . . she is so immeasurably superior to them—to everybody on earth, is she not, Nelly?'

The tone and rhythm here perfectly render both the speaker and the actions he describes: his delight wins our consent even while the last phrases place the feeling as, though true and touching, a child's.

Nelly remarks several times on the hardness and insensibility of the child Heathcliff. Actually, he feels more deeply than anyone. His vitality is an inward as Catherine's is an outward fire. Because Nelly is a biased narrator, this can sometimes be brought out only indirectly, by subtle touches: for example, the dumb, desolate poignancy of his hurt after Catherine, returning from her stay at the Lintons, first rebuffs him. Nelly finds him 'smoothing the glossy coat of the new pony in the stable, and feeding the other beasts according to custom'. He remains at the work till nine o'clock at night, then marches 'dumb and dour' to his chamber. Nelly interprets this as ill-humour. We may see in it a boy's heartbreak and loneliness.

A number of critics have thought of Nelly Dean as representing a standard of normality in **Wuthering Heights,** as indicating the writer's own attitude to the main characters and events, and as voicing the judgments upon them of conventional morality. Others have noted that neither of the two main narrators, Lockwood and Nelly, is capable of interpreting the story adequately. G. D. Klingopulos hints at this dissatisfaction: 'Nelly is conventional and . . . her moralising is rarely quite to the point'. D. A. Traversi is similarly diffident [in *The Pelican Guide to English Literature,* Vol. 6]: 'Nelly Dean, whose common sense offers throughout a necessary counterweight, a relevant though not a final comment'. Arnold Kettle makes the point more perceptively and firmly:

> The roles of the two narrators . . . are not casual. Their function (they the two most 'normal' people in the book) is partly to keep the story close to the earth to make it believable, partly to comment on it from a common-sense point of view and thereby to reveal in part the inadequacy of such common sense. [*An Introduction to the English Novel*]

That is—to develop the point more fully—the novel uses several narrators (in fact, five or six) to place the story in perspective, or in a variety of perspectives; but it also reverses the process, and the direction of interest, by making their responses to the story cast light upon the narrators themselves (even Zillah's character is richly, though economically, created). To break down resistance to its central experience, the novel must somehow overcome the reader's contrary assumptions: it does so by demonstrating the inadequacy of those assumptions in Lockwood and Nelly.

Nelly is not merely a witness. She is a creature of will, and she exerts this will to some effect. Her narrative is deeply coloured not only by her 'conventional values' but also by her private motives: her personal loyalties and her need to

protect herself. This is true of others as well. There is a constant suggestion of bias in the narration, leading at times to incompatible versions of what happened. All the narration involves recollection, selection, and emphasis; and the author shows a keen awareness of how the personality of the speaker may rearrange and even falsify what actually occurred. Catherine's quarrel with Isabella provides a simple but striking example. Isabella declares that she loves Heathcliff 'more than ever you loved Edgar'. As Catherine repeats the remark to Heathcliff, three pages further on, the insinuation against herself is transposed to Edgar. She becomes not a wife who loves weakly but one who is weakly loved: 'Isabella swears that the love Edgar has for me is nothing to that she entertains for you'. In case the reader should fail to see the discrepancy, the next sentence reads: 'I'm sure she made some speech of the kind; did she not, Ellen?'

Nelly is not an objective observer. She is an active participant in the events she describes—how often a decisive turn is given to the story through her interference or her negligence—and her feelings are deeply engaged. At the very start of her tale she reveals her indentification with the family she used to serve: 'Miss Cathy is of us—I mean of the Lintons'. Her bias against Heathcliff is manifest equally early. She admits that her conduct towards him when he first arrived was cowardly and inhuman, that she and Hindley hated him and plagued him shamefully. But she never properly faces the implications of these admissions or draws the right conclusions from them. Instead, she sums up Heathcliff's introduction to the family by saying: 'So, from the very beginning, he bred bad feeling in the house'. This, after describing his patience under Hindley's blows and her pinches.

Nelly's 'slanting' is pretty obvious at the start, and not difficult for the alert reader to cope with. Later, it demands greater attentiveness, more of looking backwards and forwards to verify what she says, than the narrative *pace* will allow. For example, at the end of chapter XVII, Nelly says:

> Hareton, who should now be the first gentleman in the neighbourhood, was reduced to a state of complete dependence on his father's inveterate enemy; and lives in his own house as a servant, deprived of the advantage of wages, and quite unable to right himself, because of his friendlessness, and his ignorance that he has been wronged.

But how has Hareton been wronged, and by whom? Nelly effectively suggests that Heathcliff has somehow cheated the boy out of his inheritance. Arnold Kettle, for one, is sufficiently impressed to write: 'Heathcliff . . . buys out Hindley and reduces him to drunken impotency. . . . He systematically degrades Hareton Earnshaw to servility and illiteracy'. The fact, however, is that Hareton's father was far gone in dissipation long before Heathcliff's return; and it was Hindley who insisted that their gambling should continue to the end:

> 'Should he offer to leave me, he's a dead man. . . . Am I to lose *all,* without a chance of

retrieval? . . . I *will* have it back; and I'll have *his* gold too; and then his blood.'

Heathcliff may have encouraged Hindley's mania, but it remains that Hareton was disinherited mainly by his own father's greed and vindictiveness. But these cross-references are four chapters apart, and in a normal reading one is less likely to see that Nelly's imputations are false than merely to feel uneasy about them.

Where two versions of the same event are given, the problem is to determine not *what* happened but, as it were, *how much* happened. For example, as Isabella relates it, when Hindley attempted to kill Heathcliff and failed, Heathcliff 'kicked and trampled on him, and dashed his head repeatedly against the flags'. On the writing in this scene, Klingopulos comments:

> The excess of vividness must be taken either as a symptom of immaturity, of insufficiently understood intensity; or as an error of judgment on the author's part, a failure to recognise that the physical violence and ruthlessness of Heathcliff had already been established. . . .

Before accepting this judgment, we need to recall that the excess of vividness, the immaturity or error of judgment, are not directly the author's. They belong first of all to Isabella. Later in the novel the episode is referred to again, more temperately. As Heathcliff relates it: 'I remember stopping to kick the breath out of him, and then hurrying upstairs'. Thus we can't be sure what we have seen: an act of gratuitous brutality by Heathcliff, or an exaggerated impression of it in the immature and prejudiced witness, Isabella.

This kind of analysis, pushed too far, could make the novel impossibly ambiguous. Effects like those I've pointed to are plentiful, but they do not obliterate the story. Rather, they make the reader vaguely mistrustful, cautious in passing judgment. And they do this especially with reference to the nastier parts of Heathcliff's conduct, making for uncertainty not only about how far his behaviour is. Judgment of him is inhibited, to a degree, by the thought that the case against him has been exaggerated by the bias of the narrators. Some sense of this appears to lie behind Kettle's comment on the narrators:

> They act as a kind of sieve to the story, sometimes a double sieve, which has the purpose not only of separating off the chaff, but of making us aware of the difficulty of passing easy judgments. One is left always with the sense that the last word has not been said.

But this effect—if, as Kettle seems content to do, we carry the analysis no further—is surely disturbing. It seems too much like a superior confidence-trick, and we may wonder whether it helps to account for the nebulousness with which critics generally refer to this side of the novel.

Everyone agrees that the most important thing in ***Wuthering Heights,*** its central experience, is the love between Catherine and Heathcliff. What to make of it is another matter. Critics often emphasise its strangeness and, in one way or another, contrive to suggest that it is not 'love' at all. Some see it as inhuman, demonic, mystical or mythical; some see it as adolescent fantasy, filled with the violence and weakness of immature passion but with the concomitant unreality. Either way, and whether in praise or in blame, the emphasis is put upon the passion's intensity: intensity for its own sake. So, according to G. D. Klingopulos, we must see the value of the novel 'in the vitality of the feelings'. And the consequence of this, whether intended or not, is a devaluation, an evacuation of significance. 'If Emily Brontë has been careful about anything,' writes Klingopulos, 'she has been most careful not to qualify whatever the Catherine and Heathcliff themes may be taken to mean. For Catherine and Heathcliff are what she set out to say'.

It is a perplexing formula: 'whatever the themes may be taken to mean'. Does this suggest that the novel must be condemned as obscure and ambiguous in its central themes? Or is it the critic's confession of failure to master his subject? Either way, we can't leave it there. For the relationship of Heathcliff and Catherine is not without meaning. The book's continuing appeal lies, I believe, precisely in the sense it gives of paying an unusually full yet legitimate recognition to a natural and normal human emotion. Catherine's most famous declaration of her feelings is an endeavour not so much to convey the strength as to define the nature of her love, and so to win a recognition from Nelly (and, in a sense, from the reader) of its value:

> 'If all else perished, and *he* remained, I should still continue to be; and if all else remained, and he were annihilated, the universe would turn to a mighty stranger: I should not seem a part of it. My love for Linton is like the foliage in the woods: time will change it, I'm well aware, as winter changes the trees. My love for Heathcliff resembles the eternal rocks beneath: a source of little visible delight, but necessary.'

She distinguishes her love for Heathcliff from her love for Linton not as more highly charged but as having a different basis. Her love for Linton grows out of the changeable surface of personality, rather like what D. H. Lawrence, in his essay on Galsworthy, called 'the social being . . . swayed . . . by the money-sway, and by the social moral'. She loves Linton because he is handsome, and pleasant, and young, and cheerful, and rich, and loves her. Her love for Heathcliff grows out of what, in the same essay, Lawrence called true humanity, the stable core of self we can know only when at one with 'the living continuum of the universe'. She loves him because she must: it is the deepest impulse of her nature, it is 'necessary'. Through her feeling for Heathcliff, Catherine discovers her own identity, her place in the world—as he does through her. The essential quality of their relationship is not its intensity but its perfect, its final, sincerity.

Beside the love of Catherine and Heathcliff all other relationships in the novel pale into insignificance, not only because it is intense and enduring but precisely because it *is* significant, it recognises important realities of our existence. A world kept in focus only by ignoring those realities would be desperately impoverished.

Lockwood's presence in the novel is best understood, I

think, as enforcing just this perception. When he has heard the first part of the story, he reflects on the contrast between these people and people like himself:

> They *do* live more in earnest, more in them-selves, and less in surface change, and frivolous external things. I could fancy a love for life here almost possible.

That 'almost' conveys the whole case. Lockwood is a pure-ly social being, all but incapable of imagining and terrified of encountering the realities of emotional life. The anec-dote about his love-affair at the sea-side plainly reveals this. He says that the reputation it earned for him of 'delib-erate heartlessness' is undeserved. In fact, however, only the one word 'deliberate' is undeserved. He is incapable of spontaneous emotion. His feelings are factitious, fashion-able, literary: 'I was thrown into the company of a most fascinating creature: a real goddess in my eyes, as long as she took no notice of me. I "never told my love" vocally . . .'. He is afraid of love. He can approach it only when it is kept at a safe distance. When it is offered, he beats a hasty retreat.

This deliberate contrast between the emotional frigidity represented by Lockwood and the vitality of the novel's central experience suggests an attempt to do more than simply present the intense emotion. The novel does not (its form ensures that it cannot) argue or exhort or philoso-phise. But into its conception there has gone a distillation of thought whose operation can be felt everywhere in the shaping of the material. Wordsworthian in quite a number of ways, **Wuthering Heights** is not the least so in its capac-ity of assimilating ideas into the presented experience.

> Blest the Babe,
> Nursed in his Mother's arms, who sinks to asleep
> Rocked on his Mother's breast; who with his soul
> Drinks in the feelings of his Mother's eye!
> For him, in one dear Presence, there exists
> A virtue which irradiates and exalts
> Objects through widest intercourse of sense.
> No outcast he, bewildered and depressed:
> Along his infant veins are interfused
> The gravitation and the filial bond
> Of nature that connect him with the world.
>   (*The Prelude*)

Heathcliff's love for Catherine is inextricably involved in the motives of his long-drawn-out struggle for mastery over his enemies. The two concerns are kept alive together until just before the end, and the survival of the love must be understood—or puzzled over—along with the perpetu-ation of the struggle. The meaning of the one provides the motive for the other.

The love begins in childhood and rebellion, and its genesis explains its nature. Heathcliff, the outcast, rejected and humiliated, is accepted only by Catherine—herself an or-phan; but by her he is accepted entirely. They recognise in each other their true humanity, their worth and dignity as persons, their right to be. Only through this relation-ship can either of them feel the vital bond with existence, the sense of belonging, the human necessity for which is

expressed in Catherine's 'surely you and everybody have a notion that there is or should be an existence of yours beyond you'. The loss of exactly this sense is at the heart of the agony in such modern novels as *Lord Jim* and *Women in Love*. And this is the loss that Catherine, through her wrong choice in marriage, must undergo:

> 'Supposing at twelve years old I had been wrenched from the Heights and every early asso-ciation, and my all in all, as Heathcliff was at that time, and been converted at a stroke into Mrs. Linton, the lady of Thrushcross Grange, and the wife of a stranger: an exile, and outcast, thenceforth from what had been my world—you may fancy a glimpse of the abyss where I grov-elled!'

Catherine's tragedy is that from deeply fulfilling relation-ship, from the sense of *community,* she is seduced by the attractive glitter of mere *society.* The point is given its full profundity in Heathcliff's image of Edgar's inadequacy:

> 'He might as well plant an oak in a flowerpot, and expect it to thrive, as imagine he can restore her to vigour in the soil of his shallow cares!'

The suggestion here is of more than Catherine's superior vitality: it points toward the need for deep roots into the processes of living, for relationship not with elements arti-ficially isolated and contained but, as it were, with the whole earth.

The singleness of Heathcliff's bond with the world is a central fact of the story. It is as well, therefore, to note that this is a condition imposed on him by the nature of the people he falls among, rather than a product simply of his own perverse will. He does have, at least for some time, a natural eagerness for a wider community of affection. As late as his homecoming after Catherine's marriage, he is disappointed by Nelly's lack of welcome and reproaches her for it: 'Nelly, you are not glad'! But Nelly is for the most part hardened against him, and he grows hard in turn. Even so, he turns to her more than once, later in the novel, as something human to share the burden of his ex-perience.

Catherine's apparent withdrawal of this fundamental rec-ognition, her rejection of himself in his degraded circum-stances, drives Heathcliff to run away. Her restoration of it, on his return, moves him to go on living instead of tak-ing revenge on Hindley, as he had planned, and then doing away with himself. He seeks revenge on Hindley, and later on Edgar, precisely because they have tried to deny him this recognition. Edgar attempts to deprive Heathcliff of Catherine. That is by far the most important point, but it is not the only one. Edgar as a child had held Heathcliff in such unthinking contempt as to refer to him, without malice, as though he were an object unfit to be directly spoken to, not a person with feelings. When they are grown up Edgar continues to see Heathcliff, despite the improvements in his appearance and bearing, as an inferi-or and interloper: a 'low ruffian'. It is difficult to see on what other grounds he can claim knowledge of Heath-cliff's 'miserable, degraded character', or why he should on such extreme terms forbid Isabella to encourage Heath-cliff's advances.

This close relationship of the love and revenge motives gives unity to Heathcliff's story—a complex unity summed up for Heathcliff in all that Hareton seems to personify:

> 'Hareton's aspect was the ghost of my immortal love; of my wild endeavours to hold my right; my degradation, my pride, my happiness, and my anguish'.

The best discussion of this part of the novel, to my mind, is in Arnold Kettle's *Introduction to the English Novel.* This is one of the rare attempts to treat of Heathcliff's revenge in human terms, and with a proper consciousness of the obligation to make unequivocal judgments; nevertheless it does not seem sufficiently clear and convincing. Like so many others, Kettle gives an overcharged and inaccurate account of Heathcliff's doings:

> Heathcliff becomes a monster: what he does to Isabella, to Hareton, to Cathy, to his son, even to the wretched Hindley, is cruel and inhuman beyond normal thought. He seems concerned to achieve new refinements of horror, new depths of degradation.

Despite these exaggerations, Kettle observes that we 'continue to sympathise with Heathcliff . . . to identify ourselves with him *against* the other characters'. His explanation is that Heathcliff's revenge has a moral force:

> For what Heathcliff does is to use against his enemies with complete ruthlessness their own weapons, to turn on them . . . their own standards, to beat them at their own game . . . we recognise a rough moral justice in what he has done to his oppressors.

Rough justice: an eye for an eye, tit for tat. Clearly, this won't do. Two wrongs don't make a right. The simple retort of ordinary morality is crushing. We need something better to explain the persistence of sympathy with Heathcliff.

Considering how much emphasis they lay on Heathcliff's ferocity, it seems odd that so little is said by critics about Hindley's. Hindley's brutality, tyranny, and murderous violence far outdo anything of which Heathcliff can be accused on the evidence. Heathcliff, of course, is at the centre of interest, and Hindley is not; but there is another, an interior, difference in the way we see them. Hindley is morally uninteresting; Heathcliff's violence and cruelty by contrast are not random and irresponsible, they are willed. Heathcliff acts with system and forethought. He has certain goals—power, money, a triumph over the circumstances and agents of his former humiliation—and he uses force and deceit to reach them. Where Hindley's violence is wild and unmeasured, Heathcliff's is controlled by purpose. He is only as harsh as the carrying out of his schemes makes necessary. Hindley used to beat Heathcliff. Heathcliff does not beat or bully Hareton. Hanging up Isabella's dog in such a way that it could neither make a noise nor follow them was an essential precaution before their elopement. His other deeds, except under extreme provocation, are likewise controlled.

Heathcliff's conduct, then, must be judged in the light of his purpose. If we do continue to sympathise with him, I suggest that it is because we see, however dimly, what his purpose is, and accept it as giving a moral theme to his actions. We do know what he means by his wild endeavours to hold his *right*. His struggle against his enemies is justified—as far as it is—by the superior right for which he strives. He strives to assert what they so cruelly, and casually, have denied: his right to exist, to hold a place in the scheme of things. So complete and complacent has been their assumption that he belongs to an inferior order of being that only the complete upheaval of their world can redress the balance. Our sympathy is drawn by the struggle of life to triumph over killing contempt.

Dr. Kettle may be right to see a reflection of the Victorian class-struggle in this part of the novel, but to emphasise it would be a mistake. Heathcliff's differences from, say, the Linton family are more than social. A fundamental distinction is suggested between different kinds of being, different kinds of men. 'Whatever our souls are made of,' says Catherine, 'his and mine are the same; and Linton's is as different as a moonbeam from lightning, or frost from fire'. The society of the novel is created in the image of the Lintons, its values and its laws are theirs (not for nothing are we told that Edgar is a magistrate), and it does not willingly tolerate the otherness of a Heathcliff. But it is in the recognition and affirmation of diversity, rather than in any emotional plangency, that the novel comes closest to what is valuable in the Romantic tradition to which it belongs. It might have taken for motto Blake's proverb: 'One law for the lion and ox is oppression'.

For all this, in Heathcliff's behaviour there is an excess from which moral sympathy does turn away: the kind of thing exemplified in: 'The more the worms writhe, the more I yearn to crush out their entrails'. As a more subtle and convincing instance we may take the savage feeling to which he admits, apropos of the younger Catherine, for anything that seems afraid of him. To regard the revenge-story as simply a moral action would be wrong, for in it the psychological effect of the enjoyment of power provides another theme. It is easy to see how Heathcliff comes by these feelings. To evaluate them, to see how they affect the implied moral judgments in the novel, is not so easy. What they show is that the author never reduces her vision to a diagram, a two-dimensional moral fable. She remains aware that the moral equations are less complex than the human agents. But that the moral judgments are not radically upset may be demonstrated by a contrast. D. A. Traversi points out that the Lintons are capable of 'a cruelty which, although very different from Heathcliff's brutality, is hardly less inhuman'. Yes; and more. Isabella, at least, has a desire for revenge that matches Heathcliff's own. Hers is truly a thirst for rough justice: 'an eye for an eye, a tooth for a tooth; for every wrench of agony return a wrench'. But this, as Isabella's spiteful impotence betrays, possesses no moral force: it is too negative. Heathcliff strives to triumph over his enemies, she only to 'reduce him to my level'. In that betraying phrase we see perhaps the subtlest variation on the novel's theme. (pp. 296-312)

F. H. Langman, "Wuthering Heights," in Es-

says in Criticism, *Vol. XV, No. 3, July, 1965, pp. 294-312.*

Charlotte Brontë on the craftsmanship of *Wuthering Heights:*

Wuthering Heights was hewn in a wild workshop, with simple tools, out of homely materials. The statuary found a granite block on a solitary moor; gazing thereon, [she] saw how from the crag might be elicited a head, savage, swart, sinister; a form moulded with at least one element of grandeur—power. [She] wrought with a rude chisel, and from no model but the vision of [her] meditations. With time and labour, the crag took human shape; and there it stands colossal, dark, and frowning, half statue, half rock: in the former sense, terrible and goblinlike; in the latter, almost beautiful, for its colouring is of mellow grey, and moorland moss clothes it; and heath, with its blooming bells and balmy fragrance, grows faithfully close to the giant's foot.

Charlotte Brontë, in her preface to the 1850 edition of Emily Brontë's **Wuthering Heights.**

John Hagan   (essay date 1967)

[*In the following essay, Hagan explores the various techniques that enable Brontë to maintain the reader's compassion for Catherine and Heathcliff in spite of their cruelty.*]

One of Emily Brontë's major achievements in *Wuthering Heights* is to keep alive the reader's sympathy for both Catherine and Heathcliff, even though their behavior after the former's marriage to Edgar Linton becomes increasingly bizarre and frighteningly akin to the demonic. From the time in Chapter X of Heathcliff's return to Thrushcross Grange after his three-year absence to the end of the novel, we are sustained in a double view: far from condoning the hideous spiritual transformation which Catherine and Heathcliff undergo, Emily Brontë evokes our moral revulsion by employing all the resources of her art to bring its viciousness into the sharpest relief; at the same time, however, she never allows her hero and heroine to forfeit our compassion. This double view is essential if the final effect of the novel is to be tragic and not merely distasteful. We must condemn the sin, but pity the sinner. The view that Emily Brontë is an amoral writer results in large part from a confusion between ethical neutrality and this pity she enlists on behalf of a hero and heroine whose behavior is allowed at the same time to shock us profoundly. (It is also a consequence of attributing to Catherine and Heathcliff a factitious metaphysical status, as I shall try to show later.) The confusion can be removed if we come to understand the precise means by which Emily Brontë accomplishes the delicate task of making us respond in this complex way.

The only critic to have specifically addressed himself to this problem in any detail is Arnold Kettle, who justly observes that "despite everything he does and is, we continue to sympathize with Heathcliff—not, obviously, to admire him or defend him, but to give him our inmost sympathy. . . ." But valuable as Kettle's discussion is for focusing attention on the issue, it is unsatisfactory both because he neglects to apply the question to Catherine as fully as her part in the novel requires and, more important, because his explanation of how this effect is achieved rests on a curious, Marxist-oriented interpretation of Heathcliff as an "outcast slummy" and a "conscious rebel." On this reading Heathcliff wins our sympathies because "he is on the side of humanity and we are with him just as we are with Oliver Twist, and for much the same reasons"; ". . . what Heathcliff stands for is morally superior to what the Lintons stand for . . . and [the] Earnshaws"; we "continue in an obscure way to identify ourselves with him *against* the other characters"; "instinctively we recognize a rough moral justice in what he has done to his oppressors . . ." Not only is this thesis quite inconsistent with the assertion that we neither "admire" nor "defend" Heathcliff (for if he is "on the side of humanity" like Oliver Twist and "morally superior" to the Lintons and Earnshaws, why shouldn't we admire and defend him?), but it is wholly unacceptable on the grounds of ordinary morality and the evidence of the text alike because it implies that Heathcliff is the moral superior of *all* his enemies. How, for instance, can it be made to apply to the second Catherine and Hareton Earnshaw? They have not been Heathcliff's "oppressors"; he has been theirs. To argue that Heathcliff's subjugation of Catherine and Hareton is only a by-product of his laudable attempt to beat Hindley and Edgar "at their own game . . . to turn on them . . . their own standards . . . their own weapons of money and arranged marriages"—in short, to get "power over them by the classic methods of the ruling class, expropriation and property deals"—still does not demonstrate these youngsters' moral inferiority. Indeed, only on the assumption of a primitive eye-for-eye morality are these tactics defensible for Heathcliff to use even against those who have really injured him. If they are proof of the corruption of whoever uses them, then Heathcliff must stand condemned as much as the "ruling class" itself. Kettle himself is uneasily aware of this, for no sooner has he spoken of Heathcliff's revenge as having "moral force" than he contradictorily concedes that it is the result of his enemies having "entrapped him in their own values."

But all of this only raises the larger question of the fairness of lumping together Isabella and Edgar Linton as mere specimens of a corrupt "ruling class" in the first place. Isabella's only "crime" against Heathcliff is her youthful and foolish infatuation. How this can cause us to feel any sympathy for Heathcliff's barbaric treatment of her after their marriage is a problem which Kettle refuses squarely to face. One would suppose that, if the moral edge had to be given to one or the other, Isabella's trust, however naive, would surely stand up as well as Heathcliff's cynical calculation. As for Kettle's excessively disparaging view of Edgar, this appears to rest not on all the evidence offered by the text, but on no better authority than the bitter, highly biased denunciations uttered by Catherine and Heathcliff in Chapters X-XII, when they are in the throes of the frustration which has followed their impassioned reunion. A far juster view of his character may be found in Mary Visick's *Genesis of Wuthering Heights* (1958). Kettle's error in handling the Lintons is to ignore almost completely the particularities of Emily Brontë's characterization and to make them mere papier-mâché representatives of a class to which he believes moral inferiority can be attributed a priori.

The critical problem which confronted us at the outset, therefore, still challenges us for a solution.

The central fact about Catherine after Heathcliff's return is that she becomes actively malignant and perverse. Her behavior between now and her death resolves itself into a succession of harrowing mad-scenes. A lesser novelist of Emily Brontë's day would have allowed the heroine gently and beautifully to pine away in unfulfilled longing. But Emily Brontë softens nothing. She carries our aversion to Catherine so far as to bring our sympathies near the breaking-point. This is the artistic risk she must run if her story is to transcend sentimental melodrama.

The first sign of Catherine's moral and psychological deterioration is her wholly unreasonable expectation in Chapter x that Edgar should welcome Heathcliff back to the Grange with open arms. When the former naturally resists this demand, she shows herself wholly unable to grasp his point of view and accuses him of being "sulky," of uttering nothing but "pettish, silly speeches," of always contriving "to be sick at the least cross," of "whining for trifles," of displaying "idle petulance," and the like. To accept these charges as a valid criticism of Edgar's character would, of course, be very wide of the mark. What Emily Brontë is rendering here, with no attempt to minimize the moral ugliness, is Catherine's blind self-pity, self-righteousness, and injustice. This state of mind becomes even more intense later in the same chapter when she discovers Isabella's infatuation with Heathcliff. Her first response, prompted by her fierce jealousy, is to slander the latter unconscionably. " 'Tell her what Heathcliff is,' " she orders Nelly; " 'an unreclaimed creature, without refinement, without cultivation; an arid wilderness of furze and whinstone. . . . He's a fierce, pitiless, wolfish man. . . . I know he couldn't love a Linton; and yet he'd be quite capable of marrying your fortune and expectations. Avarice is growing with him a besetting sin . . .'." Again, though it is easy to read this passage as if it were an interpretation of Heathcliff endorsed by Emily Brontë, the context and language alike make it clear that it is both a calculated effort to discourage Isabella by painting her idol in the most lurid colors and a kind of manic hallucination in which Catherine herself has come to half-believe. Heathcliff's roughness (for which, significantly, Catherine has never shown anything but short-lived distaste before now) is grossly overstated; his cruelty is only a presumption; and the contention that avarice is becoming his "besetting sin" is a misinterpretation of his motives for gambling with the truly avaricious Hindley. Catherine's jealous response to her discovery of Isabella's infatuation does not stop here, however. On the following day, she loses no time in brutally humiliating the girl by forcibly detaining her and exposing her passion in the presence of Heathcliff himself.

The breaking-point finally comes in Chapters XI and XII as a result of Catherine's second discovery—that Isabella's infatuation is apparently being reciprocated. In the angry confrontation with Heathcliff which follows, Catherine tries to make light of her jealousy and implies that if Heathcliff now went away she would return to a happiness with Edgar which she enjoyed before his return, but the reader sees that these are mere rationalizations. This becomes even clearer when Edgar intervenes and threatens to have Heathcliff put out of the house: instead of supporting her husband, as her remarks have led us to suppose she would, she turns on him, and, when he shows his weakness, joins Heathcliff in showering him with contempt. So confused are her emotions, however, that, immediately after Heathcliff has left, she addresses to Nelly an extraordinary speech, which concludes with her threatening to revenge herself on both men by committing suicide:

> "Well, if I cannot keep Heathcliff for my friend, if Edgar will be mean and jealous, I'll try to break their hearts by breaking my own. That will be a prompt way of finishing all, when I am pushed to extremity! But it's a deed to be reserved for a forlorn hope; I'd not take Linton by surprise with it. To this point he has been discreet in dreading to provoke me; you must represent the peril of quitting that policy, and remind him of my passionate temper, verging, when kindled, on frenzy. I wish you could dismiss that apathy out of your countenance, and look rather more anxious about me!"

In its shockingly blind and unscrupulous self-righteousness and self-pity this speech brings Catherine to a moral nadir. Almost at once she grows hysterical, locks herself in her room, falls into a fit, and, upon recovering, subjects herself to the three-day fast that fatally undermines her health. She ceases to starve herself only when she becomes maniacally suspicious that her death is precisely what Edgar desires and that everyone else in the household has become her enemy too. Thus, the vital and vivacious Catherine of childhood is transformed into a histrionic, vindictive harridan—an egomaniac and a paranoiac on the verge of insanity, reduced at last by "feverish bewilderment" to tearing the pillow "with her teeth." Emily Brontë is ruthless in systematically stripping her heroine of almost every shred of attractiveness and dignity.

She cannot, however, allow this impression to last for long. If she does, Catherine will no longer seem pitiful and tragic to us, but merely repulsive. Accordingly, from the beginning she has subtly qualified our response by leading us to see that Catherine's sense of having been betrayed by everyone, Heathcliff included, is not without a grain of truth. In Chapter XV, when she and Heathcliff are reunited for the last time and he upbraids her for having abandoned him at the prompting of her " 'poor fancy' " for Edgar, she retaliates by charging him with having abandoned *her*. Though this feeling is expressed later than the scenes I have just considered, we can hardly suppose that Catherine has hitherto been a stranger to it: the assumption that it has been rankling in her consciousness over a long period helps to account for the fierce intensity of her jealousy. Nor can we regard this feeling as wholly irrational. If we examine the account in Chapter IX of how her marriage to Edgar actually came about and correlate with it an important passage in Chapter X, we cannot avoid noticing that on the assumption of Catherine's sole responsibility for her separation from Heathcliff the plot is unnecessarily complicated. On the night she accepts Edgar's proposal and confesses her feelings to Nelly, Heathcliff is invisibly and silently present "on the other side of the settle . . . on a bench by the wall," where he can hear whatever she has to say. Since he gets up and leaves as soon as she declares that to marry him in his present state would "degrade" her, he fails to hear her confess her impassioned sense of their affinity. But he *has* heard her say that " 'I've no more business to marry Edgar Linton than I have to be in heaven'," and this is enough to assure him that her choice of Edgar is causing her deep misgivings. He runs away from Wuthering Heights, then, not in anger, but, as we learn later, to seek his fortune and thereby make himself worthy of Catherine's preference. Like Pip in Dickens's *Great Expectations,* he has been made ashamed of his low condition by the girl he loves, and he seeks to transform himself into a gentleman. Obviously, his hope was that she would not marry Edgar before he returned. But he was gone for three years, and Catherine, apparently having given up all expectation of seeing him again, went through with the marriage after all. There is a presumption, then, that if Heathcliff had come back earlier it might never have taken place. It remains true, of course, that Catherine's acceptance of Edgar's proposal is the necessary condition for all that happens subsequently, but we cannot ignore the part in her fate played, however unwittingly, by Heathcliff's wounded pride and ambition. It is her awareness that he "abandoned" her once before at a critical juncture in her life that lends plausibility as well as intensity to her fears that he may be reciprocating Isabella's love and imparts to her manic rages a measure of justification which enlists our sympathy.

An analogous method is used by Emily Brontë to modify our outraged response to Heathcliff's atrocious career of revenge. Whatever romantic glamour may have been attached to him earlier, it is dispelled by his outright savagery. No casuistry can in the least win our moral approval of his brutality, especially toward Isabella and the three members of the second generation, including his own son Linton. Nothing shows more clearly the level to which he descends than his perverse description of his pitiless behavior as " 'a moral teething'." Nevertheless, there is something in the situation which, though it does not cause us to renounce our moral judgment, does induce us to apply it with compassion. This is the way in which Heathcliff's plan of revenge actually originates. It develops only gradually—in three stages—taking shape in his mind not when he runs away from Wuthering Heights in Chapter IX, but only three years later after his reunion with the married Catherine in Chapter X. As I have just noted, he runs away only in the hope of transforming himself into a gentleman. This transformation is eventually effected, but then he discovers to his dismay that Catherine has discarded him for Edgar. His struggles now seem wholly vain, and his first plan, therefore, is simply to avenge himself in some unspecified way on Hindley (the man who caused the degradation which has cost him his happiness) and then commit suicide. The moment Catherine's ardent welcome proves she still loves him, however, he abandons this plan and adopts another—that of taking up residence again at Wuthering Heights in order to be once more in her vicinity. His third and final plan is, of course, his dual revenge against all the Earnshaws and Lintons by which he hopes to become master of the Heights and the Grange alike. Precisely when this plan occurs to him is not specified, but its evolution can easily be inferred. The crucial point is that the suggestion for it actually comes unwittingly from his victims themselves. His originally vague idea of "settling his score" with Hindley is given definite content only when the latter, out of greed for Heathcliff's newly acquired money, encourages him in that gambling at the Heights which eventually leaves Hindley stripped of his property. Similarly, Heathcliff conceives the idea and method of revenging himself upon the Linton family only after he has been made aware by Catherine that the naive Isabella has fallen in love with him.

The importance of these details cannot be ignored. They make clear that Heathcliff develops his plan of revenge against the houses of his two enemies only after they first put themselves in his power by their own volition. Though he takes the fullest advantage of the position in which they place themselves, he does not force them into this position originally. As his increasingly frequent meetings with Catherine after his return convince him that she loves him more than her husband, the need for revenge naturally grows more intense, until it reaches a climax in Chapter XI when Edgar threatens to have him thrown out of the house and strikes him in the throat. From this moment on nothing can deflect Heathcliff from his destructive course. But the essential point is that his violence has been building up only gradually and only under the stress of provocation. For this reason, though we may deplore his subsequent actions, he never entirely forfeits our sympathy.

Important though these plot manipulations are for determining our double view of Catherine and Heathcliff with its blend of moral disapproval and compassion, they are not fundamental. The decisive factor is Emily Brontë's ability to convince us that cruelty is not innate in the characters of her hero and heroine, but is the consequence of their extreme suffering. In this respect there is a very close similarity between *Wuthering Heights* and Euripides' *Medea:* in both the novel and the play the force that drives the protagonists to their outrageous behavior is their personal misery. In the case of *Wuthering Heights* this causal nexus is often obscured, as in the following interpretation by Dorothy Van Ghent:

> Whatever could happen to these two [Catherine and Heathcliff], if they could be happily together, would be something altogether asocial, amoral, savagely irresponsible, wildly impulsive: it would be the enthusiastic, experimental, quite random activity of childhood, occult to the socialized adult. But since no conceivable *human* male and female, not brutish, not anthropologically rudimentary, could be together in this way as adults, all that we can really imagine for the grown-up Catherine and Heathcliff, as "characters" on the human plane, is what the book gives of them—their mutual destruction by tooth and nail in an effort, through death, to get back to the lost state of gypsy freedom in childhood. [*The English Novel: Form and Function,* 1953]

The fallacy here is to confuse what Catherine and Heathcliff are *before* Catherine's marriage with what they are *after* it. It is implied that they are "altogether asocial, amoral, savagely irresponsible, wildly impulsive" *by nature*—nothing less, as it were, than a case of retarded development—and that this must have inevitably led to "their mutual destruction by tooth and nail" *even if a marriage between Catherine and Edgar had never taken place.* This mistake is easy to make because so much more space in the novel is given to representing Catherine and Heathcliff after the marriage than before it; but, by the same token, it is impossible to support such a reading with adequate evidence. (Indeed, Mrs. Van Ghent contradicts her thesis later when she declares that though "some alluring and astonishing destiny seems possible" for Catherine and Heathcliff, "*What that phenomenon might be or mean, we cannot know, for it is frustrated by Catherine's marriage to Edgar*" [my italics].) That Catherine and Heathcliff are wild and rebellious as children goes without saying. But Emily Brontë takes great pains to show us that the tyranny of Hindley under which they are forced to live has given them good reason to be. At this stage, there is nothing sinister in their behavior at all. On the contrary, it is their only source of consolation. Nor is it ever implied that, had circumstances been different, they would never have matured beyond the "quite random activity of childhood." Such an assumption is wholly gratuitous and runs squarely in the face of the fact that everything is done by Emily Brontë early in the novel to set forth these characters in the most sympathetic light. Indeed, it is only because she does this so well that we can accept their separation by Catherine's marriage as a calamity. The pride, hardness, and sullenness which Heathcliff displays as a child is significant only because these traits make his later violence *possible;* there is never any suggestion that they would *necessitate* it without provocation. His nature is a soil capable of nourishing violence (if this were not demonstrated early in the story the plot would be wholly implausible), but the seed of frustration has to be planted first.

What stands in the way of a clear recognition of these facts for some readers is the time-honored tradition of attributing to Catherine and Heathcliff a unique metaphysical status. They are said to be not merely human beings, with recognizably human needs, capabilities, and failings, but the embodiment of special cosmic "forces," "energies," or "principles." These views betray their weaknesses because their proponents are unable to give any consistent account of precisely what these forces or principles are supposed to be. In Lord David Cecil's famous interpretation [in his *Early Victorian Novelists,* 1935], for instance, Catherine and Heathcliff are said at one moment to incarnate a "spiritual principle" which lives on after their deaths in the form of an "immortal soul," and at another to be "a manifestation of natural forces" like a "mountain torrent," which, when it is "frustrated of its natural outlet . . . inevitably becomes destructive." What identity there is between a "natural force" and a "spiritual principle" is not explained. Similarly, Mrs. Van Ghent seems undecided whether the strange "otherness" which Catherine and Heathcliff manifest is "the raw, inhuman reality of anonymous natural energies," the unconscious mind, or some

literal demonism. The clue to the critical confusion here is the way in which each critic seems wholly unaware, as he moves from one to another, that all these different forces and principles cannot be regarded as identical, if terms are being used with any precision at all. These are not statements to the effect that Emily Brontë herself is confused; they are the inevitably confused results of trying to discover in the novel more metaphysical concreteness than it can yield.

Ultimately, the evidence on which such readings appear to rest consists of Catherine's famous utterances to Nelly Dean in Chapter IX where, in lyrical prose, she contrasts her feelings for Edgar with those for Heathcliff; the lovers' expectation of prolonging their passion for each other after death; Heathcliff's sense, near the end of the novel, of Catherine's ghostly presence; and the local legend that, after his death, the ghosts of both may be seen walking together on the moors. None of this leads to anything nearly as definite as the critics would make out. If we look closely at Catherine's speeches, for instance, and refrain from importing into them our own metaphysical preferences or those given cachet by fashionable criticism, we can hardly avoid seeing how little they lend themselves to precise formulation. They tell us simply that Catherine's feeling for Heathcliff is one of the closest, apparently most instinctive affinity—even identity; that this feeling is extraordinarily intense; that it is, indeed, the deepest kind of passion she knows; and that she experiences it as an absolute necessity of her being. All of this is perfectly intelligible and probable as an expression both of her character and of her desperate situation at the time. But, if we try to deduce from it an elaborate metaphysical doctrine, or attribute such to the author herself, we become only subjective and arbitrary.

It can be reasoned, of course, that many of Catherine's sentiments must be more than merely dramatically appropriate—that they must be endorsed to some extent by the author herself—because they are echoed in a number of Emily Brontë's lyrics. But one of the difficulties here is that since most of these lyrics themselves appear to be the dramatically appropriate utterances of characters in the Gondal saga and since the nature of this saga can only be conjectured, the lyrics offer us no more certain a guide to Emily Brontë's own metaphysical persuasions than Catherine's speeches themselves. Moreover, even allowing— what is surely likely—that the lyrics often do express ideas and attitudes endorsed by the author, they would still be largely irrelevant to the issue because they have nothing to say about that crucial conception of immortality on the basis of which the claims for Catherine and Heathcliff's unique metaphysical status seem frequently to rest. Death, revolt, moorland nature, moorland ecstasy, the grief of separated lovers, yearnings for childhood freedom and joy—these certainly are the preoccupations of Catherine and the poems alike; but on the subject of that unorthodox conception of an immortality of fierce passion which Catherine and Heathcliff anticipate for themselves the poems are quite silent. In verses like **"The Philosopher's Conclusion,"** indeed, death is conceived by the speaker simply as oblivion. And when immortality *is* envisaged, as in the famous **"No coward soul is mine,"** it is something much closer to the orthodox immortality of peace in God conceived at various times by Edgar, Nelly Dean, and Lockwood.

This raises the question of the status of the apparently supernatural elements in the novel itself. David Cecil states unequivocally that when Catherine dies "her spirit does take up its abode at Wuthering Heights. And not just as an ineffective ghost: as much as in life she exerts an active influence over Heathcliff, besieges him with her passion." But the text gives no warranty to this kind of certainty in the least. What defines Emily Brontë's method in this matter is precisely its circumspection. Catherine begins to reveal her longing for what she later calls " 'that glorious world' " beyond the grave and the " 'shattered prison' " of her body only in Chapter XII—at a time, that is, when, her mind and body alike having been wrecked by the ordeal of her hysteria and her fast, she is on the threshold of "brain fever" and already "doomed to decay." It is her remarks to the same effect in Chapter XV that also implant the idea of a transcendental reunion in the mind of Heathcliff, who heretofore has given no sign of entertaining any such notion whatsoever. After she dies he takes up the idea in earnest and feverishly prays to her that she will haunt him for the rest of his life. At first his prayer appears to be answered: no sooner is she buried than he "sees" her ghostly presence with him at the graveside. Whether he is suffering from a delusion at this time we are not, of course, explicitly told, but the point is that, in the light of his extreme grief and longing, this is left open as a distinct possibility. Indeed, in the eighteen years which follow, though he yearns continually for a repetition of his experience, none is forthcoming. Furthermore, his expectations suddenly abate at the end of this period when, upon the death of Edgar, he opens Catherine's coffin and looks upon her " 'passionless features'," for this sight persuades him that his hopes have been in vain—that, as Lockwood affirms at the end of the novel, Catherine has been for all these years only a quiet sleeper in the quiet earth. Convinced now that the only kind of reunion with her which he can expect is the purely material one of mutual dissolution, he loosens a side of her coffin and bribes the sexton " 'to pull it away, when I'm laid there, and slide mine out too'." But two months later, when Lockwood arrives at Wuthering Heights and dreams of Catherine's ghost at the window, all of Heathcliff's anguished yearning is revived. The reader knows that Lockwood has had only a nightmare, but Heathcliff is convinced that his visitor has really seen the spectre he himself had hoped to see for all those eighteen years. Most significantly, it is on precisely this delusion that Emily Brontë arranges for the dénouement of the novel to hinge, for from this point onward Heathcliff can think of nothing but joining Catherine in death (XXXIII). He now begins to see her presence again just as he did when he stood at her grave after her burial. But by this time, in order to achieve his desire, he has also begun to starve himself, and thus the possibility that he is suffering only from a hallucination is distinctly left open once more. Why, we must ask, if Emily Brontë wanted us to accept the "supernatural" in the novel as a certainty, has she so systematically hedged it round with these ironic ambiguities? There remains, of course, the local legend that Heathcliff and Catherine may still be seen walking the moors. But a less conclusive way of persuading us of their immortality than by the testimony of superstitious rustics could hardly be imagined. These tales, at any rate, are given no more authority than Lockwood's contrary conviction that Heathcliff has joined Catherine and Edgar in an eternally quiet sleep.

Finally, we cannot overlook still another objection to the metaphysical-supernaturalist reading. This is simply that it is inconsistent with the novel's total emotional effect. If Catherine and Heathcliff are merely the channels through which pour immense "spiritual" or "natural" or "demonic" energies over which they have no control, our reaction to them may be one of awe, but hardly of pity: we do not pity blind natural or supernatural forces, but only their victims. I submit, however, that this is not our principal reaction to the novel at all. On the contrary, **Wuthering Heights** is such a remarkable work partly because it persuades us so forcibly to pity victims and victimizers alike. The revealing fact about readings like those of David Cecil and Dorothy Van Ghent is that though they lay great emphasis upon Catherine and Heathcliff's power for destruction, they say next to nothing about their equally great capacity for suffering. The ultimate effect of such readings on these characters is to dehumanize them.

On our awareness of their suffering, however, and especially of this suffering as the cause of their destructive power, our entire emotional reaction to Emily Brontë's hero and heroine depends. **Wuthering Heights** is an extravagant novel, but its extravagance is not in its metaphysics. Catherine and Heathcliff are destructive not because they are blind natural forces obeying the same impersonal cosmic economy as a mountain torrent or a storm, or because they are mysterious "spiritual principles" which are not of this world, or because Heathcliff is really a demon, but because of their eminently human frustration. As we watch the step-by-step descent of these characters into their inferno and contemplate the whole ruinous process in retrospect, our dominant impression is one of tragic waste: we feel that we have witnessed the destruction of two human lives which might have been both happier and better in *this* world. The central fact of the novel is that when Catherine betrays her own and Heathcliff's deepest self by marrying Edgar Linton she creates a disorder in their souls which spreads to the entire society around them. Tragically, by her misguided choice of Edgar as her husband, she places herself and Heathcliff in a situation which exacts from each the most atrocious frustration and suffering and, in consequence, brings out the worst in both of them. Whenever Catherine and Heathcliff's cruelty threatens to drown all our sympathy in moral revulsion, this is the vital conception to which Emily Brontë returns.

A crucial matter is her timing. With great deliberation she builds up our moral aversion, carrying it (as we have already seen) to the point where it is about to stifle every other response. At this moment, however, she effects a sudden reversal: a new element is thrust into our awareness, and our horror is transformed into compassion.

Let us go back to the sequence of Catherine's mad-scenes in Chapters X-XII and take up where our earlier analysis left off. No sooner has Catherine reached the moment of "feverish bewilderment" when she is tearing the pillow "with her teeth" than there is a startling transition; the storm suddenly gives way to an almost unearthly calm. There follows for almost four pages an extremely poignant section in which, in her half-delirium, she lives again through some of the ecstasies and miseries of her childhood. The climax of this is a terrible confession of despair. Catherine tells Nelly that when she recovered from the fit into which she had fallen upon fleeing to her room at the end of the preceding chapter, the last seven years of her life became a blank. Shutting out of her mind everything connected with the Lintons and her marriage, she was, as it were, transported back over this period to the time of her father's death, when she and Heathcliff were forced by Hindley to sleep separately for the first time. The agony of being "enclosed in the oak-panelled bed" as in a coffin came back to her with all the Proustian vividness of a present reality. This sensation did not last long; her memory of the intervening years was soon restored. But then she was overwhelmed by an anguish even greater, analogous to what she would have felt seven years earlier if, instead of having merely been separated from Heathcliff in bed, she " 'had been wrenched from the Heights, and every early association, and my all in all, as Heathcliff was at that time, and been converted at a stroke into Mrs. Linton, the lady of Thrushcross Grange, and the wife of a stranger; an exile, and outcast, thenceforth, from what had been my world'." It is to this world, the world she shared with Heathcliff before her father's death, that she now longs to return. Thus, at the end of her confession, when she commands Nelly to open the window again and is refused, she leaps out of bed and, throwing it open herself, imagines that she can see in the distance the glow of lights from her old home, and that she and Heathcliff are children wandering at night on the moor. It is now that the whole section reaches its remarkable conclusion. Addressing the boy Heathcliff as if he were actually present, she challenges him to invoke the ghosts in Gimmerton churchyard and promises that if he does so she will never desert him even in death: " 'I'll not lie there by myself; they may bury me twelve feet deep, and throw the church down over me, but I won't rest till you are with me. I never will'."

Probably no words in *Wuthering Heights* are more familiar than these. But what needs to be stressed is their decisive structural significance. The essential point is their *placement:* they are the climax of a whole section which occurs at precisely that moment in the novel when Catherine's frenzied, self-righteous cruelty has threatened to cost her all our sympathy and respect. The effect of this section is to right the reader's emotional balance, both by poignantly imaging what Catherine was like before her hideous transformation and by persuading us that the cause of this transformation has been her terrible frustration. Immediately afterwards Edgar enters the room, and all her cruelty and maniacal fury revive, but now our reaction to her behavior is quite different from what it was earlier, for we cannot forget what we have just seen. This structuring of Catherine's poignant memories and yearnings between the two scenes of her greatest moral deterioration is one of the triumphs of Emily Brontë's bold fictional rhetoric.

The technique of emotional reversal is used again in Chapter XV at the critical moment of Catherine and Heathcliff's last reunion. Catherine's initial display of petulance, selfishness, and vindictiveness is only a prelude to the lovers' passionate reconciliation, which reaches its climax when Edgar's impending arrival threatens once more to separate them. In dread of this prospect Catherine falls again into delirium and dies shortly after while giving premature birth to her child. Her sufferings have literally destroyed her.

At the same time Emily Brontë is similarly controlling our response to Heathcliff. A few pages before this culminating scene a very black picture of his behavior had been painted by Isabella in her long letter to Nelly (XIII). And almost immediately after this (XIV) he was shown in Nelly's presence mercilessly reviling Edgar's "duty and humanity" and contrasting it with his own passion. Arnold Kettle takes this passage as a serious judgment on Edgar endorsed by Emily Brontë herself and finds in it a "moral passion" which "has the quality of great poetry." But this is quite unfair. If Edgar is not Heathcliff's equal for passion, neither is he so merely contemptible. Heathcliff's speech is a piece of special pleading and deplorable vainglory, particularly outrageous in the light of the fact that he has just become guilty of what Kettle himself calls "the first of his callous and ghastly acts of revenge, his marriage to Isabella." Kettle's error comes from recognizing that Emily Brontë wants to keep alive our sympathy for Heathcliff, but failing to perceive just how she succeeds in doing so; he has, therefore, to explain away passages which morally revolt us. The real corrective to our moral aversion comes not from any justice in Heathcliff's words, but from what we are shown in the two chapters which follow of his passionate reunion with Catherine and his frustration and despair in the face of her mortal illness and death. Our sympathies are enlisted by his anguished prayer that her ghost return to haunt him, his self-inflicted injuries at the tree, his cries of pain like those of "a savage beast getting goaded to death with knives and spears," his surreptitious visit to Catherine's corpse, when he substitutes his hair for Edgar's in her locket, and the testimony to his overwhelming suffering offered even by his enemy-wife.

Heathcliff performs, of course, still another action which reveals his great grief and frustration at this time: Catherine is no sooner buried than, driven to madness by the thought that only " 'two yards of loose earth . . . [are] the sole barrier between us'," he tears open her grave in the hope of holding her once more in his arms. But this episode is not described until twelve chapters later. Why? Just as our hostile response to his cruel treatment of Isabella and his unjust scorn of Edgar must be modified by the description of his anguish at the time of Catherine's illness and death and just as our response to Catherine herself was similarly modified, so too must Emily Brontë modify our hostile response to Heathcliff's fanatically brutal career of revenge—the counterpart in the second half of the novel of Catherine's infernal rages in the first. The beginning of this revenge coincides in time with the various events just mentioned, but Emily Brontë can hardly hope, as she subsequently focuses more and more exclusively on Heathcliff's cruelty to the second generation, that our memory of these events will weigh sufficiently heavy. Indeed, if Heathcliff's story is going to be truly tragic, she must render the barbarous extent of that cruelty as fully and sharply as possible. Thus, she resorts still once more to the method of sudden reversal. For almost a quarter of the novel we see and hear of Heathcliff practically nothing but his villainy, the climax of which is the outrageous marriage he forces upon Cathy and the dying Linton. It is then, in Chapter XXIX, without warning, that he discloses to Nelly the story of his violation of Catherine's grave eighteen years before. Now too he recounts how, throughout that period, he longed in vain for proof of her ghostly presence and how he has allayed this longing only by opening her grave again and gazing upon her " 'passionless features.' " But these were the eighteen years, we realize with something of a shock, during which he was also pursuing his revenge. Thus, Emily Brontë suddenly makes us see this revenge retrospectively in a wholly new light: his cruelty, in large measure, was tragically inseparable from his futile yearning.

But the technique of reversal is not Emily Brontë's only resource for making us aware of the suffering at the root of the cruelty. Its effectiveness at this point depends, in fact, on a quite different strategy. Heathcliff's vengeful actions are so protracted that if he fails to enlist our sympathy until the end and only in retrospect, he runs the risk of forfeiting it entirely. Something must be done to modify our aversion to his revenge while he is pursuing it. Emily Brontë's solution to this problem is to set before us throughout the novel a number of other characters who, when faced with circumstances analogous to his own, behave in a similar way. Because we are likely to attend only to the main functions of these characters in the plot, she can manipulate our judgment of Heathcliff very unobtrusively.

The most obvious parallel to him is, of course, Hareton Earnshaw, who is gradually transformed by his subjugation to Heathcliff into a replica of the latter as he was under the domination of Hindley. But other parallels are equally important. The chief function of Hindley himself, for instance, is to serve as Heathcliff's persecutor, and yet for one moment in the action, immediately after the death of his wife, we glimpse him as something more—the bereaved husband:

> . . . he grew desperate; his sorrow was of that kind that will not lament. He neither wept nor prayed—he cursed and defied—execrated God and man, and gave himself up to reckless dissipation.
> The servants could not bear his tyrannical and evil conduct long: Joseph and I [Nelly] were the only two that would stay.

The crucial point is that, just as in Heathcliff's case, Hindley's "tyrannical and evil conduct" is the direct result of his overwhelming sorrow. Even more sympathetic characters are transformed in this way. The mild and genteel Isabella's response to Heathcliff's cruelty is a savage desire to claim an eye for an eye. Even more startling, but no less consistent with Emily Brontë's psychological premises, is what happens to the tender and maternal Cathy as she re-

mains Heathcliff's prisoner at the Heights after the death of her father and Linton. According to the housekeeper, Zillah,

> " . . . She has no lover, or liker among us—and she does not deserve one—for, let them say the least word to her, and she'll curl back without respect of any one! She'll snap at the master himself, and as good as dares him to thrash her; *and the more hurt she gets, the more venomous she grows*" (my italics).

What could be a more distinct clue than this last sentence for our understanding of Heathcliff himself? Finally, there is the fastidious Lockwood and his surprisingly violent dream of Catherine's ghost at the window in Chapter III. Dorothy Van Ghent holds that Lockwood's action of pulling the ghost's wrist back and forth over the broken glass until it bleeds is "unmotivated" and therefore proof of some demonic element inherent in human nature itself. But the definitive answer to this fanciful interpretation has been given by Edgar F. Shannon, Jr., who shows, quite to the contrary [in "Lockwood's Dreams and the Exegesis of *Wuthering Heights*," *Nineteenth-Century Fiction* XIV (September 1959)], that the violence of Lockwood's dream is the logical result of "the physical and emotional outrages he has sustained" at the Heights during his visits of the last two days. None of these characters is evil or vicious by nature. They become so only under extreme provocation. One of their principal functions in the novel is to persuade us that the dynamics of Heathcliff's violence and cruelty are to be understood in the same way.

The dominant image of Heathcliff that emerges, then, is neither that of a "moral force" nor a "demon," but that of a tragic sufferer. And this is finally our image of Catherine too. We do not condone their outrages, but neither do we merely condemn them. We do something larger and more important: we recognize in them the tragedy of passionate natures whom intolerable frustration and loss have stripped of their humanity. (pp. 305-23)

> *John Hagan, "Control of Sympathy in 'Wuthering Heights',"* in Nineteenth-Century Fiction, *Vol. 21, No. 4, March, 1967, pp. 305-23.*

Arnold Shapiro   (essay date 1969)

[*In the excerpt below, Shapiro demonstrates how Brontë's criticism of society and treatment of characters places* Wuthering Heights *firmly within the tradition of the Victorian novel.*]

In their attempt to account for the strangeness of *Wuthering Heights* and to answer some of the difficult questions it poses—for instance, is Heathcliff a hero or villain?—critics have generally torn the novel from its Victorian surroundings and have indicated that one needs a special set of criteria to evaluate it. Thus, in his brief note on the Brontës in *The Great Tradition*, F. R. Leavis calls *Wuthering Heights* "a kind of sport," outside the main stream of the novel's development and having only a minor influence on works to follow. Lord David Cecil [in *Victorian Novelists: Essays in Revaluation*, 1958] calls Emily Brontë's outlook "pre-moral": " . . . that conflict between right and wrong which is the distinguishing feature in the Victorian view of life does not come into her view. Human nature, to her, is not a mixture of good and bad elements, as it is to Thackeray. It cannot be grouped into the virtuous and the wicked, as it is by Charlotte Brontë or Dickens. The conflict in her books is not between right and wrong. . . ." Supporting this view, Dorothy Van Ghent asserts that *Wuthering Heights* "works at a level of experience that is unsympathetic to, or rather, simply irrelevant to the social and moral reason." Emily Brontë's characters "enact their drama on some ground of the psychic life where ethical ideas are not at home, at least such ethical ideas as those that inform our ordinary experience of the manners of men. They have the 'anonymity' of figures in dreams or in religious ritual" [*The English Novel: Form and Function,* 1961].

Finally, taking a slightly different approach [in "The Brontës, or, Myth Domesticated," in *Forms of Modern Fiction,* 1948], Richard Chase accuses Emily Brontë of not having the courage of *his* convictions. To Chase, Heathcliff is "sheer dazzling sexual and intellectual force." Catherine Earnshaw fails because she does not reciprocate Heathcliff's love strongly enough and thus "comes to grasp the significance of her spiritual mission too late." According to Chase, the second generation of characters, with whom the novel ends, are only "pale replicas" of the first. The novel concludes with a dreary sort of vacillating compromise: "The happy marriages at the end of *Jane Eyre* and *Wuthering Heights* represent the ostensible triumph of the secular, moderate-liberal, sentimental point of view over the mythical, tragic point of view."

My view is that *Wuthering Heights* does not take place in some dream world. Emily Brontë is in firm moral control throughout the novel. This does not mean that she sees things in blacks and whites. She has great sympathy for her characters, but she mercilessly exposes their weaknesses, as well as the weaknesses of the society surrounding them. She has a great vision of the possibilities of love, but she also quite clearly shows how the limitations of human beings and society can make that love unattainable. She admires Heathcliff, but she condemns him when he ruthlessly accepts the values of the people he hates and seeks fulfillment through an empty revenge. She is fully aware of Catherine Earnshaw's failure to accept the challenge of Heathcliff's love. At the end, she gives us hope for the future, neither sentimentally nor compromisingly. She calls for a revolution—the reversal of the old ways of thinking and behaving. She wants society to live by the values which it has always mouthed but never yet really tried.

Wuthering Heights is in the same ethical and moral tradition as the other great Victorian novels. Its criticism of society is as fierce as Charlotte Brontë's or Dickens'. In a recent article Philip Drew has shown how Charlotte Brontë's remarks on *Wuthering Heights* are still relevant and true to the spirit of the book. I feel, in addition, that much of the same spirit interfuses the novels of Charlotte and Emily Brontë. For both writers, society and what passes for civilization are synonymous with selfishness. Both show family life as a sort of open warfare, a deadly struggle for money and power. Both see organized religion as ineffective or hypocritical or so cold and harsh as to be inhumane and deflected from true Christian ideals. The characters in Charlotte Brontë's first two novels have to face many of the same problems confronting the characters in *Wuthering Heights,* and they reach the same conclusions. Both William Crimsworth (in *The Professor*) and Jane Eyre reject the master-slave relationship as static and stultifying and come to the teacher-pupil relationship as the one that allows for growth and the fulfillment of human potential. Similarly, Catherine Linton and Hareton Earnshaw see the futility of Heathcliff's desire for revenge and domination (his seeing the world solely in terms of the master-slave relationship when love fails him) and affirm civilization and civilized values in terms of the teacher-pupil relationship.

At the outset Heathcliff is much like the orphans in other Victorian novels—Oliver Twist, or Jane Eyre, or Pip. He is alone, an outcast, as much an "alien" or "interloper" among the Earnshaws as Jane Eyre is in Gateshead Hall. The family here is defined much as Charlotte Brontë portrays it in *Jane Eyre* or in her third novel, *Shirley*. First, the family closes against the stranger. Just as the Reeds fear Jane simply because she is different from everyone else and thus seems to pose a threat, so the Earnshaws are repelled by Heathcliff's appearance. He looks like a "gypsy brat" and Mrs. Earnshaw is ready to fling him out of the house. Just as the Reeds force Jane to know her "place" by making her live with the servants, the Earnshaws attempt to dehumanize Heathcliff. He is an "it" to them, an object, not a person. He is given a first name, not a last name, as though to emphasize that he can never be part of the family.

Second, although the family acts as a unit in its opposition to Heathcliff, the members of the family act separately when their individual rights and privileges seem threatened. Heathcliff is as much a discord among the Earnshaws as Jane Eyre is among the Reeds. The children are jealous of him. Old Mr. Earnshaw brought *him* home instead of the presents they had expected. Hindley comes to regard his father as an "oppressor" because of Mr. Earnshaw's concern for the orphan. He sees "Heathcliff as a usurper of his parent's affections and his privileges." The choice of words here—"oppressor," "usurper," Hindley's "*persecuting* the poor, fatherless child"—indicates that this family is still very much a tribe, governed by power and the desire for money rather than by love. One is reminded of such other Victorian tribes as the Crawleys in *Vanity Fair* or the Yorkes in *Shirley*.

Emily Brontë broadens her attack when she indicates the failings of organized religion. In the Preface to the second edition of *Jane Eyre,* Charlotte Brontë criticizes those who confuse Christianity with sanctimoniousness: "Conventionality is not morality. Self-righteousness is not religion." Christianity is not the same thing as self-interest: "appearance should not be mistaken for truth; narrow human doctrines, that only tend to elate and magnify a few, should not be substituted for the world-redeeming creed of Christ." Preceding her sister in this sort of criticism, Emily Brontë in *Wuthering Heights* condemns the pharisaical servant, Joseph, who sees everyone damned except himself and uses his "sermonizing and pious discoursing" as a way of gaining influence. Joseph's religion is completely self-serving: he attacks those out of power in order to gain the approval of those in power. When Mr. Earnshaw is in control, he attacks Hindley. With Hindley in charge, he attacks Heathcliff and Cathy. Finally, when Heathcliff takes over, Joseph savagely criticizes the younger generation.

Among the masters, we find the same hypocrisy and the same perversion of religious values. Thus, in a telling choice of words, Emily Brontë points out that Hindley's "paradise" is his selfish idyll with Frances at the hearth, while Heathcliff and Cathy are banished to the back kitchen. As Nelly indicates, Hindley's religion, like Joseph's, is egocentric: "he had room in his heart only for two idols—his wife and himself: he doted on both, and adored one." Hindley's treatment of others follows the same selfish pattern as his "religion." He is as consistent as the Brocklehursts in *Jane Eyre,* who enjoy all the luxuries of life themselves, while advocating Spartan austerity for the poor. On the one hand, Hindley scorns Heathcliff for his lack of parentage and breeding. On the other hand, he brings home and worships a wife, Frances, who is equally without family: "What she was, and where she was born he never informed us [says Nelly]; probably, she had neither money nor name to recommend her, or he would scarcely have kept the union from his father."

The rest of the people of the novel emulate the Earnshaws in their selfishness and lack of sympathy. The Lintons presumably are good Christians, yet they are repelled by Heathcliff because he looks like a gypsy and therefore cannot be a member of their social class. Here one has only to think of *Great Expectations* or *Vanity Fair* to see that Emily Brontë is on the main road of Victorian social criticism, attacking those who judge others solely by surface appearances or money or birth. As Heathcliff bitterly notes when he tells the story later to Nelly, Cathy "was a young lady and they [the Lintons] made a distinction between her treatment and mine." The younger Lintons follow in the footsteps of the older generation. Isabella and Edgar are spoiled brats, like the young Earnshaws and the Reed children in *Jane Eyre.* They fight over their possessions. Worst of all, Edgar shows no real evidence of Christianity in his behavior toward Isabella. When his sister disobeys his orders and runs off with Heathcliff, he cuts himself off from her and self-righteously blames her for his own inability to forgive: " 'Trouble me no more about her. Hereafter she is only my sister in name, not because I disown her, but because she has disowned me'."

Nelly Dean, the chief narrator of *Wuthering Heights,* affirms the universal selfishness that pervades the world of this novel: "Well, we *must* be for ourselves in the long run," she says; "the mild and generous are only more justly selfish than the domineering." Trying to maintain a hollow peace or merely trying to keep her job, Nelly herself evidences self-interestedness: she constantly blurts out secrets that should be kept hidden or holds back things that should be told. Nelly is not, I think, the villain of *Wuthering Heights.* Rather, she is like the Brettons in Charlotte

Brontë's last novel, *Villette,* well-meaning, but sometimes unconsciously cruel. She is guilty of lack of comprehension, and, worse, almost a total lack of sympathy with the people who are supposed to be in her charge. Though she has grown up with Catherine Earnshaw, she does not understand her. When Cathy cries out in torment during her final illness, Nelly thinks she is a bad actress whose unseemly behavior is due to nothing more than "cold-water and ill-temper."

For the most part, the world of *Wuthering Heights* is hermetic. We get only one glimpse of the greater world outside Yorkshire in Emily Brontë's description of Lockwood, the first narrator. If Lockwood is typical, then the outside world too is corrupt, self-seeking, and uncomprehending. Lockwood's idea of "heaven" is misanthropy; he thinks he and Heathcliff can "divide the desolation" between them, like a pair of devils. His version of love is bashful selfishness. Confiding to Nelly about a mild flirtation he engaged in, he admits that he acted like a self-conscious child when it appeared his advances would be reciprocated: "what did I do? I confess it with shame—shrunk icily into myself, like a snail; at every glance retired colder and farther; till, finally, the poor innocent . . . persuaded her mamma to decamp." In his relations to others he simply accepts the caste system and judges by appearances. At first he assumes that Hareton is a "boor" and that he can easily sweep Cathy Linton off her feet. Like the "southerners" in Charlotte Brontë's *Shirley,* Lockwood is a man of little feeling and no profundity. Con-

Shibden Hall, near Halifax, the probable model for Thrushcross Grange.

trasting himself with the average Yorkshireman, he seems to realize his own inadequacies: "They *do* live more in earnest, more in themselves, and less in surface change, and frivolous external things. I could fancy a love for life here almost possible; and I was a fixed unbeliever in any love of a year's standing." Despite his realization, however, Emily Brontë clearly shows that Lockwood shares at least one trait with the Yorkshiremen of the novel: he too is guilty of dehumanizing other people, using them for his own ends. Just as Heathcliff was an "it" to the Earnshaws and Nelly when he first arrived, so Lockwood calls Nelly his "human fixture" and accepts her attentions to him as his due. His behavior toward Cathy during his terrible dream at the start of the novel shows that beneath even the most polished exterior there lurks a potential savage. Lockwood too can become violent, like a cornered animal, when he thinks he is threatened: "Terror made me cruel; and, finding it useless to attempt shaking the creature off, I pulled its wrist on to the broken pane, and rubbed it to and fro till the blood ran down and soaked the bedclothes." With this almost unbearable scene (one of the most painful in English literature, I think) Emily Brontë reveals how tenuous is most men's hold on civilization and civilized values.

Against this dark background of violence and weakness, hypocrisy and selfishness, the novelist depicts the love between Heathcliff and Cathy. Rereading **Wuthering Heights,** one finds that love is presented in almost completely negative terms, set forth in opposition to society and its values, in a sense defined by those values. One cannot emphasize this fact enough. Heathcliff and Cathy do not exist in some dream-like vacuum; rather, they are the products of the world that Emily Brontë clearly describes in the first part of the novel. To a surprisingly large extent they share the values of that world, and the novelist, at least by implication, criticizes their actions. It is simply not accurate to say that their relationship is "irrelevant to the social and moral reason." In the opening half of **Wuthering Heights** Emily Brontë shows how Cathy's selfishness and her attempt to compromise with society's dictates keep her from fulfilling her love for Heathcliff. In the closing half she shows how Heathcliff, in his frustration and desire for revenge, becomes the unwitting tool of the world, embodying all of society's egoism and cruelty.

Emily Brontë gives little indication of Cathy and Heathcliff's undiluted joy together. Even though critics frequently envision them frolicking happily on the moors, they are always severely limited by the narrowness and bleakness of their world. In fact, in the same paragraph (the only one in the book) where Nelly recounts their happiness, she also points out that the first thing the children did when they were set free was contrive "some naughty plan of revenge." Though Dorothy Van Ghent is correct when she states that both Heathcliff and Cathy reject ordinary concepts of human behavior, Emily Brontë does not divorce her characters from ethics and morality entirely. Cathy, for example, cannot bear the idea that Edgar has his head buried in a book while she suffers almost unutterable anguish. Heathcliff scorns Edgar's sense of *"duty and humanity . . . pity and charity"* (his italics). And rightly so. "Pre-moral" Emily Brontë does not here reject these

concepts through her spokesman, Heathcliff. She does discard the ordinary man's ordinary use of these terms. Edgar's pity and charity are directed, in the main, toward himself, since he has no real sense of what his wife is like. He has never known her. His duty and humanity toward his wife consist of his staying away from her during her final illness. He suspects, like Nelly, that she is play-acting and somehow, even though she is in the final stages of pregnancy, he never takes the trouble to find out otherwise.

In opposition to this sort of narrowness and pettiness, Cathy makes two grand positive affirmations of her love for Heathcliff, asserting at one point " 'he's more myself than I am' " and later, " 'I *am* Heathcliff' ": " ' . . . my great thought in living is himself. If all else perished, and *he* remained, I should still continue to be; and, if all else remained, and he were annihilated, the Universe would turn to a mighty stranger'." Here Cathy seems to be trying to do away with the boundaries that separate human beings and trying to live in and for another person. She seems to want freedom from the restrictions of society: " 'Oh, I'm burning!' " she tells Nelly during her illness. " 'I wish I were out of doors—I wish I were a girl again, half savage, and hardy, and free; and laughing at injuries, not maddening under them! . . . I'm sure I should be myself were I once among the heather on those hills. Open the window again wide'." Free from the world's limitations, she would be contented, she says, with a universe composed solely of herself and Heathcliff.

When Emily Brontë shows that Cathy's wishes are unattainable, she is realistic—Richard Chase notwithstanding—rather than sentimental. Cathy's failure is easier to pinpoint than is Heathcliff's: despite her noble assertions to the contrary, she is a creature of this world after all. Once she gets a taste of life at the Lintons' she decides that she enjoys gentility; like her brother, Hindley, she enjoys wielding power and she tyrannizes Edgar and Isabella who give in to all her whims. In Nelly's words, she begins "to adopt a double character," acting one way with the Lintons, another with Heathcliff. In the "catechism" on love and marriage that Nelly puts her through, she reveals that at least half her being has been given to society. She will marry Edgar because he is rich and handsome and because he loves her, not because she loves him. She thinks she can have her cake and eat it too: marrying Edgar, she will have money enough to help her true love, Heathcliff. In some ways she seems scarcely blameworthy. Like a child, she thinks she can control the world, when, in reality, the world controls her. To an extent Cathy remains a child to the very end; she is surprised when Heathcliff runs off; she no more understands Edgar than her husband comprehends her; she is shocked when Nelly finally rebels against her imperiousness. Chase's evaluation of her seems correct, then: immature and willful, Cathy is not always worthy of Heathcliff's love.

But with equal certainty, Heathcliff's pure sexual energy fails also. Where Cathy remains a child, Heathcliff shows he has been tutored only too well in the lessons taught by Hareton, Joseph, the Lintons, Cathy herself. Once deflected from his love, he turns aside blindly from the path of freedom and openness and casts himself in the iron mold of revenge: " 'I seek no revenge on you [he tells Cathy] . . . That's not the plan. The tyrant grinds down his slaves and they don't turn against him, they crush those beneath them. You are welcome to torture me to death for your amusement, only allow me to amuse myself a little in the same style'." Here Heathcliff opts for stasis rather than development, for fixity rather than growth. The whole purpose of the master-slave relationship, which he chooses quite deliberately, is to keep things always the same. The master, like the gentleman upholding the caste system, wants to maintain his superiority at all costs. He wants to keep the slave beneath his feet forever. In this way Heathcliff betrays himself and imitates the society that earlier had denied him his individuality and humanness. He ends up playing society's game because society too, as Emily Brontë has portrayed it in the novel, is based on the master-slave relationship: the Lintons and Earnshaws and Lockwoods are grasping people who like the *status-quo* because it keeps them in power.

Ironies abound in the second half of *Wuthering Heights* as Heathcliff accepts, and lives by, the values of the people he formerly detested and finds that these values are as empty for him as they were for the others. Thus, after three years away, he returns as a "capitalist," some sort of successful businessman. Using force and trickery, he gobbles up both the Earnshaw and Linton estates. But what does property mean to him? Wuthering Heights, which had at least been a home when Heathcliff entered it, is chaos and anarchy when he comes to govern it. In order to revenge himself on Edgar, he cruelly mistreats Isabella and the young Cathy Linton. Yet, scorning both females, he gets no satisfaction from his vengeance, and he remains lonely and desolate, haunted by his visions of the first Catherine.

Emily Brontë shows Heathcliff becoming a parody of his former tormentors, of Hindley especially. Reversing the golden rule, he does to his son, Linton what Hindley had tried to do to him. His words even echo those used earlier to describe him, as he calls Linton "my property," "it." He brutalizes Hareton, as he was brutalized by Hindley, by cutting him off from ordinary humanity and denying him an education. He is even more monstrous than Hindley, however, because he realizes what he is doing. Where Hindley was too savage or too stupid to understand Heathcliff, Heathcliff can empathize with Hareton, but he uses his empathy perversely, as a way of tormenting his fellow human being:

> "If he were a born fool [he says of Hareton] I should not enjoy it half so much. But he's no fool; and I can sympathize with all his feelings, having felt them myself. I know what he suffers now, for instance, exactly—it is merely a beginning of what he shall suffer, though. And he'll never be able to emerge from his bathos of coarseness and ignorance. I've got him faster than his scoundrel of a father secured me, and lower, for he takes a pride in his brutishness I've taught him to scorn everything extra-animal as silly and weak."

All Heathcliff has learned from his experience is hate.

With devastating irony, Emily Brontë shows that this hatred plays right into society's hands, as Heathcliff helps perpetuate the system that earlier he struggled against and that he knows destroyed his chance for love.

Many critics stop reading *Wuthering Heights* at the death of Catherine and see the rest of the novel as an anti-climax. But this death occurs only half-way through the book, and to neglect the second half is to neglect much of what Emily Brontë is trying to say about human existence. Symbolically, this second half begins with a birth, Catherine Linton's, which is described in much the same terms as was the entrance of Heathcliff. Nelly calls Cathy a "feeble orphan" and says she is "an unwelcomed infant it was, poor thing! It might have wailed out of life, and nobody cared a morsel, during those first hours of existence." Though the language is an echo of the past, however, Cathy turns out to be the representative of a new generation, and without the author's being foolishly optimistic, of a new set of values, an answer to the old ways.

In the concluding section of *Wuthering Heights* we trace the education of the second Catherine. She parallels her mother in her "sunshine" and in her imperiousness (and in the fact that she is spoiled by Edgar). But she differs from her mother also: as her relationship to Linton indicates, she is open to others, receptive to their needs. She responds to Linton because he is a human being and is in trouble. This is not the awesome love claimed by Heathcliff and the first Catherine, perhaps, but human sympathy—the same pity, charity, duty, humanity that Heathcliff rejected in Edgar, the difference being that Cathy practices without preaching. Like her mother, Cathy is misunderstood by Nelly, but unlike her mother, she is not simply interested in self-fulfillment; she wants to help someone else. Like Heathcliff she has the gift of empathy. Hers is a softened emotion, however, which makes her comprehend others and behave better toward them. When she is angry with Hareton because he will not share her attitude toward Heathcliff, he makes her understand by appealing to her remembrance of her relationship with her father: "he found means to make her hold her tongue, by asking, how she would like *him* to speak ill of her father? and then she comprehended that Earnshaw took the master's reputation home to himself, and was attached by ties stronger than reason could break—chains, forged by habit, which it would be cruel to attempt to loosen." Responding to Hareton's appeal, Cathy shows that a new way of life is possible. The old system need not hold sway forever, after all.

For what *Wuthering Heights* is about, finally, is what civilization is about. When Lockwood first sees it, Wuthering Heights, the place, is a "misanthropist's heaven." Bitterness and ill-will reign. The people who inhabit the house are each isolated from the other, working at cross-purposes in their hatred of, or indifference to, one another. The place has reverted to barbarism, since one of the primal laws of civilization has been revoked: the guest, Lockwood, is treated as a "stranger"; suspicion has replaced hospitality. Emily Brontë, at this point, is quite realistic in her portrayal of the young Cathy Linton. For Cathy has given in to the atmosphere of the Heights and to the prevailing customs. She has judged Hareton simply by his outward appearance. He does not look like a gentleman; therefore he cannot be her cousin: he must be a "clown." In her hatred of Heathcliff and her bitterness toward those who have not helped her in her time of need, she emulates the servant, Zillah, who quashes any impulses toward sympathy. As Zillah explains her coldness to Nelly: " 'Once or twice, after we had gone to bed, I've happened to open my door again, and seen her sitting crying, on the stairs' top; and then I've shut myself in, quick, for fear of being moved to interfere. I did pity her then, I'm sure; still, I don't wish to lose my place, you know!' " This is the attitude which supports chaos and anarchy, and keeps civilization from coming to fruition.

What saves Cathy is, in part, chance—Heathcliff's desire for revenge simply wears itself out—plus her openness and receptiveness toward Hareton, and Hareton's persistence. Emily Brontë plainly indicates that the forces of repression and hatred are always present and usually strong. If there is to be hope, it is tentative and often at the mercy of more powerful forces. Heathcliff dies; Hareton and Cathy can develop in peace. If he had not died when he did? Probably chaos would have prevailed.

George Eliot, in *Middlemarch,* points out that most people are born in "moral stupidity," taking the world as a giant "udder" from which to feed. Most of us, according to Eliot, stay fixed in this stupidity. Growing up, we remain egocentric children, thinking the world revolves around us and that there is some special providence looking out for our own interests. We usually are not even aware of the interests of other people. In general, the characters in *Wuthering Heights* are childish in this way, fixed in set positions that never change. Hindley and Frances, in their billing and cooing, treat each other as children. Neither is ready to accept adult responsibilities. Lockwood shrinks into a shell, like a snail, when he is confronted by the challenge of love. Edgar sulks and frets when he is faced by a problem that he does not know how to solve. Cathy Earnshaw thinks she can bask in the adoration of both Heathcliff and Edgar, and does not realize the effect she has on them. And when he does not get his way, Heathcliff determines, like a child who has not received an expected treat, that no one else will be happy either. He actually attempts to pervert education in order to transform Hareton from a man into a brute.

The final relationship described in *Wuthering Heights* offers a way out of this barrenness and hope for the future. The "heaven" of Hareton and Cathy, unlike that of Heathcliff and the first Catherine, remains undisturbed and they can progress from childhood to adulthood. They enter into a proper teacher-pupil relationship, which is different from any other we have seen in the novel, since it implies mutuality, respect and forbearance, development and change. Unlike the master, the teacher wants his pupil to grow until he becomes his equal. It is a truism that the teacher is taught by the pupil. The words that Emily Brontë has Nelly use at this point underlie the significance of what has taken place between Hareton and Cathy. They have signed a "treaty." The former "enemies were, thenceforth, sworn allies." The promise is that civilization, this

time based on proper actions, not on the old mouthings of the Lintons and Earnshaws, will be reaffirmed: "Earnshaw was not to be civilized with a wish [Nelly tells Lockwood]; and my young lady was no philosopher, and no paragon of patience; but both their minds tending to the same point—one loving and desiring to esteem, and the other loving and desiring to be esteemed—they contrived in the end to reach it."

This statement is not "pre-moral," dreamlike, or sentimental. The teacher-pupil metaphor is not merely "liberal" wish-fulfillment. As my analysis of *Wuthering Heights* has tried to show, Emily Brontë is totally clear-sighted about the failures of society and she is fully aware of the limitations and inadequacies of most people. Anticipating George Eliot in *Middlemarch,* she describes her characters as not completely evolved into human beings: Lockwood is a "snail," Edgar a "leveret," and Heathcliff at various times is a "cur," or "wolf," or "tiger." Like Eliot in her description of the growth of Dorothea Brooke, however, like the other major Victorian novelists, she has a sense of what society can be. About half way through the novel, Isabella Linton indirectly indicates the futility of the old way of doing things—the strict adherence to the *lex talionis:*

> "But what misery laid on Heathcliff could content me [she asks Nelly], unless I have a hand in it? I'd rather he suffered *less,* if I might cause his sufferings and he might *know* that I was the cause. . . . On only one condition can I hope to forgive him. It is, if I may take an eye for an eye, a tooth for a tooth, for every wrench of agony, return a wrench, reduce him to my level. . . . But it is utterly impossible I can ever be revenged, and therefore I cannot forgive him."

Isabella's is the system followed blindly by most of the characters in the book, including Heathcliff. It is endless—when will the desire for revenge ever stop?—and finally, as the description of Heathcliff's death shows, self-defeating. At the end of *Wuthering Heights,* Emily Brontë points to the only escape from this impasse: she describes that slow, gradual transformation of the individual which alone makes education possible and puts a better society within our reach. (pp. 284-95)

> *Arnold Shapiro, " 'Wuthering Heights' as a Victorian Novel," in* Studies in the Novel, *Vol. I, No. 3, Fall, 1969, pp. 284-96.*

Arnold Krupat   (essay date 1970)

[*Krupat is an American critic and educator. In the following essay, he contends that the strangeness of* Wuthering Heights, *commented on by critics and readers alike, is due primarily to the disparity between the novel's ordinary narrative voices and its extraordinary events.*]

Our experience of *Wuthering Heights* is now more than a hundred and twenty years old, but there still seems to be only one aspect of that experience about which there is general agreement. From "Currer Bell" to the present, readers of the book have found it strange, different somehow from other books.

Wuthering Heights must indeed seem a "rude and strange production" to those unfamiliar with the West-Riding of Yorkshire, Charlotte Brontë admitted in her 1850 Editor's Preface; yet, even to her, a native of that place, the book is "terrible and goblin-like" as well as "beautiful." The *Examiner* for 8 January 1848 began its review with the comment "This is a strange book," while other contemporary reviewers spoke of "wildness," "violence" (the *Britannia* for 15 January 1848), and "power thrown away" (the *North American Review* for October 1848). In our century, Lord David Cecil (1935) starts from the fact that *Wuthering Heights* is quite unlike other Victorian novels, and compares Emily Brontë to Blake in order to assert that some of the strangeness in her book disappears if we consider that she—like Blake—was a "mystic." Dorothy Van Ghent, indeed, finds *Wuthering Heights* unlike fiction generally, noting (1953) that the content of the book, grotesque and passionate, is more usual as the content of ballads than novels. Some similar perception of what goes on in *Wuthering Heights* is no doubt also behind F. R. Leavis's famous last word in 1954 that the book is merely a "sport." Of course, such sports, unlike many novels perhaps, may be honorable members of a prose tradition of their own. If, to approve of strangeness in fiction, we require a category for it, Richard Chase, with his interesting distinctions between "novel" and "romance," gives us just such a category (1957).

I take the nearly universal feeling that the book is strange as a central fact about it. I am not here concerned with what this strangeness may *mean;* I do not wish to interpret and translate it into statements that might constitute "Emily Brontë's philosophy." Nor am I concerned with taking sides in regard to the material of the novel as either in favor of or opposed to the odd, the violent, the demonic in fiction. Content by itself is generally neutral: murder and mutilation may amuse us, as in *Candide,* rather than horrify us. What I want to explore is how the book works to make us think it so strange. And so it is to technique— the handling of the materials—that I think we must turn for a clue to the book's effect. I want to make one suggestion as to what it might be that Miss Brontë has done to create a novel with which—even after a hundred and twenty years—we do not yet feel comfortable.

Closely attended to, all experience in fiction is strange. The worlds of *Moll Flanders, Jonathan Wild,* or *Humphrey Clinker,* taken seriously, are quite as frightening and full of anxiety as perhaps even the world of Kafka. Even so seemingly tractable a novelist as Jane Austen presents us—as the labors of recent critics have amply demonstrated—with a world full of deep-seated and unsettling ironies, fraught with dangers no less real for their domestic nature. But the world of *Wuthering Heights* is marked for its strangeness instantly and even by readers who do not attend closely nor go to the critics for help. In this respect it seems to invite comparison with the visions of writers like Hawthorne, Melville, and Faulkner, with Nathanael West and Djuna Barnes, more than with those of Defoe or Jane Austen. Fiction's more obviously strange

visions have generally been presented in a style that may seem equally strange; and critical works like Richard Poirier's *A World Elsewhere* brilliantly study the search— successful or impossible—for a style adequate to the expression of unusual and highly personal visions.

In order fully to develop the materials of *Moby Dick,* for example, Melville invented a very special style, a strikingly distinctive narrative manner. Our awareness of Ishmael's words, of the peculiar tones of his voice, looms as large, in any recollection of the novel, as the events which the voice describes. It is as if only *that* speaker could have told *that* tale; we feel throughout the novel a close compatibility of matter and manner. The same is true in the case of Faulkner, for we walk through his world only with the help of an extraordinary rhetoric, the voice full of sonority and ceremoniousness, repetitive and insistent, that is Faulkner's mature style. But, again, not only immediately strange or "gothic" worlds have made demands that they be presented in extraordinary styles. Henry James's tortuous and involuted later style is no more than the necessary vehicle for the almost maddeningly inclusive inner eye of James's later vision. And Henry Green seems to achieve his effects almost entirely in the realm of syntax and punctuation, where inversions and dislocations are not highly conventional or the sign of speech consciously invoking a tradition, but of—something else. Commas, in Green, don't do the kind of linking and separating we expect; pronouns, with great consistency, do not refer to the usual antecedents, and are replaced by nouns exactly where we have no need for that sort of help. Whatever Green may intend by all of this, we cannot miss that he does intend it; one cannot read his books—any more than one can read those of James, Melville, or Faulkner—without becoming aware of the style. In all these books, writing is, as Poirier remarks in another context, "a kind of drama of the search for clarity."

There is no such drama in *Wuthering Heights,* and Emily Brontë's peculiar achievement is precisely not to have invented a style adequate to her materials. This obviously is not an adverse judgment; on the contrary, I see her book as an extraordinarily intelligent and nearly perfect fiction with a completely absent author (ten years before *Madame Bovary*) whose existence is implied only by the literary gestures (the juxtapositions and arrangements) that call attention to it. We have really no reliable word from anyone in the book as to how to take it, and, in fact, we do not quite know how to take it; we feel it all as very strange. And this strangeness we feel is the consequence of a technical decision, the result of the consistency with which matter and narrative manner have not been joined. Where so many writers have struggled to achieve the proper style for their vision, Miss Brontë, in *Wuthering Heights,* seems to have struggled to avoid it. She has produced an uncomfortable book precisely because it is a book which suggests that no telling can properly convey this tale.

Miss Brontë first refuses the temptation to create a single narrative voice comprehensive enough for the material. There is no omniscient narrator as in *Madame Bovary,* nor is there a single character like Melville's Ishmael or Conrad's Marlow who can at least pretend to be competent to narrate. Instead, we have Lockwood, whose particular value as a narrator seems to be that he is the man least likely to be capable of telling us the story as it ought to be told. All the words not in quotation marks are Lockwood's; even those attributed to Nelly Dean come, finally, from him. But because he claims to pass Nelly's words along mostly as she herself spoke them, and on occasion "only a little condensed," we would do well to take Nelly into account as a narrator of the story.

Of Lockwood and Nelly as characters and narrators, much has been written. Nelly is a "specimen of true benevolence and homely fidelity," said Charlotte Brontë in 1850. And in 1956, John K. Mathison agrees, but with a warning: "Nelly is an admirable woman," he writes [in *Nineteenth-Century Fiction,* 11], "whose point of view . . . the reader must reject." Clifford Collins believes, however, that it is Lockwood who should be rejected. "Lockwood," says Collins [in *The Critic,* 1947], ". . . exhibits the reactions that may be expected from the ordinary reader (thereby invalidating them, for his commentary is carefully shown to be neither intelligent nor sensitive). . . . " Critics have tended to take sides between them, approving or disapproving of Nelly and Lockwood. Mathison, for instance, ultimately finds Nelly the villain of the piece, while Mary Visick, on the contrary, thinks she is "a sane narrator" [*The Genesis of "Wuthering Heights,"* 1958].

But I think we cannot quite accept any of this literally. There simply is no rejecting Nelly or Lockwood, because both are importantly present. They are the chief narrators of the book and we get at what happens in the novel only through them; there is no existence for the events of *Wuthering Heights* independent of their existence in the diction of Nelly, Lockwood, and those whom they directly and accurately (such is the convention) quote. Any "rejection" of one or another of these characters' points of view can only be an acceptance with qualifications. We cannot reject the point of view of either Nelly or Lockwood—for it is *there*—except in the sense that we judge it inadequate and inadequately expressed. We can, that is, note the considerable disparity between what is being said and the way it is being said.

In fact, rather than being opposite to one another, Nelly and Lockwood are very much alike and speak in remarkably similar fashion. To translate Lockwood into a type called City Man and Nelly into another marked Country Servant and to see them, then, as representatives of opposing principles and life styles is to ignore the evidence of their speech. Any observation we may make about Lockwood's diction is almost certain to be equally true of Nelly's. The differences in their backgrounds and education seem, therefore, quite irrelevant, for these differences have led only to sameness. In Nelly and Lockwood, country and town share a single bland speech.

The most prominent characteristic of this shared speech is its fixity. Heathcliff, Hindley, Hareton, both Catherines, and the Lintons are engaged in constant change; for them, everything—property, feeling, life itself—is always at stake; and now in greater, now in lesser degree, their

speech testifies to that fact. But for the narrators, nothing is at stake. Listening closely to Nelly and Lockwood, one would think that their vocabularies were completely determined for good some time long ago, so that no further options—experiential and linguistic—can ever exist. Yet their positions in the story do not make this necessarily so; indeed, their positions are such as to call constantly for the ability to be open to experience, open to language.

As close to everyone and everything as Nelly Dean has always been, surely on many occasions much could have been at stake for her. And yet, those events which make so great a difference in the lives of the inhabitants of Heights and Grange turn out of no great matter to Mrs. Dean. She is in no way changed by them.

As for Lockwood, his awareness of the second Catherine, a distinct temptation to involve himself in the life of the novel and to make his stay on the moors of genuine worth to him, is neutralized by his language. His words inform us that his notice of her is no more than a sentimental gesture on his part. There is nothing to indicate that she is really important to him; indeed, she finally has existence for him only as a kind of glass in which he hopes to see reflected his own high estimate of himself.

Nelly is the one who knows and first speaks of most of what happened, and the details of her story—in Lockwood's words or her own—constitute the "facts" of the novel. But these "facts," which are of various kinds and seem therefore likely to elicit various emotions from the one who recounts them, are announced always in the same tone, with no real variation at all. The emotional range displayed in Nelly's speech is extremely limited; for to display varying emotions is to change from one occasion to the next, and Nelly does not change. It is as if the world were exceedingly dangerous, so that change could only be to something unspeakable—quite literally unspeakable. And so her diction is a careful defensive construct against the unspeakable, as if to deny it words were to deny it being. To tell her story truthfully, Nelly must name the many violent upheavals in her world; but to tell her story safely, she must name them as conventionally as she can, with determined and persistent equanimity.

Nor does Lockwood, her immediate audience, feel himself in any way cheated by such a narration. On the contrary, he is an admirer of Nelly's style; mostly, I think, because it is so like his own. Lockwood's speech is also marked by fixity and a narrowness of emotional range. His, too, is a diction of enforced limitedness—and, therefore, also inappropriate for the narration of *Wuthering Heights.*

Lockwood, a gentleman sensitive to appearances, is intelligent and well-educated. His speech, perhaps more obviously even than Nelly's, is self-conscious and self-protective. Yet Lockwood's diction, for all its guardedness and premeditation, still pretends to a fitness for any occasion. Lockwood the gentleman is never actually speechless or tongue-tied, never embarrassed or surprised into complete incoherence (although his nocturnal encounter with the ghost of the first Catherine almost—but not quite—does the trick). However inappropriate his comment,

Lockwood is rarely without one; nor are his words ever without at least the possibility of irony.

There are those who find the novel structured toward "educating" Lockwood in the value of more basic or primary passions than any he has formerly known. But for this to be true—if, that is, the novel succeeds in this purpose—we should be able to find evidence of Lockwood's having learned something in his diction. We should be able to find some notable difference between the speech of Lockwood newly arrived at the Heights and Lockwood ready to depart forever. In fact, there is no such difference.

For example, early in the book, noticing the second Catherine and Hareton, Lockwood remarks:

> Here is the consequence of being buried alive: she has thrown herself away upon that boor, from sheer ignorance that better individuals existed! A sad pity—I must beware how I cause her to regret her choice.

The jocular snobbishness of these words is repeated later on in the book when the same subject prompts him to similar patronizing comment. Of Catherine he says:

> She obeyed his [Heathcliff's] directions very punctually; perhaps she had no temptation to transgress. Living among clowns and misanthropists, she probably cannot appreciate a better class of people, when she meets them.

That such talk may be indicative more of insecurity and frustration than of mere arrogance is not to the point. What is to the point is that Lockwood's experience of the world of the moors has not at all changed him. His account of his last intercourse with the characters of the novel (". . . pressing a remembrance into the hand of Mrs. Dean, and disregarding her expostulations at my rudeness, I vanished through the kitchen . . . and so should have confirmed Joseph in his opinion of his fellow-servant's gay indiscretions, had he not, fortunately, recognized me for a respectable character by the sweet ring of a sovereign at his feet") betrays him as quite as high-handed—no matter how upset he may be—as he was at the start. Lockwood appears to have learned nothing.

Not only has his behavior not improved, but so little has he been educated or changed by his experience of Heights and Grange that his imaginative capacities have not really been enlarged either. Early in the book, he remarks on Mrs. Dean's tale:

> I am too weak to read, yet I feel as if I could enjoy something interesting. Why not have up Mrs. Dean to finish her tale? I can recollect its chief incidents, as far as she had gone. Yes, I remember her hero had run off, and never been heard of for three years; and the heroine was married. I'll ring; she'll be delighted to find me capable of talking cheerfully.

Heathcliff is only the "hero" to him, and Catherine the "heroine"; all is quite ordinary—"interesting," merely. He can "recollect" the "chief incidents" of the "tale," though, so trivial is it, perhaps not its details. He invites Mrs. Dean to tell him some more as an occasion for him to talk "cheerfully."

Later, his final visit to the Heights and the Grange comes about as no more than an accident, the indulgence of a whim. His visit will, he says, "save [him] the trouble of invading the neighborhood again" to settle money matters with his landlord. His habitual, high-handed, self-regarding tone has held firm. Lockwood hears of Heathcliff's death, but his imagination is still not stirred; he is moved more by what is before his eyes, the ample evidence that Catherine has never valued him according to his own estimation, nor thought more of him than he has of her. His last words in the book, spoken at "the three headstones on the slope next the moor," find him "wonder[ing] how any one could ever imagine unquiet slumbers for the sleepers in that quiet earth." Whatever else these words may mean or intend, they state literally that Lockwood questions the imaginative powers of others. Nelly has just spoken to him of a little boy who claims to have seen the ghosts of "Heathcliff and a woman." But Lockwood, again as always, is superior to the natives of the place; he wonders how they can imagine what they do and entertain such foolish notions.

It is just because of Lockwood's habitual arrogance and superiority, in fact, that we may find it all the more curious that he does not especially value himself above Nelly Dean (though he still can, at the book's end, behave rudely to her). Commenting specifically on her diction, Lockwood says: "Excepting a few provincialisms of slight consequence, you have no marks of the manners that I am habituated to consider as peculiar to your class." Patronizing as this is, it is nonetheless intended as clear praise for her manner of narration—and Lockwood is extremely stinting of praise. The reason Nelly's narrative style pleases him so well, of course, is that it is so like his own; the "few provincialisms" are indeed of "slight consequence." Nor do they pose any threat. It should come as no surprise that Lockwood chooses to continue the story "in Nelly's own words, only a little condensed," for he finds her "a very fair narrator," and doesn't think he "could improve her style." In matters other than narration, Lockwood is usually ready enough to improve upon others' styles.

Nelly's style shows the same defensive conventionality and stubborn fixity as Lockwood's own. Her stake in the events, I have said, might well have been great, but her voice everywhere insists that nothing has mattered and nothing really can matter for Nelly Dean. Whatever may have happened to the Earnshaws and the Lintons, whatever Nelly herself may have done to advance or retard those happenings, is hardly worth getting excited about. The chief impulse behind Nelly's speech is always to calm things down and level things out. But to speak in as ordinary a fashion as possible, to proclaim by tone and diction that all is well enough, to describe even the most extraordinary occurrence as less than fit occasion for upset or worry, is not a decision on Nelly's part reflecting her judgment that a calming influence might be valuable at such and such a time, but a fixed and invariable manner. This is why Lockwood is so willing to attend to her narration, so little tempted to alter it, for he wishes only amusement and good cheer from the distinctly unamusing tale of recent life at the Heights—and nothing could be more to Nelly's taste than telling her tale amusingly.

"My history is *dree* as we say," Nelly announces in a tone quite bouncy and *dree* not at all, "and will serve to wile away another morning." This of the story of ***Wuthering Heights***! She and Lockwood are clearly made for each other. "Dree, and dreary!" intones Lockwood, ". . . and not exactly of the kind that I should have chosen to amuse me. But never mind! I'll extract wholesome medicines from Mrs. Dean's bitter herbs. . . ." To turn "bitter herbs" into "wholesome medicines" is just what Nelly Dean's style is constructed to do. Almost everywhere her tone is self-righteous and unperturbed, and her diction attuned to the single purpose of maintaining a façade of ordinariness, of conventionality, of quiet.

It is in the nature of things that there should sometimes be good reason for her doing so. When she admits, for example, to having " . . . tried to smooth away all disquietude on the subject," and the subject is Heathcliff's desire to see the mortally ill Catherine Linton, we must admit that such smoothing was surely sensible. So, too, may it have been most sensible near the end of the book where Nelly states her reason for not mentioning that Heathcliff's death may have been a suicide. She explains: "I concealed the fact of his having swallowed nothing for four days, fearing it might lead to trouble. . . ."

But there are other times when Nelly's efforts to "smooth away" are hardly so sensible, constituting, instead determined attacks on linguistic and imaginative possibilities, serving Nelly's self-protection rather more than anything else. Readers have been much moved by Catherine Earnshaw's description of her love for Edgar Linton as like "the foliage in the woods" and for Heathcliff as like "the eternal rocks beneath," but such passionate and suggestive speech is not for Nelly, who annihilates it with: "If I can make any sense of your nonsense, Miss . . . it only goes to convince me that you are ignorant of the duties you undertake in marrying; or else that you are a wicked, unprincipled girl. But trouble me with no more secrets. . . ." Nelly will not pursue such talk, will not, finally, even allow it to others, for the possibilities it hints at are more than she cares to deal with. Her response, rapid, habitual, is the definitive undercutting of self-righteousness. Such self-righteousness, arrogant in its assumptions of superiority, is of course the perfect counterpart in Nelly to Lockwood's pretensions of gentlemanly superiority to the country boors. Indeed, superiority to the events and persons around them is a marked trait in both Nelly and Lockwood, and insofar as this superiority seems fixed and unshakable it serves constantly to distance them from the material and render them unfit to speak properly of it.

There is discernible in the novel—many critics, in fact, have discerned it—a development (perhaps several developments) from one point to another. One may chiefly notice the passing of one generation and the succession of another; or, it may be the process of destruction and the promise of reconstruction that catches the attention. At any rate, something *important* seems to have taken place in ***Wuthering Heights.*** And yet we cannot find a justification for any such judgment in the speech of those who have chiefly told us what has happened. Nelly and Lockwood, as I have tried to show, have styles best suited to

the narration of the trivial, not the important. Miss Brontë has steadfastly refused us narrators with a style consistent with the material. If the vision is very special—odd, strange, whatever—most of the words are not. It is in this maintained and consistent disparity between matter and manner, I think, that our feeling of the book's strangeness may reside.

That Miss Brontë might have given us narrators with a more interesting or important style, that she could perfectly well have imagined speech more appropriate than any Nelly and Lockwood can produce is clear from the speech of almost all of the other characters, but foremost from the speech assigned to Heathcliff. Heathcliff's diction is precisely not fixed and unshakable, nor is it fully formed from the start. His style has a certain development throughout the novel.

Heathcliff's first words as a child are described as "gibberish that nobody could understand," and his last words are a curse of sorts. In between are many modulations. Almost always rough and violent, Heathcliff can nevertheless speak politely, even wittily; near the end of his life the roughness and violence begin to alternate with tones of weariness. Heathcliff's voice also has an element of unpredictability largely lacking in Nelly's and Lockwood's; we can guess the words that will accompany his responses to events rather less well than we can guess theirs.

Among the other characters, we may note briefly that Catherine Earnshaw's diction is not fixed either; yet she dies halfway through the book, before we can hear her speak to as many occasions as we would like. Hareton's diction also has a development, but in his case, similarly, we stop hearing the voice—for the book ends—just as its development seems likely to become interesting. These characters, too, tend more to occasional speechlessness than do either Nelly or Lockwood, as if to testify to the possibility that some responses to some experiences may be incapable of verbalization, that the world may not always be manageable—at least not in words. From them we hear speech often as strange as the experience it seeks to deal with.

The point, of course, is that Emily Brontë chose to give us little of Heathcliff's sort of speech and much of Nelly's and Lockwood's. One reason for this, as I have said, is that to develop at length a highly distinctive diction consistent with highly distinctive materials is always to some extent to tame those materials. Simply to maintain such a special style (like Melville's or Faulkner's, for example) at length is to assert that strangeness can be contained, shaped, and ordered—or at least survived. But this is not what Emily Brontë wished to do, nor has it been the effect of her method. The effect of what she has done has been to leave the world wild, for it is just the wildness of the world, its untamable strangeness, that all of us have felt in ***Wuthering Heights.*** To have conveyed a vast, shapeless sense of things in a thing beautifully limited and shaped is the peculiar effect of Emily Brontë's technique. And the chief strategy of her technique is the persistent split between the materials of the book and the style in which they are presented. (pp. 269-80)

Arnold Krupat, "The Strangeness of 'Wuthering Heights'," in Nineteenth-Century Fiction, *Vol. 25, No. 3, December, 1970, pp. 269-80.*

An excerpt from *Wuthering Heights*

"I pray one prayer—I repeat it till my tongue stiffens—Catherine Earnshaw, may you not rest as long as I am living! You said I killed you—haunt me, then! The murdered *do* haunt their murderers. I believe—I know that ghosts *have* wandered on earth. Be with me always—take any form—drive me mad! only *do* not leave me in this abyss, where I cannot find you! Oh God! it is unutterable! I *cannot* live without my life! I *cannot* live without my soul!"

Charles I. Patterson, Jr.   (essay date 1972)

[*In the following essay, Patterson maintains that it is the distinctly Romantic element in* Wuthering Heights—*particularly the urge to experience life on extraordinary levels—that accounts for the novel's enduring power and appeal.*]

In his monumental *History of the English Novel*, E. A. Baker makes two germinal pronouncements concerning Emily Brontë's stark and powerful novel ***Wuthering Heights.*** He proclaims that it is the first novel in English with a cosmic background, a penetrating insight obviously foreshadowed by Lord David Cecil's brilliant discussion of the ways in which the characters in their responses and actions are very largely motivated and governed by inexorable laws that are in fact the laws governing the universe [*Early Victorian Novelists*, 1935]. Also, concerning the delayed entry of the full force of Romanticism into the English novel, Baker maintains that "the deeper romanticism, the romanticism of Wordsworth and his fellows, did not enter fully into English fiction until the time of the Brontë sisters, with their deep-rooted sense of a material world transfused with spirit." But with the advent of the Brontës "imagination and instinct claimed their share" in the genre at last. Then, contends Baker, "fiction regains a place beside or only a little below poetry, dares to speak for the soul, to sound the deeps of personality, to face the enigmas of evil and death." These statements, just as do those of Lord David Cecil concerning the cosmic element in the story, point toward profound depths in this novel that can fruitfully be examined further.

The more obvious Romantic elements of ***Wuthering Heights*** are easy to recognize: the Gothic traits in the character of the hero, the Gothic aura of the house and the lonely isolated location exposed to storm winds from the moors; the suspense that stems from mystery, terror, and the supernatural; the representation of nature as an ever-present source of both the aesthetic and the spiritual; and the idea that external nature is both an influence upon the inner mind of man and an outward image of it. More deeply interfused throughout the novel as a shaping force upon the characters, upon the action, and upon the tone and atmosphere of the whole is the relentless Romantic

drive for experience more richly fulfilling than ordinary life affords. This drive manifests itself in Heathcliff and Cathy Earnshaw in two modes that continually appeared at the deepest levels of the poetry of the preceding age, especially the poetry of Coleridge, Byron, Keats, and Shelley. The first mode is the daemonic urge to pierce beyond all human limitations in the search for the heart's desire, an urge that unfortunately has been confused with the Satanic; the second is a great capacity for empathy, for what John Keats termed "Negative Capability," the capacity to become so fully united with another being or object as to feel that the self and the beloved object are one and the same. This latter capability is augmented by the emotional force of the former, and both interact upon each other throughout the story. Both have been discussed in previous criticism, but both have been considerably garbled and blurred. It is the purpose of this essay to attempt to clarify the nature and function of these two great principles of empathy and the daemonic in ***Wuthering Heights*** and to suggest that these are the elements that contribute most to its tremendous power and appeal.

Dorothy Van Ghent discusses both of these elements at some length, mentions the "daemonic character" of Heathcliff, and labels him a "demon-lover." However, she then maintains that it is difficult to define precisely the quality of the daemonic in the conception of Heathcliff. She does so in terms that at times point unmistakably toward the particular concept of the daemonic involved and reveal how it has become confused with the Satanic, which is significantly different:

> There is still the difficulty of defining, with any precision, the quality of the daemonic that is realized most vividly in the conception of Heathcliff, a difficulty that is mainly due to our tendency always to give the "daemonic" some ethical status—that is, to relate it to an ethical hierarchy. Heathcliff's is an archetypal figure, untraceably ancient in mythological thought—an imagined recognition of that part of nature that is "other" than the human soul (the world of the elements and the animals) and of that part of the soul itself which is "other" than the conscious part. But since Martin Luther's revival of the archetype for modern mythology, it has tended to forget its relationship with the elemental "otherness" of the outer world and to identify itself solely with the dark functions of the soul. As an image of soul work, it is ethically relevant, since everything that the soul does—even unconsciously, even ignorantly (as in the case of Oedipus)—offers itself for ethical judgment, whereas the elements and animals do not. Puritanism perpetuated the figure for the imagination; Milton gave it its greatest splendor, in the fallen angel through whom the divine beauty still shone. [*The English Novel: Form and Function*, 1953]

Although more is involved in this archetype than the world of the elements and animals, and although it is not as untraceable in mythology as she claims, Van Ghent clearly perceives that Heathcliff is strikingly different from those individuations of the archetype that are customarily related to ethical thought:

The exception is Heathcliff. Heathcliff is no more ethically relevant than is flood or earthquake or whirlwind. It is as impossible to speak of him in terms of "sin" and "guilt" as it is to speak in this way of the natural elements or the creatures of the animal world. In him, the archetype reverts to a more ancient mythology and to an earlier symbolism. *Wuthering Heights* so baffles and confounds the ethical sense because it is not informed with that sense at all. . . . But Heathcliff does have human shape and human relationships; he is, so to speak, caught in the human; two kinds of reality intersect in him—as they do, . . . indeed, in the other characters. Each entertains, in some degree, the powers of darkness. . . . Even in the weakest of these souls there is an intimation of the dark Otherness, by which the soul is related psychologically to the inhuman world of pure energy, for it carries within itself an "otherness" of its own, that inhabits below consciousness.

Penetrating and fruitful as these insights are, they do not offer sufficient definition and clarification of the concept of the daemonic involved, and the resort to "animism" is too vague to be helpful in particularizing it. Consequently, Van Ghent envisions the central conflicts in the novel too much as "a tension between . . . the raw, inhuman reality of anonymous natural energies, and the restrictive reality of civilized habits, manners, and codes." She is quite accurate in the latter but not so in the former. She sees the lovers as entirely too brutish and suggests that they are like animals who rend each other when they kiss. On the basis of this erroneous attribution, she then draws a conclusion quite far afield, I think: "But since no conceivable *human* male and female, not brutish, not anthropologically rudimentary, could be together in this way as adults, all that we can really imagine for the grown-up Cathy and Heathcliff, as 'characters' on the human plane, is what the book gives them—their mutual destruction by tooth and nail in an effort, through death, to get back to the lost state of gypsy freedom in childhood."

This view completely overlooks the grandeur of their mutual love and the remarkable empathy between them, which makes them nobly selfless for the most part in spite of their possessive moments and utterances. Van Ghent shows that she does not fully understand the nature of empathy when she declares their love inevitably sexless because a person cannot mate with himself and because in empathy he feels that the other person *is* himself. She thus concludes that their relationship is not an adult one. But empathy does not involve complete delusion. During empathic union one does not simply confuse his identity with another person's but feels a pronounced lessening of awareness of his separate identity and a simultaneous filling up of his selfhood by the other person's selfhood *in idea,* all the while remaining to some degree conscious of his own being. Empathy therefore enhances sexual consummation and spiritualizes it. Heathcliff and Cathy are not sexless; they are adult human lovers with high sexuality. They yearn for something far more compelling than the lost state of gypsy freedom in childhood, and they yearn forward, not backward.

Similarly, Professor John Hagan [in *Nineteenth-Century Fiction,* XXI, 1967] perceives that Heathcliff and Cathy have daemonic characteristics, but he does not differentiate between the Christian and pre-Christian conceptions of the daemonic. Hence he makes what I believe to be serious misjudgments concerning the novel and is led to assert that critics are attempting "to discover in the novel more metaphysical concreteness than it can yield." In actuality it will reveal considerable metaphysical concreteness if the particular metaphysics involved is defined and clarified. Not having this very necessary equipment in hand, Professor Hagan slips into the mistake of applying conventional moralistic standards to Heathcliff's and Cathy's actions, with critical results that are not acceptable. For example, he states, "If Edgar is not Heathcliff's equal for passion, neither is he so merely contemptible. Heathcliff's speech is a piece of special pleading and deplorable vainglory," especially outrageous because Heathcliff has just performed his horrible act of revenge, marrying Isabella. And yet Professor Hagan concludes as follows: "The dominant image of Heathcliff that emerges, then, is neither that of a 'moral force' nor a 'demon,' but that of a tragic sufferer. And this is finally our image of Catherine, too. We do not condone their outrages, but neither do we merely condemn them. We do something larger and more important: we recognize in them the tragedy of passionate natures whom intolerable frustration and loss have stripped of their humanity."

Hagan thus pares down the stature of Heathcliff and Cathy at the same time that he designates them tragic sufferers. He has ignored all the author's efforts to endow their *emotional life* with suprahuman intensity while steadily asserting that *they* are certainly within the human family. It is true that they are not motivated by "moral force" nor by the love of evil as is the case in the Christian "demonic." But surely they are markedly enhanced as tragic protagonists by the force and power of the pre-Christian daemonic, which flows through them and motivates their enormously passionate natures and fierce attachment, human beings though they are. The impetus of their daemonic search for fulfillment, centering intently upon each other alone, drives them into an empathic union as relentless as the union of two planets in orbit around each other. And this empathy then functions like the cosmic principle of inertia, the opposite of motion, resisting change of direction or separation and bringing cataclysmic eruptions when the two are forced apart.

Lord David Cecil points unerringly in this direction when he maintains with uncanny insight that their "deeds and passions do not spring from essentially destructive impulses, but impulses only destructive because they are diverted from pursuing their natural course," that Emily Brontë's outlook is neither moral nor immoral but *premoral.* This is indeed what it is, as Dorothy Van Ghent in effect perceives, and this points the way to clarification of the daemonic element in the book. In essence, the universal principles of empathy and the daemonic can be subsumed under Lord Cecil's majestic conception of a single cosmic principle of dual modes that underpins and pervades the entire novel and all its parts. The daemonic is a particular aspect of one of these dual modes and empathy an aspect of the other—the world of storm and motion as opposed to the world of inertia and stasis. Both, working together, vividly reveal how the universal principles of the cosmos operate just as unerringly within the human psyche as within a solar system.

Among the various notions of daemons in Greek mythology there is a conception, ancient but not entirely untraceable, of daemonic creatures living outside the pale of all human limitations and therefore neither good nor evil but neutral to both. Hence they were thought to dwell in joy and ecstasy without stint. And since they were not subject to human restrictions of any kind, all their emotions—even their griefs—could be considered to be stronger and more engulfing than those within the human breast. They could experience attachments and aversions with fierce intensity and total preoccupation; they could not experience what is given in human morality—obligation, duty, restraint, moderation. However, they were thought to have an important connection with human beings, for they supposedly had assisted Saturn in the creation, later ruled over men for a time and brought them great happiness, and subsequently served as messengers between gods and men. Sometimes they carried a human being away into eternal bliss and joy, as did their counterparts in fairy lore and in the medieval romances, for example, in William Butler Yeat's *The Stolen Child* and Thomas Cestre's fifteenth-century romance *Sir Launfal.* Emily Brontë probably gained much of her knowledge of such a daemonic world from fairy lore.

These daemonic creatures and their relationships with human beings are frequently mentioned in the Platonic dialogues, although Plato evidently did not believe in them literally. Knowledge of them was handed down to modern times by many of the neo-Platonists. In the dialogues "Statesman" and "Laws" the following is spoken by two of the lesser disputants:

> Blessed and spontaneous life does not belong to the present cycle of the world, but to the previous one, in which God superintended the whole revolution of the universe; and the several parts of the universe were distributed under the rule of certain inferior deities . . . and each one was in all respects sufficient for those of whom he was the shepherd . . . and I might tell of ten thousand other blessings, which belong to that dispensation.

> There is a tradition of the happy life of mankind in days when all things were spontaneous and abundant. And of this the reason is said to have been as follows: . . . God, in his love of mankind, placed over us the demons, who are a superior race, and they with great ease and pleasure to themselves, and no less to us, taking care of us . . . made the tribes of men happy and united.

In sum, such a conception is useful today only as an objective correlative to an inner proclivity within man—the relentless proclivity to seek joy, beauty, and knowledge beyond what is afforded by the ordinary human lot even at its best. This insistent drive is readily apparent in some men, though not in all, but it may be latent in all human

beings. Goethe elevates the conception into a universal principle in passages of his autobiography, *Dichtung und Wahrheit,* Part IV (first published in 1833), which sound at times as if he is speaking directly of the central characters in **Wuthering Heights** fourteen years before the novel was created. Emily Brontë could have seen the passages or heard them discussed. Goethe does more than anyone else to clarify the concept of the daemonic reflected in the novel, to distinguish it from the evil and the Satanic and to suggest the evidences of it in human conduct and human minds (Goethe is using the third person to speak of himself as a youth):

> He believed he could detect in nature—both animate and inanimate, spiritual and non-spiritual—something which reveals itself only in contradictions, and which, therefore, could not be encompassed under any concept, still less under a word. It was not divine, for it seemed without reason; not human, for it had no understanding; not diabolical, for it was beneficent; not angelic, for it took pleasure in mischief. It resembled chance, in that it manifested no consequence; it was like Providence, for it pointed toward connection. All that restricts us seemed for it penetrable; it seemed to deal arbitrarily with the necessary elements of our existence; it contracted time and expanded space. It seemed to find pleasure only in the impossible and to reject the possible with contempt.

> To this entity, which seemed to intervene between all others, to separate them and yet to link them together, I gave the name daemonic, after the example of the ancients and of those who had perceived something similar. I tried to shield myself from this fearful entity by seeking refuge, in accordance with my usual habit behind an imaginary representation. . . .

> Although this daemonic element can manifest itself in all corporeal and incorporeal things, can even manifest itself most markedly in animals, yet with man especially has it a most wonderful connection that creates a power which while not opposed to the moral order of the world still does so often cross through it that one may be considered the warp and the other the woof. . . .

> However, the daemonic appears most fearful when it becomes predominant in a human being. During my life I have observed several. . . . They are not always the most eminent men either in their intellect or their talents . . . but a tremendous power seems to flow from them; and they exercise a wonderful power over all creatures, and even over the elements; and who can say how far such influence may extend? All the combined forces of convention are helpless against them.

It is discernible at once that this passage particularizes the nature of the underlying daemonic force that imperiously motivates Heathcliff and Cathy and also that the passage suggests many of the specific manifestations of the daemonic that are apparent in their thoughts and actions. Their love for each other revealed itself continually in con-traditions—extremes of tenderness and of cruelty, great selflessness and marked possessiveness, godlike thoughtfulness for each other as well as the fierce desire to hurt and torture, condemnation of each other's actions along with soul-stirring expressions of unextinguishable devotion, tremendous joy in each other and also the most searing pain. As Van Ghent says, two realities did intersect in them, one the warp and the other the woof, according to Goethe. Moreover, they continually flouted reason, pierced through what restricts ordinary people, found pleasure in the impossible while rejecting the possible with contempt, exhibited a tremendous power over others, and indeed managed to render the combined forces of convention quite helpless against them.

For example, Heathcliff admitted neither Cathy's marriage to another nor her death nor the lapse of twenty years as a deterrent to his love, and he flung off the trammels of dire poverty and lack of status as easily as he broke through the restraints of conventional life in a rigidly hierarchical social structure. Cathy, for example, assumed that her husband, Edgar, would welcome Heathcliff into the household when he suddenly returned from his three-year absence, and she was indignant that he was not thus received. A subtle evidence of the daemonic nature of her underlying mental life and basic assumptions is that in her dreams and conceptions of the hereafter she shows no affinity whatever with the Christian Heaven nor with the world of conventional humanity but only with a metaphorical daemonic realm of freedom from restraint that has the characteristics of neither Heaven nor Hell nor earth. This realm is represented physically for her by the wild countryside surrounding Wuthering Heights and is constituted spiritually for her by her engulfing empathic union with Heathcliff, a union so complete that it very nearly blots out every other consideration. When telling Nelly Dean that she had dreamed of being in Heaven, Cathy states:

> Heaven did not seem to be my home; and I broke my heart with weeping to come back to earth; and the angels were so angry that they flung me out into the middle of the heath on top of Wuthering Heights; where I woke sobbing for joy. That will do to explain my secret as well as the other. I've no more business to marry Edgar Linton than I have to be in heaven; and if the wicked man in there had not brought Heathcliff so low, I shouldn't have thought of it. It would degrade me to marry Heathcliff now; so he shall never know how I love him; and that not because he's handsome, Nelly, but because he's more myself than I am. Whatever our souls are made of, his and mine are the same, and Linton's is as different as a moonbeam from lightning or frost from fire.

Even the imagery at the end suggests the daemonic aspects of their love and of their souls—she likens hers and Heathcliff's to lightning and fire and Linton's to pallid moonbeams and frost. Her joyous, unrestrained life on the vast heath in company with this kindred soul made of the same elemental fire as herself indicates for her the characteristics of the only heaven that she can conceive to be desirable—a neutral region, metaphorically speaking, that is

neither heaven nor earth but a place where she can be entirely free of the restrictions and limitations of conventional life. This conception of life after death appears again and again in her thoughts. She shows that she envisions something beyond this life, something to which she is related but which has no characteristics whatever of the Christian Heaven in her expression of it. She says to Nelly, "Surely you and everybody have a notion that there is, or should be, an existence of yours beyond you. What were the use of my creation if I were entirely contained here." Similarly, when her death is near, she longs for release from earthly limitations and entrance into what she calls a "glorious world," but it seems in her conception to be a world of pure energy and uninhibited life, from which her daemonic lover Heathcliff will not be absent:

> The thing that irks me most is this shattered prison, after all. I'm tired, tired of being enclosed here. I'm wearying to escape into that glorious world, and to be always there; not seeing it dimly through tears, and yearning for it through the walls of an aching heart; but really with it, and in it. Nelly, you think you are better and more fortunate than I; in full health and strength. You are sorry for me—very soon that will be altered. I shall be sorry for you. I shall be incomparably beyond and above you all. I *wonder* he won't be near me.

In sum, the metaphysical reality that Cathy expects to join after death more nearly resembles what Goethe had brilliantly described as the universal principle of the daemonic than it does the Christian Heaven, with its tranquillity, peace, and hymns of praise to the Almighty. The consistency and homogeneity of this girl's basic character, on both the conscious and subconscious levels, is remarkably well sustained throughout the book. In the light of the mighty force that motivates her being, her perversity and recalcitrance are understandable and are removed from the sphere of what we are expected to accept, condone, or blame.

Whereas Emily Brontë easily depicted Cathy as still belonging to the human family in spite of her daemonic qualities, the control of reader response to Heathcliff presented a more difficult problem. In order for his gross breaches of convention and for his sustained love beyond death to be sufficiently motivated to seem credible to readers, she repeatedly suggested that he is beyond mortality in the fierceness of his daemonic passions. Yet, in order for him still to retain enough of the reader's sympathy to appear a tragic figure, she found a way to remind readers repeatedly of his human identity at the same time. She accomplished this difficult feat through having Nelly Dean, the principal narrator, indicate in a continual dual pattern that he *seems* supramortal and yet *is* fully human, as evidenced through her own knowledge of him. By this clever manipulation of the technical narrative point of view, Emily Brontë has things both ways at once, throwing over Heathcliff the glamour of the suprahuman and at the same time maintaining reader sympathy for a very human sufferer in tragic circumstances. She keeps us ever mindful of the two kinds of reality that intersect in him. Emphasis on his pre-moral daemonic nature is carried about as far as possible without placing him beyond the pale of humanity. Even the author's sister Charlotte did so in her "Editor's Preface" to her "New Edition" of the book (1850), in which she makes the common mistake of conceiving him as basically a supramortal evil demon with little evidence of humanity. But Emily Brontë, when she created him, had masterfully projected his true lineaments through Nelly Dean.

At the very beginning of her narrative, she relates that Mr. Earnshaw found him as a deserted child on the streets of Liverpool and brought him home to be cared for in his household. Mr. Earnshaw said to the family as he unwrapped the child and set him upon his feet before them, "You must e'n take it as a gift of God, though it's as dark as if it came from the devil." His speech indicates at once that the child is to be considered within the whole human family under God and also that this child bears an aura of the extrahuman from the mystery of his origin, a mystery that is never cleared up and that continues throughout the book to suggest his difference from ordinary humanity. Earnshaw's words, "dark as if it came from the devil," are simply convenient terms for him to use for the purpose and cannot be taken to indicate serious belief in an evil origin of the boy, as the first part of Earnshaw's sentence clearly shows. Shortly afterward the other children, as well as their mother, draw away from this child and refuse to have him in their bedroom, as if he were a stranger to the human race. Nelly, who admitted hating him unjustly at first, put him on the landing of the stair, hoping he might be gone on the morrow. But the little fellow immediately asserted his humanity by creeping to Mr. Earnshaw's door during the night. They later gave him the name Heathcliff, which had been the name of a son who had died in infancy, suggesting his full acceptance in this human family. But since "Heathcliff" served him throughout life as both given name and surname, it was simultaneously a constant reminder of his difference from them. Further, he clung to Nelly in human need when seriously ill in childhood, wanting her always near. And Nelly reported, "Cathy and her brother harassed me terribly; he [Heathcliff] was as uncomplaining as a lamb." Yet he early revealed a fierce, daemonic intentness upon his own purposes regardless of powerful opposition, as shown in his getting possession of Hindley's pony to replace his own lame one. But the very human Mr. Earnshaw took to the fatherless boy inordinately, favoring him above his own children and believing all he said; Nelly reported that the boy "said precious little, and generally the truth," an ideal human trait.

The same dual pattern of human and daemonic qualities is continued throughout Nelly's account of his adult life after his and Cathy's love has locked them into an orbit together from which there could never be egress. When as a grown man, returned and well-to-do, Heathcliff appears for the first time at Thrushcross Grange, he is seen by all as an admirable blend of fine human traits with the traces of his old fire now subdued. Nelly describes him thus:

> He had grown a tall, athletic, well-formed man, beside whom my master seemed quite slender and youth-like. His upright carriage suggested the idea of his having been in the army. His countenance was much older in expression and decision of feature than Mr. Linton's; it looked intelligent, and retained no marks of former degradation. A half-civilized ferocity lurked yet in the depressed brows and eyes full of black fire, but it was subdued; and his manner was even dignified, quite divested of roughness, though too stern for grace.

> My master's surprise equalled or exceeded mine.

Shortly thereafter Cathy tells Edgar and Nelly that Heathcliff is now "worthy of any one's regard, and it would honour the first gentleman of the country to be his friend." On the other hand, after the ensuing days of terrible conflict between the two men and growing danger to Hindley, Nelly designates Heathcliff "an evil beast . . . waiting his time to spring and destroy." Later, when she sees the enormity of his anguish at Cathy's impending death, Nelly says, "I did not feel as if I were in the company of a creature of my own species." And in his terrible grief after Cathy's death, Nelly reports that he dashed his head against a knotty tree trunk and "howled, not like a man, but like a savage beast getting goaded to death with knives and spears. . . . It appalled me." By the beast imagery she does not mean actually to suggest the bestial but rather the extramortal—that is, emotion beyond the extremes of the human. Yet her human sympathies embraced him, for she says, "I was weeping as much for him as for her." To Isabella's terming him a "monster," Nelly cries out, "Hush! Hush! He's a human being. . . . Be more charitable; there are worse men." Finally at the very end just before his death she puts both strains together; two kinds of reality meet in him to the very end:

> "Is he a ghoul, or a vampire," I mused. I had read of such hideous, incarnate demons. And then I set myself to reflect how I had tended him in infancy; and watched him grow to youth; and followed him almost through his whole course; and what absurd nonsense it was to yield to that sense of horror.

> "But where did he come from, the little dark thing, harboured by a good man to his bane?" muttered superstition, as I dozed into unconsciousness. And I began, half dreaming, to weary myself with imaging some fit parentage for him.

Without thus establishing and sustaining both the human and the daemonic qualities of her lovers, Emily Brontë could never have successfully handled in the novel the elements that chiefly provide dramatic depth and power—the strong empathic union of their souls and the cataclysmic consequences of their being wrenched apart—and she could never have made credible and acceptable the stark and bare emotions in their speeches, which render forth the heights and depths of their joy and suffering. Their speeches would have seemed overladen with emotional excess, and the extent to which their consciousnesses had actually merged would not have been made palpable. But their daemonic intensity and the circumstances of their childhood, when each was everything meaningful to the other, make probable the fullness of their empathy. Therefore, we can accept unquestioningly Cathy's simple and beautiful statement of the central truth of her being, that she felt no self-identity apart from the companion of her soul, a matter which clinical psychologists could validate:

> My great miseries in this world have been Heathcliff's miseries, and I watched and felt each from the beginning: My great thought in living is himself. If all else perished, and *he* remained, I should continue to be; and, if all else remained, and he were annihilated, the Universe would turn to a mighty stranger. I should not seem a part of it. My love for Linton is like the foliage in the woods. Time will change it, I'm well aware, as winter changes the trees. My love for Heathcliff resembles the eternal rocks beneath—a source of little delight, but necessary. Nelly, I *am* Heathcliff—he's always, always in my mind—not as a pleasure, any more than I am always a pleasure to myself—but as my own being—so, don't talk of our separation again—it is impracticable.

And Heathcliff, perceiving from her wasted condition that her death is inevitable, voices with piercing directness the central fact of his existence, followed soon after her death by his anguished plea for continuance of their union beyond the grave:

> Oh, Cathy! Oh, my life! how can I bear it?
>
> . . . . .
>
> Be with me always—take any form—drive me mad! only do not leave me in this abyss, where I cannot find you! Oh, God! it is unutterable! I *cannot* live without my life! I *cannot* live without my soul!

What is expressed here occurs repeatedly in real life: the consciousnesses of two persons deeply attached to each other over a long period finally intermesh, so that each constitutes a large part of what fills up the other. When one of them is taken away, the mind of the other actually loses a significant part of its content, and the loss is felt profoundly below the levels of thought in the depths of the psyche. I remember vividly a strong and gracious lady, seventy-one years of age, who, after a lifetime of devotion to her husband, bore his death bravely and said that she would not wish to have him back suffering from disease as he was. But after a few weeks the emptiness and vacuity of her mind, divested of her thoughts of him, impelled her into a state of apathy and dejection that lasted for years. In her novel Emily Brontë has managed to present this psychological truth in the lives of two people who lived only a short span of years, not an easy task for a novelist to attempt.

In the art medium the elements of life must be heightened and emphasized for the rendering to have force and point. One great aspect of Emily Brontë's achievement is that she found a way to motivate the unleashing and expressing of the most powerful human emotions resulting from the loosening of the strongest human ties, somewhat as Shakespeare had done in *King Lear.* And in this novel, as in *King Lear,* the results of the loosening of these ties are likened and related to the workings of tremendous forces in the cosmos. Heathcliff and Cathy came to be remarkably similar to two celestial bodies in orbit round each other, like Sirius and its companion, held in orbit by interaction of the velocity of their motion and the attraction of their mass responding to the law of gravity. Their being wrenched apart, first by her marriage to another and then by her death, released into the human cosmos that energy which had been held in check as it held them together (if we may extend Lord David Cecil's conception). It had to spend its force in collisions and chaotic attractions and repulsions (such as that of Isabella to Heathcliff) before equilibrium and stasis could be restored, as it is indeed finally restored both in Heathcliff's last days before death and in the calm lives of the second generation. The deeper Romanticism had truly entered the English novel: the ways in which the instinctive, the irrational, the transcendental union of the self with the "other," the depths of the subconscious, and the human relationship to the cosmos influence our decisions and actions—all are powerfully set forth in Emily Brontë's picture of life. Her skilled use of empathy and the daemonic, which are like cosmic motion and stasis within the human sphere, are among the chief means that enabled her to emerge with admirable success in this difficult undertaking and to produce in her one novel a presentation, unparalleled in the century, of the elemental power and grandeur of human longing. (pp. 81-96)

> *Charles I. Patterson, Jr., "Empathy and the Daemonic in 'Wuthering Heights'," in* The English Novel in the Nineteenth Century: Essays on the Literary Mediation of Human Values, *edited by George Goodin, University of Illinois Press, 1972, pp. 81-96.*

Michael Black   (essay date 1975)

[*Black is an English critic. In the excerpt below, he examines the characters of* Wuthering Heights *in terms of the personal feelings and the network of relationships which define them.*]

[***Wuthering Heights***] is timeless. It was published in 1847, and scarcely noticed. Already it referred to the past: the events take place between 1770 and 1802. But there is no sense of that period: American Independence, the French Revolution, the Napoleonic Wars have no bearing on this world; they are mere passing external events, not noticed because not relevant. Jane Austen's un-interest in the great world, often commented on, is as nothing to Emily Brontë's. You are perfectly aware with Jane Austen that you are in the Bath, Hampshire, or London that she knew, at the time she knew it. It is a social world where people take colour and tone from their surroundings; and so is Flaubert's Normandy, Dickens's London and Suffolk, Tolstoy's St Petersburg and Moscow. These are actual societies, watched at a particular moment, and the people belong to them. The people of Thrushcross Grange and Wuthering Heights belong in quite a different sense to those minute spots on the map. The Heights are intensely seen and felt as a place; but the house is already a hundred years old when the action unfurls; it represents something ancestral, and the moors represent something primeval and eternal. Equally, the chief characters don't belong to 1770 and Yorkshire so much as to the human race and all time. By the end of the book things have taken place between heroic characters which the surviving inhabitants, smaller people, look back on with dread and doubtful understanding. The obsessions, the violences, the occasional births and the more frequent deaths, have been a prolonged struggle like something in an epic. In thirty years a convulsive energy has worked itself out. The people who die and are looked back on by Nelly Dean and the little boy at the very end, who sees Heathcliff and 'a woman' as ghosts, are so large in their capacity to feel one or two things, and they live out their lives with such commitment to those bare feelings, which are their personal meaning, that those who are left, not fully understanding something which transcends them, turn it into myth, or ballad or folk-tale, which are the tribute of the ordinary limited person to the men and women who go beyond those limits.

It is that tribute of the awestruck narrators (Nelly Dean, Mr Lockwood, the other characters to whom it falls to tell a chapter or two) which turns Heathcliff into a demon king, a goblin, a werewolf, an ogre or any other of the devices by which ordinariness holds off its sense of failure: failure in this case to reach a lonely, suffering and violent man. That incomprehension of Heathcliff is one of the things which the book does allow *us* to grasp and understand. Heathcliff's flashing eyes and sharp grinding teeth, the diabolic poses and gestures, are all in the reporting: they are a convention which turns misunderstanding into a more familiar kind of mystery, a romantic cliché: one that people can thrill to, which fortifies them in their sense of being normal, and enables them to write Heathcliff off as demonic, therefore not to be understood, therefore another kind of being, not akin.

Heathcliff *is* demonic, but in a way which is specifically human, and therefore fundamentally akin to us even if he is larger in scale. Nelly Dean is sometimes wiser than she knows, as well as being quite often less wise than she thinks. There is a moment in the book when Mr Lockwood, whose main function is to be told the story, be amazed by it and confirmed in his smallness, begins to ruminate over what he has been told so far. Of the people of the Heights and the Grange, he says solemnly:

> They do live more in earnest, more in themselves, and less in surface change, and frivolous external things. I could fancy a love for life here almost possible . . .

So much is true, but he makes the mistake of thinking they are for that reason, 'different' as a total group. Mrs Dean knows better than this, and replies 'Oh! here we are the same as anywhere else, when you get to know us'. She is right: the fundamental differences are not between people here and townees like Lockwood who think they have stumbled on interesting local fauna with unusually long-lasting feelings (as if the rustic crudity gave strength). It is the difference between the Heathcliffs and Catherines and people like Nelly Dean herself, who goes on to describe herself quite rightly as 'a steady reasonable kind of body'. One pattern which recurs in the book is the failure of the 'steady reasonable kind of body' to understand those who are otherwise, and the compulsion of the 'unreasonable' to bring each other down. An overall result is to cast doubt on that kind of 'reason' as a guide to the truth. The intensely-feeling are by definition beyond rea-

son. But that does not throw us into the world of the totally incomprehensible; there is no act in *Wuthering Heights* which is gratuitous. Indeed the inevitability, the comprehensibility of it in one sense, may leave us saying we should prefer not to understand, and that our reasonableness is a device for not seeing what we prefer not to face.

Heathcliff can be understood, if we ever understand anybody. So far from being a mysterious semi-mythical psychic force, he is presented with some care as a humanly conceivable evolution. Indeed he reflects a *reality* onto Dickens. It was Dickens's nightmare recurrently to imagine a small child, sensitive and totally alone, orphaned in a hideous world symbolized as a London given over almost entirely to monstrous criminals (think of *Oliver Twist*). The threat is that first you will be degraded socially, then corrupted morally, then destroyed. That nightmare is approached in *David Copperfield,* in the Murdstone and Grinby warehouse episode, followed by David's fearful journey on foot to Dover, penniless, exhausted, menaced by madmen and violent outcasts, and ignored by uncomprehending nice people. At the end of the nightmare is an equivalent heaven; you are taken in by a lovable, eccentric, middle-aged and above all rich person, who adopts you, lavishes affection on you, and leaves you a lot of money, or starts you off in life as a gentleman, and therefore secure. Evidently that is also a fantasy, but it is a powerful one, like the first. It speaks to a deep wish as the first appeals to a deep fear.

Emily Brontë deals in reality. Old Mr Earnshaw, in Liverpool one day, finds the abandoned Heathcliff; small, ugly, dirty, as repulsive as he is pathetic. He takes the child home, not to a Dickensian world of red-cheeked loving retainers and gentle eccentrics, but to an actual family capable of shock and jealousy. The result is inevitable. The adoption looks like a monstrous whim; most of the family are alienated. The old man has to stand by his action: he insists on carrying it through—hence further alienation. He is then *committed* to an affection for the foundling, to justify himself; and the conflict becomes violent. His son Hindley feels his position has been usurped, hates the newcomer and persecutes him. Apart from the old man, only his daughter Catherine and the servant Nelly Dean show any kindness to Heathcliff: Catherine because she discovers an intense affinity, Nelly because she is decent, is not involved in the family conflict, and can afford to show ordinary kindness where others can't because they are affronted or threatened.

Heathcliff is the victim in all this. He has to submit to the old man's puzzled and mostly will-driven affection, and finds himself exerting his will over him in return: his 'spoilt' behaviour as a child is a continual test of the old man's love. He is grateful to Nelly for average good nature and occasional real kindness and sympathy. He hates Hindley and anyone else who offers him hate. He responds to Catherine for giving him the only equal love, strong, unforced and natural, as from child to related child, that he has in the world—it is his only firm hold on human life. Without it he would be an animal; having strong passions and an energetic nature, he would be a wolf—something Catherine comes to realize later when the process is almost completed and she has become responsible for part of it. Describing Heathcliff to Isabella Linton, who has fallen romantically in love with him, she calls him

> an unreclaimed creature, without refinement, without cultivation; an arid wilderness of furze and whinstone.

In other words, he is like the Heights. She goes on:

> Pray don't imagine that he conceals depths of benevolence and affection beneath a stern exterior! He's not a rough diamond—a pearl-containing oyster of a rustic; he's a fierce, pitiless, wolfish man. I never say to him let this or that enemy alone, because it would be ungenerous or cruel to harm them, I say—'Let them alone, because *I* should hate them to be wronged.'

We can't accept what Catherine says as the whole truth, because Catherine is involved with Heathcliff, but also because she can't admit to herself, or doesn't yet realize, what she did at a certain moment to make him like that. Her power over him she realizes: it is displayed in that last boast: just as she could, as a child, make him 'behave', so now *she* can make him stay his hand, because he will not hurt her, and so will not hurt those dear to her. What she has not fully grasped is the reason why he is as he is.

Old Mr Earnshaw died, leaving Heathcliff and Catherine still children, and in the power of the elder child Hindley Earnshaw. Hindley persecutes Heathcliff, setting out to turn him back into the abandoned asocial unregarded being that the old man tried to save him from remaining. It's striking that Hindley doesn't turn him out; we deduce an operation of the self: that he actually wants Heathcliff in his power, wants to get a revenge, to degrade and subvert him, to make him like the trees up at the Heights—the 'range of gaunt thorns all stretching their limbs one way as if craving alms of the sun'. Hindley is the cruel wind that will work this long distortion, as naturally and without conscience as the real wind. He simply expresses his nature, his will, his sense of injury in childhood, his power to revenge it now. The sun, on the other hand, is Catherine herself. As long as Heathcliff can 'stretch his arms' to her, as long as they are all in all to each other, as they were in their unconscious childhood state, Heathcliff has a human hope and purpose, and a human nature. When the sun is removed, he becomes 'the arid wilderness'. She removes the sun by denying her love for him, by assuming he has a smaller and undemanding love for her, and by marrying Edgar Linton, the gentle, overbred, fairhaired delicate lad who lives down in the valley at Thrushcross Grange.

Catherine is less comprehensible than Heathcliff, and for that reason may be more frightening. What she seems to represent is either an immature unconsciousness, or a very tough power of the will, a thornlike hardness, a separate selfhood, a determination quite equal to Heathcliff's, far more self-confident, and far less clear about its own need. And, from first to last, he *is* clear about his one need: union with Catherine, alive or dead. She wavers, and that causes the tragedy.

Hindley's persecution merely toughens Heathcliff's exterior, his bark, and sharpens his thorns. It causes him to consecrate himself to his subsidiary aim in life: an ordinary revenge on Hindley's family. He decides to do this at a specific moment, noted by Nelly Dean. There has been a Christmas party, with the Lintons coming to the Heights. Heathcliff, conscious of his gracelessness, the uncouthness he has wilfully adopted just because it is forced upon him, but still sensitive and suffering, makes an effort to be accepted, and cleans himself up, saying 'Nelly, make me decent, I'm going to be good'. He appears; Hindley rebuffs him, and Edgar Linton in mere complacent self-superiority slights him. Heathcliff assaults Edgar, being already jealous of his attraction for Catherine, and Hindley has the pleasure of beating him pitilessly. Heathcliff vows himself to revenge:

> 'I'm trying to settle how I shall pay Hindley back. I don't care how long I wait, if I can only do it, at last. I hope he will not die before I do!'
> 'For shame, Heathcliff!' said I. 'It is for God to punish wicked people; we should learn to forgive.'
>
> 'No, God won't have the satisfaction that I shall,' he returned. 'I only wish I knew the best way.'

He hits on the best way. Hindley's wife dies, and Hindley is in his own way of the true Heights stock:

> His sorrow was of that kind that will not lament, he neither wept nor prayed—he cursed and defied—execrated God and man, and gave himself up to reckless dissipation.

So in due course Heathcliff aims at revenge by letting the drunken Hindley gamble away the house and land, winning them from him, and by taking Hareton, Hindley's son, and inciting Hareton to the loutish degradation Hindley had tried to bring Heathcliff to earlier. But this ambition, almost realized, becomes unreal at the end of the book, and this is because what Hindley had done to Heathcliff was merely an external—merely unkindness, so to speak. What Catherine did to him was worse because it went to the root of his being, what Othello called 'the fountain from the whence my current springs'. Trying to hold himself together in face of that deprivation, trying finally to win back what he had lost, becomes the true meaning of his life.

Catherine is in some sense in love with Edgar Linton; it is a somewhat conventional feeling, but there is no reason to think it is not real. He represents an opposite: graceful, gentle, pliable, cultivated. Her roots are intermingled with Heathcliff's, but that is below the surface, hard to account for, and hard to be fully conscious of. She is to some degree aware of it, but she underestimates its importance for her, and in an almost incomprehensible way takes no account of what she may be doing to him. She assumes that she can manage everything; that both Heathcliff and Edgar will be easy to manipulate, or will not even need manipulating—they will just fall in with her all-disposing will. None of the three can in fact master their variously strong natures, so this is a crucial miscalculation.

This is skilfully demonstrated, as a kind of warning prelude, on one occasion when, Hindley being away, Edgar calls. Heathcliff had hoped to have Catherine's company to himself, and says so. She is embarrassed, she wants to get rid of him so as to be with Edgar, and finally has to tell him that Edgar is coming. She is by now upset at herself for having to try to bundle Heathcliff out of the way, upset at him for being *in* the way. He makes a direct claim on her ('Don't turn me out for those pitiful silly friends of yours'), and she is further surprised and upset to find out in what degree he cares and is demanding. He has actually marked on a calendar the times she has spent with him, and those with the Lintons. Her troubled sense of being in a conflict of irreconcilable demands made on her makes her merely peevish; she snubs Heathcliff in a wounding way; he is genuinely hurt, and leaves. Edgar comes, and finds her in this turmoil, and so quite soon she pinches Nelly Dean for spying on her and Edgar, is loudly accused of doing so by Nelly, tells a lie in denying the act and boxes Nelly's ears.

> 'Catherine, love! Catherine!' interposed Linton, greatly shocked at the double fault of falsehood and violence which his idol had committed.

> 'Leave the room, Ellen!' she repeated, trembling all over. Little Hareton [Hindley's son] who followed me everywhere, and was sitting near me on the floor, at seeing my tears commenced crying himself, and sobbed out complaints against 'wicked Aunt Cathy', which drew her fury on to his unlucky head: she seized his shoulders and shook him till the poor child waxed livid, and Edgar thoughtlessly laid hold of her hands to deliver him. In an instant one was wrung free, and the astounded young man felt it applied over his own ear in a way that could not be mistaken for jest.

> He drew back in consternation—I lifted Hareton in my arms, and walked off to the kitchen with him; leaving the door of communication open, for I was curious to watch how they should settle their disagreement.

> The insulted visitor moved to the spot where he had laid his hat, pale and with a quivering lip. 'That's right!' I said to myself. 'Take warning and begone! It's a kindness to let you have a glimpse of her genuine disposition.'

> 'Where are you going?' demanded Catherine, advancing to the door.

> He swerved aside and attempted to pass. 'You must not go!' she exclaimed energetically. 'I must and shall!' he replied in a subdued voice. 'No,' she persisted, grasping the handle; 'not yet. Edgar Linton—sit down, you shall not leave me in that temper. I should be miserable all night, and I won't be miserable for you!'

> 'Can I stay after you have struck me?' asked Linton.

> Catherine was mute.

> 'You've made me afraid and ashamed of you,' he continued; 'I'll not come here again!'

> Her eyes began to glisten and her lids to twinkle.

> 'And you told a deliberate untruth!' he said. 'I didn't!' she cried, recovering her speech. 'I did nothing deliberately—Well, go, if you please—get away! And now I'll cry—I'll cry myself sick.' She dropped down on her knees by a chair and set to weeping in serious earnest. Edgar persevered in his resolution as far as the court; there he lingered. I resolved to encourage him.

> 'Miss is dreadfully wayward, sir!' I called out. 'As bad as any marred child—you'd better be riding home, or else she'll be sick only to grieve us.'

> The soft thing looked askance through the window—he possessed the power to depart, as much as the cat possesses the power to leave a mouse half-killed, or a bird half-eaten.

> Ah, I thought, there will be no saving him—He's doomed, and flies to his fate!

> And so it was; he turned abruptly, hastened into the house again, shut the door behind him . . .

Compare the assault on the child with Emma Bovary's. It is much more in good hot blood. It is equally a violent outburst of self, but is not followed by Emma's repulsive reestablishment of her self-esteem. What Catherine says here—'I did nothing deliberately'—is a powerful and disturbing truth. She flew out in that way because of the succession of pressures she had just undergone with Heathcliff and Edgar, and because she is herself. She was expressing her nature in the direct and uninhibited way which characterizes the people on the Heights. It makes them naturally powerful and dangerous people, and when they conflict with each other it leads to a fight to the death. That is the element of unconsciousness in her, of spontaneity and directness. It is bound up with her vitality and attraction. But her 'I won't be miserable for you' is bound up with her hardness.

There is something childish about it, as in 'And now I'll cry—I'll cry myself sick!' It looks like a piece of infantile blackmail, and it puts Nelly Dean's back up. She sees only the 'marred child' in that behaviour. Like *David Copperfield,* this raises questions about 'being a child' and 'being an adult' that one never gets to the end of. Perhaps the truth is that the self, directly expressing itself, is seen at its purest in the child. We say of some unacceptable behaviour that it is 'childish', meaning so to diminish it, make it seem petty, and ultimately manageable (we learn to manage naughty children by distracting their attention and other dodges. We dare not engage in the direct conflict of wills or we'd murder them. Every year a number of simple enraged people murder or brutally assault their children—usually for crying—because they don't think of sidestepping and using patience and deceit as an acceptable middle course between surrender and violence). Psychology has told us how much adults are like children, when it might be as much to the point and more salutary to show how much children are like uninhibited adults. Adults are not manageable, least of all by themselves. Nelly Dean misunderstands Catherine here, and—fatally—later. She assumes both times that Catherine is 'trying it on', when she is really at the mercy of her self and its conflicting needs in a situation she cannot manage. In the end this becomes intolerable, after she has married Edgar.

Heathcliff under Hindley's persecution has become ignoble in his overt behaviour and appearance. Catherine isn't much more than a child, nor is Heathcliff; so he has no adult pride which pulls him back from that degradation; he pushes wilfully into it in the spirit of 'I'll show them I can outdo them at their own game'; or 'it shall be *my* will that I am like this'. That inevitably disgusts her at the surface level, and she hasn't the adult judgement to see beyond. Offered Edgar Linton, handsome, rich and charming, in contrast with Heathcliff, rough, destitute and unsupported by family or wealth, there's little that she can do but accept him. She has a terrible inkling that she is wrong, but it is subdued by her youthful confidence that she can somehow manage, and that in any case it is her will to take the situation on.

In her long exchange with Nelly in chapter 9 she moves steadily away from her deep sense that in marrying Edgar she is on a false path. To Nelly's question 'where is the obstacle?' she at first replies

> 'Here! and here!' . . . striking one hand on her forehead, and the other on her breast. 'In whichever place the soul lives—in my soul and in my heart, I'm convinced I'm wrong.'

She explains herself to the listening Nelly in mysterious terms. I say 'mysterious' because the reader cannot accept them neutrally: he will either think them deeply true or dangerous self-delusion, so far as he does understand them; there is in any case an element of ambiguity in them; and the whole of the rest of the book is a commentary on them—and although at the end it is not clear whether they are endorsed or proved an illusion, our impulse is to feel them proved, or her stance vindicated.

She begins with her thematic dream about 'being in heaven':

> . . . heaven did not seem to be my home; and I broke my heart with weeping to come back to earth; and the angels were so angry that they flung me out, into the middle of the heath on the top of Wuthering Heights, where I woke sobbing for joy.

'Heaven' may offer itself as Thrushcross Grange, or marriage to Edgar, or a domesticated kind of virtuous married life of the ordinary sort; but she is bound at the roots to the Heights, and to Heathcliff. She makes the connection herself:

> That will do to explain my secret, as well as the other. I've no more business to marry Edgar Linton than I have to be in heaven; and if the wicked man in there [Hindley] had not brought Heathcliff so low, I shouldn't have thought of it. It would degrade me to marry Heathcliff, now . . .

(and Heathcliff, who has been eavesdropping, creeps out, cut to the heart, and disappears for three years)

> . . . so he shall never know how I love him; and that, not because he's handsome, Nelly, but because he's more myself than I am. Whatever our souls are made of, his and mine are the same, and Linton's is as different as a moonbeam from lightning, or frost from fire.

She goes on to show that she wants to be convinced that Heathcliff 'has no notion of these things. . . . He does not know what being in love is'. Nelly does not let her off:

> 'I see no reason that he should not know, as well as you,' I returned; 'and if you are his choice, he'll be the most unfortunate creature that was ever born! As soon as you become Mrs Linton, he loses *friend,* and love, and all! Have you considered how you'll bear the separation, and how he'll bear to be quite deserted in the world?' (*my italics*).

That is Nelly's truth, and it is here that Catherine takes off into a kind of self-deception. Or is it?

> He quite deserted! we separated! . . . Who is to separate us, pray? . . . Every Linton on the face of the earth might melt into nothing, before I could consent to forsake Heathcliff.

She goes on to say what she means, or what she has failed to grasp as a real meaning that demands she act differently:

> He'll be as much to me as he has been all his lifetime. Edgar must shake off his antipathy, and tolerate him, at least. He will when he learns my true feelings towards him.

And then she offers as bright after-thought:

> . . . if Heathcliff and I married, we should be beggars, whereas if I marry Linton, I can aid Heathcliff to rise . . .

We have a sense here that Catherine is struggling with things she can't fully realize; that she is making partly hopeful, partly wild remarks, half talking herself round into the belief that what she is doing is right, half imagining some kind of ideal relationship in which Edgars are not jealous of Heathcliffs and vice versa. Edgar shall have formal possession, and that should be good enough for him; and she will go on loving Heathcliff in the profound, wordless—perhaps actionless, gestureless—way; for words and actions and gestures are not needed when you 'are' the other person. She is struggling with an idea which comes out as a poetic utterance:

> I cannot express it; but surely you and everybody have a notion that there is, or should be an existence beyond you. What were the use of my creation if I were entirely contained here? My great miseries in this world have been Heathcliff's miseries, and I watched and felt each from the beginning; my great thought in living is himself. If all else perished and *he* remained, I should still continue to be; and if all else remained and he were annihilated, the universe would turn to a mighty stranger. I should not seem a part of it. My love for Linton is like the foliage in the woods. Time will change it, I'm well aware, as winter changes the trees. My love

for Heathcliff resembles the eternal rocks beneath—a source of little visible delight, but necessary. Nelly, I *am* Heathcliff—he's always, always in my mind—not as a pleasure, any more
than I am always a pleasure to myself—but as
my own being . . .

The question which the book poses for us, is—do we feel
that as a profound insight or as an egoistic illusion? Does
Catherine's unhappy marriage and death disprove it, or
does the ultimate course of the book, especially the end,
validate it?

One can't dismiss it; at any rate Catherine believes it as
an ultimate or higher truth. She goes on believing it even
when Heathcliff instantly disappears—thus in a practical
way proving that he is *not* her, and that he has no automatic sense of her love for him. He is deeply wounded by
her marrying Linton in preference to him; yet the trauma
also has the effect of shocking him into being his possible
social self. He comes back later, educated, self-possessed,
suave, rich and dangerous. He has, we infer, to prove to
her what he could be, what she has thrown away: something stronger than Linton and as marriageable. His plan,
he reveals in an aside, was to reappear briefly, be seen and
recognized by her, to kill Hindley and to commit suicide.
This would be a simple vengeance on Hindley and a complicated revenge on Catherine, who is (as usual) to be
sorry when he's dead, and serve her right. We recognize
that need from *Anna Karenina:* it's one of 'the rules of the
game', as Tolstoy put it.

But in any case Heathcliff's disappearance for that long
time is already a blow and a grievance to Catherine. This
sign of a separate existence is like the one James Steerforth
gave to his mother: it was Mrs Steerforth who said of her
son that he had been

> the object of my life, to whom its every thought
> has been devoted, whom I have gratified from a
> child in every wish, *from whom I have had no
> separate existence since his birth*—to take up in
> a moment with a miserable girl, and avoid me!
> (*my italics*).

Catherine and Heathcliff do later make similar jealous
charges against each other: she that he left her without a
word, to sorrow alone; he that she married Linton, forcing
him away. They offer these reproaches in all bitterness;
and we wonder, are these merely two powerful simple
predatory egos, with an equal jealous hold on each other
and an equal proud independent will? Or is that the mere
accident of their surface selfhood, incident to humanity,
and *do* they finally strike on the something deeper, the
thing that Catherine expresses as 'the eternal rocks beneath'?

On Heathcliff's disappearance, Catherine has the first of
her mysterious illnesses. This has been prepared for in the
incident where she said she would 'cry herself sick', but
also explained that she did nothing deliberately. She now
spends all night outside in the rain, watching and calling
for Heathcliff and weeping like a child; and when he
doesn't return, has a collapse which is like a breakdown,
and is also the onset of epilepsy or consumption or both.
Thereafter she must not be crossed, or she will have a fit,

the doctor says. Again, it is a curiously childish notion,
misunderstood by Nelly at the key moment, misunderstood even by Catherine. For in the end she dies, having
willed herself to die. But the odd thing is that though she
wills it, and it happens, it doesn't necessarily happen solely
because she wills it. The root of her life is cut through (at
the level of the rocks), and her death happens to coincide
with her will.

The core of the book, the lacerating part, is the succession
of violent exchanges when Heathcliff returns to find her
married, and he, she and Edgar find themselves in the classic triangle. She and Edgar have what seems to be a work-
able relationship though it is founded on his giving way
to her:

> She seemed almost over fond of Mr Linton; and
> even to his sister she showed plenty of affection.
> They were both very attentive to her comfort
> certainly. It was not the thorn bending to the
> honeysuckles, but the honeysuckles embracing
> the thorn. There were no mutual concessions;
> one stood erect and the others yielded; and who
> *can* be ill-natured, and bad tempered, when they
> encounter neither opposition nor indifference?

That is Nelly's summing up, spiced with malice. Catherine
later lets fall that her placidity and fondness is an effort
of will: underneath she was grieving for Heathcliff. Nelly
goes on to say, with some grimness:

> It ended. Well, we *must* be for ourselves in the
> long run; the mild and generous are only more
> justly selfish than the domineering—and it
> ended when circumstances caused each to feel
> that the one's interest was not the chief consider-
> ation in the other's thoughts.

The 'circumstances' were those following Heathcliff's return. He calls at the Grange, meaning not to do more than
let her see him and realize what a mistake she made, and
be off to murder Hindley:

> He took a seat opposite Catherine, who kept her
> gaze fixed on him as if she feared he would van-
> ish were she to remove it. He did not raise his
> to her, often; a quick glance now and then suf-
> ficed; but it flashed back, each time more confi-
> dently, the undisguised delight he drank from
> hers.

It's very economically stated. No more need be said. The
consequences are immediate:

> They were too much absorbed in their mutual
> joy to suffer embarrassment; not so Mr Edgar,
> he grew pale with pure annoyance, a feeling that
> reached its climax when his lady rose—and step-
> ping across the rug, seized Heathcliff's hands
> again, and laughed like one beside herself.

She does nothing deliberately, we remember. It is the natural expression of a true deep feeling that goes right back
into her childhood and is now suddenly maturing into
something else.

Edgar sees it at once. That night, according to Catherine,
he is 'childish':

> He always contrives to be sick at the least cross!

I gave a few sentences of commendation to Heathcliff, and he, either for a head-ache or a pang of envy, began to cry: so I got up and left him.

Her fatal unconsciousness, or her unwillingness to see that people are people, and therefore perhaps as 'childish' as she, or less fearless, or more sensitive, or clearer-sighted about consequences, is both her strength and her limitation. She goes on 'But does it not show great weakness? . . . I'm not envious'. She has nothing to be envious of, since she is, in the world's eyes, about to try to have her cake and eat it, or some such envious phrase. She becomes hard about Isabella and Edgar in a way which reflects back on herself:

> . . . they are spoiled children, and fancy the world was made for their accommodation; and though I humour both, I think a smart chastisement might improve them all the same.

Nelly makes the obvious retort, going on

> 'You may however, fall out at last, over something of equal consequence to both sides; and then those you term weak are very capable of being as obstinate as you.'

> 'And then we shall fight to the death, shan't we, Nelly?' she returned, laughing. 'No, I tell you, I have such faith in Linton's love that I believe I might kill him, and he wouldn't wish to retaliate.'

It is a grim prediction, for she kills herself (or 'it' kills her that she is in the situation she finds herself in) and in due course both Linton and Heathcliff appease their longing for her by following her to the grave, after eighteen and twenty years of grieving and restlessness.

It would cut the discussion unhelpfully short to say Catherine is a spoilt bitch; that she enjoys exerting her power over two men; that she cannot see why they should not be willing to be both there, in love with her, and getting from her what she is willing to grant to each of them; and that she is destroyed when they decline to accept the situation docilely but make ever-increasing jealous demands on her and fall out violently with each other. It is near enough to the truth to be disturbing, but it doesn't fully cover the case. It is a kind of innocence in her, even a purity, which insists that what she feels for the two men comes from her quite spontaneously; what she feels for each is the due of each, so what is wrong? And 'she does nothing deliberately'. Equally, though she can be made, and is made, to suffer by them, it is, she thinks, fundamentally not right that she should be 'miserable for you'. This may be the innocence of childhood, in which case our reaction, as with Emma Bovary, is to say that people who won't grow up suffer for it. Alternatively it is the glimpse of a possibility, an ideal, that people ought to be able to manage: a forbearing maturity that would permit people to accept the reality of their feelings and the feelings of those they love, and learn to make no demands. But she is the last person to be able to manage that herself, since it requires a maturity she doesn't have; indeed her charm depends on her not having it. And the last-but-one person to attempt it with is Edgar, and the last-but-two is Heathcliff.

There is a certain contrast in the behaviour of the two men. There is a moment when Edgar forces the issue in the classic terms:

> Will you give up Heathcliff hereafter, or will you give up me? It is impossible for you to be *my* friend, and *his* at the same time; and I absolutely *require* to know which you choose.

The conventionality of that—apart from the strange use once more of the word 'friend'—may blind us to its unreality. The world, in the person of the spouse exerting his or her 'rights', says 'which of these two limbs are you going to cut off?', and the victim is merely aware that she wants them both, or that even if a choice is possible it remains a violence, as any amputation must be.

It is Heathcliff who shows a gleam of realism here, even though it hardly amounts to a forbearing sympathy:

> Had he been in my place, and I in his, though I hated him with a hatred that turned my life to gall, I never would have raised a hand against him. . . . I never would have banished him from her society, as long as she desired his.

Catherine is aware of this as her *power* over Heathcliff; he is aware of it as part of his regard for her as a being with an independent existence and freedom to bestow her love on other people. It is part of his peculiar strength; and an indication of the depth of his love.

An odd reflection is cast on this capacity by Catherine's earlier asking him, more or less, whether he would like to have Isabella Linton as a kind of consolation prize ('If you like Isabella, you shall marry her'). He takes it as a profound insult, and perhaps it is. Catherine's hope is that if he will have Isabella he can live near by in his wedded bliss; and there will Catherine and Edgar be in *their* wedded bliss; and Catherine and Heathcliff can also have their wordless communion of spirit, which is satisfied by 'being' each other. But Heathcliff is profoundly faithful to his love for Catherine which for him excludes other loves; he wants her and only her. Her marriage to Edgar was a grief and a deprival, and he won't pretend otherwise. He will accept it since he must—she has done it because she wanted to, and her will is paramount. But he will not accept substitutes, or diversions or palliatives for himself, and is offended at the offer. If he then marries Isabella, it is purely because she delivers herself into his hands. He detests her, but she offers a path to his revenge and a lever on Edgar.

'The tyrant grinds down his slaves', he says to Catherine (the tyrant) '—and they don't turn against him, they crush those beneath them' (Isabella). 'You are welcome to torture me to death for your amusement, only, allow me to amuse myself in the same style—And refrain from insult as much as you are able. Having levelled my palace, don't erect a hovel and complacently admire your own charity in giving me that for a home.' We hear the real anger and bitterness there, and the violence brewing.

It is at this moment that Catherine begins to realize that she is lost. Heathcliff's violence—his urge to be revenged on those who have deprived him—threatens to be uncontrollable; Edgar's more commonplace but real jealousy is equally a threat. It turns out that people have wills as strong as hers, and the people who love her pull against her, make conflicting demands on her. Her resource is to make an even wilder, a truly childish, demand on them:

> Well, if I cannot keep Heathcliff for *my friend*— if Edgar will be mean and jealous, I'll try to break their hearts by breaking my own (*my italics*).

The threat is made to Nelly, who is resistant to that blackmail and looks stolid. She has heard it before. It is a fine touch of insight that Catherine, seeing that stolidity, is frightened. She may have to carry out her threat if she can't make people believe her and pull her back. It's in the rules of the game that you have to do it when dared:

> I wish you could dismiss that apathy out of your countenance, and look rather more anxious about me!

It sounds spoilt and self-deceiving, but is a desperate cry for help, from a child. Nelly ignores it. She understands children, but not grown-up children. Anyway, the rules of the game apply to her too, and she is convinced that she is the only sensible person in the house. If only they would all be sensible! She is the solid extrovert who tells the depressive, the neurotic, to snap out of it, to pull herself together, to make the effort of will. That too is a self-regarding role, enclosing in its limitations. But it makes Nelly a real person. Compare Dickens's Clara Peggotty, who is just a projection of David Copperfield's need for a surrogate mother, and who does nothing but radiate uncritical love for him. Nelly has a mind of her own, and a will, which she uses. She offers all the main characters affection, but also a critical judgement, and she takes decisive and sometimes disastrous steps of her own—as when she refuses to take Catherine's threat seriously.

Catherine has her fit, but doesn't die—not then. Giving up is a deeper business, prolonged, and from the whole person including the body, not the conscious will alone. This delay permits the final interview with Heathcliff, where they have their last clash, above the deep agony of their separation. It is like seeing some flayed creature still active, all the muscles moving.

What the reader remembers about this scene is how at this supreme moment the two still torture each other: each strong will reproaching the other. It symbolizes the relationship that she softens at one moment, but he cannot easily make the physical gesture which bridges the divide between them:

> I'm not wishing you greater torment than I have, Heathcliff. I only wish us never to be parted— and should a word of mine distress you hereafter, think I feel the same distress underground, and for my own sake, forgive me! Come here and kneel down again! You never harmed me in your life. Nay, if you nurse anger, that will be worse to remember than my harsh words! Won't you come here again? Do!

However that touches the heart, it is still the expression of a will; a wish to have, and a wish to be knelt to. Heath-

cliff can't submit to it, and turns his back. Catherine lets out a torrent of possessive reproach, ending

> *That* is how I am loved! Well, never mind! That is not my Heathcliff. I shall love mine yet; and take him with me—he's in my soul.

It reflects back on her thought that she *was* Heathcliff. Only it seems, 'her' Heathcliff: but there is a real one outside her, with a will of his own. This Heathcliff at last manages to cross over to her:

> 'Do come to me, Heathcliff.'
>
> In her eagerness she rose, and supported herself on the arm of the chair. At that earnest appeal, he turned to her, looking absolutely desperate. His eyes wide, and wet, at last, flashed fiercely on her; his breast heaved convulsively. An instant they held asunder; and then how they met I hardly saw, but Catherine made a spring, and he caught her, and they were locked in an embrace from which I thought my mistress would never be released alive.

The undertones would have been familiar to Racine; the spring of the predatory animal. Indeed Nelly goes on expressly, and rather luridly, to say

> . . . on my approaching hurriedly to ascertain if she had fainted, he gnashed at me, and foamed like a mad dog, and gathered her to him with greedy jealousy.

That is the myth-making tendency at work; expressing Nelly's smallness. These feelings are too big for her and too savage:

> I did not feel as if I were in the company of a creature of my own species.

But she *is* of that species; Racine knew we all were, and Nelly in her reflective moments knows it too.

That leap together, and the convulsive clinging together, express physically one kind of love, as other gestures we have seen in other books express different kinds: the prodigal's father running towards him; Lear and Cordelia kneeling to each other; Vronsky putting out an open hand which Anna will not put her hand into. Those moments and gestures are great things, and speak at the deepest level—this one among them. It is softened in its animal desperation by a specifically human touch. At the very end, Catherine holds on to Heathcliff like a child in fear of the dark, unwilling to let its father go from the bedside:

> He would have risen, and unfixed her fingers by the act—she clung fast, gasping: there was mad resolution in her face.
>
> 'No!' she shrieked, 'Oh, don't, don't go. It is the last time! Edgar will not hurt us. Heathcliff, I shall die! I shall die!'

Recurrently all the characters move into these implacably child-like postures. His response is fatherly: 'Hush, my darling! Hush, hush, Catherine! I'll stay.' They are the only humanly consoling words he speaks in the book. She needs him; he responds, glad to meet her last need. This meeting in her fear and desolation—she terrified of being alone, he comforting her in her dread—is as near as they get to a union before the end of the book. It gives them their relative stature, he larger and potentially kinder than she.

After that, the difficulty for Emily Brontë was to prevent the rest of the book being an anti-climax. It isn't one, but I don't find it strikes with the same strength partly because it moves into an equivocal kind of reality. It is meant to be a working out, an appeasement, or a laying to rest of the forces aroused in the first half. Catherine Earnshaw, who forsakes Heathcliff and marries Edgar Linton, gives birth at this mid-point to Catherine Linton, who first marries Heathcliff's son Linton Heathcliff, who dies, and then Hareton Earnshaw. She has much of her mother in her, but goes through a maturing process induced by Heathcliff. The Catherine Earnshaw we see at the end of the book is like an exorcized version of the Catherine Earnshaw we see at the beginning, and she is united to a young man who is like an exorcized Heathcliff. For Heathcliff had wanted to brutalize Hareton as Hareton's father brutalized him. He finds to his puzzlement that this has an unintended effect: Hareton does not resent it; he is not ultimately brutalized at all, nor vengeful, since he has reserves of goodness; and the isolated Catherine comes to love him as the other Catherine had loved Heathcliff. But this time the love is not self-thwarted: the second Catherine learns to subdue her will; in the process she discovers that Hareton is a separate person unlike her projected image of him, and lovable.

The searing thing in the second half of the book is Catherine's forced marriage to the weak, consumptive and dying Linton Heathcliff. She is trapped into the marriage, having never had more than childish playmate feelings for him in the first place, or protective motherly or elder-sisterly feelings in the second. But she sees him through to his death.

It is important that in a moment of clarity about himself he says to her

> You are so much happier than I am, you ought to be better . . . I *am* worthless, and bad in temper, and bad in spirit, almost always—and if you choose you may say goodbye—you'll get rid of an annoyance—Only, Catherine, do me this justice; believe that if I might be as sweet, and as kind, and as good as you are, I would be, as willingly, and more so, than as happy and as healthy. And believe that your kindness has made me love you deeper than if I deserved your love, and though I couldn't, and cannot help showing my nature to you, I regret it and repent it, and shall regret it and repent it, till I die.

That insight shines back towards the young Heathcliff, who is to some extent made what he is by what has happened to him from the beginning. The degree to which we are what we have in native strength, or are what life, especially early life, has twisted us into, like the thorns praying to the sun but twisted by the wind, is one of the mysterious issues of the book and it raises the other old question—do we do things 'deliberately'? Linton Heathcliff is a sickly child, conceived in hate, brought up by a strong-willed mother without a father, taken over by the father in scorn and hate, and used to further a will to power. He is evi-

dently entirely twisted, and it is a question which defines the nature of the onlooker whether he is more pitiful or contemptible. Catherine finds pity, and the beginnings of wisdom. It enables her to begin to see Heathcliff; she says to him:

> I know he [Linton] has a bad nature . . . he's your son. But I'm glad I've a better, to forgive it; and I know he loves me and for that reason I love him. Mr Heathcliff, *you* have *nobody* to love you, and, however miserable you make us, we shall still have the revenge of thinking that your cruelty arises from your greater misery! You *are* miserable, are you not? Lonely, like the devil, and envious like him? *Nobody* loves you— nobody will cry for you when you die! I wouldn't be you!

Even here, though, there is spite and enmity and the desire for revenge amongst the truths, which are therefore incomplete. Nobody understands Heathcliff in the novel. In the second half of the book he is working out an allotted span, bringing about the things which release him from the world, to be reunited with the first Catherine. What he is to find with her is, in the first place, peace; and that is probably all, but it may be enough. The union of two beings is achieved when, laid side by side in earth, their bodies both become part of it, their separate natures annihilated. Emily Brontë is quite carefully specific about this in a level-headed way reminiscent of the seventeenth century. She points out very early that the chapel graveyard 'lies in a hollow, between two hills—an elevated hollow— near a swamp, whose peaty moisture is said to answer all the purposes of embalming on the few corpses deposited there'. Catherine is buried there; when Edgar Linton is buried beside her, Heathcliff opens her coffin and is appeased to see that she is, so to speak, waiting for him:

> 'Disturbed her? No! she has disturbed me, night and day, through eighteen years—incessantly— remorselessly—till yesternight—and yesternight, I was tranquil. I dreamt I was sleeping the last sleep, by that sleeper, with my heart stopped, and my cheek frozen against hers.'
> 'And if she had been dissolved into earth, or worse, what would you have dreamt of then?' I said.
>
> 'Of dissolving with her and being more happy still!' he answered. 'Do you suppose I dread any change of that sort? I expected such a transformation on raising the lid, but I'm better pleased that it should not commence until I share it.'

The little patch of green, which is the graveyard in the hills, is constantly invaded by the bracken of the Heights. In due course that silent taking-over will be accomplished. Lockwood's last three paragraphs, the last in the book, envisage in sober wisdom the natural intransigence that takes over when human intransigence is stilled, the chapel dropping back to earth, the three headstones, side by side, being worked into the texture of the place by lichen, the 'sleepers in that quiet earth' reconciled by being taken into it. It is in that sense too that Catherine *is* finally Heathcliff. They become the world to each other, having always been so.

Before Heathcliff can enter that sleep he has to be formally released, to feel that Catherine's will is no longer exerted on him. It happens in the end, and, rationalizing (or perhaps I mean irrationalizing) the occurrence, we say that Catherine's spirit approves the union of the younger Catherine and Hareton and is put to rest, so releasing Heathcliff. The marriage of the young people unites the Heights and the Grange; it also unites a purified Catherine and a humanized Heathcliff; so that those two could see in this final love a happy resolution of their own unhappy love. They can let go, and leave.

So it falls out. Catherine and Hareton are at first at odds, all will and ego and pride. Both learn to subdue their pride, and so are able to give way to their tender feelings. It is a question of getting one part of oneself subdued, so that the other part may flourish (a truth young Linton Heathcliff saw, except that he also saw that it was not in *his* nature to manage that). Hareton's pride makes him gloomy and awkward, and prevents Catherine seeing what is underneath. In sheer anger he at one moment explains he has defended her to Heathcliff, and regrets it as a waste of good nature:

> 'I didn't know you took my part,' she answered, drying her eyes; 'and I was miserable and bitter at everybody; but now I thank you, and beg you to forgive me; what can I do besides?'

> She returned to the hearth, and frankly extended her hand. He blackened and scowled like a thundercloud, and kept his fists resolutely clenched, and his gaze fixed on the ground.

> Catherine, by instinct, must have divined it was obdurate perversity and not dislike that prompted this dogged conduct; for, after remaining an instant, undecided, she stooped, and impressed on his cheek a gentle kiss.

We recognize the gesture. It is touching, but pretty small in scale after the first half of the book. It is in any case overshadowed by the presence of Heathcliff still, approaching his deliverance; and his final release returns us to the people of that first half, and their unappeased longings, which are set at rest in the only possible way—by his death.

The extraordinary utterance Lockwood had overheard at the beginning of the book is, we sense, answered at the end:

> 'Come in! come in!' he sobbed. 'Cathy do come. Oh do—*once* more! Oh my heart's darling! hear me *this* time—Catherine, at last!'

We take that at the fairy-tale level by agreeing that throughout the second half of the book Catherine's ghost is awaited by Heathcliff. When she returns to him, a kind of half-compact, half-curse is fulfilled; he will be released; they will both be at peace. Emily Brontë equivocates brilliantly here; Heathcliff is clearly under the power of that obsession, and it is real for *him*. What it means for us is left to us. At the literal level we can say we don't believe in ghosts. The last sentence of the book may mean that the narrator Lockwood never *has* believed in ghosts; or that he is convinced that they are *now* both laid. But our re-

sponse to the narrative is to feel both Heathcliff's agonized expectation and the profound relaxation of his deliverance. (pp. 125-48)

Michael Black, " 'Wuthering Heights': Romantic Self-Commitment," in his The Literature of Fidelity, *Barnes & Noble Books, 1975, pp. 125-51.*

Virginia Woolf on Brontë's evocative style in *Wuthering Heights*:

It is as if she could tear up all that we know human beings by, and fill these unrecognisable transparences with such a gust of life that they transcend reality. Hers, then, is the rarest of all powers. She could free life from its dependence on facts; with a few touches indicate the spirit of a face so that it needs no body; by speaking of the moor make the wind blow and the thunder roar.

Virginia Woolf, in her The Common Reader, *Harcourt Brace Jovanovich, 1925.*

T. E. Apter   (essay date 1976)

[*In the essay below, Apter discusses Brontë's treatment of Romantic love in* Wuthering Heights, *noting that Catherine and Heathcliff's relationship is presented as "suffering love," whereas Cathy and Hareton's bond serves as "an alternative to that destructive, Romantic love."*]

A Romantic conception of romantic love can easily wilt and stew in a sickening sweet decay. When it supposes itself to be poignantly in bloom it may be stifled by an escapist's self-massaging imagination. This is the fate of Goethe's Werther who luxuriates in his pain, crying his heart out among gnarled oaks until he shoots himself in the hope that he will eventually be united with his love in the world to come. This is also the fate of Goethe's Ottilie and Eduard in *Elective Affinities* who expire through unfulfillable love (Ottilie, like Heathcliff, starves herself to death) and join one another in the grave. Goethe saw both these loves as irrational passions which could not be satisfied within the moral world and the idea of unity in death was an attempt to reconcile the passion with morality. These attempts to portray romantic passion in the language of Romanticism fail to make either the tragedy or the love convincing. Inadvertently the passion is portrayed as a weak thing, nourished for the sake of anguished ornamentation. Pain is valued because it supposedly measures intense emotion, but because the emphasis is on the self-reflecting pain, the love has no real intensity. The inclination for torment and the idea that there is depth in pain mistake themselves for the substance of tragic love. *Wuthering Heights* is a study of romantic love undertaken by a Romantic imagination, but it contains a serious study of the destructive elements within the magnetism of anguish and passion alongside a potent expression of their value and projects a far more original and useful resolution of irrational passion and morality than death while nonetheless expressing sympathy with that old Romantic solution.

The elements in the Catherine/Heathcliff theme which place it clearly within a Romantic tradition include an involvement with nature so intense, so mystical that it contains a death wish, or, more specifically, a desire to return to the mindless unity of nature, to mend the separation from nature effected by society and sophistication; also included are a love which longs for a soul unity with the beloved, a love which grows viciously single-minded when thwarted, and circumstances which prohibit the earthly satisfaction of love. But it is part of Emily Brontë's complete lack of sentimentality that she shows the prohibitive circumstances to stem from the characters' own destructive and self-destructive impulses; for although every Romantic knows that passion involves suffering, he does not often admit that the characters who enjoy the intensity of passion also enjoy, and are willing to generate, the suffering from which the intensity issues, and that it is the impulse to destroy, or rather, the capacity to value something only in its absence, or through torturous trials, that gives rise to the Romantic tragedy of love. Usually the relishing of pain takes place in the artist's imagination, spinning tales of doom and destruction which innocent characters must then enact, but Emily Brontë carries this problem of the Romantic imagination into the tale itself, and thus the meaning of that typical suffering is given a new depth and a new criticism.

The emphasis in *Wuthering Heights* is on the reality of passion. The novel insists that passion is a force with its own laws, a cosmic, inhuman thing that cannot be denied or treated lightly, and if the people who have passion disregard it, they will be divided against themselves and destroyed by their defiance. But not everyone is subject to its laws, for not everyone is able to enter the sphere in which passion is a reality. The book opens with a mistaken conception of deep feeling and deep suffering. Lockwood supposes himself to be within the world of Romantic disappointment and isolation. At first he identifies Heathcliff as a fellow member of this clan. He is in fact correct to see Heathcliff as an intriguing Romantic figure, but this correctness is ironic because Lockwood's own conception of the Romantic cult is so mistaken. When Heathcliff shouts rudely at the lovely young Cathy, Lockwood supposes his initial impression of Heathcliff to be wrong because he now sees Heathcliff as a thoroughly hard, unsentimental man; but Lockwood is mistaken in thinking that a Romantically isolated, anguished figure must have essentially a kind heart, that isolation and anguish are only surface wounds covering a good, normal nature. In short, Lockwood makes the mistake that many would-be Romantic artists make; he supposes suffering on passion's account to be a good excuse for poignant ornamentation.

Again, Lockwood is right to see Heathcliff as a misanthrope, but he is ridiculous in supposing that he shares Heathcliff's attitudes, for he does not know what it means to be misanthropic. For Lockwood misanthropy is merely an attractive posture. There is real anger directed towards Lockwood by the author not merely because he is shallow but because he is shallow and considers himself to be deep.

In this anger a jealousy of depth is felt: only those who truly suffer emotional intensity have a right to claim its glamour. Though Lockwood has an impulse to destroy love—he once fancied himself in love but grew cold when he saw that his attraction was returned, and he toys with the idea of winning young Cathy's love, but decides against it in case her temper should turn out to be as bad as her mother's—his self defeat comes from a source far inferior to the source of Catherine's or Heathcliff's destructive impulses. In Lockwood's case fear of emotion rather than emotional greed or bitter vengefulness leads him to believe he is a highly emotional person; because he tries to avoid emotional contact he assumes that his problem stems from the overwhelming intensity of his feelings; but there is no doubt in the author's mind that however horrendous Heathcliff's soul is, it is more significant than Lockwood's soul. This hierarchy of values underlines a Romantic pride in the strength of emotion, be the strength good or ill.

The good and ill, however, are not irrelevant. Early critics of the novel complained that the work was without moral design, but it is difficult to believe they actually meant that. There are numerous references to the devil and heaven and hell: Heathcliff is nearly as dark as if he came from the devil; he is prepared to defy the devil in order to protect Catherine from the Linton's dog; Hindley calls him an "imp of Satan"; in her diary the young Catherine writes that "Joseph asseverated 'owd Nick' would fetch us sure as we were living", and the sober Nelly also expresses her puzzlement as to what sort of creature Heathcliff is, implying that he might be some kind of demon. Although such references need not have a moral focus—they could be used simply for eerie effect, as in a ghost story—Emily Brontë uses them to emphasize the inhuman and demonic aspects of passion, and undoubtedly the early critics' real complaint lay not with a lack of moral design but with the particular moral design. The novel continually questions where in the human and extra-human world passion lies; and though its value is never undermined, passion is not seen to be a warm, tender thing, full of the goodness of life or neatly tied to compassionate, considerate feelings.

It is primarily the pontificating Joseph, self-righteously using religious vindictiveness as an excuse for his own sadism, and Hindley, who is afraid of his position vis-à-vis Heathcliff, who express belief in this goblin-like wickedness; but other characters, too, through fear and incomprehension, share this sense of a demon in Heathcliff. Isabella asks in her desperate letter to Nelly, written after her marriage, "What kind of man is he?" and in his last meeting with Catherine Nelly says "I did not feel as if I were in the company of a creature of my own species; it appeared that he would not understand, though I spoke to him; so I stood off, and held my tongue, in great perplexity." (XV) Heathcliff, as the embodiment of relentlessly single-minded passion, does not even speak the same language as ordinary, sociable humans. People do not fear him simply because he is cruel, but because he is unbelievably cruel while following his own moral law—passion's law. As he is dying Nelly suggests he make his peace with God, but he replies that he has done nothing wrong, and Catherine, when she is dying, admits that he has done nothing wrong. The lovers are not concerned with humanity's law, they are concerned with passion's law, and this law is shown to be startlingly different from the laws in which Joseph and Hindley and Nelly and Lockwood believe. Ordinarily love is thought to redeem destructive impulses, but in Heathcliff's case it is his love for Catherine which motivates his cruelty. He would not have minded Hindley's degradation if Catherine had stood by him; but because that degradation led to Catherine's rejection, he must destroy Hindley. He would not have bothered with Edgar Linton and his family had Catherine not married Edgar. His revenge is of primary importance and must overcome his affection for Hareton; as Hindley's child Hareton must be the object of revenge. Indeed, Heathcliff's savagery is not without sentimentality, for it is thoroughly unredeemed, indulgently consistent, and this exaggeration puts it out of focus. The more interesting factor is the love which is its cause.

What kind of love demands such destruction? Though the love between Catherine and Heathcliff is seen as a terrible and valuable force, there is no divinity or even nobility in it, no embodiment of human ideals. It is a rigidly personal, specific connection, forged by habit, without illusion, without respect, but a connection so strong that it defies the notion of separation. The dying Catherine recalls how painful it was when, at the age of twelve, Hindley prevented her and Heathcliff from sharing the same bed. Their clothes, as children, are often mingled: Catherine fastens her and Heathcliff's pinafores together to form a curtain round them, and they want a woman's cloak—one cloak—to shelter them on a scamper across the moor. Unlike Goethe's novels of love and death there is no sense here that this love would not live up to expectation. In **Wuthering Heights** the union desired in death is not an easy assertion of a nice but not quite believable connection; the union in death is seen as a point towards which inexorable forces are moving. Catherine's speech about her love for Heathcliff resembling "the eternal rocks beneath—a source of little visible delight, but necessary" (IX) has a ring of sentimentality, but the support it gets from the rest of the novel absorbs the false tone. Her language is self-indulgent, but she is fighting to understand the depth of her attachment to Heathcliff at the very moment she has tried, by promising to marry Edgar, to deny that attachment; she is not simply enjoying a Romantic pose.

Their attachment defines their world and provides their own morality. Together they can settle down comfortably to await the advent of "owd Nick" threatened by Joseph because the hell of others has no meaning to them as long as they are together. Furthermore, the heaven of others is rejected by Catherine; she dreams that she finds herself in heaven and weeps because she is separated from the Heights, and the angels, angry with her blasphemous dissatisfaction, throw her from heaven, and she awakes on the Heights, sobbing for joy. When Nelly advises Heathcliff to prepare for death he answers that he has nearly attained his heaven—and his heaven is death, and union with Catherine. No laws other than those which pertain to their attachment are binding upon them. When Isabella declares her love for Heathcliff, Catherine tells her that he

is "a fierce, pitiless, wolfish man". She never says to him "let this or that enemy alone, because it would be ungenerous or cruel to harm them, I say 'Let them alone because *I* should hate them to be wronged'." (X) And Heathcliff spurns the idea of Edgar looking after the altered, ailing Catherine on grounds of Christian charity and duty. To him such bonds are paltry things in contrast to the love which would bind him to her.

Their love, however, does go wrong; but even in the thwarting of their attachment only the laws of passion are relevant; they are not separated by an outside force—no outside force would be strong enough to eclipse their emotions. The crux of the tensions which both bind them together and tear them apart can be seen in the episode in which Catherine, having returned to the Heights after her first visit to the Lintons, is anxious to return her new friends' hospitality and quarrels with Heathcliff because he is too dirty to receive her guests. He sulks for a while, but then asks Nelly to make him look decent. She replies:

> 'High time, Heathcliff,' I said, 'you *have* grieved Catherine; she's sorry she ever came home, I dare say! It looks as if you envied her, because she is more thought of than you.'

> The notion of *envying* Catherine was incomprehensible to him, but the notion of grieving her he understood clearly enough.

> 'Did she say she was grieved?' he inquired, looking very serious.

> 'She cried when I told her you were off again this morning.'

> 'Well, *I* cried last night,' he returned, 'and I had more reason to cry than she.' (VII)

The incomprehensibility of envy comes from a complete identification of interests, and is combined with a fierce protectiveness of the other's interests. When Heathcliff watches Catherine through the window of Thrushcross Grange as the Lintons, having thrown him out, comb Catherine's hair and wash her wounded foot, his purpose is to determine whether she wants to be rescued. If she does, then he will smash the window to save her; but when he sees that she is content, he leaves. The reader is clearly aware of his loneliness, but Heathcliff does not sulk over his exclusion. He waited by the window, not to savour his unhappiness, but simply to determine whether Catherine needed him.

This lack of envy is tied to his lack of common jealousy. When Edgar becomes Catherine's husband Heathcliff refrains from killing him because he is afraid that Catherine would suffer from this loss, and he claims that he would never banish Edgar from her society as long as she desired his. But the staunch protectiveness and identification of interests implied in his inability to understand the notion of envying Catherine, is cancelled by the full meaning of "but the notion of grieving her he understood clearly enough". Nelly is remarkably insensitive to Heathcliff's attitude when she says to him, "if you be ashamed of your touchiness, you must ask pardon, mind, when she comes in", for his concern about her grief is not a straightforward concern lest she be grieved. The notion of grieving her is important to him because through the extent of her grief he can measure her attachment to him and by grieving her he can remind her of that attachment when she tries to deny it. "Well, *I* cried last night, and I had more reason to cry than she",—this is not a simple childish competition; it is a means of punishment and reassurance, pride's refuge when their union seems threatened. How can he sympathize with her pain when her pain stems from her attempt to deny him? And, in turn, Catherine is angry with him because his grief at her insults hurts her, and it is wrong for him to hurt her. Sometimes the spiral is controlled. Sometimes others wound Heathcliff more than Catherine has done, and so it is not out of place for her to comfort him; she does not have to admit herself in the wrong to do so. But the tension of their grieving one another is explosive when it survives the comparative safety of childhood behaviour. Here is Catherine at her last earthly meeting with Heathcliff:

> '. . . and should a word of mine distress you hereafter, think I feel the same distress underground, and for my own sake, forgive me! . . .
>
> Nay, if you nurse anger, that will be worse to remember than my harsh words!
>
> . . .Oh, you see, Nelly! he would not relent a moment, to keep me out of the grave! *That* is how I am loved!' (XV)

Heathcliff's anger will be worse to remember than her harsh words, but it was caused by her harsh words and she would have been furious if Heathcliff did not get angry with her (as she is furious with her husband when he does not get angry with her). She taunts Heathcliff with the image of himself visiting her grave with wife and children by his side, whom he will love more than he now loves her, and he groans at this picture, he feels how strongly it denies his love for her; yet still she is not satisfied with his love; nor is there any way he could satisfy her emotional greed.

Their naturally forged union has been broken by Catherine's marriage and now they must struggle for possession of one another. This struggle is a desperate attack; they cannot be gentle with one another; they must be ruthless in their attempt to maintain their hold upon one another:

> 'I wish I could hold you,' she continued, bitterly, 'till we were both dead! I shouldn't care what you suffered. I care nothing for your sufferings. Why shouldn't you suffer? I do! Will you forget me—will you be happy when I am in the earth? . . . '
>
> 'Don't torture me till I'm as mad as yourself,' cried he, wrenching his head free, and grinding his teeth.
>
> . . . Her present countenance had a wild vindictiveness in its white cheek, and a bloodless lip, and scintillating eye; and she retained in her closed fingers, a portion of the locks she had been grasping. As to her companion, while raising himself with one hand, he had taken her arm with the other; and so inadequate was his stock of gentleness to the requirements of her condi-

tion, that on his letting go, I saw four distinct impressions left blue in the colourless skin. (XV)

Catherine's assertion that she cares nothing for Heathcliff's sufferings does not mean that she is actually indifferent to them. She wants him to suffer; only through his suffering will she be assured of his love for her after she is dead. The "wild vindictiveness" she expresses here is not the hatred and revulsion seen in the love and death struggle between Gudrun and Gerald in *Women in Love*; it is important that Heathcliff's and Catherine's love is not ambivalent as the possessive loves Lawrence portrays; this love becomes a lurid struggle for possession because its intensity and singleness, i.e., its lack of ambivalence, has been ignored by Catherine. But their anger towards one another is never hatred, and the physical pain they inflict upon one another at this meeting is a straightforward expression of love.

This vicious struggle for possession undermines Catherine's assertion that she *is* Heathcliff; but, because she believes this herself, she thinks it safe for her to marry Edgar Linton: Heathcliff is within her soul, therefore nothing can dislodge him. Nonetheless, it is clear from the way they wound one another that each is in continual need of reassurance—something that occurs only between two separate people. Catherine thinks only of her reassurance of her own feelings. She does not consider Heathcliff's need for proof of those feelings. She does not believe she needs to behave in accordance with her feelings, and so, blind to the meaning of her action, she marries Edgar. Heathcliff demands of her:

> '*Why* did you betray your own heart, Cathy? I have not one word of comfort. You deserve this. You have killed yourself . . . You loved me— then what *right* had you to leave me? . . . Because misery, and degradation, and death, and nothing that God or Satan could inflict would have parted us, *you*, of your own will, did it. I have not broken your heart—*you* have broken it—and in breaking it, you have broken mine.' (XV)

"What *right* had you to leave me?" is the cry of outraged passion. Catherine thought she could slip beneath passion's net and take the offer of Edgar's pleasant love, but she is destroyed by her defiance. Her own emotional greed is drawn like a noose round Heathcliff's neck, but she thought he would be satisfied by her own inward assurance that they were one person. Her passion was so real that marriage to her had no reality.

The success of the Catherine/Heathcliff theme depends upon the felt potency of their love, and Mrs Leavis in her classic essay on *Wuthering Heights* [in *Lectures in America,* 1969] complains that Emily Brontë does not show their shared interests, and wonders what they conversed about during their adult companionship; but it is difficult to believe that such knowledge is actually necessary to understanding their attachment. Their shared interests are one another and one another's company. They fought and played and walked much as they had done as children. But it is true that the development and continuation of their attachment is taken for granted. The strength of their attachment is expressed not in dramatic episodes but in extremely effective Romantic rhetoric. The author achieves this rare success partly through oblique presentation of the lovers' outbursts; thus, a direct request for sympathy never embarrasses the reader. Heathcliff's first Tristanesque cry is presented through Lockwood's eyes, and at first the emphasis seems to be on the horror of Heathcliff's fascination with the spectre Lockwood has seen in a dream and which has so terrified him that the apparently ordinary man behaves towards the spectral waif with vicious cruelty. The keen sympathy then forced from the reader comes as a surprise:

> 'Come in! come in!' he sobbed. 'Cathy, do come.
> Oh, do—*once* more! Oh, my heart's darling, hear
> me *this* time—Catherine, at last!' (III)

This cry is heard only once in the novel, yet it carries the force of a relentless repetition. "Hear me *this* time," shows how many times Heathcliff has called to her. Even before the story is known (for at this point Lockwood is ignorant of his landlord's history) the hopeless longing and deadly despair are clear. And when, in Werther fashion, Heathcliff beats his head upon the knotted oak in rage and grief at Catherine's death, sentimentality is just about overcome by Nelly's response: "It hardly moved my compassion—it appalled me". The Romantic exaggeration is effective because its point is not to pull heart strings but to lay bare the inexorable strength of grief and passion.

Catherine's outbursts, on the other hand, do not belong to the Romantic tradition of *Angst*. Always her emotional fits are fits of temper and are undercut by Nelly's impatience. Of Catherine as a child Nelly says, "She beat Hareton, or any child at a good fit of passionate crying". (Imagine an old nurse of Werther's saying "He always did go on a bit much about things". In Goethe's novel passionate fits are valued for their own sake; they are signs of emotional intensity and therefore are good. It is part of the effective Romanticism in **Wuthering Heights** that intensity is seen as a harsh necessity for some natures, not as a decorative thing, and when intensity is indulgently cultivated, it is shown to be so.) And as an adult, angry with Edgar's insistence that she see no more of Heathcliff, Catherine is no more, Nelly says, than a wailing, spoiled child who works herself up to the point of illness. Indeed, Catherine's despair stems from having broken with her childhood; her childish wailing expresses a longing to return to the time when she was able to be at one with her passion. Her illness and frustration stem from the inability to absorb the deepest part of herself within her adult life:

> 'But, supposing at twelve years old, I had been
> wrenched from the Heights, and every early as-
> sociation, and my all in all, as Heathcliff was at
> that time, and been converted at a stroke into
> Mrs Linton, the lady of Thrushcross Grange,
> and the wife of a stranger; an exile and outcast,
> thenceforth, from what had been my world—.'
> (XII)

This fantasy evokes impatience rather than compassion, for Catherine herself is responsible for this harsh transformation; *she* has wrenched herself from the Heights and

from Heathcliff. Nonetheless her longing and frustration have an hypnotic pathos:

> 'Oh, I'm burning! I wish I were out of doors—I
> wish I were a girl again, half savage, and hardy,
> and free; and laughing at injuries, not madden-
> ing under them!' (XII)

The hot, closed room at Thrushcross Grange becomes a prison. Repeatedly she begs Nelly to open a window. Her sense of being stifled by illness and emotional conflict, her vision of the Heights as she leans out of the window, set her within a world impossibly out of contact with the world in which she must live. Her longing rips up reality and fires her dreams with a deathly life; but Catherine's escapism is not the author's, and though the longing is startlingly vivid, there is no suggestion that the author shares it.

Though Emily Brontë does not straightforwardly endorse a scheme of value based upon emotional intensity alone, Catherine and Heathcliff do. When Edgar, as Catherine's husband, wants to know whether she will continue her friendship with Heathcliff even after he has eloped with Isabella and threatened violence to himself, she dismisses his morality of family loyalty and asserts her own:

> 'Oh, for mercy's sake,' interrupted the mistress,
> stamping her foot, 'for mercy's sake, let us hear
> no more of it now! Your cold blood cannot be
> worked into a fever; your veins are full of ice-
> water, but mine are boiling, and the sight of such
> chillness makes them dance'. (XI)

Edgar's arguments have no point because they are not expressed with passion. Her argument against him is simply that she is passionate. Heathcliff, too, continually asserts his rights on the grounds that his feelings are the stronger. He insists, when Edgar banishes him from Catherine's company, that his own emotions are finer:

> 'and there you see the distinction between our
> feelings. Had he been in my place, and I in his,
> though I hated him with a hatred that turned my
> life to gall, I never would have raised a hand
> against him. You may look incredulous, if you
> please! I never would have banished him from
> her society, as long as she desired his'. (XIV)

He despises Edgar for the character of his concern for Catherine and believes that the lower grade of her husband's feelings gives him the right to claim her:

> 'But do you imagine that I shall leave Catherine
> to his *duty* and *humanity?* and can you compare
> my feelings respecting Catherine, to his?' (XIV)

Isabella, too, tries to play their Romantic game. When Catherine is incredulous at her declaration of love for Heathcliff, she replies, "I love him more than you ever loved Edgar". But Isabella does not really understand this Romantic universe. Like Lockwood, she merely fancies herself to be among the passionate ones. Like Lockwood, she believes that suffering for the sake of one's emotions is an attractive, glamorous thing. Her misunderstanding of passion's and cruelty's reality, destroys her.

In ordinary terms Catherine and Heathcliff are unfair in

their assessment of Edgar's feelings, for he certainly does love Catherine; but at no time do his feelings rise to the Romantic standard. After Catherine's death Nelly says of him:

> 'But he was too good to be thoroughly unhappy long. *He* didn't pray for Catherine's soul to haunt him. Time brought resignation, and a melancholy sweeter than common joy. He recalled her memory with ardent, tender love, and hopeful aspiring to the better world, where, he doubted not, she was gone'. (XVII)

How Catherine would have despised his *resignation* and *hopeful aspiring* and *melancholy sweeter than common joy*. She has, after all, said, "If I were only sure it would kill him, . . . I'd kill myself directly!" From her point of view Edgar's return to life would be a betrayal. She would feel that Edgar had no right to live because she had suffered and died. Even Heathcliff, who gives her everything, has difficulty in giving her enough. While she is dying she taunts Heathcliff with his strength and asks how many years he intends to live after she is dead. He demands of her:

> 'Is it not sufficient for your infernal selfishness, that while you are at peace I shall writhe in the torments of hell?'
>
> 'I shall not be at peace,' moaned Catherine. . . . (XV)

Catherine believes that others should die because she has to die, and she accuses both Edgar and Heathcliff of killing her; but once she has passed childhood, and her inability to integrate her emotions into her behaviour shows its poisoning effects, she actually longs for her own death. The desire to return to childhood, the wish for regression and stagnation, is a wish for death, and in her adult life this death wish becomes integrally connected with her love for Heathcliff:

> 'And,' added she, musingly, 'the thing that irks me most is this shattered prison, after all. I'm tired, tired of being enclosed here. I'm wearying to escape into that glorious world, and to be always there; not seeing it dimly through tears, and yearning for it through the walls of an aching heart; but really with it, and in it.' (XV)

She is proud of this wish to escape into death, into the glorious world of her imagination. She believes herself to be better than other people because she desires this, and because the desire will soon be fulfilled:

> 'Nelly, you think you are better and more fortunate than I, in full health and strength. You are sorry for me—very soon that will be altered. I shall be sorry for *you*. I shall be incomparably beyond and above you all.' (XV)

Her death is the means by which she can satisfy her love for Heathcliff—and it is not even the adult Heathcliff she loves, for the real Heathcliff can be so tormented by her emotional greed and accusations that he turns lividly away from her. When the real Heathcliff hurts her because she sees how much she has hurt him, she says, "Never mind, that is not my Heathcliff. I shall have mine yet".

Her love is not a longing for anything in this world; it is a longing for an impossible freedom from emotional conflict and her own excessive demands. Heathcliff shares her desire for death, but he does not want to die simply to regain a lost glorious world; he wants to die because Catherine is dying; he wants to join her in death. "Do I want to live?" he demands of her. "What kind of living will it be when you—oh, God! would *you* like to live with your soul in the grave?" (XV) Catherine does not give a straightforward answer. "Let me alone, let me alone", she sobs; for the perplexing truth is that she does want to live with her soul in the grave. With her soul in the grave she will not be encumbered by her own nature; she will be free to identify with passion alone. In death she feels that the best and deepest part of herself will come alive.

Though Catherine can in part be blamed for the thwarted love between herself and Heathcliff, there is here, as in all cases of Romantic longing, a sense of the impossibility of fulfilment *no matter what*. The intensity of the desire involves an excitement which is far from the pleasure and contentment implied in *happiness*. When Heathcliff returns after his long mysterious absence,

> Catherine flew upstairs, breathless and wild, too excited to show gladness; indeed, by her face, you would rather have surmised an awful calamity. (X)

The excited joy has to battle to find a place in reality; it seems impossible to sustain it in the ordinary world. Catherine "kept her gaze fixed on him as if she feared he would vanish were she to remove it." (X) The inability to trust the reality stems from a nervous intensity which is never resolved. The satisfaction of her longing would be explosive, annihilating. Only death is deep and dark enough to absorb the shock of fulfilment and bring the continuing peace which must follow that fulfilment.

Towards the end of his life Heathcliff becomes a Tristanesque figure, longing for the union with Catherine which will be his death. When he feels close to the realization of his desire he calls himself happy, but it is clear that he is tormented by a mingling of excitement and pain. The young Cathy describes to Hareton how he appeared:

> 'Why almost bright and cheerful—No, almost nothing—*very much* excited, and wild and glad!' (XXIV)

While Heathcliff stands at the open window, watching for Catherine, he is pale, he trembles, there is a "strange joyful glitter in his eyes", and he breathes "as fast as a cat". The description is of one possessed, demonic, but not of someone who is *happy*. The anticipation is unbearable, and he must struggle towards death. He says to Nelly:

> '. . . you might as well bid a man struggling in the water, rest within arms-length of the shore! I must reach it first, and then I'll rest . . . I'm too happy, and yet I'm not happy enough. My soul's bliss kills my body, but does not satisfy itself.' (XXXIV)

The metaphor is ironic, for Heathcliff is swimming towards death, not to a life-sustaining shore; but the irony underlines an essential element of Romanticism—the notion of death as a freer, finer form of life, the notion that death alone can sustain the exultation whose intensity and continuation are thwarted and deflected in life. Death provides for that impossible Romantic combination: ecstasy and peace. Heathcliff's longing has grown to such a pitch that only in death can he rest. His longing makes life an impossible torment. The world, without Catherine, has become a hell: her ghost fills all material objects with her image, other people mock him with their resemblance to her, the entire world is "a dreadful collection of memoranda that she did exist, and that I have lost her!" (XXXIII) Soon his "one universal idea" of joining himself with her in death triumphs; the anticipation carries a bliss of soul which kills his body; only in death is there satisfaction for this devouring Romantic passion.

The destructive, unsatisfiable, death-ridden elements of Romantic love are harshly underlined. There is no sweet nostalgic sense that the lovers might have been happy if only the world had been a bit kinder to them. This love, generated within a Romantic vision, is suffering love. But the harsh facts of such love are not related with a simple moralising tongue, and the main power of the novel does lie in the magnetism of Catherine's and Heathcliff's bond. However, Emily Brontë effectively and convincingly portrays an alternative to that destructive, Romantic love, keeping much of the vitality of the first love, but transforming it into something which can survive in this life.

Young Cathy Linton's nature is similar to that of her mother: she is lively, agile (she delights in swinging from tree branches twenty feet from the ground), pert, affectionate but not always gentle (she awakens Nelly by pulling her hair), proud of her strong emotions and healthy spirits; but the important difference between Cathy and her mother is Cathy's ability to care about hurting people in the sense of not wanting to hurt them, and her ability to suffer at the hands of others without feeling the need for revenge. When her father is ill she promises Nelly that she will not vex him:

> 'I love him better than myself, Ellen; and I know it by this: I pray every night that I may live after him, because I would rather be miserable than that he should be—that proves I love him better than myself.' (XXII)

This shows a complete reversal of her mother's feelings, for Catherine felt that others should suffer at the very least as much as herself. When young Cathy does cause a friend pain she is able to sustain a true regret. In her anger with Linton Heathcliff for insisting that her mother hated her father, she pushes his chair, and he is seized by a suffocating cough. Nelly says that Cathy then "wept with all her might, aghast at the mischief she had done." (XXIII) Nor does she subsequently, as Catherine would have done, grow angry with Linton for upsetting her with the pain she has caused him. Her mother's proud spirit is apparent, but without the vindictiveness:

> 'I'm sorry I hurt you Linton!' she said at length, racked beyond endurance. 'But I couldn't have been hurt by that little push; and I had no idea that you could, either—you're not much, are

you, Linton? Don't let me go home thinking I've done you harm! answer, speak to me.' (XXIII)

Even when faced with Linton's reply, which is a pathetic version of Catherine's morality ("you've hurt me so, that I shall lie awake all night, choking with this cough! . . . but *you'll* be comfortably asleep, while I'm in agony") she presses forward kindly and regretfully, though she fully understands his game:

> 'He's good and patient, now. He's beginning to think I shall have far greater misery than he will to-night, if I believe he is the worse for my visit.' (XXIII)

Only when she is treated with sustained cruelty, when she is separated from those who love her and is tormented by the thought that they are worrying about her, does she become cold, aloof, unhelpful. However, even during her captivity at the Heights, her hostility towards her companions does not completely separate her from them. Nelly says that she complained of loneliness and "preferred quarrelling with Joseph in the kitchen to sitting at peace in her solitude". (XXII) Cathy can work out her hostility through quarrelling whereas her mother could only work herself up. Cathy is able to notice what is happening to other people as she quarrels with them whereas Catherine's mind was devoured by rage and she could only see that people were hurting her. When Hareton is confined to the house on account of an arm injury Catherine is able to understand his pain at their mutual insults and they become friends. Her belief that people should be nice to her because it will make her happy, that they should forgive her unkindnesses because she demands it of them, has more warmth and playfulness, less "infernal selfishness" than similar demands made by her mother. Cathy is able to show gratitude rather than righteousness in the face of forgiveness; she is also able to be patient, and to forgive before forgiveness is granted her:

> 'Say you forgive me, Hareton, do! You can make me so happy, by speaking that little word.'
> He muttered something inaudible.
>
> 'And you'll be my friend?' added Catherine, interrogatively.
>
> 'Nay! You'll be ashamed of me every day of your life . . . '
>
> 'So, you won't be my friend?' she said, smiling as sweet as honey, and creeping close up. (XXXII)

The love between Cathy and Hareton, like that between Catherine and Heathcliff, is forged by habit, without illusion, without ideal. It is also nearly incestuous—they are actually cousins, and Nelly says that they were both really her children—but the close attachment will not confuse and destroy them as it did Catherine and Heathcliff. The strength of their feelings can be expressed in a playfulness which is connected to childhood play but is not simply childish. Catherine and Heathcliff destroyed the possibility of continuing such natural and easy expression of their love, and so the strength of their emotion turned into a Romantic death-ridden passion. It was not simply intense feeling which issued in this darkness; it was intense feeling which demanded to be measured in suffering, and Emily Brontë's diagnosis thus denies the debilitating aspect of the conventional Romantic picture, i.e. that intense feeling cannot survive in this world. For it is only a certain way of measuring emotion, not emotion itself, which explodes into death; it is only a certain way of demanding proof of intense attachment, not the attachment itself, which is destructive. Emily Brontë's assertion of the full-blooded reality and possible survival of emotion gives strength both to the Romantic tragedy of Catherine and Heathcliff and to the happiness of Cathy and Hareton; neither the former couple's suffering nor the latter couple's fulfilment is undercut by a conventionally benign Romanticism. Having shown the harshness and potency of Romantic passion, Brontë concludes by portraying a love which knows its measure without reference to tension and pain. (pp. 205-22)

> T. E. Apter, "Romanticism and Romantic Love in 'Wuthering Heights'," in The Art of Emily Brontë, edited by Anne Smith, London: Vision Press, 1976, pp. 205-22.

Annette R. Federico   (essay date 1985)

[In the following essay, Federico maintains that Wuthering Heights is a bildungsroman—a novel which outlines the initiation of a young character into adulthood—focusing on the development of young Cathy Linton rather than that of her mother.]

In their study of nineteenth-century women writers, The Madwoman in the Attic, Sandra M. Gilbert and Susan Gubar argue persuasively that because the story of **Wuthering Heights** is built around a central fall—generally understood to be Catherine and Heathcliff's anti-Miltonic fall from hell to heaven—"a description of the novel as in part a Bildungsroman about a girl's passage from 'innocence' to 'experience' (leaving aside the precise meaning of these terms) would probably be widely accepted."

This is an interesting interpretation, and brilliantly demonstrated. But like other views of **Wuthering Heights** as a feminine Bildungsroman, the focus of development is Catherine, and by association her male doppelganger Heathcliff. The emphasis upon the first generation of the Heights is, of course, important, and certainly Catherine and Heathcliff suffer their own peculiar rites of passage in their search for identity and wholeness. And yet it is curious that the tortured first generation of Wuthering Heights fail to develop a mature understanding of themselves and others—in fact, Catherine and Heathcliff actually shrink from full participation in adult life, regressing into the adolescent preoccupation with self and the desperate need to feel loved. Catherine, especially, is not so much struggling to grow up as she is struggling not to: it is significant that it is the "waif" not the woman who appears in Lockwood's terrifying dream.

So the critical view of Catherine and Heathcliff as Bildungsroman protagonists neglects these characters' inability to interpret experience realistically and face the limitations of adulthood. In fact, in terms of the first generation, **Wuthering Heights** is not a Bildungsroman at all, but an Entwickslungroman, a novel of mere physical passage without psychological development. Catherine and her male soul-mate remain stubbornly adolescent from beginning to end; granted, they are triumphant, rebellious, passionate characters, and Emily Brontë is obviously celebrating the untamed and undisciplined spirit of adolescent love. But in view of this first generation, **Wuthering Heights** is less a novel of development than a novel of arrested childhood. It is actually with Catherine's death in childbirth that Brontë's Bildungsroman begins. In fact, the second half of **Wuthering Heights** and the concern with young Cathy is a fascinating variation of the prototypic novel of female education in the nineteenth century, a dramatization of the struggle to relinquish childhood for the duties of womanhood in the most traditional, romantic capacity: marriage with the man of one's choice. Cathy emerges from a relatively happy childhood and a lonely adolescence as an assertive, sharing, and contented adult who is prepared to accept the responsibilities and limitations of marriage.

Cathy's marriage to Hareton is in a sense a revision of her mother's unsuccessful marriage to Edgar Linton, and a significant role reversal of the traditional feminine Bildungsroman in which a woman can achieve intellectual and social advancement only through marriage. For example, the elder Catherine looks at marriage as a means of achieving outward sophistication, as well as an escape from mental and emotional stagnation: Edgar is the man who will define her, who will shape her identity and give her status—"He will be rich, and I shall be the greatest woman of the neighborhood, and I shall be proud to have such a husband," she tells Nelly Dean. Catherine's selfish and short-sighted attitude toward marriage is not only indicative of her childish sensibilities, but underscores the traditional theme of the feminine Bildungsroman—that is, the woman must seek knowledge by attaching herself to a knowledgeable male. Brontë varies this theme in her description of young Cathy's courtship with Hareton; instead of marrying to be advanced, Brontë's true female Bildungsroman protagonist marries in order to advance the intellectual and moral status of the male. In young Cathy, Brontë gives us a woman whose acquired humility, patience, and affection yield what promises to be a satisfying marriage and a mutual broadening of experience. More than her mother, Cathy represents a successful passage through the difficult rites of adolescence: the search for self, and the sharing of self with others.

If one looks closely at the novel, it becomes clear that Cathy and Hareton are not merely watered down versions of Catherine and Heathcliff, as Richard Chase suggests. Although the strange, transcendental love of the first generation of the Heights is more stirring, more piquant than the settled affections of Cathy and Hareton, it is only because their type of frenzied passion is so rare—and so typical of adolescence. It is well to ask why Catherine marries Edgar at all, considering her feelings for Heathcliff; her naive belief that she can have both Edgar—who represents culture and security—and Heathcliff, who is the embodiment of sexual and natural energy, proves her complete inability to understand reality outside of her own narrow perspective. When Nelly Dean suggests that by marrying

High Sunderland Hall, near Halifax, a possible model for the Earnshaw residence.

Edgar, Catherine will lose Heathcliff, she is incredulous: "Oh, that's not what I intend—that's not what I mean! I shouldn't be Mrs. Linton were such a price demanded! He'll be as much to me as he has been all his lifetime. Edgar must shake off his antipathy and tolerate him, at least. He will when he learns my true feelings. . . . " It is obvious that Catherine is entering marriage with the stubborn adolescent sensibility that she can have her cake and eat it, too. Of course, this has been her spoiled way of looking at life all along; many times in the novel Brontë portrays Catherine as a selfish, demanding, manipulative child. "I demand it!" is, in fact, Catherine's favorite expression, and completely consistent with the adolescent determination to have everything.

By contrast, young Cathy gradually develops a sensitivity towards the feelings and needs of others. This is most explicit in her devotion to her father, Edgar Linton—and a complete contrast to Catherine's "naughty delight" in provoking Mr. Earnshaw. The young Cathy tells Nelly, "I fret about nothing on earth except papa's illness. . . . And I'll never—never—oh, never, while I have my senses, do anything to vex him. I love him better than myself. . . . " Cathy's comparatively happy childhood has certainly influenced her idealized view of Edgar Linton,

and she is naturally submissive to patriarchal authority. But Cathy is not without spirit; she exhibits the typical adolescent preoccupation with love intrigues, and shares her mother's rebelliousness and scorn for those who interfere with her plans. The important difference between the two generations is in the nature of the rebellion; Catherine's disregard for others—*all* others, except her other-self, Heathcliff—has a cruel, manipulative quality that takes pleasure in deceitfulness and in "punishing" others for their lack of devotion to her. Her many melodramatic "scenes" illustrate Catherine's acting talent in the service of narcissism: as a child, after an argument with Edgar Linton, she says to him, " . . . get away! And now I'll cry—I'll cry myself sick!" and she proceeds to deliver a perfect fit of weeping which softens poor Edgar's heart. Catherine never outgrows these willful displays of mad emotion, and by feigning a fit to arouse her husband's concern, she ultimately brings about her own death. She begs Nelly to tell Edgar she is "in danger of being seriously ill. . . . I want to frighten him. . . . Will you do so, my good Nelly? You are aware that I am in no way blameable in this matter." Catherine often uses Nelly Dean as an instrument for her guile: " . . . and remind Edgar of my passionate temper verging, when kindled, on frenzy." Certainly Catherine's last performance is magnificent, if unsuccessful, for even Nelly is startled by "the aspect of death" her mistress is able to assume. This undisciplined and domineering child—the little girl who wanted her father to bring her a whip from Liverpool—fails to mature at all because she never learns to control her perverse egotism. That in her last breath Catherine looks to Nelly "like a child reviving" aptly suggests the adolescent spirit of the woman's rebellion, a fatal result of Catherine's last scene of "mad resolution."

Unlike her mother's obsessiveness, young Cathy's rebellion is actually a healthy curiosity about her relatives at Wuthering Heights. Certainly it is not surprising that a young and intelligent girl who has not been beyond the range of the park before the age of thirteen, whose only companion is her nurse, and whose only amusements are rambling on the moors and reading, should be eager to make new acquaintances. And of course Cathy passes through certain predictable stages of adolescence; but unlike her mother, she does *pass* through, and restlessness, romantic love, and rebellion are only stages of her development. For example, Cathy and Linton Heathcliff's "love affair" is typical of the adolescent absorption with romantic notions, and the fact that the relationship is somehow taboo makes it all the more alluring. Cathy exaggerates the importance of her love letters, weeping and pleading to Nelly "to spare one or two." Nelly Dean's common sense reply to the mere suggestion of Cathy loving Linton is, "Loving! Pretty loving indeed, and both times together you have seen Linton hardly four hours in your life!" That Cathy is able to open her mind to this objective, adult point of view is a credit to her maturity, and something the older Catherine never learned to do.

In her relationship to Linton, Cathy begins to learn that her desires are complex and that her experience of reality must be reconciled to actual reality—in other words, *her* view of Linton Heathcliff as "a pretty little darling" must be reconciled to Nelly's less generous description: "The worst-tempered bit of a sickly slip that ever struggled into its teens!" In learning to distinguish between what she *thinks* she wants (Linton) and what she *really* wants (an energetic and empathetic companion), Cathy begins to achieve the disciplined growth and broad perspective which is the undertaking of the *Bildungsroman* protagonist. Simply the way she handles Heathcliff and her captivity at Wuthering Heights demonstrates an intelligent, unselfish, and practical kind of defiance which Catherine never displayed, because Catherine acknowledged only her own needs and desires. When Linton says, "You *must* obey my father, you *must*," Cathy replies, "I must obey my own," reflecting her growing sense of responsibility. After her forced marriage, she is prepared to accept the consequences of her situation by loving Linton in spite of Heathcliff—"You cannot make us hate each other!" Cathy remains dignified and controlled, and speaks "with a kind of dreary triumph: she seemed to have made up her mind to enter into the spirit of her future family, and draw pleasure from the griefs of her enemies."

If Nelly's narrative makes Cathy's behavior sound reminiscent of the older Catherine's vengeful fits, it should be pointed out that Cathy's "enemies" are *real,* not fancied, conspirators. Heathcliff at this point has kidnapped her, kept her from her dying father, abused her physically, and forced her to marry his sickly, peevish son. Cathy's situation is wretched, almost hopeless; when Linton dies shortly after their degenerate union, she is left at Wuthering Heights with only Hareton and Heathcliff. And here her *bildung* or education needs to be emphasized. Part of education and development is arriving at an understanding of one's value; this, I would argue, is the major undertaking of adolescence. The older Catherine never sees herself realistically. She has notions of superiority and self importance that can be justified only in terms of her exceptionally passionate nature and her extraordinary bond to Heathcliff. Catherine's immature and narrow vision cannot imagine that she is not the central concern in everyone else's life. It is almost an epiphany when she says to Nelly, "How strange! I thought, though everybody hated and despised each other, they could not avoid loving me." Despite Heathcliff's furious devotion and her husband's genuine affection, Catherine always feels unloved and undervalued. Even as she is dying, she cries, "*That* is how I am loved!" like a self-pitying child. Nor does Catherine value the love of others: "I have such faith in Linton's love," she says, "that I believe I might kill him, and he wouldn't wish to retaliate." Rarely if ever is Catherine described as a loving person, one who is willing to give the self freely to another; even her professed love for Heathcliff is strangely qualified by her claim, "I *am* Heathcliff!" He seems to be only a kind of narcissistic double.

Young Cathy of course wants to be loved, but unlike her mother she is willing to take the risks and suffer the consequences of loving another. When she kisses Hareton in an effort to make peace, she is conquering her pride and scorn—and her loneliness—in a way that truly suggests maturity. She is beginning to see herself in relation to others, beginning to develop a realistic adult perspective. For example, Cathy knows she has been unfair and cruel to Hareton, and sincerely tries to improve their relationship in the best—the most straightforward—way she knows how. "When I call you stupid, I don't mean anything—I don't mean that I despise you," she explains, and by articulating her meaning she arrives at a closer understanding of the way she affects others. By humbling herself, Cathy learns to master herself, and by offering her friendship to Hareton, she is on the verge of a new, perhaps more traditional, kind of education: marriage. But the marriage of Cathy and Hareton is not the traditional union of the male teacher/master and the female learner/servant. By reversing the roles and making Cathy the educator, **Wuthering Heights** takes on the aspects of a new feminine *Bildungsroman* in which a woman emerging from childhood and adolescence approaches marriage not merely as a means of social advancement, or knowledge, or security, but as a mutual broadening of experience in which love balances power, with "both their minds tending to the same point."

So it is with the second generation of the Heights that Brontë begins her feminine *Bildungsroman.* If Catherine and Heathcliff have a more tumultuous and exciting story, it may be because theirs is the tale of arrested childhood, a furious protest against the necessity of growing up. Perhaps Cathy's struggle is less stormy and her future too settled and neat to satisfy our lingering adolescent admiration for rebellion, stubborn self satisfaction, and emotional intensity. But in the world of *Wuthering Heights,* as in our own, the passage from innocence to experience is an awkward limbo, a thin papery wall, between two selves—between the waif outside the window, and the woman within. (pp. 26-8)

Annette R. Federico, "The Waif at the Window: Emily Brontë's Feminine 'Bildungsroman'," in The Victorian Newsletter, No. 68, Fall, 1985, pp. 26-8.

Marjorie Burns   (essay date 1986)

[*In the essay below, Burns explores the unconventional depictions of the biblical Eden throughout* Wuthering Heights.]

Images of Eden, that enclosed and favoured realm, appear throughout the novel *Wuthering Heights* in recurring patterns of innocence and unity, seduction and fall. Yet Eden itself is not mentioned directly. We have instead incidents that imitate the Eden story (though always in ways that challenge traditional accounts) and frequent references to paradise, purgatory, heaven, and hell—parallel realms associated with Eden and, like it, representative of bliss or despair, harmony or disruption.

Although Thrushcross Grange, with its walled park and cultivated fruit trees (most notably the apple tree traditionally associated with the Fall) is an easy parallel to Eden, the rough and pandemonic Heights also has its Edenic side. Only here can the bonding of Catherine and Heathcliff flourish, a bonding which is destroyed when the Grange and its mannered society come in touch with their energetic and idiosyncratic world. This does not mean, however, that we should read *Wuthering Heights* as a simple reversal, as a variation on Blake's *The Marriage of Heaven and Hell* with its idealized devils and its dissatisfying angels. Though there is clearly something of an inversion in Emily Brontë's depiction of these two households (the violent has its loyalty and innocence, the peaceful its imperfections and falsity), the entrance of Edgar into the Heights is no less disruptive than Heathcliff's entrance into the Grange. Both men serve as tempters in each other's realm, Edgar with an offer of order and civility that has no place in the restless world of Wuthering Heights and Heathcliff (more clearly a serpent figure) with unhampered energy and vengeful intent, scaling the walls of the Linton Park.

The first clear parallel to the Eden story occurs at Thrushcross Grange. This is a world that suggests peace, civilization, and adherence to established order. Tea is taken in the parlour; books are perused at leisure; servants, attentive but somewhat vaguely depicted, move in the background. There is an innocence of labour here for the ruling Lintons, not even the 'pleasant labour' of Milton's Garden of Eden. Work is carried out—trimming and planting and maintenance—but removed from sight. It is a domesticated, easeful world of ponies and lapdogs, a world named for the thrush.

We first see Thrushcross Grange from the outside, through one of Emily Brontë's recurrent windows, and it seems a haven. The children, Catherine and Heathcliff, on their night-time escape, their 'ramble at liberty', creep like two dark, wild forces 'through a broken hedge', grope their way up the path, perch on the basement, and peer into the house through the window that divides them from the Lintons.

> Ah! it was beautiful—a splendid place carpeted with crimson, and crimson-covered chairs and tables, and a pure white ceiling bordered by gold, a shower of glass-drops hanging in silver chains from the centre, and shimmering with little soft tapers. Old Mr and Mrs Linton were not there. Edgar and his sister had it entirely to themselves; shouldn't they have been happy? We should have thought ourselves in heaven! (ch. 6)

Heaven, indeed, to two berated, unloved scamps! And yet our appreciation, though drawn to the warmth and light, remains with the world that Catherine and Heathcliff have travelled through, that essence of the Heights and the moors that they carry with them, for there is pettiness in paradise, and discontent. Edgar and Isabella, the inhabitants of this Eden, are less than ideally represented. 'And now, guess what your good children were doing?' says Heathcliff. 'Isabella . . . lay screaming at the farther end of the room, shrieking as if witches were running red hot needles into her'. Edgar stood by the hearth 'weeping silently' and on a table sat yelping a little dog which 'they had nearly pulled in two between them'.

Envy and admiration for the world of the Grange fades. We see that Isabella and Edgar, the 'petted things', are pets themselves, domesticated, pampered, and soft as puppies, pale creatures who ride to church in the family carriage, 'smothered in cloaks and furs'. (ch. 7) 'When would you catch me wishing to have what Catherine wanted?' says Heathcliff, 'or find us by ourselves, seeking entertainment in yelling, and sobbing, and rolling on the ground, divided by the whole room? I'd not exchange, for a thousand lives, my condition here for Edgar Linton's at Thrushcross Grange' (ch. 6).

And yet, in a sense, this is exactly what Heathcliff will later attempt to do, for from this first confrontation comes further contact and increased and troubling interaction between the two households. Just as familiarity with the Lintons will irrevocably and unhappily alter Catherine and Heathcliff's future, bringing class consciousness and worldly values into their lives, so too will their entrance into the Grange's luxurious and sheltered world ultimately lead to the collapse of Linton privilege and Linton complacency.

Though the final effects of Grange and Heights affiliation is reciprocally destructive, the first invasion unquestionably comes from Catherine and Heathcliff. It is their action that sets the disruptive series of events into motion Edgar, when he comes to visit Wuthering Heights, will do so by invitation, by employing all the proper methods of society, and he'll visit by day. But Catherine and Heathcliff are trespassers. They invade by night, uninvited and intent on mischief, and the world they invade is clearly suggestive of paradise.

In context of the Eden story, are we expected, then, to see Catherine and Heathcliff as Satan figures? The answer, like most answers about *Wuthering Heights,* is a somewhat complicated yes and no—yes, in that they have entered the sanctum of the Grange, broken through the barrier hedge, and disturbed the stale air of that world (and disturbed it in ways that will have increasingly unpleasant repercussions). We can carry the analogy further, keeping in mind *Paradise Lost,* which, Winifred Gérin tells us, was a great favourite of Emily Brontë's father, Patrick Brontë. The night 'ramble at liberty', which brings them for the first time to Thrushcross Grange, comes after a description of Mr Earnshaw's death and Hindley's coming to power at Wuthering Heights. Heathcliff, the usurping foundling preferred by Mr Earnshaw, loses his position as the favoured, chosen son; and becomes an outsider and a rebel. In this he is like Satan, who (in Christian tradition and *Paradise Lost*) broods over 'Christ's celestial legitimacy' and becomes the rebel angel. Heathcliff, along with Catherine, now plans revenge. The two of them vow 'to grow up as rude as savages' (which is, of course, to refuse to grow up at all). Like Satan, their revolt to a large extent is a revolt against a religious regime, against Sundays spent 'reading sermons, and being catechised' or being 'set to learn a column of Scripture names' (ch. 6). The night of the ramble, these two 'unfriended creatures', like a pair of Milton's exiled angels, have been banished from the warmth and comfort of the 'sitting-room' to the 'washhouse', a place clearly chosen for its pervading discomfort. From here they escape, as the exiled Satan does from hell, and visit the paradisiacal Grange.

'We thought we would just go and see whether the Lintons passed their Sunday evenings standing shivering in corners, while their father and mother sat eating and drinking, and singing and laughing, and burning their eyes out before the fire', says Heathcliff. Now, with the door to the Heights bolted behind them, they make their way into Eden, rebellious and indifferent to what trouble they might create.

It is not that simple, of course. How seriously can we take two such small devil figures who are, in fact, nothing more than mistreated and misbehaving children, children who enter Eden in a state of revolt and resentment and whose greatest crimes are curiosity, the making of 'frightful noises' to 'terrify' the Linton children, and Heathcliff's 'recommended cursing'? As Satans they are imperfectly bad, just as the inhabitants of Paradise are imperfectly good and Paradise itself (with its quarrelling inhabitants and its 'devil' dog guarding the grounds) is a good bit less than ideal.

In this first invasion of Thrushcross Grange, Eden and the Eden story are skilfully suggested but purposely left inexact and incomplete. However, the failure of the Grange to reach perfection does not, in itself, make Wuthering Heights a paradise by contrast. When we turn to the Heights and attempt to gauge that unruly and contrary household by an Eden measuring stick of its own, we run up against a new set of complexities, a new set of contradictions. It is unquestionably easier to see the hellish qualities of that 'infernal house' than it is to see the Edenic. Though it lies on the heights above the Grange, as Milton's Eden lies above the 'subjected Plain' to which Adam and Eve are later banished, Wuthering Heights is clearly not paradisiacal in any conventional sense. 'Wuthering', we are told, is a regional adjective depicting 'atmospheric tumult', and 'the excessive slant of a few stunted firs at the the end of the house' and 'a range of gaunt thorns all stretching their limbs one way, as if craving alms of the sun' (ch. 1) in no way suggest the grace and fecundity one expects in a Garden of Eden.

Add to this an undeniable element of nastiness—beyond the wind and weather—a nastiness which has always been present at the Heights, even before Mr Earnshaw's death, and which is perhaps best exemplified by the servant Joseph, who endures almost uncannily from generation to generation, bullying and berating with 'religious curses' and prophecies of doom. In Lockwood's words, Wuthering Heights is 'a perfect misanthropist's heaven' (ch. 1). It is here, in scenes reminiscent of Goethe's 'Witch's Kitchen' (infernal and comic at once), that he is threatened by the Cerebus trio of dogs within the house and finally attacked by two of these hell hounds ('They suffer no resurrection') when he attempts to leave. Nonetheless Heathcliff's insistence that he would 'not exchange for a thousand lives' his situation at Wuthering Heights, and Catherine's girlhood dream, her rejection of Heaven in preference to the moors, must turn us back to the Heights as a rough and vivid home, a shelter of time or place that in its way too serves as an Eden. As adults, as the mistress of Thrushcross Grange or as master of both the Grange and the Heights, they never again experience the freedom of spirit and the passionate unity they knew as children. 'The greatest punishment we could invent for her', says Nelly of Catherine, 'was to keep her separate from him' (ch. 5). In the same way, Heathcliff cannot imagine wishing to be 'divided by the whole room' from Catherine, as the young Lintons are from each other when we first see them through the window of Thrushcross Grange. And though Heathcliff may covet and claim the horse belonging to the temporarily dispossessed and rather unappealing Hindley, there is no envy in his feelings for Catherine. 'When would you catch me wishing to have what Catherine wanted?'

But this assured and unquestioned loyalty cannot last. Heathcliff, after trespassing into Thrushcross Grange, is dragged away and has the door 'secured' behind him. The larger world of the Grange has invaded Catherine and Heathcliff's private world, and the two are driven apart. In the eyes of the Lintons, Heathcliff has no right to Catherine or to the privileges of her class. He is a 'gypsy', a 'castaway', a 'wicked boy, at all events . . . quite unfit for a decent house', while Catherine is 'Miss Earnshaw' (the name and status emphasized by repetition) and worthy of Linton respect and Linton attention.

Once at the Grange, Catherine is tempted by the world, and in yielding to this temptation ('for she was full of ambition') she brings about a fall from innocence as thorough as any in Genesis or *Paradise Lost,* though hers, as [Sandra] Gilbert and [Susan] Gubar point out [in *The Mad-woman in the Attic,* 1979], is not so much a religious fall *from* grace as it is a fall *into* grace in its social sense. Luxury seduces her. Catherine eats the foods of Thrushcross Grange, the 'plateful of cakes' and drinks the spiced, warm 'tumbler of negus'. And Heathcliff watches, this time separated by the window through which he and Catherine had earlier peered together. The taming of Catherine has begun, a process which will bring her to leave behind her rough girlhood ways and take up manners and clothing that require inhibited motion and artificial posturing. The girl who five weeks before raced barefoot in the dark from 'the top of the Heights to the park' (ch. 6) is now hampered by fashion and airs ('clothes and flattery') and seems to have fulfilled Mrs Linton's fearful prediction on seeing her wounded ankle, 'She may be lamed for life!' (ch. 6). When we see her next, she is no longer 'a wild, hatless little savage jumping into the house, and rushing to squeeze us all breathless'. Now there alights 'from a handsome black pony a very dignified person with brown ringlets falling from the cover of a feathered beaver, and a long cloth habit which she was obliged to hold up with both hands that she might sail in' (ch. 7).

With Catherine's return, the values of Thrushcross Grange enter Wuthering Heights. Now comes the period of Catherine's 'double character'. 'In the place where she heard Heathcliff termed a "vulgar young ruffian", and "worse than a brute", she took care not to act like him; but at home she had small inclination to practise politeness that would only be laughed at' (ch. 8). Edgar visits, bringing with him a continuation of luxury, comfort, and an artificiality of manners that allows her to say, in attempting to talk herself into accepting his proposal, 'I love the ground under his feet, and the air over his head, and everything he touches, and every word he says', unconvincing platitudes, as Nelly is quick to recognize. Edgar, Catherine sees, will be rich; and by marrying him she can become 'the greatest woman of the neighbourhood' (ch. 9).

This is the temptation Edgar presents; this is the attraction that brings Catherine to duplicity 'without exactly intending to deceive anyone' (ch. 8) and allows her to betray Heathcliff and her own heart. It is Edgar now who is the invader, whose influence disrupts an established good. As a classical figure of satanic destruction, however, Edgar makes a poor showing. His visits to the Heights are not intentionally destructive any more than Heathcliff and Catherine's first visit to the Grange had been. Edgar neither recognizes nor understands the bond that has held Catherine and Heathcliff together. He is, in fact, only minimally aware of Heathcliff's presence at Wuthering Heights. And yet we have his off-handed gibe about Heathcliff's shaggy locks, and there is as well a suggestion of predatory nastiness in Nelly's depiction of Edgar's courtship: 'He possessed the power to depart, as much as a cat possesses the power to leave a mouse half killed, or a bird half eaten' (ch. 9). But whatever his intentions, the unity of Catherine and Heathcliff is ultimately destroyed by this invasion of Grange manners and Grange opinion. Inevitably Heathcliff and Catherine grow further and further apart. There comes the night when Heathcliff over-

hears Catherine saying, 'It would degrade me to marry Heathcliff now', and the fall is complete.

It doesn't matter that Catherine goes on to confess that Heathcliff is 'more myself than I am' or that her love for Edgar is merely temporary 'like the foliage in the woods' or that by marrying Edgar, she hopes she 'can aid Heathcliff to rise'. Her argument has no more validity than the argument of the fallen Eve, assuring Adam of a 'Godhead; which for thee / Chiefly I sought' [*Paradise Lost*]. The damage is done. Heathcliff, more dramatically though less willingly than Catherine, abandons Wuthering Heights and the childhood it represents. By his own means, he will gain the wealth and outer trappings of civilization that Catherine has come to value, and in doing so, he will re-enact the tale of our first 'parents'. Like Adam, he will share in her fall—will bite the fruit she has bitten and take on with her the knowledge of good and evil.

For Catherine and Heathcliff the knowledge they acquire is the knowledge of adult society. The innocence they lose is the innocence of childhood, and their Eden has been childhood itself. To those familiar with Emily Brontë's poetry there is nothing surprising in this. Golden-haired girls and dark, melancholy boys 'all doomed alike to sin and mourn' appear throughout the poems, as does the word 'Eden' in reference to the unfallen state of childhood. It is a particularly appropriate term in the Gondal poems for the 'paradise lost' island of Ula ('Ula's Eden sky').

> I thought of many a happy day
> Spent in her Eden isle,
> With my dear comrades, young and gay,
> All scattered now so far away,
> But not forgot the while!

By specifically associating Eden with childhood Emily Brontë is following a convention of the times. In an age uneasy with adulthood, or with the sense of moral failure that comes with adulthood, only the child or childlike—Mr Dick in *David Copperfield,* for example—are seen as innocent. To put it simply (and borrowing from William Empson), 'The child has not yet been put wrong by civilization, and all grown-ups have been'.

It is only in her poetry, however, that Emily Brontë expresses the usual nineteenth-century sentiment about childhood and its Edenic nature: 'Dear childhood's Innocence', 'the pure light of childhood's morn', the 'darling enthusiast, holy child'. *Wuthering Heights* is another matter. Sentimental references to children are markedly lacking in this novel where violence and spite are the norm and where the children are as violent and spiteful as the adults. Nonetheless childhood innocence does exist in *Wuthering Heights.* It exists in Catherine and Heathcliff before their night visit to the Grange under the dairy woman's cloak. It exists in all the children figures that dominate and haunt *Wuthering Heights,* a novel full of children and the memories and ghosts of children. They come in pairs: Catherine and Heathcliff, Isabella and Edgar, young Cathy and Linton; and finally Cathy and Hareton. We have, as well, the short-lived pairing of Nelly and Hindley ('foster' siblings in their early years) and the brief coalition of Catherine and Hindley at Heathcliff's arrival. Even Frances and Hindley (though less clearly) fit this pattern in their childlike and pettish rule of the Heights, a rule more suggestive of 'playing house' than anything appropriately adult. 'Like two babies' (ch. 3) is Catherine's girlhood description of her brother and his wife.

All these children, all these pairs, begin with innocence; but innocence is not the same as docility or sweetness of temper, as Emily Brontë well knew; and she demonstrates this conviction by creating (most consistently in the first generation) children who are vivid but not particularly likeable: Catherine 'too mischievous and wayward for a favourite', Heathcliff 'not insolent to his benefactor' but 'simply insensible' (ch. 5) and those 'petted things', the pale and indulged Lintons. Our first view of the Grange children is of a weeping Edgar and a shrieking Isabella in the aftermath of the quarrel in which 'they had nearly pulled [the little dog] in two'. Nor is this behaviour simply the result of Grange indulgence. Catherine and Hindley, though less accustomed to luxury, acted much the same when the child 'dark almost as if it came from the devil' (ch. 4) arrived from Liverpool and Hindley—as weak spirited as Edgar—fell to blubbering over the loss of his violin and Catherine, for spite, made faces at the foundling. Even Heathcliff and Catherine, our main child pair and our main focus, are no improvement. We may side with these two, attributing their particular failings to high spirits and defiance in the face of tyranny, but it would be hard to make a case for their moral superiority. They, even more clearly than the others, repudiate the Victorian ideal of a sweet and compliant childhood.

More needs to be said about these child couples. By creating such matched pairs of siblings or playmates of the opposite sex, Emily Brontë is again following a nineteenth-century convention. Such boy/girl couples allowed for a type of innocent mating, small Adams and Eves in a prelapsarian state (*play*-mates, in fact), and the literature is full of examples: Tom and Maggie Tulliver in *The Mill on the Floss,* Pip and Estella in *Great Expectations,* Graham and Polly in *Villette,* or Carroll's 'Sylvie and Bruno'. In **Wuthering Heights,** however, the focus on the child or child couple is carried further than usual by both the sheer number of these pairs and also by the early loss of the adult generation. This is a world where adults seem peripheral, a world where the older generation neatly and quietly dies off before the main action begins. It is a mythopoetic world that stands for more than itself, where a small cast of players on a small stage is enough to represent the fate of the race. This is why concern for progenitors and descendants alike is so often absent in the novel; why Heathcliff, having no ties with past or future, needs no last name; and why the setting is purposefully narrow and the outside world beyond the Grange or Heights ill defined and of no real importance. (Where does Heathcliff come from? Or Frances? Where does Hindley go when he leaves the Heights? Or Heathcliff? Or Isabella?) The answers to such questions have no place in the story; they are beyond the range of our concern.

On one level it is as though the children in **Wuthering Heights** spring unaccompanied and untended into the world. Even young Cathy begins as 'an unwelcomed infant' wailing while 'nobody cared a morsel' (ch. 16). Parents are notoriously absent, indifferent, or easily lost to death. What, for example, do we see of the older Lintons? Never more than shadow figures, they are there in the background, owners of the attacking dog and servants, vague temporary support, host and hostess who conveniently take ill and fade from the picture, allowing Edgar and Isabella to come prematurely into possession of Thrushcross Grange, just as Hindley and Frances come unprepared and unguided into possession of Wuthering Heights. Inexperienced, youthful—and often thoughtless and selfish—they step into adult roles, no more ready to rule the Grange or Heights than the newly created Adam and Eve were ready to rule the Garden. For each of us, Emily Brontë seems to be saying, the world is created anew, and we ourselves are Adams and Eves alone in our Edens of childhood, and each of us alone confronts the Fall.

What follows for Catherine after Heathcliff's departure is illness and resignation. In the period of her convalescence she is invited to the Grange by Mrs Linton. 'But the poor dame had reason to repent of her kindness' (ch. 9), for Catherine's second stay at the Grange brings death to the older generation, much as Heathcliff's arrival at Wuthering Heights, though less directly or quickly, seems to herald the end of Mr and Mrs Earnshaw. Catherine marries, enters the drowsy seclusion of Thrushcross Grange and so becomes imprisoned. The Eden world of the Grange appears once again to be intact and reigned over by a new Mr and Mrs Linton. A cycle has completed itself. But once again the surface peace of this pale, complacent world is disrupted. The quiet and 'deep and growing happiness' (ch. 10), that Nelly, our somewhat unreliable narrator, claims to see in this newlywed couple, is invaded, threatened, and lost.

The story picks up again when Heathcliff reappears after a three-year absence, outwardly a gentleman 'worthy of any one's regard'. His first visit to Thrushcross Grange is based, he tells us, on a wish to have only 'one glimpse of [Catherine's] face' (ch. 10), yet again his presence will upset the status quo, and this time the effects will reach deeper and wider, collapsing the inherited structure of both households. His reappearance is clearly satanic and his subsequent visits equally so.

'On a mellow evening in September, I was coming from the garden with a heavy basket of apples', says Nelly. 'It had got dusk, and the moon looked over the high wall of the court, causing undefined shadows to lurk in the corners of the numerous projecting portions of the building' (ch. 10). A voice calls out; Nelly, fearful, turns and sees 'a tall man dressed in dark clothes, with dark face and hair'. His fingers are on the latch, 'as if intending to open for himself'. Heathcliff has returned, and a reluctant Nelly is sent to inform Catherine of his presence. The dark setting, the dark man in the garden, the apples, Nelly's strong reluctance to dispel the 'wonderously peaceful' scene in the parlour, and Heathcliff's statement that he is 'in hell' until word can reach Catherine all have echoes of the Eden story, and these echoes, especially of Satan in the garden, will continue. It is here in the garden that Heathcliff meets Isabella and from here elopes with her, and here again he hangs her dog. During Catherine's final illness, he again waits in the garden, as he will later wait for word of Catherine's death and for a chance to visit her corpse. 'Last night, I was in the Grange garden six hours, and I'll return there to-night; and every night I'll haunt the place, and every day, till I find an opportunity of entering' (ch. 14).

This emphasis on Satan and rebellious satanic figures stems from Emily Brontë's earliest literary experiences. In Byron 'Emily found the champion of unsociable man', writes Winifred Gérin, but Satan in *Paradise Lost* had an even stronger influence. 'The sense of thwarted power in the fallen angel, conscious of his lost rights, stirred her to admiration and sympathy'. From this come both the 'holy child' figure 'doomed to be / Hell-like in heart and misery' in Emily Brontë's poetry and Heathcliff in **Wuthering Heights.** From the first, as a 'dirty, ragged' foundling, Heathcliff is associated with the demonic, but after his return as an adult until the close of the novel, the Satan/devil/serpent imagery increases prodigiously. The adult Heathcliff is a 'devil', a 'hellish villain', 'a lying fiend, a monster, and not a human being'. Even Catherine recognizes this side of Heathcliff, warning Isabella that he is an 'unreclaimed creature' and adding to Nelly that the idea of offering Heathcliff a wife is 'as bad as offering Satan a lost soul' (ch. 11).

The 'vagabond', the 'gipsy', even the 'imp of Satan' that Heathcliff was called as a child had no impact like this. Now we have the conscious man, the adult, aware of the injury he inflicts and planning it with care. Nonetheless, the story that follows Heathcliff's return, though it focuses on adult characters and is seen through adult eyes, is not so removed from the earlier part. Everything relates back to the novel's primary event: Catherine and Heathcliff's separation and fall. The hopes and failures of their childhood give rise to the specific temptations and failures of their adulthood. More falls are to come, all centred on choices made by the main characters as children. There are, in fact, good reasons for feeling that we never leave the children behind even as we continue with their adult stories. Lockwood dreams of Catherine the ghost child, not Catherine the adult. The child that existed before still exists as a force or a spirit capable of manifestation and influence. Even Nelly has a vision of Hindley as a child, her 'early playmate', who some moments later seems to blend with the 'elf-locked' Hareton at the gates of Wuthering Heights. There is as well a persistent childishness in the now grown-up characters that makes it difficult to feel much has changed. Unlike the older Lintons and Earnshaws, this generation will never seem fully adult. The married Edgar and the full-grown Isabella are still referred to as 'childish'. ('Spoiled children', Catherine terms them.) And Catherine herself is 'no better than a wailing child' in her illness, engaging in what Nelly dismisses as 'baby-work' with pillow feathers. More pointedly, Catherine herself wishes to be a girl again, 'half savage, and hardy, and free' and imagines in her fevered state this is so. 'The whole last seven years of my life grew a blank! I did not recall that they had been at all. I was a child' (ch. 12). As she dies, her child self seems to return in full; Nelly

describes Catherine in her last moments as a child stretching, 'reviving, and sinking again to sleep' (ch. 16).

With Heathcliff's return the pretence of adulthood has been stripped aside. Catherine, who had assumed, 'oddly enough, that she [could] maintain the two relationships, the social and the ungoverned, the married and the passionate', now finds this impossible [Albert J. Guérard in *Twentieth-Century Interpretations of Wuthering Heights,* 1968]. Where Nelly had seen 'growing happiness' and relative stability for the new couple, Catherine now tells her of the 'very, very bitter misery' (ch. 10) she has endured. Her peace in marriage has been one of forgetting. She has denied her first and truest nature and become 'Mrs Linton, the lady of Thrushcross Grange, and the wife of a stranger; an exile, and outcast' (ch. 12). There is no return to the Eden of childhood and no further happiness where she is. To remain with Edgar is to yield to motherhood, lineage, and social position. To be again with Heathcliff is to remember (and long for) her lost independence and freedom and what Thomas Vogler calls 'the unself-conscious intensity of childlike emotions' [*Twentieth–Century Interpretations of Wuthering Heights,* 1968]. One is no longer acceptable, the other no longer possible. Catherine is held by the Grange's soft restraints, trapped by the limitations of mortal life, by her nature, her society, and her physical body, by 'this shattered prison' which binds her to this world. Death is the only release. 'You and Edgar have broken my heart', Catherine tells Heathcliff; 'You have killed me' (ch. 15). She dies, more by willing it than by any certain illness, and the infant Cathy, like an afterthought, a by-product of her mother's death, is born. This generation too will seem under-parented.

The indifference Catherine bears toward her pregnancy is striking. 'On her existence depended that of another' (ch. 13) we are told, but we are not given much indication, beyond one rather stilted statement about 'half-a-dozen nephews' (ch. 10) to erase Isabella's title as heir, ('please Heaven!') to suggest any genuine concern on Catherine's part for the next generation. Illness is not the cause of her indifference. Compare the dying Frances's concern for the infant Hareton! What seems to be behind her indifference is a rejection of her role as an adult, the role demanded by both nature and society. Eve, in her fallen state is to be 'mother of all living'. Catherine, once Heathcliff is back in her life, will have none of this.

In spite of his one comment about wishing to find Linton 'a worthy object of pride' (ch. 20), it is even more difficult to associate Heathcliff with parenthood than it is Catherine. Much of this comes from a consistent comparison of Heathcliff with winter and sterile elements in nature. He is the 'bleak, hilly, coal country' while Edgar is 'a beautiful fertile valley', (ch. 8) and even Catherine refers to him as 'an arid wilderness of furze and whinstone' (ch. 10). Yet, again following Catherine's lead, he produces a child, Linton, whom he values only as a means of enacting his revenge.

Neither Catherine nor Heathcliff wishes an existence beyond their own, beyond the one they shared together as children. To yield to parenthood is to yield the self, to yield autonomy. It is all part of the pattern of what splits apart the simple wholeness of the child, the innocence of boy and girl together, and splits them again into father or mother and offspring, into separate and opposing units. At some level, conflict is inevitable; the entrance of the new marks the end of the old. Like Heathcliff and Hindley contending throughout their lives for mastery of Wuthering Heights, the generations too must contend. They are, in a sense, in each other's way; and this in part seems to explain why so often in the novel the younger seem to bring death to the older; Heathcliff to the older Earnshaws, Catherine to the older Lintons, Cathy to Catherine, and perhaps even Linton to Isabella. This is the fate of generations, the trap of Genesis itself, Eve's curse, that 'in sorrow' she shall 'bring forth children' and that her disobedience brings death to her and Adam and to their unhappy race that follows.

'You loved me', cries Heathcliff, 'then what *right* had you to leave me? What right—answer me—for the poor fancy you felt for Linton? Because misery, and degradation, and death, and nothing that God or Satan could inflict would have parted us, *you,* of your own will, did it' (ch. 15). And yet what choice does Catherine have, and how can we blame her? Edgar Linton's attention flatters a part of Catherine that must inevitably appear; that is, she must grow up; and this may explain why Catherine can move so quickly from rough girl to apparent lady. One bite of the apple is enough, and all is changed. 'Who is to separate us?' (ch. 9) Catherine asks before Heathcliff leaves Wuthering Heights. But there is no stopping the biological clock that insists on childhood's end. And something more is at work. Catherine realizes a power in her ability to attract Edgar. Marriage being part of the inevitable requirements of life, why not marry into the comforts that Hindley and Frances hoard to themselves, into even more than Hindley and Frances have? Catherine is not insulting Heathcliff when she says 'It would degrade me to marry Heathcliff now'. This is a fact. She is becoming an adult, and degradation is an adult's concern. As two dirty, half-savage children such degradation had no effect on them, but the fall into adulthood (into sexuality and social system) wedges in between the two, and the children who lay in each other's arms 'in a union which was prior to sexual differentiation' are propelled into otherness, into class and sex roles, into inhibition and deceit [J. Hillis Miller].

Who is the villain now that enters paradise and shatters its peace? Is it so much the Linton element, Edgar's visits to the Heights tempting an Eve away from her natural and innocent state? Or is it perhaps simply the way life is in this world, caught up as we are with cycles and seasons and social standards that thrust us out of innocence into awareness, an apple of knowledge forced through our teeth, whether we choose to eat or not? The cycle of generations is a fact; social systems, hierarchies, inherited rights and all the artificialities that accompany these systems are unavoidable facts.

'Childhood's flower must waste its bloom', Emily Brontë writes in her poetry. Innocence disintegrates into awareness, experience, and—finally—adulthood. The 'iron man' of Emily Brontë's Gondal poems is no longer 'an ardent boy'. He has lost the child's sense of hope, love and

harmony with nature. The young Catherine who ran wild and free and hardy over the moors is tamed, encumbered and bound. Once she is married, we never again see Catherine outdoors but only in rooms. Her plea for open windows and her wish not to be buried 'under the chapel roof; but in the open air' (ch. 12) indicate how aware she has become of her separation from the outside and how much her girlhood freedom is lost to her. Emily Brontë is in full sympathy.

'My sister Emily loved the moors', Mrs Gaskell reports Charlotte as saying.

> Flowers brighter than the rose bloomed in the blackest of the heath for her;—out of a sullen hollow in a livid hill-side, her mind could make an Eden. She found in the bleak solitude many and dear delights; and not the least and best-loved was liberty. Liberty was the breath of Emily's nostrils; without it she perished. [*The Life of Charlotte Brontë*]

Liberty and freedom were essentials for Emily Brontë as they are for her heroine Catherine; and when freedom is the ideal, imprisonment and restriction are the greatest terror, the greatest deprivation. This explains the recurring imagery of freedom threatened and lost in Emily Brontë's writing—the 'fetters', 'chains', and 'dungeon bars' in her poetry and the enclosures and barriers and the series of characters who are exiled or imprisoned in **Wuthering Heights.** The mortal body, Catherine's 'shattered prison', is itself a form of bondage that separates her from the world of nature and unhampered spirit. 'I'm tired, tired of being enclosed here. I'm wearying to escape into that glorious world, and to be always there; not seeing it dimly through tears, and yearning for it through the walls of an aching heart; but really with it' (ch. 15). Even the enclosing wall of the churchyard is seen as a barrier to resist, so that Catherine, at her request, is buried 'neither in the chapel, under the carved monument of the Lintons, nor yet by the tombs of her own relations' but 'on a green slope, in a corner of the kirkyard, where the wall is so low that heath and bilberry plants have climbed over it from the moor' (ch. 16)

This sense of entrapment is most severe at the Heights. Gates are barred; doors are locked; Isabella, Cathy, Linton, and even Nelly all have their period of captivity there; Lockwood can neither enter the Heights nor leave it without considerable difficulty; and—most poignantly—the ghost child cannot make her way back. Yet the Grange has its own barriers and restrictions, as all limited realms must have. Catherine is the one who chafes most at the Grange's walls and closed windows, but young Cathy too recognizes the Grange's restrictions. Like a type of Sleeping Beauty, Cathy reaches the age of thirteen without once having been 'beyond the range of the park by herself' (ch. 18). Nelly tells the inquisitive girl to be content, that Penistone Crags 'are not worth the trouble of visiting' and that 'Thrushcross park is the finest place in the world'. But, says Cathy, 'I know the park, and I don't know those'. The outcome is inevitable. In a reversal of her mother and Heathcliff's earlier escape from the Heights into the Grange, she scales the walls of the Park, (her 'walled Eden', J. Frank Goodridge calls it [in *Twentieth-Century*

Interpretations of Wuthering Heights, 1968]), escaping outward to the moors and from there, urged by our Satan figure, Heathcliff, goes on to Wuthering Heights and a further enactment of the Fall.

Traditional accounts of Eden admit only to the desirability of paradise and the bitterness of its loss: driven into the wilderness, Adam and Eve lament their lot; Cherubim and sword stand at the gate; you can't go home again. This is the fate of the ghost child lost on the moors, a 'waif for twenty years' (ch. 3). But what is not spoken of directly is that other human urge, the urge to defy restriction. What, after all, is the Forbidden Tree but the urge outward, the desire to reach beyond prescribed limits, to choose for oneself, to *know*? Sooner or later Pandora will open the box; sooner or later Adam and Eve will pluck and taste the forbidden fruit; sooner or later Cathy will scale the wall.

And yet the difference between what is restriction and what is security is all a matter of perspective. One character's heaven/paradise/Eden is another's hell; one character's prison is another's longed for and likely inaccessible haven. For Catherine and Heathcliff, the freedom they knew on the moors with one another is their Eden; separation from one another is their hell. Isabella flees from Wuthering Heights 'blest as a soul escaped from purgatory' (ch. 17). For Cathy, who shows a good share of her mother's free spirit, heaven is 'the whole world awake and wild with joy', while the passive and spiritless Linton, prefers 'a hot July day' spent 'lying from morning till evening on a bank of heath'. There is no reconciling the two viewpoints. 'I said his heaven would be only half alive, and he said mine would be drunk' (ch. 24). But the most significant comment on heaven, in this book full of conflicting heavens, comes in Catherine's account of her dream. 'I dreamt, once, that I was there', Catherine tells Nelly. 'Heaven did not seem to be my home; and I broke my heart with weeping to come back to earth; and the angels were so angry that they flung me out, into the middle of the heath on the top of Wuthering Heights; where I woke sobbing for joy' (ch. 9).

Catherine's rejection of a Christian heaven is not simply a matter of Satan's 'Evil, be thou my good', but rather a way of expressing the multiplicity of character and preference in **Wuthering Heights** and the resulting conflicts which come from such differences. Left to itself the stormy Wuthering Heights could carry on as before, charged with its own Blakeian energy. Left to itself Thrushcross Grange could dream on, static and secure. But the two meet, and opposites attract (if only temporarily), Catherine to Edgar, Isabella to Heathcliff; and Cathy to Linton. And these meetings and matings of opposites have their yieldings. As Goodridge writes:

> Brontë may lead us to question whether there is any one natural and social order, the same for all men and women. The conflicting individual heavens and hells confront one another at every turn: incompatible ways of life, coupled in grotesque ways sometimes lead to violence and hysteria, sometimes to lifeless neutrality and sometimes to new and fuller forms of life. [*Twentieth*

Century Interpretations of Wuthering Heights, 1968]

When the storm of clashing extremes is cleared away, we have Cathy and Hareton, blendings of spirit and civilization, of Heights and Grange characteristics. These two, unlike Edgar and Catherine, can move toward one another, toward a union which brings closure to the book and which is best exemplified by the blending of the novel's two gardens.

Here again Emily Brontë brings us back to the underlying theme of Eden—plural Edens, Edens threatened, Edens lost, and (in this last account) an Eden regained. Cathy persuades Hareton 'to clear a large space of ground' at the Heights for 'an importation of plants' from Thrushcross Grange, and this 'importation' serves as more than a symbol of unity between the two young people and the two households they represent. Most telling is the devastation the transplanting of Grange flowers and Grange plants causes to 'the black current trees' described as 'the apple of Joseph's eye'. (A 'witty pun', Stevie Davies calls this!) The long-standing order of the garden has been disrupted, and Joseph is outraged. Cathy is a witch, a trouble-causing woman, an Eve inciting her Adam to rebel. Like an angry God, Heathcliff threatens expulsion. 'As to Hareton Earnshaw, if I see him listen to you, I'll send him seeking his bread where he can get it! Your love will make him an outcast, and a beggar' (ch. 33). The echoes of Genesis are evident.

But this is a threat that fails. Our new Cathy, our new Eve, reverses the Eden story, returning Hareton to the land and home he had lost and uniting what had previously been divided. These two, Nelly tells us, have escaped 'the sentiments of sober disenchanted maturity' (ch. 33), and the world seems renewed. When next we see the garden, it is April; and the transplanting has clearly succeeded; something of the Grange's orderly cultivation and milder climate has come to Wuthering Heights. 'The weather was sweet and warm, the grass as green as showers and sun could make it, and the two dwarf apple trees, near the southern wall, in full bloom' (ch. 34). At the barren and windy Heights a touch of the traditional Eden has taken hold, complete with apple trees (fittingly dwarf).

For a moment, Emily Brontë gives us a glimpse of peace regained, a sense of unity and continuity, as though—at last—matters have settled. But what we have is only a momentary pause in the recurring cycles and repetitions of life. It is true that an Eden—both new and rediscovered—has come to Wuthering Heights. The 'Hareton Earnshaw' of the 1500 carving over the entrance to the Heights lives again in the new Hareton Earnshaw restored to his lands; and, as well, something of Catherine Earnshaw continues in her daughter, in the similarity of their eyes, in something of their shared desire for freedom. But the particulars of any individual human spirit or any individual human form are never fully recovered; and even as we celebrate restoration and continuity in the characters and union of Cathy and Hareton, Emily Brontë requires us to feel the loss of Catherine and Heathcliff, her vivid and tempestuous rebels. With their departure, some great and wild force has gone from the earth. Wuthering Heights will be mostly 'shut up'; Cathy and Hareton will live at the Grange, and the world seems diminished.

There is only a hint or two that something of Catherine and Heathcliff's spirit still endures. Though Lockwood cannot imagine 'unquiet slumbers for the sleepers in that quiet earth', his description of the fluttering moths, the heath, the hare-bells and the 'soft wind breathing through the grass' (ch. 34) suggests a life that goes on, a slow stirring, a transmutation perhaps. And there is as well the boy who comes crying that he has seen the ghosts of 'Heathcliff and a woman, yonder, under t'Nab'. But again nothing is certain, and neither image is satisfactory. Emily Brontë chooses to leave the spirit its own mystery, and what is not offered to us, in any vision of ghost or grave, is a full return to innocence in the form we knew it first—not a transmutation into the natural world, not 'Heathcliff and a woman' (ghosts that *walk* and adult ghosts at that) but the children themselves, Catherine and Heathcliff, vivid and passionate, and running 'hardy, and free' over the moors. (pp. 31-45)

> *Marjorie Burns, " 'This Shattered Prison':*
> *Versions of Eden in 'Wuthering Heights', " in*
> The Nineteenth-Century British Novel, *ed-*
> *ited by Jeremy Hawthorn, Edward Arnold,*
> *1986, pp. 31-46.*

Winifred Gérin on the ethereal nature of *Wuthering Heights*:

Concerned with eternal principles of life, death, love and immortality, it has a timeless quality that puts it far nearer to such a work as *The Faery Queen* than to any contemporary Victorian novel. It has no concern for social questions, but is an expression of primitive passions, of the elemental forces in Man and Nature that the author shows as connecting all Creation. Hers is a cosmic vision that has little to do with nineteenth-century materialism. At the same time the narrative is firmly set in the soil. The chronological framework of the plot is precise; the seasonal changes meticulously noted, but rather as might be done by men in space who are removed from the world's orbit. The people moving in the spacious panorama of the moorlands are seen with the sharp focus of the dreamer who notes all the details of his dream but cannot account for them.

> *Winifred Gérin, in her* The Brontës, *Vol. 2,*
> *Longman House, 1974.*

Carole Gerster   (essay date 1988)

[*In the following excerpt, Gerster examines* Wuthering Heights *as an idealized depiction of characters rebelling against social gender roles.*]

We live in an imagined world. As the social critic and novelist Elizabeth Janeway notes [in her *Man's World, Woman's Place: A Study in Social Mythology,* 1971], "The social world that we share with others is a world we have imagined together and agreed to believe in. We know its inhabitants by the roles they play, and its structure is ex-

pressed in our common mythology." Observing that "the divisions of the world by sexes . . . still endures," Janeway reasons that this division is "so built into our minds and cultural background that it still produces an illusion of inevitability and revealed truth." Even though we recognize that standards of behavior change, the social roles we assume are what we most often take for granted about ourselves and our world. Even when accepted social reality is critiqued as being artificially constraining or even false to actual experience, the old patterns of thinking are slow to change. It takes writers of genius to provide new ways for us to imagine ourselves. One such writer is the Victorian novelist Emily Brontë.

Any vision of a new social structure that challenges old orthodoxies must provide what Janeway calls "a new mythology," which she defines as "a ground of shared belief on the basis of which groups of people can act together." Thus, this new vision not only must react against old codes of behavior that have lost their relevance, but also must provide positive alternatives. On this boundary, this threshold between a new social order and previous constructs, the worlds presented in such works of fantasy as Brontë's *Wuthering Heights* compete with established social reality for acceptance as an adequate register of the real.

Throughout the nineteenth century, the British novel displayed an increasing degree of "realism"; that is, it recorded more and more surface details and mirrored more precisely the dominant attitudes and values of middle-class life and society. As the novel became the dominant literary form, readers could identify with the heroes and heroines in familiar settings who exemplified prevailing social norms. This was not the case with Brontë's novel, which shocked readers when it was first published in 1847. Brontë's Victorian contemporaries characterized her novel as a powerful, imaginative vision written by someone out of touch with the social realities of the time. One reviewer termed it "a strange book . . . not without evidence of considerable power: but, as a whole . . . wild, confused, disjointed, and improbable; and the people who make up the drama . . . savages ruder than those who lived before the days of Homer." This critic found it difficult "to believe in the appearance of such a phenomenon [as Heathcliff] so near our own dwellings as the summit of a . . . Yorkshire moor." Nor could he find "any very obvious moral in the story," even though he found that "some of the incidents look like real events." In typical Victorian fashion, another reviewer found the novel so coarse, disagreeable, and vulgar that, if written by a woman, it could only have been one who had "long forfeited the society of her own sex."

In general, although modern critics disagree over what the novel is about, they have differed little from these early reviewers in their estimation of its visionary power and in their view of Brontë as secluded from and unaware of the social realities of her world. For example, David Cecil's 1935 essay judges *Wuthering Heights* to be unlike the "orthodox Victorian novel" and "distinguished by the power of its imagination." Cecil claims it is "about a different world. That bustling, prosaic, progressive world of nineteenth-century middle-class England . . . simply does not come into her view at all." He argues that Brontë does not see human beings "in relation to other human beings, or to human civilizations and codes of conduct, but only in relation to the cosmic scheme of which they form a part," that she is "a mystic . . . [whose] eyes seemed open to behold a transcendent reality usually hidden from mortal sight." Cecil attributes Brontë's visionary sensibility to her having been shut up in her father's parsonage in Yorkshire and thus "pretty well cut off from the influence of those forces that shaped the main trend of the time" [*Wuthering Heights: An Authoritative Text with Essays in Criticism*, edited by William M. Sale, Jr., 1972].

Did Emily Brontë envision "a different world"? Yes. Did she lack knowledge of the orthodoxies of thought and conduct that passed for reality in the world in which she lived? No. Both contemporary and modern readings misjudge **Wuthering Heights** in trying to measure it against standards made by and for the very social order it critiques. Even today's Marxist and feminist critics, who see the novel in terms of either class struggle or women's struggle for equality, find the fantasy a most compelling but failed vision. While both Marxist and feminist critics effectively dispel the notion that Emily Brontë was "deposited on the Yorkshire moors from some metaphysical outer space," both measure the imaginative vision in **Wuthering Heights** against the dominant ideology of the particular time and place in which it was written. Terry Eagleton finds Brontë's fantasy sufficiently "estranged from concrete existence" to show "both the splendour and the impotence of the ideal" [*Myths of Power: A Marxist Study of the Brontës*, 1975]. Sandra Gilbert and Susan Gubar argue [in *Madwoman in the Attic*, 1979] that the rebellious fantasy pair, Heathcliff and Catherine, are "exorcised" and replaced by a "proper [Victorian] couple," that Brontë's fantasy presents "powerfully disruptive possibilities" that are reduced to haunting the novel by "roaring in the distance." **Wuthering Heights** has been judged not by what it is able to offer as a counter-reality, but by how it fails to conform to accepted notions of the real. Its readers have failed to accept its challenge to reimagine the social world. **Wuthering Heights** is a female fantasy, a projected world that reveals Brontë's feelings about being a woman in a male-dominated society as it also delineates her vision of a new social structure based on relationships of equality.

Brontë's fantasy world—which contains two larger-than-life characters, Heathcliff and Catherine—breaks free from social custom in envisioning a mythic ideal that transcends social roles regulating behavior according to gender. But this fantasy is only part of Brontë's vision of a new social order. The novel's opening and closing narration is a frame for the Heathcliff/Catherine story told from the perspective of Mr. Lockwood, a civilized, literary man with the preconceived ideas that literature and life are structured according to the social codes of his time. It is through this frame that Brontë is able to expose existing social constructs as false to human realities. In the fantasy story of Catherine and Heathcliff, Brontë envisions not only a mythic ideal but also a psychic reality that is more real than the restrictive social codes with which it is at

odds and that serves as a model for a more natural, more human social order. Finally, Brontë's second generation of characters, Hareton and Cathy, realize the mythic ideal as possible in the social context of Lockwood's world; the portrayal of this second generation juxtaposes Brontë's newly imagined social world and Lockwood's unimaginative conventionalism.

Perhaps Brontë's novel is best viewed in the light of Arnold Toynbee's hypothesis that "when a civilization comes to a 'time of troubles,' individuals here and there turn from the outer world of political and social chaos to the inner world of the psyche; there come upon the vision of a new way of life; and, returning to the outer world, form the nucleus of a 'creative minority' through which that civilization may find renewal" [P. W. Martin, foreword of *Experiment in Depth: A Study of the Work of Jung, Eliot and Toynbee*, 1955]. **Wuthering Heights** begins by establishing that civilization has come to a "time of troubles." By dramatizing the dangers of conforming to the confining code of gender identity, it establishes the necessity of abandoning stereotyped roles and behavioral modes and prepares us to accept a counter-reality.

The frame occurs within time, the year 1801, and in a realistic narrative setting. A stranger to the world of Wuthering Heights, Mr. Lockwood has come to the countryside to be alone, to escape from the social world with which he identifies and yet from which he is alienated. The reader is initiated into the unfamiliar world of the novel with Lockwood and, in attempting to relate this world to the familiar world outside the novel, initially identifies with Lockwood and shares his understanding. But Brontë quickly thwarts this identification by indicating that Lockwood's conventional views, the ideas he accepts as social reality, are merely a prevailing yet false and inadequate, male-perpetuated fiction.

In his account of his arrival at Wuthering Heights, Lockwood laments that he may "never have a comfortable home" because he has recently proven himself "perfectly unworthy of one." He confesses,

> While enjoying a month of fine weather at the seacoast, I was thrown into the company of a most fascinating creature, a real goddess, in my eyes, as long as she took notice of me. I "never told my love" vocally; still, if looks have language, the merest idiot might have guessed I was over head and ears; she understood me, at last, and looked a return—and the sweetest of all imaginable looks—and what did I do? I confess it with shame—shrunk icily into myself, like a snail, at every glance retired colder and farther; till, finally, the poor innocent was led to doubt her own senses, and overwhelmed with confusion at her supposed mistake, persuaded her mamma to decamp.

Lockwood has here adopted a stereotypical male role that perpetuates an exalted ideal of what women should be and how they should behave. He sees this woman as a "goddess," rather than as a woman. His view is consonant with both the prevailing social ideal of femininity and the stereotyped characterizations of heroines in novels of the time. Neither properly socialized women nor heroines in novels were supposed to reveal their interest in a man until the man had first declared his love. Women were not viewed as human beings with human needs and desires, but as passive, asexual goddesses. When Lockwood confronts a real woman who returns his admiring glances, he dismisses her in spite of himself; she can only be a goddess as long as she takes no notice of him. Because he allows himself to be defined by a restrictive social role, Lockwood no longer knows his natural self; he is isolated from others because only certain forms of behavior are open to him. Because Lockwood is locked into custom and convention, he is locked out of a potentially loving relationship.

In allowing the reader first to identify with Lockwood and then to see that this identification is untenable, Brontë conveys her expectation that the reader will come to her novel with the same preconceptions as Lockwood—that we have been conditioned to read novels from the perspective of a male-defined reality. Lockwood's mistakes in determining male and female relationships are in line with his view of woman as goddess. Lockwood mistakes Cathy as Heathcliff's wife, as his "amiable lady" and "the presiding genius over [his] home and heart." On being corrected, he mistakes Hareton as "the favoured possessor of the beneficent fairy." Lockwood's notions about women not only are consonant with the domestic role imagined by a patriarchal society as being appropriate for women, but also are as unreal as the fictional cliches that define women as ministering angels. Rather than rely on the authority of convention and never go beyond Lockwood's view that "custom can mould our tastes and ideas," the reader is invited to trust the authority of experience. Brontë shifts the narrative perspective to offer an alternative to the demands of strict sexual polarization imposed by society. As Lockwood turns to Nelly Dean for an explanation of a world he cannot comprehend, his narrative is superseded and he becomes a reader and recorder of Nelly's tale.

Nelly's timeless, mythic tale of the bond that allows Catherine and Heathcliff to declare themselves to be one being is perhaps as old as literature itself. Plato cites the myth of primordial androgynous beings whose severance leads to humanity's desire to reunify by making one of two, and thus heal its sexual duality. In *Wuthering Heights* this mythic, androgynous state becomes both a way to redefine human nature and an alternative to sexual polarization. In Brontë's androgynous vision, traditionally defined masculine and feminine traits are not seen as products of anatomy but as independent qualities of each human psyche. The androgynous ideal posits the coexistence of masculine and feminine traits within a single, fully human individual.

Nelly's tale focuses the reader's attention on the androgynous ideal as realized by Catherine and Heathcliff when they are children. Their initial identification with each other, and through the other with the universe, is related by Nelly in Catherine's words: "If all else perished, and he remained, I should still continue to be; and if all else remained, and he were annihilated, the Universe would turn to a mighty stranger . . . Nelly, I am Heathcliff—he's always, always in my mind—not as a pleasure, any

more than I am always a pleasure to myself—but as my own being." Catherine's universe is defined by Heathcliff's presence in it, and through their union they are united with the natural universe.

Together, they represent the wholeness of an undivided self in a world divided into contraries. Wuthering Heights is the farmhouse of the dark-haired, dark-eyed Earnshaws, all of whom display the traditionally defined masculine traits of initiative and competitive activity regardless of their sex. Thrushcross Grange is the estate of the blond-haired, blue-eyed Lintons, landed gentry who all display, with equal disregard for gender, the traditionally defined feminine traits of decorum and subordinate passivity. Brontë's division of the world into masculine and feminine camps at once denies the conventional distinction that masculinity is a characteristic of men while femininity is a characteristic of women and demonstrates that such distinctions divide the world into conflicting opposites.

The oppression Catherine and Heathcliff suffer at Wuthering Heights is matched at Thrushcross Grange. Mr. Earnshaw comes under the influence of Joseph, the puritanical servant who "was relentless in worrying him . . . about ruling his children rigidly," and begins to oppress his son, Hindley, and his daughter, Catherine. When Earnshaw dies, Hindley—who by the patriarchal laws of primogeniture becomes heir and head of the house—joins Joseph in the oppression of Catherine and Heathcliff by insisting on their separation. They rebel to scamper on the moors, until they reach Thrushcross Grange and the Linton's watchdog bites Catherine; Heathcliff is sent home as a being "unfit for a decent house," while Catherine is detained for a number of weeks, until she is changed from a child into a socially acceptable young lady. The Lintons impress on her the importance of assuming the feminine role, and she willingly assumes it. Catherine returns to Wuthering Heights a "very dignified" lady to find Heathcliff reduced to the status of a rough, dirty servant. Like Lockwood, Catherine assumes a superficially conventional gender role that locks her into limited forms of behavior and denies her true self. While confessing to Nelly that "whatever our souls are made of [Heathcliff's] and mine are the same," Catherine announces that she intends to marry Edgar Linton because to marry Heathcliff would "degrade" her. On overhearing her, Heathcliff leaves Wuthering Heights to go out into the world and become a gentleman.

Their childhood paradise is shattered by their separation and their subsequent fall into conventional gender roles. Despite these transformations, however, both Catherine and Heathcliff long for a return to their original androgynous relationship. Catherine falls ill with "brain fever"; she imagines she is a child again at Wuthering Heights, the "wind sounding in the firs by the lattice," before Hindley had ordered her separation from Heathcliff and before she had become "Mrs. Linton, the lady of Thrushcross Grange." Her mind unsettled from "its right balance," she becomes like a "wailing child." Dramatizing the destructive effects of the socially divided self and the need for reintegration, Brontë depicts the dying Catherine in the same terms that characterized Lockwood's haunting vision of her at his window, which he dismisses as having occurred when he no longer had his "imagination under control." Brontë thus reveals that the natural world Lockwood would lock out is a psychic reality that cannot be contained in artificially imposed social roles. Catherine dies "like a child reviving," with "her latest ideas [having] wandered back to early pleasant days." Separated from Catherine, his "soul in the grave," Heathcliff's life in the world echoes Catherine's earlier cosmic vision of their childhood existence: "In every cloud, in every tree—filling the air at night, and caught by glimpses in every cloud, by day, I am surrounded with her image! The most ordinary faces of men, and women—my own features mock me with a resemblance. The entire world is a dreadful collection of memoranda that she did exist, and that I have lost her." Heathcliff's universe is now defined by Catherine's absence from it, by his loss.

Their relationship—the childhood oneness split asunder by gender distinctions that divide the self and the world into conflicting opposites—is resumed only in death, which is a return to their lost origins and to wholeness through immersion in primal nature. Yet, as Catherine and Heathcliff remain ever faithful, Brontë maintains the androgynous ideal in the mind of the reader. And with a second generation of characters, the "most ordinary faces" of Cathy and Hareton, Brontë imagines the ideal made real in a social context. Estranged from life in his desire to "dissolve" with Catherine into the earth, Heathcliff nonetheless remains alive until he confronts the growing love between Cathy and Hareton. They not only remind him of his loss, as does the entire world, but also reveal to him the possibility of gaining in life what he will return to only through death. Heathcliff's reunion with Catherine in death parallels Cathy and Hareton's potential union in life, the likely result of their growing intimacy.

Brontë initially portrays Cathy Linton and Hareton Earnshaw as creatures of a sexually polarized world: Cathy, kept "a perfect recluse" at Thrushcross Grange and protected from the world, is brought up to embody the feminine ideal; Hareton, taught at Wuthering Heights to "scorn anything extra animal as silly and weak," is raised an exaggerated parody of masculinity. Yet, like Catherine and Heathcliff, they cannot be contained in their roles—those of decorous young lady and rough servant, respectively—and they rebel. Each feels "stalled," artificially limited, and each is attracted to the other. But unlike Catherine and Heathcliff, who together form the mythic ideal of one androgynous being, Cathy and Hareton each awakens to her and his own androgyny. Each a separate androgyne, they harmoniously interact—rather than identify—with each other. Their marriage will take place on New Year's Day to suggest a recreation of the world as the old order gives way to the new.

As Nelly brings her tale into the present, Lockwood completes the novel to "escape" back to the city, back to the social codes to which he is accustomed. He is unchanged and has learned nothing. He flees after witnessing Cathy and Hareton together, for their behavior is at odds with convention. As when he had shrunk icily into himself on being confronted with a real woman instead of a goddess, Lockwood shrinks away again here on being confronted with a genuine relationship. Lockwood interprets Nelly's tale of Catherine and Heathcliff as the story of a "heroine" and a "hero." Lockwood can see their relationship only as a fiction to be dismissed; Brontë reveals that his social conditioning has blinded him to the human possibilities they represent, as she equates accepted social relations with the unnatural, improbable conventions of contemporary fiction. Lockwood has been attracted to Cathy, but he can imagine himself only as a romantic hero in something even "more romantic than a fairy tale" who should have rescued the fair maiden and taken her "into the stirring atmosphere of the town." In wondering why Cathy was not attracted to him, as being from "a better class of people," he continues to see male and female relationships in terms of a hierarchical arrangement. Locked into the status quo, Lockwood escapes from the novel as its meaning escapes him.

Lockwood flees after observing Cathy teaching Hareton to read the word *contrary*. Contrary to the rules of gender identity and to Lockwood's expectations, Cathy and Hareton exhibit new behavioral options that change restrictive social structures to humane ones. Lockwood has excluded himself from the world of the novel and is unable to read the lesson they master together. He first encountered a locked gate at Wuthering Heights; the now unlocked gate and open doors and lattices signify a new, nonhierarchical nonrepressive receptiveness to others, to experience, and to egalitarian relationships. As if to echo their interpersonal equality, Cathy and Hareton are also economic equals: Cathy owns Thrushcross Grange, and Hareton owns Wuthering Heights. Dismissing both literary and social convention, Brontë does not have Cathy carried off by a romance hero or dominated by her husband; instead, the young couple will settle in Cathy's home and abandon Wuthering Heights to old Joseph, who will be haunted by ghostly visions of a united Catherine and Heathcliff.

As her novel dissolves the distinction between fiction and reality—like masculine and feminine, another false duality—Brontë's vision of a new social order becomes a counter-reality juxtaposed against Lockwood's equally imaginary conventional world. J. Hillis Miller notes that "when a novel presents a fiction within a fiction within a fiction, the reality at the beginning and the ending of this series tends to be assimilated into it and to appear as itself a fiction. . . . To read a narration within a narration makes all the world a novel and turns the reader into a fictional character. . . . Imagination and reality are identical" [*The Form of Victorian Fiction*, 1968]. (pp. 71-8)

Carole Gerster, "The Reality of Fantasy: Emily Brontë's 'Wuthering Heights'," in Spectrum of the Fantastic: Selected Essays from the Sixth International Conference on the Fantastic in the Arts, *edited by Donald Palumbo, Greenwood Press, 1988, pp. 71-80.*

FURTHER READING

Bibliography

Crump, R. W. *Charlotte and Emily Brontë, 1846-1915: A Reference Guide.* Boston: G. K. Hall & Co., 1982, 194 p.

　　Annotated bibliography of essays and reviews written between 1846 and 1915 about the lives and works of Charlotte and Emily Brontë.

Biography

Gérin, Winifred. *The Brontës,* 2 vols. Essex, England: Longman Group, 1973.

　　Treats the life and works of the four Brontë siblings. Gérin divides the volumes according to "the prolific *Formative Years*" and "the accomplished *Creative Work.*"

Criticism

Adams, Ruth M. "Wuthering Heights: The Land East of Eden." *Nineteenth-Century Fiction* 13, No. 1 (June 1958): 58-62.

　　Discusses the absence of conventional morality in *Wuthering Heights.*

Barreca, Regina. "The Power of Excommunication: Sex and the Feminine Text in *Wuthering Heights.*" In her *Sex and Death in Victorian Literature,* pp. 227-40. London: Macmillan Press, 1990.

　　Contends that the female characters in *Wuthering Heights* assert their power over the patriarchal system by creating and shaping the text.

Benvenuto, Richard. *Emily Brontë.* Boston: Twayne Publishers, 1982, 148 p.

　　Includes biographical information and critical assessment of all of Brontë's known writings.

Blondel, Jacques. "Two Excerpts from '*Emily Brontë: Expérience Spirituelle et Création Poétique*'." In "*Wuthering Heights*": *Text, Sources, Criticism,* edited by Thomas C. Moser, pp. 206-13. New York: Harcourt, Brace & World, 1962.

　　Focuses on the minor characters in *Wuthering Heights,* dividing them into three categories: actors, victims, and witnesses.

Bosco, Ronald A. "Heathcliff: Societal Victim or Demon?" *The Gypsy Scholar* 2, No. 1 (Fall 1974): 21-39.

　　Rejects the critical tendency to interpret Heathcliff as a demon, emphasizing that his character "derives exclusively from the influence of his environment."

Carson, Joan. "Visionary Experience in *Wuthering Heights.*" *The Psychoanalytic Review* 62, No. 1 (Spring 1975): 131-51.

　　Applies Jungian theory to *Wuthering Heights,* analyzing the interdependence of its literal, psychological, and archetypal levels.

Davies, Cecil W. "A Reading of *Wuthering Heights.*" *Essays in Criticism* XIX, No. 3 (July 1969): 254-72.

　　Refers to Brontë's poetry and the Gondal stories in an examination of the mysticism of *Wuthering Heights.*

Dawson, Terence. "The Struggle for Deliverance from the Father: The Structural Principle of *Wuthering Heights.*" *The Modern Language Review* 84, No. 2 (April 1989): 289-304.

　　Considers the two stories of *Wuthering Heights* as parts of a single complex pattern, emphasizing thematic similarities and analyzing character traits that reappear in the second generation.

Devlin, James E. "*Wuthering Heights:* The Dominant Image." *Discourse: A Review of the Liberal Arts* V, No. 3 (Summer 1962): 337-46.

　　Discusses Brontë's imagery of restraint that "permeates every fold of her creation."

Dunn, Richard J. "The Feeling of *Wuthering Heights.*" *Research Studies* 45, No. 3 (September 1977): 160-67.

　　Describes *Wuthering Heights* as "high romantic art" in which the feelings and experiences of the characters cannot be contained in rational thought or language.

Everitt, Alastair, ed. *Wuthering Heights: An Anthology of Criticism.* London: Frank Cass & Co., 1967, 208 p.

　　Collection of essays intended to reveal the complexities of *Wuthering Heights.* Everitt includes studies by such notable Brontë critics as Dorothy Van Ghent and C. P. Sanger.

Farrell, John P. "Reading the Text of Community in *Wuthering Heights.*" *ELH* 56, No. 1 (Spring 1989): 173-208.

　　Emphasizes the importance of the novel's narrative structure in an examination of the reader's experience.

Gilbert, Sandra M. and Gubar, Susan. "Looking Oppositely: Emily Brontë's Bible of Hell." In their *The Madwoman in the Attic: The Woman Writer and the Nineteenth-Century Literary Imagination,* pp. 248-308. New Haven, Conn.: Yale University Press, 1979.

　　Argues that "the story of *Wuthering Heights* is built around a central fall . . . so that a description of the novel as in part a *Bildungsroman* about a girl's passage from 'innocence' to 'experience' . . . would probably also be widely accepted."

Gleckner, Robert F. "Time in *Wuthering Heights.*" *Criticism* I, No. 4 (Fall 1959): 328-38.

　　Examines the characters' attitudes toward the past and their reactions to the passage of time.

Goff, Barbara Munson. "Between Natural Theology and Natural Selection: Breeding the Human Animal in *Wuthering Heights.*" *Victorian Studies* 27, No. 4 (Summer 1984): 477-508.

　　Detailed examination of Brontë's belief in natural theology, which Goff describes as a "religious version of the theory of natural selection."

Gold, Linda. "Catherine Earnshaw: Mother and Daughter." *English Journal* 74, No. 3 (March 1985): 68-73.

　　Discusses Catherine Earnshaw's maturation in the novel in terms of Freud's theory of the development of the personality.

Gose, Elliott B., Jr. "*Wuthering Heights:* The Heath and the Hearth." *Nineteenth-Century Fiction* 21, No. 1 (June 1966): 1-19.

　　Analyzes *Wuthering Heights* in terms of four figurative patterns: "one stemming from the fairy tale, one from religion and the Bible, one from the traditional elements of nature, and one concerned with the process of initiation."

Haggerty, George E. "The Gothic Form of *Wuthering Heights.*" *The Victorian Newsletter,* No. 74 (Fall 1988): 1-6.

Argues that in *Wuthering Heights* Brontë "looks into the heart of Gothic fiction, . . . uncovers the most deeply rooted formal problems which Gothic novelists themselves were never able to resolve, and forges a solution to those problems out of the literary smithy of her own soul."

Kavanagh, James H. *Emily Brontë.* Oxford: Basil Blackwell, 1985, 120 p.
Freudian and Marxist reading of *Wuthering Heights* in which the novel's chief protagonists are not Heathcliff and Catherine, but Heathcliff and Nelly Dean.

Kiely, Robert. "*Wuthering Heights.*" In his *The Romantic Novel in England,* pp. 233-51. Cambridge, Mass.: Harvard University Press, 1972.
Analyzes the themes of imagination, transformation, and morality in the novel, describing it as "one of the few perfect novels in nineteenth-century English."

Klingopulos, G. D. "The Novel as Dramatic Poem (II): *Wuthering Heights.*" *Scrutiny* XIV, No. 4 (September 1947): 269-86.
Asserts that "as an Elizabethan play stands or falls by the quality of the poetry at its crises of meaning, so *Wuthering Heights* may be said to justify itself by the quality of some half-dozen or so speeches of Catherine's and Heathcliff's which are as direct and as highly organized in word and rhythm as poetry."

Knoepflmacher, U. C. "*Wuthering Heights:* A Tragicomic Romance." In his *Laughter & Despair: Readings in Ten Novels of the Victorian Era,* pp. 84-108. Berkeley and Los Angeles: University of California Press, 1971.
Suggests that *Wuthering Heights* was rejected by the Victorian public because of the "disturbing, unexplained vision of anarchy and decay" in the novel.

Lavers, Norman. "The Action of *Wuthering Heights.*" *The South Atlantic Quarterly* 72, No. 1 (Winter 1973): 43-52.
Suggests that all actions in the novel contribute to the "governing action": that of restoring power to the Earnshaw family.

Leavis, Q. D. "A Fresh Approach to *Wuthering Heights.*" In *Lectures in America,* by F. R. Leavis and Q. D. Leavis, pp. 83-138. New York: Random House, Pantheon Books, 1969.
Influential essay in which the critic points to Brontë's treatment of Catherine Earnshaw as evidence of the realistic nature and moral responsibleness of the novel.

Lenta, Margaret. "Capitalism or Patriarchy and Immortal Love: A Study of *Wuthering Heights.*" *Theoria* LXII (May 1984): 63-76.
Examines the social forces that shape the relationship between Heathcliff and Catherine.

Lettis, Richard and Morris, William E. *A "Wuthering Heights" Handbook.* New York: The Odyssey Press, 1961, 246 p.
Collection of significant Brontë studies including essays by David Cecil, C. P. Sanger, Arnold Kettle, and Virginia Woolf.

Macovski, Michael S. "*Wuthering Heights* and the Rhetoric of Interpretation." *ELH* 54, No. 2 (Summer 1987): 363-84.
Locates strategies of interpretation within the novel which act as models of understanding for the reader.

Madden, William A. "*Wuthering Heights:* The Binding of Passion." *Nineteenth-Century Fiction* 27, No. 2 (September 1972): 127-54.
Suggests that the minor character Joseph is the force that destroys the first generation, stressing that only the constructive energy of the second generation can overcome his influence.

McKinstry, Susan Jaret. "Desire's Dreams: Power and Passion in *Wuthering Heights.*" *College Literature* XII, No. 2 (Spring 1985): 141-46.
Interprets *Wuthering Heights* as a celebration of the power of desire to overthrow the obstacles to love and fulfillment.

Moser, Thomas. "What Is the Matter with Emily Jane? Conflicting Impulses in *Wuthering Heights.*" *Nineteenth-Century Fiction* 17, No. 1 (June 1962): 1-19.
A Freudian interpretation of the novel focusing on Heathcliff's role as the embodiment of sexual energy that is the driving force of the work.

Parker, Patricia. "The (Self-)Identity of the Literary Text: Property, Propriety, Proper Place, and Proper Name in *Wuthering Heights.*" In *Identity of the Literary Text,* edited by Mario J. Valdés and Owen Miller, pp. 92-116. Toronto: University of Toronto Press, 1985.
Discusses Brontë's disruption of chronology and the impossibility of a linear reading of *Wuthering Heights.*

Pittock, Malcolm. "*Wuthering Heights* and Its Critics." *The Critical Survey* 5, No. 2 (Summer 1971): 146-54.
Considers the formal techniques used to determine the meaning of *Wuthering Heights,* with an emphasis on its moral message. Pittock accuses other critics of focusing too closely on specific elements to the neglect of the novel as a whole.

Scrivner, Buford, Jr. "The Ethos of *Wuthering Heights.*" *Dalhousie Review* 54, No. 3 (Autumn 1974): 451-62.
Examines the importance in the novel of balancing social responsibility and instinct, stressing Heathcliff's failure to achieve this balance.

Senf, Carol A. "Emily Brontë's Version of Feminist History: *Wuthering Heights.*" *Essays in Literature* 12, No. 2 (Fall 1985): 201-14.
Interprets the ending of *Wuthering Heights* as a "feminizing" of patriarchal history that creates a less oppressive world for both men and women.

Solomon, Eric. "The Incest Theme in *Wuthering Heights.*" *Nineteenth-Century Fiction* 14, No. 1 (June 1959): 80-3.
Suggests that Heathcliff is Earnshaw's illegitimate son and Catherine's half-brother.

Stevenson, W. H. "*Wuthering Heights:* The Facts." *Essays in Criticism* XXXV, No. 2 (April 1985): 149-66.
Accuses other critics of extracting only those elements of *Wuthering Heights* that prove their preconceived conclusions. Stevenson focuses on the literary facts within the novel to locate what he considers to be a more authentic interpretation.

Sucksmith, H. P. "The Theme of *Wuthering Heights* Reconsidered." *Dalhousie Review* 54, No. 3 (Autumn 1974): 418-28.
Analyzes Brontë's depiction of universal themes within a Victorian context, emphasizing her concern about the

conflict between social conventions and the expression of natural instinct.

Vogler, Thomas A. *Twentieth Century Interpretations of "Wuthering Heights."* Englewood Cliffs, N. J.: Prentice-Hall, 1968, 122 p.

Collection of essays intended to illustrate Vogler's assertion that "there is no one single meaning, no single system or theory of perceptions or values which [*Wuthering Heights*] points to and stands for."

Williams, Anne. "Natural Supernaturalism in *Wuthering Heights.*" *Studies in Philology* LXXXII, No. 1 (Winter 1985): 104-27.

Compares Brontë's purpose in *Wuthering Heights* with that of Wordsworth and Coleridge in the *Lyrical Ballads,* emphasizing their common desire to uncover, in Wordsworth's phrase, "the primary laws in our nature."

Willis, Irene Cooper. *The Authorship of "Wuthering Heights."* London: Hogarth Press, 1936, 94 p.

Comprehensive analysis of the style of *Wuthering Heights.*

Wion, Philip K. "The Absent Mother in Emily Brontë's *Wuthering Heights.*" *American Imago* 42, No. 2 (Summer 1985): 143-64.

Employs psychological theories about the mother-child relationship to examine conflicts involving separation and unity in *Wuthering Heights.*

Additional coverage of Brontë's life and career is contained in the following sources published by Gale Research: *Dictionary of Literary Biography,* Vols. 21, 32 and *Nineteenth-Century Literature Criticism,* Vol. 16.

Charles Kingsley

1819-1875

English novelist, critic, historian, essayist, and poet.

INTRODUCTION

A prolific author in numerous genres, Kingsley is best known for the novels that he wrote to promote various social, philosophical, and scientific ideas. Of these works, "social problem" novels such as *Alton Locke, Tailor and Poet* (1850) and *Yeast* (1851) address the plight of laborers and rural as well as urban living conditions in Victorian England; historical romances such as *Hypatia* (1853) and *Westward Ho!* (1855) convey the author's conception of Christian ethics and patriotic virtue; and *The Water-Babies: A Fairy Tale for a Land-Baby* (1863), a children's adventure fantasy, expresses Kingsley's espousal of evolutionary theory and his endorsement of scientific exploration of natural phenomena. Kingsley has been praised for the imaginative power of his descriptive prose; due to the topical and didactic nature of most of his writings, however, few continue to attract more than scholarly interest.

Kingsley was born in Dartmoor, Devonshire, the eldest of Reverend Charles Kingsley's seven children. At age thirteen he was sent to Helston Grammar School, where he was instructed by the naturalist C. A. Johns and the noted theologian Derwent Coleridge, son of the eminent poet Samuel Taylor Coleridge. Under Coleridge's influence, Kingsley became aware of current trends in religious thought; Johns, meanwhile, fostered Kingsley's love of nature and interest in science, encouraging him to collect and study botanical and geological specimens. At Helston Kingsley also composed his first noteworthy poetry, basing his verse on Romantic traditions.

In 1838 Kingsley entered Magdalen College at Cambridge. He later described his stay there as "wicked," evidently referring to his indulgence in boating, hunting, fencing, boxing, and other sports to the detriment of his studies, as well as bouts of heavy drinking and at least one sexual liaison with an unknown woman who may have been a prostitute. Kingsley also struggled with his religious faith during these years, turning to a pantheistic love of nature for inspiration and spiritual comfort. In 1839, he met and fell in love with Fanny Grenfell. At her suggestion, Kingsley read Samuel Taylor Coleridge's treatise on religious faith, *Aids to Reflection,* along with the writings of Thomas Carlyle, who criticized what he viewed as the spiritual dissipation of the industrial age. Responding favorably to the broadly based, socially oriented religion championed in these works, and determined to settle upon a vocation that would please Grenfell, Kingsley decided to become a clergyman in the Anglican Church. To this end, he spent his last semesters at Cambridge studying earnestly and passed his examinations in 1841. He began

reading for Holy Orders the following year, and his father helped him obtain a curacy in Eversley, Hampshire. Although Kingsley was occasionally forced by ill health to reside elsewhere for extended periods of time, Eversley remained his home for the remainder of his life.

Early in 1844, Kingsley married Grenfell. Later that year he began corresponding with the noted theologian Frederic Denison Maurice, whose religious beliefs were based on a boundless love for God and all his physical creations. Maurice therefore rejected asceticism, contending that the spiritual kingdom of God would be realized in the material world. This doctrine was especially pleasing to Kingsley, who found that it justified his own insistence upon an active religion that would provide a response to, rather than an escape from, worldly strife, as well as his advocation of marriage as the divinely ordained key to a harmonious uniting of the physical and the spiritual realms. Kingsley thus rejected traditional religious suspicion of physical pleasure, abhorring especially the restrictions of celibacy. His studies of Maurice and Carlyle also fostered Kingsley's deep concern with the living and working conditions of the laboring classes. He began a series of reforms within his parish, establishing a variety of clubs, an adult evening school, a lending library, and a loan fund to assist the poor, uneducated, and largely illiterate people who comprised the majority of his congregation.

In 1846, Kingsley began rewriting a biography of Saint Elizabeth of Hungary that he had begun composing four years earlier as a wedding gift for his wife. Instead of the prose biography that he had originally planned, Kingsley constructed a blank-verse drama, completing it by the summer of 1847. *The Saint's Tragedy* relates Elizabeth's tormenting struggle to suppress natural affection for her husband in order to assume the ascetic lifestyle demanded of her by the domineering monk to whom she had turned for spiritual guidance. Published at Maurice's behest in 1848, the play presented a number of ideas that would distinguish virtually all of Kingsley's subsequent writings: it extolled married love and the sanctity of the family; attacked celibacy and monasticism as unnatural and undesirable; urged social responsibility toward underprivileged peoples; and featured in one of its heroes a Christian persona exemplifying the merits of industry, physical exertion, and courage in public service—all ideal traits associated with Kingsley's espousal of what later became known as "Muscular Christianity."

Increasingly concerned with class divisions and the "Condition-of-England" in the tumultuous years of the late 1840s, Kingsley began promoting the "Christian Socialist" views of Maurice, J. M. Ludlow, and Thomas Hughes, insisting that social, economic, and ideological reforms could best be effected through education and the application of Christian ethics. In May 1848 Maurice and Ludlow began *Politics for the People,* a periodical directed expressly to a working-class audience. The journal featured numerous contributions from Kingsley, who wrote general-interest articles as well as pungent politico-religious propaganda under the pseudonym "Parson Lot." Within three months, however, *Politics* failed. Kingsley turned to writing fiction as the best means of disseminating Christian Socialist ideals, insisting: "This is the age of books . . . a flood of books, newspapers, writings of all sorts, good and bad, is spreading over the whole land . . . now, if ever, are we bound to put holy and wise books, both religious and worldly, into the hands of all." Accordingly, Kingsley's first novel, *Yeast,* addressed many of the societal ills of the day. Serialized in *Fraser's* magazine in 1848, this story of an aristocratic young man who becomes aware of the plight of rural peasants proved controversial in its satiric treatment of contemporary religious disputations. Publisher John Parker, fearing the novel was responsible for a decline in *Fraser's* circulation, pressured Kingsley to finish it quickly. Ill health added to the strain on Kingsley at this time, and he completed the novel hurriedly in a state of exhaustion. Stanley T. Williams has written that "nowhere else has Kingsley poured himself so recklessly over the printed page" as he had in this first novel; Williams adds, however, that the work "glows with Kingsley's ardour." Early reviewers maintained that *Yeast* was marred by Kingsley's seemingly exaggerated presentation of social abuses; yet most responded favorably to the author's vehement sincerity and his pragmatic, rather than philosophical, approach. Critic Frederic Harrison, writing nearly half-a-century after *Yeast* was pub-

lished, observed that the novel's title "suggests that it is a ferment thrown into the compound mass of current political, social, and religious ideas, to make them work and issue in some new combination." Characterizing Kingsley as more a sympathetic poet than a philosopher, however, Harrison echoed a common censure of the novel when he lamented that *Yeast,* while offering an absorbing account of social abuses, "quite omits to offer a remedy."

The year 1848 marked another milestone for Kingsley: his appointment as Professor of English Literature at Queen's College, London. He resigned the post by the end of the year, however, as he struggled to maintain his duties at Eversley while meeting the demands of his publisher. Kingsley spent most of the following year personally exploring and addressing the unsanitary living conditions and poor working conditions of his parishioners. He insisted that workers' cooperatives were the best hope for a solution to these problems, and, together with his Christian Socialist colleagues, convened and sponsored a group of tailors early in 1850. The experience provided Kingsley with a wealth of first-hand knowledge about the exploitation of London tailors; he expressed his indignation in a pamphlet entitled *Cheap Clothes and Nasty* (1850), which he wrote for inclusion in a series of "Tracts by Christian Socialists." *Alton Locke,* Kingsley's second novel, followed shortly thereafter. Written in the form of an autobiography, *Alton Locke* traces the spiritual and intellectual growth of its eponymous hero, an impoverished young tailor's apprentice who aspires to be a journalist and the "People's Poet." Featuring a depth of psychological penetration uncommon in Kingsley's writings, *Alton Locke* is considered structurally and artistically superior to many of the author's other works. The novel emphasizes Kingsley's Christian Socialist ideology as it depicts its protagonist's fall into "just the same mistake as the rich of whom [he] complain[s]—the very mistake of fancying that *legislative* reform is *social* reform, or that men's hearts can be changed by act of parliament." Noted for its vivid, albeit grisly, descriptions of lamentable conditions among the laboring poor, *Alton Locke* advocates a self-sacrificing, cooperative society based upon Kingsley's conception of God's kingdom, rejecting political protest as ineffectual.

In autumn of 1850 Kingsley began contributing poetry, fiction, and theological essays to Ludlow's newly-founded *Christian Socialist: A Journal of Association.* The publication was shelved in the summer of 1852, however, and with it Kingsley's participation in Christian Socialist undertakings. Instead, Kingsley turned his attention from the "Condition of England" to historical fiction. *Hypatia,* which he completed in April 1853 and later published in two volumes, is considered the best of Kingsley's three historical novels. Its plot, centering on the struggle between mystical Christianity and classical philosophy in fifth-century Alexandria, draws specific parallels between nineteenth-century Catholicism and the asceticism and superstition that characterized early orthodox Christianity. Kingsley's readers were enthralled by the novel's vivid, sensual descriptions of pagan decadence, and by its lurid account of Hypatia's violent murder at the hands of fanatics incited by Catholic archbishop Cyril. Reviewers, however, were divided along theological lines in assessing the work's merits, many objecting to what they considered a harsh, anti-Catholic depiction of the primitive Christian church, others denouncing the novel as "immoral" and "calculated to encourage young men in profligacy and false doctrine." Later critics lamented the occasionally forced paralleling of fifth-century Alexandria with nineteenth-century London, maintaining that Kingsley's moral didacticism weakened an otherwise lively and well-interpreted description of an important historical epoch. Acknowledging *Hypatia*'s defects as typical of the author's canon, some modern critics consider the novel Kingsley's finest, praising its passionate and entertaining—if not entirely scholarly—recreation of fifth-century conflicts, while recognizing its effectiveness as an imaginative forum for the author's religious and social thought.

Kingsley spent the fall and winter of 1853 vacationing at the Devonshire seacoast, recording impressions of his explorations there while studying works on marine life. His *Glaucus; or, The Wonders of the Shore,* a portion of which appeared initially in the *North British Review,* was published in 1855. That same year, Kingsley also published *Westward Ho!,* a historical romance recounting England's sixteenth-century battle against the Spanish Armada. Kingsley was inspired to write this work both by his studies of Elizabethan history and by Britain's involvement in the Crimean War, which had begun in 1854. Written largely as motivational propaganda, *Westward Ho!* evinced a model of Christian heroism not only in the gallantry of the Elizabethans but also in their firm rejection of the papacy—affording Kingsley yet another forum for religious commentary. The novel was immensely successful in its day and for generations thereafter, being standard reading for students in England well into the twentieth century.

Kingsley's popularity reached its zenith in the years immediately following publication of *Westward Ho!.* The author fostered this growing esteem with three works that were also favorably received during the course of the next three years: *The Heroes; or, Greek Fairy Tales for My Children* (1856), a retelling of Greek myths that was later described by Lafcadio Hearn as "beyond any question the best book of Greek stories written for children in any language"; *Two Years Ago* (1857), a novel concerning the Crimean War; and *Andromeda, and Other Poems* (1858), his only published collection of poetry. Treating themes common to his novels, Kingsley's poems were well received by his contemporaries, and have been praised by modern critics for their evocative imagery and technical polish. Having become widely recognized as a poet, historical novelist, and prominent theologian, Kingsley was appointed Chaplain to the Queen in 1859. The following year, he was offered the professorship of Modern History at Cambridge, where he became tutor to the Prince of Wales. As a historian Kingsley drew criticism from colleagues who questioned his scholarship, but was held in high regard by his students, who responded favorably to his enthusiasm and candor.

In 1862, at his wife's request, Kingsley began writing a fairy tale for his youngest child; *The Water-Babies* was published the following year. Kingsley's most acclaimed

work, *The Water-Babies* anticipated Lewis Carroll's *Alice in Wonderland,* addressing adult concerns in a children's fantasy narrative. Through the life of his protagonist, a young chimney sweep, Kingsley availed himself of an opportunity to depict the deplorable conditions exposed by the Children's Employment Commission of 1861. He further used the tale to express his approval of evolutionary theory and scientific exploration, and as a vehicle for moral instruction. The playful satire and fanciful detail of Kingsley's juvenile fiction endeared the work to his reading public, and *The Water-Babies* quickly became a children's classic. However, in 1864 Kingsley became embroiled in a controversy that greatly damaged his reputation. While reviewing James Anthony Froude's *History of England* for *Macmillan's Magazine,* Kingsley commented: "Truth, for its own sake, had never been a virtue with the Roman clergy," citing the prominent Catholic convert John Henry Newman as an example. Newman's subsequent objection initiated an ongoing dispute between the two, which was carried out in a series of published letters and pamphlets. In a state of exasperation, Newman wrote his renowned autobiography, *Apologia pro Vita Sua* (1864). A passionate defense of his religious sincerity, Newman's *Apologia* opened with a brilliant attack on Kingsley's credibility, effecting a decisive end to the year-long conflict. The fiasco paved the way for widespread denigration of Kingsley's ideas, as numerous critics sarcastically maintained that the author's greatest contribution to English literature was his role in inspiring Newman's *Apologia.*

Kingsley's final novel, *Hereward the Wake: "Last of the English,"* was published in 1866 after appearing serially in the religious journal *Good Words* the previous year. Relating the eleventh-century clash between Norman France and Anglo-Saxon England, *Hereward* presents in its eponymous character a courageous and patriotic Anglo-Saxon hero. Kingsley utilized Cambridge's historical archives in preparing this novel, which is considered his most scholarly. Although less sermonizing than his earlier works, *Hereward* promotes the same "muscular Christian" ideology. In 1869, Kingsley resigned the Cambridge professorship, succumbing to ongoing criticism of his teachings, and began a lengthy journey to the West Indies, his mother's birthplace. While there Kingsley compiled a series of travel sketches entitled "Letters from the Tropics," published in the journal *Good Words* and later collected in his *At Last: A Christmas in the West Indies* (1871). The author's fascination with geology and biology inspired most of his writings during these later years, including a collection of science articles, *Madam How and Lady Why: First Lessons in Earth Lore for Children* (1870), and Kingsley's last significant published work, *Prose Idylls, New and Old* (1873). These celebrations of the natural world and its lessons for humanity convey the author's belief in the providential role of science in aiding social progress. Appointed canon at Westminster Abbey in 1873, Kingsley traveled to the United States and Canada the following year, having been advised by his doctors to take a sea voyage for his health. He returned after nearly six months abroad, still plagued by various maladies. Kingsley contracted pneumonia shortly thereafter and died early in 1875.

Known in his day as the "apostle of the flesh," Kingsley embraced and propounded a theology that reconciled divine will with Victorian ideals of the sanctity of family life, the value of vigorous industry, the ennobling influence of patriotism and public service, the inevitability of human progress, and the value of scientific inquiry. He sought through fiction and poetry to demonstrate not only the need for but the desirability of the social religion that he espoused. Though art was often subordinated to purpose and expediency in Kingsley's works, he is nevertheless praised for the power and eloquence of his descriptive prose and his poetry. The best of his hexameters are considered among the finest such poetry in English literature. Most commentators agree, however, that Kingsley's life is of greater interest to modern readers than his works, citing as evidence the relative abundance of biographical material on the author. Kingsley's works are thus presently studied primarily for their insight into the thought and temperament of a man who has become increasingly appreciated as an embodiment of Victorian attitudes and ideology. Summarizing this position, Larry Uffelman has written that Kingsley's "interest and active participation in social and sanitary reform movements, his lifelong celebration of married love and family life, his intense Protestantism and strong anti-Catholic bias, his intense pride in being British, and his passion for the natural sciences mark him in both substance and tone as one of the principal spokesmen of his age."

PRINCIPAL WORKS

The Saint's Tragedy; or, The True Story of Elizabeth of Hungary (drama) 1848
Twenty-five Village Sermons (speeches) 1849
Alton Locke, Tailor and Poet (novel) 1850
Cheap Clothes and Nasty [as Parson Lot] (pamphlet) 1850
Yeast: A Problem (novel) 1851
Phaeton: or, Loose Thoughts for Loose Thinkers (dialogue) 1852
Hypatia; or, New Foes with an Old Face (novel) 1853
Alexandria and Her Schools (lectures) 1854
Brave Words for Brave Soldiers and Sailors (essay) 1855
Glaucus; or, The Wonders of the Shore (nonfiction) 1855
Westward Ho! or, The Voyages and Adventures of Sir Amyas Leigh, Knight, of Burrough in the County of Devon, in the Reign of Her Most Glorious Majesty Queen Elizabeth (novel) 1855
The Heroes; or, Greek Fairy Tales for My Children (mythology) 1856
Two Years Ago (novel) 1857
Andromeda, and Other Poems (poetry) 1858
Miscellanies (essays and lectures) 1859
The Limits of Exact Science as Applied to History: An Inaugural Lecture (lecture) 1860
The Water-Babies: A Fairy Tale for a Land-Baby (novel) 1863
Mr. Kingsley and Mr. Newman: A Correspondence [with John Henry Newman] (essays) 1864

The Roman and the Teuton (lectures) 1864
"What, Then, Does Dr. Newman Mean?": A Reply (essay) 1864
Hereward the Wake: "Last of the English" (novel) 1866
Madam How and Lady Why; or, First Lessons in Earth Lore for Children (nonfiction) 1870
At Last: A Christmas in the West Indies (sketches) 1871
Town Geology (nonfiction) 1872
Prose Idylls, New and Old (sketches) 1873
The Works of Charles Kingsley. 28 vols. (novels, essays, poetry, speeches, letters) 1880-89

Parson Frank (essay date 1851)

[*In the following excerpt, Frank reviews Kingsley's* Alton Locke *and earlier works, contending that these are weakened artistically by the author's dogmatic approach. The critic acknowledges the timeliness of Kingsley's efforts, however, and comments appreciatively on numerous passages from the author's works that he has found to be of particular merit.*]

Magazines, like men, are subject to vicissitude in this fleeting existence of ours. Some have their exits and their entrances, coming in like a lion and going out like a lamb; others pass through a long career of ups and downs, and in their time play many parts. The Rev. Charles Kingsley, to whom we purpose devoting a page or two, is somewhat prominently connected with a magazine (*Fraser's*), the character and tone of which have, within a few years, undergone a marked alteration. For the better? Yes!— promptly reply the potent, grave, and *reverend* signiors, who form the "progress" party within the Church of England. No!—as promptly vociferate subscribers of the olden time, who loved *Fraser* for its jolly good-fellowship, and infinitely preferred the plentiful cakes and ale of its ancient régime, when Sir Toby Belches and Andrew Aguecheeks by the dozen, held mad revelry in its columns, to the Malvolio virtuousness of the new dispensation. *Blackwood*, too, is graver than of yore; but the dimness of once over-bright "Ebony" is nothing to the gloom that, as old *Fraser*ians contend, has settled on young *Fraser* since it changed its domicile from gay Regent street to the dusk offices of Mr. Parker's clerical and educational institute. Does the reader remember the clever sketches of the *Fraser*ians in 1835—the group of distinguished contributors clustered about their publisher's round table? What a change in the staff since those portraits were taken! Seated together in after-dinner companionship, we there behold—among others of kindred renown—Theodore Hook, his eye beaming with wine and a punning impromptu—Crofton Croker, merrily hob-a-nobbing with Jerdan—Lockhart, looking thoughtful, determined, and sarcastic—the Ettrick Shepherd in his plaid, tossing off a beaker with hearty good-will—John Galt, "bland and bespectacled"—Sir Egerton Brydges, like Esau, a hairy and disappointed man—Macnish, the "Modern Pythagorean" and anatomist of drunkenness—"Delta" Moir, looking, as he is, an amiable man and tender poet—Dr. Maginn, effervescent with wit and eloquence—"Father Prout," attracted ("O rare Jesuit!") to the festive board by his love of cleverness, joviality, and literature—and two other parsons, Gleig, episcopalian and novel-writing, and Irving, presbyterian and novel-denouncing—and Allan Cunningham enjoying a "crack" with Count d'Orsay—and Harrison Ainsworth cheek by jowl with venerable Coleridge—and Barry Cornwall, and Carlyle, and Sir David Brewster, and many *beaux esprits* besides. But now, *tempora mutantur.* The new editor, in the name of the old magazine, cries *peccavi!*—acknowledges truth in the charge of having dealt more than was quite becoming in personalities—pleads that the life of a magazine, like that of a nation and an individual man, has its phases, that time brings experience, and that *Fraser* will never be so boisterous again—and protests that the *Fraser*ians have quite ceased to attend imaginary *symposia,* and to drink gallons of imaginary punch, and have learned to temper their wit, that it may for the future tell on men's principles of action, without unnecessarily wounding their self-love or ruffling their tempers. Accordingly, this journal has now become the organ of that party without a name, which sympathizes with the cause of progress in church and state, and embraces among its members the accidentally differing but essentially agreeing disciples of Dr. Arnold, and Archdeacon Hare, and Professor Maurice. Under this dynasty, the contributions of Mr. Kingsley occupy a foremost place.

Of those contributions the best-known is that strange and taking story, with a strange and taking title, **Yeast**—a memoir of the sayings and doings of Launcelot Smith, gentleman—which appeared in the magazine some three years since, and has recently been *re*presented to the world with new cuffs and collars (as clergymen say when patching up an old sermon) under the name of **Yeast: A Problem.** In this, as in all his works, Mr. Kingsley is intent on a crusade against social evils. He is an enthusiastic alumnus of Mr. Carlyle, whom he is for ever quoting and for ever (*longo intervallo*) imitating. Like his master, he is clever at finding fault, quick to discern abuses, warm in intolerance of quackery. Like his master, he is vague when discussing remedies, and most foggy when off what should be Cape Clear. **Yeast** answers the purpose of producing a ferment. It is a *problem* quite capable of puzzling brains of any known consistency. But whether the author has quieted and composed his own fermenting elements into wholesome food—whether he has found the solution to his own problem—this is another question. The merit of his writings lies in their negative, not their positive character; in what is destructive rather than constructive; in exposing the weak points and vicious abuses and hollow pretences of existing systems, political, social, and religious, rather than supplying a new faith and practice. So far as he goes, Mr. Kingsley is a combatant of considerable tact and personal prowess. Not so profound as either Hare or Maurice, he is infinitely more agile, vivacious, and popular than either of those oracular gentlemen. Where they are calm and metaphysical, he is vehement and practical. The wordy paradoxes and tortuous vagaries of Professor Maurice—that able, good, but most unsatisfactory man—find little room in the pages of "Parson Lot" (as Mr. Kingsley occasionally calls himself) who is, we allow, clearness and

definiteness itself when compared with his *collaborateur* in the cause of "Christian Socialism." In fact, a competent reviewer has defined the "great merit" of **Yeast** to consist in its *clear, definite* statement of the chief questions that are fermenting in the hearts of men at the present time—its "great fault" in the passion and exaggeration of statement and inferences thence deduced. Every one can see that the author is in earnest. He is too admiring a devotee of Carlyle to be other than grimly in earnest—sometimes one-sidedly, impatiently so. Perhaps this is a necessary condition to the temperament of a Reformer. Enthusiasm may now and then cover a multitude of sins. And Mr. Kingsley's enthusiasm is always for right ends, whatever we may think of the means he adopts for their attainment. The evils of English town and country life he perceives with penetrating glance, and mourns over with no sort of do-nothing sorrow. He sympathizes in an extraordinary degree with the spirit of the age—its aspirations, hopes, fears, struggles, sufferings. He comes forward as an exponent of its "poor dumb mouth," and speaks the word it is bursting to speak, and the people waiting to hear. We might almost call him

> A latter Luther, and a soldier-priest
> To scare church-harpies from the master's feast;
>   Our dusted velvets have much need of him,

for he is no mere "Sabbath-drawler of old saws"—

> But spurred at heart with fieriest energy
> To embattail and to wall about his cause
>   With iron-worded proof,

and most heartily despises the "humming of drowsy pulpit drones," and the faded rhetoric of "worm-cankered homilies." He might have written the description of Dr. Dimsoul Darkman, with sad appropriateness termed D. D.

> So learned, he can quite dispense
> With visions and intelligence;
> He hath a creed, he hath a tongue,
> He had a heart when he was young;
> But—very melancholy fact!
> 'Tis like a bell that time hath crackt,
> Which by this certain mark is known,
> His speech is clatter without tone.

Stagnant orthodoxy of this order Mr. Kingsley cannot away with; it provokes him to rampant heterodoxy, till he breathes, if not threatening and slaughter against Dr. Dimsoul Darkman, at least what the doctor would call false doctrine, heresy, and schism.

> Oh, the mouth-man and the heart-man, different
>   they be
> As death and life, light and dark ice, and charity.

Crabbed dogmatists—Simeonite or Puseyite—are *Nehushtan* to the author of **Yeast.** As Theophilus Trinal says, there have been times and places in which, with sorrowful emphasis, it might be asked, what can be more opposite than Christ and a Christian, if such as these be Christians? and the same Theophilus, we remember, in the delirium of his last illness, cried to his mother, "Don't let those bad people come near me—those Christians"—and, on her very gently and soothingly replying, "Why, you are a Christian yourself, Theophilus!"—how significant his feverish exclamation—"What I? Take them away. They look like black goats butting at me. Let somebody stand near me that loves me." Both in *Alton Locke* and in *Yeast,* Mr. Kingsley is admirable at portraying morbid phases of religious character. Nothing can be better than Mrs. Lavington (the mother of Launcelot Smith's betrothed) a severe "evangelical" matron, who bullies her hearty fox-hunting husband after no very promising fashion—trying "to convert the old man by coldness, severity, and long curtain-lectures, utterly unintelligible to their victim, because couched in the peculiar conventional phraseology of Newton and Simeon's school. She forgot, poor, earnest soul! that the same form of religion which had captivated a disappointed girl of twenty, might not be the most attractive for a jovial old man of sixty." Another happy portrait is Vieuxbois, who considers nothing more heterodox than the notion that the poor were to educate themselves. "In his scheme, of course, the clergy and the gentry were to educate the poor, who were to take down thankfully as much as it was thought proper to give them; and all beyond was 'self-will' and 'private judgment,' the fathers of Dissent and Chartism, Trades'-union strikes and French revolutions *et si quæ ulia.*' And when this gentleman asks the agitator for educational measures, Pray what *limit* would you put to education?—mark Mr. Kingsley's reply: (Launcelot Smith *loquitur*)—"The capacities of each man. If man, living in civilized society has one right which he can demand, it is this; that the state which exists by his labors shall enable him to develope, or at least not hinder his developing his whole faculties to their very uttermost, however lofty that may be." The high-church young lady, impulsive, earnest, and devoted, is vividly represented in the person of Argemone, some of whose conversations with the hero are first-rate in matter and manner both, and are marked by the very form and pressure of the times. Launcelot, again, is powerfully depicted—one whom we cannot but watch with interest at every step of his varied and chastened career, until we leave him at the last, assumed to be "perfected through suffering." He is more truthfully and consistently drawn than his successor in the same course of probation, Alton Locke. In one turning point of his biography is concentrated the essence of Mr. Kingsley's philosophy—namely, when he (Launcelot) repents of his *laissez-faire* habits, his ignorance of society, of practical life, and the outward *present;* when he blames himself angrily for having wasted his time on *ancient* histories and *foreign* travels, to the neglect of that *wonderful living present* which weltered daily round him, every face embodying a living soul—"for now he began to feel that those faces *did* hide living souls." Mr. Kingsley recognizes the divinity that stirs within us—within this nineteenth century of ours—within our daily life and household histories; he descries something worth thinking about and writing about, even in the smoke-dried faces of factories and factory people, even in an age of mechanics' institutes, anti-corn law leagues, emigration funds, working-men's associations, ragged-schools, and such like. His heart and hope are with this rough, prosy, present time—nor with *him* does distance of centuries lend enchantment to the view. He rather sings,

> My own age! my own age! they say that thou art crude,

> Ungrateful to the former time, and wishing all renewed.
> I do not spurn that former time, but own it proud and free;
> Yet not for its heroic prime would I surrender thee!

He places his ear against the great heart of the present time—and what others declare to be the dull creaking of machinery, ironcold and dead, *he* knows to be palpitations of the mystery of Life, warm pulsations of a vital essence, dynamical and not mechanical, spiritual and not material, quickening their beat at every grand thought and noble inspiration. In sooty Manchester he sees something more than legions of operatives—he sees fellow-creatures created by the same Creator and hastening to the same awful eternity with himself, into whose daily life, and habit of thought, and cherished pursuits, he enters with unaffected sympathy—so that much of his doctrine may be expressed in Mrs. Gaskell's words [from her *Mary Barton*]:—"The vices of the poor sometimes astound us *here;* but when the secrets of all hearts shall be made known, their virtues will astound us in far greater degree. Of this I am sure,"—and of this too *he* is sure who has placed Sandy Mackay and others "of that ilk" in his Gallery of Literary Portraits.

The old Scotchman mentioned in the last paragraph, Sandy Mackay, is, we need hardly say, the presiding spirit in *Alton Locke.* Mr. Gilfillan calls him "just Thomas Carlyle *humanized.*" Certainly the quantity of Carlylese spouted by him and his author is wonderful—though the angles of the original genius are ground down or worn away, the fine gold is become dim in course of transmutation, the old wine is put into new bottles, which hardly improve its flavor or enrich its color. Mr. Kingsley is too much of a borrower and an imitator to attain a permanent place in our literature, judging at least by his latest production. We prefer Carlyle in *propria persona* to this second-hand Carlyle, vending second-hand books in a dingy shop, and discoursing second-hand Doric to Chartist visitors. Wherein consists the originality and independence often imputed to Mr. Kingsley, on the credit of *Alton Locke,* is to us unknown; it is as palpable an echo as can very well be conceived, and we are not aware that the author is likely to demur to this judgment; we rather apprehend, such is his veneration of the Latter-day pamphleteer, that he feels honored by any opinion that identifies him with, or approximates him to, the cause and person of that rugged genius. Perhaps, if he could or would shake off something of this allegiance, and allow his own inventive powers fair play, and follow the bidding of his own lively fancy, he might produce works that would miss indeed the temporary popularity of his present novels, but gain instead a solid, enduring, ever-growing reputation. As it is, he writes for a temporary purpose, as a polemic in the condition-of-England question, with the intensity and fire of an *ex-parte* churchman militant; as such, verily, he has his reward—and is probably content therewith—content to be forgotten with the social evils he yearns to destroy. It has been observed that "the materials with which he is constructing he feels to be too rough for the application of the (artist's) rule and plummet." His book is a thing thrust between the living and the dead; and the moral plague which it interprets and would help to stay, consciously mocks at the restraints of rule and the ministries of grace. In *Alton Locke* there is a negation of self on the part of the writer, an absence of all desire to stand forth as a "talented writer." Steadiness of aim and singleness of purpose are not throughout beguiled for a moment. The purpose is to arouse the attention of a wider class than that which refers to blue books and official reports, and to force them to look on the social evils that are lying at their doors. The social problems perplexing the world, as well as the social miseries that have given rise to them, are boldly grappled with by a writer who does not go into the task of moral anatomy with a box of aromatic vinegar at his nose." A question may be, and indeed has been, raised and "vexed," as to whether it is a legitimate use of *fiction,* to write stories with the purpose of illustrating an opinion or establishing a doctrine; whether polemics, be they religious, political, or metaphysical, do not lie wholly beyond its province—inasmuch as the novelist makes his facts as well as his reasonings, coins the premises from which his conclusions are drawn, and may thus coin exactly what he wants, and reject whatever would impede the circulation of his own adopted currency. However these objections may hold good in general against controversial fiction— the unfairness of which is constantly observable in the "religious novels" of all sects, of the various schools headed by J. M. Neale, Paget, Sewell, C. B. Taylor, Charlotte Elizabeth, &c.—still, we think, where evils are so rife and patent as those which Mr. Kingsley attacks, an author by the mere exposure of them, in a form adapted to arrest public attention, does the state some service; and if the manner he adopts, and the vehicle he chooses for the conveyance of his facts, be objectionable to art, and ill-according with the principles of taste, the damage is *his*— and in all probability he will have already counted the cost, and be prepared to sacrifice æsthetical reputation on the altar of the common weal. He may coin his facts to his liking; he may sometimes bind over other and contumacious facts to keep the peace, when they threaten the peace of his theory; he may be sadly partial, exclusive, deaf of one ear, and blind of one eye; but if the tendency of his agitation is to arouse sympathy with myriad sufferers previously unnoticed and uncared for—as in the instance of Hood's "Song of the Shirt"—and to reveal hidden diseases, deeds of darkness, and the "science of starving,"— why, one can hardly deny a genial and peculiar merit to his appeals.

Concerning the social and political doctrines advanced in *Alton Locke* this is not the place to speak. It may be, that the political economy, against which the diatribes of Maurice and Kingsley and their coadjutors are directed, is after all "benevolence under the guidance of science"— and that these impulsive philanthropists do exhibit in their controversial writings an intolerant, contemptuous spirit, "a restless unwillingness to submit to criticism, examination, or control, and a prompt recurrence to persecution and abuse," which calls for strong reprobation; it *may* be that they really little know, and can ill appreciate, "the strenuous effort, the stern and systematic self-control by which the votary of economic science, the benevolent *man of principle,* keeps his head cool and clear in the midst of the miseries he is called upon to contemplate; and the resolute nerve which is needed to throw cold water on the mis-

chievous schemes of sanguine and compassionate contrivers. . . . who always insist upon scrambling out of the bog on the wrong side, simply because it is the nearest." The discussion of these grave and pressing questions we leave to the *Edinburgh Review* and the *Leader,* to Parson Lot of the *Christian Socialist,* and the honorable editor of the *Economist.* Before leaving *Alton Locke,* however, let us pay our tribute of admiration to many a graphic scene and subtly-defined character in its exciting pages— willingly forgetting the mawkish affectation of a certain interview in Dulwich Gallery, and other not unfrequent blemishes, in favor of the very fine and life-like description of Alton's childhood, his "ladder to learning," erected under the auspices of Sandy Mackay, his visit of horror, under the same old Trojan's tutelage, to that memorable upper-room of female sin and shame, and starvation; and other stirring episodes in the progress of the tale. The superiority, nevertheless, of the early to the closing stages, we account very decided—and we fear that chapter the last embodies but a lame and impotent conclusion, and depicts a state of mind in the hero unwarranted by ordinary psychological laws. Here Mr. Kingsley does seem, as far as observation of man and mind in this age of *Yeast* allows us to judge, to have coined his facts as well as his reasonings in a somewhat arbitrary manner, manufacturing plastic ones that will dovetail smoothly with his religious purpose, and tossing aside those other ordinary and every-day facts which are proverbially stubborn things.

His performances in verse, dramatic and lyric, evince no insignificant fund of poetical capability. *The Saint's Tragedy* entitles him, by common consent, to a place with some of our most distinguished rising poets. If it is, like his prose, occasionally wearisome from monotony and mannerism, and also wanting in that melody and finish which no minstrel can afford to despise, it is also "tender and true," lively and picturesque, enthusiastic and dignified. It utters the same language, and introduces almost the same themes as those which characterize *Alton Locke* and *Yeast.* Thus Elizabeth, the heroine, contrasts her princely state with neighboring penury in the following strain:—

> We sit in a cloud, and sing, like pictured angels,
> And say the world runs smooth—while right
>   below,
> Welters the black fermenting heap of life
> On which our state is built; I saw this day
> What we might be, and still be Christian women:
> And mothers, too—I saw one laid in childhood
> These three cold weeks upon the black damp
>   straw,
> No nurses, cordials, or that nice parade
> With which we try to baulk the curse of Eve—
> And yet she laughed and showed her buxom
>   boy,
> And said, Another week, so please the saints,
> She'd be at work a-field.

Or take her description of a dark, noisome, crowded alley, where

>   The gaunt-haunched swine
> *Growled at their christian playmates o'er the*
>   *scraps;*
> Shrill mothers cursed; wan children wailed;
>   sharp coughs

Glared dumb reproach, *and old perplexity,*
Too stale for words; o'er still and webless looms
The listless craftsmen through their elf-locks
    scowled.

For a concise vigor in word-painting of this kind, Mr.
Kingsley frequently displays special aptitude; and being
less hampered by obligations to Carlyle than when writing
prose, he is in poetry more true to himself and to nature.
He may claim "peerage" with such of the "upper house"
as Moultrie, and R. C. Trench, and Clough, and Burbage,
and Sterling, and Patmore—and one day may possibly
command a more exalted seat—for he is Charles Kingsley
junior yet—and of him one may say, in the language of anticipation, Not as though he had already attained, either
were already perfect.

Various are the paths of literature which he has assayed
to tread. The novel—the drama—the sermon—the
tract—the review—all have been handled, and with more
or less of ease and success, by this reverend gentleman. His
Village Sermons we have never seen; but they are eulo-
gized by well qualified judges—and he is one of the few
living clerics whom we should name, *à priori,* as likely to
write effective pulpit addresses to our rural population—
the best we know being those by the late Augustus Hare.
In *Fraser's Magazine* we trace many a clever criticism to
Mr. Kingsley—replete with vivacity, earnestness, and
mannerism; like no other man's criticism—neither very
profound, nor very scholarly, nor very acute, nor very
witty—but written off in a familiar, dashing, self-sufficing
style, with a spice of humor, and a good deal of practical
English sense. And in conclusion we can but allude to his
appearances as "Parson Lot" in *Politics for the People*
(1848), and *The Christian Socialist*—in which character
he discourses graphically enough, and in unequivocal Carlylese, about **Cheap Clothes and Nasty,** the rights and
wrongs of chartism and communism, the politics of the
Old and New Testament, and multifarious topics of the
same grave order. (pp. 507-12)

    Parson Frank, "Charles Kingsley, Author of
    Alton Locke," in The Eclectic Magazine, *Vol.*
    XXIII, August, 1851, pp. 507-12.

The Saturday Review, London (essay date 1858)

[*In the following essay, the critic reviews Kingsley's* Andromeda, and Other Poems, *praising the author's sympathetic imagination, descriptive power, command of
language, and skillful use of the hexameter.*]

It is easy to understand how the great Apostle of the
Flesh, in choosing a subject for a poem, should be drawn
to the Homeric and mythic age of Greece. The high intellectual civilization of Athens, with its Socrates, its Sophists, and its Cynics, would be almost as little an object of
sympathy to him as the age of macerated monks.

Sudden she ceased, with a shriek: in the spray,
    like a hovering foam-bow,
Hung, more fair than the foam-bow, a boy in the
    bloom of his manhood,
Golden-haired, ivory-limbed, ambrosial; over
    his shoulder

Hung for a veil of his beauty the gold-fringed
    folds of the goat-skin
Bearing the brass of his shield, as the sun flashed
    clear on its clearness.
Curved on his thigh lay a falchion; and under the
    gleam of his helmet
Eyes more blue than the main shone awful,
    around him Athené
Shed in her love such grace, such state, and terri-
    ble daring.
Hovering over the water he came, upon glitter-
    ing pinions,
Living, a wonder, outgrown from the tight-laced
    gold of his sandals;
Bounding from billow to billow, and sweeping
    the crests like a sea-gull;
Leaping the gulfs of the surge, as he laughed in
    the joy of his leaping.
Fair and majestic he sprang to the rock; and the
    maiden in wonder
Gazed for awhile, and then hid in the dark-
    rolling wave of her tresses,
Fearful, the light of her eyes; while the boy (for
    her sorrow had awed him)
Blushed at her blushes, and vanished, like mist
    on the cliff's at the sunrise.
Fearful at length she looked forth: he was gone:
    she, wild with amazement,
Wailed for her mother aloud: but the wail of the
    wind only answered.
Sudden he flashed into sight, by her side; in his
    pity and anger
Moist were his eyes; and his breath like a rose-
    bed, as bolder and bolder,
Hovering under her brows, like a swallow that
    haunts by the house-eaves,
Delicate-handed, he lifted the veil of her hair;
    while the maiden
Motionless, frozen with fear, wept loud; till his
    lips unclosing
Poured from their pearl-strung portal the musi-
    cal wave of his wonder.

Compare this delicious picture with Simeon Stylites on his
pillar—with a stiff-necked picture of a saint in a painted
window—or with those monks and holy virgins who, by
the habit of going naked, became so completely covered
with hair as to require no clothes—and you have the difference between the philosophy of Mr. Kingsley and his
school, and the philosophy of those who desire to "deliver
the celestial spirit from the bondage of flesh and blood."
The spirit of the young gentleman described in the lines
we have quoted could hardly be very anxious to be released from its carnal prison-house, with the adjacent female dungeon.

Andromeda will, we believe, be thought a very successful
effort of its kind; and its success arises from its not being
a mere classical exercise, but the production of one who
enters as heartily into what is rather priggishly called the
"sensuousness" of the Homeric life as Walter Scott does
into chivalry, or Dr. Newman into the ecclesiastical life
of the middle ages. It is a glowing Etty-picture of the best
kind, but with a romance which Etty wants, or only gets
now and then by accident rather than by art. It would be
difficult indeed to find a more striking manifestation of the
common element of poetry and painting. Few have stud-

ied beauty more deeply than the author of *Andromeda*— few have such command of language and such descriptive power. The spirit of the heroic age, too, seems to us to be truly caught, and there is genuine Homeric pathos in the parting of Andromeda and her mother. As to metre, the haters of classical hexameters will probably allow that these are about the best they ever read. It seems pretty clear that had Mr. Kingsley, instead of preaching his peculiar social philosophy in novels, taken to poetry, using his philosophic sympathies merely as his guide in the choice of subjects, he would have been a very considerable poet.

It is of course almost impossible for a modern writer, by any effort of imagination, to throw himself back so completely into the feelings of the Homeric age as not occasionally to fall into an anachronism. It is an anachronism, we venture to think, when Andromeda addresses the sea thus:—

> Even as I loved thee, dread sea, as I played by
> thy margin,
> Blessing thy wave as it cooled me, thy wind as
> it breathed on my forehead,
> Bowing my head to thy tempest, and opening
> my heart to thy children,
> Silvery fish, wreathed shell, and the strange lithe
> things of the water,
> Tenderly casting them back, as they gasped on
> the beach in the sunshine,
> Home to their mother—in vain! for mine sits
> childless in anguish!
> Oh dread sea! false sea! I dreamed what I
> dreamed of thy goodness;
> Dreamed of a smile in thy gleam, of a laugh in
> the plash of thy ripple:
> False and devouring thou art, and the great
> world dark and despiteful.

This impersonation of the sea, with the "smile in its gleam," the "laugh in the plash of its ripple," certainly would find no parallel older than Apollonius Rhodius. The "opening of the heart" to the children of the sea, is a piece of modern sentimentalism which would scarcely find a parallel older than Rousseau.

The end of the poem, which makes Athene, the goddess of wisdom and heroic virtue, set aside the light Aphrodite, and claim as her own the task of rewarding and blessing the love of Perseus and Andromeda, is an excellent instance of allegorical teaching by poetry, without the smallest detriment to the poem as a work of art. This is a far more effectual, as well as more legitimate method of making art serve a moral purpose, than the thinly disguised arguments and diatribes which rouse the logical antagonism of the reader.

Of the smaller poems in the book, the principal is **"Saint Maura."** The picture of the African saint crucified beside her husband is drawn with undeniable power, but many people will be inclined to doubt whether the subject, thus worked out into detail, is not too horrible for the best purposes of art. The influence of Tennyson's historical pictures is perceptible here, as the general influence of Tennyson is perceptible throughout Mr. Kingsley's poems, no less than those of the other poets of our day. It should be noted that **"Maura,"** and one or two of the smaller poems, such as the **"Ugly Princess,"** show that Mr. Kingsley's sympathies are not cramped, but extend to types of character very different from that which he seems to love best.

The smaller pieces are mostly wild and sad, and a very large proportion of them are about the sea. The key-note of them is in the lines:—

> Scream on, ye sea-fowl! my heart echoes your
> desolate cry.
> Sweep the dry sand on, thou wild wind, to drift
> o'er the shell and the sea-weed;
> Sea-weed and shell, like my dreams, swept down
> the pitiless tide.

We are inclined to object to the **"Bad Squire,"** not because we doubt that there are bad squires enough, or that it is a good work to reform them; but we doubt whether, in such lines as these, you do not, while trying to mend one hole, make two. A poacher's widow is cursing the game-preserver by whose keeper her husband was shot:—

> In the season of shame and sadness,
> In the dark and dreary day,
> When scrofula, gout, and madness
> Are eating your race away;
>
> When to kennels and liveried varlets
> You have cast your daughter's bread,
> And, worn out with liquor and harlots,
> Your heir at your feet lies dead;
>
> When your youngest, the mealy-mouthed rec-
> tor,
> Lets your soul rot asleep to the grave,
> You will find in your God the protector
> Of the freeman you fancied your slave.

The **"Day of the Lord"** is a kind of battle hymn of Christian Socialism, or whatever the social philosophy of Mr. Kingsley and his friends is to be called, and it seems to us to be the concentrated expression of what we venture to think essentially a fallacious idea of the nature of the contest which "earnest" men have to wage with the evils of the world:—

> The Day of the Lord is at hand, at hand!
> Its storms roll up the sky:
> The nations sleep starving on heaps of gold;
> All dreamers toss and sigh;
> The night is darkest before the morn;
> When the pain is sorest the child is born,
> And the Day of the Lord at hand.
>
> Gather you, gather you, angels of God—
> Freedom, and Mercy, and Truth;
> Come! for the Earth is grown coward and old;
> Come down, and renew us her youth.
> Wisdom, Self-Sacrifice, Daring, and Love,
> Haste to the battle-field, stoop from above,
> To the Day of the Lord at hand.
>
> Gather you, gather you, hounds of hell—
> Famine, and Plague, and War;
> Idleness, Bigotry, Cant, and Misrule,
> Gather, and fall in the snare!
> Hireling and Mammonite, Bigot, and Knave,
> Crawl to the battle-field, sneak to your grave,
> In the Day of the Lord at hand.

Who would sit down and sigh for a lost age of
   gold,
   While the Lord of all ages is here?
True hearts will leap up at the trumpet of God,
   And those who can suffer, can dare.
Each old age of gold was an iron age too,
And the meekest of saints may find stern work
   to do,
   In the day of the Lord at hand.

These are spirited lines; but no such military crisis as they imply ever has occurred in the struggle between good and evil, or ever will occur till the actual day of Armageddon. It is not on a "battle-field" that the contest is really waged, nor is the victory to be gained by an almost physical effort of martial prowess for which "true hearts" may muster their energies as they would for a conflict with an enemy of flesh and blood. Nor do the two armies stand divided and arrayed over against each other in this manner. The soldier going forth to the fight will find that, whatever may be the case with "Famine, and Plague, and War," "Idleness, Bigotry, Cant, and Misrule" are not charging him front to front, but lurking beneath his own breastplate; and that it is there that the main struggle is to be carried on. It would be a long controversy to discuss whether this is the darkest hour of the night, or whether there is any particular reason at this moment to expect that the "Day of the Lord" is dawning, and that the "meekest of saints" are likely soon to be called upon to "do stern work." The "Last Day" has been pretty frequently fixed, and as often unavoidably adjourned; and possibly the "Day of the Lord" may be in the same predicament. It is better to be careful how you screw people up for that which after all may not be "at hand."

The "Early Poems" contain the germs of tendencies which have since been developed, and display a promise of power which has since been fulfilled. (pp. 594-95)

> *'Kingsley's Andromeda, and Other Poems,"* in
> The Saturday Review, *London, Vol. 5, No.
> 136, June 5, 1858, pp. 594-95.*

Henry James (essay date 1866)

[*One of the most renowned American novelists of the late nineteenth century, James is revered for his psychological acuity and skillfully wrought, complex narrative style. Throughout his career, James also wrote literary criticism in which he developed his artistic ideals and applied them to the works of others. Among the numerous dictums he formed to clarify the nature of fiction was his definition of the novel as "a direct impression of life." The quality of this impression—the degree of moral and intellectual sophistication—and the author's ability to communicate this impression in an effective and artistic manner were the two principal criteria by which James estimated the worth of a literary work. In the following review, he describes* Hereward the Wake *as one of Kingsley's best works, praising the author as a "heaven-commissioned raconteur."*]

Mr. Kingsley has written nothing better than this recital of the adventures of Hereward, son of the famous Lady Godiva of Coventry, and the "grim earl," Leofric, her husband—who as a boy, under King Edward the Confessor, was outlawed, as too hard a case for his parents to manage; who took service with foreign princes and turned sea-rover on his own account; who was the last of the Berserkers and the first of the knights-errant; who performed unparalleled feats of valor and of cunning; who on the Duke of Normandy's invasion of England felt himself, in spite of his outlawry, still an Englishman at heart, sailed over to England, and collected an army to contest the Norman rights; who contested them long and bravely, in the fen-country of Lincolnshire, but at last found the invaders too many for him and was driven for a subsistence to the greenwood, where he set the fashion to Robin Hood and the dozen other ballad-heroes whom the author enumerates; who under his reverses grew cold and faithless to the devoted wife whom he had married out of Flanders, and who had followed his fortunes over land and sea; who, repudiating Torfrida, thought to patch up his prospects by a base union with a Norman princess, for whom he had cherished an earlier but an unworthy passion, and by a tardy submission to the new king; but who at last, disappointed, humiliated, demoralized by idleness, fell a victim, in his stalwart prime, to the jealousy of the Norman knights.

Mr. Kingsley's hero, as the reader sees, is an historical figure, duly celebrated in the contemporary and other chronicles, Anglo-Saxon and Norman. How many of his adventures are fiction does not here signify, inasmuch as they were destined to become fiction in Mr. Kingsley's novel; and, as the elements of a novel by a man of genius, become animated with a more lively respectability than could ever accrue to them as parcels of dubious history. For his leading points, Mr. Kingsley abides by his chroniclers, who, on their side, abide by tradition. Tradition had made of Hereward's adventures a most picturesque and romantic story; and they have assuredly lost none of their qualities in Mr. Kingsley's hands. Hereward is a hero quite after his own heart; one whose virtue, in the antique sense, comes ready-made to his use; so that he has to supply this article only in its modern significance. The last representative of unadulterated English grit, of what is now the rich marrow of the English character, could not, with his generous excesses and his simple shortcomings, but forcibly inspire our author's imagination. He was a hero, covered with those glories which as a poet, of an epic turn, as an admirable story-teller and describer, and as an Englishman, Mr. Kingsley would delight to relate; and he was a man, subject to those masculine foibles over which, in his ecclesiastical and didactic character, our author would love to moralize. Courage has ever been in Mr. Kingsley's view the divine fact in human nature; and courage, as bravely understood as he understands it, is assuredly an excellent thing. He has done his best to make it worthy of its high position; his constant effort has been to prove that it is not an easy virtue. He has several times shown us that a man may be rich in that courage which is the condition of successful adventure, but that he may be very much afraid of his duty. In fact, almost every one of his heroes has been compelled to make good his heroism by an act of signal magnanimity. In this manner Kingsley has insisted upon the worthlessness of the greatest natural strength when unaccompanied by a corresponding strength of soul.

One of his remote disciples has given a name to this un-sanctified pluck in the title of the tale, "Barren Honors." The readers of *Two Years Ago* will remember, moreover, the pathetic interest which attached in that charming novel to the essentially unregenerate manfulness of Tom Turnall. The lesson of his history was that it behooves every man to devote his muscle—we can find no better name for Mr. Kingsley's conception of intelligence—to the service of strict morality. This obligation is the constant theme of Mr. Kingsley's teaching. It is true that, to his perception, the possibilities of human character run in a very narrow channel, and that a man has done his grandest when he has contrived not to shirk his plain duty. Duty, for him, is a five-barred gate in a hunting-field: the cowards dismount and fumble at the unyielding padlock; the "gentlemen" ride steadily to the leap.

It has been hinted how *Hereward* turns out a coward. After a long career of generous hacking and hewing, of the most heroic brutalities and the most knightly courtesies, he finds himself face to face with one of the homely trials of private life. He is tired of his wife, who has lost her youth and her beauty in his service, and he is tempted by another woman who has been keeping both for him through all the years of his wanderings. To say, shortly, that he puts away his wife and marries his unworthy temptress would be to do him injustice. This is what he comes to, indeed; but, before judging him, we must learn in Mr. Kingsley's pages how *naturally* he does so. Hereward is an instance of that "demoralization" by defeat of which we have heard so much within the last five years. He is purely and simply a fighting man, and with his enormous fighting capacity he may not unfitly be taken to represent, on a reduced scale, the susceptibilities of a whole modern army. When, at last, his enemies outnumber him, he loses heart and, by a very simple process, becomes good for nothing. This process—the gradual corrosion in idleness of a practical mind of the heroic type—is one which Mr. Kingsley is very well qualified to trace; and although he has troubled himself throughout very little with the psychology of his story, and has told it as much as possible in the simple objective tone of the old chroniclers to whom he so constantly refers, he has yet, thanks to the moralizing habit which he is apparently quite unable entirely to renounce, given us a very pretty insight into poor Hereward's feelings.

It is the absence of the old attempt at philosophy and at the writing of history which makes the chief merit of *Hereward* as compared with the author's other tales. Certain merits Mr. Kingsley has in splendid fulness, but the metaphysical faculty is not one of them; and yet in every one of his writings hitherto there has been a stubborn philosophical pretension. There is a certain faculty of story-telling as complete and, used in no matter what simplicity, as legitimate and honorable as any other; and this gift is Mr. Kingsley's. But it has been his constant ambition to yoke it with the procedure of an historian. An important requisite for an historian is to know how to handle ideas, an accomplishment which Mr. Kingsley lacks, as any one may see by turning to his lectures on history, and especially to the inaugural lecture, in which he exhibits his views on the philosophy of history. But in the work before us, as we have said, he has adhered to his chroniclers; and as there is a world of difference between a chronicler and an historian, he has not been tempted to express many opinions. He has told his story with great rapidity and vivacity, and with that happy command of language which makes him one of the few English writers of the present moment from whose style we derive a positive satisfaction. He writes in all seriousness, and yet with a most grateful suppression of that aggressively *earnest* tone which has hitherto formed his chief point of contact with Mr. Carlyle. He writes, in short, as one who enjoys his work; and this fact it is which will give to *Hereward* a durable and inalienable value. The book is not, in our opinion, what historical novels are so apt to become—a *pastiche*. It represents a vast amount of knowledge, of imagination, and of sympathy. We have never been partial to Mr. Kingsley's arrogance, his shallowness, his sanctified prejudices; but we have never doubted that he is a man of genius. "To be a master," as we were told the other day, "is to be a master." *Hereward* is simply a masterpiece, in the literal sense of the term, and as such it is good to read. This fact was supreme in our minds as we read it, and it seemed more forcibly charged than ever before with the assurance of the author's peculiar genius. What is this genius? It lies, in the first place, as it seems to us, in his being a heaven-commissioned *raconteur;* and, in the second place, in his being a consummate Englishman. Some of them are better Englishmen than others. Mr. Kingsley is one of the best. By as much as he is insufferable when he dogmatizes like a schoolboy upon the characteristics of his nation, by so much is he admirable and delightful when he unconsciously expresses them. No American can see these qualities embodied in a work of art without a thrill of sympathy. *Hereward* is an English story—English in its subject, in its spirit, and in its form. He would be a very poor American who, in reading it, should be insensible to the charm of this fact; and he would be a very poor critic who should show himself unable to distinguish between Mr. Kingsley a master and Mr. Kingsley—not a master. (pp. 115-16)

Henry James, in a review of "Hereward," in The Nation, *New York, Vol. II, No. 30, January 25, 1866, pp. 115-16.*

Sir Leslie Stephen   (essay date 1877)

[*Many scholars consider Stephen among the most important English literary critics of the Victorian era. He has been praised for his moral insight and judgment, as well as for his intellectual vigor—although some have charged that his criticism is deficient in aesthetic and formal analysis. The key to Stephen's moral criticism is his theory that all literature is nothing more than an imaginative rendering, in concrete terms, of a writer's philosophy or beliefs. It is the role of criticism, he contends, to translate into intellectual terms what the writer has told the reader through character, symbol, and event. More often than not, Stephen's analysis passes into biographical judgment of the writer rather than the work. In the following essay, he evaluates Kingsley's life and work, noting expressions of the author's temperament in the strengths and weaknesses of his writings.*

Stephen focuses especially on Kingsley's descriptive power, which he praises liberally throughout the essay.]

The Memorials of the late Canon Kingsley, published by his widow, do not constitute a biography of the normal type. In other words, the book does not profess to answer every question which the curiosity of readers might suggest; and, on the whole, one may be very glad that it does not. To many such questions the most appropriate answer is silence, not unmixed with contempt. To others, which may be taken as the expression of a legitimate interest in an eminent man, a reader of moderate intelligence may be trusted to find a sufficient answer in the ample materials placed before him. There is no great difficulty in seizing the main outlines of so strongly marked a character; and, on the whole, Mr. Kingsley well deserves the labour. Few writers of his generation gave clearer indications of power. Had he died at the age of five-and-thirty (when **Westward Ho!** was already completed) we should have speculated upon the great things which we had lost. The last twenty years of his life added little or nothing to his literary reputation. Perhaps, indeed, some of his performances—the lectures at Cambridge, and the unfortunate controversy with Dr. Newman, reflected a certain discredit upon his previous achievements. The explanation is not far to seek, when one has read the story of his life; but the fact makes it rather difficult to recall the feelings with which the rising generation of the years between 1848 and 1855 regarded the most vigorous champion of a school then in its highest vigour. The **Saint's Tragedy, Yeast, Alton Locke, Hypatia,** and **Westward Ho!** did not exactly reveal one of the born leaders of mankind; but their freshness, geniality, and vigour seemed to indicate powers which might qualify their possessor to be an admirable interpreter between the original prophets and the inferior disciples. There was the buoyancy of spirit, the undoubting confidence that the riddle of the universe had at last been satisfactorily solved, and the power of seizing the picturesque and striking aspects of things and embodying abstract theories in vivid symbols which marks the second order of intellects—the men who spread but do not originate fruitful and transforming ideas. Thinkers of the highest rank may be equally self-confident: for it cannot be denied that unreasonable trust in one's own infallibility is a great condition of success in even the highest tasks; but the confidence of great minds is compatible with a deeper estimate of the difficulties before them. They may hold that evil will be exhirpated, but they are aware that its roots strike down into the very heart of things. Kingsley's exuberant faith in his own message showed the high spirits of youth rather than a profound insight into the conditions of the great problems which he solved so fluently. At the time, however, this youthful zeal was contagious. If not an authority to obey, he was a fellow-worker in whom to trust heartily and rejoice unreservedly. Nobody, as Mr. Matthew Arnold says . . . , was more willing to admire or more free from petty jealousies. This quality gave a charm to his writings. There was always something generous in their tone; a desire to understand his antagonist's position, which was due to his own temperament as much as to the teaching of his leader, Mr. Maurice; and, in short, a warmth and heartiness which led one to overlook many defects, and rightly

attracted the enthusiasm of men young enough to look up to him for guidance.

The earlier pages in Mrs. Kingsley's volumes [Frances Kingsley, ed., *Charles Kingsley: His Letters and Memories of His Life,* 2 vols., 1877] give a vivid picture of this period of his life, or, at least, of one side of it. Something is said—as of course it is proper to say something—of the speculative doubts and difficulties through which he won his way to a more settled and happier frame of mind. But it is impossible to take this very seriously. Kingsley, as his letters prove, started in life, like other lads, with a ready-made theory of the universe. Like other lads, he was perfectly confident that it rested upon an unassailable basis and would solve all difficulties. He intended, it is true, to perfect himself in a few branches of study which he had hitherto neglected; he was to learn something about metaphysics, theology, ecclesiastical history, and other branches of knowledge; but it is quite plain that Kant and Augustine and other great teachers of mankind were to be called in, not to consult upon the basis of his philosophy, but to furnish him with a few tools for polishing certain corollaries and increasing his dialectical skill. He is quite ready to provide his correspondents immediately with a definitive philosophical system, and shows his usual versatility in applying at least some of the metaphysical phraseology caught from his intellectual idols. Many lads, however,

Kingsley's mentor, theologian F. D. Maurice.

learn to modify the speculative apparatus with which they started. Absolute conversions, it is true, are almost unknown in philosophy. No Platonist ever became an Aristotelian, or *vice versâ;* for a man's attitude in such matters depends upon intellectual tendencies which assert themselves in early youth as much as in riper years. But men of real power go through a process of development, which, though it leaves a certain homogeneity between their earlier and their later views, softens the crudeness and lessens the superficiality of the first guesses. No such process is traceable in Kingsley. His first theory is his last, except that in later years his interest in abstract speculation had obviously declined, and his declarations, if equally dogmatic in form, show less confidence than desire to be confident. He is glad to turn from speculations to facts, and thinks that his strength lies in the direction rather of the natural sciences than of speculative thought.

Probably he was quite right. It would, at any rate, be a mistake to regard any process of intellectual development as determining his career. He was no real philosopher, though capable of providing philosophical dialogues quite good enough to figure in an historical novel. He was primarily a poet, or, at least, a man swayed by the imagination and emotions. He felt keenly, saw vividly, and accepted such abstract teachings as were most congenial to his modes of seeing and feeling. The true key to his mental development must therefore be sought in his emotional history, and not in the intellectual fermentation which determines the career of a true thinker. The story of his life in this aspect, though indicated rather than directly told, seems to be simple enough. Few people, it is probable, ever had greater faculties of enjoyment than Kingsley. His delight in a fine landscape resembled (though the phrase seems humiliating) the delight of an epicure in an exquisite vintage. It had the intensity and absorbing power of a sensual appetite. He enjoyed the sight of the Atlantic rollers relieved against a purple stretch of heather as the conventional alderman enjoys turtle-soup. He gave himself up to the pure emotion as a luxuriant nature abandons itself to physical gratification. His was not the contemplative mood of the greater poets of nature, but an intense spasm of sympathy which rather excluded all further reflection. Such a temperament implies equal powers of appreciation for many other kinds of beauty, though his love of fine scenery has perhaps left the strongest mark upon his books. He was abnormally sensitive to those pleasures which are on the border-line between the sensuous and the intellectual. He speaks in an early letter of the "dreamy days of boyhood," when his "enjoyment was drawn from the semi-sensual delights of ear and eye, from sun and stars, wood and wave, the beautiful inanimate in all its forms." "Present enjoyment," he adds, "present profit, brought always to me a recklessness of moral consequences which has been my bane." The last expression must of course be taken for what it is worth, that is, for next to nothing: but he is no doubt right in attributing to himself a certain greediness of pleasures of the class described, which became more intellectual and comprehensive but hardly less intense in later years.

It is needless to point out what are the dangers to which a man is exposed by such a temperament. He describes

himself (at the age of twenty-two) as saved from "the darkling tempests of scepticism," and from "sensuality and dissipation;" saved, too, "from a hunter's life on the prairies, from becoming a savage and perhaps worse." The phrase savours of his habitual exaggeration, but it has a real meaning. Young men with a strong taste for pleasure are ruined often enough, though they do not go so far as "the prairies" to effect that consummation. We can see with sufficient clearness that during his college life Kingsley went through serious struggles and came out victorious. Partly, no doubt, he owed that victory over himself to the fact that his tastes, however keen, were not coarse. He had a genuine vein of poetry, that is to say, of really noble feeling. His intense delight in the higher forms of beauty was a force which resisted any easy lapse into degradation. The æsthetic faculties may, as has been too clearly proved, fall into bondage to the lowest impulses of our nature. In the case of a man so open to generous and manly impulses, so appreciative of the claims which outward scenery reveals to healthy and tender minds, and to them alone, the struggle against such a bondage must have been in any case prolonged and vigorous. But stronger men than Kingsley have yielded, and one may see in him the type of character which, under other conditions, produces the "diabolical" or rather the animalistic school of art and literature. An external influence, we are left to infer, had a share in saving him from so lamentable a descent. Kingsley, in short, was rescued as other men have been rescued, by the elevating influence of a noble passion. It is inevitable that this fact, tolerably obvious as it is, should be rather indicated than stated in the biography. But he was not slow to proclaim in all his writings, and we need not scruple to assume that his utterance was drawn from his own experience, that, of all good things that can befall a man in this world, the best is that he should fall in love with a good woman. It is not a new truth; indeed, most truths of that importance have an uncomfortable habit of revealing themselves to the intrusive persons who have insisted upon saying all our best things before us. Still, true as it is, many young men are apt to ignore it, or to consider it as repealed instead of limited by obvious prudential maxims. Kingsley, led to recognise it, and even to exaggerate its exclusive importance by his own history, insists upon it with an emphasis which may not only be traced through his writings, but which seems to have affected all his conceptions of life. It may almost be regarded as the true central point of his doctrine. The love of man for woman, when sanctified by religious feeling, is, according to him, the greatest of all forces that work for individual or social good. This belief, and the system of which it forms a part, give the most characteristic colouring to all his work. It appears to be decided by general consent that a novel means the same thing as a love-story. Some writers indeed have been bold enough to maintain, and even to act upon the opinion, that this view exaggerates the part played by the passion in actual life; and that men have some interests in life which survive the pairing period. Kingsley's doctrine differs from that of the ordinary novelist in another way. Love may not be the ultimate end of a man's life; but it is, as Shakspeare puts it—

The ever fixed mark
That looks on tempests and is never shaken,

It is the star to every wandering bark
Whose worth's unknown, although his height be
taken.

It is the guide to a noble life; and not only affords the discipline by which men obtain the mastery over themselves, but reveals to them the true theory of their relations to the universe. This doctrine, treated in a rather vacillating manner, supplies the theme for his earliest book, the *Saint's Tragedy.* Lancelot in *Yeast,* and even the poor tailor, Alton Locke, owe their best stimulus towards obtaining a satisfactory solution of the perplexed social problems of the time to their love for good women. Hypatia, the type of the feminine influence whose lofty instincts are misdirected by a decaying philosophy, and poor Pelagia, with no philosophy at all, excite the passions by which monks, pagans, and Goths are elevated or corrupted; and the excellent Victoria—a lady who comes too distinctly from a modern tract—shows the philosopher Raphael how to escape from a despairing cynicism. The Elizabethan heroes of *Westward Ho!* take the side of good or evil according to their mode of understanding love for the heroines. In *Two Years Ago,* the delicate curate, and the dandified American, and the sturdy Tom Thurnall, all manage to save their souls by the worship of a lofty feminine character, whilst poor Tom Briggs or Vavasour is ruined by his failure to appreciate the rare excellence of his wife. The same thought inspires some of his most remarkable poems, as the truly beautiful **"Andromeda,"** and the **"Martyrdom of Saint Maura,"** considered by himself to be his best, though I fancy that few readers will share this judgment. Lancelot in *Yeast* designs a great allegorical drawing called the "Triumph of Woman," which sets forth the hallowing influence of feminine charms upon every variety of human being. The picture is one of those which could hardly be put upon canvas; but it would be the proper frontispiece to Kingsley's works.

Such a doctrine, it may be said, is too specific and narrow to be considered as the animating principle of the various books in which it appears. This is doubtless true, and it must be taken rather as the most characteristic application of the teaching of which it is in a logical sense the corollary, though ostensible corollaries are often in fact first principles. When generalised or associated with congenial theories of wider application, it explains Kingsley's leading doctrines. Thus the love of good women is the great practical guide in life; and, in a broader sense, our affections are to guide our intellects. The love of nature, the rapture produced in a sensitive mind by the glorious beauties of the external world, is to teach us the true theory of the universe. The ultimate argument which convinces men like Tom Thurnall and Raphael Aben Ezra, is that the love of which they have come to know the mysterious charm, must reveal the true archetype of the world, previously hidden by the veil of sense. It wants no more to explain a problem which seems to have puzzled Kingsley himself, why, namely, the mystics should supply the only religious teaching which had "any real meaning for his heart." A man who systematically sees the world through his affections is so far a mystic; though Kingsley's love of the concrete and incapacity for abstract metaphysics prevented him from using the true mystical language. Still

simpler is the solution of another problem stated by his biographer. It is said to be "strange" that Kingsley should have acknowledged the intellectual leadership at once of Coleridge and Maurice and of Mr. Carlyle. The superficial difference between the two first and the last of those writers is indeed obvious. But it requires no profound reasoner to detect the fundamental similarity. They all agree in seeing facts through the medium of the imagination, and substituting poetic intuition for the slow and chilling processes of scientific reasoning. They agree in rejecting the rigid framework of dogma and desiring to exalt the spirit above the dead letter. To Kingsley, as to his teachers, and to most imaginative minds, science seemed to mean materialism in philosophy and cynicism in morals. Men of science subordinate the satisfaction of the emotions to the satisfaction of the intellect; they seek to analyse into their elements the concrete realities which alone interest the poet, and see mechanical laws where their opponents would recognise a living force. To Kingsley they seemed (rightly or wrongly) to be drying up the source of his most rapturous emotions, and reducing the beautiful world to a colourless museum of dead specimens. Instead of regulating they were suppressing the emotions. It is less remarkable that he should have opposed a doctrine thus interpreted, than that he should have gradually become less hostile to the scientific aspect of things. He accepted, instead of reviling, Mr. Darwin's teaching; and seems to have been convincing himself that, after all, science was not an enemy to the loftier sentiments. His keen eye for nature, his love of beast and bird and insect, made him sympathise with the observers, if not with the reasoners, and led him to recognise a poetic and a religious side in rightly interpreted science.

His antipathy to another kind of dogmatism is equally intelligible. To him it appeared (rightly or wrongly) to be hopelessly tainted by the evil principle which he generally described as Manichæism. It ordered him (or so he supposed) to look upon nature with horror or suspicion, instead of regarding it as everywhere marked with the indelible impress of the creative hand, and therefore calculated to stimulate the highest emotions of reverence and awe; and, still more, it set up a false and attenuated ethical standard, which condemned all natural impulses as therefore bad, and placed the monkish above the domestic virtues. It was clearly inevitable that a man who regarded human love as the very centre and starting point of all the good influences of life, and the delight in nature as the very test of a healthily constituted mind, should look upon teaching thus understood with absolute detestation. Possibly he caricatured it; at any rate he spared no pains to attack it by every means open to him, and especially by setting forth his own ideal of character. He created the "muscular Christian"—the man, that is, who, on the showing of his antagonists, is an impossible combination of classical and Christian types, and, on his own, implies the harmonious blending of all aspects of the truth. He protested, fruitlessly enough, against the nickname, because it seemed to imply that his version of the character subordinated the highest to the lowest elements. It suggested that he had used Christian phraseology to consecrate a blind admiration for physical prowess and excess of animal vigour. His indignation—expressed in an imprudently angry letter to one of his critics—was intelligible enough. The imputation was cruel, because it was at once false and plausible. It was false, for Kingsley's ideal heroes—whether properly to be called Christians or not—are certainly not mere animals. They have their faults, but they are not sensual or cynical, though in some of their literary descendants the animal side of their nature seems to have developed itself with suspicious facility. Amyas Leigh would probably have hung his Guy Livingstone from a yard-arm before the voyage was over. To readers, however, looking at Amyas from a different point of view, the likeness might be deceptive; and in asserting the value of certain qualities too much depreciated by his judges, he naturally seemed to give them an excessive value.

This is not the place to estimate the worth of Kingsley's teaching on such high matters. It may, however, be taken for granted that it would be useless to look to him for any very coherent or profound statement of his doctrine. He was, as I have said, no thinker, but a man of keen vigorous feelings, which, like other such men, he was apt to take for intuitions and to express in confident dogmas. It is the general attitude of mind, not the specific conclusions at which he had arrived, which must be appreciated in order to do justice to his writings. Without dwelling upon his philosophy, it is enough to observe that this impetuosity of temperament, which is the very antithesis of the quality most requisite in a philosopher, is prejudicial to his artistic work. Its most obvious fault is a want of repose and harmony. He can never be quiet for a moment. Every sentence must be emphatic and intense. He seizes the first aspect of a subject; dashes out a picture—sometimes of perfectly admirable vigour—in half-a-dozen lines; but cannot dwell upon a particular strain of thought or tone down the brilliant hues of fragmentary passages by the diffused atmosphere of calm reflection. He could hardly sit quiet for a moment, as one of his admirers tells us; and his strong-minded heroes, who ought to be self-sustained and tranquil, are always in as great a fever as himself. The result of this tendency is too plainly written upon his life as upon his books. He was always, in a sanitary sense, living upon his capital, and taking more out of his strength than his powers justified. He knocked himself up completely by writing *Yeast* before he was thirty, and every subsequent work seems to have involved an effort which told heavily upon his constitution. The natural consequence of such a process is to be seen in the fact already noticed that his literary productiveness rapidly declined; and that in his later works we have the emphasis which has become habitual without the force which saved it from affectation. It must, however, be said to his credit that he had the merit—a tolerably rare one—of abandoning the attempt to rival his own earlier performances when the vein no longer flowed spontaneously.

The strength and the weakness of such a temperament are illustrated by his poetry, of which some fragments will probably survive (and few, indeed, are the poets who survive by more than fragments), though we may doubt the truth of his own opinion that they would supply his most lasting claim upon posterity. He explains, however, very frankly why he can never be a great poet. He is wanting, he says, in the great poetic faculty—the "power of meta-

phor and analogue—the instinctive vision of connections between all things in heaven and earth." His mind, in other words, was deficient in the direction of philosophic imagination. He could not, like Milton, converse habitually with—

> Him that yon soars on golden wing,
> Guiding the fiery-wheeled throne,
> The cherub Contemplation.

He was too restless and impetuous to be at ease on those heights from which alone the widest truths become perceptible and excite the emotions which are at once deepest and calmest. His songs represent jets and gushes of vivid but rather feverish emotion. A pathetic or heroic story, or the beauty of some natural scene, moves him deeply, and he utters his emotion in an energetic burst of vivid language. But he is too short-winged for a long flight or for soaring into the loftiest regions of the intellectual atmosphere.

Every short lyric is the record, one must suppose, of some such mood of intense excitement. But it makes all the difference whether the excitement takes place in a mind already stored with thought, and ready to pierce instantaneously to the deepest meaning of a particular scene or incident, or in a mind incapable of sustained reflection, and accustomed to see things by brilliant flashes which reveal only their partial and superficial aspects. When, however, we do not blame Kingsley for not being somebody else, we must admit him to be excellent within his limits. The **"Andromeda"** is in every way admirable. It is probably the most successful attempt in the language to grapple with the technical difficulties of English hexameters; and he also seems to find in the Pagan mythology a more appropriate symbol for his characteristic tone of sentiment and an imagery which fits in better with his nature-worship than in regions more familiar to him. He can abandon himself unreservedly to his delight in the beautiful without bothering himself with the direct denunciation of the Manichees or showing the controversial theologian under the artistic dress. The shorter poems have generally a power for stamping themselves upon the memory, due, no doubt, to their straightforward, nervous style. They have the cardinal merit of vigour which belongs to all genuine utterance of real emotion, and are delightfully free from the flabby affectations of many modern rivals. The mark may not be the most elevated, but he goes at it as straight as he would ride at a fence. His **"North-Easter"** does not blow from such ethereal regions as Shelley's "South-west Wind." It verges upon the absurd, and is perhaps not quite free from that taint of vulgarity which vitiates all artistic reference to field sports. But given that such a sentiment was worth expressing, the tones in which it is couched are as ringing and vigorous as could be wished. He can rise much higher when he is pathetic and indignant. It would not be easy to find a better war-cry for the denouncer of social wrongs than the ballad of the poacher's widow. And to pass over the two songs by which he is best known, such poems as **"Poor Lorraine"**—first published in the biography—or the beautiful lines in the *Saint's Tragedy*, beginning "Oh, that we two were maying!" are intense enough in their utterance to make us wonder why he fell short of the highest class of song-writing. Perhaps the defect is indicated by a certain desire to be picturesque which prevents him from obtaining complete success in the simple expression of pathos. The poems have a taint of prettiness—and prettiness is a deadly vice in poetry. There is about them a faint flavour of drawing-room music. But, when we do not want to be hypercritical, we may be thankful for poetry which, if not of the highest class, has the rarest of merits at the present day—genuine fervour and originality.

The fullest expression of Kingsley's mind must be found in the works which appeared from 1848 to 1855. Those seven years, one may say, saw his literary rise, culmination, and decline. The *Saint's Tragedy* represents the period of mental agitation. It will not live longer than many other modern attempts by men of equal genius to compose dramas not intended for the stage. The form in such cases is generally felt to be an encumbrance rather than a help, and one cannot help thinking in this instance that Kingsley might have done better if he had written a picturesque history instead of forcing his story into an uncongenial framework. Nobody is now likely to share Bunsen's belief that the author had proved himself capable of continuing Shakspeare's great series of historic dramas. But one is also rather surprised that a performance which, with all its crudities and awkwardness, showed such unmistakable symptoms of power, did not make a greater impression. Perhaps the most vital fault is the want of unity, not merely in plot but in the leading thought, which was the natural result of the mode of composition. He began it in 1842—that is, at the age of twenty-three, and it was not published till 1848. As this includes the period during which Kingsley passed through his acutest struggle, it is not wonderful that the book should show signs of confusion. It has, indeed, a purpose, and a very distinct one. It is the first exposition of that doctrine which, as I have said, Kingsley preached in season and out of season. He wishes to exhibit the beauty of his own ideal of feminine meekness as compared with the monastic and ascetic ideal. And whatever may be said against books "with a purpose," it cannot, I think, be denied that this central idea was capable of artistic treatment. A dramatist might surely find an impressive motive in the conflict set up in a mind of purity and elevation by the acceptance of a distorted code of morality. There is a genuine tragic element in this interpretation of poor Elizabeth's sufferings. Nature tells her that her domestic affections are holy and of divine origin; the priests tell her that they are to be crushed and mortified. She is gradually tortured to death by the distraction of attempting to obey the two voices, each of them appealing to the loftiest and most unselfish motives. The history is probably false, but the conception is not the less powerful. The execution remains unsatisfactory, chiefly for the obvious reason that Kingsley was not quite a Shakspeare nor even a Schiller, and that his work is therefore rather a series of vigorous sketches than an effective whole; but partly also because his own sentiment seems to be vacillating and indistinct. A thorough hater or a thorough adherent of the theories impugned would have made a work more artistically telling because more coherently conceived. Kingsley is really feeling his way to a theory, and therefore undecided in his artistic attitude. The whole becomes patchy and indistinct. He is feverishly excited rather than deeply

moved, and inconsistent when he ought to be compassionate. Briefly, he wants firmness of hand and definiteness of purpose, though there is no want of spasmodic vigour.

The two novels, *Yeast* and *Alton Locke,* are far more effective; and indeed *Alton Locke* may be fairly regarded as his best piece of work. It is not creditable to the discernment of the intelligent public that Kingsley should have been taken for a subversive revolutionist on the strength of these performances. The intelligent public indeed is much given to the grossest stupidity; and as Kingsley more or less deceived himself, it is not wonderful that he should have been misunderstood. He announced himself at a public meeting to be a Chartist; and when a man voluntarily adopts a nickname he must not be surprised if he is credited with all the qualities generally associated with it. In fact, however, he was not more of a genuine radical than when in later years he declared that he would, if he could, "restore the feudal system, the highest form of civilisation—in ideal, not in practice—which Europe has yet seen." There is much virtue in the phrase "not in practice;" and perhaps Kingsley was no more of a genuine feudalist than he was of a genuine Chartist. In his earlier phase he was simply playing a part which has often enough been attempted by very honest men. Missionaries of a new faith see the advantage of sapping the old creed instead of attacking it in front. Adopting its language and such of its tenets as are congenial to their own, they can gradually introduce a friendly garrison into the hostile fort. The conscious adoption of such a method might have been called jesuitical by Kingsley, and in his mouth such an epithet would have been damnatory. But it was in all sincerity that he and his friends considered themselves to be the "true demagogues"—to quote the title of the chapter in which the moral of *Alton Locke* is embodied. They had not the slightest sympathy, indeed, with the tenets of the thoroughgoing radical. Kingsley believed in the social as much as in the ecclesiastical hierarchy; and with an intensity which almost amounted to bigotry. He would no more put down the squires than the parson; and himself a most energetic parson, he certainly did not undervalue the social importance of the function discharged by his order. In *Alton Locke* the bitterest satire is directed, not against self-indulgent nobles or pedantic prelates, but against the accepted leaders of the artisans. The "true demagogue," as is perfectly natural, holds the false demagogue in especial horror. Kingsley is the friend, not Cuffey. He hates the "Manchester school" as the commonplace version of radicalism and the analogue of the materialist school in politics. From these, he says, in 1852, "heaven defend us; for of all narrow, conceited, hypocritical, and anarchic and atheistic schemes of the universe, the Manchester one is precisely the worst. I have no words to express my contempt for it." Briefly, Kingsley's remedy for speculative error was not the rejection, but the more spiritual interpretation of the old creed; and his remedy for bad squires and parsons was not disendowment and division of the land, but the raising up a better generation of parsons and squires.

There is a superficial resemblance between this theory and that of the Young England school, who, like Kingsley, would have restored the feudal system in a purified state.

Some of his writing runs parallel to Mr. Disraeli's exposition of that doctrine. The difference was, of course, vital. He hated mediæval revivalism as heartily as he hated the demagogues; and his prejudices against the whole order of ideas represented by the *Tracts for the Times* were perhaps the strongest of his antipathies. He looked back to the sixteenth, not to the twelfth century; and his ideal parson was to be no ascetic, but a married man, with a taste for field-sports and fully sympathising with the common sense of the laity. The Young England party seemed to him to desire the conversion of the modern labourer into a picturesque peasant, ready to receive doles at the castle-gate and bow before the priest with bland subservience. Kingsley wanted to make a man of him; to give him self-respect and independence, not in a sense which would imply the levelling all social superiorities, but in the sense of assigning to him an honourable position in the social organisation. He was no more to be petted or pauperised than to be set on a level with his social superiors or set loose without guidance from his intellectual teachers.

Some such doctrines would be verbally accepted by most men; and I cannot here ask whether they really require the teaching with which Kingsley associated them. The demagogues and the obstructives were both, according to him, on a wrong tack; and he could point out the one true method of reuniting development with order. Whatever the value of his theories, the sentiment associated with them was substantially healthy, vigorous, and elevated. That part of his fictions in which it is embodied is probably his most valuable work. Nobody can read the descriptions of the agricultural labourers or of the London artisan in *Yeast* and *Alton Locke* without recognising both the strength of his sympathies and the vigour of his perceptive faculties. He was drawing from the life, and expressing his deepest emotions. "What is the use of preaching to hungry paupers about heaven?" he asks. "Sir, as my clerk said to me yesterday, there is a weight on their hearts, and they call for no hope and no change, for they know they can be no worse off than they are." The phrase explains what was the curse which rested upon Kingsley's parishioners, and in what sense he had to "redeem it from barbarism." He did his work like a man. He was daily with his people "in their cottages, and made a point of talking to the men and boys at their fieldwork till he was personally intimate with every soul, from the women at their washtubs to the babies in the cradle, for whom he had always a loving word and look." Whatever we may think of his "socialism" or "democracy," there was at least no want of depth or sincerity in his sympathy for the poor, and therefore there is no false ring in his description of their condition. He writes with his heart—not to serve any political purpose or to gain credit for a cheap display of charitable feeling.

These books, in fact, show, both by their defects and their merits, in what sense a novel may properly be subservient to a purpose. To draw a vivid picture of the life which he sees around him, or to draw it in such a way as to indicate a true appreciation of the most deeply-seated causes of the evil, is clearly as legitimate in an artistic as in a moral sense. No books can show more forcibly the dark side of the English society of the time. The side from which

Kingsley views the evil is characteristic. The root of all that is good in man lies in the purity and vigour of the domestic affections. A condition of things in which the stability and health of the family becomes impossible is one in which the very foundations of society are being sapped. Nobody could be more alive to the countless mischiefs implied in the statement that the poor man has nothing deserving the name of home. The verses given to Tregarva in *Yeast* sum up his diagnosis of the social disease with admirable vigour. Many scenes in that rather chaotic story are equally vivid in their presentation of the facts. The description of the village feast is a bit of startlingly impressive realism. The poor sodden, hopeless, spiritless peasantry consoling themselves with strong drink and brutal songs, open to no impressions of beauty, with no sense of the romantic except in lawless passion, and too beaten down to have even a thought of rebellion except in the shape of agrarian outrage, are described with singular force. Poor Crawy, the poacher, scarcely elevated above the beasts, looking to the gaol and workhouse for his only refuge, so degraded that pity is almost lost in disgust, is the significant product of the general decay. The race is deteriorating. It has fallen vastly below the standard of the last generation. All the lads are "smaller, clumsier, lower-brained and weaker-jawed than their elders." Such higher feeling as remains takes the form of the dog-like fidelity of Harry Verney, the gamekeeper. Kingsley never wrote a better scene than the death of the old man from a wound received in a poaching affray; when he suddenly springs upright in bed, holds out "his withered paw with a kind of wild majesty," and shouts, "There ain't such a head of hares on any manor in the county. And them's the last words of Harry Verney!"

Alton Locke is a more ambitious and coherent effort; and the descriptions of the London population, and of the futile attempt at a rising in the country, are in the same vigorous vein. Perhaps a more remarkable success is the old Scotchman, Mackaye, who seems to be the best of Kingsley's characters. He has some real humour, a quality in which Kingsley was for the most part curiously deficient; but one must expect that in this case he was drawing from an original. It is interesting to read Mr. Carlyle's criticism of this part of the book. "Saunders Mackaye," he says [in a letter to Kingsley], "my invaluable countryman in this book, is nearly perfect; indeed I greatly wonder how you did contrive to manage him. His very dialect is as if a native had done it, and the whole existence of the rugged old hero is a wonderfully splendid and coherent piece of Scotch bravura." Perhaps an explanation of the wonder might be suggested; but, at any rate, Mackaye is a very felicitous centre for the various groups who play their parts in the story; and not the less efficient as a chorus because he is chiefly critical and confines himself to shrewd demonstrations of the folly of everybody concerned.

Mr. Carlyle gives as his final verdict that his impression is of "a fervid creation still left half chaotic." In fact, with all the genuine force of *Alton Locke*—and no living novelist has excelled the vividness of certain passages—there is an unsatisfactory side to the whole performance. It is marred by the feverishness which inspires most of his work. There is an attempt to crowd too much into the space, and the emphasis sometimes remains when the power is flagging. Greater reserve of power and more attention to unity of effect would have been required to make it a really great book. But the most unsatisfactory part is where the author forgets to be a novelist and becomes a preacher and a pamphleteer. The admirable heroine is forced to deliver what is to all purposes a commonplace tract of two or three chapters at the end of the story, when her thoughts, to be effective, should really have been embedded in the structure of the story. Anybody can preach a sermon when no contradiction is allowed; but the novelist ought to show the thought translated into action, and not given in a raw shape of downright comment. As it is, Lady Ellerton is a mere lay-figure who can talk very edifying phrases, but is really tacked on to the outside of the narrative. The moral should have been evolved by the natural course of events; for when it is presented in this point-blank fashion we begin to cavil, and wish that the Chartist or Mackaye might be allowed to show cause against the sentence pronounced. As they can't, we do it for ourselves.

The historical novels which followed indicate a remarkable change. When he published *Two Years Ago,* Kingsley had become reconciled to the world. There is an apparent inconsistency between the denouncer of social wrongs and the novelist who sings the praises of squires, patrons, and guardsmen, with a placid conviction that they sufficiently represent his ideal. The explanation is partly that, as I have said, Kingsley never accepted the revolutionary remedy for the grievances which he described. He was quite consistent in regarding the old creed as expressing the true mode of cure. But one must still ask whether the facts had changed. Was the world regenerated between 1848 and 1855? Were English labourers all properly fed, housed, and taught? Had the sanctity of domestic life acquired a new charm in the interval, and was the old quarrel between rich and poor definitively settled or in the way to settlement? That appears to have been Kingsley's own view, if we may judge from the prefaces prefixed to later editions of his book; and the great agency to which he assigns the strange improvement was the outbreak of the Crimean war. That crisis, it seems, had taught the higher classes a deeper sense of their responsibility and roused us from the dangerous slumber of peace and growing wealth. Mr. Herbert Spencer has lately expounded a very different theory as to the results of an increased intensity of the military spirit. Without discussing so wide a question, it may, I fancy, be pretty safely assumed that the future historian will not take quite this view of recent affairs, and will attribute any improvement that may have taken place to some deeper cause than that assigned. When a whole social order is rotting, as the author of *Yeast* supposed ours to have been, it is not often cured by a little sputter of fighting; nor does the belief in the efficacy of such a remedy seem to fit in very well with a spiritual Christianity. Perhaps we may further assume, therefore, that the change was partly in Kingsley himself. If so, he was not the first man to account for an alteration in his personal outlook by a movement of the rest of the universe. His parish had been got into better order; his combative instinct had grown weaker; and, like other men who grow in years and domestic comfort, he had become more content with things in general. Fathers of families are capable, we know, of everything, and amongst other things, of softening the fervour of their early enthusiasms. There is nothing at all strange in the process; but it must be taken to illustrate the fact that, if Kingsley's sympathies were keen, his intellectual insight was not very deep. A man who holds that a social disease is so easily suppressed has not measured very accurately the constitutional disorder which it revealed.

Two Years Ago, the book in which this conclusion is plainly announced, is in some respects a painful performance. It contains, indeed, some admirable descriptions of scenery; but the sentiment is poor and fretful. Tom Thurnall, intended to be an embodiment of masculine vigour, has no real stuff in him. He is a bragging, excitable, and at bottom sentimental person. All his swagger fails to convince us that he is a true man. Put beside a really simple and masculine nature like Dandie Dinmont, or even beside Kingsley's own Amyas Leigh, one sees his hollowness. The whole story leads up to a distribution of poetical justice in Kingsley's worst manner. He has a lamentable weakness for taking upon himself the part of Providence. "After all," he once wrote in *Yeast,* "your *Rake's Progress* and *Atheist's Deathbed* do no more good than noble George Cruikshank's *Bottle* will, because every one knows that they are the exception and not the rule; that the atheist generally dies with a conscience as comfortably callous as a rhinoceros-hide; and the rake, when age stops his power of sinning, becomes generally rather more respectable than his neighbours." It is a pity that Kingsley could not remember this true saying in later years. He seems to have grown too impatient to leave room for the natural evolution of events. He gives the machinery a jerk and is fidgety because the wheels grind so slowly, though they "grind exceeding small."

Between *Alton Locke* and *Two Years Ago* there luckily intervened *Hypatia* and *Westward Ho!* They are brilliant and almost solitary exceptions to the general dreariness of the historical novel. To criticise them either from the historical or the artistic point of view would indeed be easy enough; but they have a vivacity which defies criticism. I have no doubt that *Hypatia* is fundamentally and hopelessly inaccurate, and that a sound historian would shudder at innumerable anachronisms and pick holes in every paragraph. I don't believe that men like the Goths ever existed in this world, and am prepared to give up the whole tribe of monks, pagans, Jews, and fathers of the Church. If *Westward Ho!* is (as I presume) less inaccurate because dealing with less distant ages, it is still too much of a party pamphlet to be taken for history. The Jesuits are probably caricatures, and Miss Ayacanora is a bit of rather silly melodrama. But it is difficult to say too much in favour of the singular animation and movement of both books. There is a want of repose, if you insist upon applying the highest canons of art; but the brilliance of description, the energy and rapidity of the action, simply disarms the reader. I rejoice in the Amal and Wulf and Raphael Aben Ezra, as I love Ivanhoe, and Front de Bœuf, and Wamba the Witless. The fight between "English mastiffs and Spanish bloodhounds" is almost as stirring as the skirmish of Drumclog in *Old Mortality. Hypatia,* according to Kingsley himself, was written with his heart's blood. Like other phrases of his, that requires a little dilution. But, at any rate, both books stand out for vividness, for a happy audacity and quickness of perception, above all modern attempts in the same direction.

The problems discussed in these historical novels and the solutions suggested are of course substantially the same as in his earlier books. The period of *Hypatia* bears a striking analogy to the present. In the heroes described in *Westward Ho!* he supposed himself to recognise the fullest realisation of the fundamental doctrines of his own creed. Much might be said, were it worth saying, as to the accuracy of these assumptions. Kingsley's method is in any case too much tainted by the obvious tendency to see facts by the light of preconceived theories. In the earlier writings he may be one-sided and exaggerated; but his imagination is at least guided by reference to actual observation. It seems as if in this later period he had instinctively turned away to distant periods where men and events might be more easily moulded into conformity with his prejudices. However skilful a man may be in accommodating fact to fancy, he is apt to find difficulties when he paints from the life around him. But when nobody can contradict you except a few prosaic antiquarians, the outside world becomes delightfully malleable. You do not find any fragments of rigid material in the clay which shapes itself so easily in your fingers, Kingsley has faith enough in his teaching to give a genuine glow to these hybrid beings begotten half of fancy half of the external world. But we feel too plainly that the work will not stand the test of close examination, either by the historian or the literary critic. Such a nemesis naturally overtakes men who admit too easily an appeal from fact to sentiment. They begin to lose the sense of reality, and their artistic work shows signs of flimsiness at their theories of arbitrary assumption. The great writer pierces to the true life of a period because he recognises the necessity of conforming his beliefs to realities. The inferior writer uses his knowledge only to give colouring to his dreams, and his work tries to represent what he would like to be the truth instead of showing genuine insight into what is actually true.

Whatever else in Kingsley may have been affected or half-hearted, his appreciation of nature remained true and healthy to the end. If anything it became more intense as he seemed to grow weary of abstract discussions and turned for relief to natural scenes. Nobody has ever shown a greater power of investing with a romantic charm the descriptions of bird, beast, and insect. There are no more delightful books than those which express the naturalist's delight in country sights, from the days of Izaak Walton to White of Selborne, or Waterton, or our most recent discovery, the Scotch naturalist Edward. Amongst such writers, Kingsley is in the front rank; and his taste is combined with a power of catching wider aspects of scenery, such as few of our professional describers can unravel. It would be interesting to lay bare the secret of his power. He has done for Devon and Cornwall, for the heaths and chalk-streams of the southern counties, and even for the much depreciated fens, what Scott did for the Highlands. One secret is of course the terseness and directness of his descriptions. He never lays himself out for a bit of deliberate

Fanny Grenfell Kingsley.

bombast, and deals always with first-hand impressions. The writing is all alive. There is no dead matter of conventional phrases and imitative ecstasies. And again, his descriptions are always dramatic. There is a human being in the foreground with whom we sympathise. We do not lose ourselves in mystic meditations, we surrender ourselves to mere sensuous dreaming. We are in active strenuous enjoyment; beguiling the trout of his favourite chalk-streams, sailing under the storm-beaten cliffs of Lundy, and drinking in the rich sea-breeze that sweeps over Dartmoor, or galloping with clenched teeth through the fir-woods of Eversley. One characteristic picture—to take one at random from a thousand—is the homeward ride of Zeal-for-Truth Thoresby of Thoresby Rise in Deeping Fen as he rides slowly homeward after Naseby fight along one of the fen-droves. One could swear that one had been with him, as Kingsley no doubt was merely embodying the vivid recollection of some old Cambridge expedition into the Bedford Level, a scenery which has a singular and mysterious charm, though few besides Kingsley have succeeded in putting it on paper.

Some wonder has been wasted on Kingsley's descriptions of the tropical scenery which he had never seen. Even men of genius do not work miracles; and so far as I know, they always blunder in such attempts. Johnson showed his usual sense in regard to a similar criticism upon the blind poet, Blacklock. If, he said, you found that a paralytic man had left his room, you would explain the wonder by supposing that he had been carried. Similarly, the explanation of Kingsley and of Blacklock is that they described not what they had seen but what they had read. The description in *Westward Ho!* may easily be traced to Humboldt and other sources where they are not explicable by a visit to Kew Gardens. A minute criticism would show that they are little more than catalogues of gorgeous plants and strange beasts; and show none of those vivid touches, so striking from their fidelity, which give animation to his descriptions of English scenery. In his pictures of Devonshire we can tell the time of the day and night and the state of the weather as clearly as if he were a meteorologist. In South America he leaves us to generalities. The true secret of his success is different. He describes vividly not the outward fact, but the inward enjoyment. One need not go to the tropics to imagine the charm of luxurious indolence. Perhaps we enjoy it the more because we have not really been exposed to its inconveniences. The dazzling of the eye by blazing sunlight and brilliant colours, the relief given by the cool deep streams under luxuriant foliage, the vague consciousness of wondrous forms of life lurking in the forest depths, can be realised without any special accuracy of portraiture. The contagion to which we are really exposed is that of the enthusiasm with which Kingsley had read his favourite books of travel. But of downright description there is little, and that little not very remarkable. If anybody doubts it he may read the passage of river scenery which concludes with a quotation from Humboldt, and observe how vividly the fragment of actual observation stands out from the mere catalogue of curiosities, or, again, with any of Kingsley's own Devonshire scenes, where every touch shows loving familiarity with details and a consequent power of selecting just the most speaking incidents.

We may put two passages beside each other which will illustrate the difference. Describing, after Humboldt, the mid-day calm of the forest, he says,

> The birds' notes died out one by one; the very butterflies ceased their flitting over the tree-tops, and slept with outspread wings upon the glassy leaves, undistinguishable from the flowers around them. Now and then a colibri whirred downward towards the water, hummed for a moment round some pendent flower, and then the living gem was lost in the deep darkness of the inner wood, among tree-trunks as huge and dark as the pillars of some Hindoo shrine; or a parrot swung and screamed at them from an overhanging bough; or a thirsty monkey slid lazily down a liana to the surface of the stream, dipped up the water in his tiny hand, and started chattering back, as his eyes met those of some foul alligator peering upward through the clear depths below.

This and more is good enough, but there is nothing which would not suggest itself to a visitor to the British Museum or the Zoological Gardens. It is a catalogue, and rather too full a catalogue, of curiosities, without one of those vivid touches which reveals actual observation. At the end of the same volume, we have a real sketch from nature. Amyas and his friends walk to the cliffs of Lundy:

> As they approached, a raven, who sat upon the topmost stone, black against the bright blue sky, flapped lazily away, and sank down the abysses of the cliff, as if he had scented the corpses beneath the surge. Below them, from the gull-rock rose a thousand birds, and filled the air with sound; the choughs cackled, the hacklets wailed, the great black-backs laughed querulous defiance at the intruders, and a single falcon, with an angry bark, darted out from beneath their feet, and hung poised high aloft, watching the sea-fowl which swung slowly round and round below.

That gives the atmospheric effect, and what we may call the dramatic character. Every phrase suggests a picture, and the whole description, of which I have quoted a bit, has real unity of effect, instead of being a simple enumeration of details.

When one reads some passages inspired by this hearty and simpleminded love of nature, one is sometimes half tempted to wish that Kingsley could have put aside his preachings, social, theological, and philosophical, and have been content with a function for which he was so admirably adapted. The men who can feel and make others feel the charms of beautiful scenery and stimulate the love for natural history do us a service which, if not the highest, is perhaps the most unalloyed by any mixture of evil. Kingsley would have avoided many errors and the utterance of much unsatisfactory dogmatism if he could have limited himself to such a duty. But to do so he must have been a man of narrower sympathies, less generous temper, and less hearty hatred of all evil influences. We could hardly wish him to have been other than he was, though we may wish that he had developed under more favourable circumstances. The weaknesses which marred his work and led to the exhaustion of his faculties were to be regretted, but were not such as to diminish the affection deserved by so cordial a nature. He is more or less responsible for those rather offensive persons, the Viking and the muscular Christian. The Viking, I suppose, must have been a humbug like other products of graphic history, and too much has been made of his supposed share in our ancestry. Kingsley had a feminine tenderness and an impatient excitability indicative of a different ancestry. He admires the huge, full-blooded barbarians, but only belongs to them on one side. He is as near to his delicate as to his muscular heroes, to Francis as to Amyas Leigh, and to the morbid poet, Vavasour, as to the more vigorous Tom Thurnall. In these days, when the Viking or Berserker element seems to be dying out of our literature, even this qualified and external worship of masculine vigour is valuable. There is something hectic and spasmodic about it, though it implies a homage to more healthy ideals. Kingsley, at any rate, hated the namby-pamby, and he tried, with too obvious an effort, to be simple and unaffected. His aims were thoroughly noble, though marred by his want of reserve and of intellectual stamina. He was too timid or too impatient to work out consistent theories or acquire much depth of conviction. But with all his shortcomings he succeeded in giving forcible utterance to truths of vital importance, though possibly requiring more embodiment, and brought vividly before our minds problems which most urgently press for a solution more satisfactory than he was able to reach. (pp. 424-42)

Sir Leslie Stephen, "No. XV.—Charles Kingsley," in The Cornhill Magazine, *Vol. 35, April, 1877, pp. 424-42.*

Frederic Harrison   (essay date 1895)

[*The author of many acclaimed works on historical, political, and literary subjects, Harrison was a central figure in the leading intellectual and political controversies of his day. He was attracted by the philosophical theories of Frenchman Auguste Comte, and became England's primary advocate of Comte's Positivism, a philosophy maintaining that the proper goal of knowledge is the description and not the explanation of experienced phenomena. In the following excerpt, Harrison assesses Kingsley's contributions to English art and thought, highlighting the descriptive power of his poetry as well as the passion of his argumentative prose. The critic also discusses Kingsley's central role in espousing the tenets of Christian Socialism.*]

Charles Kingsley has [a place in the evolution of British society and thought]—not by reason of any supreme work or any very rare quality of his own, but by virtue of his versatility, his *verve,* his fecundity, his irrepressible gift of breaking out in some new line, his strong and reckless sympathy, and above all by real literary brilliance. Where he failed to impress, to teach, to inspire—almost even though he stirred men to anger or laughter—Charles Kingsley for a generation continued to interest the public, to scatter amongst them ideas or problems; he made many people think, and gave many people delight. He woke them up in all sorts of ways, about all sorts of things. He wrote lyrics, songs, dramas, romances, sermons, Platonic dialogues, newspaper articles, children's fairy books, scientific manuals, philosophical essays, lectures, extravaganzas, and theological polemics. Hardly any of these were quite in the first rank, and some of them were thin, flashy, and almost silly. But most of them had the saving gift of getting home to the interests, ideas, and tastes of the great public, and he made them think even when he was very wrong himself. Such activity, such keenness, such command of literary resources, has to be reckoned with in a man of warm feeling and generous impulses; and thus, if Charles Kingsley is no longer with very many either prophet or master, he was a literary influence of at least the second rank in his own generation.

This would not be enough to make a permanent reputation if it stood alone; but there were moments in which he bounded into the first rank. It would hardly be safe to call Kingsley a poet of great pretension, although there are passages in **The Saint's Tragedy** and in the **"Ballads"** of real power; but he has written songs which, as songs for the voice, have hardly been surpassed by Tennyson himself. **"The Sands of Dee"** and **"The Three Fishers,"** if not poetry of quite perfect kind, have that incommunicable and indescribable element of the *cantabile* which fits them

to the wail of a sympathetic voice perhaps even better than any songs of the most finished poetry. A true song must be simple, familiar, musically suggestive of a single touching idea, and nothing more. And this is just the mysterious quality of these songs and the source of their immense popularity. Again, without pretending that Kingsley is a great novelist, there are scenes, especially descriptive scenes, in **Hypatia,** in **Westward Ho!** which belong to the very highest order of literary painting, and have hardly any superior in the romances of our era. No romances, except Thackeray's, have the same glow of style in such profusion and variety; and Thackeray himself was no such poet of natural beauty as Charles Kingsley—a poet, be it remembered, who by sheer force of imagination could realise for us landscapes and climates of which he himself had no sort of experience. Even Scott himself has hardly done this with so vivid a brush.

Kingsley was a striking example of that which is so characteristic of recent English literature—its strong, practical, social, ethical, or theological bent. It is in marked contrast with French literature. Our writers are always using their literary gifts to preach, to teach, to promulgate a new social or religious movement, to reform somebody or something, to illustrate a new doctrine. From first to last, Carlyle regarded himself even more as preacher than as artist: so does his follower, Mr. Ruskin. Macaulay seemed to write history in order to prove the immeasurable superiority of the Whig to the Tory; and Froude and Freeman write history to enforce their own moral. Disraeli's novels were the programme of a party and the defence of a cause; and even Dickens and Thackeray plant their knives deep into the social abuses of their time. Charles Kingsley was not professed novelist, nor professed man of letters. He was novelist, poet, essayist, and historian, almost by accident, or with ulterior aims. Essentially, he was a moralist, a preacher, a socialist, a reformer, and a theologian.

To begin with his poetry, and he himself began his literary career with verses at the age of sixteen, he began to write poetry almost as a child, and some of his earlier verses are his best. If Kingsley, with all his literary gifts, was never quite in the first rank in anything, he came nearest to being a poet of mark. Some of his ballads almost touch the high-water mark of true ballad poetry, with its abrupt fierce blows of tragedy and pathos, its simple touches of primitive, rude speech, its reserve of force, its unspoken mysteries. At any rate, Kingsley's best ballads have no superior in the ballads of the Victorian era in lilt, in massiveness of stroke, in strange unexpected turns. **"The Weird Lady"** is an astonishing piece for a lad of twenty-one—it begins with, "The swevens came up round Harold the Earl, Like motes in the sunnès beam"—and it ends with the stanza:

> A white dove out of the coffin flew;
>   Earl Harold's mouth it kist;
> He fell on his face, wherever he stood;
> And the white dove carried his soul to God
>   Or ever the bearers wist.

That little piece is surely a bit of pure and rare ballad poetry.

A **"New Forest Ballad"** is also good, it ends thus—

> They dug three graves in Lyndhurst yard;
>   They dug them side by side;
> Two yeomen lie there, and a maiden fair,
>   A widow and never a bride.

So too is the **"Outlaw,"** whose last request is this:—

> And when I'm taen and hangit, mither, a brit-
>   tling o' my deer,
> Ye'll no leave your bairn to the corbie craws, to
>   dangle in the air;
> But ye'll send up my twa douce brethren, and
>   ye'll steal me fra the tree,
> And bury me up on the brown, brown muirs,
>   where I aye loved to be.

The famous ballad in *Yeast* might have been a great success if Kingsley would have limited it to five stanzas instead of twenty. What a ring there is in the opening lines—

> The merry brown hares came leaping
>   Over the crest of the hill—

If he could only have been satisfied with the first five stanzas what a ballad it would have been!—If only he had closed it with the verse—

> She thought of the dark plantation
>   And the hares, and her husband's blood,
> And the voice of her indignation
>   Rose up to the throne of God.

That was enough for a ballad, but not for a political novel. The other fifteen stanzas were required for his story; they may be vigorous rhetoric, impressive moralising, but they are too argumentative and too rhetorical to be ballad poetry. It is curious how much of Kingsley's work, both poetry and prose, is inspired by his love of sport and his indignation at game laws!

His songs, spoiled as they are to our ears by poor music and too often maudlin voices, are as good songs and as fitted for singing as any in our time. **"The Sands of Dee,"** hacknied and vulgarised as it is by the banalities of the drawing-room, is really (to use a hacknied and vulgarised phrase) a "haunting" piece of song; and though Ruskin may pronounce "the cruel crawling foam" to be a false use of the pathetic fallacy, the song, for what it professes to be, is certainly a thing to live. I have always felt more kindly toward the East wind since Kingsley's **"Welcome, wild North-Easter!"**; and his Church Hymns such as—**"Who will say the world is dying?"** and **"The Day of the Lord is at hand, at hand!"**—are far above the level even of the better modern hymns.

We have not yet touched upon Kingsley's longest and most ambitious poem—*The Saint's Tragedy.* With all its merits and beauties it is a mistake. It was avowedly a controversial diatribe against the celibacy and priestcraft of Romanism, and was originally designed to be in prose. That is not a safe basis for a dramatic poem, and the poem suffers from the fact that it is in great part a theological pamphlet. It would have made a most interesting historical novel as a mediæval pendant to *Hypatia;* but it is not a great lyrical drama. As we have had no great lyrical drama at all since *Manfred* and *The Cenci,* that is not much in its dispraise. There are powerful passages, much poetic grace in the piece; but the four thousand lines of this elaborate polemical poem rather weary us, and a perfervid appeal to the Protestantism and uxoriousness of Britons should have been cast into other moulds.

The long poem of **"Andromeda"** almost succeeds in that impossible feat—the revival of the hexameter in English. It may be a hard saying to the countrymen of Longfellow, but the truth is that the hexameter is a metrical monster in our English speech. The paucity of easy dactyls and the absence of all true spondees in English words, the preponderance of consonants over vowels, the want of inflected forms, and other peculiarities in our language—make the hexameter incapable of transplantation; and this magnificent metre loses with us all its majesty, its ease, its beauty. The very line can hardly be printed on an ordinary page, for the immense number of letters in each English verse causes an unsightly doubling of the lines, chokes the voice, and wearies the ear. In the hexameter line of Homer there are usually about thirty letters, of which only twelve are consonants; in the English hexameter there are often sixty letters, of which nearly forty are consonants. And the Homeric hexameter will have six words where the English hexameter has twelve or fourteen. Yet having set himself this utterly hopeless and thankless task, to write English hexameter, Kingsley produced some five hundred lines of **"Andromeda,"** which in rhythm, ease, rapidity, and metrical correctness are quite amongst the best in the language. It is very rare to meet with any English hexameter which in rhythm, stress, and prosody is perfectly accurate. **"Andromeda"** contains many such lines, as for example:

> Violet, asphodel, ivy, and vine-leaves, roses and
>   lilies—
> Nereid, siren, and triton, and dolphin, and ar-
>   rowy fishes.

These lines are true hexameters, chiefly because they consist of Latin and Greek words; and they have little more than forty letters, of which barely more than half are consonants. They would be almost pure hexameters, if in lieu of the long ānd, we could put ĕt, or τε. And there are only three Saxon words in the two lines. But hexameters consisting of purely English words, especially of Anglo-Saxon words, halt and stammer like a schoolboy's exercise. The attempt of Kingsley in **"Andromeda"** is most ingenious and most instructive.

I have dwelt so much upon Kingsley's poetry because, though he was hardly a "minor poet,"—an order which now boasts sixty members—he wrote a few short pieces which came wonderfully near being a great success. And again, it is the imaginative element in all his work, the creative fire and the vivid life which he threw into his prose as much as his verse, into his controversies as much as into his fictions, that gave them their popularity and their savour. Nearly every one of Kingsley's imaginative works was polemical, full of controversy, theological, political, social, and racial; and this alone prevented them from being great works. Interesting works they are; full of vigour, beauty, and ardent conception; and it is wonderful that so much art and fancy could be thrown into what is in substance polemical pamphleteering.

Of them all *Hypatia* is the best known and the best conceived. *Hypatia* was written in 1853 in the prime of his manhood and was on the face of it a controversial work. Its sub-title was—*New Foes with an Old Face,*—its preface elaborates the moral and spiritual ideas that it teaches, the very titles of the chapters bear biblical phrases and classical moralising as their style. I should be sorry to guarantee the accuracy of the local colouring and the detail of its elaborate history; but the life, realism, and pictorial brilliancy of the scenes give it a power which is rare indeed in an historical novel. It has not the great and full knowledge of *Romola,* much less the consummate style and setting of *Esmond;* but it has a vividness, a rapidity, a definiteness which completely enthral the imagination and stamp its scenes on the memory. It is that rare thing, an historical romance which does not drag. It is not one of those romances of which we fail to understand the incidents, and often forget what it is that the personages are struggling so fiercely to obtain. No one who has read *Hypatia* in early life will fail to remember its chief scenes or its leading characters, if he lives to old age. After forty years this romance has been cast into a drama and placed upon the London stage, and it is frequently the subject of some vigorous pictures.

In any estimate of *Hypatia* as a romance, it is right to consider the curious tangle of difficulties which Kingsley crowded into his task. It was to be a realistic historical novel dated in an age of which the public knew nothing, set in a country of which the author had no experience, but which many of us know under wholly altered conditions. It was to carry on controversies as to the older and the later types of Christianity, as to Polytheism, Judaism, and Monotheism; it was to confute Romanism, Scepticism, and German metaphysics; it was to denounce celibacy and monasticism, to glorify muscular Christianity, to give glowing pictures of Greek sensuousness and Roman rascality, and finally to secure the apotheosis of Scandinavian heroism. And in spite of these incongruous and incompatible aims, the story still remains a vivid and fascinating tale. That makes it a real *tour de force.* It is true that it has many of the faults of Bulwer, a certain staginess, melodramatic soliloquies, careless incongruities, crude sensationalism—but withal, it has some of the merits of Bulwer at his best, in *The Last Days of Pompeii, Rienzi, The Last of the Barons,*—the play of human passion and adventure, intensity of reproduction however inaccurate in detail; it has "go," intelligibility, memorability. The characters interest us, the scenes amuse us, the pictures are not forgotten. The stately beauty of Hypatia, the seductive fascination of Pelagia, the childlike nature of Philammon, the subtle cynicism of Raphael Aben-Ezra, the mighty audacity of the Goths, the fanaticism of Cyril, and the strange clash of three elements of civilisation,—Graeco-Roman, Christian, Teutonic—give us definite impressions, leave a permanent imprint on our thoughts. There are extravagances, theatricalities, impossibilities enough. The Gothic princes comport themselves like British seamen ashore in Suez or Bombay; Raphael talks like young Lancelot Smith in *Yeast;* Hypatia is a Greek Argemone; and Bishop Synesius is merely an African fifth-century Charles Kingsley, what Sydney Smith called a "squarson," or compound of squire and parson. Still, after all—bating grandiloquences and incongruities and "errors excepted," *Hypatia* lives, moves, and speaks to us; and, in

the matter of vitality and interest, is amongst the very few successes in historical romance in the whole Victorian literature.

Westward Ho! shares with *Hypatia* the merit of being a successful historical romance. It is free from many of the faults of *Hypatia,* it is more mature, more carefully written. It is not laden with the difficulties of *Hypatia;* it is only in part an historical romance at all; the English scenery is placed in a country which Kingsley knew perfectly and from boyhood; and the only controversy involved was the interminable debate about Jesuit mendacity and Romanist priestcraft. So that, if *Westward Ho!* does not present us with the weaknesses and the dilemmas of *Hypatia,* on the other hand it is not so brilliant or so rich with interest. But it has real and lasting qualities. The Devon coast scenery which Kingsley knew and loved, the West Indian and tropical scenery, which he loved but did not know, are both painted with wonderful force of imaginative colour. When one recalls all that Kingsley has done in the landscape of romance,—Alexandria and the desert of the Nile, West Indian jungles and rivers, Bideford Bay, his own heaths in *Yeast,* the fever-dens of London in *Alton Locke,*—one is almost inclined to rank him in this single gift of description as first of all the novelists since Scott. Compared with the brilliancy and variety of Kingsley's pictures of country, Bulwer's and Disraeli's are conventional; even those of Dickens are but local; Thackeray and Trollope have no interest in landscape at all; George Eliot's keen interest is not so spontaneous as Kingsley's, and Charlotte Brontë's wonderful gift is strictly limited to the narrow field of her own experience. But Kingsley, as a landscape painter, can image to us other continents and many zones, and he carries us to distant climates with astonishing force of reality.

Two Years Ago has some vigorous scenes, but it has neither the merits nor the defects of Kingsley in historical romance. Its scene is too near for his fine imagination to work poetically, and it is too much of a sermon and pamphlet to be worth a second or a third reading; and as to *Hereward the Wake,* I must confess to not having been able to complete even a first reading, and that after sundry trials. Of Kingsley's remaining fanciful pieces it is enough to say that *The Heroes* still remains, after forty years, the child's introduction to Greek mythology, and is still the best book of its class. When we compare it with another attempt by a romancer of genius, and set it beside the sticky dulness of [Nathaniel Hawthorne's] *The Tanglewood Tales,* it looks like a group of real Tanagra figurines placed beside a painted plaster cast. Kingsley's *Heroes,* in spite of the inevitable sermon addressed in the preface to all good boys and girls, has the real simplicity of Greek art, and the demi-gods tell their myths in noble and pure English. The *Water Babies* is an immortal bit of fun, which will be read in the next century with *Gulliver* and *The Ring and the Rose,* long after we have all forgotten the nonsensical whims about science and the conventional pulpit moralising which Kingsley scattered broadcast into everything he said or wrote.

We have as yet said nothing about that which was Kingsley's most characteristic and effective work—his political fictions. These were the pieces by which his fame was first achieved, and no doubt they are the works which gave him his chief influence on his generation. But, for that very reason, they suffered most of all his writings as works of art. *Yeast* is a book very difficult to classify. It is not exactly a novel, it is more than a *Dialogue,* it is too romantic for a sermon, it is too imaginative for a pamphlet, it is too full of action for a political and social treatise. Incongruous as it is, it is interesting and effective, and contains some of Kingsley's best work. It has some of his most striking verses, some of his finest pictures of scenery, many of his most eloquent thoughts, all his solid ideas, the passion of his youth, and the first glow of his enthusiasm. It was written before he was thirty, before he thought himself to be a philosopher, before he professed to be entrusted with a direct message from God. Its title—*Yeast*—suggests that it is a ferment thrown into the compound mass of current political, social, and religious ideas, to make them work and issue in some new combination. Kingsley himself was a kind of ferment. His mind was itself destined to cause a violent chemical reaction in the torpid fluids into which it was projected. His early and most amorphous work of *Yeast* did this with singular vigour, in a fresh and reckless way, with rare literary and poetic skill.

If I spoke my whole mind, I should count *Yeast* as Kingsley's typical prose work. It is full of anomalies, full of fallacies, raising difficulties it fails to solve, crying out upon maladies and sores for which it quite omits to offer a remedy. But that is Kingsley all over. He was a mass of overexcited nerves and ill-ordered ideas, much more poet than philosopher, more sympathetic than lucid, full of passionate indignation, recklessly self-confident, cynically disdainful of consistency, patience, good sense. He had the Rousseau temperament, with its furious eloquence, its blind sympathies and antipathies, its splendid sophistries. *Yeast* was plainly the Christian reverse of the Carlyle image and superscription, as read in *Sartor* and *Past and Present.* Kingsley was always profoundly influenced by Frederick D. Maurice, who was a kind of spiritual Carlyle, without the genius or the learning of the mighty *Sartor,* with a fine gift of sympathy instead of sarcasm, with a genuine neo-Christian devoutness in lieu of an old-Hebrew Goetheism. Kingsley had some of Carlyle's passion, of his eloquence, of his power to strike fire out of stones. And so, just because *Yeast* was so disjointed as a composition, so desultory in thought, so splendidly defiant of all the conventions of literature and all the ten commandments of British society in 1849, I am inclined to rank it as Kingsley's typical performance in prose. It is more a work of art than *Alton Locke,* for it is much shorter, less akin to journalism, less spasmodic, and more full of poetry. *Yeast* deals with the country—which Kingsley knew better and loved more than he did the town. It deals with real, permanent, deep social evils, and it paints no fancy portrait of the labourer, the squire, the poacher, or the village parson. Kingsley there speaks of what he knew, and he describes that which he felt with the soul of a poet. The hunting scenes in *Yeast,* the river vignettes, the village revel, are exquisite pieces of painting. And the difficulties overcome in the book are extreme. To fuse together a Platonic Dialogue and a Carlyle latter-day pamphlet, and to mould this compound into a rural romance in the style of *Silas Marner,* heightened with extracts from University Pulpit sermons, with some ringing ballads, and political diatribes in the vein of Cobbett's appeals to the People—this was to show wonderful literary versatility and animation. And, after forty-five years, *Yeast* can be read and re-read still!

Alton Locke was no doubt more popular, more passionately in earnest, more definite and intelligible than *Yeast;* and if I fail to hold it quite as the equal of *Yeast* in literary merit, it is because these very qualities necessarily impair it as a work of art. It was written, we well know, under violent excitement and by a terrible strain on the neuropathic organism of the poet-preacher. It is undoubtedly spasmodic, crude, and disorderly. A generation which has grown fastidious on the consummate finish of *Esmond, Romola,* and *Treasure Island,* is a little critical of the hasty outpourings of spirit which satisfied our fathers in the forties, after the manner of *Sybil,* the *Last of the Barons,* or *Barnaby Rudge.* The Tennysonian modulation of phrase had not yet been popularised in prose, and spasmodic soliloquies and melodramatic eloquence did not offend men so cruelly as they offend us now.

As *Yeast* was inspired by *Sartor Resartus,* so *Alton Locke* was inspired by Carlyle's *French Revolution.* The effect of Carlyle upon Kingsley is plain enough throughout, down to the day when Carlyle led Kingsley to approve the judicial murder of negroes in Jamaica. Kingsley himself tells us, by the mouth of Alton Locke (chap. ix.), "I know no book, always excepting Milton, which at once so quickened and exalted my poetical view of man and his history, as that great prose poem, *the single epic of modern days,* Thomas Carlyle's *French Revolution.*" Kingsley's three masters were—in poetry, Tennyson; in social philosophy, Carlyle; in things moral and spiritual, Frederick D. Maurice. He had far more of genius than had Maurice; he was a much more passionate reformer than Tennyson; he was far more genial and social than Carlyle. Not that he imitated any of the three. *Yeast* is not at all copied from *Sartor,* either in form or in thought; nor is *Alton Locke* in any sense imitated from the *French Revolution.* It is inspired by it; but *Yeast* and *Alton Locke* are entirely original, and were native outbursts from Kingsley's own fierce imagination and intense human sympathy.

And in many ways they were amongst the most powerful influences over the thought of the young of the last generation. In the early fifties we were not so fastidious in the matter of style and composition as we have now become. Furious eloquence and somewhat melodramatic incongruities did not shock us so much, if we found them to come from a really glowing imagination and from genuine inspiration, albeit somewhat unpruned and ill-ordered. Now Kingsley "let himself go," in the way of Byron, Disraeli, Bulwer, and Dickens, who not seldom poured out their conceptions in what we now hold to be spasmodic form. It is possible that the genteeler taste of our age may prevent the young of to-day from caring for *Alton Locke.* But I can assure them that five-and-forty years ago that book had a great effect and came home to the heart of many. And the effect was permanent and creative. We may see to-day in England widespread results of that potent social movement which was called Christian Socialism, a movement of which Kingsley was neither the founder nor the chief leader, but of which his early books were the main popular exponents, and to which they gave a definiteness and a key which the movement itself sadly lacked.

I was not of an age to take part in that movement, but in after years at the Working Men's College, which grew out of it, I gained a personal knowledge of what was one of the most striking movements of our time. Nowadays, when leading statesmen assure us "we are all Socialists now," when the demands of the old "Chartists" are Liberal common form, when trades-unionism, co-operation, and state-aided benefits are largely supported by politicians, churchmen, journals, and writers, it is difficult for us now to conceive the bitter opposition which assailed the small band of reformers who, five-and-forty years ago, spoke up for these reforms. Of that small band, who stood alone amongst the literary, academic, and ecclesiastical class, Charles Kingsley was the most outspoken, the most eloquent, and assuredly the most effective. I do not say the wisest, the most consistent, or the most staunch; nor need we here discuss the strength or the weakness of the Christian Socialist reform. When we remember how widely this vague initiative has spread and developed, when we read again *Alton Locke* and *Yeast,* and note how much has been practically done in forty years to redress or mitigate the abuses against which these books uttered the first burning protest, we may form some estimate of all that the present generation of Englishmen owes to Charles Kingsley and his friends.

I have dwelt last and most seriously upon Kingsley's earliest books, because they were in many respects his most powerful, his typical works. As he grew in years, he did not develop. He improved for a time in literary form, but his excitable nerve-system, his impulsive imagination, drove him into tasks for which he had no gift, and where he floated hither and thither without sure guide. From the time of his official success, that is, for the last fifteen years of his life, he produced nothing worthy of himself, and much that was manifest book-making—the mere outpouring of the professional preacher and story-teller. Of his historical and philosophical work I shall not speak at all. His shallow Cambridge Inaugural Lecture, given by him as Professor of History, was torn to pieces in the *Westminster Review* (April 1861), it is said, by a brother Professor of History. Much less need we speak of his miserable duel with Cardinal Newman, wherein he was so shamefully worsted. For fifteen years he poured out lectures, sermons, tales, travels, poems, dialogues, children's books, and historical, philosophical, theological, social, scientific, and sanitary essays—but the Charles Kingsley of *Yeast,* of *Alton Locke,* of *Hypatia,* of *Westward Ho!* of the Ballads and Poems, we never knew again. He burnt out his fiery spirit at last, at the age of fifty-five, in a series of restless enterprises, and a vehement outpouring of miscellaneous eloquence.

Charles Kingsley was a man of genius, half poet, half controversialist. The two elements did not blend altogether well. His poetic passion carried away his reason and often confused his logic. His argumentative vehemence too

often marred his fine imagination. Thus his *Saint's Tragedy* is partly a satire on Romanism, and his ballad in *Yeast* is mainly a radical pamphlet. Hardly one of his books is without a controversial preface, controversial titles, chapters, or passages on questions of theology, churches, races, politics, or society. Indeed, excepting some of his poems, and some of his popular or children's books (but not even all of these), all his works are of a controversial kind. Whatever he did he did with heart, and this was at once his merit and his weakness. Before all things, he was a preacher, a priest of the English Church, a Christian minister. He was, indeed, a liberal priest, sometimes even too free and easy. He brings in the sacred name perhaps more often than any other writer, and he does so not always in a devout way. He seemed at last to use the word "God" as if it were an expletive or mere intensive like a Greek γε, meaning "very much" or "very good," as where he so oddly calls the North-East wind "the wind of God." And he betrays a most unclerical interest in physical torture and physical voluptuousness (*Hypatia, The Saint's Tragedy,* "*Saint Maura,*" *Westward Ho!),* though it is true that his real nature is both eminently manly and pure. (pp. 177-98)

[At] his best Charles Kingsley left some fine and abiding influences behind him, and achieved some brilliant things. Would that we always had men of his dauntless spirit, of his restless energy, of his burning sympathy, of his keen imagination! He reminds us somewhat of his own Bishop Synesius, as described in *Hypatia* (chap. xxi.), who "was one of those many-sided, volatile, restless men, who taste joy and sorrow, if not deeply or permanently, yet abundantly and passionately"—"He lived . . . in a whirlwind of good deeds, meddling and toiling for the mere pleasure of action; and as soon as there was nothing to be done, which, till lately, had happened seldom enough with him, paid the penalty for past excitement in fits of melancholy. A man of magniloquent and flowery style, not without a vein of self-conceit; yet withal of overflowing kindliness, racy humour, and unflinching courage, both physical and moral; with a very clear practical faculty, and a very muddy speculative one"—and so on. Charles Kingsley must have been thinking of his own tastes when he drew the portrait of the "squire-bishop." But he did more than the Bishop of Cyrene, and was himself a compound of squire-parson-poet. And in all three characters he showed some of the best sides of each. (pp. 198-99)

Frederic Harrison, "Charles Kingsley," in his Studies in Early Victorian Literature, *Edward Arnold, 1895, pp. 176-99.*

W. D. Howells (essay date 1901)

[*Howells was the chief progenitor of American Realism and one of the most influential American literary critics of the late nineteenth century. Through Realism he aimed to disperse "the conventional acceptations by which men live on easy terms with themselves" so that they might "examine the grounds of their social and moral opinions." In the following excerpt, Howells examines Kingsley's characterization of Hypatia, contending that his portrayal of the eponymous heroine demon-*

strates that the author is "no dramatist at all, but an exalted moralist willing to borrow the theatre for the ends of the church." Howells emphasizes, however, his respect for the author's poetic sensibility and skill, lamenting that these qualities are overshadowed by the propagandist intensity of Kingsley's ideological and moral concerns.]

One of the most striking things in Charles Kingsley's **Alton Locke: Tailor and Poet** is the modernity of the problems involved, the conditions combated, the terms of the contest, and the very language in which they are stated. The book is on this side palpitantly actual, though the literary attitude is so old-fashioned and outdated. The Chartist agitation of fifty years ago is mirrored in the Socialist aspiration of the present day; its aims are effectively the same, its means the same, its vocabulary the same, and neither the reasons nor the unreasons with which it was then met have since changed. Its quarrel is now less with aristocracy and more with plutocracy; but these were always really convertible if not identical, and now the quarrel is more directly with capital because class without capital is no longer to be feared. The one great matter in which the new industrial rebellion differs from the old is in its attitude towards religion; but this change has taken place less through the hearts of the toilers than through the hearts of the teachers. The church has risen to an ideal of Christianity which was intuitive with the world of work and need; and it was already beginning to imagine its duty in the modern industrial conditions when **Alton Locke** was written. How much that book had to do with clarifying its conception of this duty it would not be easy to say; but we can make sure of the fact that **Alton Locke** has been potent as a twofold protest: first against the cruel exploitation of labor, and second against the misdirected resentment of the sufferers. Its insurrection is on a far broader ground, and with a much wider intention than that of *Jane Eyre*. It is human and that is personal; but because humanity is still so much weaker than personality, it has probably influenced vastly fewer readers. Then, it has failed of equal influence, undoubtedly, because it is not of equal art. It is a polemic, in which all the characters, of whatever party they apparently are, are always arguing for the author. They stand for this thing or that, but they have not risen of themselves; they are where they are because he put them there. English fiction is for the most part still in the stage of allegory, though there were always masters who could teach it the higher function of drama. Charles Kingsley was not of these masters, at least in **Alton Locke,** and he was too didactic by nature and by culture ever to be simply representative. He is trying to carry a point, to enforce a truth, rather than to show it and let it enforce itself. In **Alton Locke,** the hero, who speaks for himself in the autobiographical form, is really a character, a person; Kingsley always dealt well with the literary type, its consciousness, its conceit, its self-distrust, its timid selfishness, and its bursts of enthusiasm; but the others are merely frameworks actuated directly from the author, doing the things they are expected to do. This is especially true of the two women who must stand for the heroines. Neither Lillian Winnstay, the shallow-hearted, romantic beauty, who flatters the poor poet by her pleasure in his verse and his picturesque personality, nor Eleanor Staunton, who snubs him for his good, but is really his friend, and the faithful friend of all the poor, is more than an illustration. They have their being, not in a world of law, but a world of special providences (the world of nearly all English fiction), and they do what it happens to them to do, and for the effect upon Alton Locke, whom they are to teach that if the upper classes are sometimes self-absorbed they are also sometimes self-devoted. This was a useful thing enough, and something that not only a burning-hearted orator and agitator like Alton Locke could profitably realize, but that all the struggling and suffering lower classes would do well to understand; yet it was not a thing that could give them dramatic projection, apparently, beyond the will of their creator. Lillian Winnstay was of rather more palpable substance than Eleanor Staunton, and in her more complex behavior she achieves something like the complexity of a real character. She is at least not exemplary, and so far she is saved from the worst that can befall a type in fiction, or perhaps in life. In a book so largely devoted to making it clear that the church is not the enemy but the true friend if not sole hope of the poor, it is much to have her the daughter of a dean; and it is in the interest of her reality that she is kept from anything worse than an intellectual flirtation with the sweat-shop poet, or from anything but an æsthetical appreciation of his picturesqueness.

It is a curious fact that a sort of imagination, like that of a poet, and especially such a poet as Kingsley was, can somehow give its creations greater verisimilitude by putting them back in time, where they may be posed in an arbitrary light, with a setting unquestioned by the familiar experiences and associations of the reader. For this reason Hypatia in the novel of her name is more lifelike than Eleanor Staunton, and her foil Pelagia is more lifelike than Eleanor Staunton's foil, Lillian Winnstay. Hypatia is really a young lady of the early eighteen-fifties, of the time when young ladies of her type were crudely called strong-minded. She was a sort of Alexandrian Margaret Fuller, with more good looks than our transcendental muse could pretend to; but not of a loftier ideal, a purer soul, a more "orphic utterance." She was a woman-version of Julian the Apostate, and she was born in Athens and lived and lectured at Alexandria not long after that paganizing reactionary failed to persuade the world that there was something in the old mythology or philosophy. She had a large following of cultured and gilded youth, but the mob, led on by the turbulent monks of the city, under the countenance of the patriarch Cyril, rose in tumult against her, and she was torn to pieces by the Christian zealots. So far history, with whose elements our poet (and Kingsley was a very true if not a very great poet) deals as he may and will, and reconstructs in a figure of at least as much recognizable reality as the heroines of his novels of modern life.

It cannot be said by the unprejudiced reader that his Hypatia is an attractive personality. He has somehow failed to give her charm, though he has given her a beautiful body, perfectly moulded features, with blue eyes and yellow hair, and a glorious intellect. But the truth is his Hypatia remains as cold as the baths of Apollo, and it is not going too far to say that she is rather repellent. Of course she might answer that she did not mean to be otherwise, in her poet's hands, and that what he had shown her, that she was: rather arrogant in mind, holding matrimony in high scorn, and thinking but little better, if any, of maternity. The passion of the ardent young monk Philammon for this snow-cold divinity is not made altogether credible, and his sister, poor, pretty Pelagia, who has lived the life of a wanton and is presently the paramour of the Gothic chief Amal, is more winning in some things that take the heart. She is passionately faithful to her huge, stupid, honest Goth, and she is kind to every one else, with a willingness to see people happy even if they are not virtuous. She is spiritually modest, and at least unconscious in her other immodesty. When she is awakened through the dim memories of childhood to the fact that she and Philammon are sister and brother, long ago carried captive from Athens and sold into slavery, she tries hard to let the monk bring her to a conviction of sin. But though she is good Christian enough to believe in hell, she also believes in God, and thinks He will take into consideration the peculiar circumstances under which she remains constant to Amal, whom the customs of the Goth's tribe will not suffer to marry her.

In all this Pelagia is certainly not a better woman than Hypatia; but she is a more lovable nature, and she does not make Hypatia's fatal mistake of trying to transcend her own nature. Hypatia would have married the faithless perfect Orestes in the hope of restoring the old Greek faith, though in her neoplatonism she is as passionless as he is faithless. Her author deals intelligently with her, but somehow he fails to deal impressively, and, as regards the reader's sympathy or even interest, he fails to deal successfully. It may be that he suffers himself to be too strictly trammelled by history—the historical romance must not, of all things, be historical—and does not give his imagination free play in her character. In any case she remains a woman without warmth of heart, that supreme mode of motion, without heat even of intellect. She cannot, therefore, impart movement to the figures of the drama around her and centring in her. The Alexandria of the fifth century is a great scene, with its wild monks doing the will of the bigoted Cyril, and wreaking their fanaticism now upon the Jews and now upon the pagans; with its Roman prefect seeking to hold the turbulent population in check alternately by tyranny and flattery; with its belated schools of Greek philosophy; with its church already sunk into superstition and corruption; with its swarming masses of every race and color, the prey of every lawless impulse from within and without, effete and hysterical, violent and cruel, kept from famine by public doles of food, and amused by bloody public shows at once pitiless and shameless; and *Hypatia* is Kingsley's endeavor and his failure to fuse all these warring elements into a dramatic whole. In spite of his admirable conception of the situation, his learning, his poetic insight, they will not respond to his intention. They remain dispersed, as they might not if they had been grouped about a central figure of more cohesive power. But all the different particles seem to crumble away from the repellent nature of the heroine, whose fate the spectator beholds with compassion certainly, but with more horror than compassion. On a far higher plane than Bulwer's work in *The Last Days of Pompeii,* Kingsley's work in *Hypatia* falls below it in artistic effect; for

Bulwer, cheap as he was, was at least a melodramatist, while Kingsley was no dramatist at all, but an exalted moralist willing to borrow the theatre for the ends of the church. If we realize this we shall understand why his figures seem to have come out of the property-room by way of the vestry. Orestes, the debauched Roman prefect, believing neither in the gods nor the saints, but willing to propitiate the friends of either as they shall serve the turn of his ambition; Miriam, the haggish slave-dealer, who knows the common paternity of Pelagia and Philammon, and is the mother of Orestes's boon companion, the brilliant Jewish sceptic and cynic Raphael Aben-Ezra, partner of Orestes's passion for the snow-cold Hypatia, and destined to a true Christian conversion; Theon, the Heavy Father of Hypatia, who consents for his sake as well as her own ambition to listen to the suit of Orestes; the whole tribe of monkish and prelatic fanatics; the forty Gothic barbarians stalking large and blond through the scene, and casually hewing down enough miscreants of every tradition and persuasion to satisfy the bloodthirstiest reader; the hermits and fathers of the desert; and the various soldiers, students, porters, slaves, and singing and dancing women who thickly people the scene, all affect us like old friends from beyond the foot-lights. The conception is not wanting in originality; it is the performance which seems somehow second-hand in most cases. The affair has many dramatic moments; it often promises to be a drama, but it never quite is so. As a representation of antique life closer to our own than either that of *Quo Vadis* or *The Last Days of Pompeii,* it lacks as much the brute plethora and intensity of the one as the histrionic knack of the other; and yet the message it conveys is more vital than that of either. It realizes to us that human motives and passions are immutably the same in all times and places; that philosophy perishes in spite of its beauty and truth, and that religion survives in spite of its ugliness and falsehood, because it takes account of the things of the soul and philosophy cares only for the things of the mind. It teaches that the Christianity of the nineteenth century as well as the fifth needs to be saved from itself before it can save the world, but that it alone can save the world.

Kingsley was a poet—I am always saying that—and he passionately loved the artistic presence of the antique world. He was one of those Hellenizing English minds of whom Keats was the first and finest, and he stood in some such relation to the pagan past as one of the earliest Greek Christians might, feeling the beauty of its ideality while abhorring its sensuality. He was very fit indeed to write a much better story of the zealots and sophists of Alexandria than he actually wrote in *Hypatia,* and I still think it was through his heroine that he failed. If I fail to prove this, and any reader recurring to the book after many years, or coming newly to it, shall find it greater than I have found it in my second reading, I shall rejoice, and save myself by making my critic observe that I always said the author was a poet.

Kingsley himself recognizes a difficulty in rehabilitating to the fancy the period he has chosen, and this difficulty lies in the impossibility of telling all about paganism. He could tell the worst about Christianity, but without a statement of the unnamable iniquities which the old faith suffered if

Illustration by Kingsley of himself and Fanny making love on a cross.

it did not foster there could be no sufficient contrast of the two. In paganism there could be no conviction of sin; there could be offences against the will or the dignity of the gods, but none against the spirit of righteousness, such as quicken the soul of the offender to repentance; and in like manner there could be no such meekness of heart as attributes its virtue to some source of goodness outside itself. Hypatia's enthusiasm for the pagan philosophy must ignore the foulness of the pagan life; and her stainless personal purity must rejoice in itself as the effect of her own will. She has but two passions, or rather one, for ambition includes jealousy, and she is envious of the witchery which Pelagia has for the hearts of men, and cannot bear that the dancing-woman should enjoy the triumph which she herself disdains. She has her following of those who can adore beauty that lectures and illumines, but she must have all, or at least she cannot suffer that her rival should have any.

It will have been seen that Hypatia, after all, does not escape being a woman; she is, indeed, the more a woman in failing, and it is in the throes of her self-recognized limitations that the heart warms to her a little. Hypatia angered that Pelagia should be the supreme attraction of the spectacle that the perfect is planning, is at least more tolerable than Hypatia refusing to let Pelagia profit by her teaching, even at the prayer of her beloved pupil Philammon, because she will not have her own purity contaminated by Pelagia's presence. In her former mood she is at the worst sincere, but in the latter mood she is at the best not credible even if she is sincere. It is hard to see what side of Hypatia is accessible to sympathy, but the terrible spectacle of her death must inspire compassion. This acquires reality rather from the passions of her murderers than from any quality of her own; and it is difficult to conceive of her even as a living impersonation of intellectual pride suffering martyrdom. Is not she rather a statue to a belated ideal, thrown down and broken to pieces by the sanguinary zealots of another faith? It is hard even to believe in Philammon, her pupil and lover, who has turned monk again, but who deserts his brethren to warn her of their hate, and to save her from their fury, as she appears after her lecture, in the street where they are lurking.

> At last a curricle, glittering with silver, rattled round the corner and stopped opposite him. . . . A slave brought forth an embroidered cushion, and then Hypatia herself came forth, looking more glorious than ever; her lips set in a sad, firm smile; her eyes uplifted, inquiring, eager, and yet gentle, dimmed by some great inward awe, as if her soul were far away aloft, and face to face with God. In a moment he sprang to her, caught her robe convulsively, threw himself on his knees before her. 'Stop! Stay! You are going to destruction!' Calmly she looked down

upon him. 'Accomplice of witches! Would you make of Theon's daughter a traitor like yourself?' She believed him guilty, then! It was the will of God! The plumes of the horses were waving far down the street before he recovered himself and rushed after her, shouting he knew not what. It was too late. A dark wave of men rushed from the ambuscade, surged round the car—swept forward—she had disappeared; and, as Philammon followed breathless, the horses galloped past him madly homeward with the empty carriage. Whither were they dragging her? To the Cæsareum, to the Church of God himself? Impossible! Why thither, of all places on the earth? Why did the mob, increasing momentarily by hundreds, pour down upon the beach, and return brandishing flints, shells, fragments of pottery? She was upon the church steps before he caught them up, invisible among the crowd, but he could track her by the fragments of her dress. . . . He would save her! And he struggled in vain to pierce the dense mass of parobolani and monks, who, mingled with fish-wives and dock-workers, leaped and yelled around their victim. . . . Yes! On into the church itself! Into the cool, dim shadow, with its fretted pillars and lowering domes, and candles and incense, and blazing altar, and great pictures looking from the walls across the gorgeous gloom. And right in front, above the altar, the colossal Christ watching unmoved from off the wall, his right hand raised, to give a blessing or a curse? On, up the nave, fresh shreds of her dress strewing the holy pavement, up the chancel steps themselves, up to the altar, right underneath the great still Christ, and there even these hell-hounds paused. She shook herself free from her tormentors, and, springing back, rose for a moment to her full height, naked, snow-white against the dusky mass around, shame and indignation in those wide, clear eyes, but not a stain of fear. With one hand she clasped her golden locks around her; the other long, white arm was stretched upward toward the great still Christ, appealing—and who dare say in vain?—from man to God. Her lips were open to speak, but the words that would have come from them reached God's ear alone; for in an instant Peter struck her down, the dark mass closed over her again, and then, wail on wail, long, wild, ear-piercing, rung along the vaulted roof.

But enough of this, as the novelist himself would say. Poor Hypatia, framed of such great elements by the hand of a true poet, how is it she fails of the due effect? Perhaps it is because of the double charge which the poet felt laid upon him as also a priest. He must make her at once the beautiful apostle of a creed outworn, and an example of its insufficiency to the needs at least of woman nature, if not of human nature. Hawthorne could have dealt triumphantly with such a figure, and rapt us with the mystical and thrilling charm of its contrasts; but not Kingsley, too earnest as he always was for the long patience of art, and too perfervid in that zeal for his reader's soul first of all things. The dramatist can preach and he does preach by Hamlet, by Macbeth, by Othello, who are never freed, either of them, to an absolute and single significance, but if

the preacher attempts to dramatize, we forget his lesson in our sense of his failure. The moral of *Hypatia* is, Beware of spiritual pride, and do not evil that good may come; but what is the meaning of Hypatia herself? (pp. 2-13)

> *W. D. Howells, "Charles Kingsley's Hypatia,"*
> *in his* Heroines of Fiction, Vol. II, *Harper &*
> *Brothers Publishers, 1901, pp. 1-13.*

Lewis Melville [pseudonym of Lewis Saul Benjamin] (essay date 1906)

[*In the following excerpt, Melville presents an overview of Kingsley's literary career, discussing themes and characterization in his fiction. The critic concludes his assessment of Kingsley's achievement by praising the author's "scene-painting."*]

When Charles Kingsley made his first bid for fame, Dickens was at the height of his powers and Lytton at the zenith of his popularity; Lever had done his best work and Disraeli had published the trilogy, *Coningsby, Sybil,* and *Tancred;* Charlotte Brontë had issued only *Jane Eyre;* and Thackeray was bringing out *Vanity Fair* in monthly parts; Trollope had written his earliest book, *The Macdermots of Ballycloran;* George Eliot and Mrs. Gaskell were unknown; and Wilkie Collins and Charles Reade had not entered the field. The years of Kingsley's activities as a novelist coincided with a period of great importance in the history of English fiction. During the years that intervened between the production of *Yeast* (1848) and *Hereward the Wake* (1866), Lytton produced *The Caxtons* series and *A Strange Story;* the Brontës concluded their career; Dickens added *David Copperfield, Bleak House,* and *A Tale of Two Cities;* and Thackeray, with the publication of all his great stories, satisfied the wish he had expressed that one day he might rank with classical writers. Disraeli issued no book, but he devoted the hours he could snatch from political labour to the composition of *Lothair.* Mrs. Gaskell published *Mary Barton, North and South,* and *Moorland Cottage;* and Reade, *Peg Woffington, Christie Johnstone, It is Never too Late to Mend,* and *The Cloister and the Hearth;* while all that is best of Trollope appeared. George Eliot issued *Scenes of Clerical Life, Adam Bede, The Mill on the Floss, Silas Marner,* and *Romola;* and Wilkie Collins achieved great popularity, after one or two comparative failures, with *The Woman in White* and *No Name.*

Kingsley's first serious effort was the composition, in 1842, of a poetic drama on the subject of St. Elizabeth of Hungary, which was published six years later under the title of *The Saint's Tragedy.* This never became popular. It dealt with the social problems which the author could never forget, and it was, as Maurice said in the Introduction, 'a little too bold for the taste and temper of the age.' It extorted the admiration of Bunsen, however; and, indeed, contains several fine passages, and showed much promise. His poetry, however, has never made the mark achieved by his romances; yet there are some of his shorter poems that will live for many a day. "The Sands of Dee" and "The Three Fishers" have the true poetic ring; as have the charming lyrics, "The Tide River," "The Summer

Sea," and the songs from *The Water Babies.* "**The Last Buccaneer**" is an admirable ballad; and the poem with which *Alton Locke* concludes is, in its way, second only to "**The Song of the Shirt**"; while the author was at his best in the beautiful and pathetic verses, "**When all the World is Young, Lad.**"

> When all the world is young, lad,
>   And all the trees are green,
> And every goose a swan, lad,
>   And every lass a queen!
> Then hey! for boot and horse, lad,
>   And round the world away!
> Young blood must have its course, lad,
>   And every dog its day.
>   . . . . .
> When all the world is old, lad,
>   And all the trees are brown,
> And all the sport is stale, lad,
>   And all the wheels run down:
> Creep home and take your place there,
>   The spent and maimed among;
> God grant you find one face there
>   You loved when all was young.

Kingsley held strong views on the condition of the poor, and in 1848 contributed to *Politics for the People* over the pseudonym 'Parson Lot,' adopted, so Sir Leslie Stephen has recorded, on account of a discussion with his friends, in which, being in a minority of one, he had said he felt like Lot, 'when he seemed as one that mocked to his sons-in-law.' It was under this disguise that he issued the pamphlet entitled *Cheap Clothes and Nasty* (1850), which since 1881 has been reprinted as a foreword to editions of *Alton Locke.* He learned his social philosophy from Carlyle, and there are echoes of *Sartor Resartus* in *Yeast* and of *The French Revolution* in *Alton Locke;* and he imbibed moral philosophy and the principles of religion from Frederick Denison Maurice, whom he had first met at Cambridge. Maurice was the real founder of the Christian Social Movement, but there is no name more closely associated with it than that of Charles Kingsley. Indeed, he did for Maurice what Huxley did for Spencer and Darwin: he popularised the view. Mr. Ludlow has recorded how Kingsley said to him, with his characteristic stutter: 'I am g-going to t-take a s-sermon of M-Maurice's and t-turn it into l-language understood of the p-people.'

Kingsley joined the group of men who, under the guidance of Maurice, were endeavouring to show that the socialist movement then making headway was not necessarily antagonistic to the tenets of Christianity. This view, though now generally accepted, was then somewhat of a novelty; for, in the earlier half of the century, a socialist was regarded with a feeling that was half horror and half fear. Indeed, there are still many old people who cannot be brought to believe that a socialist can be other than a rogue. But Kingsley was never actually a socialist, though he sympathised with the sufferings of the poor and did his best to assist in the upraising of the working classes. He advocated co-operation, and was a constant agitator for sanitary legislation. In later years, however, he became more conservative, more contented with things as they were; and he ceased to clamour for improvements, though

his sympathy with the London workman and the agricultural labourer was as active as ever.

It was only to be expected that when, as a young man, he devoted himself to the composition of works of fiction, he should produce novels with a purpose. Now, manners may change, habits fall out of fashion, but, *au fond,* men and women will always be, as they have always been, the same. Elemental passions will never be eliminated; and, under a veneer more or less thin, they will always hold sway. But the veneer will not stand rough usage. Scratch the Russ and you find the Tartar, is good the whole world over. The Court of Chancery was, perhaps, never so circumlocutory as Dickens made it; and to-day, when its methods of procedure have been reformed, much of the interest of *Bleak House* has disappeared. Novels with a purpose are useful, and, appealing to the public with greater force than a pamphlet, are often instrumental in bringing about desirable ends. But, because of this very success, they are for an age, not for all time; they may be valuable, but they are rarely works of art. The stories in which Dickens exposed abuses do not rank among his best; Charles Reade, the great-hearted, spoilt several of his books by attacks upon existing institutions; and many of the failures of Wilkie Collins may be traced to the same cause; while the novels of Disraeli would have been far more delightful if he had not employed them to advocate the programme of his party. *It is Never too Late to Mend* loses its *objet d'être* when prison abuses are removed; but *Tom Jones* and *Vanity Fair* will never be out of date, since they deal not with institutions but with men and women.

Yeast, though classed as a novel, is much more akin to the pamphlet. The characters are merely vehicles for the expression of different views; and the story is of the slightest. The narrative is frequently interrupted by the insertion of the author's opinions, which, interesting enough in themselves, are quite out of place in a work of this kind. There are dissertations on religion—on the young man who goes over to Rome, and on the young man who is suspected of leanings towards agnosticism—even their correspondence is inserted; on poaching; on fox-hunting; and an attack, in verse, on the preservation of game. The principal topic is the position of the poor in the country; and Kingsley has drawn a picture, terrible because of its truth, of the squalid, overcrowded, fever-haunted homes and the wretched life of the labourer.

As a contrast, he has painted a collection of landlords. Lord Minchampstead, who introduces to the farmer on his estates the latest machinery, and who is determined to make his property pay; Lord Vieuxbois, who, with the best intentions in the world, only succeeds in pauperising his tenants; and Mr. Lavington, the easy-going squire whose policy is to let things drift. There is the usual love-story, but the characterisation is weak, and the reader's interest is not aroused. It is remarked that the hero, Lancelot, might be another Mirabeau; but, though he spouts declamatory passages at every opportunity, he shows no particular cleverness. He is tedious to a degree, and may be dismissed as a prig. The heroine is Argemone Lavington, a girl with views on religion, which, however, she abandons with celerity when, to her great surprise, she finds herself devoted to Lancelot. Harry Verney is a typical old gamekeeper, unscrupulous but loyal to his master, a man that compels a reluctant admiration; but Tregarva, who talks unceasingly, and would have done good service on the agitation platform, is in a novel merely tedious, though much may be forgiven him as the author of such surprisingly good poetry for a gamekeeper as **"A Rough Rhyme on a Rough Matter,"** the ballad of a poacher's wife. In the earlier part of the book, Colonel Bracebridge, the spoilt darling of the Guards, is a well-drawn character, shrewd, capable, dissipated, feeling that he can do better things, yet muddling on in the old way. Towards the end of the story he is made to commit suicide on hearing that his mistress has borne him a son who died within a few moments of his birth. The incident is invested with other sad circumstances, but the Bracebridges do not die by their own hand for such reasons. It seems as if the suicide was introduced to point the moral that the fast-liver comes to a bad and untimely end. The moral may be good, but its application in this case spoils the book.

The sympathy shown in *Yeast* for the labourer is, in *Alton Locke* (1849), extended to the London artisan in general and to the journeyman tailor in particular. Locke is brought up among the Dissenters and, when his views broaden, he is thrown upon the world by his mother, at the instigation of a narrow-minded preacher. He works as a tailor, and sees much of the horrible trade carried on in the sweater's den. The author is so righteously incensed by the abominations about which he writes that he frequently drops the story to express his opinions. Locke educates himself and writes poems that are meritorious. A volume of his poetry is published by subscription, and it seems as if he might rise in the world. Indeed, putting his Pegasus into heavy harness, he contrives for a while to live by his pen. But he drifts back among his Chartist friends, is mixed up—though innocently enough—with the burning of a farm, and is sentenced to three years' imprisonment. The rigours of prison life affect his health, and, shortly after his release, he dies. The story is slight, but the earnestness of the author is infectious. There is one dramatic moment—the rescue of old Porter's son from the sweater's den. The book is a sermon, and the sermon had already been preached in *Cheap Clothes and Nasty.* But the sentiment is false; and people who buy their clothes from cheap tailors do not in real life pay the penalty by catching fever. The characterisation, however, shows a marked advance. The portraits of the dissenting clergymen are clearly limned; and Locke's snobbish, tuft-hunting cousin, the self-seeking, pushing *parvenu,* is well contrasted with the courteous, good-hearted Lord Lynedale; but Locke himself is merely a puppet, and his hopes and fears and his love are each and all mechanical. The success of the book is Mackaye, the second-hand bookseller, with the gruff manner and the tender heart, and the quaint, dry, kindly humour that is only to be found in the best of his race.

After these dissertations upon socialistic problems, Kingsley ventured into the field of historical romance, and produced the books, *Hypatia* (1853) and *Westward Ho!* (1855), upon which rests his fame as a novelist.

Hypatia, or, New Foes with Old Faces contains a good deal that will be painful to any reader and, as the author admitted, had much better be left unread by the young and innocent. Indeed, the story of Hypatia is one of the most terrible in Christian tradition, and it is not difficult to agree with Ruskin that this should for ever have been left in silence—at least by the novelist. Yet, *Hypatia* is a brilliant and forcible picture of life in the fifth century, when the Christian Church and the Roman Empire were struggling for mastery; but the picture is not accurate or realistic, because, for one reason, it was impossible for an English writer to show how terribly bad—from the modern standpoint—were the people of that epoch. The life of the heathens could not be described, and what it told of the Christians does not reflect glory upon them. They appear in the pages of this book to have been as cruel, as brutal, as full of tricks as their pagan antagonists; but the exceptions—Augustine, Synesius, Abbot Pambo, and Aufugus (who, before he entered the monastery, had been known in the world as Arsenius, the tutor of a king and a great statesman)—were men of whom any creed might boast.

The scene is laid in Alexandria, where Jews and Goths, Pagans and Christians, Romans and Greeks, slaves and lords, jostle one another in the streets. The city is represented as a scene of vice and abomination, and is skilfully contrasted with the peaceful monastery in the country, whence the muscular Christian, Philammon, issues forth to judge for himself of the world of which the monks talk so bitterly. The representatives of the various nations and creeds are well depicted. Philammon is an Athenian, and so, of course, is his sister, the wretched Pelagia, who, sold as a slave while still a child, has been brought up to an unnameable calling by her purchaser. Hypatia, the proud virgin, is the advocate of the gods, and to restore their worship she is willing to sacrifice herself and marry the debauched governor, Orestes. Deceived by him, and the victim of a cruel trick by Miriam, in which Philammon, all unwitting, takes part, she goes forth unflinchingly to meet death at the hands of the monks. Her friends tried in vain to save her.

> "I did what I could to die with her," said he [Eudaimon].
> "I did what I could to save her," said Philammon.
> "I know it. Forgive the words which I just spoke. Did we not both love her?"
> And the little wretch sat down by Philammon's side and, as the blood dripped from his wounds upon the pavement, broke out into a bitter agony of human tears.
> There are times when the very intensity of our misery is a boon, and kindly stuns us till we are unable to torture ourselves by thought. So it was with Philammon then. He sat there, he knew not how long.
> "She is with the gods," said Eudaimon, at last.
> "She is with the God of gods," answered Philammon: and they both were silent again.
> Suddenly, a commanding voice aroused them. They looked up, and saw before them Raphael Aben-Ezra.
> He was pale as death, but calm as death. One look into his face told them that he knew all.

"Young monk," he said, between his closed teeth, "you seem to have loved her."

Philammon looked up, but could not speak.

"Then arise, and flee for your life into the farthest corner of the desert, ere the doom of Sodom and Gomorrha fall upon this accursed city. Have you father, mother, brother, sister—ay, cat, dog or bird for which you care within its walls? . . . Then take them with you, and escape, and remember Lot's wife."

Raphael the philosopher, with his daring, his cunning, his contempt for the Gentile, his courage and self-possession, his tenderness—remember the incident of Bran and her puppies!—is one of the most striking characters in the book. The nobility of the man is shown when, without a sigh, he gives up wealth and comfort, and goes forth into the desert, penniless and alone. There he meets Victoria, the daughter of Majoricus, the perfect of a legion of Heraclian, who conquers his great heart. But his conversion to Christianity does not ring true. The history of Judaism shows that its votaries do not, even for love of a woman, abandon their faith.

Miriam, the pander, the slave-dealer, is the truest portrait ever drawn by Kingsley. Vile as she is, her lust for power, her greed, is for the child of her shame. Betrayed in her youth, in later years, while living as the humblest and poorest, she toiled, hoarded, lied, intrigued, won money for her son by every means, no matter how base. Her dying outburst is poetry itself: 'Of the house of Jesse, of the seed of Solomon; not a rabbi from Babylon to Rome dare deny that! A King's daughter am I, and a King's heart I had, and have, like Solomon's own, my son.' But it is the Goths who stand head and shoulders above the other races, for, with all their vices, they are men and heroes. Amalric is their leader, but Wulf is a prince among men. Courageous, honest, gentle, he does not care for the life in cities, and desires but to find Asgard, the ancient city of Odin, and to receive the mead-cup from the god's own hand. Later, in Spain, at the court of Adolf and Placidia, he was persuaded to accept baptism. At the last moment, however, he turned suddenly to the bishop, and asked where were the souls of his heathen ancestors. 'In hell,' replied the worthy prelate. Wulf drew back from the font. 'He would prefer,' he said, 'if Adolf had no objection, to go to his own people.' This is a true story, but it fits well into the character of this magnificent pagan. *Hypatia* is nobly planned, but it is wanting in other respects. It is sometimes stagey, and often melodramatic, and not infrequently grandiloquent. Bulwer Lytton might have written much of this book, which is to be ranked with *The Last Days of Pompeii* and *Rienzi,* or perhaps with *Romola,* rather than with the greatest historical romances.

Kingsley, who boasted that he was a West-countryman born and bred, settled at Bideford in February 1854; and in that quiet Devonshire village wrote *Westward Ho!* A great admirer of *The Faerie Queene,* it was in the spirit of Spenserian romance that he invented The Noble Brotherhood of the Rose, which consisted of a number of young men in love with Rose Salterne, the daughter of the Mayor of Bideford. Rose flirts impartially with each and all, but falls in love with a Spanish prisoner on parole, Don Guz-man Maria Magdalena Sotomayor de Soto, and when he is ransomed she elopes with him. This, it would be thought, would cause the dissolution of the Brotherhood. Instead of disbanding, however, the members seek her in the West Indies, where she is living, married, with Don Guzman; and, with the best intentions in the world, indirectly bring about her destruction. This is the framework upon which is built the story of the adventures of Amyas Leigh in the South Seas and on the Spanish Main. The book concludes with the attempted invasion of England by the Spaniards and the defeat of the great Armada. It is a stirring story of Elizabethan heroes. It would be a bold man, however, who would vouch for the historical accuracy of the book, even though it contains references to the best known events of the reign, and though numerous historical personages flit across the pages—notably the redoubtable Sir Richard Grenville, the unfortunate adventurer John Oxenham, the Jesuit Fathers Parsons and Campion (who are made unnecessarily ridiculous), Edmund Spenser, the poet, and Admirals Hawkins, Drake, and Raleigh. There is a Jesuit plot or two, and frequent mention of the Inquisition—that boon to the novelists who write of this period.

In *Hypatia,* as a matter of course, the author was on the side of the Christians in their struggle against the infidels; and in this book his sympathies are, naturally enough, with the Anglican and against the Roman Catholic Church. Indeed, the bias is very obvious. That may be right in the Protestant clergyman, but it is a defect in the novelist. The reader demands, rightly, that the romancer who goes to history for his inspiration shall not give a one-sided view of his subject. To judge from *Westward Ho!* the Protestant is a good man, the Catholic in general—with the exception of Lord Howard of Effingham, for whom Kingsley says a good word—a bad man, the Spanish Catholic in particular a vile man. This attitude is ridiculous; but Kingsley was an enthusiast, and, in these matters, hotheaded. It was these qualities that caused him to attack a man greater than he, who had 'gone over to Rome,' in the article entitled **"What, then, does Dr. Newman mean?"** that produced the world-famous *Apologia pro vita sua,* for which no admirer of exquisite English prose, whatever his creed, can be sufficiently grateful.

Of course the characters intimately connected with the story emanated from the author's imagination. Amyas Leigh, the bold-hearted—one is almost tempted to say—buccaneer; Frank Leigh, the darling of the Court, a lion-hearted dandy; the evil genius of the book, Eustace Leigh, the weak, unprincipled young man who is converted to Catholicism—than which, apparently, Kingsley cannot imagine a worse fate; the haughty, melodramatic Don Guzman; and Salvation Yeo, by far the best creation in the tale, a man who leaves England with John Oxenham a good-hearted but blaspheming sailor, and returns years after, the sole survivor of the party, a chastened, God-fearing man. One of the best scenes in the book is Yeo's interview with Sir Richard Grenvile, when he refuses, undismayed by threats, unmoved by persuasion, to tell his story upon oath—it being against his newly acquired principles to be sworn. The search of this mariner for his 'little maid' is well told, and his delight when she is found is admirably depicted.

Westward Ho! is the most successful of Kingsley's works of fiction, as certainly it is the most characteristic. Yet it is not so well conceived as *Hypatia,* nor is the picture of the age so acceptable; but it is far pleasanter to read. It is a fine work, yet far removed from the masterpieces; and perhaps it should rank a little below *Hypatia.*

Kingsley must be described rather as an eloquent writer (if the term is allowed) than as a great romancist. He was always the preacher first and the novelist afterwards. He was always in earnest, and equally sincere whether describing the sufferings of the London poor and of the country labourers, or the struggles between Christian and pagan, tyranny and freedom, knowledge and ignorance; whether telling the poor man of his birthright, or advocating the policy of *sanitas sanitatum, omnia sanitas,* or inveighing against the evils of tight-lacing. He had little pathos, and did not show himself the possessor of much humour—indeed, except in *Two Years Ago,* there is scarcely a trace of this quality in his writings. He did not realise, apparently, the importance in a work of fiction of dramatic effect, though in *Westward Ho!* he has given a vivid description of the wreck of the *Santa Catherina.* But what would not Scott have made of the scene at the inn, where the admirals are awaiting the news of the Armada? What would not the author of *Christie Johnstone* have made of the Aberalva chapters in *Two Years Ago?* Indeed, those chapters are strangely reminiscent of the former, and Lord Scoutbush and Bowie might have stepped out of them.

Kingsley's power of characterisation was weak to a degree. Generally his characters are either lay figures or unoriginal, and when original they are usually exaggerated. The only two living women he drew are both in *Westward Ho!*—Mrs. Leigh and Salvation Yeo's little maid. Rose Salterne is but a shadow, and her charms are left to the imagination, while Grace Hervey bears too strong a resemblance to the heroine of the Sunday School book to awaken much interest. Mary Armstrong does not attract attention; and Marie, with negro blood in her veins, is too obviously introduced to serve as a text upon which to hang the author's views upon the slave question; but Mrs. Mellor is bright and agreeable enough. His most successful men are Amyas and Tom Thurnall, muscular Christians, not all animal, strong, self-reliant: the sort of hero English boys and Englishmen love to read about. But what can be made of Frank Leigh, who talks in the following strain: 'Had either, madam, of that cynosural triad been within call of my most humble importunities, your ears had been delectate with far nobler melody.' On the other hand, Mark Armsworth is an agreeable figure; the blind, resigned Dr. Thurnall, though only dimly outlined, remains in the memory; and Elsley Vavasour, *alias* John Briggs, though overdrawn, might have been taken from life. It is an admirable character sketch.

Kingsley had a great command of language, and his scene painting was admirable. In few English authors can there be found finer pictures than are contained in his books, whether of English landscape, as in *Yeast,* or of wretched hovels, as in *Alton Locke,* or of Alexandria and the desert of the Nile, as in *Hypatia,* or of the downs of Devonshire and the solitude of the great South American forest which Amyas and his followers traverse, as in *Westward Ho!* or of the Fenlands, as in *Hereward the Wake.*

> All day long a careful watch was kept among the branches of the mighty ceiba-tree. And what a tree that was! The hugest English oak would have seemed stunted beside it. Borne up on roots, or, rather, walls, of twisted board some twelve feet high, between which the whole crew, their ammunition and provisions were housed roomily, rose the enormous trunk, full forty feet in girth, towering like some tall lighthouse, smooth for a hundred feet, then crowned with boughs, each of which was a stately tree, whose topmost twigs were full two hundred and fifty feet from the ground. And yet it was easy for the sailors to ascend; so many natural ropes had kind Nature lowered for their use, in the smooth lianes which hung to the very earth, often without a knot or leaf. Once in the tree, you were within a new world, suspended between heaven and earth, and, as Cary said, no wonder if, like Jack when he climbed the magic bean-stalk, you had found a castle, a giant and a few acres of well-stocked park, packed away somewhere amid that labyrinth of timber. Flower-gardens at least there were in plenty; for every limb was covered with pendent cactuses, gorgeous orchises and wild pines; and while one half of the tree was clothed in rich foliage, the other half, utterly leafless, bore on every twig brilliant yellow flowers, around which humming-birds whirred all day long. Parrots peeped in and out of every cranny, while, within the airy woodland, brilliant lizards basked like living gems upon the bark, gaudy finches flitted and chirruped, butterflies of every size and colour hovered over the topmost twigs, innumerable insects hummed from morn till eve; and when the sun went down, tree-toads came out to snore and croak till dawn. There was more life round that one tree than in a whole square mile of English soil.

Kingsley described the scenes he had never visited with no less realism than those with which he was familiar, and for this much praise has been bestowed upon him. But, after all, to describe a place one does not know requires only a small portion of imagination, and a diligent study of the works of those well acquainted with the spot. Yet it is this power of description that distinguishes him above his contemporaries, with the exception, perhaps, of Disraeli; indeed, places him in this respect above all writers since Scott, and even Scott's landscape does not always seem so spontaneous. (pp. 106-24)

> *Lewis Melville, "Charles Kingsley," in his* Victorian Novelists, *Archibald Constable and Company, Limited, 1906, pp. 106-24.*

Lafcadio Hearn (essay date 1915)

[*Hearn was an American fiction writer and critic. Often devoting his short stories and novellas to supernatural subjects, he is best known for his retellings of Japanese ghost stories. As a critic, Hearn ignored the moralistic conventions of Victorian criticism and emphasized the emotional effects of art rather than its social and ethical functions. In the following excerpt from an essay in which he addresses a Japanese audience on the subject of English literature, Hearn praises Kingsley's artistry, ranking him among the greatest of nineteenth-century authors.]*

Charles Kingsley was the son of a clergyman, became a clergyman himself, and remained one all his life. But perhaps no other name in English literature so little represents those conservative influences which we are accustomed to associate with the Church. We see a very great deal of the man, and of the soul of the man, but of the clergyman we see very little; of the Christian nothing sectarian, nothing narrow-minded, only a great broad, deep, and true religious sense, toned by idealism, but never qualified by humbug.

Kingsley was born in 1819, educated first at King's College at London, and afterwards at Cambridge. His native place was Devonshire, and in many of his stories we find charming pictures of the Devonshire coast. After entering the Church he was appointed to the rectorship of Eversley in Hampshire, where he always lived. Perhaps because of his great literary powers he was made Professor of Modern History at Cambridge in the latter part of his life. He was the brother-in-law of the great historian Froude, and what has been said of Froude, as Professor of History, has also been said of Kingsley in the same capacity. Indeed the men resembled each other in many respects, both of weakness and of strength. The faults found with the lectures of both was that they were too romantic, that they delighted the students by appealing to their imagination with vivid and emotional pictures, but at the same time gave them one-sided views of history. Romantic Kingsley's lectures certainly were, but in the most artistic sense; and it is certain that those who heard them with open minds obtained such glimpses of historic truth, and received such impulses of patriotic pride and heroism, as no merely pedantic work ever could have given.

His books represent much variety. We have pure scientific studies in natural history and geology; we have fairy tales; and we have a number of novels, both historical and romantic. The novels themselves can not be classified under one general head nor even under three. For example, **Alton Locke** is a romance of the Chartist period in England, and largely expresses personal feeling; **Hypatia** is a story of the fifth century, and the scene is Alexandria in Egypt; **Westward Ho!** is a narrative of the great naval struggle between Spain and England in the sixteenth century; **Hereward the Wake** is a romance of the time of the Norman conquest; **Yeast** embodies the theory of what was called in Kingsley's time "Christian Socialism," and **Two Years Ago** is perhaps the only novel of the lot in the strictest sense of the word—a novel of modern English life.

Perhaps because of the relation of the narratives to particular agitations of English social life, **Alton Locke** and **Yeast** are not well adapted for reading by students in Japan. I should not dare to recommend them; and yet I can not but regret that they are not likely to appeal to you

in the same way they once appealed to English readers. I do not know any pages in all Kingsley's work more politically impressive than those in which the dream of Alton Locke is described, the dream of the great migration of races from India westward, as it was imagined in the period when the new Sanskrit studies had first taught us that the English and the Hindoo were brothers in blood and kindred in speech. You will not easily forget the splendid phantasmagoria in this description—the vastness—the movement, the idea given of great space and great light, and the divisions always lessening behind the Himalayas, like a rosy dawn. More useful for your literary study, however, are almost any of his other books. Most critics say that **Westward Ho!** is his masterpiece, but I can not help believing that English patriotic feeling inspires this judgment. **Westward Ho!** is a great book with its studies of West Indian life, its drawings of the English gentlemen's adventures of Elizabeth's time, its battle scenes, its heroism, and the awful but not impossible catastrophe at the end, when Amyas Leigh is blinded by a lightning flash; but somehow or other I can not help thinking that to persons not English this story is less interesting than **Hypatia,** or even than **Hereward,** the most really English of all. I should say to the student, "Read **Hereward** and **Hypatia,** before you read any other work by Kingsley." Hereward is the old English Viking,—brother in blood and speech to the Scandinavian Berserk,—the man who took off instead of putting on his armour to fight. There was really a Hereward in history, who long resisted the power of William the Conqueror and who was called the Wake, or the Awake, because he could never be taken by surprise. Kingsley has nobly idealised this figure; he has made Hereward not merely the typical man of the North, but a model of strong and generous manhood for all time. He once and only once does wrong—he is faithless to his wife because of the fascination and the charm of another woman, and this fault brings about his ruin and death, though not before he has made, as a man should make, proper moral atonement. So much for the merely ethical side of the story. But study the artistic side! It is simply beyond praise. And here you can feel that the historian is behind the novelist. Only one who has read and studied northern literature and northern history very deeply could have made such pictures for us. As we read, we do not doubt that we really can hear the cry of the sea-kings, and the sound of the oar roll "like thunder working up from the Northeast."

I do not think that Kingsley loved the old North, the Scandinavian North, merely because he was an Englishman, but because the old North seemed to him ever the highest type of ideal manhood, combined strength of body and soul. No one, not perhaps even Mr. Swinburne, felt the beautiful side of Greek life more than Kingsley; you might be sure of that after reading the matchless volume of Greek fairy tales which he wrote for his own children, drawing the little pictures with his own hand. But he loved the North more than Greece; he loved its heroes, its scorn of death, its tremendous and ferocious energy. Therefore he introduces it to us under circumstances and in contrasts which manifest these qualities in quite a special way. **Hypatia,** you know, is the story of one of the most horrible episodes of the history of the early Christian Church. Hypatia was the last of the pagan, that is to say Greek, priestesses of note; she was also the last representative of the pagan philosophers. She was a virgin and very beautiful, and her beauty and learning had made her famous. In the universities of Alexandria she taught the philosophy of Plato in its later form, the form known as Neo-Platonism. The savage fanatics of that time regarded her as their enemy, and as the enemy of Christianity. As she went one day to lecture, they seized her, stripped her naked, scraped all the flesh off her bones with sharp shells, and burned the miserable remains. With the death of Hypatia died Greek learning in Alexandria, and fanaticism and superstition obtained supremacy by the brutal murder.

Now this was a strange subject for Kingsley to make a novel of,—I say strange, because it was so painful, so horrible a fact. But he treated it like a great artist, and he seemed to have chosen it because of the opportunity which it afforded him of introducing a Scandinavian study, or something very like it. As you know, the men of the North, under the various names of Goths or Vandals, descended upon the Roman provinces of northern Africa at an early day. Kingsley represents a small party of these terrible men entering the city of Alexandria and doing whatever they pleased by mere force of character. They avenged Hypatia. They killed four or five thousand monks just as a mere sacrifice to the soul of their chief. The contrast between the corrupted life of Alexandria and the life of these men, the study of the enervating effect of climate, luxury, and vice upon their moral character, and the magnificent sketch of the method by which they redeemed themselves triumphantly under the leadership of old Wulf,—these are the very noblest parts of the book. There are chapters which could not but appeal to the Japanese, imbued with the old Samurai spirit, which was not after all so very different from the northern spirit Kingsley describes, as you might suppose. In *Two Years Ago*—which is quite a modern English novel—we are introduced to another form of Kingsley's idealism, generally known as "muscular Christianity." At all events, it is in *Two Years Ago* that this idea is best expressed. And what is muscular Christianity? The shortest way of explaining is by stating Kingsley's strictly personal views of religion. Although a clergyman of the English Church, and in so far perfectly orthodox, Kingsley held that true religion did not consist in faith but in works,—that it was not religion merely to kneel and pray in time of trouble, or to submit to every difficulty, with the idea that the will of God makes human misfortunes. He taught that it was the duty of a man to meet and to conquer obstacles; to strive with all his might, strength of body and soul, honestly for success; to cultivate his muscles as well as his mind, to enjoy the beautiful world as much as possible without being wickedly selfish or mean or scheming. And Kingsley's readers saw in this new gospel a sort of union of the northern spirit with Christianity; they smiled at it and called it muscular Christianity. But it was good, sound teaching, no more peculiar to Christianity than to any other faith, no more English than Japanese, but simply the exposition of what religion ought to be for a gentleman of any country or any faith. *Two Years Ago* is the picture of Kingsley's ideal of an English gentleman and English university man, fighting his way through the world to success by following a few simple, noble, gentlemanly principles.

Besides the novels, Kingsley wrote a number of books for young people on scientific and other subjects, such as *Town Geology* and *Glaucus.* These might have been more successful than they were, had not Kingsley happened to live in the time of Professor Huxley. Although Kingsley's books were very good in their way, Huxley's manuals for students, written in a simple form never attempted before, took away the public attention from the juvenile scientific books of Kingsley. More noteworthy are his beautiful fairy tales, *The Heroes* and the *Water Babies.* As for *The Heroes,* it is beyond any question the best book of Greek stories written for children in any language. Kingsley has had hundreds of imitators, but none who ever approached him.

[Kingsley] was really one of the very greatest figures in nineteenth century literature, with talent of immense range. Above all, his attractiveness seems to be due to his power of exciting the emotion of heroism, of manliness, of self-confidence, of common expression,—and this by prose beyond the power of anybody but a very great poet to equal. Kingsley could also be a poet in verse. Several critics have agreed that his **"Andromeda"** is written in the very best hexameters in the whole range of English verse, Mr. Swinburne, I believe, alone dissenting from this rather generous praise. But in any case the verse of **"Andromeda"** is confessedly grand. Kingsley wrote very little poetry, but he had more success with what he did write than perhaps any of our latest poets of the century. His two songs **"The Three Fishers"** and the **"Sands of Dee"** have been translated into every European tongue, as well as into various tongues not European. Some years ago it was announced by an English traveller that the Arab women were singing the **"Sands of Dee."** (pp. 256-62)

Lafcadio Hearn, "English Fiction in the Second Half of the Nineteenth Century," in his Interpretations of Literature, Vol. I, *edited by John Erskine, Dodd, Mead & Company, Inc., 1915, pp. 248-86.*

Joseph Ellis Baker   (essay date 1932)

[*Baker is an American educator and critic who has written extensively on Victorian poetry and fiction. In the following excerpt, he elucidates Kingsley's theology as its relates to his literary method, describing the author as "the great antagonist" of the Oxford Movement.*]

The most important novels actually called forth, at least in part, by the Oxford Movement, were those of Charles Kingsley. Among the hundreds of volumes—fiction, verse, theology, scholarship,—produced by the Movement, *pro* and *con,* probably *Hypatia* is the one book which is now considered indispensable in the education of a complete gentleman. As one of the leading writers of the novel of purpose, and as the great antagonist of the Movement, whose attacks finally gave Newman an opening for the *Apologia,* Kingsley, his portrayal of the Tractarians, and his criticism of their views, deserve a central position in [the study of the novel and the Oxford Movement].

His hostility was based upon opposition in the one most fundamental question of all ethical, social, or religious thinking: Whereas Newman and the Anglo-Catholics agreed with the Calvinists in believing that human nature is sinful, unless regenerated by the Grace of God, Kingsley belonged to the third "Christian" religion, which has faith in the goodness of the Natural. The Neo-Humanists would be correct in saying that Kingsley is of the school of Rousseau. Indeed, the whole Reactionary Revolution—the Oxford Movement—New-Toryism—Neo-Catholicism—had for its avowed object of warfare just that extreme Rousseauistic faith in the goodness of the natural man and the consequent belief in democracy and moral liberty. Of the Goths, Kingsley was in his day a mighty champion, and preferred to look for true men and true worship outside the Empire of Rome. His trust in nature flows in many channels that are joined together in a common source. With reference to the external universe, it takes the form of a thorough faith in science; which means (translated into human terms), he believes that knowledge about the physical world, arrived at through experiment and speculation unfettered by *a priori* formulæ, will increase the sum of happiness. Claude Mellot [in Kingsley's novel *Yeast*], with the author's support, approves of Mechanics' Institutes. Kingsley makes sanitation a subject for romantic enthusiasm, and even shows Unsanitary Conditions as a sort of brooding evil productive of tragedy. In *Yeast,* Lancelot answers his cousin, a Tractarian curate, by saying that nature must be a revelation of God; "spiritual laws must be in perfect harmony with every fresh physical law which we discover . . . the spiritual cannot be intended to be perfected by ignoring or crushing the physical. . . . So give me the political economists, the sanitary reformer, the engineer; and take your saints and virgins, relics, and miracles." In *Alton Locke,* the Dean speaks of "the inner ideas, the spirit of Nature, which is the will of God."

Protestantism in Kingsley usually means reliance on natural instinct (as opposed to the acceptance of a celibate ideal), on the natural man's understanding of the Bible (as opposed to interpretation under guidance of the Church) and on the natural conclusions of human intellect (obedient to no previously accepted doctrine). The religion which had set up the individual three centuries before as the final judge of the meaning of the Bible had in it the seeds of Rationalism. Ultimately, the Protestant might be allowing the unrestrained reason not only to interpret but to criticize the Scriptures, as it had long ago criticized the Church. By no accident was Germany the home of Rationalism and Higher Criticism. But it is certainly old Protestant prejudice rather than reliance on human nature which speaks in *Westward Ho!* where we are told that, after the Spanish Armada was vanquished, "the everlasting war which is in heaven" between Light and Darkness was lulled for a while—a war which slowly ripens into a day of judgment once in many centuries and becomes then incarnate,

> no longer a mere spiritual fight, but one of flesh
> and blood, wherein simple men may choose their
> sides without mistake, and help God's cause not
> merely with prayer and pen, but with sharp shot

> and cold steel. A day of judgment has come,
> which has divided the light from the darkness,
> and the sheep from the goats. . . .

The devil's work collapses at the merest pin prick in these combats, and the children of Israel as of old see the Egyptians dead on the sea-shore.

But novels have for their subject matter not only brooding forces, the concepts of science, and theology, but also human problems. And here it was that Kingsley shocked the orthodox. It may seem innocent enough to say, abstractly, that you trust in nature. But when a Victorian clergyman of the "Anglican branch of the Holy Catholic Church" says that natural passions are good, when he gives this doctrine flesh and blood in dramatic narrative that women and the young will read, once again a theological proposition has shown itself to have more than scholastic meaning. Kingsley believed that we are naturally monogamous, and that the highest life involves love of one man for one woman, sanctified by—one might say a love that itself sanctifies—the sacrament of matrimony. In Victorian England there were not many who advocated the now popular dogmas of polygamous or, rather, promiscuous privileges, and those who fulminated against the sinfulness of marriage were few. In that direction not much defence was necessary, although Kingsley did put into the mouth of Raphael Aben-Ezra [in *Hypatia*] an interpretation of the Song of Solomon as a praise of monogamy, wherein the great king forgets his threescore queens and fourscore concubines and virgins without number for the pure love of one. But the arch-enemy threatening to obliterate wedded love for the Victorian clergyman was not Radicalism but the doctrine of the superiority of celibacy. When the Oxford Tracts appeared, Kingsley fiercely denounced the ascetic views which he saw would be their result. The hero of *Yeast* writes to his Tractarian cousin that God made his appetites a part of him, while "you and yours make piety a synonym for unmanliness," and later he tells his sweetheart that she has taught him "that which is most luscious is also the most pure." In *Hypatia,* Raphael, a Jew, attacks the idea that a Deity would derive pleasure from the celibacy of a girl; and he reserves his faith for some God who "takes no delight in seeing his creatures stultify the primary laws of their being." Raphael's mother speaks of herself as a nun, "fattening her own mad self-conceit upon the impious fancy that she was the spouse of the Nazarene . . . " and says that the Christians and philosophers consider it brutal to be a man and not a monk or eunuch. "Ay, and the only man who keeps his manhood, the only man who is not ashamed to be what God has made him, is your Jew." Indeed, in *Yeast,* Claude Mellot argues that Protestant clergymen should have long beards, "testifying that the essential idea of Protestantism is the dignity and divinity of man as God made him."

One of the fruits of reliance on instinct is a faith in the "lower orders," since all men are gifted with instinct, and an unusually noble conscience, according to ethical naturalists, is as likely to appear among the poor as among those who have received an expensive education. Kingsley goes so far as to say [in *Alton Locke*] that the Bible is the history of mankind's deliverance from all tyranny, the Jews then the one free constitutional people in a world of slaves, and the New Testament the good news that freedom, brotherhood, and equality, once confined to Greece and Judaea, were to become the right of all mankind. The hero of *Yeast,* a gentleman in the British sense, tells a discharged game-keeper, a Dissenter, Tregarva, "I will go [to a wake] with Paul Tregarva, whom I honour and esteem as one of God's own noblemen; who has taught me what a man can be, and what I am not." At which all advocates of decorum and taste and order might well raise a protest. But Kingsley was only a Christian Socialist, not a revolutionist. Chartism, by insisting on its own program instead of submitting to God's will, has, says Eleanor, in *Alton Locke,* "defiled itself in the eyes of the wise, the good, the gentle."

Kingsley relies on the individual conscience, and classes Catholic spiritual direction with alcohol and opium as the three best means of attaining mere peace of mind. (Anticipating Soviet Russia.) His suspicion that Catholicism is not intellectually honest became famous because his accusations against Newman were answered in the *Apologia.* But, years before, in *Yeast,* the Tractarian curate (later a convert to Rome) had written that he could not sympathize with "that superstitious reverence for mere verbal truth which is so common among Protestants." If the Protestants believed the nature of man, *including his intellect,* corrupt, they would not be so careful to tell the truth. "The proper use of reasoning is to produce opinion." Lancelot's answer is typical of Kingsley's thought: All sound intellect is divine light, and Protestants "reverence facts as the work of God."

Having sketched the ideas relative to the Oxford Movement presented in Kingsley's novels, we must speak of the novels individually before considering the author's literary method, closely related as it is to his philosophy. . . . [Immediately] after the Papal Aggression (1850), there were a number of attacks upon Catholicism. Kingsley, perhaps because he was a clergyman, and therefore closer to the Movement, had already begun his fictional opposition in *Yeast,* which ran in *Fraser's Magazine* from July to December, 1848. But this version gave less space to the attack upon the Tractarians than the revised edition of 1851, which added Chapters V, VIII, and XV, and the Epilogue. The novel in its final form is still as chaotic as most of the controversial tales of the 'forties, and its method, spirit, and interests are of the same school, though it is raised into the aristocratic circle of literature by the style, emotion, and original pictures of English life. We have a Dissenter of noble character, and, in contrast, a High Church vicar and a High Church curate, both of whom trifle with the truth. Both are finally converted to Rome. We have a lady heroine romantically concerned with being religious, who intends to enter a sort of Anglican convent, but finds that her "womanhood" cannot withstand the "manly will" of her lover, that is, as he points out, God is leading her to him. Kingsley begs the reader to remember that the author is in no way responsible for the speculations either of the hero or of his acquaintances, but if a pamphleteer is advancing certain theories,—a pamphleteer who hides his sympathies as little as Kingsley,—it is usually fairly obvious when the arguments are supposed to be convincing and when they are supposed to be ridiculous. In spite of the author's attempt to shield himself behind his *dramatis personæ, Yeast* made him enemies.

It was difficult to find a publisher for the next novel, *Alton Locke* (1850). Refused by Messrs. Parker, who thought they had suffered in reputation for publishing *Yeast* (in *Fraser's Magazine*), it was accepted by Chapman and Hall upon Carlyle's recommendation. Mrs. Locke, Alton's mother, was a thorough-going Calvinist.—Her form of Protestantism is almost as hostile to Liberalism as Catholicism itself, and Kingsley knows it.—She hated and feared Babylon (temptations of London) as she did Bishops, and believed in infant damnation, election, predestination, and the wickedness of Sunday amusements. And this in a generation when "the daily discoveries of science are revealing [God's] love in every microscopic animalcule which peoples the stagnant pool!" Her religion was an "infernal superstition which taught her to fancy . . . that God could hate His creature, not for its sins but for the very nature which He had given it." The hero is a Chartist. Some High Church figures appear as rather ineffectual. The novel concludes with arguments for Christian Socialism. Though the form is autobiographical, and Alton is more radical than Kingsley, again we feel that the author has not concealed his own voice.

Hypatia, (1853), has for a subtitle *New Foes with an Old Face.* The new foes are those nineteenth-century currents that might break up the family and the rule of the people in a nation: asceticism, scepticism, aristocracy, theocracy. The old face is the Empire of the fifth century. In 1851 Kingsley writes to Maurice [Letter to Maurice, Jan. 16, 1851. *Charles Kingsley, His Letters (etc.)*] that the notion of such a historical romance has been breeding in his head for two years. "My idea . . . is to set forth Christianity as the only really democratic creed." It opens with a young monk, Philammon, finding for the first time that women are beautiful, and that he must have liberty. In Alexandria, he plunges into the dying world of Paganism, with all its refinement, art, and learning typified in the beautiful Hypatia, but a world also cruel, sensual, sceptical, and weary. The historical imagination has seldom achieved anything so magnificent as this picture of society in decay, of a civilization that has lost heart, and devoid of unity or hope, is breaking down into cults and parties and hard ambition. Only Petronius has surpassed Kingsley in giving us a picture of Rome ageing horribly, and Petronius could not show the young Teutons as the destined heirs of the treasure whose owner was rotting away. Besides Classical decadents and splendid Barbarians, Philammon also meets with Christian monks, represented as a fanatical mob, and the leaders of the Church, bickering in petty jealously and fighting for place and power. He finds the Church with its councils rent by intrigue a travesty on Christianity. When the monks tear Hypatia to death, it is a symbol of the worst in superstition destroying the best in Classical culture. And this, according to Kingsley, was the Church of the Fathers, whose doctrine nineteenth-century Englishmen had been told to obey without question, though it might condemn Greek philosophy, supplement the teachings of Solomon and of Jesus beyond recognition, ignore the wisdom that coming centuries of Chris-

Eversley rectory, Kingsley's Hampshire home.

tian thought were to develop, disagree with the conclusions of science or scholarship, and defy the democratic hopes of a progressive nation. The Anglo-Catholics went back, not to the Bible, but to the Early Church for ideas that would be valid for all time, and Kingsley's picture of that Church was the most devastating shell that had exploded among them since the seventeenth century. It was high time for Newman's *Callista,* whose purpose was to express, "from a Catholic point of view, the feelings and mutual relations of Christians and heathens" in the third century. And it was little wonder High Churchmen should not want to give Kingsley an honorary degree, or that *Hypatia* should be called an immoral book, "and one calculated to encourage young men in profligacy and false doctrine." Nor is it surprising that, in time, he should be appointed Professor of History at Cambridge, a center of Protestantism, Platonism, and Liberalism, since before Spenser.

Westward Ho! (1855) was written during the Crimean War. In a letter to Maurice, October 19, 1854, Kingsley says that it is dreadful not to be with the army, "But I can fight with my pen still (I don't mean in controversy—I am sick of that.) . . . but in writing books which will make others fight. This one is to be called 'Westward Ho!' " Nevertheless, the novel is about the conflict between Protestant England and Catholic Spain, or, as Kingsley actually tells us in the novel, sheep *versus* goats. The religious differences receive emphasis throughout. Indeed, the novel is well designated in the High Church *Christian Re-*

membrancer as "an outburst of burly triumphant Protestantism and nationality."

Controversy has more visibly died down when we reach *Two Years Ago* (1857). The Catholic Revival is merely touched in passing, or rather *used* as any other element in English life might be. It is no longer a real key to the whole work. Such merely incidental treatment of the Oxford Movement is to be characteristic of many novels in the 'sixties and 'seventies. *Two Years Ago* illustrates, also, what is not necessarily the same thing, the new tolerance that grew all through the 'fifties. Frank Headley, a Puseyite curate, is a fine chap, though his labors among the people fail to win confidence at first because he is suspected of Popery. Frank "had nothing, save the outside, in common with those undesirable coxcombs, who have not been bred by the High Church movement, but have taken refuge in its cracks." Later, Frank learns to forget that he is a priest and to meet people "upon the commonest human grounds." The picture of the Oxford Movement in this novel, as compared with that in *Yeast* and *Alton Locke,* suggests that there has been a development towards alliance between Anglo-Catholicism and humanitarism. This is confirmed by other novels.

Even in his *Water-Babies: A Fairy-Tale for a Land-Baby* (1863) there is an attack on monks.

The key to the art, as well as to the thought, of Kingsley's novels is found in reliance on nature. The author's plots are not deterministic, like those of the later naturalists. We find little of the careful preparation of cause for consequence, little descriptive emphasis upon environment, little subjective analysis. Nor does he play upon sensational, criminal, and sexual excitement like the authors of a later day, less complacent in their philosophy. In Kingsley, "natural" must often be defined as that which is accepted by the average Englishman of the time. The plots of even *Yeast* and *Alton Locke* are built around love affairs. That is seldom true of the Anglo-Catholic novels of the same period. Granted that Kingsley is in accord with the method of the latter to the extent that the love affairs should often not culminate happily, nevertheless, he remains at the end unresigned to such an outcome, or shows it to be the result of evil forces in society. In Newman's plots, the characters are led by the voice of God. In Disraeli, they often meet a Jew, who gives them advice. In Kingsley they lead themselves, trusting their own emotions.—The same three sources of guidance were recommended, respectively, in answer to the question, "What will save England?" (not asked for the first time in the twentieth century). Kingsley, confident that the English have their source of strength in themselves, writes historical novels in praise of the national past, just as Disraeli carries his readers to Palestine, and Newman to Rome. Even in *Hypatia* the only healthy people in the Roman Empire are the Teutonic barbarians.

In motivation as in plot, sexual love is a mainspring much more important than in the Anglo-Catholic novels. Already a different dogma is leading to a different psychology. Moreover, Kingsley does at least foreshadow naturalistic determinism in showing one cause for sin and misery in a background of social conditions, for which, indeed, individuals are often responsible. Dialogue in Kingsley does not consist in logical steps intellectually developed, as in Newman, or the sparkle of programs wittily put, as in Disraeli, but in the expression of feeling or the proposal of hypotheses. His reliance on instinct is shown in the fact that the arguments do not seem to lead to definite dogmatic conclusions, but are left hanging. In constructing an outline of his philosophy, one must select somewhat insecurely from diverse statements, usually by heroes with whom the author does not entirely agree. Now there is never any doubt about what Newman means. But when it came to writing drama, or creating different characters, the man who sympathized with only one creed, was far surpassed by the one whose opinions were less definite.

There are few authors more British or more Victorian than Kingsley, with his reliance on instinct, his capacity for compromise, and his admiration for action. He holds to the Athanasian Creed and to Science. He defends a form of confession, and yet is a pugnacious Protestant— and also a "socialist." His is that national genius which is able to pass from old to new without unduly disturbing the peace of mind or of society, a genius particularly in evidence during the Victorian Age. Though Kingsley's pictures of Tractarians are so obviously prejudiced that it is hardly necessary to correct them, his comments help to reveal the core of his own vigorous mind, and the setting of the Oxford Movement within the framework of other mid-century ideas. He struck some of the most sounding blows ever dealt against the Puseyites, choosing to crush the

heads of his foes with a frank Northern stroke, thereby making the battle noisier and bloodier, and earning the gratitude of all of us today. Especially of Anglo-Catholics. Someone has said that since we have lost Satan, no one has been much interested in God. Without Kingsley, the Oxford Movement would lack epic proportions. He was not only a warrior himself, but an excuse for belligerence in others. Without Kingsley, there might have been no *Apologia Pro Vita Sua.* (pp. 88-100)

> *Joseph Ellis Baker, "Charles Kingsley: Liberal Antagonist," in his* The Novel and the Oxford Movement, *1932. Reprint by Russell & Russell, Inc., 1965, pp. 88-100.*

Crane Brinton　(essay date 1933)

[*Brinton was an American historian and critic specializing in French Revolutionary history and in nineteenth-century European political thought. In the following excerpt, he analyzes Kingsley's political ideas as they are elucidated in* Alton Locke.]

[Kingsley's] opinions were driven by his enthusiasm to that pitch of exaggeration in which the type becomes the caricature, and thereby ceases to be typical. It is tempting to select some of these opinions, and hold them up gleefully as Victorian. Here really is proof of the fact which a decent critical scepticism is constantly tempted to deny, that the Victorians were quite as bad as all that.

> "There were two Dover coachmen—twins. One drove the up-coach, the other the down, for thirty years, so that they never saw each other night or day, but when they whirled past once a day, each on his box, on their restless homeless errand. They never noticed each other in passing but by the jerk of the wrist, which is the cant sign of recognition among horse-driving men. Brutes! the sentimentalist will say—for they were both fat, jolly men! And when one of them died, the other took to his bed in a few days, in perfect health, and pined away and died also! His words were "Now Tom is gone, I can't stay." Was not that spirit love? That story always makes me ready to cry. And cases as strong are common. [Kingsley, quoted in *Charles Kingsley: His Letters and Memories of His Life,* edited by Fanny Kingsley]

Or again: "I say that the Church of England is wonderfully and mysteriously fitted for the souls of a free Norse-Saxon race; for men, whose ancestors fought by the side of Odin, over whom a descendant of Odin now rules." Finally—though the list might be prolonged indefinitely— mind makes the body, not body the mind; therefore beautiful souls like Burns, Raphael, Goethe and Shakespeare— especially Shakespeare, who combines all perfection of mind and body in himself—have beautiful faces. Raphael's is "a face to be kissed, not worshipped."

The temptation to hold Kingsley up as a Victorian must be overcome. He was a man, not a period. He had, it is true, a horror of social nonconformity. His friend, Thomas Hughes, writes that "to less sensitive men the effect of eccentricity upon him was almost comic, as when on one occasion he was quite upset and silenced by the appearance of a bearded member of Council [on Working Men's Associations] at an important deputation, in a straw hat and blue plush gloves. He did not recover from the depression produced by those gloves for days." Especially in his later years, this love of conformity makes him a useful index for the social historian. But the emotions that went into his political philosophy are strongly personal, and we shall do well not to sink him in historical generalizations. The habits into which he moulded his desires are indeed social and representative; the desires themselves are far too intense to be given a common label.

Kingsley appears in the history of thought as a Christian Socialist. He did indeed abandon the cause pretty completely after the early 'fifties. And he is by no means as profound a thinker as his master, Maurice. Yet he had a far larger audience than Maurice or any other of the group. He is a more useful figure for the student, not of the currents of professional philosophy and theology, but of ideas as they descend to the crowd. Kingsley is for our purposes an essential figure. He will stand for one kind of reaction to the problems of the industrial revolution in the mid-nineteenth century. His partial abandonment of the Socialist solution is in itself a valuable fact. It is one more contribution to an understanding of the Victorian compromise. With the caution that a large part of Kingsley belongs to the psychologist or even to the psychopathologist, and that therefore we must not take him *en bloc* as typical of an age which he often caricatures rather than represents, we may proceed to the study of what Christian Socialism meant to him.

Perhaps the best introduction to such a study will be an analysis of **Alton Locke,** a programme novel that made a great stir in its day, though it is now relegated to histories of English literature. Alton Locke is a poor tailor, orphaned of his father, a small and quite unnecessary retailer, and brought up by his mother, a hopeless, narrow Calvinist. The boy is early obliged to earn his living as a tailor. He learns from personal experience the horrors of a sweated trade, where even the best masters are forced by competition to treat their workmen not as men, but as animals. Thanks to a chance meeting with a Scotch bookseller, Sandy Mackaye, a Carlyle turned Chartist, he is able, though with great difficulties, to follow his natural bent for learning. He meets Chartist fellow workmen, is fired with the cause of the oppressed, and writes poetry under this inspiration. On a visit to the Dulwich gallery he meets the lovely Lillian and her father, the Dean. Love at first sight on his part is mingled with awe at the graces of the highly born and indignation at the social contrast between himself and these privileged beings. Locke has a cousin, son of a newly rich and selfish father. He goes up to Cambridge to see his cousin, hoping to secure help in the publication of his poems. Here he admires the dogged Anglo-Saxon qualities displayed by Cambridge oarsmen, feels something of the potentialities of the ruling classes, but is angered by their irresponsibility and sense of caste. A visit to the Dean at the cathedral town of D—— results in aid towards the publication of his poems, but only at the price of treason to his order, for he is induced to soften some of his most revolutionary expressions. In a mood of regret

at this treason, he accepts a mission from the Chartists to attend a farm labourers' meeting in East Anglia. Here his temper and unfortunate coincidences involve him in actual rioting and burning. Though he really was trying to calm the mob, he is caught, tried, and condemned to jail. Meanwhile his cousin—a mean fellow made meaner by an interested devotion to Puseyism—successfully courts Lillian. Locke, released from prison, returns to his trade. While trying to obtain the release of a farmer's son caught in a sweater's den, and held by perpetual debt to the sweater in a virtual prison, he is stricken with the typhus. He is nursed back to health by Eleanor, another member of the Dean's family, whom, in his infatuation with Lillian, he had misjudged. Eleanor is the perfect Christian Socialist. The premature death of her husband, an aristocrat with a profound sense of his obligation to his fellows, only deepened her devotion. She converts Locke—at great length—from his crude Chartist belief in the rights of man to a true appreciation of the revolutionary character of Christ's teachings. Meanwhile his cousin has ordered a wedding-coat from a sweating tailor. The workman who made the coat, destitute and unable to buy blankets, uses the garment as he works on it to keep his family warm. There is typhus in the household. Germs cling to the coat, and by an act of a just God not uninterested in melodrama, the cousin catches the typhus, communicates it to his bride, and both die. Locke, overwhelmed with grief, yet survives through his new faith. He decides to emigrate to Texas with a fellow workman, there to work out the principles of Christian Socialism. But Kingsley has not yet had enough of pathos. The industrial revolution must kill completely. Locke's confinement in the noxious atmosphere of the tailoring-shop has injured his lungs. He dies of tuberculosis on the way to Texas.

Most of Kingsley's Christian Socialism—and a great deal else—is to be found in this impassioned tract—his feeling that disease and poverty are unnecessary, the product of ignorance and social conditions, his love of sentiment, his bad taste, his hatred of religious asceticism, his interest in sanitation, his patriarchal devotion to his parishioners, even the strange mental leap by which he turned his uxoriousness into a theology. We must, however, attempt to put this chaos of emotion into some kind of order. Kingsley's Christian Socialism is far from a system. We shall most easily find out what underlies it if we make use of a method of analysis almost too obviously dictated by common sense. We shall see what in it is Christian, and what Socialism.

Of one cardinal principle Kingsley was always certain. Christianity is not an ascetic fleeing from the world of the senses. "The body the temple of the living God. . . . There has always seemed to me something impious in the neglect of personal health, strength, and beauty, which the religious, and sometimes clergymen of this day, affect." At the base of our moral code must be a frank acceptance of the fact that man is an animal. There is no opposition between the flesh and the spirit properly understood. Not even the Christian doctrine of another world may be taken as casting upon the world of the senses the reproach of impermanence. "There was a butcher's nephew playing cricket in Bramshill last week, whom I would have walked ten miles to see, in spite of the hideous English dress. One looked forward with delight to what he would be 'in the resurrection.'" Kingsley held, though he did not publish, the very heterodox belief that the delights of marriage are continued in heaven.

This acceptance of the flesh does not mean that all human desires should be requited. Kingsley was far from believing in the natural goodness of man. His doctrine here is a trifle muddled, but seems to run somewhat as follows: Man is a free agent. He can "not only disobey the laws of his being, he can also choose between them, to an extent which science widens every day, and so become, what he was meant to be, an artificial being; artificial in his manufactures, habits, society, polity—what not?" Nature is cruel and inhuman; she "kills and kills and kills" until man learns that she is only to be conquered by obeying her. (We have insisted that Kingsley was a trifle muddled.) For the higher law of Nature is really the law of God. That law has come down to us in the form of Christian morals. As to ultimate realities, we are all ignorant, the theologian as well as the scientist. All we have is "mystery and morals." It is this moral law which distinguishes for us between legitimate and illegitimate gratifications. Fornication, for instance, if natural in the lower sense, is unnatural in the higher sense. Monogamic marriage, however, is dictated by the moral law. Through this institution, our desires are disciplined into virtues. The moral law has not been revealed to us *en bloc*. From its central core of immutable truths it is constantly growing, aided by science. Between science and Christian morality there is no conflict. Kingsley welcomed the discoveries of Darwin. Though obscurantists may oppose his theories, the true Christians "find that now they have got rid of an interfering God—a master-magician, as I call it—they have to choose between the absolute empire of accident, and a living, immanent, ever-working God."

For, though we are immensely guided by our reason through science in determining our conduct, moral action is in the last resort the product of a specifically human quality, best defined—though it is incapable of being put into words—as love. "Love—truth—all are parts of that awful power of knowing, at a single glance, from and to all eternity, what a thing is in its essence, its properties, and its relations to the whole universe through all time." We distinguish between what is worth while and what is not worth while, not by any petty reasoned calculus of pleasures and pains, but by this gift of judgment. "For mankind is ruled and guided, in the long run, not by practical considerations, not by self-interest, not by compromises; but by theories and principles, and those of the most abstruse, delicate, supernatural and literally unspeakable kind; which, whether they be according to reason or not, are so little according to logic—that is, to speakable reason—that they cannot be put into speech. Men act, whether singly or in masses, by impulses and instincts for which they give reasons quite incompetent, often quite irrelevant; but which they have caught from each other, as they catch fever or smallpox."

Nature and morality are thus allied in true Christianity, the Christianity of the Protestant Church as established in England. Roman Catholicism no doubt had its historical uses. But its sacerdotal tyranny and its ascetic foundations go against the grain of those instincts we know by more than knowledge to be true. The Calvinism of English nonconformity is almost equally a denial of such instincts. True Christianity is strong, masculine, progressive, stern but not cruel, abounding in the love that creates, the Christianity of God the Father, not of the weak Virgin. It is the Christianity of the cricket field, not of the cloister, nor indeed of the factory.

Kingsley, then, meant by Christianity the whole complex of values which his character had compounded from his experience. What he meant by Socialism follows as simply from these values. Men in the England of the 'forties were not living, and could not live, the good life. "What is flogging, or hanging, King Ryence's paletot, or the tanneries of Meudon, to the slavery, starvation, waste of life, year-long imprisonment in dungeons narrower and fouler than those of the Inquisition, which goes on among thousands of free English clothes-makers at this day?" As early as 1844 he wrote, "The refined man to me is he who cannot rest in peace with a coal mine or a factory, or a Dorsetshire peasant's house near him, in the state in which they are." Here then was a definite situation, an evil thing which had to be destroyed. What were Englishmen doing about it? Some were brutes enough not to be disturbed by it. Others were turning their backs on it and seeking an anodyne in Puseyism or the Church of Rome. Others were actually justifying it in the name of economic law. The Manchester school was the enemy that must first be destroyed. "Of all narrow, conceited, hypocritical, and anarchic and atheistic schemes of the universe, the Manchester one is exactly the worst." These men say all men should be freed from artificial restraints. They talk of independence for the workers, when what they mean is "that the men shall be independent of everyone but themselves—independent of legislators, parsons, advisers, gentlemen, noblemen, and every one that tries to help them by moral agents; but the slaves of the capitalists, bound to them by a servitude increasing instead of lightening with their numbers."

The economists not only outrage human feelings, but err as scientists—though these are but two ways of saying the same thing. They maintain that "there are laws of Nature concerning economy, therefore you must leave them alone to do what they like with society. As if you were to say, you get cholera by law of Nature, therefore submit to cholera." As a matter of fact, political economy is still in a purely analytical and descriptive stage. "To be a true science, it must pass on into the synthetic stage, and learn how, by using the laws which it has discovered, and counteracting them by others when necessary, to produce new forms of society. As yet political economy has produced nothing. It has merely said 'Laissez-faire!'."

The fundamental error of the economists is that they have no conception of a society. For them, a society is a collection of selfish atoms in perpetual conflict. But "selfishness can collect, not unite, a herd of cowardly wild cattle, that they may feed together, breed together, keep off the wolf and bear together. But when one of your wild cattle falls sick, what becomes of the corporate feelings of the herd then? . . . Your Bible talks of society, not as a herd, but as a living tree, an organic individual body, a holy brotherhood, and kingdom of God." It is society that effects the miracle of morality whereby a man is actually, behaves actually, better than anything discernible in him as a human atom would lead us to believe possible. Why, a mere village lad who enlists in the army becomes "member of a body in which if one member suffers, all suffer with it; if one member be honoured, all rejoice with it. A body, which has a life of its own, and a government of its own, a duty of its own, a history of its own. . . . He [the lad] does not now merely serve himself and his own selfish lusts: he serves the Queen. His nature is not changed, but the thought that he is the member of an honourable body *has raised him above his nature."*

The problem nowadays is to recover this spirit of social discipline. We cannot turn backwards and repudiate the industrial revolution. On the contrary "it is the new commercial aristocracy; it is the scientific go-a-head-ism of the day which must save us, and which we must save." Salvation lies, as it has always lain, in the Bible. English parsons "have used the Bible as if it was a mere special constable's handbook—an opium-dose for keeping beasts of burden patient while they were being overloaded—a mere book to keep the poor in order." Actually the Bible is a charter for the true society. From the inexhaustible well of "the Poor Man's Book," Kingsley draws but a few drops: "he that will not work, neither shall he eat. . . ." "Behold the hire of your labourers which have reaped down your fields, which is by you kept back by fraud, crieth . . ." and so on. Our worldlings forget that their lives make a mere pretence of their belief in "the miracle of Pentecost, and the religion that was taught by the carpenter's Son, and preached across the world by fishermen."

The Bible does not, however, preach the French doctrine of the rights of man. The Chartists are justified in rebelling against the injustice of modern society. But they are wrong in claiming merely the same empty freedom which their opponents possess. "Englishmen! Saxons! Workers of the great, cool-headed, strong-handed nation of England, the workshop of the world, the leader of freedom for seven hundred years, men say you have common-sense! then do not humbug yourselves into meaning 'licence,' when you cry 'liberty.' " We must distinguish between false freedom, where a man is free to do as he likes, and true freedom, where a man is free to do what he ought. "True Socialism, true liberty, brotherhood, and true equality (not the carnal, deadlevel equality of the Communist, but the spiritual equality of the Christian idea which gives every man an equal chance of developing and using God's gifts, and rewards every man according to his work . . .) is only to be found in loyalty and obedience to Christ." That is, a Christian Socialist society is an hierarchical society, where a man's place is determined by his moral value, not by his capacity to cheat and grab. It is a democratic society in the only possible sense in which democracy is realizable here on earth—every member by an act of faith feels that he has the place allotted him by God.

Now all this is familiar enough, and to many will seem nonsense enough. Kingsley never accomplished what greater men have failed to do, the bringing to ground of such high abstractions as liberty and equality. But at least he has concrete notions of some of the things that must be done to realize the Kingdom of God on earth. In general, it may be said that the past of England was nearer to this Kingdom than the present. The Church, the gentry, and the old English commoner, the workman, were knit together by habits which were genuine *human* relationships. These habits may be revived against the new and inhuman relationship of employer and employed. If England is to be saved, the real battle will be between "the Church, the gentlemen, and the workman against the shopkeepers and the Manchester school." A true democracy in England "is impossible without a Church and a Queen, and as I believe, without a gentry." Kingsley's programme is singularly like that of Tory Democracy.

The first step to be taken by this alliance will be to use the law-making power to prevent the obvious abuses of the industrial revolution. Universal suffrage, not itself a right or even a good, is to be welcomed as an aid to getting such legislation through Parliament. We must have no nonsense about "vested interests." The landlords of unspeakably dirty tenements never had a right to erect them. There is little use in exhorting them to improve these tenements, and less in urging the poor tenants to try and do so. The only remedy lies in the law. Public health can be improved only by drastic sweeping away of simpler obstacles, such as inadequate houses, by the compulsory installation of proper drainage, and finally by a campaign of education among the poor. Kingsley was not to be disturbed by the reproach of paternalism. In his own parish of Eversley he played the benevolent despot in much the way Owen played it at New Lanark. He added to the duties of a conscientious parish clergyman those of teacher, doctor, lawyer, journalist, and man-of-all-work for his parishioners. Kingsley, in fact, was one of the first of the social-service parsons (a word, incidentally, that never offended him), who have since so multiplied these adjuncts of religion as to quite obscure its theological base.

Kingsley, however paternal his acts at Eversley, and however little fear he had of legislative action in itself, was far from repudiating, even in his most Socialistic period, the whole idea of competition. The economists were right enough in considering independence and self-help essential, especially to Norse-Saxon civilization. Competition was all right, if it was the right kind. Here again we must look to the cricket field. The solution to the problem of retaining the moral stimulus of competition in industry, while preventing the chaos of Manchesterism, lies in workmen's associations. With Ludlow and Maurice, Kingsley played a large part in the Society for Promoting Working Men's Associations. Their ideal was pretty close to that of modern guild Socialism. A given trade was to be, in the end, completely organized in a co-operative corporation. Competition between trades for the patronage of the consumer would prevent the dry-rot of monopoly. In a letter to Ludlow, of 1850, concerning a projected periodical to further association, he sketches a complete programme: "I. Politics according to the Kingdom of God. 2. Art and Amusements for the People. 3. Opening the Universities to the People, and Education in general. 4.

Attacking Straussism and Infidelity. 5. Sanitary Reform. 6. Association: (α) Agitation on Partnership Laws. (β) Stores and Distribution. (γ) Agricultural Schemes. . . . The five former subjects *are* connected with Socialism; i.e. with a live and practical Church."

Kingsley's Socialism began to evaporate rather early. By 1855 he could write that he would not have his children "insolent and scoffing Radicals." "I shall teach them," he continues, "that there are plenty of good people in the world, that public opinion has pretty surely an undercurrent of the water of life, below all its froth and garbage, and that in a Christian country like this, where, with all our faults, a man (sooner or later) has fair play and a fair hearing, the esteem of good men, and the blessings of the poor, will be a pretty sure sign that they have the blessing of God also." And in 1856 he wrote to a Sheffield workman: "Emigrate; but never *strike . . .* but now, I see little before the English workman but to abide as he is, and endure." It is difficult to escape concluding that Kingsley's youthful rebelliousness had its source in a feeling that he was cheated of his proper place in society. His early letters to his wife, with their romantic confession of his intent to roam the western plains of the United States and half-savage mixture of Byron and Daniel Boone, give unmistakable evidence of the kind of psychological maladjustment it is the fashion with some to detect in all revolutionaries. His success as a novelist, preacher, and lecturer made him feel that a society not unjust to Charles Kingsley was perhaps not so unjust to other men.

He did not lapse into complete conformity, and certainly not into silence. He continued to agitate for sanitary reform. He urged local governments to insist on better housing conditions and better drainage. He would have hygiene taught to boys and girls alike, though he foresees an embarrassing transition before a supply of female teachers is secured—for of course Englishwomen cannot willingly learn the facts of hygiene from men. It is of course especially important that English mothers know enough of medicine and sanitation to ensure healthy children. In particular, they must abandon the present abominable fashion of tight lacing. God—with whom, as Frederic Harrison pointed out, Kingsley was on singularly intimate terms, even for the time—does not like corsets.

Kingsley, indeed, was no man to content himself with mere submersion in the daily round of living. He had to describe the universe to himself in terms of a corporate faith. When he abandoned Christian Socialism he took refuge in an amazing form of nationalism, which again we must insist is a bit too personal to be wholly Victorian, though it certainly throws light on the Victorian state of mind. He was deeply moved by his Teutonic inheritance. His first lecture on **The Roman and the Teuton,** which he delivered from the heights of a Regius professorship at Cambridge, is called **"The Troll Garden."** It is a parable on the downfall of the Roman Empire. The vicious, clever Romans are living in a magic garden, protected by walls. The Germans, children in frankness, purity, affectionateness, come upon the garden from their forest depths, climb into it, are corrupted by the vices of the Romans, but ultimately destroy the garden and build up a new and better

one. These Germans were great boys: "very noble boys; very often very naughty boys." But they had the essential virtues; energy, beautiful bodies, honesty, courage, and a peculiar respect for female virtue. The Franks, indeed, were an unfortunate exception. They were "false, vain, capricious, selfish, taking part with the Romans whenever their interest or vanity was at stake—the worst of all Teutons." They were, in short, the ancestors of the modern French.

The English are the true heirs of Tacitus' Germans. Even Alton Locke at Cambridge felt that "the true English stuff came out there . . . the stuff which has held Gibraltar, and conquered at Waterloo—which has created a Birmingham and a Manchester, and colonized every quarter of the globe—that grim, earnest, stubborn energy, which, since the days of the old Romans, the English possess alone of all the nations of the earth." Nor is God to be left out of the matter. "For as surely as there is an English view of everything, so surely God intends us to take that view; and He who gave us our English character intends us to develop its peculiarities." Only, indeed, by casting off Rome "have we risen to be the most mighty, and, with all our sins, perhaps the most righteous and pure of nations." So great a nation cannot avoid an imperial destiny. "We have at least brought the British Constitution with us out of the bogs and moors of Jutland, along with our smock-frocks and leather gaiters, brown bills and stone axes; and it has done us good service, and will do, *till we have carried it right round the world.*" Small wonder that Kingsley welcomed the Crimean War, that he preached with deep emotion at Aldershot; nor is it strange that he saw God's hand in the punishment of France in 1870. He did not live to see the disconcerting quarrel of 1914 between the Teutonic nations.

Kingsley's achievements were by no means slight. For one thing, he helped translate Carlyle to the multitude. Certain passages of the novels, indeed, ape Carlyle's style. The sight of a butler left Locke "wondering at the strange fact that free men, with free wills, do sell themselves, by the hundred thousand, to perform menial offices for other men, not for love, but for money; becoming, to define them strictly, bell-answering animals; and are honest, happy, contented, in such a life." Kingsley actually found in Carlyle, "not a dark but a bright view of life." He himself is at times but a eupeptic Carlyle. His attacks on the industrial system sank into the English mind precisely because they were inspired by a facile optimism which never really questioned fundamentals. *Alton Locke,* like Mr. U. Sinclair's *Jungle,* really stirred the ultimate consumer, not to soulsearching discontent with society, but to an immediate discomfort. Kingsley was unquestionably an element in the downfall of *laissez-faire.*

Yet there seems singularly little transmissible, little genuinely common, in Kingsley's own faith. His Christianity was too comfortable to himself to do service in this world. Kingsley was a man of extremely simple and extremely intense desires. His energies were quite readily contained by a happy family life, an active cure of souls and bodies, an opportunity for exercise in the open air. His intellect was even more simply satisfied by a crude collection of generalizations like that of Nordic supremacy. His emotions gave him no trouble at all; he could always weep. But the great mass of men are still baulked by poverty from attaining the degree of physical comfort upon which Kingsley could base his spiritual contentment. There is no use telling them, as Kingsley told the Sheffield workman, to "endure," to console themselves with equality before God—especially when you assert, as Kingsley did, that God means his children to be healthy, well fed, beautiful, active, and contented. Traditional Christianity, which in spite of Kingsley was pessimistic, contemptuous of the flesh, offering consolation in the next world for the sufferings of this world, was a faith a poor man could hold. Kingsley's faith was not. His God, his virtue, his England, made too many promises to the flesh—promises unfulfilled to the common man. For the uncommon man, his faith was even more inadequate. Taste and intellect alike recoil from the simplicities of a universe on the pattern of Eversley. (pp. 115-30)

> Crane Brinton, "Chartism," in his English Political Thought in the Nineteenth Century, *Ernest Benn Limited, 1933, pp. 87-177.*

Edward Wagenknecht　(essay date 1943)

[*Wagenknecht is an American biographer and critic. His works include critical surveys of English and American novels and studies of Charles Dickens, Mark Twain, and Henry James, among many others. In the following excerpt from his* Cavalcade of the English Novel, *Wagenknecht surveys Kingsley's six published novels, assessing the strengths and weaknesses of each.*]

Charles Kingsley (June 12, 1819, to January 23, 1875), who once described himself as "a Church of England parson and a Chartist," but who lived to become chaplain in ordinary to Queen Victoria and tutor to the Prince of Wales, Regius Professor of Modern History of Cambridge, and canon, first, at Chester, then, at Westminster Abbey, can be said to belong to the Dickens school only in a somewhat Pickwickian sense. To speak of Kingsley as an intellectual would no doubt amuse those who recall the ineptitudes of his controversy with Newman, or his juvenile glorification of physical prowess. He was a man who lived largely in his enthusiasms and emotions, and his imagination was quite undisciplined. Nevertheless his enthusiasm went out to "ideas" as Dickens's never did. His theology was indebted importantly to Frederick Denison Maurice, his social philosophy to Carlyle. And it is perilous to sneer at his scientific studies, for they won the respect of both Darwin and Huxley, and were cited in *The Descent of Man.*

Dickens shared Kingsley's admiration for Carlyle, and he must surely have agreed with him in most of the specific reforms he advocated. He must have sympathized with his theology also, at least in a general way, though Dickens was not greatly interested in theology as such. Both men used the novel as an instrument of reform. It was not merely because Dickens was an immeasurably greater novelist that he never permitted the weight of his ideas to break down the structure of his books as Kingsley did; it

was also because he was never particularly interested in ideas for their own sake.

That Kingsley wrote novels at all is an impressive testimonial to the importance the Victorians had come to attach to this once despised branch of literature as a vehicle of discussion and reform. The novel was never more than a sideline with him: he wrote *Yeast* at night, when the work of the parish was done, *Alton Locke* between five in the morning and family prayers at seven; and his six volumes of adult fiction make up a comparatively small part of the bulk of his collected works.

Three of Kingsley's novels—*Yeast* (1848 in *Fraser's Magazine,* 1851 as a book), *Alton Locke* (1850), and *Two Years Ago* (1857)—deal with contemporary problems. In the other three—*Hypatia* (1853), *Westward Ho!* (1855), and *Hereward The Wake, "Last of the English"* (1866)—he escapes into the past but manages to carry all the problems of the present along with him.

Yeast was inspired both by the terrible condition of the agricultural laborer in England after the repeal of the Corn Laws in 1846, and by a desire to combat the drift of "the more thoughtful" among English young people "towards Rome, towards sheer materialism, or towards an unchristian and unphilosophic spiritualism."

The drift toward Rome was, of course, the result of the Oxford Movement, which Kingsley fought all his life with fanatical zeal. In the course of the book, the fox-hunting, heart-hungry hero, Lancelot Smith, has an interview with Newman, but when the priest commends him to the Blessed Virgin, he cries, "I am not a child, but a man; I want not a mother to pet, but a man to rule me." The crucified Redeemer will not do either. "I want a live Christ, not a dead one." The "unchristian and unphilosophic spiritualism" was pantheism, or, as Kingsley called it, "Emersonianism." The "sheer materialism" might have been expected to be Darwinism, but it is not, for Kingsley was a devoted Darwinian, and Lancelot is sure that "Man's scientific conquest of nature must be one phase of his Kingdom on Earth, whatever else is not," and that "If that Hebrew Bible is to be believed by me, it must agree with what I already know from science."

As a work of art, *Yeast* is very loosely constructed; as Stanley E. Baldwin puts it, "The author shoots at a variety of evils of his day with buckshot." Yet there is life in it because so much of Kingsley's self went into Lancelot. He too was a strong young man who could neither deny the imperious needs of his body nor find his heart's rest in them; he too had gone through a shattering spiritual conflict; he too had been saved by the love of a woman. Argemone is Mrs. Kingsley, but in the book there is no happy ending; Kingsley seems to have felt it would be more artistic somehow to have the heroine die during a typhus epidemic. Tregarva, the sensitive game-keeper, awakens Lancelot's social consciousness; the mysterious, unbelievable Barnakill points him finally to "Jesus Christ—THE MAN." Almost every force working for or against the Kingdom of God in England, as Kingsley understood it, appears somewhere in this book, but comparatively few of the characters involved have anything more than an ideational interest.

Alton Locke, Tailor and Poet, An Autobiography, which is based on the career of the shoemaker-poet, Thomas Cooper, author of *The Purgatory of Suicides,* whom Kingsley knew, and whom he won back to his abandoned theism, is a much better book than **Yeast,** especially in the impressive account at the beginning of the poor tailor's boy who struggles for an education in spite of poverty and Calvinism. Alton gets his poems published through the respectable patronage of Dean Winnstay, who shares Kingsley's passion for science, and who, at the end, serves as the author's mouthpiece to convince Alton that there is no necessary conflict between religion and science. But because the Dean has no social vision, the poems appear in an emasculated state, an outrage to which Alton submits only because he has fallen in love with the soulless beauty of Winnstay's daughter, Lilian. Not until the end of the book does he realize how much more he has in common with her cousin, Eleanor Staunton, and then it is too late; never was the Victorian passion for untimely death more perfectly illustrated than in Eleanor's quite needless passing!

Alton Locke centers around the Chartist crisis of April 10, 1848. The concrete demands of the Chartists were reasonable, but the method of their agitation brought up the old question of whether or not violence has a necessary share in the social struggle, and both frightened and alienated a great many people. Kingsley had an important part in this struggle.

> My only quarrel with the Charter [he said], is that it does not go far enough in reform. I want to set you *free;* but I do not see how what you ask for, will give you what you want. I think you have fallen into just the same mistake as the rich of whom you complain—the very mistake of fancying that *legislative* reform is *social* reform, or that men's hearts can be changed by act of parliament.

It is to this position that Alton comes at last through all his sufferings.

Eleanor's heroic social service is intended to show up the injustice of class discriminations. Carlyle is often referred to in ***Alton Locke*** and the Scottish bookseller, Sandy Mackaye, embodies his personality as well as his ideas. Cousin George, who sympathizes with the Tractarians, is contemptible and dishonest; his death, on the eve of his wedding, from typhus contracted through a sweated garment is as bold and sensational a piece of divine retribution as Victorian fiction knows.

The last of Kingsley's contemporary novels was ***Two Years Ago.*** The inept title recalled the Crimean War, which Kingsley, like Tennyson in *Maud,* absurdly thought of as having regenerated England! In the book itself the cholera epidemic is more important than the war. Kingsley himself had done good service during epidemics; as he grew older, his interest in politics declined, and his passion for sanitary reform grew ever stronger.

Tom Thurnall, a rolling stone who becomes a doctor, is the hero of this book. The Puseyites and the Dissenters are damned as usual, but Kingsley pours out the special vials of his wrath on Ellsley Vavasour, who sees a terrible shipwreck only as a good subject for a poem. Kingsley had grasped the important truth that if the artist is only an artist he is nothing, but the accumulation of woe he brings down on Vavasour's head seems absurdly overdone.

The schoolmistress, Grace Harvey—half mystic and saint, half unbalanced fanatic—is a strange kind of heroine; equally strange in her own way is Marie Cordifiamma, an afterthought due to Kingsley's newly-awakened interest in abolition, whose story is quite unconnected with the rest of the book. Marie is an American mulatto, a slave, but she only needs Tom to convey her to free territory in order to become an international stage celebrity, and finally the wife of a wealthy American!

No book of Kingsley's is free from absurdities, and there are probably more absurdities in **Two Years Ago** than in any other. Yet for all its infelicities the book has a strange charm, the same kind of charm as [Henry Brooke's] *The Fool of Quality,* which Kingsley adored, and by which, it is clear, he was influenced.

Of the three historical novels, ***Hypatia, or New Foes with an Old Face,*** a picture of the struggle between Christianity and paganism in fifth century Alexandria, is the one which gets farthest away from Kingsley's own time in its setting and stays closest to it in spirit. The author's own valedictory suggests the great weakness of the book: "I have shown you . . . your own likenesses in toga and tunic, instead of

Portrait of Kingsley.

coat and bonnet." He does. He even shows us Charles Kingsley's likeness as Bishop Synesius, who glorifies sportsmanship and married love. But none of this helps to take us into fifth-century Alexandria.

Kingsley was right in his feeling that, unlike religion, philosophy is always essentially aristocratic in its appeal; when Hypatia confronts the hapless Pelagia, she has "no gospel . . . for the harlot! No word for the sinner, the degraded!" And this gives him a chance to bring forward the cardinal tenet of Maurice's theology—and of his own—that the Incarnation is the answer to the human problem.

Unfortunately Kingsley was prevented from setting forth this idea very effectively by the fact that in **Hypatia** he is also trying to excoriate everything he hates most in ecclesiasticism—"those habits of doing evil that good may come, of pious intrigue, and at last of open persecution. . . ." The unfortunate result is that while paganism or "Emersonianism"—which is what Kingsley was really fighting, and which, of course, is not really paganism at all—is seen at its best in the book in Hypatia herself, the Christian party—the Bishop of Alexandria and his followers—have only a degraded Christianity to pit against it.

Critics of the past praised **Hypatia** for its elevation of tone. It has this elevation undoubtedly, and it has plenty of action also, but neither its Jews nor its Christians, its Romans nor its Goths, have any particular reality; and [W. D.] Howells was not unfair when he described the heroine [in his *Heroines of Fiction,* Vol. 2, 1901] as "a sort of Alexandrian Margaret Fuller."

To a certain extent these faults appear in **Westward Ho!** The respectability of the book is eminently Victorian, and the famous tribute to Queen Elizabeth was written with one eye on Kingsley's own sovereign. The Rose of Torridge elopes with Don Guzman, and Frank and Amyas Leigh cross the seas in pursuit. When, through an overheard conversation, Frank learns that his love is not the Spaniard's mistress, as he had feared, a great load drops from his mind. " 'Husband!' whispered Frank faintly to Amyas. 'Thank God, thank God! I am content. Let us go.' " Despite such absurdities, Kingsley understood the Elizabethan period much better than he understood Alexandria in the fifth century, and he had a much truer feeling for it. **Westward Ho!** is a highly idealized picture of the Elizabethan sea-rovers, but of its kind it is as good a picture as we are likely to get.

Morally, however, the book is open to serious objection. Kingsley's bitterness toward the Roman Catholic Church is very unpleasant, and his specific exemption, from his blanket condemnation, of "those Roman Catholics whose noble blood has stained every Crimean battlefield" is merely comic. This brings us to the second objection. **Westward Ho!** was a recruiting poster for the Crimean War, for Kingsley, forward-looking as he was on many social questions, was blind to the underlying purposes of imperialist war. So Drake, Raleigh and the others appear in his pages, though not without some historical justification, one must admit, as prophets of the modern imperialist expansion.

Hereward the Wake takes its place with Bulwer's novel and Tennyson's play about Harold as an important contribution to the Anglo-Saxon revival. Kingsley had a genuine love for the fencountry from memories of his youth, and his very limitations helped him to enter sympathetically into the experiences of the Saxon warrior. He develops his story episodically, and he is rather successful in catching the spirit of *The Anglo-Saxon Chronicle:*

> And now is Hereward to the greenwood gone, to be a bold outlaw; and not only an outlaw himself, but the father of all outlaws, who held these forests for two hundred years, from the fens to the Scottish border.

Of course it must be a woman, Torfrida, who leads Hereward into the right way, and of course when he deserts her, it must be the beginning of the end:

> But the grace of God had gone away from Hereward, as it goes away from all men who are unfaithful to their wives.

Even for that interpretation, however, there is some justification in the chronicles.

I do not wish to suggest that I consider Kingsley's achievements as a novelist altogether negligible. He was a writer of many gifts, and he knew how to tell an exciting story. But his arrows often failed to hit the mark at which he aimed them. He was right in his feeling that a man must be a good pagan before he can be a good Christian; nevertheless, it was Christianity that he wanted to preach. He can hardly be said to achieve his purpose, however, when he gives us heroes like Amyas Leigh and Tom Thurnall, who travel heroically through the books they inhabit in their pagan aspects, only to experience a hurried, offstage conversion at the close. Moreover, Kingsley's continual harping on his favorite ideas becomes very tiresome even to those who share them. To the development of the novel as such Kingsley contributed little; he applied it to social and economic problems, to be sure, but others had . . . done that before him. It is even doubtful that his novels had any important influence on the breakdown of structure so often apparent in later "novels of ideas." But certainly they themselves prefigure it. (pp. 260-67)

Edward Wagenknecht, "The Disciples of Dickens," in his Cavalcade of the English Novel, *Holt, Rinehart and Winston, 1943, pp. 234-67.*

Margaret M. Maison   (essay date 1961)

[Maison is an English educator and critic. In the following essay, she discusses religious thought in Kingsley's work, contending that while his characters lack spiritual depth, his novels do present compelling demonstrations of his Christian beliefs.]

[Kingsley] brought gusts of fresh air into the religious novel—indeed, so vigorous and breezy are these gusts that the spiritual element is often almost entirely blown away, and we are left with magnificent adventure stories and only scanty accounts of the inner life. Kingsley was a man with a message who regarded his novel-writing as a divinely-inspired vocation, but his genius for descriptions of exciting physical events exceeded his powers of portraying the adventures of the soul, and although in his own day his novels caused conversions, and brought faith and its consolations to many, the modern reader may well find the spiritual content of his novels a little shallow and schoolboyish.

Today we read *Yeast* (1851) for its superb descriptions of fishing and hunting rather than for its accounts of the hero's struggles for faith (ending in the rather nebulous conclusion of serving "Jesus Christ—THE MAN"); we read *Hypatia* (1853) for the splendid pictures of Rome ageing hideously that form a triumph of the historical imagination, for those gorgeous pagan scenes that Kingsley describes with such relish, and for the masterly account of the death of Hypatia herself rather than details of the colourless hero's search for truth and the author's intended message of warning that was the whole *raison d'être* of the book. We read *Westward Ho!* (1855) for the joy of the adventures and not for information on the spiritual progress of the characters, and we read *Two Years Ago* (1857) for nautical rather than eschatological illumination. Similarly, *Hereward the Wake* (1866) holds us by the mighty deeds of the hero, and we are far more interested in learning how he was outlawed and slew bears and performed saga-like feats than in learning how he lost the grace of God. Kingsley's gifts as a novelist are better suited to describing a man's fall from his horse than his fall from grace, and many of his best-known characters seem distinguished more by a thirst for blood than a hunger for God.

Yet, while admitting these exaggerations in the "wolf-vein", we see that Kingsley does make an interesting contribution to the religious novel. The preacher of "muscular Christianity" and the stalwart opponent of all forms of asceticism, he endeavours to show in his novels how spiritual welfare can be greatly assisted by vigorous physical activity and by encouraging rather than crushing the natural appetites and passions. True Christianity, according to Kingsley, involves an appreciation of the great importance and value of animal spirits and physical strength, and a hearty enjoyment of all the pursuits and accomplishments which are connected with them. His views are in agreement with the clerical writer who proclaimed in *The Christian World* that bodily exercise is "at once a religious duty and a means of grace".

Thus in his novels he shows us men and women developing spiritually through being toughened physically. Philammon, in *Hypatia,* who at the beginning of the story is a rather soft young monk in a deplorable state of cloistered ignorance (having never seen a woman), becomes a great Christian and a model Abbot only after he has had amazing adventures in the world, has fought hippopotamuses and Goths, has witnessed riots, murders, fires, has had hairbreadth escapes from death, has loved and lost and has scandalized his fellow monks by his astonishing confession: "Tell my brethren that I pray nightly for two women: both of them young; both of them beautiful; both of them beloved by me more than I love my soul, and tell them, moreover, that one of the two was a harlot, and the other a heathen." Thus has Philammon's spiritual education been completed. Pious schoolmistresses too have to

be shocked and battered out of their inadequate conceptions of Christianity into a higher, finer faith, and in *Two Years Ago* Grace Hervey learns from the grim horrors of an outbreak of cholera "how much of the unheroic element" is still left in her, and how narrow and untenable are her views on the doctrine of eternal damnation. True to the principles of Broad Church tolerance, Kingsley makes both Philammon and Grace Hervey have their creeds widened as well as their spiritual and physical powers developed through a more extensive acquaintance with life in the raw.

But although for Kingsley, a period of contact with the shocking and the sordid may assist in the heroifying of certain souls, yet in general it is one of his most vigorously emphasized doctrines that the soul suffers from continual exposure to bad physical conditions. Hence it is the duty of a parson to press for social, political and economic reforms, and problems of wages and sewers are as much his business as those of sacraments and prayers. Thus might Kingsley answer any critic likely to accuse him of preferring sanitation to meditation.

Bodily welfare being thus indissolubly linked with spiritual welfare, physical ills and evils cannot, in Kingsley's view, be cured by purely physical means—a lesson that Alton Locke learns to his cost. *Alton Locke* (1850), that interesting novel based on the life of Thomas Cooper, the Chartist poet whom Kingsley himself converted, shows how the hero, alienated from religion by the grim Calvinism of his mother, burns with longing to save his fellow workmen from their wretched sufferings in filthy hovels and sweatshops. He finds, however, that all his efforts fail and eventually he learns that it is Jesus of Nazareth who is the only true "People's Friend" and that nothing but Christianity can cure economic and political diseases. The souls of the lower orders, we are told over and over again, are in danger because of the vileness of their living and working conditions, and both Alton Locke and the hero of *Yeast* come through their experience of "the condition-of-the-poor question" to their first real understanding of the Christian religion.

This emphasis on one particular aspect of the faith—Christianity in its role of physician to the social ills of the Victorian working classes—gives a certain narrowness to Kingsley's notions of spirituality. His characters look outwards and downwards rather than inwards and upwards; indeed, one leaves his novels with the confused impression that the highest spiritual development can take place only through an intense and belligerent humanitarianism or else a welter of hectic and sanguinary bodily activity, wherein animal strength, spirits and courage are being tried and tested to the uttermost. Yet, inadequate as Kingsley's spiritual creations tend to be, in their strength and healthy virility they form a suitable corrective to some of the more mawkish and young-ladyish features of Oxford Movement novels as well as to some of the morbid excesses of much Evangelical fiction. (pp. 124-29)

Margaret M. Maison, "Christianity Muscular and Elastic: The Broad Church Novels," in her The Victorian Vision: Studies in the Religious Novel, *Sheed & Ward, 1961, pp. 120-37.*

Gillian Beer (essay date 1965)

[*Beer is an English educator and critic who incorporates feminist theories into her views of literature. In the following essay, she argues that Kingsley's novels express the Romantic, pantheistic ideal of nature and country common to works of the period, but also reject an entirely aesthetic appreciation of the countryside that fails to address issues of poverty and oppression among rural laborers.*]

Landscape as the epitome of aesthetic excellence reached the height of its popularity with the picturesque movement. At the same time its importance extended beyond the purely aesthetic and became linked with the belief that the natural forms of the countryside exercised a beneficent moral and spiritual influence on country people. Kenneth Maclean [in his *Agrarian Age: A Background for Wordsworth,* 1950] has pointed out that the cult of the gentleman farmer (which combined aristocratic pastoralism and advanced scientific techniques) brought with it the complementary cult of the peasant as the custodian of a simple "natural" morality. The aesthetic and the moral responses to the countryside were most profoundly fused in the poetry of Wordsworth, which creates a new kind of pastoralism: that of the native rather than the townsman. He sees country life with the sobriety of the indigenous country-dweller, responding with delight to the natural beauties of the countryside while accepting a frequent sad disparity between the country dweller of poetry and grim fact. Wordsworth uses the very plainness of the life as the basis for a kind of poetry different from that earlier pastoral in which shepherds and shepherdesses were essentially townsfolk holiday-making:

> I came not dreaming of unruffled life,
> Untainted manners; born among the hills,
> Bred also there, I wanted not a scale
> To regulate my hopes. Pleased with the good,
> I shrink not from the evil with disgust,
> Or with immoderate pain. I look for Man,
> The common Creature of the brotherhood,
> Differing but little from the Man elsewhere.

Despite the realism with which Wordsworth often treats the daily lot of the countryman, in figures such as Michael he also epitomises the virtues which he felt to be peculiarly nurtured by life close to the natural world. Moreover, his visionary perceptions of a relationship between the aesthetic and the spiritual in the natural world seem to have had the effect of preserving for his contemporaries the related moral notion that the country-dweller's lot was one of dignity and of harmony with the world about him.

The industrial encroachments on the landscape, instead of undermining the literary image of the countryside as the source of beauty and the home of morality, gave to it rather the added intensity of a vanishing world. It is as if the integral image of the countryside was an emotional and literary necessity to the reading public of the earlier nineteenth century, feeling itself perhaps newly divorced from an agrarian past. Even in the novel, where, if not in poetry, we might expect to find some record of the worsening conditions of the peasant and small farmer and of the drift to the towns which Cobbett [in his *Rural Rides*] records in the 1820's, there is no discussion of the situation. This may be accounted for partly by the genre of the popular novel at the time: the novel was still essentially entertainment reading rather than the place for serious discussions, and the Gothic romance with its emphasis on the travelogue value of landscape, retained its popularity into the 1820's. Maria Edgeworth and, to a lesser extent, Walter Scott, touched on the conditions of working-class life in the country, but they were both describing lands which, to the English reader, were picturesquely barbarous—and their novels were set back in time. The most important reason for the continued idealisation of country living was undoubtedly that the heroes and heroines of novels in the first half of the nineteenth century were almost invariably drawn from the land-owning classes. Working men are seen as figures in a landscape. They play an aesthetic, not an active role.

In the 'forties and 'fifties a new field of experience—the lot of the country-dwelling poor—was explored by a considerable number of novelists, and particularly by those who saw the novel as a means of attaining practical reforms. In *Chartism* (1840) Carlyle wrote of the working-man's England: "Is it a green flowery world, with azure everlasting sky stretched over it, the work and government of a God; or a murky-simmering Tophet, of copperas-fumes, cotton fuzz, gin-riot, wrath and toil, created by a Demon, governed by a Demon?" Now it began to be recognised in fiction that not only the townsmen but also those who lived in "a green flowery world" might be wretched. There were two main artistic difficulties inherent in the subject. The first is suggested incidentally by Mrs. Gaskell in *North and South.* The heroine tells Higgins, the North country industrial worker who wants to move south to an agricultural community, "The hard spade-work robs their brains of life; the sameness of their toil deadens their imagination; they don't care to meet to talk over thoughts and speculations, even of the weakest, mildest kind, after their work is done; they go home brutishly tired, poor creatures, caring for nothing but food and rest." The problem is to make artistically interesting the lot of those who are too weary and inarticulate to find it interesting themselves.

The second artistic problem was of a different kind. The subject matter had in it a temptation to crudity of effect. It was obviously easy to get a shock contrast between the beauty of the surroundings and the conditions of the poor—and for practical ends the novelist might even exaggerate the violence of this contrast. Disraeli, for example, does so in *Sybil:* "Beautiful illusion! For behind that laughing landscape, penury and disease fed upon the vitals of a miserable population." But his descriptive writing is so weak and conventional, so much the townsman's respectful salutation to unfelt beauty, that it vitiates his contrast. The undeniable if obscure relationship between the beauty of the countryside and the special quality of life in the country is lost, and his picture of the sufferings of the people is thereby made more shallow: their environment is simply a painted backcloth. At the other extreme, we have the sort of book which, though radical in plot structure, is so lyrical about the physical beauties of the countryside as to suggest that these are of more permanent importance than the situation of the country dwellers. Charlotte Brontë's *Shirley* is a striking example of a novel of the period which while apparently on the side of progress in effect celebrates the older way of life: and the principal reason for this contradictory effect is the way in which the countryside is treated and the attitude of the characters towards it. This is epitomised at the end of the book. Although in argument Moore's practical plans for reform conquer Caroline's love of wild solitary nature, Charlotte Brontë reserves to herself the last word. The Epilogue is spoken by the author's housekeeper, no figure in the plot. So winning are her reminiscences that they leave one with a sense not of the vitality of the new order, but of melancholy for things not to be regained:

"What was the Hollow like then, Martha?"

"Different to what it is now; but I can tell of it clean different again; when there was neither mill nor cot, nor hall except Fieldhead, within two mile of it. I can tell, one summer evening, fifty year syne, my mother coming running in just at the edge of dark, almost fleyed out of her wits, saying she had seen a fairish (fairy) in Fieldhead Hollow; and that was the last fairish that was ever seen on this countryside (though they've been heard within these forty years). A lonesome spot it was—and a bonnie spot—full of oak-trees and nut-trees. It is altered now."

This double pull between the need for development (to bring better housing and employment) and nostalgia for a primal world powerfully affected Charles Kingsley also. But of all the novelists who touched on the situation of the country-dwelling poor, he solved most interestingly the artistic problems involved while never losing sight of the practical ends for which he wrote. In his handling of literary conventions and their relationship to contemporary life, he shows greater artistry and subtlety than he is usually credited with.

Kingsley is deliberately writing tracts for the times which shall have issue in action; he sets out to shock his readers not only by narrative revelations of social conditions but by setting literary conventions against real life and then scornfully jettisoning the conventions if they are unable to contain the material he presents. He is not, like Harriet Martineau, for instance, using the novel form merely as sweetening to a pill of fact. He is quite deliberately and emphatically calling attention to the conventions of novel-writing in order to show how different from the realities of life are the expectations which books arouse. So, the Epilogue of *Yeast* is devoted to answering specifically literary objections to the book, such as its mysterious symbolic ending, the way minor characters are introduced and disappear, and its formlessness:

Readers will probably complain of the fragmentary and unconnected form of the book. Let them first be sure that this is not an integral feature of the subject itself, and therefore, the very form the book should take. Do not young men think, speak, act, just now, in this very incoherent, fragmentary way; without methodic education or habits of thought; with the various stereotyped systems which they have received by tradition breaking up under them like ice in a thaw; with a thousand facts and notions which they know not how to classify, pouring in on them like a flood?—a very Yeasty state of mind altogether, like a mountain burn in a spring rain, carrying down with it stones, sticks, peat-water, addled grouse-eggs and drowned kingfishers, fertilising salts and vegetable poisons—not alas! without a large crust, here and there, of sheer froth.

Kingsley is claiming that his concern is to show the way life is lived now, even if this means flouting accepted literary canons (though he also covers himself by invoking the principle of decorum). The imagery of the passage quoted gives some insight into the source of Kingsley's success at picturing rural life as it really was. Paradoxically, it was his love of natural beauty and his very particular gift for descriptive writing—at first sight among the most conventional elements of a Victorian novelist's art—which gave him his most artistically telling means of attack on the condition of England. The connection can be best understood through the epigraph, from Wordsworth, to the first section of *The Water Babies:*

To her fair works did Nature link
The human soul that through me ran
And much it grieved my heart to think,
What man had made of man.

It could stand as epigraph equally to *Yeast* (1851, written in 1848), *Alton Locke* (1850), and *Two Years Ago* (1857). Though scornful of the fashionable adulation of nature, the watered-down pantheism of what he calls the "barometer" hero, Kingsley nevertheless felt powerfully the real emotion which lay at the root of much rhetoric. He does not deny the beauty of landscape, or, like Disraeli, use respectful clichés about it. Instead he pictures it with freshness and fervour. His point is that the starving and sick cannot savour beauty, and that the country poor require help if their life is to become anything better than a mockery of pastoralism.

Kingsley is close to Wordsworth in his aesthetic-spiritual reaction to natural beauty, but he had ambivalent feelings about the influence of Wordworth's work in general. Kingsley, who could speak of Wordsworth as "not only poet, but preacher and prophet of God's new and divine philosophy" [F. Kingsley, ed., *Charles Kingsley, His Letters and Memories of his Life,* 1877], was powerfully drawn to a poetry of loving intimacy with the natural world and of belief in nature's power for good. What troubled him, however, was the pantheism and the passivity towards social evils which, he felt, tended to be the results of the fashionable enthusiasm which young men felt for Wordsworth's work. Recognising a core of good in any unselfconscious response to natural beauty, he objected to its systematization into a literary and social convention which blinded people to the real situation in the countryside and provided an excuse for their blindness. We see this debate in *Yeast.* Lancelot is a young man of conventional heroic aspect: good-hearted, devoted to hunting and fishing, and to Nature in a mildly pantheistic way. He thinks of himself as progressive. Through Tregarva, the game-keeper, he comes to realise his own blindness and to see the country life usually concealed from the novel-reading classes. Kingsley epitomises the contrast in the first laconic exchange between Lancelot and Tregarva:

> "Beautiful stream this," said Lancelot.
> "Beautiful enough, sir," said the keeper, with an emphasis on the first word.
> "Why, has it any other faults?"
> "Not so wholesome as pretty, sir."
> "What harm does it do?"
> "Fever, plague and rheumatism, sir."

This black-and-white exposition of the sentimental townsman's attitude as compared to the grim inhabitant's is followed a little later by Lancelot's solitary brooding by the river. Kingsley notices, with a slightly reproachful use of Wordsworthian phrases, that "All his thoughts, all his sympathies, were drowned in the rush and whirl of the water. He forgot everything else in the mere animal enjoyment of sight and sound." But he continues with a description which perfectly—and sympathetically—captures the heightened sense-impressions of Lancelot's trance-like gazing at the water, as it

> boiled up from the bottom, and dived again beneath long threads of creamy foam, and swung round posts and roots, and rushed blackening under dark weed-fringed boughs, and gnawed at the marly banks, and shook the ever-restless bulrushes, till it was swept away and down over the white pebbles and olive weeds, in one broad rippling sheet of molten silver, towards the distant sea. Downwards it fleeted ever and bore his thoughts floating on its oily stream; and the great trout, with their yellow sides and peacock backs, lounged among the eddies, and the silver grayling dimpled and wandered upon the shallows, and the may-flies flickered and rustled round him like water fairies, with their green gauzy wings; the coot clanked musically from among the reeds; the frogs hummed their ceaseless vesper-monotone; the kingfisher darted from his hole in the bank like a blue spark of electric light; the swallow's bills snapped as they twined and hawked above the pool; the swift's wings whirred like musket-balls, as they rushed screaming past his head.

At the end of the passage, as if converted by his own vivid re-creation, Kingsley answers himself through an adaptation from Wordsworth: " 'Beauty born of murmuring sound, / Did pass into his face.' Blame him not. There are more things in a man's heart than ever get in through his thoughts."

By making all his heroes primarily observers, Kingsley solves the primary artistic problem mentioned earlier in this article: that of putting country labourers in the centre of a book. Lancelot is a house-party visitor, Alton Locke is a poor townsman, and Tom Thurnall in *Two Years Ago* a stranger washed up in a shipwreck after long sojourn in foreign lands. Even Tregarva, who acts as Lancelot's guide, is in the isolated social position of gamekeeper and has been brought up in the Brazils. Each of them is embroiled of his own choice, though the extent of their commitment ranges from the guided tour which Lancelot undertakes to the active role Alton himself plays in his work of proselytising for the Chartists.

In Lancelot, Kingsley presents a hero as nearly as possible like the readers at whom the book is directed: the young at the universities. Thus Lancelot's discoveries are undergone also by the reader who is assumed to share his idea of country life as well as his mild progressivism. Kingsley uses two main methods to disillusion his readers. The more obvious is direct narrative revelation, as in the battle between poachers and game-keepers in *Yeast* (or in the description of the tailors' workshops and the presentation of Chartists in *Alton Locke,* or in the description of sanitary conditions in *Two Years Ago*). Such revelations often have a touch of the ironic. They assume false pre-conceptions rather than simple ignorance on the part of the reader. Indeed, Kingsley's most striking and characteristic method, the reversal of commonplaces, creates a collision between what the reader, and sometimes the character, is led to expect of a scene and what he is in fact offered. In the gay opening pages of *Yeast,* Kingsley uses the converse of this method, informing his reader that, as his story is to run counter to many fashions, he will conform where he can and begin with "a scrap of description." The reader is thus alerted and the ensuing description, which might have passed without remark in another novel, is subjected to new scrutiny. Kingsley flies into a pastiche of the Wertheresque writers who think that "a man's soul as well as his lungs might be saved by sea-breezes and sunshine." His extracts from Lancelot's diary illustrate the barometer hero: "Tuesday, 22nd. Barometer rapidly falling. Heavy clouds in the south-east. My heart sank into gloomy forebodings. Read *Manfred,* and doubted whether I should live long. The leaden weight of destiny seemed to crush my aching forehead, till the thunderstorm burst, and peace was restored to my troubled soul." Such literary junketings are unusual in Kingsley, but they serve to show that he was critically conscious of literary conventions. He employs some of them, nonetheless: Argemone, for example, first becomes aware of Lancelot because he uses a felicitous expression to describe some lime-trees; the thunderstorm convention Kingsley had mocked is used later in the same book in a manner quite as mechanical as any to be found in the run of Victorian novels; and in *Two Years Ago* the heroine is marked out as such by being first introduced doing good works in a rural setting.

Lancelot's discoveries culminate in the scene of the country fair. He vaguely expects that it will bear some relation to the sweet earthiness of *The Winter's Tale* even if not to the Dresden tradition, and the reader is not forewarned of anything different. What confronts both hero and reader is not the conventionally anticipated rowdiness but a far more deadly lethargy. We have expected Lancelot's idealised picture to be disappointed, but not in this manner, and Kingsley thus does not permit his readers to retreat behind an attitude of knowledgeable superiority. Within the scene he gives yet a further turn to the reversal of expectation:

> At that instant a huge hulking farm-boy rolled into the booth roaring, dolefully, the end of a song, with a punctuation of his own invention—
>
> "He'll maak me a lady. So. Vine to be zyre. And faithfully; love me. Although; I; be-e; poor-r-r."

> Lancelot would have laughed heartily at him anywhere else; but the whole scene was past a jest; and a gleam of pathos and tenderness seemed to shine even from that doggerel,—a vista, as it were, of true genial nature, in the far distance.

Through the pathos and ferocity of the songs, "Young Mary" and "I zeed a vire," the potential of the country people, as well as their plight, is dramatically realised. In his eagerness to press home his points Kingsley can rarely let well alone, and so here he continues in an ironic apostrophe to "Arcadian dreams of pastoral innocence, and graceful industry." His open proselytising must supply the lack of inherent interest in those to be saved, and *Yeast* does not avoid the taint of condescension, mainly because the hero is slumming. In *Alton Locke* Kingsley solves the dilemma by making the narrator-hero an articulate working man and poet, alienated first from his peers and later from the upper classes whose standards he for a time adopts.

Alton Locke's two "never to be forgotten" journeys to the countryside mark the stages in his progress; in the first, he discovers the beauty from which he has hitherto been shut out; in the second, after his rise and relapse from the upper classes, he sees the land's grim aspect for those who must force their living from it. The opening of the book is a powerful reversal of the convention of an introductory description which Kingsley mockingly followed in *Yeast.* The first words here are "I am a Cockney among Cockneys. Italy and the Tropics, the Highlands and Devonshire, I know only in dreams. Even the Surrey Hills, of whose loveliness I have heard so much, are to me a distant fairyland, whose gleaming ridges I am worthy only to behold afar." Having thus proudly narrowed the compass of his experience and shown the magic with which the countryside was imbued for him, Alton Locke speaks of his childhood in a suburban street where dusty lilacs were his forests and dingy sparrows his wild beasts; and his contact with the countryside was listening at night to the ceaseless rumble of the waggons bringing up to Covent Garden "the treasures of the gay green country, the land of fruit and flowers, for which I have yearned all my life in vain." This image of the little town boy in the night comforted and set dreaming by the sound of country waggons is far more powerful than any amount of author's moralising. Alton continues to describe the intensity of his childhood vision; cabbages and rhubarb, clouds and water, and the setting sun are the elements of beauty in his world. From Battersea fields he "brought home wild-flowers and chance beetles and butterflies, and pored over them, not in the spirit of a naturalist, but of a poet." They are the symbols of freedom, angels as well as objects, but when, overcome with compunction, he would regretfully return them and set them loose, they would generally have starved to death in the meantime. For once, Kingsley disciplines himself to present a symbol without a gloss, and throughout *Alton Locke* he is more content to let events speak for themselves, confident that the paradoxical nature of his hero itself points his moral.

Alton first visits the country in his young manhood when he sets off to walk to Cambridge. The description uses all the traditional elements, but it is given poignancy by being spoken by Alton, who is seeing the countryside for the first time, and finds all his expectations answered. Skylarks hang over the scene, the hills are "quivering in the green haze," and in the silence he feels "a capability of clear, bright meditation." He enters a wood with the owner's permission and injunctions not to disturb the pheasant and lies half asleep, his thoughts wavering between discovery of the delicately cut leaves of the weeds and memory of the plight of his fellow-workers to whom the countryside is "the yard where the gentlemen live when they go out of town." When Alton moralises on the plight of the poor, there can be no element of condescension as in *Yeast;* the possibility of moralising represents his newfound freedom. On this journey the only people he meets are kindly gentlefolk and the land is flowering; he is not burdened with the plight of the agricultural poor, for Kingsley is concerned to show what country life *could* be like.

Alton's second journey takes place in very different circumstances. He goes to preach Chartism in an attempt to regain his place in the class he feels he has betrayed. The landscape accords with the plight of its inhabitants: "a dreary, treeless country, whose broad brown and grey fields were only broken by an occasional line of dark, doleful firs." His encounters this time are with the poor, and the talk is not of nature's beauty but of absentee landlords and the practice of letting the cottages together with the farms, so delivering the poor man over to the tenant farmer, himself "too penurious, too ignorant, and often too poor, to keep the cottages in a state fit for the habitation of human beings." Moving across a barren landscape empty of everything but "dark curdled clouds," Alton and his companion come upon two wretched little boys whose hands are too blue with cold to turn the handle of the turnip-cutting machine. The two men stop to help them, and afterwards Alton thinks with angry repugnance of "the contrast between the highly-bred, over-fed, fat, thickwooled animals . . . and the little half-starved, shivering animals who were their slaves."

Alton Locke's journey into knowledge of the countryside is a sad one. The second journey does not negate the first, nor does it even prove the fallacy of his childhood dreams, but Kingsley forces home the terrible contrast between the promise of the landscape and the pauper conditions of the labourers. He makes the contrast the more poignant by involving its discovery in the narrator's self-discovery. It is not only a generalised literary convention which must crumble under scrutiny, but also the personal aspirations of Alton Locke, the tailor-poet.

In *Two Years Ago,* written to draw attention to the sanitary conditions in the country areas, he again draws a contrast between the romantic and the realistic countryside, this time through the persons of the two main antagonists in the story: Elsley Vavasour, the Shelleyan romantic poet, and Tom Thurnall, the doctor. Tom is the practical man, uninfluenced by fashionable attitudes, and his feeling for nature, his enjoyment of a walk through the countryside, is presented as a step on the way to God, in contrast with what we find in *Yeast,* where Lancelot merely adopts pantheism as a fashionable alternative to organised religion, and so must be weaned from it. This book reverts to the more sermonising tone of *Yeast* with an added note of strain. Apart from Tom Thurnall, there is an aura of melodrama about almost everyone. At the climaxes of the book, such as the coming of the cholera, this has its own effectiveness; and melodrama is the reason for Elsley's downfall as well as the essence of his being. At a picnic set among Welsh scenery, which is described with a happy, undidactic particularity, Elsley makes a sudden wild dash up a mountain in a fit of jealous rage. The idea is a telling one: the romantic poet who has all his life worshipped in his poetry the mountains, the mists, "Nature's melodrama," is set down alone among them. At first, he sees the mountains in their objective beauty: "From the highest saw-edges, where Moel Meich cuts the golden sky, down to the very depth of the abyss, all is lustrous darkness, sooty and yet golden still." The mist descends and Elsley rises into an ecstasy of solitariness, but then comes storm. Here Kingsley uses the conventional device of the thunderstorm to support or give an objective correlative to his hero's emotional crisis. But he uses it for his own ends: Elsley, instead of rising into the storm and glorying in it, suddenly discovers his own stature, which is that of a puny and unbelieving townsman: "Swept away helplessly, without faith or hope, by those *outward impressions of things* on which he had feasted his soul so long, he was the puppet of his own eyes and ears; the slave of glare and noise" (my italics). Into this fervent tumult come rescuers, and Kingsley comments that they are "perhaps, far more 'poetic' characters at this moment than Elsley Vavasour, or any dozen more verse-writers, because they are hazarding their lives on an errand of mercy."

To Kingsley, concern for one's fellow men was the only way to a full and lasting appreciation of both the natural beauty of the external world and the potential beauty of country life. His novels demonstrate his concern; moreover, at their best, his natural descriptions have a lyricism, a particularity, and a tactile quality, which, while renouncing didacticism, convey his sense of the inherent goodness of nature. To take an example from another of his novels, *The Water Babies:* little black Tom comes to the spring

> not such a spring as you see here, which soaks up out of a white gravel in the bog, among the red fly-catchers, and pink bottle-heath, and sweet white orchids; not such a one as you may see too here, which bubbles up under the warm sandbank in the hollow lane, by the great tuft of lady ferns, and makes the sand dance reels at the bottom, day and night, all the year round; not such a spring as either of those; but a real North country limestone fountain like one of those in Sicily or Greece, where the old heathen fancied the nymphs sat cooling themselves the hot summer's day, while the shepherds peeped at them from behind the bushes. Out of a low cave of rock, at the foot of a limestone crag, the great fountain rose, quelling, and bubbling, and gurgling, so clear that you could not tell where the water ended and the air began; and ran away under the road, a stream large enough to turn a mill; among blue geranium, and golden globe-flower, and wild raspberry, and the bird-cherry with its tassels of snow.

It is the personal apprehension of beauty in passages such as this that make us willing to listen to Kingsley when he speaks out against an exclusively aesthetic appreciation of the countryside which ignores the plight of the people who live there. (pp. 243-54)

> *Gillian Beer, "Charles Kingsley and the Literary Image of the Countryside," in* Victorian Studies, *Vol. VIII, No. 3, March, 1965, pp. 243-54.*

P. G. Scott   (essay date 1975)

[*In the following excerpt, Scott examines Kingsley's artistry, praising the author's imaginative presentation of ideas and experience in his fiction.*]

One hundred years ago, when Charles Kingsley died, it could be taken for granted, by those competent to judge, that he would be remembered as an important novelist. Matthew Arnold, for instance, wrote to Kingsley's daughter that his "fine talents and achievements in literature will now have full justice done to them again". Arnold was referring obliquely, to the theologically-laden attacks which had greeted so many of Kingsley's novels. In fact, the novels have been remembered in two different ways. One group—the "social novels", *Yeast* (1848), *Alton Locke* (1849), and *Two Years Ago* (1857)—has an academic reputation, as part of the Victorian fictional exploration of the "condition of England" question. The other group—the so-called boys' books, *The Heroes* (1855), *Westward Ho!* (1855), *The Water-babies* (1863), and *Hereward the Wake* (1866)—still has a popular reputation, and lingers decently on the shelves of the less-progressive junior libraries. Both groups, when viewed by modern critics, tend to be classed as "propaganda" novels, mere fictional vehicles through which Kingsley could propound the doctrines of, respectively, Christian Socialism and Muscular Christianity.

But this is hardly the "full justice" for which Arnold was hoping, and there is much omitted from this modern view. At least two of Kingsley's works of prose fiction get scant appreciation: his Platonic dialogue *Phaeton* (1852), and the powerful *Hypatia* (1852-3). Kingsley's contemporary reputation as a poet has been almost entirely lost sight of: who now reads *The Saint's Tragedy* (1847), or *Andromeda* (published in 1859)? All the time, too, that Kingsley was writing his novels, he was lecturing, writing literary criticism, reviewing current literature, as well as going through a marked theological and political development. The few novels, of either social propaganda or historical adventure, by which he is now remembered, are but a small part of the total published writings of the Rector of Eversley.

The modern fragmented, or selective, view of Kingsley's writings has had the result, I think, of preventing a realization of the importance which imaginative writing had in helping Kingsley to develop his own ideas, and has prevented also the realization of how imaginative even his propaganda writings really are. Re-read after a hundred years, they seem less Victorian documents than Victorian dreams. Time and again in his widow's two-volume *Letters,* one comes on some such sentence as this, of John Martineau's: "He was a poet— . . . he could not help thinking, feeling, and writing as a poet". Kingsley himself continually protests that he is "really" a poet, not a novelist: indeed, in his Inaugural Lecture at Queen's College [*Introductory Lectures Delivered at Queen's College, London,* 1849] he put forward the paradox, couched in evolutionary terms, that poetry was the more natural means of expression than prose. Even though, in his reviews in the early 1850s [collected in Kingsley's *Literary and General Lectures and Essays,* 1880], Kingsley makes the common Victorian complaint that poetry was "dying down among us year by year", and praises novelists over poets for their closer understanding of "what man is", he nowhere makes the common Victorian assertion that poetry ought to be superseded by prose. He specifically rejected the premises of the realist novel: in 1859 Kingsley wrote [in his Preface to Henry Brooke's *The Fool of Quality*], "There are those, indeed, still left on earth who believe the contemplation of the actual (easy and amusing as it is) to be pernicious to most men without a continual remembrance of the ideal". Kingley's developed view of the book he wrote was much more complicated than as merely documentary or didactic tales, even though their teaching impact was substantial during his own lifetime.

The initial impetus to Kingsley's career as a novelist *was* propagandist. In 1848, like Lancelot Smith in *Yeast,* Kingsley "felt in himself a great capability, nay an infinite longing to speak; though what he should utter or how— whether as poet, social theorist, or preacher, he could not yet decide". Significantly, his first fictional pieces were in the *persona* of Parson Lot, and it is clearly recorded how he had hoped to write a tale for the short-lived *Politics for the People,* about a young squire learning his responsibility for a neglected rural estate: "I shall be very hard on the landlords", Kingsley wrote to Ludlow in May of 1848, " . . . but I will promise *to invent nothing*" [quoted in R. B. Martin, *The Dust of Combat,* 1969]. From this odd proposal developed the novelist. The importance of literature as a moral weapon had always been clear to Kingsley: in an early sermon, "On Books" [*Twenty-five Village Sermons,* 1849], he wrote about the expanding book-market of mid-Victorian England,

> this is the age of books, the time, one would think, of which Daniel prophesied that many should run to and fro, and knowledge should be increased. A flood of books, newspapers, writings of all sorts, good and bad, is spreading over the whole land, and young and old will read them . . . now, if ever, are we bound to put holy and wise books, both religious and worldly, into the hands of all around us . . . and now, if ever, are we bound to pray to Christ, the Word of God, that He will raise up among us wise and holy writers . . . and that he may confound the devil and all his lies, and all that swarm of writers who are filling England with trash, filth, blasphemy and covetousness.

It was by no means original to utilize the novel for propa-

gating religious ideas (both Evangelicals and High Churchman had been doing it for some time), and the possibilities of the novel for publicizing social problems had been dramatically evidenced in the early work of Dickens: in his adoption of fiction in his teaching ministry Kingsley was only following in a well-trodden path. Even the tone of moralistic hectoring and brutal bonhomie, which marks so many of the authorial comments in Kingsley's novels, would have been recognizable to a Victorian reader—it is an Anglican mutation on Carlyle. If we look closely at any of Kingsley's novels, we find that his originality lies not in the propagandist element in his immediate motive, but far deeper, in the way Kingsley conveys experience.

Even the most propagandist element in Kingsley's fiction, the social criticism, achieves its impact from Kingsley's imaginative presentation, not simply from the raw material. As Dr Sheila Smith has recently pointed out, in his pictures of rural poverty in *Yeast* Kingsley was drawing not only on his own parish experience, and on the indignation of his relative-by-marriage "S.G.O." of *The Times,* but also on the findings of Parliamentary Select Committees: he was acting as a popularizer rather than a discoverer, a transmitter of facts to which the public was making an inadequate response [Sheila M. Smith, "Blue Books and Victorian Novelists", in *Review of English Studies,* n.s. XXI, 1970]. Rather similarly, in the pictures of the London tailoring trade, in *Alton Locke,* Kingsley's success came, not from the evils being unknown, but from the provoking symbolism of the tailors enslaved in Britain by debts to a system they did not understand, and from Kingsley's ability to convey to his readers his own shock and horror at urban conditions. The description, again in *Alton Locke,* of the approach to the Bermondsey hovel of Downes, the ex-sweater, will serve to illustrate his method:

> He stopped at the end of a miserable blind alley, where a dirty gaslamp just served to make darkness visible, and show the patched windows and rickety door-ways of the crazy houses, whose upper-stories were lost in a brooding cloud of fog; and the pools of stagnant water at our feet; and the huge heap of cinders which filled up the waste end of the alley—a dreary, black, formless mound, on which two or three spectral dogs prowled up and down after the offal, appearing and vanishing like dark imps in and out of the misty chaos beyond . . . the house at which we stopped was the last in the row; all its companions had been pulled down; and there it stood, leaning out with one naked ugly side into the gap, and stretching out long props, like feeble arms and crutches, to resist the work of demolition.

The whole description (based on Jacob's Island, Bermondsey, where the Christian Socialists had been engaged in sanitary agitation), is justly famous; but the impact is achieved, not by the facts, but by their literary presentation. This description, of the slum Kingsley knew best, is carefully placed at a crucial point in the novel. Downes, who had been "sweating" other workmen, is now being sweated himself; the crazy, feeble last house left alone represents his last attempt to resist the destruction of his life;

in it, his wife and children are already dead of typhus; and he goes from the animal hunting-ground among the excrement ("cinders") at the front of this last house, to annihilate himself in the disease-ridden ditch at the back, to become one with the offal and the dogs which reappear there, floating dead, on a stream so opaque that it conceals all trace of Downes's existence. As social exploration, Kingsley's prose is dissuasively over-coloured: as symbolic presentation of Downes's predicament, it is extraordinary—Kingsley saw the potential symbolism of the urban dung-heap twenty years before Dickens. Even the linguistic oddities relate to this symbolism: the spectral "dogs prowled up and down *after the offal*"—was the offal prowling? or was it alive and being hunted? Either way, men, dogs, and reject meat are terrifyingly equated. The strange literary flourish of "darkness visible" has a thematic relevance, for it links the hopelessness of the delirious Downes to Milton's fallen Satan, for whom "darkness visible, / Served only to discover sights of woe, / Regions of sorrow . . . where peace/and rest can never dwell." The force of the passage comes, not from the accuracy of its observation, but from its integration into the developing theme of the book.

At least one recent critic has suggested that Kingsley's very rhetoric led him, in the description of social conditions, into a melodramatic misunderstanding of the poor he wished to help. Dr P. J. Keating [in his *Working Classes in Victorian Fiction,* 1971] has argued that Kingsley was solely concerned to "recreate the feeling of repulsion experienced by himself", and that this hindered, rather than helped, his readers in understanding working-class life. More often in Kingsley than in other novelists the working classes not only have but are social problems. The local unreality, however, which Dr Keating rightly detects in Kingsley's portrayal of urban conditions is at least partly a concomitant of the emotional strength of the novels. Kingsley himself was sufficiently aware of the "mythic" quality of, for instance, the contest between the bluff Farmer Porter and the sweat-shop owner (ch. XXI of *Alton Locke*), to begin the chapter with his narrator reading from Lane's new translation of the *Arabian Nights*: the reader is prepared to find the release of the sweater's victims a fairy-tale ending, that he would like to but cannot, believe. Kingsley's psychedelic descriptions can be sophisticated, rather than naïve. In his descriptions of Victorian urban conditions we participate, not in the social exploration of a mid-Victorian journalist, but in the surreal visions, the mingled hell and hope, of a Victorian poet.

If this is true of the social criticism in Kingsley's novels, it is true also of the treatment of developing religious beliefs. Like many pious Victorian novelists, Kingsley risks long, prosaic discussions of theological questions: a chapter such as "Miracles and Science" (*Alton Locke,* ch. XXXVIII) hardly allows a second voice in the "conversation"—it is simply a sermon or tract, printed between quotation marks. But Kingsley's characters, like his readers, are only marginally influenced by such prose chapters, which serve mainly to give a theological context to their personal struggles. The central elements in the development of belief are represented unfailingly, as psychological, rather than as logical. Kingsley's first novel *Yeast,* be-

gins in the documentary mode, dealing with foxhunting, rural pauperism, and the dangers of celibacy, but the hero Lancelot Smith finds faith and hope, not in theological discussion, but in a "very mythical and mysterious dénouement"; deprived of his inheritance, alone in London, his fiancée dead of typhus, Lancelot takes refuge in the echoing shell of St Paul's Cathedral, and recovers faith from a Faust-like dialogue with a mysterious prophet Barnakill. Even though Kingsley wrote this conclusion while he was ill and under pressure from his publisher to conclude the novel, he did not substantially alter it when he revised the story for book publication in 1851. He tried, however, to explain it, and his explanation was that it portrayed his understanding of the Victorian mind:

> Do not young men think, speak, act, just now, in this very incoherent, fragmentary way; without methodic education or habits of thought; with the various stereotyped systems which they have received by tradition, breaking up under them like ice in a thaw; with a thousand facts and notions, which they do not know how to classify, pouring in on them like a flood?—a very Yeasty state of mind altogether, like a mountain burn in a spring rain, carrying down with it stones, sticks, addled grouse-eggs and drowned kingfishers, fertilizing salt and vegetable poisons.

This lesson, which had in a sense been forced on Kingsley by the circumstances in which he wrote his first novel, became the central insight of several of his later books. Even though Alton Locke has the problem of miracles explained to him by a Dean's daughter, his real development comes in the chapter entitled "Dreamland", where, in a delirious fever, he recapitulates the evolutionary process, and gains the hope to lead the enslaved people of the plain through the mountain pass to the good land. Kingsley's hero dreams himself to be a crab without a shell nearly seventy years before Eliot's *Prufrock*. In Kingsley's last "social novel", also, the crucial experiences of the central characters are surreal: *Two Years Ago* is a study of the hopelessness of attempting self-sufficiency; Elsley Vavasour (the druggist's apprentice, turned Shelleyan poet) struggles to evade his honest rescuers, while attempting suicide on a storm-swept Welsh mountain; and Tom Thurnall discovers his own weakness as a Turkish prisoner during the Crimean war, incarcerated by his own side. *The Water Babies,* of course, is wholly constructed as a dream-allegory. The point about such dreams, and dream-like or nightmare-like experiences, is that they form the heart of each novel, a focus for the imaginative method of the novel as a whole. For Kingsley, as he wrote in the epilogue to *Yeast,* "every human being is a romance, a miracle to himself now". It is the mysterious and the miraculous about human minds that Kingsley's visionary style was intended to represent.

The importance of dream-experience and the surreal in Kingsley's social fiction is, I think, the key to his developing interest in historical subjects. It is noteworthy that several Victorian poets made a similar development, from a direct confrontation with Victorian life to the indirect exploration of the human mind through historical narrative. Historical romance, after all, has much in common with

Under the crag where the ouzel sings,
And the ivied wall where the church-bell rings,
Undefiled, for the undefiled ;
Play by me, bathe in me, mother and child.

Dank and foul, dank and foul,
By the smoky town in its murky cowl ;
Foul and dank, foul and dank,
By wharf and sewer and slimy bank ;
Darker and darker the farther I go,
Baser and baser the richer I grow ;
Who dare sport with the sin-defiled ?
Shrink from me, turn from me, mother and child.

Strong and free, strong and free,
The floodgates are open, away to the sea,
Free and strong, free and strong,
Cleansing my streams as I hurry along,
To the golden sands, and the leaping bar,
And the taintless tide that awaits me afar.
As I lose myself in the infinite main,
Like a soul that has sinned and is pardoned again.
Undefiled, for the undefiled ;
Play by me, bathe in me, mother and child.

LEAR and cool, clear
and cool,
By laughing shallow, and dreaming pool ;
Cool and clear, cool and clear,
By shining shingle, and foaming wear ;

Song of the river in Kingsley's Water-Babies. *Illustrations by Linley Sambourne.*

the dream—its incidents both are and are not the same as in our waking, non-reading life. In historical fiction, Kingsley was able to integrate his visionary insights into a more unified style and texture.

Even in the social novels, stylistic ventriloquism had been one of the means by which Kingsley could find imaginative release: one of the most moving parts of **Yeast** borrows the form of a folk-song, and **Alton Locke** is wholly cast as Alton's own autobiography, thus allowing Kingsley the author to write as a poet, a radical, and a sceptic without compromising Kingsley the clergyman. The borrowed historical styles of **Westward Ho!** and of Hereward the Wake serve something of the same function—caught up in the romance of history, we adopt, rather than criticize, the morality of the actors. In **Hypatia,** the most under-rated of Kingsley's novels, it is in the borrowed style of an "unpublished fragment of the *Hagiologia Nilotica* of Graidiocolosyrtus Tabenniticus" that Kingsley brings off one of his boldest and weirdest strokes, when a dead monk and nun are found embracing in a desert grave:

> For in the open grave lay the body of Philammon the abbot: and, by his side, wrapt in his cloak, the corpse of a woman of exceeding beauty such as the Moors had described. Whom embracing straitly, as a brother a sister, and joining his lips to hers, he had rendered up his soul to God; not without bestowing on her, as it seemed, the most holy sacrament; for by the grave-side stood the paten and chalice emptied of their divine contents.

Clearly, Kingsley enjoys the lack of comprehension of the scene felt by his fictional monkish chronicler: clearly also there is an allegory to the scene, representing the end of the Alexandrian church, driven out by the new fanaticism: but the "legend" is far more compelling than any of Kingsley's brusque analyses of Church history earlier in the book.

In 1903, in one of the most influential books about the early Victorian novel, Louis Cazamian praised Kingsley as "a gifted writer" who "gives definitive view of the most vital aims and ideals of his time, under the guise of fiction" [Cazamian, *The Social Novel in England: 1830-1850*]. Sometimes, Kingsley himself seems to have gone along with such a propagandist view of his fiction: he wrote to F. D. Maurice in 1862, about **The Water-Babies,** "if I have wrapped my parable in seeming Tom-fooleries, it is because so only could I get the pill swallowed". But the idea of Kingsley as a healthy and strong-minded propagandist is one which will stand up to the evidence of neither his biography nor his writings: both show a strain of interesting neurosis. In 1852 he wrote that "as a child I never could distinguish dreams from imaginations, imaginations from waking impressions . . . in ill health, I had spectral illusions often . . . accompanied by frightful nervous excitability". Kingsley claimed that tobacco had released him from such spectres, but his life was plagued with ill-defined bad health (as during the writing of **Yeast**). The creative strangeness of Kingsley's fiction comes from the recurrence of such dreams and imaginations. The sugar-on-the-pill analogy so often used for "religious fiction" (and implicit in much discussion of social novels) will not do justice to the real imaginative strength of his writing. Now, a hundred years after his death, we can begin to see that the novels of Kingsley, far from being ideas "under the guise of fiction", were the medium through which he, like other Victorians, discovered the miraculous dream-world of the developing mind. (pp. 8-15)

> *P. G. Scott, "Kingsley as Novelist," in* Theology: A Monthly Review, *Vol. LXXVIII, No. 655, January, 1975, pp. 8-15.*

Henry R. Harrington   (Autumn 1977)

[*In the following essay, Harrington examines scenes involving sports as symbols of fall and redemption in Kingsley's works, focusing especially on the author's conception of the "manly Christian" who is redeemed through "feminine virtue."*]

In 1858 an anonymous reviewer for *Tait's Edinburgh Magazine* [(February 1858)] attacked Charles Kingsley (as a disciple of Thomas Carlyle) for creating a religion of physical force in his novels. The reviewer dubbed the religion "muscular Christianity." Sensing the fractious possibilities of the phrase, the Victorian reading public took it up with enthusiasm, and it continued to suggest what was considered to be an excessive emphasis on physical strength in the novels of Kingsley and his close friend, Thomas Hughes.

In applying the phrase to Kingsley's fiction, the *Tait's* reviewer focused on its most arresting scenes—those of sport and violence. He was appalled by what he interpreted in them as an open appeal to a "might makes right" morality. Kingsley, for his part, was appalled by this interpretation of his work. He subsequently disowned the phrase "muscular Christianity," calling it "utterly immoral and intolerable." What he particularly disliked about "muscular Christianity" was the license it implied: "The appetite for evil as well as good, [is] more huge, just in proportion to the native force and massiveness of the soul. The doctrine may seem dangerous, like many truths, and woe to those who, being unlearned and unstable, wrest it to their own destruction; and presume upon it to indulge their own passions under Byronic excuses of 'genius,' or 'muscular Christianity' " [Kingsley, ***The Roman and the Teuton: A Series of Lectures Delivered before the University of Cambridge***, 1875]. Kingsley's heroes are all endowed with "native force and massiveness of the soul," which he elsewhere calls "masculine virtue." This virtue is tested in his realistic fiction in the sporting scenes, and in his historical fiction in both the sporting and battle scenes. But, as he explained, such virtue has little to do with being "a gentleman, much more a Christian" [Kingsley, ***The Gospel of the Pentateuch and David***].

Distinguishing Kingsley's "manly Christian" from the "muscular Christian" is the check to his "passions" by "feminine virtue"—the "common duties of morality and self-restraint" (***The Gospel***). Thus, for Kingsley, it is not might that makes right, but the suspension of might in the name of "feminine virtue." It is not easy for the manly Christian athlete to deny the attraction of the sporting moment—escape from the frustrations of everyday social existence and from sexual anxiety. To leave the exalted sporting moment and return to these frustrating realities amounts to a fall. Finally, however, because of "feminine virtue," it is a fortunate fall. Within Kingsley's private theodicy, the fallen athlete and the manly Christian are one in a fictional world redeemed by his faith in "feminine virtue."

Three of Kingsley's six novels are set in Victorian England: *Yeast* (1848), *Alton Locke* (1850), and ***Two Years Ago*** (1857). The subject matter of each is determined largely by the purpose or social problem which it addresses. But apart from the specific social problem, there appears an occasional sporting scene distinct from the rest not only in subject matter but also in tone. The moral of the sporting scene and the novel, however, is inevitably the same—escape from the difficulties that beset Victorian society and self is impossible.

In ***Two Years Ago,*** this moral is used to distinguish two kinds of mountain climbers, one who seeks to escape his social and domestic responsibilities, the other who seeks to affirm them. Elsley Vavasour, a Romantic poet, is the escapist; Wynd and Naylor, Cambridge boating men, are his opposites. Elsley, mistakenly convinced that his wife has been unfaithful, climbs a pass in Snowdonia on his way to flee England and his family; but "he had gone out of his way for many a year to give himself up, a willing captive, to the melodramatic view of Nature, and had let sights and sounds, not principles and duties, mould his feelings for him." A victim of his own "Byronic excuses," he becomes a "puppet of his own self-created fantasies." Wynd and Naylor, the "manly Christians," pursue Elsley in order to return him to his family; they are "far more 'poetic' characters [than he] . . . because they are hazarding their lives, on an errand of mercy." Unlike Elsley, their moral perception remains clear and disinterested in the face of "Nature's melodrama."

Not only are they climbing with purposes beyond mere exercise, but also, once on the mountain, all the characters have stepped out of ordinary reality into an extraordinary topography. For Elsley the mountain becomes "the peak of Caucasus"; for Wynd and Naylor it is moral ground upon which their "errand of mercy" is accomplished. The unreality of the scene is heightened by the fact that Elsley, by any logical account, should have gone down the mountain, not up. The fact that Wynd and Naylor think at the time "that hunting a mad poet over the mountains is, on the whole, 'the jolliest lark they ever had in their lives,' " does not mitigate the moral significance of their climb. Rather, their response demonstrates their adaptation to the internal logic of the climb. It is an expression of freedom, not from "principles or duties" as Elsley thought, but for voluntary selfless activity. To call the climb a "lark" merely recognizes this quality.

The setting of the manly Christian activity establishes a special context in which moral problems within the real world can be temporarily resolved by physical exertion.

The manner in which that setting is regarded determines the ultimate success or failure of the characters acting within it. Kingsley portrays the difference between Elsley and the Cambridge pair not only in terms of physical strength, but also in terms of corresponding moral perception. Elsley is weakened both by opium and by a subjective notion of cultural rejection in the name of "Nature." Wynd and Naylor are strengthened by an "objective" (by which Kingsley means moral) notion of common humanity.

The ethical relevance of Wynd and Naylor's climb derives from two forms of commitment: the shared sense of community within the male fraternity of climbers, and the domestic ties between a man and his wife that they seek to enforce. Except for their separate names, Wynd and Naylor are indistinguishable. In part, this is no doubt the result of lazy characterization, but it also speaks to Kingsley's belief that by sport one can transcend self. What is peculiar about Wynd and Naylor is that even off the mountain they are indistinguishable. Moreover, the scene in which they pursue Elsley differs from Kingsley's usual sporting scenes in the fact that Wynd and Naylor are serving rather than escaping domestic ties.

These, then, are not ordinary sportsmen. Part of the reason for their difference lies with the fact that they are graduates of Thomas Arnold's Rugby School. Kingsley was a great friend of Thomas Hughes, the author of *Tom Brown's School Days* (1857), and in Wynd and Naylor he portrayed Hughes's kind of athlete—one who acts according to an Arnoldian sense of religious and practical duty in a social environment perfectly compatible with sport. It is as difficult to imagine Wynd and Naylor outside Snowdonia as to imagine Tom Brown, without the drastic changes that occur in his character in *Tom Brown at Oxford,* outside Rugby. Snowdonia, like Rugby, is a world unto itself, regulated by morality rather than political, economic, or sexual necessity. If Wynd and Naylor had accompanied the major characters out of Snowdonia, they would have had to confront the larger and vastly more complex world of Kingsley's novel that includes slavery, poverty, cholera, and love. Viewed in terms of this "real" world of *Two Years Ago,* Wynd and Naylor, instead of expressing social commitment, duty to one's suffering fellow man, are escaping it. Kingsley precludes this interpretation by not removing his two sportsmen from their ideal world. But elsewhere in his novels, the paradox of the socially committed athlete forces Kingsley to abandon Hughes's schoolboy idealism for a domestic realism which pits sport against necessity, escape against responsibility. The contest provokes a resolution that makes the descent from the mountain look more like a fall into "reality."

This is the case in *Alton Locke.* Gazing in an aimless way at the river Cam, Alton, the working-class poet-hero, spots Lillian Winnstay on the bank opposite. Lillian, the daughter of a cathedral dean, is far removed from Alton by her social class, and the "accursed" river which separates them symbolizes that gap. The river, however, is suddenly transformed by a University boat race: "I . . . felt my soul stirred up to a sort of sweet madness . . . by the loud fierce pulse of the rowlocks, the swift whispering rush

of the long snake-like eight oars, the whirl and gurgle of the water in their wake, the grim, breathless silence of the straining rowers." The river turns into a medium for the expression of the very things moments before it had formed a barrier against—sexual excitement and classless love ("My blood boiled over, and fierce tears swelled into my eyes; for I, too, was a man, and an Englishman.")

The key to the scene is Alton's identification with the rowers. By it he becomes a participant in the sport, where before he was a spectator alienated from the setting by his class feelings and sexual frustration. For a moment his working-class sentiments, the basis for his social self-consciousness, are overcome by empathy with the rowers before him. "I, too, was . . . an Englishman," he discovers. But beneath this democratic affirmation of his Englishness is thinly veiled sexual excitement, which complicates the otherwise simple message of the scene.

Alton's alienation from Lillian is not only the product of class differences, but also of self-created inhibitions ("I would have plunged across but there were three objections"). These inhibitions are overcome by transferring his desire for Lillian to the sporting competition before him. In identifying with the rowers, he finds release for his desire in "the loud fierce pulse of the rowlocks," "the long snake-like eight oars," and, finally, his "blood boiled over." Exciting and fulfilling as the scene may be for Alton, it is, nonetheless, an escape—escape from his desire for Lillian, from the London ghetto from which he comes and for which he is the chosen spokesman, and from "feminine virtue." It is not Alton's sexual excitement that concerned Kingsley; he regarded such excitement or "impulse" as entirely appropriate to those "rare moments of life, in which our life is not manifold, but one—body and soul and spirit working together" [Frances Kingsley, *Charles Kingsley: His Letters and Memories of His Life,* 1877]. Nor is it the image of a working man identifying with members of higher classes that bothered Kingsley; this, after all, was the ideal that Kingsley as reformer and novelist was trying to bring into existence. What concerned Kingsley was that Alton's escape could not be sustained at this point in the novel and still maintain his depth of character and the realism of his social situation. Faced with the momentary paradox of Alton's moral identification with the rowers on the one hand and his social role on the other, Kingsley forcefully returns his hero to the society that lines the banks of the Cam.

A blow on the head from an aristocrat causes Alton's fall back into society. The blow at first appears to be an ironic comment on Alton's crisis and sporting epiphany, but this interpretation does not agree with Kingsley's Christian Socialist message in the novel (translated in Alton's vision as "I, too, was . . . an Englishman"). The most likely interpretation of the blow is that it is providential; in 1862 Kingsley revised the scene so that the aristocrat hits Alton by mistake, rather than intentionally. Moreover, as a result of being hit Alton falls down the river bank into the river, a purgative ritual that appears with regularity in Kingsley's works as diverse as the fabular *Water Babies* (1863) and the scientific *Glaucus* (1855).

As he scrambles out onto the river bank, Alton receives

Lord Lyndale's apologies with bitterness because of the aristocrat's condescension: "I did not wish, of course, to be a gentleman, or an aristocrat; but I was nettled, nevertheless, at not being mistaken for one." And this, of course, is precisely the purpose of the ritual fall: to replace illusory social relationships with true ones. After the fall Alton undergoes the painful loss of Lillian, years of imprisonment, and sickness; but eventually his travails are rewarded and his manly Christianity assured by Lady Ellerton, who offers him what sport could not—"feminine virtue."

Kingsley clearly did not believe in sport as a way of life for his fellow Victorians, but used it as a means for focusing the social and moral awareness of his characters. His sporting scenes in *Alton Locke, Yeast,* and *Two Years Ago* are isolated moments of transcendence within a realistic framework. They are moments such as he himself experienced when the lifelong burden of stammering was lifted from him and he found he "could speak, not only plain but stentorially, while boxing, rowing, hunting, [and] skating." But his conscience always drew him back to the reality he might like to have left behind—troublesome family relations, financial exigency, clerical hostility, and a host of other problems that exacerbated his stammering and contributed to his several nervous breakdowns.

When he found exception with the "sporting novelists," therefore, he may well have been motivated by both conscientious social concern and well disguised envy of the escape they portrayed. Kingsley felt that R. S. Surtees, the best known of the Victorian "sporting novelists," "willfully" portrayed in *Mr. Sponge's Sporting Tour* (1853) "that uglier and baser side of sporting life" (*Two Years Ago*). Surtees created an image of field sports without defining the ethical or legal boundaries within which the sport is pursued. Mr. Sponge, a Cockney snob, moves with canny and unconscionable lawlessness across property not his own among gulled aristocrats. A descendent of the Regency buck, Mr. Sponge is, according to Kingsley at any rate, an anachronism and an escapist.

Basically, Mr. Sponge is a simple character, but to Kingsley he embodied the paradox of the sportsman. On the one hand, in his enthusiasm for the chase and disregard for class distinctions, Mr. Sponge could be interpreted as a great social unifier and a happy man. Indeed, in **"Letters to Landlords"** [in *The Plain Speaker: or, Politics for the People,* 1837], Kingsley asserts that Englishmen of all classes share an "innate love of sport." But on the other hand, Mr. Sponge, like Alton after he is bumped into the river, acts like a snob. In *Water Babies* Kingsley warns against such men: "Never touch a fish or a head of game which belongs to another man without his express leave; and people will call you a gentleman, and treat you like one . . . instead of hitting you into the river, or calling you a poaching snob." To some extent the contrast between a classless love of sport and class restrictions on the expression of that love is the consequence of Kingsley's increasing conservatism. He was a young man when he wrote **"Letters to Landlords"** and *Yeast.* Then he was far more concerned about landlord abuses and the game laws that

made them possible than about the criminality of poachers. Free trade, the New Poor Law, and a greater familiarity with the local squirearchy did much in later years to weaken the case of poachers in his mind. Behind this superficial change in his political thinking, however, is his abiding distrust of the "innate love" of sport, which can be traced back to *Alton Locke.* In reality Kingsley knew that sport could not for long be the medium for social unity without becoming a mode of escape. A man like Mr. Sponge who capitulated to "innate" desires loses his humanity; a novel like Surtees's which portrays sport as a way of life loses its realism.

Kingsley was, therefore, compelled to create a caricature of Mr. Sponge to demonstrate that not only the demands of conscience, but also of social realism, dictate a fall from the sporting life. Trebooze often "launches out . . . into the sporting conversations of that graceful and lofty stamp which may be perused and perpended in the pages of 'Mr. Sponge's Sporting Tour' " (*Two Years Ago*). But there is little that is humorous in Kingsley's caricature; Pickwickian possibilities are severely restricted by Kingsley's moral end, a retribution for the unpunished excesses of the "sporting tour." For his drunkenness and his unfeeling behavior toward his family, Trebooze finds himself the hunted in the midst of an otter hunt. As the hunt sets out, Trebooze, with a "sudden shudder, a quick half-frightened glance behind him," begins to act like the otter; at the climax of the hunt it is Trebooze, not the otter, who is run to ground and impaled in his own imaginings: " 'The world! The world upside down! . . . I'm falling, falling off into the clouds—into hell-fire'." His fall from the sporting life, however, is not into hell as he fears but, like Elsley's and Alton's, back into the reality of domestic and national life: having rejoined his wife, he signs up for service in the Army.

Trebooze's conversion raises the question that was asked by Kingsley's contemporaries: might not the military be the best place for the manly Christian? Indeed, Kingsley implied as much in his historical novels, *Hypatia* (1853), *Westward Ho!* (1855), and *Hereward the Wake* (1866), all three of which are set in wartime. In the realistic novels discussed above, the sporting scenes are extraordinary moments in which the action seems primitive and melodramatic and the characters atavistic (or "hectic and spasmodic" as Leslie Stephen said ["Charles Kingsley," in *Hours in a Library* (1909)]). The social problems set out in these novels were generally not amenable to muscular, active solutions. But the historical novels are set on the frontier of civilization, the edge of history where Victorian *sprezzatura* makes more sense: "[The perfect soldier] should be strong in body . . . ready to face the sun and rain, wind and frost; he should know how to swim for his life, to pull an oar, sail a boat, and ride the first horse which comes to hand" [Kingsley, *Glaucus; or, The Wonders of the Shore,* 1855]. In war the border between ordinary reality and sporting reality becomes less distinct.

Near the beginning of *Hypatia,* a crucial scene marks the passage of the central character, Philammon, from the repressive safety of the fifty-century monastery in which he has grown up into the "untried homeless wilderness before him." Philammon is tempted into the wilderness by dreams of "a whole world of wonders." These dreams are suddenly interrupted by "a man of gigantic stature" harpooning a hippopotamus for sport in the Nile. In this scene the sport offers Philammon not so much escape (or punishment) as initiation into the world.

At first Philammon is absorbed with the action before him, as Alton was; but, then, distracted by the women accompanying the hunters, he becomes entangled in the harpoon line, "and the monster, with its huge white tusks gaping wide, [draws] close on him as he struggle[s] in the stream." Philammon survives by attacking the hippopotamus with a small knife. Unlike Alton's, Philammon's fall into the stream marks his entry into the action rather than his withdrawal from it. Withdrawal from the sporting moment here would be equivalent to withdrawal from the world.

Once again the character's involvement in the scene is precipitated by the sight of women spectators, but the ensuing sexual imagery, a knife penetrating a monster with gaping tusks, is more clearly hostile and aggressive than the imagery in the river scene from *Alton Locke.* In the world which Philammon must face, women, for the most part, are not repositories of domestic virtue, but sexual and intellectual enchantresses. Late in the novel, Kingsley con-

Kingsley's memorial at Eversley.

verts the most infamous woman into a virtuous one and reveals her identity as Philammon's long-lost sister. With her as his companion, Philammon then performs Kingsley's typical withdrawal from the activity of the world and retreats to the desert he came from.

In his attack on John Henry Newman, Kingsley called Newman's followers "hot-headed young men." But Newman pointedly replied: "Hot-headed young men! Why, man, you are writing a Romance. You think the scene is Alexandria [the setting of most of *Hypatia*] or the Spanish main [the setting of *Westward Ho!*], where you may let your imagination revel to the extent of inveracity" [John Henry Newman, "Answer in Detail to Mr. Kingsley's Accusations" in *Apologia Pro Vita Sua: Being a History of His Religious Opinions,* edited by Martin J. Svaglic, 1967]. In terms of historicity, there is some truth to Newman's reply; but Kingsley is not writing history in *Hypatia* so much as allegory, as the subtitle, "New Foes with an Old Face," suggests. Kingsley imposes narrative—not factual—checks on his imagination, and these are in the familiar form of domestic responsibilities. Unlike those that work on the sporting scenes of the realistic novels, however, these do not come into play until the very end of the novel. In the meantime, there is indeed a "revel," and a bloody one at that.

In describing the sporting attitude appropriate to the conditions of war, Kingsley makes a distinction between two varieties of sportsmanship. The sporting bishop of *Hypatia,* Synesius, speaks for Kingsley when he states: "[While still a pagan] I followed the chase by mere nature and inclination. But now [that I am a Christian] I know I have a right to follow it, because it gives me endurance, promptness, courage, self-control, as well as health and cheerfulness." When Synesius explains his Christian "right" to follow the chase, he does so in terms of survival within the charged atmosphere of holy war. As directions for behavior, these terms make sense only on the frontier, only where warfare between man and man and between man and nature is a persistent condition. Kingsley is, therefore, asserting a connection between sport and war. The connection is both consecutive and analogical. Sport trains men for war, and war in itself is a kind of sport.

Johan Huizinga, who has commented extensively on the relationship between sport and war [in his *Homo Ludens: A Study of the Play Element in Culture,* 1966], suggests of the nineteenth century that the absence of obligatory military training then created the need and occasion for sport. Huizinga's thesis finds a good deal of indirect support in manly Christian fiction:

> "Oh you materialist English!" [says an American in *Two Years Ago*], "sporting-mad all of you, from the duke who shooteth stags to the clod who poacheth rabbits."

> "And who therefore can fight Russians at Inkerman, duke and clod alike, side by side" [answers a Pre Raphaelite painter].

Maxim Gorky put it more cynically: "In bourgeois states they utilize sport to produce cannon fodder."

Kingsley's historical novels are attempts to describe the

righteous directions in which this fodder has been aimed. Righteousness is determined by the same manly Christian values that caused the Cambridge mountain climbers to pursue Elsley. One of the crucial tests of masculine virtue Kingsley applies is the degree of playfulness with which war is undertaken. Just as the word "lark" redeems Wynd's and Naylor's motives, and "cheerfulness" redeems Synesius's from any implications of excessive self-importance, in *Westward Ho!* Salvation Yeo's good-humored response to Amyas Leigh's challenge to fight marks his side as the righteous one: " 'He'll do,' said Yeo, 'he will make a brave gamecock in a year or two.' "

The pattern by which the askesis of sport provides a model for war, however, was lost on the critics of manly Christianity: "The logic of the thing is this," said the distressed *Tait's* reviewer, "that by black eyes and bloody noses you settle the right and wrong of a case. . . . Great heroes, great soldiers and sailors, have ever been remarkable for juvenile fisticuffing." But the boyish challenge of Amyas that prefaces *Westward Ho!* clarifies the nature of the war itself; Amyas is merely doing "what a good knight errant would do." And, in that this "sanguinary book" was meant to stir the Victorian spirit during the Crimean War; the stress on competition and adventure in Amyas's challenge contains "a doctrine profitable for these times." Manly Christian sport and war are imbued with this spirit of a romantic ordeal. Kingsley called the Crimean War's effect on the English nation "discipline from heaven" (*Two Years Ago*). In *Westward Ho!* God oversees the contest between the English and Spanish, granting it a kind of seriousness that could not have come from the combatants themselves without making them suspiciously "animal" or "selfish."

Eventually, however, Amyas's wrathful pride interposes between him and God. From that point his virtuous atavism degenerates into brutal and selfish animalism, and he changes from "avenging angel" guided by Heaven to the "cruel and unjust" captain of the *Vengeance*. In the final chapters, Amyas, now blind, performs the ritual fall from the heightened atmosphere of holy war and sport and marries Ayacanora, whose songs rise with "the peaceful thoughts of the blind giant back to the Paradises of the West," where colonial wars are being fought.

In the disclaimer of "muscular Christianity" with which this essay began, Kingsley attacks those who use it to "indulge their own passions"; he almost certainly refers to the "sensation novelist" G. A. Lawrence. Kingsley had several imitators, but Lawrence was probably the most devoted and yet, the least accurate. When Lawrence was done with the manly Christian, all that remained was a male physique and an aura of sexual excitement. Reading *Guy Livingstone* (1857), one reviewer ["*Guy Livingstone*," *Edinburgh Review* (October 1858)] simply could not believe that Lawrence wrote without hidden meaning: "Physical strength [is merely] a piece of symbolism, in which the body represents the mental qualities which [Lawrence] purposes to celebrate." But even if the reviewer were correct, Lawrence supplies neither ethical nor mental coordinates by which to map the relevance of the characters' strength. There is no playfulness in his fiction, nor is there

even sport, a comprehensible context for the characters' strength. Coinciding with the absence of sport is the absence of women to define a domestic context into which his characters might fall. His women are "fair Amazons," "foolish virgins," or "Norse sorceresses," beings as unreal and unmindful of the "common duties of morality and self-restraint" as their male counterparts. But by his neglect of manly Christian constraints, Lawrence proves their value. For his *bêtes humaines* are victims of their own animal nature; their strength is the expression of innate, "blind, brutish ferocity" [George Alfred Lawrence, *Sword and Gown*, 1859] or a "fierce, wild joy [from smelling] the scent of blood" (Lawrence, *Maurice Dering*, 1864).

The relative inability of Lawrence to make sense of physical strength points up the difficulty of Kingsley's experiment in characterization. Without Kingsley's fervid belief in married love, the inducement to fall from the sporting or war-cum-sporting moment vanishes. For Kingsley, marital sex sanctified matter: "Matter is holy, awful glorious matter," Kingsley wrote to his future wife, Frances. "Let us never use those words *animal* and *brutal* in a degrading sense. Our animal enjoyments must be religious ceremonies" [quoted in Susan Chitty, *The Beast and the Monk: A Life of Charles Kingsley,* 1975]. This perhaps is the essential difference between him and an author like Lawrence, to whom the chief value of sex in fiction was the prurient interest it could arouse. Behind Kingsley's conviction that the fall from the sporting moment was desirable lay his ardent advocacy of the idea of the fortunate fall—original sin liberated and marriage saved mankind.

Walter Houghton has called Kingsley's adaptation of the fortunate fall "the liberal fallacy," because it permitted Kingsley to sanctify whatever pleased him in the natural world as he sanctified love and marriage [Walter Houghton, "The Issue between Kingsley and Newman," *Theology Today*, 4 (April 1947)]. While Houghton's analysis remains wholly convincing, it downplays the obvious moral effort it cost Kingsley to discriminate within the natural world. Consciously, Kingsley invoked the delights of marriage to justify the fall from the sporting moment, but unconsciously, this fall manifests the guilt and need for punishment that followed upon the desire to escape heterosexual and domestic reality.

As a Cambridge undergraduate, Kingsley experienced a conversion to Anglicanism; a week before his conversion Frances confessed her love for him. Linked by time, in Kingsley's imagination the two experiences were casually linked as well. Manly Christianity celebrates the coincidence of love and conversion by the fall from the sporting moment. The year prior to his conversion by love of woman, Kingsley had tried dissipating his sexual anxiety by throwing himself into athletics. Later that same year, weighed down by guilt for having gone with a prostitute, he considered becoming a Catholic monk: "I would have . . . confessed every sin of my whole life before the monks and offered my naked body to be scourged by them." After his conversion, Catholicism became oddly connected in his mind with athletics; they were opposed, extreme responses to sexuality, but both were characterized by celibacy.

Thus, when Kingsley attacked John Henry Newman, he was attacking him as a figure of his own guilt. Paradoxically, he wished to place Newman in the camp next to his soldier-athletes. "I cannot be weak enough," he wrote after the publication of the *Apologia,* "to put myself a second time, by any fresh act of courtesy, into the power of one who [acts] like a treacherous ape." Kingsley's simian interpretation of Newman's behavior recalls his own guilty judgment of himself as he tried to channel his sexual desire into sport—"utterly animal" he called it finally. According to Kingsley, Newman inhabited a haven for celibate priests who enchained you so that "you must go back again and again for self-forgetfulness." The attraction that such an all-male haven of self-forgetfulness held for Kingsley is registered in his sporting scenes. Its personal threat is in the "misery and shame [it spread] into many an English home" (Kingsley, "What, then, does Dr. Newman mean?" in Newman, *Apologia*)—that is, in its willful and sustained disregard for "feminine virtue." Thus Kingsley, as he attacked Newman for trying to circumvent "the brute male force of the wicked world which marries and is given in marriage," was describing the dangers of celibate passivity in terms similar to those he used to describe the dangers of Lawrence's love of violence. Both were extreme responses to sexuality that avoided the saving fall from celibacy and "self-forgetfulness" into marriage.

Reading Kingsley, one realizes that, estranged though he and his enemies doubtless were, the real estrangement was within himself. Opposing sides of his own personality are represented by the split between masculine and feminine virtue, sport and domesticity, instinct and responsibility. The dilemma of his life and excitement of his fiction come from his capacity to hear voices within himself from both sides of the split. The fallen athlete at peace with himself, hearing only the voice of responsibility, is an ideal his creator never attained. The sense of loss Leslie Stephen describes after Kingsley's death was shared, while he lived, by Kingsley himself: "In these days [1876], when the Viking or Berserker element seems to be dying out of our literature, even [Kingsley's] qualified and external worship of masculine vigour is valuable. . . . It implies an homage to more healthy ideals." (pp. 73-86)

Henry R. Harrington, "Charles Kingsley's Fallen Athlete," in Victorian Studies, *Vol. 21, No. 1, Autumn, 1977, pp. 73-86.*

John C. Hawley, S.J. (essay date 1989)

[*Hawley is an American educator and critic specializing in Victorian and Modern British literature. In the following essay, he examines* The Water Babies *as a vehicle for instruction designed by Kingsley to address nineteenth-century social concerns as well as the Darwinian theory of evolution. Hawley notes that Kingsley's treatment of adult themes in this children's fantasy served as a model for such later fiction writers as Lewis Carroll and J. R. R. Tolkien.*]

Does not each of us, in coming into this world, go through a transformation just as wonderful as that of a sea-egg, or a butterfly? and do not reason and analogy, as well as Scripture, tell us that transformation is not the last? and that, though what we shall be, we know not, yet we are here but as the crawling caterpillar, and shall be hereafter as the perfect fly.

(*The Water-Babies*)

Tutor to the Prince of Wales and first Professor of Modern History at Cambridge University, Charles Kingsley (1819-75) was well-known in his own day as an educator and as a strong advocate for Thomas Arnold's educational reforms. Kingsley became especially vocal as a proponent of the Greek ideal of forming a sound mind in a sound body—so vocal, in fact, that his suggestion that sports should play a major role at Eton, Harrow, and the other training grounds for the leaders of the Empire became caricatured as "muscular Christianity."

As the tag suggests, however, the goal of education for Kingsley, whether it was to be education of the mind or of the body, was ultimately religious. He was, after all, an Anglican clergyman and chaplain to Queen Victoria, and the emphasis in his pedagogy is highly moral: while granting that any knowledge, even religious, must be based on observation, he writes that the principal aim of education is to "enable us hereafter to make ourselves and all around us, wiser, better, and happier." If more empirical knowledge does not produce a better human being, it comes under Kingsley's attack.

Furthermore, like Dickens in *Nicholas Nickleby* (1839) and *Hard Times* (1854), he worries that schools have been taken over by the "reforming," statistics-minded educators—the Gradgrinds and the M'Choakumchilds. What is required to reverse this deadening trend, he feels, is not more "facts" but a love of learning, and this can best be nurtured by exploiting the child's natural inclination for the fanciful. At the same time, in preparation for the highly moralistic goal that Kingsley sets for education, the student must first be *taught* to see. While encouraging the development of the imagination, therefore, Kingsley did not conceive of children's literature as a refuge from the real world. It was to be a non-threatening, imaginative preparation for the assumption of one's Christian responsibilities in a world of real, complex, and sometimes fearsome adult problems. "Correct" perceptions in childhood—that is, perceptions that had been coached and clarified by the narrator—would prompt strong emotions in the young reader; these emotions, in turn, would compel moral actions in the same readers as adults.

Charles Kingsley was best known in his own day as a preacher and as the author of six highly polemical novels. Since he held such strong views on the philosophy of pedagogy, however, it is not surprising that he is today most widely appreciated as the author of a delightful children's book. Since it was written, in 1863, *The Water-Babies* has been dramatized, animated, filmed, and televised, and many adults, if they know nothing at all about Kingsley's other works, still fondly recall the compelling fantasy of this story, the fine original illustrations by Linley Sanbourne (who became, in 1900, the chief cartoonist for

Punch), and the even happier world that Jessie Willcox Smith evoked with her colorful drawings for the 1916 edition. Thirty-five years after its publication his tale of a little boy who plunges beneath the water into a world as colorful as Alice's Wonderland remained among the ten most popular children's books in England, and it is today still available in three editions.

The Water-Babies offers a classic example of children's literature employed to disarm and to teach. C. S. Lewis, J. R. R. Tolkien, Antoine de Saint Exupery and many others after them have used this Kingsleyan model: writing a nonsensical story supposedly for children, fully aware that it will be read aloud by adults. Since Kingsley's own earlier works had been serious and clearly tendentious, *The Water-Babies* surprised many nineteenth-century readers, who enthusiastically welcomed this remarkably light-hearted new novel. As unusual and even quirky as the watery world of Kingsley's novel may be, however, this priest/novelist somehow succeeds in showing readers young and old something very familiar and even comforting in the strange and mysterious, sugaring a pill he considers necessary medicine for his generation of readers.

Una Pope-Hennessey, one of Kingsley's biographers, contends [in "Kingsley as Children's Writer," *TLS* (15 June 1951)] that this approach to children in the literature he wrote for them was new: seeking to "awaken in (them) a sense of wonder, to call out their powers of observation, and teach them 'without their knowing that they were learning.' " Kingsley was the first to succeed in making such instructions entertaining. "Now if you don't like my story," he warns readers of *The Water-Babies,* "then go to the schoolroom and learn your multiplication-table, and see if you like that better. Some people, no doubt, would do so. So much the better for us, if not for them. It takes all sorts, they say, to make a world." This undercutting of a rationalistic reliance on statistics and his ridicule of rote recitation set the tone for much subsequent children's literature in England, and elsewhere—to the delight of many, but to the annoyance of a great many others.

While negative critics generally agree that Kingsley is a natural teacher and praise the energy he inspires in students, they consider his emphasis on sports, fantasy, and play to be distressingly nonacademic, undisciplined, and frivolous. Even his well-known popularity among college students may be naive and dangerous, such reviewers warn. As one critic, with the unfortunate name of Florence Bastard, writes [in "Mr. Kingsley," *Rambler* 3rd ser. 4 (1860)], "Mr. Kingsley's recipe for reforming the world seems to be to travestie fun into earnestness, and earnestness into fun. If any thing heroic or perilous is to be done, his model characters set about it as a matter of 'jolly fun,' whether it be attending on cholera patients or 'hunting a mad poet up Snowdon in a thunderstorm" whilst dining, fishing, or making love, are treated as stern matters of earnest duty." Such critics accuse him of carrying on as though life itself were a foxhunt—"all hard-riding and no *craning* at rights or wrongs." Several years after Kingsley's death, in fact, the *Spectator* [1882] ridiculed his edu-

cational theory as "faith, fighting, and a good digestion," code words for Muscular Christianity.

In one sense, therefore, *The Water-Babies* is a very unscientific little book—certainly it appeared that way in its advocacy of a pedagogy that sought to insure a major role for children's fantasies. Nonetheless, the topic that had preoccupied him for a number of years before he sat down to write *The Water-Babies* was the Darwinian theory of evolution; in the 1860s, in fact, Kingsley became the best-known Darwinian in Cambridge and, like many Victorian clergymen, was an amateur botanist, even calling Darwin his "Master" and sending him specimens for study. As a priest he also clearly saw the dilemma that new scientific theories were posing: "They find," he writes, "that now [that] they have got rid of an interfering God—a master magician, as I call it—they have to choose between the absolute empire of accident, and a lively, imminent, ever-working God." As frivolous as *The Water-Babies* may have seemed to some critics, Kingsley nonetheless forces this grim choice on its young protagonist. Little Tom is not off on some random adventure in nature, escaping the responsibilities of the adult world. He is searching for meaning in nature; he is exploring the possibility that there is a teleology in the world around him.

Like many of his contemporaries, Kingsley did not see that the findings of science had yet justified an untroubled belief that a "divine element" did, in fact, underlie physical nature; but, in an effort to keep the door open to that possibility, he became increasingly insistent that science and religion should at least avoid overstepping the legitimate boundaries of their respective disciplines. He seems to have found children's literature an especially appropriate forum to demonstrate these boundaries. Insisting in *The Water-Babies* that empirical knowledge and revealed knowledge could coexist in the unbiased mind—the mind of a child—he pointedly reminds readers that a lack of imagination could prejudice one's observations. Adults, in Kingsley's view, tend to see what they expect to see, but children, surprised at every turn, can use their imaginations to see the world and its possibilities anew. With the publication of this novel he offers his most attractive, deceptively simple presentation of the argument that all purely scientific explanations of reality would benefit by being placed in the larger context of Christian revelation.

The underlying message in little Tom's evolutionary adventures is that science must be especially careful not to trample on the realms of imagination and religion. "You must not say that this cannot be, or that that is contrary to nature," the narrator warns. "You do not know what nature is, or what she can do; and nobody does; not even Sir Roderick Murchison, or Professor Owen, or Professor Sedgwick, or Professor Huxley, or Mr. Darwin, or Professor Faraday, or Mr. Grove, or any other of the great men whom good boys are taught to respect. . . . That is a very rash, dangerous word, that 'cannot'; and if people use it too often, the Queen of all the Fairies, who makes the clouds thunder and the fleas bite, and takes just as much trouble about one as about the other, is apt to astonish them suddenly by showing them, that though they say she cannot, yet she can, and what is more, will, whether they approve or not." In Kingsley's view, God is ultimately this "Queen of all the Fairies," but in the meantime "the great fairy Science" was in the ascendant and "likely to be queen of all the fairies for many a year to come."

This is why the essentially religious conversion in *The Water-Babies* suggests to Kingsley the graphically physical imagery of the Darwinian theory of evolution, and also helps explain his apparent preference for a roundabout method for the "catechetics" of this novel. As a storyteller he does not wish to prove his contentions in any strictly logical way; he merely wishes to make assertions, demonstrate their import, and hope the fine points can be overlooked by those who are moved by the moral lesson. "More and more do I see daily," he writes, "the tremendous truth that all our vaunted intellect is nothing—nothing but a noble mechanism, and that the source of feeling is the *soul*. This thought begins to explain to me the mysteries of moral responsibility and moral culture." Those who were *not* in full agreement with Kingsley, of course, vehemently attacked his latitudinarian theology and his "lax" pedagogy.

Eventually, all of Kingsley's social concerns find their way into the nonsense of this children's story, including such unlikely topics as celibacy, sanitation reform, and French communism. His various biases are there, too, and he attacks lawyers, the Gothic revival, aesthetes, Roman Catholics, Jews, Americans, and the Irish. Written in a very brief time, with no apparent effort and at the virtual end of his writing career, *The Water-Babies* is therefore at least as rhetorical as any other story penned by this contentious clergyman—who entered into his disastrous encounter with John Henry Newman just one year following its publication. But the *central* story that Kingsley is telling in this novel is one that motivated his Christian Socialism: the story of personal conversion. Charting the progress of that change is Kingsley's quite serious purpose.

Conversion is described in the Judaeo-Christian tradition as a two-step process: a turning away from sin (*metanoia*) and a turning towards God (*epistrophe*). It involves a re-education and re-direction of one's life, and that process guides Kingsley's narrative. Tom begins as a little boy who has never bathed, a chimney sweep who can neither read nor write, totally oblivious to the existence of God, Christ, or prayer. His conversion begins, as did Adam's, when he discovers that he is "dirty" ("a little, ugly, black ragged figure, with bleared eyes and grinning white teeth"). The first half of the novel describes Tom's flight from this former life of enslavement to soot and filth.

Kingsley describes this metanoia as a kind of regression, however, a degradation that should not be the final end of Tom's journey. The second half of the story describes his courageous decision to re-enter the world from which he has fled and to confront his former enslaver. The true test of his conversion, in Kingsley's mind, is his ability to accept his former enemy as a brother, as one who merits Tom's forgiveness. "For you know," the novelist writes, "no enemies are so bitter against each other as those who are of the same race; and a salmon looks on a trout, as some folks look on some little folks, as something just too much like himself to be tolerated."

Kingsley's theme will impress today's reader as overly didactic and even obvious, coming from the pen of an Anglican priest. It was not only *religious* ideals, however, that assumed a more important place than rote memorization in his literature for children. True human conversion (as opposed to the degeneration that is also described in *The Water-Babies*) demanded not only a lively moral sense, but strong, healthy bodies as well. For Kingsley, it is false asceticism and heresy to conceive of the body as a burden or a distraction in prayer. It is an insult to the Creator and a perversion. So he teaches his young protagonist that it is "foolish fathers and mothers" who keep children "always at lessons . . . till their brains [grow] big, and their bodies [grow] small, and they [are] all changed into turnips, with little but water inside." Such vegetables could not fight the good fight.

Surprisingly, however, Kingsley enfleshes the mysteries and onerous responsibilities of a muscular Christian in a guiding feminine spirit, part mother, part angel, part Christ—a Mrs. Bedonebyasyoudid, who follows Tom, the little protagonist, in his various adventures. She teaches him to accept not only the beautiful diversity of the world, but also the possibilities of personal and social development, and gently reminds him of his duty to change his world for the better. Significantly, she becomes Kingsley's principal metaphor for social, religious, *and,* in the implied dialogue with scientists, physical evolution, and embodiment of the symbiosis that this naturalist and clergyman believed to be the central mystery of creation. Anticipating the twentieth-century priest/paleontologist, Pierre Teilhard de Chardin, Kingsley's Mrs. Bedonebyasyoudid shows that religious evolution is a necessary function of continued physical evolution: Jesus of Nazareth is a sign of things to come.

Written with less difficulty than any of his other novels, *The Water-Babies* demonstrates Charles Kingsley's deep-seated hope that human evolution, physical and social, will not end with everything "eternally eating everything," but leads, in fact, to the Kingdom of God. Some of Kingsley's readers would have considered such a conclusion to be naive, and he must have hoped that, through child-like "nonsense," such a possibility might be freshly entertained. "But remember always," he concludes, "as I told you at first, that this is all a fairy tale, and only fun and pretence: and, therefore, you are not to believe a word of it, even if it is true."

Kingsley tells his mentor, Frederick Denison Maurice, almost defensively, that "if I have wrapped up my parable in seeming Tom-fooleries, it is because so only could I get the pill swallowed by a generation who are not believing with anything like their whole heart, in the Living God." The message he hopes the story will convey, one which he aims not only at children but also at scientists and "laity" alike, is that "there is a quite miraculous and divine element underlying all physical nature." Without offering greater clarity than this mystical reading of nature, *The Water-Babies* embodies this central tenet of natural theology.

Despite the negative criticism of its pedagogical method, the book was generally accepted for what it is: an imaginative endorsement of contemporary evolutionary theory which seeks to leave its readers open to the possibility of divine intervention and revelation. "The publication of the above work," writes the *Anthropological Review* [1863], ends one era in British biological literature, and will open now "a new vista of contemplation." It is interesting that a book supposedly written for children would be reviewed by such a journal and would be included by them in the category of "biological literature." Nonsensical or not, the novel's science was apparently taken quite seriously by Kingsley's contemporaries.

Beyond the pleasant introduction to evolutionary theory that the novel offers, however, and serving as the rationale for the novelist's placid acceptance of a teleology in nature, is what might be called the catechetics of Christian Socialism. Far from a casuistic anticipation of every conceivable theological question, it turns its attention to the "larger" world of the individual believer. The moral of his parable, Kingsley writes, is not a set of answers to difficult theoretical questions, nor can it be summed up in an apothegm. Instead, Kingsley offers the reader one more story: this time, of newts in a pond. These helpless little creatures, he writes, are in fact the water-babies who have not yet found the courage and strength to convert first to land-babies, and then to men. "They never did anybody any harm," he writes, "or could if they tried; and their only fault is, that they do no good—any more than some thousands of their betters"; they should therefore be cared for and strengthened, not judged. If this is naive, Kingsley seems to suggest, then so be it. He concludes his catechetics of evolution with a call for mercy for those too heavily-burdened or too morally retrograde to do any better, and with an invitation to his readers to wake up to responsibilities that fall naturally on the shoulders of the strong. (pp. 19-21)

> *John C. Hawley, S.J., " 'The Water-Babies' as Catechetical Paradigm," in* Children's Literature Association Quarterly, *Vol. 14, No. 1, Spring, 1989, pp. 19-21.*

FURTHER READING

Bibliography

Harris, Styron. *Charles Kingsley: A Reference Guide.* Boston: G. K. Hall, 1981, 163 p.

> Extensive, annotated bibliography of writings about Kingsley through 1978.

Biography

Chitty, Susan. *The Beast and the Monk: A Life of Charles Kingsley.* London: Hodder and Stoughton, 1974, 317 p.

> Examines numerous previously unpublished love letters that Kingsley wrote to his wife, effecting what Chitty considers "a fuller and more intimate picture of Kingsley than any that has till now appeared."

Kendall, Guy. *Charles Kingsley and His Ideas.* London: Hutchinson & Co., 1947, 190 p.

> Examines Kingsley's life and literary career, tracing the development of his social and religious thought.

Kingsley, Fanny, ed. *Charles Kingsley: His Letters and Memories of His Life.* 2 vols. London: H. S. King, 1877.

> Compilation of Kingsley's letters and memoirs, edited by his wife.

Martin, Robert Bernard. *The Dust of Combat: A Life of Charles Kingsley.* New York: W. W. Norton & Company, 1960, 308 p.

> Highly regarded critical biography.

Pope-Hennessy, Una. *Canon Charles Kingsley: A Biography.* New York: The Macmillan Company, 1949, 294 p.

> Emphasizes Kingsley's religious ideology and his importance as a social reformer.

Rowse, A. L. "Kingsley at Eversley: Parts I, II, and III." *Contemporary Review* 221, Nos. 1282, 1283 (November 1972; December 1972): 234-38, 322-26; 222, No. 1284 (January 1973): 7-12.

> Brief anecdotal appreciation of Kingsley's life and works, occasioned by Rowse's visit to the site of the author's parish at Eversley.

Thorp, Margaret Farrand. *Charles Kingsley, 1819-1875.* Princeton: Princeton University Press, 1937, 212 p.

> Earliest scholarly biography of Kingsley. Appends an extensive, chronological bibliography "intended to indicate the extent of Kingsley's literary output year by year and also to identify the reviews, articles and poems which he published anonymously in various periodicals."

Criticism

Baker, William J. "Charles Kingsley on the Crimean War: A Study in Chauvinism." *Southern Humanities Review* IV, No. 3 (Summer 1970): 247-56.

> Examines jingoistic sentiment in *Westward Ho!,* asserting that Kingsley's "attitudes toward English involvement in the Crimean War provide not only a notable study in mid-Victorian chauvinism, but also some insight into the dominant chauvinistic themes which have persisted in the western world for the past hundred years."

Bayne, Peter. "Charles Kingsley." In his *Essays in Biography and Criticism,* Vol. II, pp. 9-51. New York: John W. Lovell, 1881.

> Balanced appraisal of Kingsley's life and writings.

Bodenheimer, Rosemarie. "The Pastoral Argument." In her *Politics of Story in Victorian Social Fiction,* pp. 115-65. Ithaca: Cornell University Press, 1988.

> Includes a discussion of *Alton Locke* as one of a number of Victorian social-problem novels in which "Romantic ideas of nature play major structural roles" as ideological alternatives to various social constructions.

Cazamian, Louis. "Kingsley: Christian Socialism." In his *The Social Novel in England, 1830-1850,* translated by Martin Fido, pp. 241-91. London: Routledge & Kegan Paul, 1973.

> Discusses Kingsley's socio-religious activity as well as

his novels *Alton Locke* and *Yeast* in relation to the intellectual movement of his day.

Cunningham, Valentine. "Soiled Fairy: *The Water-Babies* in its Time." *Essays in Criticism* XXXV, No. 2 (April 1985): 121-48.
Examines multiple meanings—particularly those "in and for its own age"—derived from *The Water-Babies*.

Dawson, Carl. "Polemics: Charles Kingsley and *Alton Locke*." In his *Victorian Noon: English Literature in 1850*, pp. 179-202. Baltimore: Johns Hopkins University Press, 1979.
Characterizes Kingsley as "a sort of mid-century Jeremiah." Dawson discusses the author's activities as a social reformer and missionary clergyman, then presents an explicatory analysis of *Alton Locke*, which he describes as "one of the oddest literary documents of nineteenth-century England."

Dowden, Edward. "Victorian Literature." In his *Transcripts and Studies*, pp. 153-236. London: Kegan Paul, Trench, Trübner & Co., 1910.
Discusses Kingsley's thought and temperament. Of the author's works, Dowden asserts: "much of the high reserve, the mystery and the pathos of art, is lost because Kingsley has an explanation to give of all the problems of life proposed in his books." Nevertheless, he considers Kingsley an important and positive influence on his age.

Hearn, Lafcadio. "Charles Kingsley as Poet." In his *Appreciations of Poetry*, pp. 280-97. New York: Dodd, Mead and Company, 1924.
Laudatory survey of Kingsley's poetry. Asserting that Kingsley wrote some of the best songs as well as the finest examples of English hexameter verse in his day, Hearn concludes that, although like other artists "there is some rubbish" among Kingsley's poetry, "the jewels among that rubbish have a peculiar colour and splendour that distinguish them from everything else written during the same period."

Hope, Norman V. "The Issue Between Newman and Kingsley: A Reconsideration and a Rejoinder." *Theology Today* VI, No. 1 (April 1949): 77-90.
Reply to Walter Houghton's essay, cited below. Hope objects to Houghton's depiction of Kingsley as "a 'whole-hog' apologist for mid-Victorian civilization in all its aspects," and also disagrees with that critic's assessment of the considerations that prompted Newman's conversion to Catholicism.

Houghton, Walter E. "The Issue Between Kingsley and Newman." *Theology Today* IV, No. 1 (April 1947): 80-101.
Contends that the controversy between Kingsley and Newman signifies "the fundamental clash, both then and now, between Protestant Liberalism and Christian Orthodoxy." Houghton examines the influence of Carlyle and Maurice, as well as Kingsley's own temperament, on the author's theology, and notes that the religion he espoused was a "liberal compromise" that sought to reconcile "marriage, business, science, progress, [and] human nature" with "the will of God."

Johnston, Arthur. "The Water Babies, Kingsley's Debt to Darwin." *English* XII, No. 72 (Autumn 1959): 215-19.
Argues that "the genesis of [*The Water-Babies*] lies in three of the topics most heatedly discussed in 1862: the employment of children, primary education and the ex-

amination system, and Darwinism." Johnston focuses especially on Kingsley's moral and religious applications of Darwin's theory of natural selection.

Mallock, M. M. "Charles Kingsley." *The Dublin Review* 107 (July 1890): 1-20.
Biographical and critical study occasioned by the publication of Fanny Kingsley's edition of the *Letters and Memories of the Life of Charles Kingsley*. Mallock asserts that his aim is to present "an examination of that special philosophy of life which has associated itself with the name of Charles Kingsley;—of its source in himself, of its influence on others, and more particularly, of the attitude towards the Catholic Church, which it was the cause of his assuming."

Maurice, F. D. "Mr. Kingsley and the *Saturday Review*." *MacMillan's Magazine* I, No. 2 (December 1859): 116-19.
Defends Kingsley against a reviewer's charges that his opinions and convictions merely mimic those of Maurice and Thomas Carlyle.

Price, J. B. "Charles Reade and Charles Kingsley." *Contemporary Review* 183, No. 1047 (March 1953): 161-66.
Assesses Kingsley's literary achievement, summarizing his works as "only half-satisfactory." Price maintains, however, that the author's "works are full of vigour, beauty, and ardent conception; and it is wonderful that so much art and fancy could be thrown into what is in substance polemical pamphleteering."

Saintsbury, George. "The Novel Since 1850." In his *History of Nineteenth Century Literature, 1780-1895*, pp. 317-41. London: Macmillan & Co., 1923.
Includes a brief survey of Kingsley's works, praising the author's powers of description as "almost unequalled and certainly unsurpassed."

Skelton, Sir John. "Poems From Eversley, By the Rector: A Spring-Tide Study." *Fraser's Magazine* 57 (June 1858): 736-47.
Reviews *Andromeda and Other Poems*, defending Kingsley's verse against charges made by other critics.

Stoddard, Francis Hovey. "The Novel of Purpose." In *The Evolution of the English Novel*, pp. 153-94. New York: The Macmillan Company, 1906.
Describes *Alton Locke* and *Yeast* as "purposeful novels" that "notably advanced the cause of freedom."

Sutherland, J. A. "*Westward Ho!*: 'A Popularly Successful Book.'" In his *Victorian Novelists and Publishers*, pp. 117-32. Chicago: The University of Chicago Press, 1976.
Details the collaborative relationship between Kingsley and the Macmillans in effecting the best-selling success of *Westward Ho!*.

Uffelman, Larry K. *Charles Kingsley*. Boston: Twayne Publishers, 1979, 162 p.
Evaluates Kingsley's literary achievement. Uffelman writes that his work is intended primarily as an introduction to the author's life and works, for those who "know little about him"; for an "audience already familiar with Kingsley and his works," the critic adds, this study is "a review and an interpretation."

Uffelman, Larry K. and Scott, P. G. "Kingsley's Serial Novels: *Yeast*." *Victorian Periodicals Newsletter* IX, No. 4 (December 1976): 111-19.

Examines revisions made in *Yeast* following its serialization in *Fraser's Magazine* and before its first publication in book form. Uffelman and Scott conclude that these revisions demonstrate changes in Kingsley's thought and attitude during this period as well as his awareness of "some of the unevennesses of plot and tone which serial composition had encouraged in his first novel."

Wolff, Robert Lee. "Broad Church." In his *Gains and Losses: Novels of Faith and Doubt in Victorian England,* pp. 251-324. New York: Garland Publishing, 1977.
　　Includes an examination of religious thought in *Hypatia.*

Young, Michael A. "History as Myth: Charles Kingsley's *Hereward the Wake.*" *Studies in the Novel* XVII, No. 2 (Summer 1985): 174-88.
　　Argues that *Hereward* is a "text dedicated to stating and proving a version of history as secular scripture."

Additional coverage of Kingsley's life and career is contained in the following sources published by Gale Research: *Dictionary of Literary Biography,* Vols. 21, 32 and *Yesterday's Authors of Books for Children,* Vol. 2.

Arthur Rimbaud

1854-1891

(Full name Jean Nicholas Arthur Rimbaud) French poet.

For further discussion of Rimbaud's career, see *NCLC*, Volume 4.

INTRODUCTION

Rimbaud is considered one of the most innovative poets in the history of French letters. Although his writing career was brief and his output small, Rimbaud's contributions to the development of the prose poem and his use of the unconscious as a source of literary inspiration anticipated the freedom of form characteristic of much contemporary poetry. Rimbaud's most celebrated works, *Une saison en enfer* (1873; *A Season in Hell*) and *Les illuminations* (1886; *Illuminations*) exemplify the artistic objectives of French Symbolism, a literary movement characterized by a desire to suggest the existence of a transcendent realm of being. Scholars have speculated that Rimbaud's elliptic style, mysterious imagery, and unorthodox metaphysics were influenced by his interest in magic and alchemy. Believing that the poet possessed supernatural powers, Rimbaud advocated the rejection of conventional notions of art and the liberation of the mind from the constraints of logic in order to penetrate the unknown.

Rimbaud was raised in Charleville, a small town near the Belgian border. His parents separated when he was six years old, and Rimbaud was thereafter raised by his mother in a strict religious environment. An overprotective woman, she accompanied her child to and from school, scrupulously supervised his homework, and would not allow him to associate with other boys. While enrolled at the College de Charleville, Rimbaud excelled in all subjects and was considered a brilliant student. His rhetoric professor, Georges Izambard, became a close friend, and under his tutelage Rimbaud avidly read the Romantic and Parnassian poets and strove to emulate their work. In 1870, Izambard abruptly left Charleville, and Rimbaud fled by train to Paris in a desperate search for his mentor but was arrested and jailed for traveling without a ticket. Although Izambard eventually rescued the youth and brought him home, Rimbaud's growing disgust with provincial life drove him away again a few months later. Scholars believe that his experiences as a runaway may have included a brutal incident which strongly altered both his personality and the tone of his work. Allusions to the event are cited in his poem "Le coeur volé," but what actually transpired is unknown, some biographers suggest that he was sexually abused by soldiers. After the incident, Rimbaud renounced his sentimental early verse and wrote poems expressing disgust with life and a desire to escape reality.

In 1871, at the age of seventeen, Rimbaud created an aesthetic doctrine, which he articulated in three letters, two to Izambard and another to a friend, Paul Démeny. The letter to Démeny, now known as the "Lettre du voyant" or "Letter of the Seer," explicates Rimbaud's concept of poetry and his own role as a poet. After tracing the history of the genre, he concluded that only the ancient Greeks and the French poets Louis Racine and Charles Baudelaire—considered the first Symbolist writer—fulfilled his ideals of visionary poetry. Castigating such authors as Alfred de Musset and Victor Hugo for their rigid and archaic writing, Rimbaud declared that the poet must "derange" his senses and delve into his subconscious in order to arrive at truths that transcend language. Rimbaud acknowledged that while this process involves much suffering and introspection, it is necessary to the development of vital and progressive poetry. Soon after writing the "Lettre du voyant," he returned to Charleville. Feeling stifled and depressed, he sent several poems to the renowned poet Paul Verlaine, whose works Rimbaud admired. Verlaine responded with praise and an invitation to visit him in Paris. Before he left, Rimbaud composed *Le bateau ivre* (published 1920; *The Drunken Boat*), a poem evoking a savage universe in which a drifting boat symbolizes Rimbaud's fate as a poet. Although the versification in *The Drunken Boat* is traditional, its daring images and complex metaphors portend the philosophical concerns and fascination with alchemy that appear in his later works.

In Paris, Rimbaud was warmly received by Verlaine's family, but the young poet found them representative of the bourgeois values he disdained and quickly alienated them with his flagrantly anti-social behavior. Verlaine, however, was strongly drawn to Rimbaud, and the two writers began a notorious and stormy liaison. They traveled together in England and Belgium from 1872 to 1873, drinking heavily and brawling constantly. Rimbaud believed that his dissipated behavior was a form of artistic stimulation, and his creativity flourished during this period. He studied Eastern religion and alchemy, denied himself sleep, and took hallucinogenic drugs. During this time, he wrote *La chasse spirituelle,* a work speculated to have later been destroyed by Verlaine's wife. According to Verlaine, this work was Rimbaud's intended masterpiece.

Overwhelmed by Verlaine's suffocating affection, Rimbaud demanded an end to the relationship. In desperation, Verlaine shot Rimbaud, wounding him in the wrist. Verlaine was sentenced to imprisonment for two years, and Rimbaud rejoined his mother at her new home in Roche, a village near Charleville. There he completed *A Season in Hell,* a volume comprising nine prose poems of various lengths. Although some commentators have characterized the work as a chronicle of Rimbaud's tumultuous relationship with Verlaine, others contend that it expresses his contempt for Western civilization and its moral system. Despite controversy concerning whether the book was written before or after *Illuminations, A Season in Hell* is often considered Rimbaud's "farewell to poetry."

In 1873, Rimbaud returned to Paris, where he completed *Illuminations,* a work thought to have been written over the course of two years. In this collection of prose poems, Rimbaud abandoned the rules of syntax and rhythm, and sought to express his radical poetic vision. Critics have proposed diverse interpretations for the unrestrained form and hallucinatory imagery of *Illuminations,* including assertions of Rimbaud's ability to recapture the innocent exuberance of youth and characterizations of the poet as a demonic purveyor of chaos and abomination. Upon completing these poems, Rimbaud gave the manuscript to Verlaine and ceased to write. At the age of nineteen, he decided to seek adventure, and he traveled throughout Europe and Africa. He finally settled in Abyssinia, Ethiopia, where he was believed to have worked as a gunrunner and slave trader. In 1886, Verlaine, assuming his friend was dead, published the manuscript Rimbaud had given him as *"Les illuminations* by the late Arthur Rimbaud." Though Rimbaud later learned of its popular reception and of the Rimbaud "cult" that was developing in Paris, he expressed no interest in returning to his former life. Instead, in an abrupt change from his earlier beliefs, he spoke enthusiastically of marrying and having a son. These dreams went unrealized, however, for he developed

cancer in his right knee and was forced to return to France for medical treatment. His leg was amputated, but the cancer continued to spread, and he died soon after.

Rimbaud is remembered as one of the most precocious talents in modern literature. Bypassing the thorough classical education and the years of imitation and apprenticeship that were typical of poets of his era, he devised an original and compelling theory of poetry and authored two acknowledged masterpieces, all before the age of twenty. This extraordinary literary career, combined with the revolutionary nature of Rimbaud's poetic innovations, his dissipated lifestyle, and his dramatic renunciation of poetry for a life of adventure in Africa, have contributed to a romantic legacy and inspired the adulation of many twentieth-century writers. The authors and artists of the Surrealist movement of the 1920s, for example, glorified both Rimbaud's anti-bourgeois stance and his exploration of the subconscious. Similarly, the novelists and poets of the Beat Generation of the 1940s and 1950s admired Rimbaud for his experimental forms, candid language, and drug-inspired imagery. Writing in 1940, Morton Dauwen Zabel remarked on the numerous and varied interpretations among admirers of Rimbaud: "No poet has invited as many incarnations in the private convenience or beliefs of his students or has become so dramatic an index of the aesthetic divergences of our time."

PRINCIPAL WORKS

Une saison en enfer   (prose poetry)   1873
  [*A Season in Hell,* 1932]
Les illuminations   (poetry and prose poetry)   1886
  [*Prose Poems from "Les Illuminations"* (partial translation), 1932; also published as *Rimbaud's "Illuminations,"* 1953]
Poésies complètes   (poetry and prose poetry)   1895
Le bateau ivre   (poetry)   1920
  [*A Drunken Boat,* 1941]
Complete Works, Selected Letters   (poetry, prose poetry, and letters)   1966

*This work was written in 1871.

George Moore   (essay date 1891)

[*An Irish novelist best known for his* Esther Waters *(1894), Moore is credited with importing the themes and techniques of French Naturalism into English literature. Also an accomplished autobiographer, poet, and dramatist, Moore was active in the Irish Literary Revival of the early twentieth century. As a critic, he sought to judge a work solely for its artistic value, maintaining that this quality was more important than any social or ideological concerns. In the following excerpt, Moore offers early commentary on the life and works of Rimbaud.*]

The poet that death has nipped in the first blossom of his talent, the girl that dies in her bridal month, the first poems, the first kisses, my soul goes out to one as to the other. And I know that I should have proved singularly capable of understanding that young Bohemian who came to Paris composing beautiful verses when he was fifteen, and who in a few years anticipated in some half-dozen prophetic poems all the poetic revolution of the last twenty years. Truly it was but the promise of May, and the blossoms fell before the fruit had begun. The blossoms fell, but those who love beautiful French verses have treasured them: *La Saison en Enfer, Le Bateau Ivre,* "Les Premières Communions," "La Mort des Petits Poux"— strange titles, strange as the poems, strange as the life of the poet—the miraculous boy who came to Paris when he was fifteen, with such a poem as *Le Bateau Ivre* in his pocket—that extraordinary boy who has fled from civilisation, and whose brief life is involved in legend and mystery, fantastic and impenetrable. We know that it befell [Rimbaud] to meet Verlaine almost immediately after his arrival; how or where there are no means of discovering. It is certain, however, that Verlaine was the hourly companion of the younger poet for some years, and it is therefore impossible not to speculate sometimes how much the genius of the poet who has since realised his æstheticism depended on the genius of him who made formal renunciation of the laurel wreath. Rumour has busied itself with this friendship, but little is known—one fact only, and that is written on the sky of palest legend in letters of blood. It is known that one night, in a house of ill-repute in Brussels, in some drunken quarrel that had suddenly sprung up between them, Rimbaud was stabbed by Verlaine. For this crime Verlaine spent two years at Mons. Rimbaud was taken to the hospital, where, after lingering some weeks between life and death, he eventually recovered. The poets only met once again. The account we have of this meeting rings strange and hollow as an old-world story. For the story is that in the years that had divided them Rimbaud had learnt to understand the immediate necessity of repentance, and it was only in the vain slight hope of inducing his friend to follow him into a purer life that he consented to see him again. But Verlaine's hour of grace had not yet come, and he sought to dissuade the young disciple from his resolve to abandon the vain glory of art, and consecrate his life to the redemption of his soul. But Rimbaud closed his eyes and ears to allurements and temptations, bade Verlaine farewell, and left Europe to immure himself for ever in a Christian convent on the shores of the Red Sea; and where it stands on a rocky promontory, he has been seen digging the soil for the grace of God.

The mediævalism of this strange story has always had a singular fascination for me. I have dreamed the meeting of the poets at Stuttgart in many an unwritten poem, and I have seen in many a picture, the desolate convent and the single figure digging in the eastern twilight. The story is singularly romantic, especially when looked at in the light of Verlaine's subsequent conversion and the beauty of his religious poems—poems that take you back to the simple unquestioning faith of mediæval Christianity. Verlaine's genius has quite lately come to be accepted even by the general reader, and we are sure, though poor and afflicted with bodily ill, that he stands on the verge of glory; but of Rimbaud few know anything. The now Christian monk, the whilom scorner of all law, human and divine, left the poetic revolution to be achieved by Verlaine, and all that remains of this Marlowe of 1870 are a few poems and a few fragments; but these are sufficient to show that he carried in his heart all the riches of a great poet. To prove decisively that my words are not vain exaggerations, I need only quote **"Les Premières Communions,"** or **"La Mort des petits Poux."** But I have no wish to prove anything. My object is rather to convey a sensation of this strange boy, and I cannot make more sure of doing this than by quoting a sonnet (never, I believe, before published), written between fifteen and sixteen, before Rimbaud came to Paris:

"Ma Bohème"

(Fantaisie)

Je m'en allais, les poings dans mes poches
    crevées;
Mon paletot aussi devenait idéal;
J'allais sous le ciel, Muse! et j'étais ton féal;
Oh! là, là! que d'amours splendides j'ai rêvées.
Mon unique culotte avait un large trou.
Petit-Poucet rêveur, j'égrenais dans ma course

Ezra Pound on Rimbaud:

After Gautier, France produced, as nearly as I can understand, three chief and admirable poets: Tristan Corbière, perhaps the most poignant writer since Villon; Rimbaud, a vivid and indubitable genius; and Laforgue,—a slighter, but in some ways a finer "artist," than either of the others. I don't mean that he "writes better" than Rimbaud; and Eliot has pointed out the wrongness of Symons's phrase "Laforgue the eternal adult. Rimbaud the eternal child". I wrote five years ago that some of Rimbaud's effects seemed to come as the beauty of certain silver crystals produced by a chemical means the name of which I have since forgotten; Laforgue always knows what he is at; Rimbaud, the "genius" in the narrowest and deepest sense of the term, the "most modern", seems, almost without knowing it, to hit on the various ways in which the best writers were to follow him, slowly. There is no use gassing about these differences; the reader can see the thing itself in the poems. In another stumbling formulation I might say "Laforgue is the last word; he, out of infinite knowledge of all the ways of saying a thing, finds the right one. Rimbaud, when right, does the thing right because he simply can't be bothered to do it anyhow else."

. . . . .

He is serious as Cèzanne is serious. Comparisons across an art are always vague and inexact, and there are no real parallels; still it is possible to think of Corbière a little as one thinks of Goya, without Goya's Spanish, with infinite differences, but with a macabre intensity, and a modernity that we have not yet surpassed. There are possible grounds for comparisons of like sort between Rimbaud and Cèzanne.

Ezra Pound, in The Little Review, *February 1918.*

Des rimes. Mon auberge était à la grande Ourse
Mes étoiles au ciel avaient un doux frou-frou.

Et je les écoutais assis au bord des routes,
Des bon soirs de Septembre où je sentais des
    gouttes
De rosée à mon front comme un vin de vigneur;
Où, rimant au milieu des ombres fantastiques,
Comme des lyres, je tirai les élastiques
De mes souliers blessés, un pied près de mon
    cœur.

Did a child ever write such verse before? I think not. (pp.
96-99)

> George Moore, "Two Unknown Poets (Lafor-
> gue, Rimbaud)," in his Impressions and Opin-
> ions, C. Scribner's Sons, 1891, pp. 95-102.

Edith Sitwell   (essay date 1932)

[*An English poet, biographer, and critic, Sitwell was extremely cognizant of the value of sound and rhythmic
structure in poetry and experimented widely in these
areas of her verse. She first received public attention as
the editor of* Wheels *(1916-21), a series of anthologies
of contemporary poetry that offered readers an alternative to the sentimental work of the popular poets of the
era. Colored with idiosyncratic imagery and highly personal allusions, her own works reflect her belief that
sound and rhythm should take precedence over meaning
in poetry. Accordingly, she composed her poetry to be
spoken aloud and often gave flamboyant recitals of her
works. The author of many volumes of verse, she infused
her later works with social commentary and a deep, religious emotion. Throughout her career, Sitwell also used
her influence to draw attention to younger writers, including Wilfred Owen, Dylan Thomas, and Allen Ginsberg. In the following excerpt from her introduction to
Helen Rootham's 1932 translation of* Les illuminations,
*she praises Rimbaud for "his invention of new prose
rhythms" and discusses his influence, quoting extensively from François Ruchon's 1929 study* Jean-Arthur
Rimbaud, sa vie, son œvre, son influence.*]

Rimbaud's own explanations of his aims are so detailed
that they leave little to be said by any critic. . . .[So] many
valuable studies of his work have been made, not only by
his fellow-countrymen, but also by Mr. George Moore,
Mr. Arthur Symons, Mr. Edgell Rickword, Mr. Peter
Quennell and Mr. Harold Nicolson, to mention only a few
names, that I feel shy about venturing my own opinion.
I can only say that I do not find Rimbaud's innovations
in verse (if they may be called innovations)—his loosening
of the formal structure—as interesting or valuable as his
invention of the new prose rhythms. In the *earlier* verses,
he uses false rhymes again and again, but, to my feeling,
if these are, in most cases, the result of conviction, they
are none the less clumsy and ineffective. The loosening
stretches the line out of its normal shape, often, and this,
again, is unfortunate, since (unless my ear is hopelessly at
fault) any disordering of rhythm is unsuitable to the material of the French language, which seems too light to support it. For this reason, if we except the strange and beautiful **Bateau Ivre,** one of the finest poems in the French

language, and that small but poignant poem, which begins
with the lines:

> Ma faim, Anne, Anne,
> Fuis sur ton âne.

Rimbaud is not to be compared, *technically,* as a poet,
with Baudelaire, although the sour out-of-tune effects of
the dissonances in

> Ma faim, Anne, Anne,
> Fuis sur ton âne.

give—to me, at any rate—the effect of a grinding hard
hunger. But, although we may not, perhaps, compare him
technically, with Baudelaire, his invention is so extraordinary, his power of concentrating visual things into a spiritual essence so high, that he is not only a great writer, but,
also, one of the most powerful influences on the rhythms,
the peculiar expressiveness and the visual sense, of our
time. It cannot, I think, be doubted that the child of sixteen, seventeen, and eighteen, who suffered the last agonies of cold, hunger, and hopeless destitution in the winter
nights of Paris, is the originator of modern prose rhythms,
and the basis from which all speculations of the kind have
arisen. His inventions on these lines are, indeed, nearly as
important as his strange, new, and acrid vision, which
owes something to the misery and destitution he had endured, something to the very fact that he was a child and
saw everything with a child's clear eyesight. His influence
has been, indeed, nothing short of extraordinary. Indeed,
it might be said that Rimbaud is, to modern English verse
and to modern English and American prose poems, what
Edgar Allan Poe was to Baudelaire and Mallarmé.

This influence is, most particularly, to be seen in the early
work of Mr. Aldous Huxley—in the prose poems included
in *Leda,* especially—in certain of my own early works
(such verses as 'Trams', 'Merrygoround', and the 'Drunkard', verses I have not included in my collected poems, because they are too derivative), and in 'Pleasure Gardens',
which comes in the 'Troy Park' section of my *Collected
Poems.* Miss Gertrude Stein has also, consciously or unconsciously, been influenced profoundly by Rimbaud's intense visual activity, and by his powers of dissociation, and
reassociation—his gift for bringing all the attributes of the
world together, irrespective of Time and Place.

If we take these separate passages of Mr. Huxley's, for instance, we shall see how deeply they are influenced both
in form, visual impressibility, and spirit, by Rimbaud.

> There are fine cities in the world—Manhattan,
> Ecbatana and Hecatompylus—but this city of
> Troy is the most fabulous of them all. Rome was
> seven hills of butcher's meat, Athens an abstrac-
> tion of marble—all the East is peopled by masks
> and apes and larvæ. But this city of Troy is most
> of all real and fabulous with its charnel beauty.

> Is not Helen the end of our search—paradisal lit-
> tle world, symbol and epitome of the Great?
> Dawn sleeps in the transparent shadow of roses
> within her ear. The stainless candour of infini-
> ty—far-off peaks in summer and the Milky
> Way—has taken marvellous form in her. The
> Little World has its meteors too, comets and

shadowy clouds of hair, stars at whose glance men go planet-struck. . . .

. . . . .

The geometry of her body had utterly outwitted Euclid, and the Philosophers were baffled by curves of a subtlety infinitely more elusive and Eleusinian than the most oracular speculations of Parmenides. They did their best to make a coherent system out of the incompatible, but empirically established, facts of her. Time, for instance, was abolished within the circle of her arms.

. . . . .

Here are pagodas of diminishing bells. The leopard sleeps in the depth of his rosy cavern, and when he breathes it is a smell of irresistible sweetness; in the bestiaries he is the symbol of Christ in his sepulchre.—The listening conch has collected all the rumours of pantheism. . . .

Miss Stein has, on her part, carried Rimbaud's system of dissociation and reassociation even further than Rimbaud, and much further than Mr. Huxley. In that most extraordinary and, to me, exceedingly beautiful book, *Geography and Plays,* and in certain other works, we find many passages which, whilst they are entirely original in phrase, meaning, thought, and image, are yet, to my belief, most clearly a development of Rimbaud's habit of creating a newer and more poignant reality by the means of dissociation.

Here is an example, for instance:

Gertrude (Mildred's thoughts). 'I have thought very much about heat. When it is really hot one does not go about in the day time. It is just as well to drink water and even to buy water if it is necessary. So many people diminish. And flowers oh how can flowers be north. They are in the air.'

. . . . .

Can it be easily seen that country life makes us realize women giants and little negresses and the colour of curtains and almost worth while.
Can a planet please. Mildred is not pleased with the heat of the sun.

. . . . .

In spite of a day a day lost in the heat a day lost in the heat of the hall, in spite of the day lost in all the heat we know, in spite of words of surprise in spite of mats and strawberries, strawberries in the woods, how prettily I have taught you to say, the woods.

He has not, however, had so fortunate an influence invariably. 'It is only necessary', says Monsieur [François] Ruchon [in his *Jean-Arthur Rimbaud, sa vie, son œuvre, son influence,* 1929], 'to turn the pages of *Pas Perdus* and the *Manifeste du Surréalisme* (Breton) to realize how much these movements are inspired by the results obtained by the **"Alchimie du Verbe."** Rimbaud wishes to soar towards invisible splendours and non-sensual delight, surrealism believes in 'the future resolution of these two states, the dream and the reality, so contradictory in appearance, into a sort of absolute reality, a super-reality . . . it is towards this conquest that I go.' But if there is identity of aim, there is a difference in the means employed. The æsthetics of the Seer has something in it

of a voluntary, active quality; it modifies, triturates, torments the real in order to transmute it, and tear its secret from it; in surrealism emphasis is laid on the passivity of the spirit, it is an *uncontrolled interrogation of the unconscious.* 'We, who have not given ourselves up to any work of filtration, we, who in our works have made ourselves the deep receptacles of so many echoes, the modern recording apparatuses which are not hypnotised by the design they trace. . . .'

Rimbaud, masculine and powerful, provoked the unconscious by perfectly voluntary methods, and at the same time remained master of the treasure-trove of his draggings; surrealism and its imitators, all of them feminine, are passive, and endure the inner word.
Surrealism is thus defined by André Breton: 'Surrealism, *n.m.*—A purely psychic automatism, by means of which it is proposed to express either verbally, in writing, or in any other manner, the real functioning of thought. It is a dictation of the thought, in the absence of any control exercised by the reason, and outside any æsthetic or moral preoccupation.'
Encycl. Philos. 'Surrealism rests upon a belief in the superior reality of certain forms of association, neglected till now, in the omnipotence of the dream-state, and in the disinterested play of thought.'
Rimbaud, in his letter of May 15th, 1871, insists continually upon the voluntary, I dare not say rational, character of his æsthetics:
'The first study of the man who wishes to be a poet is his own knowledge, in its entirety. He seeks out his soul, he inspects it, he feels, it, he learns it.'
And further:
'The poet makes himself a seer by a long, immense, and reasoned unruliness of all his senses.'
Listen to the surrealists: they raise the example of Rimbaud and also that of Lautréamont, to a theory.
'The image is a pure creation of the mind. It cannot be born of a comparison, but only of the bringing together of two realities more or less distant from each other. The more the affinities of these two realities, thus brought together, are distant and exact, the stronger the image will be, and the greater will be its motive power and poetic reality.'
This heterogeneity leads to ludicrous and queer effects. There is already a fine collection of them in *Chants de Maldoror.*
'It is, generally speaking', acknowledges Lautréamont, 'a singular thing that the attractive tendency which prompts us to seek (in order to give expression to them later) the resemblances and the differences, which are concealed, in their natural properties, in objects the most opposed to each other, and sometimes the least apt, seemingly, to this kind of sympathetically curious combination, and which, on my word of honour, gracefully gives to the style of the writer who offers himself this personal satisfaction, the impossible and unforgettable aspect of an owl serious to Eternity.' (*Revue Nord-Sud,* March, 1918, passage quoted in Breton's *Manifeste du Surréalisme.*)

The example is contained in the precept.

'He compares, not without originality, the ocean to an 'Immense blue appliqué on the body of the earth'; he will say also that 'his lower lip hung like a somniferous cable', and, finally, he will find this image which is altogether in the tone of certain cubist pictures: 'he is beautiful . . . like the fortuitous meeting of a sewing-machine and an umbrella upon a dissecting table'! or again: 'Beautiful as the law of arrested development of the chest in adults, whose propensity towards growth is not in harmony with the quantity of molecules that their organism assimilates.'

Here are some surrealist examples:

'On the harbour the cat-headed dew rocked' (André Breton).

'A little to the left in the firmament divined by me, I perceived—but doubtless it was only a mist of blood and murder—the dulled brilliancy of the perturbations of liberty' (Louis Aragon).

The sentence about the sewing-machine and the umbrella on a dissecting table seems, to me, to be so silly that it will not bear discussion. As for, 'On the harbour the cat-headed dew rocked'—if the author had said 'cat-furred' I would have known what he meant, for certain leaves, raspberry leaves, for instance, have a distinctly animal surface. If, again, he had said 'cat-voiced' it would have had great point, owing to the cold shrill sound of a cat's voice; but 'cat-headed' conveys nothing to my mind. It is invariably possible for a poet, if he does mean anything, to explain, if called upon to do so, his reasons for making even the most difficult statements—if he meant anything at all. But I doubt, in all sincerity, if 'cat-headed dew' could, or would, be explained.

Mr. Edgell Rickword, in his admirable study of Rimbaud [*Rimbaud: The Boy and the Poet*, 1924], writes of his qualities of hallucination. This hallucination consists, to my mind, not so much in transforming actualities into other actualities, as in making all things as one, in abolishing time and place, in making all times as one, all places as one. He has found a formula in which to express, with the utmost acuity of all the senses, each scene that he puts before us.

The world he describes in *Les Illuminations,* is one of luxuriance, but of a luxuriance in which he has no part. He is a traveller, seeing strange things, a wanderer, an outcast, dwelling, seeing for a moment, the 'divans upholstered in red velvet' where the popular drinks are sold, varying in price from eight hundred to eight thousand rupees—imagining, from the cold under the railway arches, those roads, luxuriant with summer, 'bordered with railings and walls which can scarcely contain their groves', for his path is on the road; and, even if he succeeded in finding his way into them, he would be brought back into family life, to the 'atrocious flowers that one is supposed to call one's brothers and sisters, damask of a damning languor'.

If we know the history of Arthur Rimbaud's life and wanderings, his vision in *Les Illuminations* is less strange to us. Many of the *Illuminations* are, actually, the records of things seen during his childhood. For instance, according to Ernest Delahaye, **'Beaten Tracks'** is a description (coloured by his genius) of the American Circus which ap-

peared at Charleville in 1868 or 1869, and is at once a circus parade, a dream, a cavalcade, and a funeral procession. The sentence in the lovely **'Childhood II'**, 'A swarm of golden leaves surrounds the general's house', refers, probably, to the villa of General Noiset, situated on the Route de Flandres, near Charleville; and the phrases 'The castle is for sale, and the shutters have dropped off. The key of the church must have been taken away by the priest', describe the countryside in the Ardennes.

'Promontory' seems to me to be a transformation of Rimbaud's strange life in London, a glorification of those rich hotels passed by the two half-starved creatures, who were among the greatest poets that France has produced. **'Towns II'** contains memories of Hampton Court and of his sightseeing in London, and **'Towns I'** is, in all probability, about Belgium. The **'Matinées d'Ivresse'**, according to Monsieur Ruchon, is a record of his experience under the influence of hashish. 'It is possible', says Monsieur Ruchon, 'that the phrase "O Palmes" ("Anguish"), with its feeling of calm, of being far away, is about the search for inspiration, for the state of ecstasy produced by the artificial paradises. . . .' But I think this is of little importance. It is of infinitely greater importance that, according to the same critic, **'Marine'** and **'Movement'** are the first poems in free verse written in France. I think this might be a debatable point, but it is not for such an unlearned reader of French as myself, to enter into an argument with such a learned, sensitive, and acute observer as Monsieur Ruchon.

> The *Illuminations,* regarded from the point of view of their formal qualities, present an attempt to render both prose and verse "more soluble in the air"; "morality and language are reduced to their most simple expression". . . . In **'Age d'Or', 'Fleurs', 'Barbare'**, and **'Mystique'**, he has refined the verbal matter, as if in a crucible, to the point of attenuation, even of extenuation. He has removed from it the "impurity of the senses", he uses happy assonances, spontaneous and gratuitous images, freed from the iron collar of logic and significance. The poem becomes an irrational thing, pure music and pure incantation. The liberation of the senses obtained by Lautréamont in the worst parts of his 'Chants de Maldoror' by abandoning himself to hallucinations, by submission to the unconscious, and by the practice of producing a sort of psychological photography, without much retouching—this liberation, Rimbaud obtained by his will, by his lucid will.

Monsieur Ruchon continues (a little too sweetly),

> The most beautiful poems in *Illuminations* are like sighs, ardent exclamations, transports of paradisaical joy which do not signify very much literally, and which, by this very fact, see their emotive and poetic power increased tenfold; they are pretences at lyrical arabesques, though our desire for music and rhythm is satisfied in them, and we murmur them to ourselves like a soothing cantilena, in those moments of dreaming when our consciousness is diffused and light as Ariel . . .
>
> And there, he follows in the tracks of Baude-

laire. He inscribes himself in the curve of pure poetry. Did not Baudelaire say, defining in advance the Rimbaldian poetics of *Illuminations;* 'Poetry, if one will descend ever so little into oneself, question one's soul, recall one's memories of enthusiasms, has no other aim than Herself; she could not have any other aim but this, and no poem will be so great, so noble, so truly worthy of the name of poem, as that which has been written solely for the pleasure of writing a poem. . . . I say that if the poet has pursued a moral purpose, he has diminished his poetic force, and it would not be imprudent to wager that his work will be bad. Poetry cannot, under penalty of death or decay, compare itself to science or morality; it has not got Truth for an object, it has nothing but Itself.'

'Baudelaire was fully under the influence of Edgar Poe when he wrote these lines, and certainly he did not realize the grave and extreme consequences that his followers would draw from this philosophy of composition. He pushed the poet towards pure song, and from there to the easy disposal of all meaning, is only a step. He did not dare to take this step, but others more audacious, Rimbaud and above all Mallarmé, crossed lightly. Both of them subscribe to the terse phrase of the poet of *Fleurs du Mal:* 'Poetry has not got Truth for her object, she has nothing but Herself', but to the first part of this phrase they add: 'not even reality'. Laforgue, so lucid and so perspicacious, also joins them when he writes in his notes upon Baudelaire: 'to write detached, short poems, without an appreciable subject (like the others, who wrote a sonnet in order to relate something poetically, to plead a point, etc.), but vague, and without any reason like the fluttering of a fan, ephemeral and equivocal as the paint on a woman's face, poems which cause the bourgeois who has just read them to say: And what then?'

With his poems and his prose in *Illuminations,* brief, equivocal (that is to say, poems in which the meaning is as fugitive and indiscernible as Proteus), musical, concentrated and concise, Rimbaud, like Verlaine, wrings the neck of that eloquence of which his first poems still bore the mark. His lyricism is no longer constructed, ordered and logical, it no longer submits to the object. Rimbaud has truly become a master in phantasmagoria.

(pp. 38-48)

> *Edith Sitwell, in an introduction to* Prose Poems from "Les Illuminations" of Arthur Rimbaud, *translated by Helen Rootham, Faber & Faber Limited, 1932, pp. 9-49.*

Morton Dauwen Zabel   (essay date 1940)

[*In the following excerpt, Zabel describes Rimbaud's mission as a poet and assesses his literary legacy.*]

Had Rimbaud never lived we should have been obliged to invent him. One is conscious of many temptations to audacity in reading the poet of *Le Bateau Ivre* and *Une Saison en Enfer.* One is conscious in reading his critics and interpreters that these temptations have seldom been re-

sisted. They have resulted in some of the boldest hypotheses and most strenuous flights of elucidation in modern criticism. Not content with the poet on his own terms, in his amazing and scarcely credible reality, his apologists have endowed him with a succession of masks that fit almost every type of spiritual and social ordeal in modern experience. Anyone approaching Rimbaud after half a century of such license and myth-making must share Miss [Enid] Starkie's feeling [in her *Arthur Rimbaud,* 1933] that it is time to call a halt to speculation and to recover the poet and his poems in terms as personal and local as possible. To do this can hardly do injustice to his achievement; it will survive the closest identification. His personality and career will always return to the larger dimensions of poetic morality and the feeling will survive that without Rimbaud the tenets of European romanticism would have lacked the sublimation by which they were recreated in contemporary art. To him Keats's sentence on Shakespeare applies with special fitness. He led a life of allegory: his works are the comments on it.

No poet has invited as many incarnations in the private convenience or beliefs of his students or has become so dramatic an index of the aesthetic divergences of our time. Rimbaud himself was fascinated by the notion of avatar and mystic possession. He read Plato, Ballanche, Cabalist texts, and Buddhist scriptures in his search for a tradition that would support his sense of endowment by powers beyond himself. From this sense of divine endowment developed his experiments in derangement and hallucination, his wish to create a new order of poetry, his effort to free himself from the confines of his family, his class, his country, from Europe itself. It crystallized in his talk of "becoming God" and in his doctrine of the poet as *voyant.* He is certainly not a poet of fixed and centered intelligence; however far his greatest poetry succeeds in resolving the discordant elements of his genius, we are wiser to refer the problem of unity in his character to psychologists, who should have no difficulty in defining a classic outline behind the pattern of hereditary and childhood influences traced by Miss Starkie. But the important thing for anyone to see who attempts to understand the real nature of Rimbaud's poetic and intellectual development is that he was more than normally conscious of his successive conflicts: of the rigid morality of his childhood with his sexual vagrancy, of his harshly rational mind with mystical illuminism, of his classical schooling with his later aesthetic doctrines, of Christian teaching with private or oriental modes of occult vision, of his precocious misanthropy with his humanitarian passion. He saw the collision between his personality as determined by nature and his identification of himself with the seer who should transcend the limits of soul and body, dissolve the arbitrary forms of European thought, and so release poetry for its highest destiny in the liberation of man. These conflicts were never obscured by the central complexity of his nature. His audacities of conduct and vision were firmly framed within his native equipment of pride, hard-headed industry, and ambition. Until he was fifteen he was a submissive son, a diligent student and prize-winner in the Collège de Charleville, an intelligence of facile energy and brilliance. Once he got to Africa he won, despite the futile outcome of most of his projects there, a reputation as a shrewd trader, bargainer, and judge of men. The intensity and anguish of his sensibility—his compulsion to sufferings that he called "inexpressible"—were lodged in a spirit of baffling toughness.

When Rimbaud's critics simplify or inflate some facet of his genius to the neglect or disparagement of others, they are not so much explaining Rimbaud as diminishing his intelligence. He was not a poet to boast of containing multitudes, but his wit and subtlety of mind were endlessly explorative. They bred and tested him in an insight that none of the violences of his career was able to brutalize or stultify. When he is used merely as a touchstone to a social, sexual, or exclusively aesthetic argument, there results a shrinking of this insight, a simplification of his powers of criticism and synthesis. His famous sentences then begin to sound ludicrous; his dynamic as a poet is curtailed. His reality as a human being is also diminished. Biographical research, commonly and often justly accused of obscuring the aesthetic virtue of a poet, is likely to have the opposite result with Rimbaud. That is what gives importance, beyond its scrupulous research and well-reasoned interpretation, to Miss Starkie's admirable book, which now supersedes other existing biographies. It is legend, theory, and the inflation of his texts in the manner of a disputed gospel that threaten to make Rimbaud a confusing and unread poet. If one must approach him in terms of parable, it is safer to see him not as the germinal source of every cult or doctrine of our age, but as the culmination of the preceding obsessions of poetic revolt and individualism in Nineteenth Century Europe. However much his abnormal nature as poet and man gives him the force of a test-case in the arguments of Marxist and Freudian critics, Catholic converts, and symbolist or surrealist apologists, he becomes far more convincing if viewed as the Messiah toward whose coming every earlier romantic poet was a signal or a prophet.

The *Rimbaud vivant* of French journalism is the mixed creation of his admirers, and there are signs that this character is becoming popularized abroad, since he is less likely to dispel the symbolic value of the poet who once lived and wrote in all too human body and "tried out the whole century to come in advance." "It is assumed," says Mr. [Delmore] Schwartz, "as with so many others, that his life interprets his poetry. One gets much more illumination by permitting our lives to interpret his text." This holds for any understanding of poetry to some degree, but it holds here with necessary qualifications. Rimbaud's text, in its fullest dimensions, is the true illumination of his genius. In that text there is much that can be recovered, understood, and translated less in terms of *our* lives and prepossessions than through the spiritual and temperamental growth of the child of Charleville. His youthful home, his study of Greek, Latin, and common-school science, his wanderings, the fantastic months in Brussels and London, his humiliating returns to Charleville, his break with republican Paris, his break with Verlaine, and his five years of obstinate struggle to break with Europe—these phases of Rimbaud's life culminate in his flight to Abyssinia, and each one made its assault on his consciousness of latent powers. In them exists the first gloss on the text of his poems; they remain antecedent to every specialized theory of his conduct or thought.

The fragmentary appearance and fitful clairvoyance of Rimbaud's pages then begin to take on a more serious unity than is commonly suspected. The fear and anguish of adolescence (**"Les Poètes de Sept Ans"**) develops into the ironical compassion of his human sympathies (**"Les Chercheuses de Poux"** and **"Les Effarés"**). The torrential imagery of *Le Bateau Ivre* indicates an outbreak of consciousness that comes to sudden maturity in *Une Saison en Enfer* and *Les Illuminations.* The large gaps in event and meaning that we find so tempting to fill up with the values and necessities of "our lives" imply a broken but continuously disintegrating and reconstructive impulse by which the poet attempted to arrive at his new conception of social happiness and human destiny and of the part poetry was to play in their attainment. "The new day industrial capitalism, an air in which all that had been holy to European man decayed," played its part in spurring Rimbaud's realization of the impasse at which humanity had arrived, but the air of his own temperament, of his personal obsessions, his social contempt generated by family discord, and his pathologically intensified emotions and insight, existed before and after his encounter with the corruptions of Second Empire and post-Commune Paris, and from this he took his strongest energy as a poet. The larger atmosphere of the historical moment came to him later. It helped him realize himself; it did not make him what he was.

For what he was we must go to the whole body of his works, every part of which bears upon the brilliant passages which often suffer the worst mangling in the hands of interpreters and translators. The picturesque Flemish charm of **"La Maline," "Au Cabaret Vert," "Le Buffet,"** and **"Les Effarés"** embodies the first exhilaration of the enchanted vagabond of **"Ma Bohême,"** whose sympathy with the poor had not yet arrived at the bitter pathos of the Paris years. The purity of **"Rêve pour l'Hiver"** expresses an adolescent emotion not yet shocked by the realities which soon overtook it and made it impossible for Rimbaud to retain the lyric simplicity that was Verlaine's enigmatic secret through the years of his worst debauchery. The peasant sympathies of **"Le Mal," "Rages de César," "Le Dormeur du Val,"** and **"L'Eclatante Victoire de Saarbroucke"**—records of the War of 1870—convey a recognition of human stupidity that tempers and subtilizes the contempt he wrote into his comments on the aftermath of that national humiliation in **"Chant de Guerre Parisien," "Les Accroupissements," "Les Assis," "Les Pauvres à l'Eglise,"** and **"Paris se Repeuple."** They also suggest that *Une Saison en Enfer* must be read with a good deal more realism than is usually brought to it. In the chapter **"L'Impossible,"** where Rimbaud records his failure in philosophical and religious belief, he recalls childhood as the most precious period in life (he again so describes it in *Les Illuminations*), the age that must be recaptured at all possible costs as the time of instinctive wisdom when God speaks directly to man. But he also sees the delusion of thinking that one can ever go back to it or recapture its innocence, for the innocence never really existed. In a momentary vision of perfect purity he realizes that it is through the spirit alone that man can reach God. The transition from the world of **"Ma Bohême"** and **"Rêve pour l'Hiver"** is suddenly revealed as a token of the poet's growth in spiritual maturity. Similarly the idea, in *Les Illuminations,* that the spirit must pass beyond its futile attempts to incarnate itself in concrete images or words which are incapable of containing it wholly, suggests the transition in Rimbaud's thought from a world of physical and practical fixities to one of symbolic words and transcendent values. He forged his way through this transition in physical terms. His struggle was not only reflected in the violences of his personal life; it is demonstrated in the changing mode and intensity of his poems and it is finally formulated as his aesthetic morality. The state of ecstasy and superhuman bliss suggested by the "spontaneous incoherence" of **"Matinée d'Ivresse"** is the extension to a metaphysical plane of the lyric happiness of **"Ma Bohême."** These signals of growth and maturity are continuous in Rimbaud's poetry. There is an organic emergence of the later thought and emotion from the earlier, and the connection, so little apparent in the surface aspect of the poems, stands out when their subordinate motives and phrases are scrutinized and their specific personal quality is understood. (pp. 268-73)

The surface values of Rimbaud's verse are not difficult to read, but because they are too often read as values of mere shock and derangement they are easily reduced to the empty eloquence and vitiating abstractness of thought that have made his influence one of the worst in modern poetry. This influence, as commonly understood, becomes an affair of sentimental and mystical pretensions and of a verbal recklessness that completely dispels the primary virtue of his art. That virtue is rooted in the rigor of his moral realism, in his lacerating study of selfhood and all that its mastery requires, and in the fact that to achieve a unity of his moral and poetic natures, he spared himself nothing. His radical criticism of the popular poets of Hugo's generation was that they had vision without realization: "La culture de leurs âmes s'est commencée aux accidents." "Musset, tenfold loathsome to a suffering generation like ours, carried away by visions of higher things which his angelic sloth only insults. Oh! these mawkish *Comédies et Proverbes!* Oh! the *Nuits!* . . . Oh! Musset! Charming his love, isn't it? That painting on enamel, what solid poetry! . . . Musset was able to achieve nothing! There were visions behind the veil that hid them, but he only closed his eyes." When Rimbaud found his first great literary passion in the work of Baudelaire, he found an aesthetic that came as a revelation of the true unity and totality of poetry and of its future in enlarging the vision and experience of man. The doctrine of correspondences, with its promise of godhead in the form of the complete poetic vision, came as the charter of a new age of truth. But it came in the work of a poet who brought the theoretic statement of the unity of art as found in Schopenhauer or Ballanche out of abstraction into the realism of the lyric experience. Baudelaire was for Rimbaud the first of the poets whose art seems "to be a complete picture of life in all its complexities, in which the highest mingles with the lowest, aspirations with failures . . . flesh and spirit, dream and nightmare all at once." He was the poet above all others of modern Europe who had a sense of the form

that poetic realization must take if it is to subsume the full experience and consciousness of man. Baudelaire was the one poet in whom Rimbaud found a dramatization of moral reality and creative ordeal:

> *Plonger au fond du gouffre, Enfer ou Ciel qu'importe?*
> *Au fond de l'inconnu pour trouver du nouveau.*

Rimbaud followed Baudelaire faithfully up to the moral crisis in his poems, the moment where Baudelaire saw that the reckless indulgence of sense and its consequence dissolution of man's standards of moral judgment meant a diminution and even a complete disintegration of human consciousness. At that point he rejected the *Paradis Artificiels* of the hallucinated intelligence; "it is in this moral conclusion that Baudelaire's real meaning is to be found and it is he himself who calls it moral." Facing in self-induced hallucination and derangement the implications of suicide, Baudelaire was thrown back on his humanity, his personal identity, the tragic conflict of his instinctive and intelligent natures. In that conflict and in the tension it imposed on his sensibility lies the specific force of his poetry. Rimbaud broke with Baudelaire in refusing to accept the conditions of human life. They must be altered. The derangement of the senses must be complete and systematic. The dissolution of conceptual reality must be as thoroughgoing as is the dissolution of sensory impressions through the correspondences and associations set up by poetic imagination. The poet as *voyant* must become the true seer, the godhead of essences.

This was Rimbaud at the outset of his career, at the threshold of Paris and at the age of fifteen. Within five years he was to learn why Baudelaire was thrown back on his conscious existence as a man, on his inescapable moral identity. The learning took so intense a form of reaction and disgust that it deprived him of the will to write, and his career as poet broke off at the age of twenty. He is a lesser poet than Baudelaire by the degree to which he delayed and finally evaded the integration of his moral nature with his creative vision. He had once written to Izambard and Démeny that "the final apotheosis of the poet would be reached only when he had acquired full knowledge of himself, of all his faculties and how best to use them"; when, too, he would realize that "he has charge of humanity" and must make his visions known to others. When he said that he had not yet learned how relentless are the claims of selfhood and of human service.

Rimbaud is the sworn enemy of sham, meanness, and every dishonesty that enslaves the dignity and vision of man, but this is not to say that the critic in him coincides with the poet or that his animus is essentially that of a critical intelligence. He would have been a dull creature had he remained blind to the impotence and brutality of his century. It hardly took a great poet to see and anathemize these. The Nineteenth Century poets had a great stock of popular sentiment and theological approval to draw on for support. Hugo and Swinburne had certain acceptable convictions in this line, but these indignations served them very slightly in strengthening or intensifying their poetic gifts. Today the indignation of social revolutionists and humanitarian poets has a similar means of success: it takes the tragedy of society, views it in its full horror of chaos and bloodthirsty anarchy, and glibly refers the problem to the abstract judgment of a social or moral theory. The whole central ground and condition of poetry—its source in private integrity and responsibility—is evaded. The large language of doctrine is set against the desperate and baffling nightmare of modern life. The two remain unanalyzed and unreconciled, and as a consequence most poetry and most social evangelism remains empty of value.

Rimbaud comes in conveniently here as a model. His imitators have become legion since 1918 and something like a public nuisance during the past decade. These self-appointed spokesmen of a new age of disillusion and cataclysm have almost succeeded in dragging his example and value down to the level of abuse and misunderstanding where they were relegated by academicians and humanist critics half a century ago. He is drawn on alternately for visionary prophecy and for Isaiahan thunders, and though he figures in the shaping of several authentic talents in our time, he is one of the most misleading of influences—misleading because he is badly read and superficially known in his fundamental quality. Hart Crane obviously brought both a high creative zeal and a strong personal recognition to his study of Rimbaud, and he made something of his example, but elsewhere Rimbaud's intensity of mind and sensibility has been vulgarized until what remains is chiefly the spectacular defiance and moral shock of his surfaces. He has been reduced either to crude diabolism or to a frantic effort to recover the spiritual meaning and energy of life from encroaching ruin. His images of search and conflict have been tumbled into meaningless avalanches of sound and sense. His influence appears to have been steadily attenuated: from the work of Salmon to that of Claudel, from Perse to MacLeish, from Crane to Prokosch, from Eluard and the more gifted surréalistes to Aragon or Dylan Thomas, from Auden to Spender to Kenneth Patchen to (finally, let us hope) Oscar Williams. It is a progress in disorganization, in accepting the fact of unrest and dissolution as the matter of poetry, in substituting the distress and irresponsibility of the modern world for the active intelligence of poetic insight, and so in retreating to the language of prophetic arrogance and hollow judgments instead of attacking the true reality of words and experience as Rimbaud hoped to create it.

To live a life like Rimbaud's and to reach the vindication he arrived at means to have his capacities for self-knowledge, truth, and endurance. To write poetry like his implies an ability to face the full truth and responsibilities of such poetry, and to combine that truth with the excitement of a new vision. It was to this responsibility that Rimbaud's *bateau ivre* returned him: "L'automne, notre barque élevée dans les brumes immobiles tourne vers le port de la misère, la cité énorme au ciel taché de feu et de boue." He refused to accept the humiliation of reconciling his sublime vision of human destiny with this *vraie vie;* a fiercer humility lay in wait for him, but outside poetry. The task of completing his work has fallen on his descendants, and only when they begin to attack it with the rigor and fearlessness of Rimbaud's character will they escape the waste and silence that overtook him and so realize the

high claims he made for the future of poetry and of mankind. (pp. 278-82)

Morton Dauwen Zabel, "Rimbaud: Life and Legend," in Partisan Review, *Vol. VII, No. 4, July-August, 1940, pp. 268-82.*

Cecily Mackworth   (essay date 1944)

[*Mackworth is a Welsh-born French critic, novelist, and biographer. In the following essay, he chronicles the development of Rimbaud's moral beliefs and documents his growth as a poet.*]

The seven-year-old child, dressed in his Sunday best, with pomaded hair and rage at his heart, read the Bible with docility and decided to love, not God, but Humanity. The precocity of Rimbaud was so astounding, his mental development so fantastic, that it is possible he really made this decision at an age when other children are absorbed in their dolls and rocking horses. After all, the letters in which he sets out the full and completely developed theory of the poet—'Voyant', were written before he was sixteen.

A passionately mystic nature observed two species of Mankind as a scientist observes two sets of cultures. The representatives of God were all around him, beginning with his mother, 'La Bouche d'Ombre'. They toned in wonderfully with the damp, grey landscape of the Ardennes. They were the Bourgeoisie, the people who understood the value of money, who stuck to their principles and kept an eye on the main chance, who were always sure to succeed because their aims in life were so small that they hardly left room for failure. They represented God smugly and vocally, parading for High Mass on Sundays as troops parade before their General. Thrift replaced love as the greatest of the virtues.

The down-and-outs of a young industrialism never thought of identifying themselves with Humanity, any more than they were conscious of 'the God in the altar of the body', but Rimbaud recognized them. The sordid workmen of Charleville, the overworked peasants of Roche were his only kinsmen. The early poems are full of a sort of mingled pity and contempt for the poor, passive herd which accepted its misery with a docility which somehow constituted an ultimate betrayal of its own potential grandure. Sometimes the note is of pure pity: 'Les pauvres Jésus pleins de givre,' sometimes it is all hatred at the unbearable humility, the acceptance of injustice, the refusal of divinity, the base gratitude to the Enemy who insults them by his indifference:

> Ces effarés y sont et ses épileptiques
> Dont on se détourait hier aux carrefours
> Et, fringalant du nez dans les missels antiques
> Ces aveugles qu'un chien introduit dans les cours;
> Et tous, bavant la foi mendiante et stupide
> Récitant la complainte infinie à Jésus
> Qui rêve en haut, jauni par le vitrail livide
> Loin des maigres mauvais et des méchants pansus.
>
> ('Les Pauvres à l'Eglise')

Rimbaud identifies himself, as he grows up, more and

more closely with this section of mankind which is alone worthy of the name of Humanity. He feels for it the horror and attraction implicit in some beloved vice:

> Pitié! Ces enfants seuls étaient ses familiers
> Qui, chétifs, front nus, oeil déteignant sur la joue
> Cachant de maigres doigts jaunes et noirs de boue
> Sous les habits puant la foire et les vieillots
> Conversaient avec la douceur des idiots.

It is the contrast between Man as he is and as he might be which rouses the extreme limits of rage and pity in the adolescent Rimbaud. There are the two visions. This picture of the poor at their servile devotions, and the vision of Mankind liberated from Christ, the 'éternel voleur des energies:'

> O! L'Homme relève sa tete libre et fière
> Et le rayon soudain de la beauté première
> Fait palpiter le Dieu dans l'autel de la chair!
> Heureux du bien présent, pâle du mal souffert
> L'Homme veut tout sonder et savoir.

It is with Mankind, in all its misery and majesty that Rimbaud identifies himself. On behalf of Mankind he decides to attain initiation, to 'penetrate and know everything', until he is capable of throwing down the final challenge to God, of waging the ultimate battle which is to free Man from his quasi-eternal fetters.

But the 'pitiés immondes' to which he indiscreetly admitted were sternly suppressed by Madame Rimbaud in the name of God and morality. Her son, after unparalleled successes at school, refused to matriculate, became sullen and unwashed and slipped from home in the evenings to drink in low-class cafés and scribble 'Mort à Dieu' on the Church walls. The daytime was occupied by the study of magic at the local library, whose shelves are unlikely to have been a fertile hunting-ground in the subject.

Rimbaud set out avowedly to penetrate the universal mysteries and become 'voyant'. 'The poet,' he explains in the famous letter addressed to his master, Monsieur Izambard, 'becomes *voyant* by the long, immense and reasoned derangement of all his senses. He seeks in himself all the forms of love, of suffering of madness. He consumes in himself all the poisons, to retain only their quintescences.'

Already he begins to suspect the possibility of destroying his own personality in order to become absorbed in a greater Personality. 'Je', he writes, '*est* un autre.' He is no longer responsible, in the ordinary, moral sense, for his own actions. He has cast aside the essential Catholic doctrine of free-will and liberated himself by one, enormous blasphemy from the trammels of his childhood.

Rimbaud's sayings about the state of 'voyance', and especially certain passages in the *Bateau Ivre,* have made some critics believe that he gradually came to think that he could identify himself with God. I believe this is wrong. Rimbaud uses the word God in many different senses, generally as some universal, abstract power. God in the religious sense, that is, the Catholic God, he took as his mortal enemy. It is not with God, but with God's adversary, Lucifer, that he finally identifies himself when the time comes to crystallize the over-vague idea of Humanity.

At this point it becomes necessary to consider the influence of Baudelaire. There is little mention of this influence in all the immense Rimbaudian bibliography, yet it seems probable that if Baudelaire had never existed Rimbaud would not have been able to carry his theory of the poet-voyant to its last, logical step. Aesthetically, Baudelaire introduced him to the idea that sound, colour and form might be transposed into a sort of divine oneness ('Les couleurs, les sons et les parfums se repondent') which Rimbaud developed in the famous vowel sonnet. Philosophically, he opened the door to a universe which might have been specially created for the younger poet.

The *Fleurs du Mal* had been published in 1857, when Rimbaud was three years old. It was promptly banned and Baudelaire himself sentenced for immorality. It is quite certain that the execrated volume can have had no place upon the meagre bookshelves of Madame Rimbaud, who had firm ideas about the facile path to hell. Equally it cannot have been available in the public library of Charleville or in the private libraries of its straitlaced and gossipy citizens. But Izambard, the advanced young schoolmaster got into trouble for lending to her son books (and notably a work of Victor Hugo) which were incompatible with the moral ideas which she worked so hard to inculcate. If the *Fleurs du Mal* had been among them the skies would probably have fallen, or at least there would have been such an almighty row that history would know all about it.

Yet Izambard must, logically, have shown a copy to his astonishing pupil, for, in the **"Lettre du Voyant,"** Rimbaud proclaims: 'Baudelaire is the first *voyant,* a king of poets, a real God.' Then, in another letter, we have Rimbaud's own estimate of the debt which he owes to his master. 'La reconnaissance que je vous ai, je ne saurais pas vous l'exprimer . . . il s'agirait de faire quelquechose pour vous que je mourrais pour le faire.' This refers ostensibly to Izambard's protection after one of his flights from Charleville, but Rimbaud was usually inclined to bite the hand that fed him and was not given to gratitude so far as material benefits were concerned. An initiation at the risk of reputation and a career was more likely to have moved him to such devotion.

Scepticism is a purely cerebral state of mind which flourishes in artificial civilizations and rarely touches the poet. Poetry which *is* poetry and not merely the product of an intellectual thesis, springs from instinct and fantasy, while the intellect fills the minor rôle of disciplinarian. The poet himself is, almost professionally, a man dominated by mysticism and imagination, the man of Myth rather than of science. His mysticism may be concentrated in the worship of an orthodox God or its edges may blur in an obsession of Celtic twilight. But it will always be there, an essential part of his make-up; poet will be poet, from St. John of the Cross to Yeats.

Running parallel to the main current of European poetry, there is the curious hierarchy of the mystics of Evil. They are the few, the outcasts, the self-destroyers, the rebels, who are seduced by the tragic majesty of Lucifer. These range themselves at the side of the defeated and reserve for the enthroned God a hatred whose violence is at the measure of its object. They are to be found almost exclusively in Catholic countries, where no one tries to deny that sin is a component part of life. They are possessed by that 'amour du sacrilege' to which Rimbaud confessed in the *Saison en Enfer.*

Among the banned poems in the *Fleurs du Mal* which Izambard must have shown to the young Rimbaud, is the Litany to Satan. Baudelaire was at least periodically a Satanist and did not fear to affirm his faith with all the passion of the Spanish mystics: 'Il n'est pas une fibre de tout mon corps tremblant, Qui ne crie—O, mon cher Belzébuth, je t'adore!' In the Litany he invokes Lucifer: 'Dieu trahi par le sort et privé de louanges', and Rimbaud instantly received—at least at my guess—the revelation of an Alternative: the God of his mother and Charleville Sundays or the mysterious and evil beauty of the Fallen Angel, the esoteric divinity reserved for the seer.

It should not be forgotten that Rimbaud had been one of the most brilliant classical scholars that the Lycée of Charleville had ever known. During the whole period of his schooldays he had literally soaked himself in classicism and shown an understanding of the classic spirit which had astonished—and even worried—his masters. Now, in a single phrase, Lucifer took shape as the very embodiment of classic tragedy, typifying more completely than Oedipus or Orestes the noble being 'betrayed by fate and denied his rightful praise'.

At the same time this Being contained his whole conception of mankind—that is, greatness and nobility reduced to beggary by successful God. 'Je est un Autre' now takes on a new meaning. Rimbaud *is* Humanity, *may become* Lucifer. His task is to make Humanity conscious of its own degradation. He cannot, being that Other, confine his experiments to mere personal experience. He is conscious of enormous and still vaguely understood responsibilities. 'Il faut que j'en aide d'autres,' he writes some years later. 'C'est mon devoir. Quoique ce ne soit guère ragoutant, chère âme.'

Now we see Rimbaud faced with the two conceptions, God and Satan. Soon these personalities become identified, as they have been through the passage of the centuries, with Construction and Destruction, with Positive and Negative. Rimbaud, brought up in the strictest tenets of the Catholic religion, realized instinctively the truth that Karl Adam was later to express philosophically, that Catholicism is Affirmation, the acceptance of life in every aspect. So with unfaltering logic, he turned to negation, denial and destruction. 'Voici le temps des assassins'—i.e. the age of destruction, of the poet-voyant.

Lucifer—Destruction. Man may become Lucifer by destruction. In one of the prose-poems contained in the collection called *Les Illuminations,* Rimbaud tells of a prince who suspected the existence of unexplored felicities. 'Il voulait voir la verité, l'heure du désir et de la satisfaction essentiels.' In order to attain this state of essential satisfaction he assassinates all the women he has known (i.e. destroys Beauty). He massacres all his hunting and drinking companions, annihilates all the beautiful beasts of his kingdom, burns his palaces. He hurls himself upon the crowd, dismembers his subjects. Yet the women, the

crowds, the golden roofs and the beautiful beasts continue to exist.

One day the Prince is galloping proudly on his horse when a Djinn appears, of incalculable and inadmissible beauty: 'De sa physionomie et de son maintien ressortait la promesse d'un amour multiple et complexe, d'un bonheur indicible, insupportable même. Le Prince et le Génie s'annéantirent probablement dans la santé essentielle. Comment n'auraient-ils pas pu en mourir? Ensemble donc ils moururent.

Mais le Prince décéda, dans son palais, à un age ordinaire. La Prince était le Génie. Le Génie était le Prince.—La musique savante manque â notre désir.'

Here Rimbaud tells in his own words of the identification by destruction of himself with Lucifer and his subsequent attainment of truth. Note that the Prince destroys not only others, but himself.

It remained to put these theories into practice—a thing which could not be accomplished in Charleville. Escape became imperative.

Several abortive attempts at flight had left Rimbaud full of bitterness and doubt. One at least, the occasion when he succeeded in joining the soldiers of the Garde Républicaine in their barracks at St. Denis, had left a lasting scar which played its part in shaping his destiny. His experiences among those who, as defenders of the adored Liberty, should have shown at least a glimpse of the divine and satanic fire, left him with a feeling of inalienable disgust. His heart has been stolen, never to be returned:

> Ithyphalliques et pioupiesques
> Leurs quolibets l'ont dépravés
> Au gouvernail on voit des fresques
> Ithyphalliques et pioupiesques
> O flots adabracadabrantesques
> Prenez mon cœur qu'il soit lavé
> Ithyphalliques et pioupiesques
> Leurs quolibets l'ont dépravé!
>
> **'Le Cœur Volé'**

This experience marks the end of the poems which retain the accent of childhood and sometimes, like **'Sensation,'** **'Ma Bohème,' 'Au Cabaret Vert,'** expresses a sort of lyric innocence and happiness.

So Rimbaud returned home, disgraced and furious. He poured his spleen into the **'Premiéres Communiantes,'** the hymn of hate for the 'eternal Thief of energies', then—the culminating point at which the theory of voyance seemed to justify itself once and for all—he produced the miracle of the prophetic and terrible *Bateau Ivre.*

'Come, dear, great soul. You are awaited, you are desired!' wrote Verlaine to the unknown poet of Charleville. He showed the *Bateau Ivre* and some of the other poems to his fellow Parnassiens, who were doubtful and perhaps uneasy, but prepared to make allowances for Verlaine's latest enthusiasm and extend a kindly welcome to its author.

A decent bohemianism characterized the artistic *milieu* of Paris in 1871. The purity or otherwise of a poet's life was still held to have some connection with his poetry, so that a few years later Verlaine was refused admission to the

pages of the *Parnasse Contemporaine* on the ground of immorality, just as Baudelaire, a few years earlier, had received a final rebuff from the Académie Française, which
disapproved of his equivocal moral standards. Leconte de
Lisle and Théodore de Banville, 'le bon maître', presided
over Parnasse and set the literary standards of the day. Art
for art's sake had become a creed and Beauty a goddess
to be worshipped with reverence and devotion. 'L'art,'
proclaimed Leconte de Lisle, 'est l'unique revelation du
Beau et il rélève uniquement'; and again, 'Le monde du
Beau, l'unique domaine de l'Art, est, en soi, un infini sans
contact possible avec tout autre conception que ce soit'. As
for dangerous innovators: 'il n'y a rien de plus inintelligent
et de plus triste que cette excitation vaine à l'originalité
propre aux mauvaises époques de l'art'.

Even the younger set, Coppée, Catulle Mendès and Hérédia, could hardly be called revolutionary. Like their elders
they approved of Beauty in neatly rhymed stanzas, sought
for 'a style as clear as the dawn' and fulminated joyously
against the Philistines; Verlaine, Charles Cros and Mérat
were the *enfants terribles* of the group. Parnasse recognized their talents but deplored their taste for absinthe.
Poets were expected to be gentlemen, although consecrated gentlemen, and these three did not always come up to
standard.

Rimbaud, the disciple of Lucifer, arrived. He was tall and
gangling, with large red hands and uncouth manners. He
spoke with a trailing provincial accent. He seldom washed
and had lice. But his worst lapse from taste lay in his
youth. The Parnassiens had expected a man and they were
offered a child and felt that they had been tricked. Even
so, they were ready to be kind, but the child mocked at
them, at their principles and at the Goddess Beauty herself. He served a different and more exigent master and
cherished a feeling of superiority which he did not attempt
to conceal.

Perhaps his manners might have been excused if his poetry
had been in any way to his credit. But he made hay of the
sacred laws of versification. 'Unknown discoveries demand new literary forms,' he had written to Izambard.
Nothing could be a clearer example of 'L'excitation vaine
à l'originalité'. His rhymes were a public scandal. When
one considers the shock which Apolinnaire administered
to French poetry more than fifty years later by refusing to
subscribe to the hallowed rule of alternating masculine
and feminine rhymes, one can understand what Hérédia,
for instance, felt about a verse like this:

> Mais moi, Seigneur, voici que mon esprit vole
> Après les cieux glacés de rouge sous les
> Nuages celestes qui courent et volent
> Sur cent Solognes longues comme un railway.

'sous les' rhymed with 'railway'! One can almost hear
Coppée, at the Café des Vilains Bonhommes squeaking
out, *'Mais c'est se moquer du monde!'*

If rudeness and dirt were the more obvious reasons for
Rimbaud's failure in Paris, there was another, less immediate, aspect of the affair. He was, and perhaps remains,
the least French of French poets. He had none of the classic restraint which controls the passion even of Baudelaire

and Verlaine and is an essential part of the French poetic
current. His style, far from being as clear as dawn, was as
obscure as the murkiest hour between dog and wolf. Later
it might be interpreted in the light of Symbolism, but Symbolism was still unheard of. Mallarmé and Laforgue, who
were to offer the key to many dark places of the mind, had
as yet made no impact on their contemporaries. Rimbaud's images outraged the very essence of Cartesian
France and the Parnassiens remained, whatever they
thought themselves, unconscious Cartesians.

One of the leaders of the Surrealist Movement recently referred, although approvingly, to Rimbaud's *'images idi-
otes'*. Literary Paris of 1871 would have agreed with him,
and so, no doubt would Rimbaud himself. 'Je m'habituai
à l'hallucination simple: je voyais très franchement une
mosquée à la place d'une usine, une école de tambours
faite par des anges, des calêches sur les routes du ciel, un
salon au fond d'une lac; les monstres; les mystères; un titre
de vaudéville dressait des épouvantes derrière moi. Puis
j'expliquais mes sophismes magiques avec l'hallucination
des mots.' (***Une Saison en Enfer.***)

As a matter of fact, Rimbaud's images are only superficially 'idiotic' in the Surrealist sense. When he says that his
hallucination is simple, he means that it is instinctive. The
completely Surrealist image is the chance product of the
subconscious, while that of Rimbaud never varies from a
sensual precision which is as rigorous in its own way as
the polished gems of Hérédia. The word 'hallucination' is
chosen *to explain* the 'magic sophism' of the instinctive
image. If the birth of the image takes place in the subconscious, the word in which it is clothed is shaped with the
care of a craftsman. It is impossible to find a meaningless
word, or one which is not intimately related to the image.
Rimbaud's consummate musicianship never falters, even
at his wildest.

But Parnasse was still too closely bound by the chains of
classicism to accept images which superficial criticism still
applauds for their glorious idiocy. The Parnassiens disapproved of Rimbaud as heartily as he despised them. His
behaviour was so bad that he was soon banned from the
weekly dinners and left to carry on a life of studied de-
bauch with Verlaine, whose own reputation suffered badly
from the association. Presently they were entirely ostra-
cized and remained on speaking terms only with Forain
and Du Cros. The two friends fled from inhospitable Paris
and commenced a carefree life of vagabondage which
eventually brought them to London.

Rimbaud's failure among the Parnassiens is important.
Whatever show of bravado he cared to put up, it is impossible that a provincial schoolboy should remain entirely
unimpressed by his first contact with the great. On some
of these men at least he had pinned his faith and their rejection of him cannot have left him indifferent. (Mérat, for
instance, although Rimbaud had granted him the honorary degree of Voyant on reading his poems, refused to figure in Fantin-Latour's picture, 'Le Coin du Table', because Rimbaud was to be among those depicted.) He had
come with a message to explain to these poets how they
might become the agency which should raise Mankind
from its state of abjection and prepare it to participate in

the Luciferian majesty. They had rejected and scorned him. In a refined and ironic way they had destroyed his illusions as completely as the Republican soldiers had destroyed them at St. Denis. His heart had been stolen again, depraved once more by jeers which no magic waves would ever wash away.

There remained Verlaine, the brother Voyant who had forsaken wife and friends, thrown off security and plunged into debauchery for his sake. Verlaine, the angelic poet and the sordidly feeble man, contained in himself all the elements of that Humanity which Rimbaud adored with such extravagance and which was proving so ungrateful. Verlaine was the stake on which he laid his last wager.

Everything went well so long as the excitement of travel and vagabondage in new countries lasted, but like many more orthodox arrangements the menage could not survive the humdrum routine of house-keeping and wage-earning. The health and nerves of both men were exhausted by systematic debauchery: 'Ma santé fut menacée,' wrote Rimbaud later. 'La terreur venait. Je tombais dans des sommeils de plusieurs jours, et, levé, je continuais les rêves les plus tristes. J'étais mur pour le trépas, et par la route des dangers ma faiblesse me menait aux confins de monde et de la Cimmérie, patrie de l'ombre et des tourbillons.' (*Une Saison en Enfer.*)

In a climate unpropitious for ardour the two men, isolated in the vacuum created by the language problem and in constant financial difficulty, were thrown entirely upon each other's society. Rimbaud, with the growing fear of madness upon him, became increasingly insupportable. He was haunted by the realization that Verlaine was incapable of following him to the logical conclusion of his poetic and philosophical system, and would remain for ever the *vierge folle*. Worse still, he was beginning to doubt the truth of his own conclusions: 'Moi! Moi qui me suis dit mage ou ange, dispensé de tout morale, je suis rendu au sol, avec un devoir à chercher, et la réalité rugeuse à étreindre! Paysan!'

His disappointment exaggerated Verlaine's failure and soon hatred began to mingle with the remains of the old love. He was driven to a frenzy of irritation by his friend's periodic fits of remorse over the wife and child he had deserted. His scruples seemed to Rimbaud symptoms of his pitiful inadequacy for the divine rôle which he should have filled. Verlaine's self-pity filled him with disgust. 'Ainsi, j'ai aimé un porc!' he wrote disdainfully at this period.

The quarrel which broke up the London home was a typical domestic tragi-comedy, pitifully and sordidly *human*. The two young men being very low in funds, Verlaine had volunteered to go out and do the day's shopping as economically as possible. Rimbaud, in a horrible temper as usual, sulked at home, wrapped in his unending nightmare. Verlaine returned, after an unsuccessful expedition which had resulted in the purchase of one large herring, which he held unwrapped and dangling from his hand. Rimbaud was watching from the window as he made his appearance and called out scornfully: 'Ce que tu peux avoir l'air cul avec un hareng à la main!' It was his epitaph to Humanity.

Rimbaud at the time of his first communion.

Verlaine, furious, hurled away the herring, turned on his heel and disappeared, not to return until the following day. His reappearance heralded a quarrel which ended in his flight to Belgium.

The story of how Rimbaud followed Verlaine to Brussels, of their tentative reconciliations and of the pistol shot which ended in a sentence of two years hard labour on Verlaine, is too well known to need repetition. Rimbaud was probably less wounded by Verlaine's bullet than by his conversion, in prison, to a singularly tearful and sentimental type of piety.

Une Saison en Enfer—Rimbaud's farewell to poetry—is one of the greatest confessions of failure in world literature. The whole of the intricate system for which he had sacrificed himself as a very real burnt offering, had broken down. Lucifer has failed him or—an even more agonizing thought—he has failed Lucifer. He had not had the strength to shoulder alone the burden of Humanity and no one had proved worthy or willing to help him in the impossible task. Destruction and negation had destroyed and denied themselves.

Rivière, Claudel and other Catholic critics have seen in the *Saison en Enfer* the proof of Rimbaud's conversion to

Catholicism. I believe that they are right in a sense. Rimbaud accepts Christ because he is constitutionally incapable of sceptism. His spirit is cut to the measure of heaven and hell and the material world has little meaning for him. When Lucifer fails he is ready, despising himself, to turn to Christ, but atheism is a solution which does not even occur to him. Without the certainty of the presence of God in one aspect or another he cannot survive.

'L'esprit est proche; pourquoi Christ ne m'aide-t-il pas en donnant à mon âme noblesse et liberté? Helas, l'Evangile, a passé! L'Evangile! Evangile! . . . J'attends Dieu avec gourmandise. *Je suis de race inferieur de toute éternité.'* He has wiped out the whole of his life as a poet and returned to the point, where, as a little child, he attended gravely at Catechism. He has made the renouncement consciously and with a certain irony, but Christ, whom he is ready to accept as a second-best, is no longer there.

In the *Saison en Enfer* Rimbaud bids good-bye to Lucifer and thus, logically, to himself. He no longer exists as a poet, having nothing to write about and no reason to write. He is gripped in the agony of enforced silence: 'Par quel crime, par quelle erreur', he cries, 'ai-je merité ma faiblesse actuelle? Vous qui pretendez que les bêtes poussent des sanglots de chagrin, que des morts revent mal, tachez de raconter ma mort et mon sommeil. Moi, je ne puis plus m'expliquer que le mendiant avec ses continuels Pater et Ave Maria. *Je ne sais plus parler.'*

Rimbaud was not quite nineteen years old when he finished *Une Saison en Enfer* and turned his back on poetry. Deliberately, as if he was in fact committing the suicide which the tenacious remnants of Catholic morality forbade him to dare, he set about destroying his old life. The earlier poems and Illuminations remain to us by chance. From now on he consecrated himself to travel, adventure and the unsuccessful pursuit of fortune, but life was, in all but the literal sense, over for him. 'Quel ennui!' he wrote from Aden. 'Quelle vie bête! Que fais-je ici, moi? . . . Et qu'irais-je chercher ailleurs?' There is nothing left but meaningless suffering, until the final humiliation of one of the most horrible deaths which can come to a human being. (pp. 180-92)

> *Cecily Mackworth, "Arthur Rimbaud," in* Horizon, *London, Vol. IX, No. 51, 1944, pp. 180-92.*

Kenneth Rexroth　(essay date 1957)

[*Rexroth was one of the leading pioneers in the revival of jazz and poetry in the San Francisco area during the 1940s and 1950s. However, it was as a critic and translator that he gained prominence in American letters. As a critic, his acute intelligence and wide sympathy allowed him to examine such varied subjects as jazz, Greek mythology, the works of D. H. Lawrence, and the cabala. As a translator, Rexroth was responsible for introducing the West to many classic works of Chinese and Japanese literature. In the following essay, originally published in* The Nation *(12 October 1957), Rexroth describes Rimbaud as "an innovator in syntax" and main-*

tains that despite his reputation as a revolutionary, he actually exemplified bourgeois values.]

Most people think of Rimbaud as the very archetype of youth in revolt, as well as the founder of modernist poetry and one of the greatest secular, that is non-religious, or in his case anti-religious, mystics. A kind of Rimbaudian orthodoxy has grown up which meets with very little protest. A few European critics have spoken in demurrer, but most interested Americans have never heard of them. I think myself that the whole Rimbaudian gospel is open to question.

The very title of his prose poems raises this question. Mrs. [Louise] Varèse discusses some aspects in her excellent introduction [to her 1957 translation of *Illuminations*]. Does it mean "illuminations," as in medieval manuscripts? The French verb is *enluminurer.* "Illuminations" is usually considered an English import into French. Does it mean mystical insights? Does it mean bits of illumination in the French sense—enlightenment? (This again in the ironic French sense; an *illuminé* is very close to being a sophisticate or, feminine, a bluestocking.) Nobody ever suggests that the first meaning to occur to an unruly adolescent boy might be "fireworks." I vote for fireworks.

The neuroses the treatment of which now consumes so much of the budget of the more fashionable members of the American upper middle class are actually, by and large, palpitations of behavior due to unsatisfied bourgeois appetites and lack of life aim. In the young, especially in the young poor, the syndrome is called delinquency. Its ravages are often attributed to television. Television has a lot to do with it all right, but not the horror serials, the Westerns, and crime shockers. The real source of corruption is the commercial. It is possible to mistake a demoralized craving for Cadillacs for "revolt." Revolutionaries hitherto have not expressed themselves by snitching the gaudier appurtenances of conspicuous expenditure. Genuine revolt goes with an all-too-definite life aim—hardly with the lack of it. Whether or not there is anything genuine about the vision, whether the visionary really sees anything, is open to dispute, but there is a wide consensus as to what the genuine experience is like, and how the genuine visionary behaves. As Baron von Hugel pointed out in one of his most penetrating observations, true illumination always results in a special sweetness of temper, a deep, lyric equanimity and magnanimity. The outstanding characteristic of the mystic's vision is that it is satisfying. He is never frustrated, at least not in our worldly sense. It would be hard to find two less suitable words in any language to apply to Rimbaud than equanimity and magnanimity. This leaves us with Rimbaud as a sort of magician of the sensibility—of that specifically modern sensibility invented by Blake and Hoelderlin and Baudelaire—and an innovator in syntax, the first thoroughly radical revealer of the poetic metalogic which is the universal characteristic of twentieth-century verse.

I think this is enough. I don't think anybody has ever demonstrated convincingly that behind the syntactic surface lay the profound content of a sort of combination Bakunin and St. John of the Cross. The content is the season in hell, the dark night of the soul, the struggle with God and the

State, of all adolescence. This, of course, has its own common profundity. I do not doubt but what the first flares to burn in the gonads of puberty do light up the ultimate questions of the fate and meaning of man, but that is not what the Rimbaudians mean. The excitement and fury is not metaphysical, it is youthful. The cocksureness is youthful too, but it is also something else. It is bourgeois. Rimbaud did not lose himself in Africa; he found himself. The average poet turns to writing because he can't compete with his schoolmates in track and football. High school dances frighten him. He never learns the proper passes that score with a chick in the back seat of a convertible. In fact, he never gets near one. But there are always a few girls, not very appetizing, most of them, who will be nice to a fellow who has made "The Lit." So, he invests in a set of Dowson, Housman, and T. S. Eliot and starts in. This was not Rimbaud's approach. He applied to literature, and to litterateurs, the minute he laid eyes on them, the devastating methods of total exploitation described so graphically in the *Communist Manifesto*. Some of them were not very applicable. He "ran" the vowels like he later ran guns to the Abyssinians, with dubious results. Usually, however, he was very successful—in the same way his contemporaries Jim Fiske and P. T. Barnum were successful. He did things to literature that had never been done to it before, and they were things which literature badly needed done to it . . . just like the world needed the railroads the Robber Barons did manage to provide.

Not for nothing is **Bateau Ivre** a schoolboy's dream of Cowboys and Indians—that's where Rimbaud belonged, on the frontier—with Cecil Rhodes. And that is where, back in his home town, he was immortalized. The old monument to Rimbaud in Charleville ignores his poetry and memorializes him as the local boy who made good as a merchant and hero of French imperialism in the Africa where the aesthetes who were never good at business think he went to die unknown, holding the Ultimate Mystery at bay. (pp. 42-5)

> *Kenneth Rexroth, "Rimbaud as Capitalist Adventurer," in his* Bird in the Bush: Obvious Essays, *New Directions, 1959, pp. 42-5.*

Yves Bonnefoy   (essay date 1961)

[*Bonnefoy is widely regarded as one of the most important French poets to emerge after World War II. Critics note in his work affinities with the Metaphysical poets of the seventeenth century for his investigation of spiritual and philosophical matters, and with the Surrealists of the twentieth century for his exploration of the subconscious rather than material reality and conscious perceptions. In the following excerpt from his biography* Rimbaud, *translated into English by Paul Schmidt in 1973, he chronicles the events of May of 1871, viewing this as a pivotal time in Rimbaud's poetic career.*]

That does not mean nothing, wrote Rimbaud to Izambard on the thirteenth of May [1871], referring to **"Le Coeur volé."** His biographers have therefore attempted to explain the poem in terms of anecdote and supposed occasions of debauchery or drunkenness, but what **"Le Coeur volé"** profoundly *means*, what it speaks of, is the self-

---

> "Rimbaud," by W. H. Auden:
>
> The nights, the railway-arches, the bad sky,
> His horrible companions did not know it;
> But in that child the rhetorician's lie
> Burst like a pipe: the cold had made a poet.
>
> Drinks bought him by his weak and lyric friend
> His senses systematically deranged,
> To all accustomed nonsense put an end;
> Till he from lyre and weakness was estranged.
>
> Verse was a special illness of the ear;
> Integrity was not enough; that seemed
> The hell of childhood: he must try again.
>
> Now, galloping through Africa, he dreamed
> Of a new self, a son, an engineer,
> His truth acceptable to lying men.
> > *W. H. Auden, in* Selected Poetry of W. H. Auden, *1958.*

disgust that for a moment came close to submerging Rimbaud's entire being. A nausea from the heart, that would have isolated him from all his former ambition, from any endeavor, any ideal. A terrible state whose outcome could only be paradox, or death.

Rimbaud chose paradox. On the thirteenth and fifteenth of May two letters, resolute, feverish, authoritative, conveyed to Izambard and to Demeny, who were hardly likely to understand them, the philosophy of the *Voyant* (visionary).

Perhaps it might be well, in order better to understand a decision that was to reveal itself so purely metaphysical, to pay attention now to . . . books read and influences undergone. Yet I can only do so incompletely here; and, leaving aside the catechism and the Gospel, crucial interventions of Christ's religion, as fascinating as it was detested, I think it is enough to evoke two or three encounters which are certain and which were essential. Many others have been supposed; but they are hardly more than fantasies. The breadth and the consistency of Arthur Rimbaud's reading have often been much exaggerated.

Of these few encounters the earliest and the one destined to remain the most important was with the writings of Baudelaire. Rimbaud surely knew him by 1871—in the 1868 edition with Gautier's preface—since we can find in *Paris se repeuple, Le Mal, Les Soeurs de charité*, even in *Les Mains de Jeanne-Marie*, the first signs of the influence of the poems of *Les Fleurs du mal*. It was, in fact, principally "Benediction" or "Le Reniement de saint Pierre" that influenced Rimbaud's rhythms or images. And how could he remain unmoved at the cry of those admirable lines by Baudelaire which recount the curse uttered by the poet's mother, the poet's will to survive, the misery he experienced with women, and at last, the transparent plenitude acquired through suffering?

Why did I not bring a nest of vipers forth

Rather than nourish such derision!
Accursed be the night of fleeting sport
When my womb conceived my retribution!
. . . . .
Yet in the invisible guard of an Angel
The Child disowned grew drunk on sunlight
. . . . .
For I know suffering is the only nobleness
That earth and hell can never destroy . . .

Rimbaud must surely have conceived an immediate passion for this magnificent faith; and if he was even then not convinced—he who could not carry forward the impulse of faith—he might hope in any case that Baudelaire was justified, for the dark horizon to be transmuted. All throughout *Les Fleurs du mal* there is an intuition of a metamorphosis of being, of a change from lead to gold, of a renovation of the spirit. Here, in this world "where action is not the sister of dreams," appears the idea of poetry as action, at one and the same time analytic intelligence and mysterious chemistry. And Rimbaud follows Baudelaire in a rapid advance along this path. Let us not doubt that it is because he had read *Les Fleurs du mal* that he was able to write **"Les Sœurs de charité"** and the admirable last sections of **"Les Premières Communions."** Never without Baudelaire could he have so soon acquired so great and so assured a knowledge of the soul, never without him could he have found this small amount of self-confidence which allowed him suddenly to judge without hatred, even with that pity which, despite his pessimistic outlook, has something of the accents of love. These are the first poems where Rimbaud appears poetically adult. In them we perceive what might have been his "victory," passage from the *atrocious scepticism* within him to a stoic serenity. But as yet they can speak only of solitude and exile. Both of them deal with the social situation of woman, who should be the mediatrix between man and reality (**"Soleil et chair"** hinted at it already), but who can no longer fulfil the role because her soul is *rotten*. Christianity has left all life desolate by ravaging the soul of woman; and woman, from now on the great absence, can provide only a sorrowful warning that Rimbaud hears with a feeling of impotence:

Do you know I have destroyed you? Turned
 your head,
And taken your heart, your life, and your
 dreams;
I am sick: Oh, lay me down among the Dead
Whose thirst is quenched by dark nocturnal
 streams!

For I was young, and Christ has soured my soul.
He filled me to the throat with sick disgust!
You kissed my hair, my hair as thick as wool,
And I lay and let you . . . Ah, you love your
 lust,

You Men! You little think the woman most in
 love,
Ruled by a conscience full of sordid terror,
Is prostituted worse than any slave,
And that all our love for you is error!

My first Communion is over and past.
I can never have understood your kisses:
For my soul and body embraced by your flesh

Crawled with the rotten kiss of Jesus!

What a distance between these serious, generous lines and the brutal stanzas of a while previously:

Oh my little lovelies,
I hate your guts!
Go stick fat blisters
On your ugly tits!

Baudelaire has now taught Rimbaud poetic responsibility. And yet what a distance still remains between Rimbaud's **"Les Premières Communions"** and Baudelaire's "Le Balcon," for example, or any poem where Baudelaire expresses his feelings about love! That difference reveals not so much the hearts, as more or less pure, of these two poets, but their original need. And how much less was the elder deprived!

Those evenings lit by glowing fires of coal,
Evenings on balconies, veiled in rosy clouds.
How sweet I found your breast! How kind your
 soul!
We whispered often imperishable words
Those evenings lit by glowing fires of coal.

There is of course in Baudelaire a good deal of mistrust of woman: he has called her "guilty" and "cold" and even once "abominable." The misery of original sin has marked her much more than man, he thought. But both man and woman, if I may put it this way, are only wounded; they can occasionally sustain each other, contemplate together "the depths of years past," attain poetry at least. There is no absolute separation between them as there is for Rimbaud.

And I believe the following to be true: the transmutation that Baudelaire attempted and the one Rimbaud desired had, without any doubt, the same goal, but for their same alchemy they did not have the same resources, and consequently the younger poet was forced from the path indicated in *Les Fleurs du mal*. Baudelaire wishes to triumph over nothingness. And in a world where being is degraded by man's yielding to fragmentation, self-dilapidation, and death, he realizes that to devote oneself to the limited object, to anything mortal, is the start of a decisive mutation, where the plentitude of existence can be reached with the help of any of its moments. And this devotion is love, which he was luckily given. He had long before been taught, in that "small white house" of his childhood's happy first years, that reciprocated love existed. Rimbaud never received this essential gift. He was thus to try to do without it, or to rediscover it through the act of poetry. But in both cases he came short of that strange happiness, exhausted but ardent, that we sense in the work of Baudelaire. Where the latter, in a word, can call upon "angels clothed in gold" as witnesses because he, like them, has been capable of love, Rimbaud, in spite of himself, knows only the anguish of Lucifer. Before being able to reinvent being he will have to *reinvent love*.

And so, unable to follow Baudelaire where the self can find salvation, he became interested in speculations that suggest more impersonal, more material means for changing lead into gold. There is no doubt that in these months he glanced through certain books on alchemy. But though he was receptive to the alchemic metaphor, he had neither the time nor the inclination to pursue it very far. He says this straightforwardly in **"Les Soeurs de charité"** and I think that his interest in both *obscure alchemy* and the *occult sciences* was of the same nature as his taste, attested at this same period, for the librettos of Favart or for oriental tales. An interest, by the way, that was not frivolous for all that, a truly poetic interest indeed, since both Alchemy, the great Art, and Favart's fantastic "dénouements" suggest the same transgression of causality, the same freedom reached through miracles, the same remission and redemption.

More important, however, were other books, as recent research has shown. Brief and scattered reading, as always. We must not exaggerate the importance of Bretagne, an amateur of occult thought whom Rimbaud saw frequently during these last months in Charleville, nor overestimate the latter's patience or even his concern for philosophical theories. All he needed were a few central ideas, a new perspective. In other words, Rimbaud may have read Eliphas Lévi or Ballanche. But even so he never became a student of some system. The ideas he had found in Illuminism or in the Kabala, floating for a while in his thoughts like distant hopes, came suddenly together only in the attempt, compounded of violence and instinct, to revolutionize his own life.

In any case, here is what occultism and Illuminism suggested to Rimbaud. An ambition, above all, close to his eternal desire—to fix man again within the fabric of being, to return him to the unity that existed at the beginning of time. Also, those ideas—contradictory perhaps, but poetically associable—of the divine: for Eliphas Lévi, a rhythm that man can and must awaken within himself; for Ballanche, a Word temporarily concealed. The world is the word of God, Ballanche teaches, following numbers of others; consequently language, which at one time preserved the substance of things, thanks to the names that Orpheus gave them, remains the key. A poet will come, a hero of the spirit, to reestablish the universal language, and in it and through it, intuitive and all-inflaming, a new reason. Rimbaud could recognize here the mysterious power he had always felt to exist in the poetic use of words. And he also loved the hope spoken of in all the traditions: that man is half-way between God and the darkness of matter; that he bears within him a spark of God; and, as well, that he is free. He is able to determine his salvation.

But to do this, Eliphas Lévi teaches, he must make himself a "voyant" (a visionary), deny the lately come social order, rediscover through an intuition of the divine law, through a kind of brutal and instinctive phenomenology of the sacred, the hidden rhythm of God's things. Ballanche also speaks of a vision, which is reached (for him) through language. Two interests: the core of reality in the one case, language in the other—and here, precisely, in its unceasing contradiction, is the double concern of poetry. Rimbaud, a poet, was acquainted with both poles. Were he to intensify the conflicting quest, would that be enough to attain at last the state of awareness; even to make him the equal of God? At this point the philosophers give him

a warning: in any case there is a price to be paid, the worst sufferings, the dismembering of the personality to be accepted; the throwing off of the individual invented by Christianity, who is nothing more than the obscure prison where life now lies, vegetating.

And it is at this point as well, probably at the beginning of May 1871, that Rimbaud conceived the extraordinary idea that decided his fate for the next two years, perhaps forever.

That an event occurred at this moment in his existence, a spiritual event, the passion of his two May letters proves amply. He feverishly records there discoveries made in rapid succession, as happens only in a state of crisis. And as for the essential nature of the first intuition, let us not doubt that it was suddenly to have identified the abjection expressed in **"Le Coeur volé"** with the price asked of the future hero of the spirit: *Right now,* he wrote to Izambard, *I'm depraving myself as much as I can. Why? I want to be a poet, and I am working at making myself a* visionary: *you will not understand at all, and I'm not even sure I can explain it. The problem is to attain the unknown by disorganizing all the senses. The suffering is immense, but you have to be strong, and to have been born a poet. And I have realized that I am a poet . . .* Rimbaud in **"Le Coeur volé"** expressed the misery of a man both rebelling and scorned. He had seen that his *heart,* his ability to love, had been taken from him, leaving him the prisoner of a fascination for base things, with only the illusory purification that facile, deceitful poetry provides—and with no other recourse, no other act to attempt. And now, skimming *per diletto* through Eliphas Lévi or Ballanche, and reading of the sufferings that have to be undergone in order to become one of the "angels" of the new spirit, but also that *I is someone else,* that one is a receptacle of knowledge without being aware of it, that one can be at the point of revealing that knowledge without being aware of it, he suddenly understands that he is in the process of paying the price, that his unhappiness is the suffering required, and that his very despair is this break-up of the personality, of its finite interests, of its too human ambitions, that the philosophers were proposing. This exhaustion of will he suffered from so much (*I am getting myself cynically kept . . .*) is simply the dissolution of an illusory, in any case degraded, subjectivity: the descent into hell whence he will return a redeemer. Just when he thought himself lost, here he is, by means of an unknown power striving in him, closer than anyone to being a witness to the Spirit. *It's not my doing at all,* he adds. *It's wrong to say: I think. Better to say: I am thought. Pardon the pun.*

Let us understand the pun and what admirable energy this new thought which dresses the wound and cures it has suddenly been able to let loose. [In a footnote, Bonnefoy explains: *"C'est faux de dire: Je pense. On devrait dire: On me pense. Penser* (to think) and *panser* (to dress a wound) are homonyms."] The more he had been in despair—and humiliated—the more now his long-frustrated pride proposes him boundless tasks. "I am the One who will create God," Verlaine makes him say later, in "Crimen Amoris." He wants at least to be *the Poet,* that is, *the great invalid, the great criminal, the great accursed—and the Supreme*

Scientist! One of those *horrible workers* who, according to Illuminism, are to prepare the return of being, which he was to call *the true life.* This desire *to remake life,* deepening—and so painfully—day after day since childhood, with what metaphysical, eschatological meaning does he now endow it!

He decides, with a courage which now seems to him quite easy, I have no doubt, to follow his destiny, deepening sufferings and torments still more, yet at the same time giving them a positive value and meaning. This estrangement that caused his suffering yesterday is now his glory . . . *But the problem is,* he wrote to Demeny, *to make the soul into a monster, like the comprachicos.* [Bonnefoy adds in a footnote: "The 'comprachicos' (in Victor Hugo's *L'Homme qui rit,* published in 1869) were kidnappers of children. They deformed them into freaks in order to exhibit them."] *Think of a man grafting warts onto his face and growing them there . . . All forms of love, of suffering, of madness; he searches, he exhausts within himself all poisons, and preserves their quintessences. Unspeakable torment, where he will need the greatest faith, a superhuman strength . . .* The *horrible worker* can take upon himself all the repudiations that Arthur Rimbaud had once pronounced so unwillingly. He can take upon himself **"Mes petites amoureuses"** with less hatred, perhaps, but more detachment—and it is not by chance that this seemingly futile poem has a place in the **"Lettre du voyant."** Estrangement has proven to be a creative ascesis. *Vice,* one of the ways of rending the veil that covers up truth. More essentially Rimbaud can now reaffirm his dark poems, **"Accroupissements,"** a *pious hymn,* he writes, or **"Le Coeur volé,"** those where the sordid is most dangerously aggressive. *I give you this: is it satire, as you would say? Is it poetry?* These poems in any case are the dissolution, the alchemists' "putrefactio", of *subjective* poetry.

I say one must be a visionary, make oneself a visionary! Rimbaud's main decision was to move from what he called *subjective* poetry to *objective* poetry.

Which is not to mention the fact, he wrote to Izambard, *that your subjective poetry will always be horribly wishy-washy.* And to Demeny, on the subject of Musset: *Oh, those insipid* Contes *and* Proverbes! *. . . Musset didn't manage to do anything worth while; there were visions within those lace window curtains; he closed his eyes.* Subjective poetry seems then to be that poetry which is satisfied with idealized figures, "artiste" aestheticism and verbalism; and that sentimental and lyrical poetry, which preserves only the tameable part of the emotions; that poetry, in a word, which shuts man up in his conventional nature without ever making him aware of the obscure layers of what is. And Rimbaud obviously has not forgotten that for a long time he conformed to this subjective poetry. **"Les Etrennes des orphelins"** and **"Soleil et chair"** are of this nature, since their dreams of plentitude so easily are part of torpid existences; and **"Ma bohème"** or **"Le Cabaret vert"** and all the sonnets written on the open road, since nothing had ever answered their hopes—these illusions; but the most recent poems are subjective poetry as well, the ones Rimbaud is still in the process of writing, **"Les Soeurs de charité"** and **"Les Premières Commu-**

nions,"** which only describe when it is necessary to transform, and **"Les Assis,"** **"Oraison du soir,"** and **"Accroupissements,"** since disgust and hate, attitudes both, fix man in the psychological framework of the analysis of alienation. All poetry until this moment has been nothing but such a void. From the point of view of the Kabala this corresponds indeed to the lower level where man vegetates, to that individuality which appeared when primordial being was fragmented. And passing beyond this deceptive poetry, Rimbaud thinks now, will be as well the dismantling of our present misfortune. He proclaims *objective* poetry as a return to the divine life, as a passage from feelings and psychological attitudes to participation regained, as an intensification of our perceptions (which provided only a partial perspective, only a particular tuning of the senses when many others are possible) until they are consumed in the substantial fire of the Unknown. Since our life compared with the life of the Greeks is no longer a harmonious existence, akin to divine rhythms, it is precisely in the burning away of what it has become that we must reinvent the real. Being becomes identified with newness, in the most radical, most *monstrous,* most destructive sense of that term; and truth with a nonmediate vision—with the emergence—of that reality that is ahead of us in the Unknown.

Thus did Rimbaud spiritualize his emotional disintegration, his horrible, martyred soul, giving them meaning and value. Vision, historically unforeseeable, is spiritually the metamorphosis of the emotional distress experienced by an adolescent.

And I will try further on to explain what techniques he attempted to devise in order to learn being, as he almost puts it; what new, hitherto unknown link between language and intuition. For the moment, in his desire for Vision, I would like simply to emphasize the enormous energy that was set to work—for profit, if I may use an expression he hated, but in a new sense, a heroic one. For the Unknown that Rimbaud obscurely senses, burning up the categories of his mind, dispels in so doing the darkness that overwhelmed him. And in a frenzy—with his usual lack of restraint—he hurls himself toward this salvation. For a long time he had tried to replace ordinary sights by fantastic glimmerings. The seven-year-old poet, seeking out Vision, *pressed his thumb against his dazzled eyes,* and the taste expressed in **"Sensation"** and elsewhere for lukewarm drinks, the odor of wet meadows, the stench of alleyways, revealed the most eager attention to whatever betrays in the familiar appearance of things, the workings of something still beyond denomination. *For a long time,* Rimbaud will say in **Une Saison en enfer,** *I boasted that I was master of all possible landscapes.* And yet nothing was extraordinary enough to foretell the two great poems that he was to write in the course of the summer; nor that he could send to Banville, whom he seemed only a few months before to respect so much, those pages filled with insolence and genius: **"Ce qu'on dit au poète à propos de fleurs."**

I consider this one of the most admirable poems Rimbaud ever wrote, and the expression probably of his energy at its purest. Banville, a *subjective* poet if there was one, had sung on and on about flowers. The soothing decor of his placid imagination was filled with lilies, carnations, and amaranths. It was now time for him to learn that such *enema bags of ecstasy* could be rather rudely insulted in Charleville:

> Always this French vegetation abounds,
> Grouchy, coughing, silly, and sick,
> Where the bellies of basset hounds
> Wallow through the growing dark;

and that someone who called himself a poet had dared to oppose the saps, glucoses, and resins of *industrious plants* to their so-called beauty, in the name of usefulness. The argument is, of course, metaphoric. The sap, coming from beyond the form, makes us think of an epiphany of being. The tangible and the nutritive found in what had been simple enjoyment stress the intoxicating strength of the Unknown. And to submerge being in usefulness and lyricism in commerce, has a polemical value in the struggle against sterile, "subjective" beauty. There seems no doubt that Rimbaud wanted to write, ironically and obliquely, a kind of *ars poetica.* The *"On,"* the persona who addresses the poet on the subject of flowers is still the same monstrous tormented being, both familiar and remote, who had spoken in the letter to Demeny, that *I* who is *someone else* and who may well have shown himself for a moment in the sarcastic and somewhat equivocal voice of that strange figure, Alcide Bava. [Bonnefoy adds in a footnote: *"Bava* means in French: *(he) slobbered,* and Alcide is of course Hercules . . ."] Yet we must not ignore the attraction that the coarsest savors may have, just for what they are, for the mind; and their straightforward poetic potency as well. The *peasant* who will step to the fore in the last lines of **Une Saison en enfer,** the *trader* and *settler* Rimbaud would one day become when he had abandoned words, deserve praise for lending their harsh knowledge of things to that kind of medium who dictated Rimbaud's poem: for from the eradication of qualities, from the destruction of forms, from this brutal intuition of substance, it is clear that a stormy light had broken forth, a lightning flash never before seen in the too-narrow skies of poetry.

The sarcasm of **"Ce qu'on dit au poète à propos de fleurs,"** its panic anti-lyricism, marks the disorganization of the old sensory approach, the overturning of the world of humanism, and for Rimbaud, the happy disappearance (yes, there is a true happiness in this savage, elusive, dancing poem) of the old self-hatred, experienced as *vomiting,* in the universal outpouring of saps. This is why I dare say I prefer this earlier poem to **Le Bateau ivre,** the other great undertaking of that summer and a more anxious ecstasy. **Le Bateau ivre** is much less the momentum of Vision than its myth; and if it manages to express its breadth and its generous immediacy, it also clearly foreshadows its failure.

It derives—and this is its only essential origin—from Baudelaire's "Le Voyage." Already a poet had wanted to test the order established by men, to advance beyond good and evil (doesn't he say so: "Heaven or Hell, what matter?") and, using words that Arthur Rimbaud was to use in turn, to plummet "the depths of the unknown to find the new." But Baudelaire, strengthened by his great capacity to love, had sought a way out by assuming his fate as a mortal being. The landscape of our odyssey, "Le Voyage" says, repeats itself, indefinitely reflecting our own image. We must not seek some truer reality in a mythical elsewhere, but in each being and each thing, by grasping them in the truth of their finiteness, that is, their death. Could Rimbaud understand this hope, at this moment at least? In any case, he makes this renovated myth of the quest his own and believes he will be able to announce that there is, right here, another way out. He mimes the movement that will cast the mind—once those who guided it from the tow-path, logical thought and sensory traditions, have been massacred—into the howling flood of profound colors which stretches out like a massive and stormy sea beyond the peaceful rivers. He affirms Vision as a *strength to come,* a higher life, a knowledge. Rimbaud says that he has *seen* and he *knows.* At least he describes with an inexhaustible appetite for images—the very hunger of our poetry so long a captive of the rational and the picturesque—the fermenting and circulating of saps, the waterspouts, all that moves from enormous potentiality to violent outbreaks, thunderous, rapid as lightning and broad as the deep. And these will remain for a long time—a long time in the optimistic first part of the poem—the happy images indeed, and the strongest ones, of the Unknown.

But they remain images and forms, that is, from our side of the real, nothing of the Unknown. And a doubt soon shows itself in **Le Bateau ivre** concerning the very location of that Unknown or the means to reach it *(Are these bottomless nights your exiled nests . . .)* and, even more seriously, concerning the very possibility of his quest and its sincerity. *True, I've cried too much,* Rimbaud writes suddenly, with extraordinary intelligence. The anguished wasting of oneself that, up to yesterday, the failure of love had caused, might well weaken any strength; or might well force desire to remain, far from the transensuous ravishment, in the more modest horizon of the original frustration that is still to be appeased. Is it certain that Rimbaud really wants to go with that boat, into the bliss of these distant seas? Is he not, in this useless exaltation, rather like that *drowned man,* absent from his own ecstasy, who passes three times in the poem? Besides, Rimbaud always knows himself, he can never refrain from saying himself, and he suddenly exposes his true desire:

> If I long for a shore in Europe,
> It's a small pond, dark cold, remote,
> The odor of evening, and a child full of sorrow
> Who stoops to launch a crumpled paper boat.

What is this still water, if not the *locus* of childhood reaffirmed? And this other boat, if not a need for something else than cosmic communion, a need for love, satisfied by the slightest of things, as long as someone who loves has given it? As a matter of fact, the child that Rimbaud evokes is *full of sorrow,* he has not known that love, and he understands obscurely that the mysterious weakness of an unfulfilled childhood will hold in check within him that *poem of the sea* which he had thought to be his future strength. **Le Bateau ivre,** like so many of Rimbaud's poems, ends as the victory of lucidity over an initial swell of hope. And Vision, just conceived, may turn out to be vain: for the kind of love it unleashes, elemental, wild, glowing above the abyss, is worth less, *is* less, than the humble love of human beings which, given freely, sanctifies. Vision leads to the inner rhythms of matter, beyond place and time, and it is not certain that it can satisfy all the exigencies of a human heart. (pp. 30-43)

> *Yves Bonnefoy, in his* Rimbaud, *translated by Paul Schmidt, Harper Colophon Books, 1973, 145 p.*

John Porter Houston   (essay date 1963)

[*Houston was an American educator and critic who specializes in French literature. In the following excerpt from his study* The Design of Rimbaud's Poetry, *he explicates* Le bateau ivre.]

Myth, whether made out of whole cloth or pieced together from classical and other sources, dominates much of romantic and modern poetry. In France the tendency toward myth is quite pronounced in various minor romantic writers, but many of them worked chiefly in prose, and often their achievements cannot be judged on any grounds other than good intentions. It was not until the mid-nineteenth century, with the later work of Hugo, Gérard de Nerval, and Lamartine, that a corpus of important myth-centered poetry accumulated. Rimbaud's evolution toward this mode of imagination is therefore part of a larger movement in French literature which, though obscure at the time—Nerval was little known and Hugo's most audacious poems, *Dieu* and *La Fin de Satan,* remained unpublished until after his death—seems, from our vantage point, of considerable scope.

The characteristics of mythopoeic poetry will emerge more clearly as we examine **Le Bateau ivre,** but we might make the distinction—which is especially pertinent in this case—that a myth is not an allegory, it is not a structure of simple, univalent symbols which can be translated into concepts. The integrity of myth refuses to be violated by reduction into abstract terms: its symbols are too rich in suggestiveness and interrelations for us to say that Rimbaud's boat represents something else. Nor is the life of a boat meaningless because boats are inanimate: we cannot press a rational order on this poem and insist that it conform. The world of myth must be understood on its own terms, and careful examination of the poem is indispensable.

> Comme je descendais des Fleuves impassibles,
> Je ne me sentis plus guidé par les haleurs:
> Des Peaux-Rouges criards les avaient pris pour
>   cibles,
> Les ayant cloués nus aux poteaux de couleurs.
>
> J'étais insoucieux de tous les équipages,
> Porteur de blés flammands ou de cotons anglais.
> Quand avec mes haleurs ont fini ces tapages,
> Les Fleuves m'ont laissé descendre où je voulais.

[As I was going down impassive Rivers, I no longer felt myself guided by the haulers: screeching redskins had taken them as targets, nailing them naked to colored stakes. I was indifferent to any crew, bearing Flemish wheat or English cottons.

When along with my haulers this uproar was over, the Rivers let me go on where I wanted.]

Le Bateau ivre is divided into a number of parts, whose discreteness and unity are assured by rhetorical devices. Several parallelisms relate the first two stanzas: the use of "Fleuves" and a form of *descendre* in lines one and eight, the mention of the haulers' massacre in the third line of each stanza, the imperfect tenses in lines one and five as contrasted with the compound tenses which follow them, and so forth. It is important to note the tenses here as elsewhere in the poem: the juxtaposition of *passé simple* and *passé composé* (lines two, seven, and eight) serves a particular function. The *passé composé,* the punctual past tense of ordinary speech, is used as a neutral, unemphatic tense, whereas the *passé simple,* with its more limited and literary usage, is reserved for dramatic effect. It is the *passé simple* which marks the sudden, magical liberation of the boat—a liberation all the more startling in that at first it is only felt and not seen (for, like a beast of burden, the boat cannot see its back). The sharply punctual, almost historical "je ne me sentis plus" cutting across the flowing durative imperfect "descendais" vividly isolates this moment of transformation when the boat gratuitously ceases to resemble other boats. Its surprise is contrasted with the rivers' attitude, since, though animate like everything else in the poem, they seem not to notice this metamorphosis. The boat's reaction to the massacre of the haulers anticipates its later adventures, where there is emphasis on colorful visual detail and indifference to suffering; thus the description of the massacre serves to set a prevailing mood. In this case, however, the boat's insouciance is quite explicable: its will is finally being asserted over the orderliness of the world represented by images of commerce. The boat and the Indians have triumphed over the shipping industry and European trade, and the fact is underscored by the emphatic position of "voulais" at the end of the second stanza.

The next three stanzas describe the boat's *physical* initiation into the sea world (as distinguished from the spiritual one, which comes later):

> Dans les clapotements furieux des marées,
> Moi, l'autre hiver, plus sourd que les cerveaux
>   d'enfants,
> Je courus! Et les Péninsules démarrées
> N'ont pas subi tohu-bohus plus triomphants.
>
> La tempête a béni mes éveils maritimes.
> Plus léger qu'un bouchon j'ai dansé sur les flots
> Qu'on appelle rouleurs éternels de victimes,
> Dix nuits, sans regretter l'oeil niais des falots!
>
> Plus douce qu'aux enfants la chair des pommes
>   sures,
> L'eau verte pénétra ma coque de sapin
> Et des taches de vins bleus et des vomissures
> Me lava, dispersant gouvernail et grappin.

[Into the furious clash of the tides I, the other winter, more heedless than children's brains, I ran! And the uprooted Peninsulas have not undergone a more triumphant hubbub. The storms blessed my maritime vigils. Lighter than a cork I danced on the waves, which they call eternal rollers of victims, ten nights, without regretting the silly eye of the lighthouses. Sweeter than the flesh of unripe apples is to children, the green water penetrated my hull of fir and washed me of spots of blue wines and vomit, dispersing rudder and grappling-hook.]

The comparison of the boat with an obstinate child brings out an important association in the poem. Earlier the Indians had evoked the world of children's books, and the word "tapage," used of the massacre, commonly designates children's uproar. The opposition between the boat and children, on the one hand, and men, on the other, is constant: eating green apples is an unwise childish penchant, and later the boat speaks of wishing to show exotic fishes to children (stanza fifteen). The boat and children are related through their common love of impetuosity and disorder: the third stanza describes the boat's entry into the sea with violent expressions. "Je courus" is opposed both by tense and energy of meaning to the peaceful "descendais" of an earlier stanza, and its rhythmically isolated place in the line heightens it. "Les Péninsules démarrées" suggests great masses in movement (the optical illusion by which, from a boat, the land seems to be moving), and the verb *subir* accentuates the triumph with which the boat imposes its will for the first time.

Stanza four, in language suddenly become gentle, confirms the benevolence of the ocean, which is hostile only to men. Their lighthouses are contemptuously called not *phares* but "falots," which means "foolish" as well as "lanterns," and their absurd fear of the sea is mocked by quoting one of their phrases: "rouleurs éternels de victimes," a parody of *le père* Hugo's sonorous verses on the perils of the deep (cf. "Oceano nox"). The grandiose Hugolian expression contrasts sharply with the simplicity of the boat's language and its homey similes. Finally the recurring *passé simple* of the fifth stanza marks the end of the boat's physical initiation into sea life: it has now become one with its element, and the last traces of the world of men are effaced. With the rudder and hook vanishes the world of orderly movement.

The long middle section of *Le Bateau ivre* (stanzas six to fourteen) opens with the boat's spiritual entrance into the ocean world, which a sudden shift of style sets into great relief:

> Et dès lors, je me suis baigné dans le Poème
> De la Mer, infusé d'astres, et lactescent,
> Dévorant les azurs verts; où, flottaison blême
> Et ravie, un noyé pensif parfois descend;
>
> Où, teignant tout à coup les bleuités, délires
> Et rhythmes lents sous les rutilements du jour,
> Plus fortes que l'alcool, plus vastes que vos lyres,
> Fermentent les rousseurs amères de l'amour!

[And from then on I bathed in the Poem of the Sea infused with stars and lactescent, devouring the green azure, where, like a pallid, ecstatic bit of flotsam, a pensive drowned man sometimes sinks down—where, dyeing suddenly the blueness, with delirium and slow rhythms under the glimmers of day, there ferments the bitter reddening of love, stronger than alcohol and vaster than your lyres!]

Vast images of space, light, and color suddenly invade the poem. These stanzas seem to describe first the night sea, milky with phosphorus, dotted with reflected stars, horizonless, and indistinguishable from the sky. Then dawn comes: "rutilements" suggests breaking day and "rousseurs" the color which "dyes" the blue sea, while the rhythms of the waves are accentuated by the long, low fingers of light. Dawn is an appropriate symbol of a new spiritual experience, and into the light imagery are woven highly emotive words which convey the boat's ecstasy. The experience is esthetic ("Poème," "lyres"), physical ("dévorant," "alcool") and so overwhelming as to be compared with death; the *noyé ravi* recalls Leopardi's famous line "E il naufragar m'è dolce in questo mar." The adjective "amères" should not surprise us: pleasure and pain are closely related and readily turn into one another. This is not an edulcorated joy but the most voluptuous self-immolation. Finally the word "amour" occurs at the climax of the passage. This term must be understood in the special sense it acquired in nineteenth-century poetic usage; the romantic pantheists employed it to describe total communion and harmony with the universe. Its connotations are at once metaphysical and sensuous. The boat's immersion in the sea perfectly exemplifies the romantics' desire to abolish the barriers between subject and object, to achieve a unity of spirit.

The stanzas we have just considered are the emotive peaks of the poem; yet many more stanzas remain, and we must now pay particular attention to Rimbaud's subtle ways of sustaining his tone and varying his images. The central part of *Le Bateau ivre* consists of six stanzas beginning with *je* or *j'ai* and also showing certain other parallelisms of sentence structure. The first three continue to elaborate light and weather imagery:

> Je sais les cieux crevant en éclairs, et les trombes
> Et les ressacs et les courants: je sais le soir,
> L'Aube exaltée ainsi qu'un peuple de colombes,
> Et j'ai vu quelquefois ce que l'homme a cru voir!
>
> J'ai vu le soleil bas, taché d'horreurs mystiques,
> Illuminant de longs figements violets,
> Pareils à des acteurs de drames très antiques
> Les flots roulant au loin leurs frissons de volets!
>
> J'ai rêvé la nuit verte aux neiges éblouies,
> Baiser montant aux yeux des mers avec lenteurs,
> La circulation des sèves inouïes,
> Et l'éveil jaune et bleu des phosphores chanteurs!

[I know the skies bursting with lightning, and the waterspouts and the surf and the currents: I know evening, dawn reaching high like a people of doves, and I have sometimes seen what man has thought to see! I have seen the low sun, spotted with mystic horrors and lighting, with long violet clots which resemble the actors of ancient dramas, the waves rolling at a distance in shutter-like quivers. I have dreamed the green night with dazzled snows, a kiss rising slowly to the sea's eyes; the circulation of unknown saps and the yellow and blue awakening of singing phosphorus.]

Only two difficulties of meaning present themselves here: the simile of the second stanza seems to mean that the long beams of light glancing on the waves move back and forth like actors in a shadow play or some other simple form of theater. The kiss and eye metaphor of the third stanza is more ambiguous; the eyes of the sea would seem to be its surface (eyes have been called "pools" after all), while the kiss, which could be in apposition to "nuit" or "neiges," might describe the approach of night from the horizon or the rising of bubbly foam to the water's surface. In any case these three stanzas deal with knowledge of the universe as symbolized by evening, dawn, sunset, and night; it is as if the boat saw the archetype of each hour. "Je *sais* le soir," says the boat with an emphatic, unusual use of *savoir*. This definitive vision is what man can only think to see (and again the boat emphasizes its difference from mankind).

Each of the preceding three stanzas contains, in simile or metaphor, a hint of living creatures: doves, actors, singing phosphorescences. Yet essentially the boat is alone in a seascape. Now lands, plants, and animals come into view:

> J'ai suivi, des mois pleins, pareille aux vacheries
> Hystériques, la houle à l'assaut des récifs,
> Sans songer que les pieds lumineux des Maries
> Pussent forcer le mufle aux Océans poussifs!
>
> J'ai heurté, savez-vous, d'incroyables Florides
> Mêlant aux fleurs des yeux de panthères à peaux
> D'hommes! Des arcs-en-ciel tendus comme des
> brides
> Sous l'horizon des mers, à de glauques
> troupeaux!
>
> J'ai vu fermenter les marais énormes, nasses
> Où pourrit dans les joncs tout un Léviathan!
> Des écroulements d'eaux au milieu des bonaces,
> Et les lointains vers les gouffres cataractant!
>
> [I followed for whole months the swell, like a hysterical dairy-stable, in its assault on the reefs, without imagining that the Maries' luminous feet could force the snout of the wheezing Oceans! I have run into, you know, unbelievable Floridas, where among the flowers are mingled the eyes of panthers with human skin! Rainbows stretched out like reins under the horizon of the seas to greenish herds! I have seen the enormous swamps fermenting, fish-traps where a whole Leviathan rots in the rushes! Avalanches of water in the middle of calms and the far distances cataracting toward the abyss!]

The cows of the sea seem at first to be merely a metaphor for the waves forced back into the sea by the headland of the Camargue (where the village of the Saintes-Maries is situated). But the green herds of the next stanza are more concrete, and the panther-men melting into the flowers are definitely more than just a figure of speech. Mythic poetry is animistic and does not know rational distinctions between animals, plants, and inert matter; it has the archaic, pre-logical vision of the world as instinct with mysterious life. In the third stanza, Leviathan is put on the same plane with gigantic whirlpools, as if they were comparable entities. In connection with animism we should also note a peculiar stylistic device which supports it: the nouns of *Le Bateau ivre* are largely in the plural, creating a blurred effect of multiplicity, pullulation, and plentitude. The so-called poetic plural is, of course, common in French, but it is seldom carried to such lengths and with so specific an effect.

In addition to the abundant plurals another distinctive stylistic trait lends a feeling of portentous life to this passage as well as to many others in the poem. The definite article is constantly used before nouns, even when, as in "pareille aux vacheries hystériques," a partitive article or other construction would be demanded by normal usage. This insistent use of the definite article ends by creating a strange class of beings, by investing almost any noun with a demonstrative particularity, as if the thing it designated were too individual to be confused with others of its kind. This curious grammar is not exclusive, furthermore, to *Le Bateau ivre* and is present in many of Rimbaud's poems.

To conclude the central part of *Le Bateau ivre* Rimbaud uses a very formal rhetorical device: an enumeration of nouns summarizing the preceding stanzas—weather and animals—and devoid of a main verb.

> Glaciers, soleils d'argent, flots nacreux, cieux de
> braises!
> Echouages hideux au fond des golfes bruns
> Où les serpents géants dévorés des punaises
> Choient, des arbres tordus, avec de noirs par-
> fums!
>
> [Glaciers, silver suns, nacreous waves, ember skies! Hideous strandings in brown gulfs where the giant serpents, devoured by bedbugs, tumble down from gnarled trees with black scents!]

We have now reached a turning point in the poem where we must once again consider the question of tenses. The central section is written in the present (for statal matters) and the *passé composé*, but the latter is ambiguous and requires some analysis. Since it may serve either as a present perfect or as a preterite, it does not clearly define the relation of past to present; it does not indicate whether the boat is still continuing its wanderings or whether they belong to an irrevocable, historical past. One's first impression is that, in contrast to the *passés simples* of the introductory stanzas, the *passés composés* indicate that the adventure is not over, that the past events are part of one continuing experience. Finally, however, by a very subtle transition Rimbaud corrects in retrospect the meaning of this tense, but not without our first having received from it a false feeling of immediacy. He slips in a conditional perfect, which implies remoteness and irremediability, and then passes into the iterative imperfect with its sense of "used to":

> J'aurais voulu montrer aux enfants ces dorades
> Du flot bleu, ces poissons d'or, ces poissons
> chantants.
> —Des écumes de fleurs ont bercé mes dérades
> Et d'ineffables vents m'ont ailé par instants.
>
> Parfois, martyr lassé des pôles et des zones,
> La mer dont le sanglot faisait mon roulis doux
> Montait vers moi ses fleurs d'ombre aux vent-
> ouses jaunes
> Et je restais, ainsi qu'une femme à genoux . . .

Presque île, ballottant sur mes bords les querel-
les
Et les fientes d'oiseaux clabaudeurs aux yeux
blonds.
Et je voguais, lorsqu'à travers mes liens frêles
Des noyés descendaient dormir, à reculons!

[I should have liked to show children those sun-
fishes of the blue wave, those golden fishes, those
singing fishes. Foams of flowers rocked my drift-
ings and ineffable winds occasionally winged me.
Sometimes when I was martyred, weary of poles
and zones, the sea, whose sob made my gentle
roll, brought up to me her shadow-flowers with
yellow suckers. And I remained like a kneeling
woman . . . Like a kind of island tossing on my
sides the quarrels and droppings of blond-eyed
noisy birds. And I sailed on, when through my
fragile ties drowned men sunk backwards to
sleep.]

As the tenses shift, the character of the boat's experiences
also changes; the energetic quest for the ocean's mysteries
yields to languor. The boat thinks, for the first time and
as if regretfully, of the existence of sympathetic creatures,
children, and is attracted more by flowers than by the rig-
ors of strange climates (vaguely categorized as the "poles
and zones"). A series of words suggests failing strength
and feeble movement: "bercer," "dérade" (a neologism
from *dérader:* "to be dragged out of harbor by winds"),
"lassé," "roulis doux," "une femme à genoux" (implying
that the boat is leaning forward to look at the flowers). The
boat has again become conscious of its physical self: the
third stanza even seems to indicate that it is topheavy with
the weight of the birds, while its hull ("frêles liens") has
become so disintegrated that drowned men may pass
through the chinks. This passage balances stanzas three to
five, which described the boat's physical sensations on entering the sea, for the form of *Le Bateau ivre* is cyclical,
and we are now returning to the original point of departure.

Another elaborate rhetorical pattern (still in the imperfect
tense) leads us further back toward the civilized world:

Or moi, bateau perdu sous les cheveux des anses,
Jeté par l'ouragan dans l'éther sans oiseau,
Moi dont les Monitors et les voiliers des Hanses
N'auraient pas repêché la carcasse ivre d'eau;

Libre, fumant, monté de brumes violettes,
Moi qui trouais le ciel rougeoyant comme un
mur
Qui porte, confiture exquise aux bons poètes,
Des lichens de soleil et des morves d'azur;

Qui courais, taché de lunules électriques,
Planche folle, escorté des hippocampes noirs,
Quand les juillets faisaient crouler à coups de
triques
Les cieux ultramarins aux ardents entonnoirs;

Moi qui tremblais, sentant geindre à cinquante
lieues
Le rut des Béhémots et les Maelstroms épais,
Fileur éternel des immobilités bleues,
Je regrette l'Europe aux anciens parapets!

[Now I, a boat lost in the foliage of coves,

thrown by the storm into the birdless ether, I,
whose water-drunken carcass would not have
been salvaged by the Monitors and the Hanseat-
ic sailing ships; free, smoking, covered with violet mists, I, who pierced the reddening sky that
looks like a wall covered with—a delicious jam
for good poets—lichens of sunlight and mucus
of blue sky; who ran, speckled with electric satellites, a wild plank, escorted by black seahorses,
when the Julys beat down with cudgels the burning funnels of the ultramarine skies; I, who trem-
bled, hearing a hundred leagues around the
moaning of the Behemoths in heat and the dense
Maelstroms, I, eternal drifter of the motionless
blue, I miss Europe and its ancient cliffs.]

The first and last stanzas of this lengthy period are related
by proper names ("Monitors," "Hanses," "Europe"), so
that it forms an elegant circle. All the stanzas are, furthermore, connected by parallel images: the boat is being
tossed into the air, pierces the sky, is thrown about by
summer storms which merge sea and sky, and runs endlessly through the "immobilités bleues," an expression
which suggests the unity of ocean and atmosphere. What
these images convey is the boat's fragile lightness and passivity, which have already been hinted at in the preceding
stanzas. However, should the boat's drunken subjugation
to the sea be interpreted as the reason for its missing Europe? That is to say, are the clauses dependent on "moi"
causal or adversative in meaning? I think the adversative
sense is a better reading, partly because it gives "Je regrette l'Europe . . . " greater dramatic relief and partly because the experiences described in the clauses dependent
on "moi" summarize the boat's original desires: to be
drunken with water, to be free, to enjoy a kind of esthetic
pleasure ("confiture exquise aux bons poètes"), to move
recklessly and irregularly, and to see the animals and phenomena of the deep. Thus, *although* the boat has done
these things, its mind returns to home. These four stanzas
are almost a résumé of the central section of the poem
(stanzas six to fourteen), and the boat expresses its surprise that, having utterly achieved its yearnings, it should
then long for Europe.

The next stanza introduces a curious new element:

J'ai vu des archipels sidéraux! et des îles
Dont les cieux délirants sont ouverts au vogueur:
—Est-ce en ces nuits sans fonds que tu dors et
t'exiles,
Million d'oiseaux d'or, ô future Vigueur?

[I have seen sidereal archipelagos! and islands
whose ecstatic skies are open to the sea-
wanderer: is it in these limitless nights that you
sleep and retire, million golden birds, O future
Vigor?]

The ecstatic sky imagery recurs but with a new nuance:
the heavens are now the symbol of conceivable but unattainable aspirations. "Vigor" is exactly what the boat has
lost—if it ever had it, for the adjective "future" has interesting implications. Has the boat's journey taken place in
real time and space, or was it merely a now fading dream,
symbolic of what is to take place in the future? We must
postpone considering this problem, for the last stanzas of

the poem are related alternatively rather than sequentially.

> Mais, vrai, j'ai trop pleuré! Les Aubes sont navrantes.
> Toute lune est atroce et tout soleil amer:
> L'âcre amour m'a gonflé de torpeurs enivrantes.
> O que ma quille éclate! O que j'aille à la mer!

> [But, truly, I have wept too much. The dawns are heartbreaking. Any moon is horrible and any sun bitter. Acrid love has filled me with intoxicating torpor. O let my keel burst! Let me dissolve into the sea!]

"J'ai trop pleuré!" abruptly places us in a new phase of the journey, for there has been no question of weeping previously. The boat suddenly realizes what has been apparent from the imagery of the preceding eight stanzas: that its sea-change leads ultimately to dissolution, that its weakness is a prelude to disgust and the desire for death. "L'âcre amour" (the noun significantly recurs just this one time to designate again the boat's total sea experience) leads to a kind of love-death.

Suddenly in a brilliant metamorphosis the boat is placed in a new perspective:

> Si je désire une eau d'Europe, c'est la flache
> Noire et froide où vers le crépuscule embaumé
> Un enfant accroupi plein de tristesses, lâche
> Un bateau frêle comme un papillon de mai.

> [If I want European water, it is the cold, black puddle where, in the sweet-scented twilight, a squatting child full of melancholy sets off a boat fragile as a May butterfly.]

The sea has dwindled to a landlocked puddle, and the boat's fragility is now understandable, since it is only a toy. The boat's bond with children is also clearer: they are its only companions, and the sea adventure was their communal dream. However, there are implications for the future in the description of the landscape with its delicate alternation of connotations (A. "noire," B. "embaumé," A. "tristesse," B. "mai"). The ground on which the child squats is cold and dark, but the evening air is fragrant with approaching spring, and the boat brings to mind a butterfly. As in the stanza on "future Vigor," height symbolizes the promise of the future, and the turn of the season reinforces the sense of expectation. The child will grow and free himself from the tyranny of the adult world.

But we must not conclude that the boat is merely a symbol of the child and his dreams, for the cycle of growing power and dissolution through which the boat passes is not identical with a child's aspirations. We must beware of the urge to make a facile epitome of the poem. The boat is to some extent equated with the child, but it is also a more general symbol and ultimately irreducible. To make clear that the poem is about a boat and not an allegory about a child, Rimbaud concludes it with a final picture of the boat's abjection:

> Je ne puis plus, baigné de vos langueurs, ô lames,
> Enlever leur sillage aux porteurs de cotons,
> Ni traverser l'orgueil des drapeaux et des flammes,

> Ni nager sous les yeux horribles des pontons.

> [I can no longer, bathed in your languor, O waves, follow close on the cotton boats, or pass haughty flags and shell-fire, or swim under the terrible eyes of the prison-ships.]

The cycle has come full swing; the boat is suddenly back in the world of organized shipping, where it had been before its magical liberation. But now the other ships are menacing and more powerful than the enervated "carcasse ivre d'eau." (There is also a symbolic correspondence here with the child's inferior position in the world of men: the stanzas interreact.)

We may define the shape and emotive content of a mythopoeic poem like *Le Bateau ivre,* but it is impossible to translate it into a coherent allegory. The association between boat and child, for example, is intermittent and most pronounced at the beginning and end of the work. The boat's voyage corresponds somewhat with the cycle of life—or love, or even artistic inspiration, if one likes—but the details of imagery (for example, that of commerce in the first and last stanzas) do not easily lend themselves to such readings. Finally, the sea is so polyvalent a symbol in literature as to defy any neat categorizing of it. Numerous allegorical interpretations are generated by the poem, but none is so definitive as to exclude the others. Such is the nature of myth: it may be used but never exhausted by ratiocination. (pp. 65-81)

> *John Porter Houston, in his* The Design of Rimbaud's Poetry, *Yale University Press, 1963, 270 p.*

"Homage to Arthur Rimbaud," by Charles Wright:

Laying our eggs like moths
In the cold cracks of your eyes,
Brushing your hands with our dark wings

—Desperate to attempt
An entrance, to touch that light
Which buoys you like a flame,
That it might warm our own lives—,

We cluster about your death
As though it were reachable.

For almost a hundred years
We've gathered outside your legend (and been afraid
Of what such brilliance affords)

And knew the while you were risen, your flight
Pneumatic and pure, invisible as a fever;
And knew the flight was forever,
Leaving us what we deserve:

Syllables, flowers, black ice;
The exit, the split cocoon . . .

Charles Wright, in his Hard Freight, *1973.*

Enid Rhodes Peschel   (essay date 1977)

[*Peschel is an American educator and critic. In the following excerpt from her* Flux and Reflux: Ambivalence in the Poems of Arthur Rimbaud, *she examines Rimbaud's ambivalence toward love and sex.*]

Ambivalence is the mainspring of Arthur Rimbaud's creative drive. Throughout his poetry he shifts between poles of affirmation and negation. With equal insistence he praises and condemns things, thoughts, his poetry, other people and himself. The flux and the reflux of his emotions are reflected not only in his ideas, language and poetic figures, but also in his self-portrayals, his implied tones and the structure of his visions.

Rimbaud's oscillations shape unresolved and unresolvable conflicts that contribute to the particular richness, complexity and energetic tension of his writings. Depicting himself as a god and a demon, a pagan and a Christian, a kind of pre-Nietzschean Übermensch and a slave, a poet-prophet-seer (the *voyant*) and a peasant, a suppliant imploring God's mercy and a rebel cursing God, he is both hopeful and despondent, omnipotent and impotent, proud and ashamed.

Toward himself and toward the world around him, Rimbaud is ambivalent. While seeking for the "harmonious Life" he craves, a life that would resolve or accept his contradictory urges, he nevertheless always feels himself dragged down again to what he bitterly calls in *Une Saison en enfer* "rugged reality". Often, the poet's images reflect his conflicting feelings: "Extase, cauchemar, sommeil dans un nid de flammes", he proclaims in **"Nuit de l'enfer."**

What may be called Rimbaud's poetic pattern follows the ever-shifting extremes of his contrary emotions, for the incentive of his poetic impulse derives from his fluctuations between antithetical desires. His poetic adventure, which generally begins with rebellion, proceeds through extraordinary hope until it reaches a momentary, sometimes apocalyptic, vision and then terminates in defeat. But the defeat itself appears at times as a new beginning, a new affirmation. Soon after exclaiming ironically in **"Adieu"** that he is not a "mage ou ange" but merely a "paysan!" who must embrace "la réalité rugueuse", he embarks on a new and hope-filled vision when he says: "à l'aurore, armés d'une ardente patience, nous entrerons aux splendides villes".

[Eugen] Bleuler's term "ambivalence", taken over by Freud, who defined it as "the sway of contrary tendencies", describes the conflict of diametrically opposed desires. "Ambivalent impulses or tendencies" either represent "simultaneously the wish and counterwish" or they serve "preponderantly one of two contradictory tendencies". Although on a human level this contest is often devastating for the person in whom the opposing tendencies are warring, on a poetic plane the conflict may generate the violent, but creative, struggle of contraries that forges dynamic, dramatic and masterful art. As Blake wrote in *The Marriage of Heaven and Hell:*

Without Contraries is no progression. Attrac-

tion and Repulsion, Reason and Energy, Love and Hate, are necessary to Human existence.

In many ways these words describe the vibrant encounters, the incessant motions and the frequent metamorphoses of persons and places that recur throughout Rimbaud's writings. His poetry is a drama of continual conflicts.

Probably the best-known form of ambivalence is the love-hate antithesis. In *Instincts and Their Vicissitudes* Freud observes: "It is particularly common to find both [love and hatred] . . . directed simultaneously towards the same object, and this phenomenon of their coexistence furnishes the most important example of ambivalence of feeling." Elsewhere he adds: "But the chronic coexistence of love and hatred, both directed toward the same person and both of the highest degree of intensity, cannot fail to astonish us." Rimbaud's love-hate feelings for himself, women, Europe, God, pagans, Christians and poetry cannot fail to astonish—and to fascinate—us.

Attraction and repulsion for the same object are also linked with taboo and dreams, according to the father of psychoanalysis. Implying concomitant dread and desire, taboo is in a sense a symbolic ambivalence: "For . . . whatever is expressly forbidden must be an object of desire." This is apparent in Rimbaud's violent rebellions against society, religion and morality; his use of scatalogical language and blasphemy; his delight in scandalizing. And since dreams tend to reduce two opposites to a unity, according to Freud, Rimbaud's propensity for dream-visions may be interpreted in the light of his warring drives. (pp. 15-17)

. . . . .

Why does Rimbaud find it necessary to reinvent love? Happiness, hopefulness and humor, along with childlike fantasy and wish-fulfillment, typify many of his first poems about eroticism, females and reverie. Dreaming that "l'amour infini" will rise in his soul as he wanders alone through nature in *Sensation,* the poet says he will be "heureux comme avec une femme". "Oh! là! là! que d'amours splendides j'ai rêvées!" exclaims the vagabonding and rather comical narrator of **"Ma Bohème."**

In several of his earliest "love" poems, Rimbaud characterizes himself or the girl he wants to win as "brutal". The lover in **"Les Reparties de Nina"** is "Brutal d'ivresse", while in **"A La Musique,"** the narrator, describing the girls who find him funny, says: "mes désirs brutaux s'accrochent à leurs lèvres." In **"Première Soirée,"** the half-naked girl had "un doux rire brutal". Suzanne Bernard is mistaken when she says that the adjective *brutal* in this poem "n'est guère heureux": on the contrary, the word is very well chosen. Brutality as a part of Rimbaud's stylization of love in his early poems emphasizes how he romanticizes lovemaking there. Furthermore, it foreshadows the poet's association of love and strength—in addition to his darker linking of love and cruelty—in his later works.

But not everything is happy, hopeful and humorous in Rimbaud's amusing poems of the debutant lover. When reverie is confronted with reality, Rimbaud the lover-dreamer portrays himself as comical and even rather ridiculous. This happens, for example, in **"A La Musique,"** **"Roman"** ("Vos sonnets La font rire") and **"Les Reparties de Nina."** In this last poem, the loquacious lover rambles on for stanzas about what he and Nina will do, see and experience. Nina talks only once, in the last line of the poem. There, silencing her ardent suitor with a prosaic question (*"Et mon bureau?"*), she returns the seductive dreamer to harsh reality. He knows that she is making fun of him. The girl's words imply a serious lack of communication between two possible lovers, a lack that will become emblematic of Rimbaud's search for the perfect partner as well as for love itself.

In **"Les Sœurs de charité"** and **"Mes Petites Amoureuses,"** poems composed only several months to a year after **"A La Musique,"** **"Roman"** and **"Les Reparties de Nina,"** the lack of rapport between the poet and women reaches aggravated proportions. As a result of the poet's amorous frustration, a dual pattern of anguish and ambivalent attack against females emerges. Since the unhappy young man in **"Les Sœurs de charité"** cannot possess the woman, he accuses her of "hanging" on him; yet at the end of the poem, when he craves Death, Death for him assumes a female form. In **"Mes Petites Amoureuses,"** the narrator blames women, whom he says he hates, for causing his suffering. One girl is even charged with wishing to perform a symbolic castration on him. She would cut off his poetic inspiration just as it was emerging from his head, he alleges: "Tu couperais ma mandoline / Au fil du front." But, he reveals in an exclamation which almost seems to surprise him, it is precisely for these girls, whom he calls derisively "these shoulders of mutton", that he has written his poetry: "Et c'est pourtant pour ces éclanches / Que j'ai rimé!"

The poignant prose-poem sketches called **"Les Déserts de l'amour"** unveil additional reasons which eventually propel the poet to proclaim that love must be invented over again. The *Avertissement,* composed in the third person, introduces the two first-person sequences, which constitute the body of this unfinished manuscript.

The would-be lover in **"Les Déserts de l'amour"** is a creature of contradictions. Part boy, part man, he is "un jeune, tout jeune *homme*". Stylistic notation here underscores the dilemma, for while "homme" is italicized, "jeune" is repeated and reinforced by "tout". This problem is reiterated in the crucial description of the adolescent's unconsummated relation with women: "N'ayant pas aimé de femmes, quoique plein de sang!—il eut son âme et son cœur, toute sa force, élevés en des erreurs étranges et tristes." What is extremely significant here is that instead of accusing women, as the poet did in earlier works, the narrator now blames the young man for his failure to achieve amorous possession. The "strange and sad errors" of his rearing may evoke sexual practices (e.g. homosexuality, masturbation) as well as erotic dreams. In the next sentence the narrator exclaims: "Des rêves suivants, ses amours! . . . de douces considérations religieuses se dégagent." The reveries (undoubtedly the two in the body of the text) are ironically called "his loves!" because this youth has only *dreamed* of possessing a woman.

Motherless and lonely, this pitiable adolescent is simultaneously cowardly and daring since he is portrayed as "fuyant toute force morale". Because of his suffering, he seems to desire death: "[il] veut la mort, ce semble." Death here, instead of presenting the kind of sensual and spiritual release that it seemed to offer in **"Les Sœurs de charité,"** now appears as a flight into guilt-tinged suffering, into terrible and fatal "shame" or inhibited "modesty". This adolescent "ne fit que s'amener à la mort comme à une pudeur terrible et fatale". But because these very words help define this youth's attitude toward women, instead of offering him a possible escape from his problems, death here presents itself in the form of his own tormented attitude toward women. Death in **"Les Déserts de l'amour"** is an ironic mirror of the young man's erotic anguish, rather than a sublimation of the poet's amorous desires, as was Death, the Sister of Charity.

The linking of love and death is the result of an "ancient ambivalence", for the Goddess of Love was "once identified with" the Goddess of Death, claims Freud. Reflecting this ambivalence, Rimbaud joins Eros with Thanatos—in **"Les Sœurs de charité"** and **"Les Déserts de l'amour,"** as has been seen—as well as in many of his later writings. Love kills, he often implies. There is, for example, the love-death embrace in **"Conte."** In *Délires I,* comparing himself to a woman who died as a result of her love, the Epoux Infernal predicts to the Vierge Folle: " 'Tu me feras mourir. . . . C'est notre sort à nous, cœurs charitables . . .' ". Elsewhere, the poet says:

> Deux amours! je puis mourir de l'amour terrestre, mourir de dévouement.
>
> (**"Mauvais Sang"**)
>
> Ah! . . . les mille amours qui m'ont crucifié!
>
> (**"Adieu"**)
>
> . . . la mort atroce pour les fidèles et les amants!
>
> (**"Solde"**)

In **"Mauvais Sang,"** he derides himself for his inability to love death: "Comme je deviens vieille fille, à manquer du courage d'aimer la mort!" Love and death sometimes join to create a setting: in **"Ville,"** the narrator portrays "la Mort sans pleurs" along with "un Amour désespéré", while in **"Fairy"** he describes "des anses d'amours morts".

Charles Mauron calls frequently associated images that tend to center around a dominating idea the poet's "obsessive metaphors". Rimbaud's joining of images of love and death may be seen as such metaphors, and the love-death union in his poetry is probably related to his simultaneous urges for creation and destruction.

In the two hallucinated dreams of **"Les Déserts de l'amour,"** the young man dramatizes his inability to make love, first with the woman servant in the country and then with the "Woman" from the city. Sexual repression and guilt are clearly associated with the youth's rearing because in both dreams he says that he is in his family's house.

Towards the mother-figure servant, he is highly ambivalent. Denouncing her as "un petit chien", he says nevertheless that she was "belle, et d'une noblesse maternelle inexprimable pour moi: pure, connue, toute charmante!" Guilt feelings compound his suffering and frustration. His unsuccessful lovemaking is searingly illustrated in the image of how he tried to kiss the woman. His mouth seized hers "comme une petite vague désespérée, minant sans fin quelque chose". The personification of the wave and the word "minant" vividly portray his physical and moral distress. Finally, the unfulfilled lover describes how he felt engulfed in amorous sadness: "ô désespoir . . . je me suis abîmé sous la tristesse amoureuse de la nuit."

In the second dream, the adolescent is no longer ambivalent about "la Femme", whom he admires and even idealizes ("Elle . . . l'Adorable"). The capital letter which he sometimes uses to designate her contrasts this "worldly" and perhaps also "fashionable" female ("elle, mondaine") with the clumsy and rather pathetic youth "en haillons". Now, even more than in his first dream, this speaker is brutally self-critical; still, as in all of **"Les Déserts de l'amour,"** he is portrayed as deserving compassion. Surprised and distressed to find the woman in his bed, the narrator describes a horrifying sequence in which he lets her fall half-naked out of his bed. In his "faiblesse indicible", he tumbles on top of her. When she disappears, he bursts into tears, and although he is exhausted, he tries hopelessly to search for her everywhere. In the closing lines, this "young, very young *man*" appears more like a child than a man, because when he realizes that she will never return, he says: "cette fois, j'ai pleuré plus que tous les enfants du monde." This unsettling theme of the child lover recurs even in the poet's search for the new love, for as the Vierge Folle will say, the Epoux Infernal "était presque un enfant . . .".

In **"Les Déserts de l'amour"** the search for a female love partner is a disaster. "Elle n'est pas revenue, et ne reviendra jamais", the wretched youth says in his second dream: "jamais". Conventional love relations between men and women are, therefore, defined by the poet as "deserts"—wildernesses, wastes, solitary places—arid for the present and barren for the future.

Elsewhere in Rimbaud's writings (in the *Album zutique*, **"Les Stupra"**, *Une Saison en enfer* and the *Illuminations*) echoes of the poet's anguish about the "deserts of love" reverberate. Insecure about himself and sex, and ambivalent towards women, the poet often blames his erotic suffering on his social and religious rearing. Although **"Les Remembrances du vieillard idiot"** is supposed to parody François Coppée's verses, it is psychologically interesting in its own right. Still agonizing about his sexual ignorance, the child speaker here who does not understand "ce long tube sanglant" reveals his feelings of shame about sexual curiosity. Confessing his youthful "crimes", calling out four times for "pardon", he admits how he wanted to hold his father's penis and how he felt guilty desire when he saw his mother's body.

Two of the three sonnets called "Les Stupra" (those beginning: "Les anicens animaux saillissaient . . . " and "Nos fesses ne sont pas les leurs . . . ") are actually pleas for freedom from moral and social restrictions on sex. The third ("Obscur et froncé . . . "), which appeared in the *Album zutique* with the title **"L'Idole: Sonnet du trou du cul,"** was signed: "Albert Mérat". Verlaine later explained in *Hombres* that he himself wrote the quatrains, while Rimbaud composed the tercets. But is this poem a sonnet about homosexual coitus, as the subtitle and Verlaine's inclusion of it in *Hombres* suggest? Probably it is,—but why do the tercets then speak of the "Chanaan féminin"? Suzanne Bernard says that we should not be deceived by these words since the sonnet was published in *Hombres*, and Enid Starkie even wonders [in *The French Mind*, 1952] if Rimbaud wrote the last six lines. As I read the sonnet, however, Verlaine's quatrains may describe homosexual intercourse, but the tercets portray the younger poet's dreams of coitus with a female. The tears, dreams and suffering described here also characterize erotic frustration with females as portrayed elsewhere by Rimbaud—in **"Les Déserts de l'amour"** and **"Mauvais Sang,"** for example. In fact, in **"Mauvais Sang"** the protagonist says: "l'orgie et la camaraderie des femmes m'étaient interdites", and he then depicts himself "weeping" before an enraged mob whose members cannot understand his sexual and emotional miseries.

Since the poet will not—or cannot—love women, he rejects them in many of his writings. "Toutes les formes d'amour" must be experienced by the *voyant,* wrote Rimbaud on May 15, 1871. And so in *Une Saison en enfer* and the *Illuminations* he describes different types of love and eroticism, including homosexual love, masturbation and amorous dreams of a perfect and powerful partner who is larger and greater than life. The poet's exploration of these types of "new love" reflects both the pattern and the problems of the *voyant*'s quest for the "*unknown*".

"Je n'aime pas les femmes. L'amour est à réinventer, on le sait", proclaims the Epoux Infernal. Here, in **"Délires I,"** may be found Rimbaud's most profound portrayal of his search for new and transcendent love.

Although he railed against women in **"Les Sœurs de charité"** and **"Mes Petites Amoureuses,"** in **"Délires I"** Rimbaud dramatizes his homosexual love affair with Verlaine in terms of a heterosexual relationship. Since the Epoux Infernal says that he does not like women and, consequently, announces that "love has to be invented over again", it is apparent, right from the beginning of **"Délires I,"** that the Infernal Bridegroom is denouncing the delirious quest for love described by his "foolish" (and sometimes "insane") female mate. Thus, because the lovers here are portrayed as male and female, their love is not really new. It will merely repeat, in unusual ways, to be sure, the problems of alienated heterosexual couples.

The main speaker, the Vierge Folle, delineates her own weak and dependent personality, while also sketching the emotional, moral and spiritual character of her infernal lover. Of course, since Rimbaud composed *Une Saison en enfer,* it is actually he who paints his portrait of Verlaine as the Vierge Folle; and through what he imagines are her eyes, he depicts himself as the Epoux Infernal.

The Vierge Folle is the "slave" of the Epoux Infernal. "Lost", "intoxicated" and "insane" ("Je suis perdue. Je suis soûle . . . Ah! je suis folle!"), she is a weak and tearful woman whose existence is "terne et lâche". Although she weepingly implores God's forgiveness for her sinful life ("moi qui . . . suis damnée"), she fears, however, that she will die if her demonic lover leaves her.

The Epoux Infernal, according to the Vierge Folle, is a "Demon" who was "practically a child". He longs to flee from reality, to live in dreams as a somnambulist. He follows his antithetical urges. A masochist who says he will cut gashes all over his body, he is also a sadist who delights in terrifying, shaming and torturing his mistress. He is both cruel and kind. "Je l'écoute faisant de l'infamie une gloire, de la cruauté un charme", relates the Vierge Folle. But she adds: "Parfois il parle, en une façon de patois attendri . . . des malheureux qui existent certainement. . . . il pleurait en considérant ceux qui nous entouraient, bétail de la misère." A demonic creature by definition, the Epoux Infernal nevertheless has a spiritual or angelic side. "Parle-t-il à Dieu?" the female wonders. And when she exlaims: "Plusieurs nuits, son démon me saisissant, nous nous roulions, je luttais avec lui!", one cannot avoid comparing this, which is, after all, a homosexual love scene, to Jacob's night-long wrestle with the angel.

In fact, many of the religious symbols in **"Délires I"** mock their spiritual sources. When he resembles the Biblical angel struggling with Jacob, the Epoux Infernal is called a "demon". In her "confession", the wretched female asks for forgiveness, but gives no promise—or even indication—that she will change her way of life. In wondering if her "petit ami" will rise to heaven in an "assomption", the Vierge Folle is comparing her infernal partner to none other than the Virgin Mary. Even the protagonists' names are parodies of religious ideas. The Vierge Folle recalls the parable about the five "foolish virgins" in *Matthew* 25: 1-13. There, the foolish virgins neglect to fill their lamps with oil; therefore, they cannot join the Bridegroom when he arrives. But here the Vierge Folle is accepted by the (Infernal) Bridegroom, who is a parody of Jesus, the Heavenly Bridegroom of the parable. In other ways, too, the Epoux Infernal partially resembles Jesus. While in *Matthew* 10 : 34-38 Jesus tells men that they must leave everything behind and follow him, the Vierge Folle exclaims about her master: "J'ai oublié tout mon devoir humain pour le suivre. . . . Je vais où il va, il le faut." Jesus in *John* 14 : 2 says that he must go away, and the Epoux Infernal says to his disciple: "il faudra que je m'en aille, très loin, un jour." For these reasons, the poet's new and supposedly peerless experience, which aims to be both erotic and spiritual, tends to degenerate into a diabolical parody of religion as well as of love.

Alienated from the society around them, the actors in **"Délires I"** reveal that they are trapped in a hellish marriage which binds them together and yet isolates them from each other. The passion that unites them, the female discloses, is based upon the "force de désespoir!". The universe they find in each other's arms is not a rapturous one, nor even a happy one. Rather, it is "un sombre ciel", where they seem like "deux bons enfants, libres de se promener dans le Paradis de tristesse". What the Vierge Folle wants from her partner is strength ("lui me rendra forte")

and a childlike adventurous life. "Oh! la vie d'aventures qui existe dans les livres des enfants . . . me la donneras-tu?" she asks. But immediately denouncing her spouse's abilities as well as her own, she answers her own question: "Il ne peut pas. J'ignore son idéal." Although linked to her lover, the mistress admits that she was "sûre de ne jamais entrer dans son monde". He, of course, recognizes this. When she says to him that she understands him, he merely shrugs his shoulders, not even bothering to refute her claim. While they find moments of tenderness and partial comprehension in their union, the two lovers are basically unable to communicate with each other. "S'il m'expliquait ses tristesses, les comprendrais-je plus que ses railleries?" she asks. Her very question highlights their essential alienation from each other.

The Foolish Virgin and the Infernal Bridegroom realize, even though they do not always admit it to each other, that their reinvented love is a failure. The fact that the mistress says her lover "feignait d'être éclairésur tout" discloses that she (as well as Rimbaud the author) knows that the Epoux Infernal does not possess the power he claims as his. "Il a peut-être des secrets pour *changer la vie*?" she used to wonder. "Non, il ne fait qu'en chercher", she would answer herself. Thus, both lovers are aware that the Infernal Bridegroom's magical and supernatural powers exist mostly in their dreams and their desires.

As the drama of **"Délires I"** develops, the Epoux Infernal, who at first seems like the antithesis of the Vierge Folle, begins to resemble her. To be sure, he disdains her for her weak and tearful manner (although he, at times, weeps, too) and because she is a woman ("Il dit: 'Je n'aime pas les femmes . . .' "). Yet, despite his contempt for females, upon occasion the Epoux Infernal appears like a woman. The Vierge Folle describes him as a "sœur aimée", a "jeune mère" and a "mère méchante". Sometimes, she says, he would go away "avec des gentillesses de petite fille au catéchisme". In criticizing women, therefore, the Epoux Infernal is not only condemning his mate; he is also denouncing certain aspects of his own personality.

Elsewhere in Rimbaud's writings, the poet in some of his roles resembles the Vierge Folle. For example, while the Vierge Folle is "damné" and tries to cope with madness, the protagonist of "Jadis . . .", who leaves to Satan his "carnet de damné", played "de bons tours à la folie". When the narrator exclaims in **"Matin"**: "*Je ne sais plus parler!*" he sounds like the Vierge Folle who declares: "Je ne sais même plus parler." Suffering in an infernal ambience, the Vierge Folle calls upon God for help and coolness, as does the protagonist in **"Nuit de l'enfer."** And just as the Vierge Folle is inferior, "ignoble", so the narrator belongs to a "race inférieure" in **"Mauvais Sang."**

Rimbaud himself sometimes resembles the Vierge Folle, too. While the tearful and repentent Foolish Virgin makes her mate promise not to leave her, in his letter of July 4, 1873, using some of the Foolish Virgin's tactics, Rimbaud himself begs Verlaine not to abandon him. "Reviens, reviens, cher ami, seul ami, reviens. . . . je m'en repens. . . . je ne cesse de pleurer. . . . Ah! je t'en supplie. . . . ô reviens, à toutes les heures je repleure." About this letter, Henri Peyre notes in his excellent study *Rim-*

baud vu par Verlaine: "Rimbaud avait essayé de retenir Verlaine, et parce que sa subsistance dépendait de lui, et sans doute parce que son attachement pour son aîné était beaucoup plus fort, et plus sentimental, que la 'vierge folle' ne semblera, quelques mois plus tard, le dire." The Vierge Folle, therefore, while being a stylization of Verlaine, and while providing a conscience which observes and judges the Epoux Infernal, is also a portrait of another aspect of Rimbaud's own personality.

Everything in **"Délires I"** points up the condemned lovers' failure to achieve the transcendence they seek: their inability to escape from themselves (or from each other) or to help themselves (or each other); their names, which are mockeries of religious concepts; and their love "invented over again", which mirrors many of the usual problems of maladjusted male-female partners, and, in addition, supplies new and diabolical dimensions to the erotic relationship. Their supposedly intoxicating love turns out to be a strangely sobering experience. Because the Epoux Infernal resembles in several significant ways the woman he desires and yet disdains, Rimbaud the author develops dramatically one of his deepest problems about love: his own contradictory ideas about himself as a person, and consequently, as a lover.

The homosexual couple's quest for the new love is frankly portrayed in **"Vagabonds,"** a prose poem from the *Illuminations* which deserves to be juxtaposed with **"Délires I."** While the Vierge Folle, observing her mate and wondering about him, kept vigils at night ("A côté de son cher corps en dormi, que d'heures des nuits j'ai veillé, cherchant pourquoi il voulait tant s'évader de la réalité"), in *Vagabonds,* the narrator, representing Rimbaud, describes the agonizing vigils he owed to his mate, his "pitoyable frère." "Que d'atroces veillées je lui dus!" he exclaims. In relating how he observed his somnambulist lover, the narrator of **"Vagabonds"** combines compassion with fascinated horror and contempt. "Et, presque chaque nuit, aussitôt endormi, le pauvre frère se levait, la bouche pourrie, les yeux arrachés,—tel qu'il se rêvait!—et me tirait dans la salle en hurlant son songe de chagrin idiot."

As in **"Délires I,"** by revealing what they think about each other, the lovers in **"Vagabonds"** also blame each other. The narrator, who attributes demonic qualities to his mate, as the Vierge Folle did to her lover, calls him "ce satanique docteur". The Satanic doctor, who ascribes to his partner "un guignon et une innocence très bizarres", accuses his lover of frivolity and cruelty. Mimicking his diabolical partner, the narrator mouths the charges against him: " 'Je ne me saisissais pas fervemment de cette entreprise. Je m'étais joué de son infirmité. Par ma faute, nous retournerions en exil, en esclavage.' "

Although much conflict exists between the lovers in **"Vagabonds,"** in this work there is more hope for attaining transcendence through love than appeared in **"Délires I."** Whereas the Vierge Folle is already the "slave" of her partner, the lovers in **"Vagabonds"** only say that if the narrator fails in his enterprise, then "nous retournerions . . . en esclavage" (implying reality). The conditional suggests that this might—and yet might not—happen. In addition, while the two lovers doubt the

"magic" skills of the Epoux Infernal, the vagabonds seem quite confident in the narrator's powers, if only he can apply them properly. "Je créais, par delà la campagne traversée par des bandes de musique rare, les fantômes du futur luxe nocturne", the narrator proclaims. And he adds that "en toute sincérité d'esprit" he had pledged to restore his pitiable companion "à son état primitif de fils du Soleil,—et nous errions, nourris du vin des cavernes et du biscuit de la route, moi pressé de trouver le lieu et la formule." Here, participating in a new type of communion, the wine and the wafer encountered during their wandering help sustain the travelers during the narrator's magical search for "the place and the formula". Did the Vierge Folle hope for much more? Thinking about her infernal spouse, she said: "lui me rendra forte, nous voyagerons, nous chasserons dans les déserts, nous dormirons sur les pavés des villes inconnues. . . . Ou je me réveillerai, et les lois et les mœurs auront changé,—grâce à son pouvoir magique . . .".

Neither work portraying the search for transcendence through the new—or homosexual—love is completely optimistic, however. Indications of unpleasantness and antagonism pervade **"Vagabonds"** (e.g. the "agonzing vigils", the narrator's snickering at his mate ["Je répondais en ricanant à ce satanique docteur"] and the pitiable brother's "chagrin idiot"), as they permeate and cloud the ambience of **"Délires I."** In fact, in these two works, the poet's homosexual "new" love is related to something demonic: the Bridegroom is "Infernal", the doctor "Satanic". The same association between homosexual love and damnation occurs elsewhere in Rimbaud's works. Writing about lesbian love in **"Dévotion,"** the poet portrays it as demonic. "A Lulu,—démon—qui a conservé un goût pour les oratoires du temps des Amies et de son éducation incomplète", he says. [In a footnote, the critic adds, "Verlaine wrote a volume of Sapphic verses called *Les Amies.*"] And, at the end of **"Adieu,"** the narrator proclaims: "j'ai vu l'enfer des femmes là-bas." With these words he may be calling lesbian love infernal (c.f. Baudelaire's *Femmes damnées*), or he may be denouncing all women.

Rimbaud in 1875, drawn by Ernest Delahaye.

Love, says the protagonist at the end of *Une Saison en enfer,* has "crucified"—has, therefore, destroyed and yet exalted—him in a physical and a metaphysical sense: "les mille amours qui m'ont crucifié!" Deriding all his past loves, including his homosexual affair, as "[les] vieilles amours mensongères", he concludes his masterwork by condemning all love that is based on the interaction between two individuals, all love that centers on the couple. Announcing that now he can "frapper de honte ces couples menteurs" ("Arrière . . . ces ménages", the Génie of new love will say in **"Génie"**), the poet proclaims his new goal in love and in life: "*to possess truth in one soul and one body.*" His words imply erotic and spiritual longings. Instead of hoping to possess the other member of the couple, the poet now wants to eliminate the separation that inevitably exists between any two people, and so he wishes to incorporate truth, which is transcendent love, within himself. This explains his quest in such poems as **"Conte,"** **"Génie"** and **"Being Beauteous"** for a perfect and powerful figure, who is larger and grander than life, with whom he can merge. Since dates of composition are not available, it is impossible to know if Rimbaud wrote these *Illuminations* before or after *Une Saison en enfer.* While "Délires I" and "Vagabonds" portrayed the new love of the homosexual couple, these three *Illuminations,* depicting another type of reinvented love, dramatize the poet's attempt—his failure, as well—to possess transcendent love in one soul and one body.

The title **"Conte,"** implying a work of fiction, downgrades the reality of the "tale", while highlighting the importance of the author's imagination. Unsatisfied with ordinary life, with "[les] générosités vulgaires", the Prince of this adventure quests for extraordinary love, which is also truth. "Il prévoyait d'étonnantes révolutions de l'amour. . . . Il voulait voir la vérité, l'heure du désir et de la satisfaction essentiels." It is significant that the poet does not state that the Prince demanded to "*possess* truth", as the protagonist dreamed of doing in **"Adieu"**; the Prince merely demanded to "see" it. The emphasis in **"Conte,"** then, as in the "Lettre du voyant", is upon seeing, not upon possessing, the vision. This Prince pré*voyait . . . il voulait voir*" (italics mine).

The Prince craves contrarieties. He wishes to see abstractions—revolutions in love and the truth—defined in terms of antithetical longings: the hour of essential desire and its simultaneous satisfaction. This erotic and spiritual endeavor, the author adds, may be an "aberration de piété", implying that although the Prince's quest is certainly a religious one, it may be, as was the search for reinvented love in **"Délires I,"** an adventure which derides or perverts its spiritual sources.

Like the poet in **"Mes Petites Amoureuses"** and like the Epoux Infernal, the Prince accuses and assails women. He "soupçonnait ses femmes de pouvoir mieux que cette complaisance agrémentée de ciel et de luxe. . . . Toutes les femmes qui l'avaient connu furent assassinées." Not all the women *he* had known (or possessed), but all *the women who had known him* were assassinated. Is it the Prince's disappointment with these women—or is it rather

their disappointment with him—that makes them candidates for his wrath?

The Prince's ecstasies of destruction and cruelty, however, are fruitless. Everyone and everything he wanted destroyed—the women, all those who followed him, the beasts of luxury, the palaces, the people he hacked to pieces—all "existaient encore", the narrator reveals. Nothing, therefore, was overcome by his power, even though he "possédait au moins un assez large pouvoir humain". What he "possessed" is not truth, of course: it is merely a "rather [not even a very] large human [and not supernatural] power". In all ways, therefore, he is limited.

"Un soir il galopait fièrement." These words, like the ones beginning with "Un soir" in "Jadis . . . " ("Un soir, j'ai assis la Beauté sur mes genoux.—Et je l'ai trouvée amère.—Et je l'ai injuriée.") introduces the climactic encounter with beauty and with bitterness. Suddenly the revolutionary love which he foresaw, the truth embodying perfect desire and satisfaction which he demanded to see, appear before him:

> Un Génie apparut, d'une beauté ineffable, inavouable même. De sa physiognomie et de son maintien ressortait la promesse d'un amour multiple et complexe! d'un bonheur indicible, insupportable même!

Evoked in terms of negation, as was the *voyant*'s "*inconnu*", the Génie, like the poet's "*unknown*", inspires overpowering—too overpowering—emotion, which can neither be stated ("ineffable", "indicible") nor "even" admitted or borne: "inavouable", "insupportable même!" And just as the *voyant* could only glimpse his visions before being overwhelmed by madness or even death (" . . . affolé, il finirait par perdre l'intelligence de ses visions. . . . Qu'il crève dans bondissement par les choses inouïes ou innommables . . . !"), so the Prince, upon encountering the object of his quest for perfect love, is overcome by intimations of destruction and death:

> Le Prince et le Génie s'anéantirent probablement dans la santé essentielle. Comment n'auraient-ils pas pu en mourir? Ensemble donc ils moururent.

The momentary conjoining of these two male figures unites the Prince in one soul and one body with perfect love. The Génie, who is truth and reinvented love, also suggest Genius, the Poetic Genius, a guardian spirit and a possible father-figure. He evokes furthermore a magical genie, for in seeming to promise "un bonheur indicible", he recalls the poet's "magique étude / Du bonheur" in "O saisons, ô châteaux!". But, as is typical of Rimbaud's poetic pattern, the Prince's ecstasy is both ephemeral and destructive. The author editorializes: "The Prince and the Genie destroyed one another probably in essential health." The adverb shades the entire sentence with ambiguity and implied doubt. *Probably* they destroyed one another in an ecstatic love-death embrace ("Peut on s'extasier dans la destruction . . . !" the narrator exclaimed earlier), and *probably* they achieved an instant of bliss, of pure being, of "essential health". The Prince, after all, craved the essence of things, "l'heure du désir et de la satisfaction essentiels". His longing, and their union in "la santé essentielle", recall the *voyant*'s desire to exhaust in himself all the poisons to keep only their "quintessences", their pure, concentrated essences. "Ineffable torture", said Rimbaud in the **"Lettre du voyant"**, before he went on to predict how the *voyant* would be destroyed after reaching the "*unknown*". How could the Prince and the Génie not have died as a result of their encounter? asks the author of *Conte* rhetorically, in a seemingly matter-of-fact way, before reaching the apparently inevitable result that they did die because of their meeting. But, of course, the narrator's conclusion is based upon his earlier premise that the Prince and the Génie "probably" destroyed one another.

Thus, the narrator of **"Conte"** is free to play with his tale, to taunt his reader, and to retract his statement of probability. Just as nothing happened when the Prince tried to destroy everything, so nothing happened during the Prince's meeting with the Génie. They did not merge to form one figure; instead, the author insinuates that they must have remained two seperate entities, for "ce Prince décéda, sans son palais, à un âge ordinaire". Either nothing happened at the moment of encounter, or everything happened and failed, the moment of death implying the loss of the vision, of love, of truth.

But no, there were not two figures, adds the author. There was only one. "Le Prince était le Génie. Le Génie était le Prince." After all, wrote Rimbaud in the **"Lettre du voyant"**: "JE est un autre." And so the love-death encounter of the Prince-Génie with himself suggests auto-eroticism as a possible pathway to the infinite. But the one being here does not possess truth in one soul and one body. Instead, he remains a solitary creature, divided from himself, who through onanism tries to make himself whole, and fails. There is no lasting love union or communion for the Prince-Génie, no enduring sense of unity, even within his own being.

"La musique savante manque à notre désir", concludes the narrator. His final words now seem to include everyone—the author, the Prince-Génie and the reader—in the gloomy closing with its echoing nasal sounds (sav*ante*, m*anque*). The "masterly music" that "disappoints our desire" evokes an art that is too contrived, too erudite, too ingenious to satisfy our basic erotic and spiritual needs or cravings. Is it ever possible to attain what the Prince demanded to see, "l'heure du désir et de la satisfaction essentiels"? Can "our desire" find "essential" satisfaction in music that is not "savante", in something like "la nouvelle harmonie" of **"A une raison"**? The final words of **"Conte"** do not preclude that possibility. But the "musique savante" is itself particularly disturbing as well as indicative of the poet's self-criticism. It condemns, as do so many other Rimbaud works, the *voyant,* who is, after all, "le suprême Savant!". Inevitably, invariably almost, the desire—for love, for truth, for the "*unknown*", for charity, for intoxication, for the infinite . . .—remains unsatisfied. While the Génie seemed to bring "la promesse d'un amour multiple et complexe!", a love that would unite soul and body, another wonderful promise, the "promesse surhumaine faite à notre corps et à notre âme créés" in **"Matinée d'ivresse,"** is denounced emphatically as "cette démence!".

The quest for the new love in **"Conte,"** therefore, follows Rimbaud's typical poetic pattern. The Prince's search begins with rebellion, progresses through visions of extraordinary hope and then reaches a moment of ecstasy before the vision vanishes. The Génie of this tale, the poet's "other" self, closely resembles the *voyant*'s "*inconnu*": both are marvelous, overpowering, dreadful and wonderful, impossible for the poet to resist, and impossible for him to possess. Like the "*unknown*", the love foreseen by the Prince in **"Conte,"** the quest for essential truth, beauty, happiness and communion, promises the poet everything—too much, even—and leaves him in the end alone with himself, either completely vanquished or agonizingly cognizant of his limited powers and his limitless desires.

Like the Génie of **"Conte,"** the Génie of **"Génie"** is a male figure who represents reinvented love incarnate: "Il est l'amour, mesure parfaite et réinventée . . . ". He, like the Génie aspect of the Prince, is a creature who brings promises ("sa promesse sonne"), a being who seems to inspire extraordinary "health" ("ô jouissance de notre santé") and a figure whom the author wishes to see ("Sachons . . . le voir"). Moreover, like the Prince's "other" self in **"Conte"** and similar to the poet's "*unknown*", the Génie of **"Génie"** and the effect he produces are described in terms of negation: e.g. "sa vie infinie . . . Il ne s'en ira pas . . . immensité de l'univers!"

Just as the Prince's craving for the Génie was a religious longing, albeit perhaps an "aberration of piety", so the author's yearning in **"Génie"** is a spiritual craving for a figure who is, in a sense, an "aberration" of Christ and of Christianity. This Génie, a new messiah who offers love and a pride more benevolent than Christian charity, has overthrown Christianity, the "old" religion with its genuflections and penalties, for his new faith based on freedom ("le dégagement rêvé") and violence ("la violence nouvelle"). "Sa vue, sa vue! tous les agenouillages anciens et les peines *relevées* à sa suite", says the poet, heeding the Génie's promise which rings out: " 'Arrière ces superstitions, ces anciens corps, ces ménages et ces âges. C'est cette époque-ci qui a sombré!' " Unlike Christ, implies the author, the Génie will not go away, nor will he have to promise a second coming. By his very presence, he has already transformed life and redeemed sin: "Il ne s'en ira pas, il ne redescendra pas d'un ciel, il n'accomplira pas la rédemption des colères de femmes et des gaîtés des hommes et de tout ce péché: car c'est fait, lui étant, et étant aimé." The Génie's religion, therefore, which aims to overthrow the "old" one, nevertheless shows, by its desire to improve upon or to "correct" Christianity, its attachment to that very religion. From the Christian foundations which the Génie overturns and seeks to surpass, he establishes his curiously contradictory spirituality. For . . . this Génie is a creature of contrasts. He is the present, the future and eternity, a "beloved engine of fatal qualities". He, who has made the house open to winter and summer, is "le charme des lieux fuyants et le délice surhumain des stations". We see him pass "dans le ciel de tempête et les drapeaux d'extase".

While he parallels in many ways the Prince's Génie and the poet's "*unknown*", the Génie of **"Génie"** "raison merveilleuse et imprévue", also resembles the Raison of **"A une raison,"** which evokes "the new love!" as well as "the new harmony", the march of "new men" and the liberation from time. The Génie, like the Reason, is at once an eternal presence and an eternal absence. "Arrivée de toujours, qui *t'en iras* partout" (italics mine), wrote the author of **"A une raison."** "Et nous nous le rappelons et il voyage . . .", admits the narrator of **"Génie,"** stressing what he had already revealed in the first paragraph: that the author and we, "standing within our rages and ennuis", are hopelessly separated from the Génie of the new love. In **"Génie,"** "Rimbaud's full identification with *nous* emerges as an admission of his defeat", notes Virginia A. La Charité [in her article: "Rimbaud and the Johannine Christ: Containment and Liberation", *Nineteenth-Century French Studies,* Vol. II, Nos. 1 & 2 (Fall-Winter 1973-1974).]

The authorial voice in **"Génie"**—unlike that of the more detached narrator of **"Conte,"** who until the last line does not link himself and the reader with the Prince's search and disappointment—portrays the quest for union with revolutionary love as both his and the reader's. Although he exults in the possibilities of the Génie's new love, he reveals throughout **"Génie"** the impossibility of such total union and communion ("Nous avons tous eu l'épouvante de sa concession et de la nôtre"). Even in the rapture of our health, the "élan de nos facultés", the narrator says, we cannot escape from our "affection égoïste" for the Génie. We cannot merge in one soul and one body with the Génie, for ours is an egotistical desire. Furthermore, the author reveals, we are too weak and too tired to merge with this Génie. Instead, he says: "Sachons, . . . forces et sentiments las, le héler et le voir, et le renvoyer, et . . . suivre ses vues, ses souffles, son corps, son jour." The word *suivre* may imply passive (let us "observe" or "watch") or active following (let us "obey"). With these closing words of the poem the author acknowledges the unbridgeable gap between himself (and, by extension, all mortals) and the fleeting figure of his reinvented charity and love. Thus, as if in a prayer, almost as if he were trying to persuade himself, he exhorts his readers as well as himself to believe in a *new* new love: a love based on liberation, on violence, on contradiction—and on separation. He seems to pray that we may know how to follow (and not to wish to possess) love, which is both a presence and an absence.

It is apparent that the poet cannot possess in one soul and one body the reinvented love personified by the male figures of **"Conte"** and **"Génie."** In **"Being Beauteous,"** he attempts to merge momentarily with a female figure who is larger than life and who promises some kind of new love. The woman here, the Être de Beauté, evokes beauty and pure "being", as did the Génie of a "*beauty* ineffable", who represented "the hour of *essential* desire and satisfaction" (italics mine), in **"Conte."** Just as the Génie in **"Conte"** and the Génie in **"Génie"** were linked with death, so is the Être de Beauté: "Des sifflements de mort et des cercles de musique sourde font monter, s'élargir et trembler comme un spectre ce corps adoré." This Incarnation of Beauty combines in her very essence the duality of the love-death embrace. Wounds, scarlet and black, erupt in her superb flesh.

Suddenly, the narrator, like the Prince of **"Conte,"** knows an instant of sublime sensual ecstasy. "Oh! nos os sont revêtus d'un nouveau corps amoureux", he declares. But the narrator's love embrace, like the Prince's, and like so many other moments of rapture in Rimbaud's writings, merges with his fall and with the disintegration of his vision. "O la face cendrée, l'écusson de crin, les bras de cristal! Le canon sur lequel je dois m'abattre à travers la mêlée des arbres et de l'air léger!" he exclaims. The Être de Beauté and the "amorous new body" are now wholly replaced by images of death, war and destruction. As in "Jadis . . .", "la Beauté" has once again proved "amére" to Rimbaud. His new love, whether personified as a male or as a female figure that is greater than life, cannot be captured. At best, as in the *voyant*'s attempt to reach the "*unknown*", the poet can only attain a momentary epiphany.

This loss of vision does not necessarily imply total failure, even in Rimbaud's search for the new love. For in his poetry of kaleidoscopic explosions, the moment often reveals everything—not serene rapture, to be sure, as in Blake's "Auguries of Innocence"—but the tragic and ambivalent perception that instantaneously links love with death, beauty with ugliness, success with failure, vision with blindness.

Dissatisfied with ordinary love, the poet tries to invent a new love which will permit him to embrace and embody truth, eroticism and charity. He tries homosexual love, onanism and imagined union with an idealized male or female figure. He craves many things in his new love, or rather, loves. He longs for a "très pur amour" (**"Matinée d'ivresse"**) as well as for freedom from guilt (as in **"Les Stupra"** and **"Matinée d'ivresse,"** where he would like to bury the tree of good and evil), for liberation from time (" 'crible les fléaux, à commencer par le temps' ", children chant in **"A une raison"**), from space (the narrator in **"Génie"** exults, "immensité de l'univers!") and from all restrictions—social, religious or moral. He craves strength, ("Amour, force!—plus haut que toutes joies et gloires!" he exclaims in **"Angoisse"**), revolutionary charity, truth and spiritual pleasure, newness, beauty, happiness and pride.

In his quest for the new love, the poet actually seeks transcendence of his earthly, human condition far more than he seeks another being—male or female—with whom he can communicate. For Rimbaud, the lover's goal, like the *voyant*'s, is to surpass himself. The Vierge Folle, the "satanique docteur", the two Génies and the Être de Beauté are all possible vehicles for helping the poet-lover reach the infinite. While these figures at times provide him with moments of power, hope, and even ecstasy, they, like the "*unknown*", ultimately torture him, escape from him or threaten to destroy him.

For these reasons, Rimbaud's search for reinvented love echoes his basic poetic pattern. Beginning with rebellion and evolving into a revolution, his quest for new love, like his attempt to reach the "*unknown*", achieves a momentary ecstasy, after which there ensues the inevitable fatal fall. But sometimes, as in **"Génie,"** for this poet who says "Je ne pourrai jamais envoyer l'Amour par la fenêtre"

("**Phrases**"), his defeat appears as a new beginning, a new affirmation.

What does the Epoux Infernal really mean when he says: "L'amour est à réinventer, on le sait"? With these words, he may be implying that love has to be found or discovered over again. Thus, in "**Vies II**," the narrator announces: "Je suis . . . un musicien . . . qui ai trouvé quelque chose comme la clef de l'amour." On the other hand, he may be inferring that love is merely *invented, made up, fabricated*. In this way, the famous pronouncement carries dual connotations of faith and of cynicism. These, of course, are basic polarities that pervade Rimbaud's poetry.

Throughout his writings, the poet longs for love's pleasures and its powers, yet he portrays love and eroticism as full of contradictions, frustrations and torments. Even in his "new love", he is not able to achieve the ecstatic strength which he craves and which he hopes love can give him; nevertheless, he often revels in his ecstatic anguish, in masochistic and sadistic erotic torments. "Rimbaud n'a jamais recherché l'amour qu'en pressentant son échec", writes Yves Bonnefoy. Despite all of the poet's disappointments and failures, or perhaps because of them, love for Arthur Rimbaud has to be "invented over [and over] again". Like the *unknown* that the *voyant* tries to reach, love for this tortured poet embodies both hope and hopelessness. Because he both loves and hates others and himself, love for him, like his poetry, is his simultaneous search for glory and for punishment, for rapture and for destruction. (pp. 87-102)

> *Enid Rhodes Peschel, in her* Flux and Reflux: Ambivalence in the Poems of Arthur Rimbaud, *Librarie Droz, 1977, 137 p.*

Lynda D. McNeil   (essay date 1983)

[*In the following essay, McNeil discusses Rimbaud's use of metaphor in "Mémoire" and* Une saison en enfer.]

Unlike his Symbolist contemporaries whose aims were to evoke the absent and abstract from Nature, Rimbaud's search engaged him in a struggle to regain the absent Totality of Being (in the Hegelian sense) in all its multifacetedness and immediacy—to make Being present and sensible, to glimpse the infinite in the finite, again and again through the magically transforming power of language. This search that he would conduct throughout his brief poetic career (1870-74 mainly) would be marked, however, by a crisis of consciousness and values (indeed a reversal) which would result in a redefinition of his poetic Self in **Une Saison en Enfer,** thereby altering the style and epistemology of his later works. Just as Nietzsche demythologized Hegel, so does Rimbaud evolve from an earlier aim to embody poetically a Hegelian-like cosmic synthesis between subject and object, poet and world, and past and present to a later abandonment and loss of faith in this project. Individual poems, such as "**Mémoire**" and "**Enfance,**" as well as his works seen synoptically, often enact thematically, phenomenologically and stylistically the dialectical play of presence and absence, play which can perhaps best be understood in relation to the conceptual framework provided by Paul Ricoeur in his phenomenological interpretation of "living" metaphor.

In *La métaphore vive* (trans. *The Rule of Metaphor*), Ricoeur extends his talent as hermeneutic phenomenologist to the study of "the truth of being" of metaphor. Rather than adopting past neopositivist or formalist views of metaphor as the substitution of signs (e.g., tenor/vehicle), Ricoeur sees it as a performative activity, or as: "that rhetorical process of transposing and transmuting semantic differences by which discourse unleases the power certain fictions have to describe reality." According to Ricoeur, the philosopher's metaphors disclose being, "since the dialectical tension of figure and concept in the living or revivified metaphor of a philosopher's text can contribute to a Platonism of the invisible or glorify the visibility of appearances." He contrasts his own concept of "living" metaphor (or "impertinent predication") with that of Derrida's "dead" metaphor (or "deviant denomination") as articulated in "White Mythology" [*New Literary History* 6 (Autumn 1974)]:

> The primitive meaning, the original figure, always sensible and material . . ., is not exactly a metaphor. It is a kind of transparent figure, equivalent to a proper meaning. It becomes metaphor when put in circulation in philosophical discourse. At that point, the first meaning and the first displacement are simultaneously forgotten. The metaphor is no longer noticed, and it

is taken for the proper meaning. This is a two-fold effacement. On this view, philosophy would be a self-eliminating process of generating metaphor. It would be of the nature of philosophy that philosophical culture be a rude obliteration.

Ricoeur counters Derrida's view of metaphor as "deformed by a metaphysics of presence" or as "nominal deviation" or substitution by adopting a tensional view: "The speculative is the very principle of disparity (inadequation) between illustrations and intellection, between exemplifications and conceptual apprehension." In this way, Ricoeur revises of notions of metaphor as the substitution of the contextually present sign ("illustration") and its implied and absent abstraction ("intellection"). Instead for Ricoeur the process involves the dialectical play between never-to-be reconciled antitheses, that is between the present sign and its absent idea or abstraction.

It is this (Ricoeur's) conceptual framework for "living" metaphor or the dialectical interplay of presence and absence, as well as metaphor as a performative activity, that serves as a tool for understanding better the phenomenological and stylistic drama at the heart of Rimbaud's poetry. Through various means, the moving force of Rimbaud's poetry would consistently remain: to transform the unsatisfactory present (tainted by alienation of self from the world, subject from object) in the Spirit of the Totality of Being. He would continuously strive to transform absence, loss and despair into pure presence, renewal and hope. In his earlier poems, this power over Being and language would temporarily satisfy a deep and insatiable need to fill the void of loneliness and the impulse for self-destruction with joy and love. In this regard, [Yves] Bonnefoy, Rimbaud's most recent biographer, reflects upon Rimbaud's sad childhood: "Robbed of love, Rimbaud was deprived of that possible communion with what is. And he saw reality, like his own mind, split into dangerous dualities" [*Rimbaud par Lui-même,* 1961]. The absent Unknown for Rimbaud was not, as the Symbolist believed, "the secret aspect of the world of appearance" or an "Idea or moral presence beyond sensory realities," rather: "the perception, of course oblique, of course fleeting and paradoxical, of the unmasked aseity of things: this aseity which, in its stupendous immediacy, is more force than form, more ravishment than spectable, more an eruption than a state." For Rimbaud the imagination held the power to disclose the fleeting "aseity" of things in the material world, their absolute self-sufficiency from man or Creator, immediate and in constant flux. And continuing, "When (Rimbaud) will attempt to describe the most profound reality, the real with all its sensory degradations plucked away, he will speak of an intense brightness, of a fire in which all things dissolve." Rimbaud's alchemical metaphor for the experience of Being expresses a view, taken up later by the Surrealists, of a "fleeting, paradoxical, yet interwoven sense of reality": "(it was) a passage from feelings and psychological attitudes to participation regained, as an intensification of our perceptions until they are consumed in the substantial fire of the Unknown." For Rimbaud, to be able even briefly to participate in this unknown, pure Being in the poetic act, must have satisfied momentarily a need to replace emptiness or absence with a sense of totality and presence. Regardless of the outcome, the major thrust of Rimbaud's poetry was to overcome the Cartesian dualism separating subject and object that served in large part as the epistemological basis for the Romantic mode of poetry he so disliked. His was a re-action against the cult of the ego, with its self-pity and morbid introspection (*mal du siècle*) isolating men from each other and from Being that the French Romantic poets had adopted from the Germans. Ironically, however, to bridge this gap between self and world, he cultivated the very fissures of consciousness that would lead to irreconcilable dualities of mind that inevitably ended his poetic silence.

While the goal of sustained communion with Being remained fairly constant throughout his short poetic career, the means to achieve it change radically as the result of his redefined sense of self in *Une Saison en Enfer* (1873). Consequently, if one views his poetry as a whole, a dialectical tension appears between the earlier (voyancy) and the later (*Saison* and after) poetry, in addition to the fact that the two modes come increasingly to co-exist in the final year.

Rimbaud's earlier voyancy poems (i.e., those prior to *Une Saison*) reflect a calculated attempt to achieve this "mystic" communion with Being through various forms of self-imposed debauchery ("le raisonné dérèglement de tous les sens"): drugs, sexual excesses, alcohol, or merely physical and mental exhaustion. In these ways, he hoped to suspend the mind's rational control over experience (and therefore of one's experience of Being) or the ego's "will to power," and thereby to maximize his subconsciousness's receptivity to the totality of Being. In doing so, he discovered a part of his consciousness very different from and seemingly opposed to the Romantic ego-and logo-centered poetry, epitomized for Rimbaud by Alfred de Musset. The newly discovered part of his mind, the irrational or subconscious, sprang forth as if an objectified poetic self, while ironically through this "dédoublement du moi" he had released the deeply subjective subconsciousness of a newly bifurcated consciousness with its natural tendency to impose its own order and "vision" on reality, he hoped to release the imagination's involuntary (often irrational) receptivity to communion with Being. This poetic process can be described in words used to explain Ricoeur's "living" metaphor: "internalizing the gaps and paradoxes, (he) repeatedly confronts in life and transforms them through the dialectic into the play of being." The "gap and paradoxes" that Rimbaud internalizes in his imagination, become translated into the radically metaphoric and ironically mythic imagery, syntax and structures seen in his voyancy poems. [In a footnote, McNeill adds: "Briefly, the term 'radical' attached to metaphor and metonymy refers (both on a figural and structural level) to those logical relationships that are based on the private associations of the poet (rather than on culturally shared experiences), such as dream, hallucination or vision; the attachment of 'ironic' to mythic refers to a poetic structure like that of *The Waste Land* where cycles of recurrency reveal change that implies contrast (rather than mythic harmony) as the contrast of the idyllic past with the corrupt present."] As [W. M.] Frohock has observed [in his *Rimbaud's Poetic Practice,* 1963], Rimbaud's capacity to experience visions of great vividness and beauty resulted from the use of artificial stimulants which served to: "loosen his ties with reality and allow his brilliant images to dissociate and then reform in new associations more or less beyond his control." He continues, "The association would seem to exist objectively and could seem more real then the phenomena of his ordinary world."

A poem that enacts the style and poetics of Rimbaud's earlier voyancy poetry, **"Mémoire"** (1872), is an autobiographical narrative poem about Monsieur (père) Rimbaud's desertion of his wife and children, the implied causes of it, and the consequent suffering it brought both to mother and son (the poet as a child), as conveyed through a series of images generally associated with the River Meuse near Charleville, his provincial home. Furthermore, from a phenomenological point of view, the poem is about his longing for mythic communion with Nature (through involuntary memory) as the poetic expression of an apparently deeper need for maternal and paternal love, as well as familial harmony. Through the processes of mythopoeic memory, the invisible past merges with the visible present and the poet and nature exchange qualities through metaphoric confusion as they attain sympathetic identification. But, before looking at the poem itself, let us see how it functions as a reaction against Romantic poetry (as it has been widely understood).

Cyrus Hamlin, who [in his "Temporality of Selfhood" *New Literary History* 6 (Autumn 1974)] hopes to revise our notions of Romantic theory and poetry in the light of Ricoeur's concept of "living metaphor," discusses the metaphoric relationship between the temporal experience of the subjective self in Romantic poetry and the Totality of time or the Infinite experience that it attempts to capture. And, like the temporal experience of the subjective self in the poem, the language of poetry, according to Hamlin, is based on a temporal experience "subject to division and difference" in contrast to the motive of such poetry as unmediated vision. Speaking on this inherently dialectical opposition both in the experience and in the language of Romantic poetry (i.e., between the subjective and temporal and the transcendent and timeless), Hamlin explains:

> Recollection of what had been lost or prediction of what was to come could only be achieved poetically in the language of metaphor, that sentimental mode of discourse where emotions and intuition must interact through dialectical opposition with reflective thought and self-consciousness. The voice which speaks in poetry can only be aware of itself within a temporal structure, just as the source for any vision of transcendence must be the mortal eye, which can only see its object by standing apart from it. Mystical communion and symbolic identity are beyond the limits of language.

Here he distinguishes between the symbolic (or naive) mode of poetry, formerly attributed to the Romantics, as the fusion of the subject and the object, and the allegorical/ironic (or sentimental) mode that more accurately characterizes Romantic poetry in practice. The later mode

is considered to be metaphoric (as opposed to symbolic), since in it there always exist those paradoxical or ironic gaps between the finite and the infinite, or between the temporal and the timeless: "The actual experience of poetry is always subject to temporal process, and self-fulfillment is never more than an aesthetic illusion. The status of the work in its relation to human experience may far more appropriately be described as metaphoric than symbolic." Hence, the metaphorical relationship between the poet as a temporal self and his transcendent experience is metaphoric *not* because they are identical (i.e., symbolic), rather because there is the same quality in the relationship as that portrayed in Ricoeur's concept of "living" metaphor, that is, the striving toward the abstract ideal while simultaneously being grounded in the finite and the temporal.

The former transcendent or "symbolic" pattern of experience—which Rimbaud uses ironically—is reflected in Abrams's definition of the Greater Romantic Lyric in which the poet's communion with nature through recollection brings enlightenment; it follows this experiential pattern: present-past-present and despair-recollection-enlightenment. If one substitutes Coleridge's idea of the "esemplastic" power of the imagination for "recollection" here (and in **"Mémoire"**), then the poem Abrams describes relies heavily upon such an imaginative power whereby the Totality of time or space (infinity could refer to both) ideally subsumes the finite and temporal. Here Abrams's theory parallels the idealistic theory of the "symbolic."

To return now to Rimbaud, **"Mémoire"** (as well as *Le Bateau Ivre,* **"Aube,"** and **"Enfance"**) enacts an *ironic* reversal of this pattern of poetic experience (rather enlightenment-recollection-despair) as well as the enactment of the loss of imaginative stamina to sustain his visionary experience. The poem is, in fact, most emphatically about the dissolution of the metaphoric relationship between the poet's goal and his actual experience as thematically and stylistically the poem "regresses" into irony, dissociated metonymies and personal alienation both from his family and nature. Perhaps one could say that these earlier poems are Rimbaud's testament to his loss of faith in the Romantic project itself, especially in its philosophical and epistemological assumptions that climaxed with Coleridge and Hegel. In the poems written in this ironically mythic mode, Rimbaud completes the curving circle of experience—the first half of which Abrams describes—by plotting the plunge from enlightenment down to despair and discontinuity. Increasingly, especially in his later voyancy poems, Rimbaud would rely upon artifical stimulants to achieve a transient vision, only repeatedly to track its loss.

The mythopoeic experience and its dissipation is enacted stylistically in **"Mémoire"** through the heavy reliance on paratactical syntatic constructions that suggest both metaphoric and dissociative relationships among images (like the tension Ricoeur describes in "living" metaphor) and through the transmutation of imagery that depicts mythical communion as well as its dissolution. Particularly with regard to the style of **"Mémoire,"** in *The Design of Rimbaud's Poetry* [1963, John Porter] Houston discusses ambiguities that arise due to the poem's paratactical syntax and its vague "symbolism." Yet, what has remained ignored in discussions of this kind, I believe, is the significant relationship of the paratactical constructions and shifting metaphoric ground of the poem to the stylistic enactment of the dissipating mythopoeic experience. In place of the "ambiguous symbols," the poem's imagery is comprised mainly of paired images that suggest interchangeably both personification and animism (the mythic harmony between man and nature) and that are themselves transmuted throughout the poem.

The first two sections (each composed of two quatrains) convey the sense of mythic communion and familial harmony, although themselves tainted with nuances of loss and sorrow. The first section is composed of ten predominant images that are isolated from each other by periods, semi-colons, colons, or syntactic disjunctures. Yet this syntactic sense of dissociation is held in tension with the implied metaphoric associations between certain pairs of images. First, here is that section:

> Clear water; like the salt of childhood tears;
> The assault of the sun by the whiteness of
>   women's bodies;
> the silk of banners, in masses and of pure lilies,
> under the walls a maid once defended.
> The play of angels—No . . . the golden current
>   on its way
> moves its arms, black and heavy, and above all
>   cool, with grass. She
> dark, having the blue sky as a canopy, calls up
> for curtains the shadow of the hill and the arch.

The first pair of such metaphorically associated images (including similies) in the first line ("Clear water; like the salt of childhood tears") establishes a mythic association, albeit played prophetically against nuances of sadness and loss, between the child and the river (as source-mother). The next cluster of images (II. 2-3) includes the white female bodies bathing in the stream, followed by those of silk banners (from the past) and pure lilies (in the present along with riverbanks) ("The assault on the sun by the whiteness of women's bodies; / The silk of banners, in masses and of pure lilies"; "L'assaut au soleil des blancheurs des corps de femme; / la soie, en foule et de lys pur, des oriflammes"). Here, Rimbaud creates an interwoven quality syntactically, so important to the association of the white bodies to lilies and silk banners, by separating the prepositional phrase, "of banners" ("des oriflammes"), from the noun it modifies, "silk" ("la soie"), thereby juxtaposing banners and lilies ("de lys pur, des oriflammes"). The image of the bathers' "assault" on the sun ("L'assaut au soleil des blancheurs des corps de femme") can be linked to Saint Joan (soldier and martyr) while simultaneously contrasting what we know of her virginity and stoic self-discipline with the open sensuality of the silken white, sun-drenched bathers. The last cluster of images in this section (II. 3-4)—lilies, banners and the wall defended by Saint Joan of Arc—introduce temporally mythic associations, that is, the simultaneous convergence of present (lilies along the still extant wall) and past (Saint Joan's fleur-de-lys bedecked banner placed on the same wall in the 15th Century). On the one hand, the pure lilies

can be seen as metaphoric substitutions both for the glistening white and silken bodies of the female bathers and for the *fleur-de-lys* on the Tricouleur gracefully undulating over the medieval wall. It appears that Rimbaud has assured one's making these associations by the syntactic positioning of "banners" at the end of the third line (rather than in the middle where it would follow more logically). There it provides a syntactic bridge between the images of lilies, banners and the wall, suggesting the child's experience of mythic simultaneity as the present and the 15th Century momentarily converge. Finally of note, this stanza introduces the central images of the poem (river, sun, and flowers) that become transmuted throughout the rest of the poem, the tenor and connotation of which will signal the decline of the mythic experience.

In the midst of this opening scene, so full of visionary awareness, appears a foreshadowing of its loss (II. 5-8) through contrastive imagery that suggests presence and absence. The first image, "the play of angels," combines the past and present in the allusion to Joan, saint and soldier, and the immediate image of girls playing in the water. But, the ejaculation, "No," follows it suggesting that the chain of associations leading to "the play of angels" had broken the magical spell of mythic continuity, by the reminder of desertion, absence, and loss. For example, the other reference to angels, in section III, compares the departing father-sun to "a thousand white angels separating on the road." Then, quickly for reassurance, the child turns to "the golden current on its way," symbol of presence and the mother, only to discover, ironically, that she (mother-river) has transmuted into a shadowy stream, "black and heavy, and above all cool, with grass." The dialectical interplay of personification (river=woman) and animism (woman=river) to enact mythic harmony of man and nature is held in tension with the evolving contrast of both river and mother first as pure presence and warm, erotic and vital source ("the golden current on its way" [I. 5] and "the water fills the prepared beds with pale bottomless gold" [I. 10]), then as cold, sluggist and shadowy absence ("She / dark, having the blue sky as a canopy, calls up / for curtains the shadow of the hill and the arch").

In the first quatrain of this section, we see another instance of the interplay of presence and absence through the "confusion" of tenor and vehicle (personification and animism) in the images of the girls in green dresses and the willow trees along the river bank ("The green faded dresses of girls / make willows out of which hop unbridled birds"). Here is the entire section:

> Ah! the wet surface extends its clear broth!
> The water fills the prepared beds with pale bot-
>   tomless gold.
> The green faded dresses of girls
> make willows out of which hop unbridled birds.
> Purer than a louis, a yellow and warm eyelid:
> the marsh marigold—your conjugal faith, O
>   Spouse—
> At prompt noon, from its dim mirror, vies
> with the dear rose Sphere in the sky grey with
>   heat.

Are the girls, possibly Rimbaud's sisters, really present

and dressed in green, brocaded with pictures of birds, or are the willow trees, alive with hopping birds, merely being compared with girls in green brocade? Yet, to be consistent with the other examples of mythic communion should not both possibilities be read as both literally and figuratively true and simultaneous? Indeed, the reciprocity of tenor and reference, of personification (willows like girls) and animism (girls like willows), stylistically enacts the child-poet's mythopoeic imagination at work. However, at the same time that the similarities may strike us as apt, clearly the tension of their differences and of the uncertainty of their presence or absence, resulting from the syntactic gaps, figures as part of his (and our) experience(s) and as a threat to maintaining the very tenuous, fleeting awareness of mythic communion.

Section III signals the decline of mythic vision as the river-wife and sun-husband image appear, not in nuptial union, but in inescapable discord. "Madame," cold and dark, stands "trop debout" (too straight or prim), while blocking out the sunlight with her parasol and stepping on the field of wildflowers. The husband, Rimbaud's father, like the now-setting sun, departs:

> Madame stands too straight in the field
> nearby where the filaments from the (harvest)
>   work snow down: the parasol
> in her fingers; stepping on the white flower, too
>   proud for her;
> children reading in the flowering grass
> their book of red morocco. Alas, he, like
> a thousand white angels separating on the road,
> goes off beyond the mountain! She, all
> cold and dark, runs! after the departing man!

Both pronouns "he" ("Lui") and "she" ("Elle") could merely refer to sun and river respectively, this is until the last image, "after the departing man." For here the natural and the human connotations merge, while also suspended in doubt, where the dark river would more aptly be seen as chasing the sun, not "the man"—as would Mme. Rimbaud. Like the sun which on its diurnal path must leave the river, thus transforming her into water, cold and dark like "the color of ash," the husband, having deserted his wife and children, leaves her, "all cold and dark, run(ning) after the departing man."

The separation completed, in section IV, Rimbaud adopts the emotional point of view of his deserted mother, as if the child, needing her more than ever, reaches out briefly in an act of sympathetic identification. Through the eyes of Vitalie Rimbaud, longing for her departed man, we witness the collapse of her marriage, now synonymous with mythic unity, as reflected in the effects of sunset on the river:

> Longing for the thick young arms of pure grass!
> Gold of April moons in the heart of the holy bed;
>   joy
> of abandoned boatyards, a prey
> to August nights which made rotting things germinate!
>
> Let her weep now under the rampart! the breath
> of the poplars above is the only breeze.
> After, there is the surface, without reflection,
>   without springs, gray:

an old dredger, in his motionless boat, labors.

Preceding images of sensuous opulence, presence, and immediacy recede into those of darkness, cold, absence, and decay; in addition, gold, the color symbolic of visionary totality and hope for Rimbaud, fades into the shadowy gray that signifies loss of vision of the child-poet's despair.

The child's poet-visionary point of view informs the final section, which turns upon the poignant irony that what is oppressively present is the realization of absence—of vision, of golden daylight (sun) and the moving current, of love of husband and father, and of mythic-nuptial communion. From the preceding merging of past and present and of man and nature in the child's memory of an idyllic state where vision, vitality and love co-existed, he is returned powerlessly to the despair of the present—visionless and stagnant—in his motionless boat.

> Toy of this sad eye of water, I cannot pluck
> O motionless boat! O arms too short, either this
> Or the other flower: neither the yellow nor
>   which bothers me
> There, nor the friendly blue one in the ash-
>   colored water.
>
> Ah! dust of the willows shaken by the wing!
> The roses of the reeds devoured long ago!
> My boat still stationary, and its chain caught
> In the bottom of this rimless eye of water—in
>   what mud?

Acting as testimony to his loss of vision, abundant images of absence and sorrow close the poem: the bright "eye" of the sun becomes the "sad eye of water"; the dust of willows is shaken by the wings of departing birds (earlier in brocaded dresses); and the roses of reeds are devoured, surrounding the immobile boat stuck in the mud.

Rimbaud's ironically mythic view of experience in **"Mémoire"** depends upon imagery and syntactic relationships that suggest metaphoric continuities in a dialectic between presences and absences, past and present. Yet, as much as he apparently needs—as an emotionally fragile child—the human and mythic harmony that his visions enact, the force of his will and his imagination fail against the forces of change in nature and in human relationships. As we witness recurrently in his poems, the ideal of experiencing the totality of Being becomes subverted by the inextricable vulnerability of Being to change and loss. The ideal of the invisible, absent underlying continuities—evoked through artificially imposed vision—inevitably gives way to the "visibility of appearances," the ever-present antipodes of experience. And in stylistic terms, the dialectical interplay of "living" metaphor gives way to the presentational imagery and dissociative metonymies that signal the loss of vision. Past and present, human and natural, mythic and mundane, all can be seen finally as much in ironic tension as in harmonious identification, further underscoring the differences, the absence of continuities, between what was merely imagined to be present and what actually was. **"Mémoire"** can be understood, then, as an early example of the loss of faith in Romantic idealism by taking the dialectical tension seen in metaphor to the limits of irony and possibly even beyond it.

Thus the subject, going beyond irony, leads us to the poetic work that enacts Rimbaud's spiritual crisis, *A Season in Hell*(*Une Saison en Enfer*).   After the **"Lettres du voyant,"** *A Season in Hell* (1873) is the most important document of Rimbaud's poetic practice, marking at its juncture a "crisis of consciousness" (anticipated in **"Mémoire"**) that would produce a radically new definition of the poetic self and of his rapport with nature and his fellowmen. In the mode of a dramatic monologue that he conducts with his past "selves" and with his immediate split-self, Rimbaud confronts in narrative unfolding the moral, poetic and epistemological contradictions that comprise his immediate self. *A Season in Hell* is a prose poem devoid of the earlier metaphorical interplay of past and present, temporal and transcendent, and yet it continues with a dialectic of various moral, poetic and epistemological points of view as if enacting through cubist-like complexity the process or *progress* of the spirit: "We are going toward the *Spirit*" ("Nous allons à l'*Esprit*"). In an attempt to free himself from the limits of subjectivity and temporality, he first strains against the boundaries of the self by delving into his origins (Ricoeur's "archeology" of the self) paradoxically in order to partake of the "pure presence" of Being, now synonymous with objectivity—to escape subjectivity as had been his plan from the beginning ("Je est un autre").

In the first poem, **"Bad Blood" ("Mauvais Sang"),** Rimbaud begins this search by recalling his ancestral past, now co-present with the modern self, both simultaneously coursing through his veins. He acknowledges the moral and epistemological dimensions of that facet of himself represented by his barbaric and idolatrous Gallic ancestors:

> I have the white-blue eye of my Gallic ancestors, their narrow skull and their clumsiness in fighting. I find my clothes as barbarous as theirs. Only I don't butter my hair.

and,

> It is quite clear to me that I have always been of an inferior race. I cannot understand revolt.

The history of France, in fact, also presently courses through his veins, engrained in his racial "memory":

> I recall the history of France, eldest daughter of the Church. A villain, I must have made the journey to the Holy Land my head is full of roads through Swabian plain, views of Byzantium, ramparts of Jerusalem: the cult of Mary, compassion for the crucified Christ awake in me among a thousand profane phastasmagoria.

While his point of view shifts from the Gallic pagan, to the medieval pilgrim to the convict, beast and "nigger," suddenly the superstition, idolatry and magic of the amoral pagan transmutes into the reason, science and selflessness of the Christian pagan-convert: "The inferior race has over-run everything—the people, as we say, the nation, reason, science." And later, "O my abnegation, O my marvelous charity! here below however!" The ebb and flow of moral and epistemological perspectives—from the bestial pagan's superstition and belief in magic to the mod-

ern Christian's faith and belief in reason and science— enacts the spiritual struggle that Rimbaud undergoes throughout the poem:

> I have never belonged to this people; I have never been a Christian; I am of the race that sang under torture; laws I have never understood; I have no moral sense, I am a brute: you are making a mistake.

and later:

> I bury the dead in my belly. Shouts, drums, dance, dance, dance! I cannot even see the time when, white men landing, I shall fall into nothingness.

The moral point of view changes:

> The white men are landing! The cannon!! We must submit to baptism, put on clothes, work. My heart has known the coup de grace. Ah! I did not foresee it.
> I have never done evil. Light will my days be and I shall not have known the torment of the soul half dead to good. . . .

This section ends, however, with Rimbaud's fall from the convert's innocence and zeal and with his distaste for blind idealism:

> I am not a prisoner of my reason. I said: God. I want freedom in salvation: how am I to seek it? Frivolous tastes have left me no more regrets for the age of tender hearts. Each of us has his reason, scorn and charity; I reserve my place at the top of that angelic ladder of common sense.

In **"Night of Hell" ("Nuit en l'enfer"),** Rimbaud is punished for his sin of pride by being plunged into Hell. What began as a moral struggle and ends as punishment for sin in **"Bad Blood,"** becomes in **"Night of Hell"** a metaphor for the self-imposed hell produced by the delirium mandated by his poetics of voyancy: "I think I am in hell, therefore I am in hell." This section of *A Season* parallels the experience of "the derangement of all the senses" spoken of in his earlier voyancy letters: the loss of innocence, morality, brotherhood (the other Christian virtues) as well as his self-destruction by fire. His is like the alchemist's deliberate destruction, albeit of the self, out of which he hoped would emerge a radiant and renewed self-in-the-world. While probably suffering the drug addict's withdrawal in his literal and figurative hell, he describes himself as a mutilated man:

> I have swallowed a monstrous dose of poison.— Thrice blessed be the counsel that came to me!— My entrails are on fire. The violence of the venom twists my limbs, deforms and prostrates me. I die of thirst, I suffocate, and cannot scream. It is Hell, eternal punishment! See how the fire flares up again! How nicely I burn. Go to it, demon!

And

> Noble ambitions!
> And still this is life!—Suppose damnation were eternal! Then a man who would mutilate himself is well damned, isn't he?

The destruction of the self in the hell fires, into a drama-tized split self, first appears subtly at the end of **"Night of Hell"** and then explicitly in the two voices that dominate **"Delirium, I and II."**

From the end of **"Night,"** the two sides of Rimbaud's split self emerge: on the one hand, the damned pagan-voyant and, on the other hand, the saved reasonable-convert. Their morally distinct points of view alternate, engaged in an internal dialogue or dialectic in the section below:

> I am going to unveil all the mysteries: religious mysteries, or natural mysteries, death, birth, the future, the past, cosmogony, nothingness. I am a master of phantasmagoria.
> Listen! . . .
> I have all the talents!—There is no one here and there is someone: I would not squander my trea-sures.—Do you want me to vanish, to dive after the *ring*? Is that what you want? I will make gold, remedies.
> Have faith in me then, faith assuages, guides, re-stores. Come, all of you—even the little chil-dren—that I may confront you, that my heart may be poured out for you, . . .
> —And what of me? All this hardly makes me re-gret the world very much. I am lucky not to suf-fer more. My life was nothing but sweet follies, it's a pity.

The moral values, the way to truth, are less locked in a battle for dominance than juxtaposed in dialectical inter-play, at once distinct facets of his personality, yet inextri-cably bound: "Ah! to rise again into life! to cast our eyes on our deformities. And that poison, that kiss, a thousand times accursed! My weakness, the cruelty of the world! My God, pity, hide me, I behave too badly!—I am hidden and I am not."

Both **"Delirium, I and II"** continue the dialectic begun in **"Night,"** but with the focus shifting to the epistemology and the poetics of voyancy, a stance he now found to be based on self-deception. In **"Delirium, I"** the repented self, the reasonable convert or "the foolish virgin," con-fesses his past sins to Christ, the Heavenly Bridegroom, telling how he had been seduced by the "infernal bride-groom," the pagan-voyant. While Rimbaud's biographical critics have established the aptness of seeing Verlaine as the foolish virgin and Rimbaud as the infernal bride-groom, his seducer, to limit the poem to this level of inter-pretation is to miss the level of dialectic that has been evolving from the beginning, that is, Rimbaud's internal struggle. The foolish virgin recalls his entrapment:

> His mysterious delicacies had seduced me. I for-got all my duty to society, to follow him. What a life! Real life is absent. We are not in the world. I go where he goes, I have to.

And he describes how they led a dream-like existence in which, as he says above, real life is absent:

> He wants to live a sleepwalker. Would his good-ness and his charity alone give him the right to live in the real world. . . . I shall awake, and the laws and customs will have changed,—thanks to his magic power,—or the world, while

remaining the same, will leave me to my desires, joys, heedless.

The effects of their cultivated derangement on poetic lan-guage are described in **"Delirium, II,"** where we learn of the poet's power of "alchemical" transformation. In his induced visionary state, the ordinary or base metals of ex-perience could magically be transformed into gold, those radiant moments of imagined totality and newness of sight. He describes one such instance here:

> I became adept at simple hallucination: in place of a factory I really saw a mosque, a school of drummers led by angels, carriages on the high-ways of the sky, a drawing-room at the bottom of a lake; monsters, mysteries; the title of a melo-drama would raise horrors before me.
> Then I would explain my magic sophisms with the hallucination of words!
> Finally I came to regard as sacred the disorder of my mind.

Yet, from the end of **"Delirium, I"** to **"Adieu,"** the final poem, Rimbaud seems to emerge from the depths of his self-imposed Hell into the light of reason—only finally to relinquish complete faith in it, too: "At last, O happiness, O reason, I brushed from the sky the azure that is dark-ness, and I lived—gold spark of *pure* light."

In **"The Impossible,"** while looking back on the poetry of voyancy he says, "how stupid it was" ("quelle sottise c'était") and tries to examine the causes of "modern wretchedness" and the alternatives open to him. We live in what he calls "the Occidental swamps," which include all the "cruel developments the spirit has suffered since the end of the Orient." Rejecting the values of the West, which include reason, science, pride and conquest ("the will to power"), Rimbaud writes:

> To the devil, I said, with martyr's crowns, the beam of art, the pride of inventors, the ardor of plunderers; I returned to the Orient and to the first and eternal wisdom.—A dream of vulgar in-dolence it would seem!
> Yet, I was hardly thinking of the pleasure of es-caping modern wretchedness. . . . But is there not real torment in this, that, ever since that dec-laration of science, Christianity, man *fools him-self,* proves to himself the obvious, puffs himself up with the pleasure of reiterating those proofs, and can live in no other way!

Edward Said's [*Orientalism,* 1978] helps us to understand Rimbaud's perception of the Orient in this section as it re-lates to his personal struggle. Within the context of 19th century French "orientalism," according to Said, "the Orient (is) less a place than a *topos,* a set of references, a congeries of characteristics" in contrast with Western "su-periority," or "a style of thought based upon an ontologi-cal and epistemological distinction made between 'the Ori-ent' and (most of the time) 'the Occident.' " Furthermore according to such a view, the Orient as it is becomes cloud-ed over by "the imaginative examination of things Orien-tal based more or less exclusively upon a sovereign West-ern consciousness out of whose unchallenged centrality an Oriental world emerged, first according to general ideas about who or what was an Oriental, then according to a detailed logic governed not simply by empirical reality but by a battery of desires, repressions, investments, and projections."

In **"The Impossible,"** Rimbaud's desired return to "the original fatherland" suggested a momentary escape to a place (that is, state of being) of eternal wisdom and purity of vision, similar to the innocence and visionary power experienced in childhood (see **"Mémoire"** and **"Enfance"**). As such it is a regressive act, a Romantic nostalgic longing for "restorative reconstruction" of a worldview whose assumptions have lost credibility. This "Eden," the Orient, stands in contrast to the repressive forces of rationalism (science and philosophy), religion (Christianity), and imperialism (French colonization of North Africa): "How far all this is from the conception, from the wisdom of the Orient, the original fatland." What Rimbaud opposes and seeks to overturn here is what we have since come to call the Western ontotheological and imperialist tradition ("the Occidental swamps") which as Heidegger would observe later has run its course, leaving Rimbaud with the dread of Nothingness or Absence (Kierkegaard) in its wake.

> Philosophers, you are of your Occident.
> My spirit, beware. No violent projects of salvation. Bestir yourself!—Ah! for us science is too slow!
> O purity! purity!
> It is this moment of awakening that has given me the vision of purity!—Through the spirit we go to God!
> Heart-breaking misfortune!

As an alternative, he searches here for the "purity of vision" freed from the will to power and its narrow ego- and logocentricity: "ever since that declaration of science, Christianity, man *fools himself,* proves to himself the obvious, puffs himself up with the pleasure of reiterating those proofs." Through the possible effacement of the self, he believed there would come about a progress of the spirit described in **"Morning"**:

> From the same desert, in the same night, always my tired eyes awake to the silver star, always, but the Kings of life are not moved, the three magi, mind and heart and soul. When shall we go beyond the mountains and the shores, to greet the birth of new toil, of new wisdom, the flight of tyrants, of demons, the end of superstition, to adore—the first to adore!

Although it is not explicit, I believe there is a movement here toward the self-less values emphasized in the last poem, **"Adieu."** While this spirit draws him toward the transcendent, "the silver star," the forces of Life (mind, heart and soul) pull him in yet another direction.

In **"Adieu,"** Rimbaud says farewell to the amorality, irrationality and poetics of the voyant, and turns to embrace "rough reality," searching for the totality of Being in the pure presence of things, in the finite and paradoxical. Rather than try to reconcile the "dangerous dualities of mind" that he cultivated as a visionary poet, Rimbaud merely abandons all subjectivity (actually the first step to-

ward his abandonment of poetry) in favor of a dream of untainted objectivity:

> I! I who called myself angel or seer, exempt from all morality, I am returned to the soil with a duty to seek and rough reality to embrace! Peasant! Am I mistaken? Would charity be the sister of death or me?
> At last, I shall ask forgiveness for having fed on lies. And now let's go.
> But no friendly hand!

Despite reverting to the other extreme of the false dichotomy (subjective/objective) to which he falls victim here, Rimbaud ends *A Season in Hell* on an optimistic note, anticipating the future when he will be able to reconcile the contradictions of his existence: "Why talk of a friendly hand! My great advantage is that I can laugh at old lying loves and put to shame those deceitful couples, . . .—and I shall be free to *possess truth in one soul and one body.*"

Any "reading" of *A Season in Hell* runs the risk of imposing coherence on its multiple themes and points of view, thereby losing sight of the struggle which it enacts. Yet, most careful readers will agree that throughout its orchestrated discord emerges a recurrent, if not a unifying, theme that reveals approximately where Rimbaud stands at the end of the poem: the idea of "charity" ("La charité"). In terms of the moral concerns in the poem, "charity" appears in several contexts to mean selflessness, self-abnegation, and brotherly love (the remnant from Christianity he saves). Then, with regard to his evolving poetics, "charity" seems to be synonymous with Kierkegaard's "interest" and Heidegger's "Care," that is, an attentiveness or openness to the pure presence of Being. And with regard to his shifting epistemological stance, "charity" signifies an objectivity akin to what he sees as the wisdom of the Orient. All three facets of his personality—the ethical, the poetic and the epistemological—appear to converge in the figure of the Peasant in **"Adieu"**: "I am returned to the soil with a duty to seek and rough reality to embrace." Quite literally, then, his search has returned him to his origins. Despite the ruggedly idyllic image with which the poem ends, one must not forget the "spiritual struggle" that we have witnessed and, in semantic terms, in which we have ourselves participated. *A Season in Hell,* finally, enacts thematically, epistemologically, and poetically "le combat spirituel" through which Rimbaud—beginning with **"Mémoire"**—has struggled to make Absence wholly present. By the end of *A Season,* "presence" has more to do with the poet's ability to apprehend the immediate and objective than with the visionary striving for communion seen in **"Mémoire."** However, the battle does not end here, for as those familiar with *The Illuminations* know, Rimbaud will return to the visionary mode intermittently in his final poems.

Included in *The Illuminations* (1873-74), **"Enfance"** traces in its five sections the birth, evolution, and abandonment of Rimbaud's poetic imagination. As such it serves as a wonderful example of the epistemological and stylistic evolution that paralleled Rimbaud's spiritual struggles from the "voyancy" poems to *A Season in Hell* and beyond to silence. **"Enfance"** deals with the theme of the child's imaginative awakening, as well as his own poetic evolution, from the visionary to the objective mode, and finally to the abandonment of poetry altogether.

For example, the first and second selections of **"Enfance"** are the most dream-like in the rapidity and density with which images produced by free association appear. The child is an orphan, yet princely, ruling over a land covered by beaches that have names that are "ferociously Greek, Slav, Celtic." The processes of radically mythic association force experiences of disparate times and locations to converge in the child's imagination. In addition to this mythic structuring, imagery emerges from improbable yoking (here synaesthetically) in his magical land where "the dream flowers tinkle, burst, illuminate" and where a girl with orange lips has "her knees crossed in the limpid flood rising up from the fields, a naked body, shadowed, penetrated, and clothed by rainbows, flowers, the ocean." For the poet-as-child, a leisurely stroll becomes a circus-like adventure (a "comédie") in which these exotic "parts" merge in a circus-collage. In addition to the figures in this "parade," a radically metonymic series of objects and people move across his sister's eyes: "their pilgrimages, sultanes, princesses of tyrannical walk and costumes, foreign girls and some others sweetly unhappy." Indeed, in this entire section, there are no common denominators drawing these disparate images together, except the magical power of free association of the child's mind.

Section II contrasts the absence suggested by death in the family and presence inherent in the visionary joy experienced in nature. For example, the little girl is dead and buried ("behind the rose bushes"), as are the mother, the small brother and the old man—all are among beautiful flowers that provoke more attention than do the memories of the deceased. The "surreality" of this section derives from the paradox in presenting these dead (absent) relatives as if really present: the girl behind the roses, dead (as if alive and present); the small brother in India, buried over there in fields of pine (as if absent in India, but alive!); the old man buried upright in the wall (as if standing up alive). It is as if Rimbaud were playfully confusing, on the one hand, the idea of physical presence and the literal (being either alive or dead) with, on the other hand, the idea of absence and the figurative level of meaning. He places two seeming contradictions in dialectical tension, thereby making it possible for one to be dead (absent), yet as if present (the little girl behind the rose bushes), or to be alive, yet absent (buried) as in the protagonist in **"Enfance, V."** However, on a metaphorical level, one might wonder: are the relatives really, literally dead, but as if present in memory, or are they literally alive, but from Rimbaud's critical point of view emotionally or imaginatively dead? Both possibilities exist and their interplay or performance makes up an important dimension of the poem's meaning.

This and other images of death and absence contrast with those of imaginative life in this section. Rimbaud describes how the "sluice (gate) opens" and suddenly: "Oh! the crosses and the windmills of the desert, the islands and the haystacks! Magic flowers were buzzing!" The claustrophobic feeling evoked in the preceding paragraph gives way to the expansiveness of the child's mind in a natural setting as his senses let in a flood of freely associated images. The imagistic quality of radical yoking continues in the final lines of this section where "The slopes rocked him like a cradle" and the clouds over the oceans were "made of warm tears of all time."

The third section muffles the tone of magical awakening, replacing it with a more sober and detached stance. In terms of Rimbaud's evolving poetics, this section best illustrates the ideas in *A Season in Hell* that the poet must reject his poetry of voyancy in favor of a complete openness to the thingness of things and the contradictions of existence. Images are vivid and concrete, yet illogical or contradictory in their relationships to one another: "The difference that the 'there is' introduces into the poem is the difference between the presence and the things present or the visibility and what is rendered visible."

> In the woods there's a bird whose singing stops you and makes you blush.
> There's a clock which doesn't strike.
> There's a clay-pit with a nest of white animals.
> There's a little carriage abandoned in the woods or rolling down the path, with ribbons all over it.
> There's a troupe of child actors, in costume, whom you can see on the road through the edge of the wood.
> And then there's someone who chases you off when you're hungry and thirsty.

The images function as pure presences in themselves, devoid of any logical or visionary associations (except through their co-presence in the poem) A. Balakian has pointed out [in her *Literary Origins of Surrealism*, 1947] a possible context uniting these disparate images, Rimbaud's remembrance of them from a child's fairytale book (inverted pictures) that take on a kind of reality of their own in the child's mind. Yet, like Rimbaud's other "epiphanies," this one too is doomed to end: "There's someone who chases you off when you're hungry and thirsty."

In section IV, anaphora, the repetition of identical sentence constructions, occurs again, but now for the purpose of ironic contrast between sections III and IV. While in section III the presentness of things emerges emphatically showing a magical harmony between self and nature, in section IV the self is alienated from others and nature:

> I am the saint in prayer on the terrace life the peaceful animals that graze as far as the sea of Palestine.
> I am the scholar in his hard armchair. Branches and rain beat against the library window.
> I am the wanderer along the main road running through the dwarfish woods. The noise of the sluices drowns my footsteps. For a long time I can see the sad golden wash of the sunset.
> I might be the child abandoned on the wharf setting out for the high seas, or the farmland following the path whose top reaches the sky.
> The pathways are rough. The slopes are covered with broom. The air is still. How far away are the birds and the springs of water! This must be the end of the world, lying ahead.

Rimbaud Wounded, in Brussels, *a painting by Jef Rosman.*

It is as if in this section, we witness the dissolution of the self (personality) in several masks (saint, scholar, wanderer, child) and the alienation of the self from nature.

The first two masks, the saint and the scholar, evoke antithetical, yet co-present, states of mind in contrast with the child-in-nature in section: "I am the saint in prayer on the terrace," and "I am the scholar in his dark armchair." While the persona in the woods in the preceding section seems a part of the natural setting, both the saint and the scholar here are physically and psychologically separated from nature (the saint on the terrace praying and the scholar immersed in his book while the rain beats on his window). The third mask, the wanderer, comes still progressively closer to nature than the first two, but regards the "sluice" mentioned earlier than connotated expansiveness and imaginative excitement now in terms that suggest enclosure (drowning) and perhaps even death. "The noise of the sluice drowns my footsteps." In fact, most of the images in this section function as negative echoes (inversions) of ones in a visionary context cited earlier. It seems fair to say that this section dramatizes the loss of the child's visionary imagination, the dissociation of his sense of self and alienation from nature. Like the child abandoned on the wharf and the farmhand wandering away

from his farm, Rimbaud may share their feelings of being isolated from nature, alienated from human society, and withdrawing from both.

In **"Adieu,"** Rimbaud had said: "Well! I must bury my imagination and my memories! An artist's and storyteller's precious flame flung away." These words are particularly salient with regard to **"Enfance, V"** where he would return to the burial metaphor to dramatize his final act of poetic suicide:

> Now hire for me the tomb, whitewashed with the lines of cement in bold relief—far underground.
> I lean my elbows on the table, and the lamp lights brightly the newspapers I am fool enough to read, and the absurd books.
> At a tremendous distance above my subterranean room, houses grow like plants, and fogs gather. The mud is red or black. Monstrous city! Endless night!
> Not so high up are the sewers. At my side, nothing but the thickness of the globe. Perhaps there are pits of azure and wells of fire? On those levels perhaps moons and comets, seas and fables meet.
> In moments of depression, I imagine sapphire

and metal balls. I am master of *silence.* Why
should the appearance of a cellar window turn
pale at the corner of the ceiling?

Here the living *and* buried (ironically absent) persona is
literally and imaginatively alienated from the rest of the
world, self-interred in a white-washed tomb. The tomb itself suggests the antithesis of the expansiveness of feeling
and mind celebrated at the end of *A Season in Hell* as well
as in **"Enfance, I."** Furthermore, the tomb image is reminiscent of the image of the boy/dredger at the end of **"Mémoire, V"** where the persona finds himself surrounded by
the terrestrial "Mud." But here at the end of **"Enfance,"**
he is no longer just stuck in it, rather he has sunk entirely
into the quagmire of hopelessness and mundanity. Whereas in **"Mémoire"** light, clarity, and movement symbolized
the poet's transient joy and harmony in nature, here the
persona merely sits immobile underground in endless
night ("la nuit sans fin"). And even his brief moments of
imagining focus upon images (radical metonymies) that
evoke his state of despair: "Perhaps there are pits of azure
and wells of fire? On these levels perhaps moons and com-
ets, seas and fables meet." In particular, the image "pits
of azure" ("des gouffres d'azur") combines symbolic antitheses in an oxymoron that recalls the extremes of both
despair and hope in Baudelaire and Mallarmé, respectively.

In the same place where Rimbaud talks about burying his
imagination in **"Adieu,"** he says: "I am returned *to the soil*
with the duty to seek and rough reality to embrace." In
a slightly different sense (an ironic pun) here in **"Enfance,"** Rimbaud finds himself "returned to the soil" and
to silence. Like the peasants from whom he has come, he
would a short time later drop his pen to become a "maitre
du silence." (pp. 187-208)

> *Lynda D. McNeil, "Rimbaud: The Dialectical
> Play of Presence and Absence," in* boundary 2,
> *Vol. XII, No. 1, Fall, 1983, pp. 187-211.*

Edward J. Ahearn (essay date 1983)

[*In the following excerpt from his critical study* Rimbaud: Visions and Habitations, *Ahearn places Rimbaud
in the tradition of "visionary-ecstatic literature" and
compares him in this respect to Samuel Taylor Coleridge, William Blake, and Friedrich Nietzsche.*]

What ecstatic poetry is and the importance of the ecstatic
poetry produced by Rimbaud have not been generally understood. For readers reared in Western cultures, altered
states of consciousness, together with their corresponding
literary forms, require a special effort of comprehension,
which is aided by the furnishing of an appropriate comparative context. Rimbaud's exuberant, searing, tragic
poems are best understood in relation both to the
nineteenth-century current of ecstatic writing (primarily
Nietzsche and Blake, but also Hölderlin, Coleridge, and
Yeats) and also to a variety of ecstatic traditions to which
some of these writers hearkened. With such materials in
mind, I shall argue that Rimbaud produced in a modern
context a poetry corresponding to central elements of several ecstatic traditions, that the striking thematic and for-

mal features of his work are thus both highly comprehensible and of great importance. (p. 104)

[Rimbaud] was most interested in altered states for the
sake of writing poetry:

> Il s'agit d'arriver à l'inconnu par le dérèglement
> de *tous les sens.*
> [It's a matter of reaching the unknown through
> derangement of *all the senses.*]
>
> . . . . .
>
> Le Poète se fait *voyant* par un long, immense et
> raisonné *dérèglement* de *tous les sens.* Toutes
> les formes d'amour, de souffrance, de folie
> [The Poet makes himself *visionary* by a long, im-
> mense, and reasoned *derangement* of *all the
> senses.* All forms of love, of suffering, of mad-
> ness]
>
> . . . . .
>
> quand, affolé, il finirait par perdre l'intelligence
> de ses visions, il les a vues!
> [even if, maddened, he ends up losing the intelli-
> gence of his visions, he has seen them!]
>
> . . . . .
>
> Le poète définirait la quantité d'inconnu
> s'éveillant en son temps dans l'âme universel-
> le.
> [The poet would define the quantity of unknown
> awakening in his time in the universal soul.]
>
> . . . . .
>
> Enormité devenant norme, absorbée par tous, il
> serait vraiment *un multiplicateur de progrès!*
> [Enormity becoming norm, absorbed by all, he
> would be truly a *multiplier of progress!*]

These phrases from the **"Lettres du voyant"** equate poetry
with the discovery, attainment and expression of altered
states of consciousness. Note that familiar elements recur
here: an intellectualist-spiritualist vocabulary, and yet the
centrality of the senses as well as, paradoxically, a materialist stance: "Cet avenir sera matérialiste" (This future
will be materialist). But all of this is mediated now by the
need to discover novel forms and language.

The issues of the self, the senses, language, form, and by
extension the ecstatic poet's communal function, are
therefore all of interest. Rimbaud's forceful view of the
"I" as other than what we normally assume can be placed
in the context of other poetic attempts to enlarge and transcend the self, from Blake's fourfold prophetic vision and
Coleridge's glimpse of some greater persona in dreams, to
doctrines of impersonality and mask in Keats, Mallarmé,
and Yeats. But it is again Nietzsche who is most relevant
to Rimbaud's assertions that "JE est un autre. Si le cuivre
s'éveille clairon, il n'y a rien de sa faute. Cela m'est évident: j'assiste à l'éclosion de ma pensée: je la regarde, je
l'écoute: je lance un coup d'archet: la symphonie fait son
remuement dans les profondeurs, ou vient d'un bond sur
la scène" (I is another. If brass wakes up trumpet, it's not
at all its fault. This is evident to me: I am present at the
birth of my thought: I watch it, I listen to it; I draw a
stroke of the bow: the symphony stirs in the depths, or
comes with a leap onto the stage). Contemporaneous with
Nietzsche, these sentences are close to his beliefs in *The
Birth of Tragedy.* Both writers re-evaluate romantic literature, asserting against common prejudice that lyric is precisely *not* subjective, but rather an *unselving.* In both, this

unselving aims at increased contact with and expression of the elemental reality of the world, which they believe has been obscured by the historical growth of narrowly subjective modes of awareness. This effort implies a dialectic between two poles of an enlarged experience. In Nietzsche, there is the Dionysian, the unconscious element, and the Apollonian, the principle of individuality. The latter, with its ultimately dreamlike structures of thought and expression, includes almost all aspects of our ordinary mental life—reason, morality, language, normal perception, plastic and visual imagery. The brief phrases from Rimbaud's letter correspond. An underlying activity of thought and expression, not originated or understood by the conscious self, is suggested by the reflexive "s'éveille," the expression "rien de sa faute," and the spontaneous actions of unconscious forces—"fait son remuement," "vient d'un bond." Second, there is an observing and structuring activity of the "I": "Cela m'est évident: j'assiste à l'éclosion de ma pensée: je la regarde, je l'écoute: je lance un coup d'archet." Through this latter process unconscious material comes to awareness. In particular, the progression *profondeurs, symphonie, scène* parallels Nietzsche's argument that consciousness originates in the depth of Dionysian reality, that it manifests itself first as music, thereafter attaining perceivable form in the Apollonian "dream spectacle."

So Rimbaud and Nietzsche sketch a model of experience involving conscious and preconscious elements, a progression to more structured forms of awareness that, however, are further removed from primitive reality. Hence the necessity of transforming these structures of the mind in favor of a more primordial kind of experience. In both writers this necessity raises questions bearing on ecstatic poetry, questions concerning sensation and reason—that is, relatively unmediated experience and the impositions of intelligence—and therefore also concerning disorder and form in the self and its expressions, indeed the unity and even existence of what we call the self.

Thus, when in the shorter **"Lettre du voyant"** Rimbaud suggests that "C'est faux de dire: Je pense. On devrait dire: On me pense" (It's false to say: I think. One should say: I am thought), he expresses in rudimentary form a radical insight that is developed in the later writings of Nietzsche, namely that the supposedly stable ego is in reality made up of half-glimpses, falsifications, illusions. Indeed, Nietzsche's critique of the soul-ego-subject superstition is most compelling when he analyzes notions like "I think" and even "it thinks" (in me) as falsifying vestiges of a primitive fetishism of language. That is, he asserts the reality of consciousness as liberated from the illusion of the subject, which in effect is a more systematic and extreme version of what Rimbaud argues from direct experience in the creation of poetry.

In the longer of the *voyant* letters Rimbaud pursues the explosion of the self in terms of enlargement and transformation—through methodical deformation of experience at the root level of sensation. His belief in the possibility of thereby arriving at full self-knowledge and a real vision of the unknown (recall "sa propre connaissance, entière"; "il arrive à l'*inconnu*!"; "il les a vues!") betrays a youthful na-

iveté alien to the mature Nietzsche's demolishing of the subject and perspectivist argument that we can never escape the prison of the senses. But Nietzsche consistently attacks intellectual consciousness as most removed from the real, and in crucial passages he insists instead on the enormous value of the senses—if not distorted then refined, perfected, thought through—as the key to the most satisfying, even the truest version of reality. Indeed he argues that the supposed objects of the senses, *things,* are as illusory as the self, and that it is only grammar that makes us believe in self, God, *and* things. Thus, the senses do not lie in revealing dynamic flux, as opposed to the fixed, illusory things that are the creations of the intellect. Altogether there is, therefore, a significant convergence of Rimbaud's and Nietzsche's ideas on consciousness and sense experience. The notions of self and thing must be transformed, even exploded; the senses are to be reconstrued as conveying a more acute, dynamic, unstable world of experience; this world may be alive with an overmastering power and beauty of which normally we are unaware but which we can come to perceive.

In fact, a text like **"Ce qu'on dit au poète à propos de fleurs"** could be read as an interpretation of Nietzsche's philosophy of the senses. That poem's disconcerting imagery subverts and enriches our sense of things; one example: flowers that are snouts and chairs, that drool pommades yet are jewellike in posssessing gem-tonsils and gem-ovaries. Such imagery also provides a starting point for the explosions of material reality and consciousness that we glimpsed in texts like **"H"** and **"Parade"**—"O terrible frisson des amours novices sur le sol sanglant et par l'hydrogène clarteux!" (O terrible shudder of new loves on the bloody ground and through the transparent hydrogen!); "Les yeux flambent, le sang chante, les os s'élargissent, les larmes et des filets rouges ruissellent" (Eyes flame, blood sings, bones expand, tears and red filaments stream). Such lines prelude the ecstatic dissolution of **"Being Beauteous"** and **"Barbare,"** and remind us that Nietzsche's and Rimbaud's demolition of self and things is motivated throughout by the attraction to states of transport and frenzy.

But the subversion of rational consciousness in favor of a sense-dominated, chaotic range of states at whose extreme we encounter ecstasy and madness inevitably raises the issues of control and form in the self and its expressions. The interaction of frenzy with lucidity is both a hallmark and a problem of visionary-ecstatic thinking, not only in Rimbaud and Nietzsche but in other poets as well, and perhaps generally in ecstatic religions. For example, shamans accede to ecstasy in part through exceptional physical and intellectual discipline, attained through years of practice. The relationship between discipline and ecstasy concerned many poets of the romantic tradition. For example, Yeats's attraction to trance and illumination is balanced by a corresponding effort to control "all Asiatic vague immensities," and his poetry is marked throughout by an ambivalent interaction of the body, spiritual trance, and sculptural-architectural motifs that suggest the coolness of art. These elements in fact characterize a certain poetic current. Earlier, not to speak of Blake or Hölderlin or Keats, there is Coleridge, whose "Kubla Khan" is similarly characterized by a mixture of orgasmic, ecstatic, musical, and visionary imagery and architectural elements. Coleridge often moves between, on the one hand, the attraction to states of trance, associated with Dionysian energy, involving absolute immediacy of perception and expression, and, on the other, his fear of the madness that such states may bring, his awareness of the difficulty the imagination has in achieving totally unified control of the full range of our experience, his more realistic emphasis on the alliance of imagination with conscious will.

Both Nietzsche and Rimbaud celebrate frenzy more wholeheartedly than Coleridge, but neither downplays the structuring activities of the mind. For Nietzsche consciousness is *constituted* by the interactions between Dionysian and Apollonian elements, the Apollonian being necessary to save us from complete dissolution by providing perceivable form; the two forces must be in strict proportion. Despite increasing attention to the value of discipline and of the lucidly self-created soul, Nietzsche never stopped insisting on the value of frenzy, on the persistence of the savage-animal element of our nature, on frenzy as in fact an *indispensable* ingredient of artistic psychology, on the persistence therefore, even in late, civilized, specialized forms of art, of the original ecstatic forces.

Throughout his career Nietzsche emphasized the persistence of the ecstatic, as well as the power of genius to combine savage elements with superior lucidity, resulting in the apparently effortless dance of the great artist-thinker. The young Rimbaud, for his part, stressed an initial penetration to the state of frenzy—which is monstrous, bordering on insanity, and which threatens to dissolve consciousness: "quand, affolé, il finirait par perdre l'intelligence de ses visions" (even if, maddened, he ends up losing the intelligence of his visions); "Qu'il crève dans son bondissement par les choses inouïes et innommables" (Let him die leaping through unheard of and unnamable things). These statements point to a severe discontinuity between exalted states and normal consciousness. In response, there is a corresponding effort to join the two realms, an insistence on the systematic effort that is necessary to attain the ecstatic illumination, and then to express it. As the passages cited at the opening of this section show, Rimbaud believed that the poet must work, by means of reasoned derangement, to make himself visionary. Similarly, he asserts: "la première étude de l'homme qui veut être poète est sa propre connaissance, entière; il cherche son âme, il l'inspecte, il la tente, l'apprend. Dès qu'il la sait, il doit la cultiver" (the first study of the man who wants to be a poet is understanding himself, complete; he searches his soul, he inspects it, he tests it, learns it. As soon as he knows it, he must cultivate it).

What emphasis, in a poet pursuing exalted states to the point of dissolution of individual consciousness, on work, method, rational control! And most revealing of all is Rimbaud's emphasis on the unknown, which is close to Nietzsche's argument on the relationship between the Dionysian chaos and the absorbing and structuring function of the Apollonian that brings it to conscious form. Let us leave aside for the moment Rimbaud's confident claim to integrate the visionary and the sociocultural (a claim un-

dermined variously by the *Saison,* "Solde" and "Génie"); still we cannot here minimize the poet's desire, having reached the unknown, to absorb it into normal consciousness, not for himself alone but especially for others.

The attempt to transcend normal consciousness, the attainment of peaks of exaltation, the problems of lucidity, discontinuity, and loss—these features in Rimbaud and other writers can be recapitulated and interrelated through arguments proposed by Roland Fischer [in *Altered States of Consciousness,* 1975]. The bipolar model of consciousness that he constructs (one element to receive experience and the other to be conscious of it, to interpret it) applies an age-old epistemological pattern to the ecstatic experience. The polarities that Fischer stresses are those between subcortical levels that register experience and cortical interpretation of it, between left and right hemispheres of the brain, and between the mutually exclusive ergotropic and trophotropic systems . . . and involving respectively increasing psychic arousal whose term is ecstasy, and decreasing arousal, to the point of attaining the ultimate peace of the yoga experience.

The value of this model lies in Fischer's attempt, based on study of many religious and drug experiences, to represent the full continuum of states of consciousness; without minimizing discontinuities, he nonetheless stresses the impulsion to psychic integration. The parallels with Rimbaud are striking: the normal, dichotomous experience of separate "I" and external world (at the center of the diagram); the creative moments of withdrawal from that normal state; the emergence, as in the *voyant* letters, of another, larger self (Fischer calls it the mental dimension of exalted states); the negative states on the way to ecstasy, corresponding perhaps to some of the painful experiences recounted in the *Saison;* the bipolarity of ecstatic excitement and the peace of *samādhi,* illuminating the contrast between the peace sought in poems like **"Fêtes de la patience," "Marine,"** and **"Mystique,"** on the one hand, and the raging energy of **"Villes I"** and **"Barbare"** on the other; and finally, the disappearance of the normal world and with it the impulse to motor activity, and the oceanic experience of unity and fulfillment, paralleling the opposition between ordinary reality and the ecstatic state in Rimbaud and particularly revealing for a text like **"Barbare"**. . . .(pp. 161-70)

Coleridge proposes for "Kubla Khan" a trance state in which reality, the content of consciousness, and expression are perfectly coincident ("all the images rose up . . . as *things,* with a parallel production of the correspondent expressions, without any sensation or consciousness of effort"), and Hölderlin in "Brod und Wein" evokes an illumination of the divine among the Greeks in which words responsively emerge with the organic necessity of natural growths ("nun müssen dafür Worte, wie Blumen, entstehn"). But Rimbaud, somewhat differently, suggests a poetic activity of two essential moments: first vision, then the devising of a language in which to express it.

Rimbaud's scheme, debatable in its supposition of the possibility of experience completely prior to language, is still apparently less idealized than the formulations by Coleridge and Hölderlin, in which words arise spontaneously, with no gap whatever between themselves and either consciousness or reality. Note, however, that Hölderlin's and Coleridge's texts evoke that ideal of language as impossible for us. Both imagine a past ecstatic experience—Dionysian–Christian for Hölderlin, a drug-initiated illumination expressed by a conflation of Greek and Asian elements for Coleridge. And both involve a more or less successful effort to move closer to the exalted state through the operation of the poem itself, but also final alienation from the ecstatic condition, return to normal consciousness (nostalgia, despondence, memory, hope, determination), return also to normal language (inadequate, arbitrary, intentional). In the *voyant* letters Rimbaud is still at the beginning, projecting the movement toward the ecstatic experience, but the potential gap between vision and expression is great, and it insinuates possibilities for serious problems and failures.

Finally, though, in Rimbaud's formulations a third moment emerges, that of the reader, to whom the vision must become palpably present, experienced, absorbed into his enriched consciousness. In "Brod und Wein" Hölderlin evokes the Dionysian possession of the Greeks, denied to us; "Kubla Khan" closes with a hypothetical imagination of a frenzied poet figure, from whom onlookers shrink in terror. Both texts therefore raise the possibility of our reaction to or involvement in the state of ecstasy, but do so in a distanced, skeptical way. Rimbaud's youthful belief in the identity of word and idea, in the approaching era of a universal language, hardly to be attained by the scholar's etymological approach, a language capable of *creating madness*, is projected toward the future and is comparably distanced. This ironically colored evocation of the ecstatic power of poetry, together with the more moderate formulations about the poet's disciplined composition and the reader's gradual absorption of the abnormal into consciousness, suggest both the ultimate goal and the recurrent limitation of Rimbaud's poetry. The *Saison* mercilessly exposes the latter, debunking Rimbaud's effort to invent new realities, ironically deflating his claim to have created a universal language: "je me flattai d'inventer un verbe poétique accessible, un jour ou l'autre, à tous les sens. Je réservais la traduction" (I flattered myself that I invented a poetic language accessible, one day or another, to all the senses. I withheld the translation). The *Saison* insists on the persistence in his work of the known resources of poetic language ("la vieillerie poétique"), which hardly seem to attain the desired immediacy.

Thus the true poetic effort is to actualize exalted states that have been inaccessible to normal consciousness, have been precisely mythic, through literary forms sufficiently original to conjure up these states in the mind of the reader, but which upon analysis appear to partake of the normal functions of language in our conscious, Apollonian world. As we shall see in the next section, a group of *Illuminations* fascinatingly reveal these ambiguities of exalted and normal consciousness and language, proposing ecstatic intensity through highly crafted and intentional imagery, structure, and convention. These *Illuminations* constitute a repertory of ecstatic forms, which we cannot see fully until we consider in a larger context the ecstatic poet's vocation and societal function, and the kinds of imagery and structures that this function might be said archetypally to generate.

For in a literal way Rimbaud reproduced features of mantic poetic activity despite his living in a modern, demythified culture. These features include: recognition of the mantic vocation; initiation involving extreme states, prolonged suffering, with the concomitant dangers of illness or madness; an extended period of study with experienced shamans, training in ecstatic techniques and in an impressive body of philosophical, religious, esthetic, and cosmological knowledge; the individual attainment of ecstasy and the conveying of it to the rest of the community; a variety of forms in which to do so, involving music, narrations of spiritual or underworld journeys, spectacles or dramatic enactments of the exalted experience.

Rimbaud's **"Lettres"** correspond closely to these mantic themes. They are first a declaration of the recognition of the poetic vocation and a realization of the necessity of painful initiation: "Les souffrances sont énormes, mais il faut être fort, être né poète, et je me suis reconnu poète" (The suffering is enormous, but it is necessary to be strong, to be born a poet, and I have recognized myself as a poet). The ecstatic techniques and the danger of madness have already been mentioned. As for training by experienced mantics, Rimbaud is in the isolated position of any ecstatic in modern Western culture. His initiation and training are represented by his reading of the poetic tradition, his judgment as to which writers are truly visionary. The phenomenon of literacy, the transformation of the communal-oral into the solitary act of reading thus characterizes the poet's situation, and the concluding portion of the second letter, with its comments on romantics, Parnassians, Baudelaire, and others, functions as Rimbaud's recognition of poetic initiation, training, and mastery.

The prestige and range of the traditional shaman's knowledge and function are only implied in Rimbaud's letters, mainly in hyperbolic statements such as "Il est chargé de l'humanité, des *animaux* même." Aside from recalling the shaman's intimate connection with the animal world, this statement introduces a strong sense of communal responsibility, expressed elsewhere in the letters as Rimbaud's desire to have a productive function in a just and responsive society. But it is the *Saison* that (ironically) demonstrates the extent of Rimbaud's pretensions—as in this previously cited description of the infernal husband in **"Délires I"**: "Il feignait d'être éclairé sur tout, commerce, art, médecine" (He pretended to be enlightened on everything, commerce, art, medicine). Even more clearly, the *Saison*'s most ecstatic chapter, "Nuit de l'enfer," expresses a global poetico-religious function of sardonically mythic proportions: "Je vais dévoiler tous les mystères: mystères religieux ou naturels, mort, naissance, avenir, passé, cosmogonie, néant. Je suis maître en fantasmagories." Earlier, in **"Nuit,"** Rimbaud spoke of being richer than poets and visionaries but of maintaining total silence; later in the chapter his pretensions lead him to a mad imagination of himself as a Christ figure. But in the sentences cited here he is closest to the underlying mantic function, revealer of all natural and supernatural mysteries, from birth to death, from time to a cosmological vision of the universe—but all finally in a cynical and negating perspective: nothingness, phantasmagories.

Thus the *Saison* indicates the full extent of the communal function that we may conceive as the outcome of the poetics of exalted states announced in the **"Lettres du voyant,"** irony being the inevitable mode concerning such a function in a desacralized culture such as ours. As for the forms of expression generated by Rimbaud's poetic goals, the **"Lettres"** provide little help. . . . The *Saison* (**"Délires II"**) is more suggestive, designating an initial *notational* effort ("je notais l'inexprimable. Je fixais des vertiges"), followed by hallucination of vision and language, the phenomenon of leaving the world and mystic fulfillment, then a kind of theatrical dissociation: "Je devins un opéra fabuleux: je vis que tous les êtres ont une fatalité de bonheur: l'action n'est pas la vie, mais une façon de gâcher quelque force, un énervement" (I became a fabulous opera: I saw that all beings have a fatality of happiness: action is not life, but a way of bungling some force, an enervation).

These indications are of less than total significance, however, since they so much concern the mystic asceticism of "Fêtes de la patience." They need to be completed by certain other kinds of art Rimbaud says he imagined, for example, "voyages de découvertes dont on n'a pas de relations, républiques sans histoires, . . . révolutions de mœurs, déplacements de races et de continents" (voyages of discovery for which we don't have the account, republics without history, revolutions in morals, displacements of races and continents). Relevant also are the overall form of the *Saison,* a narration of an ecstatic-spiritual experience explicitly called a descent to hell, and . . . forms of provocation and realization. . . . Together these elements resemble the pattern of mantic art described by [Mircea] Eliade [in *Shamanism,* 1972] and [N. Kershaw] Chadwick [in *Poetry and Prophecy,* 1952] and comparable, as we shall see, to certain features of the ecstatic *Illuminations*: celestial ascensions and underworld journeys, presentations of ecstatic states, musical and dramatic spectacles for the community. Chadwick and Eliade, like Nietzsche, locate the roots of the major art forms of music and literature in the mantic, shamanistic, or Dionysian state. The predominance of the ecstatic-lyric, of presentational-spectacular realizations, of narrative-dramatic-musical celebrations in Rimbaud comes close to these formulations, suggesting that many formal aspects of his poetry, so unique and so apparently difficult to categorize, are engendered by his ecstatic goals.

Two aspects of ecstatic form deserve further attention before we turn to the *Illuminations.* The first is the imagery, which may be viewed as archetypal in psychological terms, such as those used by Fischer, and also as a function of religious and poetic tradition; both senses bear directly on an audience's experience of ecstatic literature. . . . [We] need to summarize [this imagery] now in order to appreciate its thoroughgoing relevance for Rimbaud. As we would expect, despite certain unifying tendencies (the motif of leaving the self, or the body, or even the human), dichotomies once again are visible. In fact, in their full scope such motifs correspond to the range of conflicting traditions that we found, earlier in this chapter, to be relevant for Rimbaud's work.

In spiritual, ascensional forms, but in many drug experiences as well, the following five characteristics are of note. (1) Modification of learned perceptual constancies, with near space initially foreshortened and with spacetime progressively transformed, until in the extremes of ecstasy and *samādhi* the spatial-temporal disappears entirely. This feature is stressed as well by Baudelaire on drugs and by Blake throughout his work, and in a different form is visible in the progression of Rimbaud's **"Matinée d'ivresse," "Being Beauteous," "Barbare."** (2) The experience of heightened luminosities, complex and living geometrical patterns of an extremely absorbing sort such as Coleridge noted, that are responsible perhaps for the intense yet artificial quality of the imagery in Rimbaud's **"Fleurs,"** some of his city poems, and **"Veillées,"** especially part II—the last expressive of some initial and intermediate phases, perhaps drug-induced, of the process of altering consciousness. (3) Penetration to an archetypal area of the psyche in which one encounters the uranian imagery of heightened natural scenery, the city—cosmic mountain—palace complex, the buried precious stones and rainbows that link ancient religious and poetic traditions from Dante to Blake, and Hölderlin and Coleridge to Rimbaud and Yeats. (4) The experience of larger-than-life figures, angels, and divinities, a feature strong in Blake and remarkable in the "êtres supérieurs" engendered frequently in Rimbaud's poetry. (5) Finally, total deindividualization, transcendence of the subject-object dichotomy, the experience of undifferentiated being, expressed by the imagery of dissolution and by motifs of global, polar, universal totality (variously in **"Fêtes de la patience," "Génie," "Barbare"**).

A second group of motifs is connected with what might be called *body ecstasies.* It includes Rimbaud's strongly sexual emphasis in connection with Greek divinities such as Venus and Pan. The Dionysian is also relevant, with its motifs of intoxication, sexual abandon, a frenzy in which the god's female votaries first suckle animals and children, then rend and devour them. The savage and animal are associated as well with hunting motifs. In addition, the Dionysian penetration to the heart of reality is suggested by imagery of water and all other life-giving fluids, as well as by the attraction to nature in its most violent and powerful manifestations. Finally, Dionysus is the god of sudden appearances and disappearances; thus the orgiastic ecstasy he provokes also emphasizes the impermanence common to exalted experiences. (pp. 173-81)

In some sense Eliade's description of the symbolism of shamanistic ecstasy unites the preceding two groups, with the qualifications that shamanism downplays the specifically sexual and that it always involves individual ecstasy. The spiritual tendency of the shamans is apparent in uranian imagery, in the experience of mystic light, and especially in the insistence on the shaman's magical power of flight. The shaman also reaches the realm of the dead, encounters divine beings, and speaks to the spirits. But black shamanism follows another direction on the mystic voyage, and all shamanism, even the ascensional, emphasizes identification with the animal as a preparation for the ec-static. As in the Dionysian, hunting motifs are thus central, in combination with the exaltation of fire and the figures who control it, the smiths. Perhaps even more important is the stress on the transformation of the body—widespread symbolism of destruction of the body, numbering of the bones, introduction of painful but magical substances into the flesh, the undergoing of ritual death involving great suffering, and finally the experience of bodily rebirth, bones covered by new flesh, and the like. Once again, this motif of painful ecstatic bodily transformation (for which we will see close analogies in **"Matinée d'ivresse," "Being Beauteous,"** and **"Barbare"**) indicates the paradoxical interconnections of the bodily and the spiritual, of transcendent and immanent impulses in the ecstatic experience.

This recapitulation of imagery, all of which is relevant to Rimbaud, indicates how far-reaching are the problems of self, sensation, language, dispersion, and control discussed earlier. For the ecstatic aims at opening up *all* the domains of experience associated with such divergent imagery, and therefore raises the questions of dichotomy and unity in consciousness as well as in expression.

One final convention of ecstatic form is the theatrical in its various modalities, which involves similar complexity in that it can be viewed as actual enactment of ecstatic immediacy or as fictional imitation, as utter coherence or complete separation of ecstatic experience and language. In this connection it is interesting that **"Délires II"** describes a kind of musico-theatrical dissociation ("Je devins un opéra fabuleux") at the term of at least one phase of Rimbaud's evolution. The dramatic and the musical as ambivalently related to the immediacy of the exalted state are central to arguments about the derivation of ecstatic literature in Nietzsche, Eliade, and Chadwick. Eliade describes a range of performances, from actual trance (accompanied or induced by music) to increasingly theatrical, and finally degraded, fakiristic spectacles, the last of these a phenomenon that we linked to **"Parade"** and that is suggestive as well for **"Solde."**

Nietzsche, too, is preoccupied by the relations of actual trance and various modes of musico-theatrical performance. In *The Birth of Tragedy,* he describes the hypothetical historical stages whereby the Dionysian revelers, who supposedly once experienced themselves as literally transformed into satyrs, later became simply members of the dramatic chorus, so that the satyr comes to represent a variety of nonecstatic, or quasi-ecstatic, and also markedly *esthetic* functions: musician, poet, dancer, visionary. A later formulation derives all artistic activity from the original frenzies (both Apollo and Dionysus are now conceived as producing frenzy), placing what Nietzsche calls Dionysian histronicism, the actual physical embodying of the trance experience, at the beginning, prior to its more specialized later appearance as music.

Extremely interesting views of Rimbaud, who of course wrote no actual plays, emerge from such speculations: the literal, bodily experience of trance, giving way to musical-verbal presentations, self-conscious creations of the civilized-ecstatic, musician-poet-visionary (and fakiristic?)

writer. Ecstasies of the body, the varieties of poetic-musical-dramatic language, lyric-narrative-dramatic forms of presentation, movements toward the intensity of ecstasy and away from it to the sterility of loss, are therefore all of great importance for the study of the ecstatic *Illuminations.* (pp. 181-83)

[Blake, Nietzsche, Fischer, and Rimbaud] emphasize the continued existence of ecstatic energies, the methodical struggle to liberate them, the possibility of attaining culminating states and expressions of such states, the inevitably intermittent quality of such attainment, yet also the possibility of persistence, of overcoming amnesia, of psychic and linguistic coherence. Rimbaud expresses a lucid, tragic awareness of these issues in the longer **"Lettre du voyant,"** foreseeing the dissolution of his enterprise but insisting that this would in no way invalidate his visions, which would remain accessible in the form of poems and which would contribute to similar future experiences: "Il arrive à l'inconnu, et quand, affolé, il finirait par perdre l'intelligence de ses visions, il les a vues! Qu'il crève dans son bondissement par les choses inouïes et innommables: viendront d'autres horribles travailleurs; ils commenceront par les horizons où l'autre s'est affaissé!" (He reaches the unknown, and even if, maddened, he ends up losing the intelligence of his visions, he has seen them! Let him die leaping through unheard of and unnamable things: there will come other horrible workers; they will begin at the horizons where the other one collapsed!).

The adolescent bravado here perhaps betrays insufficient awareness of the necessity for lifelong discipline such as Blake's or Nietzsche's, but Rimbaud's insistence on suffering and derangement has its own integrity, and the price he paid for it is evident in the *Saison.* . . . [He was aware] of the difficulties of devising appropriate forms for the expression of the *innommable*—his thinking on ecstatic language, form, function, and public, and the actualizations of that thinking in the *Illuminations.* Those actualizations need to be thought of now as . . . incorporating a high degree of honesty, the ability for self-criticism, an awareness of the coexistence of failure and achievement—as intense and inherently discontinuous forms, capable of setting side by side absence and presence, possession and loss, absolute frenzy, and a comparably absolute denial of that same ecstasy.

Only such a poetry is faithful to the nature of the ecstatic for modern consciousness, as delineated in part by Blake but more by Coleridge, Nietzsche, Eliade, and Fischer, and most of all by Rimbaud himself. The struggle for the ecstatic, the resistance of the real, *simultaneous* success and failure, fragmented and fantastic forms that trouble our sense of the implacability of the world—the *Illuminations* most of all exemplify such a poetry. In their tragic way they embody Nietzsche's model of Apollonian consciousness somehow absorbing the experience of the Dionysian, Fischer's paradoxical and precious *discontinuous ecstatic totality:* "Enormité devenant norme, absorbée par tous, il serait vraiment *un multiplicateur de progrès!* " (Enormity becoming norm, absorbed by all, he would be truly *a multiplier of progress!*).

But this optimistic early formulation reintroduces a recurrent problem, that of the function of ecstatic poetry for the collectivity. The allusions to the events of the Paris Commune of 1871 in the longer *voyant* letter propose an uneasy yet idealistic view of the social function of the visionary poet, out of phase with a repressive society, hoping to be a contributing force in a future modality of political life. The poems from **"Angoisse"** to **"Génie"** are more troubling, in a way more realistically Nietzschean, in proposing an opposition between ecstatic states and social organization. The joyous collectivity of **"Villes I"** gives way to indifference or hostility toward group activity in the real world at the end of that poem and in **"Angoisse."** And the most permanent of the ecstatic realizations are comparable: **"Barbare"** involves a vast dissociation of person and reality, whereas in **"Génie"** the appeal for a collective responsiveness to immanent divinity reaches out to the extremes of nature, by-passing altogether the sociopolitical. These two poems are the most definitive and victorious of Rimbaud's achievements, and in the face of the attacks in the *Saison* and other texts, we need to recall them, recognize how astoundingly they embody the transcendent and immanent aspects of his ecstatic imagination. But if in the one we glimpse a cosmic and eternalized ecstatic reality, and if in the other we stretch toward an encounter with the generous, dynamic, divine reality of the world and of our lives, in neither can we avoid a challenge to our notions of society, to our sense of collectivity itself. (pp. 235-37)

> *Edward J. Ahearn, in his* Rimbaud: Visions and Habitations, *University of California Press, 1983, 383 p.*

Nathaniel Wing   (essay date 1984)

[*In the following essay, Wing interprets* Une saison en enfer *as autobiography, noting how the work defies the conventions of the genre.*]

> . . . ne sachant m'expliquer sans paroles païennes, je voudrais me taire.
>
>   **"Mauvais sang"**

> J'ai eu raison dans tous mes dédains: puis que je m'évade! Je m'évade! Je m'explique.
>
>   **"L'Impossible"**

> . . . il me sera loisible de *posséder la vérité dans une âme et un corps.*
>
>   **"Adieu"**

The three statements quoted above appear at significant junctures, and widely separated, in *Une Saison en enfer.* The first is in one of the opening sections of the text, **"Mauvais sang,"** in which the narrator attempts to situate a quest for self-knowledge in a specific relation to history. In the second passage, from **"L'Impossible,"** the narrator begins to refuse certain social compromises. Finally, the words in the last quotation are the final words of the entire text, about a page and a half after the narrator's statements that he has finished recounting his season in Hell, and that he is now prepared to celebrate the birth of *la sagesse nouvelle.* Each one of the quotations, though in significantly different ways, situates the narrator's quest for understanding in the register of language. The confession

in *Une Saison en enfer* is an interpretive process in which scrutiny of the poet's past and present, of history, metaphysics, love, writing, and so on, leads inevitably to an examination of the speaking subjects as a configuration in language.

The text begins within the frame of certain assumptions about the finality of the written corpus and its capacity to contain the narrated subject; these assumptions are "worked out" as they are reiterated in the course of the narrative and ultimately exhausted. A radically different understanding of the writing subject emerges as the relationship between cognition and the language of the text becomes an increasingly urgent concern of the narrator. As the narrator produces the story of the past or the present, he explicitly performs a reading which deflects the interest from the (pseudo)-referential content of the text and toward the operations of language. That shift deconstructs the Romantic self, yet is concurrent with a forceful and nostalgic resistance to the process; much of the affective tension of the text is generated by these irreconcilable forces. Various aspects of the theme of alienation constitute an important network in *Une Saison en enfer* which can be interpreted within Romantic concepts of the self, yet a far more subversive alienation is at work in the language of the text, and it is the interplay between these forms of alienation, thematic and rhetorical, which I propose to trace here.

In many respects, of course, the passages quoted above conform to the traditional patterns of an autobiographical narrative. The poem presents the narrative (*histoire*) of a season in Hell, a passage through a subterranean world of past suffering, delusion, failed strategies for re-inventing love, literature, freedom, from which the poet emerges into the clear light of truth ("Matin"); or so it would seem, as the narrated self and the narrating subject merge in the present *discours*: "Pourtant, aujourd'hui, je crois avoir fini la relation de mon enfer." To the extent that we interpret the text according to this traditional schema of autobiographical writing, as defined by Genette, Lejeune, Rousset, Starobinski and others, the development of the narrative can be traced in the passage from the verb *je fis* of the narrated past to the verb *je sais* of the narration, situated at the end point of the story. The statements quoted earlier could be read as the expression of the concurrent desires to lead the reader through the text to the truth of the conclusion and to find the language adequate to that achievement; the passages would appear, then, to situate the text securely within the boundaries of this definition of confession narrative proposed by Paul de Man in a reading of Rousseau:

> To confess is to overcome guilt and shame in the name of truth: it is an epistemological use of language in which ethical values of good and evil are superseded by values of truth and falsehood, one of the implications being that vices such as concupiscence, envy, greed, and the like, are vices primarily because they compel one to lie. By stating things as they are, the economy of ethical balance is restored and redemption can start in the clarified atmosphere of a truth that does not hesitate to reveal the crime in all its horror. [*Allegories of Reading,* 1979]

Read according to this schema, the quotations from Rimbaud would mark a progress toward truth in which the narrator had overcome the shortcomings of a deficient ("pagan") language, had countered the ruses of self-deception, and had found the happy reconciliation between desire and truth ("la liberté dans le salut," **"Mauvais sang"**) possessed in a final moment of the text. My reading thus far makes the text conform to a quite unremarkable rhetoric of autobiography, and anticipates, on the one hand, how consistently the narrator reproduces elements of that schema, which subtends the entire poem. On the other hand, the strategies of the text are quite different. They resist forcefully the implicit telos of such a rhetoric, in which the relations between *histoire* and *discours* are considered as a unity of becoming, oriented towards a final appropriation of truth in the knowledge of consciousness of self. I propose to examine the narrator's developing relations to the text by studying some of the various ways in which the self is inscribed as an effect of writing in which each utterance of the first person pronoun produces a division of the self at the very instant it is posited. As the narrator deconstructs a certain rhetoric of autobiography in a practice referred to in the text as *délire* (which can be read both as delirium and *dé-lire*), the act of writing literally forces to the surface of the text the understanding that the narrating subject is engaged less in a process of self-realization, in the manner described by de Man, than in writing the self in and as language, and deprived of any reassuring ontological ground. In this sense, the practice of writing is not the expression of a self, contained by the rhetoric of autobiography, but the exploration of effects of subjectivity in language; the subject of writing, then, becomes the autobiography of rhetoric. My study will explore the implications of the imperative set forth in the final passage of the last text, **"Adieu"**: "Il faut être absolument moderne." In this context, and in light of the problematic traced above, the statement "Je m'évade, je m'explique" takes on new resonances which suggest that self-realization in narrative necessarily gives way to an endless process of unfolding (the sense of *explicare*) and distancing.

Several references in the first two texts of **Une Saison en enfer,** the short preface which serves as a dedication to Satan, and the longer **"Mauvais sang,"** establish that the problem of language is central to the quest for self. The first act narrated in the poem is a speech act, a performative, in [J. L.] Austin's terms [from his *How To Do Things with Words,* 1975], which produces a violent break between the language of the text and the language of "Beauty." The narrator recounts having taken Beauty upon his knee one evening and, finding her deficient, curses her: "Un soir, j'ai assis la Beauté sur mes genoux. —Et je l'ai trouvée amère. —Et je l'ai injuriée." Beauty here serves rather unexceptionally as a personification for art in general, and particularly for verbal art: thus, one of the very first narrated events of this text is a specifically verbal act, a violent repudiation in which the narrator attempts to dispossess himself of the muse. As a performative, this statement is the "event" to which it refers and affirms truculently in the openings of the poem the overriding importance of the subject of language over and against non-linguistic action. Though the esthetic which Beauty personifies is not specifically characterized, as it will be later in the central section, "Alchimie du verbe," the initial refusal of her patronage is accompanied by a series of rejections which here and throughout **Une Saison en enfer** will be associated with cultural authority in general. The project of the text is twofold, set forth already in these first pages: to elaborate in detail the angry curses against Beauty, which will undo a cultural text, and to inscribe the narrator's self in a radically different relation to language.

The curse against Beauty is accompanied by a rejection of Law: "Je me suis armé contre la justice." The subject flees from the confines of defined space, in an escape which is also a flight from the self: "Je me suis enfui . . . " That displacement in space also places the subject outside hope: "Je parvins à faire s'évanouir dans mon esprit toute l'espérance humaine. Sur toute joie pour l'étrangler j'ai fait le bond sourd de la bête féroce." The refusal of Beauty, then, is followed immediately by a break between the narrator and a system of authority, the coordinates of a certain space and the confines of expectations which had defined the subject. From the outset, writing in this text is a rupture, a violent break with order, which opens the question of the nature of the alternative space and order, the outside, in which the narrator will ultimately situate himself. That question, of course, provides the motive for the entire narrative, its "resolution" deferred to the end point of the text. For the moment, however, the text explores the impasses produced by the present order; the narrator will pass from esthetic considerations to the wider problematic of the relation between the self and order in its most general sense: the law. The explicitly esthetic consequences of these rejections are indicated in the last paragraph of the dedication, in which the narrator addresses Satan:

> Mais, cher Satan, je vous en conjure, une prunelle moins irritée! et en attendant les quelques petites lâchetés en retard, vous qui aimez dans l'écrivain l'absence des facultés descriptives ou instructives, je vous détache ces quelques hideux feuillets de mon carnet de damné.

Elliptically, but no less significantly, the passage reiterates the rejection of Beauty and informs the reader about the new writing which that break makes possible; Satan's taste runs counter to mimetic or didactic writing. The relation of the narrator's text to truth, as a replication in language of a pre-existing sense, either a model reiterated in description or an ethical or epistemological meaning, is thus put in question from the outset. The consequences of this affirmation are far reaching indeed; it opens the possibility of different kinds of meaning, which would disrupt the metaphysical closure which is the condition of mimesis. The insistently absolute nature of the project must be interpreted from the beginning, however, with a certain irony, for in seeking Satan's patronage the narrator has simply reproduced the dilemma which was to be resolved by the rejection of Beauty. One patron has taken the place of another and it might be suspected that subscribing to Satan's authority is in many ways congruent to accepting the laws of beauty. This gesture of revolt then becomes symptomatic of the same dilemmas against which the narrator proposes to write. We may suspect that the narrator is not altogether mystified, for there is a note of self-mockery in this passage ("cher Satan, je vous en conjure, une prunelle moins irritée . . . ") which raises the possibility that the "solution" proposed is not as resolute as it appears. The title of the text, a ***Season in Hell,*** confirms the provisional character of this patronage, and suggests that this authority is indeed temporary and that one of the central issues of the poem will be the relation between language and the mastery over meaning. If the narrator is to emerge from the season in Hell, we may assume, it will be by rejecting any transcendental authority over meaning, whether it be a conventionally negative (Satan) or a positive figure (Beauty).

The next section of ***Une Saison en enfer,*** **"Mauvais sang,"** explores the narrator's estrangement from the dominant truths of an ideological system from which he is irrevocably excluded. The poem recounts a failed quest for origins, in which the narrator seeks a place for the self within the enclosure of a history and its metaphysics, yet repeatedly finds that his "place" lacks the desired centrality. He is constantly dis-placed towards the uncertain space of the shifting margins of the system. This marginality is figured throughout the passage, not only by the themes of bad blood, idolatry, sacrilege, idleness, vice and other similar ethically or economically determined alienations, but also as a complex relation of the narrator to language. That relation is the interplay between the language of the "real world" and the strategies which the narrator comes to discover operating in his own language. In both these registers, thematic and rhetorical, the poet is repeatedly displaced from the position of centrality which he claims to seek. This dislocation can be considered in terms of the idiom which the narrator calls a perfidious or pagan language and, concurrently, in terms of the relations of the narrating subject to past cultural and personal history and its language. This inquiry leads to an investigation of the problematic relations between *histoire* and *discours,* in this text and the attendant disruptions of the model of autobiographical narrative alluded to earlier.

In the opening lines of the poem, the narrator rejects all links between writing and any useful social activity. This anti-utilitarian stance can scarcely be taken for the idealism of Art for art's sake, however: "J'ai horreur de tous les métiers. Maîtres et ouvriers, tous paysans, ignobles. La main à plume vaut la main à charrue.—Quel siècle à mains! Je n'aurai jamais ma main." The poet violently dismisses a mode of writing which would assure the self a place in an established social order. An alternative practice of writing would subvert that order, yet neither here nor elsewhere does the poet propose a program or poetics of that mode. As we shall see, any esthetics of disruptive writing is mystified from the outset, for attempts to systematize that activity reinstate the control it seeks to undermine.

In **"Mauvais sang,"** the poet repudiates all manifestations of domesticity, including the *specular figures,* mendicity and criminality. "Après, la domesticité mène trop loin. L'honnêteté de la mendicité me navre. Les criminels dégoûtent comme des châtrés: moi, je suis intact, et ça m'est égal." The term, *intact,* here figures an (impossible) escape

from castration; the narrator supposes that he is outside the law of the Father. It is that unique position, both privileged and deficient, which he will seek to overcome, while refusing submission to the particular order of Western civilization. For the condition of being intact is the lure of *indifference* ("ça m'est égal"), as though the subject could exist outside of the constraints of any discourse whatsoever, be identical to its own undivided psychic components ("ça m'est égal"), or outside of any articulation between the subject and its relation to a lack. The possibility of this phallic plenitude is belied, however, by the narrator's persistent desire to situate the self in a relation with history, the lineage of his fathers, and language. "Si j'avais des antécédents à un point quelconque de l'histoire de France. Mais non, rien." Failing to find that link, the narrator unsuccessfully seeks a place in the continuous past of the nation, the church or in the more immediate past of personal history; he is repeatedly dislocated, thrown back into the present and into what he variously characterizes as a treacherous or pagan language. The issue is now no longer the absence or want of lack, but the relation to be assumed to that want which acknowledgement of lack makes necessary.

Pagan discourse, the narrator's alienated "language," is never explicitly defined, yet it is characterized negatively by a system of exclusions. Most importantly, pagan language is the language of the present, of *discours,* discontinuous with the past of the nation: "Je ne me souviens pas plus loin que cette terre-ci . . . " Concurrent to this amnesia is an exclusion from the language of the past. The dominant authority of the present is continuous with the "real" history of the past, and there is no break between the language of the past and that of the present. The poet, on the other hand, is excluded not only from the past and its language, and the language of the present, but he does not know the language of his own recent past: " . . . toujours seul; sans famille; même quelle langue parlais-je?" The pagan tongue is not only outside of the family, it lacks the ultimate trancendental basis: "Je ne me vois jamais dans les conseils du Christ . . . " "Freedom" from the symbolic father is presented here in several variants, as detachment from the church, law, nation, reason, science, yet the poet is nonetheless left with a powerful nostalgia for origins. "L'Esprit est proche, pourquoi Christ ne m'aide-t-il pas, en donnant à mon âme noblesse et liberté. Hélas! L'Evangile a passé! L'Evangile! L'Evangile! J'attends Dieu avec gourmandise. Je suis de race inférieure de toute éternité."

The quest for self is articulated as a quest for both an authentic past and a language capable of containing and reproducing the truth of that past. The narrator formulates this search in the remaining passages of **"Mauvais sang"** as a relation to history, in the conventional sense, and also in the more precisely linguistic sense (*histoire*) as the language which relates past events. The meaningfulness of the narrating *I,* in discourse, is not to be found here in the language of the present, for this utterance is devoid of truth. In the manner of a classical autobiography, the narrator turns to *histoire,* in an effort to reconstruct a present identity which would be produced as the subject describes and evaluates the errors of the past. By maintaining a separation between two linguistic moments, the narrated past and the present of narration, the narrator would find support for the analysis in the present and determine a coherent relation between two instances of the subject. The effort to know in the present is thus dependent upon initially maintaining a separation between discursive levels; only by traversing that space between the two levels can the analysis arrive at the abolition of that distance, in the desired unity of self-knowledge. These efforts, however, merely repeat the impasses I have been discussing; every excursion into a narrated past becomes literally ruined by the invasion of verbal and adverbial forms linked to *discours,* the present of narration. The narrator must now either turn towards exploring how the self is alienated in the language of the present, or turn towards fantasmatic solutions which deny the dilemma already uncovered. [in a footnote, Wing adds, "*Deny* is used here in the sense generally attributed to Freud's term: *Verneinung,* the negation which both denies and affirms."] Whether in recounting the past or inventing a future, the text is unable to sustain long sequences of narrative which depart from *discours,* and the narrator is quickly cast back into the inadequate language of the present. The attempts to place the self in the past should be marked by a shift from the present tense of narration to the past definite of *histoire,* but the epistemological and ontological authenticity of the past events are eroded by the use of a hypothetical mode, the past conditional: "Je me rappelle l'histoire de la France, fille aînée de l'Eglise. J'aurais fait, manant, le voyage en terre sainte . . . Plus tard, reître, j'aurais bivaqué sous les nuits d'Allemagne." Even the tenuous mimetic illusion of these narrated actions is soon undermined, as the narrator is forced to return to the time, space and language of the present: "Je ne me souviens pas plus loin que cette terre-ci . . . "

The failure of *history/histoire* to provide a stable signified as meaning in the present is echoed in a thematic register in the treatment of progress. The linear development of civilization, as a tradition of truth and development of knowledge, would be homologous to the anticipated development of the individual. That structure is also disrupted, its telos put in question: "La science, la nouvelle noblesse! Le progrès. Le monde marche! Pourquoi ne tournerait-il pas?" The confrontation between the idea of progress and the understanding of the finiteness of man and nature, a major preoccupation of 19th-century thought, is here given over to the operations of rhetoric. The narrator's rhetorical question ("Le monde marche. *Pourquoi ne tournerait-il pas?*") is more than an ironic quip which reactivates the cliché of the world striding towards progress. The sense of self is here to be found less in the full meaning of the grammatical sense of the passage than in the operations of rhetoric, which makes it impossible to decide whether the narrator is or is not posing a serious question. It is not possible to say whether the text proposes an opposition between a cyclical and a linear view of history, or whether the narrator just does not care. It has been argued that this confrontation between grammar and rhetoric opens up wide-ranging questions about the decidability of meaning in literature. Here, that shifting meaning further erodes the possibility of the narrator's finding a stable

ground for the self in history, and situates the quest in the operations of language.

In the passage immediately following this one, the self is projected into a fantasized future by means of a predictive narrative only to find that this prophetic future is symmetrical to the failed invention of a meaningful past. It is a similar deflection of the self away from a deficient present and to its diegetic space:

> Me voici sur la plage armoricaine. Que les villes s'allument dans le soir. Ma journée est faite; je quitte l'Europe. L'air marin brûlera mes poumons; les climats perdus me tanneront. . . .
> Je reviendrai, avec des membres de fer, la peau sombre, l'œil furieux: sur mon masque, on me jugera d'une race forte. J'aurai de l'or: je serai oisif et brutal. Les femmes soignent ces féroces infirmes retour des pays chauds. Je serai mêlé aux affaires politiques. Sauvé.
> Maintenant je suis maudit, j'ai horreur de la patrie. Le meilleur, c'est un sommeil bien ivre, sur la grève.
> On ne part pas. Reprenons les chemins d'ici. . . .

The movement from now and here, to another time and place fails with equal decisiveness, whether the narrative is retrospective or predictive.

A third narrative sequence recalls the narrator's recent past, the "real past" of his childhood, and it also lacks the power to provide the meaningful ground for self-presence. The wanderings in the recent past were as futile as the mythical projects just recounted:

> Sur les routes, par des nuits d'hiver, sans gîte, sans habits, sans pain, une voix étreignait mon cœur gelé: "Faiblesse ou force: te voilà, c'est la force. Tu ne sais ni où tu vas ni pourquoi tu vas, entre partout, réponds à tout. On ne te tuera pas plus que si tu étais cadavre." Au matin j'avais le regard si perdu et la contenance si morte, que ceux que j'ai recontrés *ne m'ont peut-être pas vu.*

The image of the transparent self figures the absolute lack in substance of the narrated *I,* and plays with a topos of confession narratives in a manner which forcefully undercuts its traditional function. According to the stereotype, the narrator proposes to unveil his past self in order to reveal the truth in all its nakedness, as in the opening pages of Rousseau's *Confessions.* In Rimbaud's text, however, unveiling the self fails to provide access to a plenitude of meaning. Paradoxically, the pure transparency of meaning is literally meaningless; the self which has found no place in the language of the other is utterly devoid of significance.

Further in the same sequence the narrator again rejects the laws of authority, yet the claim to absolute alterity does not produce a reassuring sense of self-sufficiency. The narrator is again cast up into a meaningless present.

> Prêtres, professeurs, maîtres, vous vous trompez en me livrant à la justice. Je n'ai jamais été de ce peuple-ci . . . Je ne comprends pas les lois; je n'ai pas le sens moral, je suis une brute: vous vous trompez.

Following this failure to establish a patrilinear link with a past origin, the narrator once again projects a proleptic narrative as a mythical future. The irony of the episode in which the poet adopts the persona of a cannibal saved by white colonialists is hardly intricate: "Les blancs débarquent. Le canon! Il faut se soumettre au baptême, s'habiller, travailler. / J'ai reçu le coup de la grâe." The uncomplex irony of the opening of this sequence, in which the savage is a figure for childlike innocence ("Vais-je être enlevé comme un enfant, pour jouer au paradis . . . ?"), becomes more problematic, however, as the allegory is abandoned. Returning to narration in the present, the narrator's pronouncements are advanced as the sole validation of his innocence: "Apprécions sans vertige l'étendue de mon innocence . . . Je ne me crois pas embarqué pour une noce avec Jésus-Christ pour beau-père." The narrator formulates his desire simply; what he wishes to attain is truth and salvation now, a pure logocentric self-presence, an absolute and unmediated origin in the present: "Je ne suis pas prisonnier de ma raison. J'ai dit: Dieu. Je veux la liberté dans le salut." The self is fully present in the closure of its own discourse . . . but it does not last. The narrator recognizes that his pronouncement, in its repetition of the inaugural moment of creation, has produced not the desired moment of pure truth, but farce: "Farce continuelle! Mon innocence me ferait pleurer. La vie est la farce à mener par tous." Farce, then, is the explosive recognition that attaining the coincidence of self and language is merely the deluded repetition of an origin which never existed. In the patterns I have been discussing, writing systematically explores the resources of certain rhetorical possibilities and plays out their deficiencies, returning the narrator to a *discours* incapable of either retrieving or producing what it seeks. Increasingly, the text will force the realization that the only language available to the narrator is one in which each articulation of *I* produces the mark of non-coincidence which deconstructs the search for meaning and presence.

I can now briefly and elliptically outline a reading of the rest of *Une Saison en enfer* in terms of the problematic discussed above. The discovery becomes increasingly explicit that desire for "absolute modernity," and the concurrent rejection of past errors, repeatedly engages the narrator in an interpretive process in which the function of language, and most specifically, the language of *discours,* is the central issue. To be "absolutely modern" will result from rejecting a deluded relation to *histoire* and posing the question of modernity in the register of *discours.* The first effort will be to demystify the poet's earlier attempts at modernity, illusions about love and about literature; only then will the way be cleared for establishing a "new modernity" as a new relation to language. It will be seen that the narrator accomplishes this by "writing himself out" of *histoire,* so to speak, primarily in the two central texts of "**Délires,**" which are presented explicitly as confession and *histoire.* Only then does he turn to the present of narration, as narrative becomes displaced by *discours.* Paradoxically, in those sections in which the narrative conforms most closely to the patterns of confession, maintaining a separation between a narrated "real" past and the present of narration, the sense of discontinuity between different moments of the subject's story becomes increasingly strong. The

radical otherness of temporally distinct moments of the story, and the lack of ontological links between the narrated and the narrating *I,* serve to erode further and further the rhetorical conventions of autobiography.

In "**Nuit de l'enfer,**" the few passages which narrate a completed past are all variants on the theme of past delusions now rejected. The shift to the level of *discours* is concurrent with an explicit judgment on the delusion of having attempted to find meaning in history, and we may assume, in attempting to find meaning *as* history. "J'avais entrevu la conversion au bien et bonheur, le salut. Puis-je décrire la vision, l'air de l'enfer ne souffre pas les hymnes. C'était des millions de créatures charmantes, un suave concert spirituel, la force et la paix, les nobles ambitions, que sais-je?". ". . . plus de foi en l'histoire." Repeatedly thrown into the space and time of the narration, the only moment and place in which meaning can be situated, the narrator interprets the conjunction of the present of discourse with the narrated self as a displacement from the world. To be outside of the world is to be outside of meaningful time: "Ah ça! l'horloge de la vie s'est arrêtée tout à l'heure. Je ne suis plus au monde." Rather than living in a continuity of becoming, the narrator knows the present as the immediacy of discontinuous moments, set adrift from temporal sequence. The subject is irrevocably fragmented, at once affirming and denying its own existence and situation: "Il n'y a personne ici et il y a quelqu'un . . ." "Je suis caché et je ne le suis pas."

The old imperatives to find truth and to fix it in the language of a vision recounted, though rejected as delusions at the beginning of this text, return in the boastful pronouncements about the narrator's genius: "Je vais dévoiler tous les mystères: mystères religieux, ou naturels, mort, naissance, avenir, passé, cosmogonie, néant. Je suis maître en fantasmagories. / Ecoutez!. . . ." Any claim to the ultimate seriousness of the statements is undercut, however, as the rantings of a still delirious narrator, suffering through the night of hell: "Bah! faisons toutes les grimaces imaginables." However, elliptically, the conclusion to this text proposes interpretation of the present as the condition for return to life; as already established, the process of interpretation engages a subject which lacks conformity to itself and must be scrutinized in its monstrous deformations. "Ah! remonter à la vie! Jeter les yeux sur nos difformités."

As I have noted above, the interpretive act will increasingly distance itself from the conventions of confession narratives, but it first exhausts that mode in a delirium of confession in the two poems entitled: "**Délires,**" "**Vierge folle,**" and "**Alchimie du verbe.**" In important ways the texts are informative not only for the content of the confessions, a bitterly ironic leave-taking from the old loves ("**Vierge folle**") and the old modernist poetics ("**Alchimie du verbe**"), but also as exercises in unlearning certain classical practices of reading: *dé-lire.* What is at stake here is the possibility of a demystified reading of existing literature and of the erotic couple. The act of perversion is itself subject to scrutiny, as mystification, whether it corrupts the esthetics of classical literature; or in a more conventional sexual sense, corrupts the stability of the heterosex-

Rimbaud on his deathbed, drawn by Isabelle Rimbaud.

ual couple by substituting the homosexual couple. The interpretation of these perversions set forth in these two texts ironically reveals the delusions reproduced in the provisional solution.

I will not comment extensively on these two texts, since their pertinence to the problematic I am discussing can be summarized briefly. The two stories recounted in **"Délires"** are two homologous aspects of the same enterprise: to displace libidinal activity, love or writing, from the determined limits of a convention. As [Shoshona] Felman has observed, Rimbaud's originality is in conceiving modernity in terms of the couple and in linking desire and language. The enterprise of perversion, of deviation and detour from the beaten path ("les chemins d'ici") bears as well upon the body as upon language. Both are charged with erotic energy which is released through the systematic infraction of interdictions. The contiguity of these two texts unmistakably underscores the interrelation between not dissimilar modes of sexual activity; language is apprehended in its erotic materiality and the production of desire viewed in terms of the operations of language.

"Vierge folle" recounts the perversion of the heterosexual couple, in which its bonds to material productivity are denounced as a domestication of erotic energy. The narrator's utopian sexual ethic is retold by a former companion in Hell:

> Il dit: 'Je n'aime pas les femmes. L'amour est à

réinventer, on le sait. Elles ne peuvent plus que vouloir une position assurée. La position gagnée, cœur et beauté sont mis de côté: il ne reste que froid dédain, l'aliment du mariage, aujourd'hui.'

The problem, as the text will reveal with bitter irony, is not that the narrator misapprehended in the past the deficiencies of the heterosexual couple, but that he reinstated the same suspect imaginary relationship in the homosexual couple. Again in the reported speech of the narrator: "Tu vois cet élégant jeune homme, entrant dans la belle et calme maison: il s'appelle Duval, Dufour, Armand, Maurice, que sais-je? Une femme est dévouée à aimer ce méchant idiot: elle est morte, c'est certes une sainte au ciel, à présent. Tu me feras mourir commee il a fait mourir cette femme." The object of the irony here is not only the narrator's companion, but the narrator as well; as the terse final comment by the narrator makes clear: "Drôle de ménage."

The effort to displace the limits of language and to redefine writing takes two forms explicitly in **"Alchimie du verbe,"** and, implicitly, a third, which relates to the problematic status of the writing subject in the present. First, literature is subverted by practices derived from sub-genres excluded from "serious" writing:

> A moi. L'histoire d'une de mes folies. / Depuis longtemps, je me vantais de posséder tous les paysages possibles, et trouvais dérisoire les célébrités de la peinture et de la poésie moderne. / J'aimais les peintures idiotes, dessus de portes, décors, toiles de saltimbanques, enseignes, enluminures populaires; la littérature démodée, latin d'église, livres érotiques sans orthographe, romans de nos aïeules, contes de fées, petits livres de l'enfance, opéras vieux, refrains niais, rhythmes naïfs.

The new writing of the recent past displaced the hierarchical distinctions which are the esthetic bases of literary genres, in favor of the excluded or marginal genres. Second is the claim to have invented a new language which would effectively overcome not only the arbitrary relation between signifier and signified, that very difference which makes meaning possible, but would also conflate the referent with the sign: "J'inventai la couleur des voyelles! . . . je me flattai d'inventer un verbe poétique accessible, un jour ou l'autre, à tous les sens. Je réservais la traduction." Beyond the subversion of traditional literary language, however, and in a manner congruous to **"Vierge folle,"** the poet here displaces the conventions of the old literature only to find certain key presuppositions relocated in the new language. The paradox here is that the invention of a radical newness is condemned to repeat the delusions of the past. The mystification which persists is the assumption that literature functions to communicate a fully retrievable meaning, available to the writing subject and susceptible to appropriation by another subject. In the poetics of the old "new" literature the narrator simply reinstates the deluded relation of the subject to language within the same circuit of exchange. The poet's refusal to "translate" in no way disrupts the underlying assumptions of the practice; it magnifies the claim to a power of control attributed to the author of the text. The writer who would be master of his own fiction in all his *authority,* inevitably becomes its dupe. Although elliptically, the final statement of the text acknowledges that mystification: "Cela s'est passé. Je sais aujourd'hui saluer la beauté."

This text marks a break with esthetics in general, whether the conventions of Literature or of the narrator's former anti-Literature, and sets up the possibility of significantly different relation between the writer and writing. We find in this last sentence of **"Alchimie du verbe"** an enigmatic echo of the earlier curse against the muse in the first page of the text . . . with the important difference that denunciation is here replaced with a respectful salutation. The precise meaning of this address, however, is impossible to determine, and that may be the most powerful meaning in this text. The salutation is either a greeting, or a leave-taking, or both a greeting and a leave-taking. In a sense it closes the text of delirium, and at the same time turns toward the possibility of a different understanding of writing. In its undecidability, both a closure and an opening, this last sentence suggests much about the meaningfulness of the new writing, which will be both the concentration and the dispersal of sense. The ultimate folly which this passage deflects is to assume that the writer can ever greet the muse without at the same time taking leave of his senses.

The predominant importance of *histoire* in these two texts produces two effects. The first underscores the break between the subject of this *histoire* and the narrating subject, conveyed most dramatically by the terse conclusion of each text in the present tense of *discours.* Second, this break prepares a subsequent and decisive shift in the discursive registers proposed already in the first three sections of the poem: the following texts will contain fewer and fewer passages written in *histoire.* What matters to the narrator in relating the two stories of the past to the present is the discontinuity of past time with that of the present, the disjunction between one of the poet's "other lives," and the present time of narration. The text thus rejects any reflection upon the possible continuity between the two subjects of the poem, the subject of the *histoire* and the narrating subject. The function of that lacuna is to produce an unbridgeable space between the two instances of the subject.

The four much briefer texts which follow reveal that the narrator desires complete difference between then and now, in order that the present self will emerge into a moment which is pure, continuous and uncontaminated by the past. These remaining pages, however, will establish the impossibility of complete separation from the past, and will scrutinize the utopian desire for unalienated presence in *discours,* as past errors are repeated in the present. The desire for an original and non-repetitive modernity, as Felman has remarked, is itself doomed to the form and paradox of repetition. The radical difference in the narrator's awareness before and after **"Délires"** is the discovery that the break with the past is never definitive, and that the very act of speaking in the present commits the subject to the alienating structures of language, whether that alienation be affirmed or denied.

A first and powerful discovery is that it is impossible to locate the quest outside of the enclosure of Western thought; in short, there is no outside. Earlier, in **"Mauvais sang,"** the narrator had situated his quest for origins firmly within the metaphoric opposition: inside/outside, simply reversing the polarities and setting the self in an "outside" to which accrues the value of centrality characteristic of the rejected "inside." Here, the issue is treated in a far more complex manner: "M'étant retrouvé deux sous de raison—ça passe vite!—je vois que mes malaises viennent de ne m'être pas figuré assez tôt que nous sommes à l'Occident. Les marais occidentaux!" The expression *se figurer,* beyond its conventional sense of to imagine, to understand, suggests a close link with the realization proposed and the acknowledgment that the self can take its "place" only in the figures, the language, of the West. Like the discovery that one can never definitively say goodbye to the muse, never leave the realm of figuration, or write a text which does not bear the traces of other texts, this understanding must be set over and against the earlier assertion that the poet was "intact." Here the narrator abandons claim to an impossibly unique and original relation to language and acknowledges that his understanding is mediated by language, which has its laws and configurations which exist prior to the individual and exceed his control.

There simply is no sense in supposing that the narrator can establish a position outside the language and the thought of the West. The dream of the absolute other, whose metaphoric vehicle in this text is the Orient, is the epitome of self-delusion: "Les philosophes: Le monde n'a pas d'âge. L'humanité se déplace, simplement. Vous êtes en Occident, mais libre d'habiter dans votre Orient, quelque ancien qu'il vous le faille,—et d'y habiter bien. Ne soyez pas un vaincu. Philosophes, vous êtes de votre Occident." This awareness is perhaps the most significant gain proposed in **"L'Impossible,"** for it is at this point that the desire for the unique, for the center, can be articulated in the language of discourse, in the recognition that language is powerless to provide the sought for guarantor of presence. The narrator now begins to think the desire for center in terms of decentering, of displacement of the subject by the language in which it is articulated. This is the point at which it becomes necessary to consider explicitly the limits of language and to affirm at the same time the self as a play of language: "je ne puis pas plus m'expliquer que le mendiant avec ses continuels *Pater* et *Ave Maria. Je ne sais plus parler.*" The poet is speechless, confounded, for the language available to him already undercuts his enterprise. It is as corrupt as the language of prayer employed in ludicrous futility by the beggar. This recognition occurs at a highly significant moment in the text, for it is the last statement preceding the pronouncement that the narrator has finished recounting his season in hell: "Pourtant, aujourd'hui je crois avoir fini la relation de mon enfer." That season is concluded when the narrator has worked out the inadequacies of the historical narrative, but the text does not end in silence, nor does it stop here. Leaving the past seasons "definitively" the narrator turns to the present and "absolute modernity," and the effort to locate the subject in a language totally contemporary to the self.

These sequences in **"Adieu,"** the last section of the text, which repeat the rejected delusions of the past, bring memories into the language of the present: "Je me revois la peau rongée par la boue et la peste, . . . " "L'affreuse évocation." This absorption of the past by the present, completed in **"Adieu,"** allows the poet to dismiss any relation of genetic continuity between the earlier narrated self and the self of the present narration. The moment of the present is the moment to get on with it: "Et allons." Stating things as they are, however, does not mark a moment of epistemological enlightenment, resulting from the appropriation of the past. The imperative here is specified as a desire to forget, and it is the act of forgetting which is burdened with rendering the poet absolutely contemporary: "Car je puis dire que la victoire m'est acquise: les grincements de dents, les sifflements de feu, les soupirs empestés se modèrent. Tous les souvenirs immodes s'effacent. Mes derniers regrets détalent, . . . / Il faut être absolument moderne." Modernity, in the very absoluteness of the desire to be modern, repeats the delusions of the past. "Adieu," as already established in **"Alchimie du verbe,"** where it is articulated as an iterative verb, is never definitive: "Je disais adieu au monde . . . " Paradoxically, the status of the modern can never be defined as absolute, for it is inevitably historical and relative, always in a differential relationship to something else.

The poet has acknowledged the divorce between literature, reality and truth: "J'ai cru acquérir des pouvoirs surnaturels. Eh bien! je dois enterrer mon imagination et mes souvenirs! Une belle gloire d'artiste et de conteur emportée!" Following the imperative to be absolutely modern, the rejection of poetry is once again linked to renunciation of its logocentric telos: "Point de cantiques: tenir le pas gagné." This refusal of poetry, significantly, produces . . . more poetry: "Et à l'aurore, armés d'une ardente patience, nous entrerons aux splendides villes," and the final words of the poem: " . . . il me sera loisible de *posséder la vérité dans une âme et un corps.*" What is perhaps so striking about this conclusion is that it repeats a desire for truth and being in a *structure* of deferral, which is to say, set in the configurations of an impossibility. The text thus does not close upon a moment of presence attained, or even in the confident assertion of a future to be gained, but articulates desire in a structure of difference and displacement. The narrator does not say: "I possess truth in a body and soul," or even "I will possess truth, etc. . . . ," but instead abandons both the present tense of assertion and the first person subject. Desire is formulated in impersonal language; the integral acting subject has been displaced by the pronoun *il* and the first person has become its object. The reader is left to consider the implications of this confident assertion in which the agent of desire disappears as a first person subject and gives over the subjective function to the "non-person" *il,* and in which the object of desire can only be attained by the narration of a new story, which in turn . . . (pp. 42-57)

Nathaniel Wing, "The Autobiography of Rhetoric: On Reading Rimbaud's 'Une Saison En Enfer'," in French Forum, *Vol. 9, No. 1, January, 1984, pp. 42-58.*

Harold Bloom on Rimbaud:

So much the worse for the wood that finds it is a violin, or the brass that finds it is a bugle, or the French boy of yeoman stock who at sixteen could write *Le Bateau ivre,* transuming Baudelaire's "Le Voyage." Rimbaud's violent originality, from *Le Bateau ivre* on, drives not against meaning but against anyone whatsoever, even Baudelaire, bequeathing Rimbaud any meaning that is not already his own. More even than the later Victor Hugo, to whom he grudgingly granted the poetic faculty of Vision, Rimbaud could tolerate no literary authority. Perhaps, if you could combine the visionary Hugo and Baudelaire into a single poet, Rimbaud would have had a precursor who might have induced in him some useful anxiety, but the Anglo-American poetic habit of creating for oneself an imaginary, composite poetic forerunner was not available to Rimbaud.

Barely two years after *Le Bateau ivre,* Rimbaud had finished *Une Saison en enfer.* Blake is supposed to have written "How Sweet I Roam'd from Field to Field" before he was fourteen, but except for Blake there is no great poet as precocious as Rimbaud in all of Western literary history. Like Blake, a poet of extraordinary power at fourteen, Rimbaud quite unlike Blake abandoned poetry at nineteen. A trader and gunrunner in Africa, dead at thirty-seven, having written no poetry in the second half of his life, Rimbaud necessarily became and remains the mythical instance of the modern poet as the image of alienation. The myth obscures the deeper traditionalism of *Saison* in particular. Despite the difference implicit in the belated Romanticism of France, Rimbaud is as High Romantic as Blake or Shelley, or as Victor Hugo.

Harold Bloom, from the introduction to Arthur Rimbaud, *1988.*

Gerald M. Macklin (essay date 1990)

[*In the following excerpt, Macklin depicts the prose poetry in* Illuminations *as a stage in Rimbaud's quest for a literary form to accomodate his vision.*]

Rimbaud's instinctive refusal to become petrified within any single poetic form is one of the most striking features of his brief and intense artistic career. Indeed the question of poetic form was one of his constant preoccupations and led to his disconcertingly rapid evolution through several distinct phases of creativity and arguably even to his controversial "silence". It is the purpose of this present study to examine certain essential elements of style and structure in the **Illuminations,** taken as the last stage in his development, and to posit as central to the collection a duality of pattern and disorder, cohesion and fragmentation, integrating principles and disunifying forces. Yet if the **Illuminations** can be viewed as a culmination for Rimbaud, a final artistic experiment with the possibilities of the prose poem, it is important to remind ourselves here of the path that brought him to such a blatant departure from conventional poetic practice.

While it is patently impossible to take the letter to Paul Demeny of May 15, 1871 as a definitive visionary manifesto or a fixed statement of Rimbaud's aesthetic assumptions and self-imposed canons, it does provide nevertheless an early indication of his reaction to the crucial question of poetic form. The imperative to "trouver une langue" is underscored not only by the audacious criticism of Baudelaire on matters of form but by this celebrated comment on the way the "voyant" will articulate his visionary discoveries:

> . . . si ce qu'il rapporte *de là-bas* a forme, il donne forme: si c'est informe, il donne de l'informe.

A related blend of form and formlessness is the major hallmark of the Rimbaldian prose poem in the *Illuminations.* Yet many of the earliest *Poésies,* for all their memorable adventures in vision and innovations in vocabulary, remain fundamentally orthodox in terms of poetic form. Rimbaud makes widespread use of the sonnet in these poems (**"Le Mal"**, **"Le Dormeur du val"**, **"Rêvé pour l'hiver"**), and, despite taking liberties with rhyme and metre in many verse poems, even in *Le Bateau ivre* manages to contain the tumbling kaleidoscope of *souvenirs de voyage* within the framework of twenty five stanzas each composed of four alexandrines. However the use of terms such as "panse", "anus", "Robinsonne" and "boulus", the oddity of the anatomical vocabulary in **"Les Assis"** ("sinciput", "caboches", "amygdales"), the disorientating formula in the first line of **"Mes petites amoureuses"** ("hydrolat lacrymal"), the multiplicity of unusual expressions in **"Ce qu'on dit au poète à propos de fleurs"** ("Oeufs de feu", "le chat Murr", "papillons électriques") and the disparity in *Le Bateau ivre* between the originality of the imagery and the orthodoxy of the form that just succeeds in accommodating it all serve notice of Rimbaud's growing subversion of normal prosody and his wish to subject common expression to new stresses and strains. Thus, in 1872, at the height of his tempestuous affair with Verlaine and no doubt under the older poet's artistic influence, Rimbaud produces the deceptively slim and engagingly fluid poems of the *Dernièrs vers,* the "prodiges de ténuité" where lightness of form is at odds with a multitude of inner tensions, emotions and aspirations as well as a complex web of reference and image. These texts clearly represent a significant graduation, a long stride away from traditional verse and in the direction of something more flexible and less rigorously defined. One thinks of the song-like refrain of **"L'Eternité"** used to convey the miracle of timelessness, of the operatic flavour of **"Comédie de la soif "** where the five divisions chart stages in the crisis of the "Moi" and of the airy lightness of **"Entends comme brame"** where one is invited to share an ineffable moment in nature. Ultimately, the prose diary of *Une saison en enfer* completes the rejection of the "ancien jeu des vers" and demonstrates once more Rimbaud's capacity to espouse and then reject particular forms as he continues his search for an elusive ideal framework with sufficient plasticity to accommodate his new vision and idiom.

As a prelude to our analysis of a series of specific formal aspects of the *Illuminations* we can make at this stage certain general observations about Rimbaud's approach to the prose poem. We have seen that his evolution as a poet is characterized by a progressive disengagement or liberation from the debilitating shackles of prosody and its many constraints. Just as the pioneering boat in *Le Bateau ivre* shakes off "gouvernail et grappin" before departing on an odyssey of acute sensory stimulation, so Rimbaud himself in the *Illuminations* gladly surrenders the security of orthodox forms and the reliable contours of verse. Leaving behind such inveterate stabilizing agents as rhyme, metre and stanza, he pursues a fluidity of expression already tasted in the *Derniers vers* with its slender and supple structures. In the prose poem the conventions and set patterns that reassure the versifier that he has control over words are replaced by the workings of a mysterious artistic intuition that prevents this new found freedom from degenerating into anarchy. In Rimbaud's case this engenders a compelling encounter between unity and dispersal, form and formlessness, pattern and disorder and Suzanne Bernard perceptively underlines this tension when she writes of what is needed in the prose poem:

> Il s'agit de trouver une forme à la fois suffisamment anarchique pour briser les conventions anciennes, les normes d'un monde inacceptable et suffisamment eurythmique pour que le poète puisse ordonner sa création poétique en un système "cosmique" et harmonieux.

One of the unavoidable problems that arise concerning the essence of the prose poem, of course, is where does prose stop and poetry begin? What ensures that a piece from the *Illuminations,* for example, attains the status of poetry and sets itself apart from ornamented prose? Rimbaud's extreme sensitivity to pace and rhythm, his exaltation of the individual word (a Pandora's box is Barthes' definition of the Word in modern poetry), his adherence to and simultaneous subversion of different types of poetic structure, the particular emphasis placed on beginnings and finales and the new role envisaged for punctuation are some of the features that characterize the collection and guarantee its unmistakable "poéticité". As we shall see, these and other elements are involved in a delicate equilibrium between order and disorder in individual poems. The impulse towards total artistic freedom reflected in Rimbaud's choice of the prose poem as a new vehicle is tempered by an assertive, disciplining artistic sense that imposes harmony and regularity in varying measures upon discontinuity and casual arrangement.

To facilitate a detailed scrutiny of these twin forces of pattern and disorder we may select three distinctive features of style and structure in the *Illuminations* that promote unity and form and contrast them with three elements that militate in favour of fragmentation and disruption. Although the prose poem discards the dependable checks and balances of verse it by no means follows that it must become shapeless and haphazard by way of a reaction to such constraints. Indeed one might well argue that it is in the process whereby the poet substitutes other formal elements for those abandoned, and this without removing the poetic "charge", that one will find the key to the prose poem. The *Illuminations* represent not random and unkempt writing but poetry into which a large measure of order has been injected through the conscious and lucid employment of a number of important and recurring techniques. Robert Faurisson's work on Rimbaud is best known for his famous erotic interpretation of the texts but it is worth remembering what this critic has to say about the composition of the *Illuminations:*

> Rimbaud a écrit les *Illuminations,* ainsi que tous ses poèmes d'apparence hermétique, avec la même application ouvrière que *Le Bateau ivre.*

We may now consider in some detail three of the techniques that suggest such careful and assiduous composition: Rimbaud's vigilant supervision of beginnings and finales, his predilection for anaphora as a structuring device and his use of the "conte" genre as a model on which to construct a number of texts.

In his discerning phenomenological study of Rimbaud's poetry Jean-Pierre Richard asserts that "le prestige unique de la poésie rimbaldienne tient en effet au marriage qu'elle opère, et qui ne sera jamais plus réalisé après elle, d'un jaillissement et d'une forme". Rimbaud's attention to beginnings and finales helps to create the formal framework in which the "jaillissement" that Richard refers to can occur. By definition, the opening and closing phases of any event enjoy a privileged position in that they respectively set the tone for the performance and condition one's ultimate impression of it. In the *Illuminations* several introductions are gentle, measured and unhurried. One recalls the cadenced opening to **"Royauté"** that leads us quietly into the fairy tale spell of the poem and the verbless first sentence in **"Being beauteous"** which raises the curtain on a scene that will burst dynamically into action:

> Devant une neige un Etre de Beauté de haute taille.

By contrast there are many examples of vigorous and arresting introductions that offer an immediate condensation of emotional power and sometimes impress upon one the prestigious presence of a character from Rimbaud's vast assembly of players. This is the case in both **"Vagabonds"** ("Pitoyable frère!") and **"Antique"** ("Gracieux fils de Pan!") and in **"Villes"** a comparable initial exclamation seems to express the poet's artistic power and his enthusiasm from the outset ("Ce sont des villes!") As further evidence that we are in the presence of a mind very much attuned to the possibilities of this area of structural arrangement we can point to a number of poems that Rimbaud starts in such a way as to break contact with a particular definition of reality and normality. **"Solde"** immediately casts Rimbaud in the role of street-crier who will not let us pass without noticing him and the poem's introductory paragraph has a rhythmical energy that creates a sense of some unprecedented revelation to follow:

> A vendre ce que les Juifs n'ont pas vendu, ce que noblesse ni crime n'ont goûté, ce qu'ignorent l'amour maudit et la probité infernale des masses; ce que le temps ni la science n'ont pas à reconnaître;

Similarly **"Vies II"** opens with a self-definition by the poet as unprecedented "inventeur" and, as in **"Solde"**, the reader is invited towards something more than his usual expectations. The first line of **"Barbare"** ("Bien après les jours et les saisons, et les êtres et les pays,") is calculated to break all links with recognizable reality and so consti-

tutes a tempting "invitation au voyage" in both an artistic and a visionary sense. The first line of **"Après le déluge"** leaves us poised on the threshold of a narrative, the beginning of **"Conte"** has the "Once upon a time" quality of the fairy tale and several poems (**"Fleurs"**, **"Métropolitain"**, **"Promontoire"**) include a splendid colour impression as visual enticement in their introductory line.

Finales in the *Illuminations* are even more distinctively fashioned by Rimbaud. Some of them involve either a challenge or a threat to the reader, a device that does not lead us out of the poem's spell but rather back to the text as a puzzle that must be solved or a haunting prophecy that cannot be lightly dismissed. In **"H"** we are invited to decipher a code or enigma ("trouvez Hortense") and in **"Parade"** the last sentence both seals and reopens the poem, distancing us from it as a completed and obscure act and simultaneously offering it to us for renewed examination:

> J'ai seul la clef de cette parade sauvage.

"Vies I" and **"Jeunesse IV"** conclude with remarks that are designed to undermine the reader's complacency, to create a sense of uncertainty about future events and to give the poem's finale a last surge of energy and what [J. P.] Houston calls [in his *Design of Rimbaud's Poetry,* 1963] "the crafty final change of direction" that is "Rimbaud's characteristic signature". In the former piece the disconcerting question at the end ("Qu'est mon néant, auprès de la stupeur qui vous attend?") is a Parthian shot aimed at the reader and the last two sentences in the latter poem are intended not to offer reassurance but to plunge one into a state of heightened apprehension and expectation:

> Quant au monde, quand tu sortiras, que sera-t-il devenu? En tout cas, rien des apparences actuelles.

An obvious feature of presentation is the manner in which Rimbaud regularly compresses his finales into a single line. Such tailpieces can offer a new metaphor, a mysterious formula to be elucidated, a detached comment on the poem proper or a quasi-philosophical *morale.* One thinks of the aphoristic ending in **"Conte"** which uses the metaphor of music, hitherto unmentioned in the poem, to stress frustration ("La musique savante manque à notre désir"), the terse postscript in **"Matinée d'ivresse"** which contains a baffling prediction revolving around an italicised term rich with etymological significance ("Voici le temps des *Assassins*") and the isolated last line in **"Aube"** ("Au réveil il était midi") that is both a counterweight to the poem's equally isolated first line and a laconic indication of the poet's ironic breaking of the spell woven in the poem. **"A une raison"**, **"Départ"**, **"Enfance 1"**, **"Parade"** and **"Guerre"** are other texts where this device is used and Bernard has pointed out how these proliferating finales are not conventional conclusions:

> Chez Rimbaud cette brève phrase de conclusion bien souvent ne "conclut" rien, elle fait au contraire repartir le poème vers de nouveaux horizons, elle ouvre des perspectives sur d'autres terrains que ceux où le poème s'était construit.

Thus, such finales are not only examples of poetic closure but also a means of reopening the text for the reader.

In the *Illuminations,* as we have seen, many poems contain a sudden reversal at the end which comes as a "sting in the tail" and radically affects one's eventual reaction to the piece concerned. In both **"Ouvriers"** and **"Soir historique"** we find an abrupt rejection of a certain lifestyle or visionary system and with startling speed the poem gravitates towards new possibilities, a reorientation as radical as it is unexpected and heralded by the exclamatory "Non!" in each case. One feels that a certain artistic and imaginative power is expressed through these defiant finales and Rimbaud is ever keen to finish his prose poems on a note of vibrant rejuvenation. Thus, the idea of a fall contained in the ending to some poems (literal in **"Aube"**, suggestive of a curtain-fall in **"Les Ponts"**) is more than compensated for by the images of apocalyptic fury and elemental upheaval encountered in the closing stages of **"Angoisse"**, **"Nocturne vulgaire"** and **"Soir historique"**. An emphasis on violence and conflict is just as marked at the end of **"Métropolitain"** where Rimbaud, in a characteristically unpredictable switch, replaces scraps of inconsequential vision with the urgency and precision of a single dramatic picture:

> Le matin où avec Elle, vous vous débattîtes parmi les éclats de neige, les lèvres vertes, les glaces, les drapeaux noirs et les rayons bleus, et les parfums pourpres du soleil des pôles,—ta force.

The pattern seen in **"Voyelles"**, where a highly unusual first line links each vowel in a most unexpected way to a certain colour and a resonant last line uses the Greek letter Omega to create impressions of infinity, shows a sensitivity to beginnings and endings that is sustained and heightened in the *Illuminations.* Rimbaud makes a potent appeal to the reader's sensibility by his indefatigable manipulation of these components of poetic structure, a feature that reminds us of how his pronounced emphasis on form and balance counteracts his equally strong impulse towards spontaneous self-expression.

Rimbaud's predilection for anaphora and the litanical format has its roots deep in his early verse. One recalls *Le Bateau ivre* where the numerous "souvenirs de voyage" are replayed in a series of stanzas beginning with the first personal form of the perfect tense ("J'ai vu . . . ", "J'ai rêvé . . . ", "J'ai suivi . . . ", "J'ai heurté . . . "), a presentation that gives order to a dazzling and frenetic retrospective. The song-like refrains of the *Derniers vers* derive at least in part from this same predilection. In the *Illuminations* anaphora has a key role in **"Solde"**, **"Dévotion"**, **"Enfance III"**, **"Enfance IV"**, **"Départ"** and **"A une raison"** and in each of these poems it creates a recognizable pattern, an incantatory rhythm and an apparently consistent and predictable verbal sequence. The repeated "à vendre" cried out by the "merchant" in **"Solde"** is a fine illustration of how anaphora operates in the collection for it engenders a sense of unity and cohesion in a poem that might otherwise be felt to be made up of many disparate elements itemised in inventorial fashion. Instead of being disjointed and piecemeal, the various abstract "treasures"

on offer take their place within a generally dependable poetic structure:

> A vendre l'anarchie pour les masses; la satisfaction irrépressible pour les amateurs supérieurs; la mort atroce pour les fidèles et les amants!
> A vendre les habitations et les migrations, sports, féeries et conforts parfaits, et le bruit, le mouvement et l'avenir qu'ils font!

So dense is the compression of elements in **"Solde"** and so rapidly do we move from one item to the next that the sale might indeed seem "sans contrôle", to borrow an expression from the text itself. The effect of the anaphora is to offset this breathless pace by placing the "à vendre" cry in a consistently prominent position so that it creates a rhythmical pulse and regularity so important in the prose poem where rhyme and verse form have been surrendered. In discussing one of the *Illuminations* ("Jeunesse II") Roger Little writes of "the care which Rimbaud took over composition" [in his *Rimbaud "Illuminations,"* 1983] and an analysis of **"Solde"** substantiates this view. In no fewer than six of the text's eight paragraphs the "à vendre" formula is present at the start. It acts as something of a trigger or curtain-raiser in the opening section by drawing our attention very dramatically to the fact that something is being put on offer which is of an unprecedented nature; in segments three to six it produces the excited pace of the sale as a stream of items are placed before us with exclamatory vigour; and in the last paragraph it returns to create the effect of a rousing reprise as Rimbaud recapitulates the "lots" that he has listed in his unique "auction". The litanical "il y a" in **"Enfance III"** which is used in a catalogue of some of the special experiences of childhood, and as a formula is so appropriately childlike and the repeated "je suis" in **"Enfance IV"**, where Rimbaud enumerates several of his many identities, are further examples of the poet's recourse to anaphora to provide a degree of continuity and stability amid the essential fluidity of his new prose form.

One could hardly fail in this connection to think of the poem **"Dévotion"** which seems to be a clear parody of the religious litany with the prepositions "à" and "pour" being the elements that give it a coherent form by setting up a network of addressess and beneficiaries. Interestingly, and this is often the case in the *Illuminations,* the anaphora is seen in its strongest and most pronounced form in the early stages of the poem. The first three paragraphs are closely bound by the devotional "à" and the fact that the addressee on each occasion is a female figure in whose name the initial "L" catches the eye adds a further degree of consistency. Yet it is noticeable that whereas the first two paragraphs have the formula "A ma soeur" in the address to Louise Vanaen de Voringhem and Léonie Aubois d'Ashby, the third segment invoking "Lulu" simply has the preposition "à". This is a salutary reminder that most of Rimbaud's anaphoric structures are subject to erosion and modification (as we have seen, "à vendre" is not present in every paragraph in **"Solde"** and it is noteworthy that the "je suis" in **"Enfance IV"** becomes "je serais"). In the middle stages of **"Dévotion"** the apparently reliable litanical format undergoes more serious stresses and strains as the stately and reverent tone of the opening paragraphs is replaced by a cavalier and ironic inventory of addresses and the previously solid "à"/"pour" arrangement breaks down. The fourth and fifth paragraphs are revealingly briefer than the first three sections and this suggests that the devotional prayer is losing its momentum as Rimbaud tires of it and seeks a new orientation for the poem. Furthermore, when we arrive at the sixth paragraph we find that the preposition "à" has lost its special place at the start and has been subsumed into a rather meandering and desultory statement:

> Aussi bien à tout culte en telle place de culte
> mémoriale et parmi tels événements qu'il faille
> se rendre, suivant les aspirations du moment ou
> bien notre propre vice sérieux.

In the seventh section the function of the preposition ("à Circeto") might be still devotional or it could be an indication of location if "Circeto" is taken as a place-name but once again the "à" is not positioned at the start of the paragraph and has been replaced by a typically Rimbaldian reference to a precise moment plucked from indeterminate time. Consequently one feels that the original litany, so confidently presented, has been subverted and transformed. Even though the finale to "Dévotion" restores "à" to its original position of prominence ("A tout prix . . . "), and thus superficially re-establishes the poem's initial pattern or arrangement, the clearly transformed function of the preposition which is now part of a near cliché shows how far the text has developed away from its original form. [Nathaniel] Wing observes [in his *Present Appearances*, 1974] that "the text thus violates . . . the structure and the substance of the convention to which it alludes" and one can conclude that **"Dévotion"** leaves us poised on the frontier between integration and fragmentation and reminds us that Rimbaud rarely remains unquestioningly faithful to any particular pattern or structure. Nevertheless, his frequent use of anaphora indicates his constant and vigilant presence as artistic supervisor in the *Illuminations.* To replace the rigorous laws of verse with his own poetic architecture it is not his practice to adhere slavishly to an adopted anaphora but rather to employ it as one of several stabilizing agents which can be challenged to create a rich structural complexity. Thus the repeated "Il est . . . " formula used to define the messianic spirit in **"Génie"** is only one component in a poetic unit that contains many changes of tempo and direction; the reverberating "Aux . . . Aux . . . Aux . . . " at the start of successive sections in **"Démocratie"** creates a pattern for the eye and rhythm for the ear but, as in **"Dévotion"**, the function of the preposition is not rigidly fixed; and the alliterative "Du détroit . . . " and "Du désert . . . " that begin the first two paragraphs of **"Métropolitain"** invest the early stages of the poem with a measure of uniformity but the anaphora is not sustained beyond the second segment.

In all areas of his poetry Rimbaud reveals a strong interest in the world of fairy tales and, more importantly in this present context, in the "conte" and "conte de fées" as literary structures. In **"Délires II"** he cites the fairy tale among a host of sources of inspiration and pleasure and at the end of **"Adieu"** he chooses to see his artistic career in retrospect as that of a "conteur" who must now relinquish his gloriously unfettered daydreams and cope with a less palatable reality. At least three poems in the *Illuminations* (**"Conte"**, **"Aube"** and **"Royauté"**) take the form of a "conte" with Rimbaud as storyteller and these pieces derive considerable structural cohesion from the choice of this particular genre as a model.

Let us consider each of these three texts briefly in turn. Advertising itself in its self-conscious title as a piece of prose fiction, **"Conte"** has numerous characteristics which guarantee that it will conform to a significant extent to the canons of the parent genre. Depicting very familiar protagonists from legend and myth in the Prince and Génie, it has a distinct narrative thread as the "hero" seeks some elusive "bonheur" not to be had in the company of his courtiers and harlots. With the encounter between Prince and Génie we seem to have the necessary ingredients for the traditional "happy ending" and the *moralité* appended to the story, which reinforces the formal contours and structural base of the poem, is what we might expect from a fable or exemplary tale. Thus we have a narrative type of prose poem with a beginning, middle and end and which moves steadily towards a particular outcome. The description of the miraculous meeting of the two central figures is a good illustration of this structured and measured presentation:

> Un soir il galopait fièrement. Un Génie apparut,
> d'une beauté ineffable, inavouable même. De sa
> physionomie et de son maintien ressortait la pro-
> messe d'un amour multiple et complexe! d'un
> bonheur indicible, insupportable même!

Yet Rimbaud is rarely satisfied with a simple and predictable pattern. As Suzanne Bernard points out "tout ce qui ressemble à une composition linéaire fait horreur à Rimbaud" and there are other features in **"Conte"** that counterbalance the unifying effect of the narrative with the result that at times the poet seems to deviate from his source at least as much as he imitates it. The poem has its own distinctive form, involving sudden changes in tempo and surprising contradictions and reorientations. The opening paragraph provides the reader with searching psychological insights into the Prince and the thicket of obscure reference used prevents this from becoming a reassuringly conventional character portrait. From the measured pace of this initial description we move to the accelerated tempo of three shorter segments which narrate the attempts of the "hero" to obliterate his associates and immediate environment. There is a strange stop/go rhythm in this sequence as the victims of the Prince's rampage obstinately refuse to be exterminated and the narrative is punctured by the authorial intervention of Rimbaud that precedes the climax:

> Peut-on s'extasier dans la destruction, se ra-
> jeunir par la cruauté!

The return to the main storyline is marked by the temporal reference "Un soir" but it is extremely significant that Rimbaud deliberately undermines the "happy ending" that the appearance of the Génie seemed to guarantee by stressing in very prosaic language the natural death of the Prince "à un âge ordinaire" and through the device of the sibylline *morale* ("La musique savante manque à notre désir") which emphasises frustration and not fulfilment. All of these features draw attention to the unusual aspects of the poem and show that it is no ordinary "conte". As a text constructed on the fairy tale model it demonstrates Rimbaud's ability to lay down a broad structural foundation for his prose poems but its many violations of the normal development of a "conte" make of it a microcosm of the balance between logical arrangement and more spontaneous expression that the present study seeks to explore.

The much briefer piece **"Royauté"** has a similar relationship with the "conte" genre. Its title, the "Once upon a time" style of the opening words "Un beau matin", the promise of happiness implicit in the deliverance from suffering spoken of by the heirs apparent in their address to the populace and the solid narrative structure of the poem with its clearly marked beginning and end—all of these features suggest close adherence to the conventions of the fairy tale. Yet **"Royauté"** is no simple imitation of a pre-existing pattern for it has several important elements of presentation which set up a fascinating play of familiarity and innovation, predictability and surprise, tradition and experimentation. As in **"Conte"** there is an ironic subversion of the motif of the "happy ending" for, while the first paragraph is positive and anticipatory, the second is cynical and retrospective. The poet deflates his myth before signing off. Moreover, the very brevity of the text is disconcerting and creates a tension between it and the model on which it is based for while the tale is usually extensive, the poem is disarmingly intensive. What presents itself as a story turns out to be little more than two juxtaposed tableaux and the brevity of the poem mirrors that of the couple's reign. The trappings of regal splendour ("tentures carminées", "palmes") are just glimpsed in what amounts to a truncated "conte" with a beginning and end but no middle section to facilitate character and plot development. Thus while the simplicity and rhythmical harmony of the poem's brief narrative again remind us of Rimbaud's search for order and pattern in the *Illuminations,* the less conventional formal aspects of **"Royauté"** serve notice of his instinctive rejection of any form that might become repressive and stifling and of his desire to exploit the flexibility of the prose poem to develop more mobile and pliable structures.

In a collection renowned for its "illisibilité", the poem **"Aube"** is often seen as a very accessible piece that describes a child's walk on a summer morning in such a way that it can be interpreted as an allegory of the search for truth and transcendence. However it is possible to assimilate **"Aube"** to the type of narrative prose poem under review here. As in *Le Bateau ivre* where the poet relates a voyage that is part of his personal mythology, so in **"Aube"** Rimbaud offers an almost exclusively first personal account of a precious imaginative experience. The special relationship between the child and the natural world produces a legendary adventure and a fairy-tale aura similar to that found in **"Conte"** and **"Royauté"**. The text has a clear and orthodox narrative structure as the child's pursuit of the "déesse" is charted through its various stages to the moment of climax:

> En haut de la route, près d'un bois de lauriers,
> je l'ai entourée avec ses voiles amassés, et j'ai

senti un peu son immense corps. L'aube et l'enfant tombèrent au bas du bois.

The generally simple language of the poem, the sequence of events leading from the initial description of the pre-dawn period to the physical contact with the goddess and the structured development of the text from the awakening of the natural world at the start to the second awakening of the child at the end all confer upon **"Aube"** a marked regularity and harmony. Nevertheless, like the other narrative pieces analysed above, this text has several special characteristics that arouse one's interest in its formal presentation. The conspicuously positioned first and last sentences frame the poem, emphasise its configuration to the reader and might remind one of the curtain going up and coming down on a stage performance; the first sentence ("J'ai embrassé l'aube d'été") seems to divulge the denouement prematurely but in retrospect withholds the ultimately ironic ending; and Rimbaud's abandonment of the first personal form in the penultimate sentence is a surprising development that introduces a note of cynical disenchantment which could not have been foreseen. Indeed each of these three poems has a factual and prosaic finale that breaks the spell of the "conte". Despite these departures from the selected source, however, the very fact that Rimbaud has decided to construct several poems on a narrative model ensures that another element of stability is injected into the *Illuminations,* a collection often so erroneously said to be devoid of any evidence of lucid composition.

The other half of the duality under consideration involves disorder, formlessness and discontinuity and here again we can identify three stylistic features of the *Illuminations* which generate these effects—the exaltation of the individual word, the spontaneous accelerations and decelerations present in many poems and the freshly revised role of punctuation that brings it more powerfully into play as a dynamic textual force. While the crucial declaration in **"Mauvais sang"** which reads "Je veux la liberté dans le salut" obviously relates in that context to the poet's spiritual crisis, it has an application to the sort of poetic structures one finds in the *Illuminations.* We have just outlined three avenues towards "salut" or security in an artistic sense and the three features that we shall now proceed to examine are corresponding paths that lead to "liberté", expression free from the inhibitions of logical and conscious arrangement and the strait-jacket of verse. Implicit in the letter to Demeny of May 15, 1871 is the idea of surprise as an aesthetic and it is a major hallmark of Rimbaud's idiom that it has the capacity to induce an acute sense of *dépaysement* in the reader through the unanticipated appearance of a perplexing term from its shifting verbal strata. One recalls the directive issued to the poet in the verse piece "Ce qu'on dit au poète à propos de fleurs":

> De tes noirs Poèmes,—Jongleur!
> Blancs, verts, et rouges dioptriques,
> Que s'évadent d'étranges fleurs
> Et des papillons électriques!

Here the poet is the conjurer who dispenses multicoloured visionary surprises from the dark depths of his poems and in the ***Illuminations*** Rimbaud continues to be the "Jongleur" who creates linguistic surprises which are no less powerful. Many individual words in the collection stand mysteriously before us as both provocation and enigma, leaving the reader uncertain about their origin, significance and relevance to their context. (pp. 248-61)

> *Gerald M. Macklin, "Aspects of the Rimbaldian Prose Poem: Pattern and Disorder in the 'Illuminations',"* in Orbis Litterarum, *Vol. 45, No. 3, 1990, pp. 248-72.*

FURTHER READING

Biography

Bianco, Joseph. "The Unvisioned Poet: Rimbaud's Middle Year." *Symposium* XLII, No. 2 (Summer 1988): 83-99.

Inquiry into the interval between September 1871 and the spring of 1872, during which Rimbaud wrote no poetry.

Bodenham, C. H. L. "Arthur Rimbaud: Poetry and After." *The Modern Language Review* 77, No. 2 (April 1982): 294-309.

Attempts to reconcile the periods of Rimbaud's life before and after 1874, the year he renounced poetry.

Ullman, James Ramsey. *The Day on Fire: A Novel Suggested by the Life of Arthur Rimbaud.* Cleveland: World Publishing Co., 1958, 701 p.

Fictionalized biography aimed at young adult readers.

Criticism

Ahearn, Edward J. "Explosions of the Real: Rimbaud's Ecstatic and Political Subversions." *Stanford French Review* IX, No. 1 (Spring 1985): 71-81.

Interprets "Fleurs," "Barbare," and "Soir historique" as poems that suggest "an elemental, prerational mode of experience."

Balakian, Anna. "A Spiritual Crisis." In her *Literary Origins of Surrealism: A New Mysticism in French Poetry,* pp. 62-97. New York: King's Crown Press, 1947.

Highlights the childlike qualities that Rimbaud brought to French literature.

———. "Verlaine, Not Rimbaud." In her *The Symbolist Movement: A Critical Appraisal,* pp. 54-71. New York: Random House, 1967.

Emphasizes Paul Verlaine's influence on French poetry, calling Rimbaud "a flash of lightning too swift and too bright to leave more than a dazzling but ephemeral impression behind."

Bays, Gwendolyn M. "Rimbaud—Father of Surrealism?" *Yale French Studies,* No. 31 (May 1964): 45-51.

Examines Rimbaud's influence on André Breton.

Behrens, Ralph. "Baudelaire and Rimbaud: Their Voyages." *Modern Language Quarterly* 18, No. 1 (March 1957): 69-71.

Focuses on the differences between Charles Baudelaire's "Le voyage" and Rimbaud's *Le bateau ivre.*

Bodenham, C. H. L. "Rimbaud's 'Poétique Sensationniste' and some Nineteenth-Century Medical Writing." *French Studies* XXXVIII, No. 1 (January 1984): 32-40.

Notes the incorporation of medical language into Rimbaud's poetry.

Chadwick, C. *Rimbaud.* Athlone French Poets, edited by Eileen Le Breton. London: Athlone Press, 1979, 151 p.

Focuses on Rimbaud's evolution as a writer.

Chisolm, A. R. *The Art of Arthur Rimbaud.* Melbourne: Melbourne University Press, 1930, 66 p.

Describes Rimbaud's revolutionary aesthetics.

Dillman, Karin J. *The Subject of Rimbaud: From Self to 'Je'.* New York: Peter Lang, 1984, 149 p.

Critical study focusing on "the problem of the subject *je* [I], its role in the creative process, and its nature and function in the text."

Ferguson, J. A. " 'Noirs Inconnus': The Identity and Function of the Negro in Rimbaud's Poetry and Correspondence." *French Studies* XXXIX, No. 1 (January 1985): 43-58.

Inquiry into Rimbaud's racial beliefs.

Fusco, Susan Wirth. *Syntactic Structure in Rimbaud's "Illuminations": A Stylistic Approach to the Analysis of Form in Prose Poetry.* University, Miss.: Romance Monographs, 1990, 177 p.

Contains chapters on "Patterns of Intensification" and "Disjunctive Patterns" in *Illuminations.*

Hackett, C. A. *Rimbaud: A Critical Introduction.* New York: Cambridge University Press, 1981, 167 p.

Includes chapters on Rimbaud's best-known works, a chronological table, and a bibliography.

Herring, Phillip. "Joyce and Rimbaud: An Introductory Essay." In *James Joyce: An International Perspective,* edited by Suheil Badi Bashrui and Bernard Benstock, pp. 170-89. Totowa, N.J.: Barnes and Noble, 1982.

Notes Joyce's admiration for Rimbaud as a rebel against tradition.

Hiddleston, J. A. "Rimbaud's 'Larme' and the 'gourde de colocase'." *Romance Notes* XXIII, No. 3 (Spring 1983): 227-31.

Asserts that the poem captures a pivotal moment in Rimbaud's career: "We are left in 'Larme' with the pitiful picture of the poet, cut off from the paradise of his childhood, disappointed with the experience of escape, defeated, and with a thirst which no drink can quench."

Houston, John Porter. "The Symbolic Structure of Rimbaud's Hell." *Modern Language Quarterly* 21, No. 1 (March 1960): 69-72.

Contradicts the idea that *Une Saison en enfer* is Rimbaud's farewell to poetry, arguing instead for an understanding of the poem as "a myth of fall and redemption."

———. "Sexual Allusions and Scholarship: Observations on Rimbaud Studies." *Nineteenth-Century French Studies* 15, Nos. 1-2 (Fall-Winter 1986-87): 162-72.

Inquiry into sexual puns and metaphors in Rimbaud's poetry.

Houston, Robert W. "Hart Crane and Arthur Rimbaud: A Comparison." In *Essays in Honor of Richebourg Gaillard McWilliams,* edited by Howard Creed, pp. 13-19. Birmingham, Ala.: Birmingham-Southern College, 1970.

Numbers among the two poets' common subjects: "waters, wings, Negroes . . . , idealized female figures . . . , Indians, cities, bridges, polar regions, intense colors, flowers—concrete, often sensual things for the most part, but always with a love for the mysterious in evidence."

Israel, Abigail. "The Aesthetic of Violence: Rimbaud and Genet." *Yale French Studies,* No. 46 (1971): 28-40.

Compares the two writers as creators of "a nightmare aesthetic."

Lawler, James. "The Unity of 'Being Beauteous'." *French Studies* XL, No. 2 (April 1986): 167-73.

Highlights the revolutionary aspects of the poem.

———. "The Poet as Self-Critic: Rimbaud's 'Jeunesse'." *The French Review* 62, No. 1 (October 1988): 11-24.

Views the poem "Jeunesse" as a radical exploration of "the bond between poetry and the world."

Little, Roger. "Rimbaud's 'Sonnet'." *The Modern Language Review* 75, Part 3 (July 1980): 528-33.

Asserts that Rimbaud's title "Sonnet" is intentionally obscure.

Macklin, G. M. "A Study of Beginnings and Finales in Arthur Rimbaud's *Illuminations.*" *Neophilologus* LXVIII, No. 1 (January 1984): 22-36.

Structural analysis of the poems in *Illuminations* finding "it is often the function of a finale to compel the reader to reassess impressions formed earlier in the poem."

———. "The Theatrical Imagination of Arthur Rimbaud." *Forum for Modern Language Studies* 23, No. 2 (April 1987): 131-50.

Interpretation of Rimbaud's poems as theatrical performances.

———. "Perspectives on the Role of Punctuation in Rimbaud's *Illuminations.*" *Journal of European Studies* 20, Part 1, No. 77 (March 1990): 59-72.

Views Rimbaud's unorthodox punctuation in the context of his larger poetic ambitions.

Metzidakis, Stamos. "Did Rimbaud Really Know His Alphabet?" *Nineteenth-Century French Studies* 14, Nos. 3-4 (Spring-Summer 1986): 278-83.

Maintains that the sequence of vowels in the sonnet "Voyelles" brings to mind the Greek alphabet as well as the French.

Minogue, Valerie. "Rimbaud's Ophelia." *French Studies* XLIII, No. 4 (October 1989): 423-36.

Surveys the critical response to "Ophélie" and offers a new interpretation of the poem.

Monroe, Jonathan. "Narrative, History, Verse Undone: The Prose Poetry of Rimbaud." In his *A Poverty of Objects: The Prose Poem and the Politics of Genre,* pp. 125-54. Ithaca, N.Y.: Cornell University Press, 1987.

Discusses the themes and techniques of Rimbaud's prose poems.

Osmond, Nick. "Rimbaud's *Illuminations:* 'Les repentires du copiste'." *The Modern Language Review* 76, No. 1 (January 1981): 60-6.

Study of Rimbaud's manuscript corrections to *Illuminations.*

Perloff, Marjorie. " 'Trouver une langue': The *Anti-paysage* of Rimbaud." In her *The Poetics of Indeterminacy: Rimbaud to Cage,* pp. 45-66. Princeton, N.J.: Princeton University Press, 1981.

Considers Rimbaud an aesthetic model for some of the most radical writers and artists of the twentieth century.

Porter, Laurence M. "Artistic Self-Consciousness in Rimbaud's Poetry." In his *The Crisis of French Symbolism,* pp. 191-252. Ithaca: Cornell University Press, 1990.

Views Rimbaud's prose poetry as politically and formally subversive.

Rhodes, Enid H. "Under the Spell of Africa: Poems and Letters of Arthur Rimbaud Inspired by the Dark Continent." *The French Review* XLIV, No. 2 (Winter 1971): 20-8.

Analyzes Rimbaud's ambivalence toward Africa and Africans.

Rhodes, S. A. "Arthur Rimbaud's Readings." *Modern Language Notes* LIII, No. 5 (May 1938): 334-40.

Speculates on Rimbaud's education during his formative years and lists the books available at the library in Charleville that may have interested him.

Rifelj, Carol de Dobay. "Rimbaud: Poetics and Politics." In her *Word and Figure: The Language of Nineteenth-Century French Poetry,* pp. 132-64. Columbus: Ohio State University Press, 1987.

Focuses on "A la musique" and "L'Orgie parisienne," noting parallels between Rimbaud's political views and poetic methods.

Riffaterre, Michael. "Interpretation and Undecidability." *New Literary History* 12, No. 2 (Winter 1981): 227-42.

Defense of semiotics as a tool for interpreting literature, using texts by Rimbaud as test cases.

Roditi, Edouard. "A French Poet and His English Critics." *The Sewanee Review* 52, No. 1 (January-March 1944): 102-17.

Surveys the early response of English critics to Rimbaud, finding that while George Moore, Arthur Symons, and Charles Whibley merely echoed romantic myths of the poet, Count S. C. de Soissons provided an intelligent and thoughtful response in his article in the *Contemporary Review* of April 1912.

Ross, Kristin. *The Emergence of Social Space: Rimbaud and the Paris Commune.* Theory and History of Literature, Vol. 60, edited by Wlad Godzich and Jochen Schulte-Sasse. Minneapolis: University of Minnesota Press, 1988, 170 p.

Biographical and critical study of Rimbaud informed by Marxism and spatial theory.

"The Malady of Rimbaud." *The Saturday Review* (London) 138, No. 3,593 (6 September 1924): 235.

Discusses Rimbaud's renunciation of poetry at the age of nineteen.

Saurat, Denis. "A Portent—Rimbaud: 1854-73-91." In his *Modern French Literature: 1870-1940,* pp. 8-10. Port Washington, N.Y.: Kennikat Press, 1946.

Describes the quality that Rimbaud brought to French

literature: "something hard, cruel, unjust, unromantic, a new departure of genius cutting off the past."

Smith, Madeleine M. "The Theme of the Hunt in Rimbaud: *La chasse spirituelle.*" *PMLA* 64, No. 3, Part 1 (June 1949): 325-39.

Explores instances of violent death in Rimbaud's poetry.

Spicer, Jack. "A Fake Novel about the Life of Arthur Rimbaud." In *The Collected Books of Jack Spicer,* edited by Robin Blaser, pp. 149-67. Santa Barbara, Calif.: Black Sparrow Press, 1980.

Series of vignettes—some satirical, some enigmatic—pertaining to Rimbaud's life and works.

St. Aubyn, F. C. *Arthur Rimbaud.* Updated edition. Boston: Twayne Publishers, 1988, 176 p.

General introduction to Rimbaud's life and works.

Weinberg, Bernard. "*Le Bateau Ivre,* or the Limits of Symbolism." *PMLA* LXXII, No. 1 (January 1959): 165-93.

Discusses the literal and symbolic meaning of the poem.

Zimmermann, Eléonore M. "Mallarmé and Rimbaud in Crisis." In *Writing in a Modern Temper: Essays on French Literature and Thought in Honor of Henri Peyre,* pp. 102-16. Saratoga, Calif.: Anma Libri, 1984.

Argues that the two poets experienced similar periods of "trial and initiation" in their quests for enlightenment.

Additional coverage of Rimbaud's life and career is contained in the following sources published by Gale Research: *Nineteenth-Century Literature Criticism,* Vol. 4 and *Poetry Criticism,* Vol. 3.

Thomas William Robertson

1829-1871

English dramatist.

INTRODUCTION

A dramatist best known for his romantic comedies, Robertson is associated with the transitional period in English theater during which playwrights began to incorporate greater realism into a genre previously noted for its extravagant artificiality and melodramatic style. Robertson's plays feature realistic characterizations and dialogue as well as meticulous directions concerning details of staging and production. Although some have dismissed Robertson's innovations as being of an extremely limited nature, his move toward a more realistic theater heralded a trend which later culminated in the works of Henrik Ibsen and Bernard Shaw and is widely viewed as a significant contribution to the development of modern drama.

Robertson was born in 1829 in Newark, Nottinghamshire, to a theatrical family. His parents were both actors—his father was a stage manager as well—and his youngest sister became a leading Victorian actress under the name Madge Kendal. Robertson made his stage debut at the age of five in the musical drama *Rob Roy*. In 1836 he began his formal education at a boarding school, but he returned to Newark after only seven years to help support his family. Working as an assistant to his father, he learned much about various aspects of the theater including scene-painting, prompting, stage-managing, acting, singing, and song-writing. In 1849 his father's theater company disbanded and Robertson went to London, where he began writing plays while continuing to act in minor productions. In 1856 he married an actress named Elizabeth Burton, and together they performed at the Theatre Royal, Dublin, where Robertson also worked as stage manager. In the late fifties he gave up acting and began writing dramatic reviews with W. S. Gilbert for the periodical *Fun*. He also contributed to the *Illustrated Times, London Society, Comic News,* and other publications, eventually becoming the drama critic for the *Illustrated Times* under the pseudonym "Theatrical Lounger." He gained additional writing experience adapting and translating French plays, most of which were sold to Thomas Haile Lacy, the leading theatrical publisher. After achieving minor success with *David Garrick,* an adaptation of a French play by Mélesville (the pseudonym of Anne-Honoré-Joseph Duveyrier), Robertson was introduced to Squire Bancroft and his wife Marie Wilton, actors who owned the Prince of Wales's Theatre. The Bancrofts produced and acted in Robertson's most successful plays—*Society, Ours, Caste, Play, School,* and *The M. P.*—between 1865 and 1870. Robertson died of heart disease in 1871, at the height of his career.

Intended as entertainments for a middle-class audience, most of Robertson's plays are romantic comedies that treat social issues of the day in an idealized manner. Many concern issues of class, satirizing the pretensions of the aristocracy and the nouveau riche and ultimately upholding the values of the middle class. *Society,* for example, depicts a poor but honest man who achieves a title, property, and a seat in Parliament as the result of his moral character. His morality is sharply contrasted with that of the upper class, which is depicted as valuing only wealth. Similarly, in *Caste,* Robertson's best-known play, a young actress earns the respect and affection of her aristocratic husband's family by patiently enduring hardship and censure. In other plays, Robertson depicted conflicts between the aristocracy, with its devotion to tradition, and the rising middle class, which favors social change. Robertson was one of the first English dramatists to bring timely social issues to the stage, yet critics note that his treatment of those issues was similar to that of earlier Romantic dramatists in its reliance upon the redeeming power of worthwhile sentiments.

Although conventional in sentiment, Robertson's plays were markedly different from those of his predecessors in terms of dialogue, characterization, and staging. Seeking to avoid the exaggeration and bombast of earlier Victorian acting methods, he created characters who spoke in a realistic manner and provided his actors with elaborate directions concerning facial expression, hand gestures, and vocal intonation. In addition, his dialogues are composed of short speeches that require the actors to address one another, thus avoiding the prevailing declamatory style. Robertson augmented this dramatic realism by insisting on authenticity in his stage sets, which included furniture and backdrops that clearly depicted the settings of his plays, and making extensive use of props, including real food. Robertson's combination of stage realism with a focus on themes drawn from English life of the period is considered his most significant contribution to the English drama.

Robertson's plays were extraordinarily successful with contemporary audiences who enjoyed their depiction of middle-class values and concerns. Although some nineteenth-century critics derided his plays as "cup and saucer comedies" for their attention to physical detail, most praised his attempt to mirror reality on the stage. His unique use of stage directions was appreciated by later playwrights who acknowledged their debt to his innovations. W. S. Gilbert offered this tribute: "Most pieces are now stage-managed on the principles he introduced. I look upon stage-management, as now understood, as having been absolutely invented by him." Although many critics praised Robertson's contributions to dramatic production methods, they did not see any literary value in the plays, which were rarely performed after the 1890s. In addition, the dramatic changes subsequently brought to the stage by such Realists as Ibsen and Shaw overshadowed the efforts of Robertson and many of his contemporaries. Recent scholarship, however, has brought renewed awareness of Robertson's contributions to the theater, and William Tydeman has commented: "[Robertson's] plays do convey something of the quality of everyday existence where meals are eaten, watches consulted, pipes smoked, peas shelled, half-crowns borrowed, and galoshes fetched. . . . In introducing even a hint of these factors into his pieces Robertson cautiously unbolted a door which bolder spirits were to fling wide."

PRINCIPAL WORKS

Castles in the Air (drama) 1854
Faust and Marguerite (drama) 1854
The Half Caste; or, the Poisoned Pearl (drama) 1856
Peace at Any Price (drama) 1856
David Garrick [adaptor; from the drama *Sullivan* by Mélesville] (drama) 1864
Society (drama) 1865
Ours (drama) 1866
Caste (drama) 1867
Play (drama) 1868
Progress [adaptor; from the drama *Les ganaches* by Victorien Sardou] (drama) 1869
School [adaptor; from the drama *Aschenbrödel* by Roderick Benedix] (drama) 1869

Birth (drama) 1870
The M.P. (drama) 1870
War (drama) 1871
Principal Dramatic Works. 2 vols. (drama) 1889
Six Plays (drama) 1980

John Oxenford   (essay date 1867)

[*The following essay, originally published in* The Times *in 1867, is a favorable review of* Caste *which praises Robertson's distinctive style.*]

Mr. T. W. Robertson's new comedy, entitled **Caste,** belongs exactly to the class of drama, of which we have already had specimens in **Society** and **Ours,** and which the experience of two years has led us to associate with one particular author and one particular theatre. The 'sensational' melodrama called **Shadow Tree Shaft,** recently brought out at another house, though likewise written by Mr. Robertson, was no type of his manner, and might be regarded as an interruption to the series, which began at the Prince of Wales's with **Society,** and which is now continued in **Caste.** An epigrammatic tendency, which not only shows itself in the dialogue, but points the entire fable; a predilection for domestic pathos, which is ever kept in check by a native abhorrence of twaddling sentimentality; a firm, steady hand, and a freedom from convention in the delineations of character; an eye to picturesque effects, that arise less from the employment of accessories than from the arrangement of groups that are the natural result of the action, and a connexion with the realities, which, perhaps, must not be too closely scrutinized, but which, to a certain extent, makes the stage reflect the world with more than usual accuracy—these are the characteristics which distinguish the best works of Mr. T. W. Robertson, and which have made each of them one of the leading pieces of its season. Nor is there any reason to surmise that the success of **Caste** will prove inferior to that of **Ours.**

As might be inferred from its title, the comedy **Caste** treats of that distinction between various grades of society which, among the Brahmins, is marked by express law, and which among the more western representatives of the great Aryan race, is drawn by a prejudice which has scarcely less than legal force. Since all modern plays must have some reference to love, the question of *mésalliance* naturally presents itself as offering the ground on which the social battle is to be fought. King Cophetua must marry his beggar girl, and the point for artistic discussion is how far he is right and how far wrong.

A play being a work of art addressed to a very mixed assembly the debate will of necessity take a somewhat democratic turn. The brutal way of handling the subject is boldly to revert to what the French call the principles of '89, and to declare that the beggar girl, *qua* beggar girl, was quite as good, if not better, than his Ethiopian Majesty. A more 'shirky' method is to clothe the beggar girl with all the exceptional attributes proper to birth and cultivation, and then dexterously to insinuate that she is a fair average type of mendicity in general. But Mr. Robertson, while impelled by the theatrical Parcæ towards a democratic goal, which he is likewise forced to reach, provides himself with a good conservative snaffle, and is scrupulously careful that his audience shall not mistake a sentiment for a principle. The Hon. George d'Alroy, with the commingled blood of French and English aristocracy in his veins, and with infinite pecuniary resources, marries the Columbine of a minor theatre, and the union proves to be one which gods might sanction, as they did the nuptials of Peleus and Thetis, but he is anxious to show that the example of George d'Alroy is not to be followed without a vast deal of circumspection. Even the model condition of *mésalliance* which is presented in his history is fraught with obstacles which cannot be regarded as exceptional, and which constantly threaten to destroy every chance of felicity. If Columbine is one of nature's ladies, she has a father whom nature, as well as convention, would shrink from acknowledging as a gentleman, and he is sure to be manifest when his appearance is least desirable.

The plot is excellently constructed for the purpose of exhibiting and grasping the various characters. The Hon. George d'Alroy (Mr. Frederick Younge), son of the Marquise de Saint-Maur (Miss Larkin), an English lady of high birth, married to a French nobleman, has fallen in love with Esther (Miss Lydia Foote), daughter of Eccles (Mr. George Honey), a dissipated specimen of the working man, who does no work, and during the absence of his mother on the Continent visits the humble residence of the plebeian in the character of an honourable suitor. He is accompanied by his friend Captain Hawtree (Mr. Sydney Bancroft), who lectures him from a worldly point of view on the danger he is encountering by entering into a family so much below him in rank. Old Eccles is simply detestable, his two daughters support themselves and him by dancing at the 'Theatre Royal Lambeth' (wherever that may be), and, though Esther, the object of his choice, is a girl of superior manners, the same cannot be said of her sister, Polly (Miss Marie Wilton), who is a damsel of very blunt manners, engaged to Sam Gerridge (Mr. Hare), a worthy gasfitter, who neither tries nor even desires to elevate himself above his order. The reasoning of Captain Hawtree, specious as it is, has no effect on his fascinated friend, who to prevent his beloved Esther from accepting an engagement at Manchester proposes a speedy marriage, leaving to the destinies the office of settling difficulties with his mother as best they may.

When the second act begins the union has taken place, and eight months have elapsed. The scene of action is now removed from the 'little house in Stangate' to an elegant apartment in Mayfair, the residence of George d'Alroy and his young wife. A gloom is on the brow of the husband, which, however, arises not from regret at the matrimonial step he has taken, but from the fact that the regiment to which he and his friend Hawtree are attached is ordered to India on account of the Sepoy mutiny. This fact he has feared to communicate to Esther, thinking that the shock may be too great for her, and he would gladly transfer the unpleasant office to Hawtree, who in his turn is of opinion that the task of breaking the ice had best be con-

fided to Polly, whose opportune call seems to promise a solution of the difficulty. But in a few moments another visit of a more portentous kind is paid. The formidable Marquise has returned unexpectedly from the Continent, totally ignorant of her son's marriage, and comes prepared to take leave of him prior to his departure for the wars. The announcement of her arrival is a signal for the two sisters to conceal themselves in an ante-room, and the Marquise finding herself alone with George commences a maternal lecture. As becomes an unquestionable daughter of the Plantagenets, whom, with lofty pedantry, she prefers to call the 'Plantagenistæ', the favourite author of the good old lady is Froissart, whole passages from whose chronicles she pours into her son's ear, who finds himself pelted by their aristocratic tendency, and 'bored' by their length. At last there is a beam of sunshine. The old lady, after exhorting her boy to distinguish himself by the most chivalrous valour, changes the topic, and preaches in eloquent terms against the sin of seduction, extolling the love of a woman as something that soars high above all social distinctions. Poor George begins to fancy that this is just the right moment to confess his *mésalliance,* but unfortunately his mother's words have conveyed the first intimation of his approaching departure to the sisters hidden in the adjoining room, and a scream from Esther, who has fainted, causes the truth to be revealed without due preparation. The marquise is not a little displeased so suddenly to find herself the mother-in-law of a young person of whose existence she was not aware a minute before, and the conduct of Polly, who has a rough spirit of independence, does not tend towards conciliation. Still, as Esther is a most presentable person, and Polly is tolerably free from offence when her temper is not ruffled, matters would not be altogether desperate, did not the horrible old Eccles stagger into the room sodden with drink, accompanied by Sam Gerridge, who, though gifted with every virtue, has been niggardly in his worship of the Graces, and who in his best clothes looks even more plebeian than in his working attire. Horrified at the company by which she is surrounded, the Marquise seizes the arm of Captain Hawtree and sails from the room, while poor Esther takes leave of her husband and falls senseless to the ground. We may here pause to remark that this second act is a masterpiece of constructive skill. Every movement that takes place occurs naturally, and answers a definite purpose, the whole act being, indeed, one situation gradually developed till it reaches its highest point of effectiveness.

Eighteen months have elapsed, and when the third act begins Esther is again at the 'little house in Stangate', her father having lost all her money by low gambling. She wears a widow's dress, for news has arrived of the death of George in India, and at the back of the room is a crib, containing an infant to whom she had given birth since her husband's departure, and who, while the delight of his mother and aunt, is execrated by his hateful grandfather as an oppressive young aristocrat. The chief tyranny of the child consists in wearing a gold coral during a period of distress, when spirituous liquor is scarce in the establishment, and old Eccles thinks that he does but assert the rights of man when he detaches the 'gaud' from the baby's neck, with the intent to convert it into ready cash at the nearest pawnbrokers. The little operation is prevented by

Esther, who immediately becomes a Goneril in the eyes of her father, and she has presently another battle to fight with the Marquise, who, hearing of her distressed condition, calls upon her, offering to take upon herself the care of the child, and who, indignantly repulsed, indignantly retires, much to the disgust of old Eccles, whose democratic proclivities have entirely vanished, and who now jumps at an alliance which promises to be lucrative as well as aristocratic. Captain Hawtree, who has returned from India, proves a kind friend to Esther, and at last happiness is restored by the reappearance of George d'Alroy, who, of course, was not really dead, but escaped from the Sepoys, and who is amazed to find his wife a widow and himself a father. The joy felt by the Marquise at her son's return is too great to allow her to retain any feeling of resentment against Esther, and the curtain drops on a general condition of happiness, the long duration of which may be surmised from the fact that old Eccles, in consideration of an annuity, promises to live in Jersey, and there, liquor being cheap, to do his best to drink himself to death.

As a specimen of construction the third act is not to be compared with the second. We feel that George is killed and brought to life again just as his death or life happens to be useful, and that the change in the temper of the Marquise is due rather to the necessity of bringing the story to a happy close than to the operation of any moral law. A little compression, too, might be effected with advantage.

Nevertheless, the defects of the third act are more than compensated by the admirable character of old Eccles, which here reaches its fullest development. It is not impossible that the hint of this character was taken from the father of the 'Dolls' dressmaker' in Mr. Charles Dickens's *Mutual Friend,* but Mr. Robertson by endowing the sot with political attributes has given him an aspect which is peculiarly significant at the present time. Eccles is a degraded mortal, who is always howling about the rights of labour, but who has scarcely been known to do a 'stroke of work' within the memory of his best friends. He hates the aristocracy in theory, but is ready to lick the shoe of a person of quality if anything is to be made by the degradation. That democratic claptrap which is among the leading nuisances of the day is satirized in this character with the most unsparing severity, and the moral effect of the part is heightened by the contrast of Eccles with Sam Gerridge, intended as a good specimen of the operative class. A less conservative writer would have found an opportunity for putting a little claptrap into the mouth of honest Sam, but such operations are not to the taste of Mr. Robertson. Sam is not at all idealized, nor are his uncouth appearance or the vulgar Terpsichorean feats which he performs under the influence of excessive joy accompanied by the possession of lofty sentiments. He is honest, industrious, and good-natured, has an eye ever directed to the main chance, and respects his own 'caste' without less respecting that of others. He has a fitting partner in Polly Eccles, whose character is in the main similar to his own, though a tinge of feminine coquetry gives her somewhat the tone of a fine lady. These three parts are as well played as they can possibly be by Mr. George Honey, Mr. Hare, and Miss Marie Wilton.

In the treatment of those of his personages who belong to the other 'caste' Mr. Robertson still preserves his independence. The reader of the plot given above will probably imagine that George is a romantic youth intended to charm all the young ladies in the stalls—a noble creature with a soul too big for conventional bondage. He is nothing of the sort, but a slow, 'spooney' youth, with a thickness of utterance which, totally distinct from a fashionable lisp, suggests a density of intellect. Luck, not wisdom, has guided him to the choice of such an excellent person as Esther. Had Fortune been less kindly his career might have been similar to that of the young man whose eccentricities proved so profitable a few years since to the members of the legal profession. He has an excellent heart and a high spirit, but these can only show themselves under the influence of some pressure from without, the general manner being stolid and heavy. Let us add that he is intrusted to an essentially comic actor, Mr. F. Younge, who thoroughly understands his qualities, as Mr. Bancroft does those of the more decided 'swell', Captain Hawtree, who is marked by an ungainliness of another kind, and who is intended to show that a man is not necessarily hateful, even though he becomes almost boorish in his desire to be aristocratically exclusive. Neither is the loftiness of the Marquise to be rebuked with a scowl. She is not raised on a pedestal to be knocked down, but represents a social principle, and is to be respected accordingly. This is a part exactly in the line of Miss Larkin, and is represented to the life by Miss Larkin.

The one ideal personage of the play is Esther, who is entirely distinct from her sister Polly, and in whom the boundary marks of 'caste' vanish, though it is on her account that the battle of 'caste' is fought. The author has even given her an aristocratic tinge, and when her spirit is roused she does not assert plebeian independence like Polly, but speaks as Mrs. George d'Alroy, mother of a child of ancient lineage. To Esther belong the strong situations, and generally what may be called the hard work of the piece. The part is most efficiently filled by Miss Lydia Foote.

The success of *Caste* is indubitable, and there is one fact to which we would draw attention before bringing our somewhat lengthy notice to a close. Not only are the characters typical of a lower 'caste', entirely free from claptrap, as we have already remarked, but Old Eccles, with his humbug Jacobinism, would be a positive offence to an audience composed of fanatical levellers, nor would the solid unshining virtues of Sam Gerridge be much more acceptable. Nevertheless, the occupants of the gallery, who are numerous, sanction the author's work, regarding Eccles as a proper object of derision and Sam as a person to be respected. Let it be remembered, too, that the Prince of Wales's Theatre, though it has been fashionable for two years, is by no means in a fashionable neighbourhood, and that the gallery must be peopled by many of those working men who patronized it when it was the humble 'Queen's'. That such an assembly is pleased with an exhibition which is of a most anti-demogogic kind is a fact worth noting by those who take an interest in the study of the real operative of London. (pp. 132-41)

John Oxenford, in a review of "Caste," in Specimens of English Dramatic Criticism XVII—XX Centuries, *edited by A. C. Ward, Oxford University Press, London, 1945, pp. 132-41.*

J. Hain Friswell   (essay date 1870)

[*Friswell was an English novelist and essayist. In the following excerpt, he discusses Robertson's background as an actor and his success at the Prince of Wales's Theatre.*]

There is no approval so delightful as a full house; no criticism so damning as a beggarly account of empty boxes. Hence the decline of the Drama, and hence the merit of the courageous endeavour of Mr. Robertson to render one English theatre at least worthy of the name, and to present a comedy which reflected the manners of the age, and justly satirised the follies of the day. This, too, at a time when almost all the plays that we have are stolen or taken from the French, without leave often, frequently with the consent of the authors; dramas which cannot possibly picture English manners, which have almost all of them a stain of original sin so deep that it cannot always be washed away by any amount of English cleansing powder, and which if washed away leaves the adaptation weak, colourless, and worthless.

Mr. Thomas William Robertson is one of those few dramatic authors who have been originally actors. The great name of Shakespeare heads the list; those of Carrick, Tobin, Colley Cibber, Buckstone, and a few others have to be included; but it follows that either the author is a bad actor, or, if a good actor, he is a poor and weak author. The one *rôle* must subordinate the other. Colley Cibber succeeded in both if we take his *Careless Husband* as a specimen, but in general the actor-author is a mistake. Dramatic literature has a despotic Muse who will not be conciliated with a merely partial courtship. Shakespeare taught one actor how to read his Ghost in *Hamlet,* and himself made but a lame representative of old Adam in *As You Like it.* Mr. Robertson, we believe, never achieved distinction as an actor, and indeed was, we have been told, little better than a second-rate walking gentleman at second-rate theatres. But he gained therefrom an immense knowledge of stage business and effect, and that chief part of knowledge, to know what to say and to say no more. He never overloads his parts; he writes with excessive neatness, and taking the measure of his audience, never treats it—whatever may be its component parts—to any deep reflections, poetical rhapsodies, long lengths of verse or measured prose, or pathos of any depth. What he means is always transparent, and hence his jokes never miss fire. He has been seconded by such good actors and actresses that, although by no means acute, they seem to be so, for while his plays really display their own merit more than any other writings that we know of, and in a very clever way too, they have the singular merit of persuading the actors that they are profoundly clever. When a man or a woman has to say for a hundred consecutive nights a piece of flat English to which the situation gives point, and finds that the sympathetic audience always grins, giggles, or applauds the platitude, he or she, insensibly at least, becomes persuaded that the words contain a deep meaning, a recondite wit, which escapes or is above the ordinary perception. Hence the author has a sort of doubly-reflected fame. The merit which was at first denied him is forced upon the actor's mind, and by him, by extra point, upon the audience. (pp. 346-48)

[Robertson] has not flown at very high game in literature, but it is due to him to say that he very rightly, in one sense, despises the pompous assumption of the larger magazines and reviews. *London Society* is perhaps the most advanced magazine that he has contributed to; but previously to his great success as a dramatic writer, he worked very hard as a journalist; he contributed to *Fun;* edited, with Mr. Hingston, the lecture of Artemus Ward; contributed to the "Savage Club Papers," and wrote more than one truthful and pathetic story in the Christmas numbers of various magazines.

It is, however, especially as a dramatist that Mr. Robertson must be viewed, and, curiously, as a successful dramatist at *one* theatre. Never was the policy of getting a good working company, and of keeping it together, more thoroughly proved to be the right one. At the Prince of Wales's Theatre, under the management of Mrs. Bancroft, and with the London company managed by Mr. Frederick Younge, there is absolutely nothing to be desired. So well do the actors and actresses enter into the parts played, that each one seems to have been born for the character. Mrs. Bancroft (Marie Wilton), her husband, and Mr. Hare, act so well that all trace of acting disappears. The style is simply that of the drawing-room; the theatre is so small and yet so elegant that it *looks* like a drawing-room; the actors and actresses like ladies and gentlemen indulging in very pointed conversation. And, wondrous to relate, when we repeat that very pointed conversation the next day, it is dull and pointless; yet so well is it given by the company, so thoroughly is every cue taken up, that what is actually dull enough to be real conversation, becomes burnished and glows with theatric polish on the stage. And this fact will account for the failure of all, or nearly all, of Mr. Robertson's pieces when produced at any other theatre but that in Tottenham Street. Look, for instance, at the fate of **A Rapid Thaw, Shadow Tree Shaft, For Love, Dreams, A Breach of Promise,** and the **Nightingale,** produced at other theatres, compared with that of **Society, Ours, Caste, Play, School,** and **M.P.,** produced by Miss Marie Wilton. The suggestion which carries with it an accusation of dishonesty, namely, that the author keeps all his best pieces for his favourite theatre, is untrue. **Dreams,** for instance, played at Marie Wilton's theatre would have run as long as **School.** The fact is, that one company in London knows how to appreciate and to play Mr. Robertson's works, and the others do not; and this is proved by the actual dulness of the dialogue in reading, which on the stage appears so brilliant. (pp. 351-53)

To conclude, Mr. Robertson is the dramatist of the age, and reflects the artificial manners of society. He has no depth, little pathos, small humour; but he knows his business and his audience, his time, stage, and actors thoroughly. Well mounted, his pieces have a freshness, a cleverness, and a charm which belongs to a fine piece of art *a la* Watteau, or in Dresden or Sevres china. **School** has even more; it has the effect of the prettiest little idyll on the stage, but we must not compare its idyllic force with that of *As You Like It,* but rather with that of one of those old English operas, *Love in a Village; or, the Mountain Sylph,* now too seldom acted. Robertson has not high art nor high feeling, but he very successfully assumes a tone of high-breeding and well-bred cynicism. His pieces are not highly moral, but they are not immoral, and are quite up to the morality of the age. He has been accused of sneering at everything: this he does not do, he only sneers at what he and society does not believe in. He is exceedingly artificial, but then so are the times; he appreciates Tennyson, whom he quotes; he is at any rate on the side of virtue and of manliness so far as that is consistent with kid gloves and an evening dress. He dares to satirise what is weak and foolish in John Stuart Mill, and to give a wholesome opinion of the silly burlesques which are vitiating the taste of society. (pp. 355-56)

> *J. Hain Friswell, "Mr. T. W. Robertson," in his* Modern Men of Letters Honestly Criticised, *Hodder and Stoughton, 1870, pp. 345-59.*

Temple Bar (essay date 1875)

[*In the following excerpt, the critic praises Robertson's innovations in Victorian drama, examining his work as a reflection of changes in contemporary art and poetry.*]

It is hardly ten years ago that comparative chaos reigned in things theatrical, and darkness brooded over the face of the stage. From time to time some shooting star lit up the dull opaque, or some sensational drama galvanized an audience into some special theatre. But literature and art had nearly left the stage, and educated men could only smile at the mention of an exhibition which was almost beneath their notice. With Charles Kean dead, Macready gone, and Phelps banished to Islington, burlesque and melodrama reigned undisturbed. Intellect was, for the most part, reduced to rant, and poetry was chiefly represented by physical exhibitions of humanity.

How, under these circumstances, in November, 1865, was produced, at the Prince of Wales's Theatre, the comedy of **Society** by Mr. Robertson; how for the next five or six years he brought out there successively **Ours, Caste, Play, School,** and **M.P.;** how during these years burlesque gave way gradually to intelligence, and theatrical enterprise so improved, that instead of two or three theatres being constantly to let, some six or eight new ones were built and others rehabilitated; how, in spite of all remonstrance and demonstrance, the modern school was founded upon human nature and natural acting; how educated audiences were brought back to the theatre;—all this is matter of notoriety. And, further, how, after the death of Robertson, another theatre took up the torch and carried the revival into the higher region of poetical drama, proving, in the success of *Charles I.* and *Hamlet,* that modern audiences would listen to modern blank verse and Shakespeare revived, if only it was presented to them as it should be, and

not as dead sea fruit. All this is more than a twice-told tale. Is it not written in the chronicles of the daily press?

But what is not there written, because not yet sufficiently recognised, is the fact that in this revival the theatre was only undergoing the revolution which other branches of art had already exhibited in England. The wave of the nineteenth century renaissance had reached the stage!

To understand this movement, we must go back a step or two and obtain a clear view of contemporary art and its tendencies. What had poetry and painting been doing, and other arts? For the stage is not now the only "abstract and brief chronicle of the time." The first great awakening of art and truth is due to the influence of modern German thought, and the first definite *general* movement in this country was the creation of the Præraphaelite School some twenty years ago, which came to us through France from Germany, and which, with all its extravagance and prejudice, contained within itself the germ of greater things. The group of men who led that movement have, for the most part, emancipated themselves from the thraldom of their own dogmas, and have imparted a new life to all art. But rightly to understand even that movement we must go back to the earlier art of poetry.

The batch of poets—Shelley, Burns, Byron, Wordsworth, and others—whose genius lifted and lighted the first quarter of this century, represented the infancy of our modern poetry—the new birth or revival of poetical art after nearly two hundred years of silence;—yes, of silence; for, notwithstanding Milton, Dryden, Pope, and the pseudo-poets of their generation, the cold Latinity of the classical renaissance had taken all the soul out of English poetry. But it was not till the time of Tennyson that the lisping muse spoke out in articulate speech. Whether Tennyson be himself a cause or a consequence, it is bootless to inquire; he is probably both; but that in lyric poetry he first struck the full chords of passion and pathos that Shakespeare had left vibrating, will have some day to be acknowledged by posterity. For the first time for two hundred and fifty years the ring of Shakespeare's sonnets is recalled in *Maud* and *In Memoriam.* For the first time since those immortal songs were written, 'Oh, mistress mine,' 'Freeze, freeze, thou bitter sky,' or 'Fear no more the heat of the sun,' they are matched in sweetness and soul by such verses as 'Come not when I am dead,' or 'My life is full of weary days,' or 'A Dirge.' And to go a step farther, there are lines in the *Idylls,* such as Arthus's dying speech, or his parting with Guinevere, that will bear comparison with some of the finest passages in *Henry V.* or *Henry VIII.* Whereas Shakespeare was essentially a dramatic poet, Tennyson is of course a lyric, or, more strictly, an idyllic poet; but he is the first who has touched these tones: and albeit the older poet has the more masculine power, the younger one fairly rivals him in lyric pathos and intensity.

These may be bold statements in an age when the critic has almost usurped the place of the creator; but it is time they were said. Tennyson and Carlyle have but to die for us to appreciate them at their real worth. Who knows but that we shall one day have a Tennyson Society, or a Carlyle Club, making dry-as-dust disquisitions to our posterity. Why not? This generation has already produced a

Shakespeare Society and a Tennyson Concordance. But however that may be, the same vivid tone, with a stronger grasp of reality and truth (almost imperceptible fifty years ago, except in some flashes of Defoe and Hogarth), is what now leavens the works of our principal artists, such as Millais, Watts, and Leighton; and has pervaded and renewed our literature in such writers as Thackeray, Ruskin, and Carlyle. And this same quality is moulding the Art and Thought of the Future in every branch.

Or, to speak more analytically, and in the critical diction of the day, the revival is specially characterised by these features:—

1. Truth and freedom, with closer fidelity to human nature.

2. Intensity and pathos, with a certain realism.

3. The combination in a higher degree than heretofore of the rational and the æsthetic, that is, form and colour.

For Christianity was in one sense a great æsthetic revolution, and the sixteenth century its development; and whereas the two greatest periods of art known to us, namely, the Greek of the time of Phidias, and the European of the sixteenth century, are characterised by Form and Colour, the expression of the Rational or Intellectual, and the Æsthetic or Imaginative respectively, the Art of the Future (at least in this England), expressive as it must be of the mind of the age, will be a combination of those two elements, tinctured with a certain realism, which is the Physical.

But not only in poetry and painting, and in the works of our greatest writers, but in more general literature, in architecture, and in the arts of decoration, the same qualities now appear. The writings of a Hume or a Smollett seem insipid beside the vivid intensity of a Macaulay or a Kinglake. The newspaper of fifty years ago seems written by a child compared with the incisive diction of to-day. Then, again, the dull, meaningless architecture of even twenty years ago looks bald and ugly by the side of some of those lofty, graceful, red-brick structures which are rising up all over London, especially such as the School Board are erecting far and wide in every district, like lamps of architecture in the structural revolution imminent. The hideous wall-papers and carpets of our grandfathers, the senseless decoration, the gold and the plaster, the veneer and the stucco, are giving way to artistic decoration of a sober and exquisite beauty. The great god Sham, the creation of a plutocracy, the almighty idol of Materialism and Convention, must prepare for dissolution.

Now the same dead levelment which had depressed all other art pervaded the theatre when Robertson began to write; the same cobwebs of conventionality and vulgarity had to be cleared away by a more vital expansion and drastic renaissance; and a careful study of his comedies will exhibit the same qualities that had characterised all other Art in its emancipation, namely, Truth and freedom, Poetry and pathos; delicate artistry with a certain realism. In human nature and character, there is no dramatist of this century that will compare with him. To find even that you must go back to Sheridan and Goldsmith, with whom

(*pace* contemporary critics) he will one day range; but in some qualities he is their master. He may be wanting in their power and brilliancy, but in pathos and in absence of conventionality he is their master, and in the portrayal of human nature, the great touchstone of dramatic art, he is their equal, if not their superior. It is the fashion of those who cannot appreciate him to decry what they call "the cup and saucer school," as the fox once aspersed the grapes; but his very detractors are sometimes his imitators, and only show their own inability to reproduce the delicate poetry of his conceptions.

It must not be supposed that these comedies were sudden inspirations or the only offspring of his brain. For many years he wrote before the power came. In his earlier pieces, chiefly one-act translations from the French, there is hardly a trace of the scintillating dialogue that first appears in *Society.* In this he was not unlike Gluck, Offenbach, and others who produced for many years quite inferior works. And even after he had obtained the power, Robertson failed whenever he attempted drama. Most of the pieces produced elsewhere than at the Prince of Wales's Theatre were either failures or but indifferent successes, with the exception of *David Garrick, Home,* and *Dreams;*—a careful examination of these, however, shows considerable inferiority. And nothing to extenuate, be it said that the rest, excepting a touch here and there, are not worthy of his reputation: *Shadow-Tree Shaft, For Love, The Nightingale, Rapid Thaw, Progress,* and *War,* were failures in London.

Besides these, however, he wrote a piece called *Birth,* for Mr. Sothern, produced in the country without success; also a translation of 'On ne badine pas avec l'amour,' entitled *Passion Flower,* produced likewise in the country without success; or rather the last act proved too much for the stolidity of a British country audience. During his last illness he was occupied on a comedy called *Faith,* intended for the Prince of Wales's Theatre. It was a mere sketch of character, in which a starving curate, a rich rector, and a strolling player, with their respective belongings, are brought into contrast. The outline left is too shadowy to hope that any adequate coadjutor could finish it into a play, but there is reason to believe that *Passion Flower* and *War* might, with judicious alterations, be successfully revived, if presented with the careful stage management that has distinguished the Prince of Wales's Theatre.

It has been said that all these successful comedies can be traced to foreign sources, and that Robertson was an imitator of Emile Augier and Sardou. No doubt his familiarity with the French stage taught him the value of dialogue as apart from physical action; that is, the higher importance of movement of mind to movement of body, which our melodramatists had lost sight of. It was also said that he studied Thackeray to some purpose, and drew inspiration from the Præraphaelites, with some of whom he was intimate; but if all this be true, it does not detract one jot from his position or fame, rather the contrary. Were not the plots of all Shakespeare's dramas taken from stories already extant? but it required the solvent of his genius to mould them into those immortal plays. What then was the secret of Robertson's superiority? While others were copying stage humanity and lay figures, he was drawing from the life.

Of the six successful comedies here mentioned, the two first, *Society* and *Ours,* though both containing special and intrinsic beauties, show some signs of immaturity. *Caste* and *School* are his best. *Play* (written, however, before *School*) and *M.P.* show some signs of decadence, chiefly in the repetition of situations. They are all entirely free from impropriety in word or motive, and so far betray no Gallic origin. His central idea seems to be that of a young girl, eminently pure and beautiful, surrounded by every untoward and discordant circumstance; and it was the tare and tret of such situations that produced some of his most delicate poetry. His judgment of his own writings was not always correct: he believed strongly in the success of *Shadow Tree Shaft,* and *A Rapid Thaw.* The latter will be remembered as a complete *fiasco,* which its author himself delighted to describe.

There are two points that must not be overlooked in accounting for the success of Robertson's comedies—first, his power of contrast; secondly, his knowledge of the stage. This power of contrast (to recur to a former simile), was his sense of form, or light and shade, and it is what gives, in fact, the strength where the plot seems so slight. He generally contrasts two social conditions, as Bohemianism and conventionality, or old families and new, or else opposite characters. It is this quality (namely, the contrast of the laughing girls with the misanthropic usher and ponderous doctor, the old beau with the young loungers), that gives the interest to *School,* otherwise without backbone or plot; and every one of his successful pieces, especially *Caste, Society, School,* and *M.P.,* contain that distinctive element. The theoretical critic who believes in nothing but physical action and anecdotic plot, is puzzled when he encounters a piece like *School,* absolutely without story, which had one of the greatest runs on record, and has to confess that there may be more things in art than are dreamt of in his philosophy. But here also was revolution and a return to a higher phase of stage art.

It was, however, in his stage management that lay the chief secret of Robertson's success; the power he had of conveying to the players his conceptions, not treating them as mechanical dolls, but incensing them with his own spirit, and leaving to their intelligence the portrayal of the character. It is certain that the delicacy and poetry of his conceptions would have been almost lost by incompetent stage management and bad acting. But the absence of this knowledge is what makes so many dramatic failures. Authors, as a rule (except those who have learnt it by long experience), have no sufficient appreciation of this necessity, and it is probably that Shakespeare's office of stage-manager at the Globe Theatre was what gives his plays their remarkable vitality as acting pieces. He, too, as Robertson, was a great realist. Let no one doubt of that, after comparing his writings with those of his contemporaries. But a wide distinction must be made between Realism and Realisticism, which is its dull, stale, and unprofitable imitation—the one is art, the other is not. There is more poetry in the reality of Shakespeare and Robertson than in the actual poetry of many versifiers. There have

been players, and there are to-day, who can exhibit this power in an extraordinary degree, but it is never unaccompanied by something of the ideal; and this is also the essential quality of Robertson's comedies. (pp. 199-205)

This notice would be incomplete without a glance at the future of our stage. Its decline in intellectual power during these last thirty years has been owing partly to the pseudo-importance given to opera: æsthetic taste has overbalanced rational intelligence; form has been sacrificed to colour; and this, permeating downwards into music halls, has struck root upwards, and borne its fruit in our execrable and vulgar burlesque. But we are coming to our bearings now; the rational is asserting its position, not by the sacrifice of the æsthetic, but rather by its subordination and harmony. It is probable that any farther advance will depend more on the appearance of a new author than on any internal evolution. He will probably come, as Shakespeare and Robertson came, rather from the theatre itself than from the closet. We want the practical dramatist, not the literary author; but it would be well if our poets could be brought to regard the stage with more favour, and acquaint themselves with its necessities and practical requirements. We have playwrights dexterous in stage effects, but incapable of sustained poetry; and we have poets for the most part unversed in stage requirements. If the two could collaborate, perhaps something might be effected pending the coming of some more perfect genius. With such an opening as there is now at the Lyceum for poetical drama, some capability should be evolved.

The great feature and curse of this age is its Materialism, arising partly from the unprecedentedly rapid accumulation of wealth, and partly from a decay or flux in the higher aspirations that have kindled humanity in former times. Against this spirit of Materialism there is no more apt and antagonistic influence than the spirit of art and the education of the higher instincts. The power once possessed by the pulpit and the stage has, by disuse, failure, and other causes, permeated into other channels. Literature and the daily press have a larger influence to-day among educated men. It may some time be acknowledged that literature is but the crystallisation of the highest thoughts of humanity, and religion rightly so called the sum of that crystallisation. Meanwhile the dormant power of the Stage lies comparatively idle and unevoked by modern writers. But no one can have seen the audiences that have filled the Prince of Wales's Theatre, especially on a first representation, no one can have watched the crowds that night after night have been thronging the Lyceum, without feeling that the Stage is still a great factor in our civilization; an instrument for evil or for good, whether it minister to the physical tastes or lower passions like much of the French theatre, or addresses a more intellectual level like the old Greek and modern German drama, or whether it appeals to the higher senses in the universal poetry of a Shakespeare. (pp. 208-09)

"Thomas William Robertson and the Modern Theatre," in Temple Bar, *Vol. 44, June, 1875, pp. 199-209.*

W. Wilding Jones   (essay date 1879)

[*In the following essay, Jones examines what he describes as Robertson's "new school of comedy" which addresses social problems within the comic form.*]

I propose to make a few remarks on the principal works of Robertson, and on his position as a dramatist. I need not touch upon his life, as it has already been given with sufficient fulness to the public. Its events resemble those which happen in the career of every literary man nowadays, except a favoured few who do not suffer the buffets of fortune before they taste her sweets. But perhaps it is wrong to call them favoured, for these buffets really constitute the discipline of art; they prevent the young author from throwing his immature productions before the world, and give him that experience which is absolutely necessary to enable him to see and correct the errors of youth and inflated ambition. There are but few authors who have succeeded in making a success at an early age, and fewer still whose successes have received the subsequent approval of posterity; indeed, this world would be a sad place if we had to pass through it without experiencing some of its misery as well as some of its happiness. I leave it to my readers to conjecture how many of our great literary works, even the humorous ones, would have been written, if their authors had never been acquainted with one or another of the various phases of misfortune.

Comedy has been frequently defined; it is the holding up to view the lighter follies and vices of humanity, and satirising them with a gentle hand. The love of money; the littlenesses of what is called, by those who belong to it, "society;" the artificial barriers raised by rank and wealth; the follies of parvenus; the grotesqueness and hauteur of a portion of the aristocracy; any peculiar manners and customs of the time opposed to common sense; all these are legitimate game for the shafts of humorous satire, and are subjects for comedy. Now, comedy requires that the subject should be exhibited in the form of a well-constructed story, that the story should be made up of the acts of different persons, and that these persons should talk. Thus, we see that comedy is composed of three ingredients, Plot, Character, and Dialogue.

Robertson may be styled the author of a new school of comedy, for his plays differ altogether in character from those of other celebrated authors up to his time. His comedies bear the same relation to the older ones that ginger-beer bears to strong ale; while his are of a sketchy and sometimes weak nature, the others are robust, and even intoxicating in the fulness of their flavour. Of the old school—which began with the dramatists of the Restoration and ended with Boucicault—I must needs write briefly; with the exception of Sheridan's, the plays were generally of an artificial character, owing their success chiefly to the sprightliness of the dialogue and the ingenuity of the plot. Although they may have to some extent represented life in the reign of Charles II, yet when they professed to portray our own time their artificiality became apparent, and they speedily lost the public favour. This style then died out, and for a time a void occurred in the annals of the stage, until it was filled by Robertson, the founder of the new school.

Society was produced in 1865. This piece ridicules in a mild fashion the efforts of parvenus to enter the polite world. No character stands out prominently in the play, and they are all of them mere sketches, written, as it were, in ink and water. Sydney is represented to be a writer, but if he wrote at all after the fashion in which he acts, his opinions would not be greatly esteemed by his readers. He is a petulant, ill-conditioned young fellow, and no amount of jealousy could make a well-bred man behave as he behaves in the second act. Maud is equally inconsistent in her conduct. She breaks off her acquaintance with Sydney, not on account of his conduct at the ball, which would have justified the act, but on account of an absurd misconception, and professes herself willing to do what is most hateful to her, namely, to become Mrs. John Chodd. Lady Ptarmigant is slightly more natural, but her manner of throwing cold water on Johnny's suit when she learns that Sydney has succeeded to the baronetcy is a little too barefaced even for a match-making woman of rank. One can hardly understand a woman of her position thrusting upon society so vulgar a brute as the younger Chodd. There may be young men of his stamp, but if so they are either extremely rare, or are content to remain in the obscurity in which their youthful days have been passed. The only character really deserving of mention is Tom Stylus. He is a warm-hearted, good-natured, self-indulgent, happy-go-lucky, possessing a fund of mild humour to which he frequently treats his companions. If he had money it would be at the service of his friends; as he has none, he offers his advice, which is fairly good, and, *mirabile dictu,* sometimes taken. The best scenes in which he appears are his introduction of John Chodd to the "Owl's Nest," and his own introduction into society. In the latter scene, there is a small incident—dropping his pipe—taken from Augier's comedy *Les Effrontés,* which fits in very well with his character. Some of his sayings are pithy and neat, if not very witty. Here is one, for example: "Love is an awful swindler, always drawing upon Hope, who never honours his draughts—a sort of whining beggar, continually moved on by the maternal police, but 'tis a weakness to which the wisest of us are subject—a kind of manly measles which this flesh is heir to, particularly when the flesh is heir to nothing else—even I have felt the divine damnation—I mean emanation. But the lady united herself to another, which was a very good thing for me, and anything but a misfortune for her. Ah! happy days of youth! Oh! flowering fields of Runnington-cum-Wapshot, where the yellow corn waved, our young loves ripened, and the new gaol now stands!'"

On the whole, the play is a weak specimen of a weak school, and yet, like most of Robertson's pieces, it is effective on the stage. This result is due to various causes. In the first place, the length of the play is proportionate with the interest, *i.e.,* it ends before the patience of the audience begins to fail them. This remark applies to all of Robertson's pieces, and in my opinion accounts in a great measure for their success. He is never diffuse; he recognises the meagreness of his plots, and wisely confines them within reasonable limits. Again, the dialogue, if not so witty and full of epigrammatic sparkle as the dialogue of some other writers—and, to tell the truth, even wit and epigram become wearisome if forced down one's throat by the bucketful—is bright and animated, and, like the structure of the piece, concise. A third reason is that we are so deluged with adaptations from the French, full of mawkishness and sentimentalism, and only borne with because they have the stupendous advantage of coming from Paris, that it is refreshing to see a play of home manufacture, even if it is not quite a masterpiece.

The next play in order of production, *Ours,* shows an improvement upon *Society.* The characters are drawn with a firmer hand, and the plot is more elaborated. *Ours* is typical of the follies of wealth; and its principal characters may be divided into two classes, those who are rich, and those who are poor. The character that catches the spectator's attention the most is Hugh Chalcot. He is a cynic, and yet a really good-natured one. He suffers from a plethora of wealth; he is afraid to do a generous act lest it should figure in the newspapers as the "extraordinary munificence of Hugh Chalcot, Esquire," and he cannot summon up courage to propose to a girl, for fear that his riches, and not love, should be the cause of her accepting his offer. He has had one experience of this kind; and you, my readers, and I know how in our days mothers preach at their daughters to marry for money. Money! money! Yes, so it is, and a hang for love! Well, it's an ill wind that blows nobody any good, and these unions bring business to the lawyers, and make the judgeship of the Divorce Court no sinecure. Here is Mr. Chalcot's experience, as related to Angus, who is lamenting his poverty:—

> At last I met a woman I thought I could love, and who I thought loved me. She was eighteen—blue eyes, sweet as a dream—with yellow hair, with a ripple on it like cornsilk when the breeze gently blows over it under the sunbeams. Her mother made much of me; her connections *fêted* me. Indeed I loved her, if ever I loved. They all knew it, and she had always showed delight on seeing me. One day I heard her speak when she thought I was not by; she said—her voice said—that voice to which I had lent my charmed ear so many times, "I don't care for him, but of course I shall marry him; he is so very rich!" I left her for ever, and I plunged on the nearest downward road. I sank deeper and deeper still, till I had reached the lowest hell. I was but thought a prize pig, fattened in a golden sty. You bemoan the lot of the poor! Pshaw! rather pity the rich, who have no natural feelings gratified,—who are barren of love and bankrupt in hopes.

Mary Netley is the next to attract us. She is a high-spirited, free-spoken girl; even poverty does not damp her spirits, and she gives the reins to her thoughts on every possible occasion, in spite of Lady Shendryn's snubs. Angus and Blanche are what they are intended to represent, a pair of every-day lovers, and nothing more. It is difficult to write a love scene for the stage that shall not appear ridiculous in the action, but Robertson manages to make his lovers talk as naturally and insipidly as they would do in real life. We can pardon the improbability of all the characters meeting in the Crimea; it is necessary to the successful winding-up of the piece, although the scene in which Blanche and Mary play at soldiers is childish,

and more fitted for a charade than a comedy. Played by skilful actors, the piece will probably continue to suit the tastes of the public until a more robust school of comedy—not so much depending upon the strength of the acting as upon the inherent strength of the play—comes into fashion.

I proceed to discuss the merits of *Caste,* which play is in the opinion of many Robertson's *chef-d'œuvre,* and in this opinion I concur. The author's powers have matured, and although it is possible to find many faults in the play, yet these faults are inseparable from the new school of comedy. The characters are more ably sketched. The story is more interesting, and is not encumbered with any improbabilities, and the motive is one eminently suited for comedy. It is, as its name suggests, an invective against those prejudices which animate society when its members marry out of their own sphere. But in this case the author rather overreaches his mark, for while endeavouring to prove that these prejudices are degrading and absurd, he shows us that the concomitants of such a union are of a character to make most men choose to remain single rather than to defy the laws of "caste." All the characters are naturally drawn, but none of them, with the exception of Eccles, are of sufficient importance to merit a full description. It is not Robertson's forte to paint strong characters that live in the memory of the spectator after he has seen them upon the stage. When it is said that Esther is an affectionate wife, Polly a warm-hearted, vulgar girl, the Marquise an aristocrat among aristocrats, D'Alroy and Hautree two commonplace "swells," and Sam Gerridge an honest and generous young tradesman, enough has been said of them. But Eccles merits a more detailed description. He is an agitator by trade and a drunkard by disposition. With the pence which he wrings from the fools who listen to his declamations on the rights of the working man he gets decorously drunk. Whenever he procures a gratuity from his son-in-law, D'Alroy, he has a friend outside waiting for "him;" and when he returns from the interview his speech is thick and his gait unsteady. On one occasion, when he is set to rock his [grandson's] cradle, he bursts forth into the following characteristic soliloquy:—

> I'm as dry as a limekiln! Of course, there's nothing in the house fit for a human being to drink! (Looking into jug) Milk! milk for this aristocratic young pauper! Everybody in the house is sacrificed for him. To think of me, member of the Committee of Banded Brothers, organized for the regeneration of human kind by an equal diffusion of labour, and an equal division of property!—to think of me without the price of a pot of beer, while this aristocratic pauper wears round his neck a coral of gold—real gold! Oh, Society! Oh, Governments! Oh, class-degradation! Is this right? Shall this mindless wretch enjoy in his sleep a jewelled gaud while his poor old grandfather is thirsty? It shall not be! I will resent this outrage on the rights of man! In this holy crusade of class against class; of (very meekly) the weak and lowly against the (loudly, pointing to cradle) powerful and strong! I will strike one blow for freedom (stoops over cradle and takes coral).

When, at the conclusion of the play, he is asked whether, with two pounds a week, he could not manage to drink himself to death within a year, he modestly answers that he will try and doubtless he will succeed. He is one of the few characters in Robertson's plays which are drawn with any vigour, and, few as they are, they sufficiently indicate what he might have accomplished had he cultivated a style in which something more than mere elegance of action and elegance of diction were required. But we must judge him, not as he might have been, but as he was.

No one will deny the cleverness of Robertson's work, but its sketchiness is apparent to all. The style of comedy he introduced has been called "Milk-and-water comedy," and there is a good deal of correctness in the term, but it is milk and water of a kind not easily imitated. Imitators have of course appeared, in the same way as imitators of all men who strike out a new path for themselves appear; but their success has generally been in an inverse ratio to the success of their master. The chief merit of his plays consists in the conciseness of the dialogue; the sentiments are uttered in the fewest words possible, and never weary the audience by being repeated. But this single merit cannot outweigh the obvious demerits of plots possessing little interest, frequency of incidents of a childish nature, and characters natural in their way, but lacking vigour and finish.

I do not think I shall be wrong in prophesying that the days of the old comedy, which was last attempted by Boucicault, are gone, and that English comedy, at any rate of the immediate future, will be of an essentially different character. It will be modelled on the present French system, that is, it will partake both of comedy and tragedy. The plot will be more elaborately constructed than has hitherto been the case, and will frequently serve to illustrate social problems; and, to this end, it will be admissible occasionally to allow Thalia to put on the mask of her more sober sister. It will have this great advantage, that no writer will succeed in it unless he be a man of culture and thought, as well as versed in the art of dramatic construction. Whether this class of comedy will last for any length of time I dare not conjecture, for fashion is so constantly changing that no one can speak with confidence of what may happen at any distant period; but I doubt not that it will produce one effect which every true lover of the drama will hail with infinite pleasure, that of inaugurating a new era of prosperity to the English stage. (pp. 355-60)

> *W. Wilding Jones, "Robertson as a Dramatist," in* The Theatre, *No. 12, July 1, 1879, pp. 355-60.*

Henry James   (essay date 1881)

[*James was an American-born English novelist, short story writer, critic, and essayist of the late nineteenth and early twentieth centuries. He is regarded as one of the greatest novelists of the English language and is also admired as a lucid and insightful critic. In the following excerpt from an essay originally published in 1881 in* Scribner's Monthly, *he condemns the simplicity of Robertson's work.*]

Among the three or four best theatres there has lately been a changing of hands. The company of the Prince of Wales's have lately established themselves at the Haymarket, which has been "done up," as they say in England, with great magnificence; and that of the Court has transferred itself to the St. James's, where, for a long time, no such promise of prosperity had reigned. The two forsaken theatres have meanwhile re-opened their doors in creditable conditions. The Prince of Wales's, indeed, has been the scene of an interesting performance, of which we shall presently speak. The Haymarket has gained by being taken by Mr. and Mrs. Bancroft, but we are not sure that this humorous couple have bettered themselves with the public by leaving the diminutive play-house to which they taught the public the road. The Prince of Wales's is a little theatre, and the pieces produced there dealt mainly in little things—presupposing a great many chairs and tables, carpets, curtains, and knickknacks, and an audience placed close to the stage. They might, for the most part, have been written by a cleverish visitor at a country-house, and acted in the drawing-room by his fellow-inmates. The comedies of the late Mr. Robertson were of this number, and these certainly are among the most diminutive experiments ever attempted in the drama. It is among the habits formed upon Mr. Robertson's pieces that the company of the Prince of Wales's have grown up, and it is possible that they may not have all the success they desire in accommodating themselves to a larger theatre. Upon this point, however, it is quite too early to pronounce; and meanwhile Mr. Bancroft has transformed the Haymarket—which was an antiquated and uncomfortable house with honourable traditions, which had latterly declined—into the perfection of a place of entertainment. Brilliant, luxuriant, softly cushioned and perfectly aired, it is almost entertainment enough to sit there and admire the excellent device by which the old-fashioned and awkward proscenium has been suppressed and the stage set all around in an immense gilded frame, like that of some magnificent picture. Within this frame the stage, with everything that is upon it, glows with a radiance that seems the very atmosphere of comedy.

So much for the house, but for the rest, there is less to say. As soon as we come to speak of a theatre of which the specialty is the comedy of contemporary manners, our appreciation stumbles into the bottomless gulf of the poverty of the repertory. There can be no better proof of such poverty than the fact that the *genius loci* at the Prince of Wales's was always the just-mentioned Mr. Robertson. This gentleman's plays are infantile, and seem addressed to the comprehension of infants. Mr. and Mrs. Bancroft's actors and actresses could not go on playing them for year after year without falling into the small manner. It is not incumbent on us to say that this manner has been found wanting on being applied to larger things, for the simple reason that it has been rarely put to the test. (pp. 147-48)

> *Henry James, "The London Theatres, 1880," in his* The Scenic Art: Notes on Acting & the Drama, 1872-1901, *edited by Allan Wade, Rutgers University Press, 1948, pp. 133-61.*

William Archer   (essay date 1882)

[*A Scottish dramatist and critic, Archer is best known as one of the earliest and most important translators of Henrik Ibsen's plays and as a critic of the London stage during the late nineteenth and early twentieth centuries. Archer valued drama as an intellectual product and not as simple entertainment. For that reason he did a great deal to promote the "new drama" of the 1890s, which dealt largely with pressing social and moral concerns. Throughout his career he protested critical overvaluation of ancient drama and asserted that modern works were in many ways equal to or better than Elizabethan and Restoration drama. In the following excerpt, he claims that although Robertson was once "the ruling spirit of English comedy," his work has no lasting importance and that on re-examination the plays are simplistic and overly contrived.*]

Of the playwrights of yesterday the first in point of merit and influence is undoubtedly Mr. T.W. Robertson. For the past twenty years he has been the ruling spirit of English comedy. He has had many direct imitators, and even those writers who have not precisely imitated him, such as Mr. Albery and Mr. Byron, have been indirectly influenced by the taste he fostered among audiences and the style he created among actors. The story of his short career of success is soon told. After years of chequered fortune he produced *Society* at the Prince of Wales's in November, 1865, and the success of that famous work changed the fortunes of the theatre, converting it from a burlesque house into the home of drawing-room comedy. *Society* was succeeded by *Ours* in September, 1866, by *Caste* in April, 1867, by *Play* in February, 1868, and by *School* in January, 1869, while *M.P.,* the last of the series, produced in April, 1870, could not, despite the charming Cecilia Dunscombe of Mrs. Bancroft, be included among the Robertsonian successes. All these pieces, except perhaps *Play* and *M.P.,* may be said to belong to the living drama, and yet it is distinctly the drama of yesterday. Not long ago *Society* was revived at the Haymarket, and the performance was altogether melancholy. It confirmed the observation that it is not always pleasant to meet an old friend after a lapse of years. Time has probably changed both him and you, and pleasant recollections are apt to be rudely effaced. There was still much to be amused at in *Society,* but there was more to be wondered at, if not mourned over. There were touches of dialogue and character still fresh and true, but it was quite evident that the play as a whole was to be regarded mainly as a curiosity. It is at least half-way on its journey towards that haven of rest for theatrical *invalides,* Mr. Hollingshead's "educational" repertory. Anything more threadbare in the matter of construction it is hard to conceive. As no one ever did or ever will remember the plot of a Robertsonian comedy for more than a week after having seen it, a sketch of the plot of *"Society"* may have the charm of novelty.

Sydney Daryl, younger brother of a baronet, is in love with Maud Hetherington, niece and ward of Lord and Lady Ptarmigant. The latter wishes her to marry Mr. John Chodd, Junior, whose character may be guessed from his name, and a paragraph to the effect that a marriage has been arranged between them finds its way into the newspapers. Daryl, on reading this, goes to a party at the Ptarmigants', insults Maud, and wins 1000*l.* of Chodd at cards, by the most extraordinary run of luck on record. Just then a dissolution of Parliament takes place, and Chodd stands for the seat which has long been an heirloom in the Daryl family. Daryl opposes him on the strength of his own 1000*l.*, wins the election, which, so far as I can make out, takes place on the day after the dissolution, succeeds to the baronetcy, and is accepted by Maud, who, a few minutes before, has formally accepted Chodd. Such is the plot, and Mr. Byron himself could scarcely have invented a balder one.

I have said nothing of the child episode, which has the advantage of being unpleasant as well as absurd. Sydney Daryl secretly pays for the board and lodging of a little girl, innocently unconscious of the injurious suspicions to which this very secrecy must give rise. One fine morning his Bohemian friend Tom Stylus conceives the bright idea of calling at Lady Ptarmigant's along with the child. When asked who she is, he naively, not to say fatuously, replies, "Daryl's little girl." Lady Ptarmigant and Maud at once jump at the only possible conclusion, and by this ingenious device the author explains Maud's consent to receive the addresses of Chodd. Could anything be more deliciously simple in the way of dramatic construction? Of course we learn in the end that the child is really Lady Ptarmigant's own grand-daughter, her only son, now dead, having contracted a private marriage and left his child to Daryl's care.

The scenes in the Owl's Roost remain genuinely amusing, though the sort of life represented, or rather caricatured, in them is more or less a thing of the past. In the scenes between Lord and Lady Ptarmigant and Tom Stylus, on the other hand, the action degenerates into mere farce. Lady Ptarmigant's perseverance in calling Stylus "Mr. Silenus" becomes in the end amusing; but is there any so-called comedy in any other European language, in which such tricks as this are tolerated for the sake of a laugh? Or is there any comedy, farce, or burlesque, from Cadiz to Archangel, in which one of the leading characters has nothing whatever to do but to drag a chair after him wherever he goes and to fall asleep on every possible occasion, leaving his legs sticking out for the other characters to tumble over?

I dwell on *Society* partly because it was the play which made Robertson's reputation, partly because it is the last of his I happen to have seen. The last revival of *Caste,* however, was an almost equally melancholy performance. The crudity of its construction, especially in the scenes where the Marchioness is brought into contact with the Eccles-Gerridge family, is almost incredible; and only the character of Eccles, which is really finely observed and strongly drawn, raises the play above the level of the merest commonplace. *School,* on the other hand, is to my mind the very pleasantest of all Robertson's works. It has not the strong character-drawing of *Caste,* but neither has it the glaring faults of that unequal play. It lacks the picturesque military element of *Ours,* but its story is much more evenly developed. Its morality, as I shall afterwards have occasion to remark, is questionable, but fortunately no one thinks of drawing a moral from it. In fine, it is a charming woodland and garden comedy, full of grace, and with an atmosphere of freshness and health about it.

Yet withal what a trifling and flimsy work it is! It takes no hold of real life, it illustrates no point in dramatic art, except the possibility of keeping an audience of Britons amused for two hours with cleverly flippant and feebly sentimental small-talk. As Mr. Ruskin has aptly said:— "Its 'hero' is a tall youth with handsome calves to his legs, who shoots a bull with a fowling-piece, eats a large lunch, thinks it witty to call Othello a 'nigger,' and having nothing to live on, and being capable of doing nothing for his living, establishes himself in lunches and cigars for ever, by marrying a girl with a fortune. The heroine is an amiable governess, who, for the general encouragement of virtue in governesses, is rewarded by marrying a lord." And this is the best work, or one of the best, of the founder of modern English comedy! The fact is wonderful but undeniable; and another undeniable and sad fact is that this dramatist of yesterday lives again in a degenerate and time-hardened form in more than one prominent dramatist of to-day—"for what we have been makes us what we are." (pp. 21-6)

> *William Archer, "Playwrights of Yesterday,"*
> *in his* English Dramatists of To-Day, *Sampson Low, Marston, Searle, & Rivington, 1882, pp. 19-48.*

T. W. Robertson   (essay date 1889)

[*The following tribute was written by Robertson's son.*]

If eloquent testimony were needed to prove the value of the work contributed by Thomas William Robertson to the British stage, coming as it did when foreign drama had the first call on the attention of the theatre-going public, one has only to point to the *renaissance* of interest in English plays, bred and born of native talent which, commencing with his own brilliant career, has steadily asserted itself since his lamented death.

Robertson's ultimate success after struggles, which would have wearied, if not actually killed, most men, ere they had received some sort of recognition, assuredly stimulated many now famous dramatists, who, fondly lingering on the attractive threshold of the theatre were doubting the wisdom of casting their literary eggs in so risky a basket; but he, with a full knowledge of the power within him, cheerfully set himself to the task of facing the storm and strife incidental to breaking through ancient prejudices connected with all theatrical enterprises, and though it cost him dear and burdened him with shattered health, terminating in an early death, yet he won his life's wager in clearing the way of the seemingly impassable barrier set up against a dramatist daring to wander from the beaten track.

Simplicity of plot, brilliancy of dialogue, a wealth of characterisation beautifully blended into a perfect every day realism were the ingredients of plays which revolutionised the existing state of things theatrical.

An eminent critic in writing of *Caste* the morning after its first production said:

> *Society* and *Ours* prepared the way for a complete reformation of the modern drama and until the curtain fell on Saturday night it remained a question whether Mr. Robertson would be able to hold the great reputation which those pieces conferred upon him. The production of *Caste* has thrown aside all doubt. The reformation is complete, and Mr. Robertson stands preeminent as the dramatist of this generation. The scene-painter, the carpenter, and the *costumier* no longer usurp the place of the author and actor. With the aid of only two simple scenes—a boudoir in Mayfair and a humble lodging in Lambeth—Mr. Robertson has succeeded in concentrating an accumulation of incident and satire more interesting and more poignant than might be found in all the sensational dramas of the last half century. The whole secret of his success is—truth!

Pieces which reflected the form of existing society, devoid of the adventitious aid of the scene-painter and wholly destitute of mechanical effects, were received by lovers of the drama as a breath of air in a vitiated atmosphere. Such an innovation created a whirlpool of wonderment in the traditional minds of the very traditional managers whose economical ideas of novelty consisted in a clever pirated version of a successful French play.

Relying on a foreign market, they suddenly discovered a strong demand for goods of home manufacture, and had to venture, cap in hand, and beg from the men they had as translators reduced to the level of literary-thinkers, that which they had hitherto refused with ignorant scorn, an original play!

Here was a change!

The author, like the willing horse, had quietly allowed the managerial jockey to ride him to a standstill, but the stable had now changed hands, and the whip and spurs transferred to the author, who in his turn jockeyed the management.

The ice once broken, a feeling of independence soon permeated all sections of the theatrical world, and the speedy growth of theatres, together with the gradual decay and downfall of those petty provincial tyrants (owners of the bitter school of adversity in which actors were then reared much as Smike at Dotheboys Hall) opened up a new field and gave fresh impetus to the growing concern with which the public eagerly watched the advent of a new era in English dramatic literature.

Speaking of the days of "stock companies," so often described by actors, with weak and forgiving memories, as "palmy days," (how Henry J. Byron was wont to shiver when he heard the term) Robertson remarked: "Those were the days when I had one meal a day and three parts a night to play—now I have three meals a day and no part to play, and for this relief Providence has my most heartfelt thanks." And he meant it.

His acting experiences were indeed a sore point, and no more satirical expressions ever fell from his lips than when referring to the hardships and cruelties to which actors were subject from a certain class of country managers then existing. In his own words, in a manuscript of a one act play, he describes a character beloved of "John Coleman, Esq.," and easily recognisable as this individual of the past, viz., "His manner to be pompous and vulgar like a country manager. A stomach, and the manner of an elderly young man: an old-fashioned light comedian run to seed."

Robertson's plays were founded on the simple principle of virtuous intentions. His heroes were manly, his heroines were pure. A spirit of chivalry pervaded his whole composition, and nothing in word or action can be found in any indicative of a contrary meaning. The philosophy of human nature in its highest form was the star that guided him across the trackless desert of the drama! No vermilion-coloured vice thinly veneered with a camel-hair touch of dramatic ingenuity was used to evolve a moral—the paradoxical French fashion of teaching a lesson in morality—by presenting immorality in a tissue-paper wrapper of false logic and gilded romance.

The comedies which made Robertson's name famous represented events and emotions as expressed by men and women of the day with the most remarkable fidelity and minute skill—holding up the mirror to society and reflecting it in its kindliest phases.

He told his story in his own inimitable way, the predominating features being neatness in construction, absolute freedom from conventionality, and an intellectual vivacity developing itself in the most delightful and epigrammatic dialogue, which may well be balanced against the absence of the old intricacy of plot and prosy verbosity which the play-goer had been taught were the first principles of comedy writing. His methods were his own, and he entirely eschewed the common and tricky devices, so long a stock-in-trade of play-builders, and his masterly handling of detail in all matters appertaining to stagecraft as an art is readily acknowledged by those, who following in his footsteps, are only too pleased to say the source of their own inspirations.

As a stage manager Robertson was *facile princeps*.

It was he, and he alone, who insisted that rehearsal should embrace the effects, usually kept secret until the first performance, when actors would selfishly disconcert each other and destroy an author's *motif* by the introduction of some eccentric "bits o' business," in many instances perfectly out of keeping with the demands of the piece or the exigencies of the characters they were enacting. His notion was that a play, like a plant, should be carefully cultivated and trimmed, ere it is put on show for exhibition, and no one, least of all those who were intimately associated with him in the presentation of the ever-to-be-remembered series at the little house in Tottenham street, will grudge to his memory the credit of the system due to his initiation.

In treating of this subject the opinion of W.S. Gilbert may be quoted as an authority. An intimate and affectionate friend of Robertson's from the year 1862 when he first met him at the dinner given to the literary staff of *Fun* at its institution, and to which they were both attached, Gilbert

had very great and exceptional opportunities of judging. He writes—"I frequently attended his rehearsals and learnt a great deal from his method of stage-management which, in those days, was quite a novelty, although most pieces are now stage-managed on the principles he introduced. I look upon stage-management, as now understood, as having been absolutely 'invented' by him." This outspoken acknowledgment is the more valuable emanating, as it does, as a totally independent and unfettered opinion, and from one who has built up success in his own original sphere, similar, in more ways than one, to that of his departed comrade.

Again, John Hare, a master of this particular and necessary branch of the collective arts of the theatre, sends this valuable criticism: "My opinion of Robertson as a stage-manager is of the very highest. He had a gift peculiar to himself, and which I have never seen in any other author, of conveying by some rapid and almost electrical suggestion to the actor an insight into the character assigned him. As Nature was the basis of his own work, so he sought to make actors understand it should be of theirs! He thus founded a school of natural acting, which completely revolutionised the then existing methods, and by so doing did incalculable good to the stage."

To a great extent the executive genius which Robertson brought to bear in the exposition of his work has not been historically recognised by those who have pardonably and possibly in ignorance, credited others with the ease and grace characteristic of the productions at the original Prince of Wales's Theatre—then looked upon as the home of perfection in regard to stage detail. In alluding to this detail, it must not be supposed that it has any reference to a lavish or tasteful display of bric-á-brac, but rather to the natural movements and realistic methods of arriving at "situations" as against many old and objectionable stage traditions one of which may be looked upon as a fair sample—it being of all the most "familiar," not to say annoying, viz., that every impressive speech or scene should be spoken or acted in the centre of the stage, and the actor, or actress, whose scene "it was" (as if a scene was not part and parcel of the play) should "take the corner" on each and every occasion possible.

An actor appearing in one of Robertson's pieces for the first time at the finish of rehearsal suggested to him that at a certain point he should "take the corner." "Certainly," said Robertson, "take it when and where you please, but don't bring it back again." The actor left the corner and took the hint.

The lack of concentration in many of the productions of the day had originated a school whereby the play was a secondary consideration so long as a celebrated "Mr.," "Mrs.," or "Miss" was suited, and the *ensemble* was entirely spoilt by an absence of that persuasive and uniform style of acting usually the outcome of a combination of ideas whereby everyone concerned was treated as a jewel in a setting. Robertson, in the construction of his comedies, recognised this decided drawback, and to counteract it, wrote no "leading" parts, inasmuch as they were all equal in their importance individually and collectively, and against the old and pernicious system of subordinating a piece to the players—a fatal error in production—he adopted a stringent *vice versâ* principle to which the public owe much for the extra value of the performances they have since witnessed.

The little band of actors of the Prince of Wales's Theatre set an example in the development of their master's methods—knowing to a nicety each other's capacity—that finally their performances, not only of his works but of all comers who had the good fortune to obtain the advantage of their cultured art, became "the pattern to go by." The subsequent careers of many who had the privilege of connection with the memorable days of this happy combination of "all the talents" go a long way to prove the stability of their early training.

Speaking of stage *technique,* the fact that Robertson had breathed the atmosphere of a theatre from the day of his birth and, as an actor, had probably played the whole range of the British drama, it is not surprising with such an experience, together with a strongly inventive and imaginative mind, brought into an active force by a long period of consistently fighting the odds of adversity, that he should have created new departures standing out in bold relief against the background of worn-out old technicalities and silly anachronisms with which the English stage then abounded. For the rest, what Carlyle wrote of Schiller may well be said of Robertson.

> One virtue, the parent of many others, and the most essential of any in his circumstances, he possessed in a supreme degree; he was devoted with entire and unchanging ardour to the cause he had embarked in. . . . His resources, his place of residence, his associates, his worldly prospects, might vary as they please, his purpose did not vary; it was ever present with him, to nerve every better faculty of his head and heart, to invest the chequered vicissitudes of his fortune with a dignity derived from himself. The zeal of his nature overcame the temptations to that loitering and indecision, that fluctuation between sloth and consuming toil, that infirmity of resolution with all its tormenting and enfeebling consequences to which a literary man working as he does at a solitary task, uncalled for by any pressing tangible demand, and to be recompensed by distant and dubious advantage, is especially exposed.

These truthful sentiments apply in every particular to Robertson who from the time he received his first encouragement to the day of his death, barely six short years, contrived to regenerate a class of literature which of all others is the most prone to evil.

In his endeavours to raise the drooping standard of English dramatic literature he exceeded the fondest anticipations of the faithful friends who felt that he must conquer in the end, and though we still have among us the Stigginses and the Carpetbaggers of the literary world, ever ready to throw a stone, they can never dim the memory of Robertson, which shines out as a beacon light in the great sea of letters, where so many are wrecked on the quicksands of early disappointments.

Tom Robertson was held in the greatest affection by his brother workers in literature, indeed by all his friends. He was a brilliant conversationalist, and he told a story with a rich unction and appreciation (particularly anecdotes of his theatrical experiences) which made him invaluable as a companion and a treat at a dinner table. His so-called cynicism was, after all, only a pretty affectation. Everyone could see through it. No one with such a beaming and good-natured face, which was for ever running over with smiles; no one with such a generous disposition or such an affectionate heart could be a cynic in the true sense of the word. He made no enemies. He was beloved in private as much as he was appreciated in public. No one envied him his success for which he struggled with such untiring energy, though all regretted that he died with the laurel-wreath only just planted on his head. The winter of Tom Robertson's life was a long and cold one, and he died when the happy summer time had only just begun. The work of the clever author, the touch of the delicate artist will live after him, while the name of the man, yes, and the man himself, will be affectionately remembered by all who had the privilege of knowing him.

This charming tribute appeared in a London newspaper, and was evidently written by one who knew Robertson intimately. (pp. ix-xvi)

> *T. W. Robertson, in an introduction to* The Principal Dramatic Works of Thomas William Robertson, *Vol. I, Sampson Low, Marston, Searle & Rivington, Limited, 1889, pp. ix-xvi.*

Bernard Shaw   (essay date 1897)

[*Shaw is generally considered to be the greatest and best-known dramatist to write in English since Shakespeare. He is closely identified with the intellectual revival of the British theater, and in his dramatic theory he advocates eliminating Romantic conventions in favor of a theater of ideas, grounded in realism. During the late nineteenth century, Shaw was a prominent literary, art, music, and drama critic, and his reviews were known for their biting wit and brilliance. In the following excerpt from an essay originally published in* The Saturday Review *(London) in 1897, he reviews a revival of* Caste *and reminisces about his first impressions of the Robertsonian movement.*]

The revival of **Caste** at the Court Theatre is the revival of an epoch-making play after thirty years. A very little epoch and a very little play, certainly, but none the less interesting on that account to mortal critics whose own epochs, after full deductions for nonage and dotage, do not outlast more than two such plays. The Robertsonian movement caught me as a boy; the Ibsen movement caught me as a man; and the next one will catch me as a fossil.

It happens that I did not see Mr. Hare's revival of **Caste** at the Garrick, nor was I at his leave-taking at the Lyceum before his trip to America; so that until last week I had not seen **Caste** since the old times when the Hare-Kendal management was still in futurity, and the Bancrofts had not left Tottenham Court Road. During that interval a great many things have happened, some of which have changed our minds and morals more than many of the famous Revolutions and Reformations of the historians. For instance, there was supernatural religion then; and eminent physicists, biologists, and their disciples were 'infidels.' There was a population question then; and what men and women knew about one another was either a family secret or the recollection of a harvest of wild oats. There was no social question—only a 'social evil'; and the educated classes knew the working classes through novels written by men who had gathered their notions of the subject either from a squalid familiarity with general servants in Pentonville kitchens, or from no familiarity at all with the agricultural laborer and the retinues of the country house and west end mansion. Today the 'infidels' are bishops and church-wardens, without change of view on their part. There is no population question; and the young lions and lionesses of *Chronicle* and *Star*, *Keynote* and *Pseudonym*, without suspicion of debauchery, seem to know as much of erotic psychology as the most liberally educated Periclean Athenians. The real working classes loom hugely in middle-class consciousness, and have pressed into their service the whole public energy of the time; so that now even a Conservative Government has nothing for the classes but 'doles,' extracted with difficulty from its preoccupation with instalments of Utopian Socialism. The extreme reluctance of Englishmen to mention these changes is the measure of their dread of a reaction to the older order which they still instinctively connect with strict applications of religion and respectability.

Since *Caste* has managed to survive all this, it need not be altogether despised by the young champions who are staring contemptuously at it, and asking what heed they can be expected to give to the opinions of critics who think such stuff worth five minutes' serious consideration. For my part, though I enjoy it more than I enjoyed *The Notorious Mrs Ebbsmith*, I do not defend it. I see now clearly enough that the eagerness with which it was swallowed long ago was the eagerness with which an ocean castaway, sucking his bootlaces in an agony of thirst in a sublime desert of salt water, would pounce on a spoonful of flat salutaris and think it nectar. After years of sham heroics and superhuman balderdash, *Caste* delighted everyone by its freshness, its nature, its humanity. You will shriek and snort, O scornful young men, at this monstrous assertion. 'Nature! Freshness!' you will exclaim. 'In Heaven's name [if you are not too modern to have heard of Heaven], where is there a touch of nature in *Caste?*' I reply, 'In the windows, in the doors, in the walls, in the carpet, in the ceiling, in the kettle, in the fireplace, in the ham, in the tea, in the bread and butter, in the bassinet, in the hats and sticks and clothes, in the familiar phrases, the quiet, unpumped, everyday utterance: in short, the commonplaces that are now spurned because they are commonplaces, and were then inexpressibly welcome because they were the most unexpected of novelties.'

And yet I dare not submit even this excuse to a detailed examination. Charles Mathews was in the field long before Robertson and Mr Bancroft with the art of behaving like an ordinary gentleman in what looked like a real drawing room. The characters are very old stagers, very thinly 'humanized.' Captain Hawtrey may look natural now in the hands of Mr Fred Kerr; but he began by being a very near relation of the old stage 'swell,' who pulled his moustache, held a single eyeglass between his brow and cheekbone, said 'Haw, haw' and 'By Jove,' and appeared in every harlequinade in a pair of white trousers which were blacked by the clown instead of his boots. Mr Henry Arthur Jones, defending his idealized early impressions as Berlioz defended the forgotten Dalayrac, pleads for Eccles as 'a great and vital tragi-comic figure.' But the fond plea cannot be allowed. Eccles is caricatured in the vein and by the methods which Dickens had made obvious; and the implied moral view of his case is the common Pharisaic one of his day. Eccles and Gerridge together epitomize mid-century Victorian shabby-genteel ignorance of the working classes. Polly is comic relief pure and simple; George and Esther have nothing but a milkcan to differentiate them from the heroes and heroines of a thousand sentimental dramas; and though Robertson happens to be quite right—contrary to the prevailing opinion among critics whose conception of the aristocracy is a theoretic one—in representing the 'Marquizzy' as insisting openly and jealously on her rank, and, in fact, having an impenitent and resolute flunkeyism as her class characteristic, yet it is quite evident that she is not an original study from life, but simply a ladyfication of the conventional haughty mother whom we lately saw revived in all her original vulgarity and absurdity at the Adelphi in Maddison Morton's *All that Glitters is not Gold*, and who was generally associated on the stage with the swell from whom Captain Hawtrey is evolved. Only, let it not be forgotten that in both there really is a humanization, as humanization was understood in the 'sixties: that is, a discovery of saving sympathetic qualities in personages hitherto deemed beyond redemption. Even theology had to be humanized then by the rejection of the old doctrine of eternal punishment. Hawtrey is a good fellow, which the earlier 'swell' never was; the Marquise is dignified and affectionate at heart, and is neither made ridiculous by a grotesque headdress nor embraced by the drunken Eccles; and neither of them is attended by a supercilious footman in plush whose head is finally punched powderless by Sam Gerridge. And if from these hints you cannot gather the real nature and limits of the tiny theatrical revolution of which Robertson was the hero, I must leave you in your perplexity for want of time and space for further exposition. (pp. 250-54)

Bernard Shaw, "Robertson Redivivus," in his Plays & Players: Essays on the Theatre, *edited by A. C. Ward, Oxford University Press, Oxford, 1952, pp. 250-56.*

A. E. Morgan   (essay date 1924)

[*In the following essay, Morgan praises Robertson's perception of social changes in Victorian England.*]

[The] most important work of [dramatic] reform was to be brought about by a young man who began life as an actor. This was Tom Robertson, the unsuccessful dramatist and thoroughgoing bohemian. In 1865 Marie Wilton, the darling of the Strand Theatre, where she was the life of H. J. Byron's empty but popular burlesques, boldly took and opened The Prince of Wales's Theatre. Byron was her coadjutor in the venture, but things went ill. The autumn came and with it a piece of good fortune. T. W. Robertson, who had eaten out his heart in despair and disappointment through a long period of years, at length wrote a play which succeeded in the provinces. Marie Wilton obtained it, and in November 1865 was produced at The Prince of Wales's Robertson's first famous comedy, *Society.* This was an epoch-making event in English drama. The success was immediate. It is not a great play, but it contained qualities which were novel and at the same time not so much beyond the public that they could not appreciate them. The dialogue is bright: there is a quickness of wit and smartness of repartee. A sufficient flavouring of satire gave it spice. High life is ridiculed, vulgar wealth is held up to laughter, and that bohemianism, which Robertson knew from personal acquaintance, was included in the picture. The whole was skilfully overlaid with a coating of thin sentiment and at the finish all ended well.

Society was a striking success and it was quickly followed by *Ours,* which had a still longer run in the years 1866 and 1867. This play is less sentimental than its predecessor, but it is marred by an absurdly impossible plot. Another triumph was *Caste,* which ran in 1867 and 1868, whilst *School* (1869) surpassed all its forerunners and was played for nearly 400 consecutive performances.

Robertson stands out distinctly in the mid-Victorian period as one who made a very real attempt to bring the stage into closer touch with life. In the light of later developments his colours may appear faded; but in his own day he was undoubtedly a pioneer. To us his characters seem feebly drawn, but his attempts at characterization are remarkable when we compare them with what was usual at that date. His plays have the further merit of being recognizably English,—a very healthy sign at a time when foreign domination of the stage was so strong. Satire is perhaps his chief quality. Even to-day, in reading or seeing Robertson's comedies, one cannot fail to appreciate the cleverness of his satirical thrusts, so pointed but yet not unkind. He did not confine his satire to one particular class. All sorts and kinds of people are held up to ridicule; many sections of society are subjected to his laughter.

Like all good satire, Robertson's comedies are valuable and interesting to the student of manners and of social evolution. In the middle of the last century a new stratification of society resulted from the important economic changes which were taking place or which had taken place earlier and were then producing their effect. The middle class was becoming wealthier and more powerful politically and socially. The new rich have for centuries provided the satirist with material, and Robertson was not slow to see the absurdity of that gross belief in wealth which marked not only the vulgar parvenus who were invading the more select circles of society, but also the more firmly established members of the aristocracy.

In *Society* the following conversation takes place between Lady Ptarmigant, whose position in society was assured by birth and marriage, and her daughter. Maud rebels against the plans of her mother who designs that she shall marry the graceless son of the vulgar but immensely wealthy manufacturer, Mr. Chodd.

> MAUD. Mr. Chodd again?
>
> LADY PTARMIGANT. Yes, Mr. Chodd again.
>
> MAUD. I hate him.
>
> LADY PTARMIGANT. You wicked thing! How dare you use such an expression in speaking of a young gentleman so rich!
>
> MAUD. Gentleman!
>
> LADY PTARMIGANT. Yes, gentleman!—at least he will be!
>
> MAUD. Nothing can make Mr. Chodd—what a name!—anything but what he is.
>
> LADY PTARMIGANT. Money can do everything.

Thus the aristocratic lady. The aforesaid young Mr. Chodd has his own views on wealth, but they are scarcely grosser than Lady Ptarmigant's, though he may express them more bluntly. He is conversing with Maud's accepted but impoverished lover.

> CHODD JUNIOR. . . . Capital commands the world. The capitalist commands capital, therefore the capitalist commands the world.
>
> SIDNEY. But you don't quite command the world, do you?
>
> CHODD JUN. Practically, I do. I wish for the highest honours—I bring out my cheque book. I want to go into the House of Commons—cheque book. I want the best legal opinion in the House of Lords—cheque book. The best house—cheque book. The best turn-out—cheque book. The best friends, the best wife, the best-trained children—cheque book, cheque book and cheque book.

Crude it may seem, but was its brusqueness unjustified?

It is a startling change to find oozing out of this harsh stuff the sweet tricklings of sentimentality which was no less truly Victorian. The conversation proceeds:—

> SIDNEY. But "honour, love, obedience, troops of friends"?
>
> CHODD JUN. Can buy 'em all, sir, in lots as at an auction.
>
> SIDNEY. Love, too?
>
> CHODD JUN. Marriage means a union mutually advantageous. It is a civil contract, like a partnership.
>
> SIDNEY. And the old-fashioned virtues of honour and chivalry?
>
> CHODD JUN. Honour means not being a bankrupt. I know nothing at all about chivalry, and I don't want to.
>
> SIDNEY. Well, yours is quite a new creed to me, and I confess I don't like it.

The stalls would have needed a good dose of *Idylls of the King* to restore their equanimity after such a rude shock.

The feminist movement is reflected in Robertson's works. In *School* he satirized the man-made ideal of the doll-wife. Lord Beaufoy says:

> My wife must be a woman . . . not a regulation doll of the same pattern as the other dolls—the same absence of thought, the same simper, same stupid dove-like look out of the eyes. "I love papa, I love mamma. I go to church on Sunday; I can walk, and talk, and play . . ."

The iconoclastic nature of such notions is emphasized by the pained cry of Farintosh: "Did you ever hear? It's profane—quite profane." On the other hand he could gird at the extreme feminists, women who thought that the equality of the sexes was to be found in a bold imitation of the male and who consequently desired to have "their clothes made by a he tailor instead of a she milliner. How pleasant for a man and wife to be measured together; or, at an election, for him to walk arm-in-arm to the hustings with a wretched, half-mad, whole-mannish creature, who votes for the creature you wish to exclude." The sting in the tail shows that he meted out his satire impartially. The final touch is emphasised by Jack's reply:

> I agree with you there; if women were admitted to electoral privileges, they'd sell them for the price of a new chignon; man, as a nobler animal, has the exclusive right to sell his vote—for beer!

Robertson perceived the social changes which were going on around him. Here too he dealt out satire with generous impartiality. If he was in sympathy with the spirit of his times it was in the belief that each class should be wisely content to remain in the place where a higher providence had placed it. He implicitly pleads for the virtue of the convenient stratification of society which Victorian England in the main accepted. He ridicules the rebels who strive to climb out of their class. He meets with laughter the bourgeois who intrudes into the aristocracy, and also the proletarian who strives to enter the bourgeoisie. In *Caste* he strives to show what a mistake it is to attempt to mix the classes, though he is obviously not without traces of that sentimental fiction which had peopled the earlier nineteenth century stage with the virtuous poor. The older melodrama had thriven on the pretty theme of the virtuous poor, the whiteness of whose innocence was accentuated by the dark background of the wicked rich. Nothing would bring down the house so easily as the reward of humble innocence by marriage with the wealthy profligate converted in a fifth act repentance by the strength of virgin purity. However much the Victorians believed in the poor "keeping their place," they were always ready (in fiction) to applaud the chivalry of the high-born youth, even the greatest scoundrel, who stooped to promote injured or merely innocent poverty in the shape of a lovely girl. *Caste* is not unmarked by this influence in the marriage of George D'Alroy, a young aristocrat (untrue to type in that he does not seem to be tainted by the customary villainy of his antetypes), with Esther, the daughter of a boozing old workman who never works. It is Sam Gerridge, the artisan, who "knows his place," who

expresses Robertson's view on the inadvisability of attempting to break down class distinctions:

> People should stick to their own class. Life's a railway journey, and mankind's a passenger—first class, second class, third class. Any person found riding in a superior class to that for which he has taken a ticket will be removed at the first station stopped at, according to the bye-laws of the company.

Surely that ought to have pleased the stalls. But here again Robertson's satire is double-edged. The fact is that Sam himself who is a third class worker has just taken a second class ticket as a master plumber.

In the person of Eccles, the proletariat came in for its lashing. Eccles is depicted as ostentatious, wordy and worthless. We hear his drunken wailing over the ills of the oppressed "working man"—he who never did a stroke—his bibulous bragging as a member of "The Committee of the Banded Brothers for the Regeneration of Human Kind, by means of equal diffusion of intelligence and equal division of property." But when it comes to helping his daughter or minding the baby all his brutality and selfishness stand out in coarse contrast to his pretended principles. Eccles is perhaps the greatest creation which Robertson has achieved. The character is, however, marred by an exaggerated grossness which inspires so much disgust that one is not capable of fully appreciating the dramatic creation.

The stalls also came in for their flagellation in the good natured man-about-town, Captain Hawtree, who is not overburdened with brains, but whose heart is in the right place; and still more in the marchioness. She is a consummate old snob, and in her treatment of the lovable girl Esther, whom her son has married, she shows as much brutality as the bestial Eccles. His drunken incoherence is indeed no more absurd than her idiotic babblings of Plantagenets and the doughty deeds of her ancestors in whose praise she repeats pages from the Chronicles of Froissart.

Robertson was, however, not concerned with maintaining a social thesis, nor indeed was satire his only aim. The chief merit of the play and the quality which makes *Caste* so important an event in the development of English drama was that the play definitely attempted to depict life. It was, within somewhat narrow limits, a real attempt to restore nature to the drama, and one must believe that it was largely for this reason that the public gave the play so warm a welcome.

Did Robertson then create real characters in the sense that we understand the expression to-day? One is bound to admit that he did not. Eccles is the only character which is not a stage puppet; and as time went on Robertson tended more and more to write parts suitable for the actors and actresses of the Prince of Wales's Theatre, with the result that his characterization became stereotyped. At the same time there was a truer psychology in his plays than in those of his contemporaries. Furthermore, the life which he depicted was English. His plays have a certain homely atmosphere which is refreshing. This was produced largely by the "business" for which his plays are remarkable, and which by giving scope to the accomplished actors for whom he wrote—men like Hare and Bancroft—went a long way to assuring success. There was no danger of an old man's rôle not being successful in the hands of Hare. Bancroft with his perfect polish and blasé superiority was certain to make the part of such a character as Hawtree. A frolicsome and vivacious girl would always be popular with Marie Wilton's acting.

By this time Marie Wilton had become Mrs. Bancroft, and she and her husband as managers had contributed not a little to dramatic development by careful attention to the details of stagecraft and properties. In this they collaborated closely with Robertson, who introduced properties with rare novelty. It was a pleasing innovation for an audience to see on the stage a real bassinette (although the baby was a sham), a real rolling pin and actual tea things. The managers did their share and improved the dresses; real furniture was introduced; and they strove to make the scenery more realistic.

It would be easy to point out many respects in which Robertson remained a slave to other conventions. But we must remember that the stage always must be conventional, and it is only a question as to whether the conventions are compatible with illusion. To-day we dislike asides, soliloquies and separate conversations spoken by people who are on the stage together but are supposed to be unconscious of each other. Robertson uses all these devices, and presumably his public accepted them.

Such criticisms are not vital. What is fundamental is that despite many signs of progress and many good qualities in his work Robertson is essentially theatrical. The great ideal beyond which neither he nor his contemporaries could see was *la piéce bien faite*. His plays were therefore popular. Improbability of plot, weak sentimentality, and dialogue, which though smart and quick, consisted of repartee for its own sake, were faults which were covered or overlooked because the plays were well made.

Robertson's plays are exceedingly interesting documents. They reflect very accurately the outlook of the rising Victorian middle class of England. Snobbery is satirized in all classes. "Everybody," says Filon, "cries out in them against money, but as against a master." Well might the mid-Victorian thus cry out. They are respectable and sufficiently sentimental. But love is a sorry second to money. To quote again the criticism of that acute Frenchman, "Love cuts but a poor figure in comparison, though for form's sake it may triumph for five minutes before the curtain falls." (pp. 13-20)

> *A. E. Morgan, "A Mid-Victorian (Robertson)," in his* Tendencies of Modern English Drama, *Charles Scribner's Sons, 1924, pp. 13-20.*

Frank Rahill (essay date 1929)

[*In the following essay, Rahill assesses Robertson's lasting impact on theater, crediting his innovative style as representing the inauguration of realistic, socially conscious drama.*]

Back in the mouldy gloom of the 60's, when Ibsen was not even a remote, scandalous rumor, modern social comedy made its bow on the English stage. The experiment flourished for a while in a single London playhouse, but failed to take root; a decade later scarcely a trace of its influence remained. Largely the creation of one man, T. W. Robertson, it did not survive him, and the realistic theatre had to await other times and other men for its complete realization.

Robertson's name means little to the present generation of theatre-goers. His plays are no longer exhibited, and chroniclers of the drama, with the exception of William Archer, have done little to preserve his fame. Even his own profession has so far forgotten his memory as to permit his Centenary, which occurred this year, to pass unmarked by a revival of any of his comedies. Robertson deserved a better fate. His brief years at The Prince of Wales were crowded with achievement, and our theatre today in many important respects dates quite as legitimately from *Society* and *Caste* as from *Ghosts* and *A Doll's House*.

One tribute he inspired, however, goes far to atone for popular and critical neglect. [Pinero's] *Trelawney of the Wells* is as happy a memorial as any man of the stage could wish for. *Trelawney* is his story, cast in the mould of his beloved theatre, the work of a man whose early efforts in the drama were patterned after Robertson's own. Pinero's pretentious social dramas have lost much of the glitter that fascinated an earlier generation in the theatre; this simple, unperplexed *comedietta* with its delightful Robertsonian archaisms of speech and sentiment gives promise of outliving them all. It quite disarmed the acid young critic on *The Saturday Review* when it was mounted in 1896; Shaw, no Pinero partisan, confessed that *Trelawney* touched him as nothing else its author had ever done.

Trelawney reanimates the uphill struggle of Robertson to bring to fruition his dream of a drama that would introduce ordinary people, employing everyday speech and acting out contemporary problems against settings of recognizable reality. If that sounds like a modest and commonplace program to make a commotion about, it is only because Robertson's reforms have become the accepted conventions of our modern stage—conventions whose aesthetic validity has only of recent years been called into question by zealous advocates of simplification and suggestion. In the middle years of Victoria's reign they were daring innovations, flouting traditions of acting, playwriting and production.

When Tom Robertson wandered in the early acts of *Trelawney* about London, as Wrench, peddling his manuscripts and eking out a bare livelihood from fugitive reviewing and play-adaptation from the French, the serious theatre in England had sunk into a deplorable rut. The drama, dominated by a degenerate romanticism, was an extravagant, unreal thing, wholly out of touch with contemporary life—or any life, for that matter. Dialogue oscillated between cheap verbal "wit" and inflated rhetoric; technique had hardened into a stiff, mechanical, lifeless formula; subject matter and situations were far-fetched and operatic. Of character delineation there was none, properly speaking; stock types like the ingenue and sou-

The Prince of Wales's Theater.

brette were jerked about puppet-wise in accordance with the exigencies of an elaborate intrigue, after the prescription that had proved so successful with Sardou. Men of letters, Tennyson and Browning among them, continued to write blank verse tragedies on historical subjects, but these closet dramas belong to literary rather than theatrical history and were dismal failures on the stage. Bulwer's *The Lady of Lyons* and one or two things of Charles Reade won popular success only by stooping to the current level of sentimentality and sensationalism. Acting shared in the general demoralization. The huge auditoriums of the patent houses had conspired with the declamatory drama in driving all subtlety from the art; the shouting, gesticulating school of Kemble flourished virtually unchallenged. But it was the scenic investiture of the day that was the prize exhibit in ineptitude. Flapping canvas backdrop, wings and borders were the meagre materials available; on these, hack daubers were turned loose to do their worst in atrocious color and puerile perspective.

It was this sorry stage that Robertson set about reforming at all points, restoring human nature to the drama, breathing life into stage management and introducing settings and properties that would create an illusion of reality. He was not without brilliant forerunners in several depart-

ments of the theatre, whose contributions to naturalistic reform he could study, imitate and develop. For nearly a generation, the gifted Charles Matthews, a sort of Victorian Menjou, had been familiarizing Londoners with the possibilities of under-emphasis and nuance in acting; Boucicault had found time between writing his numerous melodramas to introduce some salutary improvements in stage business at the Adelphi; and at the Lyceum the French Actor-Manager Charles Fechter was even then in the midst of extensive experiments which were to revolutionize the mechanical side of play production. It was Fechter who constructed the first built-up sets and solved the complicated engineering problem of adapting it to rapid change of scene. He abolished the unwieldy flats that slid—and often stuck—in grooves, the trapdoors and other encumbering paraphernalia inherited from the eighteenth century, building his floors in removable zig-zag sections, manipulating his scenery perpendicularly and doing his shifting below the stage on the mezzanine.

Robertson availed himself freely of the work of these pioneers and added his own ideas—always prolific in matters of the theatre—synthesizing the various elements of production into a harmonious whole, the ancestor of our modern realistic theatre. In the scope and organization of his work, he distinctly foreshadowed the *regisseur* who was to come into prominence much later on the continental stage. By training and associations, he was admirably fitted for the task he had set for himself. A member of a famous English stage family, he had been successively actor, prompter, hack-adapter, playwright, reviewer, stage manager. The theatre was a part of him, and he thought, worked and planned in terms of the physical playhouse which he had come to know so well.

From Marie Wilton (later Mrs. Bancroft) and J. H. Byron his opportunity came to translate his theories into practice—they were theatrical folk who had taken over a small, ancient, run-down playhouse in Tottenham Court Road and labelled it importantly The Prince of Wales. Here on November 11, 1865, *Society* had its metropolitan debut. This comedy is many removes from being a masterpiece, but historically it ranks with the most important works of our modern English speaking theatre. Realism had its birth that night on the stage of The Prince of Wales. The dialogue was crisp and colloquial; the characters at least approximated recognizable human types; and the theme of the play, a clash of interest between a nouveau riche and an impoverished member of the gentry, was some sort of attempt to grapple with a problem growing out of the contemporary scene, however naive its premises and projection. *Society* introduced practicable property and scenic accessories on a large scale. One set was a faithful reproduction of a famous Bohemian resort of the period, accurate down to the detail of its habitues—drawn from cronies of the author, well known about town. A refreshing change from the extravagance and artificiality of the current theatre, *Society* scored a notable hit.

Ours, brought out at the same house in 1866, marked another step forward in synthesizing play, setting, direction and scenery in the interest of a greater illusion. Falling leaves, the patter of rain and the slow dimming of lights to suggest the coming of darkness, reveal a widening application of Robertson's theories to stage effects.

But it was in *Caste,* produced in 1867, that Robertson was able to give complete expression to all his ideas of a realistic comedy. The play itself is by far the best of the dozen or more which he turned out in the brief six years of active production granted him before his early death at forty-five. The characters were types to be encountered in a day's walk about London. There was Gerridge, the cockney gasman, mouthpiece of the author's fixed ideas on the unwisdom of attempting to go out of one's class; Polly, the ballet girl; Captain Hawtrey, a new, human sort of "swell"; and Eccles, Robertson's happiest piece of portraiture, a delightful old drunken reprobate, quite Dickensian. The action did not confine itself to the stock London drawing room and stately country house, but flowed over into shabby Stangate lodgings, reproduced with characteristic fidelity—tea things on the table, a bassinet in view, and a kettle on the grate.

It was this preoccupation with commonplace detail that suggested the derisive epithet, "cup and saucer comedy," flung at Robertson by his critics, a numerous body, recruited largely from within the theatre. Actors could never forget that Robertson had said, "I do not want actors, but men and women who will do as I tell them." Accustomed to impersonate fine ladies and noble lords much as their individual whims dictated, it was quite a shock to be reduced to demeaning themselves as ordinary human beings behind the footlights, as Robertson's methods forced them to. It was an affront to the dignity of their art they resented deeply. Like the players of Colman's day who refused to perform in *She Stoops to Conquer,* they considered such pieces, "ungenteel."

Robertson's comedies, considered apart from their milieu, are at most merely effective theatre. We ransack them in vain for any vigor or originality of conception, any genuine insight into character or creative handling of technique. The dialogue is pedestrian; the satire, so freely indulged in at the expense of snobbish aristocrats and presumptuous upstarts, never rises above the superficial; and the point of view throughout is pure, unadulterated Victorian cant. Robertson did much to free the drama of the barnacles of romanticism, but some of the worst excesses of that tradition cling to his comedies, disfiguring his motivation, his plots, his situations and even his language.

But, for all their shortcomings, there is freshness about them, a naturalness, an abundance of homely detail. In these comedies, life—like the nondescript bohemians crowding into the Gower Mansion in *Trelawney*—finally effects an entrance into the musty theatre of the day.

The movement Robertson inaugurated had begun to wane while he was yet alive, and at his passing its days were numbered. He founded no school, launched no living tradition. The Bancrofts, his noble allies while he lived, carried on for a while without him, but had a change of heart, noticeably after *Ours,* revived under their management at The Haymarket, failed on that huge arena to duplicate its success on the intimate stage of The Prince of Wales. The impulse seemed definitely exhausted in the 70's.

But the realistic theatre was too well attuned to the needs and temper of the times to disappear permanently. Its resuscitation was inevitable. Socialism, feminism, the whole moral and intellectual ferment of the nineteenth century cried out for dramatic expression that the older theatre could not supply. A decade or two later, an adult, intellectualized Robertsonism of independent, continental origin made its appearance on the English stage. This time, vitalized by a mind of the first order and reinforced with a brilliant, resourceful new technique, it did not stop until it had penetrated and transformed the theatre. At the turn of the century, thanks largely to Ibsen, realism of theme and treatment were everywhere firmly entrenched behind the footlights.

In our own times, minute, factual reproduction of reality has lost prestige. The new theatre has arisen from the theories of Appia and Craig. Atmosphere has supplanted actuality, with the evocation of a mood the object of stagecraft. Furthermore, the stage has burst through the four walls with which Robertson, his heirs and assigns, had bound it, and surges over into the audience, demolishing the proscenium in its path—its ideological sponsors envisioning a mystical union of actor and audience, not unlike that achieved between priest and worshippers through the sacrifice of the Mass in the ages of faith.

It is a development Robertson, workaday man of the theatre, would not have understood. Yet if he were to return today, he would not feel an utter stranger in the playhouse. The popular stage, at least in English speaking countries, has only been slightly modified by this modernistic radicalism, adhering in the main to the lines which he laid out for it. His contemplative ghost might justifiably regard George Kelly as a disciple, applaud Belasco as a successor, and—if the current Broadway season came within scope of the visitation—heartily approve of the set of *Journey's End* as quite in his tradition. Whatever its future, our theatre is still a realistic one—a Robertsonian one. That is his monument. (pp. 838-44)

> Frank Rahill, *"A Mid-Victorian Regisseur,"* in Theatre Arts Monthly, *Vol. 13, November, 1929, pp. 838-44.*

Maynard Savin   (essay date 1950)

[*In the following excerpt, Savin examines the social content of Robertson's plays, claiming that he accepted the dominant modes of thinking and sought to affirm the status quo.*]

That [Robertson's] innovations were limited is, I think, a fact manifest even in terms of Victorian drama. Contemporary Continental drama had certainly gone far beyond Robertson in facing up to the truths of society. Within a few short years, English dramatists, such as [Sir Arthur Wing] Pinero and [Henry Arthur] Jones, were to take the Robertsonian advances very much for granted, and move on to richer pastures. . . . I wish to pay particular attention to the cause of the abortive nature of the so-called Robertsonian revolution. Why was his work so quickly eclipsed, even though the realistic elements he released fed the atmosphere of all subsequent drama?

The reason is fairly simple. Robertson hit upon some interesting ways of saying things (ways, it is true, which were not new and mysterious to the drama, but which playwrights had lost sight of), but unfortunately he had nothing very much to say.

His period was one of tremendous conflict in which the artists of the first rank were forced to define their position. It was an era challenged by the onslaughts of science, by a militant bourgeoisie seeking wider political expression, by the disruptions of a sprawling industrialism. It was a world through which the intellectual élite walked, menaced on the one side by crass materialism and on the other by the specters of Jacobinism.

The leading writers of the century fell athwart the compelling issues of the times. They took sides, of course,—becoming apologists of the old order or prophets of a new. But the literature of the age, regardless of particular partisan approach, is remarkable for its penetrating recognition of the issues at stake—so penetrating, in fact, that the student must marvel at how Victorians have crystallized for him the disturbances implicit in capitalism of the twentieth century. Victorian writers explored the implications of factory life, class conflict, and suburbanism, tracing their influence on the thinking and behavior of society.

To move from the poets, novelists, and essayists of the Victorian period to the playwrights is to move from the complex to the simple, from analysis to shibboleth. It is fascinating to watch the intellectual conflicts of the age filter down to the level of the footlights, where they resolve into large, bold patterns.

To catch this process, we have merely to visualize for ourselves the vast numbers of Englishmen whose insight into their environment was no deeper than that they received from over the footlights. The drama insists on direct and immediate communication of ideas. If a society responds enthusiastically to the plays of its day, we can take those plays as a reasonably safe gauge of its thinking. The drama corrals the attitudes and aspirations of its audience. It reaches out for the common denominator; it epitomizes the social philosophy of a period.

A great measure of Robertson's success lay in his putting contemporary life on the stage. At least he deluded himself and his audience into thinking that he had. Actually, Robertson fell prey to the pervasive myths and wishful thinking of his era—he fell prey to what we have come to designate as the smug, complacent aspect of Victorianism. It is his unquestioning acceptance of the dominant modes of thinking which accounts for the limited extent of his pioneering, for the sameness of his plays, and for the short duration of his place on the playbill.

I should like to take up the points of view to which he subscribed. We shall discover them checking at every point his dramatic inventiveness. They lie at the root of his failure to invest his plots and characters with honesty. Prominent among these guiding ideas appears the acceptance of the frailty of woman, a conception which led to her idealization. Her apotheosis was a heritage from the romantic revival at the beginning of the century. But the original flowering of the ideal, emerging from a romantic matrix of platonism, humanitarianism, and the exciting discovery of intuition, wilted into a fainting, helpless creature. The decadent residue of romanticism, of course, harmonized readily with bourgeois values; the rising nation of shopkeepers, keen on respectability and quick to capitalize on a marriageable commodity, took to its collective heart the sentimental heroine whose reputation must at all costs be sheltered.

The fact that audiences instinctively preferred the vivacious roles of Marie Wilton, which hinted audaciously at independence, suggests that below the surface forces were gathering for the overthrow of an impossible enslavement. For the time being, however, the Noras, the Mrs. Tanquerays and Ebbsmiths were unheard from, and playwrights led the nation's anthem to an idealized conception.

In the following description of Mademoiselle Favart of the Comédie Française Robertson gives explicit expression to his embodiment of the feminine ideal:

> She seems to be exactly the sort of woman who would take a delight in sacrificing herself for somebody—a lover, a brother, a husband, a child, or a father—and make no sign. If the

world knew of her sacrifice, or even guessed at it, she would feel robbed of half her sentimental pleasure. To charm her thoroughly, there must be something stealthy in her goodness and her love. She takes delight in being an anonymous benefactor. She is too high-minded to advance a step. She conceals emotion, but not under a smile. She is the antagonistic thing to a coquette. The heart of the man she loves must be as keen and prescient as her own, and must guess at her affection. Their love must be too high and holy to be spoken of. Always ready to perform her share of the duties of the household, her love is a thing apart from contact with the world.

And this ideal lies behind his tender characterizations: Blanche Haye in *Ours,* Esther Eccles in *Caste,* Rosie in *Play,* Bella Marks in *School,* Ruth Deybrooke in *M. P.* Where society transforms woman into a passive, delicate ideal, we encounter on the stage an even more heightened stereotype, from which there is no deviating species.

A second guiding idea in Robertson's plays is the acceptance as inevitable and desirable of the division of society into social classes. In truth, his ideology summarizes, only more bluntly, the cautious rationalization of the liberal humanitarians of the age. We can bring to mind Tennyson's distrust of the masses and Arnold's implicit retreat from the full implications of democracy. The Chartist novelists, Kingsley, Disraeli, Dickens, voluntary spokesmen for the oppressed, after delivering themselves of diatribes against capitalist exploitation, stop short with a word to the wise and a plea for paternalism.

The fears of the French Revolution had not played themselves out. Social thinkers still looked to the aristocracy as a wholesome check on excessive inroads of the proletariat. The middle classes, persistent enough in their struggle with the lords of the realm on the economic and political fronts, eyed wistfully the scutcheons of established, stable position. Throughout his plays, Robertson shows a sentimental attachment to *noblesse oblige* and the other romantic qualities of a decaying class. While touched by the currents of democratic feeling, he remains aloof from the proletariat. Caught between humanitarian sympathy and distrust of the masses, his position is thus basically akin to that of the Chartist novelists. Because he made no incursions into the problems of the dispossessed, his work does not even display the lively understanding and sympathy of the Chartists.

Robertson's one representative of a militant proletariat, Eccles in *Caste,* is a distasteful caricature. I find it impossible to agree with Ernest Reynolds when he says [in *Early Victorian Drama, 1830-1870,* 1936] that *Caste* "succeeded admirably in describing social conditions as they were, without prejudice and without propaganda." Robertson, in creating Eccles, was allying himself with those who deplored the thrust of the working class towards suffrage and unionism. Robertson makes Eccles detestable, but does not so much as hint that his environment has produced his deficiencies. The following, by Bulwer-Lytton, strikes the dominant chord in Victorian social thinking with regard to the working class. The important element to be noticed in such statements is the emphasis, which is not one of vig-

orous progressivism, but a tacit, defeatist acceptance of an inevitable condition:

> The working class have virtues singularly noble and generous, but they are obviously more exposed than the other classes to poverty and passion. Thus in quiet times their poverty subjects them to the corruption of the rich; and in stormy times, when the State requires the most sober judgment, their passion subjects them to the ambition of the demagogue.

(pp. 104-08)

Two statements in *Caste,* taken in conjunction, express the theme of that play and the sentiment behind all of Robertson's plays. Sam Gerridge, with characteristic directness, supplies one half of the formula:

> People should stick to their own class. Life's a railway journey, and Mankind's a passenger—first class, second class, third class. Any person found riding in a superior class to that for which he has taken his ticket will be removed at the first station stopped at, according to the bye-laws of the company.

George D'Alroy, quoting from Tennyson's "Lady Clara Vere de Vere," supplies the other half:

> True hearts are more than coronets,
> And simple faith than Norman blood.

The arbitrary representatives of the class in *Caste* are permitted a lesson in mutual understanding. There is a general awakening to the universal qualities of goodness; class lines, yes, but not barbed-wire fences, bristling with ugly hostility. Rather useful, protective lines tying the nation into one benevolent, peaceful entity. Hawtree, after his exposure to the Eccles family, confesses in an aside: "'Pon my word, these are very good sort of people. I'd no idea—." Sam, the belligerent gas-fitter, after being forced to observe Hawtree at close quarters, grudgingly admits in an aside: "Now who'd ha' thought that long swell 'ad it in 'im?" The reconciliation between Hawtree and Sam is handsomely democratic:

> HAW. . . .Mr. Gerridge, I fear I have often made myself very offensive to you.
>
> SAM. Well, sir, yer 'ave!
>
> HAW. . . .I feared so. I didn't know you then. I beg your pardon. Let me ask you to shake hands—to forgive me, and forget it. *(offering his hand)*
>
> SAM. *(taking it)* Say no more, sir; and if ever I've made myself offensive to you, I ask your pardon; forget it, and forgive me.

In spite of this outburst of brotherhood, the play ends on a more sober, practical note:

> HAW. . . .A gentleman should hardly ally himself to a nobody.
>
> GEO. My dear fella, Nobody's a mistake—he don't exist. Nobody's nobody! Everybody's somebody.
>
> HAW. Yes. But still—Caste.

GEO. Oh, Caste's all right. Caste is a good thing if it's not carried too far. It shuts the door on the pretentious and the vulgar; but it should open the door very wide for exceptional merit.

In this proposition Robertson finds the material for his drama. Henry Arthur Jones [in *The Renascence of the English Drama,* 1895] was later to decry the falsehood and abortive nature of such a starting point in dramatic art:

> The question has an aspect of expediency that it may be well to deal with first. Obviously as a matter of expediency and worldly prudence, a dramatist will do wisely to avoid giving offence to the prejudices and susceptibilities of any great portion of his possible audiences. Indeed, so perfectly has this rule been understood upon the recent English stage, so eager have we been to exclude everything that might be offensive or tedious or incomprehensible to any possible spectator, that by a process of continual exhaustion and humble deference to everybody's prejudices we have banished from the stage all treatment of grave subjects but what is commonplace and cursory and conventional. The course of the drama has been diverted and hopelessly cut off from the main current of modern intellectual life. While the companion arts—painting, poetry, and music—are allowed to present every aspect of human life, on the stage only the narrow, ordinary, convenient, respectable, superficial contemplation and presentation of human affairs is allowed. Though off the stage the gravest matters have been in heated prominence, on the stage nothing of much greater importance has been bruited than how a tradesman's family may prepare itself for alliance with the aristocracy. And such tradesmen! And such aristocrats!

The aristocracy comes in for a good deal of sympathy. Traditions harking back to the Restoration stage, of course, afforded stock comic types: those who failed to carry the mantle of their class gracefully invited ridicule: the snobbish dowager (Lady Ptarmigant in *Society,* Lady Shendryn in *Ours,* and Marquise de St. Maur in *Caste*), the eccentric, doddering old man (Lord Ptarmigant in *Society* and Beau Farintosh in *School*). But such are the obvious deviations from the norm, recognized and tagged in the canons of Restoration drama and bequeathed as fair game.

Thus it was according to Hoyle that Lady Ptarmigant so betray her class as to pander to the Chodds. Since she was an accepted theatrical type, anything might be expected from her.

> As the "owls" were so much diverted by the faithful portrayal of their resorts and of their customs, thus presented for the first time upon the stage, there was no reason that Society would take offence over the extraordinary and incongruous proceedings at the establishment of Lord and Lady Ptarmigant. This kind of comic libel was not unknown;—Bulwer, for instance, had set himself to depict the union of the old aristocracy with the new, the naive veneration displayed by Riches for Rank, and on the other hand, the prostration of Rank before Riches. No

one showed astonishment at seeing Lady Ptarmigant smilingly take the arm of old Chodd, though his language and his manners were those of a costermonger, and though his lordship's valet would probably have hesitated about letting himself be seen with him in a public-house.

From the school of early and mid-Victorian melodrama comes the slippery-tongued villain of Bond Street. The progenitor of *Raffles,* though at this point in his evolution unredeemed by altruism, the villain of birth afforded a titillating variation in melodrama. Enjoying entrée everywhere and possessed of devilishly good manners, he dismayed audiences by his apparently undetectable villainy. Robertson utilized the type in the Chevalier Browne in *Play,* but at the final curtain, it will be remembered:

> My repentance is sincere. Indeed I meant to seek you at your hotel, confess all, and implore your pardon. It is now too late. I have been dazzled, but I am not bad at heart.

With the exception of these smoothed theatrical coins, Robertson treats the upper class with respect tantamount to reverence. They become the responsible guardians of all that is noble and pure in the stream of English tradition, protecting their charge against the vulgar, elbowing encroachments of the middle class. At the final curtain of *Progress,* the characters suddenly assume symbolic garb. Eva becomes England; Ferne, the bourgoisie; Lord Mompesson, the aristocracy:

> EVA. A few more minutes to thank you so much for all your goodness to me. I shall get better; I feel I shall! When the snow melts from the grass, I shall be stronger; and when the summer covers those black branches with green leaves, I shall be able to walk down the avenue.
>
> FER. With me by your side?
>
> LORD M. You, on one side—me on the other. Left to yourself your pace would be too fast, and mine would be too slow. You have youth, strength, and speed; I have age, judgment, and experience. Let Eva walk between us.
>
> EVA. *(as they are going round door R.)* My path must lead to happiness when love and hope conduct me, and affection and experience guide me—*(smiling)*—That's Progress!

Those in the plays on whom Robertson heaps ridicule are the upstart bourgeois, those who have made their money in trade and manufacturing and now expect to buy their way into society.

The class types which emerged from the Industrial Revolution provided Robertson with material for writing Victorian comedies of manners. Robertson did focus his attention, albeit superficially, on the special foibles of the *nouveaux riches,* their *faux pas,* vaulting ambition, and crass values. Certainly, one would say, abundant riches for a revitalized comedy of manners. He took seriously, however, the defensive disdain of the rich; he sentimentalized conservatism. In his depiction of the social-climbing parvenu, he introduced an acrid note. Thus Robertson was incapable of assuming the disinterest necessary to the genre. Sentimentality strained to the breaking point the thin strand of objectivity, and objectivity is a prime requisite for the creation of a comedy of manners.

In *Society,* the ogres begot by the Industrial Revolution are the Messrs. Chodd, Junior and Senior. With unblinking arrogance they set out to buy their way into polite circles. Equipped with cash, their first step is to pave the way of John Chodd, Junior, into Parliament by investing in a newspaper. And with this aim they approach Sidney Daryl, a writer in straitened circumstances. The chrysalid socialite unloads his philosophy on Daryl:

> CHODD, JUN. . . .The present age is, as you are aware—a practical age. I come to the point—it's my way. Capital commands the world. The capitalist commands capital, therefore the capitalist commands the world.
>
> SIDNEY. . . .But you don't quite command the world, do you?
>
> CHODD, JUN. Practically, I do. I wish for the highest honours—I bring out my cheque-book. I want to go into the House of Commons—cheque-book. I want the best legal opinion in the House of Lords—cheque-book. The best turn out—cheque-book. The best friends, the best wife, the best trained children—cheque-book, cheque-book, and cheque-book.
>
> SIDNEY. You mean to say with money you can purchase anything.
>
> CHODD, JUN. Exactly. This life is a matter of bargain.
>
> SIDNEY. But "honour, love, obedience, troops of friends"?
>
> CHODD, JUN. Can buy 'em all, sir, in lots, as at an auction.
>
> SIDNEY. Love, too?
>
> CHODD, JUN. Marriage means a union mutually advantageous. It is a civil contract, like a partnership.
>
> SIDNEY. And the old-fashioned virtues of honour and chivalry?
>
> CHODD, JUN. Honour means not being a bankrupt. I know nothing at all about chivalry, and I don't want to.
>
> SIDNEY. Well, yours is quite a new creed to me, and I confess I don't like it.
>
> CHODD, JUN. The currency, sir, converts the most hardened sceptic.

In *Ours,* Hugh Chalcot, genteel, indifferent to the commercial success which has made possible his moving in aristocratic circles, comments cynically on the *mariage de convenance.* The institution dominated bourgeois thinking, reducing the training and indoctrination of a daughter to something like the promotion of a saleable commodity. The institution likewise took hold of aristocratic families, as a desperate measure to uphold fast-fading grandeur.

Accordingly Sir Alexander Shendryn had smiled on the possible union of his daughter Blanche with Chalcot.

> CHAL. . . .You know that I proposed to her?
>
> ANGUS. Yes.
>
> CHAL. But I'm proud to say that she wouldn't have me. Ah! she's a sensible girl; and her spirited conduct in saying "No!" on that occasion laid me under an obligation to her for life.
>
> ANGUS. She declined?
>
> CHAL. She declined very much. I only did it to please Sir Alick, who thought the two properties would go well together—never mind the two humans. Marriage means to sit opposite at table, and be civil to each other before company. Blanche Haye and Hugh Chalcot. Pooh! the service should have run: "I, Brewhouses, Malt-kilns, Public-houses, and Premises, take thee, Landed Property, grass and arable, farm-houses, tenements, and Salmon Fisheries, to my wedded wife, to have and to hold for dinners and evening parties, for carriage and horseback, for balls and presentations, to bore and to tolerate, till mutual aversion do us part"; but Land, grass and arable, farm-houses, tenements, and Salmon Fisheries said "No"; and Brewhouses is free.

Chalcot is a rare specimen of a sympathetically-drawn bourgeois. Disillusioned by match-making matrons and sensitive about his income, he effects a mocking, cynical air. Wishing to give a poor sergeant, who has become the father of twins, fifty pounds, he hesitates before a display of conspicuous consumption:

> There's the sergeant. I must tip him something in consideration of his recent domestic—affliction. *(takes out pocket-book)* I'll give him a fiver—eh? Here's Angus's fifty, I'll give him that. *(pausing)* No; he'll go mentioning it, and it will get into the papers, and there'll be a paragraph about the singular munificence of Hugh Chalcot, Esq., the eminent brewer!—eminent!—as if a brewer could be eminent! No; I daren't give him the fifty.

(pp. 109-15)

Robertson, then, stacked the cards in favor of the old order. The working man drank and grumbled. The bourgeoisie pushed and elbowed. The landed aristocracy, alone, had a sense of responsibility.

A third restricting point of view to which Robertson subscribed is the glory of militarism. He joined his voice to the hosannas which were swelling in intensity to greet the *fin de siècle* revival of imperialism. Sidney Daryl has been a lancer, Chalcot wins glory in the Crimea, George D'Alroy and Harold Fane become heroes in India. Frank Price is tricked into a duel with a Prussian officer because the villain in the piece is able to appeal to Price's patriotism: "Do not be under the least misapprehension nor fear that the reputation of England, Ireland, and Scotland, or of Englishmen abroad, will suffer at my hands." Before the duel, Price reassures himself that "military rank, wrinkles, medals, and all told, he is only a foreigner." Jack Poyntz finds it "hardly worth while" to mention his service at the

Battle of Inkerman. Talbot Piers has been an army officer. The whole of *Ours* is drenched in a romantic glow of militarism. Rittmeister Harfthal in *Dreams* rises to a rhapsodic outburst:

> There is no finer art than fighting—than the habit of obedience and command. What melody like a gallop? What harmony like a charge? What music like a trumpet or a drum?

In *The Nightingale,* Keziah holds Mary's baby to the window: "Look at the pretty soldiers, dear, who go out to fight and die in cold weather and hot weather, that pretty babies like you may lie soft and warm, and have no fear of nasty foreigners."

War makes no inquiry into the right and wrong in the Franco-Prussian war, resting with praise for the patriotic mobilization in both countries. Captain Sound, the Englishman, encourages his Continental friends, "I say I hate war; but when once you begin to fight, fight it out—you're better friends after." There is sentimental pathos over the forced separation of lovers, but after all, Oscar's supposed death proves a mistake, and he returns to Lotte, wearing a medal and reinforced in his conviction that "the truest glory is the glory of war." This enchantment, unrelieved and unreserved, precluded the slightest inquiry into the march of historical events. It constituted the acceptance of and contribution to the growth of chauvinism at its uncritical worst.

Thus three stifling currents of Victorian orthodoxy—the glorification of woman, caste, and war—combined to smother the creative energy of Robertson. The limitation of his intellectual grasp on his milieu forced him to fall back on melodrama and on a conventional, sentimentalized treatment of love. Robertson was a rebel against theatrical convention, not against Victorianism. The only instrument he provided for arbitration in the class struggle was the love seat.

Where his advance lay was in the transformation of stagnant bombast into delicate, lyric-tinged dialogue, of shabby staging into a realistic, intimate *mise en scène.* Through his direction, the solo performance yielded to the ensemble. Under the combined aegis of Robertson and the Bancrofts, dramatic presentation attained a new unity, with the proper subordination of the parts to the whole.

This new unity, in turn, generated new impulse. His domestication of drama quickened the evolution of both actor and audience towards the play of discussion. Having rid the stage of rant and rave, he facilitated the approach of his immediate followers towards the problem play. He died, unmindful of the ultimate consequences of the tempest he had raised; had he lived out his four score, he would have witnessed the naturalness he introduced evolve into naturalism. (pp. 116-18)

> *Maynard Savin, in his* Thomas William Robertson: His Plays and Stagecraft, *Brown University, 1950, 146 p.*

John Russell Taylor   (essay date 1967)

[*Taylor is an English educator, critic, and editor. In the following excerpt, he evaluates Robertson's historical importance, focusing on his realistic reforms of nineteenth-century theater.*]

It has long been normal to date the realistic reform in the English theatre from the advent of T. W. (Tom) Robertson. And while this is on nearly all counts an oversimplification, it remains all the same a reasonable one to start with, mainly because, whether on strict and careful study of Robertson's predecessors and how he differed from them we conclude that his 'revolution' was as radical as people thought, the important thing is that at the time many influential in the theatre thought so and acted accordingly.

What Robertson was (and is) famed for above all is having introduced on to the mid-Victorian stage a realistic picture of everyday middle-class life. Well, of course the term is relative. To us, now, Robertson's plots seem often hardly less improbable and melodramatic than those of the unashamed melodramas he was reacting against, while his plays abound in such conventions as soliloquy, aside and simultaneous conversations on stage by characters who are supposed not to be aware of each other's presence. Nor was Robertson the first dramatist of his age to deal with current social problems in what was meant to be a realistic way—even Lord Lytton, author of the most phenomenally successful romantic melodrama of the period, *The Lady of Lyons* (1838), also dabbled, according to his lights, with everyday realism in plays like *Money* (1840), the very title of which has a Robertson-like ring.

But undoubtedly Robertson went further in this direction, wrote better while doing so, and hit exactly the right moment for doing so—hence his historical importance, even if as a dramatist he remains very much in the minor league. He was born in 1829, his family background including a number of actors, writers, painters and professional artists of various sorts. He himself went on the stage in early childhood, and continued to act with modest success for some years. He also had the itch to write, however, and seemed all set for early success when a play of his, *A Night's Adventure,* was accepted for production by a major London company in 1851.

But though this piece of period flummery about Jacobites, Hanoverians and a romantic highwayman in disguise was in no way challenging and was by all accounts in general rather better than the run of such plays at the time, it had no success at all, and its unfortunate author was reduced to churning out innumerable adaptations, mainly 'from the French'. Among those he wrote in the mid-1850s were, significantly perhaps, *The Ladies' Battle* from *La bataille des dames,* by Scribe and Legouvé, and *A Glass of Water,* from Scribe's *Un Verre d'eau.* Thus the great innovator-to-be was thoroughly familiar with Scribe's work and methods some years before his own major original successes were written, and no doubt learnt from them quite a lot about Scribe's concept of the *pièce bien faite,* which was . . . above all the art of telling a story to maximum effect in specifically theatrical terms.

Robertson's first success with a play of his own did not come until 1864, by which time he had completely given up acting for writing and spent some time as a drama critic, of the *Illustrated Times*. And even the first play to make any sort of a name for him, *David Garrick,* was in fact an adaptation, admittedly free, from a French play, de Melesville's *Sullivan,* which in its turn was only one of many variations on the old notion of a stage star deliberately disenchanting an infatuated young admirer by cutting a very unflattering figure off-stage. The main thing which distinguishes the play from any number of others cast in a similar mould is the love-scene in the last act, which though inevitably sentimental has a lightness and charm which convinced audiences at the time that it was very true to life—or at any rate a good deal truer than most of what they were currently offered on the stage.

Girded with this success Robertson went on almost at once to offer an original play of his own: *Society,* written in 1864 and produced in November 1865. This had a resounding success, and marked Robertson's definitive arrival as the dramatist of the day, especially when confirmed by the success of *Ours* in 1866 and *Caste,* his most famous play, in 1867. These slight, graceful, rather silly plays do not look much like the start of revolution, and it does not seem to have been a vital part of Robertson's purpose to call anyone in the theatre to arms. Indeed here even Pinero's funny, nostalgic and not essentially inaccurate picture of Robertson in *Trelawny of the Wells* errs somewhat; Robertson wrote what his nature made him write, not in response to any doctrinaire programme.

Certainly *Society,* for all its air of novelty in 1865, does not now seem very revolutionary unless we think ourselves back carefully into the historical context. The story itself is full of devices straight out of Scribe. The Chodd family, rich but far from aristocratic, decide to enter society—as a first step towards which John Chodd Jr. is to get elected to Parliament. With this in view his father hires a 'literary barrister' called Sidney Daryl to run a newspaper supporting the candidate, and this brings on to the scene Daryl's sweetheart Maud Hetherington, who immediately attracts Chodd Jr's attentions. Her aunt, Lady Ptarmigant, supports Chodd's suit, since he is rich and Daryl is poor; Maud does not oppose her because, owing to a conveniently contrived misunderstanding, she has taken it into her head that Daryl's ward is in fact his daughter. Daryl in his turn, hearing at a gathering in the Owls' Roost, a bohemian pub, that Maud is engaged to Chodd, is first reduced to quiet despair and then, in a rousing second-act curtain scene, accuses her of shameless double-dealing during a ball at Lady Ptarmigant's house and leaves her fainting. To fight back he enters the election in competition with Chodd and wins. At last all is revealed: the mysterious ward is really Lady Ptarmigant's granddaughter, orphan child of a scapegrace son, nobly protected by Daryl. Moreover, he comes in for a last-minute legacy, and so all obstacle to his marriage with Maud is removed.

The machinery is quite obviously that of the *pièce bien faite:* the very slightly-based misunderstanding—Maud, hearing little Maud refer to herself as 'Mr. Daryl's little girl', automatically assumes the bachelor Daryl must be her father, and makes no further inquiries—the secret about parentage, the 'strong' curtain tableau, even the *deus ex machina* with a bequest of money out of the blue. But audiences and critics who believed they were seeing something new in the British theatre were not mistaken. First, and most importantly, there is Robertson's way with dialogue. In *Society* he has not yet perfectly mastered his style, but it is still plain enough what he is doing: in place of the prevalent rhetorical style—of Scribe as much as of the normal British drama at the time—he adopts a light, intimate style of short speeches, each one taking up the thread of what has gone before in an easy, natural-seeming way. The characters seem, in fact, to be listening to and answering each other rather than speaking to the audience or at least primarily for the audience's benefit.

This imposes a natural, unemphatic style of acting on the players, and, moreover, requires them to play as an ensemble rather than as so many individuals waiting to deliver their big speeches. The style is not quite consistently maintained: the opening exposition is a little clumsily managed, and big effects like Daryl's denunciation of Maud in the second act fall into melodrama. But enough is there to signal the arrival of a new voice in the theatre and indeed a whole new approach to the business of drama. Even conventions like the simultaneous presentation of two actions independent of each other in the same scene are turned to account: the cross-cutting of Daryl's electoral address with a duologue between Maud and Chodd Jr. broadly but effectively breaks up any possibility of a big rhetorical effect, and points the way to Robertson's far subtler use of the same device in later plays. And if Robertson shows in it little originality as a social thinker, at least he does manage to come up with rough but believable exchanges like this, between rich and poor suitors:

> CHODD JR.. . . . Capital commands the world. The capitalist commands capital, therefore the capitalist commands the world.
>
> SIDNEY. But you don't quite command the world, do you?
>
> CHODD JR. Practically, I do. I wish for the highest honours—I bring out my cheque-book. I want to go into the House of Commons—cheque book. I want the best legal opinion in the House of Lords—cheque book. The best house—cheque book. The best turn-out—cheque book. The best friends, the best wife, the best-trained children—cheque book, cheque book and cheque book.

The great success of *Society* went far to type Robertson as writer of the sort of play by which he is now (if at all) remembered: the romantic comedy-drama of middle-class life, with the upper and lower orders impinging from time to time. As to how far it went in ruthless realism, *The Daily Telegraph* reviewing the first production of *Society* reached a conclusion which still seems fair and valid:

> Those who demand a subtle analysis of human motives, and require an elaborate dissection of the various component parts of the social body,

must seek opportunities for acquiring knowledge elsewhere; but people who care about seeing a clever, sketchy picture of modern men and manners, dashed off in a spirited style, and giving, perhaps, a new view of some gradations in the social scale, may include themselves among the throng who nightly gather round the portals of the cheerful little theatre in Tottenham Street, and make sure of not coming away disappointed.

That is a reasonable judgement: the plots of Robertson's plays may be full of contrivance, and nothing in them goes very deep, but they are constantly illuminated by little insights, strokes of irony which give an edge to the sentiment and do after all remind us of a reality beyond the walls of the theatre. In *Society* the key scene as far as the play's success was concerned was the least conventional: that at the Owls' Roost, which surprised audiences both by the detailed realism of its setting and by the way that its final dramatic effect was underplayed. Here is the opening direction:

> Parlour at the 'Owls' Roost' public house. Cushioned seats all round the apartment; gas lighted on each side over tables; splint boxes, pipes, newspapers, etc., on table, writing materials on table (near door); gong bell on another table; door of entrance near centre; clock above door (hands set to half past nine); hat pegs and coats on walls.

And the action within this setting is equally realistic—or so at any rate the journalists who were feared likely to take offence at it found—and the conclusion is a sharp break with melodramatic tradition. Daryl, one of the revellers, gathers from something which is said that Maud is engaged to his rival, Chodd. Admittedly later, at the ball, he is to have his moment of melodrama over this, but for the moment nothing could be quieter and more restrained. He just starts slightly at the news, and when asked by a friend what is wrong he says 'Nothing'. Then, as the attention of the other club-members switches elsewhere, with a song about how fickle women are, he sits silently at a table and then sinks his head on his hands in a despairing gesture as the curtain falls.

This way of building drama by underplaying it, so novel in the theatre of the 1860s, scored such a success that Robertson knew he was on the right track and exploited it further in *Ours,* the first play he wrote specifically for the Bancroft company. This is a more expertly written play, but suffers from much more improbability in the overall plot. It takes place during the Crimean War, which provides a lightly sketched-in background for three romantic stories: those of Blanche Haye, a young woman being pressed by her guardian Lady Shendryn to marry a rich Russian prince but in love with a poor and diffident Scot; Blanche's friend Mary Netley, who has a sparring love-relationship with the initially effete but eventually heroic Hugh Chalcot; and Lady Shendryn, an unreasonably jealous woman who constantly suspects her husband of infidelity. The plots are set up in England and resolved in the Crimea, when the ladies turn up in conditions of unlikely comfort and convenience to care for their menfolk and see them through unscathed. It may seem curious to us that

the play's original audiences, many in which had personal reason to see the Crimea in a grimmer light, should have accepted this all so readily (the play was more profitable than any Robertson except *Caste*). But no doubt the reason for this was largely the great skill with which Robertson disposed the elements of his comedy, and particularly the ease with which he varied its pace, using to great effect the technique of the election scene in *Society* to set the timid young lovers Blanche and Angus against the bickering of Blanche's guardians in the first act and against the easy bonhomie of Chalcot with the rest in the third.

In *Caste,* the most famous of all Robertson's plays, the method was developed still further. For one thing, there is rather less in the way of plot, so that the characters of the principals can expand at will. Esther Eccles, a young actress, has married George d'Alroy, a handsome young aristocrat who promptly goes off to war and gets himself killed. Most of the play is occupied with the battle of Esther to keep her child and to keep her from d'Alroy's insufferably snobbish mother, the Marquise de St. Maure. In this she is sorely tried by her reprobate father, a boozy old monster who won't work and does nothing but make trouble for everybody—the character is one of Robertson's liveliest. Meanwhile her sister Polly is engaged in a contrasting romance with Sam Gerridge, a respectable workman who believes that everyone ought to keep to his place. In the end George comes back, unharmed, Esther and her child are welcomed into the family by the Marquise, and everything ends in a welter of charmingly sentimental contrivance. But even here, right at the end of the piece, the happy girl and his sister soliloquize thus:

> ESTER. (*aside*) And she will live in a back room behind a shop. Well—I hope she will be happy.
>
> POLLY. (*aside*) And she will live in a fine house, and have a carriage, and be a lady. Well—I hope she will be happy.

The whole play, with its adroit mixing of comedy and sentiment, its light, easy movement and its air of naturalness even when most obviously contrived, has a sort of Mendelssohnian grace and charm which keeps it obstinately alive and fresh when by any reasonable judgment it should be hopelessly faded by now. It is perhaps the high point of Robertson's career—certainly most people then and since have agreed in finding it that. Apparently Robertson thought so too; in any case, having found his style and company, and having confirmed his hold on his audience, he went on writing in much the same vein. Not exclusively, though. So far was he from being doctrinaire about his realistic revolution that in various plays after *Ours,* he showed every willingness to try his hand at old-style melodrama: in *Shadow Tree Shaft* (1867), for instance, in *For Love, or, The Two Heroes* (1867), which was suggested in part by the wreck of the Birkenhead, and in *The Nightingale* (1870), a demented fantasy involving scheming orientals, sopranos inclined to insanity while under stress and a full-scale flood for the sake of stage spectacle—all irresistibly pilloried by W. S. Gilbert in the pages of *Fun.* But try as he might, this sort of play was just not in his line: his graceful love-scenes, subtleties of characterization and occasional shafts of satirical wit—everything in fact which went to make up what one of his biographers called, not unfairly, his 'delicate and scholarly style'—went for nothing and less than nothing, proving positively destructive to the sturdier pleasures which might be expected from melodrama.

His realistic comedy-dramas, however, continued to show a ripening and maturing of the style he had made his own. His next piece for the Bancrofts, *Play* (1868), wandered a little away from it, setting its slightly melodramatic plot in a German gambling resort and varying the simple central love-story with touches of spectacle and interludes of comedy broad to the verge of farce. But *School* (1869) retrieved the situation: it is the slightest, most delicate and tender of all Robertson's plays, a spring-song by Mendelssohn with hardly any plot to speak of and its realism dissolved into a haze of romantic enchantment. It is based remotely on a German play, Roderick Benedix's *Aschenbrödel,* a rather heavy rehandling of the Cinderella story. In Robertson's hands it becomes a romantic comedy about Bella and Naomi, two teachers in a girls' school, and the romantic confusions they produce in the hearts of the neighbouring young gentry. Lord Beaufoy is encouraged by his uncle Percy Farintosh to cultivate their company in the hope that he will fall for Naomi, who happens to be an heiress. But of course instead romance blossoms between him and Bella. The romance gets Bella sent away from the school, but Lord Beaufoy goes after her to London, marries her and brings her back—to the news that she has all along been Farintosh's longlost granddaughter.

Nothing to it at all, in fact, except that Robertson, by now completely master of his craft, lets it run along almost entirely on atmosphere, on the unforced charm of the relations between the young people, and on the knowing touches of eccentric characterization among their elders. Nowhere else is his dialogue so simple and natural: he carefully took the advice of his eleven-year-old son on what sort of answers he would give a teacher if meaning to be pert, and had the astuteness to break up the looming melodrama of a scene in which Bella receives an unwelcome proposal from the odious tutor Krux by having her scream 'Oh, don't!'—and then add, more realistically '—on such a nice day as this!'

By this time Robertson came to write his last play for the Bancrofts, *M.P.* (1870), he was already ill and exhausted from his busy life as a writer, which had included during the five years of his association with the company at least fourteen other plays, several of them adaptations from the French and none at all comparable with his six Bancroft plays. The last few scenes of *M.P.* had to be dictated, as he was too ill to write, and the rehearsals were conducted in his home as he could not come to the theatre. In the circumstances it might be expected that the play would show no advance, and it does not show any very noticeably, though one or two scenes bring Robertson's technique of cutting back and forth from one conversation to another to a new degree of complexity. On the other hand *M.P.* shows no falling off: the rather involved plot is handled with great skill and the characterization, if like all Robertson's characterization based on the modification in detail

of clearly recognizable stereotypes, is as accomplished as ever in ringing the necessary changes.

The story is again one of social degree and romantic impulses which cut across. The Dunscombe estates are passing to a rich parvenu, Isaac Skoome, and to make matters worse Dunscombe Dunscombe's son Chudleigh falls in love with Skoome's ward Ruth instead of his cousin Cecilia, the choice of his father. Meanwhile Cecilia falls in love with Talbot Piers, Skoome's opponent in a parliamentary election, and pays from her own bank account a necessary bribe which he is too high-principled to countenance. Finding that £2,000 of her money has gone Piers at once assumes that Dunscombe has taken it to aid Skoome; Cecilia finds this unforgivable and they quarrel. Meanwhile Chudleigh runs away with Ruth, who was destined to be Skoome's bride; Skoome loses the election to Piers, and Piers and Cecilia are reunited.

So ended, prematurely, Robertson's career as a dramatist. . . . [His] revolution, if such it may be called, was less a full-scale attack on the sort of theatre then in vogue than a significant refinement, a modification of detail. He had learnt technical adroitness from Scribe, and there is no doubt that in the art of telling a story in dramatic terms, keeping the audience *au fait* with what had gone before and panting to know what would happen next, he had few if any rivals in the contemporary English theatre. But by temperament he was not fitted to the wilder flights of melodrama, and so instead he applied this talent to altogether quieter, more everyday material than his mentor usually chose, paying more attention to atmosphere and individual characterization. The result of these two small modifications—the systematic application of Scribe-like technique and the concentration on contemporary middle-class British life for subject-matter—taken together was a new and influential genre: the British realistic well-made play. Perhaps, as has been suggested, Robertson himself imagined that his plays were a brusque English answer to the *pièce bien faite* as established by Sardou, but if so this would be yet another example of how little authors tend to know about the precise nature and sources of their art.

But the influence Robertson was to have in the next couple of decades came only partly from his writing *per se.* For Robertson was perhaps even more influential as a 'stage manager'—director, as we would now say—than as a writer. Though at this time the director in the modern sense was unknown in Britain, Robertson made a point—as long as his health allowed him, which was to within a year or so of his death in 1871—of supervising the production of his own plays in very close detail. To begin with the physical setting of the production did not always match the realistic intentions of the text. The *Pall Mall Gazette,* reviewing *Society* in 1865, remarked that

> In a comedy which aims at realism, and the essential character of which demands *vraisemblance,* the furniture and accessories are of great importance. For these the author is not altogether accountable. Few dramatists are allowed to be stage-managers, and one does not expect to find in Tottenham Court Road the elegance which Madame Vestris exhibited at the Lyceum; but we may reasonably expect to see a fashionable

drawing-room in the 'noble mansion' of Lord Ptarmigant furnished with more than one chair and with a carpet of visible proportions, especially as there are some allusions to the wealth of the British nobleman.

How far this particular deficiency was the result of carelessness and how far simple lack of funds does not seem to be recorded. But what is certain is that Robertson determined that there should be no ground for criticism of this sort again. In *Ours,* the following year, a particular impression seems to have been created by the effect of snow driving into a hut in the Crimea (the background was nothing if not topical) every time the door was opened, but this sort of obtrusive special effect was no great novelty in the theatre. On the other hand *Caste,* the year after, had such refinements on current theatrical practice as sets with ceilings, doors with locks and windows with glass. The advantages, if any, of this can be, and have been, endlessly debated, but undoubtedly at the time such details were considered important, a great stride towards greater stage realism. And this, not because individually they were entirely without precedent, but because they were introduced less as obtrusive production-gimmicks than as part of the whole production's fabric of realism.

Allied with these visual refinements was Robertson's close concern for the style in which his pieces were played. The company for which most of his best plays were written, that run by the Bancrofts, was at this time young, forward-looking, admiring of their author and unusually amenable when it came to instruction. So he found himself in a position to instruct, and his methods at rehearsal have been constantly cited as exemplary by other writers and actors who worked with him. In the 1890s W. S. Gilbert wrote that he regarded 'stage-management as now understood, as having been absolutely "invented" by Robertson', and John Hare, a distinguished alumnus of the Bancroft company who specialized in the portrayal of old men, said that 'As nature was the basis of his own work, so he sought to make actors understand it should be theirs. He thus founded a school of natural acting which completely revolutionized the then existing methods, and by so doing did incalculable good to the stage.'

Thus it was that Robertson's impact on the theatre was as concentrated as it was: the modifications he introduced might be small enough taken one by one, but they all hung together and represented a novel way of looking at the theatre. His own style of writing worked well only in his own kind of play, and his own kind of play worked well only with his own kind of player. But when everything was favourable, as it was especially in his happy association with the Bancrofts, it all worked so spectacularly well that it imposed itself as a model for intelligent English drama for some time to come, and even when Robertson came to seem as old-fashioned to Pinero as Lytton had seemed to him and as Pinero seemed to Shaw, his example was still revered as the only begetter of the realistic English drama which flourished in his wake.

Not that, as far as the writing side of drama was concerned, this flourished very spectacularly for nearly twenty years after Robertson's death. His way of writing was too personal and idiosyncratic to find many followers, and the Bancrofts, while always on the look-out for a new Robertson, found themselves compelled to keep reviving Robertson's plays as the centrepieces of their modern repertory. But something at least did rub off on the dramatists of the 1870s and 1880s: Robertson's plays, and the way the Bancrofts played them, had done much to abolish for ever the rigid categorization of roles in British drama, with the hero, heroine, villain, soubrette, low comedian, old father, etc. each the province of a particular player in a stock company, and each played in much the same rigidly stereotyped way from play to play. Robertson, whatever his drawbacks as a depictor of character, at least believed that every character in a play should be written as an individual, and played as such, without any automatic reference to 'the usually recognized lines of business'. This the Bancroft company put triumphantly into effect, and from 1870 on the concept of every role a character role became standard, at least in the respectable, 'serious' theatre. (pp. 19-31)

> *John Russell Taylor, "Tom Robertson and the 1870s," in his* The Rise and Fall of the Well-Made Play, *Methuen & Co. Ltd., 1967, pp. 19-34.*

Errol Durbach   (essay date 1972)

[*In the following essay, Durbach maintains that Robertson's contribution to drama has been greatly exaggerated and that his minor innovations have been superseded by the greater achievements of Henrik Ibsen and Anton Chekhov.*]

The centenary of Tom Robertson's death passed scarcely noticed by anyone. No one in 1971 could reasonably be expected to acquiesce in George Bernard Shaw's judgment [in "Robertson Redivivus," *Saturday Review* (London) 19 June 1897] of *Caste* as "epoch-making" (albeit a very little epoch) or of Robertson's innovations as a "theatrical revolution" (albeit a very limited one). Reviewing a revival of *Caste* in 1897, some thirty years after its première, Shaw's critique itself reads as a rather fond commemoration of Robertson—a sometimes facetious, sometimes admiring backward glance over the more momentous revolutions and reformations of mind and morals to a minor, quaintly anachronistic triumph of theatrical style.

> After years of sham heroics and superhuman balderdash, *Caste* delighted everyone by its freshness, its nature, its humanity. You will shriek and snort, O scornful young men, at this monstrous assertion. "Nature! Freshness!" you will exclaim, "In Heaven's name (if you are not too modern to have heard of Heaven) where is there a touch of nature in *Caste*?" I reply, "In the windows, in the doors, in the walls, in the carpet, in the ceiling, in the kettle, in the fireplace, in the ham, in the tea, in the bread and butter, in the bassinet, in the hats and sticks and clothes, in the familiar phrases, the quiet, unpumped, everyday utterance: in short, the commonplaces that are now spurned because they are commonplaces, and were then inexpressibly

welcome because they were the most unexpected novelties."

The vital innovations of previous decades appear all too often as the clichés of the modern theatre, and the more scornful may even be inclined to echo Max Beerbohm's dismissal of such period-piece dramatics [in a review dated 25 February 1899 and reprinted in *More Theatres,* 1969]: "Robertson's plays [are], *as plays,* dead as door-nails, but might, properly produced, stimulate the archaeologist and touch the sentimentalist to the quick." It was clearly to the archaeologist in Shaw that Robertson's fussy sense of domestic realism most appealed. But his sentimental inclination saw another admirable element in Robertson's style: a naturalness of character, a humanization, "as humanization was understood in the 'sixties: that is, a discovery of saving sympathetic qualities in personages hitherto deemed beyond redemption. . . . And if from these hints you cannot gather the real nature and limits of the tiny theatrical revolution of which Robertson was the hero, I must leave you in your perplexity for want of time and space for further exposition." What apologist for Tom Robertson, writing in the age of Ibsen, could do more than beg the question when praising the dramatic qualities which a new epoch could simply take for granted and supersede? Such strict domestic verisimilitude is converted by Ibsen into symbol and visual metaphor; and the superficial humanization of Robertson becomes the psychological complexity of Chekhov. There can be no doubt where the greater revolution in nineteenth-century drama is to be found.

Robertson's innovations in theatrical style, in spite of Shaw, were scarcely radical or even novel. The "revolution" had been initiated in France years before by Scribe and Sardou, those forerunners of the bourgeois domestic theatre and the well-made play. In England, Madame Vestris was staging plays with a scrupulous concern for realistic detail, and Bulwer Lytton was already writing the sort of play that would later be called "Robertsonian." It may even be argued that his "humanizing" influence was a consequence rather than a cause of the naturalistic style of the sixties' actors—of Edward Sothern, for instance, or of Charles Mathews to whom Robertson had served as prompter in his apprentice days. To present Robertson as the avant-gardist of a revolution would be to overstate his claims to dramatic importance. One must distinguish between the revolutionary genius who creates new forms and new directions for the drama, and the talented innovator who takes what is available to him in his own effete tradition, adapting it and refining it to some new purpose. The images of "Robertson the Pre-Raphaelite of the Theatre" concerned with practicable stage-equipment, and "Robertson the Revolutionary" creator of natural characterization both misrepresent the nature of his achievement and the spirit of novelty he brought to The Prince of Wales. They were, as Ernest Watson suggested, "a spirit of freshness in utilizing accumulated advantages, and a spirit of war upon imitation and tradition." Well-worn melodramatic situations still form the basis of his plots—but inverted, parodied, and reshaped to wonderfully comic or bathetic effect. In similar fashion, the stock-types of the burlesque stage undergo a metamorphosis in Robertson's

plays without losing contact with the positive element of the earlier tradition. Mrs. Bancroft, we are told, "looked back with horror at her successes at the Strand; she wanted never again to play a *gamin's* part (as we should call it) or to appear in burlesque. Robertson wrote her a succession of *gamin's* parts and burlesque scenes. But the *gamin* was petticoated and the burlesque scenes set in comedy." It is as well to remember that nearly a century elapses between the cup-and-saucer and the kitchen-sink. Indigenous innovations in English drama are few and far between, and a public which mistakes talent for revolutionary genius may surely be forgiven its enthusiasm.

Robertson's "cup-and-saucer" drama was clearly a reaction against melodramatic excess, an attempt to domesticate the overprotested emotional displays of the first half of the century. "An actor," as Maynard Savin says [in *Thomas William Robertson: His Plays and Stagecraft,* 1950], "cannot vibrate with emotion while balancing a tea-cup on his knee." Yet this is precisely the feat that Robertson obliged him to perform. Domestic objects in his comedies serve both to inhibit the demonstration of passion and to deflate its expression. The paraphernalia of bourgeois economy simply overwhelm human pretension, the conventions of the genre imposing upon the action a deliberate restraint, an underplaying of gesture. A single scene from *Caste* will suffice as an example of "cup-and-saucerism" at its most comically absurd and technically perfect. Potential melodrama is held in check by a style of ludicrous understatement. George D'Alroy, presumed killed in action, is mourned for months by his widow and friends; and then, in what ought to be the climax of Act III, he returns to the bosom of his family alive and well—an entrance which has all the shock value of Victorian sensation drama. It occurs in the midst of the inevitable Robertsonian tea-party, fraught with its usual undercurrents of domestic tension.

> *Polly meantime has poured out tea in two cups, and one saucer for Sam, sugars them, and then hands cup and saucer to Hawtree, who has both hands full. He takes it awkwardly and places it on table. Polly, having only one spoon, tastes Sam's tea, then stirs Hawtree's, attracting his attention by doing so. He looks into his tea-cup. Polly stirs her own tea, and drops spoon into Hawtree's cup, causing it to spurt in his eye. He drops eye-glass and wipes his eyes.*

> POLLY. (*Making tea*) Sugar, Sam! (*Sam takes tea and sits facing fire*) Oh, there isn't any milk—it'll be here directly, it's just his time.

> VOICE. (*Outside; rattle of milk-pails*) Miaoow.

> POLLY. There he is. (*Knock at door*) Oh, I know; I owe him four-pence. (*Feeling in her pocket*) Sam, have you got four-pence? (*Knock again, louder*)

> SAM. No (*His mouth full*)—I ain't got no four-pence.

> POLLY. He's very impatient. Come in!

> *Enter George, his face bronzed, and in full*

health. He carries a milk can in his hand, which, after putting his hat on piano, he places on table.

GEORGE. A fellow hung this on the railings, so I brought it in.

Sensation is splendidly undercut by comedy. Men returning from the dead announce their presence with a cat-noise, and enter as if on an errand for the milk-man; and the expression of high-wrought emotionalism and astonishment is rendered impossible by mouths crammed with bread and butter or hands clutching teacups. Sentiment is undermined by deftly handled bathos and nonchalant anticlimax neatly inverts the incipient melodrama. The elaborate stage-directions in the opening sequence, moreover, demonstrate another characteristic feature of Robertson's "cup-and-saucerism": the convention by means of which the tensions of a social group are made to reverberate within the narrowly confining structure of a familiar domestic ritual. By superimposing the staid and genteel English tea-ceremony upon the strained class differences of the pompous military captain and the contemptuous working-class Sam, and by playing both off against the indecorous teasing of Polly, Robertson manages to juxtapose the superficially civilized ritual and the antagonism which it holds in check. This comic interplay between opposing social and emotional impulses is one of Robertson's major contributions to the comic style of English domestic realism.

The pity of Robertson's career is that his style of "Mendelssohnian grace and charm," [in the words of John Russel Taylor, in *The Rise and Fall of the Well-Made Play,* 1967] his sensitivity to the delicate contrapuntal effects of divided action and his novel use of stage properties as vehicles of emotions or conductors of tension, should have been lavished on such small-minded dramatic theses. In spite of the fact that his most successful plays purport to deal with momentous social issues and ideas—the rise to social and political power of the nouveau riche in *Society,* the Crimean War in *Ours,* class differences in *Caste,* the displacement of the aristocracy by a moneyed bourgeoisie in *M. P.*—the governing abstraction inevitably leads towards a conventional ratification of the status quo or loses itself completely in the romanticism of the plot. There is never in Robertson's view of society, as there is in Shaw's, that impression of a great moral intelligence being brought to bear on middle-class values. Social analysis gives way to social observation, and Robertson's view is usually charmingly benign, seldom disturbing the cosy equanimity of his middle-class audience. Love ultimately levels all ranks for him, and his philosophy of conservative social benevolence is summed up in *Caste* (with a little help from Tennyson):

HAWTREE. Yes, best to marry in your own rank of life.

GEORGE. If you can find *the* girl. But if ever you find *the* girl, marry her. As to her station,—

"True hearts are more than coronets,

And simple faith than Norman blood."

HAWTREE. Ya-as. But a gentleman should hardly ally himself to a nobody.

GEORGE. My dear fella, Nobody's a mistake— he don't exist. Nobody's a nobody! Everybody's somebody!

HAWTREE. Yes. But still—Caste.

GEORGE. Oh, caste's all right. Caste is a good thing if it's not carried too far. It shuts the door on the pretentious and the vulgar; but it should open the doors very wide for exceptional merit. Let brains break through its barriers, and what brains can break through love may leap over.

True hearts and simple faith are wretchedly inadequate answers to the problems engendered by a caste system; nor is a supercilious condescension to exceptional intellectual merit likely to win much sympathy. These are the attitudes which W. S. Gilbert was later to parody in the Savoy operas.

Robertson died at an early age, and his achievement remained relatively unassessed for nearly thirty years. Many, of course, acknowledged their own particular understanding of the Robertsonian contribution to the theatre: Gilbert praised his invention of stage-management; John Hare, the actor, saw his "revolution" as one in acting methods; and Shaw acknowledged an indebtedness to the new stage-types that Robertson had created in his comedies. But it was not until the turn of the century that Robertson's work attracted any really significant attention. It was the revival of *Caste* at the Court Theatre in 1897 that produced two memorable reassessments in Shaw's commemorative critique and, a year later at the same theatre, in the production of a charming piece of sentimental biography by Pinero called *Trelawny of the "Wells"*. In this play, Pinero looked back with great nostalgia to the heyday of the Bancrofts, to the period in which he really belonged, and wrote an anachronistic period-piece which delighted even Shaw. Archaeology and sentiment blend most ingeniously in the plot, which not only traces a chapter of theatrical history but presents Robertson's "revolution" in the only form which can make it theatrically viable: through the dramatic metaphor of the theatre, through the actor's medium. The play concerns the fortunes of Rose Trelawny, leading-lady of a theatrical troupe dedicated to pantomime and sentimental melodrama, whose experience of life's little tragedies makes it impossible for her to falsify her feeling in the declamatory style of the old drama. The gulf between human passion and the unreality of theatrical emotion is too wide for her to bridge, and her company cannot now accommodate her newly discovered talents. But waiting in the wings is a young actor-dramatist, thinly disguised as Tom Wrench, who for years has been writing "ordinary" plays in an attempt to "revolutionize" the Victorian stage:

I strive to make my people talk and behave like live people, don't I—? . . . To fashion heroes out of actual, dull, every-day men—the sort of men you see smoking cheroots in the club windows in St. James's Street; and heroines from simple maidens in muslin frocks. Naturally, the managers won't stand that.

Pinero, of course, is popularising the myth of Robertson the revolutionary, making the Tom of his play a far more doctrinaire theorist than Robertson seemed conscious of being. But the truly ingenious enactment of Robertson's contribution to English drama occurs in the final act. By this time Tom has managed to finance a small theatre in which to stage his realistic character-plays, providing Rose Trelawny with a dramatic style which finally corresponds to her experience of life's reality. Act III ends as Tom begins to read aloud from his new play; and Act IV opens with the play being rehearsed in the new theatre: *"The scene represents the stage of a theatre, with the proscenium arch and the dark and empty auditorium in the distance. The stage extends a few feet beyond the line of the proscenium, and is terminated by a row of old-fashioned footlights with metal reflectors."* The play in rehearsal, with a typically monosyllabic Robertsonian title, is aptly entitled *Life;* for even in its sketchy, incomplete form it seems to be a dramatized biography of its romantic leads. They are mirrored by its theme as art mirrors life, the theatrical medium perfectly suited to Pinero's dramatic idea. The theatre-within-a-theatre and the play-within-a-play become devices for the exploration of the various levels of illusion and reality which anticipate Pirandello in their sophistication. And in the rehearsal which becomes a reality, the play which becomes a "life," Pinero produced the most memorable, if not the most accurate, commemorative tribute to Robertson's theatrical achievement.

It is one of the ironies of the English stage that while *Trelawny of the "Wells"* is revived from time to time, Robertson is now almost completely forgotten. There is a rather poignant little interchange in Pinero's play which confronts such unpredictable vicissitudes of theatrical taste and style with a sense of stoical inevitability. The Telfers, two "hams" of the old drama, find themselves lost and bewildered in the new drama:

> TELFER. [*Pointing towards the Green-room*] And so this new-fangled stuff, and these dandified people, are to push us, and such as us, from our stools!
>
> MRS. TELFER. Yes, James, just as some other new fashion will, in course of time, push *them* from their stools.

The push, in Robertson's case, was almost immediate. In spite of the Bancrofts' revivals, his memory seems not to have survived the impact of Ibsen and Shaw upon the *fin de siècle* stage. But although he cannot be said to have influenced the masters of nineteenth-century naturalism, Robertson did, at least, provide a point of departure from which significant European drama might develop. (pp. 284-88)

> *Errol Durbach, "Remembering Tom Robertson (1829-1871)," in* Educational Theatre Journal, *Vol. 24, No. 3, October, 1972, pp. 284-88.*

Michael R. Booth   (essay date 1980)

[*In the following excerpt, Booth considers Robertson's successful collaboration with the Bancrofts and his depiction of middle-class values and themes.*]

Robertson's ideas about the performance of his plays so well accorded with the notions of the Bancrofts that the theatrical union of both parties was a perfect example of a marriage between a dramatist in search of a company and a company in search of a dramatist. One must not think, however, that the debt and the good fortune were all on Robertson's side. The playwright was well acquainted with all aspects of production from his experience on the Lincoln circuit, and had been both a prompter and a stage-manager, jobs that combined much of the function of the modern director. He had very clear ideas as to how his plays should be produced, and the principles of artistic restraint and truth to nature, which were also those of the Bancrofts, were of prime importance to him. At several points in the stage directions of his plays he warned the actor against what he considered exaggerated effect but what an actor nurtured for years on stock company stereotypes might believe to be a standard and acceptable performance. For instance, on the first appearance of the Earl of Eagleclyffe in **Birth** Robertson declares, "It is requisite that no foppery, or swelldom of dress or manner be assumed." At the final curtain of **M.P.** "DUNSCOMBE *masters his emotion."* Robertson glosses this direction: "The actor playing Dunscombe is requested not to make too much of this situation. All that is required is a momentary memory of childhood—succeeded by the external phlegm of the man of the world. No tragedy, no tears, or pocket-handkerchief." Even in the melodrama **The Nightingale** the actor playing the sinister Eastern villain Ismael is instructed that his manner should be " . . . amiable and agreeable, perpetually smiling (no Iago-glances at the pit, and private information to the audience that he is a villain, and that they shall see what they shall see)." In his last play, **War,** the part of a French colonel is to be played " . . . with a *slight* French accent. He is not to pronounce his words absurdly or shrug his shoulders, or duck his head towards his stomach, like the conventional stage Frenchman." A German in the same piece is "to be played with a slight German accent, and not to be made wilfully comic." Robertson does not avoid caricature and comic eccentricity in his plays, for they were essential ingredients of nineteenth-century drama, but he was obviously concerned to set limits which the actor should not overstep.

In performance it is clear that at least at the Prince of Wales's Robertson had artistic control over his plays. The Bancrofts were happy to turn the stage management over to him, and the results much impressed contemporaries. Looking back from the 1880s, W. S. Gilbert thought that stage management "as now understood"—that is, the direction of plays—was absolutely invented by Robertson. Sir John Hare, who acted in all the Prince of Wales's comedies, remembered the playwright's gift in rehearsal of " . . . conveying by some rapid and almost electrical suggestion to the actor an insight into the character assigned him." Hare believed that Robertson founded a natural school of acting. To decide what was or was not "natural" on the stage is very difficult. Every apparently new "natural" actor proves to have antecedents. It is doubtful if Robertson was as much of an innovator here as Hare claimed, considering what had been done previously by actors in comedy like Charles Mathews and Alfred Wigan, but there is no doubt that together with Dion Boucicault he was the first nineteenth-century dramatist to exercise a significant influence on the staging of his plays and the performance of his actors: Gilbert, Pinero, Shaw, and Granville-Barker were followers in this respect rather than leaders.

The restraint and scaling-down of effects evident in Robertson's writing was matched by the style of the Bancrofts. The size of the Prince of Wales's with a seating capacity in 1866 of 814, one of the smallest in London, meant two things: first, that actors did not have to be much larger than life, or strain to produce an impression, and secondly, that a detailed domestic realism of setting was possible in a playhouse where all spectators could observe this detail. The critic Dutton Cook made the first point in reviewing **School:**

> A story gains in strength and significance by being brought so close to the view of the spectators; and the players are not constrained to unnatural shouting and grimacing in order that their speeches may be heard and the expression of their faces seen from the distant portions of the house. Both author and actors are thus enabled to avoid exaggeration of language and manner which has long been a prominent failing in dramatic writing and representation.

When Robertson was too ill to attend rehearsals of **M.P.** the Prince of Wales's company came to rehearse in his house; it was their longest rehearsal period for a Robertson play—six weeks. Henry James probably did not know this, but interestingly he developed the idea of household domesticity in a disparaging remembrance in 1881 of the Prince of Wales's as a "little theatre":

> The pieces produced there dealt mainly with little things—presupposing a great many chairs and tables, carpets, curtains, and knick-knacks, and an audience placed close to the stage. They might, for the most part, have been written by a cleverish visitor at a country house, and acted in the drawing-room by his fellow inmates. The comedies of the late Mr. Robertson were of this number, and these are certainly among the most diminutive experiments ever attempted in the drama.

The Times, reviewing **M.P.,** noted that the actors are ". . . almost at arm's length of an audience who sit, as in a drawing-room, to hear drawing-room pleasantries, interchanged by drawing-room personages." This intimacy and domesticity of decor was matched on the Bancrofts' part by an intimate and quietly domestic acting style. During rehearsals of **Caste** Bancroft (playing Hawtree) told Frederick Younge (who was playing the hero, D'Alroy) that Hawtree should be dark and D'Alroy fair. This surprised Younge, who was accustomed to the conventional dark hero and the fair eccentric swell with long flaxen whiskers and an exaggerated acting style, the sort of stereotyped character represented by E. A. Sothern as Lord Dundreary in Tom Taylor's *Our American Cousin* and by H. J. Byron in several of his own comedies. In the event,

although there is something of the traditional stage fop in the character of Hawtree, Bancroft acted him as a pale man with short, straight black hair, and was praised for his quiet realism and departure from convention. The careful stage furnishing at the theatre was all the more noticed in combination with the care and restraint of the ensemble performance with which it was perfectly in accord. The real doors, the real locks, the snow blowing into the hut of **Ours**—these were not such innovations as critics like Clement Scott and Shaw claimed, since impeccable stage furnishing and realistic stage effects went back in the former case to the management of Madame Vestris at the Olympic in the 1830s and in the latter at least to the well-mounted melodramas of several managements in the fifties and early sixties. However, together with domestic realism of the writing and acting in many of the parts, the staging (after **Society**) impressed many contemporaries. It was the combination of these elements that was in some way revolutionary, not their separate existence.

"Domestic and commonplace" were the adjectives H. Barton Baker applied to Robertson's plays in 1878, plays which he believed required little more from actors than the ". . . tame emotions of everyday existence." He did not exactly mean it as a compliment, but nevertheless this very domesticity and commonplaceness is at the heart of Robertson's appeal, especially as the dramatist was able to bathe them both with washes of sentiment and charm. When Hawtree says in **Caste** that "I suppose I'm about the average standard sort of thing" he typifies much about Robertsonian character that was fundamentally attractive to ordinary, decent middle-class audiences. The juxtaposition of strong emotion and sentiment with extreme domesticity can be seen in the miraculous return from the dead of George D'Alroy in **Caste** in the middle of a front parlour tea, or the smothering of the Crimean War in a mass of detailed kitchen business, including the making of a real roly-poly pudding on stage a few yards from the battlefield, in **Ours.** In instances of this kind Robertson makes a virtue of ironing out great moments of human emotion and great events so smoothly that they seem but wrinkles on the brow of comedy and domestic incident.

There is, however, an aspect of Robertson completely antagonistic to quiet sentiment and domestic restraint—although coexistent—and that is an incipient tendency to melodrama. Robertson certainly did not eschew the conventional plot mechanisms of the nineteenth-century stage, the initial expositions, soliloquies, asides, and strong curtains; the exposition at the beginning of **Caste** and **Progress,** for example, is clumsy. It was especially with act endings that Robertson showed his love of melodramatic effect and his adherence to the traditional conventions of strong curtains that dictated stage grouping and moments of both verbal and wordless climax. The Act II curtain of **Society** is an instance of this familiar method, when Sidney Daryl makes his speech denouncing Maud, which is followed by a crash of music, the near collapse of Maud, and Daryl reeling through a ballroom full of dancers as the curtain falls. Another is the end of the second act of **Play** when the heroine Rosie badly misunderstands the situation when Frank Price appears in the picturesque ruins searching for a trivial box of lozenges and

"AMANDA *reels backwards, and falls fainting into his arms.* MRS KINPECK *sees all this from her perch, and gesticulates with her parasol to those above and below her. Enter* FANQUEHERE, ROSIE, BROWNE, *and* TODDER, *from different points, to form picture.*" Mrs. Kinpeck is, admittedly, a comic figure, but there is no such admixture of comedy at the end of Act II of **Progress,** when Eva staggers suicidally out into the bitter wind and falling snow as "*music—piano*" sounds till the curtain. Nor is it easy to accept Robertson's instruction about **Dreams** (1869)— "The Author requests that this Drama may be played after the style and manner of Comedy, and not after the manner of Melodrama"—when emotionally the play is intensely melodramatic, as at the conclusion of the first act when Rudolf departs for England, leaving his mother and his devoted Lina on stage:

> FRAU. My son—my pride—my life! [*sobbing*] My home will be desolate without thee—what shall I do? I who have watched thee from thy childhood. My noble boy, away in a new world, among new faces, who will keep thee from harm, who watch over thee?
>
> > [*The stage gradually darkens. Vespers sound till end of scene at intervals. Organ heard until end of scene.*]
>
> LINA. Heaven! dear mother, I love him too. [*Bell. The women embrace and sob together.*] We are but two poor women, but we can pray together for his safety and his happiness [*falling on her knees near chair; bell*]—bear up, bear up, your Rudolf, my Rudolf is away [*bell*], but he is watched and guarded, as all are here on earth. [RITTMEISTER *appears at window.*]
>
> RITTMEISTER. Is he gone?
>
> > [INA, *who is kneeling at chair, sobs and hides her face in her hands.* FRAU *points to her.* RITTMEISTER *at window. Bell at intervals as Act Drop descends.*]
>
> (pp. xi-xv)

Birth and **Progress** have the most overtly melodramatic character; that neither was done by the Bancrofts perhaps tells us something about their restraining influence on their author. Contrariwise, the lurid melodrama of **The Nightingale** (though apparently not lurid enough for Adelphi audiences) contains a character from pure Robertsonian comedy in Jack Chepstowe. Yet although the melodrama in the comedies performed at the Prince of Wales's may on the whole be more controlled, it is still there, and breaks out from time to time. A mixture of comedy and melodrama or strong pathetic emotion in the same play was not, however, some awkward compromise or new amalgam of dramatic form arrived at by Robertson, but inherent and traditional in comedy from the beginning of the nineteenth century. It is one illustration of Robertson's indebtedness to his predecessors, but not, as we shall see, the only one.

Robertson's domesticity, the freshness, humour, and sincerity of his writing at its best, to which is joined a genuine delicacy and restraint in feeling and expression, especially in love scenes, all this, curiously mixed with a fondness for the purple passage and the melodramatic climax, is utterly typical of the better comedies. Yet Robertson is not only interesting as the creator of a distinctive style as well as of a range of very human, amusing, and likeable characters, but he also deals in interesting ways with ideas of considerable social significance.

For the historian of attitudes to social class in entertainment, Robertson is absorbing material. The audience of the Prince of Wales's, the Haymarket, and most of the West End theatres was in the 1860s and 1870s primarily middle-class. The Prince of Wales's in particular, with its repertoire, its antimacassars on the seats, its elegance and refinement, and its ten-shilling stalls, deliberately appealed to what would now be called an up-market audience. This audience did not seek to have its comfortable middle-class values challenged, nor was it sceptical and looking for the faith of honest doubt; that sort of comic territory was uniquely the property of Gilbert, not Robertson. What it got from Robertson was reassurance, the comic exploitation but not the discrediting of an unshakeable class position, and the fulfilment of class dreams related to money, ambition, and love; there is much fantasy in Robertson. In performance style and in the handling of character and theme both the Bancrofts and Robertson were extraordinarily skilful at suiting their product to the tastes of their consumers.

The class contrasts and economic antagonisms of the first Prince of Wales's comedy, **Society,** are obvious. Sidney Daryl may be poor, but he is well-born, and by the end of the play comes into his inheritance: the lady, a title, property, and—most respectably—a seat in Parliament. The audience was therefore able to have its cake and eat it. Daryl is both beneath the audience in respectability, income, and position, and above it; he can be both patronised and admired, and his final elevation is a satisfying fantasy common to the nineteenth-century theatre. The Chodds, on the other hand, are newly moneyed vulgarians, generally the most disliked and satirised class of character in Robertson. The Chodds' only value, their only morality, is money, and this is clearly wrong. Chodd Junior declares that with his cheque-book he can purchase anything: friends, a wife, honours, a House of Commons seat. Of course he must receive his comeuppance and lose wife, seat, and possible influence and status. The third side of the triangle is the unabashed and haughty aristocrat Lady Ptarmigant. Her refusal to understand and forgive would carry more dramatic weight if it were not based on the feeble plot devices of coincidences and off-stage events which Robertson could never avoid; similarly, her partial reformation and reconciliation with Daryl is suspiciously coincident with his sudden good fortune—but that may be the point. In any case, like her comically eccentric husband she proves to be good at heart, like all the principal characters except the Chodds, and that is often the main thing in Robertson. The Ptarmigant view of wealth and luxury is little different from that of Chodd Junior, only more aristocratic, and there seems to be little satire of such a view when it is held in the right quarters.

In **Ours** the class position is somewhat more complex. The aristocracy is represented by the quarrelsome and unyielding Lady Shendryn, the brave, harassed, and altruistic Sir Alexander, and the dignified Prince Perovsky. There is no fundamental antagonism to Hugh Chalcot, the representative of a rich brewing family, because he is neither a vulgarian nor too obviously a man of commerce. All the same, his alliance is not with the heiress Blanche Haye, but with Mary Netley, a lady in reduced circumstances. "I know my place," she says, "and if I didn't, Lady Shendryn and the world would make me." The Prince of Wales's audience, one feels, would have approved that sentiment. The heiress is reserved not for the Russian prince, which would have been patriotically unthinkable, but for the brave Scottish officer who goes to war for a change of scene. To be a soldier and an officer is in Robertson to be brave, virtuous, and deserving of good fortune; he admired war and was fascinated by it. In the comedies it is glorified because it is romantic and exciting, because it proves the innate superiority and heroism of the British soldier, and because it makes a man of the likes of Hugh Chalcot. Daryl, Angus MacAlister in *Ours,* D'Alroy, Oscar de Rochevannes in *War*—these are all heroes (in the dramatic sense) and all soldiers. Mary and Blanche in *Ours* even play at soldiers, and the curtain to Act II falls on one of the most rousing and theatrically effective expressions of patriotic feeling on the nineteenth-century stage. The debate in *War* between the jingoism of Colonel de Rochevannes and Karl Hartmann's hatred of war is never resolved, but is evenly balanced while it lasts. It was the nearest Robertson came to the serious examination of a subject that colours the background of several of his plays. *War,* however, is drama, and none of the comedies has anything like even this degree of commentary on war and the concepts of honour and glory. *Ours* is much more typical of the dramatist's attitudes.

War is a remote but romantic background to *Caste,* the one play of Robertson's overtly about class and its "inexorable law". This law can be broken by love but by nothing else; at the end of the play D'Alroy says, "Caste is a good thing if not carried too far. It shuts the door on the pretentious and the vulgar: but it should open the door very wide for exceptional merit. Let brains break through its barriers, and what brains can break through love may leap over." An examination of the comedies reveals that although the door is certainly shut on the pretentious and vulgar and although love certainly leaps over barriers, the breakthrough of merit and brains is not so noticeable— only *Birth* and *Progress* deal with these aspects of ambition and achievement. In *Caste* the class war is carried on purely by comic means. The *prima donna* of the aristocracy is the arrogant Froissart-spouting Marquise, and the radical working-class agitator is the drunken Eccles; any class conflict here is merely ludicrous. More serious is the Marquise's (and initially Hawtree's) attitude to Esther and Polly and to D'Alroy's marriage into the Eccles family, but this problem is overcome by the judicious application of a warm poultice of sentiment and heroism to the wound; as in so much Robertson the main theme fritters away, unresolved and almost forgotten. The lower middle-class tradesman Sam Gerridge is also comic, and his aspirations, though as strong in their way as Chodd Junior's, are rendered socially harmless to the audience by their very nature. Men of trade and commerce are almost invariably funny in Robertson—the exception being Chalcot, who, as mentioned above, does not actually seem to work at the business and is perfectly well bred. A manufacturer like Paul Hewitt in *Birth* is different, and excepted from this kind of comic disparagement because he actually *makes* things rather than too obviously *selling* them. The class division between trade and manufacturing in nineteenth-century comedy was well established before Robertson; in Douglas Jerrold's *Retired from Business* (1851) there are even gulfs of snobbery fixed between the wholesale and retail trades: "Raw wool doesn't speak to halfpenny ball of worsted—tallow in the cash looks down upon sixes to the pound, and pig iron turns up its nose at twopenny nails." The comedy of Sam Gerridge and Polly usefully controls and sometimes ironically undercuts the elements of romantic love and the gravitation to melodrama in the D'Alroy-Esther relationship. In fact the strength of *Caste* lies in this ingenious contrapuntal structure and the rich comic vigour of situation and character, as well as in the detailed and loving observation of a lower middle-class setting used for purposes both comic and serious, ironic and tender.

The elements of dream and fantasy fulfilment in Robertson's comedies are most marked in *School,* based on the German *Aschenbrödel* by Roderich Benedix, a dramatic treatment of the Cinderella story. The eight young women are treated dreamily and sentimentally; their collective sweetness and romanticism may be cloying to our taste, but to the audience of 1869 they represented the beauty of feminine innocence and girlhood, a Victorian ideal of purity and sanctity; the fairy-tale element is strong in the dramatisation of this particular Victorian myth. (*Cinderella* was a very popular pantomime in the last half of the nineteenth century.) Marie Bancroft's reasons for preferring Naomi Tighe to all her other parts are instructive. She admired her "artless simplicity and sunny nature" and "the utter ignorance of any sadness in the whole world except what school discipline enforces, her fearless and open avowal of her romantic adoration"—qualities very necessary to the Victorian image of young womanhood. This ideal is bifurcated in Robertson; half of it was acted by Marie Bancroft: Mary Netley in *Ours,* Polly Eccles in *Caste,* Naomi Tighe in *School,* Cecilia Dunscombe in *M.P.*—characters of intelligence, spirit, activity, and fun. The other half was played by Lydia Foote or Carlotta Addison: Blanche Haye in *Ours,* Esther Eccles in *Caste,* Bella in *School,* Eva in *Progress,* Ruth Deybrooke in *M.P.*—the quieter, more passive, romantic, passionate, and domestic heroine. "I am a woman—I am a wife—a widow—a mother!" Esther Eccles tells the Marquise proudly; of course she is not a widow—the return of the noble husband untouched by war is part of the fantasy— but the other things she is constitute the entire pattern of the ideal. Bella, on the other hand, is purely a fairy-tale character, elevated and rewarded like Cinderella with a prince and a fortune. The opening scene of *School,* with all the girls distributed languorously around a woodland glade, is pure pictorial fantasy, the sort of subject matter not uncommonly found in Victorian oil paintings and watercolours. The plot of *School* is as remote from reality as anything Robertson devised, and there is no hint of contact with the real world, which is somewhere outside the bounds of the enchanted wood—even the evil Krux is a fairy-tale ogre. The appeal of the fairy-tale to the Victorian mind was extremely powerful. By 1869 dozens of editions of English translations from the brothers Grimm and Hans Christian Andersen had been published; the genre of fairy painting had flourished; several notable productions of *The Tempest* and *A Midsummer Night's Dream* had strongly emphasised the fairy elements, as did Christmas pantomime; *Giselle* and *La Sylphide* were popular romantic ballets; *The King of the Golden River, The Rose and the Ring, The Water Babies,* and *Alice's Adventures in Wonderland* had already appeared. It is not surprising that **School** had the longest initial run of any Bancroft production, 381 nights. (pp. xv-xix)

Play and **M.P.** were never revived and must be counted among the weaker effusions of Robertson's pen. Repetition of character, theme, structure, and technique is obvious; despite this the Bancrofts managed to bring off a successful opening run in each case. **Play** is set in a German spa and concerns unscrupulous attempts at fraud and double-dealing which are frustrated, mostly by coincidence. The plan of an already married man to marry the heroine and obtain her fortune, which nobody but he knows she possesses, goes awry through the timely revelation of marital and financial truths. Malicious intent and dark characterisation are nullified and lightened by the sudden reformation of the pseudo-villain. The comic figure of the commercial man appears again, this time in the person of the bourgeois Todder of "Todder's Original Patent Starch", and once again there is the juxtaposition of two simultaneous but very different love scenes, a favourite technique of Robertson's and used with great skill in **Ours** and **Caste.** In the last of the comedies, **M.P.,** the upright and honourable Talbot Piers takes both the girl with a fortune and the seat in Parliament from the *nouveau-riche* schemer Isaac Skoome, whose name betrays his nastiness. Plot structure and themes echo **Society,** but **M.P.** has neither the charm nor the delicate touch of that play. From the evidence of **M.P.** it is clear that Robertson had nothing new to say in comedy, nor any new ways in which to say the old things.

Thematically, the two most potentially interesting Robertson comedies are not those the Bancrofts produced but **Progress** (1869) and **Birth** (1870). Like **Society,** the first was written for the Buckstone company at the Haymarket and, like **Society,** not performed by them. The original destination of **Progress** is indicated by the large part for Bunnythorne, the sort of character Buckstone had been playing for years, and for Bob Bunnythorne, meant for Buckstone's son. **Birth** was written for Sothern—thus the substantial and distorting part for the largely irrelevant Jack Randall—and was successful in the provinces. Sothern, however, did not have the courage to bring the play in its present form into London, and Robertson was too ill for rewriting. The first acts of both plays are promising. In **Progress,** adapted from Sardou's *Les Ganaches,* the clash is between the old aristocracy and the new technocracy, between the values of tradition and the values of technological innovation and radical social change; in **Birth** the conflict is between the aristocracy of the old landowner and the manufacturing power of the new in-

dustrialist. In **Progress** the railway and the Abbey come face-to-face; in **Birth** the castle glowers down at the new ironworks. Class antagonism is initially bitter in both plays. **Progress** also contains the character of a retired tradesman who is the object of amusement not unconnected with his devotion to all things old and tested.

Yet these striking themes dwindle into triviality after the first acts of both plays. Unlike some of his predecessors Robertson was never able to sustain the serious dramatic development of socially significant themes, despite the titles of the plays, which suggest more in content than they deliver. This did not much bother his contemporaries, although they noticed it. They frequently employed terms like "truth to nature" and "realism" to describe his achievement, but several recognised the fact that this was nature and realism on a small scale. John Oxenford praised **Caste** in *The Times* for " . . . a connection with the realities, which, perhaps, must not be too closely scrutinised, but which, to a certain extent, makes the stage reflect the world with more than usual accuracy." Baker thought that Robertson dealt only with "the superficial phases" of civilisation, and Henry James disdainfully dismissed the comedies as "infantile" and "addressed to the comprehension of infants". The problem that we can recognise, although it did not disturb Victorian audiences, is that as in so much Victorian comedy the subject matter of ambition, pride, wealth, class conflict, social position, commercialism, privilege, and so on, is finally either resolved (if one can call it a resolution) or pushed aside by the pressing claims of love and marriage. This is particularly true in Robertson, and **Birth** and **Progress** are examples of the impulse in his work to cover the initial and potentially vital social themes with a thick candy-floss of sweet sentimentality and romantic entanglements. Thus in **Progress** Ferne the engineer falls in love with the stricken Eva; there is no more talk of the subject matter of the first act, and at the end Eva says to *"music, piano,"* "My path must lead to happiness when love and hope conduct me, and affection and experience guide me—(*smiling*)—That's Progress!"—a rather different notion of progress from that propounded in the dialectic of Act I. Similarly, in **Birth** the gulf of class hostility between industry and aristocracy is easily bridged by the intermarriage of the rival families. Even in the drama **War** the theme of war itself and the antagonism of opposing views are forgotten and subordinated to romantic sentiment and the triumph of love. Economic difficulties and humble status are not overcome by effort—the people who make that sort of effort and are successful, the Chodds, the Skoomes, the Bunnythornes, the Todders of the Robertson world, are vulgarians and are to be laughed at or vanquished, or both—but by the *deus ex machina* of a fortune or a title, as in the case of Sidney Daryl, Rosie Fanquehere in **Play,** and Bella in **School.** Potentially serious themes may not exactly be abandoned, but are developed through love relationships and romantic sentiment. In this development, however, they become diluted and enervated. Yet it may be unfair to criticise Robertson in the 1860s for not writing the sort of play we might want him to write, and for not fulfilling the thematic potential of the early acts of his plays. They were, after all, light comedies written to entertain and reassure a pleasure-seeking middle-class audience; it was not

Robertson's responsibility to be a Shaw a generation ahead of his time.

In using romance and endings that brought happiness, marriage, and wealth to his main characters, Robertson was only following the standard pattern of development in several preceding generations of stage comedy. Thematically he was no innovator. All his theme material is inherited from older writers. The coexistence of the melodramatic and pathetic with the ludicrous and comically satiric has already been noted, and this mixture, characteristic of English drama, had immediate antecedents in the early nineteenth-century comedy of George Colman, Thomas Morton, Frederic Reynolds, and others. The ambitious parvenu is satirised in the person of a retired stationer aspiring to Parliament and a baronetcy in Mrs. Gore's *Quid Pro Quo* (1844) and in the wife of the retired grocer in Jerrold's *Retired from Business*. The relationship of wealth to social ambition and class standing is satirically explored by a really important and influential comedy, Bulwer-Lytton's *Money* (1840), although this may have owed something to an especially savage attack upon the corruption engendered by money in Jerrold's *The Golden Calf* (1832). Several of *Money*'s ideas of position and fortune and the lengths people will go to obtain them are picked up by Boucicault in *The School for Scheming* (1847), which is much concerned with the world of commerce, capitalist speculation, and "progress". The play sustains the serious themes for four acts but collapses in the fifth; Robertson was not the only Victorian playwright who would not or could not pursue his intellectual concepts to the final curtain. Another author of comedies who failed to do this was Jerrold, despite *The Golden Calf*. *Retired from Business* veers off into love and sentimentality in the same way as does Robertson. The bright ideal of womanhood, the innocence and purity of Victorian girlhood, the apotheosis of wifehood and motherhood—these shine through and dominate so many Victorian comedies and dramas before Robertson that it would be pointless to enumerate them. Idealism about life so intense that it almost becomes—and sometimes does become—fantasy is strong in Robertson as in his progenitors, and nowhere is his idealism stronger than in his depiction of young love between serious characters; it is really no wonder that love usually sinks the thematic freight of other concerns without a bubble. Robertson's skill in making this love interesting and dramatically credible through seemingly ordinary conversation and a quiet, hesitant, coming together of mutually attracted couples is considerable, and here he had no predecessors.

Since Robertson came toward the end of a long and developing tradition of English comedy, he represents an end rather than a beginning. One can easily trace the varied influences of the past upon his work, but it is harder to say how significant was his impact upon succeeding dramatists. Certainly his immediate contemporaries quickly absorbed his techniques. Tom Taylor's *New Men and Old Acres*, which appeared in the same year as *School* and *Progress*, is a less rumbustious comedy than others Taylor had written before; the love scenes are restrained and quietly sentimental somewhat in Robertson's manner. The themes of the vulgar *nouveau-riche* pitted against the

proud aristocrat, of technology clashing with tradition, are close to Robertson as well as to the substance of Victorian comedy. James Albery intensifies Robertson's sweetness and sentimentality in *Two Roses* (1870), a story of idealised love as well as melodramatic intrigue and low comedy derived from the character of a travelling salesman. Gilbert was undoubtedly influenced by Robertson in his duet for two lovers, *Sweethearts* (1874), a graceful, controlled, and delicate comedy, written for the Prince of Wales's and for Mrs. Bancroft. Later he went his own way into realms of cruel satire and topsy-turvydom that Robertson could never have created.

Robertson's influence on the next generation of playwrights was probably small. Pinero drew on the techniques of French dramatists, the themes of social guilt and fear of social exposure in the Mayfair society around him, and the determinism of Ibsen. The comedies of Henry Arthur Jones were closer to Pinero than to Robertson, with a strong admixture of melodrama and the old stock company stereotypes which he and Pinero and Shaw transformed but never abandoned. (It should not be forgotten that Robertson wrote for a stock company, and there are traditional character stereotypes in his plays too.) It is true that much English comedy developed in the direction of rather ordinary middle-class domestic reality after Robertson, and this may be his most significant dramatic legacy; there were, however, firm indications of this direction before *Society.* In 1897 all that the sympathetic Shaw could really advance in favour of Robertson was the domestic reality of his settings, the novel domestic commonplaces of his dialogue, and the humanity of his observation and characterisation. This is much, but it does not constitute the *oeuvre* of an original and influential dramatist; these characteristics can be found—though not in combination—in previous drama and staging. Yet even taking into account all influences and indebtedness, conscious or unconscious, Robertson's dramatic territory is his very own and nobody else's. This makes him unique, and to be unique is to be important. The humanity to which Shaw draws attention, the charm, the domesticity, the style, the peculiar fairyland of his dramatic vision, the very Englishness of his work, all these make him a dramatist to be respected, valued and prized. (pp. xix-xxiii)

Michael R. Booth, "T. W. Robertson," in Six Plays *by T. W. Robertson, Amber Lane Press, 1980, pp. vii-xxiii.*

William Tydeman (essay date 1982)

[*Tydeman is an English educator and critic who is interested in "the inter-relationship between the playtext on the printed page and its realization on the stage." In the following excerpt, he examines Robertson's major plays and surveys their changing critical reception.*]

It has never been a simple matter to deal justly with even the best plays of Tom Robertson. Excessively admired and lavishly praised in their own generation, often for features whose lasting merit has proved dubious, they have since that time been sadly undervalued and harshly denigrated for lacking qualities to which they never made pretence.

If Robertson's popularisation of certain fruitful innovations in the character and presentation of English stage plays once led effusive disciples to link his name with Ibsen's, his role in establishing a vogue for genteel, amiable, optimistic comedies of respectable middle-class life has frequently doomed him to unjustified dismissal. Yet, if both attitudes seem misguided, it is equally mistaken to ignore Robertson's place as both pioneer and influence.

To appreciate the work of Tom Robertson truly, we have to reconstruct not only the prevalent tendencies of the stage he helped to reform, and the constitution of the principal dramatic company for which he wrote his best plays, but also the changing preferences of the age in which he lived. His brief life coincided with a transition in British theatrical taste from a penchant for the heroic and exotic to a preoccupation with the native and domestic, from a love of the overtly histrionic to an obsession with the ostensibly lifelike, and his personal share in bringing about this significant shift in public demand must not be forgotten. Like Bernard Shaw, who was later to commend Robertson's novelty of approach, he too endeavoured to replace the extravagant and outworn conventions of the drama of his day with portrayals of human behaviour and conditions more closely related to actuality. Admittedly, unlike Shaw's, Robertson's intellect was unoriginal, his moral and social thinking orthodox, but at his best he established the dramatic validity of placing unextraordinary people in recognisably mundane settings, of involving them in everyday situations to which they responded in credible ways while conducting their affairs through convincingly authentic conversation. His is still far from being a literal imitation of life, but if with hindsight Robertson's 'revolution' seems only a timid step in the evolution of the naturalistic movement in the theatre, it should not be written off as unsound in principle.

To cater for the new predilections of Victorian theatregoers, the playwright was in one sense amply equipped, his impeccable theatrical pedigree supplementing possession of an intimate personal knowledge of current stage practice and popular requirements. But this familiarity did not bestow on Robertson those automatic advantages which some commentators have claimed for him. His experience of the early nineteenth-century equivalent of 'provincial rep' exposed him to the tried and tested formulae of dramatic literature at a young age, so that he might have been forgiven for remaining inhibited for ever by the conventions accepted by many of his contemporaries. As it is, given the number of Victorian authors from outside the playhouse who professed an interest in 'reviving the drama', it is curious that perhaps the most successful individual 'reformer' of nineteenth-century English plays not only emerged from within the ranks of the profession, but achieved his results by promulgating the ideal of a theatre which would take its subject-matter and artistic criteria from contemporary life rather than from hallowed stage tradition.

In this he was neither unique nor alone: we should never forget that there were precedents for Robertson's practices, or that he was supported in his aims by a 'production team' whose concern for accuracy, refinement, and detail was fully equal to his own. It was his good fortune to have his first play with any genuine claim to originality accepted by an enterprising and youthful management prepared to take risks in pursuit of high standards of theatrical artistry, and all his subsequent triumphs were gained through adherence to the same principles and allegiance to the same personnel which had unexpectedly made *Society* the talk of London in 1865. The complaisance and gentility of proceedings at the Prince of Wales's Theatre should not be allowed to detract from the courage and integrity with which the Bancrofts carried through their reforms in stage management and playhouse procedure, just as the obviousness and popularity of Robertson's comedies should not obscure their innate stageworthiness or their author's instinctive understanding of what makes for satisfying theatre.

For it is not enough merely to urge the historical importance of what Robertson accomplished; any true assessment of his quality as a playwright must depend eventually on the intrinsic pleasure and satisfaction obtained from his plays when viewed from the auditorium or recreated in the imagination. Apart from periodic revivals of *Caste,* the modern stage has largely elected to pass Robertson's work by, yet many of his pieces possess immense latent theatrical appeal, and would repay respectful (which is not the same as pedantically reverential) revival. Most of them feature 'well-made' if slender plots with watertight *dénouements,* a broad range of personages memorable for their distinctive characteristics and vitality, and a wealth of effective and pleasing scenes encapsulating fundamental aspects of Victorian society, its values, conduct, and beliefs. If it be objected that they also abound in dramatic contrivances and coincidences, in trivial fooling or sentimental banter, in tritely sententious maxims, in arbitrarily achieved conclusions, and in facile solutions to complex problems, it must be remembered that these are also the weaknesses of much Victorian writing, even outside the playhouse. Affronted zealots have never been slow in sneering at Robertson's 'teacup-and-saucer' or 'bread-and-butter' school of playwriting; what they tend to ignore is that Robertson's wholesome bread-and-butter enraptured a public surfeited with cheap cake, and his homely brew, if oversweetened, can still prove distinctive enough to placate even today's sophisticated taste-buds. (pp. 1-2)

With the passage of time it is impossible to say whether what struck *Society's* early audiences as novel was truly so: certainly many inaccurate claims have since been made for Robertson on the grounds that his was the first English piece in which box-sets and real ceilings, actual doorknobs or coat-hooks or genuine food for stage meals, were employed. In productions at the Prince of Wales's no doubt part of the attraction lay in the good taste of the management in supplying 'everything of the best', but that *Society* was innovatory or even satisfactory in this particular is belied by the *Pall Mall Gazette's* tart observations of 17 November 1865:

> In a comedy which aims at realism, and the essential character of which demands *vraisemblance,* the furniture and accessories are of great importance. For these the author is not altogether accountable. Few dramatists are allowed to be

stage managers, and one does not expect to find in Tottenham Court-road the elegance which Madame Vestris exhibited at the Lyceum; but we may reasonably expect to see a fashionable drawing room in the 'noble mansion' of Lord Ptarmigant furnished with more than one chair and with a carpet of visible proportions, especially as there are some allusions to the wealth of the British nobleman . . .

Yet, setting aside financial limitations on *Society*'s budget, perhaps the reviewer, in drawing adverse comparisons with Vestris, was missing the point: Vestris had been required to make her art one of diversion; Robertson aimed to do a little more than amuse and give pleasure. Despite its romantic interest, *Society* seems intended to offer some serious observations on modern civilisation: that hard cash is no substitute for generous impulse and considerate behaviour; that snobbery and hypocrisy are to be despised at whatever class-level they occur; that the press wields immense power for good or evil; that good fellowship and loyalty count for more than social prestige. Sidney with his hatred of pretensions, folly, and cant, Tom Stylus with his deflationary horse-sense, are descendants of the men of honesty and honour from Restoration comedy, while the collision between the vulgar *nouveaux riches* and a scion of the old aristocracy prefigures dramas yet unborn, including Galsworthy's *The Skin Game* of 1920. Robertson's plays are not High Art, but they are not mere *jeux d'esprit* either. Moreover, although Vestris had introduced a measure of realism to her presentations, practically all her dramatic material was highly unrealistic: in *Society* and its successors not only were set, costumes, and properties 'lifelike', but dialogue, situations, stage business, theme, and character usually combined harmoniously with the mounting of the production to achieve a total effect, namely that of conveying the illusion that spectators were witnessing a faithfully recorded, unexaggerated series of events taken from ordinary life in all its flat normality. The size of Lord Ptarmigant's carpet was a detail.

But verisimilitude was not the only key to *Society's* success: partisans such as Clement Scott [in *The Drama of Yesterday and To-day,* 1899] were inclined to regard the freshness and youth of the company as significant:

> the young, good-looking, well-dressed actors and actresses on the stage were a change indeed after the . . . old fossils who persisted in playing young lovers and dashing sparks when they were rapidly qualifying for the role of grandfather . . . *Society* was never intended for the fossils of the old school, but for the bright young fellows of the new . . .

Scott was notoriously prone to overstate the novelty of Robertson's methods and achievements, yet playwright, management, and public certainly came to believe that *Society*'s success heralded a new movement in the English theatre; whatever the secret of its appeal, it held the stage for over 150 performances and paved the way for Robertson's other Prince of Wales's ventures. Bancroft himself accounted for the dramatist's impact in the following terms:

> In those now far-off days there had been little at-

tempt to follow Nature, either in the plays or in the manner of presenting them. With every justice was it argued that it had become a subject of reasonable complaint with reflective playgoers, that the pieces they were invited to see rarely afforded a glimpse of the world in which they lived . . .

> The Robertson comedies appeared upon the scene just when they were needed to revive and renew intelligent interest in the drama. Nature was Robertson's goddess, and he looked upon the bright young management as the high-priest of the natural school of acting. The return to Nature was the great need of the stage, and happily he came to help supply it at the right moment.

It is easy now to smile at Bancroft's earnest assertions: the belief that Robertson's plays, with their fortunate coincidences and lucky contrivances, their just deserts and happy endings, constitute 'a return to Nature' seems ludicrous. He may have persuaded the denizens of Mayfair that it was safe to re-enter a playhouse, but it would be several decades before even society's more intelligent and perceptive elements would accept an unvarnished portrait of *true* social and economic conditions on the stage. Yet Robertson unwittingly paved the way to that goal: his plays do convey something of the quality of everyday existence where meals are eaten, watches consulted, pipes smoked, peas shelled, half-crowns borrowed, and galoshes fetched; behind the fiction some of the domestic and ethical pressures of the age can be dimly discerned, and in his far from facile characterisations intimations of psychological complexity filter through. In introducing even a hint of these factors into his pieces Robertson cautiously unbolted a door which bolder spirits were to fling wide. *Society* and its sequels are no more 'like life' than the plays Robertson strove to displace, but they are a little less 'unlifelike' and that is part of their claim on posterity's attention.

When *Society* was produced in London Robertson had just over five years left to live, and into this period he crammed a fierce amount of work. In addition to his labours as a playwright, he also directed a number of those pieces he composed, becoming the virtual founder of a new school of organised, authoritative, meticulous 'stage management', and an important forerunner of today's director of plays. The fact that he was thus able to dictate, not only what was said on stage, but how it was spoken, not only what was done but the manner of doing it, obviously ensured for him a greater degree of control over his work than most dramatists could command. It also enhanced the reputation of the Prince of Wales's as the home of tastefully homogeneous productions and polished ensemble playing where egocentricity was not tolerated. Because they found such carefully-presented fare to their liking, the well-to-do and better-educated continued to be the Bancrofts' chief patrons, notwithstanding the presence in the gallery of the former clients of the 'Dust Hole', and it was their preferences and prejudices that Robertson seems increasingly to have catered for. Gradually prices were raised, the pit eroded by successive extensions of the stalls, and the 'smart little bandbox' refurbished on more than one occasion. The 'carriage trade' also expected the dra-

Playbill for Robertson's first play at the Prince of Wales's Theater.

matic accent to be placed on restfulness and respectability: the harrowing or vulgar was to be avoided at all costs, and Robertson's later work tends to be, like his dress circle, 'lined with rose-bud chintz'.

He wrote five more comedies for the Prince of Wales's company after *Society: Ours* (1866), *Caste* (1867), *Play* (1868), *School* (1869), and *MP* (1870). All enjoyed enormous acclaim, although *Play* and *MP* were generally felt to be less satisfactory than the others, even if their popularity with the public was only slightly less marked. Robertson's plays for other theatres are, however, a different matter: he achieved little success with old-fashioned melodramas such as *Shadow-Tree Shaft, For Love,* and *The Nightingale,* and while there are effective and typical episodes in *Home, Dreams, Progress,* and *Birth,* none of them possesses the sustained power of the Prince of Wales's comedies by which Robertson must stand or fall. It is certainly difficult to deny the suggestion that he never obtained his best results away from the Bancrofts' intimate, miniature playhouse, however sternly Bancroft might point to *Caste*'s popularity at the vast Standard Theatre, Shoreditch, in 1873, or John Hollingshead claim that *Dreams* did excellent business at the Gaiety. As Dutton Cook remarked in his review of *School:*

> It may be noted that the limited size of the Prince of Wales Theatre is of real advantage to the class of plays Mr. Robertson is fond of producing; a story gains in strength and significance

by being brought so closely to the view of the spectators; and the players are not constrained to unnatural shouting and grimacing in order that their speeches may be heard and the expression of their faces seen from distant portions of the house. Both author and actors are thus enabled to avoid the exaggeration of language and manner which has long been a prominent failing in dramatic writing and representation.

The preparations for *Ours,* the sequel to *Society* completed during the summer of 1866, did not augur well: the piece, said to have been inspired by Millais's Academy picture *The Black Brunswicker,* was certainly infused with Robertson's perennial fascination with things military, a brother having actually served in the Crimea, but dissension followed the initial reading of *Ours* to the Prince of Wales's company who were to give the play its pre-London try-out in Liverpool themselves. The part of Hugh Chalcot (assigned to John Clarke) was felt to be too dominant; Hare only agreed to play the 'insignificant' role of Prince Perovsky as a personal favour to the author; Marie Wilton was disappointed with the character of Mary Netley, and much of the 'business' developed during act III was devised by her with Robertson's consent in order to 'flesh out' a figure which, as a result, tends to eclipse that of the more mature Blanche. Furthermore, in her efforts to sparkle, Marie Wilton resorted to the somewhat pointless techniques of burlesque, a fault critics were quick to reprove. On the other hand, the device of matching a quiet, introverted girl with a more mercurial, 'sparky' companion is effective, and Robertson was often to repeat it, so much so that these female pairs became something of a trademark, whose influence lingers in James Albery's *Two Roses* (1870), Gilbert's *Engaged* (1877), Pinero's *Dandy Dick* (1887), and even *The Importance of Being Earnest.*

It is not surprising, in view of the preliminary unrest, that Robertson supervised rehearsals for *Ours* in a state of some anxiety, or that by the opening night in Liverpool he was in a condition of high nervous tension as to the play's fate, which was only dispelled when it became clear that *Ours* was a hit. Before the production opened in London on Saturday 15 September 1866, alterations were made to the troublesome third act, and Frederick Younge, a long-standing friend of the playwright, replaced Fred Dewar as Sergeant Jones. The capital's response to the new piece was overwhelming: *The Times* for 19 September, in describing it as 'an exact specimen of the ultra-real school of comedy', singled out for particular praise examples of 'the minute regard for detail which is so indispensable to this species of comedy', which included the pattering of the rain on the leaves of the trees in act I, the sounds of bands and marching columns off stage in act II, and the military and domestic paraphernalia in the hut for the final act. Most remarked upon, however, were the now-legendary 'realistic' flurries of driven snow which accompanied the opening of the hut-door, which startled with their novelty. In summing up, *The Times* gave its opinion that 'the success of *Ours* is complete beyond the shadow of a doubt'.

For all but the most captious, *Ours* retains its charm and

appeal, though it is a more markedly 'period piece' than *Society,* where the bluff humour of the Bohemians and the satirical exposure of the vulgar *parvenus* can still be relished. In *Ours* genteelly flirtatious romance is made more of, and the *ambience* is high Victorian, without those Regency touches which enliven *Society* with its duns and drunks, its prize-fighters and its Pickwickian election. The pictorial element in *Ours* often appears posed: the lovers under the great trees of an English park, the *Black Brunswicker* tableau and 'The Girl I Left Behind Me' off stage, the song at the piano, the captured colour, all are reminiscent of Victorian book-illustrations or song-covers, stimulating an unthinking response by their picturesque blandness. Even the very real hardship of the Crimean winter is rendered merely piquant, its miseries almost flippantly transformed into petty irritations, while war is glamourised, yet trivialised too. To be just, *Ours* is romantic comedy whatever its pretensions to realism; for the military heroes Hugh and Angus love finds a way, just as the resource of British womanhood rises superior to the rigours of the Crimean campaign and the urgent necessity for roly-poly pudding.

In terms of construction, however, *Ours* represents a considerable advance on *Society* with its episodic development, laboriously interwoven narrative threads, and diffuse cast: the three couples introduced in act I of *Ours* retain the centre of the stage throughout, with Sergeant Jones and the enigmatic Perovsky acting as foils rather than distractions; the dialogue often has real pace, and Robertson's ingenious method of juxtaposing the exchanges of his paired protagonists for the purpose of ironic comment arouses an interest not unlike that found in *Much Ado About Nothing* or *A Midsummer Night's Dream.* Admittedly, Scribean tactics are once again clumsily employed to set Lady Shendryn and her husband at loggerheads in acts I and II, in order to effect their tearful reconciliation in act III, and some of the extraneous foolery jars, but these are minor flaws, even the apparent improbability that a trio of women could be brought to within a short distance of so much as a skirmish with the Russians being rendered less damaging by the knowledge that some serving officers *were* joined in the Crimea by their wives. Not that *Ours* is in any sense literal documentary: it is rather a set of interrelated contrasting love stories, coloured by some fairly realistic tints, and it must be judged as a piece of light fiction in a non-fictional setting. Discrepancies were perhaps inevitable. (pp. 13-19)

Although based on Robertson's short story '**The Poor-Rate Unfolds a Tale**', *Caste* also appears to owe a debt to a true story of the courtship of one of Robertson's innumerable sisters in similar circumstances to Esther's, although the final details remind us once again that his purposes never involved the direct transcription of actuality. Whatever the spark which kindled *Caste*'s cheerful flame, there can be little doubt that this honest-to-goodness, plain comedy remains the high point of Robertson's achievement, and that he never wrote as good a play again: it is the only one of his pieces even remotely familiar to theatregoers today, and the reasons are not difficult to comprehend. Firstly, it is an extremely economical play in terms of plot and characters, even the utter simplicity

of its basic narrative making for a coherent and craftsman-like structure where the resolution of one problem creates the next. Each memorably-etched character may only be a modification of a stock type, as Shaw was later to stress, but nonetheless each is clearly defined, nicely discriminated from its associates, and forms part of an attractive pattern of contrasts and conflicts, of which the combinations are endless: George and Hawtree; Esther and Polly; Polly and Hawtree; George and Esther; Sam and Hawtree; Eccles and the Marquise; the Marquise and Esther. Moreover, in true ensemble spirit the acting honours are equally divided, and the rich quality and variety of the characters unequalled in the entire Robertson canon: Polly, Sam, Eccles, and the Marquise (with a little help from Froissart) are interesting as much for what they say as what they do, and their distinctive speech styles divert attention from the occasional plunge into the older grandiloquent manner, of which the injured Esther is the most frequently guilty. But such lapses are rarer in *Caste* than elsewhere in Robertson's works: here he perfected the apparently natural, semicolloquial, telegraphic conversational manner which in *Society* and *Ours* was sometimes at the mercy of the declamatory highfalutin' strain considered *de rigueur* at moments of great emotional tension, and the idiom of Eccles, however Dickensian at base, is unforgettable. Finally, there is in *Caste* genuine comedy, chiefly but not exclusively emanating from Eccles whose comic rascality can be richly savoured still; the sparring of Polly and Sam may be only mildly amusing, but there is Hawtree who is caricatured just sufficiently for the purposes of laughter, but never to the point of ridicule, so that his deeper qualities are revealed as a surprise but not as a flagrant impossibility. The Marquise, too, while a figure of fun for much of the action, retains a measure of justification for her conduct and attitude, so that the final reconciliation can be endorsed and not sneered at.

Naturally, it is not hard to sneer at *Caste* if one chooses: Robertson does not really close with the question of class distinctions and their validity: he prefers to drown any exploration of the issues in a sea of sentimental tears over a bassinet. His faith in emotional outpouring and the impulses of the tender heart to overcome awkward social and moral problems is typical of countless writers of his day, not always excluding Dickens, and his admiration for Sam is symptomatic of an age prepared to tolerate working-class aspirations so long as the artisan 'knew his place'. *Caste* and plays like it helped to hypnotise the Prince of Wales's clientele into the comforting illusion that a class system which permitted society's Georges and Esthers to marry and live happily ever after was in little need of restructuring or abolishing, and that the maintenance of the *status quo* was the best guarantee of a healthy and contented populace.

But we do not have to endorse a play's premises in order to admire it, and as a technical accomplishment for the theatre of any age one must admire *Caste.* Granted the permissible objection that George is reported killed rather than merely missing, there is little that cannot be accepted as credible; there are few artificial contrivances of a Scribean nature, and if the finale with its mock-ballet seems unnecessarily protracted, it may perhaps be attributed chiefly to Polly's sense of theatre. In its geniality, its economy, its domesticity, *Caste* is the happy apotheosis of the new comedy.

Robertson's next work for the Bancrofts was *Play,* staged on 15 February 1868; in the interim he had married for a second time, his new wife being of German origin (his first wife died in 1865), and *Play* is set in a German watering-place amid gamblers and tourists. It was the least well-liked of the Prince of Wales's pieces, never being revived, and a reading soon makes it clear why. For one thing Robertson had reverted to the looser type of construction eschewed in *Ours* and *Caste,* and peopled the stage with a heterogeneous cross-section of society engaged in miscellaneous adventures not all of which coalesce. The sole function of several farcical figures of a kind Robertson had been at pains to humanise elsewhere seems to be not so much to supplement the main action as to distract attention from it. Even the principals are not built on the natural lines of their predecessors, but are mostly unconvincing clichés: rich brave young man; sweet apparently penniless girl; heartless philandering aristocrat; devoted, deserted actress-wife. One can understand Robertson's desire to produce a more panoramic canvas than had been possible in *Ours* or *Caste,* but in so doing he betrayed the principles that had brought him success. Hawes Craven's sets were highly commended as capturing the essence of the German landscape, but the only episode in the play to match them for delicacy and 'truth to life' was the love scene between Frank Price and Rosie in the castle ruins.

The relative failure of *Play* was however redeemed by the runaway commercial success of *School,* the most popular of the Prince of Wales's group of comedies, which opened on Saturday 16 January 1869 and ran to crowded houses for an amazing 381 performances. This fact is an interesting comment on Robertson's work, for, though less sprawling than *Play, School* is only a little more distinguished as a dramatic creation; the difference is basically that *School* is more typically 'Robertsonian'. It embodies the most characteristic aspects of his art: an idealised English setting; sharp characterisations and flowing dialogue; gentle humour; pretty stage pictures; the sentimental charm of schoolgirl heroines; a whiff of aristocracy to satisfy the sycophantic instincts of middle-class spectators. *The Times* for 18 January 1869 once more led the chorus of critical approbation, observing that the presentation of a new play by Robertson at a theatre which had now become one of the most fashionable in London was to be regarded as one of the most important events of the dramatic year. It was acknowledged that *School*'s plot was of the slightest, yet this was felt to be no defect: 'four pictures, all striking and full of significance, though of unequal merit, are connected with an artistic hand, and when all is over an unwearied audience is aware that a perfectly organized whole has been contemplated with uninterrupted pleasure'. Particular praise was bestowed on the lovers' moonlit duologue in act III:

> by the mere force of treatment it is worked into an episode which for simple gracefulness is altogether unique. The dialogue between the young lord and Bella, while they converse in the moonlight, contemplating their own strongly-cast

shadows, and fancifully commenting upon them, is replete with the prettiest conceits, in which it is hard to say whether wit or sentiment has the mastery, and the effect of the situation is heightened by the perfect arrangement of the decoration and the contrivance of dioramic effect . . . the peculiarity of *School* is a certain idyllic character, to which it would be difficult to find a parallel in any other work. The first scene in the wood, the interview between the two pairs of lovers in the grounds of the school, seem pervaded with a spirit which suggests a reminiscence of Watteau, though employed not on the conventions of an imaginary Arcadia, but on the manners of the period to which we belong . . .

The *Athenaeum* of 23 January was equally generous, believing *School* to be in point of dialogue and situation 'its author's masterpiece', though it both criticised the slowness of the concluding act and censured the classroom riot which ends act II as 'unnatural and farcical', involving a sacrifice of 'both art and probability to obtain a situation which is out of keeping with the rest of the play'. However, the overall impression was approved of, and Robertson's works summed up as

> simple almost to baldness in plot, and altogether free from improbable incident or melodramatic situation. Their hold upon an audience is due to three gifts which Mr. Robertson possesses in a remarkable degree,—power of characterization, smartness of dialogue, and a cleverness in investing with romantic associations commonplace details of life. Mr. Robertson's plays are brilliant, epigrammatic, and amusing. They fall short of greatness, but their cleverness is remarkable.

The general enthusiasm of *School*'s critics was scarcely cooled by the allegation that the author had annexed without acknowledgement a play entitled *Aschenbrödel* (Cinderella) by the prolific German playwright Roderick Benedix, and merely supplied it with an English colouring. A long article in *The Times* for 1 February 1869 endeavoured to arbitrate in the matter, pointing out that while there were certainly resemblances between the German play and Robertson's—the Cinderella motif, the school setting, the orphan-pupil heroine, the examination, the jealous wife, frustrated usher, and noble suitor—*School* had enough original elements and omitted sufficient of Benedix's ingredients to be deemed, if not an independent invention, at least as much Robertson's creation as his mentor's. *The Times* pointed to the different spirit of the English work whose comicality and wit contrasted with *Aschenbrödel*'s more Germanic sentiments and mystery, to the prominence given Naomi and Jack whose counterparts are mere sketches in the German play, to Robertson's invention of Beau Farintosh, and to his failure to make the parallel with *Cinderella* more than an incidental feature of *School.* The writer concluded that Benedix's piece was 'very pretty and romantic' while Robertson's comedy was 'extremely smart'.

Whatever its origins, *School* contains the quintessence of Robertson, however inferior to *Society, Ours,* and *Caste* it may be adjudged to be. Here we meet in their most undisguised form his blend of fairy tale and everyday life, his mixture of sweetness and mild satire, the latter chiefly conveyed in Beaufoy's somewhat contradictory strictures on women, and in the ridicule of the antiquated Beau. Unfortunately, in **School** the two contrasting elements do not coexist happily, so that the revelation of Bella's ultimately impeccable antecedents seems more contrived than it should, while Beaufoy's worldly cynicism renders the awe and deference his presence inspires even more uncongenial. Indeed, one's sense of justice as well as credibility is strained when at the end of act III the chivalrous lord calmly permits Bella to be dismissed at the vindictive Krux's instigation, without attempting to defend her moonlight activities to which he was (to say the least) a party: clearly his non-intervention is tolerated simply to engineer the laboriously-contrived *peripateia* of act IV with its orange-blossom tableau and comforting reassurance that Lord Beaufoy has not only not seduced Bella, but has not allied himself to a penurious waif either. Even by Victorian standards Beaufoy and Jack Poyntz are clearly the least satisfactory heroes in Robertson; Krux may be despicable, and deserve his final thrashing, but it is difficult to resist the conclusion that Jack is a Philistine hearty whose sole talents appear to be throwing his weight about, eating other people's food, and fortune-hunting, while Beaufoy seems little more than an opinionated and useless British peer with little consideration for the feelings of others, even those of his bride. Add to these a pair of heroines embarrassing in their archness, and the implausibly jealous Mrs Sutcliffe, and one senses that **School**'s weaknesses of motivation and characterisation were only masked from its early audiences by the somewhat facile charm of its schoolgirlish romping, and the 'idyllic character' of its staging which owed much to the artistry of Hawes Craven. As in **Ours,** atmosphere and youthful innocence, quiet humour and naturally-moving dialogue, compensated for inconsistencies of character and contrivances of plotting, but **School** remains not for all time but of an age, a flaw several reviewers emphasised when the piece was revived at the end of the century. (pp. 20-4)

Even the earliest criticisms of his work had been far from universally approving, and it was hardly to be expected that the newer school of drama critics, most of them apostles of the naturalistic faith which exalted Ibsen, Hauptmann, and others, would be content to leave Robertson's reputation unassailed, particularly when they sensed that the public preference for 'cup-and-saucer' pieces was preventing Ibsen and the modernists from obtaining a fair hearing. Clement Scott revered Robertson and reviled Ibsen; therefore Robertson had to be toppled from his plinth. Yet there were others who blamed Robertson for starting the trend towards realism which had permitted *Ibsen* to write as he did! Robertson had steered a middle course: now he was shelled from both banks, by radicals who belittled his modest attempts at naturalism because they did not go far enough, and by conservatives who despised his brand of homely truth and still hankered after fire and passion.

Of those commentators who condemned the lack of incident and significant action in the plays, contending that the commonplace and everyday might at first stimulate a *frisson* occasioned by recognition, but rapidly became dull and trite, Thomas Purnell who wrote in the *Athenaeum* under the pseudonym of 'Q' is typical:

> In our day 'stagey' has become a word of reproach. An audience no longer enjoys the representation of what is beyond its reach. The present and the near now best satisfies it. In the drama, as in prose fiction, realism is wanted. Every man judges what is laid before him by his own experience. Truth to current existence is the criterion of merit he applies to a drama . . . Mr. Robertson is a realist; the artificial and the ideal he eschews. Just as another dramatist introduces on the stage the real cab in which he has ridden to the theatre, so Mr. Robertson gives us the real conversation he has heard at the 'Owl's Roost', or in the West End Square where people come out at night to enjoy the evening breeze under a weeping ash in front of their houses. I cannot say we do not want the commonplace artistically represented on the stage, for it finds an appreciative public; I can only express my surprise that people pay to hear other men say behind footlights what they hear in their own houses.

Others were less charitable than Purnell: there were complaints about 'superficiality' and 'triviality', charges of a lack of robustness, dignity and even grandeur, from advocates of the old-fashioned modes Robertson had supplanted; Henry James deplored the concentration at the Prince of Wales's on 'little things . . . a great many chairs and tables, carpets, curtains and knickknacks', and took no pains to conceal his contempt for plays which 'seem addressed to the comprehension of infants'. The stern William Archer, too, as early as 1882 found Robertson's work sadly behind the times, finding the construction of *Society* and *Caste* primitive, seeing *School* as both trifling and flimsy, and adding of the latter that 'it takes no hold on real life, it illustrates no point in dramatic art, except the possibility of keeping an audience of Britons amused for two hours with cleverly flippant and feebly sentimental small-talk'. John Coleman accused the dramatist of deliberately pandering to the tastes of his patrons:

> The author knew what his public wanted, and he gave it them. Whenever he suffered his dramatic instincts to carry him away, whenever he was in sight of a great situation, he pulled up and reduced his art to the standard of his auditor's intelligence.

Even more severe were those who felt that Robertson had not carried his revolution far enough towards full-blown naturalism: typical was the young Max Beerbohm who not only castigated John Hare for reviving Robertson's plays in modern dress and so exposing their antiquated character, but attacked the snobbery of *School,* the silliness of *Ours,* and the mental limitations revealed in all the works. For this critic the plays 'were, *as plays,* dead as door-nails, but might, properly produced, stimulate the archaeologist and touch the sentimentalist to the quick'.

Others were swift to concur, yet there remained at least one notable critic prepared to give Robertson his fair measure of credit for his reforms, however much he might qualify his remarks. Whether stimulated as an archaeologist or touched as a sentimentalist, George Bernard Shaw gave due recognition to his predecessor in a notice of *Caste* at the Court Theatre for the *Saturday Review* on 19 June 1897; Shaw's judicious generosity is evident in every line:

> I do not defend it. I see now clearly enough that the eagerness with which it was swallowed long ago was the eagerness with which an ocean castaway, sucking his bootlaces in an agony of thirst in a sublime desert of salt water, would pounce on a spoonful of flat salutaris and think it nectar. After years of sham heroics and superhuman balderdash, *Caste* delighted everyone by its freshness, its nature, its humanity. You will shriek and snort, O scornful young men, at this monstrous assertion. 'Nature! Freshness!' you will exclaim. 'In Heaven's name (if you are not too modern to have heard of Heaven), where is there a touch of nature in *Caste*?' I reply, 'In the windows, in the doors, in the walls, in the carpet, in the ceiling, in the kettle, in the fireplace, in the ham, in the tea, in the bread and butter, in the bassinet, in the hats and sticks and clothes, in the familiar phrases, the quiet, unpumped, everyday utterance: in short, the commonplaces that are now spurned because they are commonplaces, and were then inexpressibly welcome because they were the most unexpected of novelties.'

Immediately after this appreciative paragraph Shaw does admit that Robertson was anticipated by others, and that his characters were simply thinly humanised versions of the stock figures beloved of the older drama, whose natures he rendered more credible only by the implantation of redeeming traits. Yet modest as the alteration was, Shaw himself did not scorn to profit from it when he came to write *You Never Can Tell* where the former stereotypes of traditional farce are transformed very much on Robertsonian principles.

Of course, Shaw's artistic purposes went far beyond those of Tom Robertson; a faithful imitation of the surfaces of life was never his goal, and paradoxically he wished to restore to the stage that overt theatricality and bravura which in Robertson's work had been supplanted by 'toned-down' acting, drawing-room manners, and the creation of a partial illusion of actuality. Robertson's tentative innovations were to be brushed aside, not only by the floodtide of 'total' naturalism, but by those forces inimical to naturalism which were to contend with it for possession of the twentieth-century stage. Yet Robertson helped to blaze a trail: he challenged the cherished premises on which the drama of the past had been founded, and he replaced them with a new set of artistic principles which more daring creators were free to develop and eventually to outgrow. While he might undermine the old conventions, it was beyond his intellectual scope to question the attitudes and assumptions of his age, or to probe those social, economic, political, and moral realities underlying its surface appearance. His plays merely sketched the obvious features of everyday existence; they did not analyse its bases as Shaw was to do. But Robertson's assertion that drama could legitimately present, if not an exact transcription of men's daily lives, then at least an impression of events and behaviour consistent with normal experi-

ence, was timely and invaluable. It is surely an indication not only of Robertson's attraction but also his importance that the greatest and most gifted of Britain's 'Ibsenite' dramatists should pay reluctant tribute to his work, even as he sought to transcend it. (pp. 26-9)

William Tydeman, in an introduction to Plays by Tom Robertson, *edited by William Tydeman, Cambridge University Press, 1982, pp. 1-30.*

FURTHER READING

Biography

Goldfarb, Alvin. "Thomas William Robertson: Actor." *Theatre Survey* XX, No. 2 (November 1979): 64-7.
> Surveys Robertson's acting career and suggests that it had an impact on his writing.

Pemberton, T. Edgar. *The Life and Writings of T. W. Robertson.* London: Richard Bentley and Son, 1893, 320 p.
> Contains information about the theater, Robertson's early struggles, and his personal relationships.

Criticism

Archer, William. "The Adaptive Age." In his *The Old Drama and the New: An Essay in Re-valuation,* pp. 252-79. Boston: Small, Maynard and Co., 1923.
> Addresses the inconsistent quality of Robertson's work, concluding that the success of his plays was due to the staging and acting rather than the writing.

Armstrong, Cecil Ferard. "Thomas William Robertson." In his *Shakespeare to Shaw: Studies in the Life's Work of Six Dramatists of the English Stage,* pp. 168-205. 1913. Reprint. Freeport, N. Y.: Books for Libraries Press, 1968.
> A biographical sketch that includes a lengthy discussion of early productions of Robertson's plays.

Barrett, Daniel. "Freedom of Memory *v.* Copyright Law: The American Première of *Caste.*" *Theater Research International* 8, No. 1 (Spring 1983): 43-52.
> Recounts the copyright infringement by an American actor who memorized *Caste* when it was performed in London and attempted to stage it in New York without Robertson's permission.

Dale, Harrison. "Tom Robertson: A Centenary Criticism." *The Contemporary Review* CXXXV (March 1929): 356-61.
> Celebratory essay surveying Robertson's major work and praising his contributions to the theater.

Filon, Augustin. "Chapter IV." In his *The English Stage: Being an Account of the Victorian Drama,* translated by Frederic Whyte, pp. 114-37. London: John Milne, 1897.
> Recounts Robertson's early success at the Prince of Wales's Theater and discusses his unique method of characterization.

Meier, Erika. "Thomas William Robertson." In her *Realism and Reality: The Function of the Stage Directions in the New*

Drama from Thomas William Robertson to George Bernard Shaw, pp. 7-40. Bern: Francke Verlag, 1967.

A detailed analysis of Robertson's increasing use of stage directions as the source of his originality.

Pinero, Sir Arthur. "The Theatre in the 'Seventies." In *The Eighteen-Seventies: Essays by Fellows of the Royal Society of Literature,* edited by Harley Granville-Barker, pp. 135-63. New York: Macmillan, 1929.

Discusses Robertson's role in the theater of the period and explains the characterization of Robertson as Tom Wrench in Pinero's play *Trelawny of the "Wells."*

Scott, Clement. "The Success of Tom Robertson." In his *The Drama of Yesterday and Today,* Vol. 1, pp. 492-531. London: Macmillan, 1899.

Contains the author's personal reminiscences of Robertson and opinions about his work.

Walkley, A. B. "T. W. Robertson." In his *Pastiche and Prejudice,* pp. 264-69. New York: Alfred A. Knopf, 1921.

Praises Robertson's plays as historical documents and discusses why he was forgotten despite his contributions to theatrical production.

Watson, Ernest Bradlee. "At the Prince of Wales's." In his *Sheridan to Robertson: A Study of the Nineteenth-Century London Stage,* pp. 402-28. Cambridge, Mass.: Harvard University Press, 1926.

Studies Robertson's work in relation to earlier developments in English drama, claiming that his achievement was not an innovation but a refinement of prior changes.

Vasily Zhukovsky

1783-1852

(Full name Vasily Andreyevich Zhukovsky; also transliterated as Zhukovskiy, Zhukóvskiy, and Joukovski) Russian poet and translator.

INTRODUCTION

Second in importance only to Alexander Pushkin among early nineteenth-century Russian poets, Zhukovsky is widely regarded as the first Russian exponent of Romanticism in literature. He created poems and verse translations that explore idealistic themes, evoke moods and emotions, and express other subjective impressions through the innovative use of descriptive language. Many of his translations have been praised as artistic equivalents to the originals; in some instances, his versions are even perceived as superior. Through his renderings and adaptations of works by literary figures such as Johann Wolfgang von Goethe, Friedrich von Schiller, Ludwig Uhland, Robert Southey, Lord Byron, and Sir Walter Scott, Zhukovsky helped introduce Russian readers to Western European literature, particularly German and English Romantic poetry. Russian critic V. G. Belinsky declared Zhukovsky "our country's Columbus who discovered for it German and English literatures, the existence of which it had never suspected."

Zhukovsky was born in the province of Tula, the illegitimate son of a wealthy landowner and his Turkish servant. He received his early education in the home of his father's legal wife and reportedly began to write verse at the age of seven or eight. In 1797 Zhukovsky matriculated at a school for the nobility affiliated with the University of Moscow and published numerous articles, poems, and translations of several works by the German dramatist August Kotzebue before graduating in 1800. The following year, he formed a short-lived literary circle with several other young writers, including Andrei and Nikolai Turgenev, who shared an interest in pre-Romantic German and English literature. In 1802 Zhukovsky published a noted translation of Thomas Gray's "Elegy Written in a Country Churchyard" in Nikolai Karamzin's literary journal *Vestnik Evropy*. Zhukovsky continued to work on the journal with Karamzin, who—as the leader of the Sentimentalist movement in Russian literature—advocated the reform of Russian literary language in order to facilitate the depiction of emotions and feelings in literature. Published in 1806, the original poem "Vecher" ("Evening") garnered additional respect for Zhukovsky. In 1808 he became the editor of *Vestnik Evropy;* the publication that year of his ballad "Lyudmila," a free adaptation of Gottfried Bürger's "Lenore," solidified his reputation as an accomplished poet.

For the next three years, Zhukovsky lived with his sister's

family and tutored her daughters. He fell in love with his eldest niece, but a request for her hand in marriage in 1812 was denied by her mother. Subsequently, Zhukovsky served with the militia and was stationed close to Borodino, the site of a bloody encounter with Napoleon Bonaparte's troops; the battle is the subject of his poem "The Bard in the Camp of the Russian Warriors," which was famed for its patriotic fervor. He retired from military service in 1813 and was appointed in 1815 to the position of Russian-language tutor to the German wife of Czar Nicholas I. He also co-founded Arzamas, an avant-garde literary society comprised mostly of young liberal poets who, as proponents of Romanticism in literature, supported many of Karamzin's stylistic reforms. Characteristics of the nascent movement of Romanticism included a reverence for nature, a belief in the innate goodness of the individual, a tendency toward idealism, and an attraction to things beyond human knowledge: the spiritual, the supernatural, the mystical, and the mythical. Zhukovsky was briefly considered a leader among early Romantics in Russia, but was soon succeeded by Pushkin as the most prominent figure of the movement. While at court, Zhukovsky translated Schiller's tragedy *The Maid of Orleans;* he also produced such experimental works as the poem "The

Twelve Sleeping Maidens" (1817), which comprises two ballads derived from a romance by the German novelist C. H. Spiess, and a blank verse version of Prosper Mérimée's short story "Mateo Falcone." Beginning in 1826, Zhukovsky served as tutor to Alexander II, the heir to the Russian throne. He created very few more original works and, by this point in his career, his writing was already considered dated by a younger generation. Retiring from his position at court in 1839, Zhukovsky settled in Germany in 1841 and worked on a translation of Homer's *Odyssey* during the years 1842 to 1848. He died in 1852.

Zhukovsky was a pioneer in attempting to express the influence of personal experience on the perception of surroundings, thereby deviating from the objective depiction of the external world that was traditional in Russian literature. He employed anthropomorphic descriptions and impressionistic details and images—often of natural settings—to suggest the state of mind or mood of the poet. Kazimierz Waliszewski described Zhukovsky as "the first Russian writer who gave ideal expression to the subjective life of the human heart." This quality was first evinced in his free translation of "Elegy Written in a Country Churchyard," which has been commended for its sincerity, depth of emotion, and lyricism. The ballad "Lyudmila" is considered by some critics the first Russian Romantic work because it conflated the method of Zhukovsky's earlier poetry with such idealistic subjects as unconditional love, knightly medieval lore, and supernatural and fantastic elements. Zhukovsky also experimented with new rhythms, meters, and themes, eliminated many Slavonic words, and introduced foreign terms into Russian literary discourse. Scholars have observed that his poetry contains a current of melancholy, sometimes appearing as longing, and many critics attribute this motif to Zhukovsky's disappointment in love and his sense of loss after the sudden death of his good friend Andrei Turgenev. Others have noted that, while composing little original poetry after the 1820s, Zhukovsky began to translate with greater fidelity to the original, as evinced by his 1839 translation of "Elegy Written in a Country Churchyard," which is a far more literal rendering than his 1802 version. His style also became more formal and classically oriented as he turned to translating such epics as the *Odyssey,* the Persian poem *Shah-nameh,* and the episode of Nala and Damayanti in the Indian poem *Mahābhārata.*

Commentators have asserted that Zhukovsky's work is impaired by its sentimental and dreamy quality, its tone of weak and pious resignation, or a preoccupation with the terrible and the fantastic. Furthermore, some scholars have disparaged Zhukovsky's poetry as derivative and have described his later poetry as moralistic. Despite these criticisms, he is considered largely responsible for hastening the development of modern poetry through his stylistic and technical experiments. Zhukovsky's translations not only brought Romantic literature to Russian audiences, they are judged important works in their own right. As William Edward Brown attested, Zhukovsky "treated the art of translation not as a task of slavishly turning an original into another language with as great accuracy as possible, but as an almost alchemistic procedure whereby the metal of the original becomes the gold of a Russian poem, itself just as true an original."

PRINCIPAL WORKS

Sobranie rushkikh stikhotvorenii. 5 vols. (poetry) 1810-11
Sochineniaa. 6 vols. (poetry and essays) 1878
Sobranie sochinenii. 4 vols. (poetry and essays) 1959-60

Selections of Zhukovsky's poetry have appeared in the following publications: John Bowring, ed., *Specimens of the Russian Poets,* part 1 (1821) and part 2 (1823); Charles F. Coxwell, ed., *Russian Poems* (1929).

V. G. Belinsky   (essay date 1834-36)

[*Belinsky is considered the most influential Russian literary critic of the nineteenth century. His insistence that literature both mirror life and promote social reform established the theoretical basis of the Natural school in Russian literature and directed the change from Romanticism to Realism. He encouraged the early efforts of Nikolai Gogol and Fyodor Dostoevsky and is credited with establishing Pushkin's preeminence in the history of Russian literature. Belinsky's critical estimates of his contemporaries are accepted without qualification, though his judgments on foreign authors are deemed prejudicial and overly emotional. In the following excerpt, written sometime between 1834 and 1836, he describes Zhukovsky's talent and importance as a translator, hailing him as "our country's Columbus who discovered for it German and English literatures, the existence of which it had never suspected."*]

Zhukovsky's appearance amazed Russia, and not without reason. He was our country's Columbus who discovered for it German and English literatures, the existence of which it had never suspected. Moreover, he completely transformed the language of poetry, and excelled Karamzin in prose [The critic adds in a footnote: "I have in mind the minor pieces of Karamzin."]: these are his chief merits. He has few original works of his own; his productions are either translations, or adaptations or imitations of foreign works. A style that was bold, vigorous, though not always concordant with feeling, and a one-sided romantic tendency said to be the outcome of personal experience—such are the characteristics of Zhukovsky's works. It is a mistaken notion that he was an imitator of the Germans and the English: he would not have written otherwise had he not been familiar with them, if he only wished to be true to himself. He was not a son of the nineteenth century, but was, so to speak, a *proselyte;* add to this that his works were perhaps really the outcome of his personal experiences, and you will understand why they do not contain world ideas, ideas of humanity, why *Karamzinian* ideas frequently seem to lurk under the most gorgeous forms (for example **"My friend, protector, angel mine!"** etc.), why his finest works (as, for example, **"The Poet in the**

Camp of the Russian Warriors") contain a number of purely rhetorical passages. He was self-contained, and that is the reason for his one-sidedness, which in his case was supreme originality. In the profusion of his translations Zhukovsky is related to Russian literature as Voss or August Schlegel were related to German literature. Authorities assert that he did not translate but assimilated to Russian literature the works of Schillers, Byrons, etc.; that, I believe, is beyond a shadow of doubt. In short, Zhukovsky is a poet with a remarkably vigorous talent, a poet who has rendered Russian literature an inestimable service, a poet who will never be forgotten, who will never cease to be read; but nonetheless, not the kind of poet one would call a genuine Russian poet whose name could be proclaimed at a European tournament where *national* fames contend for supremacy. (pp. 50-1)

> *V. G. Belinsky, "Literary Reveries," in his* Selected Philosophical Works, *Foreign Languages Publishing House, 1948, pp. 3-97.*

K. Waliszewski   (essay date 1900)

[*Waliszewski is the author of works on Russian historical figures and literature. In the following excerpt, he objects to Zhukovsky's reputation as a representative and significant early Russian Romantic poet, though he agrees that Zhukovsky's life and work provide an example of an essentially Romantic concept—the inextricability of poetry and human experience.*]

The glory of having introduced Romanticism into Russia was claimed by Vassili Andréievitch Joukovski (1786-1852). This was a mere illusion. Can my readers imagine a writer of the Romantic school who winds up his literary career with a translation of the *Odyssey*? The only features of that school which Joukovski was capable of understanding and assimilating, were those which, as exemplified by Tieck, Novalis, or Fouqué, corresponded with the dreamy melancholy of his own temperament. The great aims and objects attributed to the new poetry by the two Schlegels escaped him entirely, and the scepticism of Byron and the irony of Heine, in later years, were both sealed books to him. His love of vague distances, of the terrible and the fantastic, his intense mysticism, which betokened an excessive development of feeling at the expense of reason, closed his eyes to these horizons of contemporary thought.

Practically, he simply carried on the work of Karamzine, whose political ideas and didactic and moralising tendency he shared. Thus it came about that in 1830 he found himself left out of the current on which the younger generation of literary men was floating. He misjudged Gogol, and only met the author of *Dead Souls* after the period of his intellectual bankruptcy, on the common ground of a pietism not far removed from madness. The only quality of the Romantic poet which he possessed was his subjectivity, but this was his to a remarkable degree, and in such a manner as to make him the first Russian writer who gave ideal expression to the subjective life of the human heart. In his eyes, poetry and real life were one—the external

world and the intellectual world mingled in one matchless sensation of beauty and harmony.

The very birth of Joukovski was a page of romance. A country land-owner, Bounine, of the obsolete type of the ancient Russian Boyard, owned a Turkish slave named Salkha. A child was born, and adopted by a family friend, Andrew Grigorovitch Joukovski. The boy was afterwards entrusted to the care of his natural father's sister, Mme. Iouchkov, who resided at Toula. She lived in a literary and artistic circle, in which concerts and plays were frequently organised. Before young Joukovski had thoroughly mastered the principles of Russian grammar, he had become a dramatic author, having written two plays, *Camilla, or Rome Delivered,* and *Paul and Virginia,* both of which were duly performed. In 1797 Mme. Iouchkov sent him to the University School at Moscow, and not long afterwards his first verses began to appear in the literary miscellanies of the day. They were sad and melancholy even then. The death of Mme. Iouchkov, which occurred just at this time, inspired the youthful poet with an imitation of Gray's "Elegy" under the title of **"Thoughts on a Tomb."** But verses had a poor sale. The editors gave translations a far warmer welcome. To bring in a little money, Joukovski translated all Kotzebue's plays and several of his novels. After this he tried the administrative career, and failing in it, took refuge for a while with his adoptive family, returning to Moscow in time to undertake the editorship of the *European Messenger.* According to the custom of the period, he filled the whole paper with his own work—literary criticisms, more translations from Schiller, Parny, and Dryden, and a few original compositions, romances, epistles, and ballads. In 1810, the generosity of Bounine enabled him to buy a small landed property to which he retired, and there, for a while, he lived a splendid idyl. His near neighbour, Pletchéiev, a rich land-owner with a mania for music, was the possessor of a theatre and an orchestra. Joukovski wrote verses, which Pletchéiev set to music, and Mme. Pletchéiev sang. There was an uninterrupted series of concerts, plays, and operas.

Suddenly the idyl turned to elegy. The melancholy poet fell in love with one of his nieces, Marie Andréievna Protassov, and soon he was fain to shed genuine tears. The young girl's mother would not hear of an illegitimate son as her daughter's husband. The terrible year 1812 opened, and she insisted on his entering a regiment of the National Guard. He did not distinguish himself at the Borodino, but after the battle he wrote his first great poem, **"The Bard in the Russian Camp,"** which opened the gates of glory to him.

It was only an imitation, and a somewhat clumsy one, of Gray's "Bard," with a strange medley of romantic sentiment and classic imagery—lyres that rang warlike chords and warriors dressed in armour. But the public did not look too closely at such trifles, and its enthusiasm was increased, after the taking of Paris in 1814, by the appearance of an Epistle of five hundred lines addressed to the victorious Tsar. The Empress, surrounded by her family and intimate circle, desired to hear it, and the reader, A. I. Tourguéniev [Turgenev], could hardly get to the end of his task. His voice was drowned in sobs and plaudits; he was sobbing himself; and throughout the country the cry went up that another great poet had risen in the footsteps of Lomonossov, and there would be fresh master-pieces for all men to admire.

But the country waited long. Tourguéniev even went so far as to chide Lomonossov's poetic heir. "You have Milton's imagination and Petrarch's tenderness—and you write us ballads!" At that moment Joukovski was forced to play the great man rather against his will. In spite of himself, he was pushed to the head of the Karamzine party, then in full warfare with Chichkov's *Biéssiéda,* and became the pillar of the rival society of the *Arzamas.* He drew up its reports in burlesque hexameters, which seem to indicate that, in his case, melancholy was much more a matter of fashion than of temperament. But the great work which was obstinately demanded of him came not. Settled at court, first as reader to the Empress, and later as tutor to her children, Joukovski gradually built up his reputation as an excellent pedagogue, and continued to prove his ability, conscientiousness, and good taste as a translator. From 1817 to 1820 he superintended the education of Alexander II. Between 1827 and 1840 he translated, from Rückert's German version, Magharabati's Indian poem, *Nal and Diamaianti.* In 1841, overwhelmed with kindnesses, and considerably enriched in pocket, he went abroad, married, at sixty, the daughter of the painter Reutern—she was nineteen—fell into a nest of pietists, was on the brink of conversion to the Catholic faith, and finally plunged into mysticism. His ill-starred passion for Mdlle. Protassov may have had something to do with this catastrophe.

In 1847, nevertheless, he gave the world his fine translation of the *Odyssey,* and two years later that of an episode in Firdusi's Persian poem (*Shah Mamet*), **"Rustem and Zorav"**—this also after Rückert. Death overtook him at Baden-Baden, just as he was beginning work upon the *Iliad.*

He was a distinguished scholar and a noble-souled man. Joukovski's was the hearth at which the flame which burnt and shone in the heart of the "Liberator Tsar" during the earlier part of his reign, was kindled. Did he possess and conceal a poetic genius the revelation of which was prevented by some unexplained circumstance? This has been believed. I doubt it. Joukovski's lack of originality amounted to an entire absence of national sentiment. The ancient chronicles of his country inspired him with only one feeling—horror; the Slavonic language of the sacred books, "that tongue of mandarins, slaves, and Tartars," exasperated him; and even that he used, with its crabbed *chas* and *chtchas,* sometimes struck him as barbarous.

He wrote no master-piece, but by interpreting and disseminating those of English and German literature, he largely contributed to the literary education of his country. And Alexander II was not his only pupil. Pouchkine [Pushkin], after having risen in revolt against the blank verse adopted by this master, adopted it, in later years, as his favourite method of expression, and Batiouchkov owed more than mere instruction to the great poet, who never made his mark, but who was something better than

a genius—a kind, and generous, and helpful friend. (pp. 142-47)

K. Waliszewski, "The Transition Period—Karamzine and Joukovski," in his A History of Russian Literature, *1900. Reprint by D. Appleton and Company, 1910, pp. 128-53.*

A. Brückner   (essay date 1905)

[*A German educator and critic, Brückner published extensively on Slavic language and literature. In the following excerpt from his* Geschichte der russischen litteratur *(1905;* A Literary History of Russia), *he notes a pervading dreamy melancholy in Zhukovsky's poetry, and commends him for the originality of his translations and the sincerity of his verse.*]

The real representative of the sentimental, æsthetical tendency in literature was first found in [Nikolai Karamzin's] young protégé and friend Zhukovsky, the most Germanophil of Russian poets; no arch-romanticist as he has often been labelled, but a dreamer and a thinker. His dreaming and thinking, however, were no poetical mask, but the real mirror of a rarely pure soul. Absolutely unselfish, ready to renounce and sacrifice everything for others, to mitigate their misfortunes (the Decembrists), to avert their dangers (as with Púshkin), and for his friends (Voêykov, who repaid him but ill, Gógol, and others), himself unpretending, modest, gentle, chaste—thus did he move through life. No energetic nature, it is true, he was not formed for fighting; in vain did his friends seek to stir in him the vein of a social poet and then dread for him the enticements of the Court; the epigrams coined thereupon did not wound him. He remained ever conscious of the purity of his intentions. This want of energy brands his imaginative writing also, which is simply imitative. He is the most highly esteemed translator in the Literature, from Gray's "Elegy" in 1802 to the *Odyssey* in 1848. One main theme runs through all these creations and translations, in their choice and in their interpretation—the theme of renunciation and resignation such as his own experience of life instilled.

Búnin Zhukovsky, in whose veins Oriental blood flowed, was at Moscow brought into touch with German and English poetry by his school friends the sons of the Freemason Turgénev. It was a circle of cultivated, high-striving, idealistic young men: Andrew, the bosom friend of Zhukovsky, died early; Nicholas went into exile because of his Liberal opinions; Alexander did not share the fate of his brother though he held his opinions. They all took a lively interest in literature, and Zhukovsky's first attempts went back to his boyhood. To a wider circle his name became known by his imitation of Gray's "Elegy"; by his **"Bard's Song at the Grave of Victorious Slavs"** (1806, to celebrate Austerlitz), a rhetorical patriotic ode, and by his **"Ludmíla,"** the first Russian ballad, copied from Bürger's "Leonore," which was simply of epoch-making significance to the Slav literatures. Not only in Russian was it the first to wake a long array of skeletons and dances of death, screech-owls, and all sorts of spectres; for Kámenev's "ballad," "Gromvál" (1803), is as little a ballad as, say, Mrs. Radcliffe's gruesome romances are romantic. Thus did Zhukovsky evolve full-blown all Russian devils, witches, and ghostly apparitions. The fame of the "Balladkin" was enhanced by prose stories like **"Mariana's Grove,"** insufferably namby-pamby to us but enchanting to his contemporaries, bitter earnest to the poet; for his Uslàv, the singer of primeval times who mourns by the bier of his Mariana, was Zhukovsky himself in deep sorrow for his Màsha.

Expecting little of life, he devoted himself exclusively to poetry, convinced that in thus serving all that was noble and good he discharged a high social duty. His ideal was Schiller, not Goethe; he did not go back to Bürger again, but to Uhland and Hebbel, by whom he put later Herder's "Cid" and Fouqué's "Undine," and still later Halm's "Camoens." Schiller's Ballads and Greek Songs, as also the "Maid of Orleans," are among the triumphs of his art as a translator. Conscientiously as in his renderings he tried to adhere to the original, we often come upon intentional alterations which gave the whole that ideally fantastic, dreamily elegiac tone which is his own. He recast the poems till they were his. That was how he proceeded with **"Ludmíla,"** whom he garbed in the Russian *sarafán.* Thus he drew from the novel of Spiess his subject, which, however, he materially recast in his **"Twelve Sleeping Maids"**; the Gromobóy of the first part (1810) sells his soul to Asmodeus, who entraps him and sacrifices to him instead of his own the souls of his twelve virgin daughters, who await in deep sleep their deliverance. In the second part (1817) this is achieved by Vadím, whom an inexplicable longing ("What to seek and where? To what direct my desire?") drives out into the world. The poet weeded out sensual episodes and plunged the whole in a purposely dim light which does not allow us to distinguish the outlines clearly. In these epical attempts and in the ballad of **"Svetlana,"** as a pendant to the **"Ludmíla,"** we find the only concessions to Russian antiquity—*i.e.,* to the Utopias that people made of them, a mixture of pagan and classical mythology and troubadourism which the "Livy of the North" was to be the first to dissipate. His contemporaries expected with certainty of Zhukovsky such a Russian heroic epic: he set to work several times on a "Vladímir" and the Heroes of a Round Table, but never got farther than the first drafts—not only because the vision of the ages was lacking to him in spite of his "Livy," but above all because he was no epic, always only a lyric, poet.

His greatest poetical success he achieved with a very questionable performance which years later was no longer to satisfy himself. If the **"Bard's Song"** of 1806 was couched in the conventional style, by 1812 he himself had taken his place among the defenders of his country and had brought back with him from the campaign the **"Singer in the Camp of the Russian Warriors."** This heroic Ode, though much too long, was received with enthusiasm everywhere, from the Court downwards; all that was really poetical in it were some sentimental tirades and a heaping up of effective antitheses. All else was conventional, from the singer Bayán, the delight of years gone by, who with his harp sped in arms before the ranks of the Slavs, and poured forth the sacred hymn, and the helms and shields to the daring defiance, "Seek, O enemy, to tear from us the shield which the hand of our beloved gave, on which gleams a

sacred vow, 'Thine even beyond the grave.' " Still more frigid and rhetorical was the following ode, **"The Singer in the Kremlin,"** for the anniversary of the "Explusion of the Gauls and twenty Tribes," but both brought the poet nearer to the Court, where he became first teacher of Russian to a German Grand Duchess and then tutor to the Cesarévich Alexander II. Nor did the years 1812 and 1813 awaken any more potent echo elsewhere; things did not get further than the official lyrics of Derzhávin; not even the guerilla Davýdov brought any variation into this paper or tinfoil poetry.

It was only for the time being, as he did again in 1831 in rivalry with Pushkin, that Zhukovsky performed this lyrical *corvée,* into which nevertheless he managed to smuggle small particles of himself—for instance, in the closing verses of the **"Kremlin"** the allusion to what is beyond and the rising once more of what the hour of death has torn from us. Other poems far more amply expressed his nature, such as **"Theon and Æschines,"** where Theon proclaims to the latter, only disappointed by life and its gifts, Zhukovsky's philosophy: "Not in swift pleasure, not in deceitful dreaming, did I see earthly happiness. What Fate can in a moment destroy, that is not ours in this world; the imperishable treasure of the heart, Love, the sweetness of lofty thoughts, that is happiness . . . To the heart only, what has passed away is eternal"—the thought most often quoted and expatiated on by him. "Sorrow at parting is also a way of love: over the heart loss has no power. Is not mourning for what is lost the promise of infallible hope, that in a known but mysterious country our loss will be made good to us?" This belief the grown-up child retained for ever; in the course of years his religiousness waxed stronger, the mystic vapour grew thicker.

His power of poetical invention often ceased for whole years; friends and disciples like Pushkin hoped for a new life for the poet, but his unaccustomed duty, taken in earnest in an exceptional way—in Alexander's mind he implanted for ever humane impulses—claimed all his powers; he did not rise above occasional poems, and dallyings in verse, and even his activity as a translator came to a stop. Not until his service at Court was ended and he was his own man again did he become, in spite of his advanced years, more active, his imitations increased in number, notably his **"Nala and Damayanti,"** which is far more poetical than Rückert's original, and he braced himself to translating the *Odyssey.* (pp. 168-71)

[Nikolai Gnêdich] was the first of the Russians to penetrate into Homer's magic world. The fruit of many years' labour was the translation of the *Iliad,* begun in Alexandrines, but at Uvárov's urgent instances carried out in hexameters; it made no impression at all on the Russian public, impervious like everything Slavonic to the truly classic; you cannot deny it precision and force, but it lacked naturalness; the solemnity, *i.e.,* forcedness of the diction, was arrived at by superfluous "Slavisms" and obsolete constructions; not for a moment can you get rid of the feeling that you have only a translation before you.

It was otherwise with Zhukóvsky's **Odyssey,** which appeared in 1848 and 1850. When he had put into the quiet haven of family life for his declining years, the "choice spirit" grew to hate "the modern, convulsive, hysterical, sense-confusing poetry" of a Herwegh and his satellites, the spirit which stood unsympathising and uncomprehending in face of social and political conflicts, with its childlike faith and its deliberate subordination of understanding and will to grace and providence; in return it was powerfully drawn towards the primitive pastoral poetry of the Bible and Homer, "which brightly and gently cheers and calms, peacefully beautifies all that surrounds us, and neither troubles us nor draws us away into misty distances. Homer's Muse gilded the hours of my diclining life." Even in the **Odyssey** Zhukóvsky remained true to himself. Truly did Varnhagen say of it: "The effect of this translation comes very near to that of the original; the same charm of language, the same simplicity and clearness, the same epic flow and sonorousness of the hexameter. The poet has reproduced the Ionian charm and brilliancy in Scythian sounds, which, indeed, are more akin to the Hellenic than one commonly thinks." The inestimable qualifications of Russian for such rendering Zhukóvsky's genius has used with the greatest success: his mastery of the art of verse handled the alien form with the happiest grace. At bottom, however, it is Zhukóvsky's **Odyssey,** not Homer's: for all the fidelity and literalness the keynote is different; a sentimental and didactic strain has been brought in by the translator, who managed in the same way to soften down the complaint of Byron's "Prisoner of Chillon." And with all his simplicity and smoothness the translator could not escape obsolete and inconvenient forms and words. Like Gnêdich, he met with only a cool and indifferent reception.

In any case he remains the most original translator in the world's literature; what other translator made whatever foreign work he touched into his own mental property by mere omission of some traits and emphasising of others? Translations became adaptations, and in these he showed himself an unrivalled master. His merits, then, lay in the final deliverance of Russian literature from the exclusive French spell; no other like him enlarged its scope by an abundance of masterpieces, especially from German and English literature; like child's play he overcame the difficulties of versification and language; for this Pushkín particularly admired him. Russian poetical diction attained through him a far higher perfection than that of prose through Karamzin. This backwardness of prose was again specially felt by Pushkín. What attracts us in Zhukóvsky is the sincerity of his tone, the genuineness of his sentiment; we do not share his flight from the world, his consolings of himself with what is beyond, or his resignation, but we honour them, for they came from his heart and were not cunningly devised or affected. (pp. 173-74)

> *A. Brückner, "The Age of Alexander I," in his* Literary History of Russia, *edited by Ellis H. Minns, translated by H. Havelock, T. Fisher Unwin, 1908, pp. 139-77.*

Prince Kropotkin   (essay date 1905)

[*Kropotkin was a Russian sociologist, philosopher, geographer, essayist, and critic. Born of an aristocratic family, he became an anarchist in the 1870s and later fled*

to Europe. Among other works, Kropotkin composed several literary histories, including Ideals and Realities in Russian Literature *(1905; reprinted 1915), which was drawn from a series of lectures he gave in the United States in March 1901. In the following excerpt from that work, he praises Zhukovsky as a poet suffused with the Romantic spirit, and hails his poetry translations.*]

Zhukóvskiy was a romantic poet in the true sense of the word, and a true worshipper of poetry, who fully understood its elevating power. His original productions were few. He was mainly a translator and rendered in most beautiful Russian verses the poems of Schiller, Uhland, Herder, Byron, Thomas Moore, and others, as well as the *Odyssey,* the Hindu poem of Nal and Ramayanti, and the songs of the Western Slavonians. The beauty of these translations is such that I doubt whether there are in any other language, even in German, equally beautiful renderings of foreign poets. However, Zhukóvskiy was not a mere translator: he took from other poets only what was agreeable to his own nature and what he would have liked to sing himself. Sad reflections about the unknown, an aspiration towards distant lands, the sufferings of love, and the sadness of separation—all lived through by the poet—were the distinctive features of his poetry. They reflected his inner self. We may object now to his ultra-romanticism, but this direction, at that time, was an appeal to the broadly humanitarian feelings, and it was of first necessity for progress. By his poetry, Zhukóvskiy appealed chiefly to women. . . . Altogether, Zhukóvskiy appealed to the best sides of human nature. One note, however, was missing entirely in his poetry: it was the appeal to the sentiments of freedom and citizenship. (pp. 33-4)

> *Prince Kropotkin, in an introduction to his* Ideals and Realities in Russian Literature, *Alfred A. Knopf, 1915, pp. 3-36.*

D. S. Mirsky   (essay date 1949)

[*Mirsky was a Russian prince who fled his country after the Bolshevik Revolution and settled in London. While in England, he wrote two important histories of Russian literature,* Contemporary Russian Literature *(1926) and* A History of Russian Literature *(1927). In the following excerpt from the 1949 volume combining these two works, Mirsky briefly sketches Zhukovsky's influence and his style, noting that he was the "first . . . personal and subjective Russian poet."*]

Up to about 1820 Zhukóvsky was the leader of the advanced literary movement, and the extent of his influence may be compared with that of Spenser's or Ronsard's. He created a new poetical language on the basis of the Karamzinian reform. Both his metrical methods and his diction remained the standard for all the nineteenth century. Besides these formal innovations Zhukóvsky reformed the very conception of poetry. In his hands it became, for the first time in Russia, the direct expression of feeling. There is no trace in his poetry of raw, unmastered, merely recorded, emotion: the sentimental experience is always completely transformed. But it was a step in the direction of expressive, emotional poetry. The next step was made by Lérmontov. It was not made by Púshkin; the subjective element in Púshkin's poetry is less prominent and more subordinate to the creative design than in Zhukóvsky's.

It is one of the curios of literary history that this first, and for some time to come most, personal and subjective Russian poet was almost exclusively a translator. His original work is small in extent, consisting of a few humorous epistles, occasional elegies, and lyrics. But these last are alone sufficient to give Zhukóvsky a place in the first rank of poets. The æthereal lightness, the melodiousness of his verse and the exquisite purity of his diction reach in them their highest perfection. Romantic melancholy and the resigned hope in a better beyond have never spoken in nobler or more exquisite accents. But it is characteristic of Zhukóvsky that even these lyrics have sources in foreign poetry. Thus the wonderful lyric on the death of Marie Móyer (**"19th March 1823"**) closely resembles in meter and construction a poem of the German romanticist Brentano. It is the actual words, cadences, and intonation, the very texture of the verse, that make the poem what it is— and those slight touches which are at the hand of only the great poet. Zhukóvsky's poetry of 1808-21 charmed the public by its atmosphere of romantic sensibility, daydreams, optimistic religiosity, and sweet resignation, with a touch of the mildly fantastic paraphernalia of the balladry of terror. But what the initiated most admired was the poet's supreme mastery, his metrical inventiveness, and, above all, the absolutely unheard-of purity, sweetness, and melodiousness of his verse and diction, which were such a contrast to the splendidly barbaric ruggedness of Derzhávin.

The poets Zhukóvsky translated in this period were the romantic, pre-romantic, and even classical poets of Germany and England. His special favorites in Germany were Uhland and Schiller, whose Greek ballads (*Die Siegesfest* and others) are, owing to Zhukóvsky, quite as much classics in Russia as they are in Germany (if not more so). The English poets translated by him were Dryden (*Alexander's Feast*), Thomson, Gray (the "Elegy"), Southey, Scott, Moore, Campbell, and Byron ("The Prisoner of Chillon"). After what I have said of Zhukóvsky's supreme and impeccable mastery in Russian verse it will scarcely be startling if I add that certain of his translations from his English contemporaries (none of whom was really a great craftsman) are very often superior to the original. Southey's "Queen Urraca," Campbell's "Lord Ullin's Daughter," Moore's "Death of the Peri," Scott's "Eve of St. John," and Byron's "Prisoner of Chillon" have both relatively and absolutely a higher place in Russian than they have in English poetry.

After 1830 Zhukóvsky gradually abandoned the too fluent sweetness that had made him popular. Like Púshkin in the same years he strove after greater objectivity, a more Doric outline and more epic manner. Almost all his later work is either in hexameters or blank verse. He uses both forms with the utmost freedom and variety, placing his words in the most "unpoetical" order, using the most destructive overflows, attaining a style that is *"beau comme de la prose"* and (in blank verse) reminiscent of the later Shakspere. Among the principal works of this period are the adaptations (from the German) of *Rustam and Sohrab* and *Nala and Damayanti.* In both he succeeded in eschewing all sentimentality. In the former, the effect is one of grand, primæval, rude majesty; in the latter, of genuinely Indian wealth and color. Still more remarkable is his adaptation, in very free and enjambed hexameters, of the German romanticist Fouqué's prose romance *Undine.* The atmosphere of the poem is one of optimistic religiosity and romantic fantasy, and akin to that of his early lyrics and elegies, but the story is told with majestic leisure and has a true epic tone. The most extensive task of his old age was the translation of the *Odyssey,* completed in 1847. Though he knew no Greek, and translated Homer from a word-for-word German translation, it is a masterpiece of exactness and reliability. Zhukóvsky's ***Odyssey*** was intended to complete the Russian Homer, and is, as it were, a sequel to Gnédich's translation of the *Iliad* (1829).

Nikoláy Ivánovich Gnédich (1784-1833) was a poet of considerable merit who wrote a few exquisite lyrics and a much-admired Russian idyl in the style of Theocritus. His *Iliad* is high-sounding and magnificent, full of splendid Slavicisms, with a Virgilian accompaniment of sonorous trumpets and with wonderfully invented composite epithets. It is the most splendid example in Russian poetry of the grand classical style.

The ***Odyssey*** of Zhukóvsky is very different. He deliberately avoids Slavicism. He makes the *Odyssey* a homely, leisurely, Biblical story of the daily life of patriarchal kings. But Zhukóvsky does not sentimentalize Homer, and, though perhaps it is in the Telemachos and Nausicaa cantos that he is at his best, even in the cruelest parts of the *Mnesteroktonia* he gives a faithful reflection of the true Homer. The two Russian Homers are in a most happy way mutually complementary, and if Gnédich's *Iliad* is our highest achievement in the grand manner, Zhukóvsky's ***Odyssey*** is unsurpassed as a heroic idyl. (pp. 74-7)

> *D. S. Mirsky, "The Golden Age of Poetry," in his* A History of Russian Literature comprising "A History of Russian Literature" and "Contemporary Russian Literature," *edited by Francis J. Whitfield, Alfred A. Knopf, 1949, pp. 71-121.*

William Edward Brown   (essay date 1974)

[*Brown is an American professor of comparative literature and critic who has written, among other works, histories of Russian literature that focus, respectively, on the literature of the seventeenth century, the eighteenth century, and the Romantic period. In the following excerpt, he surveys the career of Zhukovsky, whom he regards as the first major Russian figure of the Romantic literary movement, and examines his particular brand of Romanticism.*]

Although Zhukovsky's earliest poetry belongs to the eighteenth century, all the best of it was composed after 1800, and his career marks a very definite new trend in Russian literature, coinciding with the appearance of the new century—romanticism. It will be well therefore to consider briefly the nature of this new tendency before undertaking a detailed study of its first major Russian representative.

Nikolai Karamzin may be characterized as the most typical representative in Russia of "sentimentalism," that late eighteenth-century literary fashion which immediately precedes romanticism. Some of the salient characteristics of this fashion are: a cult of "nature," represented in English poetry by such a writer as James Thompson, whose *Seasons* was so widely imitated; the cultivation of the qualities of "sensibility" and "virtue," as exemplified in English literature by Laurence Sterne; an interest in the "ordinary man" rather than the "hero" of the classical age; here one may think most readily of Lillo's *London Merchant* and Richardson's *Clarissa Harlowe*. Sentimentalism, although evidently a step in the direction of full romanticism, still retains a great deal of the rationalistic outlook of the eighteenth century enlightenment, and most notably, although already beginning to delve into the mysteries of individual psychology, as for example Richardson in depicting his heroines' affairs of the heart, or Sterne in opening up glimpses of the noble feelings of his Tristram Shandy or his Parson Yorick, yet continues to view the psychology of the individual as primarily an exemplification of universal and generalized types of character—that is, the same description of feelings, sensibilities, and the like, may be carried without falsification from one person to another. Thus in Karamzin's "Poor Liza," a typical production of the movement, several of these general tendencies may be isolated: the feeling for nature, but still so remote from individualization that it would be very difficult to point out any qualities of the real scenery of the Moscow environs in the background; the feeling for the "ordinary man," in that the heroine is a peasant-girl: yet so generalized that virtually nothing of her social position is depicted realistically; and a sympathetic description of her sensibilities, which again are those of any girl in any age and any social environment, and totally devoid of the particular coloration that might in reality be expected from an eighteenth-century Russian peasant girl. Her love for Erast, her feelings of abandonment, her despair before her suicide are all shown in ready-made emotional cliches that could just as well apply to a heroine of Crabbe, or Haller, or of Salomon Gessner.

The nineteenth century in Europe begins politically with the tremendous upheaval of the French revolution and the decade of the Napoleonic wars, which shook to its foundations the entire "old order." The naively unquestioned and God-given authority of monarchy was never again a possibility; even though monarchy was to be restored, even in France, and maintained by a liberal application of force almost everywhere, yet the "restoration" was quite evidently only a facade. In the same way the unquestioned authority of the literary legislators was everywhere undermined and toppled; and this constitutes the essence of romanticism. Just as politically various tendencies arose in Europe and America, united only in their hostility toward absolute monarchy, so in the literary world a number of "romanticisms" evolved, often apparently contradictory to one another, but united in the negative aspect of their common hatred of "rules" and of rationalism. Marxist critics are wont to distinguish two fundamental varieties

A detail of an oil painting by G. G. Chernetsov that depicts a group of writers—Ivan Krylov, Alexander Pushkin, Vasily Zhukovsky, and N. Gnedich—in the Summer Garden, St. Petersburg.

of romanticism, which although not generally recognized by Western criticism, are too useful to overlook. The differentiating criterion is—naturally for a Marxist—attitude toward reality. The one wing, which is called "passive" in the terminology of Maxim Gorky, is characterized by a withdrawal from real life, a passive acceptance of things as they are, and the creation of a kind of "ivory tower." The other, "active" romanticism, is the romanticism of revolution, of vehement protest against the world as it is.

In defining the characteristics of the so-called "passive" romanticism, Marxist critics emphasize the rejection of the world of reality as the primary feature of the movement. The romanticist attempts to withdraw from a present which he finds repellent. He is repelled by the reality surrounding him for many reasons—the general Philistinism of his fellow men, the cruelty and repression of the social system, the senselessness of a political order, the encroachments of a drab and unattractive industrialism, and the like. Whatever the reasons for his rejection, the "passive" romantic finds his refuge in either a retreat into a more roseate past, or into a wholly imaginary world of fantasy. The rejection of the "enlightened" rational world of the *philosophes* brings with it a return to religious faith, especially of the aesthetically satisfying Catholic variety. A rejection of the monarchic system of the present may lead to a wistful recreation of the world of chivalry; and since both a naive faith and a picturesque world of knightly prowess are to be found in the popular conceptions of the middle ages, that era proves the most attractive for escape. We may note in this connection the early tales in verse of Sir Walter Scott—*The Lady of the Lake* and *Marmion,* particularly—and the ballads of Robert Southey and such Germans as Uhland. Of all the "passive romantics" perhaps the German Novalis, and his medieval novel *Heinrich von Offerdingen,* are the most typical. If escape is not sought in the middle ages, it may be sought equally well in the irrational and fantastic, especially as these are seen in the conceptions of popular superstition. Here the tendency is reinforced by the already noted interest of the sentimentalists in the ordinary man. The common people have always created naively terrifying beings, episodes, and beliefs, wholly irrational and remote from reality— ghosts, vampires, were-wolves, will-o'-the-wisps, witches, and the like. It should be noted that in German one of the monuments of romanticism is the great collection of popular tales by the Brothers Grimm, *Kinderund Hausmärchen.* The middle ages, that great "age of faith," flowered most luxuriantly with this kind of tale, and from this sprang what is perhaps the most peculiar variety of preromantic literary creation, the "Gothic novel," of horror and mystery. Besides the English creators of this genre, Horace Walpole and Mrs. Ann Radcliffe, the most distinguished author of these thrillers is the great German E. T. A. Hoffmann. In poetry, as well as in the novel, this retreat from rationalism into popular superstition can be traced; here its typical representative is the ballad, a form which is popular by definition, and which most commonly deals with the supernatural in some form or other, and revels in blood and terror. It should be noted that one of the most popular of all single poems from the early romantic period was Gottfried August Bürger's "Lenore." Coleridge's "Ancient Mariner" and "Christabel" are monuments of the same kind. The French seem to have been less attracted to this area of escape than the Teutonic peoples, but for medieval horror Victor Hugo's *Han of Iceland* could scarcely be surpassed, while many of his *Odes et Ballades* follow the Teutonic ballad pattern.

The "active" branch of romanticism, as the Marxist critics define it, is characterized by an equal rejection of present reality, but in the Rousseauist direction of a return to the primitive, to the "noble savage." This would be exemplified by Chateaubriand, with his "noble savages" Atala and Chactas, and his world-weary European Rene, seeking to lose himself in the primitive world of the Mississippi Indians. "World-weariness" is the earmark of this romantic genre, and the primitive world into which the world-weary hero attempts to escape may be that of the American Indian, or of the exotic east. Byron is the chief representative of this romantic trend in English poetry, with Shelley a rather unclassifiable second. It is to be noted that according to the Marxist definitions, the "active" romantic does not passively retire into his ivory tower to avoid reality: he attempts to change what he detests. Thus Byron not only creates his "world weary" hero Childe Harold, or his exotic protesting "Giaour" and "Corsair," but he himself ends his life as a fighter for Greek independence. Shelley not only writes his passionate protests against tyranny in *Hellas* and *Prometheus Unbound,* but is an active advocate of anarchism, free love, and atheism. Victor

Hugo, the embittered foe of "Napoleon the Little" would be a French example of the "active" type, although, as already noted, he shows some qualities of the "passive" type as well. The clear and unequivocal separation of the two types is impossible; they merge with one another in a most confusing way. Nevertheless, the distinction seems to be a valuable one to make, and it is usually possible to assign a poet at any particular time of his career to one or the other type.

In Russian literature the great "activists" are Pushkin and Lermontov, preceded by the minor but interesting poets of the Decembrist group, especially Küchelbecker and Ryleev. It is in these that the "retreat" from reality is least noticeable. As for the "passive" class, Zhukovsky is its coryphaeus, to be followed by such lesser poets as Delvig, Vyazemsky, Baratynsky and Yazykov.

The first generation of Russian romantic poets belongs to the first two decades of the nineteenth century, and it is possible, although not particularly useful, to classify this group as "pre-romantic." Of the four outstanding poets of this group, Ozerov's creative life ends in 1814, Batyushkov's in 1822 (both men became deranged); Gnedich carries on until his death in 1833, but mainly occupied with his masterly translation of the Greek *Iliad;* and Zhukovsky outlives the entire romantic period, continuing to maintain its traditions into the very height of realistic prose fiction; he died in 1855. He can therefore scarcely be considered a "pre-" romantic in the temporal sense; yet many aspects of the fully developed romantic style are absent from his work, and he is most important in literary history as a mediator.

Vasily Andreevich Zhukovsky was born in 1783, the illegitimate son of a Russian nobleman of the Bunin family and a Turkish woman taken captive during the first of Catherine's wars with the Ottoman Empire. The boy was given a nobleman's rank and name by a gentleman retainer of Bunin, and educated in a school for noblemen's sons connected with the University of Moscow, from which he was graduated in 1800. At school he was closely associated with the director, I. P. Turgenev, and the director's two sons, Andrei and Alexander I. Turgenev, especially with the former. Upon graduation, Zhukovsky and the two younger Turgenevs formed a literary society which they called with typical romantic effusiveness "The Friendly Literary Society." Other members of it were the later university professor Merzliakov, the satirist A. F. Voieikov, and other lesser lights. The literary influence of this short-lived society (it terminated its existence after only a few months in 1801) was considerable, for Andrei Turgenev turned Zhukovsky's interest toward the modern German literature of the day, especially toward Goethe, whose *Werther* Andrei translated, and Schiller. This attraction for things German remained with Zhukovsky to the end of his days; he eventually married a German lady named Reutern (1841), and spent the last ten years of his life entirely in Germany.

In spite of their interest in the German pre-romantic literature of the *Sturm und Drang* period, Zhukovsky and his friends remained at this time still faithful to the eighteenth century modes of Lomonosov and Derzhavin. The earliest of Zhukovsky's verses, which date from 1797, still reflect this influence; at this period he was also translating some typically classical pieces—fables of La Fontaine, and elegies of De Lille and Alexander Pope.

The first "modern" influence to reach Zhukovsky was that of his countryman Karamzin, the leader of Russian "sentimentalism." The smooth "salon style" of the author of "Poor Liza" appealed to the young poet, and the genre represented by that sentimental story for a moment weaned Zhukovsky away from verse. It was during these years that he wrote, thoroughly in Karamzin's vein, the story **"Maria's Grove"** (1809), with its purely imaginative reconstruction of the ancient past of Moscow. Zhukovsky's own view of life coincided rather closely with that of the sentimentalists, and he never outgrew it, although his native good taste led him soon to avoid the more extreme exaggeration of the sensibilities which some other adherents of the mode were guilty of. He did not continue to develop his view of life in the prose story, as his model Karamzim had chiefly done, but soon went over entirely to verse as a medium. One story of the earlier period, however, deserves some attention. It was published during the years (1808-09) when the poet was editor of the journal *European Herald,* and is in the form of a letter under the title of **"Sad Occurrence that Took Place in the Year 1809."** The "sad occurrence" is the tragedy of a peasant girl, who through the ostensible beneficence of her master, has been educated to a degree incompatible with her continued servitude, without thereby losing servile status. The incident is obviously founded on actual fact, and in part at least shows a realistic treatment that is unusual with Zhukovsky; the central love story, however, is developed in the traditional sentimental style, even the names of the lovers—Liza and Liodor—betraying their conventionality.

Zhukovsky's personality, from all we can determine, was in full harmony with the attitudes of sentimentalism. His was an extremely indrawn and dreamy nature, passive in the extreme. His profound love for his niece, doomed to frustration from the opposition of the girl's mother to their marriage on the supposedly religious grounds of consanguinity, is the emotional center of his life, and this affair took the form of complete self-denial and resignation to "the will of heaven." There was no protest from Zhukovsky over the denial of his love, only a deep melancholy, tempered only by a religious faith that the imperfections of this world would be remedied in the world beyond the grave. It is this religious faith, usually absent from the rationalistic world outlook of the sentimentalists, that makes it necessary to classify Zhukovsky rather with the passive wing of early romanticism. It is notable that in his later years the Russian poet, who resided long in Germany, became very deeply influenced by the German romantic Friedrich Hardenberg, or "Novalis." Novalis, a strange combination of practicality (he was a mining engineer!) and mysticism, lost his sweetheart to an early death and in his last years developed an intensely personal and "other-worldly" kind of Christianity in association with the Moravian Brethren. Zhukovsky's wistful yearnings for the rest of the grave, for an eternal reuniting with his beloved in a happy "other world" are of the same kind, although there is no evidence that Zhukovsky shared the intellectual brilliance and philosophical acuteness of Novalis.

The first really significant poetical piece published by Zhukovsky, and that which was celebrated fifty years later (the year of his death) as the quasi-official entry of the poet into the world of literature (see Vyazemsky's "Song on the Birthday of V. A. Zhukovsky") was a translation (1802) of Thomas Gray's "Elegy Written in a Country Churchyard." This work, although a translation, is very free, and is actually a poetical transmutation of the original rather than a faithful rendering. The mood of Gray's famous poem, gently wistful and melancholy, is perfectly conveyed in the Russian version, although in a different metrical form and with considerable freedom. This, incidentally, is generally true with the "translations" for which Zhukovsky is more famous than for his original verse. He treated the art of translation not as a task of slavishly turning an original into another language with as great accuracy as possible, but as an almost alchemistic procedure whereby the metal of the original becomes the gold of a Russian poem, itself just as true an original. He was phenomenally successful in this almost unique task, and in a very large number of cases the "translation" is a far better poem than the original. This is not true with the "Country Churchyard," of course, but the Zhukovsky rendering must be considered as a fully independent and original work. It is interesting to note that in later years Zhukovsky for unknown reasons retreated from his earlier view of the translator's art, and began to render with far greater faithfulness—and much less poetry—than before. In 1839 he retranslated the "Elegy"—this time in Russian dactylic hexameters, popularized by Gnedich's great translation of the *Iliad,* and later used by Zhukovsky himself in his translation of the *Odyssey.* A comparison of the two versions shows the much greater faithfulness of the 1839 poem, which none the less, although a good translation, lacks the emotional impact of the version from 1802. Among other things may be noted the manner in which the elements of Gray's original, unfamiliar to the Russian scene, are transmuted; thus the "drowsy tinklings" become "the cheerless sound of horns"; the "ivy-mantled tower" becomes "the ancient vault of yonder tower"; the line "beneath those rugged elms, that yew-tree's shade" is rendered "Under the shelter of black pines and bent elms."

How closely the mood of Gray's poem coincided with Zhukovsky's own poetic temper may be seen by a comparison of the final portion of the "Elegy in a Country Churchyard"—the account of the rustic youth whose epitaph ends the piece—with Zhukovsky's original **"The Singer"** (1811). Gray's epitaph on the frustrated village singer records that "He gave to Misery all he had, a tear, He gained from Heaven ('twas all he wished) a friend." Very similar is the fate of the "poor singer" in Zhukovsky's poem, except that Gray's rustic, although "A youth to Fortune and to Fame unknown," and marked by Melancholy "for her own," lived content; Zhukovsky's hero, before hanging up his lyre and garland forever, sings his farewell song: "O lovely world, where I have vainly come to bloom—farewell forever. With soul deceived I await happiness—an end to dreams. Everything has perished; be silent, lyre. Quickly, quickly, to the abode of peace, poor singer!" The singer, too, had known friendship: "He sang of friendship, giving a friend his tender hand—but his loyal friend was snuffed out in the flower of his years." The cult of friendship is of course one of the most prominent traits of sentimentalism. Gray's hero is described in his epitaph: "Large was his bounty, and his soul sincere." Zhukovsky's "was simple of heart, he was tender of soul—but in the world he was but a moment's wanderer." Rather surprisingly, for Zhukovsky, the religious note on which the "Elegy" ends: "No farther seek his merits to disclose, Or draw his frailties from their dread abode (There they alike in trembling hope repose) The bosom of his Father and his God," has no corresponding passage in **"The Singer."** The last strophe of that poem relates: "And the singer is no more; his lyre is silent, his traces have vanished. Sorrowful is everything in the plain and on the hills, and everything is silent. Only the quiet breezes, swaying the withered wreath, are wafted sometimes over the grave, and the lyre gloomily repeats to them: 'Poor singer'."

The language which Zhukovsky employs in these early poems is a variant of Karamzin's "salon style." The brooding, intimate subjects which he chiefly exploits are precisely such as Lomonosov would have marked as appropriate to the "middle style," and the solemn and elevated "high style," with its many Slavonicisms, would have been completely unfit for the intensely personal and subjective content of the Zhukovsky elegies. But at the time when these were written Russian literary circles were beginning to be torn by a violent and sometimes undignified controversy over the merits of the "salon style" and the "high style." Lomonsov's eminently sensible formulation was lost sight of, and literary matters became entangled with ultra-nationalistic attitudes coinciding with the wars between Russia and the Napoleonic Empire. The battle began with an attack by the fiery nationalist Admiral Alexander Semenovich Shishkov (1754-1841), entitled "Considerations on the Old and the New Styles of the Russian Language" (1803). In this treatise the Admiral, who was a passionate advocate of the use of the Church Slavonic, which he regarded as a pure and ancient form of Russian, blasted the modernists such as Karamzin, who in his opinion had corrupted the mother tongue by the introduction of all sorts of needless Gallicisms. In Shishkov's belief the future of the Russian language lay in a return to the truly Slavonic past, and in a renewal and enrichment of vocabulary through coinages, if necessary, using purely Slavonic roots, to express ideas for which foreign—German, French, even English—words were being borrowed. Karamzin, although the principal object of the attack, did not reply, and remained throughout the controversy quite aloof. Zhukovsky did reply, not with a treatise, naturally, but in satires and polemic epigrams; so did a good many of the other younger poets. Following the crystallization of two literary parties, unions were formed for each. In 1807 the followers of the "Russo-Slavonic" line began to meet regularly in the Admiral's house, and a society took shape, not officially organized until 1811, under the title: *Beseda liubitelie russkogo slova,* or "Society of Lovers of the Russian Word." Among the adherents of

the *Beseda,* besides Shishkov himself, were Prince Sergei Alexandrovich Shirinsky-Shikhmatov (1783-1837), Semen Sergeevich Bobrov (c. 1767-1810), the poetess A. P. Bunina, the satiric poet D. I. Khvostov, and—most significant of all—the satirist and fable writer Ivan Krylov and the leading poet of Catherine's age, Gavrila Romanovich Derzhavin, at whose home the later meetings of the *Beseda* took place. The period of the final organization of the group, 1811, was marked by a wide growth throughout Russia of an anti-French feeling, aggravated by the economic disadvantages resulting from the Peace of Tilsit, and reaching its acme during the War of 1812. It was easy to transfer hatred of Napoleon and the "continental system," suspicion of the ideas of the French Revolution, which he was supposed to be disseminating throughout Europe, and frustration at the hardships imposed by the blockade of England, to a linguistic area, and to decry Gallicisms in language as unpatriotic. Thus the *Beseda,* many of whose members were high government officials, attained a quasi-official sanction. Shishkov became president of the Russian Academy in 1816, at which time the *Beseda* terminated its existence.

The modernists, mostly young poets, after years of deadly sniping through satire and epigram, organized themselves into a counter group, calling itself "The Arzamas Society of Obscure Men." The town of Arzamas was famous for its geese, and the Boeotian stupidity of its townsmen. The title was intentionally parodistic and humorous, and the "society," which began to meet in 1815 and continued for only a few years, was scarcely serious in conception. Its rituals were farcical, and the whole procedure of its meetings was marked by high-spirited fun of a not particularly subtle or elegant variety. Members of this group were first and foremost Vasily Zhukovsky, who became its permanent secretary; Batyushkov, next to Zhukovsky the most important poet of the period; the "hussar poet" Denis Davydov; Prince Peter Vyazemsky; Vasily Lvovich Pushkin, a satirist and writer of elegant Anacreontic poems, and, in the last year of its existence, the brilliant young nephew of the last-named, Alexander Sergeevich Pushkin, at the age of eighteen already one of the leading poets of Russia.

The polemical literature emanating from this curious literary feud was considerable. Prince Alexander Alexandrovich Shakhovskoi (1777-1846), one of the *Beseda* group, justifiably ridiculing the execrable sentimentalist dramas of the German Kotzebue and his Russian imitators, wrote his comedy (1805) *The New Sterne,* the butt of which was Karamzin and his negligible imitator P. I. Shalikov. Another comedy, appearing in 1815, the year the *Arzamas* was organized, entitled *The Baths of Leipzig,* by the same Shakhovskoi, ridiculed Zhukovsky himself under the caricature of the poet Fialkin (from *fialka,* "violet"). Blasts from the liberal side were equally numerous and even more devastating. The most famous of these is probably "A Vision on the Banks of Lethe" (1809) in which the poet Batyushkov subjects most of the *Beseda* group, especially Shishkov himself, to a sousing in the beneficient waters of the river of eternal forgetfulness. Vasily Pushkin also entered the fray, and in his "Epistle to V. A. Zhukovsky" (1810) subjected the whole *Beseda* movement to merciless and well-founded criticism. After the year 1816 the polemics began to die away, and the controversy may be considered to have been by that time pretty thoroughly settled. Derzhavin died in that year, and with him passed away the only *Beseda* poet of merit except Krylov, whose position was always ambivalent, since he remained in spite of his membership in the *Beseda* on the best of terms also with the *Arzamas* group, and was idolized for his vigorous popular fables by such poets as Batyushkov, Vyazemsky, and Alexander Pushkin. The victory remained with the modernists, and the "high style" with its antiquated Slavonic vocabulary became an anachronism, to be finally given the *coup de grace* by the genius of the younger Pushkin.

One of the most prominent features of the romantic style popularized by Zhukovsky is the semantic shift involved in the romantic poet's subjective approach to the world of reality. Because this semantic innovation has become as familiar to the modern world as the air we breathe, it is extremely difficult for us even to appreciate the magnitude of the change involved. In reading poets of the eighteenth century, in any European language, we are vaguely aware of what we are likely to call a "dry" and abstract quality in their work, but without further analysis and comparison with typical works of the romantic period we are unlikely to realize that the essence of the difference lies in a completely different attitude toward the word. The eighteenth century classicist followed a formula which, whether explicitly so stated or not, amounted to this: the word is an unchanging symbol of a single and definite reality; and it must be used in both prose and poetry only in such a way that its precise and objective meaning is applicable. There are, to be sure, such things as "figures of speech," especially metaphors, in which the precise meaning of a word is used in a "transferred" sense: but these figures must be used with great restraint, and never slipped unobtrusively and as it were illicitly into the verse. The romantic poet, on the other hand—and in the present discussion this means preeminently Zhukovsky, who first introduced into Russian poetry this long suspect innovation—utilized words not so much as precise and definite symbols of the objective world, as he did to mirror certain states of the writer's own mind. The word thus is employed to tell about the subjective world of the poet almost as much as about the objective world which he senses about him. To the classicist such a procedure is wholly illegitimate, and the most indignant protests were raised over turns of phrase which to us seem completely natural and innocuous, simply because we have become so habituated to this mode of writing that it is rather the classicist prejudices that have to be reconstructed for us. Perhaps an illustration of what is meant here will serve to throw light on the whole difference.

Let us use for this illustration two descriptive portions of poems, each called "Evening," [by] A. F. Merzliakov (1797) and V. A. Zhukovsky (1806) respectively. The dates are not particularly significant, for many "classical" poems continued to be written long after 1806; but we may note that Zhukovsky's poetical career really started only a year before this date, with his translation of Gray's "Elegy." Merzliakov, although in some aspects—notably

his interest in the "popular" element of folk-song—akin to the pre-romantics, is in his use of words without subjective color, completely a product of the eighteenth century. . . . Translated into the most literal English, [his description of the coming of evening, which opens a long meditative poem], says:

> Already the paling day was becoming hidden in the purple western regions and darkness was being poured out in streams upon the pale-blue fields of the heavens. The tempests have fallen asleep (and) the violent winds, upon the bosom of the deeps, upon the cliffs of the mountains; billowing on the gold-red seas evening was revealing his purple gaze. Taking leave of the gentle luminary of day, resting upon the breast of Morpheus, in a dreary frenzy tender Nature was silent, drowsing beneath the cover of silence; and I, having taken leave of the swift day, am going with avid solicitude, with fuss, to wash away the bloody sweat, to cool the burning heart with the streams of sweet rest.

Here we will first be struck by the common figure of speech "personification," very frequently employed by classical poets. The "tempests have fallen asleep upon the bosom of the deeps." "Evening" (because of the Russian gender, a masculine figure) "Was revealing his purple gaze" upon the seas; "tender nature" (feminine) "was silent, resting upon the breast of Morpheus, drowsing beneath the cover of silence." Nature has to be pictured as a relaxed female figure reclining upon the sleep-god's breast, and drowsing beneath a metaphorical blanket of silence! Metaphor is involved in the last phrase of the first quatrain: "Upon the pale-blue fields of the heavens"—the sky is clearly being equated with the earthly plains below. The dark is a river, which "was being poured out in streams"; rest is also a stream, with which the poet can "cool his burning heart." The adjectives employed with the personified natural phenomena are such as to apply equally well to their literal and to their figurative existence: the "violent" winds have fallen asleep; "tender" Nature has taken leave of the "gentle" sun; the poet, in turn has taken leave of the "swift" day. Other adjectives, however, are as precise and unambiguous as possible. Here they are mostly terms of color: "paling," "purple," "pale-blue," "gold-red," and "purple" again. Each of these conveys a perfectly definite and precise meaning. The total effect of the picture is that of an objective painting of the scene; until the poet overtly introduces himself, in the last five lines quoted, and, again metaphorically (e.g., "bloody sweat," "burning heart," "streams of sweet rest") explicitly refers to his emotional condition, the reader can make no judgement of the mood with which Merzliakov views the evening, only of his skill in catching the appropriate words for conveying the color and quietness of the sunset.

Now let us look at three strophes (6-8) from Zhukovsky's elegy "**Evening**." . . .

> Already it is evening . . . The edges of the clouds have become dark, the last ray of sunset is dying on the towers; in the river the last shining stream is going out with the heaven that is quenched. All is still; the groves are asleep; all

around there is quiet; upon the grass beneath the bending willow I note, as I lie reclined, how the brook, shaded with bushes, murmurs as it flows together with the river. How the incense of the plants merges with the coolness! How sweet in the stillness is the plashing of the streams on the shore! How still is the wafting of the zephyr on the waters, and the trembling of the pliant willow!

Here the personifications are very unobtrusive: "the groves are asleep" (perhaps metonymy—the groves for the birds that inhabit them); "the last ray of sunset is dying," etc. There is no precise and definable color—only that implied in the verb "have become dark" and that equally implied in the word *zaria,* "sunset." But note the words that apply much more to the mood of the observer than to the objective reality of the scene observed: "last"—there is a melancholy in this word, even when it can be considered precise, as here—and it is twice repeated; "is dying"—one can say that here is no more than a metaphor, just like that of Merzliakov's "the tempests have fallen asleep"; but no, that is different, because "dying" conveys a mood, while "sleeping" does not. The participle "shining" conveys a mood also, of quiet happiness; but this is almost at once cancelled by the slanted word *ugasaet,* "is going out"—the verb specifically used of a guttering candle. We seem then to have a slightly mixed metaphor, since what "goes out" here is not a candle, but a "shining stream." What is more, the same metaphoric figure is applied also the sky, with another synonymous word, *potukhshim;* and in both cases the idea of "quenched," "gone out" is a mournful one. Then there is the adjective *tikhii* and its noun, *tishina.* Literally applied, this should be the antonym of "noisy"; but the word, more in Russian than in English, implies "peace." Not only is everything "still," but everything is "peaceful"; not only is the plashing of the streams sweet in the "stillness" by the shore, but in the "peace" by the shore. But "peace" is a value word, and means much more as describing the mood of the observer than as describing the scene. *Tishina,* it may be remembered, is in Merzliakov's poem only a metaphorical coverlet beneath which "tender Nature" drowses. A direct comparison between the methods of the two poets is possible also with the words *pokoi* ("rest") and *sladkii* ("sweet"). By itself *pokoi* means "quiet," "repose," "peace of mind," sometimes indeed even the "peace of the grave," as well as a literal "sleep." Merzliakov clearly has the literal meaning in mind, when he speaks of "cooling his burning heart with the streams of sweet rest,"—in plain prose, he is eager to forget his troubles in a good night's sleep. Zhukovsky's phrase *v okrestonosti pokoi,* "all around there is *pokoi,*" is certainly more than an otiose repetition of the idea that all nature is asleep—it conveys much more the quieting and restful effect which the natural surroundings have on the poet himself. And finally, when the classical poet employs the word "sweet" as an epithet of *pokoi,* it must be remembered that *pokoi* is here a stream, and that "sweet" is a habitual epithet for water, originally distinguishing fresh from salt. With Zhukovsky, however, the adjective can most certianly not be understood literally of the word "plashing"; it does not describe the noun it is grammati-

cally associated with, but the mood of the observer. Similarly the word "trembling," although it may literally describe the vibrations of a "pliant willow" in the breeze, inevitably also conjures up a mood of fear. And finally, it is surely not an over-subtlety to see even in the noun *iva* ("willow") a melancholy association; the *plakuchaia iva,* "weeping willow," is as familiar in Russian as in English.

Lastly, we should not be oblivious of the strange effect, for the classicist, of the first line of the last strophe quoted of Zhukovsky's poem: "How the incense of the plants is mingled with the coolness!" The literal-minded reader must protest: "This is impossible, sheer nonsense. Incense (*fymiam*) means 'fragrance' (the word would be an example, if you will, of metonymy); and how can 'fragrance,' which belongs to the sense of smell, be 'mingled' with 'coolness,' which belongs to the sense of touch?" The classicist is of course perfectly correct from the point of view of his rules for word use; but the romanticist uses these words *not* to describe an objective reality, but to convey a subjective experience; and since both "fragrance" and "coolness" are pleasurable sensations in the subject, they can perfectly well "mingle."

In sum, when we read the quoted strophes of Zhukovsky's poem, we are less aware of a concrete picture than of a mood; we do not know a great deal about how the evening actually looked—a few "moody" symbols stand out, such as the "weeping willow" beside a river—but what comes through is rather how the evening affected Zhukovsky: an aura of peace and pleasant melancholy pervades the poem. With Merzliakov, on the other hand, the picture is clear and bright, but there is little intimation of how it affects the poet's feelings.

It was this new use of words which Zhukovsky introduced into Russian, probably having learned it from the German romantics, that puzzled and infuriated the classicists. Apropos of Zhukovsky's translation of Goethe's ballad "The Fisherman," Orest Somov writes: "*The soul* (one must guess, that of the fisherman) *is full of cool stillness.* In a transferred sense one may say that rapture, reverence, fill the soul; because this is proper to the analogy of these concepts with certain visible actions; but neither to stillness nor to sound is attributed the capacity for filling the soul. And what sort of quality of stillness is 'cool'? Is there also then a 'warm stillness' and a 'hot noise' and the like?" Of course "warm stillness' would not seem at all out of place to us, habituated as we are to the romantic semantics; and even a "hot noise" might convey something to a jazz addict.

Zhukovsky's innovation, then, consisted in introducing into Russian the *subjective* use of words; instead of impersonally observing and reporting the scenes and incidents described in words as precisely fitted to their objects as possible, the poet—with his eye on the object, to be sure—reports in words that while applying to the object in a formal, syntactical sense, actually convey more information about the subject, and thus establish a mood which is communicated to the reader. This is why eighteenth century classical verse seems to us "dry" and colorless; this is exactly what it is meant to be, and this is exactly the area in which the romantic poet made his greatest innovation.

We may note in passing the prevalence in Zhukovsky's poetry of such "mood" words as *unylo* ("gloomy"), *sladko* ("sweet"), *tomno* ("weary, languid"), and the like. And the innovation caught on with other writers of the same generation and literary direction. Thus, Batyushkov, despite his classical plasticity, indulges in romantic mood-fixing just as does Zhukovsky.

As was earlier mentioned, Zhukovsky's school friend Andrei Turgenev had initiated him into German sentimentalism (the *Sturm und Drang*). One of the most famous productions of this movement in Germany was G. A. Bürger's ballad "Lenore" (1773). The ballad form itself was at this time something of a novelty in Germany—the artificial creation of a narrative poem on a theme of terror from popular superstition. The enthusiasm for popular balladry came in with Herder, but Bürger's attempts to create "art ballads" antedate Herder's great collection of the "Voices of Peoples." Bürger's poem narrates the fate of a young girl whose sweetheart has gone off to war. She waits impatiently for his return, and when he fails to come, complains bitterly of the injustice of God. In answer to her wicked discontent her lover appears one night on a black horse and carries her off with him to their "wedding," which turns out to be entombment together in the churchyard as the bells toll midnight. The whole is told in a quasi-popular style, with a constantly repeated refrain line, "Hurra! Die Toten reiten schnell!" Whether or not any genuinely popular ballads ever employed this motif, Bürger's creation achieved its effect, and became immensely popular. In 1808 Zhukovsky recreated this in a manner much freer than he had employed in the "Elegy." His version is entitled **"Lyudmila."** His heroine is thus given a Slavic name, and her circumstances are changed accordingly: the war in which her lover is involved is the Livonian War of Ivan IV, and the setting is made entirely Russian. The style, however, is less "popular" in **"Lyudmila"** than in Bürger's original; Zhukovsky did not yet realize the power of the popular language, and still chose to employ the elegant, and here rather inappropriate "salon style."

Karamzin's ballad *Raisa* is the first example of the genre in Russian literature, but **"Lyudmila,"** a far better poem and far more widely appreciated, is the first real success of the new type, which comes to be one of the chief forms of the early romantic verse. So significant was the success of **"Lyudmila"** that in the quaint ritual of the *Arzamas* Zhukovsky himself was given the name of his most famous heroine! He thereupon continued on this fruitful path, and began to translate from English as well as from German originals. Subjects were furnished by Sir Walter Scott, whose "St. John's Eve" became Zhukovsky's **"Castle of Smalholm"**; by Robert Southey, and by lesser poets. Schiller's ballads particularly attracted Zhukovsky, and the German poet's "Ritter Toggenburg" is one of Zhukovsky's best recreations. Goethe's "Erlkönig" was successfully transmuted into Russian, as were several of Uhland's ballads. But what is without a question one of the most signal triumphs of Zhukovsky in the ballad genre, as well as in the art of remaking poems from one language into another, is the ballad of the Austrian poet Joseph Christian von Zedlitz, "Die nächtliche Heerschau." The original is in the usual ballad form, quatrains of four-beat iambic lines; it narrates the "review" of Napoleon's spectral army which the ghost of the fallen Emperor carries out at midnight. There is nothing in the original to mark it out from a host of other minor German ballads. Von Zedlitz was not a great poet, and although his conception is striking and original, the execution lags far behind. Zhukovsky's "translation" is an original poem of the greatest distinction. In it he demonstrates his unparalleled skill in fitting sound to sense. The poem begins with the rousing of the drummer boy from his grave to beat the tattoo for the assembly of the infantry. The banal ballad meter of the original has been replaced by a strongly rhythmical amphibrachic meter which startingly reproduces the muffled sounds of the ghostly drum. . . . Zhukovsky's poem, it should be noted, compresses the sixty lines of the German into forty-eight; even without this difference the Russian is more a paraphrase than a translation. . . . The Von Zedlitz original reads: "Nightly at twelve o'clock the drummer leaves his grave, goes the rounds with his drum, walks briskly up and down. With his fleshless arms he plies the two drum-sticks together, strikes many a good roll, reveille and tattoo." Zhukovsky turns this:

> At twelve o'clock at night the drummer rises from his grave, walks back and forth, and briskly beats the alarm. And in their dark graves the drum arouses the mighty infantry; the young chasseurs rise up, the old grenadiers rise up; they rise from beneath Russian snows, from the lush plains of Italy; they rise from the African deserts, from the burning sands of Palestine.

The muffled drum is almost audible in the first line: *V dvenadtsat' chasov po nocham;* with almost as vivid an onomatopoetic effect the trumpeter for the cavalry rises in the second strophe: *i gromko trubit on trevogu* ("And loudly he trumpets the alarm"). In the last strophe, when the ghostly emperor himself rides down the line giving the watchword, the muted whisper is audible in the sibilants of the Russian lines: *I blizhnemu na ukho sam On shepchet parol' svoi i lozung* ("And himself in his neighbor's ear whispers his countersign and watchword"). After the thunderous last line, with its magnificently placed Slavonicism: *Vstaet imperator usopshii* ("rises the deceased emperor!") Von Zedlitz's German "original" sounds strangely tame and tawdry.

During the period of Schiller's close collaboration with Goethe, both poets wrote ballads on subjects from classical antiquity—for example Goethe's "Bride of Corinth" and Schiller's famous "Crane of Ibycus," on a story taken from Herodotus. It may be questioned whether this procedure was appropriate, whether, that is, the "popular" ballad form was inherently suited to the retelling of tales from the Greek past; but it resulted in some notable poems. Macaulay's "Lays of Ancient Rome" are an English attempt along the same lines. Zhukovsky translated Goethe's ballad "The Fisherman," and Schiller's "Cranes of Ibycus," "Ring of Polycrates" (again from Herodotus), "The Complaint of Ceres," "The Eleusinian Festival" (the translation that Mitya Karamazov quotes in the chapter "Confession of a Passionate Heart—in Verse"). There is an evident kinship between the later Schiller (not the poet of "The Robbers") and the melancholy and mystical Zhukovsky.

After **"Lyudmila,"** Zhukovsky's most successful ballad was **"Svetlana,"** published in 1812. His theme is here a combination of the "Lenore" motif and a popular Russian superstition (utilized also by Tolstoy in *War and Peace*), an unmarried girl's attempted divination of her future husband. The popular element in **"Svetlana"** is far greater than in any previous ballad of Zhukovsky; his heroine goes through the rigmarole of trying to find out who her future husband is to be, but falls asleep and dreams that she sees in the mirror the features of her lover's ghost, who has come to carry her off as Lenore and Lyudmila were carried. She awakes from her nightmare to find that her lover has actually arrived to take her away, but happily in flesh and blood. The description of the divination is thoroughly popular in style, but Zhukovsky still cautiously avoids the real peasant speech. It is interesting to note that some of the more extreme of the younger poets were at this time beginning to become dissatisfied with Zhukovsky's leadership, and Pavel Alexandrovich Katenin (1792-1853), himself incidentally a member of the *Beseda* group, created still another "Lenore" poem in his "Olga" (1816), greeted by Griboedov as a more truly popular poem than Zhukovsky's **"Lyudmila"** or **"Svetlana."** Katenin's language is far more genuinely colloquial than Zhukovsky's.

The last important piece of balladry which Zhukovsky wrote is the long poem **"The Twelve Sleeping Maidens"** (1817). He took his subject again from the German, this time from a prose romance by Christian Heinrich Spiess (1755-1799), a well-forgotten *Sturm und Drang* composer of "horror tales," one of which is his three-volume *Die zwölf schlafenden Jungfrauen* (1794-96). Zhukovsky's version is entitled "A Poem in Two Ballads." The first ballad, "Gromoboi," is a Russianization of a common western folklore motif, a variant of the Faust legend—of the man who sells his soul to the devil. Gromoboi sells his soul to the demon Asmodeus for wealth and sensual happiness; when the demon comes to collect his prize, Gromoboi bargains for an extension of his life at the price of the ultimate sacrifice of his twelve innocent daughters. The sinner repents of his wickedness, and spends his last years in good works; at the second appearance of Asmodeus to claim him, an unnamed saint whose picture has adorned the chapel built by Gromoboi descends from heaven, puts the twelve maidens into an enchanted slumber in the miraculously protected castle, and sends their repentant father to his grave, in which he is to be temporarily tormented and restless until the destined deliverer of his daughters shall appear. The second ballad, "Vadim," continues the tale with the adventures of the young Novgorodian of that name (apparently wholly unconnected with the legendary hero who opposed the "tyranny" of Riurik), who is, of course, the heaven-appointed deliverer of the twelve maidens. Vadim sees a vision of the protective saint and of one of the maidens, enchantingly beautiful, and inspired by the saint's words, sets out on his journey south through the trackless forests. Arrived at length in the territories of Kiev, he rescues a lovely maiden from the clutches of a giant who is abducting her, and spends the night with her

in a cave in the forest. In the original version of Spiess this adventure is filled with eroticism; but Zhukovsky, true to his other-worldly orientation, allows Vadim only to be tempted by the seductive beauty of his protégée; a far-away vision of his guardian saint and the ringing of the bell that symbolizes the lady of his dreams bring him safely away, and he conveys the princess to her father, the prince of Kiev. At the festivities attending her recovery, Vadim is destined by her grateful father to be his son-in-law and heir; but the young hero wanders off to the shore of the Dniepr at the height of the celebration, and gets into an unmanned boat, which whisks him off down the river to the deserted and eery region where is located the long-forgotten castle of Gromoboi. Here Vadim succeeds without much supernatural opposition in scaling the cliff, entering the castle, and waking the maidens. The tormented spirit of Gromoboi has peace at last, Vadim and his princess (still unnamed) are united in marriage in the miraculously regenerated chapel, and the unlucky eleven sisters of his bride, for whom no husbands have been provided, retire into a nunnery to pray for the probably still insufficiently redeemed soul of their father.

The piece is Zhukovsky's longest attempt in the purely romantic line, and is marked by both the excellencies and the deficiencies of his style. It is exceptionally melodious and sweetly flowing, and the narration is given in a spirited and interesting way; the landscapes are sketched with particular skill, and all of Zhukovsky's magical art of utilizing the effects of nature to mirror or contrast with psychological conditions is shown to the full. Of particular note is the description of the fateful evening on which Asmodeus makes his first appearance to carry off his victim; the natural background most effectively conveys the horror of the situation:

> And lo—the last day has come. And now the sun is behind the mountain. The evening shadow is spreading out in a transparent pall; and now it is twilight . . . It is dark . . . Behold the moon shining from behind the cloud. Silence has descended upon the hills; the deep wood has grown still. The river has made itself smooth within its banks; the candles of night have been kindled. There is profound slumber upon the fields, and near is the hour of midnight. . . . Everything was in a terrible silence; all around was like a tomb. Behold, a raven croaked on the wall. Behold, a pack of dogs began to howl. And suddenly, lingeringly, midnight struck. Clouds began to cover the sky. The river swelled, the forest roared, and scudding dust swept past. Alas! The last terrible stroke ceased to resound behind the hills. The clang grew quieter. . . . it died away . . . And Gromoboi beheld the devil before his eyes.

But the witchery of the verse conceals a great emptiness; the figures which move through the poem are unreal and puppet-like, and have no character. The ballads themselves are far too long-winded: greater concision would have undoubtedly made them more impressive. The denouement of the poem is strangely tame—the demon Asmodeus disappears altogether from the second ballad, presumably totally overawed by the domineering saint. And perhaps most seriously of all, the entire atmosphere of the story, despite the mentions of Novgorod and Kiev and of the River Dniepr, is totally un-Russian. There is not the slightest degree of Slavic inspiration in it, everything is a most transparent derivation from western story. It is perhaps worth noting that Gogol too, although far closer to a popular inspiration in his turbid horror tale "A Dreadful Vengeance," suffers from the same defects as Zhukovsky. It is simply not convincing to find medieval castles, tenanted by ghosts, vampires, and the un-dead, located on the Dniepr! All these creations of Germanic fantasy are grotesquely out of place in a Russian locale, and even the art of Zhukovsky or Gogol does not suffice to naturalize them there.

Zhukovsky's ballads no doubt constitute his best and most typical work; but for long he was known almost as much for a single patriotic poem as for these. In 1812, during Napoleon's invasion of Russia, the poet joined a regiment of reserves, and was actually present at Tarutino with other reservists when the decisive battle of the campaign was fought at Borodino, no great distance away. He seems to have sensed the importance of this action, and almost immediately after the battle wrote his poem, **"The Bard in the Camp of the Russian Warriors."** Here we have a curious mixture of types: in form the piece is perhaps closest to an old-fashioned triumphal ode of the Lomonosov or Derzhavin variety, filled with elements of the "high style"; at the same time, where the "bard" sings of the loved ones left at home, the poem takes on a decidedly elegiac tone; and finally the situation, in which the "bard" presumably calls upon his warrior audience to drink to their generals, the emperor, victory, and the fatherland, is reminiscent of the light "hussar poetry" of Denis Davydov, with its constant refrains urging deep drinking on all possible occasions. Besides the mixture of types—not an entirely successful experiment—Zhukovsky's poem evidences some rather grotesque features of conventionality in diction. In addressing his "warriors" the bard has occasion to refer to their armament—and this consists, it seems, rather improbably of shields, spears, swords and helmets! The effect is as incongruous as that of Batyushkov's poem "My Penates," of which Pushkin complained that the collocation of classical *mores* with a realistic Russian situation was absurd. But it will be long before the poet can feel free to depict an actual contemporary situation without tricking it out in classical paraphernalia.

"The Bard in the Camp of the Russian Warriors," although from the point of the poetical art a quite inferior poem, made Zhukovsky famous as a patriot, and from this fame sprang an unexpected effect: he was drawn into service by the emperor himself, eventually becoming the tutor of Alexander Nikolaevich, the emperor's nephew and second successor (as Alexander II). Thus for a long period of his middle life Zhukovsky almost entirely abandoned poetry and occupied himself with his duties as a tutor, which he took very seriously, in the hopes of inculcating "virtue" in his charge such as befitted an autocrat. During this period Zhukovsky's position as leader of the modernist school was more and more definitively lost to Alexander Pushkin. Zhukovsky translated a number of longer poems during this time (1820-1840)—for example,

the ancient Russian "epic" *The Tale of the Campaign of Igor,* Schiller's poetic drama *The Maid of Orleans,* and Lord Byron's famous "Prisoner of Chillon." From evidences in in his letters, it is clear that Zhukovsky had a great admiration for Byron, and even contemplated making a series of translations of his tales; but there was such a temperamental lack of harmony between the melancholy, retiring, resigned and passive Russian poet and the rebellious, tempestuous English activist, that the project came to nothing. The translation of the "Prisoner of Chillon" incidentally is of some significance in Russian literature from the influence which it had on the young Lermontov in creating his masterpiece *The Novice (Mtsyri);* both the external form of the stanza and the inspiring passion for freedom of the central characters are features common to both poems. During the summer of 1831 Zhukovsky was with Pushkin at Tsarskoe Selo and underwent strong influence from that quarter. While Pushkin created at this time his magnificent *skazki* (popular narrative tales) the "Golden Cockerel" and "Tsar Saltan," Zhukovsky composed a much tamer *skazka* entitled in full: **"Tale of the Tsar Berendeia, of his Son Ivan-Tsarevich, of the Crafts of Koshchei the Deathless and of the Wisdom of Maria-Tsarevna, Koshchei's Daughter."** The title nearly gives away the plot.

Zhukovsky's last poetical achievements show a new attitude toward the art of translation. We have noted his earlier translations as "transmutations" of originals which are themselves in every sense original poems, sometimes far superior to those which inspired them. The second translation of Gray's "Elegy" (1839) is a true "translation,"

A lithograph of Zhukovsky, dated 1820.

faithful to its original in every regard. So is the translation of Bürger's "Lenore" (1831), written after Zhukovsky had twice in famous poems treated the same theme more freely. Of the translations of this period mention may be made of fragments of the second book of Virgil's *Aeneid,* of portions of Homer's *Iliad* and of the pseudo-Homeric *Battle of the Frogs and Mice,* as well as the whole of the *Odyssey.* To these translations from the Greek we shall return presently. In his later years Zhukovsky was attracted also to the literatures of the ancient east, which he read in translations made by German scholars of the romantic period. This interest led him to make in the years 1837-1841 a "translation" of an episode, "Nal and Damayanti," from the Sanskrit epic *Mahabharata,* worked into Russian blank verse (iambic pentameter unrhymed) from the prose of the Sanskrit scholar Franz Bopp and a poetical version by the poet Friedrich Rückert. From Rückert's partial translation of Firdausi's Persian epic the *Shah-Nameh* Zhukovsky also worked out a Russian version "Rustem and Zorab" (the same story which Matthew Arnold was to treat in English some years later).

It has been mentioned that Zhukovsky employed a prose—and rather frivolous and pornographic—romance for his "tale in two ballads," **"The Twelve Sleeping Maidens."** This unusual procedure, which Zhukovsky continued throughout his life, led to some rather odd results. Few poets have been attracted to the possibilities of "translating" prose of one language into verse in another. Zhukovsky's exploits in this field brought into existence: a version, in "popular" (*skazka*) form of the famous western "fairy tale" *Puss in Boots,* as retold by Perrault in French (*Le Maître chat, ou le Chat botté*); the blank verse version of Prosper Mérimée's powerful *conte Matteo Falcone;* and a dactylic hexameter version of the prose *Märchen* of the German romantic Friedrich de la Motte-Fouqué, *Undine.* The last mentioned is the best of this group, and indeed may be considered one of Zhukovsky's finest pieces.

Zhukovsky's last great work was his masterly translation of Homer's *Odyssey.* This project he seems to have conceived as early as the 20s, but he did not actually begin work on it until January, 1842. The work was carried on with many interruptions until April, 1849. It appeared first in complete form in Volumes VIII and IX of Zhukovsky's complete works, published in 1849.

Perhaps no great translation from the ancient Greek was ever made under such peculiar conditions as Zhukovsky's **Odyssey.** The poet himself in a letter (12 [24] September, 1847) to S. S. Uvarov, the Minister of Education (1833-1849) describes these conditions most fully:

> You will ask: how did I get it into my head to busy myself with the *Odyssey,* when I do not know Greek, and convert myself from a mysteriously arrogant German romantic into a meek classicist? There is a simple answer to this: having come in my old age to the peaceful haven of family life, I took a notion of gladdening my soul with primeval poetry, which is so bright and quiet, so life-giving and restful, which so peaceably beautifies everything that surrounds us, is so un-alarming, and strives toward no murky

distances. Old age is a second childhood; on the eve of old age one likes stories. And so I took the notion to join myself with that most simple-souled of all story-tellers, and, since I had not any tales of my own in store, to repeat in Rus' his ancient Greek fables. In a word, my goal was: to amuse myself in idleness with poetical garrulity; and in this I have succeeded.

> So far my chief purpose has been attained; Homer's Muse has turned to gold many an hour of my senility; but that which has diverted me myself so sweetly, so light-heartedly, I know not whether it will be a diversion also for the readers among my fellow-countrymen, with whom I want to share the treasures which I have taken from Homer. If this shall happen, the thought will gladden me that in Rus' will remain a solid memorial of my poetic life. To be a faithful presenter of Homer. . . . But how, you will ask, without knowing Homer's language, can I speak his language in Russian? This I must explain to you. I have had the assistance of conscientious, laborious, German scholarship. In Düsseldorf I found Professor Grashof, a great Hellenist, who is occupied in particular with explaining Homer. He took it on himself to assist my ignorance. In his own hand, and very distinctly he copied out for me in the original the whole 'Odyssey'; under each Greek word he put the German word, and under each German the grammatical sense of the original. In this way I was able to have before me the entire literal sense of the 'Odyssey' and to have before my eyes the entire order of the words; in this chaotic faithful translation, inaccessible to a reader, there were gathered, so to speak, before me all the materials of knowledge; there was lacking only beauty, shapeliness and harmony. And here is what, properly, my labor consisted of: from the given awkwardness I had to divine the shapeliness concealed in it, by means of a poet's intuition to seek out beauty in ugliness, and to create harmony from sounds that offended the ear—and all this not to the detriment of, but with the faithful preservation of the ancient physiognomy of the original. In this respect my translation can be called an original production. But the question is: have I succeeded? For myself, I cannot be my own judge, because I cannot compare. You are able to hear Homer himself—ask him whether he is satisfied with his Hyperborean presenter, and let me know his opinion. I have tried to translate word for word, so far as this was possible without violence to the language (servile fidelity often becomes servile betrayal!); I pursued every word, and in particular I tried to keep *their place in the verse* for those words which in this place produce a special poetical effect. I repeat here that which I have said of my labor in another place [he cites here his letter to I. V. Kireevsky **'On the Translation of the Odyssey,'** printed in *Moskvitanin,* 1845, no. 1]:

> "A translation of Homer cannot be like any other. In every other poet, not primitive, but already an artist, you encounter his natural inspiration and a work of art. In Homer there is none of this art; he is a babe, who has seen in dream

everything that is wondrous on earth and in the heavens, and who babbles about this in a sonorous, childish voice on the bosom of nature his nurse. This is a quiet, broad, bright stream without waves, which purely and faithfully reflects both the sky and its banks and everything that lives and moves on its banks. You see only the faithful reflection, but the bright crystal that reflects has, as it were, no existence—the eye does not feel it. In translating Homer (and in particular the *Odyssey*), you will not get far if you pay attention to the fortune of each verse separately, because with him—Homer, that is—there are no individually striking lines: there is their flow, which one must capture entire, in all its fullness and brightness; one must preserve every word and every epithet, and at the same time forget every particular for the whole. And in the choice of words one must observe a peculiar kind of caution: often the most poetical, picturesque, overpowering word for this very reason is unsuited to Homer; anything that has an appearance of novelty or the ingeniousness of our age, everything out of the ordinary, has no place here; it is, so to speak, an anachronism; one must return to a primeval language, which has already lost its freshness because all have been using it; in borrowing from the primal father of poetry, one must return to this stale, worn-out language its primitive freshness and newness, and eschew all the novelties with which poetical language, departing from primitive simplicity, has of necessity replaced this childish simplicity. In a word, in translating Homer, one must eschew every kind of affectation, every kind of embellishment, every kind of striving for effect, every kind of coquetry. . . . This task is very difficult; there are no clear rules for it; one must be guided by feeling alone. For me this task was the more difficult in that in this regard I was unable to come to an agreement with the original, because I do not know it, and could only guess."

Let me add: I have tried everywhere to keep a simple, folk-tale language [*skazochnyi iazyk*], avoiding every kind of strain, avoiding every kind of Slavonicism, and as far as possible I have kept an agreement between the forms of the original (which were preserved in everything material in the interlinear translation) and the forms of the Russian language, so that the Homeric verse should be felt in the Russian verse, without the latter's being forced into a distortion to match the Greek.

Zhukovsky's *Odyssey* is indeed a model of simple, direct, unaffected language, in these respects closely approximating Homer's Greek. A great deal of what he has to say about Homer's artlessness and childishness is of course an echo of Schiller's *Uber naive und sentimentalische Dichtung,* and based on a misconception. The Homeric poems are anything but artless, and what appeared to the romantic era to be their "primeval" character we now know to be a quality of their *oral* mode of composition and transmission. But Zhukovsky's poetical sensitivity hit most accurately upon certain musts and must nots of translating Homer. Most emphatically what he says about "eschewing all affectation," or anything smacking of modern "in-

geniousness," and of keeping an eye always on the movement of the whole, forgetting the effect of individual lines, are the most fundamental—and most often neglected—of all rules for the art. "Cute" modernisms, whether of T. E. Shaw or of Dudley Fitts—or of Pope, for that matter—are more surely calculated than anything else to pervert and vulgarize and destroy the noble and timeless simplicity of the Greek.

In one respect, we may note, the translator felt certain qualms about his unabashed reproduction of the original. "The language of my translation, it seems to me, is so simple that the Russian *Odyssey* will be accessible to all ages, and may, if certain omissions are made, be put into the hands of every youth who is beginning to read *to himself.* . . . thus the *Odyssey* may be made a most attractive and at the same time most instructive children's book." The cautious poet then points out to the Minister of Education that he has designated in red ink in his manuscript such passages in the poem as he deems should be excised for youthful readers. (It must be remembered that the *Odyssey* contains, in Demodocus' story of the adultery of Ares and Aphrodite, in Book VIII, the earliest bawdy story in European literature). Zhukovsky proposes two editions of his *Odyssey,* one for adults and one for youth. To Uvarov's everlasting credit, he vetoed this proposal; in a letter (10 November 1847) he wrote Zhukovsky: "As regards a *cleaning up* of the edition of the *Odyssey,* there is in my opinion no need to resort to this. Everywhere and always the youth read Homer in *complete* editions, and it has never been noted that this reading produced the slightest temptation." (The present writer would add his own postscript: when he first encountered the *Odyssey,* c. A. D. 1919, first in English and then in Greek, both texts had been thoroughly emasculated).

The tortuous method of translation which Zhukovsky describes is certainly not a normal or frequently used one; but in this case it was phenomenally successful. The Russian *Odyssey* is a splendid poem, and without undue awkwardness is startlingly close to its original even in such relatively minor regards as the placing of words in the line. This is of course a far easier matter in a highly inflected language such as Russian than it is in English, where the absence of case endings prohibits all such flexibility. Where Zhukovsky is least successful—and it must be said that Gnedich's *Iliad* is somewhat better in this regard—is in the treatment of the hexameter. The Greek quantitative meter can, by its freedom to substitute a spondee (two longs) for a dactyl (long and two shorts), achieve endlessly different effects and avoid monotony. The German and Russian (and English) *accentual* hexameter can utilize occasional accentual trochees, with somewhat the same effect. Without this kind of variation the reader is faced with an interminable succession of accentual dactyls, broken only by the obligatory trochee that marks the end of a line, and by variations of caesura. Monotony is built into such a line, and neither Voss in German, Longfellow in English, nor Zhukovsky in Russian has been able to avoid it. In this respect, indeed, it almost seems as though Zhukovsky's *Odyssey* represents a regression, for a rather casual inspection of the hexameters of the "Nal and Damayanti" translation reveals a far greater proportion of accentual trochees, which tends to offset this monotony, than are to be found in the *Odyssey.*

Before taking leave of Russia's first great Romantic, we must pause for a moment to consider one further and significant contribution which his verse made to the age which followed him. A feature common to romanticism in general, seen in Zhukovsky most notably and for the first time in Russian literature, is the creation of a literary duplicate of the poet who may be called the "lyric hero." In this connection it is necessary to go back for a moment to consider the nature of eighteenth-century classical practice. Such a poet as for example Sumarokov, who ambitiously attempted to distinguish himself in tragedy, comedy, satire, fable-writing and lyric verse, is a different person in each one of these genres. This results from the fact that in classical literary theory a different style was required in each kind of writing, and *"le style, c'est l'homme même."* The lyric verses may reveal a languishing lover or a roistering *bon vivant* according as they are amatory or Anacreontic; the satires will show a bitter and caustic critic of society, perhaps of the very foibles which are glorified in the lyrics—love and wine and women. The fables may show to view a sly, worldly-wise and sometimes rather stuffy "poor man's philosopher," while the tragedies will show a pompous and unbending and exalted poet, completely different from the wit who finds expression in the comedies. All this may be seen even in such an untypical eighteenth-century poet as Derzhavin; powerful as is the personality of this splendid poet, there can be no question that the poetic image which he conveys in his Anacreontic lyrics, in his great state odes, such as "The Waterfall," or in his satiric and playful odes such as "Felitsa" and "The Magnate," and again in such an intimate, bantering piece as "Life at Zvanka," is in every case a different image. We may be able to read through the conventions of the genre some indication of the "real" Derzhavin, whom we come to know from his personal letters, but he makes no attempt to reveal this "real" personality, nor to be consistent as a person in all his works. The eighteenth century did not care for "personality" in this sense; given the leading conception that all "passions" are universal, regardless of historical time, geographical location or social background, the poetic "I" is irrelevant, and becomes a mere mask, different for each variety of literature undertaken.

The romantic movement is often characterized as preeminently the "revolt of the individual" from this levelling universalism. The romantic poet does not recognize the binding force of the genre conventions, and whatever kind of verse or prose he undertakes to write becomes in his hands a vehicle for the expression of his own individuality. But this individuality is not necessarily identical with the poet's "real" personality; it will of course share certain leading traits with it, but it will normally be an idealized creation, an abstract of the poet as he desires to be regarded by his audience. Not only will the poet quite naturally attempt to avoid showing qualities of his personality of which he is ashamed for one reason or another, but he will attempt to color more highly those traits which he regards as most "poetic" and attractive to his audience. A most obvious example of this romantic innovation may be found in the English poets Wordsworth and Byron. There

will be no doubt that Wordsworth really was an enthusiastic lover of nature, but must we take as actual childhood experiences all the pantheistic meditations that fill *The Prelude?* And again, Lord Byron was no doubt not being a simple *poseur* in pouring forth the torments of his lacerated heart in *Childe Harold,* yet the poetic image which he gives is certainly not a photographic portrayal of the "real" Byron, any more than that of Wordsworth is of him. Moreover we may note the consistency in Byron's poetry of this poetic image: it was said by Pushkin that Byron in all his works depicted only one hero—himself; and this is to this extent true, that the image he reveals is always that of his idealized personality, whether it is the Prisoner of Chillon or the Giaour or Manfred or Childe Harold or Don Juan, or the lover of the "Maid of Athens" whom he is formally portraying.

Zhukovsky is the first Russian poet to develop and reveal to the world such a "poetic hero." And as with Byron, it makes no difference whether the genre employed is formally objective or subjective, whether it is such an elegy as **"Evening,"** or **"The Moth and the Flowers,"** or such a "translation" as that of Gray's "Elegy" in the first rendition, or a narrative ballad such as **"The Aeolian Harp"** or **"The Castle of Smalholm"**—behind each poem lies the same reality, a *persona* who is unquestionably related to the "real" Zhukovsky, but who is an idealized and heightened and refined version of this poet who creates him. We can readily pick out the salient features of this *persona:* he is gentle and submissive and melancholy, extremely sensitive to nature, brooding and introspective, with few and tenuous connections with other men; he is emotionally religious and mystical—and completely humorless. If in only this last trait we may see a striking difference between the "poetic hero" and the "real" Zhukovsky, for from all we know of his character as his friends of the *Arzamas* have revealed it in their reminiscences, he was extremely high-spirited and witty and a great joker. But evidently these were features which he felt were inconsistent with the desired poetic image, so they were suppressed, while other features, such as the pervasive and all-encompassing melancholy were deliberately accentuated and made most prominent. And here again the novelty of this procedure commended itself to other poets of the age, and other poetic images were created in bodies of lyric verse which are sometimes even less harmonious with the objective reality. Such, for example, is that of the partisan poet Denis Davydov, whose own verse is almost exclusively built up around the image of a bold, devil-may-care, roistering, hard-drinking, hard-fighting hussar—a personality which coincides in only a small degree with the real character of this rather unhappy and quite painstaking and deliberate poet. In this case the image was so infectious that not only did Davydov himself perpetuate it in a large part of his verse, but even his friends, such as Prince Vyazemsky, in writing epistles to him, took care to copy the same tone. Such versified epistles are almost invariably couched in terms of flowing bowls and hussars' shakos and sabres and black-eyed beauties loved for a night and exciting cavalry charges. And even a painter could be caught up in the same image, as we can see from the wonderful "portrait" of Davydov by Kiprensky, which idealizes the handsome, black-moustached young cavalry officer as he wished his image to be in his verse, but as, according to contemporaries, he certainly was not in "real life." The "romantic hero" will appear later in all his glory in the poems and prose stories of Mikhail Lermontov, and from such a prose figure as that of Pechorin in his *Hero of Our Time* we shall see an an easy transition to the novelistic hero of later decades. The creation of such a "poetic hero" in a body of lyric is only a step on the way to the creation of a hero of similar kind in the novel.

Zhukovsky's great achievement was the introduction of romanticism (in its "passive" variety) into Russian literature. In this achievement his translations, especially of German and English ballads, played a particularly significant part. The Russian public were educated to the new world outlook, already partially familiar from the similarities between it and eighteenth century sentimentalism. As an original poet and as a translator, Zhukovsky's outstanding qualities are his ability to picture in languishingly beautiful melodic form the intimate psychological experiences of a wistful, dreamy, other-worldly individual, the passive victim of a fate against which he feels it impious to struggle. In the matter of form, Zhukovsky introduced into Russian literature and popularized the typical romantic form of the "ballad," and popularized the subjective elegy as a vehicle for self-revelation of feeling. But his chief contribution—and one that it is impossible to appreciate outside of his own language—is his superlatively musical verse. He introduced many meters into common use in Russian for the first time, and tamed the stiff and refractory language of Lomonosov and his contemporaries into a flexible and melodious medium which only Pushkin could carry to a still further degree of perfection. (pp. 295-327)

> *William Edward Brown, "Vasily Andreevich Zhukovsky," in* Russian Literature Triquarterly, *No. 9, 1974, pp. 295-328.*

Zhukovsky on Romantic developments in poetry:

In the poetry of the ancients the subject-matter dominated the poet; in the poetry of the moderns, the place of subject-matter is, to the greatest extent, taken over by the poet himself. The former is occupied more with material nature, the latter more with spiritual nature: the former does not look for anything that could make its subject more attractive in extraneous spheres, but finds everything in the subject itself; the latter unites the extraneous with the subject—emotions, ideas; the former, finally, presents to us the subject just as it is; the latter mostly presents to us only reflections on the subject and actions undertaken by it.

> *Vasily Zhukovsky, in the journal* Vestnik Evropy, *1811.*

Michael R. Katz   (essay date 1976)

[*An American critic and educator, Katz has translated works by the Russian authors Alexander Herzen, Nikolay Chernyshevsky, and Fyodor Dostoevsky and has published several works on Russian literature, including*

The Literary Ballad in Early Nineteenth-Century Russian Literature *(1976). In the following excerpt from that study, he characterizes Zhukovsky as the most influential Russian balladeer, examining Zhukovsky's theory of translation and discussing examples of his work to provide insight into his method of composition.*]

The name of Zhukovsky and the genre of the literary ballad are inseparable. It was Zhukovsky who made the first theoretical statements about the genre and who influenced all subsequent attempts at definition. Zhukovsky considered himself, and was considered by his contemporaries, primarily as a writer of ballads. Moreover, the content and the style of Zhukovsky's forty ballads established the model for all future Russian literary ballads.

The first written description of the genre is contained in an unpublished translation of J. J. Eschenburg's *Entwurf einer Theorie und Literature der schönen Wissenschaften* (1783). In 1804 Zhukovsky completed his free rendition of this treatise, to which he added copious notes referring to other French and German literary theories. In the section on lyrical poetry, the 'romance' and the 'ballad' are defined as 'light, lyrical narratives of important or unimportant, touching or uplifting, tragic or comic occurrences'. The source of such works could be mythology, history, chivalry, monasticism, everyday social life, or poetic fantasy. The plot should be 'simple, natural, light, pleasant, and should correspond to the material'. For example, the narrative was to be *zhivopisen* whenever the poet describes something *chudesnoe, mrachnoe, uzhasnoe ili neobychainoe.*

The earliest published description of the ballad genre also belongs to Zhukovsky and was included in the preface to his ***Sobranie russkikh stikhotvorenii*** (1810-11). He wrote that the ballad belongs simultaneously to two sorts of poetry since it is 'narrative' in content but 'lyrical' in form. Therefore in his anthology Zhukovsky includes short ballads in the section of lyrical poetry (Karamzin's "Raisa," Murav'ev's "Boleslav," Dmitriev's "Starinnaya lyubov"), and long ballads in the section of narrative poetry (Kamenev's *Gromval*).

By 1816 Eschenburg's entire book had been translated and published anonymously. In the appropriate section the ballad is defined as a genre of 'lyric-epic' poetry, the content of which is *pechal'noe, chudesnoe, romanicheskoe, inogda zabavnoe.* Zhukovsky is mentioned as the Russian poet who had demonstrated the 'outstanding attractions of this genre'.

One year earlier excerpts from N. F. Ostolopov's *Slovar' drevnei i novoi poezii,* including one on the characteristics of the ballad, had been published in *Vestnik Evropy.* In 1821 the entire *Slovar'* was published; it contains a long article on the genre which begins with the derivation of the word 'ballad' and is followed by a discussion of the French *ballade* and by a definition of the German *Ballade* as a narrative about 'amorous or unfortunate adventures', always based on the *chudesnoe.* In the section on the Russia *ballada,* Ostolopov needed to mention only one name, Zhukovsky. He quotes the entire text of **"Svetlana,"** and then lists the first stanzas of nine other ballads to demonstrate the variety of Zhukovsky's skills as a ballad-writer.

In 1822 N. I. Grech, in one of the first attempts at writing a history of Russian literature [*Opyt kratkoi istorii russkoi literatury*], referred to the ballad as a 'new genre', 'created by Zhukovsky'. When in 1832 N. I. Nadezhdin surveyed [in *Teleskop* VII (1832)] the state of Russian poetry for the previous year and wrote that 'ballads . . . have replaced the ode as reigning genre', he was of course referring almost exclusively to Zhukovsky's achievement. During the first few decades of the nineteenth century the ballad genre attained the popularity and the literary status which the ode had enjoyed during the mid-eighteenth century.

[Literary critic Vissarion] Belinsky's articles written during the 1840s show the most perceptive understanding of Zhukovsky's transformation of the ballad. In his series on Pushkin (1843) Belinsky describes the genre as it existed before Zhukovsky: 'a short story about love, usually unhappy; graves, crosses, ghosts, night-time, moonlight, and sometimes *domovye* and witches.' Then he alludes to the 'deeper meaning' with which Zhukovsky had endowed his literary ballads, but does not elaborate. However, in an earlier article on poetic genres (1841) Belinsky's definition of the ballad clearly indicates his view of the transformation which Zhukovsky had effected: 'In the ballad the poet takes some sort of fantastic and popular legend, or he himself invents an episode of this kind. But the main feature in it is not the episode, but the experience (*oshchushchenie*), which it awakens, the thoughts which it suggests to the reader.' Thus Belinsky implies that the 'deeper meaning' of Zhukovsky's ballads is contained in their total subjectivity: they all express private emotional experience shared by the poet with the reader.

Zhukovsky's own words demonstrate that he considered himself primarily as a ballad-writer. As early as 1813 he admitted in a letter to A. I. Turgenev: 'My chosen genre of poetry is the ballad.' And in 1849, almost at the end of his literary career, he referred to himself in a letter to A. S. Sturdza as 'the father of German romanticism in Russia and the poetic uncle (*dyad'ka*) of German and English demons and witches'.

The most famous portrait of Zhukovsky as a young poet painted by O. Kiprensky in 1815 and engraved by F. Vendramina two years later undoubtedly portrays him as a *balladnik*. The background of stormy sky, steep cliffs, rough sea, wind-blown trees, and medieval castle is the typical setting of his literary ballads. The poet himself is pictured as a youthful, melancholy visionary with tousled hair, gazing into the distance.

Zhukovsky was virtually identified with his ballads by most of his contemporaries, poets and critics alike. Batyushov begins his *poslanie,* "K Zhukovskomu" (1812) with the lines: 'Prosti, balladnik moi,/ Beleva mirnyi zhitel'.' An anonymous review published in 1821 of an anthology of verse contains a portrait of Zhukovsky with the inscription 'Germaniya! tvoya s toboyu chest':/ Na beregakh Nevy—Balladnik est' . . .'. Belinsky, in the same article on Pushkin (1843), also states that it was Zhukovsky who created and established the genre of the ballad, and that contemporary readers thought of him almost exclusively as a *balladnik*. In 1855 N. G. Chernyshevsky, referring to Zhukovsky's translations from Schiller, wrote that

'Zhukovsky interested his readers as a *balladnik,* and not as a translator of Schiller'. Finally, an unintentionally amusing tribute to Zhukovsky was penned by Ieronim Trofimovsky, a pupil at the No. 2 Gymnasium in Kiev in 1883, Zhukovsky's jubilee year. . . . (pp. 37-40)

What was it that attracted Zhukovsky to the genre of the ballad? The question is ultimately unanswerable, but several theories have been advanced. One postulates that the ballad offered the poet an escape from the subjectivity of his lyrics, since it enabled him to objectify lyrical situations and characters. This explanation was implied as early as 1825 by A. I. Galich [in his *Opyt nauki izyashchnago*], whose definition of the ballad is based on Zhukovsky's poetic practice: 'a romantic elegy in which the internal condition of the soul is expressed indirectly, namely by means of some story or adventure'. All but the most superficial reading of the ballads eliminates this theory. Zhukovsky was not really interested in objective characters or events, in time or place, or even in the psychology of his heroes. Zhukovsky's ballads are an extension of his lyrical poetry: a lyrical effusion of the poet's soul.

It has also been suggested that Zhukovsky's choice of the ballad genre was related to a larger trend in Russian literature towards *narodnost'*. According to this explanation, the ballad provided the poet with a means for expressing his interest in popular legends, beliefs, customs, and so forth. This theory, propounded by Yu. M. Lotman and R. I. Iezuitova, ignores several facts. Only three of Zhukovsky's forty ballads contain so-called 'Russian motifs'; the vast majority are translations from Western European sources; and 'Russification' in these translations is conventional and artificial. Lotman has also suggested that the length of the ballad could have provided Zhukovsky with the potential for more significant thematic statements than could either the lyric or the elegy. However, some of the ballads are shorter than some of the lyrical poems, and both the *poslanie* and *povest'* also offered the possibility of writing a larger work.

Finally, N. V. Izmailov has suggested [in *Istoriya russkoi poezii* I (1968-69)] that Zhukovsky chose the ballad for thematic reasons: his sympathy for human suffering and man's compulsory submission to Fate caused him to reject the external world and create an ideal dream world of inner experience. Izmailov has erroneously transformed Zhukovsky into a social critic who deliberately created the ballad genre in order to escape the horrors of nineteenth-century Russian reality. Zhukovsky was neither a Decembrist nor even a social critic; he spent a large part of his life at court, as tutor to the imperial family, and particularly to the future Alexander II.

There is reason to believe that the real explanation for Zhukovsky's choice of the ballad genre lies elsewhere. Firstly, the ballad was undergoing a revival throughout Western Europe, and was, for a time, the most popular genre in English and German poetry. Secondly, the ballad form was new, exciting, and exotic. It opened up a whole new world to the imagination: a world of nature and supernature; of strong passions, secret affairs, and extraordinary characters. The Russian memoirist F. F. Vigel' captures the novelty of the genre in his reminiscences:

Nourished on the classics and on French literature, and on submissive imitations of the
same, . . . we saw something monstrous in his
[Zhukovsky's] choices. Corpses, visions, demons, murders by moonlight; all this belongs to
the *skazki* and even to English novels; instead of
Hero awaiting his drowning Leander, he presented us a madly passionate Lenora with her galloping corpse of a lover! His [Zhukovsky's] miraculous talent was needed to force us not only
to read the ballads without repugnance, but also,
finally, to fall in love with them. I do not know
if he spoiled our taste; but at least he created new
sensations, new enjoyments for us. That was the
beginning of our romanticism [*Zapiski* III
(1891-93)].

An important component of the 'new sensations' was the
Gothic element of fear and the pure emotional excitement
of being frightened. Zhukovsky was not unaware of this
new delight in fear. . . . Belinsky describes the appeal of
the ballads as 'some sort of sweetly-horrible pleasure, and
the more they horrified us, the more passionately we read
them'.

In all probability it was the ballad's popularity in Western
Europe, the novelty of its exotic world, and the delight
in the emotional experience of fear which attracted Zhukovsky to the genre. . . . [Let] us look at
Zhukovsky's theory of translation and an example of that
theory put into practice.

Zhukovsky expressed his views on the principles of translation at the beginning of his literary career in two critical
articles and in a translation of a French work, all published in *Vestnik Evropy* (1809-10); close to the end of his
life, in 1848 he once again set forth his ideas on the subject.
Zhukovsky's basic aesthetic principles remained the same
throughout his career. The only difference between his
earlier and later statements is the more philosophical, almost mystical, language of the 1848 pronouncements.

One of Zhukovsky's first articles (1809) was devoted to the
genre of the fable, and in particular to Krylov. He begins
with a brief discussion of Krylov's debt to La Fontaine,
and then defines Krylov's originality as his ability to adapt
the original author's thoughts, feelings, and genius, and to
express all this in his own style. Then Zhukovsky develops
his general views on translation, beginning with a motto
which could well serve as a justification for his own poetic
career: 'A translator of prose is a slave; a translator of
verse is a rival.' Zhukovsky contrasts the 'poet-imitator',
who is inspired by the actual model, with the 'original
poet', who is inspired by 'an ideal contained within his
own imagination'. Therefore the translator must have the
same imagination, style, intelligence, and emotions as the
creator of the original work. He must find in his own imagination the corresponding beauty to serve as a replacement
for the original beauty, and it should be equal or even superior to it. Thus, according to Zhukovsky, the translator
is a creator, and must possess talent equal in all respects
to that of the original author.

This theory was further developed in Zhukovsky's review
[reprinted in ***Polnoe sobranie sochinenii***] of S. Viskovatov's translation of P. J. de Crébillon's tragedy *Rhada-*

miste et Zénobie. The article begins with the bold assertion
'Only a poet can translate a poet' and goes on to condemn
Viskovatov's poor attempt. Zhukovsky explains that to
translate poetry, in addition to understanding rhyme, cae-
suras, grammar, and so forth, the translator must possess
'poetic talent', which is defined as 'the ability to imagine
and feel vividly, combined with the ability to find in one's
own language those expressions which would correspond
to that which one feels and imagines'. Zhukovsky once
again emphasizes the originality of the translator as a 'creator of expressions'; he can create only if he is filled with
the ideal of the original work, which he then transforms
into a creation of his own imagination. The final goal of
the translator, then, is not a literal equivalent; rather it is
to translate 'so that the translated verse produces the same
total impression on the soul of the reader as does the original verse'.

In 1810 Zhukovsky published a translation [in *Vestnik
Evropy* No. 3 (1810)] of an anonymous French article on
the same subject. The author of this article states categori-
cally: 'I consider excessive fidelity [of a translation to its
source] as excessive infidelity'; then he specifies some of
the cases in which alterations are necessary to achieve the
same effects in the translation as in the original. An example relevant to Zhukovsky's own work concerns the issue
of local colour. If the original contains geographical details or references to the customs of a particular nation,
this information is of interest only to that nation; such details would seem strange in a translation and must be
avoided. The main responsibility of the translator is to
'produce that effect which the original produces'. The article concludes with some curious advice to aspiring translators—in order to partake of the sources of the original
poet's inspiration, they should observe the natural landscape of that poet's native land. Thus the skilful translator
must be well-travelled!

Such were Zhukovsky's views on the theory of translation
in 1810, at the beginning of his literary career: the translator as creator, possessing talents equal to those of the original author; the translator as inspired by the ideal of the
original, contained within his own imagination; and the
translator trying to achieve the equivalent effect on the
soul of the reader, rather than striving after a literal rendition. (pp. 40-4)

After a life's work of writing, *i.e. translating,* poetry,
Zhukovsky returned to his theory of translation in order
to provide it with a philosophical foundation. In an article
on *Faust* (1848) he analyses the scene preceding the appearance of Mephistopheles, in which Faust attempts to
rewrite the *Logos* passage from the Gospel of St. John,
substituting for *Logos* the German words *Sinn, Kraft,* and
Tat. Zhukovsky soundly disapproves of Faust's alternatives, asserting that no human mind could possibly conceive of anything more sublime or more encompassing
than *Logos.* He defines the Russian *Slovo* as both a 'spiritual embodiment of thought', conceived at the same time as
the thought, and as the 'material clothing of this spiritual
embodiment', or the sound which expresses it. Then
Zhukovsky lapses into 'proto-symbolist' mysticism: 'All
our thoughts, unexpressed and expressed, separate and

unified, are only fragments of something whole (*otryvki chego-to tselogo*) . . .'

Zhukovsky's article entitled **"On the Poet and his Contemporary Significance"** (1848) was intended as a reply to Gogol's treatment of the 'word' in his *Correspondence with Friends* (1847). Zhukovsky borrows Pushkin's aphorism 'Slova poeta sut' uzhe dela ego' and elaborates on it. He starts with Rousseau's statement that 'Il n'y a de beau que ce qui n'est pas', which Zhukovsky interprets as implying that, although beauty exists, man can neither seize it nor understand it. Art is defined as the 'experience and expression of the beautiful', and the artist as a creator; the means of creation are the forms of art (poetry, music, painting), while the materials of creation are words, sounds, colours, and so forth. The poet's materials are words; Pushkin's aphorism, therefore, is substantiated.

These two articles, although concerned with the 'word' in general, really provide the foundation of Zhukovsky's theory of translation. The crucial importance of the 'word' for the poet-creator and the relationship between the 'word', the thought, and the 'something whole' underlie his earlier, more practical, pronouncements on the translation of verse.

Another of Zhukovsky's letters clearly summarizes the views expressed in these later articles. In February 1848 he wrote to Gogol':

> I have often noticed that I have my most lucid thoughts when I have to improvise them to express or to supplement others' thoughts. My intellect is like steel which must be struck against flint in order that a spark might leap out. In general that is the nature of my authorial work; almost everything of mine is either someone else's or apropos of someone else's; but it is still all mine.

Additional evidence to substantiate the claim for the 'originality' of Zhukovsky's translations is provided by his method of publication and by the reactions of contemporary readers to his works. In preparing his poetry for publication, Zhukovsky rarely specified whether a given work was a translation from a foreign source, or whether it was an original composition. Furthermore his contemporaries received his translations as if they were original works, and in their reviews usually emphasized Zhukovsky's independence from his source.

In an article [in *Sorevnovatel' prosveshcheniya i blagotvoreniya*, No. 2 (1822)] on Zhukovsky's translation of Byron's "Prisoner of Chillon," Pletnov wrote: 'We even dare to state emphatically that to translate as Zhukovsky translates, is the same as creating.' Bestuzhev, in his survey of Russian literature for 1823 [*Polyarnaya zvezda*, 1824], noted: 'Many of Zhukovsky's translations are better than their originals, since euphony and versatility of language adorn the accuracy of his expression.' In articles written in the early 1840s, Belinsky developed the same theme:

> They say that Zhukovsky has little of his own, that it is almost all translation: a mistaken opinion! Zhukovsky is a poet, and not a translator.

As children, having no clear idea as yet of what was a translation and what an original, we learned his renditions by heart as the *works of Zhukovsky*.

Pletnev had the final say in his sketch of Zhukovsky's life and works:

> Zhukovsky imparted to his translations the life and inspiration of their originals. Therefore each of his translations was accorded the value and force of an original composition. This original talent afforded him the means for transforming our literature. [*O zhizni i sochineniyakh V. A. Zhukovskogo* (1853)]

An example of Zhukovsky's theory of translation put into practice is his ballad **"Rybak"** (1818), a translation of Goethe's "Der Fischer" (1778). The theme of Goethe's ballad is the irrational attraction of the natural elements and their power over rational beings. Although Goethe disparaged any attempts to analyse his work, "Der Fischer" is much plainer in rhythm and more complex in meaning than a simple folk ballad. The fisherman can be seen as a symbol of rational self-sufficiency, of non-resistance to the fatal attraction of the elements, and perhaps of a narcissistic attraction to his own reflection. The mermaid's colloquial speech, the narrator's sophistication, the sensual imagery, and the hypnotic repetitions all contribute to the ballad's charm.

Zhukovsky's translation transforms Goethe's original into a very different work. In the first stanza Goethe's unemotional *ruhevoll* (peacefully, tranquilly) becomes *zadumchlv* (plunged in thought, reflection), one of Zhukovsky's most important emotional epithets. *Kühl bis ans Herz hinan* (implying spiritual serenity and rationality) is rendered as *dusha polna/ Prokhladnoi tishinoi,* in which the phrase *prokhladnaya tishina* attempts to combine the two German epithets *kühl* and *ruhevoll*. Goethe's *Und wie . . . er lauscht* (with its temporal conjunction and standard punctuation) is replaced by *V drug . . . pritikh . . .: vdrug* is Zhukovsky's favourite temporal adverb, most often used to interrupt the narrative, and usually followed by three dots to indicate expectation; *pritikh* returns to the motif of silence introduced in line 4 (*tishina*). Goethe's stanza ends with the words *rauscht/ Ein feuchtes Weib hervor* (the verb expresses the sound "rushing", and is repeated from line I; *feuchtes Weib* is a poetic expression for mermaid). Zhukovsky's rendition, *I vlazhnaya vsplyla glavoi/Krasavitsa . . .* , employs a less forceful, more poetic verb, translates Goethe's *feuchtes* literally as *vlazhnaya,* and supplies the more literary *krasavitsa* to identify the mermaid.

In the second stanza *Sie sang zu ihm, sie sprach zu ihm* is rendered as *Glyadit ona, poet ona:* instead of 'speaking', Zhukovsky's mermaid will 'sing' her fifteen lines. Her monologue contains numerous epithets which are introduced by Zhukovsky and which have no equivalents in Goethe's original. Zhukovsky translates *Todesglut* as *kipuchii zhar,* and then combines *rodnoe dno* to form its opposite, probably by analogy with *rodnaya strana* or *zemlya.* The colloquial speech of Goethe's mermaid (*wie's Fischlein ist/ So wohlig*) is replaced by the neutral expression *Kak rybkoi zhit'/ Privol'no.* The second stanza ends with another of Zhukovsky's unusual combinations, *znoinaya vyshina,* a synonym for *kipuchii zhar,* both of which are in contrast to the fish's *rodnoe dno* and to the fisherman's *prokhlada.*

The syntax of Goethe's third stanza is varied (*nicht* occurs in initial, medial, and final positions) and the word order is reasonably logical. Zhukovsky's syntax is monotonous: the negative particle is fixed in the initial position; the word order, however, leads to some confusion. Goethe's epithet *feuchverklärte Blau* is rendered as *prokhladno-goluboi:* Zhukovsky avoids the idea of moisture, returns to the motif of *prokhlada,* and invents a compound epithet combining temperature and colour, but with vague spiritual overtones. He ignores Goethe's other, more difficult epithet *wellenatmend.*

The final stanza of the German original begins with a vivid sensual image: *Netzt' ihm den nackten Fuss;* Zhukovsky's modesty was probably responsible for his abstract, poetic replacement: *Na bereg val plesnul!* The exclamatory intonation not only of this line, but of the entire fourth stanza, and the use of three dots in lines 1 and 7, replace Goethe's declarative intonation and standard punctuation. The order of the clauses in line 5 is the reverse of that in the second stanza (*Sie sprach zu ihm, sie sang zu ihm*); Goethe's mermaid 'sings' to lure the fishermen into the sea. Zhukovsky's mermaid is still 'singing' (*Ona poet, ona manit*), and the second verb demonstrates his propensity to make the meaning more explicit, to explain rather than to depict. Line 7 in the original is another vivid physical image (*Halb zog sie ihn, halb sank er hin*), which contains the complex resolution of Goethe's theme, namely, the fisherman enters the sea, partly dragged by the mermaid and partly of his own free will. Zhukovsky's abstract version (*K nemu ona, on k nei bezhit*) lacks the force of the German and resembles a conventional meeting of two lovers.

This juxtaposition of one of Zhukovsky's translations with its original source indicates that his poetic practice conforms in full to his own theory of translation. Inspired by some ideal of the original in his own imagination, Zhukovsky creates an equivalent work rather than a literal rendition. But the original is not replaced by some objectively equivalent imagination, style, intelligence, and emotion, but rather by Zhukovsky's own individual interpretation of the original, influenced by his criteria of good taste, and expressed in his own subjective language. For example, he freely alters the epithets of his source, combining, eliminating, or inventing others as he pleases. He introduces elaborate verbal leitmotives (*tishina, prokhlada*). His syntax is characterized by parallelism, exclamatory and interrogative intonation, and inverted word order; the action is frequently interrupted by dots, dashes, and temporal adverbs (*vdrug*). Concrete images of the original ballad become generalized in translation; physical, sensual ones become abstract and poetical. The colloquial tone of certain passages is transmuted into one that is neutral or elevated; themes are made more explicit in some cases, and in others the sense is sacrificed for the total emotional effect.

One can only speculate on the impression which Zhukovsky's translations made on his readers; what is clear both from this comparison of source with translation and from the testimony of his contemporaries is that Zhukovsky was not a 'translator' in the ordinary sense of the word. He created original works, equivalents of foreign sources, and his contemporaries were justified in perceiving those works as original creations.

Throughout his literary career, Zhukovsky's principles and practice of translation never altered. His techniques evolved as he gained more experience and greater linguistic facility. His later translations and revisions of earlier ones tend to be more accurate with respect to the source, although this is not always the case. In 1831, for example, Zhukovsky retranslated Bürger's "Lenore," which he had rendered in 1808 as **"Lyudmila."** The manuscript of the second translation demonstrates how difficult it was for the poet to get any closer to the German original. . . . Both the manuscript and the final published version of the new translation bear a stronger resemblance to Zhukovsky's own **"Lyudmila"** than to Bürger's "Lenore." Any 'translation' by Zhukovsky must indeed be considered as the creation of an original poet.

Zhukovsky wrote forty literary ballads between 1808 and 1833. Of these, twenty-two were translated from German sources: two each from Bürger and Goethe, and nine each from Schiller and Uhland. Eleven ballads were translated from English sources: one each from Goldsmith, Mallet, and Campbell; two from Scott, and six from Southey. One ballad was translated from a French source: F. A. de Moncriff. Of the remaining six so-called 'original' ballads: **"Svetlana"** is a reworking of Bürger's "Lenore"; **"Akhill"** is strongly influenced by Schiller's Trojan cycle; **"Eolova arfa"** may have originated as a translation from another of Bürger's ballads; "Gromoboi" and "Vadim" [which comprise **"The Twelve Sleeping Maidens"**] are based on a novel by the German author C. H. Speiss; and **"Uznik"** has its source in an elegy by Chénier.

In addition to the forty ballads, Zhukovsky also translated from balladic sources and employed balladic techniques in other genres. Among his lyrics, **"Teon i Eskhin"** (1814) is an original balladic elegy; **"Tri putnika"** (1820) is a translation of Uhland's balladic "Der Wirtin Töchterlein"; and **"Nochnoi smotr"** (1836) is a translation of J. C. F. von Zedlitz's "Die nächtliche Heerschau." Among Zhukovsky's *povesti,* **"Perchatka"** (1831) is a translation of Schiller's ballad "Der Handschuh", and **"Dve byli i eshche odna"** (1831) includes translations of two Southey ballads, "Mary, the Maid of the Inn" and "Jaspar." Zhukovsky's early prose tale **"Mar'ina roshcha"** (1809) also employs balladic techniques and language. (pp. 45-51)

Zhukovsky's first ballad **"Lyudmila"** (1808) created something of the same excitement in Russia that Bürger's "Lenore" (1773) had caused in Germany and later in England. Zhukovsky's version was finished in April 1808 and published in *Vestnik Evropy* with the sub-title "Russkaya ballada" and with the note: *Podrazhanie Birgerovoi Leonore* [sic]. The sub-title and the note demonstrate the twofold importance of **"Lyudmila"**: the former established the genre of the Russian literary ballad as an original form of poetry; and the latter indicated that the content of this first ballad was derivative, being an 'imitation' of a Western European work adapted for Russian readers.

The ballad begins with a description of the heroine's anxiety at her lover's long absence in the war. When the men return, Lyudmila's *milyi* is not among them. She laments her fate and rejects her mother's religious consolation. Late that night her lover returns to claim his sweetheart and to carry her off to their bridal bed. They ride through the night and arrive in the morning at their destination: the lover turns out to be a corpse, and his home a grave. The ballad ends with Lyudmila's death, presented as proof of God's justice.

Although the subject of **"Lyudmila"** and "Lenore" is basically the same, Zhukovsky's 'imitation' contains numerous deviations from the original which both illuminate his method of adapting foreign sources and demonstrate the most typical characteristics of his literary ballads. Bürger's "Lenore" begins with a reference to a particular historical setting: the hero had gone off to fight with the Prussian army against the Austrians at the Battle of Prague (1757). The armistice and the victorious homecomings of both armies are treated satirically. In contrast, Zhukovsky's **"Lyudmila"** has no definite period or location. The situation is abstract and generalized, in spite of a vague hint at Old Russian local colour (*rat', druzhina*).

Bürger's characters are called Lenore and Wilhelm: the heroine demonstrates genuine courage; her dramatic lament begins and ends with violent physical gestures (tearing her hair, throwing herself to the ground, and beating her breast). The hero is presented as a real man of action whose few utterances are terse and rapid. In contrast, Zhukovsky's heroine is given the Slavonic name Lyudmila and is transformed into a sentimental, melancholy character. The narrator describes her in the first stanza with verbs which express emotion, not action: *priunyv, vzdykhala, mechtala*. Her physical gestures differ considerably from those of Bürger's heroine: *K persyam ochi prekloniv* (I:7) and *Tikho v terem svoi idet,/ Tomnu golovu sklonila* (3:8-9). Whereas Lenore rants and raves against her cruel fate, Lyudmila accepts hers and submits to its decrees. Unlike Bürger, Zhukovsky intervenes directly in the narrative to express his emotional sympathy for the heroine. . . . The alternation of interrogative and exclamatory intonation [is evident] . . . in Lyudmila's extended lament. Zhukovsky's hero is transformed into an anonymous melancholy character, referred to only as *milyi*, whose speech, even to his horse, is saturated with sentimentality. . . . (pp. 51-3)

The lament in Bürger's ballad is based on a series of symmetrical alternations between mother and daughter, gradually increasing in length as the statements become more serious. Zhukovsky dispenses with both the symmetry and the gradual expansion, and greatly reduces the number of lines spoken by the mother. While she expresses herself almost entirely in aphorisms, Lyudmila echoes elegiac motifs from Zhukovsky's lyrics. The syntax of the lament also recalls that of the lyrics in its alternation of interrogative

and exclamatory intonation, its use of rhetorical questions, negative constructions, repetition, and parallelism.

The lament is followed by the dramatic midnight appearance of the lover. Bürger has only three lines of transition in which he describes the sunset and nightfall. Zhukovsky expands the transition to nineteen lines (7:9-9:3); the passage contains no fewer than thirteen epithets. These epithets, characterized by their emotional overtones, inundate the reader's senses with a multitude of vague visual and aural impressions in order to create a mood of uncanny mystery.

Bürger's midnight ride is famous for its dramatic sound effects: *trapp trapp trapp; klinglingling; hurre hurre hop hop hop;* and so on. Zhukovsky's ride, reduced from 104 to 83 lines, has no equivalent onomatopoeic expressions. Furthermore, the dynamic description in stanzas 14-15, which contains no epithets but numerous verbs, is not original but a literal translation of Bürger's stanzas 19-20.

Bürger introduces his refrain in stanza 17:6, 'Wir und die Toten reiten schnell', which is repeated with increasing frequency to heighten the dramatic tension. Zhukovsky introduces his refrain in stanza 15:2, 'Mertvyi s devitseyu mchitsya', and it is repeated only once, in 17:2. Its meaning anticipates the climax of the ballad and consequently lessens the dramatic tension. Neither Bürger's weird funeral procession (stanza 21) nor the haunting dirge (stanza 22) has any equivalent in Zhukovsky's version. Whereas the grotesque transformation of Wilhelm into a skeleton is graphically depicted in "Lenore," Zhukovsky's description is expressed in his favourite epithets. . . . (pp. 53-4)

The moral of Bürger's ballad is fairly straightforward: 'Mit Gott im Himmel hadre nicht!' (32:6), which refers back to Lenore's transgression as defined earlier by her mother: 'Sie fuhr mit Gottes Vorsehung/ Vermessen fort zu hadern' (12:3-4). Bürger implies that whether God is just or unjust one must accept his will with forbearance ('Geduld! Geduld!'). Lenore would not; therefore she was punished.

Zhukovsky's conclusion is more difficult to interpret. . . . The poet implies that protest is imprudent because God is unquestionably just; therefore his will must be accepted. Rather than a punishment, Lyudmila's death seems to be a release from her sufferings, granted by a merciful Creator.

Thus while Zhukovsky's **"Lyudmila"** is in fact an 'imitation' of Bürger's "Lenore," the differences are far more important than the superficial similarity of the subject. Zhukovsky's generalization of time and place, his sentimental heroine and her melancholy *milyi*, the modifications in the lament, the descriptive transition, the ride, the refrain, and the concluding moral lesson demonstrate the degree to which Zhukovsky deviated from his original source. The greatest contrast between the two works lies in the style of each. Bürger's colloquialisms, conversational expressions, vivid physical descriptions, and dynamic verbs are replaced by Zhukovsky's literary syntax and vocabulary, particularly by an increase in the use of emotion-

An oil painting entitled A Saturday at V. A. Zhukovsky's.

al epithets. There are few traces of popular language in either dialogue or description.

An entry in one of Zhukovsky's early notebooks provides an interesting perspective on his attitude towards Bürger. First he praises both the tone and the simple narrative in his ballads; then he continues with a list of Bürger's other virtues, including 'his successful use of popular expressions both in descriptions and in the expression of feelings; brevity and vividness; simplicity and variety in his rhythms'. He also approves of Bürger's depiction of the *uzhasnoe,* which results from his successful description of *mrachnye* subjects and themes. Zhukovsky contrasts Bürger's style with that of Schiller; he finds Schiller's style less 'picturesque' than Bürger's, less 'colloquial', and far more 'poetic'. He concludes: 'Schiller is more the philosopher, and Bürger—the simple narrator, who, occupied with his own subject, does not concern himself with anything peripheral.'

There is a significant disparity between these theoretical views on Bürger and Zhukovsky's poetic practice. The qualities which he praises in Bürger's style are precisely those which he so radically altered or eliminated in his ballad **"Lyudmila."** Furthermore, in spite of his professed admiration for Bürger and his disdain for Schiller, during his lifetime Zhukovsky translated only one ballad from Bürger and nine from Schiller. In spite of these critical views, the poet in Zhukovsky recognized that the subjects and style of Schiller's ballads were more suited to his own taste. Schiller became one of Zhukovsky's most important models in the creation of the Russian ballad genre.

Bürger's "Lenore" also provided the impetus for Zhukovsky's **"Svetlana"** (1808-12). This ballad, a very free reworking of its original source, was one of Zhukovsky's most popular and most influential works. During the 1810s the poet was continually referred to by his contemporaries as "the creator of **'Svetlana'** "; during the 1820s, as criticism of his poetry and his politics increased, even the most ardent Decembrists approved of **"Svetlana,"** considering it Zhukovsky's most *narodnyi* ballad. And it was **"Svetlana"** which exerted the strongest influence on Pushkin, particularly apparent in *Evgenii Onegin* and *Metel'.*

The ballad has been the subject of considerable research by Soviet scholars. The most detailed analysis is [an unpublished Candidate's Thesis by R. V.] Iezuitova, who considers it proof of Zhukovsky's 'profound interest' in Russian folklore, namely rituals, superstitions, and legends. As evidence of this new interest she quotes Zhukovsky's letter to A. P. Zontag, written in 1816 (i.e. three years after the publication of **"Svetlana,"**), in which he asked that he be sent Russian *skazki* and legends. But when Iezuitova investigates the immediate sources of Zhukovsky's folkloric material, she rejects I. P. Lupanova's suggestion that the *skazka* is the basis of **"Svetlana,"** since it is not clear how Zhukovsky had access to *skazki* until 1816. Similarly, Iezuitova rejects the influence of traditional Russian folk ballads, since Zhukovsky could not have had any models to imitate. Her theory is that the manuscript plans for **"Svetlana"** show definite borrowings of detail and diction from the works of M. Chulkov; she admits, however, that it has never been established that Zhukovsky actually knew Chulkov's collections.

The earliest manuscript plan of the ballad, first called "Svyatki," is a simple enumeration of the main scenes. It deviates from Bürger's original in its inclusion of the heroine's dream; but, unlike the final version, the dream here turns out to be true and the ballad was to end tragically.

The happy ending was introduced in a later manuscript plan called "Gadan'e," which is a detailed, stanza-by-stanza, summary of the action. Iezuitova, who ignores the earlier plan, compares the later plan to Chulkov's chapter on fortune-telling in his *ABC of Russian Superstitions* (1786), and finds close similarities in the description of the mirror divination; she also discovered that the *podblyudnaya pesenka* in **"Svetlana"** (1:9-14) was borrowed from Chulkov's *Sobranie raznykh pesen* (1770-4).

Other critics emphasize different aspects of the ballad. N. V. Izmailov pays particular attention to Zhukovsky's philosophical optimism as reflected in **"Svetlana,"** citing the intervention of beneficient forces which supply a happy solution to the tragic subject [*Istoriya russkoi poezii* I]. On the other hand, Gukovsky emphasizes [in *Pushkin i russkie romantiki*] the playfulness of the work, arguing that it has no real theme, and is nothing more than an invented fairy-tale. Ts. S. Vol'pe suggests the most interesting interpretation. He maintains that in **"Svetlana"** Zhukovsky applied the principles of parody to the poetics of the Gothic ballad, and that by setting the frightening tale within the framework of a dream he created a parody of his own **"Lyudmila,"** and thus a parody of the whole literary ballad genre.

It must be admitted that the *narodnost'* of **"Svetlana"** has been overemphasized; in fact, it is limited to a very few stylistic elements and folk motifs. Zhukovsky uses diminutive forms (*podruzhen'ka, slovechko, legokhon'ko*), colloquial expressions (*vraz, krasa*), and folk epithets in a conscious attempt at stylization of folklore. The epithets occur primarily in the first stanza, relating specifically to the fortune-telling (*yaryi vosk, chistaya voda, zolotoi persten', belyi plat*), and again in the hero's speech in the seventh stanza (*shirokii dvor, tesovye vorota, shelkovy povoda*). *Belyi* is employed most frequently as a folk epithet with such substantives as *plat, pelena, zapona, polotno,* and *golubochek,* and in the compound form *belosnezhnyi golubok.* The popular motifs which appear in **"Svetlana"** include the fortune-telling, the song (stanza 2), the description of the church (stanza 9), the *chernyi vran* (stanza 10), and the dove (stanza 13).

Certainly there are more *narodnyi* elements in **"Svetlana"** than in **"Lyudmila,"** or, for that matter, than in any of Zhukovsky's other literary ballads. But the *narodnost'*, which may conceivably be derived from Chulkov, is stylized and conventional. Folkloric language is restricted to the expression of the few folkloric motifs. Most of **"Svetlana"** is written in Zhukovsky's individual literary style at its most original because there was no foreign model in immediate proximity to restrain him.

Zhukovsky's heroine is described as 'molchaliva i grustna/ Milaya Svetlana', epithets which characterize a sentimental heroine, certainly not a folk heroine. Svetlana's timidity (*robost'*) is her most emphasized 'spiritual' trait. This characteristic is demonstrated in her acceptance of Fate and in her gentle apostrophes to her guardian angel: 'Mne sud'bina umeret'/ V grusti odinokoi' (3:3-4) and 'Utoli pechal' moyu,/ Angel uteshitel' (3:13-14), both of which replace Lenore's *Hader* and Lyudmila's milder *ropot* against God's providence. The hero's remark to Sve-

tlana, 'Tvoi uslyshan ropot' (6:14), is illogical since there has been no *ropot*. Zhukovsky himself was right when he admitted in the nineteenth stanza that his ballad contains *ochen' malo skladu*. The poet's sympathy for the heroine is obvious from the very beginning of the ballad (*milaya Svetlana*, 2:4), and in the various apostrophes to her: 'Akh! Svetlana, chto s toboi!/ V ch'yu zashla obitel'?' (12:5-6), and 'Chto zhe tvoi, Svetlana, son,/ Proritsatel' muki?' (18:1-2).

The hero of **"Svetlana"** is characterized by the epithets *blednyi* and *unylyi* (8:14, 9:14). He is the perfect sentimental hero, whose summons to his Svetlana ('Radost', svet moikh ochei/ Net dlya nas razluki', 7:3-4) provides a striking contrast to Wilhelm's first words to his Lenore ('Holla, holla! Tu auf, mein kind!', 14:1). Zhukovsky's thoughtful hero also describes to his bride-to-be the elaborate arrangements made for their formal church wedding (stanza 7).

The atmosphere in **"Svetlana"** is created in part by the frequent repetition of the word *strakh* in its various forms: *strashno* (5:10, 15:6), *strakh* (5:11, 6:9), *strashnyi* (11:7, 12:6-7, 13:6, 20:1); this makes the horror of the story explicit, rather than demonstrating it implicitly. The dramatic tension which reaches its climax in stanza 15 is suddenly released in the final verb ["to awaken"]. . . . With this verb the *strakh, uzhas,* and *mrak* dissipate momentarily; light and the sounds of morning flood the senses (*V se blestit*). Just as one of Svetlana's friends predicted (stanza 4), her *milyi* returns to her. The amorous delights which await her are described in conventional eighteenth-century language: *priyatny vzory, sladostnye usta, mily razgovory,* and *vernye obety.*

Zhukovsky's epilogue places the whole subject in its proper perspective. The ballad is indeed frightening, but it is only a bad dream, the creation of poetic fantasy, full of *bol'shie chudesa* (19:3). **"Svetlana"** is Bürger's "Lenore" and Zhukovsky's **"Lyudmila"** turned upside down, mocked, or parodied. Zhukovsky concludes with his usual moral, 'Vera v providen'e' (19:11), but it is of little importance. The meaningful experience has been in the contrast between two moods: between the loneliness, anticipation, and terror of the dream world, and the 'clarity', 'pleasures', and 'brightness' (stanza 20) of the real world which promises love and happiness for all.

"Svetlana" is one of Zhukovsky's most original works. In spite of its conventional *narodnyi* language and stylized motifs, the poet succeeds in producing a balladic atmosphere of fear and mystery within the dream framework. Zhukovsky demonstrated that he was the undisputed master of the Russian literary ballad, who could both create its *strakh* and write a brilliant parody of it. (pp. 34-9)

> *Michael R. Katz, "Zhukovsky's Literary Ballads," in his* The Literary Ballad in Early Nineteenth-Century Russian Literature, *Oxford University Press, London, 1976, pp. 37-75.*

Irina M. Semenko   (essay date 1976)

[*Semenko is a critic specializing in the history of Russian lyric verse whose numerous studies of Russian literature include* Poets of the Pushkin Epoch *(1970). In the following excerpt, she examines stylistic elements of Zhukovsky's poetry that contribute to his "disclosure of the inner world of the individual," an essentially Romantic motif which often recurs in his poetry.*]

Zhukovsky is credited with the aphorism: "With us, a writer of genius might achieve more than Peter the Great!" . . . [The] poet attached exceptional importance to the content, the aim of art. "Poetry is virtue"; "the poet's words are his deeds"; "poetry should influence the soul of the whole people": these phrases expressed Zhukovsky's understanding of the aims of literature as aims of a primarily moral nature.

From the very beginning this attitude defined Zhukovsky's particular position among the poets who had begun writing at the same time as he. It distinguished Zhukovsky from the elegant epicureanism of his friend and contemporary Konstantin Batyushkov; from the "wild" "Hussar's" muse of the poet partisan, Denis Davydov; from the libertine poetry of the younger Vyazemsky. The best of these poets, Batyushkov, whose talent may be compared with Zhukovsky's own, represented that hedonistic, erotic tradition of eighteenth-century poetry which enjoyed a particularly luxuriant flowering in France. Batyushkov's "pagan" epicureanism, the civic enthusiasm of Davydov and Vyazemsky (and, later, of the Decembrist poets), contrast directly with Zhukovsky's Christian self-denial.

> I see the castles of the rich
> With gardens girt around . . .
> But my road is another which
> Leads me where care is found.
> Yet of good fortune I'm not shy,
> I keep my grief apart;
> Bidding the gay—as I go by—
> "God speed you!" from my heart . . .
> ("The Song of the Poor Man")

Zhukovsky was a logical and uncompromising thinker. For Batyushkov, with his harmonious, aesthetic ideal, life was acceptable only as a blaze of beauty and happiness, opposed to destruction and despair. Batyushkov's poetry is not without dissonances, the bitter awareness of a life passing irretrievably. Zhukovsky's poetry is a poetry of reconciliation, of the dissolution of man in a world that is full of the breath of the Divinity. It is not surprising that Zhukovsky was so struck by Gogol's phrase that art is "reconciliation with life." Zhukovsky always strove to create a harmonious, lofty, specifically poetic world, firmly rooted in the Ideal, a world in which such human moral concepts as "virtue," "truth," "greatness," and "beauty" were expressed in sublimated form. For him, "the good" and "the beautiful" were inseparable.

Zhukovsky's poetry, like his life, was far from idyllic. Naively idealistic notes are to be found only in his very earliest poems (even in some of his masterpieces, such as the **"Village Churchyard"** and **"Evening"**). On the whole, however, Zhukovsky's poetry provides us profound insight into the complexity of human experience, man's striving after the moral and aesthetic ideal, and his sorrow

at the awareness of the imperfection of a life "where all, my friend, is victim or destroyer" (**"To Turgenev, In Answer to His Letter"**). Given this choice, Zhukovsky preferred the role of victim. The sadness which pervades his lyric poetry and almost all his work is invariably colored by an element of self-limitation, self-denial.

Zhukovsky remained aloof from the spirit of Romantic individualism which affected his contemporaries in varying degree. Nothing in him responded either to vividly expressed "demonism" or to the milder forms of individualism in poetry.

The principal feature of Zhukovsky's artistic manner was his lyricism. It would be incorrect to say that his poetry, for all its concentration on feelings and experiences, was psychological in the sense that the poetry of Pushkin, Lermontov, Baratynsky or Tyutchev was psychological. The image of the poet in Zhukovsky's poetry is still somewhat abstract, devoid of individual or psychological features. Yet the atmosphere of poetic, lofty lyricism is a typical characteristic not only of his poetry as a whole, but also of each separate work.

The principle of the poetic "confession" is alien to Zhukovsky's artistic manner. He prefers a summarized description of his emotion to analysis, dissection, or detailed description. But the lyric tenor of every image, of every poetic word serves to enlarge the perspective of the content, semantically enriching the imagery. A special hidden emotionalism—natural to lyricism, as a genre of the art of the word, and differing essentially from the more "open," more obvious emotions of the epic and drama—is particularly characteristic of Zhukovsky's style. It is this trait that invests his poetry with the unfading enchantment and power of the highest flights of poetry.

Zhukovsky uses words in such a way as to render them capacious, rich in implications and associations. Zhukovsky did much to bestow upon the word that wealth of profound association which distinguishes the word as employed in poetry from the same word used in prose.

This multisignificance is rooted in Zhukovsky's understanding of the complex relationships of man with the world around him. Since the days of Petrarch, the problem of "man and the world" has been understood throughout European lyric poetry as the problem of "man and culture." This concept, of course, had its origins in the remote past and, in Zhukovsky's poetry (as also, incidentally, in Petrarch's), is closely linked with his conception of the divine "creation" of nature. Hence the veneration of nature so especially characteristic of Zhukovsky.

"We would overlook one of Zhukovsky's most important features," wrote Belinsky [in his *Polnoe sobranie sochinenii*], "if we failed to mention that poet's divine gift for describing scenes from nature and imbuing them with romantic life." Among Zhukovsky's lyric verses we will scarcely find one in which the lyrical subject is not developed against the background of a landscape. Even the word "background" is misleading. It does not convey the essence of Zhukovsky's manner, by which the world (the landscape, the natural setting) and man are always presented in a kind of unity.

Zhukovsky was the first Russian poet to introduce not only the colors, sounds, and smells of nature into his work (all of which helps form its "material" charm), but also, as it were, to endow nature with the thoughts and feelings of the human beings who view it. This concept constitutes the basic framework (despite all the differences between them) of such poems as **"The Village Churchyard," "Evening," "Slavyanka," "A Sentiment of Spring," "Desire" ("Zhelanie"), "To the Moon" ("K nesyatsu"), "The Inexpressible" ("Nevyrazimoe"), "The Moth and the Flowers" ("Motylyok i tsvety")**, and many other masterpieces of Zhukovsky's lyric poetry.

Let us first examine the original elegy **"Evening"** (1806), which has received a generous share of critical study by scholars, but which still remains a never-failing source of appreciative enthusiasm on the part of the reader:

> Already evening . . . and the clouds' bright rims
> Have faded. On high towers the last ray slowly
>   dies,
> The last faint-gleaming ripple on the river dims
> And flickers out beneath dulled skies.
>
> All's quiet; trees sleep sound; around me all is
>   still,
> And, stretched out on the grass beneath a bend-
>   ing willow,
> I hear the chuckling haste of a leaf-hidden rill
> To mingle with the river's shallows.
>
> How mingled with the cool the incense of the
>   leaves!
> How sweet in stillness here to listen to the river!
> How quietly o'er the waters wafts the soft-blown
>   breeze
> The supple willow branches quiver!

In the first verse quoted here, the dominant words are all colored by a similar emotional mood: "have faded," "last," "dies," "last," "dulled,' "flickers out". Yet Zhukovsky does not resort to simple—positive or negative—parallelism in his evocation of nature and man. In the second verse, where the poet depicts himself, the dominant words are emotionally neutral, almost prosaic: "stretched out," "bending," "I hear," "chuckles," "to mingle." In this way the poet is neither brought into too close contact with the fading landscape, nor set at too great a distance from it. And in this way, too, the state of contemplation, of meditation, is expressed not only thematically ("stretched out . . . I hear"), but also by the very character of the words employed. A profound emotion infects the reader and renders him, as it were, a participant in the creative act.

The words in this elegy have more than one level of meaning; they include an objective meaning and a psychological meaning (melancholy). In the Russian original, there is a deliberate, musical use of assonance in *pomerknuli-poslednii, luch-potukhshii,* and in the semantically and morphologically homogeneous rhymes *umiraet-ugasaet.* The beauty, the poetic worth of the words also become a part of their content. The semantics of these words however, are somewhat loose: Zhukovsky is not seeking precision or differentiation. Through this multiple meaningfulness and associative evocativeness he achieves an effect of

things left unsaid, of spacious scope for possible reinterpretation. Zhukovsky's use of words is remarkable for this ability to leave his reader in possession of a *semantic reserve.*

Owing to the "deliberate complexity of meaning" in his use of words [B. A. Larin in *Russkaia rech'*], Zhukovsky is able to convey the deepest stirrings of the heart. For instance, the stillness in the poem **"Evening"** is at once a real stillness and a stillness of the heart. Later it would become one of the poet's favorite images. It is not "dying" or "fading," but this complex image of "stillness" that provides, in this elegy, the link between man and nature. To depict a state of being harmoniously at one with the natural world is undoubtedly a part of Zhukovsky's basic concept. Even the twice-repeated use of the word *slivat'sia* ("to mingle") contributes to this impression: the little rill "mingles" with the river, and the scent of growing things is "mingled" with the cool of evening in the famous line "How mingled with the cool the incense of the leaves."

Just as complex and semantically weighted is the epithet "sweet." Zhukovsky was the first poet in Russian literature to make wide use of it in the psychological, Petrarchan sense (*dolce*). The "sweetness" of the contemplation of nature as a material expression of the beauty of this present life is, for Zhukovsky, a most important aspect of the life of the soul, not only in **"Evening,"** but in many other works as well (e.g., **"Sentiment of Spring," "Slavyanka,"** and **"To the Moon"**).

The lyrical emotionalism found in Zhukovsky's lyric poetry has much in common with music. Perhaps no other Russian poet's work was so organically connected with music. The room Zhukovsky always left for "unexpressed" associations creates an inner connection with the principles of the art of music, a connection confirmed by "exterior" elements.

In Zhukovsky's poetry, a particularly significant place is occupied by the song the romance. Many of his poems are actually called "Song": these include **"My Friend, My Guardian Angel," "O, Dearest Friend! Now Thou Art Joyful," "The Charm of Days Gone By."** If we comprehend Zhukovsky's conscious use of music to lend greater expressiveness to his verse, we will understand the great significance of sound-painting in Zhukovsky's poetic method, the composition of many of his verses (the use of couplets, refrains, etc.), and, finally, the actual way in which he uses words. "The whole of Nature was a song to me"—these words from the introduction to *Undine* do not, of course, refer in any literal sense to what we have been saying, but they do reveal a great deal about Zhukovsky's poetry.

In his verse Zhukovsky pays much attention to the elaboration of mood. The interrogative approach, another typical characteristic of the song, is the mood he makes use of most often. In this connection, it is interesting to point out the purely songlike system of exclamations and exhortations which always lend a characteristic intonation to Zhukovsky's poetry. It is no wonder his verses have so often been set to music; for the potentiality of a musical interpretation was already organically contained within them. For example, the first three lines of the elegy **"Evening,"** set to music by Tchaikovsky, are immediately recognizable as musically organized, even if we detach ourselves from the familiar melody. The compositional symmetry characteristic of the song and the uniformity of musical periods here find their counterpart in the pattern of the exclamations: "kak slit," "kak sladko," "kak tikho" ("how mingled," "how sweetly," "how softly"). From the point of view of sound effects, we perceive clearly the melodic shifts in the accented vowels *i, e,* and *a,* which are sounded successively once again, with increased emphasis, in the last line: "*I gibkoi* vy tr*e*petan'*e*. . . ."

A remarkably rich variety of rhythms distinguishes Zhukovsky's poetry. It contains the most varied forms and combinations of iambic meter: blank iambic pentameter, hexameter, four-foot iambic lines with masculine rhymes throughout (a verse form later given high poetic standing by Lermontov in his narrative poem *Mtsyri*), the trochee with dactylic endings, not to mention the wide use of trisyllabic meters (dactyls, amphibrachs, anapests). Use of such a wide variety of meters enabled Zhukovsky to convey complex shades of mood and emotion, not only through words and their meanings, but also phonetically. "What cannot be said in words, whisper to the soul in sounds"—these words, by which Afanasy Fet sought to express the essence of his poetry in the poem "No, I've No Song of Passion for Thee" ("Net, ne zhdi ty pesni strastnoi"), are equally applicable to Zhukovsky's lyrics.

"Romances" and "songs": thus Zhukovsky himself entitled an important section of the editions of his collected verse published during his lifetime. His "songs" include both original and translated works. It is noteworthy that in some of Zhukovsky's translations the subtitle "Song" appears when it was not present in the original (cf., for example, the subtitle to Zhukovsky's translation of Schiller's "Die Ideale" ["Mechty"]). It is also characteristic of Zhukovsky that he actually transforms the phonetic structure of the verse to make it more songlike; in Schiller's original there is less phonetic symmetry. For example the correspondence between the exclamations in the first and the second lines is lacking.

It is not only the phonetic structure and meter, but also the principle of the construction of an image, the principle of the use of words themselves, which often . . . invest Zhukovsky's poetry with its songlike, lyric quality. The word-image in the song possesses its own specific characteristics, and in this field Zhukovsky was a great master. To a certain extent, his achievement stemmed from his association with the tradition of sentimental songwriting and poetry of the late eighteenth and early nineteenth centuries; Nikolay Lvov, Yury Neledinsky-Meletsky, and Ivan Dmitriev may be cited. This association was particularly noticeable in the poetry written between 1800 and the early 1810s. Their songlike quality here assumes a conventionalized elegiac form:

> When that I was beloved, in ecstasies, in pleasure,
> The days of life flowed by like an enchanting dream.

Later, the "musicality" of Zhukovsky's poetry attained

ever greater perfection, while remaining the basic element of his lyricism. This development sprang from that generalized descriptive quality of his use of words which we have already mentioned.

The vital words of Zhukovsky's poetic lexicon are those conveying general, rather than individual, emotions, for instance "memory," "sorrow," "joy," "stillness," "life," "love." But in Zhukovsky's poetry these words have several dimensions of meaning. Possessed of great "reserves" of significance, they call up a whole chain of associations that lead into the very depths of man's emotional life. This type of word-image, closely akin to music, in many ways defines the specific grace of Zhukovsky's lyricism, and is evident not only in his original works, but also in his translations.

As an example, we may quote the poem **"To the Moon"** (1817):

> Once again the wood and vale
> Drown in misty gleam;
> In your stillness sweet my soul
> Melts as in a dream.
>
> You appeared—and quietly
> Meadows dark grew bright,
> As a smile, quite suddenly,
> Floods our life with light.
>
> Grief and joy of far-off years
> Echo back to me,
> In the stillness I can hear
> Call of memory.
>
> Down, my stream, go gushing by!
> Life has lost its bloom;
> So my hopes went rushing by
> So my love is gone. . . .

Here, no single word suggests any sharply individual shade of meaning in "sorrow" and "joy"; yet the torrent of emotional "information" released by these lines is very powerful.

The opening chord for the entire poem is the phrase "Once again." Placed as it is at the very beginning, in the position where it will assume the greatest possible metric weight, it acquires a heightened semantic intensity, expressing the resurrection of a past experience of the heart. In this way, the poem's time setting is enlarged to include what happened long ago.

"To the Moon" is a translation of a poem by Goethe of the same title, "An den Mond," in which the emotions are clearly defined and depicted in more detail. In Goethe's poem, for all the melancholy that pervades it, the dominant mood is one of calm, even as the moon's gaze is "calming" to the poet. From the beginning, Goethe is concerned with the elegiac problem of the impossibility of recalling the past. Zhukovsky, however, does recall this past, to experience once again with full intensity the sorrow of his loss (he hears "an echo" and "a salutation" from bygone days). The soul is wide open to impressions from the past. Goethe, in this same passage, speaks of bidding farewell to the past and even of finding release from it. Zhukovsky does not diminish the original: he simply creates different images.

In the Russian word *rastvoril* ("melted") we again discover the multiplicity of meaning so characteristic of the Russian poet. One of the word's meanings is "opened," but the basic idea is connected with Zhukovsky's concept of the mingling of the "inner" and the "outer," of the "dissolving" of the one in the other. As in **"Evening,"** "sweet stillness" is once again both stillness in nature and a state of the soul. It is not so much the expression "sweet stillness" as such as the fact that it opens or "dissolves" the soul (*rastovoriaet dushu*); this is the great discovery of Zhukovsky as lyric poet, all the greater for the fact that he is translating no less a poet than Goethe.

One of the specific characteristics of Zhukovsky's lyric poetry is his talent for investing conventional literary themes with life and conviction. He varies and combines the same themes, reworking them into complete, original compositions. Thus "times gone by" (*minuvshee*) is one of Zhukovsky's favorite word-themes. He is always looking back to the past. But this conventional, almost banal, theme of elegiac poetry achieves in his poetry, as we have seen, profound emotional significance.

In Zhukovsky's poetry, words are oriented toward evocation of emotional *experience,* not of new and untried sensations. This orientation is also reminiscent of the principles of classical music.

The word "chord" used earlier is a common enough metaphor, but it is singularly apt when applied to Zhukovsky's style. The musical organization of the line cited above and of those that followed it is of a very high caliber. In them, as in **"Evening,"** are dominant full-voiced, melodious passages of ringing sound. In the first verse, the harmonious diphthongs (the *"i-vowels"*) occur within both the rhymes, and, in each case, also preceding the rhymes: *tumannyi tvoi; sladkoi tishinoi.* The monosyllabic words *les, dol,* and *blesk* emphasize by way of contrast the long-drawn-out *tumannyi. Les* and *blesk* are assonances.

This vividly expressed phonetic musicality has a function of meaning, for it creates a more immediate and convincing sense of real experience. (pp. 42-50)

Although never an advocate of "confession," Zhukovsky nevertheless contrived a perfect means of conveying human feeling through poetry. In Zhukovsky's scheme of things, man's place in the world was a very important one. As he saw it, the human mind was an ultrarefined instrument for contact with the outer world in its most varied manifestations, whether the "secret" life of that world not usually immediately apprehensible by man; or signals emanating from this "secret" world—its sounds, scents, colors; or, beyond all this, its "eternal" values of goodness and beauty.

Zhukovsky's poetry does not distinguish between individual characters and feeling. On the contrary, it is remarkable because it constantly evokes and reevokes one and the same "state of soul": inspiration, animation, a controlled but exalted intensity of reaction to the impressions of the exterior world, enabling the subject to penetrate its "mysteries."

This power of evocation is the outstanding feature of Zhukovsky's lyric poetry and one that distinguishes it from the lyricism of Sentimentalism (although the poet was undoubtedly indebted to the latter). Sentimentalism cultivated *mood* and the mature Zhukovsky, *state of soul,* which is not the same thing at all. "Mood" in poetry is a forerunner of subjectivism. It colors the exterior world according to its own whim and thus often deprives it of its independent, material reality.

In this way, Zhukovsky himself introduces into his translation of Gray's "Elegy" such expressions as "grows pale" and "sunk in thought" which we do not find in the original, thereby independently creating the "mood," but at the same time detracting from the real, material detail of the descriptions.

The other form of Zhukovsky's lyricism—the conveyance of a "state of soul"—does not detract from the material quality of descriptions but, on the contrary, presupposes the power of obseration and acute reaction to the surrounding world. The realism of Zhukovsky's description of material objects is, of course, quite different from Derzhavin's. Derzhavin describes what can be—and should be—visible to anybody at all times; Zhukovsky, that which is only perceptible through that controlled exaltation of soul which permits the poet to hear the silence being broken by the falling of a leaf, as in the poem **"Slavyanka."**

In Zhukovsky's languorously landscaped elegies (**"The Village Churchyard," "Evening,"** and, again, **"Slavyanka"**), there are descriptions of country life abounding in material detail in the spirit of Derzhavin. Naturally, this style was not Zhukovsky's own discovery, although in some contexts it took on a new coloration.

Some of Zhukovsky's insights into the material world are very interesting and complex. Derzhavin saw the way the sky is reflected in the water and the way birds flying in the sky seem to be "flying in the meadow" ("A Walk in Tsarskoe Selo"); he saw the brilliant colors of the banquet table: "green sorrel soup," "glowing red ham" ("To Evgeny. Life at Zvanskoe"); he saw how "through blue veins courses the rosy blood" ("Russian Girls"). All this is materially, sensually real. Yet the following verses from Zhukovsky cannot be denied a certain material, sensual reality:

> I walk a winding path beneath the forest eaves;
> Each step—and a new scene is to my eyes unfolding;
> Now, gleaming sudden through the trees, as though all wreathed
> In smoke—a bright vale I'm beholding.
> Then all is gone again. . . . The forest thickens now;
> Here all is wild and strange, the twilight, and the silence;
> Save when, from time to time, through the dark, vaulted boughs,
> There steal diurnal shafts of radiance.

> To gild the roots and pallid, thrusting plants
>   with light;
> Save when some breath of wind, a little leaf loose
>   shaking,
> Sends it a-fluttering down, against the dimness
>   bright,
>   So, by its fall, the stillness breaking.

This sound of a falling leaf, heard by a poet, marked the beginning of a new era in the Russian lyric. Derzhavin had heard the roar of the waterfall: "An avalanche of diamonds falls . . ." ("The Waterfall"), but the gleam of the leaf "against the dimness," the sound of its falling, the sudden ripple on the water, the swan hidden among the low shrubs and "shining" there—all these were new, real, material aspects of a world that Zhukovsky was the first "to see."

He applied an analogous technique in describing mountain scenery in his free translation of Goethe's "Der Morgen kam," and of the moonlit night in his **"Inventory of the Moon" ("Podorobnyi otchet o lune")**.

> Beneath the drowsy, opiate ray
> The world itself, it seemed, was drowsing—
> Save for the whispering waters' play,
> Save for some day-bird's sleepy rousing,
> Save when, along the empty road,
> His shadow close beside him keeping,
> Belated, some lone traveler strode
> And broke the stillness of the evening.

As we can see, Zhukovsky did not merely use the concept of "mist" as a background to emphasize the melancholy mood of the poet, and his moon is not just "sorrowful and pale." In the moonlit night he saw the shadow of the lonely traveler keeping pace with him along the road and sensed the startled rousing of a sleepy bird.

The monotonous melancholy of sentimental lyricism was predominant in early nineteenth-century poetry, and it did not lend itself to detailed perception of material reality. The range of words used to convey a sustained emotional atmosphere severely limited the scope of things to be described. Pushkin disliked "monotony" in this sense, calling it "uniformity" (for instance, he disliked Lamartine's elegies for their "insupportable uniformity"). But of Zhukovsky he wrote [in his *Polnoe sobranie sochinenii*]: "No one ever has had or will have a style to equal his power and variety."

The lofty dreaminess of Zhukovsky's verses did not strike Pushkin as "monotonous," precisely because this quality was not felt as an obstacle to a sweeping and penetrating view of the surrounding world. Zhukovsky obtained the effect of unity of the state of soul without resorting to monotony of emotional coloring. He obtained his goal by endowing the very objects he described with *animation*. This animation of outward things is sometimes directly connected with the Romantic conception of nature, but at other times the link is extremely tenuous. In the poem **"The Light Has Dawned"** (*"Vzoshla zaria . . ."*), the mist "flies up" like a live being, the mist is "winged." In the same poem, the breath of dawn is said to have "lured" sleep away.

> And day had sprung, a fiery-winged Spirit!

And to the living heart all things were living.

The general "aliveness" of nature, in which man is organically included—such is the Romantic concept, and a most fruitful one it is for poetry.

All these "leaves" of Zhukovsky's are alive, "stirring." Typical in this respect is the epithet in "a sleepy leaf is stirring" (**"Slvyanka"**). Zhukovsky's feeling for the "aliveness" of living creatures was particularly intense (let us once more recall the way Zhukovsky, in all the vast world of life, notices one tiny creature—the sleepy bird aroused). His swan is not merely observed from without as a "shining" object, but it has "hidden" in the bushes. Here we have at one and the same time a remarkable refinement of the poetic "instrument" and a profound sympathy with all living things, not only in the Romantic but also in the more everyday sense of the word. This refinement and sensitivity explain why these elements of Zhukovsky's poetry were adopted by Pushkin and by Russian poetry after him.

The peculiar emotional quality of Zhukovsky's poetry is intimately linked with the foregoing observations. His poetry is characterized not only by the melancholy reflectiveness of Sentimentalism, but by something else as well: exaltation of soul, inspiration, an awakened consciousness, swift to record and to interpret all it sees. Pushkin, for all the distance separating him from Zhukovsky, seems to be restating in his own words the fundamental experience of the latter's poetry in "The Prophet":

> And then I heard the sky gongs stricken,
> And angels soaring in the height,
> And monsters move through ocean night,
> And vines in mountain-valleys quicken.

The elegy **"Slavyanka"** is one of Zhukovsky's most remarkable poems along these lines. Here the poetry is extremely rich, and this richness it owes above all to its awareness of the external world, perceived through an acutely sensitive human consciousness. In **"Slavyanka,"** Zhukovsky interweaves in a single, complex whole his impressions of the countryside, his dreams of glory and the fatherland, sorrowful memories and astonishingly sharp-eyed observations. The picture he paints of the visible, external world is at once poeticized and extraordinarily accurate.

> And here a church is glimpsed through birch
>   with maple twining;
> And there a swan, safe-hidden on the shrub-
>   grown bank,
> Stands still amid the dimness shining.

Through this combination of thoughts, observations, and emotions, through this sensitivity to almost imperceptible "signals" from without, the poem is built up to its culmination: the Romantic contact between the poet's "soul" and the "soul" of the world:

> So stillness everywhere extends her sovereign
>   law;
> All sleeps . . . save when some voice on distant
>   darkness drifting
> Sounds indistinct . . . or else some ripple laps
>   the shore . . .
> Or when a sleepy leaf is stirring. . . .

. . . As though, concealed beneath the bark of
  these young trees,
Through this enchanted stillness welcome sound
  dispersing,
A voice, a soul unseen were reaching out to me,
And with this soul of mine conversing. . . .

The "state of soul" of which we have been speaking, and which is so personally Zhukovsky's, is invariably present not only in his original poetry but also in his translations. This is the secret of their capacity to endure as works of art in their own right. A striking instance of this ability is the manner in which Zhukovsky reorganizes the system of images in Goethe's "Der Fischer" (translated as **"Rybak"**). Here, quite independently of the original, Zhukovsky creates a complex image of "stillness." Once again, this is both a real stillness and a stillness of the soul. Zhukovsky introduces an original image: "the soul is full of cool stillness." There is nothing of this kind in Goethe's original. His fisherman "saw calmly to his rod and line, cool to the depths of his heart." In the same way, as we have already shown, Zhukovsky introduced his beloved image of "stillness" into the poem **"To the Moon."**

Zhukovsky was a great master of imagery. Sometimes these images are formed not so much by the words themselves as by mood and syntax. A characteristic example is the poem **"Desire"**:

Valley, melt your mists in fire!
Scatter, gloom, and get ye gone!
Where's the land of heart's desire?
Where shall my soul rise again?

There the stillness keeps her cloister,
There the lyres have well-tuned strings,
There from whence the gentle zephyrs
Waft me sweet scents of the spring.

There the golden fruits hang glistening
From the spreading, leafy bough;
Spiteful blizzards come not whistling
Over grassy hill and howe. . . .

Our first response to these verses is an awareness of their beat and rhythmic structure, the symmetry of identical syntactic forms, as exhibited in the repeated imperatives "Receive," "Scatter"; the repeated question "where?"; and the fourfold answer: "There. . . ." Thanks to the emphatic imperatives and the strong rhythm, the "desire" appears rather as an incantation, the invocation of a miracle.

In the original of this poem (Schiller's "Sehnsucht"—literally "longing"), the tonal and syntactic system are quite different; they are more passively descriptive.

Ach, aus dieses Thales Gründen,
Die der kalte Nebel drückt,
Könnt' ich doch den Ausgang finden,
Ach, wie fühlt' ich mich beglückt.

Although the theme of miracle is present in the original—"Only miracle might bear you to the lovely wonderland"—its linguistic imagery, the sense of expectation and invocation, are entirely Zhukovsky's creation. Through the "incantational" rhythm the metaphors come alive: we feel the misty valley must be filled with light and the thick darkness must scatter and disperse—not just figuratively, but in the literal sense of the word.

Another example closely akin to this is to be found in Zhukovsky's translation of Goethe's ballad "Mignon" (Zhukovsky calls her "Mina"). In this translation, textually quite close to the original, two changes have been introduced. In the first place, instead of the descriptively real "die Citronen blühn" ("the lemons bloom"), Zhukovsky has "the golden lemon glows amid the darkness of the trees." In the second place, the interrogative and descriptive tone is replaced by an exclamatory note (the only use of the exclamatory form by Goethe is in the refrain "Dahin! Dahin!"). In Zhukovsky's version, instead of the opening "Know'st thou the land?" we have "I know the land!" And so on right through to the end: "There a fair house stands!" "There is a mountain!" "The rock falls!" This exclamatory note pervades the whole poem, creating an impression of prophetic ecstasy, and again, as it were, suggesting "wonders." Because of this "prophetic" tone we perceive, here as well, the poet's animation of the direct, literal meaning of the word. In the line "The golden lemon glows amid the darkness of the trees" "golden" is not simply a conventional, decorative epithet, a substitute for "yellow," but a symbol of the wonderful. Added animation is achieved by the metaphor "burns"; this truly "golden" lemon seems indeed to burn in an enchanted forest.

In the finale, the exclamatory mood to which we have become accustomed is suddenly replaced by the interrogative: "But shall I ever be there?"; and this shift, as much as the actual question, emphasizes still more the unattainability of this legendary land. Without diluting in any way the formal accuracy of his translation, Zhukovsky has wrought a fundamental change of image. Simply by altering the tone he has transformed Goethe's image of a beautiful but real country into that of a kind of fairyland.

Both in his translations and in his original poetry, Zhukovsky achieves profound effects of meaning through his skill in discovering ever new combinations of words, mood, and rhythm. In the poem **"Sentiment of Spring,"** it is again mood that plays the chief part. In eight verses out of twelve, questions are addressed to abstract and inanimate objects. The singsong smoothness of the rhythm gives lyrical feeling to this interrogative mood while at the same time the direct form of address to the wind, the torrent, and the spring "animate" them. Adjectives and adverbs such as "light," "sweetly," "softly," "enchanted" lend this animation a romantic significance. The torrent "plays," the clouds "fly," the "migrant spring" returns; amid the common life of nature the soul of man reawakens too. A pantheistic feeling for the world is conveyed by the poet's material, sensual image of this life of nature. (pp. 59-66)

Irina M. Semenko, in her Vasily Zhukovsky, *Twayne Publishers, 1976, 167 p.*

FURTHER READING

Gronicka, André von. "Goethe and His Russian Translator-Interpreter V. A. Zhukovski (1783-1852)." *PMLA* LXX, No. 1 (March 1955): 145-65.

Declares of Zhukovsky: "His place in Russian literary history as the greatest of the early champions, interpreters, and translators of Goethe is secure for all time." However, Gronicka notes that "Zhukovski has placed before his Russian audience a Goethe image, reflected and refracted in the medium of his own predominantly sentimental, romantic, mystical nature, his own elegiac, nostalgically retrospective mood and, in the end, devoutly pietistic faith."

Katz, Michael R. *The Literary Ballad in Early Nineteenth-Century Russian Literature*. London: Oxford University Press, 1976, 248 p.

Includes chapters on such topics as: the use of epithet in Zhukovsky's ballads, "the polemics in Russian literary criticism which surrounded the ballad genre and its creator [Zhukovsky]," the ballads of Zhukovsky's imitators, and Zhukovsky's influence on Alexander Pushkin and Mikhail Lermontov.

Ober, Kenneth H., and Ober, Warren U. "Marginalia. Percy's Nancy and Zhukovsky's Nina: A Translation Identified." *The Slavonic and East European Review* 57, No. 3 (July 1979): 396-402.

Observes the relationship between Thomas Percy's poem, "A Song," and Zhukovsky's two translations of "A Song," both entitled "K Nine" ("To Nina"): "By avoiding the easy and obvious phrase and choosing the sharp and fresh image, Zhukovsky the translator-as-maker once again in 'To Nina' takes a promising original and gives it new life."

————. "Marginalia. Two Bards: Zhukovsky and Bowring." *The Slavonic and East European Review* 62, No. 4 (October 1984): 560-66.

Claims that when translating Zhukovsky's "Pevets" ("The Bard") into English, the early nineteenth-century scholar John Bowring "reworked Zhukovsky's poem to its detriment as he tried to fit it to his own concept." Both Zhukovsky's poem and Bowring's translation are reprinted.

Passage, Charles E. "The Influence of Schiller in Russia, 1800-1840." *The American Slavic and East European Review* V, No. 12-13 (May 1946): 111-37.

Credits Zhukovsky with popularizing Friedrich Schiller's lyric poetry in Russia. Passage states that Zhukovsky's translations of Schiller's poetry "began by being over-free, but gradually increased in fidelity to the originals, until they stand as masterful transferences of masterpieces from the German into the Russian language."

Pushkin, Alexander. *Pushkin on Literature*, edited and translated by Tatiana Wolff. London: Methuen & Co., 1971, 554.

Contains scattered references to Zhukovsky in various letters by Pushkin.

Slonim, Marc. "The New Era." In his *The Epic of Russian Literature: From Its Origins through Tolstoy*, pp. 49-64. New York: Oxford University Press, 1964.

Surveys Zhukovsky's career, noting that the significance of his translations lies in their originality and their role in introducing European poetry into Russia. Slonim also discusses the subject matter and innovative style of Zhukovsky's poetry.

Nineteenth-Century
Literature Criticism

Cumulative Indexes
Volumes 1-35

This Index Includes References to Entries in These Gale Series

Children's Literature Review includes excerpts from reviews, criticism, and commentary on works of authors and illustrators who create books for children.

Classical and Medieval Literature Criticism offers excerpts of criticism on the works of world authors from classical antiquity through the fourteenth century.

Contemporary Authors Series encompasses five related series. *Contemporary Authors* provides biographical and bibliographical information on more than 97,000 writers of fiction and nonfiction. *Contemporary Authors New Revision Series* provides completely updated information on authors covered in *CA*. *Contemporary Authors Permanent Series* consists of listings for deceased and inactive authors. *Contemporary Authors Autobiography Series* presents specially commissioned autobiographies by leading contemporary writers. *Contemporary Authors Bibliographical Series* contains primary and secondary bibliographies as well as analytical bibliographical essays by authorities on major modern authors.

Contemporary Literary Criticism presents excerpts of criticism on the works of novelists, poets, dramatists, short story writers, scriptwriters, and other creative writers who are now living or who have died since 1960.

Dictionary of Literary Biography encompasses four related series. *Dictionary of Literary Biography* furnishes illustrated overviews of authors' lives and works. *Dictionary of Literary Biography Documentary Series* illuminates the careers of major figures through a selection of literary documents, including letters, interviews, and photographs. *Dictionary of Literary Biography Yearbook* summarizes the past year's literary activity and includes updated entries on individual authors. *Concise Dictionary of American Literary Biography* a six-volume series, collects revised and updated sketches on major American authors that were originally presented in *Dictionary of Literary Biography*.

Drama Criticism provides excerpts of criticism on the works of playwrights of all nationalities and periods of literary history.

Literature Criticism from 1400 to 1800 compiles significant passages from the most noteworthy criticism on authors of the fifteenth through eighteenth centuries.

Nineteenth-Century Literature Criticism offers significant passages from criticism on authors who died between 1800 and 1899.

Poetry Criticism presents excerpts of criticism on the works of poets from all eras, movements, and nationalities.

Short Story Criticism compiles excerpts of criticism on short fiction written by authors of all eras and nationalities.

Something about the Author Series encompasses three related series. *Something about the Author* contains well-illustrated biographical sketches on juvenile and young adult authors and illustrators from all eras. *Something about the Author Autobiography Series* presents specially commissioned autobiographies by prominent authors and illustrators of books for children and young adults. *Authors & Artists for Young Adults* provides high school and junior high school students with profiles of their favorite creative artists.

Twentieth-Century Literary Criticism contains critical excerpts by the most significant commentators on poets, novelists, short story writers, dramatists, and philosophers who died between 1900 and 1960.

Yesterday's Authors of Books for Children contains heavily illustrated entries on children's writers who died before 1961. Complete in two volumes.

Literary Criticism Series
Cumulative Author Index

This index lists all author entries in the Gale Literary Criticism Series and includes cross-references to other Gale sources. References in the index are identified as follows:

AAYA: *Authors & Artists for Young Adults,* Volumes 1-7
CA: *Contemporary Authors* (original series), Volumes 1-136
CAAS: *Contemporary Authors Autobiography Series,* Volumes 1-14
CABS: *Contemporary Authors Bibliographical Series,* Volumes 1-3
CANR: *Contemporary Authors New Revision Series,* Volumes 1-35
CAP: *Contemporary Authors Permanent Series,* Volumes 1-2
CA-R: *Contemporary Authors* (first revision), Volumes 1-44
CDALB: *Concise Dictionary of American Literary Biography,* Volumes 1-6
CLC: *Contemporary Literary Criticism,* Volumes 1-70
CLR: *Children's Literature Review,* Volumes 1-25
CMLC: *Classical and Medieval Literature Criticism,* Volumes 1-8
DC: *Drama Criticism,* Volume 1-2
DLB: *Dictionary of Literary Biography,* Volumes 1-112
DLB-DS: *Dictionary of Literary Biography Documentary Series,* Volumes 1-9
DLB-Y: *Dictionary of Literary Biography Yearbook,* Volumes 1980-1990
LC: *Literature Criticism from 1400 to 1800,* Volumes 1-19
NCLC: *Nineteenth-Century Literature Criticism,* Volumes 1-35
PC: *Poetry Criticism,* Volumes 1-4
SAAS: *Something about the Author Autobiography Series,* Volumes 1-13
SATA: *Something about the Author,* Volumes 1-66
SSC: *Short Story Criticism,* Volumes 1-9
TCLC: *Twentieth-Century Literary Criticism,* Volumes 1-44
YABC: *Yesterday's Authors of Books for Children,* Volumes 1-2

A. E. 1867-1935 . . . . TCLC 3, 10
See also Russell, George William
See also DLB 19

Abbey, Edward 1927-1989 . . . . . . CLC 36, 59
See also CANR 2; CA 45-48;
obituary CA 128

Abbott, Lee K., Jr. 19??- . . . . CLC 48

Abe, Kobo 1924- . . . . CLC 8, 22, 53
See also CANR 24; CA 65-68

Abell, Kjeld 1901-1961 . . . . CLC 15
See also obituary CA 111

Abish, Walter 1931- . . . . CLC 22
See also CA 101

Abrahams, Peter (Henry) 1919- . . . . . CLC 4
See also CA 57-60

Abrams, M(eyer) H(oward) 1912-... CLC 24
See also CANR 13; CA 57-60; DLB 67

Abse, Dannie 1923- . . . . CLC 7, 29
See also CAAS 1; CANR 4; CA 53-56;
DLB 27

Achebe, (Albert) Chinua(lumogu)
1930- . . . . CLC 1, 3, 5, 7, 11, 26, 51
See also BLC 1; CLR 20; WLC 1; CANR 6,
26; CA 1-4R; SATA 38, 40

Acker, Kathy 1948- . . . . CLC 45
See also CA 117, 122

Ackroyd, Peter 1949- . . . . CLC 34, 52
See also CA 123, 127

Acorn, Milton 1923- . . . . CLC 15
See also CA 103; DLB 53

Adamov, Arthur 1908-1970 . . . . . . CLC 4, 25
See also CAP 2; CA 17-18;
obituary CA 25-28R

Adams, Alice (Boyd) 1926- . . . CLC 6, 13, 46
See also CANR 26; CA 81-84; DLB-Y 86

Adams, Douglas (Noel) 1952- . . . CLC 27, 60
See also CA 106; DLB-Y 83

Adams, Francis 1862-1893 . . . . . . NCLC 33

Adams, Henry (Brooks)
1838-1918 . . . . TCLC 4
See also CA 104; DLB 12, 47

Adams, Richard (George)
1920- . . . . CLC 4, 5, 18
See also CLR 20; CANR 3; CA 49-52;
SATA 7

Adamson, Joy(-Friederike Victoria)
1910-1980 . . . . CLC 17
See also CANR 22; CA 69-72;
obituary CA 93-96; SATA 11;
obituary SATA 22

Adcock, (Kareen) Fleur 1934- . . . . . . CLC 41
See also CANR 11; CA 25-28R; DLB 40

Addams, Charles (Samuel)
1912-1988 . . . . CLC 30
See also CANR 12; CA 61-64;
obituary CA 126

Addison, Joseph 1672-1719 . . . . LC 18
See also DLB 101

Adler, C(arole) S(chwerdtfeger)
1932- . . . . CLC 35
See also CANR 19; CA 89-92; SATA 26

Adler, Renata 1938- . . . . CLC 8, 31
See also CANR 5, 22; CA 49-52

Ady, Endre 1877-1919 . . . . TCLC 11
See also CA 107

Afton, Effie 1825-1911
See Harper, Francis Ellen Watkins

Agee, James 1909-1955 . . . . TCLC 1, 19
See also CA 108; DLB 2, 26;
CDALB 1941-1968

Agnon, S(hmuel) Y(osef Halevi)
1888-1970 . . . . CLC 4, 8, 14
See also CAP 2; CA 17-18;
obituary CA 25-28R

Ai 1947- . . . . CLC 4, 14, 69
See also CAAS 13; CA 85-88

Author Index

Becker, Walter 1950- . . . . CLC 26

Beckett, Samuel (Barclay)
　　1906-1989 . . . . . CLC 1, 2, 3, 4, 6, 9, 10,
　　　　　　　　　　　　11, 14, 18, 29, 57, 59
　　See also WLC 1; CA 5-8R; DLB 13, 15

Beckford, William 1760-1844 . . . . NCLC 16
　　See also DLB 39

Beckham, Barry 1944-
　　See also BLC 1; CANR 26; CA 29-32R;
　　　DLB 33

Beckman, Gunnel 1910- . . . . CLC 26
　　See also CANR 15; CA 33-36R; SATA 6

Becque, Henri 1837-1899 . . . . NCLC 3

Beddoes, Thomas Lovell
　　1803-1849 . . . . NCLC 3

Beecher, Catharine Esther
　　1800-1878 . . . . NCLC 30
　　See also DLB 1

Beecher, John 1904-1980 . . . . CLC 6
　　See also CANR 8; CA 5-8R;
　　　obituary CA 105

Beer, Johann 1655-1700 . . . . LC 5

Beer, Patricia 1919?- . . . . CLC 58
　　See also CANR 13; CA 61-64; DLB 40

Beerbohm, (Sir Henry) Max(imilian)
　　1872-1956 . . . . TCLC 1, 24
　　See also CA 104; DLB 34

Begiebing, Robert J. 1946- . . . . CLC 70
　　See also CA 122

Behan, Brendan
　　1923-1964 . . . . CLC 1, 8, 11, 15
　　See also CA 73-76; DLB 13

Behn, Aphra 1640?-1689 . . . . LC 1
　　See also WLC 1; DLB 39, 80

Behrman, S(amuel) N(athaniel)
　　1893-1973 . . . . CLC 40
　　See also CAP 1; CA 15-16;
　　　obituary CA 45-48; DLB 7, 44

Beiswanger, George Edwin 1931-
　　See Starbuck, George (Edwin)

Belasco, David 1853-1931 . . . . TCLC 3
　　See also CA 104; DLB 7

Belcheva, Elisaveta 1893-
　　See Bagryana, Elisaveta

Belinski, Vissarion Grigoryevich
　　1811-1848 . . . . NCLC 5

Belitt, Ben 1911- . . . . CLC 22
　　See also CAAS 4; CANR 7; CA 13-16R;
　　　DLB 5

Bell, Acton 1820-1849
　　See Bronte, Anne

Bell, Currer 1816-1855
　　See Bronte, Charlotte

Bell, James Madison 1826-1902 . . . TCLC 43
　　See also BLC 1; CA 122, 124; DLB 50

Bell, Madison Smartt 1957- . . . . CLC 41
　　See also CA 111

Bell, Marvin (Hartley) 1937- . . . . . CLC 8, 31
　　See also CA 21-24R; DLB 5

Bellamy, Edward 1850-1898 . . . . . . NCLC 4
　　See also DLB 12

Belloc, (Joseph) Hilaire (Pierre Sebastien
　　Rene Swanton)
　　1870-1953 . . . . TCLC 7, 18
　　See also YABC 1; CA 106; DLB 19

Bellow, Saul
　　1915- . . . . . CLC 1, 2, 3, 6, 8, 10, 13, 15,
　　　　　　　　　　　　　　25, 33, 34, 63
　　See also WLC 1; CA 5-8R; CABS 1;
　　　DLB 2, 28; DLB-Y 82; DLB-DS 3;
　　　CDALB 1941-1968

Belser, Reimond Karel Maria de 1929-
　　See Ruyslinck, Ward

Bely, Andrey 1880-1934 . . . . TCLC 7
　　See also CA 104

Benary-Isbert, Margot 1889-1979 . . . CLC 12
　　See also CLR 12; CANR 4; CA 5-8R;
　　　obituary CA 89-92; SATA 2;
　　　obituary SATA 21

Benavente (y Martinez), Jacinto
　　1866-1954 . . . . TCLC 3
　　See also CA 106

Benchley, Peter (Bradford)
　　1940- . . . . CLC 4, 8
　　See also CANR 12; CA 17-20R; SATA 3

Benchley, Robert 1889-1945 . . . . . . TCLC 1
　　See also CA 105; DLB 11

Benedikt, Michael 1935- . . . . CLC 4, 14
　　See also CANR 7; CA 13-16R; DLB 5

Benet, Juan 1927- . . . . CLC 28

Benet, Stephen Vincent
　　1898-1943 . . . . TCLC 7
　　See also YABC 1; CA 104; DLB 4, 48

Benet, William Rose 1886-1950 . . . TCLC 28
　　See also CA 118; DLB 45

Benford, Gregory (Albert) 1941- . . . CLC 52
　　See also CANR 12, 24; CA 69-72;
　　　DLB-Y 82

Benjamin, Walter 1892-1940 . . . . . . TCLC 39

Benn, Gottfried 1886-1956 . . . . TCLC 3
　　See also CA 106; DLB 56

Bennett, Alan 1934- . . . . CLC 45
　　See also CA 103

Bennett, (Enoch) Arnold
　　1867-1931 . . . . TCLC 5, 20
　　See also CA 106; DLB 10, 34

Bennett, George Harold 1930-
　　See Bennett, Hal
　　See also CA 97-100

Bennett, Hal 1930- . . . . CLC 5
　　See also Bennett, George Harold
　　See also DLB 33

Bennett, Jay 1912- . . . . CLC 35
　　See also CANR 11; CA 69-72; SAAS 4;
　　　SATA 27, 41

Bennett, Louise (Simone) 1919- . . . . CLC 28
　　See also Bennett-Coverly, Louise Simone
　　See also BLC 1

Bennett-Coverly, Louise Simone 1919-
　　See Bennett, Louise (Simone)
　　See also CA 97-100

Benson, E(dward) F(rederic)
　　1867-1940 . . . . TCLC 27
　　See also CA 114

Benson, Jackson J. 1930- . . . . CLC 34
　　See also CA 25-28R

Benson, Sally 1900-1972 . . . . CLC 17
　　See also CAP 1; CA 19-20;
　　　obituary CA 37-40R; SATA 1, 35;
　　　obituary SATA 27

Benson, Stella 1892-1933 . . . . TCLC 17
　　See also CA 117; DLB 36

Bentley, E(dmund) C(lerihew)
　　1875-1956 . . . . TCLC 12
　　See also CA 108; DLB 70

Bentley, Eric (Russell) 1916- . . . . . . CLC 24
　　See also CANR 6; CA 5-8R

Beranger, Pierre Jean de
　　1780-1857 . . . . NCLC 34

Berger, John (Peter) 1926- . . . . . . CLC 2, 19
　　See also CA 81-84; DLB 14

Berger, Melvin (H.) 1927- . . . . CLC 12
　　See also CANR 4; CA 5-8R; SAAS 2;
　　　SATA 5

Berger, Thomas (Louis)
　　1924- . . . . CLC 3, 5, 8, 11, 18, 38
　　See also CANR 5; CA 1-4R; DLB 2;
　　　DLB-Y 80

Bergman, (Ernst) Ingmar 1918- . . . . CLC 16
　　See also CA 81-84

Bergson, Henri 1859-1941 . . . . TCLC 32

Bergstein, Eleanor 1938- . . . . CLC 4
　　See also CANR 5; CA 53-56

Berkoff, Steven 1937- . . . . CLC 56
　　See also CA 104

Bermant, Chaim 1929- . . . . CLC 40
　　See also CANR 6; CA 57-60

Bernanos, (Paul Louis) Georges
　　1888-1948 . . . . TCLC 3
　　See also CA 104; DLB 72

Bernard, April 19??- . . . . CLC 59

Bernhard, Thomas
　　1931-1989 . . . . CLC 3, 32, 61
　　See also CA 85-88,; obituary CA 127;
　　　DLB 85

Berriault, Gina 1926- . . . . CLC 54
　　See also CA 116

Berrigan, Daniel J. 1921- . . . . CLC 4
　　See also CAAS 1; CANR 11; CA 33-36R;
　　　DLB 5

Berrigan, Edmund Joseph Michael, Jr.
　　1934-1983
　　See Berrigan, Ted
　　See also CANR 14; CA 61-64;
　　　obituary CA 110

Berrigan, Ted 1934-1983 . . . . CLC 37
　　See also Berrigan, Edmund Joseph Michael,
　　　Jr.
　　See also DLB 5

Berry, Chuck 1926- . . . . CLC 17

Berry, Wendell (Erdman)
　　1934- . . . . CLC 4, 6, 8, 27, 46
　　See also CA 73-76; DLB 5, 6

Berryman, John
　　1914-1972 . . . . . CLC 1, 2, 3, 4, 6, 8, 10,
　　　　　　　　　　　　　　13, 25, 62
　　See also CAP 1; CA 15-16;
　　　obituary CA 33-36R; CABS 2; DLB 48;
　　　CDALB 1941-1968

Bertolucci, Bernardo 1940- . . . . CLC 16
　　See also CA 106

Bertrand, Aloysius 1807-1841 .... **NCLC 31**

Bertran de Born c. 1140-1215 ..... **CMLC 5**

Besant, Annie (Wood) 1847-1933 ... **TCLC 9**
See also CA 105

Bessie, Alvah 1904-1985 .... **CLC 23**
See also CANR 2; CA 5-8R;
  obituary CA 116; DLB 26

Beti, Mongo 1932- .... **CLC 27**
See also Beyidi, Alexandre
See also BLC 1

Betjeman, (Sir) John
  1906-1984 .... **CLC 2, 6, 10, 34, 43**
See also CA 9-12R; obituary CA 112;
  DLB 20; DLB-Y 84

Betti, Ugo 1892-1953 .... **TCLC 5**
See also CA 104

Betts, Doris (Waugh) 1932-.... **CLC 3, 6, 28**
See also CANR 9; CA 13-16R; DLB-Y 82

Bialik, Chaim Nachman
  1873-1934 .... **TCLC 25**

Bidart, Frank 19??-............. **CLC 33**

Bienek, Horst 1930- .... **CLC 7, 11**
See also CA 73-76; DLB 75

Bierce, Ambrose (Gwinett)
  1842-1914? ...... **TCLC 1, 7, 44; SSC 9**
See also WLC 1; CA 104; DLB 11, 12, 23,
  71, 74; CDALB 1865-1917

Billington, Rachel 1942-.......... **CLC 43**
See also CA 33-36R

Binyon, T(imothy) J(ohn) 1936- .... **CLC 34**
See also CA 111

Bioy Casares, Adolfo 1914-.... **CLC 4, 8, 13**
See also CANR 19; CA 29-32R

Birch, Allison 1974?- .... **CLC 65**

Bird, Robert Montgomery
  1806-1854 .... **NCLC 1**

Birdwell, Cleo 1936-
See DeLillo, Don

Birney (Alfred) Earle
  1904- .... **CLC 1, 4, 6, 11**
See also CANR 5, 20; CA 1-4R

Bishop, Elizabeth
  1911-1979 ..... **CLC 1, 4, 9, 13, 15, 32;
                                PC 3**
See also CANR 26; CA 7-8R;
  obituary CA 89-92; CABS 2;
  obituary SATA 24; DLB 5

Bishop, John 1935-............... **CLC 10**
See also CA 105

Bissett, Bill 1939-................ **CLC 18**
See also CANR 15; CA 69-72; DLB 53

Bitov, Andrei (Georgievich) 1937-... **CLC 57**

Biyidi, Alexandre 1932-
See Beti, Mongo
See also CA 114, 124

Bjornson, Bjornstjerne (Martinius)
  1832-1910 .... **TCLC 7, 37**
See also CA 104

Blackburn, Paul 1926-1971 ...... **CLC 9, 43**
See also CA 81-84; obituary CA 33-36R;
  DLB 16; DLB-Y 81

Black Elk 1863-1950 .... **TCLC 33**

Blackmore, R(ichard) D(oddridge)
  1825-1900 .... **TCLC 27**
See also CA 120; DLB 18

Blackmur, R(ichard) P(almer)
  1904-1965 .... **CLC 2, 24**
See also CAP 1; CA 11-12;
  obituary CA 25-28R; DLB 63

Blackwood, Algernon (Henry)
  1869-1951 .... **TCLC 5**
See also CA 105

Blackwood, Caroline 1931- .... **CLC 6, 9**
See also CA 85-88; DLB 14

Blair, Eric Arthur 1903-1950
See Orwell, George
See also CA 104; SATA 29

Blais, Marie-Claire
  1939- .... **CLC 2, 4, 6, 13, 22**
See also CAAS 4; CA 21-24R; DLB 53

Blaise, Clark 1940-............... **CLC 29**
See also CAAS 3; CANR 5; CA 53-56R;
  DLB 53

Blake, Nicholas 1904-1972
See Day Lewis, C(ecil)

Blake, William 1757-1827 .... **NCLC 13**
See also WLC 1; SATA 30

Blasco Ibanez, Vicente
  1867-1928 .... **TCLC 12**
See also CA 110

Blatty, William Peter 1928-........ **CLC 2**
See also CANR 9; CA 5-8R

Blessing, Lee 1949-............... **CLC 54**

Blish, James (Benjamin)
  1921-1975 .... **CLC 14**
See also CANR 3; CA 1-4R;
  obituary CA 57-60; DLB 8

Blixen, Karen (Christentze Dinesen)
  1885-1962
See Dinesen, Isak
See also CAP 2; CA 25-28; SATA 44

Bloch, Robert (Albert) 1917-....... **CLC 33**
See also CANR 5; CA 5-8R; SATA 12;
  DLB 44

Blok, Aleksandr (Aleksandrovich)
  1880-1921 .... **TCLC 5**
See also CA 104

Bloom, Harold 1930- .... **CLC 24, 65**
See also CA 13-16R; DLB 67

Blount, Roy (Alton), Jr. 1941- ..... **CLC 38**
See also CANR 10; CA 53-56

Bloy, Leon 1846-1917............ **TCLC 22**
See also CA 121

Blume, Judy (Sussman Kitchens)
  1938- .... **CLC 12, 30**
See also CLR 2, 15; CANR 13; CA 29-32R;
  SATA 2, 31; DLB 52

Blunden, Edmund (Charles)
  1896-1974 .... **CLC 2, 56**
See also CAP 2; CA 17-18;
  obituary CA 45-48; DLB 20

Bly, Robert (Elwood)
  1926- .... **CLC 1, 2, 5, 10, 15, 38**
See also CA 5-8R; DLB 5

Bochco, Steven 1944?- .... **CLC 35**

Bodenheim, Maxwell 1892-1954 ... **TCLC 44**
See also CA 110; DLB 9, 45

Bodker, Cecil 1927- .... **CLC 21**
See also CLR 23; CANR 13; CA 73-76;
  SATA 14

Boell, Heinrich (Theodor) 1917-1985
See Boll, Heinrich
See also CANR 24; CA 21-24R;
  obituary CA 116

Bogan, Louise 1897-1970..... **CLC 4, 39, 46**
See also CA 73-76; obituary CA 25-28R;
  DLB 45

Bogarde, Dirk 1921-.............. **CLC 19**
See also Van Den Bogarde, Derek (Jules
  Gaspard Ulric) Niven
See also DLB 14

Bogosian, Eric 1953- .... **CLC 45**

Bograd, Larry 1953-.............. **CLC 35**
See also CA 93-96; SATA 33

Bohl de Faber, Cecilia 1796-1877
See Caballero, Fernan

Boiardo, Matteo Maria 1441-1494 .... **LC 6**

Boileau-Despreaux, Nicolas
  1636-1711 .... **LC 3**

Boland, Eavan (Aisling) 1944-... **CLC 40, 67**
See also DLB 40

Boll, Heinrich (Theodor)
  1917-1985 ... **CLC 2, 3, 6, 9, 11, 15, 27,
                                39**
See also Boell, Heinrich (Theodor)
See also WLC 1; DLB 69; DLB-Y 85

Bolt, Robert (Oxton) 1924-........ **CLC 14**
See also CA 17-20R; DLB 13

Bonaventura.................... **NCLC 35**
See also DLB 90

Bond, Edward 1934-....... **CLC 4, 6, 13, 23**
See also CA 25-28R; DLB 13

Bonham, Frank 1914-............. **CLC 12**
See also CANR 4; CA 9-12R; SAAS 3;
  SATA 1, 49

Bonnefoy, Yves 1923-........ **CLC 9, 15, 58**
See also CA 85-88

Bontemps, Arna (Wendell)
  1902-1973 .... **CLC 1, 18**
See also BLC 1; CLR 6; CANR 4;
  CA 1-4R; obituary CA 41-44R; SATA 2,
  44; obituary SATA 24; DLB 48, 51

Booth, Martin 1944-.............. **CLC 13**
See also CAAS 2; CA 93-96

Booth, Philip 1925-............... **CLC 23**
See also CANR 5; CA 5-8R; DLB-Y 82

Booth, Wayne C(layson) 1921- ..... **CLC 24**
See also CAAS 5; CANR 3; CA 1-4R;
  DLB 67

Borchert, Wolfgang 1921-1947 ..... **TCLC 5**
See also CA 104; DLB 69

Borges, Jorge Luis
  1899-1986 ... **CLC 1, 2, 3, 4, 6, 8, 9, 10,
                        13, 19, 44, 48; SSC 4**
See also WLC 1; CANR 19; CA 21-24R;
  DLB-Y 86

Borowski, Tadeusz 1922-1951 ...... **TCLC 9**
See also CA 106

Borrow, George (Henry)
  1803-1881 .... **NCLC 9**
See also DLB 21, 55

Buzzati, Dino   1906-1972 .... **CLC 36**
See also obituary CA 33-36R

Byars, Betsy   1928- .... **CLC 35**
See also CLR 1, 16; CANR 18; CA 33-36R;
SAAS 1; SATA 4, 46; DLB 52

Byatt, A(ntonia) S(usan Drabble)
1936- .... **CLC 19, 65**
See also CANR 13, 33; CA 13-16R;
DLB 14

Byrne, David   1953?- .... **CLC 26**

Byrne, John Keyes   1926-
See Leonard, Hugh
See also CA 102

Byron, George Gordon (Noel), Lord Byron
1788-1824 .... **NCLC 2, 12**

Caballero, Fernan   1796-1877 ..... **NCLC 10**

Cabell, James Branch   1879-1958 ... **TCLC 6**
See also CA 105; DLB 9, 78

Cable, George Washington
1844-1925 .... **TCLC 4; SSC 4**
See also CA 104; DLB 12, 74

Cabrera Infante, G(uillermo)
1929- .... **CLC 5, 25, 45**
See also CANR 29; CA 85-88

Cade, Toni   1939-
See Bambara, Toni Cade

CAEdmon   fl. 658-680 .... **CMLC 7**

Cage, John (Milton, Jr.)   1912- ..... **CLC 41**
See also CANR 9; CA 13-16R

Cain, G.   1929-
See Cabrera Infante, G(uillermo)

Cain, James M(allahan)
1892-1977 .... **CLC 3, 11, 28**
See also CANR 8; CA 17-20R;
obituary CA 73-76

Caldwell, Erskine (Preston)
1903-1987 .... **CLC 1, 8, 14, 50, 60**
See also CAAS 1; CANR 2; CA 1-4R;
obituary CA 121; DLB 9, 86

Caldwell, (Janet Miriam) Taylor (Holland)
1900-1985 .... **CLC 2, 28, 39**
See also CANR 5; CA 5-8R;
obituary CA 116

Calhoun, John Caldwell
1782-1850 .... **NCLC 15**
See also DLB 3

Calisher, Hortense   1911- .... **CLC 2, 4, 8, 38**
See also CANR 1, 22; CA 1-4R; DLB 2

Callaghan, Morley (Edward)
1903-1990 .... **CLC 3, 14, 41, 65**
See also CANR 33; CA 9-12R;
obituary CA 132; DLB 68

Calvino, Italo
1923-1985 .... **CLC 5, 8, 11, 22, 33, 39;**
SSC 3
See also CANR 23; CA 85-88;
obituary CA 116

Cameron, Carey   1952- .... **CLC 59**

Cameron, Peter   1959- .... **CLC 44**
See also CA 125

Campana, Dino   1885-1932 .... **TCLC 20**
See also CA 117

Campbell, John W(ood), Jr.
1910-1971 .... **CLC 32**
See also CAP 2; CA 21-22;
obituary CA 29-32R; DLB 8

Campbell, Joseph   1904-1987 .... **CLC 69**
See also CANR 3, 28; CA 4R;
obituary CA 124; AAYA 3

Campbell, (John) Ramsey   1946- .... **CLC 42**
See also CANR 7; CA 57-60

Campbell, (Ignatius) Roy (Dunnachie)
1901-1957 .... **TCLC 5**
See also CA 104; DLB 20

Campbell, Thomas   1777-1844 .... **NCLC 19**

Campbell, (William) Wilfred
1861-1918 .... **TCLC 9**
See also CA 106

Camus, Albert
1913-1960 ... **CLC 1, 2, 4, 9, 11, 14, 32,**
63, 69; DC 2; SSC 9
See also CA 89-92; DLB 72

Canby, Vincent   1924- .... **CLC 13**
See also CA 81-84

Canetti, Elias   1905- .... **CLC 3, 14, 25**
See also CANR 23; CA 21-24R; DLB 85

Canin, Ethan   1960- .... **CLC 55**

Cape, Judith   1916-
See Page, P(atricia) K(athleen)

Capek, Karel
1890-1938 .... **TCLC 6, 37; DC 1**
See also CA 104

Capote, Truman
1924-1984 ..... **CLC 1, 3, 8, 13, 19, 34,**
38, 58; SSC 2
See also CANR 18; CA 5-8R;
obituary CA 113; DLB 2; DLB-Y 80, 84;
CDALB 1941-1968

Capra, Frank   1897- .... **CLC 16**
See also CA 61-64

Caputo, Philip   1941- .... **CLC 32**
See also CA 73-76

Card, Orson Scott   1951- .... **CLC 44, 47, 50**
See also CA 102

Cardenal, Ernesto   1925- .... **CLC 31**
See also CANR 2; CA 49-52

Carducci, Giosue   1835-1907 ...... **TCLC 32**

Carew, Thomas   1595?-1640 .... **LC 13**

Carey, Ernestine Gilbreth   1908- .... **CLC 17**
See also CA 5-8R; SATA 2

Carey, Peter   1943- .... **CLC 40, 55**
See also CA 123, 127

Carleton, William   1794-1869 ...... **NCLC 3**

Carlisle, Henry (Coffin)   1926- ...... **CLC 33**
See also CANR 15; CA 13-16R

Carlson, Ron(ald F.)   1947- .... **CLC 54**
See also CA 105

Carlyle, Thomas   1795-1881 ...... **NCLC 22**
See also DLB 55

Carman, (William) Bliss
1861-1929 .... **TCLC 7**
See also CA 104

Carpenter, Don(ald Richard)
1931- .... **CLC 41**
See also CANR 1; CA 45-48

Carpentier (y Valmont), Alejo
1904-1980 .... **CLC 8, 11, 38**
See also CANR 11; CA 65-68;
obituary CA 97-100

Carr, Emily   1871-1945 .... **TCLC 32**
See also DLB 68

Carr, John Dickson   1906-1977 ...... **CLC 3**
See also CANR 3; CA 49-52;
obituary CA 69-72

Carr, Virginia Spencer   1929- .... **CLC 34**
See also CA 61-64

Carrier, Roch   1937- .... **CLC 13**
See also DLB 53

Carroll, James (P.)   1943- .... **CLC 38**
See also CA 81-84

Carroll, Jim   1951- .... **CLC 35**
See also CA 45-48

Carroll, Lewis   1832-1898 .... **NCLC 2**
See also Dodgson, Charles Lutwidge
See also CLR 2; DLB 18

Carroll, Paul Vincent   1900-1968 .... **CLC 10**
See also CA 9-12R; obituary CA 25-28R;
DLB 10

Carruth, Hayden   1921- .... **CLC 4, 7, 10, 18**
See also CANR 4; CA 9-12R; SATA 47;
DLB 5

Carter, Angela (Olive)   1940- ..... **CLC 5, 41**
See also CANR 12; CA 53-56; DLB 14

Carver, Raymond
1938-1988 ... **CLC 22, 36, 53, 55; SSC 8**
See also CANR 17; CA 33-36R;
obituary CA 126; DLB-Y 84, 88

Cary, (Arthur) Joyce (Lunel)
1888-1957 .... **TCLC 1, 29**
See also CA 104; DLB 15

Casanova de Seingalt, Giovanni Jacopo
1725-1798 .... **LC 13**

Casares, Adolfo Bioy   1914-
See Bioy Casares, Adolfo

Casely-Hayford, J(oseph) E(phraim)
1866-1930 .... **TCLC 24**
See also BLC 1; CA 123

Casey, John   1880-1964
See O'Casey, Sean

Casey, John   1939- .... **CLC 59**
See also CANR 23; CA 69-72

Casey, Michael   1947- .... **CLC 2**
See also CA 65-68; DLB 5

Casey, Patrick   1902-1934
See Thurman, Wallace

Casey, Warren   1935- .... **CLC 12**
See also Jacobs, Jim and Casey, Warren
See also CA 101

Casona, Alejandro   1903-1965 ...... **CLC 49**
See also Alvarez, Alejandro Rodriguez

Cassavetes, John   1929-1991 .... **CLC 20**
See also CA 85-88, 127

Cassill, R(onald) V(erlin)   1919- ... **CLC 4, 23**
See also CAAS 1; CANR 7; CA 9-12R;
DLB 6

Cassity, (Allen) Turner   1929- .... **CLC 6, 42**
See also CANR 11; CA 17-20R

Castaneda, Carlos   1935?- .... **CLC 12**
See also CA 25-28R

Copeland, Stewart (Armstrong)
1952- .... CLC 26
See also The Police

Coppard, A(lfred) E(dgar)
1878-1957 .... TCLC 5
See also YABC 1; CA 114

Coppee, Francois   1842-1908 ...... TCLC 25

Coppola, Francis Ford   1939- .... CLC 16
See also CA 77-80; DLB 44

Corcoran, Barbara   1911- .... CLC 17
See also CAAS 2; CANR 11; CA 21-24R;
SATA 3; DLB 52

Corman, Cid   1924- .... CLC 9
See also Corman, Sidney
See also CAAS 2; DLB 5

Corman, Sidney   1924-
See Corman, Cid
See also CA 85-88

Cormier, Robert (Edmund)
1925- .... CLC 12, 30
See also CLR 12; CANR 5, 23; CA 1-4R;
SATA 10, 45; DLB 52

Corn, Alfred (Dewitt III)   1943- ..... CLC 33
See also CA 104; DLB-Y 80

Cornwell, David (John Moore)
1931- .... CLC 9, 15
See also le Carre, John
See also CANR 13; CA 5-8R

Corso, (Nunzio) Gregory   1930- ... CLC 1, 11
See also CA 5-8R; DLB 5, 16

Cortazar, Julio
1914-1984 ..... CLC 2, 3, 5, 10, 13, 15,
33, 34; SSC 7
See also CANR 12; CA 21-24R

Corvo, Baron   1860-1913
See Rolfe, Frederick (William Serafino
Austin Lewis Mary)

Cosic, Dobrica   1921- .... CLC 14
See also CA 122

Costain, Thomas B(ertram)
1885-1965 .... CLC 30
See also CA 5-8R; obituary CA 25-28R;
DLB 9

Costantini, Humberto   1924?-1987... CLC 49
See also obituary CA 122

Costello, Elvis   1955- .... CLC 21

Cotter, Joseph Seamon, Sr.
1861-1949 .... TCLC 28
See also BLC 1; CA 124; DLB 50

Couperus, Louis (Marie Anne)
1863-1923 .... TCLC 15
See also CA 115

Courtenay, Bryce   1933- .... CLC 59

Cousteau, Jacques-Yves   1910- ...... CLC 30
See also CANR 15; CA 65-68; SATA 38

Coward, (Sir) Noel (Pierce)
1899-1973 .... CLC 1, 9, 29, 51
See also CAP 2; CA 17-18;
obituary CA 41-44R; DLB 10

Cowley, Malcolm   1898-1989 .... CLC 39
See also CANR 3; CA 5-6R;
obituary CA 128; DLB 4, 48; DLB-Y 81

Cowper, William   1731-1800 .... NCLC 8

Cox, William Trevor   1928- ...... CLC 9, 14
See also Trevor, William
See also CANR 4; CA 9-12R

Cozzens, James Gould
1903-1978 .... CLC 1, 4, 11
See also CANR 19; CA 9-12R;
obituary CA 81-84; DLB 9; DLB-Y 84;
DLB-DS 2; CDALB 1941-1968

Crabbe, George   1754-1832 .... NCLC 26

Crace, Douglas   1944- .... CLC 58

Crane, (Harold) Hart
1899-1932 .... TCLC 2, 5; PC 3
See also CA 127; brief entry CA 104;
DLB 4, 48; CDALB 1917-1929

Crane, R(onald) S(almon)
1886-1967 .... CLC 27
See also CA 85-88; DLB 63

Crane, Stephen
1871-1900 ..... TCLC 11, 17, 32; SSC 7
See also YABC 2; CA 109; DLB 12, 54, 78;
CDALB 1865-1917

Craven, Margaret   1901-1980 ...... CLC 17
See also CA 103

Crawford, F(rancis) Marion
1854-1909 .... TCLC 10
See also CA 107; DLB 71

Crawford, Isabella Valancy
1850-1887 .... NCLC 12
See also DLB 92

Crayencour, Marguerite de   1903-1987
See Yourcenar, Marguerite

Creasey, John   1908-1973 .... CLC 11
See also CANR 8; CA 5-8R;
obituary CA 41-44R; DLB 77

Crebillon, Claude Prosper Jolyot de (fils)
1707-1777 .... LC 1

Creeley, Robert (White)
1926- .... CLC 1, 2, 4, 8, 11, 15, 36
See also CANR 23; CA 1-4R; DLB 5, 16

Crews, Harry (Eugene)
1935- .... CLC 6, 23, 49
See also CANR 20; CA 25-28R; DLB 6

Crichton, (John) Michael
1942- .... CLC 2, 6, 54
See also CANR 13; CA 25-28R; SATA 9;
DLB-Y 81

Crispin, Edmund   1921-1978........ CLC 22
See also Montgomery, Robert Bruce
See also DLB 87

Cristofer, Michael   1946- .... CLC 28
See also CA 110; DLB 7

Croce, Benedetto   1866-1952 ...... TCLC 37
See also CA 120

Crockett, David (Davy)
1786-1836 .... NCLC 8
See also DLB 3, 11

Croker, John Wilson   1780-1857 .. NCLC 10

Cronin, A(rchibald) J(oseph)
1896-1981 .... CLC 32
See also CANR 5; CA 1-4R;
obituary CA 102; obituary SATA 25, 47

Cross, Amanda   1926-
See Heilbrun, Carolyn G(old)

Crothers, Rachel   1878-1953....... TCLC 19
See also CA 113; DLB 7

Crowley, Aleister   1875-1947 .... TCLC 7
See also CA 104

Crowley, John   1942-
See also CA 61-64; DLB-Y 82

Crumb, Robert   1943- .... CLC 17
See also CA 106

Cryer, Gretchen   1936?- .... CLC 21
See also CA 114, 123

Csath, Geza   1887-1919........... TCLC 13
See also CA 111

Cudlip, David   1933- .... CLC 34

Cullen, Countee   1903-1946 ..... TCLC 4, 37
See also BLC 1; CA 108, 124; SATA 18;
DLB 4, 48, 51; CDALB 1917-1929

Cummings, E(dward) E(stlin)
1894-1962 .... CLC 1, 3, 8, 12, 15, 68
See also CANR 31; CA 73-76; DLB 4, 48;
CDALB 1929-1941

Cunha, Euclides (Rodrigues) da
1866-1909 .... TCLC 24
See also CA 123

Cunningham, J(ames) V(incent)
1911-1985 .... CLC 3, 31
See also CANR 1; CA 1-4R;
obituary CA 115; DLB 5

Cunningham, Julia (Woolfolk)
1916- .... CLC 12
See also CANR 4, 19; CA 9-12R; SAAS 2;
SATA 1, 26

Cunningham, Michael   1952- .... CLC 34

Currie, Ellen   19??- .... CLC 44

Dabrowska, Maria (Szumska)
1889-1965 .... CLC 15
See also CA 106

Dabydeen, David   1956?- .... CLC 34
See also CA 106

Dacey, Philip   1939- .... CLC 51
See also CANR 14; CA 37-40R

Dagerman, Stig (Halvard)
1923-1954 .... TCLC 17
See also CA 117

Dahl, Roald   1916- .... CLC 1, 6, 18
See also CLR 1, 7; CANR 6; CA 1-4R;
SATA 1, 26

Dahlberg, Edward   1900-1977... CLC 1, 7, 14
See also CA 9-12R; obituary CA 69-72;
DLB 48

Daly, Elizabeth   1878-1967......... CLC 52
See also CAP 2; CA 23-24;
obituary CA 25-28R

Daly, Maureen   1921- .... CLC 17
See also McGivern, Maureen Daly
See also SAAS 1; SATA 2

Daniken, Erich von   1935-
See Von Daniken, Erich

Dannay, Frederic   1905-1982
See Queen, Ellery
See also CANR 1; CA 1-4R;
obituary CA 107

D'Annunzio, Gabriele
1863-1938 .... TCLC 6, 40
See also CA 104

Dante (Alighieri)
See Alighieri, Dante

Danvers, Dennis 1947- .... CLC 70

Danziger, Paula 1944- .... CLC 21
See also CLR 20; CA 112, 115; SATA 30, 36

Dario, Ruben 1867-1916 .... TCLC 4
See also Sarmiento, Felix Ruben Garcia
See also CA 104

Darley, George 1795-1846 .... NCLC 2

Daryush, Elizabeth 1887-1977.... CLC 6, 19
See also CANR 3; CA 49-52; DLB 20

Daudet, (Louis Marie) Alphonse
1840-1897 .... NCLC 1

Daumal, Rene 1908-1944 .... TCLC 14
See also CA 114

Davenport, Guy (Mattison, Jr.)
1927- .... CLC 6, 14, 38
See also CANR 23; CA 33-36R

Davidson, Donald (Grady)
1893-1968 .... CLC 2, 13, 19
See also CANR 4; CA 5-8R;
obituary CA 25-28R; DLB 45

Davidson, John 1857-1909 .... TCLC 24
See also CA 118; DLB 19

Davidson, Sara 1943- .... CLC 9
See also CA 81-84

Davie, Donald (Alfred)
1922- .... CLC 5, 8, 10, 31
See also CAAS 3; CANR 1; CA 1-4R;
DLB 27

Davies, Ray(mond Douglas) 1944- .. CLC 21
See also CA 116

Davies, Rhys 1903-1978 .... CLC 23
See also CANR 4; CA 9-12R;
obituary CA 81-84

Davies, (William) Robertson
1913- .... CLC 2, 7, 13, 25, 42
See also CANR 17; CA 33-36R; DLB 68

Davies, W(illiam) H(enry)
1871-1940 .... TCLC 5
See also CA 104; DLB 19

Davis, Frank Marshall 1905-1987
See also BLC 1; CA 123, 125; DLB 51

Davis, H(arold) L(enoir)
1896-1960 .... CLC 49
See also obituary CA 89-92; DLB 9

Davis, Rebecca (Blaine) Harding
1831-1910 .... TCLC 6
See also CA 104; DLB 74

Davis, Richard Harding
1864-1916 .... TCLC 24
See also CA 114; DLB 12, 23, 78, 79

Davison, Frank Dalby 1893-1970 ... CLC 15
See also obituary CA 116

Davison, Peter 1928- .... CLC 28
See also CAAS 4; CANR 3; CA 9-12R;
DLB 5

Davys, Mary 1674-1732 .... LC 1
See also DLB 39

Dawson, Fielding 1930- .... CLC 6
See also CA 85-88

Day, Clarence (Shepard, Jr.)
1874-1935 .... TCLC 25
See also CA 108; DLB 11

Day, Thomas 1748-1789 .... LC 1
See also YABC 1; DLB 39

Day Lewis, C(ecil)
1904-1972 .... CLC 1, 6, 10
See also CAP 1; CA 15-16;
obituary CA 33-36R; DLB 15, 20

Dazai Osamu 1909-1948 .... TCLC 11
See also Tsushima Shuji

De Crayencour, Marguerite 1903-1987
See Yourcenar, Marguerite

Deer, Sandra 1940- .... CLC 45

De Ferrari, Gabriella 19??- .... CLC 65

Defoe, Daniel 1660?-1731 .... LC 1
See also SATA 22; DLB 39

De Hartog, Jan 1914- .... CLC 19
See also CANR 1; CA 1-4R

Deighton, Len 1929- .... CLC 4, 7, 22, 46
See also Deighton, Leonard Cyril
See also DLB 87

Deighton, Leonard Cyril 1929-
See Deighton, Len
See also CANR 19; CA 9-12R

De la Mare, Walter (John)
1873-1956 .... TCLC 4
See also CLR 23; CA 110; SATA 16;
DLB 19

Delaney, Shelagh 1939- .... CLC 29
See also CA 17-20R; DLB 13

Delany, Mary (Granville Pendarves)
1700-1788 .... LC 12

Delany, Samuel R(ay, Jr.)
1942- .... CLC 8, 14, 38
See also BLC 1; CANR 27; CA 81-84;
DLB 8, 33

de la Ramee, Marie Louise 1839-1908
See Ouida
See also SATA 20

De la Roche, Mazo 1885-1961 ..... CLC 14
See also CA 85-88; DLB 68

Delbanco, Nicholas (Franklin)
1942- .... CLC 6, 13
See also CAAS 2; CA 17-20R; DLB 6

del Castillo, Michel 1933- .... CLC 38
See also CA 109

Deledda, Grazia 1871-1936 ...... TCLC 23
See also CA 123

Delibes (Setien), Miguel 1920- ... CLC 8, 18
See also CANR 1; CA 45-48

DeLillo, Don
1936- .... CLC 8, 10, 13, 27, 39, 54
See also CANR 21; CA 81-84; DLB 6

De Lisser, H(erbert) G(eorge)
1878-1944 .... TCLC 12
See also CA 109

Deloria, Vine (Victor), Jr. 1933- .... CLC 21
See also CANR 5, 20; CA 53-56; SATA 21

Del Vecchio, John M(ichael)
1947- .... CLC 29
See also CA 110

de Man, Paul 1919-1983 .... CLC 55
See also obituary CA 111; DLB 67

De Marinis, Rick 1934- .... CLC 54
See also CANR 9, 25; CA 57-60

Demby, William 1922- .... CLC 53
See also BLC 1; CA 81-84; DLB 33

Denby, Edwin (Orr) 1903-1983 ..... CLC 48
See also obituary CA 110

Dennis, John 1657-1734 .... LC 11

Dennis, Nigel (Forbes) 1912- .... CLC 8
See also CA 25-28R; obituary CA 129;
DLB 13, 15

De Palma, Brian 1940- .... CLC 20
See also CA 109

De Quincey, Thomas 1785-1859 ... NCLC 4

Deren, Eleanora 1908-1961
See Deren, Maya
See also obituary CA 111

Deren, Maya 1908-1961 .... CLC 16
See also Deren, Eleanora

Derleth, August (William)
1909-1971 .... CLC 31
See also CANR 4; CA 1-4R;
obituary CA 29-32R; SATA 5; DLB 9

Derrida, Jacques 1930- .... CLC 24
See also CA 124, 127

Desai, Anita 1937- .... CLC 19, 37
See also CA 81-84

De Saint-Luc, Jean 1909-1981
See Glassco, John

De Sica, Vittorio 1902-1974 .... CLC 20
See also obituary CA 117

Desnos, Robert 1900-1945 .... TCLC 22
See also CA 121

Destouches, Louis-Ferdinand-Auguste
1894-1961
See Celine, Louis-Ferdinand
See also CA 85-88

Deutsch, Babette 1895-1982 .... CLC 18
See also CANR 4; CA 1-4R;
obituary CA 108; SATA 1;
obituary SATA 33; DLB 45

Devenant, William 1606-1649 .... LC 13

Devkota, Laxmiprasad
1909-1959 .... TCLC 23
See also CA 123

DeVoto, Bernard (Augustine)
1897-1955 .... TCLC 29
See also CA 113; DLB 9

De Vries, Peter
1910- .... CLC 1, 2, 3, 7, 10, 28, 46
See also CA 17-20R; DLB 6; DLB-Y 82

Dexter, Pete 1943- .... CLC 34, 55
See also CA 127

Diamano, Silmang 1906-
See Senghor, Leopold Sedar

Diamond, Neil (Leslie) 1941- .... CLC 30
See also CA 108

Dick, Philip K(indred)
1928-1982 .... CLC 10, 30
See also CANR 2, 16; CA 49-52;
obituary CA 106; DLB 8

Dickens, Charles
1812-1870 .... NCLC 3, 8, 18, 26
See also SATA 15; DLB 21, 55, 70

Author Index

Dickey, James (Lafayette)
    1923- .... CLC 1, 2, 4, 7, 10, 15, 47
    See also CANR 10; CA 9-12R; CABS 2;
    DLB 5; DLB-Y 82; DLB-DS 7

Dickey, William 1928- .... CLC 3, 28
    See also CANR 24; CA 9-12R; DLB 5

Dickinson, Charles 1952- .... CLC 49

Dickinson, Emily (Elizabeth)
    1830-1886 .... NCLC 21; PC 1
    See also SATA 29; DLB 1;
    CDALB 1865-1917

Dickinson, Peter (Malcolm de Brissac)
    1927- .... CLC 12, 35
    See also CA 41-44R; SATA 5; DLB 87

Didion, Joan 1934- ..... CLC 1, 3, 8, 14, 32
    See also CANR 14; CA 5-8R; DLB 2;
    DLB-Y 81, 86; CDALB 1968-1987

Dillard, Annie 1945- .... CLC 9, 60
    See also CANR 3; CA 49-52; SATA 10;
    DLB-Y 80

Dillard, R(ichard) H(enry) W(ilde)
    1937- .... CLC 5
    See also CAAS 7; CANR 10; CA 21-24R;
    DLB 5

Dillon, Eilis 1920- .... CLC 17
    See also CLR 26; CAAS 3; CANR 4;
    CA 9-12R; SATA 2

Dinesen, Isak
    1885-1962 .... CLC 10, 29; SSC 7
    See also Blixen, Karen (Christentze
    Dinesen)
    See also CANR 22

Ding Ling 1904-1986 .... CLC 68

Disch, Thomas M(ichael) 1940- ... CLC 7, 36
    See also CAAS 4; CANR 17; CA 21-24R;
    SATA 54; DLB 8

Disraeli, Benjamin 1804-1881 ..... NCLC 2
    See also DLB 21, 55

Dixon, Paige 1911-
    See Corcoran, Barbara

Dixon, Stephen 1936- .... CLC 52
    See also CANR 17; CA 89-92

Doblin, Alfred 1878-1957 .... TCLC 13
    See also Doeblin, Alfred

Dobrolyubov, Nikolai Alexandrovich
    1836-1861 .... NCLC 5

Dobyns, Stephen 1941- .... CLC 37
    See also CANR 2, 18; CA 45-48

Doctorow, E(dgar) L(aurence)
    1931- ..... CLC 6, 11, 15, 18, 37, 44, 65
    See also CANR 2, 33; CA 45-48; DLB 2,
    28; DLB-Y 80; CDALB 1968-1987

Dodgson, Charles Lutwidge 1832-1898
    See Carroll, Lewis
    See also YABC 2

Dodson, Owen 1914-1983
    See also BLC 1; CANR 24; CA 65-68;
    obituary CA 110; DLB 76

Doeblin, Alfred 1878-1957 .... TCLC 13
    See also CA 110; DLB 66

Doerr, Harriet 1910- .... CLC 34
    See also CA 117, 122

Domini, Rey 1934-
    See Lorde, Audre

Donaldson, Stephen R. 1947- .... CLC 46
    See also CANR 13; CA 89-92

Donleavy, J(ames) P(atrick)
    1926- .... CLC 1, 4, 6, 10, 45
    See also CANR 24; CA 9-12R; DLB 6

Donnadieu, Marguerite 1914-
    See Duras, Marguerite

Donne, John 1572?-1631 ...... LC 10; PC 1

Donnell, David 1939?- .... CLC 34

Donoso, Jose 1924- .... CLC 4, 8, 11, 32
    See also CA 81-84

Donovan, John 1928- .... CLC 35
    See also CLR 3; CA 97-100; SATA 29

Doolittle, Hilda 1886-1961
    See H(ilda) D(oolittle)
    See also CA 97-100; DLB 4, 45

Dorfman, Ariel 1942- .... CLC 48
    See also CA 124

Dorn, Ed(ward Merton) 1929- ... CLC 10, 18
    See also CA 93-96; DLB 5

Dos Passos, John (Roderigo)
    1896-1970 ... CLC 1, 4, 8, 11, 15, 25, 34
    See also CANR 3; CA 1-4R;
    obituary CA 29-32R; DLB 4, 9;
    DLB-DS 1

Dostoevsky, Fyodor
    1821-1881 .... NCLC 2, 7, 21, 33; SSC 2

Doughty, Charles (Montagu)
    1843-1926 .... TCLC 27
    See also CA 115; DLB 19, 57

Douglas, George 1869-1902 ...... TCLC 28

Douglas, Keith 1920-1944 .... TCLC 40
    See also DLB 27

Douglass, Frederick 1817?-1895 ... NCLC 7
    See also BLC 1; SATA 29; DLB 1, 43, 50,
    79; CDALB 1640-1865

Dourado, (Waldomiro Freitas) Autran
    1926- .... CLC 23, 60
    See also CA 25-28R

Dove, Rita 1952- .... CLC 50
    See also CA 109

Dowson, Ernest (Christopher)
    1867-1900 .... TCLC 4
    See also CA 105; DLB 19

Doyle, (Sir) Arthur Conan
    1859-1930 .... TCLC 7, 26
    See also CA 104, 122; SATA 24; DLB 18,
    70

Dr. A 1933-
    See Silverstein, Alvin and Virginia B(arbara
    Opshelor) Silverstein

Drabble, Margaret
    1939- .... CLC 2, 3, 5, 8, 10, 22, 53
    See also CANR 18; CA 13-16R; SATA 48;
    DLB 14

Drayton, Michael 1563-1631 .... LC 8

Dreiser, Theodore (Herman Albert)
    1871-1945 .... TCLC 10, 18, 35
    See also CA 106; SATA 48; DLB 9, 12;
    DLB-DS 1; CDALB 1865-1917

Drexler, Rosalyn 1926- .... CLC 2, 6
    See also CA 81-84

Dreyer, Carl Theodor 1889-1968 .... CLC 16
    See also obituary CA 116

Drieu La Rochelle, Pierre
    1893-1945 .... TCLC 21
    See also CA 117; DLB 72

Droste-Hulshoff, Annette Freiin von
    1797-1848 .... NCLC 3

Drummond, William Henry
    1854-1907 .... TCLC 25
    See also DLB 92

Drummond de Andrade, Carlos 1902-1987
    See Andrade, Carlos Drummond de

Drury, Allen (Stuart) 1918- .... CLC 37
    See also CANR 18; CA 57-60

Dryden, John 1631-1700 .... LC 3

Duberman, Martin 1930- .... CLC 8
    See also CANR 2; CA 1-4R

Dubie, Norman (Evans, Jr.) 1945- .. CLC 36
    See also CANR 12; CA 69-72

Du Bois, W(illiam) E(dward) B(urghardt)
    1868-1963 .... CLC 1, 2, 13, 64
    See also BLC 1; CA 85-88; SATA 42;
    DLB 47, 50, 91; CDALB 1865-1917

Dubus, Andre 1936- .... CLC 13, 36
    See also CANR 17; CA 21-24R

Ducasse, Isidore Lucien 1846-1870
    See Lautreamont, Comte de

Duclos, Charles Pinot 1704-1772 ..... LC 1

Dudek, Louis 1918- .... CLC 11, 19
    See also CANR 1; CA 45-48; DLB 88

Dudevant, Amandine Aurore Lucile Dupin
    1804-1876
    See Sand, George

Duerrenmatt, Friedrich
    1921- .... CLC 1, 4, 8, 11, 15, 43
    See also CA 17-20R; DLB 69

Duffy, Bruce 19??- .... CLC 50

Duffy, Maureen 1933- .... CLC 37
    See also CA 25-28R; DLB 14

Dugan, Alan 1923- .... CLC 2, 6
    See also CA 81-84; DLB 5

Duhamel, Georges 1884-1966 .... CLC 8
    See also CA 81-84; obituary CA 25-28R;
    DLB 65

Dujardin, Edouard (Emile Louis)
    1861-1949 .... TCLC 13
    See also CA 109

Duke, Raoul 1939-
    See Thompson, Hunter S(tockton)

Dumas, Alexandre (Davy de la Pailleterie)
    (pere) 1802-1870 .... NCLC 11
    See also SATA 18

Dumas, Alexandre (fils)
    1824-1895 .... NCLC 9; DC 1

Dumas, Henry 1918-1968 .... CLC 62

Dumas, Henry (L.) 1934-1968 .... CLC 6
    See also CA 85-88; DLB 41

Du Maurier, Daphne 1907- ... CLC 6, 11, 59
    See also CANR 6; CA 5-8R;
    obituary CA 128; SATA 27

Dunbar, Paul Laurence
    1872-1906 .... TCLC 2, 12; SSC 8
    See also BLC 1; CA 124;
    brief entry CA 104; SATA 34; DLB 50,
    54, 78; CDALB 1865-1917

Freeman, Judith 1946-............ CLC 55

Freeman, Mary (Eleanor) Wilkins
    1852-1930 .... TCLC 9; SSC 1
    See also CA 106; DLB 12, 78

Freeman, R(ichard) Austin
    1862-1943 .... TCLC 21
    See also CA 113; DLB 70

French, Marilyn 1929-...... CLC 10, 18, 60
    See also CANR 3; CA 69-72

Freneau, Philip Morin 1752-1832.. NCLC 1
    See also DLB 37, 43

Friedman, B(ernard) H(arper)
    1926- .... CLC 7
    See also CANR 3; CA 1-4R

Friedman, Bruce Jay 1930-.... CLC 3, 5, 56
    See also CANR 25; CA 9-12R; DLB 2, 28

Friel, Brian 1929-........... CLC 5, 42, 59
    See also CA 21-24R; DLB 13

Friis-Baastad, Babbis (Ellinor)
    1921-1970 .... CLC 12
    See also CA 17-20R; SATA 7

Frisch, Max (Rudolf)
    1911- .... CLC 3, 9, 14, 18, 32, 44
    See also CA 85-88; DLB 69

Fromentin, Eugene (Samuel Auguste)
    1820-1876 .... NCLC 10

Frost, Robert (Lee)
    1874-1963 ... CLC 1, 3, 4, 9, 10, 13, 15,
               26, 34, 44; PC 1
    See also CA 89-92; SATA 14; DLB 54;
    DLB-DS 7; CDALB 1917-1929

Fry, Christopher 1907-....... CLC 2, 10, 14
    See also CANR 9; CA 17-20R; DLB 13

Frye, (Herman) Northrop
    1912-1991 .... CLC 24, 70
    See also CANR 8; CA 5-8R;
    obituary CA 133; DLB 67, 68

Fuchs, Daniel 1909-........... CLC 8, 22
    See also CAAS 5; CA 81-84; DLB 9, 26, 28

Fuchs, Daniel 1934-.............. CLC 34
    See also CANR 14; CA 37-40R

Fuentes, Carlos
    1928- ...... CLC 3, 8, 10, 13, 22, 41, 60
    See also CANR 10; CA 69-72

Fugard, Athol 1932-... CLC 5, 9, 14, 25, 40
    See also CA 85-88

Fugard, Sheila 1932- .... CLC 48
    See also CA 125

Fuller, Charles (H., Jr.)
    1939- .... CLC 25; DC 1
    See also BLC 2; CA 108, 112; DLB 38

Fuller, John (Leopold) 1937-...... CLC 62
    See also CANR 9; CA 21-22R; DLB 40

Fuller, (Sarah) Margaret
    1810-1850 .... NCLC 5
    See also Ossoli, Sarah Margaret (Fuller
    marchesa d')
    See also DLB 1, 59, 73; CDALB 1640-1865

Fuller, Roy (Broadbent) 1912-.... CLC 4, 28
    See also CA 5-8R; DLB 15, 20

Fulton, Alice 1952-.............. CLC 52
    See also CA 116

Furabo 1644-1694
    See Basho, Matsuo

Furphy, Joseph 1843-1912....... TCLC 25

Futabatei Shimei 1864-1909...... TCLC 44

Futrelle, Jacques 1875-1912 ..... TCLC 19
    See also CA 113

Gaboriau, Emile 1835-1873...... NCLC 14

Gadda, Carlo Emilio 1893-1973 .... CLC 11
    See also CA 89-92

Gaddis, William
    1922- .... CLC 1, 3, 6, 8, 10, 19, 43
    See also CAAS 4; CANR 21; CA 17-20R;
    DLB 2

Gaines, Ernest J. 1933-...... CLC 3, 11, 18
    See also BLC 2; CANR 6, 24; CA 9-12R;
    DLB 2, 33; DLB-Y 80;
    CDALB 1968-1988

Gaitskill, Mary 1954-............. CLC 69
    See also CA 128

Gale, Zona 1874-1938 .... TCLC 7
    See also CA 105; DLB 9, 78

Gallagher, Tess 1943-.......... CLC 18, 63
    See also CA 106

Gallant, Mavis
    1922- .... CLC 7, 18, 38; SSC 5
    See also CA 69-72; DLB 53

Gallant, Roy A(rthur) 1924- .... CLC 17
    See also CANR 4; CA 5-8R; SATA 4

Gallico, Paul (William) 1897-1976 ... CLC 2
    See also CA 5-8R; obituary CA 69-72;
    SATA 13; DLB 9

Galsworthy, John 1867-1933...... TCLC 1
    See also CA 104; DLB 10, 34

Galt, John 1779-1839........... NCLC 1

Galvin, James 1951-.............. CLC 38
    See also CANR 26; CA 108

Gamboa, Frederico 1864-1939..... TCLC 36

Gann, Ernest K(ellogg) 1910- ...... CLC 23
    See also CANR 1; CA 1-4R

Garcia Lorca, Federico
    1898-1936 ..... TCLC 1, 7; DC 2; PC 3
    See also CA 131; brief entry CA 104;
    DLB 108

Garcia Marquez, Gabriel (Jose)
    1928- ... CLC 2, 3, 8, 10, 15, 27, 47, 55,
               68; SSC 8
    See also CANR 10, 28; CA 33-36R;
    AAYA 3

Gardam, Jane 1928-.............. CLC 43
    See also CLR 12; CANR 2, 18; CA 49-52;
    SATA 28, 39; DLB 14

Gardner, Herb 1934- .... CLC 44

Gardner, John (Champlin, Jr.)
    1933-1982 .... CLC 2, 3, 5, 7, 8, 10, 18,
               28, 34; SSC 7
    See also CA 65-68; obituary CA 107;
    obituary SATA 31, 40; DLB 2; DLB-Y 82

Gardner, John (Edmund) 1926-..... CLC 30
    See also CANR 15; CA 103

Gardons, S. S. 1926-
    See Snodgrass, W(illiam) D(e Witt)

Garfield, Leon 1921-.............. CLC 12
    See also CA 17-20R; SATA 1, 32

Garland, (Hannibal) Hamlin
    1860-1940 .... TCLC 3
    See also CA 104; DLB 12, 71, 78

Garneau, Hector (de) Saint Denys
    1912-1943 .... TCLC 13
    See also CA 111; DLB 88

Garner, Alan 1935-............... CLC 17
    See also CLR 20; CANR 15; CA 73-76;
    SATA 18

Garner, Hugh 1913-1979 .... CLC 13
    See also CA 69-72; DLB 68

Garnett, David 1892-1981 .... CLC 3
    See also CANR 17; CA 5-8R;
    obituary CA 103; DLB 34

Garrett, George (Palmer, Jr.)
    1929- .... CLC 3, 11, 51
    See also CAAS 5; CANR 1; CA 1-4R;
    DLB 2, 5; DLB-Y 83

Garrick, David 1717-1779 .... LC 15
    See also DLB 84

Garrigue, Jean 1914-1972 .... CLC 2, 8
    See also CANR 20; CA 5-8R;
    obituary CA 37-40R

Garvey, Marcus 1887-1940 .... TCLC 41
    See also BLC 2; CA 124; brief entry CA 120

Gary, Romain 1914-1980.......... CLC 25
    See also Kacew, Romain

Gascar, Pierre 1916-.............. CLC 11
    See also Fournier, Pierre

Gascoyne, David (Emery) 1916- .... CLC 45
    See also CANR 10; CA 65-68; DLB 20

Gaskell, Elizabeth Cleghorn
    1810-1865 .... NCLC 5
    See also DLB 21

Gass, William H(oward)
    1924- .... CLC 1, 2, 8, 11, 15, 39
    See also CA 17-20R; DLB 2

Gates, Henry Louis, Jr. 1950-...... CLC 65
    See also CANR 25; CA 109; DLB 67

Gautier, Theophile 1811-1872 ..... NCLC 1

Gaye, Marvin (Pentz) 1939-1984 ... CLC 26
    See also obituary CA 112

Gebler, Carlo (Ernest) 1954-....... CLC 39
    See also CA 119

Gee, Maggie 19??- .... CLC 57

Gee, Maurice (Gough) 1931-....... CLC 29
    See also CA 97-100; SATA 46

Gelbart, Larry 1923?-........... CLC 21, 61
    See also CA 73-76

Gelber, Jack 1932-........ CLC 1, 6, 14, 60
    See also CANR 2; CA 1-4R; DLB 7

Gellhorn, Martha (Ellis) 1908- .. CLC 14, 60
    See also CA 77-80; DLB-Y 82

Genet, Jean
    1910-1986 ... CLC 1, 2, 5, 10, 14, 44, 46
    See also CANR 18; CA 13-16R; DLB 72;
    DLB-Y 86

Gent, Peter 1942-................. CLC 29
    See also CA 89-92; DLB 72; DLB-Y 82

George, Jean Craighead 1919-...... CLC 35
    See also CLR 1; CA 5-8R; SATA 2;
    DLB 52

George, Stefan (Anton)
    1868-1933 .... TCLC 2, 14
    See also CA 104

Gerhardi, William (Alexander) 1895-1977
    See Gerhardie, William (Alexander)

Gerhardie, William (Alexander)
1895-1977 .... CLC 5
See also CANR 18; CA 25-28R;
obituary CA 73-76; DLB 36

Gerstler, Amy 1956-.............. CLC 70

Gertler, T(rudy) 1946?- .... CLC 34
See also CA 116

Gessner, Friedrike Victoria 1910-1980
See Adamson, Joy(-Friederike Victoria)

Ghelderode, Michel de
1898-1962 .... CLC 6, 11
See also CA 85-88

Ghiselin, Brewster 1903- .... CLC 23
See also CANR 13; CA 13-16R

Ghose, Zulfikar 1935-............. CLC 42
See also CA 65-68

Ghosh, Amitav 1943- .... CLC 44

Giacosa, Giuseppe 1847-1906 ...... TCLC 7
See also CA 104

Gibbon, Lewis Grassic 1901-1935... TCLC 4
See also Mitchell, James Leslie

Gibbons, Kaye 1960- .... CLC 50

Gibran, (Gibran) Kahlil
1883-1931 .... TCLC 1, 9
See also CA 104

Gibson, William 1914-............ CLC 23
See also CANR 9; CA 9-12R; DLB 7

Gibson, William 1948-........ CLC 39, 63
See also CA 126

Gide, Andre (Paul Guillaume)
1869-1951 .... TCLC 5, 12, 36
See also CA 104, 124; DLB 65

Gifford, Barry (Colby) 1946-...... CLC 34
See also CANR 9; CA 65-68

Gilbert, (Sir) W(illiam) S(chwenck)
1836-1911 .... TCLC 3
See also CA 104; SATA 36

Gilbreth, Ernestine 1908-
See Carey, Ernestine Gilbreth

Gilbreth, Frank B(unker), Jr.
1911-....................... CLC 17
See also CA 9-12R; SATA 2

Gilchrist, Ellen 1935-.......... CLC 34, 48
See also CA 113, 116

Giles, Molly 1942- .... CLC 39
See also CA 126

Gilliam, Terry (Vance) 1940-
See Monty Python
See also CA 108, 113

Gilliatt, Penelope (Ann Douglass)
1932-.............. CLC 2, 10, 13, 53
See also CA 13-16R; DLB 14

Gilman, Charlotte (Anna) Perkins (Stetson)
1860-1935 .... TCLC 9, 37
See also CA 106

Gilmour, David 1944-
See Pink Floyd

Gilpin, William 1724-1804....... NCLC 30

Gilroy, Frank D(aniel) 1925-........ CLC 2
See also CA 81-84; DLB 7

Ginsberg, Allen
1926- ..... CLC 1, 2, 3, 4, 6, 13, 36, 69;
PC 4
See also CANR 2; CA 1-4R; DLB 5, 16;
CDALB 1941-1968

Ginzburg, Natalia
1916-1991 .... CLC 5, 11, 54, 70
See also CANR 33; CA 85-88

Giono, Jean 1895-1970......... CLC 4, 11
See also CANR 2; CA 45-48;
obituary CA 29-32R; DLB 72

Giovanni, Nikki 1943- ..... CLC 2, 4, 19, 64
See also BLC 2; CLR 6; CAAS 6;
CANR 18; CA 29-32R; SATA 24;
DLB 5, 41

Giovene, Andrea 1904-............ CLC 7
See also CA 85-88

Gippius, Zinaida (Nikolayevna) 1869-1945
See Hippius, Zinaida
See also CA 106

Giraudoux, (Hippolyte) Jean
1882-1944 .... TCLC 2, 7
See also CA 104; DLB 65

Gironella, Jose Maria 1917- .... CLC 11
See also CA 101

Gissing, George (Robert)
1857-1903 .... TCLC 3, 24
See also CA 105; DLB 18

Gladkov, Fyodor (Vasilyevich)
1883-1958 .... TCLC 27

Glanville, Brian (Lester) 1931- ...... CLC 6
See also CANR 3; CA 5-8R; SATA 42;
DLB 15

Glasgow, Ellen (Anderson Gholson)
1873?-1945................. TCLC 2, 7
See also CA 104; DLB 9, 12

Glassco, John 1909-1981 .... CLC 9
See also CANR 15; CA 13-16R;
obituary CA 102; DLB 68

Glasser, Ronald J. 1940?- .... CLC 37

Glendinning, Victoria 1937-........ CLC 50
See also CA 120

Glissant, Edouard 1928-........ CLC 10, 68

Gloag, Julian 1930- .... CLC 40
See also CANR 10; CA 65-68

Gluck, Louise (Elisabeth)
1943- .... CLC 7, 22, 44
See also CA 33-36R; DLB 5

Gobineau, Joseph Arthur (Comte) de
1816-1882 .... NCLC 17

Godard, Jean-Luc 1930-.......... CLC 20
See also CA 93-96

Godden, (Margaret) Rumer 1907-... CLC 53
See also CLR 20; CANR 4, 27; CA 7-8R;
SATA 3, 36

Godwin, Gail 1937-.... CLC 5, 8, 22, 31, 69
See also CANR 15; CA 29-32R; DLB 6

Godwin, William 1756-1836...... NCLC 14
See also DLB 39

Goethe, Johann Wolfgang von
1749-1832 .... NCLC 4, 22, 34
See also DLB 94

Gogarty, Oliver St. John
1878-1957 .... TCLC 15
See also CA 109; DLB 15, 19

Gogol, Nikolai (Vasilyevich)
1809-1852 ..... NCLC 5, 15, 31; DC 1;
SSC 4
See also CAAS 1, 4

Goines, Donald 1937?-1974
See also BLC 2; CA 124; obituary CA 114;
DLB 33

Gokceli, Yasar Kemal 1923-
See Kemal, Yashar

Gold, Herbert 1924-....... CLC 4, 7, 14, 42
See also CANR 17; CA 9-12R; DLB 2;
DLB-Y 81

Goldbarth, Albert 1948-......... CLC 5, 38
See also CANR 6; CA 53-56

Goldberg, Anatol 1910-1982 .... CLC 34
See also obituary CA 117

Goldemberg, Isaac 1945- .... CLC 52
See also CANR 11; CA 69-72

Golding, William (Gerald)
1911- ..... CLC 1, 2, 3, 8, 10, 17, 27, 58
See also CANR 13; CA 5-8R; DLB 15

Goldman, Emma 1869-1940....... TCLC 13
See also CA 110

Goldman, William (W.) 1931- .... CLC 1, 48
See also CA 9-12R; DLB 44

Goldmann, Lucien 1913-1970 ...... CLC 24
See also CAP 2; CA 25-28

Goldoni, Carlo 1707-1793 .... LC 4

Goldsberry, Steven 1949-......... CLC 34

Goldsmith, Oliver 1728?-1774....... LC 2
See also SATA 26; DLB 39

Gombrowicz, Witold
1904-1969 .... CLC 4, 7, 11, 49
See also CAP 2; CA 19-20;
obituary CA 25-28R

Gomez de la Serna, Ramon
1888-1963 .... CLC 9
See also obituary CA 116

Goncharov, Ivan Alexandrovich
1812-1891 .... NCLC 1

Goncourt, Edmond (Louis Antoine Huot) de
1822-1896 .... NCLC 7

Goncourt, Jules (Alfred Huot) de
1830-1870 .... NCLC 7

Gontier, Fernande 19??-........... CLC 50

Goodman, Paul 1911-1972.... CLC 1, 2, 4, 7
See also CAP 2; CA 19-20;
obituary CA 37-40R

Gordimer, Nadine
1923- .... CLC 3, 5, 7, 10, 18, 33, 51, 70
See also CANR 3, 28; CA 5-8R

Gordon, Adam Lindsay
1833-1870 .... NCLC 21

Gordon, Caroline
1895-1981 .... CLC 6, 13, 29
See also CAP 1; CA 11-12;
obituary CA 103; DLB 4, 9; DLB-Y 81

Gordon, Charles William 1860-1937
See Conner, Ralph
See also CA 109

Gordon, Mary (Catherine)
    1949- . . . . CLC 13, 22
    See also CA 102; DLB 6; DLB-Y 81

Gordon, Sol   1923-. . . . . CLC 26
    See also CANR 4; CA 53-56; SATA 11

Gordone, Charles   1925- . . . . CLC 1, 4
    See also CA 93-96; DLB 7

Gorenko, Anna Andreyevna   1889?-1966
    See Akhmatova, Anna

Gorky, Maxim   1868-1936 . . . . TCLC 8
    See also Peshkov, Alexei Maximovich

Goryan, Sirak   1908-1981
    See Saroyan, William

Gosse, Edmund (William)
    1849-1928 . . . . TCLC 28
    See also CA 117; DLB 57

Gotlieb, Phyllis (Fay Bloom)
    1926- . . . . CLC 18
    See also CANR 7; CA 13-16R; DLB 88

Gould, Lois   1938?- . . . . CLC 4, 10
    See also CA 77-80

Gourmont, Remy de   1858-1915. . . . TCLC 17
    See also CA 109

Govier, Katherine   1948-. . . . . CLC 51
    See also CANR 18; CA 101

Goyen, (Charles) William
    1915-1983 . . . . CLC 5, 8, 14, 40
    See also CANR 6; CA 5-8R;
        obituary CA 110; DLB 2; DLB-Y 83

Goytisolo, Juan   1931- . . . . CLC 5, 10, 23
    See also CA 85-88

Gozzi, (Conte) Carlo   1720-1806 . . NCLC 23

Grabbe, Christian Dietrich
    1801-1836 . . . . NCLC 2

Grace, Patricia   1937-. . . . . CLC 56

Gracian y Morales, Baltasar
    1601-1658 . . . . LC 15

Gracq, Julien   1910- . . . . CLC 11, 48
    See also Poirier, Louis
    See also DLB 83

Grade, Chaim   1910-1982 . . . . CLC 10
    See also CA 93-96; obituary CA 107

Graham, Jorie   1951-. . . . . CLC 48
    See also CA 111

Graham, R(obert) B(ontine) Cunninghame
    1852-1936 . . . . TCLC 19

Graham, W(illiam) S(ydney)
    1918-1986 . . . . CLC 29
    See also CA 73-76; obituary CA 118;
        DLB 20

Graham, Winston (Mawdsley)
    1910- . . . . CLC 23
    See also CANR 2, 22; CA 49-52;
        obituary CA 118

Granville-Barker, Harley
    1877-1946 . . . . TCLC 2
    See also CA 104

Grass, Gunter (Wilhelm)
    1927- . . CLC 1, 2, 4, 6, 11, 15, 22, 32, 49
    See also CANR 20; CA 13-16R, DLB 75

Grau, Shirley Ann   1929- . . . . CLC 4, 9
    See also CANR 22; CA 89-92; DLB 2

Graver, Elizabeth   1965-. . . . . CLC 70

Graves, Richard Perceval   1945- . . . . CLC 44
    See also CANR 9, 26; CA 65-68

Graves, Robert (von Ranke)
    1895-1985 . . . CLC 1, 2, 6, 11, 39, 44, 45
    See also CANR 5; CA 5-8R;
        obituary CA 117; SATA 45; DLB 20;
        DLB-Y 85

Gray, Alasdair   1934- . . . . CLC 41
    See also CA 123

Gray, Amlin   1946- . . . . CLC 29

Gray, Francine du Plessix   1930-. . . . CLC 22
    See also CAAS 2; CANR 11; CA 61-64

Gray, John (Henry)   1866-1934 . . . . TCLC 19
    See also CA 119

Gray, Simon (James Holliday)
    1936- . . . . CLC 9, 14, 36
    See also CAAS 3; CA 21-24R; DLB 13

Gray, Spalding   1941-. . . . . CLC 49

Gray, Thomas   1716-1771 . . . . . . LC 4; PC 2

Grayson, Richard (A.)   1951- . . . . CLC 38
    See also CANR 14; CA 85-88

Greeley, Andrew M(oran)   1928- . . . . CLC 28
    See also CAAS 7; CANR 7; CA 5-8R

Green, Hannah   1932-. . . . . CLC 3, 7, 30
    See also Greenberg, Joanne
    See also CA 73-76

Green, Henry   1905-1974 . . . . CLC 2, 13
    See also Yorke, Henry Vincent
    See also DLB 15

Green, Julien (Hartridge)   1900- . . CLC 3, 11
    See also CA 21-24R; DLB 4, 72

Green, Paul (Eliot)   1894-1981 . . . . . . CLC 25
    See also CANR 3; CA 5-8R;
        obituary CA 103; DLB 7, 9; DLB-Y 81

Greenberg, Ivan   1908-1973
    See Rahv, Philip
    See also CA 85-88

Greenberg, Joanne (Goldenberg)
    1932- . . . . CLC 3, 7, 30
    See also Green, Hannah
    See also CANR 14; CA 5-8R; SATA 25

Greenberg, Richard   1959?- . . . . CLC 57

Greene, Bette   1934- . . . . CLC 30
    See also CLR 2; CANR 4; CA 53-56;
        SATA 8

Greene, Gael   19??- . . . . CLC 8
    See also CANR 10; CA 13-16R

Greene, Graham (Henry)
    1904-1991 . . . CLC 1, 3, 6, 9, 14, 18, 27,
                                                    37, 70
    See also CANR 35; CA 13-16R;
        obituary CA 133; SATA 20; DLB 13, 15,
        77, 100; DLB-Y 85

Gregor, Arthur   1923-. . . . . CLC 9
    See also CANR 11; CA 25-28R; SATA 36

Gregory, J. Dennis   1925-
    See Williams, John A.

Gregory, Lady (Isabella Augusta Persse)
    1852-1932 . . . . TCLC 1
    See also CA 104; DLB 10

Grendon, Stephen   1909-1971
    See Derleth, August (William)

Grenville, Kate   1950-. . . . . CLC 61
    See also CA 118

Greve, Felix Paul Berthold Friedrich
    1879-1948
    See Grove, Frederick Philip
    See also CA 104

Grey, (Pearl) Zane   1872?-1939 . . . . . TCLC 6
    See also CA 104; DLB 9

Grieg, (Johan) Nordahl (Brun)
    1902-1943 . . . . TCLC 10
    See also CA 107

Grieve, C(hristopher) M(urray)   1892-1978
    See MacDiarmid, Hugh
    See also CA 5-8R; obituary CA 85-88

Griffin, Gerald   1803-1840 . . . . NCLC 7

Griffin, John Howard   1920-1980. . . . CLC 68
    See also CANR 2; CA 2R; obituary CA 101

Griffin, Peter   1942- . . . . CLC 39

Griffiths, Trevor   1935-. . . . . CLC 13, 52
    See also CA 97-100; DLB 13

Grigson, Geoffrey (Edward Harvey)
    1905-1985 . . . . CLC 7, 39
    See also CANR 20; CA 25-28R;
        obituary CA 118; DLB 27

Grillparzer, Franz   1791-1872. . . . . . NCLC 1

Grimke, Charlotte L(ottie) Forten   1837?-1914
    See Forten (Grimke), Charlotte L(ottie)
    See also CA 117, 124

Grimm, Jakob Ludwig Karl
    1785-1863 . . . . NCLC 3
    See also SATA 22; DLB 90

Grimm, Wilhelm Karl   1786-1859 . . NCLC 3
    See also SATA 22; DLB 90

Grimmelshausen, Johann Jakob Christoffel
    von   1621-1676 . . . . LC 6

Grindel, Eugene   1895-1952
    See also brief entry CA 104

Grossman, David   1954- . . . . CLC 67

Grossman, Vasily (Semenovich)
    1905-1964 . . . . CLC 41
    See also CA 124, 130

Grove, Frederick Philip
    1879-1948 . . . . TCLC 4
    See also Greve, Felix Paul Berthold
    Friedrich

Grumbach, Doris (Isaac)
    1918- . . . . CLC 13, 22, 64
    See also CAAS 2; CANR 9; CA 5-8R

Grundtvig, Nicolai Frederik Severin
    1783-1872 . . . . NCLC 1

Grunwald, Lisa   1959-. . . . . CLC 44
    See also CA 120

Guare, John   1938- . . . . CLC 8, 14, 29, 67
    See also CANR 21; CA 73-76; DLB 7

Gudjonsson, Halldor Kiljan   1902-
    See Laxness, Halldor (Kiljan)
    See also CA 103

Guest, Barbara   1920-. . . . . CLC 34
    See also CANR 11; CA 25-28R; DLB 5

Guest, Judith (Ann)   1936-. . . . . . . CLC 8, 30
    See also CANR 15; CA 77-80

Guild, Nicholas M.   1944- . . . . CLC 33
    See also CA 93-96

Guillen, Jorge   1893-1984. . . . . CLC 11
    See also CA 89-92; obituary CA 112

Guillen, Nicolas   1902-1989 . . . . CLC 48
    See also BLC 2; CA 116, 125;
    obituary CA 129

Guillen y Batista, Nicolas Cristobal
    1902-1989
    See Guillen, Nicolas

Guillevic, (Eugene)   1907- . . . . CLC 33
    See also CA 93-96

Guiney, Louise Imogen
    1861-1920 . . . . TCLC 41
    See also DLB 54

Guiraldes, Ricardo   1886-1927 . . . . . TCLC 39

Gunn, Bill   1934-1989 . . . . CLC 5
    See also Gunn, William Harrison
    See also DLB 38

Gunn, Thom(son William)
    1929- . . . . CLC 3, 6, 18, 32
    See also CANR 9; CA 17-20R; DLB 27

Gunn, William Harrison   1934-1989
    See Gunn, Bill
    See also CANR 12, 25; CA 13-16R;
    obituary CA 128

Gunnars, Kristjana   1948- . . . . CLC 69
    See also CA 113; DLB 60

Gurganus, Allan   1947- . . . . CLC 70

Gurney, A(lbert) R(amsdell), Jr.
    1930- . . . . CLC 32, 50, 54
    See also CA 77-80

Gurney, Ivor (Bertie)   1890-1937 . . . TCLC 33

Gustafson, Ralph (Barker)   1909- . . . . CLC 36
    See also CANR 8; CA 21-24R; DLB 88

Guthrie, A(lfred) B(ertram), Jr.
    1901- . . . . CLC 23
    See also CA 57-60; DLB 6

Guthrie, Woodrow Wilson   1912-1967
    See Guthrie, Woody
    See also CA 113; obituary CA 93-96

Guthrie, Woody   1912-1967 . . . . CLC 35
    See also Guthrie, Woodrow Wilson

Guy, Rosa (Cuthbert)   1928- . . . . CLC 26
    See also CLR 13; CANR 14; CA 17-20R;
    SATA 14; DLB 33

Haavikko, Paavo (Juhani)
    1931- . . . . CLC 18, 34
    See also CA 106

Hacker, Marilyn   1942- . . . . CLC 5, 9, 23
    See also CA 77-80

Haggard, (Sir) H(enry) Rider
    1856-1925 . . . . TCLC 11
    See also CA 108; SATA 16; DLB 70

Haig-Brown, Roderick L(angmere)
    1908-1976 . . . . CLC 21
    See also CANR 4; CA 5-8R;
    obituary CA 69-72; SATA 12; DLB 88

Hailey, Arthur   1920- . . . . CLC 5
    See also CANR 2; CA 1-4R; DLB-Y 82

Hailey, Elizabeth Forsythe   1938- . . . CLC 40
    See also CAAS 1; CANR 15; CA 93-96

Haines, John   1924- . . . . CLC 58
    See also CANR 13; CA 19-20R; DLB 5

Haldeman, Joe   1943- . . . . CLC 61
    See also CA 53-56; DLB 8

Haley, Alex (Palmer)   1921- . . . . . . CLC 8, 12
    See also BLC 2; CA 77-80; DLB 38

Haliburton, Thomas Chandler
    1796-1865 . . . . NCLC 15
    See also DLB 11

Hall, Donald (Andrew, Jr.)
    1928- . . . . CLC 1, 13, 37, 59
    See also CAAS 7; CANR 2; CA 5-8R;
    SATA 23; DLB 5

Hall, James Norman   1887-1951 . . . TCLC 23
    See also CA 123; SATA 21

Hall, (Marguerite) Radclyffe
    1886-1943 . . . . TCLC 12
    See also CA 110

Hall, Rodney   1935- . . . . CLC 51
    See also CA 109

Halpern, Daniel   1945- . . . . CLC 14
    See also CA 33-36R

Hamburger, Michael (Peter Leopold)
    1924- . . . . CLC 5, 14
    See also CAAS 4; CANR 2; CA 5-8R;
    DLB 27

Hamill, Pete   1935- . . . . CLC 10
    See also CANR 18; CA 25-28R

Hamilton, Edmond   1904-1977 . . . . . . CLC 1
    See also CANR 3; CA 1-4R; DLB 8

Hamilton, Gail   1911-
    See Corcoran, Barbara

Hamilton, Ian   1938- . . . . CLC 55
    See also CA 106; DLB 40

Hamilton, Mollie   1909?-
    See Kaye, M(ary) M(argaret)

Hamilton, (Anthony Walter) Patrick
    1904-1962 . . . . CLC 51
    See also obituary CA 113; DLB 10

Hamilton, Virginia (Esther)   1936- . . . CLC 26
    See also CLR 1, 11; CANR 20; CA 25-28R;
    SATA 4; DLB 33, 52

Hammett, (Samuel) Dashiell
    1894-1961 . . . . CLC 3, 5, 10, 19, 47
    See also CA 81-84; DLB-DS 6

Hammon, Jupiter   1711?-1800? . . . . NCLC 5
    See also BLC 2; DLB 31, 50, 31, 50

Hamner, Earl (Henry), Jr.   1923- . . . CLC 12
    See also CA 73-76; DLB 6

Hampton, Christopher (James)
    1946- . . . . CLC 4
    See also CA 25-28R; DLB 13

Hamsun, Knut   1859-1952 . . . . . . TCLC 2, 14
    See also Pedersen, Knut

Handke, Peter   1942- . . CLC 5, 8, 10, 15, 38
    See also CA 77-80; DLB 85

Hanley, James   1901-1985 . . . CLC 3, 5, 8, 13
    See also CA 73-76; obituary CA 117

Hannah, Barry   1942- . . . . CLC 23, 38
    See also CA 108, 110; DLB 6

Hansberry, Lorraine (Vivian)
    1930-1965 . . . . CLC 17, 62; DC 2
    See also BLC 2; CA 109;
    obituary CA 25-28R; CABS 3; DLB 7, 38;
    CDALB 1941-1968

Hansen, Joseph   1923- . . . . CLC 38
    See also CANR 16; CA 29-32R

Hansen, Martin   1909-1955 . . . . TCLC 32

Hanson, Kenneth O(stlin)   1922- . . . . CLC 13
    See also CANR 7; CA 53-56

Hardenberg, Friedrich (Leopold Freiherr) von
    1772-1801
    See Novalis

Hardwick, Elizabeth   1916- . . . . CLC 13
    See also CANR 3; CA 5-8R; DLB 6

Hardy, Thomas
    1840-1928 . . . TCLC 4, 10, 18, 32; SSC 2
    See also CA 104, 123; SATA 25; DLB 18,
    19

Hare, David   1947- . . . . CLC 29, 58
    See also CA 97-100; DLB 13

Harlan, Louis R(udolph)   1922- . . . . . CLC 34
    See also CANR 25; CA 21-24R

Harling, Robert   1951?- . . . . CLC 53

Harmon, William (Ruth)   1938- . . . . . CLC 38
    See also CANR 14; CA 33-36R

Harper, Frances Ellen Watkins
    1825-1911 . . . . TCLC 14
    See also BLC 2; CA 125;
    brief entry CA 111; DLB 50

Harper, Michael S(teven)   1938- . . CLC 7, 22
    See also CANR 24; CA 33-36R; DLB 41

Harris, Christie (Lucy Irwin)
    1907- . . . . CLC 12
    See also CANR 6; CA 5-8R; SATA 6;
    DLB 88

Harris, Frank   1856-1931 . . . . TCLC 24
    See also CAAS 1; CA 109

Harris, George Washington
    1814-1869 . . . . NCLC 23
    See also DLB 3, 11

Harris, Joel Chandler   1848-1908 . . . TCLC 2
    See also YABC 1; CA 104; DLB 11, 23, 42,
    78, 91

Harris, John (Wyndham Parkes Lucas)
    Beynon   1903-1969 . . . . CLC 19
    See also Wyndham, John
    See also CA 102; obituary CA 89-92

Harris, MacDonald   1921- . . . . CLC 9
    See also Heiney, Donald (William)

Harris, Mark   1922- . . . . CLC 19
    See also CAAS 3; CANR 2; CA 5-8R;
    DLB 2; DLB-Y 80

Harris, (Theodore) Wilson   1921- . . . . CLC 25
    See also CANR 11, 27; CA 65-68

Harrison, Harry (Max)   1925- . . . . . . CLC 42
    See also CANR 5, 21; CA 1-4R; SATA 4;
    DLB 8

Harrison, James (Thomas)   1937- . . . CLC 66
    See also Harrison, Jim
    See also CANR 8; CA 13-16R

Harrison, Jim   1937- . . . . CLC 6, 14, 33
    See also Harrison, James (Thomas)
    See also DLB-Y 82

Harrison, Kathryn   1961- . . . . CLC 70

Harrison, Tony   1937- . . . . CLC 43
    See also CA 65-68; DLB 40

Harriss, Will(ard Irvin)   1922- . . . . . . CLC 34
    See also CA 111

Hart, Josephine   1942?- . . . . CLC 70

Hart, Moss   1904-1961 . . . . CLC 66
    See also Conrad, Robert Arnold
    See also obituary CA 89-92; DLB 7

Harte, (Francis) Bret(t)
1836?-1902......... **TCLC 1, 25; SSC 8**
See also brief entry CA 104; SATA 26;
DLB 12, 64, 74, 79; CDALB 1865-1917

Hartley, L(eslie) P(oles)
1895-1972 .... **CLC 2, 22**
See also CA 45-48; obituary CA 37-40R;
DLB 15

Hartman, Geoffrey H. 1929-....... **CLC 27**
See also CA 117, 125; DLB 67

Haruf, Kent 19??-................. **CLC 34**

Harwood, Ronald 1934-........... **CLC 32**
See also CANR 4; CA 1-4R; DLB 13

Hasegawa Tatsunosuke 1864-1909
See Futabatei Shimei

Hasek, Jaroslav (Matej Frantisek)
1883-1923 .... **TCLC 4**
See also CA 104, 129

Hass, Robert 1941-............ **CLC 18, 39**
See also CANR 30; CA 111

Hastings, Selina 19??- .... **CLC 44**

Hauptmann, Gerhart (Johann Robert)
1862-1946 .... **TCLC 4**
See also CA 104; DLB 66

Havel, Vaclav 1936-........ **CLC 25, 58, 65**
See also CA 104

Haviaras, Stratis 1935- .... **CLC 33**
See also CA 105

Hawes, Stephen 1475?-1523?........ **LC 17**

Hawkes, John (Clendennin Burne, Jr.)
1925- ...... CLC 1, 2, 3, 4, 7, 9, 14, 15,
27, 49
See also CANR 2; CA 1-4R; DLB 2, 7;
DLB-Y 80

Hawking, Stephen (William)
1948- .... **CLC 63**
See also CA 126, 129

Hawthorne, Julian 1846-1934 ..... **TCLC 25**

Hawthorne, Nathaniel
1804-1864 ... **NCLC 2, 10, 17, 23; SSC 3**
See also YABC 2; DLB 1, 74;
CDALB 1640-1865

Hayashi Fumiko 1904-1951....... **TCLC 27**

Haycraft, Anna 19??-
See Ellis, Alice Thomas
See also CA 122

Hayden, Robert (Earl)
1913-1980 .... **CLC 5, 9, 14, 37**
See also BLC 2; CANR 24; CA 69-72;
obituary CA 97-100; CABS 2; SATA 19;
obituary SATA 26; DLB 5, 76;
CDALB 1941-1968

Hayman, Ronald 1932-........... **CLC 44**
See also CANR 18; CA 25-28R

Haywood, Eliza (Fowler) 1693?-1756.. **LC 1**
See also DLB 39

Hazlitt, William 1778-1830 ...... **NCLC 29**

Hazzard, Shirley 1931- .... **CLC 18**
See also CANR 4; CA 9-12R; DLB-Y 82

H(ilda) D(oolittle)
1886-1961 .... **CLC 3, 8, 14, 31, 34**
See also Doolittle, Hilda

Head, Bessie 1937-1986....... **CLC 25, 67**
See also BLC 2; CANR 25; CA 29-32R;
obituary CA 119

Headon, (Nicky) Topper 1956?- .... **CLC 30**
See also The Clash

Heaney, Seamus (Justin)
1939- .... **CLC 5, 7, 14, 25, 37**
See also CANR 25; CA 85-88; DLB 40

Hearn, (Patricio) Lafcadio (Tessima Carlos)
1850-1904 ....**TCLC 9**
See also CA 105; DLB 12, 78

Hearne, Vicki 1946-.............. **CLC 56**

Hearon, Shelby 1931-............. **CLC 63**
See also CANR 18; CA 25-28

Heat Moon, William Least 1939-... **CLC 29**

Hebert, Anne 1916- .... **CLC 4, 13, 29**
See also CA 85-88; DLB 68

Hecht, Anthony (Evan)
1923- .... **CLC 8, 13, 19**
See also CANR 6; CA 9-12R; DLB 5

Hecht, Ben 1894-1964 .... **CLC 8**
See also CA 85-88; DLB 7, 9, 25, 26, 28, 86

Hedayat, Sadeq 1903-1951........ **TCLC 21**
See also CA 120

Heidegger, Martin 1889-1976 ...... **CLC 24**
See also CA 81-84; obituary CA 65-68

Heidenstam, (Karl Gustaf) Verner von
1859-1940 .... **TCLC 5**
See also CA 104

Heifner, Jack 1946- .... **CLC 11**
See also CA 105

Heijermans, Herman 1864-1924 ... **TCLC 24**
See also CA 123

Heilbrun, Carolyn G(old) 1926-..... **CLC 25**
See also CANR 1, 28; CA 45-48

Heine, Harry 1797-1856
See Heine, Heinrich

Heine, Heinrich 1797-1856 .... **NCLC 4**
See also DLB 90

Heinemann, Larry C(urtiss) 1944- .. **CLC 50**
See also CA 110

Heiney, Donald (William) 1921-..... **CLC 9**
See also Harris, MacDonald
See also CANR 3; CA 1-4R

Heinlein, Robert A(nson)
1907-1988 ...... **CLC 1, 3, 8, 14, 26, 55**
See also CANR 1, 20; CA 1-4R;
obituary CA 125; SATA 9, 56; DLB 8

Heller, Joseph
1923- .... **CLC 1, 3, 5, 8, 11, 36, 63**
See also CANR 8; CA 5-8R; CABS 1;
DLB 2, 28; DLB-Y 80

Hellman, Lillian (Florence)
1905?-1984..... CLC 2, 4, 8, 14, 18, 34,
44, 52; DC 1
See also CA 13-16R; obituary CA 112;
DLB 7; DLB-Y 84

Helprin, Mark 1947- ..... **CLC 7, 10, 22, 32**
See also CA 81-84; DLB-Y 85

Hemans, Felicia 1793-1835 ...... **NCLC 29**

Hemingway, Ernest (Miller)
1899-1961 ... **CLC 1, 3, 6, 8, 10, 13, 19,
30, 34, 39, 41, 44, 50, 61; SSC 1**
See also CA 77-80; DLB 4, 9; DLB-Y 81,
87; DLB-DS 1; CDALB 1917-1929

Hempel, Amy 1951- .... **CLC 39**
See also CA 118

Henley, Beth 1952-............... **CLC 23**
See also Henley, Elizabeth Becker
See also CABS 3; DLB-Y 86

Henley, Elizabeth Becker 1952-
See Henley, Beth
See also CA 107

Henley, William Ernest
1849-1903 .... **TCLC 8**
See also CA 105; DLB 19

Hennissart, Martha
See Lathen, Emma
See also CA 85-88

Henry, O. 1862-1910 ... **TCLC 1, 19; SSC 5**
See also Porter, William Sydney
See also YABC 2; CA 104; DLB 12, 78, 79;
CDALB 1865-1917

Henry VIII 1491-1547.............. **LC 10**

Henschke, Alfred 1890-1928
See Klabund

Hentoff, Nat(han Irving) 1925-..... **CLC 26**
See also CLR 1; CAAS 6; CANR 5, 25;
CA 1-4R; SATA 27, 42; AAYA 4

Heppenstall, (John) Rayner
1911-1981 .... **CLC 10**
See also CANR 29; CA 1-4R;
obituary CA 103

Herbert, Frank (Patrick)
1920-1986 .... **CLC 12, 23, 35, 44**
See also CANR 5; CA 53-56;
obituary CA 118; SATA 9, 37, 47; DLB 8

Herbert, George 1593-1633 .... **PC 4**

Herbert, Zbigniew 1924- .... **CLC 9, 43**
See also CA 89-92

Herbst, Josephine 1897-1969....... **CLC 34**
See also CA 5-8R; obituary CA 25-28R;
DLB 9

Herder, Johann Gottfried von
1744-1803 .... **NCLC 8**

Hergesheimer, Joseph
1880-1954 .... **TCLC 11**
See also CA 109; DLB 9

Herlagnez, Pablo de 1844-1896
See Verlaine, Paul (Marie)

Herlihy, James Leo 1927-.......... **CLC 6**
See also CANR 2; CA 1-4R

Hermogenes fl.c. 175-............ **CMLC 6**

Hernandez, Jose 1834-1886...... **NCLC 17**

Herrick, Robert 1591-1674 .... **LC 13**

Herriot, James 1916-............. **CLC 12**
See also Wight, James Alfred
See also AAYA 1

Herrmann, Dorothy 1941-........ **CLC 44**
See also CA 107

Hersey, John (Richard)
1914- .... **CLC 1, 2, 7, 9, 40**
See also CA 17-20R; SATA 25; DLB 6

Lustig, Arnost 1926-.............. CLC 56
    See also CA 69-72; SATA 56; AAYA 3

Luther, Martin 1483-1546.......... LC 9

Luzi, Mario 1914-............... CLC 13
    See also CANR 9; CA 61-64

Lynch, David 1946- .... CLC 66
    See also CA 129; brief entry CA 124

Lynn, Kenneth S(chuyler) 1923-.... CLC 50
    See also CANR 3, 27; CA 1-4R

Lytle, Andrew (Nelson) 1902-...... CLC 22
    See also CA 9-12R; DLB 6

Lyttelton, George 1709-1773........ LC 10

Lytton, Edward Bulwer 1803-1873
    See Bulwer-Lytton, (Lord) Edward (George
      Earle Lytton)
    See also SATA 23

Maas, Peter 1929- .... CLC 29
    See also CA 93-96

Macaulay, (Dame Emilie) Rose
    1881-1958 .... TCLC 7, 44
    See also CA 104; DLB 36

MacBeth, George (Mann)
    1932-...................... CLC 2, 5, 9
    See also CA 25-28R; SATA 4; DLB 40

MacCaig, Norman (Alexander)
    1910- .... CLC 36
    See also CANR 3; CA 9-12R; DLB 27

MacCarthy, Desmond 1877-1952 .. TCLC 36

MacDermot, Thomas H. 1870-1933
    See Redcam, Tom

MacDiarmid, Hugh
    1892-1978 .... CLC 2, 4, 11, 19, 63
    See also Grieve, C(hristopher) M(urray)
    See also DLB 20

Macdonald, Cynthia 1928-...... CLC 13, 19
    See also CANR 4; CA 49-52

MacDonald, George 1824-1905..... TCLC 9
    See also CA 106; SATA 33; DLB 18

MacDonald, John D(ann)
    1916-1986 .... CLC 3, 27, 44
    See also CANR 1, 19; CA 1-4R;
      obituary CA 121; DLB 8; DLB-Y 86

Macdonald, (John) Ross
    1915-1983 ...... CLC 1, 2, 3, 14, 34, 41
    See also Millar, Kenneth
    See also DLB-DS 6

MacEwen, Gwendolyn (Margaret)
    1941-1987 .... CLC 13, 55
    See also CANR 7, 22; CA 9-12R;
      obituary CA 124; SATA 50, 55; DLB 53

Machado (y Ruiz), Antonio
    1875-1939 .... TCLC 3
    See also CA 104

Machado de Assis, (Joaquim Maria)
    1839-1908 .... TCLC 10
    See also BLC 2; brief entry CA 107

Machen, Arthur (Llewellyn Jones)
    1863-1947 .... TCLC 4
    See also CA 104; DLB 36

Machiavelli, Niccolo 1469-1527 ...... LC 8

MacInnes, Colin 1914-1976...... CLC 4, 23
    See also CANR 21; CA 69-72;
      obituary CA 65-68; DLB 14

MacInnes, Helen (Clark)
    1907-1985 .... CLC 27, 39
    See also CANR 1, 28; CA 1-4R;
      obituary CA 65-68, 117; SATA 22, 44;
      DLB 87

Macintosh, Elizabeth 1897-1952
    See Tey, Josephine
    See also CA 110

Mackenzie, (Edward Montague) Compton
    1883-1972 .... CLC 18
    See also CAP 2; CA 21-22;
      obituary CA 37-40R; DLB 34

Mac Laverty, Bernard 1942-....... CLC 31
    See also CA 116, 118

MacLean, Alistair (Stuart)
    1922-1987 .... CLC 3, 13, 50, 63
    See also CANR 28; CA 57-60;
      obituary CA 121; SATA 23, 50

MacLeish, Archibald
    1892-1982 .... CLC 3, 8, 14, 68
    See also CANR 33; CA 9-12R;
      obituary CA 106; DLB 4, 7, 45;
      DLB-Y 82

MacLennan, (John) Hugh
    1907-...................... CLC 2, 14
    See also CA 5-8R; DLB 68

MacLeod, Alistair 1936- .... CLC 56
    See also CA 123; DLB 60

Macleod, Fiona 1855-1905
    See Sharp, William

MacNeice, (Frederick) Louis
    1907-1963 .... CLC 1, 4, 10, 53
    See also CA 85-88; DLB 10, 20

Macpherson, (Jean) Jay 1931-...... CLC 14
    See also CA 5-8R; DLB 53

MacShane, Frank 1927-.......... CLC 39
    See also CANR 3; CA 11-12R

Macumber, Mari 1896-1966
    See Sandoz, Mari (Susette)

Madach, Imre 1823-1864........ NCLC 19

Madden, (Jerry) David 1933- .... CLC 5, 15
    See also CAAS 3; CANR 4; CA 1-4R;
      DLB 6

Madhubuti, Haki R. 1942-.......... CLC 6
    See also Lee, Don L.
    See also BLC 2; CANR 24; CA 73-76;
      DLB 5, 41; DLB-DS 8

Maeterlinck, Maurice 1862-1949 ... TCLC 3
    See also CA 104

Mafouz, Naguib 1912-
    See Mahfuz, Najib

Maginn, William 1794-1842...... NCLC 8

Mahapatra, Jayanta 1928-......... CLC 33
    See also CAAS 9; CANR 15; CA 73-76

Mahfuz Najib 1912-........... CLC 52, 55
    See also DLB-Y 88

Mahon, Derek 1941-.............. CLC 27
    See also CA 113, 128; DLB 40

Mailer, Norman
    1923- ...... CLC 1, 2, 3, 4, 5, 8, 11, 14,
                           28, 39
    See also CANR 28; CA 9-12R; CABS 1;
      DLB 2, 16, 28; DLB-Y 80, 83;
      DLB-DS 3; CDALB 1968-1987

Maillet, Antonine 1929-.......... CLC 54
    See also CA 115, 120; DLB 60

Mais, Roger 1905-1955 .... TCLC 8
    See also CA 105, 124

Maitland, Sara (Louise) 1950-...... CLC 49
    See also CANR 13; CA 69-72

Major, Clarence 1936-........ CLC 3, 19, 48
    See also BLC 2; CAAS 6; CANR 13, 25;
      CA 21-24R; DLB 33

Major, Kevin 1949- .... CLC 26
    See also CLR 11; CANR 21; CA 97-100;
      SATA 32; DLB 60

Malamud, Bernard
    1914-1986 ..... CLC 1, 2, 3, 5, 8, 9, 11,
                       18, 27, 44
    See also CANR 28; CA 5-8R;
      obituary CA 118; CABS 1; DLB 2, 28;
      DLB-Y 80, 86; CDALB 1941-1968

Malcolm X 1925-1965
    See Little, Malcolm
    See also BLC 2

Malherbe, Francois de 1555-1628..... LC 5

Mallarme Stephane
    1842-1898 .... NCLC 4; PC 4

Mallet-Joris, Francoise 1930-...... CLC 11
    See also CANR 17; CA 65-68; DLB 83

Maloff, Saul 1922-................. CLC 5
    See also CA 33-36R

Malone, Louis 1907-1963
    See MacNeice, (Frederick) Louis

Malone, Michael (Christopher)
    1942-....................... CLC 43
    See also CANR 14; CA 77-80

Malory, (Sir) Thomas ?-1471....... LC 11
    See also SATA 33, 59

Malouf, David 1934- .... CLC 28

Malraux, (Georges-) Andre
    1901-1976 ...... CLC 1, 4, 9, 13, 15, 57
    See also CAP 2; CA 21-24;
      obituary CA 69-72; DLB 72

Malzberg, Barry N. 1939-.......... CLC 7
    See also CAAS 4; CANR 16; CA 61-64;
      DLB 8

Mamet, David (Alan)
    1947-................ CLC 9, 15, 34, 46
    See also CANR 15; CA 81-84, 124;
      CABS 3; DLB 7; AAYA 3

Mamoulian, Rouben 1898-......... CLC 16
    See also CA 25-28R; obituary CA 124

Mandelstam, Osip (Emilievich)
    1891?-1938?................ TCLC 2, 6
    See also CA 104

Mander, Jane 1877-1949 .... TCLC 31

Mandiargues, Andre Pieyre de
    1909-....................... CLC 41
    See also CA 103; DLB 83

Mandrake, Ethel Belle 1902-1934
    See Thurman, Wallace

Mangan, James Clarence
    1803-1849 .... NCLC 27

Manley, (Mary) Delariviere
    1672?-1724.................... LC 1
    See also DLB 39, 80

McCaffrey, Anne 1926- . . . . CLC 17
See also CANR 15; CA 25-28R; SATA 8;
DLB 8

McCarthy, Cormac 1933- . . . . CLC 4, 57
See also CANR 10; CA 13-16R; DLB 6

McCarthy, Mary (Therese)
1912-1989- . . . CLC 1, 3, 5, 14, 24, 39, 59
See also CANR 16; CA 5-8R;
obituary CA 129; DLB 2; DLB-Y 81

McCartney, (James) Paul
1942- . . . . CLC 12, 35

McCauley, Stephen 19??- . . . . CLC 50

McClure, Michael 1932- . . . . CLC 6, 10
See also CANR 17; CA 21-24R; DLB 16

McCorkle, Jill (Collins) 1958- . . . . . . CLC 51
See also CA 121; DLB-Y 87

McCourt, James 1941- . . . . CLC 5
See also CA 57-60

McCoy, Horace 1897-1955 . . . . TCLC 28
See also CA 108; DLB 9

McCrae, John 1872-1918 . . . . TCLC 12
See also CA 109; DLB 92

McCullers, (Lula) Carson (Smith)
1917-1967 . . CLC 1, 4, 10, 12, 48; SSC 9
See also CANR 18; CA 5-8R;
obituary CA 25-28R; CABS 1; SATA 27;
DLB 2, 7; CDALB 1941-1968

McCullough, Colleen 1938?- . . . . CLC 27
See also CANR 17; CA 81-84

McElroy, Joseph (Prince)
1930- . . . . CLC 5, 47
See also CA 17-20R

McEwan, Ian (Russell) 1948- . . . CLC 13, 66
See also CANR 14; CA 61-64; DLB 14

McFadden, David 1940- . . . . CLC 48
See also CA 104; DLB 60

McFarland, Dennis 1956- . . . . CLC 65

McGahern, John 1934- . . . . CLC 5, 9, 48
See also CANR 29; CA 17-20R; DLB 14

McGinley, Patrick 1937- . . . . CLC 41
See also CA 120, 127

McGinley, Phyllis 1905-1978 . . . . . . CLC 14
See also CANR 19; CA 9-12R;
obituary CA 77-80; SATA 2, 44;
obituary SATA 24; DLB 11, 48

McGinniss, Joe 1942- . . . . CLC 32
See also CANR 26; CA 25-28R

McGivern, Maureen Daly 1921-
See Daly, Maureen
See also CA 9-12R

McGrath, Patrick 1950- . . . . CLC 55

McGrath, Thomas 1916- . . . . . . CLC 28, 59
See also CANR 6; CA 9-12R, 130;
SATA 41

McGuane, Thomas (Francis III)
1939- . . . . CLC 3, 7, 18, 45
See also CANR 5, 24; CA 49-52; DLB 2;
DLB-Y 80

McGuckian, Medbh 1950- . . . . CLC 48
See also DLB 40

McHale, Tom 1941-1982 . . . . CLC 3, 5
See also CA 77-80; obituary CA 106

McIlvanney, William 1936- . . . . CLC 42
See also CA 25-28R; DLB 14

McIlwraith, Maureen Mollie Hunter 1922-
See Hunter, Mollie
See also CA 29-32R; SATA 2

McInerney, Jay 1955- . . . . CLC 34
See also CA 116, 123

McIntyre, Vonda N(eel) 1948- . . . . . CLC 18
See also CANR 17; CA 81-84

McKay, Claude
1889-1948 . . . . TCLC 7, 41; PC 2
See also BLC 3; CA 104, 124; DLB 4, 45,
51

McKay, Claude 1889-1948
See McKay, Festus Claudius

McKay, Festus Claudius 1889-1948
See also BLC 2; CA 124; brief entry CA 104

McKuen, Rod 1933- . . . . CLC 1, 3
See also CA 41-44R

McLuhan, (Herbert) Marshall
1911-1980 . . . . CLC 37
See also CANR 12; CA 9-12R;
obituary CA 102; DLB 88

McManus, Declan Patrick 1955-
See Costello, Elvis

McMillan, Terry 1951- . . . . CLC 50, 61

McMurtry, Larry (Jeff)
1936- . . . . CLC 2, 3, 7, 11, 27, 44
See also CANR 19; CA 5-8R; DLB 2;
DLB-Y 80, 87; CDALB 1968-1987

McNally, Terrence 1939- . . . . CLC 4, 7, 41
See also CANR 2; CA 45-48; DLB 7

McNamer, Deirdre 1950- . . . . CLC 70

McNeile, Herman Cyril 1888-1937
See Sapper
See also DLB 77

McPhee, John 1931- . . . . CLC 36
See also CANR 20; CA 65-68

McPherson, James Alan 1943- . . . . . CLC 19
See also CANR 24; CA 25-28R; DLB 38

McPherson, William 1939- . . . . CLC 34
See also CA 57-60

McSweeney, Kerry 19??- . . . . CLC 34

Mead, Margaret 1901-1978 . . . . CLC 37
See also CANR 4; CA 1-4R;
obituary CA 81-84; SATA 20

Meaker, M. J. 1927-
See Kerr, M. E.; Meaker, Marijane

Meaker, Marijane 1927-
See Kerr, M. E.
See also CA 107; SATA 20

Medoff, Mark (Howard) 1940- . . . CLC 6, 23
See also CANR 5; CA 53-56; DLB 7

Megged, Aharon 1920- . . . . CLC 9
See also CANR 1; CA 49-52

Mehta, Ved (Parkash) 1934- . . . . CLC 37
See also CANR 2, 23; CA 1-4R

Mellor, John 1953?-
See The Clash

Meltzer, Milton 1915- . . . . CLC 26
See also CLR 13; CA 13-16R; SAAS 1;
SATA 1, 50; DLB 61

Melville, Herman
1819-1891 . . . . . . NCLC 3, 12, 29; SSC 1
See also SATA 59; DLB 3, 74;
CDALB 1640-1865

Membreno, Alejandro 1972- . . . . CLC 59

Mencken, H(enry) L(ouis)
1880-1956 . . . . TCLC 13
See also CA 105, 125; DLB 11, 29, 63;
CDALB 1917-1929

Mercer, David 1928-1980 . . . . CLC 5
See also CANR 23; CA 9-12R;
obituary CA 102; DLB 13

Meredith, George 1828-1909 . . . . . . TCLC 17
See also CA 117; DLB 18, 35, 57

Meredith, George 1858-1924 . . . . . . TCLC 43

Meredith, William (Morris)
1919- . . . . CLC 4, 13, 22, 55
See also CANR 6; CA 9-12R; DLB 5

Merezhkovsky, Dmitri
1865-1941 . . . . TCLC 29

Merimee, Prosper
1803-1870 . . . . NCLC 6; SSC 7

Merkin, Daphne 1954- . . . . CLC 44
See also CANR 123

Merrill, James (Ingram)
1926- . . . . CLC 2, 3, 6, 8, 13, 18, 34
See also CANR 10; CA 13-16R; DLB 5;
DLB-Y 85

Merton, Thomas (James)
1915-1968 . . . . CLC 1, 3, 11, 34
See also CANR 22; CA 5-8R;
obituary CA 25-28R; DLB 48; DLB-Y 81

Merwin, W(illiam) S(tanley)
1927- . . . . . . CLC 1, 2, 3, 5, 8, 13, 18, 45
See also CANR 15; CA 13-16R; DLB 5

Metcalf, John 1938- . . . . CLC 37
See also CA 113; DLB 60

Mew, Charlotte (Mary)
1870-1928 . . . . TCLC 8
See also CA 105; DLB 19

Mewshaw, Michael 1943- . . . . CLC 9
See also CANR 7; CA 53-56; DLB-Y 80

Meyer-Meyrink, Gustav 1868-1932
See Meyrink, Gustav
See also CA 117

Meyers, Jeffrey 1939- . . . . CLC 39
See also CA 73-76

Meynell, Alice (Christiana Gertrude
Thompson) 1847-1922 . . . . TCLC 6
See also CA 104; DLB 19

Meyrink, Gustav 1868-1932 . . . . TCLC 21
See also Meyer-Meyrink, Gustav

Michaels, Leonard 1933- . . . . CLC 6, 25
See also CANR 21; CA 61-64

Michaux, Henri 1899-1984 . . . . . . CLC 8, 19
See also CA 85-88; obituary CA 114

Michelangelo 1475-1564 . . . . LC 12

Michelet, Jules 1798-1874 . . . . NCLC 31

Michener, James A(lbert)
1907- . . . . CLC 1, 5, 11, 29, 60
See also CANR 21; CA 5-8R; DLB 6

Mickiewicz, Adam 1798-1855 . . . . . NCLC 3

Middleton, Christopher 1926- . . . . . . CLC 13
See also CANR 29; CA 13-16R; DLB 40

Middleton, Stanley 1919- . . . . CLC 7, 38
See also CANR 21; CA 25-28R; DLB 14

Migueis, Jose Rodrigues 1901- . . . . . CLC 10

Nexo, Martin Andersen
        1869-1954 .... TCLC 43

Nezval, Vitezslav 1900-1958 ...... TCLC 44
    See also CA 123

Ngema, Mbongeni 1955- .... CLC 57

Ngugi, James Thiong'o 1938-
    See Ngugi wa Thiong'o

Ngugi wa Thiong'o 1938-... CLC 3, 7, 13, 36
    See also Ngugi, James (Thiong'o); Wa
        Thiong'o, Ngugi
    See also BLC 3

Nichol, B(arrie) P(hillip) 1944- ..... CLC 18
    See also CA 53-56; DLB 53

Nichols, John (Treadwell) 1940-.... CLC 38
    See also CAAS 2; CANR 6; CA 9-12R;
        DLB-Y 82

Nichols, Peter (Richard)
        1927- .... CLC 5, 36, 65
    See also CANR 33; CA 104; DLB 13

Nicolas, F.R.E. 1927-
    See Freeling, Nicolas

Niedecker, Lorine 1903-1970.... CLC 10, 42
    See also CAP 2; CA 25-28; DLB 48

Nietzsche, Friedrich (Wilhelm)
        1844-1900 .... TCLC 10, 18
    See also CA 107, 121

Nievo, Ippolito 1831-1861 .... NCLC 22

Nightingale, Anne Redmon 1943-
    See Redmon (Nightingale), Anne
    See also CA 103

Nin, Anais
        1903-1977 ...... CLC 1, 4, 8, 11, 14, 60
    See also CANR 22; CA 13-16R;
        obituary CA 69-72; DLB 2, 4

Nissenson, Hugh 1933-.......... CLC 4, 9
    See also CANR 27; CA 17-20R; DLB 28

Niven, Larry 1938-............... CLC 8
    See also Niven, Laurence Van Cott
    See also DLB 8

Niven, Laurence Van Cott 1938-
    See Niven, Larry
    See also CANR 14; CA 21-24R

Nixon, Agnes Eckhardt 1927-...... CLC 21
    See also CA 110

Nizan, Paul 1905-1940.......... TCLC 40
    See also DLB 72

Nkosi, Lewis 1936-............... CLC 45
    See also BLC 3; CANR 27; CA 65-68

Nodier, (Jean) Charles (Emmanuel)
        1780-1844 .... NCLC 19

Nolan, Christopher 1965-......... CLC 58
    See also CA 111

Nordhoff, Charles 1887-1947...... TCLC 23
    See also CA 108; SATA 23; DLB 9

Norman, Marsha 1947- .... CLC 28
    See also CA 105; CABS 3; DLB-Y 84

Norris, (Benjamin) Frank(lin)
        1870-1902 .... TCLC 24
    See also CA 110; DLB 12, 71;
        CDALB 1865-1917

Norris, Leslie 1921-............. CLC 14
    See also CANR 14; CAP 1; CA 11-12;
        DLB 27

North, Andrew 1912-
    See Norton, Andre

North, Christopher 1785-1854
    See Wilson, John

Norton, Alice Mary 1912-
    See Norton, Andre
    See also CANR 2; CA 1-4R; SATA 1, 43

Norton, Andre 1912- .... CLC 12
    See also Norton, Mary Alice
    See also DLB 8, 52

Norway, Nevil Shute 1899-1960
    See Shute (Norway), Nevil
    See also CA 102; obituary CA 93-96

Norwid, Cyprian Kamil
        1821-1883 .... NCLC 17

Nossack, Hans Erich 1901-1978..... CLC 6
    See also CA 93-96; obituary CA 85-88;
        DLB 69

Nova, Craig 1945-............. CLC 7, 31
    See also CANR 2; CA 45-48

Novak, Joseph 1933-
    See Kosinski, Jerzy (Nikodem)

Novalis 1772-1801 .... NCLC 13

Nowlan, Alden (Albert) 1933-...... CLC 15
    See also CANR 5; CA 9-12R; DLB 53

Noyes, Alfred 1880-1958 .... TCLC 7
    See also CA 104; DLB 20

Nunn, Kem 19??-.................. CLC 34

Nye, Robert 1939- .... CLC 13, 42
    See also CANR 29; CA 33-36R; SATA 6;
        DLB 14

Nyro, Laura 1947- .... CLC 17

Oates, Joyce Carol
        1938- ..... CLC 1, 2, 3, 6, 9, 11, 15, 19,
                        33, 52; SSC 6
    See also CANR 25; CA 5-8R; DLB 2, 5;
        DLB-Y 81; CDALB 1968-1987

O'Brien, Darcy 1939-............. CLC 11
    See also CANR 8; CA 21-24R

O'Brien, Edna
        1932- .... CLC 3, 5, 8, 13, 36, 65
    See also CANR 6; CA 1-4R; DLB 14

O'Brien, Fitz-James 1828?-1862.. NCLC 21
    See also DLB 74

O'Brien, Flann
        1911-1966 ...... CLC 1, 4, 5, 7, 10, 47
    See also O Nuallain, Brian

O'Brien, Richard 19??-............ CLC 17
    See also CA 124

O'Brien, (William) Tim(othy)
        1946- .... CLC 7, 19, 40
    See also CA 85-88; DLB-Y 80

Obstfelder, Sigbjorn 1866-1900.... TCLC 23
    See also CA 123

O'Casey, Sean
        1880-1964 .... CLC 1, 5, 9, 11, 15
    See also CA 89-92; DLB 10

Ochs, Phil 1940-1976............. CLC 17
    See also obituary CA 65-68

O'Connor, Edwin (Greene)
        1918-1968 .... CLC 14
    See also CA 93-96; obituary CA 25-28R

O'Connor, (Mary) Flannery
        1925-1964 ... CLC 1, 2, 3, 6, 10, 13, 15,
                        21, 66; SSC 1
    See also CANR 3; CA 1-4R; DLB 2;
        DLB-Y 80; CDALB 1941-1968

O'Connor, Frank
        1903-1966 .... CLC 14, 23; SSC 5
    See also O'Donovan, Michael (John)
    See also CA 93-96

O'Dell, Scott 1903-.............. CLC 30
    See also CLR 1, 16; CANR 12; CA 61-64;
        SATA 12; DLB 52

Odets, Clifford 1906-1963 .... CLC 2, 28
    See also CA 85-88; DLB 7, 26

O'Donovan, Michael (John)
        1903-1966 .... CLC 14
    See also O'Connor, Frank
    See also CA 93-96

Oe, Kenzaburo 1935-.......... CLC 10, 36
    See also CA 97-100

O'Faolain, Julia 1932-........ CLC 6, 19, 47
    See also CAAS 2; CANR 12; CA 81-84;
        DLB 14

O'Faolain, Sean
        1900-1991 .... CLC 1, 7, 14, 32, 70
    See also CANR 12; CA 61-64;
        obituary CA 134; DLB 15

O'Flaherty, Liam
        1896-1984 .... CLC 5, 34; SSC 6
    See also CA 101; obituary CA 113; DLB 36;
        DLB-Y 84

O'Grady, Standish (James)
        1846-1928 .... TCLC 5
    See also CA 104

O'Grady, Timothy 1951-.......... CLC 59

O'Hara, Frank 1926-1966 ..... CLC 2, 5, 13
    See also CA 9-12R; obituary CA 25-28R;
        DLB 5, 16; CDALB 1929-1941

O'Hara, John (Henry)
        1905-1970 .... CLC 1, 2, 3, 6, 11, 42
    See also CA 5-8R; obituary CA 25-28R;
        DLB 9; DLB-DS 2; CDALB 1929-1941

O'Hara Family
    See Banim, John and Banim, Michael

O'Hehir, Diana 1922-............. CLC 41
    See also CA 93-96

Okigbo, Christopher (Ifenayichukwu)
        1932-1967 .... CLC 25
    See also BLC 3; CA 77-80

Olds, Sharon 1942-............ CLC 32, 39
    See also CANR 18; CA 101

Olesha, Yuri (Karlovich)
        1899-1960 .... CLC 8
    See also CA 85-88

Oliphant, Margaret (Oliphant Wilson)
        1828-1897 .... NCLC 11
    See also DLB 18

Oliver, Mary 1935-............. CLC 19, 34
    See also CANR 9; CA 21-24R; DLB 5

Olivier, (Baron) Laurence (Kerr)
        1907- .... CLC 20
    See also CA 111, 129

Olsen, Tillie 1913- .... CLC 4, 13
    See also CANR 1; CA 1-4R; DLB 28;
        DLB-Y 80

Raeburn, John 1941- . . . . CLC 34
  See also CA 57-60

Ragni, Gerome 1942- . . . . CLC 17
  See also CA 105

Rahv, Philip 1908-1973 . . . . CLC 24
  See also Greenberg, Ivan

Raine, Craig 1944- . . . . CLC 32
  See also CANR 29; CA 108; DLB 40

Raine, Kathleen (Jessie) 1908- . . . CLC 7, 45
  See also CA 85-88; DLB 20

Rainis, Janis 1865-1929 . . . . TCLC 29

Rakosi, Carl 1903- . . . . CLC 47
  See also Rawley, Callman
  See also CAAS 5

Ramos, Graciliano 1892-1953 . . . . . TCLC 32

Rampersad, Arnold 19??- . . . . CLC 44

Ramuz, Charles-Ferdinand
  1878-1947 . . . . TCLC 33

Rand, Ayn 1905-1982 . . . . CLC 3, 30, 44
  See also CANR 27; CA 13-16R;
  obituary CA 105

Randall, Dudley (Felker) 1914- . . . . . . CLC 1
  See also BLC 3; CANR 23; CA 25-28R;
  DLB 41

Ransom, John Crowe
  1888-1974 . . . . CLC 2, 4, 5, 11, 24
  See also CANR 6; CA 5-8R;
  obituary CA 49-52; DLB 45, 63

Rao, Raja 1909- . . . . CLC 25, 56
  See also CA 73-76

Raphael, Frederic (Michael)
  1931- . . . . CLC 2, 14
  See also CANR 1; CA 1-4R; DLB 14

Rathbone, Julian 1935- . . . . CLC 41
  See also CA 101

Rattigan, Terence (Mervyn)
  1911-1977 . . . . CLC 7
  See also CA 85-88; obituary CA 73-76;
  DLB 13

Ratushinskaya, Irina 1954- . . . . CLC 54
  See also CA 129

Raven, Simon (Arthur Noel)
  1927- . . . . CLC 14
  See also CA 81-84

Rawley, Callman 1903-
  See Rakosi, Carl
  See also CANR 12; CA 21-24R

Rawlings, Marjorie Kinnan
  1896-1953 . . . . TCLC 4
  See also YABC 1; CA 104; DLB 9, 22

Ray, Satyajit 1921- . . . . CLC 16
  See also CA 114

Read, Herbert (Edward) 1893-1968 . . CLC 4
  See also CA 85-88; obituary CA 25-28R;
  DLB 20

Read, Piers Paul 1941- . . . . . . CLC 4, 10, 25
  See also CA 21-24R; SATA 21; DLB 14

Reade, Charles 1814-1884 . . . . NCLC 2
  See also DLB 21

Reade, Hamish 1936-
  See Gray, Simon (James Holliday)

Reading, Peter 1946- . . . . CLC 47
  See also CA 103; DLB 40

Reaney, James 1926- . . . . CLC 13
  See also CA 41-44R; SATA 43; DLB 68

Rebreanu, Liviu 1885-1944 . . . . . . TCLC 28

Rechy, John (Francisco)
  1934- . . . . CLC 1, 7, 14, 18
  See also CAAS 4; CANR 6; CA 5-8R;
  DLB-Y 82

Redcam, Tom 1870-1933 . . . . TCLC 25

Reddin, Keith 1956?- . . . . CLC 67

Redgrove, Peter (William)
  1932- . . . . CLC 6, 41
  See also CANR 3; CA 1-4R; DLB 40

Redmon (Nightingale), Anne
  1943- . . . . CLC 22
  See also Nightingale, Anne Redmon
  See also DLB-Y 86

Reed, Ishmael
  1938- . . . . CLC 2, 3, 5, 6, 13, 32, 60
  See also BLC 3; CANR 25; CA 21-24R;
  DLB 2, 5, 33; DLB-DS 8

Reed, John (Silas) 1887-1920 . . . . . . TCLC 9
  See also CA 106

Reed, Lou 1944- . . . . CLC 21

Reeve, Clara 1729-1807 . . . . NCLC 19
  See also DLB 39

Reid, Christopher 1949- . . . . CLC 33
  See also DLB 40

Reid Banks, Lynne 1929-
  See Banks, Lynne Reid
  See also CANR 6, 22; CA 1-4R; SATA 22

Reiner, Max 1900-
  See Caldwell, (Janet Miriam) Taylor
  (Holland)

Reizenstein, Elmer Leopold 1892-1967
  See Rice, Elmer

Remark, Erich Paul 1898-1970
  See Remarque, Erich Maria

Remarque, Erich Maria
  1898-1970 . . . . CLC 21
  See also CA 77-80; obituary CA 29-32R;
  DLB 56

Remizov, Alexey (Mikhailovich)
  1877-1957 . . . . TCLC 27
  See also CA 125

Renan, Joseph Ernest
  1823-1892 . . . . NCLC 26

Renard, Jules 1864-1910 . . . . TCLC 17
  See also CA 117

Renault, Mary 1905-1983 . . . . CLC 3, 11, 17
  See also Challans, Mary
  See also DLB-Y 83

Rendell, Ruth 1930- . . . . CLC 28, 48
  See also Vine, Barbara
  See also CA 109; DLB 87

Renoir, Jean 1894-1979 . . . . CLC 20
  See also CA 129; obituary CA 85-88

Resnais, Alain 1922- . . . . CLC 16

Reverdy, Pierre 1899-1960 . . . . CLC 53
  See also CA 97-100; obituary CA 89-92

Rexroth, Kenneth
  1905-1982 . . . . . . CLC 1, 2, 6, 11, 22, 49
  See also CANR 14; CA 5-8R;
  obituary CA 107; DLB 16, 48; DLB-Y 82;
  CDALB 1941-1968

Reyes, Alfonso 1889-1959 . . . . TCLC 33

Reyes y Basoalto, Ricardo Eliecer Neftali
  1904-1973
  See Neruda, Pablo

Reymont, Wladyslaw Stanislaw
  1867-1925 . . . . TCLC 5
  See also CA 104

Reynolds, Jonathan 1942?- . . . . . . CLC 6, 38
  See also CANR 28; CA 65-68

Reynolds, Michael (Shane) 1937- . . . CLC 44
  See also CANR 9; CA 65-68

Reynolds, Sir Joshua 1723-1792 . . . . . LC 15

Reznikoff, Charles 1894-1976 . . . . CLC 9
  See also CAP 2; CA 33-36;
  obituary CA 61-64; DLB 28, 45

Rezzori, Gregor von 1914- . . . . CLC 25
  See also CA 122

Rhys, Jean
  1890-1979 . . . . . . CLC 2, 4, 6, 14, 19, 51
  See also CA 25-28R; obituary CA 85-88;
  DLB 36

Ribeiro, Darcy 1922- . . . . CLC 34
  See also CA 33-36R

Ribeiro, Joao Ubaldo (Osorio Pimentel)
  1941- . . . . CLC 10, 67
  See also CA 81-84

Ribman, Ronald (Burt) 1932- . . . . CLC 7
  See also CA 21-24R

Ricci, Nino 1959- . . . . CLC 70

Rice, Anne 1941- . . . . CLC 41
  See also CANR 12; CA 65-68

Rice, Elmer 1892-1967 . . . . CLC 7, 49
  See also CAP 2; CA 21-22;
  obituary CA 25-28R; DLB 4, 7

Rice, Tim 1944- . . . . CLC 21
  See also CA 103

Rich, Adrienne (Cecile)
  1929- . . . . CLC 3, 6, 7, 11, 18, 36
  See also CANR 20; CA 9-12R; DLB 5, 67

Richard, Keith 1943- . . . . CLC 17
  See also CA 107

Richards, David Adam 1950- . . . . CLC 59
  See also CA 93-96; DLB 53

Richards, I(vor) A(rmstrong)
  1893-1979 . . . . CLC 14, 24
  See also CA 41-44R; obituary CA 89-92;
  DLB 27

Richards, Keith 1943-
  See Richard, Keith
  See also CA 107

Richardson, Dorothy (Miller)
  1873-1957 . . . . TCLC 3
  See also CA 104; DLB 36

Richardson, Ethel 1870-1946
  See Richardson, Henry Handel
  See also CA 105

Richardson, Henry Handel
  1870-1946 . . . . TCLC 4
  See also Richardson, Ethel

Richardson, Samuel 1689-1761 . . . . . . LC 1
  See also DLB 39

Richler, Mordecai
   1931- ...... **CLC 3, 5, 9, 13, 18, 46, 70**
   See also CLR 17; CANR 31; CA 65-68;
   SATA 27, 44; DLB 53

Richter, Conrad (Michael)
   1890-1968 .... **CLC 30**
   See also CANR 23; CA 5-8R;
   obituary CA 25-28R; SATA 3; DLB 9

Richter, Johann Paul Friedrich   1763-1825
   See Jean Paul

Riddell, Mrs. J. H.   1832-1906..... **TCLC 40**

Riding, Laura   1901- .... **CLC 3, 7**
   See also Jackson, Laura (Riding)

Riefenstahl, Berta Helene Amalia
   1902- .... **CLC 16**
   See also Riefenstahl, Leni
   See also CA 108

Riefenstahl, Leni   1902- .... **CLC 16**
   See also Riefenstahl, Berta Helene Amalia
   See also CA 108

Rilke, Rainer Maria
   1875-1926 .... **TCLC 1, 6, 19; PC 2**
   See also CA 104, 132; DLB 81

Rimbaud, (Jean Nicolas) Arthur
   1854-1891 .... **NCLC 4, 35; PC 3**

Ringwood, Gwen(dolyn Margaret) Pharis
   1910-1984 .... **CLC 48**
   See also obituary CA 112

Rio, Michel   19??- .... **CLC 43**

Ritsos, Yannis   1909-........ **CLC 6, 13, 31**
   See also CA 77-80

Ritter, Erika   1948?- .... **CLC 52**

Rivera, Jose Eustasio   1889-1928... **TCLC 35**

Rivers, Conrad Kent   1933-1968..... **CLC 1**
   See also CA 85-88; DLB 41

Rizal, Jose   1861-1896......... **NCLC 27**

Roa Bastos, Augusto   1917- .... **CLC 45**

Robbe-Grillet, Alain
   1922- ...... **CLC 1, 2, 4, 6, 8, 10, 14, 43**
   See also CA 9-12R; DLB 83

Robbins, Harold   1916- .... **CLC 5**
   See also CANR 26; CA 73-76

Robbins, Thomas Eugene   1936-
   See Robbins, Tom
   See also CA 81-84

Robbins, Tom   1936-........ **CLC 9, 32, 64**
   See also Robbins, Thomas Eugene
   See also CANR 29; CA 81-84; DLB-Y 80

Robbins, Trina   1938- .... **CLC 21**

Roberts, (Sir) Charles G(eorge) D(ouglas)
   1860-1943.............. **TCLC 8**
   See also CA 105; SATA 29; DLB 92

Roberts, Kate   1891-1985 .... **CLC 15**
   See also CA 107; obituary CA 116

Roberts, Keith (John Kingston)
   1935- .... **CLC 14**
   See also CA 25-28R

Roberts, Kenneth   1885-1957 ...... **TCLC 23**
   See also CA 109; DLB 9

Roberts, Michele (B.)   1949-........ **CLC 48**
   See also CA 115

Robertson, Thomas William
   1829-1871 .... **NCLC 35**

Robinson, Edwin Arlington
   1869-1935 .... **TCLC 5; PC 1**
   See also CA 104; DLB 54;
   CDALB 1865-1917

Robinson, Henry Crabb
   1775-1867 .... **NCLC 15**

Robinson, Jill   1936- .... **CLC 10**
   See also CA 102

Robinson, Kim Stanley   19??-....... **CLC 34**
   See also CA 126

Robinson, Marilynne   1944-........ **CLC 25**
   See also CA 116

Robinson, Smokey   1940- .... **CLC 21**

Robinson, William   1940-
   See Robinson, Smokey
   See also CA 116

Robison, Mary   1949- .... **CLC 42**
   See also CA 113, 116

Roddenberry, Gene   1921-........... **CLC 17**
   See also CANR 110; SATA 45

Rodgers, Mary   1931- .... **CLC 12**
   See also CLR 20; CANR 8; CA 49-52;
   SATA 8

Rodgers, W(illiam) R(obert)
   1909-1969 .... **CLC 7**
   See also CA 85-88; DLB 20

Rodman, Howard   19??- .... **CLC 65**

Rodriguez, Claudio   1934-......... **CLC 10**

Roethke, Theodore (Huebner)
   1908-1963 ...... **CLC 1, 3, 8, 11, 19, 46**
   See also CA 81-84; CABS 2; SAAS 1;
   DLB 5; CDALB 1941-1968

Rogers, Sam   1943-
   See Shepard, Sam

Rogers, Thomas (Hunton)   1931-.... **CLC 57**
   See also CA 89-92

Rogers, Will(iam Penn Adair)
   1879-1935 .... **TCLC 8**
   See also CA 105; DLB 11

Rogin, Gilbert   1929-.............. **CLC 18**
   See also CANR 15; CA 65-68

Rohan, Koda   1867-1947......... **TCLC 22**
   See also CA 121

Rohmer, Eric   1920- .... **CLC 16**
   See also Scherer, Jean-Marie Maurice

Rohmer, Sax   1883-1959.......... **TCLC 28**
   See also Ward, Arthur Henry Sarsfield
   See also CA 108; DLB 70

Roiphe, Anne (Richardson)
   1935- .... **CLC 3, 9**
   See also CA 89-92; DLB-Y 80

Rolfe, Frederick (William Serafino Austin
   Lewis Mary)   1860-1913...... **TCLC 12**
   See also CA 107; DLB 34

Rolland, Romain   1866-1944...... **TCLC 23**
   See also CA 118; DLB 65

Rolvaag, O(le) E(dvart)
   1876-1931 .... **TCLC 17**
   See also CA 117; DLB 9

Romains, Jules   1885-1972 .... **CLC 7**
   See also CA 85-88

Romero, Jose Ruben   1890-1952 ... **TCLC 14**
   See also CA 114

Ronsard, Pierre de   1524-1585........ **LC 6**

Rooke, Leon   1934-............ **CLC 25, 34**
   See also CANR 23; CA 25-28R

Roper, William   1498-1578......... **LC 10**

Rosa, Joao Guimaraes   1908-1967... **CLC 23**
   See also obituary CA 89-92

Rosen, Richard (Dean)   1949-...... **CLC 39**
   See also CA 77-80

Rosenberg, Isaac   1890-1918...... **TCLC 12**
   See also CA 107; DLB 20

Rosenblatt, Joe   1933-............. **CLC 15**
   See also Rosenblatt, Joseph

Rosenblatt, Joseph   1933-
   See Rosenblatt, Joe
   See also CA 89-92

Rosenfeld, Samuel   1896-1963
   See Tzara, Tristan
   See also obituary CA 89-92

Rosenthal, M(acha) L(ouis)   1917-... **CLC 28**
   See also CAAS 6; CANR 4; CA 1-4R;
   SATA 59; DLB 5

Ross, (James) Sinclair   1908-....... **CLC 13**
   See also CA 73-76; DLB 88

Rossetti, Christina Georgina
   1830-1894 .... **NCLC 2**
   See also SATA 20; DLB 35

Rossetti, Dante Gabriel
   1828-1882 .... **NCLC 4**
   See also DLB 35

Rossetti, Gabriel Charles Dante   1828-1882
   See Rossetti, Dante Gabriel

Rossner, Judith (Perelman)
   1935- .... **CLC 6, 9, 29**
   See also CANR 18; CA 17-20R; DLB 6

Rostand, Edmond (Eugene Alexis)
   1868-1918 .... **TCLC 6, 37**
   See also CA 104, 126

Roth, Henry   1906-........... **CLC 2, 6, 11**
   See also CAP 1; CA 11-12; DLB 28

Roth, Joseph   1894-1939......... **TCLC 33**
   See also DLB 85

Roth, Philip (Milton)
   1933- ...... **CLC 1, 2, 3, 4, 6, 9, 15, 22,**
                        31, 47, 66
   See also CANR 1, 22; CA 1-4R; DLB 2, 28;
   DLB-Y 82; CDALB 1968-1988

Rothenberg, James   1931-.......... **CLC 57**

Rothenberg, Jerome   1931-........ **CLC 6, 57**
   See also CANR 1; CA 45-48; DLB 5

Roumain, Jacques   1907-1944...... **TCLC 19**
   See also BLC 3; CA 117, 125

Rourke, Constance (Mayfield)
   1885-1941 .... **TCLC 12**
   See also YABC 1; CA 107

Rousseau, Jean-Baptiste   1671-1741 ... **LC 9**

Rousseau, Jean-Jacques   1712-1778... **LC 14**

Roussel, Raymond   1877-1933 ..... **TCLC 20**
   See also CA 117

Rovit, Earl (Herbert)   1927-........ **CLC 7**
   See also CANR 12; CA 5-8R

Rowe, Nicholas   1674-1718.......... **LC 8**

Service, Robert W(illiam)
1874-1958 .... TCLC 15
See also CA 115; SATA 20

Seth, Vikram 1952-.............. CLC 43
See also CA 121, 127

Seton, Cynthia Propper
1926-1982 .... CLC 27
See also CANR 7; CA 5-8R;
obituary CA 108

Seton, Ernest (Evan) Thompson
1860-1946 .... TCLC 31
See also CA 109; SATA 18; DLB 92

Settle, Mary Lee 1918- .... CLC 19, 61
See also CAAS 1; CA 89-92; DLB 6

Sevine, Marquise de Marie de
Rabutin-Chantal 1626-1696..... LC 11

Sexton, Anne (Harvey)
1928-1974 ... CLC 2, 4, 6, 8, 10, 15, 53;
PC 2
See also CANR 3; CA 1-4R;
obituary CA 53-56; CABS 2; SATA 10;
DLB 5; CDALB 1941-1968

Shaara, Michael (Joseph) 1929- .... CLC 15
See also CA 102; obituary CA 125;
DLB-Y 83

Shackleton, C. C. 1925-
See Aldiss, Brian W(ilson)

Shacochis, Bob 1951-.............. CLC 39
See also CA 119, 124

Shaffer, Anthony 1926- .... CLC 19
See also CA 110, 116; DLB 13

Shaffer, Peter (Levin)
1926- .... CLC 5, 14, 18, 37, 60
See also CANR 25; CA 25-28R; DLB 13

Shalamov, Varlam (Tikhonovich)
1907?-1982................... CLC 18
See also obituary CA 105

Shamlu, Ahmad 1925- .... CLC 10

Shammas, Anton 1951-............ CLC 55

Shange, Ntozake 1948-....... CLC 8, 25, 38
See also BLC 3; CANR 27; CA 85-88;
CABS 3; DLB 38

Shapcott, Thomas W(illiam) 1935- .. CLC 38
See also CA 69-72

Shapiro, Karl (Jay) 1913- .. CLC 4, 8, 15, 53
See also CAAS 6; CANR 1; CA 1-4R;
DLB 48

Sharp, William 1855-1905 .... TCLC 39

Sharpe, Tom 1928-.............. CLC 36
See also CA 114; DLB 14

Shaw, (George) Bernard
1856-1950 .... TCLC 3, 9, 21
See also CA 104, 109, 119; DLB 10, 57

Shaw, Henry Wheeler
1818-1885 .... NCLC 15
See also DLB 11

Shaw, Irwin 1913-1984....... CLC 7, 23, 34
See also CANR 21; CA 13-16R;
obituary CA 112; DLB 6; DLB-Y 84;
CDALB 1941-1968

Shaw, Robert 1927-1978 .... CLC 5
See also CANR 4; CA 1-4R;
obituary CA 81-84; DLB 13, 14

Shawn, Wallace 1943- .... CLC 41
See also CA 112

Sheed, Wilfrid (John Joseph)
1930- .... CLC 2, 4, 10, 53
See also CA 65-68; DLB 6

Sheffey, Asa 1913-1980
See Hayden, Robert (Earl)

Sheldon, Alice (Hastings) B(radley)
1915-1987
See Tiptree, James, Jr.
See also CA 108; obituary CA 122

Shelley, Mary Wollstonecraft Godwin
1797-1851 .... NCLC 14
See also SATA 29

Shelley, Percy Bysshe
1792-1822 .... NCLC 18

Shepard, Jim 19??-................ CLC 36

Shepard, Lucius 19??-............. CLC 34
See also CA 128

Shepard, Sam
1943- .... CLC 4, 6, 17, 34, 41, 44
See also CANR 22; CA 69-72; DLB 7

Shepherd, Michael 1927-
See Ludlum, Robert

Sherburne, Zoa (Morin) 1912-...... CLC 30
See also CANR 3; CA 1-4R; SATA 3

Sheridan, Frances 1724-1766........ LC 7
See also DLB 39, 84

Sheridan, Richard Brinsley
1751-1816 .... NCLC 5; DC 1
See also DLB 89

Sherman, Jonathan Marc 1970?-.... CLC 55

Sherman, Martin 19??-............ CLC 19
See also CA 116

Sherwin, Judith Johnson 1936-... CLC 7, 15
See also CA 25-28R

Sherwood, Robert E(mmet)
1896-1955 .... TCLC 3
See also CA 104; DLB 7, 26

Shiel, M(atthew) P(hipps)
1865-1947 .... TCLC 8
See also CA 106

Shiga, Naoya 1883-1971.......... CLC 33
See also CA 101; obituary CA 33-36R

Shimazaki, Haruki 1872-1943
See Shimazaki, Toson
See also CA 105

Shimazaki, Toson 1872-1943....... TCLC 5
See also Shimazaki, Haruki

Sholokhov, Mikhail (Aleksandrovich)
1905-1984 .... CLC 7, 15
See also CA 101; obituary CA 112;
SATA 36

Sholom Aleichem 1859-1916 .... TCLC 1, 35
See also Rabinovitch, Sholem

Shreve, Susan Richards 1939-...... CLC 23
See also CAAS 5; CANR 5; CA 49-52;
SATA 41, 46

Shue, Larry 1946-1985............ CLC 52
See also obituary CA 117

Shulman, Alix Kates 1932- ...... CLC 2, 10
See also CA 29-32R; SATA 7

Shuster, Joe 1914- .... CLC 21

Shute (Norway), Nevil 1899-1960... CLC 30
See also Norway, Nevil Shute
See also CA 102; obituary CA 93-96

Shuttle, Penelope (Diane) 1947- ..... CLC 7
See also CA 93-96; DLB 14, 40

Sidney, Mary 1561-1621 .... LC 19

Sidney, Sir Philip 1554-1586....... LC 19

Siegel, Jerome 1914- .... CLC 21
See also CA 116

Sienkiewicz, Henryk (Adam Aleksander Pius)
1846-1916 .... TCLC 3
See also CA 104

Sigal, Clancy 1926-............... CLC 7
See also CA 1-4R

Sigourney, Lydia (Howard Huntley)
1791-1865 .... NCLC 21
See also DLB 1, 42, 73

Siguenza y Gongora, Carlos de
1645-1700 .... LC 8

Sigurjonsson, Johann 1880-1919... TCLC 27

Sikelianos, Angelos 1884-1951 .... TCLC 39

Silkin, Jon 1930- .... CLC 2, 6, 43
See also CAAS 5; CA 5-8R; DLB 27

Silko, Leslie Marmon 1948- .... CLC 23
See also CA 115, 122

Sillanpaa, Franz Eemil 1888-1964... CLC 19
See also CA 129; obituary CA 93-96

Sillitoe, Alan
1928- .... CLC 1, 3, 6, 10, 19, 57
See also CAAS 2; CANR 8, 26; CA 9-12R;
DLB 14

Silone, Ignazio 1900-1978 .... CLC 4
See also CAAS 2; CANR 26; CAP 2;
CA 25-28, 11-12R,; obituary CA 81-84

Silver, Joan Micklin 1935- .... CLC 20
See also CA 114, 121

Silverberg, Robert 1935- .... CLC 7
See also CAAS 3; CANR 1, 20; CA 1-4R;
SATA 13; DLB 8

Silverstein, Alvin 1933- .... CLC 17
See also CANR 2; CA 49-52; SATA 8

Silverstein, Virginia B(arbara Opshelor)
1937- .... CLC 17
See also CANR 2; CA 49-52; SATA 8

Simak, Clifford D(onald)
1904-1988 .... CLC 1, 55
See also CANR 1; CA 1-4R;
obituary CA 125; DLB 8

Simenon, Georges (Jacques Christian)
1903-1989 .... CLC 1, 2, 3, 8, 18, 47
See also CA 85-88; obituary CA 129;
DLB 72

Simenon, Paul 1956?-
See The Clash

Simic, Charles 1938-... CLC 6, 9, 22, 49, 68
See also CAAS 4; CANR 12, 33;
CA 29-32R; DLB 105

Simmons, Charles (Paul) 1924-..... CLC 57
See also CA 89-92

Simmons, Dan 1948- .... CLC 44

Simmons, James (Stewart Alexander)
1933- .... CLC 43
See also CA 105; DLB 40

Sophocles
   c. 496? B.C.-c. 406? B.C. . . . . . . CMLC 2;
                                         DC 1

Sorrentino, Gilbert
   1929- . . . . CLC 3, 7, 14, 22, 40
   See also CANR 14; CA 77-80; DLB 5;
   DLB-Y 80

Soto, Gary 1952- . . . . CLC 32
   See also CA 119, 125; DLB 82

Soupault, Philippe 1897-1990 . . . . . . CLC 68
   See also CA 116; obituary CA 131

Souster, (Holmes) Raymond
   1921- . . . . CLC 5, 14
   See also CANR 13; CA 13-16R; DLB 88

Southern, Terry 1926- . . . . CLC 7
   See also CANR 1; CA 1-4R; DLB 2

Southey, Robert 1774-1843 . . . . NCLC 8
   See also SATA 54

Southworth, Emma Dorothy Eliza Nevitte
   1819-1899 . . . . NCLC 26

Soyinka, Wole
   1934- . . . . CLC 3, 5, 14, 36, 44; DC 2
   See also BLC 3; CANR 27; CA 13-16R;
   DLB-Y 86

Spackman, W(illiam) M(ode)
   1905- . . . . CLC 46
   See also CA 81-84

Spacks, Barry 1931- . . . . CLC 14
   See also CA 29-32R

Spanidou, Irini 1946- . . . . CLC 44

Spark, Muriel (Sarah)
   1918- . . . . CLC 2, 3, 5, 8, 13, 18, 40
   See also CANR 12; CA 5-8R; DLB 15

Spencer, Elizabeth 1921- . . . . CLC 22
   See also CA 13-16R; SATA 14; DLB 6

Spencer, Scott 1945- . . . . CLC 30
   See also CA 113; DLB-Y 86

Spender, Stephen (Harold)
   1909- . . . . CLC 1, 2, 5, 10, 41
   See also CA 9-12R; DLB 20

Spengler, Oswald 1880-1936 . . . . . . TCLC 25
   See also CA 118

Spenser, Edmund 1552?-1599 . . . . LC 5

Spicer, Jack 1925-1965 . . . . CLC 8, 18
   See also CA 85-88; DLB 5, 16

Spielberg, Peter 1929- . . . . CLC 6
   See also CANR 4; CA 5-8R; DLB-Y 81

Spielberg, Steven 1947- . . . . CLC 20
   See also CA 77-80; SATA 32

Spillane, Frank Morrison 1918-
   See Spillane, Mickey
   See also CA 25-28R

Spillane, Mickey 1918- . . . . CLC 3, 13
   See also Spillane, Frank Morrison

Spinoza, Benedictus de 1632-1677 . . . . LC 9

Spinrad, Norman (Richard) 1940- . . . CLC 46
   See also CANR 20; CA 37-40R; DLB 8

Spitteler, Carl (Friedrich Georg)
   1845-1924 . . . . TCLC 12
   See also CA 109

Spivack, Kathleen (Romola Drucker)
   1938- . . . . CLC 6
   See also CA 49-52

Spoto, Donald 1941- . . . . CLC 39
   See also CANR 11; CA 65-68

Springsteen, Bruce 1949- . . . . CLC 17
   See also CA 111

Spurling, Hilary 1940- . . . . CLC 34
   See also CANR 25; CA 104

Squires, (James) Radcliffe 1917- . . . . CLC 51
   See also CANR 6, 21; CA 1-4R

Stael-Holstein, Anne Louise Germaine Necker,
   Baronne de 1766-1817 . . . . NCLC 3

Stafford, Jean 1915-1979 . . . CLC 4, 7, 19, 68
   See also CANR 3; CA 1-4R;
   obituary CA 85-88; obituary SATA 22;
   DLB 2

Stafford, William (Edgar)
   1914- . . . . CLC 4, 7, 29
   See also CAAS 3; CANR 5, 22; CA 5-8R;
   DLB 5

Stannard, Martin 1947- . . . . CLC 44

Stanton, Maura 1946- . . . . CLC 9
   See also CANR 15; CA 89-92

Stapledon, (William) Olaf
   1886-1950 . . . . TCLC 22
   See also CA 111; DLB 15

Starbuck, George (Edwin) 1931- . . . . CLC 53
   See also CANR 23; CA 21-22R

Stark, Richard 1933-
   See Westlake, Donald E(dwin)

Stead, Christina (Ellen)
   1902-1983 . . . . CLC 2, 5, 8, 32
   See also CA 13-16R; obituary CA 109

Steele, Sir Richard 1672-1729 . . . . . . LC 18
   See also DLB 84, 101

Steele, Timothy (Reid) 1948- . . . . . . CLC 45
   See also CANR 16; CA 93-96

Steffens, (Joseph) Lincoln
   1866-1936 . . . . TCLC 20
   See also CA 117; SAAS 1

Stegner, Wallace (Earle) 1909- . . . CLC 9, 49
   See also CANR 1, 21; CA 1-4R; DLB 9

Stein, Gertrude 1874-1946 . . . TCLC 1, 6, 28
   See also CA 104; DLB 4, 54, 86;
   CDALB 1917-1929

Steinbeck, John (Ernst)
   1902-1968 . . . . . CLC 1, 5, 9, 13, 21, 34,
                                      45, 59
   See also CANR 1; CA 1-4R;
   obituary CA 25-28R; SATA 9; DLB 7, 9;
   DLB-DS 2; CDALB 1929-1941

Steinem, Gloria 1934- . . . . CLC 63
   See also CANR 28; CA 53-56

Steiner, George 1929- . . . . CLC 24
   See also CA 73-76; DLB 67

Steiner, Rudolf(us Josephus Laurentius)
   1861-1925 . . . . TCLC 13
   See also CA 107

Stendhal 1783-1842 . . . . NCLC 23

Stephen, Leslie 1832-1904 . . . . TCLC 23
   See also CANR 9; CA 21-24R, 123;
   DLB 57

Stephens, James 1882?-1950 . . . . TCLC 4
   See also CA 104; DLB 19

Stephens, Reed
   See Donaldson, Stephen R.

Steptoe, Lydia 1892-1982
   See Barnes, Djuna

Sterchi, Beat 1949- . . . . CLC 65

Sterling, George 1869-1926 . . . . . . TCLC 20
   See also CA 117; DLB 54

Stern, Gerald 1925- . . . . CLC 40
   See also CA 81-84

Stern, Richard G(ustave) 1928- . . . CLC 4, 39
   See also CANR 1, 25; CA 1-4R; DLB 87

Sternberg, Jonas 1894-1969
   See Sternberg, Josef von

Sternberg, Josef von 1894-1969 . . . . . CLC 20
   See also CA 81-84

Sterne, Laurence 1713-1768 . . . . LC 2
   See also DLB 39

Sternheim, (William Adolf) Carl
   1878-1942 . . . . TCLC 8
   See also CA 105

Stevens, Mark 19??- . . . . CLC 34

Stevens, Wallace 1879-1955 . . . . . TCLC 3, 12
   See also CA 104, 124; DLB 54

Stevenson, Anne (Katharine)
   1933- . . . . CLC 7, 33
   See also Elvin, Anne Katharine Stevenson
   See also CANR 9; CA 17-18R; DLB 40

Stevenson, Robert Louis
   1850-1894 . . . . NCLC 5, 14
   See also CLR 10, 11; YABC 2; DLB 18, 57

Stewart, J(ohn) I(nnes) M(ackintosh)
   1906- . . . . CLC 7, 14, 32
   See also CAAS 3; CA 85-88

Stewart, Mary (Florence Elinor)
   1916- . . . . CLC 7, 35
   See also CANR 1; CA 1-4R; SATA 12

Stewart, Will 1908-
   See Williamson, Jack
   See also CANR 23; CA 17-18R

Still, James 1906- . . . . CLC 49
   See also CANR 10, 26; CA 65-68;
   SATA 29; DLB 9

Sting 1951-
   See The Police

Stitt, Milan 1941- . . . . CLC 29
   See also CA 69-72

Stoker, Abraham
   See Stoker, Bram
   See also CA 105; SATA 29

Stoker, Bram 1847-1912 . . . . TCLC 8
   See also Stoker, Abraham
   See also SATA 29; DLB 36, 70

Stolz, Mary (Slattery) 1920- . . . . CLC 12
   See also CANR 13; CA 5-8R; SAAS 3;
   SATA 10

Stone, Irving 1903-1989 . . . . CLC 7
   See also CAAS 3; CANR 1; CA 1-4R, 129;
   SATA 3

Stone, Robert (Anthony)
   1937?- . . . . CLC 5, 23, 42
   See also CANR 23; CA 85-88

Stoppard, Tom
   1937- . . . CLC 1, 3, 4, 5, 8, 15, 29, 34, 63
   See also CA 81-84; DLB 13; DLB-Y 85

Storey, David (Malcolm)
    1933- .... CLC 2, 4, 5, 8
    See also CA 81-84; DLB 13, 14

Storm, Hyemeyohsts 1935- .... CLC 3
    See also CA 81-84

Storm, (Hans) Theodor (Woldsen)
    1817-1888 .... NCLC 1

Storni, Alfonsina 1892-1938 .... TCLC 5
    See also CA 104

Stout, Rex (Todhunter) 1886-1975 ... CLC 3
    See also CA 61-64

Stow, (Julian) Randolph 1935- .. CLC 23, 48
    See also CA 13-16R

Stowe, Harriet (Elizabeth) Beecher
    1811-1896 .... NCLC 3
    See also YABC 1; DLB 1, 12, 42, 74;
    CDALB 1865-1917

Strachey, (Giles) Lytton
    1880-1932 .... TCLC 12
    See also CA 110

Strand, Mark 1934- .... CLC 6, 18, 41
    See also CA 21-24R; SATA 41; DLB 5

Straub, Peter (Francis) 1943- ...... CLC 28
    See also CA 85-88; DLB-Y 84

Strauss, Botho 1944- .... CLC 22

Straussler, Tomas 1937-
    See Stoppard, Tom

Streatfeild, (Mary) Noel 1897- ..... CLC 21
    See also CA 81-84; obituary CA 120;
    SATA 20, 48

Stribling, T(homas) S(igismund)
    1881-1965 .... CLC 23
    See also obituary CA 107; DLB 9

Strindberg, (Johan) August
    1849-1912 .... TCLC 1, 8, 21
    See also CA 104

Stringer, Arthur 1874-1950 .... TCLC 37
    See also DLB 92

Strugatskii, Arkadii (Natanovich)
    1925- .... CLC 27
    See also CA 106

Strugatskii, Boris (Natanovich)
    1933- .... CLC 27
    See also CA 106

Strummer, Joe 1953?-
    See The Clash

Stuart, (Hilton) Jesse
    1906-1984 ...... CLC 1, 8, 11, 14, 34
    See also CA 5-8R; obituary CA 112;
    SATA 2; obituary SATA 36; DLB 9, 48;
    DLB-Y 84

Sturgeon, Theodore (Hamilton)
    1918-1985 .... CLC 22, 39
    See also CA 81-84; obituary CA 116;
    DLB 8; DLB-Y 85

Styron, William
    1925- .... CLC 1, 3, 5, 11, 15, 60
    See also CANR 6; CA 5-8R; DLB 2;
    DLB-Y 80; CDALB 1968-1987

Sudermann, Hermann 1857-1928 .. TCLC 15
    See also CA 107

Sue, Eugene 1804-1857 .... NCLC 1

Sukenick, Ronald 1932-..... CLC 3, 4, 6, 48
    See also CAAS 8; CA 25-28R; DLB-Y 81

Suknaski, Andrew 1942- .... CLC 19
    See also CA 101; DLB 53

Sully Prudhomme 1839-1907..... TCLC 31

Su Man-shu 1884-1918.......... TCLC 24
    See also CA 123

Summers, Andrew James 1942-
    See The Police

Summers, Andy 1942-
    See The Police

Summers, Hollis (Spurgeon, Jr.)
    1916- .... CLC 10
    See also CANR 3; CA 5-8R; DLB 6

Summers, (Alphonsus Joseph-Mary Augustus)
    Montague 1880-1948....... TCLC 16
    See also CA 118

Sumner, Gordon Matthew 1951-
    See The Police

Surtees, Robert Smith
    1805-1864 .... NCLC 14
    See also DLB 21

Susann, Jacqueline 1921-1974....... CLC 3
    See also CA 65-68; obituary CA 53-56

Suskind, Patrick 1949-........... CLC 44

Sutcliff, Rosemary 1920- .... CLC 26
    See also CLR 1; CA 5-8R; SATA 6, 44

Sutro, Alfred 1863-1933........... TCLC 6
    See also CA 105; DLB 10

Sutton, Henry 1935-
    See Slavitt, David (R.)

Svevo, Italo 1861-1928........ TCLC 2, 35
    See also Schmitz, Ettore

Swados, Elizabeth 1951- .... CLC 12
    See also CA 97-100

Swados, Harvey 1920-1972 .... CLC 5
    See also CANR 6; CA 5-8R;
    obituary CA 37-40R; DLB 2

Swan, Gladys 1934- .... CLC 69
    See also CANR 17; CA 101

Swarthout, Glendon (Fred) 1918- ... CLC 35
    See also CANR 1; CA 1-4R; SATA 26

Swenson, May 1919-1989..... CLC 4, 14, 61
    See also CA 5-8R; obituary CA 130;
    SATA 15; DLB 5

Swift, Graham 1949- .... CLC 41
    See also CA 117, 122

Swift, Jonathan 1667-1745.......... LC 1
    See also SATA 19; DLB 39

Swinburne, Algernon Charles
    1837-1909 .... TCLC 8, 36
    See also CA 105; DLB 35, 57

Swinfen, Ann 19??-............... CLC 34

Swinnerton, Frank (Arthur)
    1884-1982 .... CLC 31
    See also obituary CA 108; DLB 34

Symonds, John Addington
    1840-1893 .... NCLC 34
    See also DLB 57

Symons, Arthur (William)
    1865-1945 .... TCLC 11
    See also CA 107; DLB 19, 57

Symons, Julian (Gustave)
    1912- .... CLC 2, 14, 32
    See also CAAS 3; CANR 3; CA 49-52;
    DLB 87

Synge, (Edmund) John Millington
    1871-1909 .... TCLC 6, 37; DC 2
    See also CA 104; DLB 10, 19

Syruc, J. 1911-
    See Milosz, Czeslaw

Szirtes, George 1948-............. CLC 46
    See also CANR 27; CA 109

Tabori, George 1914-............. CLC 19
    See also CANR 4; CA 49-52

Tagore, (Sir) Rabindranath
    1861-1941 .... TCLC 3
    See also Thakura, Ravindranatha
    See also CA 120

Taine, Hippolyte Adolphe
    1828-1893 .... NCLC 15

Talese, Gaetano 1932-
    See Talese, Gay

Talese, Gay 1932-................. CLC 37
    See also CANR 9; CA 1-4R

Tallent, Elizabeth (Ann) 1954- ..... CLC 45
    See also CA 117

Tally, Ted 1952-.................. CLC 42
    See also CA 120, 124

Tamayo y Baus, Manuel
    1829-1898 .... NCLC 1

Tammsaare, A(nton) H(ansen)
    1878-1940 .... TCLC 27

Tan, Amy 1952- .... CLC 59

Tanizaki, Jun'ichiro
    1886-1965 .... CLC 8, 14, 28
    See also CA 93-96; obituary CA 25-28R

Tarbell, Ida 1857-1944 .... TCLC 40
    See also CA 122; DLB 47

Tarkington, (Newton) Booth
    1869-1946 .... TCLC 9
    See also CA 110; SATA 17; DLB 9

Tasso, Torquato 1544-1595 .... LC 5

Tate, (John Orley) Allen
    1899-1979 .... CLC 2, 4, 6, 9, 11, 14, 24
    See also CA 5-8R; obituary CA 85-88;
    DLB 4, 45, 63

Tate, James 1943-............ CLC 2, 6, 25
    See also CA 21-24R; DLB 5

Tavel, Ronald 1940-.............. CLC 6
    See also CA 21-24R

Taylor, C(ecil) P(hillip) 1929-1981 .. CLC 27
    See also CA 25-28R; obituary CA 105

Taylor, Edward 1642?-1729........ LC 11
    See also DLB 24

Taylor, Eleanor Ross 1920-......... CLC 5
    See also CA 81-84

Taylor, Elizabeth 1912-1975 ... CLC 2, 4, 29
    See also CANR 9; CA 13-16R; SATA 13

Taylor, Henry (Splawn) 1917-...... CLC 44
    See also CAAS 7; CA 33-36R; DLB 5

Taylor, Kamala (Purnaiya) 1924-
    See Markandaya, Kamala
    See also CA 77-80

Taylor, Mildred D(elois) 1943- ..... **CLC 21**
See also CLR 9; CANR 25; CA 85-88;
SAAS 5; SATA 15; DLB 52

Taylor, Peter (Hillsman)
1917- .... **CLC 1, 4, 18, 37, 44, 50**
See also CANR 9; CA 13-16R; DLB-Y 81

Taylor, Robert Lewis 1912- .... **CLC 14**
See also CANR 3; CA 1-4R; SATA 10

Teasdale, Sara 1884-1933. .... **TCLC 4**
See also CA 104; SATA 32; DLB 45

Tegner, Esaias 1782-1846. .... **NCLC 2**

Teilhard de Chardin, (Marie Joseph) Pierre
1881-1955 .... **TCLC 9**
See also CA 105

Tennant, Emma 1937- .... **CLC 13, 52**
See also CAAS 9; CANR 10; CA 65-68;
DLB 14

Tennyson, Alfred 1809-1892 ..... **NCLC 30**
See also DLB 32

Teran, Lisa St. Aubin de 19??- ..... **CLC 36**

Teresa de Jesus, St. 1515-1582 ...... **LC 18**

Terkel, Louis 1912-
See Terkel, Studs
See also CANR 18; CA 57-60

Terkel, Studs 1912- .... **CLC 38**
See also Terkel, Louis

Terry, Megan 1932- .... **CLC 19**
See also CA 77-80; CABS 3; DLB 7

Tertz, Abram 1925-
See Sinyavsky, Andrei (Donatevich)

Tesich, Steve 1943?- .... **CLC 40, 69**
See also CA 105; DLB-Y 83

Tesich, Stoyan 1943?-
See Tesich, Steve

Teternikov, Fyodor Kuzmich 1863-1927
See Sologub, Fyodor
See also CA 104

Tevis, Walter 1928-1984 .... **CLC 42**
See also CA 113

Tey, Josephine 1897-1952 .... **TCLC 14**
See also Mackintosh, Elizabeth

Thackeray, William Makepeace
1811-1863 .... **NCLC 5, 14, 22**
See also SATA 23; DLB 21, 55

Thakura, Ravindranatha 1861-1941
See Tagore, (Sir) Rabindranath
See also CA 104

Tharoor, Shashi 1956- .... **CLC 70**

Thelwell, Michael (Miles) 1939- .... **CLC 22**
See also CA 101

Theroux, Alexander (Louis)
1939- .... **CLC 2, 25**
See also CANR 20; CA 85-88

Theroux, Paul
1941- .... **CLC 5, 8, 11, 15, 28, 46**
See also CANR 20; CA 33-36R; SATA 44;
DLB 2

Thesen, Sharon 1946-............. **CLC 56**

Thibault, Jacques Anatole Francois
1844-1924
See France, Anatole
See also CA 106

Thiele, Colin (Milton) 1920- .... **CLC 17**
See also CANR 12; CA 29-32R; SAAS 2;
SATA 14

Thomas, Audrey (Grace)
1935- .... **CLC 7, 13, 37**
See also CA 21-24R; DLB 60

Thomas, D(onald) M(ichael)
1935- .... **CLC 13, 22, 31**
See also CANR 17; CA 61-64; DLB 40

Thomas, Dylan (Marlais)
1914-1953 ..... **TCLC 1, 8; PC 2; SSC 3**
See also CA 104, 120; SATA 60; DLB 13,
20

Thomas, Edward (Philip)
1878-1917 .... **TCLC 10**
See also CA 106; DLB 19

Thomas, John Peter 1928-
See Thomas, Piri

Thomas, Joyce Carol 1938- .... **CLC 35**
See also CLR 19; CA 113, 116; SAAS 7;
SATA 40; DLB 33

Thomas, Lewis 1913- .... **CLC 35**
See also CA 85-88

Thomas, Piri 1928-............... **CLC 17**
See also CA 73-76

Thomas, R(onald) S(tuart)
1913- .... **CLC 6, 13, 48**
See also CAAS 4; CA 89-92; DLB 27

Thomas, Ross (Elmore) 1926- ...... **CLC 39**
See also CANR 22; CA 33-36R

Thompson, Ernest 1860-1946
See Seton, Ernest (Evan) Thompson

Thompson, Francis (Joseph)
1859-1907 .... **TCLC 4**
See also CA 104; DLB 19

Thompson, Hunter S(tockton)
1939- .... **CLC 9, 17, 40**
See also CANR 23; CA 17-20R

Thompson, James Meyers 1906-1976
See Thompson, Jim

Thompson, Jim 1906-1976 .... **CLC 69**

Thompson, Judith 1954-.......... **CLC 39**

Thomson, James 1700-1748. .... **LC 16**
See also DLB 95

Thomson, James 1834-1882...... **NCLC 18**
See also DLB 35

Thoreau, Henry David
1817-1862 .... **NCLC 7, 21**
See also DLB 1; CDALB 1640-1865

Thurber, James (Grover)
1894-1961 .... **CLC 5, 11, 25; SSC 1**
See also CANR 17; CA 73-76; SATA 13;
DLB 4, 11, 22

Thurman, Wallace 1902-1934 ...... **TCLC 6**
See also BLC 3; CA 104, 124; DLB 51

Tieck, (Johann) Ludwig
1773-1853 .... **NCLC 5**
See also DLB 90

Tilghman, Christopher 1948?- ...... **CLC 65**

Tillinghast, Richard 1940- .... **CLC 29**
See also CANR 26; CA 29-32R

Timrod, Henry 1828-1867 ...... **NCLC 25**

Tindall, Gillian 1938-............. **CLC 7**
See also CANR 11; CA 21-24R

Tiptree, James, Jr. 1915-1987... **CLC 48, 50**
See also Sheldon, Alice (Hastings) B(radley)
See also DLB 8

Tocqueville, Alexis (Charles Henri Maurice
Clerel, Comte) de 1805-1859.. **NCLC 7**

Tolkien, J(ohn) R(onald) R(euel)
1892-1973 .... **CLC 1, 2, 3, 8, 12, 38**
See also CAP 2; CA 17-18;
obituary CA 45-48; SATA 2, 24, 32;
obituary SATA 24; DLB 15

Toller, Ernst 1893-1939 .... **TCLC 10**
See also CA 107

Tolson, Melvin B(eaunorus)
1898?-1966. .... **CLC 36**
See also BLC 3; CA 124;
obituary CA 89-92; DLB 48, 76

Tolstoy, (Count) Alexey Nikolayevich
1883-1945 .... **TCLC 18**
See also CA 107

Tolstoy, (Count) Leo (Lev Nikolaevich)
1828-1910 ..... **TCLC 4, 11, 17, 28, 44;
SSC 9**
See also CA 104, 123; SATA 26

Tomlin, Lily 1939- .... **CLC 17**

Tomlin, Mary Jean 1939-
See Tomlin, Lily
See also CA 117

Tomlinson, (Alfred) Charles
1927-............. **CLC 2, 4, 6, 13, 45**
See also CA 5-8R; DLB 40

Toole, John Kennedy
1937-1969 .... **CLC 19, 64**
See also CA 104; DLB-Y 81

Toomer, Jean
1894-1967 ..... **CLC 1, 4, 13, 22; SSC 1**
See also BLC 3; CA 85-88; DLB 45, 51;
CDALB 1917-1929

Torrey, E. Fuller 19??-............ **CLC 34**
See also CA 119

Tosei 1644-1694
See Basho, Matsuo

Tournier, Michel 1924- ...... **CLC 6, 23, 36**
See also CANR 3; CA 49-52; SATA 23;
DLB 83

Townsend, Sue 1946- .... **CLC 61**
See also CA 119, 127; SATA 48, 55

Townshend, Peter (Dennis Blandford)
1945- .... **CLC 17, 42**
See also CA 107

Tozzi, Federigo 1883-1920. ...... **TCLC 31**

Traill, Catharine Parr
1802-1899 .... **NCLC 31**
See also DLB 99

Trakl, Georg 1887-1914........... **TCLC 5**
See also CA 104

Transtromer, Tomas (Gosta)
1931- .... **CLC 52, 65**
See also CA 129; brief entry CA 117

Traven, B. 1890-1969........... **CLC 8, 11**
See also CAP 2; CA 19-20;
obituary CA 25-28R; DLB 9, 56

Treitel, Jonathan 1959- .... **CLC 70**

Tremain, Rose 1943-............. **CLC 42**
See also CA 97-100; DLB 14

Vazov, Ivan   1850-1921 . . . . **TCLC 25**
See also CA 121

Veblen, Thorstein Bunde
1857-1929 . . . . **TCLC 31**
See also CA 115

Verga, Giovanni   1840-1922 . . . . **TCLC 3**
See also CA 104, 123

Verhaeren, Emile (Adolphe Gustave)
1855-1916 . . . . **TCLC 12**
See also CA 109

Verlaine, Paul (Marie)
1844-1896 . . . . **NCLC 2; PC 2**

Verne, Jules (Gabriel)   1828-1905 . . . **TCLC 6**
See also CA 110; SATA 21

Very, Jones   1813-1880 . . . . **NCLC 9**
See also DLB 1

Vesaas, Tarjei   1897-1970 . . . . **CLC 48**
See also obituary CA 29-32R

Vian, Boris   1920-1959 . . . . **TCLC 9**
See also CA 106; DLB 72

Viaud, (Louis Marie) Julien   1850-1923
See Loti, Pierre
See also CA 107

Vicker, Angus   1916-
See Felsen, Henry Gregor

Vidal, Eugene Luther, Jr.   1925-
See Vidal, Gore

Vidal, Gore
1925- . . . . **CLC 2, 4, 6, 8, 10, 22, 33**
See also CANR 13; CA 5-8R; DLB 6

Viereck, Peter (Robert Edwin)
1916- . . . . **CLC 4**
See also CANR 1; CA 1-4R; DLB 5

Vigny, Alfred (Victor) de
1797-1863 . . . . **NCLC 7**

Vilakazi, Benedict Wallet
1905-1947 . . . . **TCLC 37**

Villiers de l'Isle Adam, Jean Marie Mathias
Philippe Auguste, Comte de
1838-1889 . . . . **NCLC 3**

Vinci, Leonardo da   1452-1519 . . . . . . **LC 12**

Vine, Barbara   1930- . . . . **CLC 50**
See also Rendell, Ruth

Vinge, Joan (Carol) D(ennison)
1948- . . . . **CLC 30**
See also CA 93-96; SATA 36

Visconti, Luchino   1906-1976 . . . . **CLC 16**
See also CA 81-84; obituary CA 65-68

Vittorini, Elio   1908-1966 . . . . . . **CLC 6, 9, 14**
See also obituary CA 25-28R

Vizinczey, Stephen   1933- . . . . **CLC 40**

Vliet, R(ussell) G(ordon)
1929-1984 . . . . **CLC 22**
See also CANR 18; CA 37-40R;
obituary CA 112

Voight, Ellen Bryant   1943- . . . . **CLC 54**
See also CANR 11; CA 69-72

Voigt, Cynthia   1942- . . . . **CLC 30**
See also CANR 18; CA 106; SATA 33, 48;
AAYA 3

Voinovich, Vladimir (Nikolaevich)
1932- . . . . **CLC 10, 49**
See also CA 81-84

Voltaire   1694-1778 . . . . **LC 14**

Von Daeniken, Erich   1935-
See Von Daniken, Erich
See also CANR 17; CA 37-40R

Von Daniken, Erich   1935- . . . . **CLC 30**
See also Von Daeniken, Erich

Vonnegut, Kurt, Jr.
1922- . . . . . . **CLC 1, 2, 3, 4, 5, 8, 12, 22,
40, 60; SSC 8**
See also CANR 1, 25; CA 1-4R; DLB 2, 8;
DLB-Y 80; DLB-DS 3;
CDALB 1968-1988; AAYA 6

Vorster, Gordon   1924- . . . . **CLC 34**

Voznesensky, Andrei   1933- . . . **CLC 1, 15, 57**
See also CA 89-92

Waddington, Miriam   1917- . . . . **CLC 28**
See also CANR 12, 30; CA 21-24R;
DLB 68

Wagman, Fredrica   1937- . . . . **CLC 7**
See also CA 97-100

Wagner, Richard   1813-1883 . . . . . . **NCLC 9**

Wagner-Martin, Linda   1936- . . . . **CLC 50**

Wagoner, David (Russell)
1926- . . . . **CLC 3, 5, 15**
See also CAAS 3; CANR 2; CA 1-4R;
SATA 14; DLB 5

Wah, Fred(erick James)   1939- . . . . . . **CLC 44**
See also CA 107; DLB 60

Wahloo, Per   1926-1975 . . . . **CLC 7**
See also CA 61-64

Wahloo, Peter   1926-1975
See Wahloo, Per

Wain, John (Barrington)
1925- . . . . **CLC 2, 11, 15, 46**
See also CAAS 4; CANR 23; CA 5-8R;
DLB 15, 27

Wajda, Andrzej   1926- . . . . **CLC 16**
See also CA 102

Wakefield, Dan   1932- . . . . **CLC 7**
See also CAAS 7; CA 21-24R

Wakoski, Diane
1937- . . . . **CLC 2, 4, 7, 9, 11, 40**
See also CAAS 1; CANR 9; CA 13-16R;
DLB 5

Walcott, Derek (Alton)
1930- . . . . **CLC 2, 4, 9, 14, 25, 42, 67**
See also BLC 3; CANR 26; CA 89-92;
DLB-Y 81

Waldman, Anne   1945- . . . . **CLC 7**
See also CA 37-40R; DLB 16

Waldo, Edward Hamilton   1918-
See Sturgeon, Theodore (Hamilton)

Walker, Alice
1944- . . . . . . **CLC 5, 6, 9, 19, 27, 46, 58;
SSC 5**
See also BLC 3; CANR 9, 27; CA 37-40R;
SATA 31; DLB 6, 33;
CDALB 1968-1988; AAYA 3

Walker, David Harry   1911- . . . . **CLC 14**
See also CANR 1; CA 1-4R; SATA 8

Walker, Edward Joseph   1934-
See Walker, Ted
See also CANR 12; CA 21-24R

Walker, George F.   1947- . . . . **CLC 44, 61**
See also CANR 21; CA 103; DLB 60

Walker, Joseph A.   1935- . . . . **CLC 19**
See also CANR 26; CA 89-92; DLB 38

Walker, Margaret (Abigail)
1915- . . . . **CLC 1, 6**
See also BLC 3; CANR 26; CA 73-76;
DLB 76

Walker, Ted   1934- . . . . **CLC 13**
See also Walker, Edward Joseph
See also DLB 40

Wallace, David Foster   1962- . . . . **CLC 50**

Wallace, Irving   1916- . . . . **CLC 7, 13**
See also CAAS 1; CANR 1; CA 1-4R

Wallant, Edward Lewis
1926-1962 . . . . **CLC 5, 10**
See also CANR 22; CA 1-4R; DLB 2, 28

Walpole, Horace   1717-1797 . . . . **LC 2**
See also DLB 39

Walpole, (Sir) Hugh (Seymour)
1884-1941 . . . . **TCLC 5**
See also CA 104; DLB 34

Walser, Martin   1927- . . . . **CLC 27**
See also CANR 8; CA 57-60; DLB 75

Walser, Robert   1878-1956 . . . . **TCLC 18**
See also CA 118; DLB 66

Walsh, Gillian Paton   1939-
See Walsh, Jill Paton
See also CA 37-40R; SATA 4

Walsh, Jill Paton   1939- . . . . **CLC 35**
See also CLR 2; SAAS 3

Wambaugh, Joseph (Aloysius, Jr.)
1937- . . . . **CLC 3, 18**
See also CA 33-36R; DLB 6; DLB-Y 83

Ward, Arthur Henry Sarsfield   1883-1959
See Rohmer, Sax
See also CA 108

Ward, Douglas Turner   1930- . . . . **CLC 19**
See also CA 81-84; DLB 7, 38

Warhol, Andy   1928-1987 . . . . **CLC 20**
See also CA 89-92; obituary CA 121

Warner, Francis (Robert le Plastrier)
1937- . . . . **CLC 14**
See also CANR 11; CA 53-56

Warner, Marina   1946- . . . . **CLC 59**
See also CANR 21; CA 65-68

Warner, Rex (Ernest)   1905-1986 . . . . **CLC 45**
See also CA 89-92; obituary CA 119;
DLB 15

Warner, Susan   1819-1885 . . . . **NCLC 31**
See also DLB 3, 42

Warner, Sylvia Townsend
1893-1978 . . . . **CLC 7, 19**
See also CANR 16; CA 61-64;
obituary CA 77-80; DLB 34

Warren, Mercy Otis   1728-1814 . . . **NCLC 13**
See also DLB 31

Warren, Robert Penn
1905-1989 . . . **CLC 1, 4, 6, 8, 10, 13, 18,
39, 53, 59; SSC 4**
See also CANR 10; CA 13-16R, 129, 130;
SATA 46; DLB 2, 48; DLB-Y 80;
CDALB 1968-1987

Warshofsky, Isaac   1904-1991
See Singer, Isaac Bashevis

Warton, Thomas   1728-1790 . . . . **LC 15**

Washington, Booker T(aliaferro)
1856-1915 . . . . **TCLC 10**
See also BLC 3; CA 114, 125; SATA 28

Wassermann, Jakob   1873-1934 . . . . . **TCLC 6**
See also CA 104; DLB 66

Wasserstein, Wendy   1950- . . . . . **CLC 32, 59**
See also CA 121; CABS 3

Waterhouse, Keith (Spencer)
1929- . . . . **CLC 47**
See also CA 5-8R; DLB 13, 15

Waters, Roger   1944-
See Pink Floyd

Wa Thiong'o, Ngugi
1938- . . . . **CLC 3, 7, 13, 36**
See also Ngugi, James (Thiong'o); Ngugi wa
Thiong'o

Watkins, Paul   1964- . . . . **CLC 55**

Watkins, Vernon (Phillips)
1906-1967 . . . . **CLC 43**
See also CAP 1; CA 9-10;
obituary CA 25-28R; DLB 20

Waugh, Auberon (Alexander)   1939- . . **CLC 7**
See also CANR 6, 22; CA 45-48; DLB 14

Waugh, Evelyn (Arthur St. John)
1903-1966 . . . **CLC 1, 3, 8, 13, 19, 27, 44**
See also CANR 22; CA 85-88;
obituary CA 25-28R; DLB 15

Waugh, Harriet   1944- . . . . **CLC 6**
See also CANR 22; CA 85-88

Webb, Beatrice (Potter)
1858-1943 . . . . **TCLC 22**
See also CA 117

Webb, Charles (Richard)   1939- . . . . . . **CLC 7**
See also CA 25-28R

Webb, James H(enry), Jr.   1946- . . . . **CLC 22**
See also CA 81-84

Webb, Mary (Gladys Meredith)
1881-1927 . . . . **TCLC 24**
See also CA 123; DLB 34

Webb, Phyllis   1927- . . . . **CLC 18**
See also CANR 23; CA 104; DLB 53

Webb, Sidney (James)
1859-1947 . . . . **TCLC 22**
See also CA 117

Webber, Andrew Lloyd   1948- . . . . . . **CLC 21**

Weber, Lenora Mattingly
1895-1971 . . . . **CLC 12**
See also CAP 1; CA 19-20;
obituary CA 29-32R; SATA 2;
obituary SATA 26

Webster, John   1580?-1634? . . . . **DC 2**
See also DLB 58

Webster, Noah   1758-1843 . . . . **NCLC 30**
See also DLB 1, 37, 42, 43, 73

Wedekind, (Benjamin) Frank(lin)
1864-1918 . . . . **TCLC 7**
See also CA 104

Weidman, Jerome   1913- . . . . **CLC 7**
See also CANR 1; CA 1-4R; DLB 28

Weil, Simone   1909-1943 . . . . **TCLC 23**
See also CA 117

Weinstein, Nathan Wallenstein   1903-1940
See West, Nathanael

Weir, Peter   1944- . . . . **CLC 20**
See also CA 113, 123

Weiss, Peter (Ulrich)
1916-1982 . . . . **CLC 3, 15, 51**
See also CANR 3; CA 45-48;
obituary CA 106; DLB 69

Weiss, Theodore (Russell)
1916- . . . . **CLC 3, 8, 14**
See also CAAS 2; CA 9-12R; DLB 5

Welch, (Maurice) Denton
1915-1948 . . . . **TCLC 22**
See also CA 121

Welch, James   1940- . . . . **CLC 6, 14, 52**
See also CA 85-88

Weldon, Fay
1933- . . . . **CLC 6, 9, 11, 19, 36, 59**
See also CANR 16; CA 21-24R; DLB 14

Wellek, Rene   1903- . . . . **CLC 28**
See also CAAS 7; CANR 8; CA 5-8R;
DLB 63

Weller, Michael   1942- . . . . **CLC 10, 53**
See also CA 85-88

Weller, Paul   1958- . . . . **CLC 26**

Wellershoff, Dieter   1925- . . . . **CLC 46**
See also CANR 16; CA 89-92

Welles, (George) Orson
1915-1985 . . . . **CLC 20**
See also CA 93-96; obituary CA 117

Wellman, Mac   1945- . . . . **CLC 65**

Wellman, Manly Wade   1903-1986 . . **CLC 49**
See also CANR 6, 16; CA 1-4R;
obituary CA 118; SATA 6, 47

Wells, Carolyn   1862-1942 . . . . **TCLC 35**
See also CA 113; DLB 11

Wells, H(erbert) G(eorge)
1866-1946 . . . . . . **TCLC 6, 12, 19; SSC 6**
See also CA 110, 121; SATA 20; DLB 34,
70

Wells, Rosemary   1943- . . . . **CLC 12**
See also CLR 16; CA 85-88; SAAS 1;
SATA 18

Welty, Eudora (Alice)
1909- . . . . **CLC 1, 2, 5, 14, 22, 33; SSC 1**
See also CA 9-12R; CABS 1; DLB 2;
DLB-Y 87; CDALB 1941-1968

Wen I-to   1899-1946 . . . . **TCLC 28**

Werfel, Franz (V.)   1890-1945 . . . . . . **TCLC 8**
See also CA 104; DLB 81

Wergeland, Henrik Arnold
1808-1845 . . . . **NCLC 5**

Wersba, Barbara   1932- . . . . **CLC 30**
See also CLR 3; CANR 16; CA 29-32R;
SAAS 2; SATA 1, 58; DLB 52

Wertmuller, Lina   1928- . . . . **CLC 16**
See also CA 97-100

Wescott, Glenway   1901-1987 . . . . . . **CLC 13**
See also CANR 23; CA 13-16R;
obituary CA 121; DLB 4, 9

Wesker, Arnold   1932- . . . . **CLC 3, 5, 42**
See also CAAS 7; CANR 1; CA 1-4R;
DLB 13

Wesley, Richard (Errol)   1945- . . . . . . **CLC 7**
See also CA 57-60; DLB 38

Wessel, Johan Herman   1742-1785 . . . . **LC 7**

West, Anthony (Panther)
1914-1987 . . . . **CLC 50**
See also CANR 3, 19; CA 45-48; DLB 15

West, Jessamyn   1907-1984 . . . . . . **CLC 7, 17**
See also CA 9-12R; obituary CA 112;
obituary SATA 37; DLB 6; DLB-Y 84

West, Morris L(anglo)   1916- . . . . . **CLC 6, 33**
See also CA 5-8R; obituary CA 124

West, Nathanael
1903-1940 . . . . **TCLC 1, 14, 44**
See also CA 104, 125; DLB 4, 9, 28;
CDALB 1929-1941

West, Paul   1930- . . . . **CLC 7, 14**
See also CAAS 7; CANR 22; CA 13-16R;
DLB 14

West, Rebecca   1892-1983 . . **CLC 7, 9, 31, 50**
See also CANR 19; CA 5-8R;
obituary CA 109; DLB 36; DLB-Y 83

Westall, Robert (Atkinson)   1929- . . . **CLC 17**
See also CLR 13; CANR 18; CA 69-72;
SAAS 2; SATA 23

Westlake, Donald E(dwin)
1933- . . . . **CLC 7, 33**
See also CANR 16; CA 17-20R

Westmacott, Mary   1890-1976
See Christie, (Dame) Agatha (Mary
Clarissa)

Whalen, Philip   1923- . . . . **CLC 6, 29**
See also CANR 5; CA 9-12R; DLB 16

Wharton, Edith (Newbold Jones)
1862-1937 . . . . **TCLC 3, 9, 27; SSC 6**
See also CA 104; DLB 4, 9, 12, 78;
CDALB 1865-1917

Wharton, William   1925- . . . . **CLC 18, 37**
See also CA 93-96; DLB-Y 80

Wheatley (Peters), Phillis
1753?-1784 . . . . **LC 3; PC 3**
See also BLC 3; DLB 31, 50;
CDALB 1640-1865

Wheelock, John Hall   1886-1978 . . . . **CLC 14**
See also CANR 14; CA 13-16R;
obituary CA 77-80; DLB 45

Whelan, John   1900-
See O'Faolain, Sean

Whitaker, Rodney   1925-
See Trevanian

White, E(lwyn) B(rooks)
1899-1985 . . . . **CLC 10, 34, 39**
See also CLR 1; CANR 16; CA 13-16R;
obituary CA 116; SATA 2, 29, 44;
obituary SATA 44; DLB 11, 22

White, Edmund III   1940- . . . . **CLC 27**
See also CANR 3, 19; CA 45-48

White, Patrick (Victor Martindale)
1912-1990 . . **CLC 3, 4, 5, 7, 9, 18, 65, 69**
See also CA 81-84; obituary CA 132

White, T(erence) H(anbury)
1906-1964 . . . . **CLC 30**
See also CA 73-76; SATA 12

White, Terence de Vere   1912- . . . . . . **CLC 49**
See also CANR 3; CA 49-52

White, Walter (Francis)
    1893-1955 .... TCLC 15
    See also BLC 3; CA 115, 124; DLB 51

White, William Hale   1831-1913
    See Rutherford, Mark
    See also CA 121

Whitehead, E(dward) A(nthony)
    1933- .... CLC 5
    See also CA 65-68

Whitemore, Hugh   1936- .... CLC 37

Whitman, Sarah Helen
    1803-1878 .... NCLC 19
    See also DLB 1

Whitman, Walt
    1819-1892 .... NCLC 4, 31; PC 3
    See also SATA 20; DLB 3, 64;
    CDALB 1640-1865

Whitney, Phyllis A(yame)   1903- .... CLC 42
    See also CANR 3, 25; CA 1-4R; SATA 1,
    30

Whittemore, (Edward) Reed (Jr.)
    1919- .... CLC 4
    See also CAAS 8; CANR 4; CA 9-12R;
    DLB 5

Whittier, John Greenleaf
    1807-1892 .... NCLC 8
    See also DLB 1; CDALB 1640-1865

Wicker, Thomas Grey   1926-
    See Wicker, Tom
    See also CANR 21; CA 65-68

Wicker, Tom   1926- .... CLC 7
    See also Wicker, Thomas Grey

Wideman, John Edgar
    1941- .... CLC 5, 34, 36, 67
    See also BLC 3; CANR 14; CA 85-88;
    DLB 33

Wiebe, Rudy (H.)   1934- ...... CLC 6, 11, 14
    See also CA 37-40R; DLB 60

Wieland, Christoph Martin
    1733-1813 .... NCLC 17

Wieners, John   1934- .... CLC 7
    See also CA 13-16R; DLB 16

Wiesel, Elie(zer)   1928- ..... CLC 3, 5, 11, 37
    See also CAAS 4; CANR 8; CA 5-8R;
    SATA 56; DLB 83; DLB-Y 87

Wiggins, Marianne   1948- .... CLC 57

Wight, James Alfred   1916-
    See Herriot, James
    See also CA 77-80; SATA 44

Wilbur, Richard (Purdy)
    1921- .... CLC 3, 6, 9, 14, 53
    See also CANR 2; CA 1-4R; CABS 2;
    SATA 9; DLB 5

Wild, Peter   1940- .... CLC 14
    See also CA 37-40R; DLB 5

Wilde, Oscar (Fingal O'Flahertie Wills)
    1854-1900 .... TCLC 1, 8, 23, 41
    See also CA 119; brief entry CA 104;
    SATA 24; DLB 10, 19, 34, 57

Wilder, Billy   1906- .... CLC 20
    See also Wilder, Samuel
    See also DLB 26

Wilder, Samuel   1906-
    See Wilder, Billy
    See also CA 89-92

Wilder, Thornton (Niven)
    1897-1975 ..... CLC 1, 5, 6, 10, 15, 35;
                                DC 1
    See also CA 13-16R; obituary CA 61-64;
    DLB 4, 7, 9

Wiley, Richard   1944- .... CLC 44
    See also CA 121, 129

Wilhelm, Kate   1928- .... CLC 7
    See also CAAS 5; CANR 17; CA 37-40R;
    DLB 8

Willard, Nancy   1936- .... CLC 7, 37
    See also CLR 5; CANR 10; CA 89-92;
    SATA 30, 37; DLB 5, 52

Williams, C(harles) K(enneth)
    1936- .... CLC 33, 56
    See also CA 37-40R; DLB 5

Williams, Charles (Walter Stansby)
    1886-1945 .... TCLC 1, 11
    See also CA 104

Williams, Ella Gwendolen Rees   1890-1979
    See Rhys, Jean

Williams, (George) Emlyn
    1905-1987 .... CLC 15
    See also CA 104, 123; DLB 10, 77

Williams, Hugo   1942- .... CLC 42
    See also CA 17-20R; DLB 40

Williams, John A(lfred)   1925- .... CLC 5, 13
    See also BLC 3; CAAS 3; CANR 6, 26;
    CA 53-56; DLB 2, 33

Williams, Jonathan (Chamberlain)
    1929- .... CLC 13
    See also CANR 8; CA 9-12R; DLB 5

Williams, Joy   1944- .... CLC 31
    See also CANR 22; CA 41-44R

Williams, Norman   1952- .... CLC 39
    See also CA 118

Williams, Paulette   1948-
    See Shange, Ntozake

Williams, Sherley Anne   1944-
    See also BLC 3; CANR 25; CA 73-76;
    DLB 41

Williams, Shirley   1944-
    See Williams, Sherley Anne

Williams, Tennessee
    1911-1983 .... CLC 1, 2, 5, 7, 8, 11, 15,
                           19, 30, 39, 45
    See also CA 5-8R; obituary CA 108; DLB 7;
    DLB-Y 83; DLB-DS 4;
    CDALB 1941-1968

Williams, Thomas (Alonzo)   1926- ... CLC 14
    See also CANR 2; CA 1-4R

Williams, Thomas Lanier   1911-1983
    See Williams, Tennessee

Williams, William Carlos
    1883-1963 ... CLC 1, 2, 5, 9, 13, 22, 42,
                                67
    See also CA 89-92; DLB 4, 16, 54, 86;
    CDALB 1917-1929

Williamson, David   1932- .... CLC 56

Williamson, Jack   1908- .... CLC 29
    See also Williamson, John Stewart
    See also DLB 8

Williamson, John Stewart   1908-
    See Williamson, Jack
    See also CANR 123; CA 17-20R

Willingham, Calder (Baynard, Jr.)
    1922- .... CLC 5, 51
    See also CANR 3; CA 5-8R; DLB 2, 44

Wilson, A(ndrew) N(orman)   1950- .. CLC 33
    See also CA 112, 122; DLB 14

Wilson, Andrew   1948-
    See Wilson, Snoo

Wilson, Angus (Frank Johnstone)
    1913- .... CLC 2, 3, 5, 25, 34
    See also CANR 21; CA 5-8R; DLB 15

Wilson, August
    1945- .... CLC 39, 50, 63; DC 2
    See also BLC 3; CA 115, 122

Wilson, Brian   1942- .... CLC 12

Wilson, Colin   1931- .... CLC 3, 14
    See also CAAS 5; CANR 1, 122; CA 1-4R;
    DLB 14

Wilson, Edmund
    1895-1972 .... CLC 1, 2, 3, 8, 24
    See also CANR 1; CA 1-4R;
    obituary CA 37-40R; DLB 63

Wilson, Ethel Davis (Bryant)
    1888-1980 .... CLC 13
    See also CA 102; DLB 68

Wilson, Harriet   1827?-?
    See also BLC 3; DLB 50

Wilson, John   1785-1854 .... NCLC 5

Wilson, John (Anthony) Burgess   1917-
    See Burgess, Anthony
    See also CANR 2; CA 1-4R

Wilson, Lanford   1937- .... CLC 7, 14, 36
    See also CA 17-20R; DLB 7

Wilson, Robert (M.)   1944- .... CLC 7, 9
    See also CANR 2; CA 49-52

Wilson, Sloan   1920- .... CLC 32
    See also CANR 1; CA 1-4R

Wilson, Snoo   1948- .... CLC 33
    See also CA 69-72

Wilson, William S(mith)   1932- ..... CLC 49
    See also CA 81-84

Winchilsea, Anne (Kingsmill) Finch, Countess
    of   1661-1720 .... LC 3

Wingrove, David   1954- .... CLC 68
    See also CA 133

Winters, Janet Lewis   1899-
    See Lewis (Winters), Janet
    See also CAP 1; CA 9-10

Winters, (Arthur) Yvor
    1900-1968 .... CLC 4, 8, 32
    See also CAP 1; CA 11-12;
    obituary CA 25-28R; DLB 48

Winterson, Jeannette   1959- .... CLC 64

Wiseman, Frederick   1930- .... CLC 20

Wister, Owen   1860-1938 .... TCLC 21
    See also CA 108; DLB 9, 78

Witkiewicz, Stanislaw Ignacy
    1885-1939 .... TCLC 8
    See also CA 105; DLB 83

Wittig, Monique   1935?- .... CLC 22
    See also CA 116; DLB 83

Wittlin, Joseph   1896-1976 .... CLC 25
    See also Wittlin, Jozef

Literary Criticism Series
Cumulative Topic Index

This index lists all topic entries in the Gale Literary Criticism Series *Contemporary Literary Criticism, Literature Criticism from 1400 to 1800, Nineteenth-Century Literature Criticism,* and *Twentieth-Century Literary Criticism.*

Topic Index

NCLC Cumulative Nationality Index

Nationality Index

Title Index to Volume 35

ISBN 0-8103-5835-2